ARIZONA'S NAMES
(X Marks the Place)

by

BYRD HOWELL GRANGER

Foreword by
Sen. Barry Goldwater

Illustrations by
Connie Asch

Maps by the Author

Arizona's Names (X Marks the Place)

ISBN 0-91 8080-18-5

Set in Helvetica and Times Roman Type Face by
Sunrise Graphics, Inc., Tucson, AZ

THE FALCONER PUBLISHING COMPANY

Distributed by

Treasure Chest Publications, Inc.
P.O. Box 5250
Tucson, Arizona 85703

Table of Contents

Foreword

Those of us who are Arizona natives, particularly those of us who were born in Arizona when it was still a territory, have had a lifelong and intense interest in the names of the counties, the towns, and the various locations of scenic and historic places in our state. There have been several excellent books published on this subject, beginning with the first *Barnes' Place Names* and followed up in 1960 by the current available publication from the University of Arizona.

These volumes were deeply researched, excellently presented and, at the time of their publication, served as right-hand mentors to those of us interested in the history of Arizona. This new book, however, I believe will – at least for a long time –satisfy the growing interest in the details of Arizona history because it includes thousands of names not mentioned in the other books and this is done in an alphabetical way instead of a county manner, which required more time to find a name in the 1960 volume.

In addition locations are noted by township and range, with useful and very clear maps which cover the entire state. Also, as you will immediately notice, this book is of standard size, more easily kept in the library and more acceptable to one who will find it in constant use.

I know the research on this publication was deep because it went, as all solid research must, into Arizona maps, military records, postal records, and others available in the National Archives.

Frankly, I don't know how anyone interested in the history of Arizona and the territory that preceded it, and just the plain part of the country which went before all of that, can get along without this book as a handy guide. I heartily recommend it as good reading and as excellent research material. I am very happy that Dr. Granger has seen fit to bring into publication the result of her research which I know personally has gone back many, many years.

Barry Goldwater
United States Senate

Introduction

Arizona's Names (X Marks the Place) epitomizes an interest which dates to my first setting foot on the solid ground of my adopted state in 1943. The occasion was an emergency landing made at Davis-Monthan Air Force Base during WW II. My query which started it all was, "What's the name of those mountains?" This book answers that question and 17,999 others.

An "Introduction" should live up to its name, so allow me...

Entries

Using this volume is easy. Place names are listed alphabetically and most contain information like this:

NAME OF THE PLACE   pronunciation: /what it is/
Derivation: Language: word origin = "its translation"
County   Township & Range   Elevation
Pertinent information about the place. Other places having the same name (with T & R, if different from that of the place featured); variant names (having various spelling; Indian names; archaic or obsolete names for the place). Post office information.   References.

When several places have the same designation, such as *Red* or *Brushy*, they are under a single classification and are listed alphabetically with specific information whenever it is known or necessary.

Appendix

The *Appendix* lists alphabetically all names contained in the major entries except those heading such entries. Further, all names in the *Appendix* are cross referenced to major entries. It contains (1) associated names, which have the same name as that of a main entry, but they are geographically different (a village may have the same name as a creek or valley); (2) variant names, which includes non-American names, archaic and obsolete names, and so on; (3)... but let's keep it simple: if a name does not appear as a main entry, then it is probably in the *Appendix*.

Pronunciation

Many entries have no pronunciation noted, for the simple reason that it seems to me that the way to say the name is rather obvious. Others which have a local way of wrapping one's tongue around them may have pronunciation noted. As for Indian place names, pronunciations are cited more for their inherent interest than an expectation that any person other than a Native American can possibly say them "correctly." A careful reader will note that some Indian names have a pronunciation guide which wobbles above and below the line, this being an indication of the inflectional quality of the particular language. This volume has no complete pronunciation guide, but those interested in it are referred to my 1960 volume, which contains a special guide prepared for my use.

For present purposes, the following may prove helpful:

Printed as	Sounds like
/ ə /	uh, a "swallowed" sound as in above
/ ʌ /	like the u in up
/ æ /	like the a in "sap" or "corral"
/ iy /	as in "sweet" or "mesquite"
/ ay /	like the i in "kite"
/) /	the sound of aw as in "awful"
/ č /	ch as in Charles
/ š /	sh as in "sure"

Derivations

Derivations speak for themselves. For example: Spanish: *charco* = "pond"

Locations

All major entries contain the name of the county in which the place is, but in the *Appendix* the county name is cited only if different from that of the major entry to which it is cross referenced.

As for Township and Range designations, they are based on the fact that deeds to Arizona land are so recorded. The T/R system arrives at Townships by dividing the state into quadrants measured north-to-south or south-to-north from an established baseline, hence Township North or Township South. Ranges have been determined from an imaginary baseline splitting Arizona from north to south, hence Range East and Range West.

Locations cited are as accurate as desk-top research with a magnifying glass and dividers used on all available maps can make them. Place locations are not exactly pin-pointed, nor are they intended to be. (NB: On any state map, place a pencil dot and then estimate how much "ground" it covers. Quite a sizeable area, isn't it?) On the other hand, the T/R given can be used in locating the place on other maps. That is why only one T/R is given for places which of course cover or extend over more than a single township. (See **Maps** below.)

Elevations

The figures speak for themselves, but for stream beds, canyons and other features where elevation varies, the cited elevation can be taken as a general indication. It is not intended to be more than that. Elevations for highest points in mountain ranges may be taken at face value.

Post Office Information

Accurate dating of when place names arose and when they ceased to be extant is a major problem in onomastics. Post office information frequently not only eliminates doubts, but also provides absolute knowledge about place name origins. Such information was found in the National Archives, which houses original post office applications and p.o. site maps. The latter label surrounding terrain, another clue to place names. For instance, one site map eliminated a gnawing doubt that a particular creek really existed: on the postal site map an illiterate postmaster had scrawled "nokrknrhr." It took some decipering to arrive at its meaning: "No creek near here."

Dates of postal service termination provide a now-distant death knell for many place names.

A word of caution: information in the National Archives may not always jibe with that in John and Lillian Theobald's excellent *Arizona Territory: Post Offices and Postmasters* (see Bibliography), as dates in this volume are as recorded in Washington, D.C.

References

References are either oral, printed or manuscript. Where a family name is cited, the reference is to information learned during visits with "old timers" or those knowing local history. During the early years of research, the oral sources were most important, for the true pioneers were increasingly being silenced by time. Information about people named in the "References" is in the section on *Contributors*. Some recollections in this book, by the way, reflect events now a century deep in the past. The extent of this volume has permitted me to include much hitherto unpublished information. Some of it comes from family histories, and some has been sent to me by letter. In each instance, letters are so noted.

Newspaper references or books and periodicals which supplied only one or two items are cited, not in the *Bibliography,* but under main-entry references. Readers may at first be puzzled by noting the use of numbers, followed by the designation for page references. The numbering system is duplicated in the *Bibliography.*

Bibliography

Numbers occurring in "References" sections correspond to items listed in the *Bibliography*, which of course furnishes information about the source in the usual way. Thus "218, p. 49" is a reference taken from James Marshall, *Santa Fe: The Railroad That Built an Empire.* The reference to "58," however, is to a manuscript by Kirk Bryan, and "242" refers to the National Archives, where hundreds of military maps and manuscripts (not to mention printed reports) were scrutinized, as were postal records and maps. The number "329" is that of the United States Geological Survey headquarters at Reston, Virginia, where I spent weeks abstracting otherwise unavailable information.

Maps

Citing Township and Range locations in *Arizona's Names* would, I believe, be useless without immediate access to suitable maps. This book has them. Some counties required several (Coconino County has five). Not only do the maps show T/R coordinates, but also major water courses, selected major landmarks, and railroads.

Acknowledgments

Unlike Venus, *Arizona's Names (X Marks the Place)* did not suddenly appear on the half-shell. It holds the contributions of many. I am indebted to the Arizona State Highway Department for its T/R computer listing, and to the highly professional staffs of the National Archives, the Huntington Library, and of the Map and Special Collections Divisions of the University of Arizona Library. I am indebted for having had access to files in the Arizona Historical Society in Tucson, and access to the Arizona files of the USGS in Reston, Virginia.

Thanks are due to the many who contributed information for this volume, and to those who helped with research. Members of my family (who live on the outskirts of Washington, D.C.) stood in my stead when things had to be rechecked at the National Archives, and they spent many hours at the USGS offices helping abstract information. Specific appreciation is due Mrs. Jeanne Younggren, an able and willing research assistant, and also to my old friend Mrs. G.C. Kindig of Phoenix, an expert typist without whose diligence I doubt the work would ever have been done. I do not know quite how to express my gratitude to Oscar T. Branson, but it is surely owed: at a time when seeing *Arizona's Names* in print seemed very remote, he offered advice and expertise which have resulted in the book I had planned.

Most particularly I wish to offer appreciation to The Hon. Barry Goldwater, United States Senator for Arizona, for his many years of interest and support — and for preparing a fine Foreword for *Arizona's Names.*

Byrd Howell Granger
Carefree, Arizona
January 1983

A

A'AI STO
Papago: *a'ai sto* = "white on both sides"
Pima   c. T14S R2E
The name describes the valley of the community.   Ref.: 58

ABBIE WATERMAN PEAK
Pima   T12S R9E   Elev. 3825'
Surveyor George Roskruge named the peak for the Abbie Waterman Mine, in operation as early as 1880 at a mining camp known originally as Silver Hill, but the name was changed by J. C. Waterman to honor one of his daughters.
Ref.: 18a; AHS, Emerson O. Stratton *ms.*

ABRA   pro.: /ábrə/
Spanish = "gorge"
Yavapai   T18N R20W   -   Elev. 4439'
This location was a small railroad station near a deep canyon, hence the name.
Ref.: 18a

ABRA PLAIN, LA
Pima   T17S R7W
This name was in use in 1892 for this small valley on the International Boundary.

ABRA VALLEY, LA
Pima   T17S R7W
This is a small open valley west of the old headquarters of the Organ Pipe Cactus National Monument. The name probably comes from that of the former Abra Ranch. See Abra Plain, La, Pima Ref.: Henson

ABYSS, THE
Coconino (Grand Canyon)   T31N R2E   Elev. c. 6000'
This is the descriptive name first used by James for the deep gorge here.
Ref.: 178, p. 31

A C HILL
Greenlee   T4S R29E
The *A*rizona *C*opper *C*ompany owned this hill.   Ref.: Donna Olney (Morenci, 1961)

ACHI   pro.: /ačə/
Papago = "ridge"
Pima   T13S R4E   Elev. c. 1500'
This small Papago village is named because of its location. Here a special prayer stick ceremony takes place, based on the legend that during the Great Migration, I'itoi (Elder Brother) stopped to place such prayer sticks. The location is also spelled as follows: Aatci; Achie; Archi. Ref.: 262, p. 5; 92

ADAIR

Navajo   T10N R21E   Elev. c. 5000'

George Bagnall, a shoemaker, settled and stayed at Bagnall Hollow from about 1881 to 1885. After he left, Aaron Adair moved in. Considering the poor soil, his move was so foolish that his neighbors called his place "Fools Hollow." Gradually a settlement formed, but all traces of it are now gone.

P.O. est. March 2, 1899, Jesse Jackson Brady, p.m.; disc. July 14, 1906
Ref.: 242; 18a

ADAIR SPRING

Navajo   T38N R16E   Elev. 6680'

This spring feeds about one million gallons a day into the lake at Lakeside. Both the spring and wash were named for Wesley Adair, who settled here c. 1878, according to Barnes. However, the location is that used by Aaron Adair. See Adair, Navajo
Ref.: 18a; 5, p. 450

ADAMANA

Apache   T18N R14E   Elev. 5600'

With Jim Cart, Adam Hanna raised cattle, with the ranch headquarters also containing the post office. The name is a contraction of Adam Hanna. It was also the name of a railroad stop for tourists en route to the nearby Petrified Forest. Hanna moved to Farmington, New Mexico, where he later died.

P.O. est. Jan. 31, 1896, Adam Hanna, p.m.; disc. 1910, but reest.; disc. Jan. 1, 1969; Wells Fargo 1904 Ref.: Grigsby; 18a; *Arizona Times* (Feb. 18, 1947), State Library Files; 242

ADAMS MESA

Maricopa   T4N R7E   Elev. 2515'

In the early 1900s Jeff Adams, a cattleman, maintained a ranch at this mesa.
Ref.: 18a

ADAMS TANK

Coconino   T20N R9E

This watering place was named for William Adams, a rancher, who created the stock tank. In April 1964 the USGS eliminated the name Cabin Tank for this location. Also see Foster Tank, Coconino Ref.: 329

ADAMSVILLE

Pinal   T5S R9E   Elev. 1440'

In 1866 Charles S. Adams (b. Ohio, 1834) surveyed a townsite named for himself, where he built and operated a store and saloon. In 1869 William Bichard & Company (consisting of brothers William and Nick) established a second store and a flour mill, the only one between Tucson and California. Pima Indians supplied it with vast quantities of corn, a source of supply for many Arizona forts. Adams left the thriving town of four hundred and moved to Prescott. The town name was oficially changed to Sanford for Capt. George B. Sanford, 1st U.S. Cavalry, in 1870, but local people continued to use the original name. Sanford was gone by 1871. The town fell into a gradual decline and the adobe stores, hotel and homes melted under the rains so that by 1920 only a row of roofless buildings remained, and these too have vanished.

P.O. est. as Sanford, Jan. 24, 1871, Larkin W. Carr, p.m.; disc. Jan. 26, 1876. Carr remained at the post office only thirteen days, after which William Dumont became p.m.
Ref.: AHS, Emerson O. Stratton *ms.*; 62; *Arizona Miner* (April 29, 1871), and (June 17, 1871); *Arizona Citizen* (March 2, 1872); 206, p. 343; 163, p. 43; 224, p. 175; 57, p. 386; Theobald

ADAMS WELL

Yuma   T5S R17W

In 1863 Samuel Adams (b. 1828, Pennsylvania; d. 1915) settled at the south end of the Castle Dome Mountains, digging a ninety-foot well to supply water for travelers along the adjacent desert trail. He was so enthusiastic about the possibilities of developing the

Colorado River for ocean-going vessels that he earned the nickname "Steamboat." Adams asserted he was the first to make a Grand Canyon voyage.
Ref.: AHS, Mercer, "Desert Scrapbook," *Yuma Daily Sun* (Oct. 30, 1954)

ADOBE: The name *adobe* has been applied to several place names in Arizona. In some instances it has been so used because of the presence of an adobe structure at the location, but in others the name derives from the fact that large clay adobes were made at such places. Instances follow:

Adobe (Town)	Maricopa	T4N R2E	Elev. 1393'
Adobe Canyon	Cochise	T13S R23E	
Adobe Canyon	Santa Cruz	T20S R15E	
Adobe Creek	Yavapai	T17N R10W	
Adobe Flats	La Paz	T3N R11W	
Adobe Lake	Yuma	T4S R23W	
Adobe Mountain	Maricopa	T4N R2E	Elev. 1700'
Adobe Spring	Santa Cruz	T24S R13E	
Adobe Well	Pima	T13S R6W	Elev. 1633'

ADOBE WASH
Maricopa/Pima   T13S R6W   Elev. 1600'
The name for this location came from a house called "The Adobe" with its well (Adobe Well), both constructed by a man named Cameron c. 1904. Although the name is well established locally, it is referred to as Daniels Arroyo in 1937 USGS Professional Paper #209. However, Daniels Arroyo actually has another location (T11S/-R8W). Ref.: 329; 58

ADONDE
Spanish = "where"
Yuma   T9S R19W   Elev. c. 500'
A stage station, this became a railroad stop when the expanding Southern Pacific R.R. tracks reached it in January 1879. Steam engines filled their water tanks from the wells here. The place is today a railroad siding. Ref.: 206, p. 311; Lenon

AGASSIZ
Coconino   T21N R8E
Agassiz was a railroad station. Its name was changed to Milton. See Agassiz Peak, Coconino

AGASSIZ PEAK
Coconino   T22N R7E   Elev. 12,356'
Jean Louis Rodolphe Agassiz (1807-1873), a geologist and zoologist, reported on fossils for the Pacific Railroad surveying expedition of 1855-1860. In 1869 Gen. W. J. Palmer in his *Report on Surveys of 1867-1868* named the peak in the San Francisco group for Louis Agassiz, the famous Swiss-born Harvard professor. The peak is known also as San Francisco Mountain and, according to Harold S. Colton (in a 1933 communication), since c. 1890, as Fremont Peak.
Ref.: 32, p. 316; 346, p. 175, Note 16; 285, p. 1; 329

AGATE BRIDGE
Apache   T17N R24E   Elev. 5575'
This is the largest petrified log in the Petrified Forest National Monument. It is one hundred and eleven feet long and lies partially buried, forming a forty-four foot agate bridge supported by concrete. Ref.: 5, p. 312

AGATE CANYON
Coconino (Grand Canyon)   T32N R1E   Elev. 3250'
Richard T. Evans, with the USGS in 1903, named the canyon. It is one of several canyons in the Grand Canyon region named for semi-precious stones.
Ref.: Kolb

AGATE HILL
Mohave   7 mi. n. of Katherine Landing

Agates found on this hill give it the name. Ref.: Burns

AGATE HOUSE
Apache   T16N R23E

A prehistoric seven-room apartment, this structure is built of petrified wood, hence its name. Constructed c. 1000 A.D., it is one of more than three hundred such sites. Ref.: 13, Jepson, "Trees of Stone," p. 4; Branch

AGATHLA NEEDLE
Navajo: *aghaele* = "much wool"

Navajo   T40N R20E   Elev. 7100'

According to the Navajo Bead Chant, Indians killed an antelope herd here and scraped so many hides against the volcanic rocks that the needle rock was called "The Place of Wool and Hair." On the Macomb map of 1860, it is named Lana Negra (Spanish = "black wool"). Navajo Indians are said to translate the name as the "Place of the Scraping of Hides," because hides were scraped against the volcanic rough rocks of this great black shaft. It rises like a needle 1255' above its sloping base, which in turn is one hundred feet high. Because of its shape it has been called Needle Rock. Because it commands the entrance to Monument Valley, its first name of El Capitan (Spanish = "the captain" or "commander") was given it by Kit Carson. It is also called El Agathla Peak. Capitan Wash is nearby. Ref.: Burcard; 129, p. 18; 143, p. 205; 191, p. 6; 326, p. 51; 331, p. 53; 232a, p. 24

AGENCY PEAK
Pinal   T4S R6E   Elev. 2009'

The name is due to its location close to the Gila River Indian Reservation agency headquarters.

AGUA CALIENTE   pro.: /agwəkaliᴧente/
Spanish: *agua* = "water"; *caliente* = "hot"

Maricopa   T5S R10W   Elev. 454'

The hot springs here were called *xakŭpi'nc* by Pima Indians (= "hot water"), who used them to soothe "aches and swellings as well as to destroy vermin." Fr. Jacobo Sedelmayr visited in 1744 and noted they were near the Cocomaricopa Indian settlement of Dueztumac and named the springs Santa Maria del Agua Caliente, calling it a fine site for a mission. When in 1775 Fr. Francisco Garcés visited here, he called the place San Bernardino. It was also known as San Bernardino del Agua Caliente and as Ojo Caliente, the word *ojo* (= "eye") being used for the springs.

     King S. Woolsey (b. Alabama, 1832; d. June 29, 1879) was the first American to settle here, arriving from California in 1860 with a horse, a rifle, a pistol, and five dollars. For awhile he drove mules, then supplied hay to army posts until enlisting in Confederate forces in 1862. On the march east he fell ill and saw no active service, but returned to Arizona. After being in the Prescott region for a time, with George Martin he bought the Agua Caliente Ranch c. 1865. Martin c. 1868 sold his portion to Woolsey, who took charge of the nearby stage station (see Burkes, Maricopa). By 1873 Agua Caliente had become a prominent health resort. Woolsey sold his holdings to David Neahr, withholding the important water rights for Woolsey's heirs.

P.O. est. March 12, 1867, Patrick McKannon, p.m.; disc. June 24, 1867; reest. as Agua Caliente, Aug. 3, 1887, George W. Wilson, p.m. Ref.: *Arizona Graphic* (March 24, 1900), p. 1; *Arizona Star* (March 21, 1920), pp. 1, 2; *Tucson Citizen* (May 31, 1873), pp. 1, 5, 7; 15, pp. 365, 366, 367; 77, p. 118; 287, p. 40; 206, pp. 138, 139; 242

AGUA CALIENTE CANYON
Pima/Santa Cruz   T19S R13E

                                T13S R16E

This canyon heads next east to Madera Canyon. Its name probably comes from that of the Agua Caliente Ranch in 1879. By 1889 Ed Bullock, a breeder of fine horses, owned this location. The ranch had served as a way station in 1876 for the mail route from Tucson to Fort Buchanan. Ref.: *Arizona Star* (July 2, 1889), p. 4; 277, p. 39; 242

AGUA CALIENTE CANYON
Pima   T13S R16E
This was the original name of a resort located at Hot Mineral Springs. See Tanque Verde Hot Springs, Pima Ref.: 81, p. 238

AGUA CERCADA CANYON
Spanish: *cercada* = "walled up"; *agua* = "water"
Pima/Santa Cruz   T23S R10E
The name probably derives from a watering place used by cattle owned by H. M. Bryan. Ref.: 58

AGUA DULCE MOUNTAINS   pro.: /ágwə dúwlsey/
Spanish: *agua* = "water"; *dulce* = "sweet"
Pima   T15–16S R8–9W   Elev. 2850'
The name derives from that of Agua Dulce Spring (T16S/R9W), which has sweet tasting water. When Lt. Michler visited the spring in 1854, his men dug to reach the water level. These mountains also extend over the border into Mexico and are called the Sonoyta Mountains, taking their name from the nearby Sonoyta River in Mexico. See also Quitobaquito Hills, Pima Ref.: Ketchum; Hensen; 106, p. 115; 329

AGUA DULCE PASS
Pima   T16S R9W
Fr. Eusebio Kino made at least seven trips through this pass in the Ajo Mountains, but did not name it. The name derives from the mountains in which it is located. (See Agua Dulce Mountains, Pima.) Through translation of the Spanish name, this place is also known as Sweet Water Pass. Ref.: Hensen

AGUA DULCE SPRING
Yuma   T16S R9W
In 1951 the Fish and Wildlife Service developed this spring, naming it for the Agua Dulce Mountains. It is not the same as the spring in Mexico. See Agua Dulce Mountains, Pima Ref.: Monson

AGUA FRIA   pro.: /ágwə friyə/
Spanish: *agua* = "water"; *fria* = "cold"
Maricopa   T5N R1E   Elev. c. 1000'
At this stage station, owner-operator Martin Heald Calderwood (see Calderwood Butte, Maricopa) was building a residence in 1879. By August 1884 Calderwood had sold this property. See Agua Fria River, Maricopa/Yavapai, and Mirage, El, Maricopa Ref.: *Arizona Miner* (Aug. 29, 1879); *Prescott Courier* (Aug. 15, 1884)

AGUA FRIA RANCH
Yavapai
King S. Woolsey established his Agua Fria Ranch in the 1870s on the Agua Fria River. He sold it in 1879 to Nathan S. Bowers and his brothers, who were among the first cattle ranchers in Arizona Territory. Part of the ranch headquarters used stones from a prehistoric building on the ranch. Under their ownership the ranch was called Bowers Ranch. By 1921 it was called the Smetter Ranch. See also Litchfield Park, Maricopa Ref.: 107, II, 263; 49, pp. 165-165; *Arizona Sentinel* (May 24, 1879), p. 1

AGUA FRIA RIVER   pro.: /águə friyə/
Spanish: *agua* = "water"; *fria* = "cold"
Maricopa/Yavapai   T14N R1W   Elev. c. 3800'
A letter in the Sharlot Hall Museum (Dec. 5, 1921) states this stream was named "because of the cold water at the old King Woolsey Ranch." The creation of Carl Pleasant Dam stopped its former violent flooding. Ref.: 329; 5, p. 356

AGUAJITA SPRING   pro.: /águə hiytə/
Spanish: *agua* = "water"; *jita* = "little" (diminutive)
Pima   T17S R7W
The name describes a little seep, barely a spring. Ref.: Hensen; Supernaugh

AGUA SAL CREEK   pro.: /ágwə sə́l/
Spanish: *agua* = "water"; *sal* = "salt"
Apache   T7N R8E to T11N R10E   Elev. c. f000'
This intermittent creek is noted for its unpalatable salty taste.
Ref.: 18a; 141, p. 91

AGUA VERDE CREEK
Spanish: *agua* = "water"; *verde* = "green"
Pima   T16S R17E
This name was used by Lt. John G. Parke in 1854. Agua Verde Wash joins it. Roskruge
on his map of 1893 called it Agua Verde Wash. Ref.: 254, p. 26

AGUILA   pro.: /əgilə/
Spanish: *aguila* = "eagle"
Maricopa   T7N R9W   Elev. 1800'
A nearby eminence, Pico del Aguila (Spanish = "eagle's beak"), lent its name to a small
settlement (on the railroad), which was planned and promoted by F. H. Kline in June
1909, with little result.
P.O. est. Jan. 28, 1910, Frank Sperger, p.m. Ref.: *Arizona Gazette* (June 11, 1909);
Willson; 242; Lenon

AGUILA MOUNTAINS   pro.: /əgiylə/
Maricopa/La Paz   T9N R10W   Elev. 1655'
A rock formation looks like an eagle's eye and beak, hence the name. See also Aguila,
Maricopa Ref.: Monson; 58

AGUILA VALLEY
Maricopa/La Paz   T7N R8W
This valley lies at the east end of the Aguila Mountains, from which it takes its
name. See Aguila Mountains, Maricopa/La Paz Ref.: 329

AGUIRRE   pro.: /agiyriy/
Pima   T15S R13E
This was the name of the railroad station at Emery Park. See Emery Park, Pima
Ref.: 242

AGUIRRE LAKE   pro.: /agiyriy/
Pima   T21S R8E
Pedro Aguirre in 1886 constructed a dam which created a large lake here (named for
him), for years a favorite duck hunting location. Indian ranchers now use the lake. See
Aguirre Peak, Pima Ref.: Kitt; 279, p. 53; 5, p. 32; 242

AGUIRRE PEAK   pro.: /agiyriy/
Pima   T15S R9E   Elev. 4947'
This peak was named for Pedro Aguirre (b. June 21, 1835, Mexico), who came to
Arizona in 1859. With his brothers he operated various stage lines (including the one
which passed through the custom-station village of Sasabe (see that entry). In 1870 he
established the Buenos Ayres Ranch where he had a large dam constructed c. 1886, thus
creating Aguirre Lake. (see Aguirre Lake, Pima) Barnes says that the peak is named
for Pedro's brother Epifanio. He, however, was slain by Apaches south of the border
many years prior to the first appearance of the name Aguirre (for the ranch vicinity) in
1892 on a GLO map. To further confuse the issue, a letter dated July 13, 1917, in the
USGS files says it is named for Don Tesorio Aguirre, on whom further information is
lacking. Ref.: Kitt; AHS; 18a; 329

AGUIRRE STATION
Pima
On the stage road from Tucson to Quijotoa in 1884 the Aguirre brothers changed horses
at this dry camp. See Aguirre Peak, Pima

AGUIRRE VALLEY
Pima   T11S R5E
Probably named for Pedro Aguirre, as it was on the route of the stage line run from
Tucson to Quijotoa. See Aguirre Peak, Pima Ref.: 262, p. 18

AGUIRRE VAYA   pro.: /agiyrəwáha/
Pima   T13S R7E   Elev. c. 3000'
This temporary Papago village is named for a Mexican ranger. Ref.: 262, p. 12

AGUIRRE WASH
Pima   T11–12S R6E
This wash flows northwest by Aguirre Vaya and derives its name from that of the
settlement. See Aguirre Vaya, Pima Ref.: 262, p. 27

AGUSTIN DE OIAUR, SAN
Pima
This location was visited by Fr. Eusebio Kino on October 23, 1697. See Tucson, Pima
Ref.: 77, p. 541

AHA KITCHA KUKAVO
Mohave   T14N R12W
Hualapai: A type of laurel tree growing in this region is called *Kitha'ela*. Combined
with *aha* ("water") and *Kukavo*, it is a locative designating where Black Canyon enters
Burro Creek. It is typical of Indian place names to be geographically and descriptively
specific, applying to a precisely limited location, i.e. where the Burro Stream meets
Sandy River. It is also spelled Ha Kitchi Kavo'o.
Ref.: Dobyns, citing Dick Grover

AHAN OWUCH
Papago = "feather lies"
Pima   T15S R1W
This is a small permanent Papago village, but why it is so named is not known to the
editor. Ref.: 262, p. 10; 329

AHAPOOK CREEK
Hualapai: *Aháa* = "water"; *pook* = "head"
Mohave   T15–18N R11W
Appearing on the GLO 1892 as Ah-ah-pook Creek, the Indian name designates its
heading near Cygnus Peak, from which it flows south to Spencer Creek.
Ref.: Dobyns

AHE VONAM   pro.: /aˀey ownəm/
Papago: *aai* = "sides"; *vonam* = "hat"
Pima   T13S R2E   Elev. 2500'
The name is descriptive of the fact that the site of this Papago village has a view of one of
the Brownell Mountains which appears like a hat when viewed from either side. The
village is near, but is not part of, the town of Brownell. See Brownell, Pima
Ref.: 58; 262, p. 5

AJAX HILL
Cochise   T22E R21S   Elev. 5327'
An undated clipping from the *Bisbee Review* states the hill was named during the 1880s
for a prospector holding several claims on it. Ref.: State Library Archives

AJO   pro.: /áho/
Papago: *au'auho* = "paint"
Pima   T12S R6W   Elev. 1751'
Some believed the name Ajo derived from wild onions here, but it comes from a Papago
word *au'auho* ("paint"), the red ore Indians used to decorate their bodies. Mexican

miners contracted it to the sound of Spanish *ajo*. Copper ore was first noticed here in 1853 by Capt. Peter R. Brady, with the surveying party for the 32° parallel railroad route. Later he organized a group to explore mining possibilities. Easily smelted ores were sparse. The rich but unworkable ores remained for more efficient technology to reduce. By the early 1900s, ore reduction was feasible and the New Cornelia Copper Company was formed. In 1911 only about fifty people lived in Old Ajo, but by 1916 the population in the new town of Cornelia, a mile north, increased to over five thousand. Too close to rich deposits, Old Ajo was doomed. In fact, it burned to extinction. (See also Clarkstown, Pima) The Papago name for Ajo is *Muy Vavi* (= "many wells" or "warm water"). The name Ajo is shared by the following: North Ajo Peak (Elev. 2776'), Mount Ajo (Elev. 4829'), Ajo Mountains or Range (T18S/R5W, Elev. 4808'; a.k.a. Sierra del Ajo, 1854 Gadsden Purchase Map and Sierra de la Esperanza, Mil. Map, 1859, derived from La Laguna de la Esperanza, found there by the Gadsden Survey party), Little Ajo Mountains, and Valley of the Ajo.
P.O. est. Aug. 29, 1900, John Henry Hovey, p.m. Ref.: 58; 138, p. 59; 205, p. 80; 57, p. 367; 5, p. 90; *Ajo Copper News* (Oct. 21, 1954); 93, p. 157; AHS, Castillo File

AJO PEAK
Pima   T12S R6W   Elev. 2617'
Ajo Peak is one of three sharply pointed hills in the Little Ajo Mountains.
Ref.: 58

AKABA, MOUNT
Coconino (Grand Canyon)   T34N R3W   Elev. 4865'
This butte was named in 1925 for a local Havasupai Indian family.
Ref.: 18a; 295, p. 184

AKCHIN
Pinal   T5S R3E   Elev. 1200'
This small Maricopa village is not the same location as Ali ak Chin, Pima, also known as San Serafin. In 1941 the USGS eliminated the spelling Aktjin for this location. See Serafin, San, Pima Ref.: 329

AK CHUT VAYA   pro.: /ak tit vʷaha/
Papago = "well in wash"
Pima   T21S R5E   Elev. 2425'
This descriptive name applies to a small Papago village. Ref.: 262, p. 3

AKEE'MULL
This is the Pima Indian name for the Salt River. Ref.: 203, p. 3

Á'KIMÛLT
Maricopa
Prior to 1904 this was the Pima Indian name for the Salt River and also for a Pima village on the north side of the Salt River about three miles from the present community of Mesa. See Pima Villages, Pinal/Maricopa

AK KOMELIK
Papago = "flat channel"
Pima   T19S R2E
The reason for the name of this location is not known to the editor. Ref.: 262

ALAMO   pro.: /ǽləmow/ or /áləmo/
Spanish = "cottonwood"
Alamo occurs in many Arizona place names and probably denotes the presence of such trees in the past or contemporaneously. Examples follow:

Alamo   Pima
See Nawt Vaya, Pima

Alamo   Maricopa
In 1881 Viall Ransom operated a stage station called Alamo between Phoenix and Maricopa Wells, exact location unknown. Ref.: 18a

Alamo	La Paz	T11N R13W	Elev. c. 1500'

This was the location of Alamo Crossing on the Bill Williams River.
P.O. est. as Alimo, Nov. 23, 1899, Joseph B. Tappan, p.m.; resc. Dec. 15, 1900; reest. as Alamo, March 30, 1911, Vincent M. Devine, p.m.; disc. Dec. 31, 1918 Ref.: Dobyns; Willson; 242

Alamo Canyon	Pima	T12S R14W	

Also known as Tres Alamos Canyon because of three cottonwoods here. Ref.: Henson; Supernaugh

Alamo Canyon	Pinal	T2S R11E	

Alamo Canyon	Santa Cruz	(1) T21S R16E	(2) T21S R14E

Alamo Crossing	Mohave	T11N R13W	Elev. 1050'

Alamo Crossing is now one hundred feet beneath the surface of Alamo Lake at Alamo Lake State Park. See Alamo, Yuma

Alamo Dam	Mohave	T5N R27E	Elev. 1200'

This location serves a summer residential community.

Alamo Lake	Mohave	T11N R13W	

The name was changed by the USGS in March 1972 from Alamo Reservoir.

Alamo Muerto, Picacho del   Pima

Spanish: *picacho* = "peak"; *alamo* = "cottonwood"; *muerto* = "dead"
In 1869 this was the name given to peaks near the north end of the present Baboquivari range, as shown on the 1878 Boyle map.

Alamo Reservoir	Mohave/La Paz	T11N R12W	

This water hole is not the same as Alamo Lake. Ref.: 329

Alamo Reservoir Wild Life Area	Mohave/La Paz	T11N R13W	Elev. 1400'

About five hundred acres of this 22,856 acre wild life and fishery recreational area is water. The place is managed by the Arizona Game and Fish Department. Ref.: 9, p. 3

Alamo Springs	Apache	T7N R25E	
Alamo Spring	Mohave	T13N R12W	
Alamo Spring	Pima	T12S R17E	
Alamo Spring	Santa Cruz	(1) T21S R16E (2) T24S R12E	
Alamo Spring	La Paz	T1N R16W	
Alamo State Park	Mohave	T10N R13W	
Alamo Wash	Apache	T11N R27E	
Alamo Wash	Pima	T15S R5W	
Alamo Wash	La Paz	T3N R15W	

ALARÇON TERRACE   pro.: /ǽlersán/

Coconino (Grand Canyon)   T33N R2W   Elev. 4750'

Capt. Juan Hernando de Alarçon left the harbor at Acapulco, Mexico, on May 9, 1540, carrying on his boats supplies intended for the Coronado Expedition, then en route overland. Alarçon was the first white man to journey by water beyond the mouth of the Colorado River. The name for this land spur was suggested by Francois E. Matthes in 1915 to the USGS geographer for the Shinumo quadrangle.
Ref.: 244 (June 30, 1929), p. 2; 357, p. 403; 329

ALCHESAY CANYON

Maricopa   T3N R12E

In naming places along the Apache Trail to Roosevelt Lake, Prof. Aubrey Drury in 1917 gave this location the name of a famous White Mountain Apache leader and scout. Bourke describes the Indian as follows: "Alchesay ('The Little One') was a perfect Adonis in figure, a mass of muscle and sinew, of wondrous courage, great sagacity, and as faithful as an Irish hound." Ref.: Schmelzer; 48, p. 15; 329

ALCOVE CANYON

Apache   T39N R27E   Elev. c. 6000'

Gregory wrote that this canyon has "precipitous edges ... elaborately carved into alcoves," hence the name. Ref.: 141, p. 31

ALDER: Alder trees grow abundantly in some parts of Arizona, hence several place names, as follows:

Alder Box Spring	Pima	T11S R16E
Alder Canyon	Coconino	T13N R14E
Alder Canyon	Pima	T11S R16E
Alder Creek	Gila	(1) T9N R9E (2) T2N R18E
Alder Creek	Greenlee	T1S R30E

Fred Fritz, Sr. (d. 1916) named this canyon because of its many alder trees when he homesteaded in it in 1890. He used alders for his cabin, some logs being a foot square after dressing. In accordance with his wishes, Fritz is buried at a bend of this creek. Ref.: Mrs. Fred Fritz, Sr.

Alder Creek	Maricopa	T3N R10E
Alder Lake	Coconino	T12N R13E

Following the battle with Apaches at Big Dry Wash on July 17, 1882, soldiers carved their names and regiment on alder trees along this lake. Ref.: 18a

Alder Peak	Greenlee	T13 R30E	Elev. 6743'
Alder Saddle	Maricopa	T4N R10E	Elev. 6447'
Alder Wash	Pima/Pinal	T11S R17E	

ALDONA

Pima   Elev. 2800'

Formerly a railroad stop named for Alfred S. Donau, a cattleman, merchant, and real estate man who arrived in Arizona in 1883, this place now is in the city of Tucson. Ref.: 18a

ALDRICH

Cochise   T12S R26E

This railroad switch was probably named for Mark Aldrich (b. New York), who moved from Illinois to Tucson in 1855. He was its first American merchant as well as its first postmaster and mayor. He owned a ranch on the San Pedro River near Tres Alamos. Ref.: AHS, Chambers File; Kitt

ALEXANDER, CAMP

Mohave   T21N R22W   Elev. c. 700'

In 1867 this location was a mile and one-half north of Hardyville on the Colorado River. Capt. George M. Wheeler reported in 1871 that it was the point farthest north on the river which could be crossed by ferry. This suggests that the camp operator may have been named Alexander, but no proof has been found to support the conjecture. Ref.: 335, p. 52; 345, I, 157

ALEXANDER CANYON

Coconino   Between Camp #18 and #19

Beale in 1857 named this canyon for one of his men. Ref.: 23, p. 61

ALEXANDRA

Yavapai   T11N R1E   Elev. c. 5500'

Thomas Matthew Alexander (b. 1822; d. Nov. 10, 1910) with Ed Peck and Col. H. A. Bigelow located and named a mine and its townsite for Mrs. Alexander (b. 1828; d. 1898), feminizing it to Alexandra.

P.O. est. as Alexandra, Aug. 6, 1878, Joseph F. Drew, p.m.; disc. March 25, 1896 Ref.: AHS, Alexander File; Sharlot Hall Museum; 242

ALGERT

Coconino   T1N R7W

Charles H. Algert, a trader to the Navajo Indians, had this post office in Blue Canyon named for him. See Blue Canyon, Coconino
P.O. est. March 27, 1900, Cirrilla E. Needham, p.m.; disc. Sept. 2, 1903
Ref.: 18a; 242

ALGODON   pro.: /ælgədówn/
Spanish = "cotton"

Graham   T21N R28E   Elev. 3124'

The former small settlement existed on land originally a part of the Goodspeed Ranch, bought in 1900 by John A. and William Franklin Lee, Mormons. They were soon joined by other Mormons. Although one source says Lebanon is a separate community, the first name proposed for the post office here was Lebanon, probably because it would have been easier to re-establish an older office, but the Post Office Department pencilled out "Lebanon" and wrote in "Algodon." Why the latter name was selected is not known. Today the older names of Algodon, Lebanon, or Lebanon Hot Springs are not used, having given way to the specifically descriptive name Cactus Flat. See Lebanon, Graham
P.O. est. Dec. 27, 1914, Effie Lee, p.m.; disc. Dec. 30, 1921
Ref.: Jennings; 242; 353, pp. 48, 56

ALHAMBRA

Maricopa   T2N R2E   Elev. c. 1000'

Josiah Harbert (b. Alhambra, California) named both that community and the one in Arizona. He owned the land on which each took shape. His reason for the name is not known.
P.O. est. Nov. 11, 1892, Arthur Elmer Hinton, p.m.; disc. Nov. 15, 1918; Wells Fargo 1903 Ref.: 18a; 242

ALI AK CHIN   pro.: /awaᵏčin/
Papago = "little mouth of wash"

Pima   T18S R3W   Elev. 1800'

The name describes the location of this small Indian community at the small mouth of a wash in the La Quituni Valley, a name which is probably a corruption of a Papago appellative. A more important Ak Chin is on the Maricopa Indian Reservation. See Serafin, San, Pima Ref.: 58; 262, p. 17; 329

ALI CHUKSON   pro.: /ali čuksówn/
Papago = "foot of little black hills"

Pima   T17S R3E   Elev. 2589'

Also called Tucsoncito (Spanish = "little Tucson"), a corruption, this large Papago village has fields cultivated at the base of a small black lava hill. The name has also been spelled Alitjukson, Al Cukson, and Chumatjuikson. Ref.: 58; 57, p. 407; 262, p. 1

ALICE GULCH

Gila   T1N R15E

At the head of this gulch was the Alice mining claim, which the Old Domining Mining Company later bought. Ref.: Woody

ALICIA

Maricopa   T4E R2S   Elev. c. 1000'

This stop on the Maricopa and Phoenix R.R. was named for Alice Masten, daughter of N. K. Masten, first president of the railroad. Ref.: 18a

ALI MOLINA
Papago = "Little Magdalena"

Pima   T18S R6E   Elev. 2674'

The name derives from that of Magdalena, Mexico. It applies to other locations in the area. Ref.: 329; 57, p. 24

ALI OIDAK
Papago = "little field"
Pima   T16S R2E
The name describes the locality of this small Papago town.
Ref.: 329; 57, p. 5

ALISO SPRING   pro.: /ali′so/
Spanish = "alder tree" or "sycamore tree"
Santa Cruz   T21S R12E   Elev. c. 4000′
The presence of alder or sycamore trees here resulted in the descriptive name. It is a
large spring, capable of watering about three hundred and fifty head of stock.
Ref.: 59, p. 417

ALI WUA PASS
Papago = "little pond pass"
Pima   T17S R3W
Papago Indians apply this name to the pass in the Ajo Range. See also Gusano Pass,
Pima (name used by local ranchers) Ref.: 329

ALKALI: Any reader of western novels is familiar with reference to alkali dust choking
travelers. The word *alkali* is often used to refer to light colored and salt-impregnated
ground which pulverizes to a choking, salty tasting dust. The following place names are
examples of the word *alkali*, which may refer to such ground or to the alkaline taste of
water at the locations:

Alkali Canyon	Gila	T8N R11E
Alkali Canyon	Yavapai	T10N R2E
Alkali Flats	Cochise	
See Willcox, Cochise		
Alkali Spring	Mohave	(1) T15N R12W (2) T18N R19W
Alkali Valley	Apache/Navajo	T34N R22E
Alkaline Seep	Mohave	T39N R13W
There are two such seeps in this section.		
Alkaline Spring	Yavapai	T15N R16W

ALLAH (R.R. STN.)
Maricopa   T7N R4W   Elev. c. 1100′
Brill's Ranch on the Hassayampa River (and a stop on the Ashfork-Phoenix railroad
branch) had many cottonwoods and was a favored picnic spot. It so resembled the desert
oasis described in *The Garden of Allah* (a novel) that it became known by that name,
shortened by usage to Allah.
P.O. est. Nov. 16, 1917, Frances E. Sanger, p.m.; resc. Jan. 22, 1919
Ref.: 18a; AHS, G.E.P. Smith; 203, p. 10; 242

ALL-AMERICAN CANAL
Yuma
This canal, first proposed in 1931 and completed in 1940, lies entirely within the U.S. It
is about eighty miles long. Ref.: Williams; 5, p. 273; 242

ALLAN LAKE
Coconino   T17N R9E   Elev. c. 8000′
The lake takes its name from that of "Bronco Jim" Allan, a pioneer horseman in the
region. Ref.: 18a

ALLEN FLAT
Cochise   T14S R22E
This flat is named for a ranch owned by a pioneer named Allen. Ref.: Bennett

ALLEN SPRING

Yavapai   T15N R2E

The spelling is probably an error, as the spring was named for "Bronco Jim" Allan and his family. This large spring supplies water for the area of Jerome. See Allan Lake, Coconino Ref.: Allan

ALLENVILLE

Maricopa   T1S R3W   Elev. 840'

This small community is south of Buckeye.

ALLIGATOR, THE

Coconino (Grand Canyon)   T31N R2E   Elev. c. 5700'

The name describes this low-lying ridge below Mohave Point. Ref.: Kolb

ALMA

Maricopa   T1N R5E   Elev. c. 850'

The first settlers here were Henry and William N. Standage, members of the Mormon Battalion. First called Stringtown because its houses were strung along a country road, this place took shape from 1880 to 1884, being in the latter year declared a ward of the Mormon Church and named for a prophet in *The Book of Mormon*. Today it is part of Mesa. Ref.: 322, p. 9; 225, p. 218; 18a; 329

ALMA

Pinal   Elev. c. 2500'

Frank M. Doll founded this location in 1891, on the San Pedro River near its juncture with Aravaipa Creek. The name may be a corruption of Alamo (Spanish = "cottonwood"). The place with its post office went out of existence following the murders of Doll and his son by an unknown person. Mrs. Doll survived the attack.
P.O. est. May 12, 1891, Frank M. Doll, p.m.; disc. Aug. 22, 1898
Ref.: 18a; 238, pp. 44-45; 264

ALMA MESA

Greenlee   T1N R32E   Elev. c. 6000'

Lying close to the New Mexico border and the town of Alma, New Mexico, this mesa takes its name from the town, which in turn was named by Morris E. Coates for the town in Colorado from which he came. Ref.: 18a

ALPINE

Apache   T12N R25E   Elev. c. 8000'

Apparently the location of this community has changed, for on the Post Office Site Location dated April 5, 1892, it is given as T11N/R30E, Sec. 11, moving to the east 1350' in 1934. Alpine lies in Bush Valley, named from a log house called Fort Bush by its builder–owner Anderson Bush, who arrived in 1876. Bush sold his land c. 1879 to William Maxwell and Fred Hamblin, Mormons, who then sold to Mormon settlers from Alpine, Utah. For a brief time the settlers called their new community Frisco, as it is near the head of the Frisco (San Francisco) River, but the elevation and pine trees led to an easy transfer of the name Alpine from Utah to Arizona. The Mormon explorer Jacob Hamblin (d. Aug. 31, 1886) is buried at Alpine.

    Bush Valley is said to be the highest place in the United States for successful farming.
P.O. est. Jan. 7, 1885, William G. Black, p.m. (An error in reading the date is a possibility. See text above). Ref.: Noble; 225, pp. 186, 187; 5, p. 429; AHS, Evans Coleman File and "Record of Heber Ward, Luna, New Mexico" *ms.*; 242

ALSAP BUTTE

Coconino (Grand Canyon)   T33N R4E   Elev. c. 7000'

Frank Bond of the USGS in 1930 named this butte for John Taber Alsap (b. Kentucky 1832; d. 1886), who in 1861 settled near what was to become Phoenix. A farmer, lawyer, district attorney and first treasurer for Arizona Territory, Alsap was often called "the Father of Maricopa County." Ref.: 18a; 62; 329

ALTAR VALLEY   pro.: /altar/
Spanish = "altar"; "sacred"
Pima   T15–21S R9–10E   Elev. c. 4000'
In 1693 when Fr. Eusebio Kino and Juan Mateo Manje stopped at the place where the
Altar River disappeared into the sand, Kino dubbed the spot El Altar. From here the
river flows south farther into Mexico, but the valley extends north. The present road goes
from the valley to the town of Altar, Mexico. The valley was named for the mission
there. Pumpelly called this valley Baboquivera Plain. Ref.: 329; 269, p. 228; Kitt; 43,
p. 278

ALTO
Spanish = "high"
Santa Cruz   T21S R14E   Elev. 4650'
This mining community had an on-again-off-again existence, having been worked
intermittently by Spaniards or Mexicans from c. 1687 until c. 1857 when Apaches drove
them away, and by Americans until troops were removed from the region to serve in the
Civil War. In 1875 Mark Lully reopened the workings under the name Goldtree Mine
(named by Joseph Goldtree), a venture which also faded. Spaniards called the hill
location El Plomo (= "lead") because the ore contained lead. Its community was also
called El Plomo. The next developer was Joseph Bond, a well educated mining engineer,
who settled here with his wife, Minnie. Both are buried near the old workings. As of the
1970s, nothing other than a ranch was at the location.
P.O. applied for Aug. 2, 1901, U.L. Logan, p.m.; p.o. est. March 6, 1907, A. W. Larson,
p.m.; resc. June 10, 1907; reest. June 6, 1912, Minnie A. Bond, p.m.; disc. Dec. 30,
1933 Ref.: Kitt; 286, pp. 196-197, 198, 209; Seibold; 242; Lenon

ALUM CANYON
Santa Cruz   T22S R15E   Elev. c. 4000'
Alum in the creek water flowing through this canyon gives the water a bitter taste. This
led to naming the Alum Mine, developed during the late 1850s and abandoned during the
Civil War because of Apache attacks in the region. The canyon is also called Alum
Gulch. Ref.: 286, pp. 22, 23

ALVAREZ, CHARCO DE   pro.: /ælvərez/
Pima   T19S R4E
The name for this watering place, now reflected in that of the Alvarez Mountains in
which it is located, was among the very earliest recorded on regional maps of the mid-
1850s. Both the *charco* and the mountains were named for a Mexican rancher.
Ref.: Ketchum; 242

AMADO   pro.: /əmádo/
Santa Cruz   T20S R12E   Elev. 3070'
In 1910 Manuel H. Amado established a store with a post office at a station on the
Tucson-Nogáles branch of the S.P.R.R. How long his family had been in the region may
be reflected in the name of a mine in existence nearby in 1857: La Mina de Amado. See
also Pattison Siding, Santa Cruz
P.O. est. as Amadoville, April 5, 1910, Manuel H. Amado, p.m.; name changed to
Amado, April 3, 1920 (The first P.O. location was at T20S/R13E, Sec. 5); disc. March
7, 1958 Ref.: 18a; AHS; 242

AMARGOSA WASH
Spanish = "bitter"
Pima   T18S R12E
The USGS in 1965 so named this wash because dissolved minerals give a bitter taste to
its water. Ref.: 329

AMARILLA, CIENEGA   pro.: /siénə æmariy'yə/
Spanish = "yellow marshy place"
Apache   T26N R31E   Elev. c. 6000'
Rain at this spot dampens it so that native grass grows luxuriantly. It dries to a golden
shade among a multitude of golden flowers. See Michaels, Saint, Apache
Ref.: 141, p. 133

AMBERON FLAT pro.: /əmberan/

Apache   T4N R27E   Elev. 8300'

Amberon Anglevson, a freighter, in 1877 built a corral on this flat and kept his horses in it. In 1880 his horses stampeded and killed him, after which the name came into use. Ref.: Butler; Wentz

AMBOY

Mohave   Elev. c. 500'

In early 1865 Charles Debrille Poston suggested that a military post be established on this point at the mouth of the Bill Williams River. Why the name was chosen is not known. Ref.: 18a

AMERICAN FLAG

Pinal   T10S R16E   Elev. 4842'

Isaac Lorraine (b. Martinique) in the late 1870s located and developed the American Flag Mine and also c. 1882 a cattle ranch called the American Flag Ranch, where he lived for about eight years. He then moved to Phoenix, where he had a real estate business. In 1881 The Richardson Mining Company bought the American Flag Mine. P.O. est. Dec. 28, 1880, Peter H. Loss, p.m.; disc. July 16, 1890 Ref.: AHS, Emerson O. Stratton *ms.*; 264; 238, pp. 24-25

AMERICAN GULCH

Gila   T10N R9E

This gulch takes its name from the American Flag Mine on the gulch. Ref.: Pieper (through Woody)

AMERICAN MINE

Mohave   T11N R12W   Elev. c. 4000'

In 1874 W. M. Shoulters located the American Mine near the summit of the highest peak on the southern slope of the Hualapai Mountains. He sold it in 1878 to W. M. Richards, John Covin, John Pemberton, and Joseph Frish, Cornishmen. No traces remain of this mining camp. Ref.: Babcock; Harris; 215, p. 110

AMERICAN PEAK

Santa Cruz   T23S R16E   Elev. 5254'

In the early 1860s the American Mine was in operation. The peak took its name from that of the mine. Ref.: 286, p. 277

AMERICAN RANCH

Yavapai   c. T12½N R3W   Elev. c. 5000'

On the road from Ehrenberg to Prescott, James Harrison Lee (d. 1915) operated a ranch and stage stop as early as 1875. He sold out in 1898. Ref.: 314, p. 74; Kitt; AHS; *Southwest Stockman* (Jan. 28, 1898), p. 5

AMERICAN VALLEY

Yavapai

In this valley was the American Ranch. Here Jacob Smith was killed by Indians in early March 1870. This fact may have given rise to the story cited by Barnes in his 1935 *Arizona Place Names* that a man named Lee was slain by Indians, his stage station then being leased to a man who left poisoned flour in the empty store — flour which caused the deaths of twenty-four Indians whose bodies were found there. The story is interesting, but not true. Ref.: *Arizona Miner* (March 5, 1870), p. 3; 18a

AMERIND FOUNDATION MUSEUM

Cochise   T16S R22E

This privately owned and operated museum in Dragoon is devoted to southwestern American Indian culture and artifacts. It was founded by Mr. and Mrs. W. S. Fulton. Not regularly open to visitors because its staff is devoted to full-time research, the museum can be visited by making an appointment in advance. Its name is a contraction of *AMER*ican *IND*ian.

AMOLE   pro.: /əmówliy/
Spanish = "soap root"
Pima   T17S R18E   Elev. 3917'
Innumerable elata yucca cactus (*amole*) grow in the vicinity, hence this descriptive
name for this point on the railroad. Ref.: 18a; 246, p. B-157

AMOLE PEAK   pro.: /əmówliy/
Spanish = "soap root"
Pima   T13S R12E
This highest peak in the Tucson Mountains is one-half mile east of Wasson Peak. A
prospector told Eldred D. Wilson and his partner Jenkins, U. of A. geologists, that
Amole was the name for this peak. Natives in the area use yucca cactus (amole) to make
soap, but the growth of amole is no more abundant here than elsewhere.
Ref.: 10, p. 33; G.E.P. Smith, Letter to USGS Board on Geographic Names (Nov. 3,
1939)

AMSTER
Gila   c. T2N R16E
This small community (northeast of Globe about seven miles) was named for N. L.
Amster, president of the Shannon Copper Company. Ref.: 203, p. 10; Kitt

AMUS-OVI
Navajo   Elev. c. 6000'
Amus-ovi is, according to Harold C. Colton (founder of the Museum of Northern
Arizona), the Hopi name of long standing, replaced by the more recent Navajo name of
Zillesa Peak for this round butte. The USGS has further confused the name by officially
deciding on Little Black Mountain. Ref.: 329; Letter, Colton to Frank Bond (March 12,
1932)

ANASAZI RUINS
Apache   T27N R9W
The name *anas* means "the old ones" and refers to ancient peoples formerly inhabiting
this part of the Southwest.

ANCHA, SIERRA   pro.: /siyerə ančə/
Spanish: *ancha* = "broad"; *sierra* = "mountains"
Gila   T7N R12E   Elev. 6263'
The base of these mountains is uncut by canyons, thus making it appear broad before it
separates into peaks, which include McFadden, Baker, Aztec, and McFadden Horse
Mountain. These mountains have been known by their name since c. 1860. Indians
called them *Ewee-Tha-Quaw-Ai* ("wide ranges of rocks"). The range concealed many
Indian bands, as reflected in the number of skirmishes with Apaches listed in army
records, the first occurring in 1864 and the last in 1875.
Ref.: 159, pp. 441, 447, 692; 107, III, 304; *Weekly Arizona Miner* (Aug. 13, 1864),
State Library Archives; Woody

ANCHA EXPERIMENTAL FOREST, SIERRA
Gila   T5N R14E
Its 13,150 acres were set aside in 1938. See Ancha, Sierra, Gila

ANCHA FOREST RESERVE, SIERRA
Gila
This reserve was established following a recommendation in 1900 to do so. See Ancha,
Sierra, Gila Ref.: 116, p. 729

ANCHA MINES, SIERRA
Gila
White spots on the Sierra Ancha are caused by ore dumps of the asbestos mine there.
Gradually accumulated dust is altering its snow-like appearance. See Ancha, Sierra,
Gila Ref.: 5, p. 365; Woody

ANDERSON CANYON
Cochise   T15S R29E
In the early 1900s a settler named Anderson had his home here near Anderson Spring, also named for him. Ref.: Riggs

ANDERSON CANYON
Coconino   T18N R10E
Jim Anderson came with his partner W. H. Ashurst and their stock from California. Anderson settled on a point named Anderson Point for him, but the Forest Service altered the name to Truman Point. Anderson Gap and Anderson Mesa also carry his name. Anderson Mesa, which is pine covered, merges with the rough volcanic area near the San Francisco Peaks. Ref.: Mrs. Anderson; 18a

ANDRADE'S RANCH
Pima   T17S R17E   Elev. 3800'
In the early 1870s Jose Andrade (b. 1853, Mexico; d. Sept. 27, 1902; spelled "Andrada" in 1880 Territorial census) homesteaded a ranch in Davidson Canyon, a spot favored by Apaches, who attacked travelers on this route from Tucson to Fort Crittenden and, after 1879, to Tombstone. In 1880 a mine was located here. This led to the establishment of California Camp at the California or Mann Mine. By 1880 Andrade was living in Tucson. Ref.: *Arizona Star* (Sept. 30, 1902), p. 1; Kitt; 286, pp. 141, 150; 63

ANDRUS CANYON
Mohave   T33N R11W
This canyon, also called Andrus Draw and Donsill Canyon, takes its name from that of Capt. James Andrus, a stockman, who developed a seep into Upper Andrus Spring and Lower Andrus Spring, at least as early as 1909. The date may be earlier, as Andrus led pursuers of Indians who had killed Dr. James M. Whitmore and Robert McIntire near Pipe Springs in 1866. Ref.: 18a; 329

ANEGAM
Papago: *an* = "slender tree" (desert willow); *gam* = "many"
Pima   T12S R3E   Elev. 1761'
This Papago village was called Anagam by Kino in 1698 and Tocodoy Onigam in 1699. Hodge in 1910 called in Anicam. Lumholtz spelled the name Anekam, noting that the name meant "where the *an* tree grows, the *an* having long leaves and the pink flowers of the desert willow." It has also been called Francisco del Adid.
Ref.: 58; 262, p. 16; 57, p. 191; 43, I, 205, 398, 399

ANGELICA WASH
Spanish = "angelic"; "heaven-born"
Pima   T17S R12E
This wash was named by the USGS because early miners believed a silver lode underlay the headwaters of the wash, hence finding it was "heaven-born." Ref.: 326

ANGELL
Coconino   T21N R10E   Elev. 5000'
On the A. & P.R.R. this was a watering stop for steam engines. It was named for the first assistant railroad superintendent. A siding today serves for loading red cinders from a volcanic mountain for use on the roadbed. The entire mountain is gradually disappearing. A small workers' settlement is here. Ref.: 18a; Edward C. Smith, Letter (Jan. 20, 1960)

ANGEL'S ALCOVE
Coconino (Grand Canyon)
George Wharton James named this place because it is a "vast double-cornered recess ... on the right side going down the Bright Angel Trail." Ref.: 178, p. 60

ANGEL, SAN
Mohave   T38N R9W
Fr. Silvestre Vélez de Escalante in 1776 named this small mesa.
Ref.: 42, p. 60

ANGLE MONUMENT
Santa Cruz   T24S R13E
The name describes the point about twelve miles west of Nogales where the angle occurs in the boundary between the United States and Mexico. A small monument lies one-half mile east and another one-half mile west of this point. Ref.: Ketchum

ANGORA
Gila   T11N R10E   Elev. c. 6000'
The postmaster here raised goats, hence the name.
P.O. est. May 6, 1900, John F. Holder, p.m.; disc. Feb. 5, 1908 Ref.: 18a; 242

ANGOSTURA, LOS CERRITOS DE
Spanish: *cerritos* = "little hills"; *angostura* = "narrow"
Pima
These *cerritos* connect at their northwesterly tip with the Ajo Mountains, forming a low narrow lava ridge not at any point more than two hundred feet high. They are on the Mexico-U.S. border. The name is that used by Mexicans for the gap in which is Menager Dam (1915). See Artesia Mountain, Pima Ref.: 57, p. 409

ANIMAS MOUNTAINS, LAS
Pima   T20S R5E   Elev. 3043'
This small mountain mass was called Sierra las Animas by Roskruge in 1893. It has also borne the following names: Las Animas Range (1912 Lumholtz); Animas Mountain (1939 Douglas Aeronautical Chart). Ref.: 329

ANITA
Coconino   T29N R1E   Elev. c. 6000'
The railroad line which now extends to the Grand Canyon originally terminated here. The line was created, not to serve tourists, but the Anita Mines (T22N/R2E) east of what came to be called Anita Junction after completion of the railroad to the Grand Canyon in 1901. The mines, opened c. 1898, were named for a relative of Fred Nellis, their owner.
P.O. est. Dec. 25, 1913, Grace E. Lockridge, p.m.; disc. Aug. 331, 1918
Ref.: 18a; 333, p. 41; 178, p. 15; 242

ANITA
Pima
In 1926 this was a small village on West Grant Road, then outside Tucson city limits. It included the Yaqui settlement, site of annual Indian Easter ceremonies. Anita now is a part of Tucson.

ANKRIM'S LANDING
Probably Yuma
Ankrim's Landing on the Colorado earned a place in history when the Colorado steamer *Uncle Sam* sank there on June 22, 1853. As Ankrim was then in business with Jaeger, the fact suggests that the landing was near the present Yuma. Capt. William Ankrim (d. March 1859) was a partner with William Jaeger, ferrying emigrants across the Colorado River prior to 1859 when Ankrim became a steamboat captain on the river. Later Ankrim bought Capt. George A. Johnson's interest in the ferry company. Ankrim also ran sheep to California, at one time herding twenty-two thousand to the West Coast market. He once reported battling Apaches en route, killing forty and losing five of his own men. The fact that he said the Indians used clubs suggests they may have been Mohave, who used clubs as a favored weapon. Ankrim also asserted that the Indians used gold bullets. Ref.: 315, pp. 213, 258, 262, 269; *Daily Alta California* (April 4, 1859)

ANNADALE
Mohave
On old Hwy 66, just east of Hackberry
Elev. c. 2500'

Mrs. Anna McCaw, whose first name was used for this small settlement, lived here from c. 1940 until she sold out her property in c. 1951. Ref.: Schaefer

ANNEX RIDGE
Yavapai
T20N R10W

In 1972 this name was proposed to the USGS as being descriptive of a ridge which appears annexed to a dome here. Ref.: 329

ANTARES pro.: /ænteyriys/
Mohave
T24N R15W
Elev. 3608'

It is not known why this railroad section house was named for the brightest star in the constellation Scorpio. No town remains here. Ref.: 18a; Harris; 203, p. 11

ANTELOPE: The word *antelope* occurs in many Arizona place names. At one time antelope were abundant and they are still to be found in several locations. Examples of such locations are as follows:

Antelope Canyon	Coconino	T41N R9W
Antelope Canyon	Greenlee	T11S R32E
Antelope Creek	Yavapai	(1) T9N R5W (2) T11N R2E
Antelope Creek	La Paz	In Cullen Valley

This location was named by A. H. Peeples in 1863 after he had killed five antelope here. Ref.: 224, II, 111

Antelope Dam	Yavapai	T18N R4W
Antelope Draw	Coconino	T15N R10E
Antelope Flat	Coconino	T27N R4E
Antelope Flat	Graham	T1N R21E
Antelope Hill	Coconino	(1) T23N R5E Elev. 8234'
		(2) T25N R7E Elev. 7008'
Antelope Hill	Yavapai	

See Black Canyon Hill, Yavapai

Antelope Hill	Yuma	T8S R17W Elev. 816'

On November 22, 1775 Fr. Garcés called this location Cerro de Santa Cecelia. The Indians, however, called it Cerro del Metate, derived from the Nahuatl word *metlatl*, referring to a grinding stone for corn. This is probably the same place referred to as Las Metates on early American-made maps of the region. In 1854 Lt. N. Michler wrote that while his group was camped here, about thirty Yuma Indians arrived to collect stones suitable for hewing into metates. He said that Maricopa and Pima Indians also arrived for the same purpose. See Tacna, Yuma Ref.: 77, p. 128, Note 40, and p. 129, Note 41; 105, p. 105

Antelope Hills	Apache	T9N R24E
Antelope Hills	Pima	T14S R10W Elev. 1532'
Antelope Hills	Yavapai	T17N R2E
Antelope Hill Stage Station	Yuma	T8S R17W

This stage station was built in 1857 by John Kilbride, whose place is not noted on the original Butterfield Route map of 1858, although it is on the 1859 itinerary. See Antelope Hill, Yuma

Antelope House	Apache	T5N R27E Elev. c. 6000'
		(In Canyon del Muerto)

The name derives from red and white pictographs of antelope on the canyon wall above the ruin. Navajo Indians made the painting in the mid-19th century. Ref.: 5, p. 420; 331, p. 23

Antelope Island	Coconino/Utah	T42N R9E	

This location is also known as Lake Powell Island and as San Carlos Island. Ref.: 329

Antelope Lake	Apache	T24N R28E	

Antelope Lake	Coconino	T21N R2E	Elev. c. 7000'

In 1934 to help assure its water supply, the town of Williams dammed this site about seven miles southeast. It was named to honor James Kennedy, but by 1936 the local name had taken hold and it was also evident that the typically sieve-like volcanic bottom would not hold water, and the project was abandoned. Ref.: 124, p. 147

Antelope Mesa	Greenlee	T2S R31E	

Antelope Mesa	Navajo	T28N R20E	

See Kawaioku, Navajo

Antelope Mountain	Apache	T8N R27E	Elev. 9003'

Antelope Mountain	Yavapai		

See Antelope Peak, Yavapai

Antelope Park	Coconino	T19N R8E	

Antelope Pass	Coconino	T38N R7E	

Antelope Peak	Pinal	T6S R2E	Elev. 3121'

ANTELOPE PEAK
Yavapai   T10N R5W   Elev. 5786'

In 1863 A. H. Peeples, a member of the Pauline Weaver prospecting party, killed three antelope in the nearby valley and made jerky. He called the creek west of the hill Antelope Creek. A man named Alvaro took time to climb to the top of the peak while others looked for gold in the creek. At the top of the hill Alvaro found a one-acre basin containing many gold nuggets. Meanwhile, men in the arroyo also found gold. The party called the hill both Rich Hill and Antelope Hill. They named the site of their prospecting Weaver Gulch. Ref.: 226, p. 17, 224, III, 111; 168, pp. 64, 65; 163, p. 98; AHS

Antelope Plains	Mohave		

See Uinkaret Plateau, Mohave

Antelope Point	Apache	T5N R10W	

Antelope Point	Coconino	T31N R3W	

Antelope Ravine	Pinal	T9S R13E	

Antelope Ridge	Apache	T39N R24E	

Antelope Spring	Cochise	T20S R24E	

Antelope Spring	Coconino		

See Flagstaff, Coconino

Antelope Spring	Mohave	T41N R9W	

This spring is in Antelope Valley, the eastern part of Wonsits Valley north of Toroweap Valley. Mohave Indians call the spring Aha'a Chi or Ha'a Chi, the name referring to long bunch grass (*ichi*) which grows near water. See Wonsits Valley, Mohave
Ref.: Dobyns; G.E.P. Smith

Antelope Spring	Mohave	T26N R18W	

Antelope Springs	Navajo	T29N R18E	

See Jadito, Navajo

Antelope Station	Yavapai		

See Cordes, Yavapai, and Antelope Valley, Yavapai

Antelope Valley	Mohave	T37N R6W	

Maj. John Wesley Powell mapped it as Wonsits Valley (Piute = "antelope"). In the late 1800s when there were many, many antelope in this broad region, the entire area was called Antelope Valley, but today it is sectioned into Wild Bank Valley, Upper Clayhole Valley, Little Clayhole Valley, and Cabin Valley. Ref.: 329; 140, p. 37; Schellbach File, G.C.

ANTELOPE VALLEY
Yavapai   T10N R5W   Elev. 3450'
For the discovery of gold which resulted in the development of this small community, see Antelope Peak, Yavapai. To serve prospectors and miners who rushed to the place, a stage station (Antelope Station) was established in 1863 by William Partridge near a store owned by G. H. Wilson. Wilson's pigs broke into Partridge's place, leading to vicious enmity between the men. In the early 1870s, Charles C. Stanton arrived, after whom the growing community was first named. He played up the feud by bribing Mexicans to tell Partridge that "the owner of the pigs is out to get you," even though Wilson had said in public he would pay for the damage. Partridge shot Wilson on sight and was jailed. Stanton, who wanted to run things by himself, then contrived to get rid of the only store owner left — Timmerman. With him also gone, Stanton took over all trade and stage operations, setting up a new post office under his name. This was more than the citizens could take, and they soon had the name changed to Antelope Valley. Stanton did not last much longer than his post office, for in 1886 he was killed by a Mexican avenging his sister, whom Stanton had insulted. Mining activities dropped off, then discontinued, but were renewed c. 1896. Today Stanton is a ghost town. In 1959 *The Saturday Evening Post* bought it, intending to use it as a prize in an advertising contest. In late 1978 it was bought by the Lost Dutchman Mining Association for use by members only. P.O. est. as Stanton, March 5, 1875, Charles C. Genung, p.m.; disc. Dec. 13, 1890; reest. as Stanton, Sept. 24, 1894; disc. May 23, 1905 Ref.: 359, p. 72; *Daily Arizona Miner* (Dec. 20, 1897), p. 4; *Arizona Daily Star* (May 25, 1959); Varney

Antelope Wash	Coconino	T26N R12E
Antelope Wash	Mohave	T19N R13W
Antelope Wash	Yavapai	T18N R4W

ANTISELL RIDGE
Graham   T5S R17E
Unnamed until 1954, this ridge was named for Dr. Thomas Antisell, who served as a geologist with the railroad surveying party in the 1850s. He was the first to geologically describe this area. Ref.: 329

ANTLER SPRING
Mohave   T12N R11W   Elev. 5000'
The spring takes its name from the Antler Mine about two thousand feet lower on Arrastra Mountain. Ref.: 329

ANTONIO, RIO SAN
This was the name given by explorers to one branch of the Verde River which was north of the present Prescott. It was so called by Oñate in 1604. Ref.: 15, I, 155, 348

ANVIL MOUNTAIN
La Paz   T1N R11W   Elev. 2340'
Barnes says this place looks like a blacksmith's anvil. Ref.: 18a

ANVIL ROCK
Yavapai   T19N R8W   Elev. 5700'
In use at least as early as 1869, the name describes this huge volcanic rock, which looks like a blacksmith's anvil. A stage station near its base was owned and operated by C. P. Wilder. Ref.: 18a; 163, p. xxiv; *Arizona Miner* (Sept. 30, 1871), p. 2

A ONE MOUNTAIN
Coconino   T21N R6E   Elev. 8300'
The A 1 brand reflected in this name was used here by the Arizona Cattle Company in the early 1890s. A former insurance fire patrol chief from Chicago, Capt. Ben Bullwinkle, was company manager. An inexperienced and wild rider, Bullwinkle in 1896 rode a horse to death on the road into Flagstaff, being killed in the animal's death plunge. The mountain name was changed in 1934 from A One Crater and Crater Hill (a five hundred foot volcanic cone at north end of mountain). Ref.: 18a; Slipher

A 1 RANCH SPRING

Coconino   c. T29N R9E

The spring is on the Little Colorado River, about five miles above Tanner Crossing. See
A One Mountain, Coconino Ref.: 141, p. 158

APACHE: Unquestionably the Apache Indians have made more impact on place names
in Arizona than that of other Indian tribes in the state. Although referred to as though they
were members of a single cohesive group, in fact Apache Indians gradually came to be
recognized as particular groups. The Apaches as such did not use that name for
themselves, but — as is relatively common — used a term meaning "the people." The first
reference to these Indians by name occurs in the record of the 1581 Espejo expedition, in
which they were termed *Apichi*. How little Spaniards realized they were dealing with a
variety of tribes is reflected in a name used somewhat later: *Apachu de Nabahu* (the
Spanish *j* has roughly the effect of *h*, hence *Navajo*.) The source citing that fact notes that
Indians of the Jemez pueblo called the tribe *Apachu*, a word meaning "Strangers." A later
study (1971) notes that the Zuñi word for "enemy" is *aabachu*. Still another source asserts
that the Maricopa Indians called these Indians *Apache*, a word again meaning "enemy." A
variant on the same concept is that the name *Apache* derives from Cuchan (Yuma) *apa* (=
"man"), *ahwa* (= "war, fight"), and *tche* (nominal suffix to form plurals), thus resulting in
Apahuatche (= "hostile man, warrior"), contracted to *Apache*.

As for what groups were believed by the Spaniards in 1799 to be Apache Indians, they
include the following recognized divisions: Tonto; Chiricaguis (Chiricahua); Gilenos
(Gila); several in New Mexico (Mimbrenos, Taracones, Mescaleros, Lipanes), and the
Llaneros and Navajos. The names are familiar to Arizonans, except for Llaneros, who
were associated with what is today the Pinal Mountains region. Included by later people
among Apaches are also the Apache-Yuma, Apache-Mohave, Apache-Yavapai. By
whatever name they were known, Apache Indians were enemies to others, whether by their
own desire or by being forced into conflict through the necessity of defending themselves
and their territory. Ref.: 49, p. 122; 326, p. 91; 77, p. 457, Note 14; 103, p. 72

The following are examples of place names with the designation *Apache*:

Apache   Cochise   T20S R31E   Elev. 4382'

The monument, about all that remains here, was dedicated on April 29, 1934, to commemorate
Geronimo's surrender in 1886. That event, however, took place several miles to the southeast (see
Skeleton Canyon, Cochise). For a discussion of Apache Indians, see entry on *Apache*.
P.O. est. Feb. 26, 1908 (The first name proposed was Lusk, but the village was already named
Apache), J. W. Richhart, p.m.; disc. Aug. 15, 1943 Ref.: 18a; 242

Apache   Yavapai

See Apache, Fort, Navajo
P.O. est. Jan. 7, 1873, John A. Meredith, p.m.; disc. Aug. 11, 1875 Ref.: 242

Apache Butte   T6N R25E   Elev. 9773'

Apache Butte   Navajo   T18N R18E   Elev. 5186'

Apache, Camp   Navajo

See Apache, Fort, Navajo

APACHE CAMP   Pima

This was the Apache Mine camp owned by E. O. Stratton and Bob Leatherwood in
1881. Following a quarrel, both men lacked funds to buy the other out, so Stratton
turned over his entire interest for one silver dollar. He then developed the Stratton Mine
nearby. The Apache Mine failed in 1882. See Oracle, Pinal Ref.: AHS, Emerson O.
Stratton *ms.*, and Chambers Collection, Box 12

Apache Canyon   Cochise   T18S R19E

Apache Canyon   Gila   T2N R13E

The USGS named this two-mile canyon in 1965 to clarify its location relative to Campaign Creek,
the name deriving from the fact that the latter was associated with Apache Indian wars in southern
Arizona. Ref.: 329

Apache Canyon   Graham   T11S R25E

Apache Canyon   Pima   T21S R11E

Apache Cave   Maricopa   T3N R10E   Elev. 4619'

This cave, sometimes called Skull Cave or Skeleton Cave, was named Apache Cave following a fierce battle on December 27, 1872, against Yavapai-Apache Indians hiding there with their leader Nanichaddi. The battle was under way with an officer named Ross commanding. An Apache scout called Nantaje led Maj. William Brown with troops to the battle. Bullets ricocheting off the cavern roof struck women and children in this cave. Their wailing led Brown to cease fire, giving the Indians a chance to surrender. To the contrary, the wails changed to the half-exultant death chant and about twenty Indians leaped over the cave rampart at the troops. Seven Yavapai were killed and the rest retreated. Meanwhile a third contingent of troops with officers Burns and Thomas in command had arrived at the top of the cliff above the cave. Burns harnessed two men with suspenders from other soldiers and lowered them so they could and did shoot directly at the Indians in the cave while other soldiers rolled boulders onto the Indians who attempted escape. When Maj. Brown once again called a halt to the fierce attack, the noise of crashing boulders, guns, and screams fell into silence. Thirty Yavapai survived. The bodies of the slain were left in the cave. Ref.: 5, pp. 367, 368; 49, pp. 190, 191, 196, 197, 199

Apache Chief   Gila   T9N R13E

This is a rock formation at Potato Butte, southeast of Young about four miles. About sixty feet high, it bears a remarkable resemblance to a hawk-nosed Indian profile. Ref.: McKinney

APACHE COUNTY

On February 24, 1879 Apache County was separated from Yavapai County, one of the four originally in Arizona Territory. In turn, the new county was destined to lose portions in the formation of additional counties. In 1881 that part between the Black and Gila Rivers went to form part of Graham County, and a great stretch of the original Apache County went into the formation of Navajo County. (For specific information see Navajo County.) Apache County was, of course, named for the Apache Indians.

Apache Creek   Greenlee   T6S R31E

See Apache Gulch, Greenlee

Apache Creek   Yavapai   T18N R6W

Apache de Xila

See *Apache*, and Gila River

Apache Flat   Maricopa/Yuma   T5S R9W

In 1869 this name was in use for the flat south of the overland stage route, between Oatman Flat and Burke's Station. See Oatman Flat, Maricopa.

APACHE, FORT

Navajo   T5N R22E   Elev. 5200'

Malaria prevalent at Camp Goodwin caused Maj. John Green, commanding officer of the First Cavalry stationed there, to seek a healthier camp site. He found such a place on the south bank of what was then called the White Mountain River (today East Fork, White River). The camp lay in territory traditionally Apache, but adjacent to Navajo country. Troops moved there on May 16, 1870, naming it Camp Ord to honor the departmental commander, Gen. Edward Otho Cresap Ord (d. July 22, 1883). The designation was short lived, for on August 1 it changed to Camp Mogollon, possibly because the mesa extended to the plateau forming the first portion of the Mogollon range. The second name lasted six weeks, giving way to the name Camp Thomas. As Maj. Gen. George Henry Thomas had died on March 28, 1870, the change was probably in his honor. "J.H.M." writing on September 10, 1870, refers to it as Fort Mogollon. Officially the name became Camp Thomas on September 12, 1870. The camp was then expanding, having its own sawmill, operated by steam generated by coal mined in the vicinity. The name again changed, becoming Camp Apache on February 2, 1871, having justly earned the name from the number of military forays being made against Apache Indians.

Camp Apache became headquarters for the Indian reservation established by Executive Order on November 9, 1871. The Indian Agency, however, was not at the same location as the military establishment, but was on the opposite side of the stream. On April 5, 1879 the name of the military location was changed to Fort Apache. The post continued to expand, with permanent buildings being erected, gradually encompassing the agency headquarters as well. The military withdrew in 1924, turning its facilities over to the agency.

P.O. est. as Apache, Jan. 7, 1873, John A. Meredith, p.m.; disc. Aug. 11, 1875; name changed to Fort Apache, Aug. 13, 1879, Frank Staples, p.m.

Ref.: 49, pp. 123, 147; 82, p. 165, Note 7; 224, III, 156; 206, p. 97; 345, III, 218; *Weekly Arizona Miner* (Oct. 1, 1870) and (Feb. 25, 1871), p. 2; *Tucson Citizen* (Feb. 8, 1873), p. 3, and (Dec. 10, 1870), p. 3; 242; 116, p. 538

APACHE INDIAN RESERVATION, FORT

Navajo   T5N R22E   Elev. 5200'

In 1870 Maj. John Green (see Apache, Fort, Navajo) reported that a reservation near the new military encampment would be feasible. An Executive Order on November 9, 1871 established a 1,681,920 acre reservation for Arivapai, Chiricahua, Coyotero, Mimbreno, Mogollon, Piñaleno, and Tsiltaden Apaches. Among these groups was no unity, for they contained subdivisions with linguistic differences and separate leaders, the cohesive unit usually being comprised of perhaps thirty households related by membership in a clan or by marriage. Such groups were frequently mutually hostile, a fact which led to trouble on the reservation. Initially the agency was called the White River Indian Reservation. Later a portion of it was cut off to form the San Carlos Indian Reservation.

The agency headquarters was on the opposite side of the East Fork of the White River (then called White Mountain River) from the military post. The army post was turned over to the agency in 1924. Ref.: 167, II, 374; 65, p. 155

Apache Gap   Maricopa   T2N R9E   Elev. 4510'

The S.P.R.R., seeking to develop a tourist attraction, asked Prof. Aubrey Drury to name points along the Apache Trail. He gave this place the name in 1917, asserting that Lt. Lawton with men of the 7th Cavalry had fought Apaches nearby. Ref.: 329

Apache Grove   Greenlee   T6S R31E   Elev. 3560'

See Apache Gulch, Greenlee

Apache Gulch   Greenlee   T6S R31E   Elev. 3800'

Indian ruins dot the mountainside and Apache Creek, which runs through this gulch. They are notable at Apache Grove in the gulch, hence the name. See also Stargo Gulch, Greenlee

Apache Hill   Gila   T2N R13E

Apache Junction   Pinal   T1N R8E   Elev. 1715'

The name derives from the fact that this thriving community lies at the junction of the Apache Trail with the main highway from Phoenix to Superior.

P.O. est. Aug. 15, 1950, Mrs. Marie L. Porter, p.m. Ref.: 264

Apache Lake   Gila/Maricopa   T3N R10E

Following the completion of Horse Mesa Dam in 1927, this seventeen-mile-long lake gradually formed by its impounded waters. The lake is adjacent to the Apache Trail, hence its name. Ref.: 5, p. 367

Apache Lake   Navajo   c. T5N R22E

The fact that it was in the vicinity of Fort Apache led to the naming of this intermittent lake by a member of the Wheeler expedition in 1873. It was said to be near the north fork of what was then called White Mountain River (today: East Fork, White River). Ref.: 345, III, 538; 163, p. 382

Apacheland (Site)   Pinal   T1S R8E

This was the original site of what is today Apache Junction.

Apache Leap   Pinal   T2S R12E   Elev. 4833'

According to legend, in the 1870s a cavalry detachment from Camp Pinal trapped seventy-five Apaches on the cliff here. Rather than surrender, the Apaches leaped to their deaths, hence the name. Ref.: 5, p. 349

APACHE MAID MOUNTAIN

Coconino/Yavapai   T16N R8E   Elev. 7315'

The name appears simply as Apache Maid on an 1875 military map, a fact lending some support to the assertion that c. 1873 Camp Verde troops battled Indians here, killing an Apache woman and taking her baby to the fort. However, Saxton Seth ("Boss") Acker, who moved to this location in 1884, said that a young Apache girl came from Camp Verde c. 1874 to this mountain, and it was decided to name the mountain for her. A third version of how the name originated says that emigrants en route through this area sent a scout ahead with instructions to send up smoke when he had found a route. The scout's fire signal attracted a lost and starving young Apache girl, whom one of the emigrants adopted. The name for the mountain has resisted attempts to change it, including one in 1908 by the Forest Service, which suggested substituting Bronco Mountain. It appears as Bronco Mountain on GLO 1896, 1903, and 1921. Ref.: 18a; Bunch

Apache Mine   Pinal
See Oracle, Pinal

Apache Mountains   Gila   T2N R16E
See Apache Peaks, Gila

Apache National Forest Apache/Green-   T4S R31E
                            lee/N.M.

First known as the Black Mesa Forest Reserve after its location partially on Black Mesa, this forest was established on August 17, 1898. The name was changed on July 1, 1908. The Arizona portion of this high timber country with its clear streams and deep ravines covers 677,823 acres. Ref.: 243, pp. 34, 36

APACHE PASS
Cochise   T15S R28E

In 1873 the Apache name for this pass was *Se-art-deits-art* (= "rocky country"). The Fremont Association party passed through this narrow and deep gorge in 1849, noting it was called Puerto del Dado, a name also reported by Lt. John G. Parke in 1854 during the survey for a railroad route to the Pacific Coast. Three years later the Butterfield Overland Stage established a station here, of which nothing now remains. Apache Pass was well named, for it was a spot favored by bands of Apache Indians to waylay emigrants and miners. Sometimes Apache bands numbered over one hundred. It was said that the four miles through the pass and the road beyond at either end held the bones of horses, mules, and oxen, and wreckage of wagons so thickly that travelers were never out of sight of them or of graves along the trail. At one time the pass was called Ewell's Pass, probably after Capt. Richard S. Ewell (see Buchanan, Fort, Santa Cruz). Fort Bowie was in Apache Pass. See Bowie, Fort, Cochise
P.O. est. as Apache Pass, Dec. 11, 1866, George Hand, p.m.; disc. (?)
Ref.: 351 (Smithsonian); 101, pp. vii and 18e, Note 20; 73, II, 132; 198, p. 41; 224, II, 169, 170; 4, p. 149; *Arizona Miner* (Oct. 22, 1870), p. 2; 242

Apache Pass	Santa Cruz	T22S R11E	
Apache Pass Dam	Santa Cruz	T22S R11E	
Apache Peak	Cochise	T18S R19E	Elev. 7680'
Apache Peak	Maricopa	(1) T2N R6E	
		(2) T6N R3E	Elev. 3219'
Apache Peak	Pima	T13S R11E	Elev. 3100'

APACHE PEAKS
Gila   T2N R16E   Elev. c. 4500'

The first name recorded for these individual peaks in 1869 was Apache Mountains, a name in use when the Wheeler expedition made its survey in 1873. This was a translation of Sierra Apache. (See Rockinstraw Mountain, Gila). However, as the USGS noted in 1931, *sierra* indicates a ridge or range, and hence is not applicable to this group of several peaks. Several military engagements with Apaches occurred in this locale in 1870 and 1871, underscoring the application of the name.
Ref.: 159, pp. 435, 436; 18a; 329; 345, III, 107, 221

Apache Peak	Pinal	T10S R16E	
Apache Point	Coconino	T33N R2W	Elev. 5850'
	(Grand Canyon)		

APACHERIA
Gila

This was a name in general use in the 18th century for territory occupied by Apache Indians. It was also the name used for a mushroom town which developed on the south side of Roosevelt Reservoir during its construction period.

Apache Ridge	Gila	T10N R12E

See Battleground Ridge, Gila

Apache Ruins, Fort   Gila

See Kinishba, Gila

Apache, Sierra   Gila

See Apache Peaks, Gila, and Rockinstraw Mountain, Gila

Apache Spring	Apache	T27N R26E
Apache Spring	Cochise	T14S R27E

See Apache Pass, Cochise

Apache Spring	Coconino	T24N R2W
Apache Spring	Gila	(1) T2N R13E (2) T4S R16S
Apache Spring	Graham	T11S R25E
Apache Spring	Maricopa	T6N R3E
Apache Spring	Pima	T18S R18E
Apache Spring	Santa Cruz	T20S R16E
Apache Spring	Yavapai	T17N R6W
Apache Spring Ranch	Santa Cruz	

See Gardner Canyon, Santa Cruz

Apache Springs	Navajo	T9N R21E

These springs on the Fort Apache Indian Reservation at the head of Forestdale Creek were named by Mormons who settled here in 1879 but were required to leave in 1880 because they were on reservation land. Ref.: 18a

Apache Terrace   Coconino (Grand Canyon)   T33N R2W

Named because it is just below Apache Point.

APACHE TRAIL
Maricopa/Gila   T3N R10E

This "trail" was developed in part by construction crews needing to take supplies and to work at Roosevelt Dam in 1905. In part the Southern Pacific Railroad developed it as a tourist attraction. The route followed the older Tonto Trail (so named because of Tonto Creek). It was also called the Yavapai Trail because it was used by tribe members who lived along Tonto Creek. The first part of the Apache Trail was cleared in 1904-05 by the Reclamation Service from Mesa to the dam site settlement of Roosevelt. It was literally carved in the sides of mountains and gorges, under the supervision of Louis C. Hill. On October 8, 1914, the Apache Trail Stage Company was incorporated, its purpose being to haul railroad passengers from the station at Globe over the Apache Trail to the station at Phoenix where they again boarded the train. To make the overland stage journey as interesting as possible, the company erected road signs bearing place names which stage drivers explained with fabulously interesting and wholly inaccurate stories. Many names were suggested by Prof. Aubrey Drury, whom the S.P.R.R. employed to help develop the Apache Trail itinerary. The charter for the stage line expired on October 8, 1939. Today the Apache remains a fascinating but hair-raising journey, particularly for those not accustomed to driving around hairpin curves in mountains. The drive is, however, one of the most beautiful in the United States. Ref.: Woody; State Library Archives; 329

Apache Wash	Graham	T2S R19E
Apache Wash	La Paz	T3N R18W
Apache Wash	Maricopa	T6N R3E

APEX

Coconino   T30N R2E   Elev. c. 6000'

The name derives from the fact that this is the highest point on the Grand Canyon branch of the railroad. There is a siding here. Ref.: 18a

APIARY WELL

Maricopa   T4S R8W   Elev. c. 250'

Wild bees at times were noticeably thick around the many wells in this area, but no more so at any one well than at others. Ref.: Parkman

APOLLO TEMPLE

Coconino (Grand Canyon)   T32N R5E   Elev. 6261'

The classical name is one of those applied by Mr. and Mrs. Francois E. Matthes c. 1902, a period when such names were a fad in the United States.
Ref.: Grand Canyon Archives

APOSTOLES, RIO DE LOS SANTOS

This is the name Fr. Kino applied to the Gila River on February 27, 1699 because of its four major tributaries. The name was still in use on the map dated April 7, 1805, sent by Capt. Clark to Pres. Jefferson. See Gila River Ref.: 77, p. 136, Note 48

AQUA LAVARIA

Pima

The name Lavaria (Spanish: *lavar* = "to wash, launder") suggests a possible use for this location, but who can say where the Indians did their laundry? See Nawt Vaya, Pima

AQUARIUS CLIFF

Mohave   T16N R11W

This almost continuous cliff rim extends along the Aquarius Mountains on the Bill Williams River to the Colorado River. The name is said to derive from the abundance of water along it. Ref.: 329, G.E.P. Smith, Letter

AQUARIUS MOUNTAINS

Mohave   T20N R11W   Elev. c. 4500'

In 1854 Capt. Amiel W. Whipple named this range because of the many streams flowing from it. There is another Aquarius Range to the northeast.
Ref.: 346, pp. 201, 202; Dobyns

AQUARIUS PLATEAU

Mohave/Yavapai   T19N R12W   Elev. c. 6000'

Powell says that his exploring party named this tableland Aquarius Plateau, noting that it was "dotted by numerous lakes." Ref.: 266, p. 139

AQUARIUS RANGE

Mohave   T16N R11W

Whipple is said to have named it this in 1853 because of the rainfall. It is not the same as Aquarius Mountains. Ref.: 346, p. 201, Note 6

ARABY

Yuma   T8S R22W   Elev. 141'

Prior to 1888 Hiram W. Blaisdell constructed the Araby Canal about fifteen miles east of Yuma at Araby and extended it to East Araby, nine miles east of Yuma. A railroad station was at Araby, later replaced by a siding. The region was called Araby Valley. On a postal site map locating the Blalock post office (1926), Araby is shown as the railroad station and site of the post office. Lloyd suggests the name Araby refers to the desert character of this land. See Blalack, Yuma Ref.: Mercer; 203, p. 12; 242

ARAVAIPA   pro.: /ǽrəváypə/

Graham   T6S R19E   Elev. 4563'

The first post office at the cattle ranch headquarters owned in 1883 by Burt Dunlap (b. Ohio; d. Dec. 26, 1930) was named Dunlap, changed in 1892 to Aravaipa because of

there being another Dunlap post office. The Dowdle family bought the ranch c. 1916.
See Aravaipa Canyon, Pinal
P.O. est. as Dunlap, March 22, 1883, Burt Dunlap, p.m.; name changed to Aravaipa,
April 18, 1892; disc. Sept. 15, 1893; reest. March 26, 1903, Rosa Firth, p.m. (loc.:
T5S/R20E); disc. Sept. 15, 1933 Ref.: Jennings; 18a; 242

ARAVAIPA, CAMP

Pinal   T6S R16E
Fort Aravaipa was established on May 8, 1860 at the junction of Aravaipa Creek with
the San Pedro River. The name was changed on August 6, 1860 to Fort Breckenridge.
On May 18, 1862 Col. James H. Carleton changed the name to Fort Stanford to honor
Gov. Leland Stanford of California. On November 1, 1865 the name was changed
again, this time to Camp Grant. The location of this post was changed during the early
part of 1873. See Grant, Old Camp, Pinal Ref.: 311, pp. 1,2; 238, p. 8

ARAVAIPA CANYON   pro.: /ærəváypə/

Nevome Pima: *aarivapa* = "girls"
Pinal/Graham   T7S R17E
The name of this canyon derives from that of the Indians living along the creek which
runs through it. Why the nickname "girls" was applied to Arivaipi Apaches is unknown
today. What "unmanly act" may have resulted in their name is not known. There is,
however, a possibility that it arose after they drove out the Sobaipuri Indians c. 1792 and
moved into their territory here, merging with Pima Indians to form a formerly unknown
group — Arivaipa Apaches — the name perhaps attributable to their having merged with
Indians whose way of life differed so from that of their conquerors. However, the
question is an open one, as the name Aribabia occurs nearly a century earlier (1700) on a
map. Kino in 1697 called the same location Babiteoida and also Busac. Lt. John Bourke
spelled the name Aravypa Canyon. The Arivaipa Apaches can scarcely be thought of as
unmanly, judging by the fact that prior to 1853 they had erased most towns in what was
then northern Mexico all the way to the Gila River and continued their depredations
after the Gadsden Purchase. The group was nearly wiped out by the Old Camp Grant
massacre (see Grant, Old Camp, Pinal), and in 1872 the survivors were moved to the
San Carlos Reservation, leaving their ruggedly beautiful canyon home.   It took some
San Carlos Reservation, leaving their ruggedly beautiful canyon home.
king
    It took some time for the name to settle down to its current spelling, meanwhile making
its way through the following: Aribabia (Kino 1697; map 1700); Aribaiba (Hodge,
Handbook); Aravaypa; Arayaipa; Arivapah; Arivapai; Arivaypa.
Ref.: 167, I, 83, 87; 224, III, 92; 163, p. 234

ARAVAIPA SPRINGS

Pinal   T6S R18E
These springs at the head of Aryvapai Canyon (*sic*) were the site of a camp used by
Troop I under 1st Lt. Reilly, with ten men each from Troops M and L, 5th Cavalry,
under 1st Lt. Jacob Almy. The contingent set up a camp on February 3, 1872 and
occupied it for the next two months. It had been used in August 1871 by Gen. Crook.
Ref.: *Citizen* (March 23, 1872), p. 1

ARCADIA

Maricopa   T2N R4E
This was formerly a distinct and separate group of handsome residences on the lower
part of Camelback Mountain in Scottsdale. Ref.: 5, p. 354

ARCH CANYON

Pima   T16S R4W
A double arch in Organ Pipe Cactus National Monument gave rise to this descriptive
name. One is one hundred twenty-five feet long by thirty feet high, with a smaller arch
topping it, measuring ten feet long by six high. Ref.: Hensen

ARCH IN THE SKY

Coconino   T40N R13E
The name describes a natural arch one hundred and seventy-seven feet high by two
hundred and thirty-five feet wide, named by Frank E. Masland, the first white

"discoverer," who viewed it through binoculars in July 1952. In 1954 he made an expedition to it, noting that it is of Navajo sandstone and that when one looks directly up at it, only the arch in the sky can be seen, hence the name. Ref.: 329

ARCH TANK
Yuma   T3S R19W   Elev. c. 1500'
A natural arch about seven feet high faces this natural waterhole. Said to be "the most beautiful natural tank in the world," it is difficult to visit because it is in a narrow, steep-walled canyon. Ref.: Monson

ARCOSANTI
Yavapai   T11N R22E
Architect Paolo Soleri has since 1971 been creating an architecturally interesting and radically different concrete city at this location. His students help devise plans and create the building. As of May 1981, no residences had been completed.

AREY
Coconino   On Grand Canyon R.R. branch   Elev. c. 7000'
R. J. Arey, an engineer for the Albuquerque and Arizona division of the S.P.R.R., had his headquarters at Williams c. 1905. This small station bore his name.
Ref.: James R. Fuchs, Letter (April 30, 1956)

ARIEL POINT
Coconino (Grand Canyon)   T32N R4E   Elev. 6430'
In 1906 Francois E. Matthes named this point where the Bright Angel Canyon trail begins. Ref.: 329

ARIPINE
Navajo   T12N R18E   Elev. 6500'
A Mormon settlement began here in 1883. First called Joppa at the suggestion of Mrs. Lucy O. Flake, this Mormon settlement was at the edge of pine timberland. Its name results from combining the first three letters of the state plus the word *pine*, and thus is descriptive. The post office application says that locally it was known as "Joppa" or "Flake." In September 1912 Mrs. Flake noted it was also called Decker Wash. From c. 1913 to c. 1921 there was little activity here, new settlers in the later year applying the new name. In 1932 "Joppa" was still being used locally.
P.O. est. as Joppa, March 4, 1913, Mrs. Lucy O. Flake, p.m.; disc. May 15, 1913; reest. as Aripine, Aug. 25, 1922, Grace F. Turley, p.m.; disc. Jan. 1, 1964
Ref.: 203, p. 12; 242; 225, p. 148

ARITOAC
Maricopa
This flat area was either the present Oatman Flat or near it. Fr. Jacobo Sedelmayr was here in 1744, using the name cited. Garcés, at this former Maricopa Indian settlement in 1775, called it Aritoac. Because it lay near the great bend of the Gila River, both de Anza and Font in 1775 referred to it as Rinconada (Spanish = "elbow").
Ref.: 167, I, 86, 87; 77, p. 118, Note 25

ARIVACA   pro.: /ærivakə/ or /ærivækə/
Pima: *alivapk* = "little reeds"
Papago: *a-ar-e-wai-pi* = "children's wells" or *are vaxr* = "small swamp"
The origin of the name Arivaca remains obscure, but many explanations have been advanced for it. Mrs. Mary B. Aguirre, who arrived in Arizona c. 1869, said it was a Papago Indian name, *hijovajilla* (= "son of the great valley"), and the great valley being the wide "avri" valley. On the other hand, Isaac D. Smith in his manuscript history said the name was an Indian one meaning "rotten ground." Kirk Bryan advanced the hypothesis that the name was a Mexican corruption of the Indian *Alivapk*, in which *vapk* indicated "reeds," plus *ali*, meaning "little." Riggs says Ali-Bac means "where little people dig holes," the "people" being the way Papago refer to animals. Whatever its origin, the name is very old, appearing as the Indian village of Aribac (or Arivaca) on a map dated 1773. As a direct result of the Pima Indian revolt in 1751, it was deserted. Mines near it continued to be worked by the Spanish until 1767. In 1812 Agustin Ortiz petitioned for two farming lots of the Aribac Ranch. His petition having been granted, the land was surveyed and

auctioned on October 10, 1812. Ortiz was the successful bidder at $799.59. He never received title to the land, but his sons obtained title in 1833 by proving their father had paid for the land. The place was deserted in 1835. Tomas sold his share to his brother Ignacio on June 7, 1856 for $500.00. In December 1856 Charles Debrille Poston noted in his *Journal* that he had bought the place from Tomas and Ignacio Ortiz for $10,000. The reduction works for the Heintzelman (Cerro Colorado) Mine were then erected at Arivaca. Later still the Court of Private Land Claims disallowed the Arivaca Land Grant, sometimes called the Arivaca Ranch. The community, at one time termed a ghost town, is today a thriving settlement. See Colorado, Cerro, Pima
P.O. est. April 10, 1878, Noah M. Bernard, p.m. Ref.: 58; 167, I, 87; 142, p. 118; 106, p. 119; 275, p. 6; 133; 242; AHS, Kitt; 33, pp. 62, 74, 93; 228; 126 (July 1897), n.p.

ARIVACA LAKE WILD LIFE AREA
Pima   T21S R11E
In 1969 the Arizona Game and Fish Department acquired the one hundred ninety-five acre area of which eighty-eight acres are the lake itself. It is used as a fishery and for recreation. See Arivaca, Pima Ref.: 9, p. 2

ARIVAYPA MOUNTAINS
Pinal/Graham
At least two military fights with Indians took place in these mountains. Although the name has not been found on maps, it seems safe to assume it refers to the north end of the present Galiuro Mountains through which Arivaipa Canyon extends.
Ref.: 159, pp. 443, 440

ARIZMO
Cochise   T22S R29E
Homesteaders from Missouri coined the name from *Ariz*ona and *Mo* (Missouri).
P.O. est. Sept. 9, 1903, Louis A. Gregory, p.m.; disc. Aug. 17, 1906
Ref.: 18a; 242

ARIZOLA
Pinal   T7S R6E   Elev. 1451'
The first settler, a man named Thomas from Carthage, Missouri, coined the name from the first four letters of *Ariz*ona plus Ola, his daughter's name. Had it not been for the "Baron of Arizona," the place might never have come to public notice. However, here "Baron" Peralta-Reavis had his headquarters for his vast "holdings," claiming ownership by right of an old Spanish land grant to all water and mineral rights over a huge area. The fraud was ultimately exposed, but not before the "Baron" had garnered millions from railroads and mines for quit-claim deeds.
P.O. est. April 29, 1892, Julia S. Fishback, p.m.; disc. Sept. 26, 1904
Ref.: 18a; *Arizona Enterprise* (Jan. 3, 1891), p. 3; 225, p. 30; Powell

ARIZONA
From 1540 to 1820 what is now southern Arizona and Sonora, Mexico, was known as Pimeria Alta (*q.v.*) and was under Spanish dominion. During those centuries what is now northern Arizona was explored by Catholic missionizing priests and was viewed as being part of New Mexico. Sonora was a rich mining region, so large that to distinguish separate areas, district names were applied. Among them was the "District of Arizonac," today occupied by parts of northern Sonora and southern Pima County, Arizona. Arizonac was a station of Saric Mission, near which were rich silver mines. Ores from the vicinity of Arivaca were first taken to Arizonac for further transshipment to Mexico. McClintock says that in 1754 Padre Ortega referred to the Real de Arizona as "the town in whose district were silver mines." He adds that Spaniards dropped the *c* to accord with their phonetics. Recent scholarship suggests that the name *Arizona* may have a Basque origin, noting strong Basque influence in the region. However, the name first appears on a map prepared by Fr. Pfeffercorn, who was missionizing among Indians prior to what amounted to visits by those having Basque associations. However, the possibility exists as suggested. On the other hand, McClintock notes that *arizonac* derives from Papago *ali* (= "small") and *shonak* (= "place of the spring"). He also reports that an Arizona pioneer named Isaac D. Smith said Indians here used a small spring they called *Aleh-zon* (= "Young spring"), and that Spaniards destroyed the village of Arizonac c. 1790. William Kurath, a

linguist, said that a "Spanish" *r* is not unusual for Papago *l* since the latter is a sound somewhere between European *r* and *l*," and that it is possible that strangers, not understanding the Papago language, fit what they thought they heard into something which was more familiar to their ears. As for Arizonac, it was about eight miles west of Old Sasabe, south of the international border about a mile at a place called Banera.
Ref.: 224, p. 3; 15, I, 344, 345; Frank C. Lockwood, Letter from Fr. Bonaventure Oblasser (May 5, 1935); 195, pp. 20-22; 94, pp. 217-231

ARIZONA: As is to be expected several place names reflect their location in Arizona. Examples follow:

Arizona   Yuma
See Yuma, Yuma

Arizonac
See main entry on Arizona

Arizonac, Real de
See main entry on Arizona

Arizona City   Maricopa
See Gillespie Dam, Maricopa

Arizona City   Pinal   T8S R7E   Elev. 1500'

Arizona City   Yavapai
Barnes says Arizona City was a small mining camp on Big Bug Creek, but it does not appear on any of many maps examined.

Arizona City   Yuma
See Yuma, Yuma

Arizona County
In 1860 the present state of Arizona was part of the Territory of New Mexico. In that year Arizona County was created west of the boundary line of Doña Ana County "through a point one mile distant easterly from what is called the Overland Stage mail station, to the Apache caves...." Ref.: 18a

Arizona Dam Butte   Maricopa   T2N R6E

Arizona Divide   Coconino   T21N R6E

Arizona Gulch   Graham   T5S R19E

Arizona Mountains   Santa Cruz
See Pajarito Mountains, Santa Cruz

Arizona, Plateau of   Coconino
See Coconino Plateau, Coconino

Arizona Spring   Mohave   T25N R18W

Arizona Sun Bowl   Coconino   T23N R6E   Elev. 9640'

Arizona-Sonora Desert   Pima   T14S R11E
Museum
Named because it contains living desert flora and fauna of Arizona and Sonora, Mexico

Arizona Strip   Coconino/Mohave
See Strip, The, Coconino/Mohave, and Mohave County

ARKANSAS MOUNTAIN

T12S R6W   Elev. 2080'

This name was in use at least as early as 1914, but for what reason is not known. The town of Old Ajo was on its east side. Ref.: 58; Ketchum; *Ajo Copper News* (Oct. 21, 1954), p. B-5

ARK BASIN

Mohave   c. T22N R19W   Elev. 3800'

This basin takes its name from the Ark Mine, located and owned prior to 1906 by the Ark and San Antonio Mining Company. Ref.: 200, p. 87

ARKILLS

Graham   Elev. c. 4000'

This former stop on the Arizona Eastern R.R. fourteen miles north of Bowie was named for Seth T. Arkills, a pioneer locomotive engineer during its construction (1894-1899) and thereafter. He took the first train into Globe. Its service was so irregular that it earned the name of "Try-weakly." Ref.: AHS, Arkills File; Woody

ARLINGTON

Maricopa   T2S R5W   Elev. 800'

Both this community and Arlington Valley were named by the wife of its first postmaster. She said she had no reason other than liking the sound of the name. P.O. est. Aug. 28, 1899, Moser (*sic*) E. Clanton, p.m. Ref.: Parkman; 242

ARMER

Gila   T4N R15E   Elev. c. 3000'

J. H. Armer came to Arizona in 1877 and established a cattle ranch where he later had a post office. It was at the mouth of Armer Gulch (a.k.a. Armer Wash). The place is now covered by Roosevelt Lake. Armer and Tanner, his partner, had a winter livestock camp on Armer Mountain.
P.O. est. March 2, 1884, Mrs. Lucinda Armer, p.m.; disc. May 13, 1895
Ref.: 18a; 329; 242

ARMISTEAD CREEK

Mohave

On July 4, 1859 "somewhere west of Truxton Springs" (Barnes), Lt. Edward Fitzgerald Beale said his party named this creek for Maj. Lewis Addison Armistead (d. July 3, 1863, at Gettysburg), who had been breveted a major in 1847 for gallant action in the war with Mexico. Ref.: 18a; 159, p. 1

ARNETT CREEK

Pinal   T2S R12E   Elev. c. 2600'

This creek is named for the Arnett Ranch, belonging to the Arnett family c. 1885. In 1886 William L. was registered at Pinal, and James B. at Silver King.
Ref.: 18a; Craig; *Gila Co. Great Register*

ARNOLD CANYON

Yavapai   T12N R4E

Wales Arnold settled here with his family, hence the name. Ref.: Dugas

ARNTZ

Apache   T18N R22E

Now a section house stop, this place on the S.F.R.R. was named for the Albuquerque Division trainmaster, W. P. Arntz. Ref.: 18a; 218, p. 353

ARRASTRA   pro.: /aræstrə/ or /əræstrə/

Spanish: *arrastre* = "drag mill"

This is a Spanish term for drag mills for grinding ores. A huge flat granite rock was dragged over a pit by an animal going in a circle around the pit. The remains or existence of such mills led to the naming of several places. Examples follow:

Arastra (*sic*) Gulch	Gila		
See Single Standard Gulch, Gila			
Arraster (*sic*) Gulch	Maricopa	T5N R10W	
Arrastra Canyon	Mohave	(1) T13N R13W	(2) T13N R13W
Arrastra Creek	Yavapai	T11N R1W	
Arrastra Creek Spring	Yavapai	T11N R1W	
Arrastra Lake	Yuma	T5S R23W	

The wash has an arrastra at its mouth. It is also called Island Lake because the arrastra resembles an island. Ref.: Monson

Arrastra Mountain	Mohave	T13N R11W	Elev. 4807'
Arrastra Spring	Maricopa	T7N R5E	
Arrastre (*sic*) Creek	Yavapai	(1) T11N R3W	(2) T9N R2E
Arrastre (*sic*) Gulch	Gila	T10N R9E	

ARROWHEAD TERRACE
Coconino (Grand Canyon)   T34N R1W   Elev. c. 5000'
This spur has the shape of an arrowhead, hence the name. Ref.: 18a

ARROYO: The word *arroyo* signifies a gulch and thus identifies the kind of location. For locations bearing the designation, see entry under main name: For example, Arroyo Chico, see Chico, Arroyo

ARTESA   pro.: /artiyža/
Pima   T18S R5E   Elev. 2490'
This town on the Papago Indian reservation was established about 1907. Its water comes from wells. However, the name was in existence prior to digging the well. It was first used by a Mexican for a waterhole in the Artesa Mountains and then transferred to the name of a dam built by the same man. It then came to be applied to Menager's store and the entire area. At the time the post office was established at Indian Oasis a mile west, the name Artesa was given to this small community. Bryan says that the Mexican who first used the name applied it to his big watering trough, as the word *artesa* locally indicates such a trough. Variant: Komoktetuvavosit (Papago = "where the turtle was caught"). This place is not identical with Sells, which is a mile west. See also Sells, Pima Ref.: 58; 57, p. 352

ARTESA MOUNTAINS
Pima   T18S R5E   Elev. 3384'
Two brothers — Joseph and Louis Menager (both b. Tucson) — homesteaded six square miles in this vicinity, with a ranch sometimes known as La Quituni. They began constructing Menager's Dam in 1917 and completed it c. 1920, in a gap which local Mexican-Americans called Angostura. In 1930 the brothers sold their land to the Papago Indian Reservation. Joseph died in July 1979 and Louis in August 1982. Ref.: Ketchum; Mrs. R. C. Livingston (Louis' granddaughter), Letter (Sept. 1982)

ARTESIA
Graham   T8S R26E   Elev. 3278'
A deep artesian well gave the name to this place.
P.O. est. Sept. 29, 1904, William Randolph, p.m.; resc. Feb. 8, 1905; reest. Sept. 18, 1911, Charles A. Angle, p.m.; disc. May 14, 1926 Ref.: Jennings; 242

ARTILLERY MOUNTAINS
Mohave   T12N R13W   Elev. 3213'
In 1854 Lt. Amiel W. Whipple noted a volcanic cone which he called Artillery Peak. The name was transferred to the range, which is described as having "massive volcanic battlements," reminding one of artillery in position. In March 1967 the USGS eliminated the name Artillery Peak and now uses only Artillery Mountains. On some GLO maps the range is termed Rawhide Mountains, which, however, are a separate group. See Rawhide Mountains, Mohave Ref.: 347, pp. 103, 217; 329

ASBESTOS CANYON
Coconino (Grand Canyon)   T31N R5E   Elev. c. 4000'
William Bass found an asbestos vein in this canyon, hence the name.
Ref.: Kolb

ASBESTOS POINT
Gila   Southern edge of the Sierra Ancha
                                            Elev. 6652'
Asbestos mined from this point has left a huge tailings dump on the south side of the Sierra Ancha Mountains peak here. Mining began c. 1915. Ref.: McKinney

ASENCION, RIO DE
Yavapai

On a map dated 1849 are noted three rivers very close together. The Rio Azul lies east and the Rio Verde is shown flowing into the Rio de Asencion, all of which then enter the Gila River.

ASHBURN MOUNTAIN
Santa Cruz   T22S R17E   Elev. 5444'

Oscar F. Ashburn (d. 1924) with Walter Vail and Gates owned the ranch here, formerly called Monkey Springs Ranch. The town of Patagonia is on the old Ashburn homestead. See also Hughes Mountain, Santa Cruz, and Patagonia, Santa Cruz
Ref.: Lenon; Kitt

ASH: The designation *ash* indicates the presence of ash trees at the location so named. Examples follow:

Ash Canyon	Cochise	T24S R20E	
Ash Canyon	Santa Cruz	T22S R15E	
Ash Canyon Spring	Yavapai	T15N R2E	
Ash Creek	Cochise	(1) T12S R23E	(2) T16S R19E
		(3) T18S R27E	
Ash Creek	Gila	T11N R10E	
Ash Creek	Graham	(1) T1N R22E	(2) T6S R25E
Ash Creek	Maricopa	T3N R10E	
Ash Creek	Pima	(1) T18S R11E	(2) T15S R18E
Ash Creek	Pinal	T5S R16E	
Ash Creek	Yavapai	(1) T11N R3E	(2) T12N R2W
Ash Creek Canyon	Cochise	T13S R22E	
Ash Creek Station	Yavapai		

In 1875 John Stemmer managed this stage station half way between Prescott and Verde.
Ref.: *Weekly Arizona Miner* (April 2, 1875), p. 2

Ash Creek Ridge	Cochise	T18S R26E	
Ash Creek Spring	Gila	T5N R10E	
Ash Creek Spring	Mohave	T26N E18W	
Ash Creek Valley	Gila	T5N R10E	
Ashdale	Maricopa	T7N R5E	
Ash Flat	Graham	T2S R24E	
Ash Gulch	Cochise	T13S R26E	
Ash Peak	Cochise		

See Montezuma Peak, Cochise, and Bob Thompson Peak, Cochise

Ash Peak	Graham/Greenlee	T8S R30E	Elev. 5585'

At Ash Spring was a particularly beautiful ash tree grove (a natural ambush pocket) and an Apache waterhole. Here Indians killed Horatio Merrill and his fourteen-year-old daughter on December 3, 1895. Ref.: Cosper; Empie; 68, p. 70

Ash Peak Canyon	Greenlee	T7S R30E	

This location is also called Sheldon Canyon.

Ash Spring	Cochise	T24S R29E	
Ash Spring	Greenlee	T4S R30E	
Ash Spring	Yavapai	(1) T15N R2E	(2) T12N R3E
		(3) T10N R2W	(4) T9N R5E

Ash Spring Canyon	Greenlee	T4S R30E
Ash Spring Creek	Yavapai	T9N R5E
Ash Spring Wash	Gila	T2N R15E
Ash Timber Spring	Graham	T4S R25E
Ash Wash	Pima	T18S R10E

ASHER HILLS
Maricopa   T4N R6E   Elev. 2050'
These hills were named for the Asher Ranch, on which they are located.

ASH FORK
Yavapai   T21N R2W   Elev. 5140'
Freighters taking supplies to Jerome journeyed along Ash Creek, named for ash trees there. Near its mouth the creek separates into three branches and they rejoin at a stage depot called Ash Fork, which was constructed under the ash trees. Freighters and stage passengers had to drive from there to the railroad at Williams. They agitated for a more convenient railroad terminal, and in 1882 a second siding was established west of Williams. One source says the first name suggested for the new railroad stop was Ash Canyon, but the name Ash Fork transferred to the siding and its developing community. The settlement burned in 1893 and the present town was begun. The name is acceptable both in the single or two-word form.
P.O. est. as Ash Fork, April 2, 1883, Henry W. Kline, p.m.; name changed to Ashfork, Sept. 17, 1894; Wells Fargo 1885; name changed to Ash Fork, June 1, 1950
Ref.: Kelly; 242; 124, p. 39

ASH FORK RIDGES
Coconino
The Hualapai name for this place is Kthil Kisob Gova. See Ash Fork, Yavapai
Ref.: Dobyns

ASHLEY FALLS
Coconino (Grand Canyon)   Location uncertain
Maj. John W. Powell named this falls for Ashley because they are where Ashley carved his name. Ref.: 266, p. 217

ASHURST
Graham   T5N R23E   Elev. 2829'
Although locally this area was called Redlands, when the farmers applied for a post office in 1918, residents suggested calling it Pershing to honor Gen. John Pershing of W W I fame. However, postal authorities crossed out that name, substituting Ash. Residents then altered it to Ashurst to honor U.S. Senator Henry Fountain Ashurst (b. Sept. 13, 1874, Nevada; d. 1960).
P.O. est. Jan. 8, 1919, Gilbert S. Richardson, p.m.; disc. Aug. 31, 1955
Ref.: Jennings; 5, p. 343; 242

ASHURST RUN
Coconino   T18N R9E   Elev. c. 7000'
A sheepman, William Henry Ashurst located near Bill Williams Mountain in 1877 and later at this location, which he called Ashurst Run. Ashurst was detained by a snow storm while away from his ranch. During his absence his daughter choked to death of diphtheria.Mrs. Ashurst prepared the child for burial, making the coffin herself. After a bitter struggle through snow, he arrived home in time to help dig the small grave.
    Years later in 1900 while prospecting in the Grand Canyon, Ashurst was pinned under a sliding stone and, remaining calm, died there. His friend Niles Cameron found his body and transported it to the Rim of the Grand Canyon where it remained until the 1940s. His remains were finally removed for burial in Grand Canyon cemetery. See Williams Lake, Coconino Ref.: Henry Fountain Ashurst, Letter (Dec. 12, 1955); Slipher; 166, p. 77

ASPEN: Aspen trees grow in the mountains of Arizona, notably where other trees have been burned off. With their light-colored bark they look not unlike birch trees. In autumn their leaves turn bright gold. Their beauty probably underlies many of the following place names:

Aspen Butte	Apache	T5N R26E	Elev. 9215'
Aspen Canyon	Apache	(1) T27N R6W	(2) T34N R23E
Aspen Creek	Yavapai	T13N R3E	

Locally this is often called Mike's Place. Ref.: Gardner

Aspen Creek Spring	Yavapai	T13N R3W
Aspen Grove Wash	Navajo	T34N R22E
Aspen Hill	Coconino	T21N R2E	Elev. 7650'
Aspen Lake	Coconino/Navajo	T11N R14E
Aspen Ridge	Apache	T6N R25E
Aspen Spring	Apache	T9N R25E
Aspen Spring	Coconino	T20N R6E
Aspen Spring	Navajo	T35N R23E
Aspen Wash	Apache	T33N R23E
Aspen Wash	Navajo	T35N R21E

ASUMPCION, RIO DE LA
In 1538 two friars, Pedro Nadal and Juan de la Asuncion (*sic*), discovered the Salt River and gave this name to its "principal branch." See Salt River
Ref.: 77, p. 136, Note 48

ASUNCION RIVER
Gila
This is said to be the name given by Padre Ignacio Javier Keller of Suamca in 1736-37 to the stream formed by the junction of the Verde and Salado Rivers. Ref.: 15, I, 362

ATASCOSA MOUNTAINS   pro.: /atəskósə/
Santa Cruz   T23S R12E   Elev. 6440'
These mountains, which extend south to the Mexican border where they become the Pajarito Mountains, take their name from a spring on the Bear Valley Ranch called the Atascosa (Spanish = "muddy" or "boggy"). In wet seasons the spring forms a *cienega* (swampy area) at the base of these mountains. The name was in use in 1854. Atascosa Peak is the highest point in these mountains. See Bear Valley Ranch, Santa Cruz
Ref.: 329, Noon, Letter, and Sykes, Letter; 106, pp. 118, 119

ATCHESON RESERVOIR
Apache   T7N R28E
This reservoir was named for an early settler. It is near the Slade Reservoir and with it is sometimes called the Cahon Reservoirs. Ref.: 329

ATHOS
Mohave   T18N R18W   Elev. 2150'
A siding on the S.F.R.R., this place was first called Signal, then in 1912 Tungsten, and in 1913 Athos, probably for ease in keyboard telegraphy. Ref.: 18a

ATIL MISSION
Pima   Location uncertain
At this mission in the Altar Valley, Fr. Antonio Gonzales served from 1837 to 1841. Ref.: 263, p. 22

ATOSCACITA SPRINGS
Apache   T9N R27E
The name for this group of springs may have derived from the word *atasoca* (Spanish: *atasoca* = "boggy place"), plus the diminutive *cita*. The spelling is as on a sign posted at these springs. Ref.: 329

AUBINEAU CANYON
Coconino   T23N R7E
Julius Aubineau (1852-1903) served as mayor of Flagstaff in 1898. He was a member of
the Grand Canyon Electric Power Company, which planned to construct a dam as a
power source at the foot of Bright Angel Creek. Aubineau owned Aubineau Spring, the
source of Flagstaff's first water supply system. It is on Aubineau Peak.
Ref.: 329; Slipher

AUBREY
Yavapai   T23N R7W
Barnes said the name of this location on the railroad was changed because there was
already another Aubrey on the line. The name is sometimes given as Augley. This name
appears on only two maps: GLO 1869 and "Map of Arizona Territory" prepared by
authority of Maj. Gen. O. B. Willcox, 1879. Ref.: 18a

AUBREY CLIFFS
Coconino   T30N R8W
These cliffs derive their name because Aubrey sandstone is "their most conspicuous
stratographic member." This is probably the same range that Beale called the Aulick
Range on Oct. 6, 1857. See Aubrey Landing, Mohave Ref.: 23, p. 66; 345, III, 47

AUBREY HILLS
Mohave   T11N R17W
In 1961 the name Williams Mountains was changed to Aubrey Hills by the USGS. The
Hualapai name is *Wi Sukohautave* (= "cone shaped mountain, brown"). See Aubrey
Landing, Mohave Ref.: Dobyns; 329

AUBREY LANDING
Mohave   T11N R18W   Elev. c. 500'
According to the Kern Report o October 23, 1851, the settlement here was called
Williams Fork. The report says, "The branch receives its name from Old Bill
Williams." Leroux says he met him "at the mouth below the Amajave in 1837." The
location continued to be known as Williams on the Parke map of 1851, and by 1870
there was an election precinct here. The presence of the Miners Hill Mine and the Planet
Mine on Williams Fork led to the establishment of Aubrey Landing, which in 1876 was
still called Williams Fork or Sand Creek. A misspelling of the name is Abray Landing.
Aubrey Landing was an important shipping point at the mouth of Bill Williams River. A
town meeting here on August 4, 1864 selected the name Aubrey to honor the "Skimmer
of the Plains," Francois Xavier Aubrey, who had earned his nickname by galloping
eight hundred and eighty miles in five days and thirteen hours from Independence,
Missouri, to Santa Fe, New Mexico. Aubrey (b. Dec. 4, 1824, Canada; d. Aug. 20,
1854) was a famous freighter. In 1852 he drove thousands of sheep across Arizona to
California, returning via the Mohave River to Arizona where in 1853 he found gold in a
gulch near the Colorado River. A year later he was the first to explore for a wagon route
along the 35th Parallel, driving a wagon from San Jose, California, to Santa Fe, New
Mexico. At the end of the journey he was killed by Maj. R. H. Weightman in a barroom
brawl.
    The landing was also sometimes called Aubrey City. When the market for copper fell
badly, the place was abandoned after 1865 and by 1878 only a post office, a saloon, and
hotel — all under one roof — remained, along with a unique ship's cabin converted into a
residence where William J. Hardy, agent for a steamboat company, held open house.
(Lake Havasu now covers this location.)
P.O. est. as Aubrey, Oct. 2, 1866, Henry J. Lightner, p.m.; disc. Nov. 3, 1886
Ref.: *Arizona Miner* (Sept. 7, 1864), p. 4; *Arizona Sentinel* (June 15, 1878), p. 4; 206,
p. 198; 224, p. 119; 107, I, 353; 335, p. 10, Note 15; 200, p. 44

AUDLEY
Yavapai   T23N R7W
This point on the railroad is an adjustment of its original name of Aubrey, the change
being made in 1879. See Aubrey, Yavapai

AUGUSTÍN, (MISSION OF) SAN

Pima   T14S R13E

The Mission of San Augustin, the patron saint of Tucson, was originally on the west bank of the Santa Cruz River about three miles from the section of the city referred to as the Old Pueblo (the walled section now occupied by governmental buildings.) Hinton wrote that a mile due east of it was what appeared to be "an old town in ruins, but no clue can be obtained as to its origin ... history...." The mission was founded in 1769, according to one source, but on a map dated 1857 S. Augustin is located on the east side of the Santa Cruz River, northeast of San Cosme. Other names include the following: San Augustin de Oaiur and Augustin de Pueblicito de Tucson. See Tucson, Pima Ref.: 163, pp. 264, 265; 168, p. 19

AULTMAN

Yavapai   T14N R4E   Elev. c. 4000'

The Conger Mill in the Middle Verde section of Yavapai County required postal service and a post office was established for it in 1885. It was named for a resident.
P.O. est. July 9, 1885, Charles A. Bush, p.m.; disc. Feb. 21, 1923
Ref.: R. W. Wingfield; Goddard; 18a

AVIE MIL-LI-KET

Yuma   20 mi. N. of Yuma (1871)

Emory noted that this peak, a.k.a. Chimney Peak and called San Pablo by old Jesuits, was named to honor a "wise chief" who became a deity after his death.
Ref.: 106, p. 104

AVONDALE

Maricopa   T1N R1W   Elev. 3969'

Near a ranch called Avondale, Billy Moore maintained a freight station on the west bank of the Agua Fria River. Because the river name in translation meant "cold water" and because he had a well which gave clear cold water, Moore called his place Coldwater. Old timers, however, called it simply Billy Moore's. The railroad established a station a mile west of Coldwater on the Avondale Ranch, but called the stop Litchfield. A community developed around it, and Moore's lost its importance so that the name Coldwater was gradually abandoned.
P.O. est. as Coldwater, July 2, 1896, Mary V. Jones, p.m.; disc. Oct. 3, 1896 (never in operation); reest. as Cold Water, Oct. 21, 1897, John M. Van Hores, p.m.; disc. July 11, 1905; reest. as Avondale, March 15, 1911, Henry E. Weaver, p.m.
Ref.: Parkman; 18a; 279, p. 13; 242

AVRA VALLEY pro.: /ævrə/

Pima   T14S R10E   Elev. 2205'

Avra Valley is the northern portion of the Altar Valley (q.v.). The name is said to mean "open." The southern section of this valley is sometimes called Arivaca Valley. It is actually a broad plain with an indefinite boundary to the south, with the Tucson-Ajo road usually considered the arbitrary boundary line. A post office existed under the name Avra at one time (T13S/R11E). The first name suggested on the post office application was Hinson, but the Post Office Department substituted Avra.
P.O. est. as Avra, July 30, 1931, Mrs. LaVera Lacey, p.m.; disc. Jan. 20, 1933
Ref.: George C. Martin, U.S. Board on Geographic Names, Letter to G.E.P. Smith (Dec. 31, 1936); AHS, Mrs. Mary B. Aguirre File; 242

AWATOBI pro.: /àwat'owbiᴧ/

Hopi = "High place of the Bow People"
Navajo   T27N R19E   Elev. 6480'

The name for these ruins derives from the fact that the Bow Clan of the Hopi Indians lived here. Fewkes first used the name. When Pedro de Tobar and Lopez de Cardenas in 1540 visited this Hopi village, it was an active community, but today drifting sands cover it. However, it long remained important as evidenced by the fact that on August 20, 1629, Fr. Francisco de Porras started a Franciscan mission here with the help of Andres Gutierrez, Cristobal de la Concepcion, and Francisco de San Buenaventura. They named their mission San Bernadino for the saint's day on which they began constructing the mission.

Hopi resistance to Christianization and to Spanish oppression resulted in the poisoning of Fr. Porras in 1629. Efforts to Christianize continued until 1680 when the Pueblo Indian revolt occurred. Fr. Figueroa was murdered. Missionizing vanished until about 1700 when Fr. Garaycoechea baptized seventy-three of the nearly eight hundred living at Awatobi. The residents were friendly to the missionaries, a fact that alarmed Hopi living in Walpi and Mishongnovi, who in November 1700 attacked Awatobi at night and killed most of its inhabitants. Thereafter the drifting sands began to take over. When Fewkes gave it its name, he was not the first to name it, for Espejo in 1583 called it by the following names: Aguato, Ahuato, and Zaguato. In 1878 Hinton used the name Zuguato. Mindeleff in 1886 called it Talla-Hogan (Navajo = "house at the water") because a hogan (Navajo home) was at Talla-Hogan Spring near Awatobi Spring.
Ref.: Bartlett; 111, p. 617, 22, p. 51; 141, pp. 134, 154, 190, 195; 167, I, 119, 120, 561; Museum of Northern Arizona

AYER POINT

Coconino (Grand Canyon)   T31N R4E   Elev. c. 5000'
Mrs. Edward Everett Ayer, whose husband was a prominent Flagstaff lumber dealer, in 1883 was the first white woman to visit the Grand Canyon and certainly the first white woman to go down into the Canyon from this point via the Hance Trail. With her were her daughter and a Miss Sturgis. Ref.: Slipher; 333, p. 19

AZANSOSI MESA   pro.: /asdzā:ts?ośí/

Navajo = "slim woman"
Navajo   T41N R17E
Gregory named this mesa to honor Mrs. Louise (John) Wetherill. The Wetherills established the first trading post in this locality and the Navajo called Mrs. Wetherill "Asthonsose." Gregory's name for it is a phonetic corruption. Ref.: 141, p. 47

AZATLAN

Yavapai
This is a community that never came into existence. Its possibility was founded on a battle in 1864 in the first Arizona Territorial Legislature, which concerned the insistence by delegates from the First District to establish the new territorial capital anywhere but in Prescott. These gentlemen insisted that a capital be elsewhere, even suggesting building a town at the juncture of the Verde and Salt Rivers, to be called Azatlan. Barnes says, however, that there was a mining camp so called six miles south of Prescott in 1866. Ref.: 18a; 116, p. 420

AZTEC

Santa Cruz   T22S R16E   Elev. 4850'
The post office at this location served employees of the mill and also the Aztec Mining prospect in Aztec Gulch.
P.O. est. Dec. 6, 1878, Christian Foster, p.m.; disc. June 6, 1883
Ref.: Lenon; 286, p. 263; 18a

AZTEC

Yuma   T7S R12W   Elev. c. 800'
This is a transfer name taken from the nearby Aztec Hills. The S.P.R.R. established a watering stop for its steam engines here in 1881.
P.O. est. Sept. 12, 1889, Charles A. Dallman, p.m.; disc. July 30, 1900; Wells Fargo 1890 Ref.: Johnson; 279, p. 78

AZTEC MOUNTAIN

Mohave   c. T23N R18W
In 1906 this was the name used for a mountain about three miles south of Mineral Park, where turquoise was being mined. See Aztec Peak, Gila Ref.: 200, p. 219

AZTEC PASS

Yavapai   T18N R6W
This pass between the Santa Maria and Juniper Mountains in 1853 was called Aztec Pass by the Whipple exploring expedition. Here on January 23 they had time to explore Indian ruins rather extensively and, to quote Whipple "From a fancy founded on having

antiquity of these ruins, we have given the name of Aztec Pass to this place." The pass became an important route from the Colorado River to the east. An enterprising citizen in the 1860s put in a toll gate which commanded access or egress to and from the pass. It was called quite simply Tollgate. See Tollgate, Yavapai
Ref.: 348, pp. 91, 94; 347, pp. 192, 194 (Note 11), 198, 199; Dobyns

AZTEC PEAK
Gila   T6N R14E   Elev. 7694'
This peak in the Sierra Ancha is a narrow rock chimney. Obvious signs indicate that Indians used it as a point of defense against attackers. The name "Aztec" derives from the fact that it was commonly believed prior to archeological investigation that the prehistoric Indians of Arizona were largely Aztec. The eminent historian Prescott supported the idea. In consequence settlers who arrived in Arizona in the 1860s and 1870s used the name Aztec in association with ancient ruins. Ref.: McKinney

AZTEC RANGE
Yavapai
This is the name Whipple gave to the mountains in which Aztec Pass is located. See Aztec Pass, Yavapai Ref.: 348, p. 192

AZURE RIDGE
Mohave (Lake Mead)   T33N R16W
The name describes the appearance of this ridge.

AZURITE
Pima   T17S R15E
From 1899 to c. 1902 there was a small mining town by this name about eighteen to twenty miles south of Tucson. Its residents were employed at the Azurite Mine.
Ref.: *Oasis* (March 11, 1899), p. 7; *Tucson Directory* (1902), p. 18

B

BABBITT BILL TANK

Coconino   T21N R1E   Elev. c. 6000'
Formerly called by its corrupted name of Rabbit Bill Tank, this location came into use
through the cattle ranching of the five Babbitt brothers. William and David arrived in
Arizona in 1886, later being joined by Charles J., Edward J., and George Babbitt.
Several tanks share the name Babbitt Tank. Associated names include the fol-
lowing: Babbitt Lake (T25N/R5E), Spring (T20N/R8E), Babbitt Tank Canyon
(T17N/R17E), Wash (T21N/R11E), and Water (T14N/R14E). Ref.: Kelly; 218, III

BABBITT SPRING

Coconino   T20N R8E
First known as Elden Spring because it is south of Elden Mountain, the name was
changed by railroad officials who established Babbitts, a station here on the Central
Arizona R.R. See Babbitt Bill Tank, Coconino, and Elden Mountain, Coconino
Ref.: 18a; Sykes

BABOCOMARI LAND GRANT   pro.: /barbakómǝriy/ or /barbǝkóma/

Papago: "*Vav-ko-multh* = "stone dish for making tortillas"
Cochise   T19S R19E   Elev. 46" – 38"
On December 25, 1832 the Mexican government granted title to San Ignacio del
Babacomari (*sic*) to Ignacio Eulalia Elias. The spelling changes on the map of the
Gadsden Purchase. When Boundary Survey Commission surveyors were here in 1851,
Apache raids had destroyed the fine hacienda on the banks of Babocomari Creek (or
River). United States courts confirmed 34,707 acres of the grant. By 1855 the remaining
walls served as a settlers' stronghold and thereafter for an encampment for a military
detachment from Camp Wallen. Capt. Richard Ewell and Capt. John Tevis wrote of
passing this old hacienda in 1857, calling it Fort Babocomari.
Ref.: 131, p. 42; 201, p. 51; 18a; 107, V, 195; 51, p. 322; 116, p. 428; AHS Names File
(Lockwood); 242; 228, n.p.

BABOCOMARI RANCH

Santa Cruz/Cochise   T20S R21E
This ranch, one of the oldest in the Southwest, is said to have been visited by Fr. Eusebio
Kino in 1697, at which time it was a Sobaipuri Indian village called Huachuca. Fr.
Francisco Garcés also was here, calling it Santa Cruz de Gaybaniptea. A Mexican
walled fort erected here was still in existence in 1857. See also Huachuca, Fort,
Cochise, and Babocomari Land Grant, Santa Cruz Ref.: 43, p. 248, Note 2; 319, pp.
71, 75; 206, p. 40

BABOCOMERI CREEK

Santa Cruz/Cochise   T19S R19E
This was Bartlett's name for Babocomari Creek (or River). Bartlett described it as "A
pretty little stream, which I learned from the Mexican hunters ... called the Ba-
bacanora...." See Babocomari Land Grant, Santa Cruz Ref.: 20, p. 185

[41]

BABOQUIVARI PEAK   pro.: /babokiyvəriʌ/
Papago: *vav* = "mountain"; *kovolik* = "narrow about the middle" (seen from south)
Pima   T19S R6E   Elev. 7730'
Fr. Eusebio Kino's lieutenant, Juan Mateo Manje, wrote that this highest peak in the
Baboquivari Mountains looked like a "tall castle ... on ... a high peak," and was called
Noah's Ark. In 1854 Lt. Michler of the Boundary Survey Commission party said that its
Indian name meant "water on the mountains," an error possibly attributable to his
misunderstanding the Papago explanation about a waterhole near its top. On the original
Gadsden Purchase map, it is called Papago Peak. Babuquiburi is the name used in
Tanner's *American Atlas*, 1823. In Papago culture the peak is important, being
considered the center of the Papago world. Associated names include the fol-
lowing: Baboquivari (P.O.), Baboquivari Camp (T19S/R7E), Baboquivari Canyon
(T19S/R7E), Baboquivari Forest Reserve, and Baboquivari Mountains (T18S/R7E),
Baboquivari Plain, Baboquivari Valley, Baboquivari Wash, and Babuquivera Plain.
Ref.: 58; 105, p. 119; 208, p. 31; 242

BABY CANYON
Yavapai   T9N R2–4E
The 1880 Eckhoff map of Arizona Territory shows this canyon five miles north of
Willow Creek. At the mouth of Baby Canyon is the Baby Canyon Indian Ruins
containing the crumbling remains of well over one hundred rooms. Ref.: 5, p. 306

BABY MUMMY CAVE
Navajo   5 mi. s. of Tyende Mesa
In 1914 Prof. Byron Cummings excavated a cave overlooking the confluence of
Dogoszhi Biko and Nagashi Biko. He unearthed two infant burials at the site, hence the
name which he applied to the cave. Ref.: 87, p. 619

BABY ROCKS
Navajo: *Tse asee* (or: *Tse awe*) = "baby rocks"
Navajo   T39N R22E
The name is descriptive of a group of rocks. The individual rocks resemble little children.
In 1912 severe flooding destroyed a Navajo farming community here. As a result, the
residents were led by Old Crank, a Navajo, to establish Dinnehotso, which has a natural
dam site. Ref.: 41, p. 51

BACA FLOAT GRANT (NO. 3)   pro.: /bákə/
Santa Cruz   T21S R13E
The correct name for this twelve-mile-square area is Luis Maria Baca Land Grant No. 3.
In the 1500s the King of Spain granted land in what is now New Mexico to Alvar Nuñez
Cabeza de Vaca. Disputes arose because others settled on it and at Las Vegas took up
claims to some five hundred thousand acres of it. They were settled on June 21, 1860 by
an Act of Congress which permitted the lineal descendants of the original grantee to
select land elsewhere from the public domain. They were given tracts of one hundred
thousand acres. No. 3 is in Santa Cruz County, No. 1 and No. 5 in Yavapai County, No.
4 in Colorado, and No. 2 in New Mexico. In Santa Cruz County in 1866 a surveyor's
error caused overlapping with other land ownership. The Supreme Court decided in
Baca's favor. His heirs have long since sold their land grant, which has changed hands
several times, most recently in 1967 to develop Rio Rico. That development snarled in
an unsavory land fraud which had sixty sales representatives. Their force was down to
three by mid-1975. Over forty-four thousand purchasers were involved. Today a small
community of the "model home" type survives and a multitude of bare dirt ribbons scars
the uninhabited desert landscape.
Ref.: Lenon; Glannon; 5, pp. 371-372; *Daily Arizona Journal-Miner* (Dec. 15, 1898);
AHS, Pendleton File; *Arizona Sunday Star* (June 1, 1975), p. C-5

BACA FLOAT NO. 5
Yavapai   T18N R7W
The ranch at the Float south of Seligman was also known as the Oro Ranch because of its
O R O brand. (*R O* on left hip; *O* on left shoulder). It was bought in 1911 by Charles E.
Wiswall, a cattleman. See Baca Float Grant No. 3, Santa Cruz
Ref.: 289, pp. ix, ix, 2, 4

BADGER CREEK

Coconino   T31N R6E   Elev. c. 3000'

A noted Mormon missionary, Jacob Hamblin, killed a badger on this creek, hence the name. He then took the animal to a nearby creek where he boiled it. Alkali in the water combined with animal fat, forming soap, hence the name of the second creek, Soap Creek. Badger Creek is also called Clear Creek and Spring Creek. It is in Badger Canyon below Badger Butte. Ref.: 18a; 5, p. 158

BADGER CREEK RAPIDS

Coconino   T39N R7E

In 1924 the Birdseye Grand Canyon Expedition noted that these were the first rapids downstream in Marble Canyon, with a "fall of thirteen feet in about one hundred yards." Ref.: 36, p. 183

BADGER DEN WELL

Graham   T10S R29E, Sec. 20

Cattlemen used this name because a slovenly cowboy stayed in a cabin near the well, which in turn borrowed the name. The name was also spelled Badger Din Well. Ref.: 329

BADGER, FORT

Maricopa   33°30'/111°35'

Hartley's map of Arizona (c. 1866) shows this name just below the junction of the Verde and Salt Rivers. Ref.: Kitt

BADLANDS

Gila   T5N R15E

The area is thick with manzanita, hence the name. Ref.: Woody

BAGDAD

Yavapai   T14N R9W   Elev. 4100'

When John F. Lawler bought a mining claim here (then known as Copper Creek) in 1883 from its 1882 locators, W. J. Pace and J. M. Murphy, Lawler's brother William renamed the place Bagdad because he was a "diligent reader of the *Arabian Nights*." P.O. est. Jan. 5, 1910, Henry A. Geisendorfer, p.m.; disc. July 15, 1913; reest. July 12, 1944 Ref.: Helen Lawler; 242

BAGNAL WASH

Navajo   T12N R18E

Despite the spelling, the wash probably is named for George Bagnall. See Adair, Navajo

BAILEY PEAK

Pima   T18S R2W

This peak in Thomas Canyon, part of the Baboquivari Mountains, was named for Walter Bailey, owner of a cattle ranch here until 1917. Ref.: *Arizona Cattleman* (March 10, 1917), p. 8

BAILEY WELL

Graham   T10S R8E

Joshua Eaton Bailey (b. Nov. 4, 1834, New York; d. April 9, 1900) arrived in Yuma in 1870. He supervised several stage stations in Yuma County. In 1872 he and others founded Safford and he was its first postmaster. He moved to 1882 to Bailey's Wells, living there until 1899 when he moved to Eaton Rapids, Michigan. Ref.: AHS, Bailey File; 62

BAKABI   pro.: /bakavwi/

Hopi = "place of the jointed reed"

Navajo   T29N R15E   Elev. 6583'

Jointed reeds grow at nearby Bakabi Spring. Bakabi is the name given in the Hopi Constitution. The village (also spelled Bacabi or Bacobi) came into being when

dissidents from Oraibi who lived in Hotevilla wanted to return to their mother village. They were refused permission and settled here at Bakabi (or Bakavi) Spring.
Ref.: 71, p. 47; 153, p. 7

BAKER BUTTE
Coconino   T12N R9E   Elev. 8074'
Lt. John G. Bourke, aide to Gen. George Crook, said the correct spelling should be Baecker, the name of an army engineer. Locally it is said a man named Baker worked a mine nearby. Baker Lake and Baker Spring are here.   Ref.: 18a; 329

BAKER MOUNTAIN
Gila   T6N R14E   Elev. 7700'
John H. Baker, a cattleman, built the first cabin on the east side and raised potatoes c. 1885. Another (legendary) origin says that Indians in 1868 ambushed Ned Baker, a packmaster, at the "jumpoff" on this mountain. Ref.: 329; McKinney; 107, V, 81; AHS

BAKER PEAKS
Yuma   T9S R17W   Elev. 1416' and 1409'
Charles Baker (b. 1835, New York) was farming in Yuma County in 1870 and established a ranch with a natural waterhole called Baker's Tanks. His ranch lay on the old trail from Mexico which followed a pass between the two pyramid-shaped peaks (a.k.a. Baker Butte). Baker employed an unsavory character named Chavez, who broke horses without pay until he was recognized as a bandit sought by King S. Woolsey. Woolsey sent a cohort named Colvig to capture Chavez. Colvig shot Chavez in the back. In revenge Chavez' band attacked Woolsey's ranch.   Ref.: 355, p. 169; *Weekly Arizona Miner* (Dec. 3, 1875), p. 4 and (Dec. 3, 1875), p. 4, and (Dec. 17, 1875), p. 1; Mrs. Kelland

BAKER TANKS
Yuma   T9S R17W
Also called La Poza. A number of potholes are here. The name on Chain & Hardy's 1881 map is Los Posos, rendered by Pumpelly in 1870 Los Pozos. See Baker Peaks, Yuma

BAKERVILLE
Cochise   T23S R24E
At this small station on the S.P.R.R. Jake Pirrung, a Dutch baker, settled and built a hotel-roominghouse in the 1880s. Apparently a post office distribution office existed at one time, for postal records note that in 1907 the place was "to be served by the Warren post office."   Ref.: C.E. Mills, Letter (April 14, 1956); 242

BALAKAI MESA   pro.: /balókay/
Navajo: *baalok' asi* = "reeds under the rim"
Apache/Navajo   T30N R22E   Elev. 7630'
Cattails grow around springs at the south end of this mesa, hence the name is descriptive. It is also spelled Balukai, Salah-Kai, or Tselagai.   Ref.: 331, p. 129; 143, p. 49; 329

BALANCED ROCKS
Coconino   T31N R11E
A truncated boulder on a narrow base is the cause for the name.

BALD: The word *bald* is used descriptively for a number of locations which stand out prominently because of their baldness. The following are examples:

Bald Hill	Santa Cruz	T21S R18E	Elev. 5050'
Bald Hill	Yavapai	(1) T14N R7E	Elev. 6182'
		(2) T8N R1E	Elev. 3801'
		(3) T12N R4E	Elev. 6089'
See Glassford Hill, Yavapai			
Bald Knob	Cochise	T22S R28E	Elev. 5035'

Bald Mesa	Coconino	T14N R10E	
Bald Mountain	Coconino	T22N R3E	
Bald Mountain	Yavapai	(1) T14N R5E	
		(2) T17N R6W	Elev. 5900'
Bald Mountain Spring	Yavapai	T17N R6W	
Bald Point	Navajo	T11N R19E	Elev. 6805'
Bald Ridge	Cochise	T12S R21E	

BALDY, MOUNT
Apache   T6N R26E   Elev. 11,590'
Capt. George M. Wheeler in 1873 established camp here on what he called Thomas Peak to honor Gen. Lorenzo Thomas (d. March 2, 1875). Wheeler wrote that the view from the summit was "the most magnificent and effective of any ... Outstretched before us lay the tributaries of seven principal streams ... four main mountain peaks ... valley lands far surpassing any I have before seen ... Mountain, forest, valley, and stream are blended in one harmonious whole...." Wheeler's view was unobstructed, for the mountain top is bald, a fact which has led to the gradual substitution of its current name for that used by Wheeler. Ref.: 345, I, 63, 64; 329

BALDY MOUNTAIN
Greenlee   T3S R32E   Elev. 6415'
Descriptive of mountain as a whole.

BALLARD, MOUNT
Cochise   T23S R23E   Elev. 7200'
Promoters who never saw Bisbee (W. H. Martin and John Ballard) sent Ben and Lewis Williams to act for them in purchasing the option for the Copper Queen claims, bought on April 5, 1880. This mountain is named for John Ballard. Ref.: Burgess

BALLY BROPHY
Cochise
In the late 1950s the S.P.R.R. established a stop to be used for shipping livestock. It is near the headquarters of the Babocomari Ranch at Milepost 1069 and honors ranch owner Frank C. Brophy. The name comes from that of Ballybriphy (sic) R.R. station in County Leix, Ireland. The Arizona sign is bright green against white. Ref.: Frank C. Brophy, letter (Jan. 21, 1960)

BANDED CANYON
Mohave
The walls of this canyon, also known as Williams Canyon, have conspicuous banding of gneisses and schists, hence its preferred local name. Ref.: 200, p. 29

B AND M WILDLIFE AREA
Maricopa   T1N R1E   Elev. c. 1100'
In the bottom lands of the Gila River, this one hundred and twenty-three acre wildlife area is owned and managed by the Arizona Game and Fish Department. Ref.: 9, p. 2

BANDY TANK
Yuma   T3S R19W
Named for Henry Bandy, who in 1956 was a farmer at Bard, California. He prospected at Bandy Tank. Ref.: Monson

BANFIELD SPRING
Coconino   T15N R8E
John Banfield (b. 1835, New York) raised horses, using this spring. Ref.: Hart; 63

BANGHARTS
Coconino
This was a stage station run by George L. Banghart (d. July 1895) in 1866. See Del Rio, Coconino Ref.: 18a

BANGS, MOUNT

Mohave   T38N R15W   Elev. 8012'

Clarence King, an eminent geologist, named this highest peak of the Virgin Mountains for James E. Bangs, a clerk with King's party. Ref.: 88, p. 194; 18a

BANJO BILL

Coconino   T18N R6E

Banjo Bill had his place here, but played his banjo in Flagstaff saloons c. 1890. Ref.: Hart

BANNING CREEK

Yavapai   T13N R2W

Although some say the name should be spelled Bannon, this creek may have been named for William F. Banning (b. 1837, Illinois), who in 1870 was farming in this vicinity. Furthermore, locally the name is Banning. Ref.: Gardner; 62

BANNING WASH

Gila   T5N R15E

Named for Jim Banning, an early-day rancher who later had a cabin at the McFadden Circle Ranch. Ref.: Woody

BANNON

Apache   T10N R24E   Elev. 7000'

Named for an early settler and cattleman.

P.O. est. Dec. 20, 1919, Elizabeth S. Marble, p.m.; disc. Dec. 31, 1942 Ref.: Hayden; 242

BANTA POINT

Coconino (Grand Canyon)   T33N R5E   Elev. 5250'

Formerly called Apache Point, this location was named by Will C. Barnes in 1931 for Albert Franklin Banta (b. 1846, Indiana; d. June 21, 1924), who under the name Charles A. Franklin in 1863 came to Arizona with territorial governor John N. Goodwin's party (see Navajo Springs, Apache). From 1865 to 1871 Banta was a scout for Gen. George Crook, and in 1871-1873 was a guide for the Wheeler Expedition. Later he lived in Apache County, serving as an attorney and judge and a member of the 10th Arizona Legislature. A teller of extraordinarily tall tales, Banta was the Kilroy of Arizona, claiming to have been everywhere.

Ref.: 107, VIII, 31, 32; 182; AHS, Chambers File; 63

BAPCHULE   pro.: /bǽpčúwliy/

Pima = "hook nose" or "long pointed nose"

Pinal   T3S R4E   Elev. c. 1500'

The first Catholic church on the Gila River Indian Reservation was established in this Papago town.

P.O. est. Jan. 24, 1931, Mrs. Myra Martin, p.m.

Ref.: AHS, Castillo Collection; 242

BARAGAN MOUNTAINS   pro.: /baragán/

Yuma   T4S R11–14, 18W   Max. Elev. 1289'

Frank Baragan, a Mexican rancher, dug a well here to water his stock. "Baragon" is a misspelling. Ref.: Lenon; 279, p. 201

BARBARA, SANTA

Mohave   T41N R1W

This was named by Fr. Escalante. Ref.: 42, p. 66

BARBENCETA BUTTE   pro.: /bárbnsiytə/

Coconino (Grand Canyon)   T34N R5E

Jacob Hamblin, a noted Mormon missionary and explorer, met Barbenceta, a principal leader of the Navajo. In 1871 Hamblin introduced the Indian to Maj. John Wesley

Powell and asked the Indian to help enlist Indians in aiding the 1872 Grand Canyon exploration. Later Powell named the butte for the Indian leader.
Ref.: Schellbach File (Grand Canyon)

BARBERSHOP CANYON

Coconino   T13N R11E   Elev. c. 7000'
Dick Hart Ridge and Dick Hart Draw were named for a stockman who had a sheep-shearing location on its east slope at Barbershop Spring, named for a member of Hart's crew who served as barber for the men. This canyon is a.k.a. Dick Hart Draw.
Ref.: 18a

BARDGEMAN WASH

Navajo   T23N R16E
The wash takes its name from two shallow wells dug here by Joe Bardgeman c. 1888. Navajo Indians, who considered the range theirs, resented Bardgeman's running cattle in the area. Ref.: 41, pp. 39, 161; 182

BARFOOT PEAK

Cochise   T17S R30E
The peak takes its name from that of the park (i.e., a natural open park-like area) where the Barfoot family ran goats. The name is their own, and not a brand. Barfoot was also a freighter. Ref.: Riggs; Burrall

BARKERVILLE

Pinal   T7S R13E
Here A. F. Barker had a cattle ranch with a ranch post office on the old stage road from Tucson to Florence. On the post office application, the name suggested is Black Mountain. Post office officials wrote in Barkerville.
P.O. est. May 12, 1923, Mrs. Ruth E. Barker, p.m.; disc. Dec. 15, 1933 Ref.: Kitt; 242

BAR M CANYON

Coconino   T17N R8E   Elev. c. 6000'
Matthew Burch (b. 1859, Prussia) lived at Camp Huachuca prior to 1880, moving from there to establish a cattle ranch which used the Bar M Spring for many years. Bar M was his brand. Ref.: 63; 18a

BARNES BUTTE

Maricopa   T2N R4E
In 1937 this butte was named to honor Will C. Barnes (b. June 21, 1858; d. Dec. 17, 1936), a noted pioneer, stockman, legislator, and historian. Barnes, who was awarded the Congressional Medal of Honor for his part in the Indian wars, was first editor of *Arizona Place Names* (1935). Ref.: State Library Files; 329

BARNES PEAK

Gila   T2N R14E   Elev. 5028'
In 1903 F. L. Ransome in USGS Paper No. 12 named a geological formation here after a local prospector, A. M. Barnes (b. 1833, Pennsylvania). The Barnes Mine was at Barnes Spring. Ref.: Barnes (no relation); 62; 270, p. 30

BARNEY FLAT

Coconino   T21N R2E   Elev. c. 5000'
George Barney, a homesteader, started the Bar Heart cattle ranch here c. 1905.
Ref.: Benham

BARNEY PASTURE

Coconino   T19N R5E
James Mitchell Barney (b. 1838, New York) had a horse ranch here. He constructed a fence about four miles long between Oak Creek Canyon and Sycamore Canyon to confine his horses to this grazing range. Ref.: Earl C. Slipher, Letter (Feb. 29, 1956)

BARNEY STATION

Cochise

This was an Overland Mail Company stage station a few miles east of Stein's Pass near Doubtful Canyon. Ref.: 147, p. 25; 56, p. 292

BARNHARDT CANYON

Gila   T9N R9E

Probably named for Marshall B. Barnhart (b. 1846, Ohio) or for another early settler named Barnhardt who had a ranch here prior to 1915. Ref.: 18a; 63; Pieper

BARRETT, FORT

Pinal

At the Pima Villages (about six miles northwest of Sacaton), Capt. Calloway of the California Column (organized to march east and take part in the Civil War) learned that a Confederate detachment under Lt. Jack Swilling (see Gillette, Maricopa) was nearby. Calloway assigned Lt. James Barrett and twelve men to capture Swilling and his men. In a battle at Picacho on April 15, 1862 Barrett and two of his men were killed, as were two Confederates, two others being captured. (see Picacho, Pinal) By that time the California Column had arrived at Ammi White's flour mill on the Overland Stage route, and there they threw up earthworks to defend if attacked. They named it Fort Barrett in honor of the dead officer. The column of the First California Infantry under Lt. Col. Joseph R. West moved on, but left a detachment in charge. Fort Barrett was officially established May 31, 1862 and abandoned July 23, 1862. Ref.: 145, p. 124; 206, p. 87; 73, II, 167; 107, II, 88

BARRIER ISLANDS

La Paz   T5N R22W

Joseph Christmas Ives named these high rocks in the middle of the Colorado River because they somewhat blocked easy passage of his party in 1854. In 1866 Browne called them The Barriers, noting they were about halfway between the town of Yuma and La Paz. On the Hartley map the name is Barrie Islands. Rhodes (see Rhodes Ranch, Yuma) drowned near the rapids created by these "islands." Ref.: 245, p. 10

BARTLETT DAM

Maricopa   T6N R7E

The highest reclamation dam of its type, Bartlett Dam was completed in 1939. It has multiple-arch construction, impounding the waters of Bartlett Reservoir with a normal high water elevation of 1798'. Ref.: 5, pp. 55, 147

BARTLETT MOUNTAIN

Santa Cruz   T23S R11E   Elev. 4566'

This mountain is named for "Yank" Bartlett, who was a packer for the Boundary Survey party. He lived nearby at Yank's Spring in Bear Valley, where he was shot through the shoulder by marauding Indians under Geronimo's leadership. Bartlett was still ranching here in the 1890s. By 1941 the peak was often being referred to locally as Sentinel Peak. It should not be confused with Sentinel Peak in the Santa Rita Mountains. Ref.: 329; Gilbert Sykes, Letter (1941)

BASALT CLIFFS

Coconino (Grand Canyon)   T32N R5E

Dark basaltic formations below the plateau gave rise to the name for the cliffs, for the canyon walls, and for Basalt Creek (or Basalt Canyon Creek). Ref.: Kolb; 182

BASIN RANGE

The Basin Range, an area of about 68,000 square miles, has two major divisions. The first is the Plains, about 27,000 square miles in southern Arizona, extending to the eastern border. The second is the Mountain District, which lies between the Plains and the high northern Arizona Plateau. Range upon range of mountains slice across it. The Plains, on the other hand, contains both mountains and desert.

BASKIN TANK CANYON

Gila   T3N R21E

An Indian family named Baskin maintained a stock tank here, hence the name of the canyon. Ref.: 329

BASS CANYON

Coconino (Grand Canyon)   T33N R1W

William Wallace Bass (b. Oct. 2, 1841, Shelbyville, Indiana; d. March 7, 1933) settled near Williams in 1883. In 1884 he made a hunting trip to the head of the Havasupai Indian trail to Mount Huethawali, and Capt. Burro (an Indian) showed Bass hidden springs. Because they lay undiscovered where Bass believed he had already searched out everything, Bass called the place Mystic Spring, possibly also because it was sacred to the Havasupai tribe. Bass found an old Indian trail nearby and extended it into the Grand Canyon. He named it Mystic Spring Trail, completing it prior to 1900. Bass set up tents for tourists, many of whom he met at Bass Station, about four miles south of the end of the Grand Canyon branch railroad and about twenty-five miles from the camp where Bass had moved in 1889. George Wharton James, who visited Bass Camp, calls it Surprise Lookout. Although Bass sold his Grand Canyon property and moved in December 1925, he left orders so that his body was cremated and the ashes dropped in a copper box from an airplane onto Bass Tomb, also now known as Holy Grail Temple (elev. 6710') in the Grand Canyon.

The name of Mystic Trail changed to Bass Trail. Those who used it were ferried over the Colorado River in a cage on a strong cable — strong enough to carry horses, cattle, and sheep as well as people — from whence they climbed to the North Rim. The cable was the Bass Ferry or Bass Cable Ferry Crossing. It was also the site of Bed Rock Camp. Bass Canyon contains Bass Rapids. Ref.: W. W. Bass Materials (Wickenburg); Schellbach File (Grand Canyon); 5, pp. 485-486; 178, pp. 77, 78, 181; 333, p. 77

BASSETT PEAK

Graham   T11S R20E   Elev. 7650'

Named for Bob Bassett, a pioneer cattleman with holdings nearby. Ref.: 18a

BATAMOTE MOUNTAINS   pro.: /bátamówtey/

Pima   T11S R5-6W   Elev. 3202'

A natural rock tank near the base of these low mountains was called *batamote* (Batamote Well) after a local plant which grows where it has permanent moisture. The tank is on the site of a ranch which was described as *old* in the early 1900s. Thomas Childs and his father maintained the watering place, which was also called Temmile Well, its distance by road northeast of Ajo. Ref.: Ketchum; 58; 57, p. 359

BAT CANYON

Navajo: *tse jaa abani* = "bat rock"

Apache   T4N R28E   Elev. c. 6000'

Said to be infested with bats, Bat Rock is at the foot of the canyon and at the end of Bat Trail, an important Navajo horse trail. This scenic spruce-lined canyon and the trail take their name from that of the rock. Ref.: 331, p. 22

BAT CANYON

Greenlee   T5S R29E   Elev. c. 4000'

The canyon derives its name from the presence of a bat-infested cave (Bat Cave of course) on Eagle Creek southwest of Morenci.

BAT CAVE

Greenlee   T5S R29E

The cave is a source of bat guano fertilizer. See Bat Canyon, Greenlee
Ref.: Simmons

BATES-GROWLER MOUNTAINS

Pima   T15S R6 and 7W

This is the name given on the blueprint of 1915 for the "Nomadic Papago Surveys," at a time when men named Bates and Growler were known here. See Bates Well, Pima, and Growler Mountains, Pima Ref.: 329

BATES PEAK
Mohave   T20N R15W
This peak in the Hualapai Mountains was named for J. Wells Bates (b. 1847, New York), a mining operator, who was living in New Virginia mining settlement in 1880. Ref.: 329; 63

BATESVILLE
Pinal   T5S R18E
The *Tucson Enterprise* (July 27, 1893) carried an advertisement for lots to be sold in the proposed mining company town of Batesville. J. Wells Bates (see Bates Peak, Mohave) was a partner with Bates, Newman and Company, the mining concern seeking to create the community. It is not known whether a village came into being here, but the name of Bates became attached to the canyon where the town was to be. Ref.: 18a; 329

BATES WELL
Pima   T14S R6W   Elev. c. 1700'
The original well which lends its name to the current small village here was one of two in the pass between a conical peak and the Growler Mountains. Mexicans, who could not pronounce *Bates* Well, called it El Veit, and Papago Indians referred to it as *Tjuni Káatk* (= "where there is sahuaro fruit"). The east well, dug by a man named Bates in the 1890s, and the west by C. A. Puffer in 1913 (see Growler Mountains, Pima) is called the Growler Well. The east well was taken over by Ruby Daniels, who ran about two thousand cattle in the region until forced to leave by a severe drought in 1920. The wells and region are sometimes called Daniel's Ranch. Today Bates' name is reflected in the Veit Wild Life Area of one hundred and sixty acres, established in 1948. Ref.: 58, 57, p. 418; 9, p. 1

BATH FALLS
Coconino (Grand Canyon)   T31N R2E
These falls were used as a natural shower by men in Hermit Creek Canyon. Ref.: Kolb

BATTLE FLAT
Yavapai   T11N R1W   Elev. 5740'
In May 1864 Fred Henry, Stuart N. Wall, DeMarion Scott, Samuel Herron, and Frank Binkley camped here on a small open area. Attacked by an estimated one hundred and fifty Indians, the men battled for three hours. Fred Henry, wounded in the arm, escaped and sought help. Before he returned, the Indians abandoned their attack. Frank Binkley lost an eye and Herron died of wounds nine days later. Ref.: 116, p. 385; *Arizona Star* (Feb. 4, 1889), p. 1

BATTLEGROUND CREEK
Apache   T3N R27E   Elev. c. 7500'
Imprisoned for years for cattle rustling, Bill Smith escaped. Later he visited Crosby's store with his brothers Al, George, and Floyd. When they left, Crosby rode sixteen miles to Springerville to form a posse. The group tracked Smith to Battleground Creek where, in a sunken marshy area, two posse members and Bill Smith were killed. Ref.: Thompson

BATTLEGROUND RIDGE
Coconino   T13N R10E
This ridge on the edge of Gila County was the site of two Apache battles. In the first, all the soldiers but one were slain, and in the second (July 1882) all fifty marauding Apaches died in the last major Indian battle in Arizona. Ref.: 261, p. 6; 168, pp. 381, 389

BATTLESHIP, THE
Apache   Elev. 5530'
This butte in the Petrified National Forest has petrified logs jutting from it like cannon, hence the name. Ref.: Branch

BATTLESHIP, THE
Coconino (Grand Canyon)   T31N R2E   Elev. 5867'
Known as the Battleship *Iowa*, and so referred to by Emery Kolb in 1914, the name was in use shortly after the Spanish-American War (1898). The butte resembles an old-style battleship. Its early name has been truncated to The Battleship.
Ref.: Verkamp; Kolb; 178, p. 59

BATTLESHIP MOUNTAIN
Mohave   T20N R20W   Elev. 4165'
This place looks like a huge battleship. It is not the same location as Mount Nutt (T20N/R19W). Ref.: 18a

BATTLESHIP PEAK
La Paz   T9N R15W   Elev. c. 2500'
This peak in the Buckskin Mountains resembles a battleship. Ref.: Willson

BAYARD
Yavapai   T10N R1W   Elev. c. 5000'
This was a mining camp named for James A. Bayard, secretary of Arizona Territory in 1887.
P.O. est. May 25, 1888, William B. Long, p.m.; disc. April 24, 1897 Ref.: Barnes

BEACON ROCK
Mohave (Lake Mead)   T40N R15W
This place was named for a beacon light near its summit. In 1946 Elzada U. Clover suggested the name Callville Islands because of its location near that place in Utah, but in 1948 the USGS assigned the current name. Ref.: 329

BEAL CANYON
Coconino   T21N R8E
Named for the Beal family, early settlers in this canyon, its rough terrain has now been filled in and the Flagstaff sewer system runs through it. Ref.: Paten

BEALE POINT
Coconino (Grand Canyon)   T33N R2W   Elev. 6695'
This location was named in honor of Lt. Edward Fitzgerald Beale, USN (d. 1893) who left San Antonio, Texas, on June 25, 1857 to survey for a wagon route from Fort Defiance to the Colorado River. Beale had twenty-five camels to carry supplies and equipment. In 1851 the Sitgreaves Expedition had followed the route, and Lt. Amiel W. Whipple surveyed it for a railroad route in 1853-54. Beale crossed the Colorado River at Beale's Crossing on October 18, 1857. As for Beale's camels, they were eminently satisfactory from the military standpoint, but they panicked miners' burros which bucked their loads on sight of the hump-backed beasts. The camels aroused the ire of miners and prospectors to such an extent that public furor followed. See also Mohave, Fort, Mohave Ref.: 159, p. 479; 335, pp. 5, Note 5, and p. 50

BEALE'S PASS
Mohave
This location is on the Jacob Blickenderfer blueprint map dated February 1872. See Mojave, Fort, Mohave Ref.: 242

BEALES SPRINGS
Mohave   T21N R7W
These two springs were found by Lt. Edward Fitzgerald Beale on October 8, 1857, but he did not name them. They became important when Hualapai Indians began skirmishing in the area. There were fights with the military in 1867, at which time there was a

mail route station here where Lt. Col. William Redwood Price said the Indians had attacked on December 10, 1867, shooting all the mail company livestock. As a result, on March 25, 1871 a small "tent fort" commanded by Capt. Thomas Byrne, 12th Infantry, was established at Beal's (*sic*) Springs. Byrne, a red-headed Irishman with a " 'deludherin' tongue," controlled the Indians without battles. J. A. Toner, agent for the Indians on the Colorado River Reservation, reported in 1873 that the Hualapais were settled, not on the reservation, but on the direct route used by miners and travellers at Camp Beale Springs, and should be made to move to the reservation. By July the military camp was ordered removed. It was abandoned on April 6, 1874. The mail station was omitted from the stage route on January 8, 1875. See Mojave, Fort, Mohave
P.O. est. as Beale Spring, March 17, 1873, Benjamin S. Spear, p.m.; disc. March 30, 1875 Ref.: *Weekly Arizona Miner* (Sept. 30, 1871), p. 2, and (Jan. 8, 1875), p. 3; 159, p. 479; 335, pp. 50-52

BEAN CANYON
Cochise   T14S R27E
The canyon borrows its name from that of Bean Station on the nearby railroad. The station, now gone, was established by Superintendent Bean of the Southern Pacific R.R. on September 28, 1881, but the name was only briefly in use, and never officially so. See Bowie, Cochise
P.O. est. under name Bean, Sept. 28, 1881, Henry A. Smith, p.m.; changed to Teviston, Dec. 27, 1881

BEAR: Many place names carrying the appellative *Bear*, which may be attributed to one of the following in the majority of cases: (1) presence of bear; (2) resemblance of a formation to a bear; (3) landmarks associated with being used by bear (e.g. a wallow); (4) an incident concerned with bear; (5) a family name. The following are instances of "Bear" place names in Arizona, with comment about the origin where it is known or is interesting enough to assign space. In most cases the origins may never be recovered.

Bear, The	Navajo	In Monument Valley	
Bear	Yavapai	T18N R1E	

During the construction of the railroad, a bear was shot here. The place is a major shipping point for flagstone. Ref.: 18a

Bear Basin	Graham	T8S R23E	
Bear Camp	Coconino		

The *Arizona Miner* (Nov. 20, 1869), p. 2, says Henry Clifton reported it was named by Joseph Walker on August 17, 1861.

Bear Canyon	Apache	T27N R8W	
Bear Canyon	Cochise	(1) T13S R28E	(2) T19S R30E
Bear Canyon	Coconino	T19N R2E	

Bear used to be numerous in this region. The informant killed one in 1900. Ref.: Hart

Bear Canyon	Gila	(1) T11N R10E	(2) T5N R22E
Bear Canyon	Graham	(1) T4S R26E	(2) T6S R19E
		(3) T10S R25E	(4) T11S R20E
Bear Canyon	Greenlee	T1S R28E	
Bear Canyon	Navajo	T6N R22E	
Bear Canyon	Pima	(1) T20S R7E	(2) T13S R15E
Bear Canyon	Yavapai	T18N R1E	
Bear Canyon Lake	Coconino	T12N R13E	
Bear Cienega	Apache	T5N R27E	
Bear Creek	Cochise	(1) T12S R21E	(2) T24S R19E
Bear Creek	Gila	T9N R15E	
Bear Creek	Greenlee	(1) T2S R30E	(2) T4N R28E

John H. Toles Cosper killed over four hundred bears along #1 above. Ref.: Cosper (nephew)

Bear Creek	Navajo	T8N R15E	
Bear Creek	Pima	T14S R18E	
Bear Creek	Yavapai	T11N R1W	
Bear Fall Point	Coconino (Grand Canyon)	T32N R2W	
Bear Flat	Gila	T11N R12E	

Oak mast attracts bears to this flat. Ref.: Woody

Bear Flat	Yavapai	T15N R7W
Bear Flat Creek	Apache/Navajo	T7N R23–24E
Bear Flat-Hellgate-Pleasant Valley Trail	Gila	

Occasionally bears appear along this trail, hence the first part of its name. Second, the terrain is "rough as the gate to hell." The section in Pleasant Valley is opposite Hellgate. Ref.: Woody

Bear Gulch	Cochise	T15S R29E
Bear Head Canyon	Gila	T7N R12E
Bear Headland	Coconino (Grand Canyon)	T33N R3W

Because of its fancied resemblance to the outline of a bear head, Frank Bond named this location c. 1930. Ref.: 18a

Bear Head Mountain	Gila	T7N R12E	Elev. 6650'
Bear Hills	La Paz	T4N R16W	Elev. 2188'

These hills were named for William Bear, first postmaster at Harrisburg. Following his death, his body was carried to its grave on a burro, as Bear had requested. Ref.: Willson

Bear Lake	Coconino	T34N R2E	
Bear Jaw Canyon	Coconino	T23N R7E	
Bear Mountain	Gila	T6N R17E	Elev. 6424'
Bear Mountain	Greenlee	T2N R30E	Elev. 8550'

From certain angles, this mountain resembles a bear lying down. There are many bears in this region. Ref.: Paton; Sweeting

Bear Mountain	Yavapai	(1) T18N R7W	Elev. 7200'
		(2) T18N R4E	Elev. 6276'
Bear Park	Coconino	T17N R9E	

This area used to be called Little Horse Park because the skeletons of three very small horses were found here. Navajo Indians were said to have such horses. Ref.: 329

Bear Paw Spring	Coconino	T23N R7E
Bear Playground Spring	Navajo	T7N R21E
Bear Ridge	Navajo	T9N R18E
Bear's Ears	Navajo	

(Formation in Monument Valley)

Bear Seep	Coconino	T18N R8E	
Bear Sign Canyon	Coconino/Yavapai	T19–18 R5E	
Bear Sign Creek	Yavapai	T18M R5E	
Bear Spring	Apache	(1) T5N R30E	(2) T6N R28E
Bear Spring	Cochise	(1) T15S R29E	
		(2) T18S R30E	(3) T23S R20E
Bear Spring	Gila	T6N R22E	
Bear Spring	Graham	(1) T4S R26E	(2) T5S R26E
Bear Spring	Greenlee	(1) T2S R31E	(2) T2N R31E

Bear Spring	Coconino	(1) T18N R8E

See Elden Spring, Coconino

Bear Spring	Coconino	(2) T42N R14E

The name is a translation of its Navajo name: *shuah-betoh* (= "bear spring").

Bear Spring	Maricopa	T6N R9E
Bear Spring	Navajo	T6N R22E
Bear Spring	Pima	(1) T19S R18E (2) T15S R18E (3) T14S R18E
Bear Spring	Santa Cruz	T20S R15E
Bear Spring	Yavapai	(1) T12N R5E (2) T15N R5W
Bear Springs	Cochise	T15S R29E

In 1854 Lt. Parke noted that these six springs (Spanish: *Ojos de los Osos* = "springs of the bears.") "rising from the plain ... The water is abundant and agreeable to the taste." Apache Indians frequently attacked ranchers and travellers who dropped by to share the water with the Indians. Here Lt. Howard B. Cushing, three soldiers, and several civilians were killed by the Chiricahua leader Cochise in May 1871. In 1887 an earthquake did away with the springs, which had supplied water for Fort Bowie. Ref.: 254, pp. 26-27; *Citizen* (March 2, 1872), p. 2; 49, p. 105; *Tombstone Prospector* (May 9, 1887), p. 3

Bear Spring Canyon	Graham	T5S R27E
Bear Spring Canyon	Pima	T19S R18E
Bear Springs Canyon	Pinal	T6S R18E
Bear Springs Pass	Cochise	T15S R29E
Bear Springs	Coconino	T20N R2E
Bear Springs	Graham	T7S R23E
Bear Springs	Navajo	T11N R18E

During a roundup in the mid-1880s a bear was roped and killed here. Ref.: 18a

Bear Springs Draw	Navajo	T11N R18E
Bear Springs Flat	Graham	T6S R23E
Bear Springs Knoll	Graham	T7S R23E
Bear Springs Wash	Graham	T7S R23E
Bear's Wells	Pima	c. T19S R7E

The name translates the Papago name, *Tjotom vaxia* (= "bear wells"). One well is twenty feet deep and the other, twenty-nine. Ref.: 58

Bear Tank Canyon	Pinal	T1S R23E
Bear Thicket Creek	Pinal	T1N R12E
Bear Track Canyon	Yavapai	T13N R2E
Bear Trap Spring	Yavapai	T16N R6W
Bear Valley	Greenlee	T2N R31E
Bear Valley	Santa Cruz	T23S R11E

See Bartlett Mountain, Santa Cruz

Bear Valley Ranch	Santa Cruz	T23S R11E

This ranch was owned by "Yank" Bartlett's partner, a man named Shanahan, who was killed at Yank's Spring by Apaches. They shot him in the stomach. See Bartlett Mountain, Santa Cruz Ref.: 329; Sykes, Letter (Aug. 8, 1941)

Bear Valley Mountains	Santa Cruz	T23S R11E

See Bear Valley, Santa Cruz; Bartlett Mountain, Santa Cruz, and Pajarito Mountains, Santa Cruz

Bear Valley Ranch	Santa Cruz	T23S R11E

This ranch was owned by Shanahan. See Bear Valley, Santa Cruz

Bear Wallow	Pima	T12S R16E
Bear Wallow Campground	Pima	T12S R16E

It seems likely that this is the place Emerson O. Stratton used as a camp site "at the bear wallow." Ref.: AHS, Emerson O. Stratton *ms*.

Bear Wallow Canyon	Coconino	T17N R6E
Bear Wallow Canyon	Navajo	T8N R19E
Bear Wallow Creek	Graham/Greenlee	T3N R27–28E

When Pete Slaughter drove cattle into this valley in 1894, bear wallows were common here. Bears sought wallows to rid themselves of pesky biting flies. Ref.: 18a

Bearwallow Spring	Graham	T8S R24E
Bear Wallow Spring	Pima	T12S R16E

BEARDSLEY
Maricopa   T4N R1W   Elev. 1265'

In 1888 Will H. Bearsley planned irrigation here. A community named for him has developed. Ref.: 279, p. 202; 18a

BEARDSLEY (R.R. SPUR)
Maricopa   T3N R2W   Elev. 1250'

This place was probably named for nearby Beardsley (T4N/R1W). It had a post office. P.O. est. Jan. 28, 1936, Bess Simmons, p.m. Ref.: 242

BEARGRASS BASIN
Graham   T4S R21E

This location is named because of the abundant growth of so-called "bear grass." It is not the same as the bear grass of Montana and nearby states (which is used in Sioux and other tribal sacred ceremonies).

BEASLEY LAKE
Coconino   T20N R6E

An earlier name for this location was Lost Tank or Lost Lake. It was also known as Lowlander Lake or Tank. It is near Beasley Park, formerly Lowlander Park. The Forest Service renamed this place for Al Beasley c. 1950. Ref.: Dietzman

BEAST, THE
Apache   T1N R5W

Gregory c. 1915 named this volcanic neck because of its shape. Ref.: 141, p. 190

BEAUCHAMP PEAK
Apache

On July 25, 1864 J. W. Beauchamp left the Woolsey expedition camp to take sightings from this "high, round mountain, at the end of a range," southwest of Black River. He was ambushed by Indians who shot, lanced and stripped him, leaving him dead. The expedition members buried him at the foot of the mountain, naming it for him. Ref.: *Arizona Miner* (Sept. 21, 1864), p. 1

BEAUFORD, MOUNT
Maricopa   T8N R5E   Elev. 5239'

Barnes gives the name for this location as Buford (a clue to its pronunciation), but notes it was named for Clay Beauford (b. 1846, Virginia; d. 1905), a cavalry captain in charge of Indian scouts operating out of San Carlos. The name "Mount Buford" occurs on a 1869 military blueprint map at a time when Beauford was leading his scouts on forays in the region northwest of Fort McDowell. After his honorable discharge in 1873, Beauford established a ranch in Arivaipa Canyon. His legal name was Welford Chapman Bridwell. For an unknown reason, the peak name also appears as Humboldt Mountain. Ref.: 98, pp. 48, 49, 66; 242

BEAUTIFUL MOUNTAIN
Navajo: *zitkéh* = "mountain top"; *xóžóne* = "beautiful"
Coconino   T28N R15E   Elev. 6314'
The American name is a translation of the Navajo.

BEAUTIFUL VALLEY
Apache   T3N R10W
So called by first whites here.
Ref.: 18a

BEAUTY, CAMP
Apache   T5N R10W
A trail led from Fort Defiance to this spot in Canyon de Chelly, near Spider Rock, a
photograph of which is in Capt. Wheeler's report. The canyon walls are about one
thousand feet high. Ref.: 345, I, 75

BEAVER: The word *Beaver* occurs in at least two dozen Arizona place names. Beaver
were once so plentiful in Arizona streams, particularly the Gila River, that fur trappers
were here as early as 1830. Thanks to conservationists, in the 1970s beaver began making
a comeback. The following incorporate *Beaver* in their names:

Beaver Branch   Navajo
See Reidhead Crossing, Navajo

Beaver Canyon   Coconino (Grand Canyon) T33N R4W
See Wall Creek, Coconino (Grand Canyon), and Havasu Canyon, Coconino (Grand Canyon)

Beaver Canyon   Coconino   T13N R11E
See Houston Draw, Coconino

Beaver Canyon   Greenlee   T1N R32E

Beaver Canyon   Navajo   T8N R22E

Beaver Creek   Coconino   T13N R11E
See Houston Draw, Coconino

Beaver Creek   Greenlee   T4N R29E
On the 1918 post office site map for the Espero post office, the name of this creek is Willow Creek, but
by 1924 the newer name was firmly entrenched. Ref.: 242

Beaver Creek   Yavapai   T14N R5E

Beaver Dam   Mohave   T40N R15W
Bonelli moved here in 1864 when a flood washed away his Santa Clara, Utah, home. See Beaver
Dam Wash, Mohave, and Bonelli entries, Mohave

Beaver Dam Mountains   Mohave   T41N R14W
See Beaver Dam Wash, Mohave, and Littlefields, Mohave

Beaver Dam Park   Apache   T8N R25E

Beaver Dams   Apache   T6N R25E   Elev. 8800'

Beaver Dams   Mohave
See Littlefields, Mohave

Beaver Dam Wash   Mohave (& Utah) T41N R16W
Numerous beaver dams were found along this wash by the first Mormon settlers c. 1863, hence the
name. It is now a dry wash. Ref.: 322, p. 12; 329

Beaver Falls   Coconino   T33N R4W
                                  (Grand Canyon)
See Havasu Canyon, Coconino (Grand Canyon)

Beaver Island   La Paz   c. 230 mi. N. of Yuma (1870)

Beaver Park   Coconino   T12N R12E

Beaver Point   Mohave   T12N R19W

BEAVERHEAD

Yavapai   T16N R6E

Beaverhead Station was on the route from Camp Verde to Brigham City in 1880, but by 1895 only a deserted cabin marked the spot. Fewkes called it Beaver Head. By transfer the name was applied to Beaverhead Flat. Ref.: 111, p. 548

BEBERTON

Yavapai   T17N R2W

The name derives from that of M. Beber, its owner in January 1918. Ref.: AHS Names File

BECKER CREEK

Apache   T7N R26E   Elev. c. 8500'

Because stakes were at one time used here to measure snow depth, this creek was first known as Snowstake Creek. It is now called Becker after the Becker family of Springerville. Ref.: Davis; Wentz

BECKER LAKE

Apache   T9N R29E   Elev. c. 8000'

Julius and Gustav Becker (brothers) in 1882 dammed a natural spring to create a lake used for irrigation. Several outlaws are buried at the bottom of the lake. Ref.: Becker (Gustav's son); Willson; Wiltbank

BECKERS BUTTE

Gila   T5N R18E

This butte, capped by redwall limestone, may have been named for P. Becker (b. 1843, Germany), a farmer in the valley in 1870. The butte overlooks the junction of Flying V Canyon with the Salt River. Ref.: 329; 62

BEDIVERE POINT

Coconino (Grand Canyon)   T33N R1E   Elev. 7750'

Maj. John Wesley Powell, who explored the Grand Canyon in the 1870s, established the precedent of assigning names of mythological deities and heroes to canyon locations. Nomenclature drawn from the Arthurian legends was introduced by Richard T. Evans in 1902, inspired by the magnificent scenery, which aroused in him thoughts of the Holy Grail legends. Among names so introduced are the following: Elaine Castle, Galahad Point, Gawain Abyss, Gunther Castle, Guinevere Castle, King Arthur Castle, Lancelot Point, Merlin Abyss, and Modred Abyss. Ref.: Francois E. Matthes File, Letter to Geographic Board (May 6, 1925) (Grand Canyon)

BEDROCK RAPIDS

Coconino (Grand Canyon)   T34N R2W

The name describes the appearance of these rapids as they tumble over rocks in the bed of the Grand Canyon. In 1932 Frank Bond applied the name to this canyon west of the rapids. Ref.: 329

BEE CANYON

Gila   T9N R10E

A cave high on the cliff face has honeycombs hanging from it and the bluffs in this canyon hum with myriads of wild bees, hence the name. Ref.: Pieper

BEEHIVE PEAK

Pima   T15S R13E   Elev. 2712'

This sharp peak in the northeast corner of the San Xavier Indian Reservation bears a name descriptive of the shape of its volcanic neck.

BEGASHIBITO WASH   pro.: bégašibəto/

Navajo: *begashi* = "cow", "cattle"; *bito* = "water"

Navajo/Coconino   T37N R15E T32N R13E

As the name indicates, cattle find water along the upper portion. According to Gregory, rains result in a series of lakes and pools joined by streams. Ref.: 141, p. 92

BEKIHATSO LAKE
Navajo: *beekid* = "lake"; *hatso* = "large in area"
Coconino   T33N R7E
Gregory calls this the largest of the dry lakes in the vicinity of Chinle Wash.
Ref.: 141, pp. 118, 190

BELGRAVIA
Pinal   T4S R14E   Elev. c. 1500'
The post office here served the mill for the Belgravia Mine. The first name for this
location was Hercules, at the time the name of the Ray-Hercules Mining Company,
changed by Mr. Adams to Belgravia. He named it for a suburb of Johannesburg, South
Africa, his home.
P.O. est. Nov. 15, 1918, Frederick O. Locks, p.m.; disc. June 19, 1930
Ref.: 242; 18a

BELL BUTTE
Maricopa   T1N R4E   Elev. 1369'
This butte has a bell shape, hence its name. Ref.: 18a

BELL BUTTE
Navajo   T25N R19E   Elev. 6342'
The name describes the shape of this butte.

BELL BUTTE
Pinal   T3S R12E   Elev. c. 2000'
The butte borrowed the name from the nearby Silver Bell Mine. Ref.: 18a

BELLEMONT
Coconino   T22N R5E   Elev. 7132'
The first name for this location was Volunteer (see Volunteer Mountain, Coconino),
which in September 1882 was changed by the A.T. & S.F.R.R. to Bellemont. Prior to
the coming of the railroad the location had been a stage and relay station on the northern
Arizona route. The name "Bellemont" was coined to honor Belle Smith, daughter of F.
W. Smith, in charge of railroad construction in the early 1880s.
P.O. est. March 2, 1887, Frank W. Payne, p.m.; disc. Aug. 1, 1957; Wells Fargo 1887
Ref.: Fuchs, quoting *Prescott Weekly Courier* (Sept. 9, 1882), p. 2; 242; AHS Names
File

BELLEVUE
Gila   T1S R14E
The Whelan brothers named this location because of its fine view. The first name
suggested — Summit — was rejected by the postal department.
P.O. est. May 14, 1906, Edward P. Whelan, p.m.; disc. April 7, 1927
Ref.: Woody; 242; 18a

BELLOTA CANYON   pro.: /beyótə/
Spanish: *Bellota* = "sweet acorn"
Santa Cruz   T23S R12E
Edible sweet acorns fall from oak trees in this canyon, hence the name. Ref.: Seibold

BELLOWS CANYON
Graham   T8S R22E
This canyon was also called Tripp Canyon. It was named for an old forge and mine
bellows formerly in it. Ref.: 329

BELL ROCK
Yavapai   T16N R5E   Elev. 4919'
"Old Man" James, who settled near here in 1876, named this location because of its bell
shape. Ref.: Schnebly; 18a

BELL'S CANYON

Yavapai   T12N R5W

This canyon, described as "in one of the roughest granite mountains on earth," forms a natural ambush pocket. Its name comes from the fact that on May 3, 1865, Richard Bell was killed by Indians here along with Cornelius Sage and Charles Cunningham. Bell was the first to be killed. A year later George W. Leihy, successor to Charles D. Poston as Superintendent of Indian Affairs, and his clerk W. H. Evarts, were also ambushed here by Indians. Ref.: 107, II, 2, 128; *Weekly Arizona Miner* (April 16, 1875), p. 2; *Arizona Miner* (Nov. 30, 1866), p. 2; 224, pp. 188, 189

BELL WELL

Yuma   T12S R8W

This old well in the Growler Mountains is named for Charlie Bell, an old-time cowman. It is sometimes called Charlie Bell Well. Ref.: Monson

BELMONT

Santa Cruz   T24S R16E

This was a community proposed at Washington Camp in early 1880. It was named for the Belmont Mine.

BELMONT CANYON

Pinal   T2S R12E

This canyon takes its name from that of Belmont Mine, which is in the canyon.

BELMONT MOUNTAINS

Maricopa   T4N R6W   Elev. 3137'

This group was named in March 1963 by the USGS because there are "two wells and a mine nearby," which used the name Belmont. Ref.: 329

BENCHMARK MOUNTAIN

Yavapai   T8N R4E

There is a surveyor's benchmark on this mountain, hence the name.

BENEDICT, MOUNT

Santa Cruz   T23S R15E   Elev. 4565'

John Benedict settled with his brother at this ranch on the Santa Cruz River near Helmet Mountain, as Benedict called it c. 1870. At a later date the location was called Gold Hill, possibly because gold was discovered on its slope. Ref.: Lenon; 329; *Arizona Citizen* (Aug. 24, 1872), p. 2

BEN NEVIS MOUNTAIN

Pima   T15S R2E   Elev. 4013'

Papago Indians call this mountain *Kia Hoa Toak* for one section, and *Gah-Kotch* for the other. American miners soon applied other names, such as Peer Mountain for a mining claim there held by Alexander McKay. S. A. Manlove called it Ben Nevis to honor McKay, a Scotsman, the first white man to climb the mountain. Manlove found the name in Wordsworth's poetry which refers to rugged and precipitous heights. See Quijotoa, Pima Ref.: 308, pp. 17, 18, 24; 57, p. 392

BENNY CREEK

Apache   T7N R27E   Elev. c. 8000'

Parallel creeks — Benny and Rosey Creeks — memorialize a romance which did not materialize. Prior to 1900 Rosey Thompson was engaged to marry Benny Howell, or so he thought. While he was getting the license, she ran off with Fred Hoffman and married him. Ref.: Wentz

BENSON

Cochise   T17S R20E   Elev. 3580'

Benson was founded in 1880 with the coming of the S.P.R.R. It soon became the overland rail shipping point for booming Tombstone. Benson was named for Judge

William B. Benson of California, friend of Charles Crocker, president of the S.P.R.R. How close Benson was to Tres Alamos may be judged from the fact that in 1897 the Papago name for Benson was rendered as *Vai k'au'pä* (= "three cottonwoods"). Benson Pass is east of Benson. See also Ohnesorgen Stage Station, Cochise
P.O. est. July 26, 1880, John Russ, p.m.; Wells Fargo 1885
Ref.: *Arizona Miner* (April 16, 1880); AHS; *The Oasis* (April 4, 1896), p. 1; 126, n.p.

BENTON
Greenlee   T1N R30E
This location, which is today known as the Rail H U Ranch, is about three and one-half miles above the junction of the Little Blue and the Blue River. It was named for a cattle rancher (first name unknown) killed in the first Apache raid on the Blue River c. 1889. The small settlement here was a lumber center where Ira Harper had his sawmill. It also had a school, important because ranchers customarily moved into towns to send their children to school during the winter. Floods from 1904 through 1906 washed most of the place away. When the Balke family left, the post office closed.
P.O. est. Aug. 15, 1903, Max A. Balke, p.m.; disc. Oct. 10, 1907
Ref.: Mr. & Mrs. Eddie Fritz; Mrs. Fred Fritz, Sr.; Mrs. Fred Fritz, Jr.; Sweeting; 242

BENTON SPRING
Santa Cruz   T24S R5E
The spring here was named for the Benton Mine (T24S/R16E).

BERGEMEYER COVE
Mohave   T21N R21W
This deep cove one-mile south of the power line at Katherine Boat Landing was named for Frederick R. Bergemeyer (b. 1913, Mason City, Iowa; d. Aug. 23, 1953), the first ranger in charge of the National Park Service activities at Katherine Wash District near Bullhead City. While en route to a forest fire in Zion National Park, he was killed in an automobile accident. This location was named in his honor.
Ref.: Burns; Paul R. Franke, Superintendent, Zion and Bryce Canyon National Park, Letter (March 23, 1956)

BERNADINO
Cochise   T22S R30E   Elev. 4500'
In 1921 the name of this location was changed from San Bernadino. The place name was one of the oldest in Arizona, as it was applied at least as early as 1697 to this location (now on the international boundary) by those making the journey between the garrisons of Janos and Fronteras, Mexico. When the Mexican government took over from Spain (1820), the San Bernardino Land Grant was awarded (in 1822) to Ignacio Perez. The grant consisted of 73,240 acres. The ranch which developed was an important one, said to run about eighty thousand head. After the dissolution of the missions in 1828, the ranch was abandoned and the cattle reverted to the wild state. By 1846 the ranch buildings were in ruins. In 1853 the Gadsden Purchase placed 2,336 acres of the San Bernardino Land Grant within the United States. A visitor to the ruins in 1854 noted that from fifteen to twenty families had probably lived at the location prior to its being deserted. Because of Apache activities, the place remained deserted until John Horton Slaughter (b. Oct. 2, 1841, Louisiana; d. Feb. 15, 1922) bought the rights of the Perez descendants and drove cattle into the area in 1883. It is possible that the house constructed there in 1848 by Maj. Lawrence P. Graham was still in existence. Sheriff Slaughter in turn leased it to A. T. Kirkendall in 1918.
    A post office was established to serve the area at a station by the same name on the railroad close to the ranch headquarters (T24S/R30E).
P.O. est. Sept. 15, 1906, Elizabeth McAllister, p.m.; disc. March 16, 1918 (apparently at ranch headquarters); Bernadina P.O. est. March 5, 1915, W. B. Claunch, Jr., p.m.; disc. Dec. 15, 1917 Ref.: 242; 26, pp. 304 and 304, Note 1; *Arizona Cattleman* (April 8, 1918), p. 6; 43, p. 245; 224, p. 3; 269, pp. 295, 296, 302, 306; 116, p. 428; *Arizona Star* (May 2, 1878), p. 3

BERT LEE PARK
Coconino   T18N R8E
In December 1966 the USGS altered this name from Lee Park, as it was named for Bert Lee. Ref.: 329

BESH-BA-GOWAH PUEBLO
Apache = "camp for metal"
Gila   T1N R15E
These restored ruins were occupied c. 1225 to 1375 AD.

BETATAKIN   pro.: /b̥itát⁷ahkin/
Navajo: *bita'sh kin* = "house on the edge"
Navajo   T38N R17E   Elev. 6600'
Betatakin is the most accessible of the three spectacular cave pueblos of the Navajo
National Monument. They are Inscription House, Keet Seel, and Betatakin. The initial
view of Betatakin from the Sandal Trail is breathtaking. Far below and set well back in a
wind-carved cave (large enough to house the United States capitol building) rests a
magnificent two-hundred room cliff dwelling. It is about seven centuries old. This
second largest ruin in the Monument was first seen by white men when visited in 1909 by
Dr. Byron Cummings and John Wetherill. It is located in a canyon known both as
Betatakin Canyon and as Tsegi Branch of Laguna Canyon. The old Navajo name for this
place was *Kin Lani* (= "many houses"). The post office application said that it was
known locally as Shonto Trading Post.
P.O. est. Aug. 20, 1931, Mrs. Elizabeth Rorick, p.m.; disc. Feb. 28, 1934
Ref.: 141, p. 190; 331, p. 140; 13, Brewer, "Navajo National Monument," pp. 3, 4; 5,
pp. 38, 422; 242

BIBO
Apache   T19N R25E   Elev. c. 5800'
This was a trading post run by Sol Bibo from 1880 to 1890. It was also a railroad stop.
Ref.: 18a; 85, Sheet 16

BIDAHOCHI BUTTE   pro.: /b̥idáho:čiyʌ:⁷/
Navajo = "many red streaks up its slope"
Navajo   T23N R21E   Elev. 5750'
The name comes from the fact that behind the trading post (run by Julius Wetzler from
1882-92) the mountain has a red rock slide scar. The name gradually extended to
include the valley and nearby pueblo ruins. Its name has been rendered as fol-
lows: Biddehoche; Bita Hache; Bitahochee; Biddahoochee, and Bitahotsi. At Bi-
dahochi Spring, Navajo Indians dug a well, for they camped regularly here en route to
Keams Canyon and to Holbrook. It came to be known as Indian Wells. See Indian
Wells, Navajo Ref.: 141, pp. 153, 190; 331, p. 77

BIG: The descriptive designation *Big* occurs in many Arizona place names, listed below.
In addition, other place names incorporate *Big* with another name, e.g. Big Ship Corral.
The latter are listed individually, with no cross reference to *Big*.

Big Bend	Mohave	(1) T40N R16W	
		(2) T20N R22W	Elev. 520'
Big Bend	Maricopa		
See Gila Bend, Maricopa			
Big Bend Creek	Cochise	T21S R29E	
Big Blue Mountains	Greenlee		
See Big Lue Mountains, Greenlee			
Big Canyon	Coconino	T32N R7E	
Big Canyon	Gila	T11N R12E	
Big Canyon	Graham	T6S R27E	
Big Canyon	Navajo	T7N R22E	
Big Cove	Mohave	T33N R7W	
Big Cove Canyon	Coconino	T37N R3W	

When Tom Pollock owned this location, it was called Cold Springs. He took it over from Hi Fuller.
Ref.: Hart

Big Creek	Graham	T9S R24E	
Big Dome	Pinal	T3S R13E	
Big Draw	Cochise	T16S R22E	
Big Dry Fork	Coconino		

See Chevelon Creek, Coconino/Navajo

Big Dry Lake	Navajo		

See Zeniff, Navajo, and Mormon Lake, Coconino

Big Dry Wash	Coconino/Navajo		

See Chevelon Creek, Coconino/Navajo

Big Fields	Pima	T17S R3E	Elev. 2044'

See Gu Oidak, Pima

Big Fields Valley	Pima		

See Gu Oidak, Pima

Big Fields Wash	Pima		

See Sells Wash, Pima

Big Hands	Maricopa		

See Gila Bend, Maricopa

Big Hands	Navajo		

See Mitten Butte, Navajo

Big Hill	Yavapai	T14N R7E	
Big Hogan	Apache	T41N R21E	

This hill looks somewhat like a Navajo hogan (round or rectangular home).

Big Lake	Apache	T5N R28E	Elev. 9415'

In the early 1900s Ted Wentz patented the land where Big Lake now is. In 1923 the place was a slough, but was being called Big Lake. The constructing of a dam in 1934 created a true lake. During the time it had been a slough, wild game stood in it to find relief from stinging insects. Wentz sold it in 1954. It is today a fishing and recreation area. Ref.: Wentz; Becker; Wiltbank

Big Lake Knoll	Apache	T5N R28E	Elev. 9415'
Big Mesa	Greenlee	T6S R31E	
Big Mountain	Navajo	T8N R22E	Elev. 7144'

The American name is a translation of the Navajo name. In 1968 the USGS replaced the following names: Zihi-Dush-Jhini Peak, Ziltah Jini Mesa, and Zilth Dush-Jin. Ref.: 331, p. 52; 329

Big Moqui Spring	Coconino	T14N R11E	

Not really a spring, but a stock tank, this place takes its name from its location on the Moqui Ranch owned by the Clear Creek Cattle Company in the early 1900s. Ref.: Hart

Big Oak Flat	Gila	T4N R10E	
Big Pine Spring	Gila	T5N R10E	
Big Pocket	Coconino	T40N R4E	
Big Point	Mohave (Grand Canyon)	T33N R7W	
Big Point	Navajo	T40N R18E	Elev. 7990'
Big Point Canyon	Mohave (Grand Canyon)	T33N R7W	
Big Point Valley	Navajo	T33N R20E	
Big Pond	Pinal	T9S R13E	
Big Prairie	Graham	T1N R25E	
Big Ridge	Coconino	T38N R2E	
Big Ridge	Gila	T10N R13E	

Big Saddle	Coconino	(Grand Canyon)	

See Nankoweap Butte, Coconino (Grand Canyon)

Big Saddle	Maricopa	T4N R10E	Elev. 5448'
Big Saddle Point	Coconino (Grand Canyon)	T35N R1W	
Big Sand Wash	Coconino	T16S R6W	
Big Sand Wash	Mohave	T39N R6W	
Big Spring	Coconino	(1) T30N R9W	(2) T21N R3E
Big Spring	Graham	(1) T6S R25E	(2) T5S R26E
Big Spring	Maricopa	(1) T7N R3E	(2) T5N R3W
Big Spring	Mohave	T34N R8W	

This place is also called Whitmore Spring.

Big Spring	Navajo	T8N R22E	
Big Spring	Yavapai	(1) T13N R7E	(2) T17N R9W
Big Springs	Navajo	T9N R22E	
Big Spring	Gila		

See Goldtooth Smith Spring, Gila

Big Spring Canyon	Coconino	T20N R3–4E	Elev. 7850'

This location was named in 1882 by Maj. Clarence Dutton, who said that it was in Stewart's Canyon. Big Spring Canyon heads at Big Spring, hence the name. In April 1964 the USGS changed the name of Shinumo Creek (also known as South Big Spring Canyon) to the current Big Spring Canyon. Ref.: 100, p. 130; 329

Big Springs	Coconino	T37N R1E	Elev. 7850'

This place now has a small community.

Big Springs	Navajo	T9N R22E	
Big Springs Wash	Graham	T5–6S R25E	

This wash heads at Big Spring, hence its name. It is also called Peck Wash. Ref.: 329

Big Valley	Mohave	T41N R12W	
Big Valley	La Paz		

See McMullen Valley, for which "Big Valley" was used in the 1860s.

Big Wash	Coconino	T30N R12E	
Big Wash	Mohave	T23N R19W	
Big Wash	Pima	(1) T19S R3E	(2) T11S R14E
Big Wash	Pinal	T10S R14E	

See Box O Wash, Pinal

BIG BUG

Yavapai   T12N R1W   Elev. c. 4300'

In 1863 John Marion named this creek because prospectors found numerous large bugs here. These insects, which still abound, are large, dark brown, shiny flying beetles about the size of a walnut. The mining community of Big Bug borrowed its name from that of the creek, as did also the famous Big Bug Mining District with its Big Bug Lode.
P.O. est. as Bigbug, March 1, 1879, William A. Munch, p.m.; changed to Red Rock, Nov. 28, 1879, Amos C. Stedman, p.m.; changed to Big Bug, March 29, 1881; changed again to Bigbug, Aug. 22, 1895; disc. March 1, 1910 Ref.: Thompson; Merritt; 242; *Weekly Arizona Miner* (June 5, 1865), p. 3

BIG CASA BLANCA CANYON

Santa Cruz   T21S R15E

Renamed from Casa Blanca Canyon by USGS in 1959. This was done to differentiate it from Little Casa Blanca Canyon.

BIG CAVE RUINS

Apache   T6N R28E

These are Indian ruins in a large cave in Canyon de Chelly, hence the name.

BIG CHAIR

Navajo   T14N R21E

This is a chair-like rock formation.

BIG CHINO VALLEY

Yavapai   T2N R5W

In 1975 the USGS added the term *big* to Chino Valley to distinguish the valley from the settlement, which is not in Big Chino Valley.

BIG EYE MINE

Yuma   T4S R18W

This gold mine is named for a natural window in the mountain. Big Eye Wash is at T7S/R17W. Ref.: Monson

BIG HORN

Maricopa   T2N R10W

This was the post office on the Buzzard Ranch. According to one informant, the owner of this ranch rustled cattle and was killed at the ranch. The signs of habitation here have almost completely disappeared. The post office took its name from that of the nearby Big Horn Mountains.

P.O. est. April 4, 1930, Wesley W. Watson, p.m.; disc. June 29, 1925

Ref.: Johnson; 242

BIG HORN MOUNTAINS

Maricopa   T5N R9W   Elev. 3480'

In 1854 Antisell noted that mountain sheep were abundant on the Big Horn or Goat Mountains. Ref.: 4, p. 131

BIG JOHNEY CANYON

Gila   T1N R15E

This canyon, which is sometimes erroneously spelled Big Jonnie or Big Johnnie, was named for the Big Johney Gold Mine, located in 1876 by Henry Ramboz. He named it for a miner nicknamed Big Johney. Ref.: Woody; 18a; Willson

BIG LUE CANYON

Greenlee   T4S R32E

This canyon took its name from the LUE brand used by the Big Lue Ranch (T4S/R32E). It was owned by Eugene Johnson, in the area at least by 1884. "Stuttering Charlie" Johnson settled on the lower Blue River in 1886. Although his first brand was 333, he also later used the LUE brand. He sold out to Abe and Dick Boyles c. 1906. They in turn sold in 1911 to Bud Stacey. See Johnson Canyon, Greenlee

Ref.: Fred Fritz, Sr., Notes; Mrs. Fred Stacey; Mrs. Fred Fritz

BIG LUE MOUNTAINS

Greenlee   T4S R31E   Elev. 7047'

In August 1963 the USGS eliminated the following names for this location: Big Blue Mountains, Black Jack Rim, and Big LEU Mountain. See Big LUE Canyon, Greenlee

BIG SANDY RIVER

Mohave/La Paz   T18N R13W   Elev. c. 1400'

The stream runs through a sandy valley called Big Sandy Valley, naturally. Big Sandy River forms the boundary line between La Paz and Mohave Counties. In 1604 Juan Mateo de Oñate called this stream Rio de San Andres, as he came to it on Saint Andrew's Day (November 30). In 1744 Jacobo Sedelmayr called it Rio Azul. In 1854 Lt. Amiel Whipple said that Capt. Joseph R. Walker descriptively named this stream. Whipple called it Williams River, proceeding along to its juncture with the Santa Maria

River (to form Bill Williams River). The portion Whipple traveled is now called Little Sandy, and its lower section Big Sandy River.
Ref.: 346, pp. 211 and 211, Note 19; 200, pp. 50, 52

BIG WATER

Navajo: *Totosoh* = "big water"
Apache   T35N R29E
This place is also called Debebekid (= "sheep lake"), but that name can be applied to many in the area. In 1968 it was also being called Forest Lake, a descriptive name as it is the only spot having big trees. Ref.: 331, p. 88; 329

BIGELOW, MOUNT

Pima   T12S R16E   Elev. 8550'
This name first appears on a 1917 Forest Service map. According to Mrs. Edith Kitt, the name was in use years before that date. There is some doubt about the origin, one possible source being that it was named for Dr. J. M. Bigelow, who served with the Boundary Survey Commission for the Gadsden Purchase and who was with the railroad survey group under Lt. Amiel W. Whipple. There is also a possibility that Bigelow Peak was named for Lt. John Bigelow, Jr., who led a command in 1885 to Stockton Gap (Graham, *q.v.*). He had been a cavalry scout in the Santa Rita Mountains in the early 1870s. Ref.: 347, pp. 10 and 10, Note 5; 18a

BILL ARP CREEK

Yavapai   T10N R1E
This creek, also known as Rock Creek, is named for the Bill Arp Mine.

BILLINGS GAP

Apache   T18N R25E
This gap was so named for the Billings Cattle Company, established here c. 1883 by A. E. Henning.

BILL McCLINTOCK DRAW

Coconino   T12N R11E
This draw is named for a man who raised horses here c. 1900. Ref.: Hart

BILL WILLIAMS MOUNTAIN

Coconino   T21N R2E   Elev. 9256'
This is a double-peaked, lava-cone formation. The name first appears in 1851 on Richard H. Kern's Sitgreaves' survey map. Williams was a rugged mountain man whom Antoine Leroux met in 1837 when Williams was on the river which has his name, after journeying across Arizona trapping beaver. William Sherley Williams (b. Jan. 3, 1787, North Carolina; d. March 14, 1849) for nine years was an itinerant preacher, living for twelve years thereafter on the frontier, plus an additional seven as a plainsman and mountain man. Zebulon Pike said Williams was a tall, gaunt, red-headed man. While transporting baggage for the Fremont Expedition in 1849, he was killed by Ute Indians. Kern in 1851 told Leroux they were memorializing Williams by naming a mountain and river for Williams. Other mountain names are as follows: *Jock-Ha-We-Ha* (Mohave = "covered with cedar"); *Hue-Ga-Woo-La* (Havasupai = "bear mountain"); Ives Mountain; Santa Maria Mountain (Disturnall map, 1847).
Ref.: 177, pp. 379, 380; 109, pp. 18, 77, 107, 144; 107, III, 292; 5, p. 321

BILL WILLIAMS SKI AREA

Coconino
This skiing area is on Bill Williams Mountain. The first course was established here in 1939. Ref.: 124, pp. 148, 149

BILLY CREEK

Navajo   T9N R22E
This creek was named for William T. Corse, whom Barnes describes as "an eccentric Englishman" living on its banks for several years. The USGS corrected the spelling from Billie to Billy in April 1964. Ref.: 18a; 329

BINGHAM PEAK

Greenlee   T1N R29E   Elev. 7070'
This peak was named for Lt. Theodore Alfred Bingham. In the early 1880s he traversed this area with troops en route to Fort Apache. Ref.: 18a

BIRCH MESA

Gila   T11N R10E
This was the name of an old ranch homesteaded by the Pieper family.
Ref.: Pieper

BIRD SPRINGS   pro.: /tsidiyⱽ:toʔi/
Navajo: *Tsidiito'i* = "bird spring"

Navajo   T22N R16E
This spring between Moqui Butte and Leupp was an important landmark and stopping point for travellers until the Indian Service developed other water facilities.
Ref.: 331, p. 9

BISBEE

Cochise   T23S R24E   Elev. 5300'
John Dunn, an Army scout, was in pursuit of Apaches in 1877 when he found samples of rich ore in Mule Pass. Unable because of his military duties to take up a claim, Dunn grubstaked George Warren, notable not only as a pick-and-shovel man, but as a first class alcoholic. They named their mine the Copper Queen, an allusion to the fame of the Silver King in Pinal County, which they hoped the Copper Queen would rival. In 1880 Phelps Dodge & Company, then a small mining firm, sent Dr. James Douglas to buy copper prospects in Arizona. He bought property on the boundary of the Copper Queen. Rather than enter litigation, the two companies merged as the Copper Queen Consolidated Mining Company. Among its promoters were Ben and Lewis Williams. One shareholder was Judge DeWitt Bisbee, father-in-law of one of the Williams brothers. Bisbee, Williams & Company developed the Copper Queen Mine, naming the community after Judge Bisbee, who never visited there. In 1929 Bisbee became county seat for Cochise County.
P.O. est. Sept. 7, 1880, Horace C. Stillman, p.m.; incorp. Jan. 9, 1902
Ref.: 7, p. 9; 5, p. 174; "Arizona Days and Ways," *Arizona Republic* (Aug. 8, 1854), p. 23

BISBEE JUNCTION

Cochise   T24S R24E
The first name for this location was Osborne, for William Church Osborne of the Phelps Dodge Corporation. It was sometimes also called New Osborne. See Bisbee, Cochise Wells Fargo 1907

BISCUIT MOUNTAIN

Santa Cruz/Cochise
The name denotes that this mountain looks very much like a Parker House roll, as it is "folded over" at the top. See Bruce, Mount, Santa Cruz Ref.: Lenon

BISCUIT PEAK

Graham   T8S R19E   Elev. 6539'
The peak looks like a biscuit. Ref.: Jennings

BISHOP CREEK

Yavapai   T10N R3E
This location was named for a saloon-keeper named Bishop, who had a wooden leg. He owned the Four Mile House saloon near Prescott. Ref.: Dugas

BISHOP KNOLL

Gila   T9N R10E   Elev. 4848'
This knoll was named for the young Mormon bishop in charge of the settlement at Gisela. Ref.: 18a

BISHOP LAKE

Coconino   T24N R3W

John Bishop (b. 1855, Maryland) maintained a ranch near this location where Bishop had homesteaded in 1886. Ref.: Rothwell; 62

BISHOP NOSE

Gila   T9N R11E   Elev. 4423'

This is the local name for a peak at the south end of Red Hills. It is sometimes called Red Mountain. Ref.: 329

BISHOP SPRINGS

Coconino   T32N R4W

As this location is near Bishop Lake, there is a possibility it was named for John Bishop. On the other hand, Samuel A. Bishop (d. 1877) in 1859 left California and made his way to where he met the party under Lt. Edward Fitzgerald Beale at San Francisco Mountain. There Bishop became camel master. Needing supplies cached at the Colorado River, Beale and Bishop went to the spot, but discovered the supplies had vanished and that they must hasten to Los Angeles for more. Years later Bishop died of heat exhaustion and exposure on the upper Colorado River. He is buried at Kenyon Station. Ref.: AHS, Samuel Bishop File; *Weekly Alta California* (May 21, 1859), "Arrival of Lt. Beale"

BISMARK CANYON

Mohave   T23N R17W

Bismark was a prospector and miner who afterwards became a barger. Ref.: Harris

BISSEL'S POINT

Coconino (Grand Canyon)

This name was in use in 1897. See Comanche Point, Coconino (Grand Canyon)

BITSIHUITOS BUTTE   pro.: /bətzi^{h}wit^{d}ẕ^{ʔ}a ʌs/

Navajo: *Bitsu'h hwits'os* = "tapered formation at its base"

Apache   T35N R23E

The Navajo name describes this formation. In 1932 the name was spelled Pitsehytse. Ref.: 141, pp. 138, 190

BITTER: The use of the word *Bitter* in place names in Arizona usually refers to the taste of water. Occasionally such water is poisonous.

Bitter Creek	Greenlee	T6W R32E
Bitter Creek	Yavapai	T7N R2W

Named by a party of Navajo prospectors in 1876, including John O'Dougherty and Capt. John Boyd. Ref.: 359, p. 102

Bitter Spring	Coconino	T33N R13E
Bitter Well Wash	Pinal	T9S R3E

See Sif Vaya, Pinal

Bitterwell Mountains	Pinal

See Vekol Mountains, Pinal

Bitterweed Springs	Navajo

See Chilchinbito, Navajo

BLACK: Over one hundred place names in Arizona use *Black*. Frequently the word designates a volcanic area. Examples follow:

Black Butte	Graham	T7S R19E	Elev. 4568'
Black Butte	Maricopa	(1) T8S R4W	Elev. 1772'
		(2) T2S R7W	Elev. 3612'
		(3) T6N R7W	

Black Butte	Mohave	T29N R21W	

Named by Wheeler in 1871.

Black Butte	Pima	T15S R2E	Elev. 2838'
Black Butte	Pinal	T5S R7E	Elev. 1786'
Black Butte Spring	Yavapai	T16N R2E	
Black Canyon	Graham	(1) T15S R19E	(2) T10S R21E
		(3) T5S R27E	
Black Canyon	Mohave	T37–38N R7W	

This canyon on the Colorado River was named by Lt. Joseph Christmas Ives.

Black Canyon	Navajo	(1) T7N R23E	(2) T16N R16E

Not volcanic, the second location was named because of black gumbo in which army wagons mired. It was also called McCauley Sinks.

Black Canyon	Yavapai		

This is an Arizona Game and Fish Department shooting facility of one thousand five hundred forty nine acres of state land and one hundred and sixty acres of federal land. It is in Black Canyon (see below).

BLACK CANYON

Yavapai   T15N R2E

The route connecting the military forts for stage lines and freighting companies followed this canyon, and Black Canyon Highway follows the old route but cuts through the high sides of the canyon. At points one can see wagon wheel scars on the canyon floor. Black Canyon Hill was a dangerous one-way grade with few turn-outs. Here stage drivers announced their coming by blasts on long tin horns. A two-blast reply warned of someone coming from the opposite direction. Occasionally the thunderous noise of the stages blanked out the horns, and if two stage coaches met at an impassable place, "the 'up team' was unhitched, two men grasped the tongue of the vehicle and rolled it downhill until reaching a place where it could be passed."

The current community of Black Canyon is on this highway. A post office was established here under the name Cañon in 1894. It was also called Goddard's, for its first postmaster. The area was served briefly by a post office at Rock Springs, but when it closed, a new post office was opened under the name Black Canyon. This location is also known both as Bumble Bee Canyon and as Black Canyon Station. The latter was in operation in 1875 where the Agua Fria River crossed the Black Canyon road.

P.O. est. as Cañon, May 19, 1894, Charles A. Goddard, p.m.; disc. Oct. 17, 1906; reest. Sept. 24, 1902, Morris Fuller, p.m.; name changed to Rock Springs, 1932; name changed to Black Canyon City, June 1, 1955, Mrs. Alma Amann, p.m.; name changed to Black Canyon, Jan. 1, 1966 Ref.: Amann; Schnebly; Slipher; Theobald; 5, p. 306, 329; 242

Black Canyon City	Yavapai	T8N R2E	Elev. 2228'

See Black Canyon, Yavapai

Black Canyon Hill	Yavapai		

This location was also called Antelope Hill. Not currently on the main highway, it is on the old road still used by miners and ranchers. See Black Canyon, Yavapai Ref.: Schnebly

Black Canyon Lake Wild Life Area	Navajo	T11N R15E	

This seventy-eight acre lake is a wild life area maintained by the Arizona Game and Fish Department. Ref.: 9, p. 4

Black Canyon Range	Mohave	T25S R21W	
Black Canyon Spring	Graham	T5S R19E	
Black Canyon Spring	Mohave	T13N R11W	Elev. 2800'
Black Canyon Spring	Navajo	T7N R23E	
Black Canyon Spring	Yavapai	T15N R2E	

Black Canyon Station   Yavapai
See Black Canyon, Yavapai

Black Cave   Yavapai   T7N R1W

Black Circle Mountain   Pima   T13S R2W   Elev. 2368'

Black Creek   Apache/New Mexico   T22N R30E

This creek originally flowed from its source in Black Lake at the west end of the Chusca Mountains. Later its waters were diverted into the present Red Lake Reservoir. Ref.: 141, pp. 33, 87, 88, 89; 331, p. 9

Black Creek   Apache   T1N R5W

Black Creek Canyon   Apache   T22N R30E

Black Creek Valley   Apache   T2N R7W
See Red Valley, Apache

Black Cross Butte   Maricopa   (1) T3N R10E   Elev. 3351'
    (2) T2N R11E   Elev. 4806'

Black Draw   Cochise   T23S R30E

Black Holes   Coconino   T25N R11E

Tongues of *malpais* (volcanic terrain) extend from the San Francisco Mountain group to several falls on the Little Colorado River. At Black Holes the river runs over several black lava tongues. Ref.: 141, pp. 42, 43

Black Forest   Yavapai   T20N R3W

This area was named by Whipple in 1857 because of the densely growing juniper forest. Ref.: 346, p. 180, Note 23

Black Gap   Cochise   T23S R24E

Black Gap   Maricopa   T8S R6W

Black Hill   Apache   T41N R26E

Black Hill   Pima   (1) T12S R2E   (2) T15S R13E

Black Hill   Pinal   T3S R10E

Black Hill   Yavapai   T8N R1W   Elev. 2948'

Black Hills   Graham/Greenlee   T7–6S R29E

Black Hills   Graham   (1) T4S R23E   Elev. 3642'
    (2) T9S R21E

Black Hills   Pima   (1) T12S R2E   Elev. 2706'
    (2) T18S R10E   Elev. 4421'

Black Hills   Pinal   T8S R15E   Elev. 4357'

Black Hills   Yavapai   T16N R2E   Elev. 6000'

Black Hills   Yuma   T5S R17W   Elev. 1633'

Black Hill Wash   Yavapai   T11N R3E

Black Knob   Cochise   T23S R25E   Elev. 5837'

Unfortunately for this listing, the name is not descriptive. Why it is so called is not clear. Ref.: Burgess

Black Knob   Coconino (Grand Canyon)   T32N R5E

In 1906 Frank Bond named this location Lava Butte. Ref.: 329

Black Knob   Coconino   T29N R9E

This location also carries the following names: Pogue Butte, Black Peak, and Lava Butte. Ref.: 141, pp. 43, 190

Black Knoll   Apache   T18N R25E   Elev. 5964'

Black Knolls   Mohave   (1) T40N R7W   (2) T41N R13W

| **Black Little Hill** | Pima | T16S R1W | Elev. 2000' |
| **Black Mesa** | Apache | T12N R24E | |

Navajo: *Dziti'jiin* = "mountain extends black"
The name is a translation of the Navajo. In 1932 the USGS changed it to the current form from the following spellings: Zilh-le-jini Mesa and Zilthe-le-jini. Ref.: 141, pp. 40, 190; 329

| **Black Mesa** | Coconino/Apache | T26N R9E | Elev. 5315' |

This is a variant name for the Mogollon Rim (*q.v.*).

| **Black Mesa** | Gila | T4N R14E | Elev. 4355' |

The name derives from a dense growth of black oak. Ref.: Woody

| **Black Mesa** | Graham | T2S R26E | |

| **Black Mesa** | Maricopa | (1) T7N R4E | Elev. 4698' |
| (2) T6N R9E | Elev. 3832' | (3) T2N R9E | Elev. 2991' |

| **Black Mesa** | Mohave | (1) T25N R14W | Elev. 5675' |
| | | (2) T12N R14W | |

In 1967 the USGS changed the name of this mesa from Manganese Mesa, a clue to the descriptive name — its dark color. Ref.: 329

| **Black Mesa** | Navajo | T12N R21E | |

In 1858 Capt. John G. Walker called it Mesa de las Vacas (Spanish = "mesa of the cows"). In 1921 the USGS changed the name from Mesa la Vaca. Spanish explorers had called it Tusayan. Black Mesa is similar to a huge island, two hundred and fifty miles in circumference. On the "fingers" of this roughly hand-shaped mesa are the Hopi Villages.
Ref.: 326, p. 106; 331, p. 10; 5, p. 58

Black Mesa	Pima	T22S R9E	Elev. 4650'
Black Mesa	Yavapai		
Black Mesa	La Paz	T3N R17W	
Black Mesa Canyon	Gila	T2N R19E	
Black Mesa Forest Reserve	Coconino		

See Coconino National Forest, Coconino

Black Mesa Wash	Navajo	T34N R16E	
Black Mesa Wash	Yavapai	T11N R8W	
Black Mesquite Spring	Gila		

See Mesquite Spring, Gila

Black Mountain Store	Navajo	T31N R22E	Elev. 6400'
Black Mountain	Gila	T9N R10E	Elev. 3969'
Black Mountain	Graham	(1) T1N R22E	
		(2) T4S R25E	Elev. 4880'
Black Mountain	Greenlee	T1S R29E	Elev. 6876'
Black Mountain	Maricopa	(1) T6N R4E	Elev. 3398'
(2) T2N R13E		(3) T6N R1E	Elev. 2460'
(4) T7N R6W	Elev. 3066'	(5) T5N R8E	Elev. 2992'
		(6) T6N R4E	Elev. 3398'
Black Mountain	Navajo		

See Black Mesa, Navajo. This is a variant name.

Black Mountain	Pima	(1) T1S R6W	Elev. 3008'
		(2) T15S R13E	Elev. 3703'
Black Mountain	Pinal	T7S R13E	Elev. 5587'

See Barkerville, Pinal

| **Black Mountain** | Yavapai | (1) T18N R3E | Elev. 6038' |

This was named for George Black, a successful cattleman, saloon-keeper, and pioneer Flagstaff settler. Ref.: Slipher

| **Black Mountain** | Yavapai | (2) T11N R3W | Elev. 4972' |

This name has no particular reference to tint. Ref.: 18a

Black Mountain	La Paz	T9N R19W	Elev. 1665'
Black Mountain Canyon	Yavapai	T13N R6E	
Black Mountains	Apache	T5N R22E	

BLACK MOUNTAINS
Mohave   T29N R22W

This range of mountains extends like a black barrier along the westernmost part of Mohave County. The blackness derives from forbidding looking hills extending from the northern region south to Union Pass. From the pass to Sacramento Wash, the name Black Mesa has often been applied because here the range is an ancient volcanic plateau sliced by erosion into individual hills. Formerly the name Ute Mountains was given to the entire length of the range, but in 1932, the name having fallen into disuse, the USGS eliminated it entirely. Fr. Francisco Garcés was the first white man to name this range in 1775, calling it Sierra de Santiago. Lt. Amiel W. Whipple (1854) called the eastern portion Blue Ridge Mountains. Lt. Joseph Christmas Ives while struggling up the turbulent Colorado River in the *S. S. Explorer*, had passed through a twenty-mile-long rock gorge with walls of black rhyolite, thus causing him to name it Black Canyon. Lt. Mallory (1865) extended the name to include the Black Mountains, calling it the Black Canyon Range. In Mallory's time, however, the range was usually called Sacramento Range because it bordered Sacramento Valley. Wheeler in his report called it the Colorado Range. Gradually Ives' name was extended to the entire mountain range. Ref.: 200, pp. 25, 27; 335, p. 5; 346, p. 302; 89, p. 167; 77, p. 315; 324; 245, p. 74

Black Mountain Trading Post	Apache	T32N R23E	
Black Mountain Wash	Apache	T6N R24E	
Black Mountain Wash	Gila	T9N R10E	
Black Pass	Coconino	T20N R6E	

Named for George Black, who owned a ranch and Black Spring (T20N/R7E). Ref.: Frier; Slipher

| **Black Peak** | Coconino | T33N R9E | Elev. 5879' |

See Black Knob, Coconino

Black Peak	Gila	T1N R15E	Elev. 4780'
Black Peak	Pima/Santa Cruz	T22S R10E	Elev. 5091'
Black Peak	La Paz	T9N R19W	Elev. 1656'
Black Pinnacle	Apache	T6N R28E	Elev. 7938'

Navajo: *Chezhini* = "black rock"

The American name is a translation of the Navajo. The Navajo also called this location *Shashdit' Inih* (= "where the bear lived"). It is a volcanic ridge towering above a pine forest. Other spellings for the name are as follows: Sajini Butte, Sezhini Butte, Mal-pais Butte. Ref.: 141, pp. 34, 190, 195; 331, p. 11

Black Point	Coconino	T27N R10E	Elev. 4930'
Black Point	Graham	T4S R22E	Elev. 2800'
Black Point	Pinal	T1S R10E	
Black Range	Mohave	T18N R20W	

This post office existed only on paper. It was supposed to serve a mining camp which also had a brief life. See Black Mountains, Mohave
P.O. est. Feb. 10, 1917, Mrs. Pansy Maud Keyes, p.m.; disc. Oct. 15, 1917 Ref.: 242

Black Range	Mohave	

See Black Mountains, Mohave

Black Range	Pinal	

See Slate Mountains, Pinal

Black Ridge	Apache	T13N R27E
Black Ridge	Maricopa	T7N R8E
Black Ridge	Yavapai	T11N R6E
Black River	Apache	T23N R4E
Black River	Graham	T2N R24E
Black River	Gila	T4N R20E
Black River	Navajo	T3N R22E

James Ohio Pattie explored eighty miles above the mouth of the Black River in 1826 and called the middle or upper Salt River the "Black River." The Black River of today heads on Mount Baldy and tumbles through canyons from one thousand two hundred feet to one thousand five hundred feet deep, the sides of which are lined with black volcanic precipices. It traverses country so wild that the river is crossed by only two roads. On October 26, 1846 Lt. William Emery called it Prieto River (Spanish = "black" or "dark"). Obviously impressed by the same blackness, King S. Woolsey in his report (September 21, 1864) called it Negrita, which the editor of the *Arizona Miner* translated to "Black River" because Col. Woolsey believed that the *Black* and *Negrita* were actually identical. The same editor said the river was also sometimes called Prieta.

Ref.: Schroeder; *Arizona Miner* (Sept. 21, 1864), p. 1; Wentz; 163, p. 284; 49, p. 440

Black River	Greenlee	T24N R28E
Black River	Gila/Maricopa	

See Salt River, Gila/Maricopa

Black River, East Fork	Apache	T5N R29E

See Black River, Gila/Apache/Navajo/Graham

Black River, East Fork	Greenlee	T4N R28E
Black River Springs,	Apache	T6N R28E

Head of

See Black River, Gila/Apache/Graham/Navajo

Black River Mountains	Apache	
Black River West Fork	Apache	T5N R29E

See Black River, Gila/Apache/Graham/Navajo

Black River West Fork	Greenlee	T4N R28E	
Black Rock	Apache	T37N R30E	Elev. 6664'

See Fluted Rock, Apache

Black Rock	Apache	T5N R28E	Elev. 7618'

In December 1960 the USGS approved this name, thus eliminating Sezhini Butte and Black Rock. See Black Pinnacle, Apache

Black Rock	Coconino	T30N R7E	Elev. 5773'
Black Rock	Graham	T6S R21E	Elev. 4784'

Despite its name, this is "a great barren monolith of red sandstone."

Black Rock	Yavapai	T8N R3W	
Black Rock Canyon	Apache	T5N R27E	
Black Rock Canyon	Graham	T6S R21E	
Black Rock Canyon	Mohave	T41N R10W	
Black Rock Gulch	Mohave	T40N R13W	
Black Rock Hill	La Paz	T3N R13W	Elev. 1414'

Black Rock Mountain	Mohave	T39N R14W	Elev. 7375'
Black Rock Point	Apache	T40N R29E	Elev. 7521'
Black Rock Pond	Navajo	T34N R18E	
Black Rock Ridge	Coconino	T35N R7E	
Black Rocks, The	Mohave	T38N R8W	
Black Rock Spring	Mohave	(1) T39N R13W (2) T25N R14W	
Black Rock Spring	Navajo	T20N R20E	

This location is also known as Smith Spring.

Black Rock Spring	Yavapai	T14N R2E	
Black Rock Standing	Navajo	T39N R19E	Elev. 5868'
Black Rock Wash	Graham	T5S R22E	
Black Rock Wash	Mohave	T19N R17W	
Black Rock Wash	Navajo	T34N R20E	
Black Rock Wash	La Paz	T4S R23W	

This was named for the Black Rock Mine (T3N/R13W). By 1881 it was producing well enough to sell for $125,000., a considerable sum in those days. Ref.: 355, p. 67

Black Soil Wash	Apache	T1N R8W
Black Spot Reservoir	Coconino	T35N R6E
Black Spring	Coconino	T20N R7E

See Black Pass, Coconino

Black Spring	Pinal	T1N R12E
Black's Station	Cochise	T19S R25E

In early 1909 this station was two and one-half miles southeast of Courtland. Ref.: 242

Black Stump Valley	Apache	T34N R22E	
Blacktail Canyon	Cochise	T22S R19E	Elev. 4800'

Several Arizona place names refer to blacktail deer, presumably at such places.

Blacktail Canyon	Coconino (Grand Canyon)	T33N R2W

See Blacktail Canyon, Cochise

Blacktail Spring	Cochise	T22S R19E

See Blacktail Canyon, Cochise

Blacktail Valley	Coconino (Grand Canyon)	T34N R1W

See Blacktail Canyon, Cochise

Black Tank	Yuma	T3S R19W

Black metamorphic rocks here led to the name.

Black Tanks	La Paz	T9N R18W

Named by Charles C. Genung in 1863.

Black Tank Wash	Coconino	T29N R3W
Black Top Mesa	Pinal	T1N R9E
Black Wash	Mohave	T34N R16W
Blackwater	Cochise	T5S R8E

See Douglas, Cochise

Blackwater Creek	Yavapai	T10N R4W
Black Spring	Yavapai	T10N R4W
Black Well	Cochise	T18S R20E

BLACK BILL PARK

Coconino   T22N R8E   Elev. c. 6200'

William West (d. c. 1927) was a logger and saloon-keeper known locally as Black Bill. He homesteaded one hundred and sixty acres and built an 8' x 8' cabin where he thought the railroad to Grand Canyon would pass by. The project failed to materialize and Black Bill moved on. It is also called Black Bill Flat. See Doney Park, Coconino
Ref.: Colton

BLACK DIAMOND

Cochise   T18S R24E   Elev. 5000'

The Black Diamond Mine was in operation in 1880, taking its name from the color and nature of the ore. Its post office served a mining camp of about one hundred.
P.O. est. Dec. 9, 1901, William Hamilton Schofield, p.m.; disc. Aug. 7, 1908
Ref.: 242; Larriau

BLACKHORSE CREEK

Apache/Navajo   T37N R32E

In 1915 Herbert Gregory noted that Black Horse was the name of a long-time Indian resident of the Navajo Indian Reservation. The name is also Blackhorse Wash.
Ref.: 329, Gregory, Letter

BLACK JACK CANYON

Greenlee   T5S R31E

Two outlaws were called Black Jack. One was Black Jack Christian, who in the early 1890s led a gang operating near and in Tombstone. He was shot fatally by a deputy sheriff at Cave Springs near Clifton. He called his gang the High Five. Among its members were Tom Anderson, Bob Hayes, Jess Williams, and "Code" Young.

 The other outlaw was Black Jack Ketcham, who in 1899 murdered two storekeepers named Rogers and Wingfield at Camp Verde. Ketcham had a hide-out in a cave at Black Jack Spring (T4S/R31E) and continued his depradations. Among them were many robberies, including one of a train in New Mexico. He was caught, tried, convicted, and hanged at Clayton, New Mexico, on April 26, 1901. The canyon is said to be named for Black Jack Ketcham by some, and by others after Black Jack Christian.
Ref.: Patterson; Mrs. Fred Fritz, Sr.; AHS, Chambers Collection, Box 7-8; Scott; 116, p. 694

BLACK JACK POINT

Yavapai   T8N R5E   Elev. 5404'

The origin of this name is not known, but it may be for one of the Black Jacks. See Black Jack Canyon, Greenlee

BLACK WARRIOR

Gila   T1S R14E

The post office here was established to serve employees at the Black Warrior Mine (T1N/R15E) located by Silas Tidwell. The Inspiration Mining Company bought the claim. A small community is under the tailings dump here.
P.O. est. Jan. 4, 1900, Charles S. Fleming, p.m.; disc. Feb. 29, 1912
Ref.: Woody; 242

BLACKWATER

Pinal   T5S R7E

The Blackwater Stage Station was in existence as early as 1875. According to Russell, the name of Blackwater first appears on Indian calendar sticks in 1851-52. It is noted on a manuscript map of 1870 as a location where William Bichard lived. (See Casa Grande, Pinal) In 1879 this name was on the map of the Pima Agency in Arizona Territory at a railroad stop. The Pima name for the location was *Os Kuk* (= "tree standing"). Another source gives the Pima name as *Chukma-Shu-dk* (= "black water"). There was an old Pima Indian man named Blackwater living near here in the early 1900s. In 1940 the name Uhs Kug was changed to Blackwater Chapel by action of the Gila River Pima-Maricopa Indian Council.
P.O. est. Jan. 22, 1907, O. J. Green, p.m.; disc. Feb. 28, 1931 Ref.: 329; 242; *Weekly Arizona Miner* (June 18, 1875), p. 3; 281, p. 45; 351 (Smithsonian Institution), p. 23

BLADDER CANYON

Gila   T5N R15E

Cowboys used the narrow entrance here to help them build a holding corral. When the owner saw the corrals, he said they looked like a bladder with a narrow neck, hence the name. See Heffner Canyon, Gila

BLAISDELL

Yuma   T8S R21W   Elev. 186'

Hiram W. Blaisdell engineered two canals in this vicinity, and hence the small railroad station here was probably named for him. However, Ira Blaisdell, in Yuma in 1879, succeeded in getting the S.P.R.R. to let him manage the water pump to supply Yuma with water. The station may have been named for him.

P.O. est. March 23, 1896, John E. McIver, p.m.; disc. Dec. 18, 1905; Wells Fargo 1903 Ref.: Kline; Huntington Library, Fr. Figueroa *ms.*, pp. 68, 69; 242

BLALACK   pro.: /blélæk/

Yuma   T8S R22W

The post office application lists Gila Center as the first name for this place, no doubt because the post office was to be in the Gila Center Store. It in turn was at a stop on the railroad named Araby. Blalack is reported to be the name of a local land owner.

P.O. est. Dec. 30, 1926, L. F. Moyer, p.m.; disc. Oct. 31, 1933 Ref.: 242

BLANCA MOUNTAINS, SIERRA

Spanish: *Blanca* = "white"; *Sierra* = "mountains"

Pima   T14S R1E   Elev. 3727'

This oval mass of mountains rises abruptly with its main portion consisting of white and grey granite gneiss, hence the name. This is a curious place name, meaning in literal translation "mountains white mountains," as given in Barnes but contemporarily the name is simply Sierra Blance. There was also a Papago village named Sierra Blanca with fifty inhabitants in 1858. Ref.: 57, p. 231; 167, II, 565

BLANCHARD

Yavapai   T13N R1W

This was the name of the post office at Iron King (*q.v.*).

P.O. est. July 7, 1903, Annie M. Williams, p.m.

BLANKENSHIP VALLEY

Mohave   T15N R20W

Blankenship was a pioneer cattleman in this valley, hence the name.

Ref.: Housholder

BLANKENSHIP WELL

Pima   T18S R5W

This well was named because Lon Blankenship dug it in 1917 for his cattle.

Ref.: 57, p. 425

BLAZE RIDGE

Coconino   T13N R10E   Elev. 7200'

Trees on this ridge were blazed to mark the site of one of the last Indian fights to take place near Pine. Ref.: Hart

BLIND: A few place names are so named because the locations are hard to find. Examples follow:

Blind Canyon	Cochise	(1) T20S R30E	(2) T23S R20E
Blind Lake	Coconino	T17N R9E	
Blind Spring	Navajo	T8N R23E	

BLIND INDIAN CREEK

Yavapai   T11N R2W

According to Charles Genung, this creek was named because the first prospectors here

in the 1860s met an old blind Indian who camped along the creek.
Ref.: 329 (as reported by Genung's daughter)

BLOODY BASIN
Yavapai   T11N R6E   Elev. 3077'
Bloody Basin is said to have earned its name because of the many Indian battles which
took place in it. It is reported that Fred Henry and four other prospectors were attacked
here by Apaches in May 1864 and all were wounded. Henry went for help despite having
been wounded in both legs.

Another legend says that where the town of Bloody Basin is, there used to be a bridge
over a gorge used by sheepherders taking bands of sheep to fresh grazing areas, from
southern to northern Arizona. During one of these crossings, the suspension bridge
collapsed and the sheep fell to a bloody death in the "basin" below. Many Indian ruins
are in this area. It is topographically extremely rough country where it is not uncommon
to become lost. Ref.: Schnebly; Antonio Gonzalo, collected by Frances Gonzalo
(1965); 329

BLOODY TANKS
Gila   T1N R14E
Bloody Tanks is at the head of Bloody Tanks Wash, also called Miami Wash. The
original name of the wash was West Branch of Pinal Creek. On January 24, 1864 King
S. Woolsey and his party from Prescott, which included fifteen Maricopa Indians,
pitched camp just above the tanks. Woolsey was convinced that Apaches camped at a
nearby hill were hostile. He persuaded them to enter camp for a parley. Without
warning, the Woolsey party opened fire and massacred the Apaches, whose blood
mingled with the water in the creek, hence the name Bloody Tanks.

According to another story, the Indians were not shot, but were murdered by eating
poisoned *piñole* (= "flour"), hence the reference to the Pinole Treaty. There is no
evidence to support the story beyond the fact that the Indians were given flour. On the
contrary, after the massacre the Woolsey expedition members trailed the fleeing
survivors, picking up tobacco and *piñole* handed to Indians before the massacre. There
is little likelihood that Woolsey's men would have tried to find poisoned *piñole*.
Ref.: Woody; 56, p. 121; 5, p. 348

BLOODY TANKS WASH
Gila   T1N R14E
Another name for this is The Canal. It runs through the town of Miami. See Bloody
Tanks, Gila

BLOWOUT: This term is used in the following place names to indicate a *blowout* or
volcanic action:

Blowout Creek	Yavapai	T16N R2E	
Blowout Mountain	Yavapai	T10N R4W	Elev. 4700'
Blowout Tank	Coconino	T23N R6E	

This lake, also known as Dry Lake, is a cattle waterhold. See Walker Lake, Coconino

BLOXTON
Santa Cruz   T22S R15E
This station on the Benson-Nogales branch of the S.P.R.R. was named by Denton G.
Sanford (see Sanford, Santa Cruz) for Robert B. Bloxton, his brother-in-law. Bloxton
was a sheepman near here in 1881. As late as 1915 Bloxton Siding was used to load ore
from the 3-R Mine. The railroad line ran through Sanford Ranch, now the Circle Z
Ranch (*q.v.*). Ref.: AHS; Kitt

BLOXTON, MOUNT
Santa Cruz
This is the round mountain near Bloxton Siding, Santa Cruz (*q.v.*).
Ref.: Seibold

BLUE

Greenlee   T3N R31E   Elev. 5680'

The first name for this location was Whittum, the site of the third ranch owned by Fred Fritz, Sr. He lived with Nat Whittum, who had been an Indian scout. Upon returning from Clifton where he had gone for supplies in 1891, Fritz found Nat Whittum by the bed in the cabin. He had apparently been murdered, for a trail of blood led from the spring and horse corral. The Apache Kid, a renegade Indian, was believed to be the murderer. Whittum was buried at a place now called Old Base Line because it is on the Forest Service boundary line.

The original post office at Whittum was at T4N/R31E. While C. D. Martin was postmaster, he circulated a petition to change the name to Blue because everyone knew where the Blue River was, but few where Whittum might be. It should be noted that this is apparently not the same place as Boyles (*q. v.*). In 1899 the post office at Blue was moved to T3N/R31E.

P.O. est. as Whittum, July 21, 1894, Isaac F. Castro, p.m.; name changed to Blue, Nov. 3, 1898 Ref.: Cosper; Mrs. Fred Fritz, Sr.; *Arizona Bulletin* (April 28, 1899), p. 2; 242

BLUEBELL

Yavapai   T11N R1E   Elev. 4620'

The location given is that for the Bluebell Mine, but the name Bluebell applies to a siding on the power-plant railroad tracks a mile east of the mine. Ores were carried from the mine to the siding by an aerial tramway and the ore transshipped for smelting at the Humboldt smelter. Ref.: Glannon; 5, p. 305

BLUE: The use of the designation *blue* in many place names indicates the presence of that color. Sometimes it occurs in geologic formations and sometimes from the hazy atmosphere and the color of the locality as seen from a distance. Except where otherwise noted, the following place names are so derived:

Blue Canyon   Apache   T1N R7W
See Quartzite, Apache

BLUE CANYON

Coconino   T32N R14E

This is the name of a trading post, the name being derived from the canyon where it is located. The first name for the post office here was Algert, after Charles H. Algert.

P.O. est. Jan. 7, 1899, Cirrilla E. Needham, p.m.; disc. Dec. 15, 1904
Ref.: 242; 5, p. 42; Museum of Northern Arizona; 141, pp. 88, 190, 191; 331, p. 13

BLUE CANYON

Coconino/Navajo   T33–32N R15–14E

This canyon name is a translation of its Navajo name: *Guku* = "canyon"; *dotklish* = "blue," derived from the presence of blue clay formations that have resisted erosion. In September 1968 the USGS eliminated the following names for this location: Bukudotklish, Dotklish, Moenkapi Wash, Algert.

Blue Canyon	Yavapai	T15N R8W	
Blue Creek	Greenlee	T1N R31E	
See also Francisco River, Greenlee			
Blue Canyon Trading Post Ruin	Coconino	T32N R13E	
Blue Clay Hill	Apache	T36N R28E	Elev. 6004'
Blue Clay Reservoir	Coconino	T39N R4E	
Blue Forest	Apache		

This portion of the Petrified Forest National Monument was named by John Muir because of its blue (bentonite) clay. Petrified wood is never blue. In this location petrified logs and pieces are scattered in blue sand. Ref.: Branch; 5, p. 312

Blue Gap   Apache   T32N R22E

Blue Holes Spring	Greenlee	T3S R31E	
Blue House Mountain	Gila	T7N R17E	Elev. 6417'

The origin of this name is uncertain.

Blue Jay Peak	Graham	T8S R23E	Elev. 8889'

Arizona blue jays are abundant here. Ref.: Jennings

Blue Jay Ridge	Graham	T8S R23E	
Blue Knolls	Mohave	T41N R4W	
Blue Lake	Navajo	T10N R16E	
Blue Mesa	Apache	T18N R24E	

This location is in the Petrified National Monument.

Blue Mountain	Apache	T8N R24E	Elev. 7789'
Blue Mountain	Cochise	T16S R31E	Elev. 5783'
Blue Mountain	Coconino	T26N R9W	
Blue Mountain	Maricopa	T6N R6E	Elev. 3169'
Blue Mountain	Mohave	T30N R11W	
Blue Mountain	Yavapai	T15N R8W	Elev. 5550'
Blue Mountain Canyon	Coconino	T27N R10W	
Blue Mountain Spring	Maricopa	T6N R6E	
Blue Peak	Greenlee	T3N R29E	Elev. 9346'

The name for this peak was suggested by the presence of a lookout station here called Blue Lookout. It was adopted by the USGS in 1969. Ref.: 329

Blue Peaks	Navajo		

See Hopi Buttes, Navajo

Blue Plateau	Maricopa	T7S R3W	Elev. 3921'
Blue Point	Coconino	T27N R14E	Elev. 6094'
Blue Point	Maricopa	T3N R8E	Elev. c. 1500'

This steep bank at the end of the Tonto Sheep Trail (see Bloody Basin, Yavapai) has a blue clay face. The sheep bridge is a short distance from this point. Ref.: 18a

Blue Range	Apache/Greenlee	T1–3N R28E	Elev. c. 8000'

This range is between the White Mountains and Escudilla Mountain. It may be identical with the Sierra Azul of the early Spanish explorers. Ref.: Becker

Blue Ridge	Coconino	T14N R10E	
Blue Ridge	Graham	T7S R21E	
Blue Ridge	Maricopa	T2N R8E	Elev. 2497'
Blue Ridge	Mohave	T24N R21W	

This is the western range of the Black Range which the Mohave Indians called Hamook-häbî. See Mohave Ref.: 345, II, 30, 96

Blue Ridge	Pinal	T1N R8E	
Blue Ridge Mountain	Navajo	T9N R23E	Elev. 7656'
Blue Ridge Mountains	Mohave		

See Blue Ridge, Mohave

Blue Ridge Peak	Navajo	T9N R23E	
Blue River	Gila	T1N R19E	

The upper portion of this river has blue-tinged water. Ref.: Woody

Blue River	Greenlee	T2N R30E	Elev. c. 6000'

Spaniards called this stream Rio Azul (= "blue river") because the water is a clear blue. It heads in the Sierra Azul or Blue Mountains. Whipple noted that the name may have come from the bluish cast of the basaltic formation. Ref.: 329

Blue Rock	Mohave	T12N R12W
Blue Rock Tank	Mohave	T23N R16W
Blue Spring	Coconino	T32N R6E

The water of this spring is indigo. Although this spring is only three feet deep, it is reputed to produce more water than most other springs in Navajo country. Ref.: 331, p. 173

Blue Spring	Maricopa	T3N R9E
Blue Spring	Navajo	T8N R19E
Blue Spring	Pinal	T1N R12E
Blue Stem Wash	Coconino	T28N R3E

Much blue-stem grass grows here, hence the name. Ref.: 329

Blue Tank Canyon	Maricopa	(1) T3N R9E (2) T3N R10W (3) T7N R5W
Blue Tank Canyon	Maricopa	T5N R10W
Blue Tank Wash	Mohave	T19N R15W
Blue Tank Wash	Yavapai	T8N R4W
Blue Vista	Greenlee	T3N R31E
Blue Wash	Maricopa	(1) T6N R5E (2) T4N R6W

BLUE WATER
Pinal   T7S R7E   Elev. c. 1500'

In the latter part of 1859 the Butterfield Overland Stage company sank a well here and established a stage station called Blue Water. Ownership of the location changed hands several times. Samuel B. Wise sold in 1870 to a stage driver named Baker, whose route lay between Blue Water and Tucson. In 1871 a Mexican employee murdered Baker and his family here. The stage station was active until at least 1879. It has completely disappeared. Ref.: 116, p. 448; 73, II, 164, 165; 51, p. 25; 224, p. 276; *Weekly Arizonan* (June 11, 1870), p. 3

BLUFF: The descriptive term *bluff* occurs in the following place names and is indicative of the location:

Bluff Cienega Creek	Apache	T4N R27E
Bluff Hollow	Graham	T6S R25E
Bluff Spring	Apache	T9N R26E
Bluff Spring	Graham	T9S T29E
Bluff Spring	Pinal	T1N R10E

Although the name Crystal Spring is also used for this location, it is an error because Crystal Spring is a little to the south and is a temporary spring whereas Bluff Spring is permanent. Ref.: 329

Bluff Spring Canyon	Pinal	T1N R10E	
Bluff Spring Mountain	Pinal	T1N R10E	Elev. 4041'

BLY
Coconino   T28N R3E

This railroad siding and Bly Tank were named for Fletcher D. Bly, a sheepman whose ranch extended from Williams to the Grand Canyon.
Ref.: AHS, Mrs. Nathan S. Bly, Notes

BOARD CABIN DRAW
Gila   T9N R12E

There was formerly a board cabin in this location, hence the name. Ref.: Woody

BOARDINGHOUSE CANYON
Gila   T10N R8E

A boardinghouse existed here at one time, hence the name. Ref.: Woody

BOARDSHACK KNOLL
Apache   T7N R27E   Elev. 9524'

This knoll takes its name from the former presence of a board shack.

BOARD TREE SADDLE
Gila   T7N R14E   Elev. 6007'

At this saddle in the Sierra Ancha Mountains the trees were large enough to make boards from them, hence the name. Ref.: Bob Foris

BOBCAT: Bobcats are native to Arizona. The following place names may be presumed attributable to incidents in which a bobcat featured:

Bobcat Butte	Navajo	T24N R18E	Elev. 6472'
Bobcat Creek	Graham	T1N R24E	
Bobcat Hills	Greenlee	T10S R31E	Elev. 4784'
Bobcat Reservoir	Mohave	T38N R8W	Elev. 4950'

BOB THOMPSON PEAK
Cochise   T24S R21E   Elev. 7259'

Both the park and this peak were named for a Forest Service Ranger in this area in the 1920s and early 1930s. The peak is also known as Ash Peak and was so named by Harry Van Horn, but the name is not used locally. Ref.: 329

BODOWAY MESA   pro.: /bəʔádiwey/
Coconino   T34N R7E   Elev. c. 6000'

The spelling as given above has been used in various documents from the earliest Arizona explorations. *Ba awoe*, a Piute Indian leader, arrived with his band c. 1850 in the Arizona Strip area. His name was thereafter applied to this entire area. The American spelling is an anglicized form of the Navajo pronunciation. The name Broadway Mesa is a corruption. Ref.: 141, p. 42; 331, p. 14

BOG CREEK
Apache   T8N R25E   Elev. 8825'

Boggy during the wet season, this creek crosses the old road between Springerville and Fort Apache. A round trip from Springerville to Fort Apache in good weather took six days and in bad sometimes more than twelve. More than one freighter cursed as he struggled with teams and wagons mired in gummy mud. The Becker brothers of Springerville, who accepted barter from local farmers for store goods, saved the merchant firm the possibility of getting stuck at Bog Creek by having farmers deliver their oats and hay directly to Fort Apache. Ref.: Wentz; 24, pp. 4, 5, 7

BOGGS RANCH
Yavapai   T12N R1E

The great grandson of Daniel Boone and the son of Gov. Liburn W. Boggs of Missouri, Theodore W. Boggs (b. c. 1836, Independence, Missouri; d. June 7, 1905) arrived in Arizona in 1862. He worked on the Big Bug Mining claim and later discovered the Mexican Gulch Mine (origin of the name of Mexican Gulch (T10N/R2E). His ranch headquarters also served as a stage station. Ref.: AHS Files

BOLEN WASH
Pima/Graham   T11S R19E

This is named for the Bolen family, which had a farm here.

BOLTON MESA
Mohave   T37N R7W

In 1928 the men of historian Bolton's party renamed it for Bolton. Fr. Escalante called it Mesa de la Shalona, for cloth (*shaloon*) given the Indians. Ref.: 42, p. 61

BON
Pinal   T9S R4E   Elev. 1298'
This location on the S.P.R.R. was named by taking the first three letters of the last name
of H. G. Bonorden, chief dispatcher for the railroad. Ref.: 18a

BOND CANYON
Santa Cruz   T21S R14E   Elev. c. 5000'
Josiah Bond, a mining engineer who c. 1910 relocated mines at Alto Canyon (where his
wife was postmistress), named this location for his wife. She was also the first
postmistress at Ajo. She was killed by lightning. Ref.: Lenon

BONELLI LANDING
Mohave (Lake Mead)   T31N R21W   Elev. 1258'
This is a recreational community on Lake Mead above the point where Bonelli's
Crossing was. It is now under water. See Bonelli's Crossing, Mohave

BONELLI'S CROSSING
Mohave   T31N R21W   Elev. c. 1100'
On September 29, 1871 Capt. George M. Wheeler noted that two settlers had just
arrived at the mouth of the Virgin River where they were establishing a ferry on the
Colorado River to permit access from Utah to northwestern Arizona. One of these men
was probably Jim Thompson, who sold the ferry c. 1875. The buyer was Daniel Bonelli
(b. Switzerland; d. 1904). Bonelli, a stone mason converted to the Mormon faith in
Switzerland, traveled with Brigham Young to Salt Lake City by ox team, was sent to
colonize an unsuccessful community in southern Utah, and from there was sent by his
church to colonize Muddy Valley in 1864. Not only did he establish and make a success
of the ferry, but he built a fine rock house and had a productive farm. He supplied the
mining camps of White Hills, Arizona, and Eldorado Canyon, Nevada, as well as the
traveling public, with hay, meanwhile prospecting, and mining salt, which he shipped to
cattlemen in Arizona. The salt was used for fluxing ores in the stamp mills of the region.
After his death he was buried on the mesa overlooking the ferry. (His body was removed
to Kingman when the waters of Lake Mead were impounded.) The ferry was sold, but
during a flood the single flat used for it disappeared down the raging river and the
ferry was abandoned. Bonelli's farm was also abandoned. His house was still in
existence when the waters of Lake Mead closed over it. Another name for the place was
Rioville. Ref.: Harris; Housholder; 345, I, 160; 55; 259, pp. 32, 34, 36

BONER CANYON
Mohave   T16N R13W
This canyon was named for five Boner brothers who lived in it from 1880 to about 1930.
The spellings *Bohner* and *Banner* are errors. Ref.: 329

BONES CANYON
Apache   T5N R24E
This canyon was named for an Apache Indian nicknamed "Bones" because he often
asked for soup bones from soldiers and officers at Fort Apache.
Ref.: James Dale (Whiteriver, Jan. 22, 1971)

BONEYARD, THE
Apache   T6N R29E   Elev. c. 9000'
The Chriswell family from Arkansas arrived in the fall of 1887. They found abundant
grass, water, and timber in this little valley where they built a two-room log cabin and
moved in just before Christmas. Then came the snow and it was very heavy. With only a
few cattle and no salt, the family lived through the severe winter by consuming their
cattle. They threw bones out through a hole cut in the side of the cabin, closing the hole
with a clapboard shutter. When spring came and the snows melted, the bones began their
bleaching on the hill north of the cabin. Since the spring of 1878 the place has been called
the Boneyard. Ref.: AHS, Evans Coleman File, Box 2

BONEYBACK PEAK
Gila   T6N R12E
This peak is sometimes called Harrahs Peak for a family which settled in Greenback

Valley in the 1870s. However, they themselves called it Boneyback Peak, a name which has been in use at least since 1890. It is descriptive. Ref.: 329

BONIFACIO DEL COATE Y DEL SIBUOIDAG, SAN
Pinal
This is apparently the location visited by Fr. Eusebio Kino in 1698, referring to two villages he called El Coati and El Sibuoidag. See Kohatk, Pinal Ref.: 43, p. 397

BONITA   pro.: /boníytə/
Spanish = "pretty"
Graham   T10S R23E   Elev. 4531'
On payday soldiers from Fort Grant poured into this little community and made the place really roar. About one thousand people then lived there: merchants, cow punchers, Mexicans, and families of black soldiers stationed at the post. The families owned "hog ranches," indicating that they kept places with hogsheads of whiskey. Officers and their wives stayed away from Bonita, going to Hooker's Sierra Bonita Ranch instead. Payday occurred three times a year. At that time the population of Bonita increased when the girls flocked in from Willcox. Both the girls and the ten saloons did a rush business. Today Bonita is quiet and sleepy, almost deserted.
P.O. est. Feb. 25, 1884, Edward Hooker, p.m.; disc. Sept. 30, 1955
Ref.: Jennings; AHS, "Bonita, the One-Time Rip-Roaring Camp," *Arizona Daily Star* (no date)

BONITA: The descriptive term *bonita* (Spanish = "pretty") is used for various locations which are indeed pretty. Examples follow:

Bonita Canyon   Apache
See Bonito Canyon, Apache

Bonita Canyon   Cochise   T16S R29E

Bonita Canyon   Santa Cruz   T23S R10E

Bonita Creek   Apache
This creek now goes under the name Little Bonita, which joins the Big Bonita. See Little Bonita Creek, Apache

Bonita Creek   Coconino   T34N R2W

Bonita Creek   Gila   T12N R11E
This creek is also known as Fuller Creek or as Pearly Creek. However, Fuller Creek actually enters Bonita Creek. Ref.: 329

Bonita Creek   Graham   T6S R28E (at Gila River)
This creek is also known as Gila Bonita Creek and as Rio Bonita. When running, it supplies some water to the town of Safford. Its course was followed by Indians who in April.1882 broke out of the San Carlos Indian Reservation. Ref.: Jennings

Bonita Lava Flow   Coconino
See Yaponcha Crater, Coconino

BONITA RANCH, SIERRA   pro.: /siyérə boníytə/
Spanish = "pretty mountains"
Graham   T11S R23E   Elev. c. 4400'
Henry C. Hooker (b. Jan. 10, 1828, New Hampshire; d. Dec. 5, 1907) arrived in Arizona in 1866. As a government contractor supplying Camp Goodwin, he made more money than was legal. Thereafter he went to California but returned to resume profitable contracting. While he was camped at Oak Grove in 1872 with a herd of cattle "left over after he had filled his government contracts," the herd stampeded. Hooker's cowboys trailed them to a spring so beautiful that Hooker homesteaded there, calling his ranch Sierra Bonita. Hooker was also famous for his blooded stock, both cattle and horses, bought with his contracting profits. Sierra Bonita was the Mexican name for the Pinaleno Mountains. In the days before fencing, the government owned the land, but Hooker controlled a range nearly thirty miles square. The ranch headquarters were a social cynosure, visited by officers and their wives from Fort Grant.
Ref.: AHS, Henry C. Hooker File; 116, p. 585; 206, p. 231

Bonita, Rio	Graham	
See Bonita Creek, Graham		
Bonita, Sierra	Graham	
See Graham, Mount, Graham		
Bonita Spring	Apache	T1N R6W
Bonita Spring	Cochise	T16S R30E
Bonita Spring	Graham	T4S R27E
Bonita Spring	Mohave	T14N R14W

BONITO, CANYON

Apache   T1N R6W   Elev. c. 8000'

Capt. James H. Simpson referred to the "beautiful stratified walls of 'Cañoncito Bonito' " where his party camped on September 11, 1849. Soldiers, however, called this place "Hell's Gate" during the campaign against the Navajo. A battle between Indians and mounted rifle men occurred in the canyon on October 17, 1858. In 1932 the USGS changed the name from Bonita Canyon to its more historical name of Bonito. Bonito Creek runs through this canyon. Ref.: 141, p. 33, Note 2, and p. 190; 143, p. 42; 292, p. 84; 159, p. 404; Burcard

Bonito Canyon	Pinal	T10S R16E
Bonito Cienega	Apache	T6N R26E
Bonito Creek	Apache	T2N R6W

This creek which flows through Bonito Canyon had such a good flow of water that it was one reason for establishing Fort Defiance on its banks. Ref.: 141, p. 89

Bonito Prairie	Navajo	T4N R23E
Bonito Rock Cienega	Apache	T5N R26E
Bonito Trading Post	Apache	T27N R31E

BOOT HILL

Cochise   T20S R22E   Elev. 4400'

In the West men who died with their boots on were frequently buried in "Boot Hill" cemeteries. That name gradually replaced the earlier name of Tombstone Cemetery. In such cemeteries the names of the dead were painted on headboards and as weathering took place, the painted portions were embossed by the wearing away of the board. All but one of the original wooden grave markers have disappeared at this Boot Hill. Ref.: 5, pp. 250, 251

BOOT HILL CEMETERY

La Paz

This cemetery, established in 1856, is at the end of the Trail of Graves. Embedded in the monument placed here by the Arizona Highway Dept. are guns, burro shoes, spurs, branding irons, miners' candles, picks, dutch ovens, etc. See Boot Hill, Cochise, and Trail of Graves, La Paz Ref.: 5, p. 363

BOOT LAKE

Coconino   T19N R10E   Elev. c. 8000'

The first name for this location was Borne Lake, but it was changed in 1921 to Boot Lake because the lake is shaped like a long hip boot. Ref.: 18a

BOOTLEGGER SPRING

Gila   T7N R11E

During prohibition, water from this spring was used by bootleggers, hence the name. Ref.: 329

BOOT PEAK

Yuma   T7S R21W   Elev. c. 1500'

Lt. Joseph Christmas Ives named this location Boot Mountain in 1857. It looks like a huge boot. Ref.: 245, p. 21

BOQUILLAS   pro.: /bokiyəs/
Spanish = "little mouths"
Cochise   T19S R21E   Elev. 4200'
This railroad location borrowed its name from the adjacent San Juan de Boquillas y
Nogales Land Grant. The name comes from the fact that several streams come together
on Babocomari Creek. In 1853 Ignacio Elias Gonzalez and Nepomuceno Felix bought
this grant. The U.S. Land Grant Court recognized 17,355 acres of the total 47,076 acre
grant. Ref.: Bennett; 18a

BORIANA CANYON
Mohave   T18N R6W
This canyon was so named because in it is the Boriana Mine, discovered c. 1904,
Arizona's first tungsten mine. There is a settlement here also.
Ref.: Harris; 215, p. 77; 5, p. 325

BOSQUE   pro.: /boskey/
Spanish = "forest grove"
Maricopa   T5S R3W   Elev. c. 1000'
The Phoenix Wood and Coal Company established a shipping point on the railroad here
in 1895. The company was then cutting ironwood and mesquite, hence the name "Forest
Grove." Because the company was cutting wood on government land, the government
entered suit and received a payment of $0.25 per acre for "cutting timber on public
lands." Ref.: 18a

BOSTON MILL
Cochise   T19S R19E   Elev. c. 4000'
In 1882 eighty-six eligible voters were at this location three miles above Fairbank on the
San Pedro River. The name may derive from Bostonians having erected the mill. It was
also called Emery City. Ref.: Larriau; Macia; *Tombstone Epitaph* (July 15, 1882), p. 3

BOTKIN
Yavapai   T16N R1E   Elev. 6000'
A now abandoned switch on the Union Verde & Pacific R.R. at this location was named
for Robert Botkin, a section foreman. Ref.: 18a

BOTTLE CANYON
Graham   T8S R20E
The name derives from the fact that there are several bottlenecks or narrow places in this
canyon. The name Squaw Creek is also applied to it. Ref.: 329

BOTTLE SPRING
Coconino   T15N R9E
Water gurgles from this spring much as it does when being poured from a bottle, hence
the name. Ref.: McKinney

BOTTOMLESS PITS
Coconino   T21N R8E   Elev. c. 5000'
When the A.& P.R.R. tracks were being laid here in the early 1880s, engineers did not
construct a culvert for draining under the tracks. Trash gradually accumulated,
evidently forming a dam. Consequently waters backed up behind it to form a lake south
of the road bed. One night in 1885 Stanley Sykes camped near here. He was awakened
by hearing a weird sucking sound. In the morning he noted that the lake level had
dropped about two feet and it continued dropping rapidly. The accumulated water had
dissolved the limestone basin. Using lengths of rope, Sykes attempted to find the bottom
of the new pit but could not do so. He thereupon gave the name to the locality.
Ref.: Sykes; 276, p. 16

BOUCHER CREEK   pro.: /búwčer/ or /buwšéy/
Coconino (Grand Canyon)   T31N R1E   Elev. c. 4000'
Louis D. Boucher (b. Sherbrook, Canada) arrived at the Grand Canyon in 1891 and

established a tourist camp. He maintained two tents and a corral. He created the Boucher trail on which Dripping Springs (which he also named). Boucher Trail was the last to be constructed (c. 1902-05). The USGS c. 1945 eliminated this name in favor of Long Creek. Ref.: Schellbach File (Grand Canyon); 178, pp. 46, 47, 48

BOUCHER'S GARDEN
Coconino (Grand Canyon)   c. T31N R1E
At this location on the Boucher Trail at the bottom of Boucher Creek (*q.v.*) Louis Boucher had a fruit and vegetable garden as well as seventy-five trees, including oranges, figs, and peaches. Ref.: 178, pp. 47, 115

BOUCHER TRAIL
Coconino (Grand Canyon)   T31N R1E
This trail is today called the Dripping Springs Trail. See Boucher Creek, Coconino (Grand Canyon)

BOULDER BASIN
Mohave (Lake Mead)   T31N R23W
In June 1946 Edward Schenk and Elzada U. Clover proposed this name to replace the following, then in use: Callville Basin, Lower Basin, and Lower Lake. The change was made by the USGS in June 1948. A further change was later made, to Lower Lake Mead (*q.v.*). The name Boulder Basin applies between Hoover Dam and Boulder Canyon, hence the name. Ref.: 329

BOULDER: The use of the word *boulder* in place names indicates the presence of boulders unless otherwise noted in the following examples:

Boulder Canyon	Cochise	T14S R26E
Boulder Canyon	Maricopa	T2N R9E
Boulder Canyon	Mohave	T40N R15W
Boulder Canyon	Yavapai	(1) T14N R3E (2) T12N R7E
Boulder Canyon Dam	Mohave (Lake Mead)	

See Hoover Dam, Mohave (Lake Mead)

Boulder Creek	Coconino (Grand Canyon)	T31N R3E
Boulder Creek	Maricopa	T4N R9E

This is now called La Barge Creek (*q.v.*).

Boulder Creek	Yavapai	(1) T8N R1E (2) T15N R10W

This was the name of a mining town, now vanished. Ref.: 18a

Boulder Creek	Coconino	T19N R13E
Boulder Dam	Mohave	(Lake Mead)

See Hoover Dam, Mohave (Lake Mead)

Boulder Dam Spring	Yavapai	T10N R2W
Boulder Islands	Mohave	(Lake Mead)

The USGS approved this name suggested by Elzada U. Clover for islands at the lower end of Lake Mead and nearer to Boulder City and Boulder Dam than other islands. Ref.: 329

Boulder Mountain	Maricopa	T5N R9E	Elev. 6320'

The Forest Service called this location Pine Ridge in 1943, but that name was unknown to residents. Ref.: 329

Boulder Mountain	Pinal	T7S R18E	Elev. 5339'
Boulder Mountain	Yavapai		

See Genung Mountain, Yavapai

Boulder Mountain Spring	Maricopa	T5N R9E
Boulder Narrows	Coconino (Grand Canyon)	T38N R6E

Boulder Pass	Maricopa	T6N R9E
Boulder Pass Peak	Yavapai	T9N R2W
Boulder Rapids	Coconino	(Grand Canyon)

This was the name given by Birdseye to a "mass of rock that had recently tumbled into the center of the channel" in Marble Canyon about forty-three miles below Lee's Ferry. Ref.: 36, p. 183

Boulder Spring	Mohave	T20N R17W
Boulder Wash	Mohave	T31N R9W

BOUNDARY BUTTE
Apache   T41N R25E   Elev. 9263'

This butte is at the northwestern boundary of the Treaty Reservation established in 1868. Ref.: 331, p. 99

BOUNDARY CONE
Mohave   T19N R20W   Elev. 3430'

This huge white rhyolitic cone was so named by Lt. Joseph Christmas Ives in 1857 because the 35th Parallel lies about a mile from the center of the cone. Additionally, it is an angle point for the Mojave Reservation Boundary. Ref.: Harris; Housholder 245, p. 70; Lenon

BOUNDARY CONE WASH
Mohave

This wash takes its name from the Boundary Cone Mining District. It is separated from the Vivian Mining District to the north by Boundary Cone Wash. Both locations take their name from Boundary Cone, Mohave (*q.v.*). Ref.: 200, p. 180

BOUNDARY HILL
Mohave/Nevada   T32N R16W

This hill is on the boundary between Arizona and Nevada, hence the name.

BOUNDARY POINT
Mohave (Lake Mead)   T32NR16W

This name was approved by the USGS in 1948. See Boundary Hill, Mohave/Nevada

BOUNDARY RIDGE
Coconino (Grand Canyon)   T34N R4E   Elev. 7000'

Richard T. Evans proposed the name because the ridge follows the northern boundary of the Grand Canyon National Park. Ref.: Ed McKee, Park Naturalist, Letter to Francois Matthes, in Matthes' File (Grand Canyon)

BOURKE POINT
Coconino (Grand Canyon)   T33N R4E   Elev. 6542'

In 1931 Will C. Barnes suggested naming this location to honor Lt. John Gregory Bourke (b. 1842, Delaware), aide to Gen. George Crook in the 1870s. Bourke wrote several books about his experiences in Arizona. Ref.: 18a

BOUSE
La Paz   T7N R17W   Elev. 942'

On the post office application the first name proposed for this location was Brayton, but the post office wrote "Bouse" in red ink on the application. The name Brayton was that of John Brayton, merchant owner of the Brayton Commercial Company, a store one mile southeast. His store supplied the Harqua Hala (*sic*) Mine. The name Bouse is probably that of George Bouse. In 1909 the Bouse Townsite Land and Improvement Company "secured about sixteen hundred acres" for agricultural purposes and announced plans for creating a winter resort. Thomas Bouse, a contractor and storekeeper, was George's brother.

P.O. est. March 6, 1906, William E. Enos, p.m.; name changed from Brayton to Bouse, Nov. 22, 1927; Wells Fargo 1907 Ref.: 242; *Arizona Star* (Jan. 15, 1909), p. 3

BOWIE   pro.: /Búwiy/

Cochise   T13S R28E   Elev. 3762'

This town borrows its name from that of Fort Bowie (*q.v.*). A Mexican settlement, its first name was Tres Cebollas (Spanish = "three onions"). A second name was imposed on the location when Capt. James H. Tevis (b. July 11, 1835, Wheeling, West Virginia; d. Aug. 29, 1905) took up his homestead here. He had spent two years (1857-1859) at the Overland Butterfield stage station in Apache Pass at what was later Fort Bowie.

After serving with the Confederate forces with the Arizona Scouts in New Mexico, Tevis was mustered out in 1869 as a 2nd Lt. In 1879 he planned his return to Arizona and arrived at Fort Bowie November 1, 1880. There he opened a sutler's store. He donated land for the mill and offices of the Cochise Mining and Milling Company. A member of that company, Capt. John Hancock, said a post office should be established at the mill so that mail would not have to be brought in each day from Fort Bowie. The new post office, at first in a tent, was moved later to Tevis' new store when it was completed. Hancock named the new post office Teviston.

Tevis took up his homestead where he believed the railroad would go through, and it did. In late 1881 railroad superintendent Bean discussed with Tevis naming the railroad station Bean City. Tevis replied that the residents ate beans three times a day every day and were sick of the word. Insulted, Bean walked out, saying he would call the place Bowie's Station. Until 1910 the place was known both as Bowie Station and as Teviston, and Bean carried out his anger by establishing the post office as Bean.

P.O. est. Sept. 28, 1881, Henry A. Smith, p.m.; changed to Teviston, Dec. 27, 1881, William L. Martin, p.m.; changed to Bowie, June 11, 1908, Jomer Henrich, p.m.; Wells Fargo 1885 Ref.: Riggs; 242

BOWIE, FORT

Cochise   T15S R28E

Because the Butterfield Overland stage station in Apache Pass was often attacked by Apaches, the stage line president requested federal protection in 1858, but a post was not set up until a year after Butterfield ceased business, on July 28, 1862. The site was selected by Capt. L. E. Mitchell of the California Column and was named for Gen. George W. Bowie, Fifth California Cavalry. Water for the post was obtained from nearby Bear Spring. Initially, members of the Fifth Infantry and of Company A, First Cavalry, California Volunteers, garrisoned the post, under Brig. Gen. James H. Carleton. Bowie was then a regimental colonel.

The post had a limited garrison and not until after the War Between the States were sufficient troops available for a concentrated and organized campaign against Apaches. Fort Bowie rapidly gained importance in warfare against Apache Indians. The graveyard soon filled with men tortured to death by Indians. During Gen. Nelson A. Miles' campaign, Fort Bowie was his headquarters and station No. 1 on the heliograph system. In 1872 a truce was achieved with the Apache leader, Cochise. When he died in 1874, his band of Chiricahua Apaches was sent to San Carlos Reservation, but they soon left because of their great discontent. As a result they were shipped out of Arizona. Following that fact, Fort Bowie went into decline, its usefulness ended.

Curiously, the name of Camp Bowie did not become Fort Bowie officially until April 5, 1879. It was abandoned as an army post on October 17, 1894. In June 1911 the Federal government sold the twenty-four hundred acres of the Fort Bowie Military Reservation at public auction. The Fort Bowie National Historic Site was established in August 1964, and dedicated in 1972 to preserve the Apache Pass stage station and the fort complex.

P.O. est. as Apache Pass, Dec. 11, 1866, George Hand, p.m.; name changed to Fort Bowie, June 22, 1880, Sidney R. Delong, p.m.; disc. Nov. 30, 1894
Ref.: 73, II, 138, 139; 319, p. 94; 224, pp. 154, 155; 107, II, 121; 15, p. 515; 176, p. 28

BOWLEY

Pima   T16S R10E   Elev. c. 3600'

In 1883 Bowley Ranch served as a stage station and eating place for travelers en route to the Quijotoa Mines. The name was sometimes erroneously spelled Bawley, hence the name Bawley Wash. It was further corrupted to Brawley.
Ref.: 308, p. 78; 57, p. 376; 329, G.E.P. Smith, Letter (Dec. 9, 1936)

BOWYER PEAK

La Paz   T5N R20W   Elev. 2125′

This peak took its name from the Bowyer Mine owned by Joe Bowyer. The spelling "Boyer" is erroneous. Ref.: 18a

BOX: The term *box* is often used in connection with canyons having an entry which is also the only exit, thus forming a box. Examples follow:

Box Camp Canyon	Pima	T12S R15E
Box Canyon	Cochise	T21S R28E
Box Canyon	Coconino	T13N R10E
Box Canyon	Gila	T1N R15E
Box Canyon	Graham	T4S R24E
Box Canyon	Greenlee	T4N R32E
Box Canyon	Maricopa	T3N R10E

See also Fish Creek Canyon, Maricopa

Box Canyon	Mohave	T25N R12W
Box Canyon	Pima	T19S R15E

This is the same location as Madera Canyon; the name Box was used locally at least as late as the 1940s. See Madera Canyon, Pima

Box Canyon	Pinal	T3S R11E
Box Canyon	Santa Cruz	T22S R17E
Box Canyon	Yavapai	(1) T8N R4W (2) T12N R2W (3) T8N R1W
Box Spring	Coconino	T24N R11E
Box Spring	Graham	(1) T11S R22E Elev. 4725′ (2) T5S R21E
Box Spring	Mohave	T22N R21W
Box Spring	Navajo	T9N R20E
Box Spring	Yavapai	T10N R2W

BOX O HILLS

Pinal   T6S R12E   Elev. 3080′

This location takes its name from the Box O Ranch. Ref.: 329

BOX O WASH

Pinal   T7–4S R13–11E

This wash heads near the Box O Ranch. The wash is also called Big Wash and on GLO 1892 Grant Wash. Ref.: 329

BOYCE THOMPSON SOUTHWESTERN ARBORETUM

Pinal   T2S R12E

William Boyce Thompson established this experimental station for plant research. Ref.: 5, p. 349

BOYER CANYON

Gila   T6N R12E

The Boyer cabin was in this canyon, hence the name. Boyer Gap is nearby.

BOYLES

Greenlee   T3N R30E

At the mouth of the Blue River, Dick and Abe Boyles established a ranch. After Benton was flooded out of existence, Mr. and Mrs. Dick Boyles started a saloon and little store which contained the post office. It was first called Carpenter after the name of its

postmistress. (Boyles had bought out the old Carpenter Ranch.) The name was later changed to Boyles Ranch. Cowboys and travelers could not expect the usual hospitable cup of coffee and a meal, as Mrs. Boyles was very tight-fisted. The cowboys evened the score by roping a Boyles' maverick and putting a neighbor's brand on it.
P.O. est. as Carpenter, Feb. 12, 1903, Rada H. Carpenter, p.m.; new post office started as Boyles, April 4, 1906, Laura L. Boyles, p.m.; disc. Oct. 31, 1906
Ref.: 242; Mrs. Fred Fritz, Sr.; Fred Fritz Notes

BOYSAG POINT
Piute: *boysag* = "bridge"
Mohave (Grand Canyon)   T34N R4W   Elev. 5589'
This point on the North Rim was so named because it could be reached only by a small man-made bridge. Ref.: 329

BRADLEY POINT
Coconino (Grand Canyon)   T31N R3E
G. Y. Bradley was with Maj. John Wesley Powell's first expedition through the Grand Canyon in 1869. Ref.: 18a

BRADSHAW CITY
Yavapai
P.O. est. July 1, 1874, Noah C. Sheckells, p.m.; disc. Dec. 15, 1874 See Bradshaw Mountains, Yavapai

BRADSHAW MOUNTAINS
Yavapai   T9N R2E
This range was first known as the Silver Range because of the discovery of silver ores in 1863. Their current name is taken from that of William D. Bradshaw (see Olive City, Yuma). While Bradshaw's brother Isaac was running the Bradshaw ferry at Olive City, Bill Bradshaw prospected and on one of his excursions led a small party into the mountains which now bear his name. There in the fall of 1863 Bradshaw made a strike and the new mining district was named in his honor. In 1871 miners and prospectors laid out a town site on top of Bradshaw Mountain above Poland's cabin (see Poland, Yavapai). The community of Bradshaw, or Bradshaw City, was on the trail from Prescott to the Tiger and Eclipse Mines. In its one-year existence it managed to attract five thousand residents. All that remains today is a signpost.
Ref.: *Arizona Miner* (Sept. 21, 1864), p. 2; and (April 29, 1871), p. 2; 163, p. 254; 107, III, 88, 89; 5, p. 307

BRADY BUTTE
Yavapai   T12N R1W   Elev. 6400'
The name comes from that of Francis Brady, who worked a mine here c. 1881. Ref.: 18a

BRADY PEAK
Coconino (Grand Canyon)   T33N R4E   Elev. 8009'
In 1931 the supervisor of the Grand Canyon National Park suggested that this peak be named for Peter Rainesford Brady (b. Aug. 4, 1828, Washington, D.C.; d. May 2, 1902), who arrived in Tucson in 1853. Brady was a graduate of the Naval Academy (1844), resigning his commission in 1846 to serve with the Texas Rangers in the war with Mexico. He was four times a member of the Territorial Legislature.
Ref.: 62; 224, III

BRADY WASH
Pinal   T7S R11E
A son of Peter R. Brady (see Brady Point, Coconino [Grand Canyon]) established a ranch on this wash c. 1880. He was Richard Garnett Brady (b. 1864, Sonora, Mexico). Brady left his ranch to move to Tucson in 1890.
Ref.: AHS, Emerson O. Stratton File; 224, III

BRAHMA TEMPLE

Coconino (Grand Canyon)　　　　　T32N R4E　　　　　Elev. 7554'
In April 1906 the USGS approved this name for one of the many fantastic buttes in the
Grand Canyon. The name was among others suggested by Francois E. Matthes. Brahma
was "the first of the Hindu Triads, the name of the Supreme Creator" and the butte was
so named to correspond with Shiva Temple nearby.
Ref.: 178, p. 30; 329

BRANAMAN (R.R. STN.)

Pinal　　　　　　　　　　　　　　T4S R14E
This location on the Phoenix & Eastern R.R. was seven miles east of Ray Junction. The
name is occasionally incorrectly spelled Brannaman. It took its name from that of the
Branaman Ranch owned by Jack M. Branaman (b. 1827, Kentucky). He was in charge
of the horse corral at Riverside Stage Station in November 1889 when his ranch was said
to be "up the river" a few miles. In 1887 with his partner George Scott, he located the
Pioneer Mine on the south side of the Pinal Mountains. He died of a beating after a fight
in 1889, leaving his widow with four sons. For awhile she kept a boarding house in
Globe. Then she married George Scott. With her sons they sold their mine and bought a
ranch on the Gila River, later called the Crescent Ranch. Ref.: Woody

BRANDENBERG MOUNTAIN

Pinal　　　　　　　　　　　　　　T6S R17E　　　　　Elev. 4367'
In the early 1880s James William Brandenberg established a farm on Aravaipa Creek
where he farmed and raised fruit until 1912. He hauled and peddled his produce on the
streets of Mammoth, Oracle, Florence, and Tucson.
Ref.: Mrs. Annie E. Forbach, Letter (Nov. 30, 1973)

BRANNOCK

Cochise　　　　　　　　　　　　　T16S R29E
Brannock Riggs (b. 1829, Missouri) arrived in Arizona in 1879 and homesteaded within
a mile of Fort Bowie. Although there was a post office on the military reservation, he
established another in his home, headquarters of the Riggs Ranch. The red tape proving
too much for him, he wrote several times telling the Post Office Department he wanted
none of their business. Failing to receive any reply whatsoever, he simply one day put the
key into the mail bag, locked it up, and sent it to Washington with a notice saying he was
through.
P.O. est. Aug. 16, 1887, Brannock Riggs, p.m.; disc. April 1, 1891 Ref.: Riggs

BRECKENRIDGE SPRING

Coconino　　　　　　　　　　　　　　　　　　　　　Elev. c. 8000'
On September 13, 1857 Lt. Edward Fitzgerald Beale passed north of Mount Sitgreaves
en route to Mount Kendrick. He passed two springs on the north side of Mount
Sitgreaves, naming the first Breckenridge and the second Porter for members of his
party. Breckenridge was the same one that Mormons referred to as Bear Spring,
according to Floyd Breckenridge, Jr., who was in charge of Beale's camels at the outset.
Ref.: 23, pp. 51; 52; Floyd ms. (April 1859) (Huntington Library)

BREEZY POINT

Coconino (Grand Canyon)　　　　　T31N R2E　　　　　Elev. 3500'
Emery C. and Ellsworth Kolb named this location because here the breeze is so strong
that it blows gravel. Ref.: Kolb

BREON

Mohave　　　　　　　　　　　　　T25N R11W
Paul M. Breon in 1880 was living at Fort Mohave where he was a grocer. The 1870
census lists him as Paul M. Breon (b. 1840, France) but the 1880 census lists him as
having been born in 1844 in New York, thus throwing some doubt either on the census
taker or on Mr. Breon's veracity. The papers were sent to Hackberry when the Breon
post office was discontinued. This also throws some doubt on the usually accepted rather
loose location.
P.O. est. April 6, 1883, Allan H. Grant, p.m.; disc. Feb. 19, 1885 Ref.: 62; 63; 18a

BREWERY GULCH

Cochise   In Bisbee   Elev. 5900'
This gulch is the second most important canyon in Bisbee, where it joins the main Mule Pass (or Mule Gulch) at a right angle. There was formerly a brewery in this gulch, not to mention numerous places where "experiments were carried on with the products of malt and grain and hops." There were also several places where the girls were.
Ref.: 5, p. 173; Don Dedra, "Arizona Days and Ways," *Arizona Republic* (Feb. 11, 1962); 78a, pp. 21, 22

BRIDGE CANYON

Mohave (Grand Canyon)   T27N R12W
The name derives from the fact that this is the proposed location of a hydroelectric dam to help prevent Lake Mead from loading with silt. Ref.: AHS, Colorado River Files

BRIGGS

Yavapai   T9N R3W
The post office at this location was established to service the mining camp three and one-half miles south of Crown Point and ten miles northwest of Hot Springs.
P.O. est. Dec. 30, 1890, Emory W. Fisher, p.m.; disc. March 20, 1907
Ref.: Gardner; 242; 18a

BRIGHAM CITY

Navajo   T19N R16E
Among Mormon emigrants who arrived near the present Joseph City on March 24, 1876 was Jesse O. Ballenger. He established Ballenger Camp or Ballinger. In September 1878 residents changed the name to Brigham to honor Mormon leader Brigham Young. The colony flourished, having nearly three hundred residents. Some ran a grist mill donated by Utah Mormons. The flooding Little Colorado River literally washed the place off the map, possibly some time in early 1881, the year in which the settlement was finally broken up. By 1890 only one family still lived at the site.
P.O. est. April 10, 1878, James T. Woods, p.m.; disc. May 5, 1882
Ref.: 242; Richards; 225, p. 146; 341, pp. 1, 2; Huntington Library

BRIGHT ANGEL CAMP

Coconino (Grand Canyon)   T32N R3E
In September 1901 the S.F.R.R. used twenty acres (as specified under the Act of 1875) at the Grand Canyon in planning to build tourist accomodations. The first building to go up was a log cabin to serve as a hotel, with ten other cabins around it. This was at the head of Bright Angel Creek and was called Bright Angel Camp. See Bright Angel Creek, Coconino (Grand Canyon)

BRIGHT ANGEL CREEK

Coconino (Grand Canyon)   T32N R3E
During his 1869 Grand Canyon expedition, Maj. John Wesley Powell on August 16 reported that "four days of rain had just ended and as a result great floods were pouring over the canyon walls. The Colorado River was exceedingly turbid." That same day they encountered a clear little creek or river. Powell called it Silver Creek, but in a lecture given in Detroit in December 1869, Powell called it Bright Angel because it was a sharp contrast to the dirty Devil River in Utah.
    Bright Angel Creek runs through Bright Angel Canyon, which in turn drops from the lip of the North Rim to the Colorado River where the suspension bridge crosses that stream. Ref.: 266, p. 86; 100, p. 173; 178, pp. 33, 63

BRIGHT ANGEL PLATEAU

Coconino (Grand Canyon)
This is part of the Tonto platform from Indian Gardens to Plateau Point. See Bright Angel Creek, Coconino (Grand Canyon)

BRIGHT ANGEL TRAIL

Coconino (Grand Canyon)   T32N R3E
The Bright Angel Trail, originally known as Cameron Trail, was created in 1891 by P.

D. Berry, Robert Ferguson, C. H. McClure, and Niles J. Cameron, who needed access to their mines deep in the canyon. Berry filed for a toll road here. Ralph H. Cameron and Berry had acquired all mines nearby in 1890 and sold out in 1902 to the Canyon Copper Co.

Conflict over the Bright Angel Trail endured from 1901 through 1928, spreading four ways. It involved the citizens of Coconino County, the S.F.R.R., the county government, and the federal government. Part of the conflict was the battle by the railroad officials with Ralph Cameron (b. Oct. 21, 1863, Southport, Maine), who owned a hotel on the Canyon Rim. In an attempt to force Cameron to sell, the railroad moved its station, the site of Bright Angel Camp, one thousand feet east in order to attract tourists away from Cameron's Trail. The dispute ended on May 22, 1928 with the sale of the trail by Coconino County to the United States government. On December 2, 1937 the name Cameron Trail was officially changed to Bright Angel Trail.

One portion of the trail used to wind and twist so abruptly downward for twelve hundred feet that it was called Devil's Corkscrew. Ref.: 333, pp. 29, 30, 44, 45, 50, 59, 60

BRONCO: The noun *bronco* means "a wild horse." Several places in Arizona bear the designation *bronco*, possibly indicating the presence of wild horses. At one time wild horses were so abundant on the vast plains in northern Arizona that they had to be destroyed before they destroyed the land. The following are examples of the use of the word *bronco*:

| Bronco Butte | Maricopa | (1) T3N R11E | Elev. 4349' |

This is at the eastern end of Horse Mesa and is sometimes referred to as Horse Mountain. The name Bronco Butte was suggested by Aubrey Drury to retain "the 'wild west' flavor." It is doubtful that wild horses ever were here. Ref.: 329

Bronco Butte	Maricopa	(2) T7N R5E	Elev. 4840'
Bronco Canyon	Gila	T6N R15E	
Bronco Creek	Gila	T3N R11E	
Bronco Creek	Maricopa	T7N R5E	
Bronco Gulch	Graham	T1N R21E	
Bronco Mountain	Coconino/Yavapai	T17N R8E	

The local name for wild horses is "broom tails." There were many broom tails in this vicinity. See Apache Maid Mountain, Coconino

| Bronco Wash | Mohave | T15N R13W | |

BROOKBANK CANYON
Navajo   T11–14N R15–17E

This location derives its name from that of J. W. Brookbank, who settled here in 1884. He later moved to Holbrook. Ref.: Richards

BROOKLINE
Cochise   T20S R20E   Elev. 4100'

A small community formerly existed at this location on the Fairbank branch of the S.P.R.R. where it crossed a brook, hence the name. Ref.: Macia; 18a

BROOKLYN PEAK
Yavapai   T9N R4E   Elev. 5379'

The peak took its name from that of the Brooklyn Mine. Ref.: 18a

BROPHY WELL
Cochise   T20S R26E

Brophy Well is the site of the Soldier Hole Ranch owned by Jim and Frank Brophy. Jim (b. 1859, Ireland) arrived in the United States several years ahead of his younger brother Frank (b. 1863, Ireland). Ultimately they met in Tucson and Jim took his brother to the ranch where they began digging what is now generally called Brophy Well. The name for the ranch came from the fact that troops had formerly stopped at what they called Soldier Hole because there water was found very close to the surface. The spot was also used by

teamsters hauling materials to and from the sawmills in the Chiracahua Mountains to Tombstone and Bisbee. While they were digging the well, the brothers took turns shoveling or holding a rifle on the lookout for Apaches. The man with the rifle also operated the windlass. Frank soon decided that a cowman's life was not for him and he went to Bisbee. In 1892 a post office was established at the ranch headquarters. Postal authorities were somewhat staggered by the request for a post office to be named Soldier Hole. The authorities asked for an explanation and when it arrived, a Mr. Wannamaker seized a Spanish dictionary, thumbed through the pages, and came upon *descanso*, meaning "a haven of rest." The name was thereupon substituted for Soldier Hole.
P.O. est. as Descanso, May 23, 1892, William O. Abbott, p.m.; disc. May 2, 1894
Ref.: Frank C. Brophy, Jr., Letter (May 25, 1956); 277, p. 131; Riggs; *Weekly Arizona Enterprise* (1892); AHS Files

BROWN CANYON
Pima   T19S R8E   Elev. c. 3000'
Rollin Carr Brown (b. Oct. 24, 1844, Rushville, Indiana; d. May 5, 1937) after his arrival in Tucson on March 6 began working for John Wasson at the Tucson *Citizen* in 1873. He was editor for more than ten years and was twice editor-owner. He later moved to his ranch in this canyon. Ref.: AHS, Chambers Collection, Box 7, and Rollin C. Brown File

BROWN CREEK
Apache/Navajo   T11N R23E
This creek takes its name from the first homesteader, Charles Brown. It heads at Brown Spring. Ref.: 329

BROWNELL
Pima   T13S R2E
Frank Brownell gave his name to the post office at this location, which serviced the Brownell Mine. Brownell, a Civil War veteran, kept the post office in his store. The mine became inactive and the post office was discontinued. Nothing remains here today. See Ahe Vonam, Pima
P.O. est. April 3, 1903, Frank Brownell, p.m.; disc. Dec. 15, 1911
Ref.: 242; 58; 262, p. 5; 18a

BROWNELL PEAK
Pima   T14S R2E   Elev. 3573'
This name, rather than Brownell Mountain, is approved by the USGS. See Brownell, Pima

BROWN'S COVE
Coconino (Grand Canyon)   T39N R7E
Frank Mason Brown, a member of the Stanton party, drowned in a riffle here on July 10, 1889. "His companions cut an inscription in a rock ledge."
Ref.: P.T. Reilly, Letter (Oct. 1974); 329

BROWN'S RAPID
Coconino (Grand Canyon)   T38N R7E
This location is also called Rapid No. 108. See Brown's Cove, Coconino (Grand Canyon)

BROWN'S SPRING
Yavapai   T12N R3E
This spring is in the gap on Gap Creek. It is named for sheepmen from the Dakotas who patented land here. See Gap Creek, Yavapai Ref.: Dugas

BRUCE, MOUNT
Santa Cruz   T20S R18E   Elev. 6087'
On July 22, 1893 both the canyon and this mountain were named for Charles Morelle Bruce, Secretary of the Territory of Arizona (1893-1897) and also manager of the Babocomari Cattle Company. The canyon is on an old Indian trail into Mexico. Bruce

had settled at the mouth of the canyon c. 1880. The Pima County Board of Supervisors named the mountain for him and placed a bronze tablet on its northern face in 1922. Biscuit Peak (*q.v.*) is a variant name.

Ref.: AHS Charles M. Bruce, Interview; 18a; Lenon

BRUNCKOW MINE

Cochise   T20S R22E

Although well over one hundred years old, the adobe ruin of the cabin built by Frederick Brunckow c. 1858 is still in existence in the 1980s. Brunckow (b. Germany) was an engineer and scientist exiled from Germany. At this location he developed a mine. He did not live to enjoy profits because Mexicans murdered him in his cabin and threw his body down the mine shaft. After his death his cabin on a little mound became an outlaws' rendezvous, earning a reputation as "the bloodiest cabin in Arizona history." Reports that his mine was rich led to claim jumping, but the mine never paid off.

Ref.: Macia; H.D. Stillman, Letter to George H. Kelly (Dec. 8, 1942), (State Library Files); 206, p. 282; 359, p. 99

BRUSH AND BRUSHY: Thick undergrowth in many locations in Arizona led to the use of the terms *brush* and *brushy*. Examples follow:

Brush Canyon	Cochise	T12S R21E	
See also Brushy Canyon, Cochise			
Brush Canyon	Graham	T9S R19E	
Brush Corral Canyon	Gila	T10N R12E	
Brush Corral Canyon	Maricopa	T6N R8E	
Brush Corral Creek	Maricopa		
See Davis Wash, Maricopa			
Brush Mountain	Gila	T8N R17E	
Brushy Basin	Gila	T13N R4E	
Brushy Basin	Maricopa	T4N R9E	
Brushy Basin	Yavapai	T13N R4E	
Brushy Basin Canyon	Gila	T10N R11E	
Brushy Canyon	Cochise	(1) T22S R19E	(2) T16S R30
Brushy Canyon	Gila	(1) T8N R12E	(2) T11N R9E
Brushy Canyon	Graham	T5S R27E	
Brushy Canyon	Greenlee	T5S R30E	
Brushy Creek	Cochise	T19S R29E	
Brushy Creek	Cochise	T19S R29E	
Brushy Creek	Graham	T3S R27E	
Brushy Creek	Yavapai	T10N R5E	
Brushy Flat	Apache	T9N R24E	
Brushy Hollow	Gila	(1) T9N R11E	(2) T8N R11E
Brushy Knoll	Coconino	T15N R10E	
Brushy Mesa	Gila	T11N R8E	
Brushy Mountain	Apache	T8N R25E	Elev. 8461'
Brushy Mountain	Graham	T3S R27E	Elev. 6914'
Brushy Mountain	Greenlee	T4S R31E	Elev. 6495'
Brushy Mountain	Maricopa	T6N R6E	Elev. 3533'
Brushy Mountain	Yavapai	(1) T14N R5W	Elev. 6189'
		(2) T17N R5W	Elev. 6000'

Brushy Prong	Yavapai	T12N R6E	
Brushy Spring	Apache	T9N R24E	
Brushy Spring	Graham	T5S R19E	
Brushy Spring	Maricopa	T4N R9E	
Brushy Spring	Yavapai	T4N R5W	
Brushy Springs	Graham	T2S R27E	
Brushy Top Mountain	Gila	T7N R15E	Elev. 5900'
Brushy Wash	Graham	T5S R21E	
Brushy Wash	Yavapai	T13N R2E	

BRYAN MOUNTAINS
Yuma   T12S R11W   Elev. 1794'
In 1930 Eldred D. Wilson of the University of Arizona Department of Geology named
these mountains for Kirk Bryan, author of several works on the geology of southwestern
Arizona. The north half of T12S is also known as the Mohawk Mountains.
Ref.: 355, p. 155

BRYCE
Graham   T6S R25E   Elev. 2831'
Ebenezer Bryce and his sons in January 1883 began creating a ditch where they had
established squatters' rights. A settlement developed thereafter. The name also applies
to a knoll and a mountain. The latter is sometimes called Bryce Peak.
P.O. est. Oct. 9, 1895, Alma N. Bryce, p.m.; disc. Feb. 28, 1922
Ref.: 242; 225, p. 249; 353, p. 60; Jennings

BRYCE WASH
Graham
This location is also called Peck Wash for reasons unknown. See Bryce, Graham

BUCARELI, PUERTO DE
Coconino
Fr. Francisco Garcés in 1776 named this location for the then Viceroy of New Spain. It
is just below the juncture of the Little Colorado River and the Colorado River. See Little
Colorado River.

BUCHANAN, FORT
Santa Cruz   T20S R16E   Elev. c. 4500'
Troops arriving in Tucson in the late fall of 1856 remained only long enough to receive
orders. Following these orders, they proceeded to establish a camp called Camp Moore,
and in November Maj. Enoch Steen left Lt. I. N. Moore in command. The place bore his
name briefly, however, for on November 17 the name was changed to Fort Buchanan in
honor of James Buchanan, then President of the United States.
   In 1856 Tucson was insignificant and the plan to have a post office in "Tucson" was
associated with the military establishment, hence moving the post office to Fort
Buchanan rather than having it at Tucson. Its first postmaster was Elias Brevoort, who
had come from New Mexico specifically to serve as a sutler for the troops. The name of
the post office was changed to Fort Buchanan within six months.
   In the late 1850s Secretary of War Breckenridge placed as many military and other
stores as he could at posts which might conceivably fall into the hands of southern
sympathizers. Southern Arizona was notably in sympathy with the Confederate cause.
For that reason Fort Buchanan was made a depository for more than $1,000,000. in
military supplies. The Confederate Column planned to march from Texas to lay hands
on such supplies and on the rich silver mines of Arizona and the gold of California, but
found itself thwarted. The first step was the closing of the Fort Buchanan post office on
October 21, 1860. Early in July 1861, Moore – now a captain – received orders to burn

Fort Breckenridge and then Fort Buchanan. On July 21, 1861 under the command of Lt. Richard Lord, Fort Buchanan was completely destroyed.
P.O. est. as Tucson, Dec. 4, 1856, Elias Brevoort, p.m.; name changed to Fort Buchanan, July 5, 1857; disc. Oct. 21, 1860
Ref.: 159, pp. 483, 525; AHS, Richard S.C. Lord (Lt.) File; 224, p. 150; 206, p. 90

BUCKBED WASH
Yavapai   T13N R3E
According to the informant, the name derives from the fact that many buck deer used to water and bed down at this spot. Ref.: Allan

BUCKEYE
Maricopa   T1S R3W   Elev. 890'
The name of this community came from that of the Buckeye Canal built by M.M. Jackson, who named it for the nickname of his home state of Ohio. Thomas Newton Clanton donated a quarter section (160 acres) for a town site along the canal. Jackson was a native of Sydney, Ohio, and the new town was called Sydney (misspelled Sidney). By 1889 the town site was laid out, and two years later the post office was established in Clanton's home (with his daughter as postmistress). Although by 1895 the town was being called Buckeye, real estate deeds continued to be made out under the name of Sydney until Buckeye was incorporated c. 1931. A special order of the State Supreme Court changed the name to Buckeye. The name applies also to Buckeye Hills (T2S/R5W, Elev. 1782'), and Valley.
P.O. est. March 10, 1888, Mrs. Cora J. Clanton, p.m.
Ref.: Parkman; *Arizona Star* (May 17, 1889), p. 4

BUCKEYE MOUNTAIN
Gila   T1N R15E   Elev. 4694'
The Buckeye Mine, located in 1876 by S. R. and A. R. Epley, was on this mountain, hence the name. Ref.: Woody

BUCK FARM CANYON
Coconino (Grand Canyon)   T35N R5E
This canyon was named for George W. Buck (b. 1848, Kentucky), in this region c. 1880. Ref.: 62

BUCK HEAD: A few place names in Arizona appear to memorialize the finding of the skull of either a buck deer or a buck sheep. Examples follow:

Buckhead Canyon	Gila	T11N R9E
Buck Head Draw	Gila	T11N R9E
Buck Head Mesa	Gila	T11N R9E
Buckhead Point	Coconino	T19N R6E
Buckhead Ridge	Coconino	T19N R6E

BUCK HORN: Several place names in Arizona appear to memorialize the finding of horns of either a buck deer or a buck sheep. Examples follow:

Buckhorn   Maricopa   T1N R6E
This is a suburb of Mesa. P.O. disc. Jan. 1, 1974

Buck Horn Basin   Cochise   T16S R29E

Buck Horn Basin   Gila   T4N R11E
See Buck Horn Creek, Gila

Buck Horn Creek   Gila   T4N R11E
Before 1870 a hunter found two bucks, their horns in a death lock, hence the name of the creek through Buck Horn Basin. It is the location of a mythical "massacre" of miners by Indians. Such rumors were rife in Arizona near the end of Gen. George Crook's assignment. He ordered every rumor investigated and as in many cases, there was no basis for the story. Ref.: 49, pp. 454, 455; 18a

Buck Horn Mountains	Coconino	T14N R8E	Elev. 6674'
Buck Horn Mountains	Maricopa	T4N R10E	Elev. 6612'
Buck Horn Mountains	Yavapai	T8N R2W	Elev. 6612'
Buck Horn Ridge	Maricopa	T4N R10E	
Buck Horn Spring	Mohave	(1) T34N R5W (2) T34N R16W	
Buck Horn Spring	Yavapai	T8N R2W	
Buck Horn Tank	Yuma	T14S R15W	

The Fish and Wild Life Service developed this tank in 1949, naming it after finding the horns of a buckhorn sheep at the site. Ref.: Monson

Buck Mountain	Coconino	T24N R3E	Elev. 7412'
Buck Mountain	Gila	T4N R15E	Elev. 3544'

Here bucks separate from does after they have bred in the fall. Ref.: Woody

Buck Mountains	Mohave	T16N R18W	
Buck Mountain Tank	Yuma	T12S R16W	

This is near the Buck Mountains, Mohave, hence its name.

Buck Mountain Wash	Mohave	T16N R18W	
Buck Pasture Canyon	Coconino	T41N R2E	
Buck Peak	Gila	T7N R13E	Elev. 6142'

This place is also known as Lauffer Mountain, for a pioneer homesteader and cattleman. Possibly Lauffer was the original owner of the J R Ranch. Ref.: 329

Buck Peak	Yuma	T12S R16W	Elev. 2629'

In this instance the bucks are those of mountain sheep.

Buck Ridge	Coconino	(1) T19N R4E (2) T38N R1E	
Buck Ridge Point	Coconino	T38N R1E	Elev. 7560'
Buck Spring	Coconino	T21N R3E	

This spring was named for Billie Buck, but who he was has not been learned. Ref.: Hart

Buck Spring	Navajo	T11N R16E	
Buck Spring Canyon	Coconino	T12N R12E	
Buck Springs Ridge	Coconino	T13N R11E	
Buck Tank	Coconino	(1) T23N R2–3W (2) T22N R2W (3) T21N R1W	
Buck Tank Canyon	Gila	T8N R11E	

BUCKMAN FLAT
Yavapai T14N R3W

John J. Buckman (b. June 28, 1820; d. June 28, 1900) arrived in Arizona in 1862. He lived near Prescott until 1880 when he moved to southern Arizona. On the way he camped overnight at this spot and since then the location has borne his name. On his birthday in 1900 a bull attacked and killed him. Ref.: Vernon Scott (Prescott)

BUCKSKIN MOUNTAINS
La Paz T9N R18W

These mountains are described as being "virtually the southward continuation of the Aubrey Hills." Buckskin Mountain State Park is on the banks of Lake Havasu. Ref.: 329; 200, pp. 25, 28

BUCKSKIN WASH
Navajo T11N R17E

In 1879 Lehi Heward (b. Aug. 7, 1851; d. Dec. 2, 1926) settled in St. Joseph. In 1883 he moved to this wash near Heber. Its name comes from the fact that Heward dressed in buckskin. He moved again, this time in 1887, to Pine and still later to Tuba City. His final move was to a homestead on Dry Lake c. 1906. Ref.: Glen Heward, Letter (1956)

BUCK TAYLOR SPRINGS
Coconino   T22N R11E
Buck Taylor was an old logger and bullwhacker who lived north of Flagstaff c. 1895. Ref.: Hart

BUCKY O'NEILL HILL
Cochise   T23S R24E
This hill is in the center of Bisbee. It was named for Capt. William O. O'Neill (1860-1896), who arrived in Arizona in 1880. His nickname was earned because he was addicted to "bucking the tiger" at the game of faro. He was the first Arizonan to enlist in the Spanish-American War, in which he lost his life in the charge up San Juan Hill. Ref.: 5, p. 240

BUDDHA TEMPLE
Coconino (Grand Canyon)   T32N R3E   Elev. 7203'
This formation in the Grand Canyon was named in 1906 by Henry Gannett, who also at the same time named the Ottoman Amphitheater and Zoroastra Temple. The fashion of naming geologic formations for deities and for founders of ancient religions was then in vogue. Ref.: 329

BUEHMAN CANYON
Pima   T12S R17E
This location was named for Henry Buehman (b. May 14, 1851, Bremen, Germany; d. Dec. 19, 1912), who was twice mayor of Tucson as well as being a mine owner, cattleman, rancher, and outstanding photographer. Ref.: AHS, Chambers Collection, Box 3

BUELL MOUNTAIN
Apache   T2N R6E   Elev. 8171'
This mountain and Buell Park were both named for Maj. Buell, called by Mexicans Don Carlos Buell (b. 1818, Ohio; d. 1898), who camped in this area during the Navajo campaign. Buell resigned from the Volunteers as a major general in 1862. The park is a rock-walled basin about ten miles square.
   Navajo Indians regard this as a sacred place where they begin their Wind Ceremony. Their name for it is *Nizhaldzis* (= "basin sunk in the ground"). The name has been misspelled as follows: Bule, Yule, and Newell. Ref.: 141, pp. 33, 112, 190; 331, p. 14; 97, p. 26, Note 2; 329

BUENA
Cochise   T22S R20E
The name suggested on the post office application was Fairview. See Pomerene, Cochise
P.O. est. Feb. 2, 1913 as Buena, John H. Downer, p.m.; disc. Oct. 31, 1919 Ref.: 242

BUENA ESPERANZA, RIO GRANDE DE
This was the name for the Colorado River used in 1626 by Zarate. See Colorado River

BUENA VISTA LAND GRANT   pro.: /bweynə viystə/
Spanish: *buena* = "good"; *vista* = "view"
Santa Cruz   T24S R16E
On October 24, 1831 the Mexican government made this grant of eighteen thousand six hundred forty acres to Doña Josefa Morales, under the title Maria Santissima del Carmen Land Grant. Following the Gadsden Purchase, the U.S. Land Grant Court confirmed seven thousand one hundred twenty-eight acres to Maish and Driscoll. The original grant was first mapped in 1820. Ref.: 18a; 116, p. 428

BUENA VISTA PEAK pro.: /bweynə viystə/

Spanish: *buena* = "good"; *vista* = "view"

Cochise   T17S R30E   Elev. 8823'

Prior to 1921 this peak was named by a USGS surveying party because there is a beautiful view from the peak. Ref.: 18a

BUENO pro.: /bweyno/

Spanish = "good"

Yavapai   T12N R1W   Elev. 5258'

Bob Groom located the Bully Bueno Mine here c. 1872. The post office provided mail service for miners.

P.O. est. June 27, 1881, Marion A. Vickroy, p.m.; disc. June 1, 1893

Ref.: AHS, William Fourr Collection, Books 5, 6; 18a; 242

BUENO FAIRVIEW

Cochise

A curious overlapping of information suggests that this was where a local struggle occurred over who was to have the post office, a fact which throws its location into doubt. For clarification, see Buena, Cochise, and Pomerene, Cochise

BUENOS AYRES

Pima   T21S R7E   Elev. 3050'

Buenos Ayres (*sic*) was the name of both the ranch and the post office at this location. See Aguirre Ranch, Pima, and Osa, La, Pima

BUFFALO GULCH

Gila   T1N R15E

On April 4, 1876 John Devine, Joseph Collinswood, and John Anderson located the Buffalo Mine in this gulch. Buffalo Hill (or Ridge) has the same origin. Ref.: Woody

BUFORD HILL

Graham   T7S R21E   Elev. 6456'

This hill is the site of the Spring Gardens Ranch owned by Clay Buford, who was an Indian agent at San Carlos. Ref.: 18a

BUGGELN HILL

Coconino (Grand Canyon)   T30N R4E

This location takes its name from that of Martin Buggeln, who built one of the first tourist accommodations at the Grand Canyon.

BULLARD PEAK

Greenlee   T1S R31E   Elev. 7847'

Jim Bullard (d. Nov. 1870), a cousin of the Shannon brothers and a retired cavalry lieutenant and Indian scout, was among the first miners and prospectors to arrive near the present-day Clifton. A solitary man, Bullard built a small cabin and began prospecting around what was then called Galinas Peak. Apaches killed him while he slept. He may be buried either at the base of this peak or in the Shannon plot at Silver City, New Mexico. Ref.: Shannon; Mrs. Fred Fritz

BULLARD PEAK

Yavapai   T8N R10W   Elev. 3124'

According to Barnes, a prospector named Bullard had a mine five miles south of this peak, hence the name.

BULL BASIN

Coconino   T24N R5E

This location was probably named for John Bull (b. 1840, England), although there was another John Bull (b. 1850, Maryland), who may have been in this vicinity in the 1880s. Ref.: 62; 63

BULL: Although it may not be the case in some of the instances listed below, in the majority the presence of a *bull* or *bulls* probably accounts for the use of the word in the place name:

Bull Basin	Pinal	T1N R12E	
Bull Basin Canyon	Yavapai	T17N R1W	
Bull Basin Mesa	Coconino	T24N R5E	
Bull Butte	Gila	T19E R5N	

This location is also called Cowboy Butte or Tank Butte. Ref.: 329

Bull Canyon	Apache	T5N R30E

This location may take its name from that of John Bull (b. 1850, Maryland).

Bull Canyon	Gila	T5N R15E
Bull Canyon	Graham	T1N R26E
Bull Canyon	Greenlee	T3S R31E
Bull Canyon	Mohave	(1) T18N R15W
		(2) T16N R13W
Bull Canyon	Navajo	T8N R20E
Bull Cienega	Apache	T6N R26E
Bull Cienega Creek	Navajo	T8N R23E
Bull Cienega Spring	Navajo	T8N R23E
Bull Creek	Apache	T3N R26E
Bull Creek	Greenlee	T1N R30E
Bull Creek	Navajo	T7N R23E
Bull Creek	Yavapai	T16N R8W
Bull Flat Canyon	Gila/Navajo	T10N R15E
Bull Hill	Gila	T2N R15E
Bull Hole	Yavapai	T14N R7E
Bull Hollow	Navajo	T12N R21E
Bull Hollow Canyon	Navajo	T12N R21E

Bull Mountain	Maricopa	T5N R9E	Elev. 6604'
Bull Mountain	Mohave	T22N R17W	
Bullock Canyon	Pima	T12S R17E	

The Bullock Ranch is at the entrance to this canyon, hence the name.

Bullock Corrals Spring	Pima	T12S R17E
Bullpasture Spring	Pima	T16S R4W

BULL RUN

Cochise   c. T17S R20E

In 1847 when the Mormon Battalion under Gen. Philip St. George Cooke came to Babocomari Creek, a tributary of the San Pedro River, they stopped to give thanks for finding water. However, wild bulls also drank there. Provoked by the intruders, the bulls attacked fiercely and the battle which followed between men and the bulls has been dubbed Arizona's "Battle of Bull Run." Ref.: Macia; 107, I, 140

Bull Run Creek	Yavapai	T12N R6E
Bull Run Spring	Yavapai	T10N R1W
Bull Spring	Cochise	T22S R23E
Bull Spring	Gila	T10N R7E

Bull Spring	Pima	T12S R17E
Bull Springs	Graham	T4S R25E
Bull Spring Canyon	Gila	T10N R7E
Bull Spring Wash	Yavapai	T15N R9W

BULLDOG MINE
Pinal   T1N R8E

This mine was near a rock formation resembling an enormous bulldog. The rock was blown up in 1895, a fact that led to confusion in mining claims, many having been located with reference to their distance and direction from the "Bulldog."
Ref.: Barnes Notes; State Library Files, *Phoenix Gazette* (Nov. 20, 1895)

BULLFROG CANYON
Gila   T10N R8E

The Bullfrog Mine was in this canyon, hence its name. Ref.: Woody

BULLHEAD CITY
Mohave   T20N R22W   Elev. 525'

The name of this community comes from its proximity to Bullhead Rock, which is largely concealed by waters impounded by Davis Dam. See Bullhead Rock, Mohave
P.O. est. Nov. 28, 1945, Mrs. Ethel M. Pryor, p.m. Ref.: Hornbuckle; 242

BULLHEAD ROCK
Mohave   T21N R21W

Before being covered by waters impounded by Davis Dam, this rock bore a strong resemblance to a bull head. However, the "horns" are now under water.
Ref.: Ranger Barnes, Lake Mohave Resort

BULLRUSH WASH
Mohave   T38N R5W

Correctly spelled, this name would be Bulrush, for this formerly swampy area had a notable growth of cattails or bulrushes. Ref.: 18a

BUMBLE BEE
Yavapai   T10N R2E   Elev. 2573'

In 1863 the first prospector here found a bumblebee nest in the cliffs along the creek. The bees objected to being disturbed and the prospector named the place for that fact. A Mr. Bobs had a stage station where Bumble Bee is now and a Mr. Snyder bought the place from him c. 1887. By 1945 the buildings were privately owned. Its community consisted of about sixty people. It was put up for sale in April 1949. The place is now closed to the public (1980) by a fence while it is being reconstructed as a tourist attraction. In common with such places, it appears to be shaping up as a kind of western town which never was, certainly not the old community of Bumble Bee.
P.O. est. as Bumblebee, Feb. 3, 1874, William D. Powell, p.m.; disc. Feb. 1, 1888 Ref.: G.E.P. Smith; Sharlot Hall Museum Files; 18a; Varney; 242

BUMBLEBEE CREEK
Gila   T5N R10E

Many bumblebees are along this creek. Ref.: Woody

BUNCH RESERVOIR
Apache   T7N R27E

In 1887 Tom Bunch, a farmer, put this reservoir into use.
Ref.: C.H.W. Smith, Letter (April 26, 1956); Wiltbank

BUNDY PONDS
Mohave   T37N R6W

Settlers who attempted farming here were forced by drought to abandon the place and by 1971 only four families still farmed in the vicinity. See Trumbull, Mount (Town), Mohave Ref.: 317, p. 26; Patey

BUNKER HILL
Coconino   T19N R4E
Edward Bunker, who created Bunker Trail in the Grand Canyon, settled here at Bunker
Spring. Ref.: 329

BUNKER HILL
Pinal   T8S R18E
During the mining of the Bunker Hill Mine here, about fifty people lived in a small
community named for the mine. See Sombrero Butte, Pinal Ref.: 329

BUNKERS
Greenlee   1/2 way between Clifton & Morenci
This place was named for C. E. Bunkers, a railroad engineer. Here on October 5, 1917,
Sheriff Slaughter and his deputies met a gang of striking miners who were on their way to
drive strike breakers from Clifton. Facing more than three hundred in the mob, the
sheriff pretended that the mesquite trees concealed many deputies rather than the half
dozen with him. When he demanded that the mob give in, some began running, the
deputies fired at their feet, and that ended the matter.
Ref.: 257, pp. 64, 65; 329

BURCH
Gila   T1N R15E
In 1876 there was a small trading post, the site of a mining camp, on the banks of Pinal
Creek. It was named for Kenyon Burch. This area is now covered by tailings dumps.
Ref.: 5, p. 364; Craig *ms.*, p. 4

BURCH MESA
Gila   T11N R9E
This mesa takes its name from that of William Burch, who first settled in the Big Green
Valley and later moved to this mesa. The name is sometimes erroneously spelled Birch
Mesa. Ref.: 18a

BURCH PEAK
Mohave   T17N R15W   Elev. 6840'
Tom Burch (b. 1838, Missouri), a prospector, had several mining claims in this locality
in 1873. He was living in Charleston, Cochise County, in the mid-1880s.
Ref.: Harris; 63

BURCH PUMPING STATION
Gila   T1N R15E
This location on Miami Flat is named for Kenyon Burch, an early mining company
engineer. See Burch, Gila Ref.: Woody

BURGER
Yuma   T7S R14W
Only a sign board now marks this former station on the Yuma-Phoenix railroad. See
Burger Well, Maricopa Ref.: Mercer

BURGER WELL
Maricopa   T1N R8W
John Henry Burger (b. 1830, Maryland) dug this now abandoned and caved in well. It
was on the old stage route to Agua Caliente. Ref.: 279, p. 204; 62; 18a

BURKE'S STATION
Maricopa   T10S R5W   Elev. c. 500'
In September 1858 Patrick Burke (b. 1837, Ireland) established this station on the
Butterfield Overland stage route. With the discontinuance of the stage through Arizona,
the station fell into disuse and in 1864 J. Ross Browne noted that the only building still
there was occupied by two soldiers taking care of stored government hay. By July 1874
G. R. Whistler had bought the station from Billy Fourr (see Oatman Flat, Maricopa). A

stable hand, Ventura Nuñez, murdered Whistler. Nuñez then fled, but was caught by King S. Woolsey, brought to the station, and hanged. His body was left dangling as a warning to other potential malefactors. When the remains finally dropped, Mexican traders buried them. The coming of the railroad ended Burke's station, which reverted to being part of a ranch. In 1900 its name was changed to Alpha, but for what reason is not known.

P.O. est. as Alpha, May 1, 1894, Tennie Cameron, p.m.; disc. March 8, 1898
Ref.: 56, p. 99; 224, pp. 273, 274; 73, II, 181; 77, p. 119, Note 26; 62

BURNED PUEBLO

Coconino   T24N R11E   Elev. c. 5000'

This prehistoric ruin contains adobe melted by intense heat, the result of burning stored corn. It is so black that visitors often take it to be lava rather than adobe.
Ref.: 71, p. 41

BURNS

Gila   T5S R15E

This railroad station in 1916 was immediately west of Winkelman. It was named for a cattleman and rancher here c. 1898. Ref.: 18a

BURNT: The use of the word *burnt* in place names usually indicates a bad fire having occurred at the location. The following are examples:

Burnt Canyon   Yavapai   T15N R2E

A forest fire occurred along this canyon and burned off the young timber c. 1900, hence the name. The name Burns is erroneous. Ref.: Allan

Burnt Corral Canyon	Coconino	T36N R1W
Burnt Corral Creek	Apache	T3N R24E
Burnt Corral Creek	Maricopa	T3N R12E
Burnt Corral Draw	Greenlee	T2N R29E
Burnt Corral Point	Coconino (Grand Canyon)	T36N R1W
Burnt Corral Ridge	Coconino (Grand Canyon)	T36N R1E
Burnt Corral Rim	Coconino (Grand Canyon)	T36N R1W
Burnt Corral Spring	Apache	T3N R25E
Burnt Corral Spring	Mohave	T41N R4W
Burnt Mountain	Apache	T6N R26E	Elev. 9970'
Burnt Mountain	Maricopa	T2N R8W	Elev. 2917'

The name Turtle Back is in error for this location.

BURNT RANCH

Yavapai   NNE of Prescott c. 7 mi.   Elev. 5125'

In 1865 Jake Miller built a small log cabin at this location so he could spend time here making pine shakes for use in Prescott. Because the area was grassy, Judge E. W. Wells asked Miller to care for Wells' cattle, corraling them at night. While out bringing in the cattle one night, Miller noticed ravens flying up from the brush. Looking intently at it, Miller saw an Indian's head. He rounded up the cattle and as he headed for the corral, several Indians broke out in pursuit. Miller shot the first one. His bulldog at once began worrying the body of the dead Indian. The others stopped to fight it off and killed it. Miller got the cattle into the corral and went into the cabin where a friend helped him prepare for an attack. It came swiftly. Miller was down to his last bullet. The practice in those days was to use the last shot on one's self. Miller, however, decided to risk it, trying to kill the Indian leader. If he succeeded he knew the Indians would run. Cautiously he poked his rifle through a bit of chinking. An Indian immediately grasped the barrel. Jumping back, Miller recovered the rifle and also laid his hand on a forgotten horse pistol

loaded with buckshot. He then looked through a hole higher up. The Indian leader was directly below, watching the hole in the chinking. Miller fired the pistol, the Indian leader sprang up and backward about twenty feet, and fell dead. The others took to their heels. Miller defiantly fired his last bullet at their retreating backs. That evening when the mail carrier passed by and stopped to water his mules, Miller sent word through him to Wells to come and get his cattle. The cattle and Miller both went into Prescott. During the same night the Indians burned Miller's cabin and corral, hence the name Burnt Ranch. The place last earned fame when Gen. George Crook was assigned a new command and a farewell gathering was held at Burnt Ranch. Hundreds walked from Prescott to hear Gen. August V. Kautz, the new commander, bid Crook farewell.
Ref.: 116, V, 311, 315; 49, p. 239

Burnt Spring	Yavapai	T12N R6E
Burnt Springs Canyon	Mohave	T30N R13W
Burnt Piñon Wash	Apache	T26N R9W
Burnt Place Valley	Navajo	T35N R20E
Burnt Stump Mesa	Greenlee	T3S R31E
Burnt Trees Wash	Navajo	T38N R19E
Burnt Wash	Yavapai	T15N R4W
Burnt Wash Spring	Yavapai	(1) T15N R5W (2) T15N R4W
Burnt Wells	Maricopa	T2N R9W

BURRIS LAKE
Coconino   T18N R7E
This lake was named for F. Burris (b. 1846, New York), who was a miner before he retired to this location. Ref.: 62

BURRO: Many place names in Arizona derive from the fact that burros, wild or tame, were at the places so named. When prospectors and miners decided to call it quits, as they were frequently forced to do by lack of supplies, luck, or health (to say nothing of encounters with Indians), they frequently turned their burros loose. Their wild burro descendants are considered a nuisance today as in some places they exist by the thousands. This is true of Burro Canyon, Coconino (Grand Canyon). Except where specific mention is made otherwise, the following place names are so derived:

Burro Basin	Pima	T12S R17E
Burro Canyon	Coconino (Grand Canyon)	T33N R1W
Burro Canyon	Mohave (Grand Canyon)	T38N R7W
Burro Canyon	Santa Cruz	T23S R14E
Burro Canyon	Yuma	T1N R17W
Burro Canyon Wash	Coconino	T28N R8E
Burro Creek	Mohave/Yavapai	T14N R11W
Burro Creek	Pima	T12S R17E
Burro Creek	Yavapai	T15N R10W
Burro Creek Spring	Apache	T6N R27E
Burro Flats	Yavapai	T7N R1W
Burro Gap	Pima	T12S R4W
Burro Hills See Tombstone Hills, Cochise	Cochise	
Burro Mesa	Greenlee	T3S R31E
Burro Mesa Dam	Yavapai	T17N R9W

Burro, Mount	Coconino	T32N R3W	Elev. 5684'
	(Grand Canyon)		

This location was named for a Havasupai leader, Capt. Burro, who was here in 1914. The name was approved by the USGS in 1925. Ref.: 329; Susie Verkamp

Burro Mountain	Yavapai	T14N R7W	Elev. 3578'
Burro Point	Mohave	T31N R23W	
Burro Pond Village	Pima		

The name translates the Papago name. See Vopolo Havoka, Pima

Burro Saddle	Graham	T5S R27E	
Burro Spring	Apache	T35N R23E	
Burro Spring	Cochise	T18S R31E	
Burro Spring	Coconino	(1) T23N R1W	(2) T40N R3E
		(3) T19N R10E	
Burro Spring	Maricopa	T6N R1W	
Burro Spring	Mohave	(1) T33N R16W	(2) T34N R16W
	(3) T30N R18W	(4) T22N R20W	(5) T18N R12W
Burro Spring	Navajo	T27N R15E	

The name is a translation of the Navajo *Tielii Bito*. See Chilchinbito, Navajo

Burro Spring	Pima	T17S R7W	
Burro Spring	Pinal	T1N R13E	

This location has also been called Burro Water.

Burro Spring Wash	Apache		
Burro Wash	Navajo		

See Chilchinbito Canyon, Navajo

BURRO TOWN

Yuma

This little section north of Somerton had a predominantly Mexican population and at one time as many burros as children. Local legend says that people in Somerton objected to the burros' braying and killed some, but because the burros were not blessed before being killed, their ghosts now appear at about midnight.

Ref.: Cecil Stone (Informant), Edith Leonard (Collector, 1964); David Coronado (Informant), Mrs. Meryl Jacquest (Collector, 1964)

Burro Wallow	Yavapai	T12N R3W
Burro Wash	Apache	T36N R23E
Burro and Cottonwood Wash	Greenlee	T9S R32E
Burro Wash	Mohave	T10N R12W
Burro Water Spring	Pinal	T5S R17E

BUSHY: The following place names derive from the presence of thick brush at these locations:

Bushy Canyon	Gila	T11N R9E	
Bushy Mesa	Gila		
Bushy Mountain	Maricopa		Elev. 3525'
Bushy Top Mountain	Gila		

BUTLER CANYON

Apache   T7N R27E   Elev. 8000'

Jacob Noah Butler (b. April 26, 1852, Iowa; d. May 7, 1919) in 1888 moved to this

location with his nineteen children, hence the name. Butler came from Salt Lake City and also St. Joseph, where he had helped build Mormon temples.
Ref.: Mollie Butler, Letter (May 28, 1956)

BUTLER MOUNTAINS
Yuma   T12S R19W   Elev. 1169′
Eldred D. Wilson named this range in 1930 for Dr. G. M. Butler, then Dean of the College of Mines, University of Arizona. Ref.: 355, p. 179

BUTLER VALLEY
La Paz   T8N R13E
In 1888 Samuel A. Butler (b. 1845, Illinois) and his brothers, miners, were living in this valley, hence its name. Butler Valley is also sometimes called Cunningham Valley or Cactus Plain. Ref.: 279, p. 205; 18a; 63

BUTTE
Pinal   T3S R11E   Elev. 4293′
This butte east of Florence is sometimes called San Carlos Butte. The post office here was established for miners who started a community in late December 1881 or early January 1882. The Pinal Consolidated Mining Company had reduction works here.
P.O. est. April 16, 1883, Maurice B. Fleishman, p.m.; disc. June 23, 1886
Ref.: *Arizona Weekly Enterprise* (Jan. 7, 1882), p. 2

BUTTERFLY PEAK
Pima   T11S R16E   Elev. 7360′
The Butterfly Peak Natural Area of about one thousand acres is at this location. It was established on July 25, 1935. The name *butterfly* derives from the fact that butterflies can be seen here by the thousands at certain times of the year.
Ref.: 76, p. 14

BUZZARD: The presence of *buzzards* has led to the use of the word in the following place names:

Buzzard Canyon	Greenlee	T1S R32E	
Buzzard Knoll	Coconino	T20N R2E	Elev. 666′
Buzzard Ranch See Big Horn, Maricopa	Maricopa		
Buzzard Ridge	Coconino	T19N R5E	
Buzzard Roost Canyon	Gila	T7N R13E	

This camping place was used by "men on the dodge who flopped there to hide." Cowpokes also camped here. As they referred to each other and to themselves as "buzzards," the name stuck.
Ref.: McInturff; Packard

Buzzard Roost Mesa See Buzzard Roost Canyon, Gila	Gila	T8N R13E	
Buzzard Spring	Greenlee	T4S R31E	
Buzzard Roost Spring	Pinal	T7S R18E	
Buzzard Roost Wash	Yavapai	T12N R2W	
Buzzard Spring	Coconino	T19N R5E	
Buzzard Spring	Yavapai	T12N R3W	
Buzzards Roost Spring	Pinal	T1N R10E	Elev. 3754′

BYLAS   pro.: /báyləs/
Apache = "one who does all the talking"
Graham   T4S R22E   Elev. 2620′
In 1882 Bylas, whose name was also spelled By-Lass, was an Apache leader. During Geronimo's outbreak with a Chiracahua band, Bylas tried to warn people at the agency headquarters that the telegraph wires were cut, but they scoffed, thinking he was drunk. The town of Bylas is today a San Carlos Apache community.
P.O. est. May 26, 1917, Theodore E. Reed, p.m. Ref.: 242; Jennings; 5, p. 344

C

CABABI
Papago: *ka-p-va-vi* = "badger well"
Pima   T16S R4E
There was a mine at this location in 1850. By 1883 it had a post office. See Ko Vaya, Pima
P.O. est. March 12, 1883, Robert H. Coat, p.m.; disc. June 4, 1884
Ref.: 163, p. 227; 228, n.p.

C A BAR CANYON
Greenlee   T6S R31E
The name derives from that of an old ranch which used this brand prior to 1910.
Ref.: 329

C A BAR RANCH
Greenlee   T6S R31E
This was a cattle outfit owned by Warden and Courtney. Ref.: Fred Fritz, Notes

CABEZA PRIETA   pro.: /kəbéysə priéytə/
Spanish: *cabeza* = "head;" *prieta* = "black"
Yuma   T12S R6W   Elev. 2559'
This is a black lava-capped peak near the center of the Cabeza Prieta Mountains. The old trail from Mexico went through Cabeza Prieta Pass. Ref.: Mercer; Lenon; 355, p. 162

CABEZA PRIETA NATIONAL WILD LIFE REFUGE
Yuma/Pima
This 860,000 acre refuge was established in 1939. On March 21, 1975, it became a National Wild Life refuge, the home of big horn sheep and the endangered Sonoran prong horn and other wild life. It extends from Tinajas Altas Mountains to Childs Mtn. See Cabeza Prieta, Yuma   Ref.: "Final Environmental Statement," U.S. Fish and Wild Life Service Brochure, p. A-2

CABEZA PRIETA TANKS
Yuma   T13S R15W
These are natural tanks where Indians formerly lived. See Cabeza Prieta, Yuma
Ref.: Monson

C A CREEK
Greenlee   T6S R31E
This name as well as C A Bar Creek is not used locally. Residents use the term C A only with reference to the canyon. Ref.: Fred Fritz

CACTUS
Maricopa   T3N R3E   Elev. 2500'
The first name suggested on the post office application for this location was Pass City.

As is the case in many locations, this area contains much cactus.
P.O. est. May 14, 1918, William C. Hyatt, p.m.; disc. Jan. 1, 1964 Ref.: 242

CACTUS: The word *cactus* occurs in many place names. The variety of cactus may be prickly pear, saguaro, cholla, or some other, but where the name has been used, the cactus growth is usually dense. Listed below are examples with some exceptions:

Cactus	Maricopa	T3N R3E	Elev. 2500'

The first name suggested on the post office application for this location was Pass City. This area contains much cactus.
P.O. est. May 14, 1918, William C. Hyatt, p.m.; disc. Jan.1, 1964 Ref.: 242

Cactus Basin	Yavapai	T11N R3E	Elev. c. 4000'
Cactus Butte	Gila	T5N R12E	Elev. 3668'
Cactus Butte Spring	Gila	T5N R12E	
Cactus Canyon	Coconino	T31N R2W	

See Cataract Canyon, Coconino

Cactus Dam	Graham	T12N R20E	
Cactus Flat	Graham	T12N R20E	

See Lebanon, Graham

Cactus Flat	Navajo	T12N R2E	
Cactus Forest	Pinal	T5S R10E	Elev. 1808'
Cactus Mountain	Mohave	T17N R17W	Elev. 2600'
Cactus Mountain	Yavapai	T13N R6E	Elev. 4256'
Cactus Pass	Coconino		

The pass over Elden Mountain to Flagstaff was known formerly by this name, given to it c. 1849 by a botanist named Dudley. Ref.: 166, p. 107

Cactus Pass	Mohave	T20N R13W	Elev. c. 5000'

Dr. Bigelow, a botanist, urged Lt. Amiel W. Whipple on January 30, 1854 to name this pass because Bigelow had found there "numerous specimens of this, his favorite plant."
Ref.: 232, II, 214; 346, pp. 98, 208, and 208, Note 14

Cactus Plain	La Paz	T8N R17W	Elev. 2000'

See Butler Valley, Yuma

Cactus Ridge	Gila	T8N R9E	Elev. 6799'
Cactus Spring	Gila	T5N R12E	
Cactus Tank	Pima	T17S R8E	

CALABASAS pro.: /kǽləbæsəs/ or /kaləbasəs/
Spanish: *calabaza* = "gourd" or "pumpkin"

Santa Cruz		T22S R13E	Elev. c. 3500'

Fr. Eusebio Kino on his map of 1701 called this place San Gaetan. It was probably a Sobaipuri Indian village. Another name for it was San Cayetano de Calabazas. The use of the name *calabasas* years prior to the construction of the "yellow building" (at least a century later), gives credence to assuming that gourds and other melons grew abundantly in this region. They still do. The location until 1784 was a *visita* of Guevavi (*q.v.*). A church and house for the friars were built in 1797. Meanwhile, however, Apache attacks had been severe. Guevavi ceased to be the head mission and Tumacacori became head mission. By 1777 Indians had burned the community at Calabasas and it was deserted. It was never again a mission. Under a Spanish land grant Calabasas Ranch was created on December 4, 1786. In 1842 the government of Mexico sold the grant to Francisco Aguilar, who in turn sold it to Gov. Manuel M. Gandara. By 1850 Calabazas Ranch was a stock farm. Its corral covered four acres. Instead of a fence it had a four-foot-high adobe wall. Only a year later (1851) the Boundary Survey Commission visited here and Bartlett noted that the so-called hacienda was an old one "which seems to have been abandoned many years before as much of its adobe walls was washed away." The hacienda was possibly the friar's house. The ruins may, of course, have been those of the church. Bartlett also noted that the name Calabasas may have come from the quantity of wild pumpkins and gourds in the valley nearby. To Reid must be attributed the following concerning the name: "Calabasas ... so called from an old yellow adobe, named from its color, which stands on the right bank of the river near the above noted junction with the Sonoita Creek."

Because of Apache depradations, by early 1857 four companies of the First Dragoons were stationed at Rancho de las Calabasas at the juncture of Sonoita Creek and the Santa Cruz River. Many sources cite it as the location of Calabasas, thus reinforcing the report that Fort Mason was at Calabasas. In 1864 Fort Mason was established (see that entry) and a year later M. H. Calderwood, who says that Calabasas and Fort Mason were identical, noted that the fort was on an elevated plateau. Troops were withdrawn for service elsewhere during the War Between the States, and Apache attacks increased. Fort Mason was abandoned in 1866. Life at Calabasas continued at a slow pace, being interrupted by Apaches from time to time. In November 1871 the last two settlers — Blanchard and Sanders — were killed by Apaches as the two men were working in their fields.

The coming of the railroad from the north (to join that in Mexico inching toward the international boundary) brought new life to Calabasas. Convinced that Calabasas would become the Port of Entry, many rushed to build a tent city almost overnight. One tent was called the "Palace Hotel," under the aegis of orientals named Cum Sing, Hi Sing, and Lo Sing. The renewed existence of Calabasas met an early demise when Nogales was declared the Port of Entry.

In 1898 Calabasas returned to life as a military post with Maj. Nowlan commanding a troop of cavalry. Communications with other military posts was achieved via the telegraph line in Calabasas. As the threatened troubles with revolution in Mexico subsided, so did the life of Calabasas.

Although the name of the post office on the Pete Kitchen Ranch was Calabazas (among others), it should not be confused with the postal service which existed briefly near Fort Mason, largely for the convenience of the military.

P.O. est. as Calabasas, Oct. 8, 1866, Edwin N. Fish, p.m.; disc. June 24, 1867; reest. as Calabazas, April 26, 1880, William G. Campbell, p.m.; disc. May 10, 1880; name changed to Calabasas, Sept. 11, 1882; disc. date unknown; re-instated as "a new post office" March 28, 1903, G. W. Atkinson, p.m.; disc. Aug. 15, 1913; Wells Fargo 1885

Ref.: 224, pp. 136, 137; 167, I, 187; 15, I, 369, 383 (Note 21), 385; 51, pp. 327, 328; 272, pp. 187, 188; 107, .., IV, 190, 191; 277, pp. 74, 76; 206, pp. 341, 342; *Weekly Arizona Miner* (Nov. 4, 1871), p. 1; *Oasis* (May 21, 1898), p. 8; 242; Lenon; Huntington Library *ms.* (1878)

CALAHAN DRAW

Gila   T11N R10E

A blacksmith named Jim Calahan lived in this draw, hence its name. Ref.: Gillette

CALAMITY CAVE

Navajo   c. T41N R27E Near head of Nakai
                                          Canyon, southern fork

This cliff pueblo ruins was visited by Charles L. Bernheimer c. 1923, who named it Wild Rose Cave. As it has four kivas (ceremonial rooms), this location may have served as a ceremonial center. Ref.: 87, p. 632, Figure 1

CALDERWOOD PEAK

Maricopa   T5N R1E   Elev. 1703'

M. H. Calderwood (d. May 15, 1913) served with the California Volunteers in 1865-66. Subsequently he bought a stage station from Darrel Duppa on the Agua Fria where it intercepted the road from Phoenix to Wickenburg. (See Agua Fria, Maricopa.) The post office was at the station. In 1884 he sold to M. H. (Johnny) Elder.

CALERA CANYON   pro.: /kaléra/

Spanish = "lime kiln"

Pima   T20S R10E   Elev. c. 3500'

A lime kiln formerly in this canyon results in the name. It is also known as Lime Kiln Canyon and Calera Draw. Ref.: Lenon

CALICO PEAK

Mohave   T24N R18W   Elev. 5129'

It is possible that this is a transfer name from Calico, California, a good silver mining location, as is also this location in Arizona. Many miners came into this section of Arizona from California Ref.: Harris

CALL OF THE CANYON

Coconino   T17N R6E   Elev. 4000'

At this location Zane Grey had a log cabin in which he wrote the *Call of the Canyon*. At that time the place was called the Lola Maw Lodge and it was not on property owned by the Call of the Canyon resort. That resort is across the creek.
Ref.: Schnebly; Mrs. Florence Smithe, Call of the Canyon Resort, Letter (June 11, 1957)

CALLOWAY LAKE

Yavapai/Coconino   T13N R8E   Elev. 6860'

A farmer named Calloway had a farm at the mouth of Beaver Creek c. 1910.
Ref.: Hart

CALUMET

Cochise   T24S R27E   Elev. 3958'

This railroad siding for loading ore cars was named for the Calumet and Arizona Mining Company, which constructed a smelter northwest of the Copper Queen Mine. Martin Costello of Tombstone owned the Calumet claims. He leased them to the Calumet and Hecla Mining Company of Calumet, Michigan, in March 1889. It developed into the Calumet and Arizona Mining Company, which in late 1931 and early 1932 merged with Phelps Dodge. Ref.: *Douglas Dispatch*, "50th Anniversary Edition," Section 4, p. 4; 197, p. 62

CALUMET

Gila   T2N R14E

In 1907 this post office was applied for to serve two hundred and twenty-five working at a nearby mine. There is no record the application was approved.
P.O. est. May 4, 1907, James Lightfoot, p.m.; disc. (?) Ref.: 242

CALVA

Graham   T3S R21   Elev. 2579'

This station on the Arizona Eastern R.R. was established in the late 1890s under the name Dewey (probably for Admiral Dewey), prominent in the Spanish-American War. A flood washed this location away but it was rebuilt and renamed, this time Calva. Calva was the name of a San Carlos Indian leader who lived and farmed near here. His name was probably Calvario. It was believed that waters impounded by Coolidge Dam would cover Calva and it was temporarily abandoned. However, the waters never came and the people came back. When Coolidge Dam overflowed, Calva was flooded temporarily.
P.O. est. March 1, 1938, Chalmers Brown Paul, p.m.; disc. June 30, 1941
Ref.: 242; 18a; Jennings; 5, p. 344; Lenon

CAMELBACK MOUNTAIN

Maricopa   T2N R3E   Elev. 2704'

This mountain outline resembles the hump and head of a camel.

CAMELBACK MOUNTAIN

Pima   T12S R6W   Elev. 2572'

This mountain hump resembles that of a camel.

CAMEL BUTTE

Navajo   T41N R21E   Elev. 5680'

This location resembles a camel lying down.

CAMEL FRANCIS LAKE

Coconino   T20N R9E

The name Camel Francis derives from that of two sheepherders formerly in the region. The name Youngs Lake is not known locally although that is what the USGS has used in the past. The name "Camel" is undoubtedly a corruption, as it should be Campbell, named for a partner in the Campbell-Francis Sheep Company. Ref.: 329

CAMEL ROCK

Yavapai   S. end of Oak Creek

There is a huge hump-back rock, hence the name. From its top there is a magnificent view of Oak Creek in which this formation is. It is also called the Camel. Ref.: Schnebly; 71, p. 52

CAMEL'S BACK

Cochise   T13S R26E   Elev. 6344'

The name describes the appearance of this location.

CAMERON

Coconino   T29N R9E   Elev. 4201'

Cameron is a trading post and tourist stop where the bridge crosses the Little Colorado River. The Navajo name *Nasna'ah* (= "little span across") indicates that fact. In 1911 when the original bridge was constructed Scott Preston, a Navajo, maintained a store here. In the same year Hubert Richardson began a settlement, naming it for then U.S. Senator Ralph Cameron (b. Oct. 21, 1863, Southport, Maine), last territorial delegate for Arizona to the U.S. Congress.

P.O. est. May 2, 1917, Elizabeth F. Haldeman, p.m.; disc. Dec. 31, 1919; reest. April 24, 1924, S. K. Borum, p.m. Ref.: 242; 331, p. 16; 5, p. 285; Verkamp

CAMERON, CAMP

Santa Cruz   31° 50'/110° 50'

Following the closing of the post at Calabasas (*q.v.*), Camp Cameron was established on October 1, 1866, sixteen miles east-northeast of Calabasas, where Madera Canyon debouches onto mesa land. It was named for Simon Cameron, Secretary of War under President Abraham Lincoln. Cameron was an uncle of the Cameron brothers (see Rafael Valley, San, Cochise). The camp was abandoned March 7, 1867 when troops were transferred to Camp Crittenden. Ref.: 145, p. 127; 35, p. 473; AHS; 52, p. 25; Lenon

CAMERON PASS

Santa Cruz   T22S R18E   Elev. c. 6000'

This pass was named for Colin and Brewster Cameron, who raised cattle in the San Rafael Valley from 1882 to 1890. Ref.: 18a

CAMERON TANK

Yuma   T13S R7W

Created by the Fish and Wildlife Service in the 1930s, this tank was named for the man who had the grazing allotment here. Ref.: Monson

CAMINO DEL DIABLO   pro.: /kam^no del diyáblo/

Spanish = "Devil's Highway"

The first white man to use this route from eastern Arizona to near the mouth of the Colorado River was Fr. Eusebio Kino, in 1697. Later it was used by emigrants seeking a route to California, who knew it as the Yuma Trail. Such travellers set out from the vicinity of Tubac and went roughly via Arivaca to Sasabe, dipping there into Mexico and following the border from Sonoyta to Monument 179, whence the trail followed the *Playas* to Tule Well. At that point they chose whether to go on to Cabeza Prieta Tank or west to Tinajas Altas. If they chose the latter, their route proceeded from that point north to the Gila River or west through a mountain gap to the Colorado River near Yuma. As for the name of the route, it was justly applied because many who followed it suffered the tortures of the damned from heat and thirst. The route meandered from water hole to water hole, and it was always problematic whether such holes would be holding water. Further, at times shifting sands made portions of the trail impassable so that far too often travellers perished before finding their way or water to sustain them. Ref.: 227, p. 129; 5, pp. 389, 390; 355, pp. 178, 179; 57, p. 413; Ketchum

CAMOTE pro.: /kamotiy/
Spanish = "sweet potato"
Pima   T18S R1W
Papago call this village on their reservation Shaotkam (= "sweet potato": pro.: šowətkm[SV]) because of edible roots which grow abundantly in the vicinity. The name has also been rendered Camoti, and the Papago as Shaatkam (1912, Lumholz). See Shaotkam, Pima Ref.: 58; 262, p. 7

CAMP: Place names preceded by the word *camp* will be found in this volume under the major identifying word. For instance, Camp Verde is listed under Verde, Camp, and Camp Verde Hills is listed under Verde Hills, Camp. The only exceptions are the following:

Camp Creek   Maricopa   T6–7N R5E   Elev. c. 2500'
This is a summer camping location. Ref.: 18a

Camp Gulch   Gila   T11N R7E

Camp Well   Mohave   T19N R13W

CAMPAIGN CREEK
Gila/Maricopa   T3N R13E
In naming and explaining names on the Apache Trail in 1917, Aubrey Drury said, "This creek ... commemorates one of the early expeditions against the Apache." According to Barnes, locally it was believed that Gen. George Crook had his headquarters somewhere on this creek in 1873. Ref.: 329; 18a

CAMPANILE, THE
Mohave (Lake Mead)   T32N R19W
Reclamation officials gave this name to a point Daniel Bonelli in 1870 called Napoleon's Tomb because of its fancied resemblance to Napoleon Bonaparte's profile. Ref.: 329

CAMPBELL CREEK
Gila   T7N R15E
This location was named for Campbell, the son-in-law of Jesse Ellison, who had a ranch on this creek. Ref.: Woody

CAMPBELL DRAW
Coconino   T16N R8E
Dan and Hugh Francis and Sen. Thomas E. Campbell operated the Campbell-Francis Sheep Company in this area. See Campbell Springs, Coconino Ref.: Hart

CAMPBELL FLAT SPRING
Yavapai   T10N R2W
This location may have been named for Colin Campbell, who settled in this region as a sheepherder about 1885. Ref.: Hart

CAMPBELL'S BLUE CREEK
Apache/Greenlee   T4N R29–30E   Elev. c. 7000'
In 1888 William Campbell, a cattleman and one-time sheriff of Apache County, ranged cattle along this stream, hence its name. (Campbell established the V T Ranch in 1883).It is sometimes called Blue River, as attested to by a post office site location map for Espero post office in 1924. Ref.: Noble; 18a; AHS, Coleman Collection, Box 1, "Diary"; 242

CAMPBELL'S PASS
Apache
Albert H. Campbell, topographer for Whipple's expedition of 1853-1854, located this potential railroad pass at the west end of the Rio Puerco, on the south face of the Dutton Plateau. Whipple named it in his honor. Ref.: 346, pp. 12, 14

CAMPBELL SPRINGS

Coconino   T16N R8E

This location is named for Thomas Edward Campbell (b. Jan. 18, 1878, Prescott, Arizona), who with Dan Francis had the Campbell-Francis Sheep Company. Campbell was governor of the state of Arizona twice. He has the distinction of having been the first native Arizonan to be elected to the legislature. Ref.: Hart

CAMP CREEK

Maricopa   T7–5N R5–7E   Elev. 3400'

A small community has developed on the creek, which flows southeast to the Verde River at Needle Rock. The rock is so named because of its shape. The community was formerly a summer camping place, hence the name. Ref.: 18a

CAMP VERDE INDIAN RESERVATION

Yavapai

This reservation was established for about five hundred Yavapai Indians in 1914. See Verde, Camp, Yavapai

CANAAN DAM

Mohave   T38N R5W

This dam was constructed by Mormons on Temple Road (*q.v.*). See Gertrudis, Arroyo de Santa, Mohave Ref.: 42, p. 65

CAÑADA DEL ORO   pro.: /kanyádə del oro/

Spanish: *cañada* = "ravine"; *del oro* = "of gold"

Pima/Pinal   T11S R13E

The first mention of this name, which is an old one, is in reports by Capt. C. R. Sellman of his military operations from June to November 1862. The canyon, which was part of the route from old Fort Grant to Tucson, was the scene of many Apache encounters. Typical was the attack by three hundred Apaches on a Tully and Ochoa wagon train on May 10, 1872. Five men were killed, seven wounded, the wagons were burned and all the mules taken. Apaches were very fond of roasted mule meat. Of further interest is the fact that in 1877 Hiram C. Hodges reported finding rich placer gold deposits and that he had found evidence of mining for gold years before American occupation. That fact probably led to naming this canyon Gold Canon on the 1879 Willcox map of Arizona Territory. Ref.: AHS, William Whelan, "Log"; 168, p. 62; 49, p. 53; 224, p. 166

CAÑADA DEL ORO

Pinal   Location unknown

See Cañada del Oro, Pinal/Pima

P.O. est. March 28, 1881, Jose de Camacho, p.m.; disc. Oct. 12, 1882 Ref.: 242

CANBY, FORT

Apache   c. 18 mi. s.w. of Holbrook

Kit Carson in 1863 selected the site for an operations base in the campaign against the Navajo tribe. It was abandoned in 1864. Some assert it was in New Mexico. Ref.: 338, p. 71

CANE: The presence of cattails or wild cane has led to the following place names (see also Cane Beds, Mohave). Wild cane was used by Indians for making arrow shafts because it was light, straight and strong.

Cane Beds   Mohave   T41N R6W   Elev. 5090'

Seeking places for Mormon settlements, John D. Lee in 1852 explored along the bottom lands of the Virgin River, the Virgin Bottoms, and thence to the junction of the Virgin River with Ash Creek. As a result of his explorations, by 1868 a small settlement was forming at the Virgin Bottoms locations. The presence of wild cane or cattails led to the designation Cane Beds.

P.O. est. March 14, 1917, Cora Height Cox, p.m.; disc. April 18, 1945 Ref.: 242; 140, pp. 25, 42

Cane Canyon   Coconino   T36N R3E

Cane Creek   Gila

The Woolsey Expedition of 1864 named this creek because of the huge stands of cane grass along its banks. Indians used the cane for arrows because of its straight and light lengths. The creek is near Aliso Creek, lying southeast of the east branch of Agua Fria. Ref.: *Arizona Miner* (May 11, 1864)

Cane Spring   Gila   T7N R11E

The heavy growth of cane around the spring gives it the name used locally since 1914. A little used variant name is Pasture Spring. Ref.: 329

Cane Spring	Graham	T5S R26E
Cane Spring	Maricopa	T3N R9E
Cane Spring	Mohave	(1) T26N R18W (2) T18N R13W
Cane Spring	Navajo	T37N R21E
Cane Spring	Pinal	T3S R14E
Cane Spring Canyon	Gila/Maricopa	T7N R9E

This location was named by Charlie Chilson and Dick Robbins (both of whom ranched in this area for over thirty years) because of the abundant growth of wild cane. Ref.: Woody

Cane Spring Canyon	Maricopa	T3N R9E
Cane Springs	Graham	T3S R22E
Cane Springs	Mohave	(1) T38N R14W (2) T32N R9W
Cane Springs Mountain	Gila	T11N R8E	Elev. 5364'
Cane Spring Wash	Mohave	T18N R13W

See Bull Canyon, Mohave

Cane Valley	Apache	T40N R23E
Cane Valley Wash	Apache	T40N R23E
Cane Wash	Navajo	T37N R21E

CANEBRAKE CANYON

Yuma

The Ives map of 1857 gives this name to a bend swinging southeast on the Colorado River.

CANELO

Santa Cruz   T22S R18E   Elev. 5000'

The name for this post office was borrowed from that of the hills in the vicinity. Through a misunderstanding of the word, the Post Office Department first spelled it Canille. See Canelo Hills, Santa Cruz

P.O. est. as Canille, June 16, 1904, Robert Andrew Rodgers, p.m.; name changed to Canelo, Aug. 22, 1904; disc. April 10, 1924 Ref.: 242

CANELO HILLS   pro.: /kəniʌlo/ or /kənélo/

Spanish = "cinnamon"

Santa Cruz   T22S R18E   Elev. 6257'

The name for these hills first appears on GLO 1896 as the Canille Mountains. The Gadsden Purchase maps give the name Sierra de la Santa Cruz for what probably was later divided into the Patagonia Mountains and the Canille Mountains. Their early name probably came from the community of Santa Cruz in Sonora, Mexico.

As for the origin of the name, it has been in some dispute. A letter from Addie Parker, p.m. of the community in 1923 and a member of a family who pioneered in this area, notes that the local name for these hills was at that time "La Sierra de las Osos Canellos," or "The Mountain of the Cinnamon Bears." She further notes that that species of bear once infested the hills. By curious coincidence the hills themselves have a cinnamon color and, further, Mexicans used the word *canelo* in describing a "bluish roan cow." By 1941 the Forest Service reported, "Our local officers feel certain that . . .

it was derived from the cinnamon color of the vegetation at certain times of the year on the Canelo Hills and that the true Spanish name would be La Lomas de Canelo ... the spelling Canille is a rather willful perversion of the word." Anyone wishing to have a strong opinion one way or the other about this name is entitled to do so. Ref.: 329; Addie Parker, Letter (Jan. 27, 1923), and Forestry Service (June 10, 1941); AHS, G.E.P. Smith, Letter to Board on Geographic Names (July 16, 1941)

CANOA pro.: /kanówə/
Spanish-American = "a trough for carrying irrigation water"
Pima   T19S R13E   Elev. c. 3200'
The Canoa Ranch is one of the oldest in Arizona. In 1775 Fr. Francisco Garcés noted that a Papago rancheria was at this place. In 1821 Tomas and Ignacio Ortiz took over from the Mexican government the Canoa Land Grant under the name San Ignacio de la Canoa. The word *canoa* means "canoe" and it is possible that irrigation was conducted over broken ground here by means of hollowed out logs which resemble canoes. It seems beyond question that there was a settlement called Canoa on the east bank of the Santa Cruz River, whereas the Canoa ranch was on its west side at a later date, close to Sopori Creek. The location of the Canoa settlement on the river was called Canoa Crossing. The quarters for travelers at the settlement began with a house and corral constructed by men whip-sawing lumber in the nearby Santa Rita Mountains. The lumber was carried across the river at Canoa Crossing and used in the Heintzelman Mine. In 1860 Canoa had a stockade house which also served as an inn. It was the scene of a fierce battle in 1861 between the lumbermen, Mexicans, and Apaches. The Apaches were defeated but returned within a month. When they left the stockade, it was in total ruins. No one had been left alive at the inn. In 1869 the ranch was sold to Maish and Driscoll. The "new ranch house" was probably erected shortly thereafter. Ref.: AHS, John Spring Collection, p. 11 and map; 58; 167, ..I, 201; 269, p. 7; 107, II, 54, 55, 56; *Arizona Star* (Feb. 19, 1880); AHS

CANOVA
Pima
This name, a corruption, appears on a single map. See Canoa, Pima

CANYON: In many place names the word *canyon* is used as a generic designating the kind of location. For that reason such entries will be found under the identifying word. For instance, for Canyon Diablo, the entry will be found under Diablo, Canyon. The following are exceptions based on a rather remarkable lack of imagination on the part of those who named the locations:

Canyon Butte	Navajo	c. T16N R22E	Elev. c. 5000'
Canyon Creek	Apache	T5N R30E	
Canyon Creek	Gila	(1) T10N R15E (2) T5N R15E	
Canyon Creek	Greenlee	T4N R31E	
Canyon Creek	Maricopa	T6N R8E	
Canyon Creek	Navajo	T8N R15E	
Canyon Creek Butte	Gila	T15N R16E	Elev. 4059'
Canyon Creek Point	Coconino	T11N R14E	
Canyon Creek Ruin	Navajo	c. T8N R17E	

The Canyon Creek Ruin has been investigated by the University of Arizona. It is a fourteenth century, fifty-eight room cliff dwelling. Ref.: 345, I, p. 43; Davis; 159, pp. 437, 447; 223a, p. 4

Canyon Creek Spring	Maricopa	T16N R8E
Canyon Lake	Maricopa	T2N R9E

This lake was formed in 1925 by waters impounded by Mormon Flat Dam. The waters now cover Mormon Flat. See Mormon Flat, Maricopa

Canyon Lodge	Coconino	T20N R12E	Elev. c. 6000'

This lodge, no longer in existence, was built on the then new Route 66 (National Old Trails Highway)

in 1924. It was named because of its proximity to Canyon Diablo.
P.O. est. June 23, 1924, Earl M. Cundiff, p.m.; disc. May 14, 1926 Ref.: 242

Canyon Meadow	Apache	T35N R28E	
Canyon Mouth Dam	Yavapai	T2N R27W	
Canyon Ridge	Mohave	T32N R22W	Elev. 3917'
Canyon Spring	Mohave	T25N R17W	
Canyon Rapids	Coconino/Mohave		

See Roadrunner Rapids, Coconino/Mohave

Canyon Viewpoint	Mohave	T27N R13W	Elev. 4720'

CAPE: See following entries:

Final, Cape	Coconino	(Grand Canyon)
Royal, Cape	Coconino	(Grand Canyon)
Solitude, Cape	Coconino	(Grand Canyon)

CAPITAN, EL pro.: /el kæpitæn/
Spanish = "The Captain"

Gila   T2S R15 E   Elev. 6564'

The post office at this location served El Capitan Mine, which may have been named for the commanding peak nearby, El Capitan Mountain (a.k.a. Capitan Mountain or Peak). Associated names include Capitano Creek, Pass, Pass Spring, and Capitan Trap Spring. P.O. est. July 7, 1919, Mrs. Mary Mabel Greer, p.m.; disc. Sept. 15, 1924 Ref.: 242; 18a

CAPITOL BUTTE
Yavapai   T17N R5E   Elev. 6355'

This butte in Oak Creek Canyon resembles the capitol building. A former name for it was Judge Otey's Tombstone (on land plats dated 1879). It said the gentleman wished to be buried on it. By 1889 it was being called Gray Mountain. In 1956 it was being referred to as Grayback. In 1928 the earliest name was officially dropped. The name "Capital" Butte is erroneous. Ref.: 329; 18a

CAPTAINS, THE
Apache

This name has sometimes been used for Spider Rock. See Spider Rock, Apache

CARBON BUTTE
Coconino (Grand Canyon)   T32N R5E   Elev. c. 4000'

Charles E. Wolcott named this butte because it lies between the Colorado River and the fork of Carbon Creek. The East Fork and the West Fork of Carbon Creek form arms that lie on either side of Carbon Butte, hence the name Carbon Canyon. Ref.: Francois Matthes, Letter to Geographic Board on Names (Nov. 27, 1926), Grand Canyon Files

CARDENAS AISLE
Coconino (Grand Canyon)

On September 13, 1915 Francois E. Matthes suggested the Cardenas Aisle and Alarçon Aisle because they "constituted together one unit, namely that portion of the Canyon lying between the two Granite Gorges." However, he further suggested that as they formed a unit, a more appropriate name might be Explorer's Canyon. Matthes also suggested naming Cardenas Terrace. See Cardenas Butte, Coconino (Grand Canyon) Ref.: Matthes Papers, Grand Canyon Files

CARDENAS BUTTE pro.: /kardéynəs/
Coconino (Grand Canyon)   T31N R5E   Elev. 6269'

This location and Cardenas Creek are named for Garcia Lopez de Cardenas, second son of a Spanish nobleman, who arrived in South America in 1535. He later went to Mexico

City where Mendoza, a distant relative by marriage, was viceroy. A member of the Coronado Expedition of 1540, Cardenas was commissioned to investigate an Indian story that a great canyon lay west of the Hopi villages. In doing so, Cardenas became the first white man known to have viewed the great gorge of the Grand Canyon.
Ref.: 41, p. 55

CARDIGAN PEAK
Pima   T12S R6W   Elev. 2922'
This location is the highest in the Little Ajo Mountains. A man named Cardigan had a mine and well here in 1914. The name Corrigan Well is a corruption.
Ref.: 58; Netherlan

CAREFREE
Maricopa   T6N R4E
Two realtors named Tom Darlington and K. T. Palmer, motivated by their disappoint-ment in Scottsdale's lack of civic planning and the surrounding of the Camelback Resort area by urban development, in 1955 bought four hundred acres to develop a resort community. Its name is euphemistic. Ref.: "The Carefree Caper," pp. ;46, 47; *The Phoenix Republic* (Oct. 1967)

CARLOS, SAN
Gila   T1S R18E   Elev. 2635'
This location must be differentiated from a former community called San Carlos, but now referred to as Old San Carlos, which is completely out of existence. The first name for the post office on the railroad was Rice. It seems probable that its name came from that of 1st Lt. William F. Rice, who was near here in 1874 when Crook named him to be one of those in charge of the Verde Reservation. The Indian school was built several years after the establishment of the post in 1880. Just prior to 1900 a separate post office was opened under the name Talklai. It was close to, but not identical with Rice. Talklai (or Tau-el-Cly-ee) (b.c. 1860; d. March 4, 1930) served in the Indian police unit developed by John P. Clum. He was a half-brother of a San Carlos leader called Distalin. On December 22, 1875 Distalin went berserk and attacked Clum and other agency officials. Talkai and another Indian policeman killed Distalin.
   The Talklai post office, judging by its location on GLO 1903, may have been in Tiffany's store. On GLO 1909 Talklai is shown on the west bank of the San Carlos River almost contiguous to Rice which, however, is on the east bank. This suggests that Talklai served for private mail whereas Rice was the name of the railroad station and was the address used for the Indian school and the San Carlos Apache Reservation. When the original post office at Tiffany's Store was closed (June 12, 1908), its mail was simply handled by Sadie E. Davis, its postmaster, in the Rice office under the continuing name of Talklai. The name was eliminated in favor of Rice, with Sadie E. Davis continuing as postmaster, on February 16, 1909. The date of official discontinuance of the Talklai post office is recorded as May 19, 1909.
   It was believed that waters impounded by Coolidge Dam would cover Old San Carlos, as it is now referred to. Therefore in 1930 the name of Rice was changed to San Carlos. The original San Carlos never vanished under impounded waters and hence its current name of Old San Carlos. By 1940 at San Carlos a new agency and school had been completed.
P.O. est. at Rice, Sept. 7, 1900, James H. Stevens, p.m. (NB: A file in the National Archives gives two dates and postmasters for the first post office at Talklai, as follows:) p.o. est. at Talklai, Nov. 19, 1900, R. A. Cochran, p.m.; *and* est. Dec. 19, 1900, James W. Balmer, p.m. Mail transferred from Talklai to Rice, June 12, 1908; name changed to Rice and Talklai disc. Feb. 16, 1909, Sadie E. Davis, p.m.; name changed to San Carlos, Sept. 1, 1930 Ref.: 67, pp. 66-68; 5, p. 447; Woody, Theobald; 242

CARLOS DAM, SAN
Pinal
On June 7, 1924 the United States Congress authorized the construction of San Carlos Dam, later renamed Coolidge Dam. See Carlos, Old San, Gila

CARLOS, FORT SAN

Gila   T3S R19E

Directly responsible for the creation of Fort San Carlos Military Reservation was the Camp Grant massacre conducted aginst Eskiminzin and his tribal followers, a peaceful group supposedly under the protection of the military at old Camp Grant. Gen. O. O. Howard in 1872 promised that a peaceful spot would be found for the group. Maj. William B. Royall, Lt. Jacob Almy, and the Indian agent named Jacobs reconnoitered and by June 1872 found a "spot on the east bank of the San Carlos, about three miles above its confluence with the Gila." The first name given to the location was San Carlos Picket, but when more troops arrived it became Fort San Carlos, a sub-post of Fort Grant. It became a "permanent" post on May 29, 1873 when I Company, 5th Cavalry, reinforced later by F Company, 5th Cavalry, and M Company also, were sent to garrison the post. It was garrisoned until July 16, 1900 when a small detachment took over and ultimately abandoned the post. Ref.: *Weekly Arizona Miner* (June 29, 1872), p. 2; Farmer; 242; 311, p. 79; 15, p. 564

CARLOS INDIAN RESERVATION, SAN

Gila

In c. 1869 the San Carlos District was created by carving it out of the White Mountain Indian Reservation and changing its name to San Carlos Indian Reservation. Plans were already under way to create such a place for several Apache tribal groups. (See Carlos, Fort San, Gila) The San Carlos Indian Reservation came into official existence by Executive Order on December 14, 1872. It is surrounded on all but the south side by the White Mountain Apache Reservation. Elevations on the reservation vary from 2290' on the Gila River below Coolidge Dam to 8200' in the northeast corner of the reservation. The San Carlos Agency was constructed on the river opposite the military headquarters and there was much rivalry between the military and the Indian agent about which should control the Indians and their activities. As for the Indians, their name for this location was *Toot-laden-le* (= "at the junction of two rivers").

There was bound to be trouble because far too many Apache tribal groups were brought together and there was rivalry and enmity among the groups. They included the Coyoteros, Pinals, Aravaipas, Tontos, Apache-Yuma, Apache-Mohave, and Chiracahus. The last group included the Cochise Indians. Gen. Crook, who had protested strongly against bringing these groups together, was ordered out of Arizona Territory in March 1875 to take command of the Department of the Platte. If the problems of confining freedom-loving Indians were not enough, some white citizens in Arizona disgraced their citizenship by proposing to wipe out the Apaches on the San Carlos Indian Reservation. To quote John Bourke, the "Tombstone Toughs" were thoroughly disreputable and "represented all the rum-poisoned bummers of the San Pedro Valley." Bourke noted that the Tombstone Toughs managed to fire upon a single old Indian who had been living in peace. Then they ran away, leaving the white settlers, who had been getting along well with the Indians, subject to the vengeance that was bound to come from the Indians. Fortunately, John P. Clum served as Indian agent for the San Carlos Indian Reservation from 1874 to 1877. To his eminent good sense must be credited the ultimate success of the San Carlos Apaches in raising livestock, for to keep the Indians busy and out of trouble Clum bought four thousand two hundred sheep, two hundred cows, two hundred goats, and two hundred burros. He kept the Indians so busy that troops were no longer needed and on October 9, 1875 Gen. Kautz ordered the military camp abandoned. Unfortunately, other and subsequent Indian agents lacked Clum's good sense. Discord between army officers and the Indian agent increased. The San Carlos agency gradually dropped the name "agency." With the creation of Coolidge Dam, Old San Carlos, as it came to be known, was abandoned. The historic Apache Indian agency at San Carlos was destroyed by blasting on February 16, 1930. See Carlos, San, Gila

P.O. est. Oct. 22, 1875, George Stevens, p.m.; disc. Jan. 15, 1877; reest. Sept. 22, 1880, Reuben Wood, p.m.; disc. May 9, 1883; reest. June 20, 1882, p.m. unknown; Wells Fargo 1903; name transferred to p.o. at Rice, Sept. 1, 1930

Ref.: 242; 206, p. 183; 168, p. 163; 49, p. 456; 349; (Smithsonian Institution); 67, p. 164; 66, p. 59

CARLOS LAKE, SAN

Gila/Pinal/Graham   T3S R18E

These are the waters impounded by Coolidge Dam. The name derives from the fact that the lake was expected to cover the site of Old San Carlos. See Coolidge Dam, Pinal

CARLOS PROJECT, SAN

Gila/Pinal

The San Carlos project includes several works, the most important of which are the Coolidge Dam, the Picacho Reservoir, the Sacaton Diversion Dam and Bridge, and several canals. Among them are the following canals: Old Florence, North Side, San Tan, Casa Blanca, Southside, and Southside Storm Water Channel. See Coolidge Dam, Pinal Ref.: 185, p. 40

CARLOS RESERVOIR, SAN

Gila/Pinal/Graham

This is an alternate name of San Carlos Lake. See Carlos Lake, San, and Coolidge Dam, Pinal

CARLOS RIVER, SAN

Gila   T3N R20E   Elev. 2635'

On November 4, 1775 Fr. Francisco Garcés named this stream the Rio San Carlos because he encountered it on Saint Charles Day. Coincidentally, Carlos III was then king of Spain. Garcés also referred to this location as the Rio de Carlos. In the late 1840s Maj. William H. Emory renamed the location San Francisco River, a name that appears on subsequent military and GLO maps until 1869 when it appears as Williams Creek. Its original name persisted, however, reinforced by the establishment of the San Carlos Military District, the establishment of San Carlos Indian Agency, and the authorization of the San Carlos Indian Reservation. As a result, by 1874 the name Rio San Carlos was formally established and the military map of 1875 names it the San Carlos River. Ref.: 77, p. 139; Maps: (1) Parke 1851; (2) Territory of New Mexico 1859; (3) Map of Arizona ... to Accompany Surveyor General's Report, 1874; (4) Willcox 1879; (5) Mallory 1875

CARL PLEASANT LAKE

Maricopa   T6N R1E

This lake is formed by waters impounded by Carl Pleasant Dam, named for Carl Pleasant (b. 1886, Kansas; d. 1930), the engineer who designed and constructed the dam. On maps in 1875 the location had been called Frog Tanks, designating a place on the Agua Fria River where frogs of a mighty size held court. Somewhat later William B. Pratt operated a mine here which had a post office with his name. During the construction period of the dam, it was called Frog Tanks Dam. On the post office application form for the construction camp, the first name suggested for the location was Camp Pleasant, but the post office was named Lake Carl Pleasant. The dam was dedicated on November 14, 1927. On September 24, 1964, the board of directors of Maricopa County Municipal Water Conservation District changed the name of the dam to Donal W. Waddell Dam to honor its financier. The lake was officially named on November 14, 1967.

P.O. est. as Pratt, May 5, 1890, Eugene E. St. Claire, p.m.; disc. Aug. 25, 1896; p.o. est. as Lake Carl Pleasant, July 15, 1926, James G. Tripp, p.m.; disc. Feb. 27, 1928 Ref.: 242; 5, p. 356; 329

CARMEN

Santa Cruz   T21S R13E   Elev. 3242'

This location is named for Mrs. Carmen Zepeda, who in November 1918 homesteaded here and set up a store. At that time she was the sole resident. The place has since developed into a small community. Ref.: Mrs. Carmen Zepeda

CARNERO LAKE   pro.: /karnéro/
Spanish = "sheep"

Apache   T8N R27E   Elev. 9033'

The name derives from the fact that Apaches watered sheep here. Below the creek fork Henry Barrett raised alfalfa, leading to the name Green Spot Draw. Ref.: Davis; 18a

CARNEY SPRING
Pinal   T1N R10E

This location was named for Thomas Carney (b. 1856, Holland). Ref.: AHS; 63

CAROL SPRING MOUNTAIN
Gila   T4N R17E   Elev. 6629'

This location is also called Timber Camp Mountain because of logging here at one time. Why it is called Carol Spring Mountain is not known. The name Corral Spring Mountain is a corruption. Ref.: 326

CARR CANYON
Cochise   T23S R20E   Elev. 6000'

The name comes from that of James Carr, a horse rancher in this canyon in 1886. Ref.: AHS; *Arizona Star* (June 6, 1866)

CARRISO, SIERRA
Apache

This is the name used on the Macomb map of 1860. See Four Corners, Apache

CARRIZO
Spanish = "cattails" or "rushes"
Gila   T7N R19E   Elev. 4960'

This is a small community and railroad station on the S.F.R.R.

CARRIZO BUTTE
Apache   T18N R23E   Elev. 5435'

Cattails grow in this vicinity, hence the name. The butte overlooks Carrizo Creek, Apache.

CARRIZO CREEK
Apache   T17N R26E

In December 1853 Lt. Amiel W. Whipple applied this name to the creek, as did also Lt. Edward Fitzgerald Beale, who camped on it on September 2, 1857. The name indicates the presence of cattails in the then swampy areas along the stream, although the majority of the course of the creek was dry. This creek today is called the Dead River (T20N/R25E). The name was sometimes spelled Carisso or Carriso Creek. See Lithodendron Creek, Apache, and Dead River Wash, Apache Ref.: 346, pp. 152, 153, Note 6; 23, p. 40; 107, VIII, 55

CARRIZO CREEK
Gila/Navajo   T6N R19E

This creek has cattails along its banks at some spots, hence the name. Several important Apache events occurred along this stream, the most important being a conclave of many Apache groups here in 1881 under the fanatic leader Noch-ay-del Klinne, who instituted the Ghost Dance among his tribesmen. Ref.: 18a

CARRIZO MOUNTAINS
Apache   T39N R29E   Elev. 9420'

The elevation cited is that for Carrizo Mountain, which in Navajo is called *Dzil naozill* (= "whirling mountain"), indicating that this solitary peak is surrounded by other mountains. The name Sierra de Carriso appears on the Macomb map of 1860. The first name, recorded on the DominguezEscalante map of 1776, was Sierra de Chegui. The name *Carrizo* in this instance is associated with that of a band of Navajo Indians living in the vicinity in 1799. See also Chuska Mountains, Apache Ref.: 141, p. 96; 331, p. 7; 167, I, 208

CARRIZO RIDGE
Navajo   T10N R17E
This ridge overlooks the railroad location of Carrizo, from which it borrows its name.

CARRIZO WASH
Apache   T14N R27–28E
This wash currently has two branches: Big Carrizo Wash and Little Carrizo Wash. See Carrizo, Apache

CARRIZO WASH
Navajo   T18N R22E
This wash runs at the base of Carrizo Butte, Apache. See Little Lithodendron Wash, Navajo

CARR LAKE
Coconino   T11N R13E   Elev. c. 6000'
Originally this lake was called Lake No. 2, but cowboys renamed it c. 1886 for the general manager of the Waters Cattle Company, E. P. Carr. Ref.: 18a

CARR LAKE
Navajo   T17N R23E
In 1899 E. W. Carr constructed a dam here, and thus created the lake bearing his name. It has since filled in and the lake no longer exists. Ref.: Branch; Grigsby

CARR PEAK
Gila   T6N R14E   Elev. 7604'
This peak is adjacent to Carr Mountain. Both locations are on the Carr Ranch. Ref.: Woody

CARROLL, CAMP
Maricopa
In 1869 the military en route from Fort McDowell to Camp Reno pitched camp at this location. It was sixteen and one-half miles in a direct line northeast of McDowell. Ref.: 242

CARSON MESA
Apache   T33N R24E   Elev. c. 6000'
In the fall of 1863 Col. Christopher (Kit) Carson assumed command of the Navajo campaign. This mesa is named for Carson. See Chelly, Canyon de, Apache Ref.: 141, p. 190

CARSON PLAINS
Because Col. Christopher (Kit) Carson crossed the Arizona desert following the course of the Gila River, this name was formerly used for that section of the desert in southern Arizona. Ref.: 18a

CART RIDGE
Coconino   T14N R12E
The name derives from the fact that formerly a man named Cart had a cabin in this vicinity. Cart Cabin Tank is at T13N/R9E.

CARTER CANYON
Pima   T11S R15E
Carter and William Reed homesteaded in this canyon in 1882 but failed to prove up their homestead, which means that they did not make improvements necessary to take possession. A variant name is Carter Gulch. Ref.: AHS, Emerson O. Stratton *ms.*, p. 63

CASA BLANCA
Spanish = "white house"
Pinal   T3S R4E   Elev. 1200'
The name for this place was borrowed from that of the nearby Casa Blanca ruins. At this

location in 1858 Ammi White (b. Maine) built the first flour mill in Arizona and opened a trading post. He maintained a stage station for the Butterfield Overland route at his store. In 1863 White was appointed Indian agent. The location was called White's Mill.

Following the battle of Picacho Peak during the Civil War, Capt. Hunter of the Confederate forces captured White, who was taken as a captive to New Mexico. Soon thereafter the Bichard brothers took over the mill operation. William Bichard (b. 1841, Guernsey, England), and Stephen Bichard (b. England), had their operations washed out by a flood in 1868. They built a new mill at Adamsville. Many years later on the post office application is the following: "Known only as Casa Blanca or Vake (Vah-Ki) by Indians." See Vah Ki, Pinal, and Pima Villages, Pinal

P.O. est. as Vah Ki, March 16, 1916, S. J. Martin, p.m.; disc. Dec. 31, 1926
Ref.: 242; AHS, Crampton Collection; 62; 281 (Smithsonian Institution), p. 23; 167, I, 11, 104, 167, 168, 209, 211; 73, II, 167, 168

CASA BLANCA RUINS

Pinal   T4S R5E   Elev. 1200'

This small prehistoric ruin should not be confused with Casa Grande, another and far more substantial ruin. The Pima Indian name is Vah Ki (= "ancient house"), sometimes spelled Va-aki or Va Vak. The Maricopa name is A-vuc-hoo-mar-lish. In 1884 Bandelier used the term *ho ho qom*, a word today spelled Hohokam, which refers to "the ancient ones." Bandelier notes that the term was the Pima name for the ruins. Casa Blanca was sometimes called Montezuma's Castle or Casa Montezuma, the reason being that prior to 1900 many people believed that the Aztecs of Mexico had made their way as far north as this location. In fact there are several legends in Arizona which refer to Montezuma's Treasure. He is supposed to have brought it with him on his journeyings north. See Casa Blanca, Pinal (T3S/R4E) for other names associated with this location.

CASA GRANDE pro.: /kasa grandiy/ or /kasa grand/
Spanish = "big house"
Pinal   T6S R6E   Elev. 1398'

When the railroad established a station at this location, the company borrowed the name of the nearby Casa Grande Ruins. See Casa Grande National Monument, Pinal
P.O. est. Sept. 10, 1880, Jere Fryer, p.m.; Wells Fargo 1885 Ref.: Prather

CASA GRANDE NATIONAL MONUMENT pro.: /kasa grandiy/ or /kasa grand/
Spanish = "big house" or "great house"
Pinal   T5S R8E   Elev. 1045'

Prior to 1900 archeologists believed that the Casa Grande Ruins were among those occupied by Aztecs in their migration northward. For that reason the name used for this location was sometimes Casa Montezuma or Montezuma Castle. The Pima Indian legend about how the ruins came to be is as follows: Civano, either a chief or a Pima deity, built these structures and from that comes the Pima name Civano or House of Civano for the location. Fr. Eusebio Kino visited here in 1694 and called it Casa Grande. To preserve these interesting ruins from weathering and vandalism, a national reservation was created on June 22, 1892. On March 2, 1889 the location was classified as a National Park, and it was made a National Monument on August 3, 1918 (four hundred seventy-two acres). Various names have been applied to this location, including the following: Chivano-ki (Bandelier, 1886); Great Houses (Bartlett, 1854); Hall of Montezuma (Doniphan's Expedition, 1848); Tco-oltuk (Pima = "corner").
Ref.: 167, I, 209, 210, 211; 43, p. 369; 5, pp. 403, 404; 13, Frances Elmore, "Casa Grande National Monument," p. 1

CASA PIEDRA
Spanish = "stone house"
Santa Cruz   T23S R11E

This location is a stock watering place where the remains of a stone house still exist.
Ref.: 59, p. 420

CASCABEL   pro.: /kǽskəbel/
Spanish = "rattlesnake's rattles"

Cochise   T13S R19E   Elev. 3080'

Alex Heron wanted to call the post office at his ranch and store after Joseph Pool. Pool had maintained a ranch post office until 1913 and it would have been a simple matter to transfer the papers. However, post office regulations required that a new name be found for the new post office. En route to Benson, Heron met a Mexican who had just killed a large rattlesnake. The man told Heron the snake was called "Cascabel" and Heron thereupon selected that name.

P.O. est. Jan. 4, 1916, Alexander Heron, p.m.; disc. July 15, 1936
Ref.: 242; AHS Files

CASHION
Maricopa   T1N R1E   Elev. 991'

Jim Cashion (b. Canada) arrived in Arizona in 1900 as a superintendent of railroad construction. Soon thereafter he bought a section of land (640 acres) and as the railroad passed through his land, the depot on it took on the name Cashion. The settlement came into existence c. 1910.

P.O. est. Nov. 24, 1911, Fred L. Bush, p.m. Ref.: 242; Parkman; 224, III

CASNER MOUNTAIN
Yavapai   T18N R4E   Elev. 6843'

G. R. (Bill) Casner and Moses Casner raised sheep at or near locations bearing their name in the early 1880s. Ref.: Slipher

CASNER PARK
Coconino   T18N R8E

The Casner brothers grazed their sheep at a sheep spring in this location. See Casner Mountain, Yavapai

CASSADORE MESA   pro.: /kǽsədor/
Gila   T1N R19E   Elev. c. 4000'

In 1873 at the height of the Apache troubles, Cassadore and his band of San Carlos Apaches fled from the San Carlos Reservation. Federal troops pursued them into the hills. Of their own volition, the Indians reported to the army camp and surrendered. They told Capt. J. M. Hamilton that they were starving, that their moccasins were so worn their feet left blood on the rocks, and that they preferred to die by bullets rather than to go hungry. Capt. Hamilton thereupon fed them and refused to carry out his orders to take no prisoners. The order was rescinded and the surrender accepted officially on February 18, 1874. Apache descendants of Cassadore spell their name as given here. The word Cazadero is a corruption, as is also Cazador. Ref.: Jennings; Woody; 5, pp. 446, 447

CASSIDY SPRING
Gila   T10S R21E

This spring, also misspelled Cathey Spring, was named for an early settler. Ref.: 329

CASTERSEN SEEP
Gila   T20N R9E

A rancher by this name owned this section. On current maps, Young's Lake is here.
Ref.: 329; Mrs. Grace Castersen (widow), Letter (1972)

CASTLE: Because many geologic formations resemble castles, the term is frequently used in place names:

Castle	Coconino	T22N R19E	
Castle	Navajo	T22N R18E	Elev. 6491'
Castle See Dilkon, Navajo	Navajo	T22N R19E	Elev. 5800'
Castle Butte	Santa Cruz	T22S R15E	Elev. c. 5000'

Castle Butte Wash	Coconino/Navajo	T21N R15E	

See Coyote Wash, Coconino/Navajo

Castle Canyon	Coconino (Grand Canyon)	T34N R1W	

Castle Canyon, South Fork	Coconino (Grand Canyon)	T36N R2E	

Castle Creek	Greenlee	T4N R31E	

Castle Creek	Yavapai	(1) T9N R2W	

This creek flows in part through a canyon with castellated walls. The Wickenburg stage road used to use this creek bed. Ref.: 18a

Castle Creek	Yavapai	(2) T10N R2E	

Castle Dome	Cochise	T21S R28E	Elev. 5809'

Castle Dome	Maricopa	T2N R11E	Elev. 5308'

Castle Dome	La Paz		

See Castle Dome Peak, La Paz

CASTLE DOME (TOWN)

Yuma   T4S R19W

In 1863 Jacob Snively and a man named Conner found signs of ancient mine excavations in the area around this location. The size of slow-growing trees showed that the workings were very old. The two men then filed for the Castle Dome Mining District. By April 1864 many other prospectors had arrived and Castle Dome City, also known simply as Castle Dome, was an actuality. It did not last long because the ores proved to be not worth very much. Most of them left, but in 1875 activities resumed briefly when Colorado steamboat captains tried shipping ores from Castle Dome Landing on the Colorado River. The mining community was at the mining locations in the hills. The coming of the railroad caused the cessation of steam boating on the Colorado, and it was consequently the end of Castle Dome Landing and pretty much of Castle Dome as a community. The name Castle Dome was borrowed from that of a nearby peak. See Castle Dome Peak, La Paz

P.O. est. as Castle Dome, Dec. 17, 1875, William P. Miller, p.m.; disc. Dec. 4, 1876; reest. as Castle Dome Landing, Aug. 6, 1878, Andrew H. Cargill, p.m.; disc. June 16, 1884 Ref.: Lenon; 355, pp. 85, 86; *Arizona Miner* (April 6, 1864), p. 2; 279, p. 205; 146, p. 72; 242

Castle Dome Mountain	Maricopa	T2N R11E	Elev. 5316'

CASTLE DOME MOUNTAINS

La Paz/Yuma   T1N–7S R18W   Elev. 3788'

In 1775 Fr. Francisco Garcés called these mountains the Cerros del Cajon. Their Mohave Indian name in 1859 was Sierra Mo-Quin-To-ara. The Chocolate Mountains are a part of this range. See Castle Dome Peak, La Paz

CASTLE DOME PEAK

La Paz   T2N R11E   Elev. 3763'

Fr. Francisco Garcés in 1775 called it Cabeza del Gigante (Spanish: *cabeza* = "head"; *del gigante* = "of the giant"). This formation, the highest in the Castle Dome Mountains, is hundreds of feet square and at a distance appeared to soldiers at Fort Yuma in the late 1850s to look like the nation's capitol dome, whence their name of Capitol Dome. The name quite easily and naturally shifted to Castle Dome. Among local Mexican and Spanish settlers the peak has long been called La Pelota (= "the ball").

Ref.: 77, p. 162, Note 4; 168, p. 234; Col.: M. Cabrera; inf.: Marian Mayer (1964)

Castle Dome Plain	La Paz/Yuma	T3S R20W	

Castle Dome Range	La Paz/Yuma		

See Castle Dome Mountains, La Paz/Yuma

Castle Dome Wash   La Paz/Yuma
See Castle Dome, Yuma

Castle Hill   Cochise
See Castle Rock, Cochise

CASTLE HOT SPRINGS
Yavapai   T8N R1W   Elev. 1980'

Although not documented, possibly true is the story that Charles Craig and his men discovered the springs on November 4, 1867, calling them Hot Springs. In 1874 George Monroe (b. 1835, Indiana; d. Dec. 23, 1897) and Ed Farley not only found the springs, but made a trail to them. Hinton refers to them as Monroe Hot Springs. Jesse Jackson relocated these same springs on May 27, 1877. The mineral springs contain waters which at their source measure 150° to 160° F. The water flows over a six-foot high rock into a rock pool about ten feet long and four feet wide. From the first information about the temperature to one reported in 1940, either the thermometers improved or the water temperature dropped, for in 1940 the maximum temperature was reported as 122° F. Further, the single pool had been developed into several with various temperatures.

During pioneer days the ranch at this location was a stage stop where passengers were furnished with towels and invited to enjoy the mineral waters. Thereafter it developed into a fine resort with buildings that became historic and worthy of preservation. Unfortunately, some burned in Dec. 1976. Arizona State University now owns the property.

P.O. est. as Hot Springs, May 22, 1891, Minnie Grove, p.m.; name changed to Castle Hot Springs, May 1, 1936, Clyde Douglas, p.m.; disc. Jan. 1, 1966
Ref.: 62; 242; *Arizona Magazine*, "Apaches and the Magic Water" (Feb. 1914), p. 6; *Weekly Arizona Miner* (June 15, 1877), p. 1; 163, pp. 334, 335; *Arizona Journal Miner* (Dec. 27, 1897), p. 4; 5, p. 356

Castle Hot Springs   Maricopa
Junction
See Morristown, Maricopa; see also Castle Hot Springs, Yavapai

Castle Lake   Coconino   T34N R1E
                         (Grand Canyon)

Castle Mountains   Pima   T12S R1E   Elev. 6287'

Castle Peak   Gila   T7N R15E   Elev. 6287'

Castle Point   Coconino   T37N R1E
                          (Grand Canyon)

Castle Reef   Mohave   T31N R23W
                         (Lake Mead)

This location was named in 1947 "because of the castle-like rocks along the shore." Ref.: 329

Castle Rock   Cochise   T23S R24E   Elev. c. 5100'

This name has been in use since the beginning of Bisbee, in which it is located. It dominates the road through Mule Canyon.

Castle Rock   Greenlee   T4N R30E   Elev. 8861'

Castle Rock   Mohave   T14–15N R20W

This place is also known as Mohave or Pulpit Rock. According to the informant, when the Colorado River used to be here, "The rock stuck up at low stages and looked like a castle." Ref.: Housholder

Castle Rock   Santa Cruz   T23S R12E   Elev. 4503'

Castle Rock   Yavapai   (1) T15N R6W (2) T10N R1W

Castle Rock   La Paz   T11N R18W

Castle Rock Bay   Mohave   T13N R20W
                             (Lake Mead)

See Castle Rock, Mohave (Lake Mead)

Castle Rock Canyon   Santa Cruz   T23S R12E   Elev. 4400'

Castle Rock Dam   Yuma   T4S R17W

This dam was built by the Fish and Wild Life Service in 1952. It was named for a nearby rock formation. Ref.: Monson

Castle Rocks   Mohave   T22N R17W   Elev. 4634'

Charley Metcalf, who owned this place, called it Garden of the Gods. The name Castle Rocks was. not used locally. Despite this fact, it has made its way onto maps. Ref.: Housholder

Castle Rock Tank   Pima   T21S R9E

Castle Spring   Coconino   T37N R1W

Castle Temple   Coconino
                    (Grand Canyon)

See Castor Temple, Coconino (Grand Canyon)

CASTOR TEMPLE

Coconino (Grand Canyon)   T32N R1E   Elev. 6215'

Prior to 1937 the name for this location was Castle Temple, possibly derived from its small, elongated top, which may resemble a castle. However, the USGS on March 28, 1938 decreed the name to be Castor Temple. Ref.: 329

CATALINA (COMMUNITY)

Pima   T11S R14E   Elev. 3138'

This community is near the Santa Catalina Mountains, hence its name. In 1949 A. B. Garner opened the Oracle Mercantile store at this location and began sub-dividing lots in the early 1950s. He sold out in 1957. The community has continued to develop, but is restricted by the Tortolita area plan to a population of six thousand.
Ref.: *Arizona Star* (July 6, 1975), Section A, p. 5

CATALINA

Pima   T17S R13E

P.O. est. Feb. 9, 1917, Edwin P. Bernard, p.m.; disc. Jan. 19, 1926 Ref.: 242

CATALINA

Pinal   T10S R14E

This post office served a mining camp near the American Flag Mine.
P.O. est. Jan. 4, 1881, John T. Young, p.m.; disc. June 19, 1896 Ref.: 242

CATALINA FOOTHILLS

Pima   T12S R14E

These Tucson foothills are named because they are at the base of the Santa Catalina Mountains.

CATALINA FOREST RESERVE, SANTA

Pima

Presidential proclamation established this as a forest reserve on July 2, 1902.
Ref.: 116, p. 730

CATALINA MOUNTAINS, SANTA   pro.: /santə catəliynə/ or /sæntə cætəliynə/

Pima/Pinal   T12S R15E   Elev. 9100'

While visiting a now vanished Papago rancheria in this area near what is today Tucson, Fr. Eusebio Kino called these mountains Santa Catalina Cuitchibaque, but earlier he had called the nearby mountains bordering the valley to the north and east Sierra de la Santa Catarina, a name still in use for the range in 1865. The name Santa Catarina apparently became well established, for in 1854 Lt. John G. Parke used that name and Lt. N. Michler referred to them as the Sierra de Santa Catarina. Until at least 1900 the name continued to be used, sometimes rendered Santa Catrina.
Ref.: 167, I, 371; 45, p. 24; 106, p. 118

CATALINA NATURAL AREA, SANTA

Pima

These four thousand four hundred and fifty acres were set aside on March 23, 1927 to provide a natural area for study and use by foresters, stockmen, scientists, and the general public. Ref.: 76, p. 13

CATALINA RAVINE
Pinal   T10S R14E
Named for the Catalina Mountains.

CATALINA WASH
Pinal   T10-11S R17E
This wash is in the Catalina Mountains, hence the name.

CATALPA
Gila   T4N R13E   Elev. c. 2500'
This location, now under the waters of Theodore Roosevelt Lake, was the name of a post office established at The Grove of Robinson, probably a corruption (it was owned by Peter Robertson). In 1877 he drove the first sheep into the Little Salt River area, as it was then known. The name of the post office came from the fact that a row of catalpa trees grew at Robertson's place.
P.O. est. Dec. 4, 1885, Peter C. Robertson, p.m.; disc. Oct. 17, 1888
Ref.: Woody; 329, Mrs. Dudley I. Craig, Letter (1928); 242

CATARACT CANYON
Coconino (Grand Canyon)   T32N R4W
This canyon is so named because of a series of beautiful waterfalls along Cataract Creek, which runs through it. In December 1964 the USGS eliminated the following as variants: Cactus Canyon, Cedar Creek, Havasu Canyon. The creek may be the same location which Fr. Francisco Garcés in 1774 called the Rio de San Antonia. On June 19, 1775 he called the creek Rio Jabesua. Cataract Creek is now called Havasu Creek. The name given to it by Lt. Joseph Christmas Ives in 1858 — Cascade Creek — appears only on Ives' map. See Havasu Canyon, Coconino (Grand Canyon) Ref.: 329; 335, p. 11; 18a; 224, pp. 69, 70; 77, p. 11, Note 20

CATARACT PLAINS
Coconino
According to a local informant, this area extends from Red Butte west and north to Frazier's Well and then north to Cataract Canyon. It takes its name from that of Cataract Canyon and Cataract Creek. Ref.: Morris

CATARINA, SANTA
Pinal
In 1701 this village, also known as Santa Catarina de Cuitabagum, existed near the present Picacho Peak. See Picacho Mountains, Pinal Ref.: 43, p. 503

CATARINA, SANTA
Pima
This was the name of a mining camp post office near American Flag.
P.O. est. April 21, 1882, Louis Goodman, p.m.; disc. Sept. 11, 1882 Ref.: 264

CATHEDRAL: Fancied resemblance to that of a cathedral has led to the use of the descriptive term in several place names. Examples follow:

Cathedral Cave   Mohave   T32N R21W
                                           (Lake Mead)
In 1948 the USGS changed this name to Wishing Well Cave. Because of "the cathedral-like aspect of the surrounding topography," Edward Schenk had suggested the name Cathedral Cave in 1946, but the name was not officially accepted. Ref.: 329

Cathedral Peak   Gila
See Two Bar Mountain, Gila

Cathedral Peak   Pima
See Kimball Peak, Pima

[127]

Cathedral Rock	Cochise	T18S R31E	Elev. 6985'
Cathedral Rock	Coconino	T40N R7E	Elev. 3760'

This name was used prior to 1900, but the names Sunset Rock and Five Mile Point have also been used since that time. Ref.: 329

Cathedral Rock   Gila

See Two Bar Mountain, Gila

Cathedral Rock   Maricopa

See Court House Butte, Maricopa

Cathedral Rock	Mohave	(1) T19N R20W	Elev. 2945'
		(2) T15N R21W	

This location is the same as Castle Rock, Mohave.

Cathedral Rock	Pima	T12S R15E	Elev. 7952'

See Kimball Peak, Pima

Cathedral Rock	Pinal	T10S R2E	
Cathedral Rock	Yavapai	T17N R5E	Elev. 4964'
Cathedral Rock	Yuma		

Judging from its position on maps, this location is probably identical with Coronation Peak.

Cathedral Stairs	Coconino	T31N R2E
	(Grand Canyon)	

As the trail on which this location existed has been abandoned, the USGS has sought to eliminate the name. They were on the Hermit Trail.

Cathedral Wash	Coconino	T40N R7E

CATHOLIC PEAK

Gila   T8N R15E   Elev. c. 6000'

This peak resembles a crude cross, hence the name. Ref.: 18a

CAT MOUNTAIN

Pima   T15S R123E   Elev. 3854'

The resemblance of this mountain to a cat lying down with its back somewhat hunched has led to its being known also as Catback Mountain or as El Gato (= "the cat").

CATOCTIN

Yavapai   T12N R3W   Elev. c. 5000'

The post office at this location served employees at the Catoctin Mine.

P.O. est. Sept. 17, 1902, Harry N. Tharsing, p.m.; disc. July 15, 1920 Ref.: 242

CAUFMAN DAM

Coconino   T28N R8W

Prior to 1902 Jacob Caufman and R. J. Arey with their partner John Freeman constructed this dam on a branch of Cataract Creek. Arey sold his rights to his partners in May 1902. To help supply the town of Williams with water, a pipe line was begun to it in 1909. Ref.: 124, pp. 89, 91, 110

CAVALRY HILL

Santa Cruz

This was the local name for the hill in Nogales, Arizona, where the Baptist church is. It earned its name when the U.S. Cavalry camped on it at various times. In March 1913 Col. Kostelisky, a Russian commanding Mexican *rurales*, was defeated in a battle in Nogales, Sonora, by Mexican revolutionary forces and surrendered to United States forces to escape the Mexican troops. His men were imprisoned on this hill for several months. Ref.: Mrs. Ada Jones

CAVE: The presence of one or several caves has led to the use of the descriptive term *cave* in several place names. Examples follow:

Cave Canyon	Cochise	T24S R19E	Elev. 5350'

Cave Canyon	Gila	T3N R12E

This location is also known as Cholla Canyon, a name approved by the USGS in 1917. Ref.: 329

Cave Canyon	Mohave	T31N R15W
	(Lake Mead)	

Because Columbine Falls is in this canyon, it is also known as Columbine Canyon, although the latter name was not adopted officially. There are yellow columbine growing here. However, the caves in this vicinity are more prominent. Ref.: 329

Cave Canyon	Navajo	T9N R15E
Cave Canyon	Pinal	T6S R18E
Cave Creek	Cochise	(1) T27S R32E	Elev. 4396'

At the head of this creek is Crystal Cave, a large cavern which is responsible for the name of Cave Creek. The canyon through which this creek runs consists of stone bluffs with smoothly eroded faces in pink, red, green, buff, and gold, pock-marked with caves from fist-size to cavernous.

Cave Creek	Cochise	(2) T18S R30E
Cave Creek	Gila	T4N R20E
Cave Creek	Graham	T8S R25E
Cave Creek	Greenlee	T3S R29E

CAVE CREEK
Maricopa T6N R4E Elev. c. 2500'

The name probably derives from the presence of a few rather large caves which Indians used. However, another possibility is that it was named for "Edward Cave, a prospector ... in the early days," probably after 1879. A community gradually developed, named for the creek. In October 1872 John H. Marion wrote about traveling through here with Col. George Stoneman's party. At least three skirmishes with Indians occurred along this creek.

P.O. est. April 28, 1890, William B. Gillingham, p.m.; disc. Nov. 20, 1895; reest. as Cavecreek, Aug. 29, 1896, E. J. Bonsall, p.m.; name changed to Cave Creek, Feb. 1, 1962. It should be noted that on the post office application site map for the 1896 office, a post office named Tyrol with McCormick shown as its postmaster, is three-quarters of a mile south-southeast of Cave Creek. Ref.: 329; 242

Cave Creek	Santa Cruz	T20S R15E
Cave Creek	La Paz	T2N R18W
Cave Creek Canyon	Cochise	

See Cave Creek (1) Cochise

Cave Creek Dam	Maricopa	c. T6N R4E

This flood control dam is a subsidiary to Theodore Roosevelt Dam.

Cave Creek Wash	Maricopa	

See Cave Creek, Maricopa

Cave Draw	Gila	T11N R11E
Cave Hill	Coconino	

See Old Caves Crater, Coconino

Cave Mountain	Navajo	T25N R19E	Elev. 6557'
Cave Mountain	Pima	T12S R1E	Elev. 2920'
Cave Ridge	Coconino	T14N R12E	
Cave of the Bells	Santa Cruz	T20S R15E	
Cave Rapid	Coconino		
	(Grand Canyon)		

This was the name given by Lewis Freeman in 1923 to what is now called Cave Spring Rapids, Coconino (Grand Canyon). Ref.: 123, p. 511

Cave Spring	Coconino	T19N R6E

Cave Spring	Cochise	(1) T17S R23E (2) T22S R20E
Cave Spring	Mohave	T20N R19W
Cave Spring	Navajo	T28N R17E
Cave Spring Rapids	Coconino (Grand Canyon)	T37N R5E

See Cave Rapid, Coconino (Grand Canyon)

| Cave Wash | Mohave | T11N R17W |

CAYETANO MOUNTAINS, SAN

Santa Cruz   T22S R29E   Elev. c. 5400'

These mountains were named because they are at the center of the San Cayetano Land Grant. Ref.: Glannon

CAYETANO DEL TUMAGÁCORIC

Santa Cruz

This is the name used in 1695 by Fr. Eusebio Kino. See Tumacacori National Monument, Santa Cruz

CAYETANO TUMAPACORE, SAN

Santa Cruz

This location was also called San Cayetano. See Tumacacori National Monument, Santa Cruz

CAZADERO MOUNTAIN

Gila   T2N R19E

This is a misspelling of the name of an Apache leader, Cassadore. The mountain, also sometimes called Cassadora, is on the San Carlos Apache Indian Reservation. See Cassadore Mesa, Gila Ref.: Woody; 18a

CAZADOR

Cochise   T22S R29E

This railroad stop was named for Cassadore, the Apache leader. See Cassadore Mesa, Gila

CCC CANYON

Santa Cruz   T22S R16E

This canyon was named because of activities of the Civilian Conservation Corps in the 1930s.

CEBADILLA MOUNTAIN   pro.: /sebədiyə/

Spanish = "wild lily"

Pima   Elev. c. 5000'

The name for this rounded mountain between the end of the Rincon Mountains and the adjacent Santa Catalina Mountains was in use in the early 1870s, a fact attested to both by Clum's account of the route taken by the Camp Grant massacre marauders and by a newspaper article stating that the Board of Supervisors had ordered surveys for a wagon road over Cebadilla Pass to the San Pedro Valley. The name first appears on the Roskruge Pima County map in 1893. Apparently the name derives from the fact that small wild lilies called *cebadilla* grow around springs at the base of this mountain, as well as elsewhere following rains. This wild lily has an edible bulb which looks not unlike a spring onion. The lily produces a single tubular green leaf approximately eleven inches long, tipped by a small blue flower. A corruption of the name is Ceballeta Mountain. Ref.: 67, pp. 67, 68; *Weekly Citizen* (April 11, 1885), p. 2

CEDAR: The dark green of cedar trees with their shaggy bark dots the high landscape of Arizona and it is not surprising that the word *cedar* occurs in many place names. Stockmen have discovered that the intrusive cedar trees will rapidly take over high range country and

their attempts to uproot them frequently results in double and triple overgrowth. The following are examples of place names carrying the word *cedar*:

| **Cedar** | Mohave | T16N R14W | Elev. 4450' |

This location, sometimes called Cedarville, was a post office established to service the many mines in the Cedar Mining District at the southern end of the Hualapai Mountains. In 1874 the community had thirty-five residents, but by 1907 about two hundred lived nearby in Cedar Valley. The community has vanished.
P.O. est. June 27, 1895, Ira M. George, p.m.; disc. July 21, 1911 Ref.: 242; 215, pp. 77, 111; Babcock; 200, p. 25

Cedar Basin	Gila	T10N R7E	
Cedar Basin	Maricopa	T2N R12E	
Cedar Basin	Mohave	T24N R17W	Elev. 5200'
Cedar Basin	Yavapai	(1) T11N R6E	(2) T7N R2W
Cedar Basin Canyon	Pinal	T1N R10E	
Cedar Bench	Gila/Yavapai	T11–12N R7–5E	
Cedar Canyon	Coconino	T31N R6E	
Cedar Canyon	Mohave	T24N R17W	
Cedar Canyon	Navajo	T8N R20E	
Cedar Canyon	Pima	(1) T21S R11E	(2) T18S R17E
Cedar Canyon	Santa Cruz	T22S R11E	
Cedar Canyon	Yavapai	T11N R1E	
Cedar Creek	Coconino	(1) T19N R3E	(2) T32N R4W

See Cataract Canyon, Coconino

| **Cedar Creek** | Gila | (1) T6N R21E | |

This post office was established to service about three hundred residents nearby.
P.O. est. May 29, 1946, Virginia Ann Kirkpatrick, p.m.; disc. Dec. 15, 1949 Ref.: 242

Cedar Creek	Gila	(2) T7N R19E	
Cedar Creek	Pima	T21S R11E	
Cedar Creek	Coconino/Yavapai	T19N R3E	
Cedar Creek	Yavapai	T11N R1E	
Cedar Dam	Coconino	T20N R10E	
Cedar Dam	Pima	T21S R11E	
Cedar Flat	Gila	T11N R9E	
Cedar Flat	Graham	T10S R20E	
Cedar Flat	Yavapai	T14N R7E	
Cedar Knoll	Coconino	T39N R1W	Elev. 5706'
Cedar Knoll	Mohave	T39N R5E	
Cedar Lake	Navajo	T13N R20E	
Cedar Lake Reservoir	Apache	T15N R27E	
Cedar Lake Wash	Apache	T15N R27E	
Cedar Mesa	Coconino		

See Howell Mesa, Coconino

Cedar Mesa	Gila	T11N R10E	
Cedar Mesa	Yavapai	T15N R6W	
Cedar Mesa Canyon	Gila	T15N R6W	

Cedar Mountain	Coconino		
Cedar Mesa Canyon	Gila	T15N R6W	
Cedar Mountain	Coconino (Grand Canyon)	T32N R3E	Elev. 7053'
Cedar Mountain	Graham	T8S R22E	Elev. 6688'
Cedar Mountain	Pinal	T6S R14E	
Cedar Mountain	Yavapai	T14N R6E	Elev. 5472'
Cedar Pocket Reservoir	Mohave	T33N R11W	
Cedar Pocket Wash	Mohave/Utah	T33N R11W	
Cedar Pond	Mohave	T36N R9W	
Cedar Ridge	Coconino	(1) T31N R3E (2) T35N R8E	Elev. 6289' Elev. 6000'

This is the location of the Cedar Ridge Trading Post, named because it is on a high ridge covered with juniper and piñon. Ref.: 331, p. 28

Cedar Ridge	Mohave	T40N R6W	
Cedar Ridge Reservoir	Coconino	T40N R1W	
Cedar Salt Ground	Yavapai	T15N R6W	
Cedar Spring	Coconino	T31N R2E	
Cedar Spring	Graham	T10S R20E	
Cedar Spring	Greenlee	T3N R31E	
Cedar Spring	Mohave	(1) T37N R16W (2) T32N R10W (3) T28N R16W (4) T24N R17W	
Cedar Spring	Navajo	T6N R22E	
Cedar Spring	Pima	T12S R17E	
Cedar Spring	Yavapai (3) T12N R6E	(1) T13N R3E (4) T15N R3W	(2) T12N R5E (5) T10N R2W
Cedar Spring Canyon	Greenlee	T3N R31E	
Cedar Springs	Cochise	T14S R26E	
Cedar Springs	Graham	T7S R21E	

Cedar Springs was the name of a headquarters ranch of the Norton and Stewart Cattle Company. Here on October 2, 1882 after escaping from the San Carlos Indian Reservation, Nachez and Juh with their band attacked a wagon train and killed Bartoles Samaniego and six of his teamsters. While the plundering was going on, troops of cavalry arrived. This led to the location being called the Battle Ground. The Indians retreated and managed to escape into Mexico.
P.O. est. Sept. 20, 1887, Bernard E. Norton, p.m.; disc. April 8, 1892
Ref.: 116, pp. 691, 692; 18a; 264

Cedar Spring	Navajo	T24N R18E	

The first trading post was established here by Jake Tobin in the 1880s. When the original trading post was abandoned, the office was moved five miles north to Tees To. See Tees Toh, Navajo
P.O. est. April 1, 1910, Charles Hubbell, p.m.; name changed to Tees to, June 18, 1930

Cedar Springs Butte	Graham	T8S R21E	Elev. 5157'
Cedar Tank Canyon	Coconino	T17N R7E	
Cedar Tank Canyon	Yavapai	T16N R7E	
Cedar Tree Bench	Coconino	T39N R12E	
Cedar Tree Hills	Coconino	T36N R8E	Elev. 6825'
Cedarville	Mohave		

See Cedar, Mohave

Cedar Wash	Coconino	(1) T25N R6E	(2) T29N R6E
See Tappan Wash, Coconino			
Cedar Wash	Mohave	T37N R16W	
Cedar Well	Pima	T21S R11E	

CEMENT: The word *cement* often indicates that the location — frequently a water hole — had been cemented by tufa or other conglomerate having cement-like qualities. Such cementing is frequently natural. Examples follow:

Cement Canyon	Cochise	T14S R27E
Cement Spring	Navajo	T7N R17E
Cement Spring	Pinal	T1N R12E

CEMENT TANK: The word *tank* indicates a watering place. In country where the presence of potable water frequently means the difference between life or death for men and animals, the combination of *cement* with *tank* indicated that the water hole so named could be counted on in all probability to hold water.

Cement Dam Tank	Coconino	T26N R9E	
Cement Dam Tank	Navajo	T14N R17E	
Cement Dam Tank	Pima	T11S R15E	
Cement Tank	Coconino	(1) T24N R3E	(2) T26N R1E
Cement Tank	Greenlee	T3S R28E	
Cement Tank	Pima	(1) T14S R18E	(2) T13S R18E
		(3) T17S R4W	
Cement Tank	Yavapai	T19N R5W	
Cement Tank Spring	Coconino	T32N R7W	
Cement Trough Canyon	Navajo	T8N R17E	
Cement Troughs Spring	Yavapai	T16N R6W	
Cement Well	Maricopa	T2N R5W	
Cementosa Tanks	Yuma	T1S R14W	

CEMETERY RIDGE
Yuma   T1S R11W   Elev. 2184'

A series of small hills along the top of the ridge is called Cemetery Hills, a name in use since before 1900. Its highest point is Nottbusch Butte. The name for the ridge and hills derives from the killing of several prospectors here in the 1870s. Their bodies are said to be buried on the ridge. Ref.: 18a; 355, p. 142

CENTENNIAL WASH
La Paz/Maricopa   T5N R10W

The name was supposed to have been given to this wash because it is about one hundred miles long. It drains Harrisburg Valley and the following mountains: Harquahala, Eagle Tail, Bighorn, and Gila Bend, as well as much of Arlington Valley. See Harrisburg, La Paz Ref.: 279, p. 39

CENTENNIAL WELLS
La Paz

In 1879 this was a stage station in Centennial Valley on the road between Yuma and Prescott. Ref.: *Arizona Sentinel* (Feb. 15, 1879), p. 3

CENTER MOUNTAIN
Gila   T6N R14E   Elev. 6789'

The name comes from the fact that this mountain in the Sierra Ancha is midway between McFadden Horse Mountain and Baker Mountain. See also Ancha, Sierra, Gila

CENTEOTL POINT
Coconino (Grand Canyon)   T32N R2W

This name of this point, given on some maps as Centeoti, has a Nahuatl derivation, but what its meaning is is unknown. It is one in the group of geologic formations carrying Aztec names. See Ceyotl, Coconino (Grand Canyon)

CENTRAL
Graham   T6S R25E   Elev. 2880'

This community was settled in 1882 by Joseph Cluff, George Clemens, John Young, Daniel Whitbeck, and A. Lambson, Mormons who named their community for the Central Canal, which carried water from the Gila River to their agricultural area. Furthermore, the new community was about half way between Thatcher and Pima.
P.O. est. Nov. 15, 1897, Joseph Cluff, p.m.
Ref.: 225, p. 249; 116, p. 592; 15, p. 533; 242

CENTRAL CANYON
Cochise

In 1876 this canyon was so named because it is in the center of the east slope of the Huachuca Mountains. Today it is called Huachuca Canyon. See Huachuca, Fort, Cochise, which was established in this canyon. Ref.: 159, p. 510

CERBAT   pro.: /serbæt/ or /serbət/
Coconino-Maricopa and Mohave = "bighorn mountain sheep"
Mohave   T22N R17W   Elev. c. 4000'

At one time this now vanished mining community was very important. It began as the site of the Golden Gem, Esmeralda, and Vanderbilt Mines in 1860. Its name derived from that of the Cerbat Range in which it was located. By 1869 a small mill was in operation here in Cerbat Canyon. Because of the increasing importance of the community, in 1871 it became the Mohave County seat, replacing Hardyville (*q.v.*). It lost that honor in 1873 when the county seat was removed to Mineral Park (*q.v.*).
P.O. est. as Cerbat, Dec. 23, 1872, William Cary, p.m.; name changed to Campbell, June 25, 1895, John H. Campbell, p.m.; name changed to Cerbat, Oct. 24, 1902; disc. June 15, 1912 Ref.: 200, pp. 13, 19, 91; 346, p. 212; AHS, Charles Metcalf, Letter (March 10, 1906)

CERBAT MINE
Mohave   T23N R16W

This mine about a mile northeast of Cerbat opened in 1869. Its operations increased when a large mill was installed in the gulch below the mine c. 1880. However, it did not remain operative for very long. Ref.: 200, p. 97

CERBAT MOUNTAINS
Mohave   T24N R18W

In 1854 Lt. Amiel W. Whipple applied the name Cerbat Range. It is the range described by Fr. Francisco Garcés on June 9, 1775 as the Sierra Morena (Spanish = "blackish" or "blackish mountains"). See Cerbat, Mohave

CEREUS TANK
Yuma   T1S R18W

This tank, developed by the Fish and Wild Life Service in 1959, was named because of the large number of night-blooming cereus here. Ref.: Monson

CERRO: The Spanish word *cerro* means "hill" and the word *cerrito* means "little hill."
For entries using *cerro* as a word indicating the type of location, the information is listed under the major word of the entry. For instance, for Cerro Montoso, see Montoso, Cerro.

CEYOTL
Coconino (Grand Canyon)   T32N R2W

This is the name of one of several geologic formations bearing Aztec names. "Ceyotl" is probably a misprint for the Nahuatl Coytl, from which we derive our transfer word "coyote." The probability is made even stronger by the fact that Coyote is an important figure in North American Indian mythology, being a noted trickster. However, this name may be a cartographer's error for Centeotl or vice versa.

CHAGIT VO
Papago = "in-between charco"

Pima   T14S R3W

This is the name of a temporary village on the Papago Indian Reservation. It should not be called either Josquin Village, Jaquin Village, or Joaquin's Village, although Joaquin, a principal Indian of Pozo Redondo, settled here with his family. Ref.: 262, p. 7; 58

CHAIN TANK
Yuma   T4S R17W

The name for this tank derives from the fact that many years ago prospectors fastened a thirty-foot length of chain to another forty feet long so they could use water from this twenty-foot deep hole. They fastened a rope over a rock projection on the lip of the tank and then pulled the chain up over the projection and the men climbed hand over hand by the chain to put in a pipe and siphon the water. The sides of this tank are so steep that it used to be a death trap for game. The Fish and Wild Life Service dug a tunnel to the tank so that game which falls into it can escape. It is also possible for game to enter safely at the lower level to get water. Ref.: Monson

CHAISTLA BUTTE
Navajo   T39N R19E   Elev. 6098'

The Navajo name for this location means "beaver corner," a clue to the fact that beaver congregated here. In 1932 the USGS changed the spelling from Cha-ez-kla Rock to Chaistla Butte. Ref.: 141, pp. 152, 191; 329

CHAKPAHU
Hopi = "little water"

Navajo   T27N R20E   Elev. 6360'

It is reported that the spring at this location produced little water, hence its Hopi name. The location is at the site of Bat House, a large ruin first investigated by archeologists in 1901. Hodge says that the name Bat House probably derives from the ruins having been built and occupied by the Bat clan. Ref.: 152, pp. 18, 19, 20; 164, I, 135, 232, 564

CHALCEDONY PARK
Apache

This is the third park in the Petrified Forest National Monument (q.v.). Chalcedony, a variety of translucent quartz which is frequently grayish, occurs at this location. Ref.: 177, p. 114

CHALENDER
Coconino   T22N R3E   Elev. 6880'

This location was named for George F. Chalender, a superintendent of the A. & P. R.R. In 1883 it was a lumbering center on Chalender Lake (a.k.a. Mineral Lake) with one hundred residents, but it declined after 1900. The spelling Challendar is a corruption. P.O. est. May 2, 1883, Harry L. Harris, p.m.; disc. Aug. 27, 1897 Ref.: 124, p. 45; 242; 18a

CHALK: A presence of soft white limestone has led to the designation *chalk* in several place names, examples of which follow:

Chalk Canyon	Maricopa	T7N R4E	
Chalk Creek	Gila	T4N R15E	
Chalk Creek	Pima/Pinal	T11–10S R13E	
Chalk Mountain	Gila	T8N R12E	
Chalk Mountain	Yavapai	T8N R12E	Elev. 2783'
Chalk Peak	Greenlee	T4S R30E	Elev. 5274'

Chalk Point Spring	Yavapai	T13N R7E
Chalk Spring	Maricopa	T7N R8E
Chalk Spring	Mohave	T23N R21E
Chalk Spring	Yavapai	(1) T11N R5E (2) T12N R6E
Chalk Tank	Maricopa	T7N R8E
Chalk Tank	Yavapai	T12N R5E
Chalk Tank Canyon	Yavapai	T12N R4E
Chalk Wash	La Paz	T4N R17W
Chalky Spring	Maricopa	T6N R1W

CHAMBERLAIN TRAIL
Gila
The Civilian Conservation Corps in the 1930s did the original construction of this trail to connect Gordon Canyon and the vicinity of the town of Young. It was named for Harry A. Chamberlain, killed in World War I. Ref.: Woods; McKinney

CHAMBERS
Apache   T21N R27E   Elev. 5750'
The name Chambers comes from that of Charles Chambers, who had a trading post at this location prior to 1881. He remained at least until 1888 and the railroad named its station here for him. It seems likely that the post office was out of existence for a time, because on December 29, 1926, the name was changed to Halloysite, possibly because of the Post Office Department policy of rejecting re-opening offices under their original name. Halloysite, a bentonite clay, was mined four miles northeast of the railroad station. It is used in manufacturing fine white china.
P.O. est. as Chambers, June 22, 1907, Frank P. Hathorn, p.m.; resc. Nov. 27, 1907; Joseph Root appointed p.m., Dec. 5, 1907; name changed to Halloysite, Dec. 9, 1926, Spencer Balcomb, p.m.; name changed to Chambers, May 10, 1930; Wells Fargo 1908
Ref.: Grigsby; Richards; 242; 331, p. 36; 141, p. 34; Museum of Northern Arizona

CHAMISO   pro.: /kəmiyso/
Spanish = "half-burned wood"
Cochise   T17S R19E   Elev. c. 4000'
The name is the result of the burning of a cord of mesquite wood here c. 1890.
Ref.: 18a

CHANDLER
Maricopa   T1S R5E   Elev. 1213'
This community is named for Alexander John Chandler (b. July 15, 1859, Canada; d. May 8, 1950). After arriving in Arizona in August 1887, Chandler was appointed first veterinarian surgeon for the Territory of Arizona. He arrived at a time of severe drought and cattle were dying all over the landscape. After only thirty days Chandler resigned, deciding to head for California. He set out, but the night he arrived in Phoenix the rains came and Chandler changed his mind. He rescinded his resignation and kept his job as the state's veterinarian surgeon until 1892. In the early 1890s he took up land holdings which later comprised the Chandler ranch of nearly eighteen thousand acres. An irrigation expert, he surveyed his acreage into agricultural plots of ten to one hundred and sixty acres. In 1911 he put up his land for sale and had an immediate response, one result being the establishment of the town of Chandler.
P.O. est. April 2, 1912, Ernest E. Morrison, p.m.; incorp. Feb. 16, 1920
Ref.: 242; 309, pp. ;17, 19, 20, 42, 48

CHANDLER HEIGHTS
Maricopa   T2S R6E   Elev. 1500'
In the late 1920s Alexander Chandler, C. A. Baldwin, and others incorporated to grow citrus on this location southeast of Chandler. It was also called Citrus Heights.
P.O. est. Jan. 24, 1938, Theresa M. Binner, p.m. Ref.: 309, p. 126; 242

CHAOL CANYON
Navajo = "piñon"
Coconino   T39N R11E
Gregory suggested the name Dortch Canyon to honor a local man but in 1932 the USGS
officially removed the name in favor of Chaol Canyon. Ref.: 329

CHAPERAL pro.: /šæpərǽl/
Spanish = "bramble bushes"
Yavapai   T13N R1W
A post office was established here to serve employees at a mine which was located in
dense chaparral. The post office was at a shipping point on the railroad.
P.O. est. Chaperal, May 24, 1894, Harmon B. Hanna, p.m.; disc. Dec. 31, 1917
Ref.: 242; 18a

CHAPARRAL GULCH
Yavapai   T13N R1W
This gulch was named c. 1870 by Allan Doyle and Fred Plum, his partner, "because of
rough brush along the hillside." Ref.: 329

CHARCO: The generic designation *charco* persists in a few place names of southern
Arizona. The term indicates a pool of standing water in a clay (i.e. adobe) flat or wash filled
by run-off. Size is variable, being anything from a pool three feet by six feet and perhaps
eighteen inches deep, to one which may be thirty feet wide, one thousand feet long and as
much as six feet deep. The existence of charcos on the Papago Indian Reservation made
possible the raising of certain crops tended by Indians in so-called "temporary" villages
near the pools. In fact, Hodge notes that such a village existed in 1858 under the name
Charco, which was "probably identical with Chioro." The following exemplify the use of
the term *charco* in place names. (Note the following: *Charco Tank* = "Tank Tank")

Charco	Coconino	T19N R7E	
Charco	Navajo	T4N R23E	
Charco	Pinal	T6S R10E	
Charco	La Paz	(1) T3N R14W (2) T2N R16W	
Charco de la Piedra See Hotasan Vo, Pima	Pima		
Charco en Medio See Chagit Vo, Pima	Pima		
Charco de la Roche	Pima		
Charco 27 (Town)	Pima	T13S R3W	Elev. 2091'
Charcos de los Pimos	Pima		

See Point of Mountain, Pima, and Cienega de los Pimos, Pima Ref.: 279, p. 42; 167, I, 235

CHARCOAL CANYON
Mohave   T22N R17W
Charcoal was essential in blacksmithing, required by miners to maintain sharp picks. In
this canyon charcoal was prepared. Some other Charcoal Canyon names have an
identical origin. Ref.: Harris

CHARCOAL GULCH
Yavapai   (1) T13N R1W
                                                (2) T10N R1W
A variant name for #1 is Juniper Gulch. See Charcoal Canyon, Mohave

CHARLEBOIS TANKS
Coconino   T19N R11E
Lou Charlebois, a cattleman, was a partner with LaBarge and established herds in La
Barge Canyon. The intersecting canyon with it is called Charlebois Canyon. He retired
to California. Ref.: 261, p. 123

CHARLESTON

Cochise   T21S R21E   Elev. 3980'

In March 1879 A. W. Store of Tombstone laid out a plat and named it Charleston. The community owed its existence to the fact that Tombstone had no water to work ore reduction facilities, so Charleston was established on the San Pedro River banks. Charleston was a mill town with reduction works which in 1880 served the Tombstone Milling and Mining Company. Smaller and tougher than Tombstone, Charleston was a center for rustlers as well as for soldiers on a tear from Fort Huachuca. An abundance of water in the wrong place – in the mine shafts of Tombstone – put an end to Charleston as the ores were no longer available for milling. The location was also known as Millville, but that place was actually across the river and hence north of Charleston and had its own post office.

P.O. est. April 17, 1879, Charles D. Handy, p.m.; disc. Oct. 24, 1888; Wells Fargo 1885 Ref.: 146, p. 32; 359, p. 98; 241, p. 235; Macia; *Arizona Sentinel* (March 1, 1879), p. 1

CHARLIE BELL WELL

Pima   T12S R8W

Charlie Bell of Ajo dug this well c. 1928. Ref.: Monson

CHARLIE DAY SPRING

Coconino   Elev. c. 5000'

This spring on the outskirts of Tuba City was near the hogan of Charlie Day, a blind Navajo who c. 1880 served as a scout. Among Navajo, the name for this location is *Na'editsoi* (= "bottomless hole"). In 1928 this spring was cleaned out and walled with concrete. Workers found fossils of bison, camels, and elephants at that time.
Ref.: 324, pp. 1, 2; 331, p. 163

CHARMINGDALE

Yavapai

Charmingdale was about a mile northwest of old Camp Hualapai. When the military camp closed, the post office was transferred to this point. On January 30, 1879 the post office name was changed from Hualapai to Charmingdale. See Hualapai, Camp, Yavapai

P.O. est. as Camp Hualapai, Jan. 13, 1873, D. T. Foster, p.m.; name changed to Charmingdale, Jan. 30, 1879, Samuel C. Rogers, p.m.; disc. Nov. 18, 1880
Ref.: *Weekly Arizona Miner* (March 14, 1879), p. 3

CHAROULEAU GAP

Pinal   T10S R15E

This location takes its name from that of Anna Charouleau (b. 1823, France), a retail merchant in Tucson in 1870, who later established a ranch near this saddle. He sold out in 1917 to Frank Sutherland. The name has been misspelled in a variety of ways.
Ref.: 62; 329; *Arizona Cattleman* (March 10, 1917), p. 3

CHASE CREEK

Greenlee   T4S R29E   Elev. c. 5000'

This location was named, not for George Chase (a prospector), but for a Capt. Chase who left Silver City, New Mexico, in 1870 to pursue Apaches. His party, including Bob and Jim Metcalf, camped near Clifton, perhaps on this creek. In the late 1870s Henry Lezinsky (*sic*) financed the construction of the Stone House, the site of a small Mexican smelter. Gradually Chase Creek was engulfed in the town of Clifton as buildings were constructed along this narrow, twisting canyon.
Ref.: Farnsworth; 257, pp. 7, 8; 68, p. 36

CHASM CREEK

Yavapai   T12N R5E

According to the informant, who pronounced the name "ch-asm," a deep gorge at this location resulted in the name. Ref.: Dugas

CHAVES PASS RUINS

Coconino   T16N R11E

The large ruins in Chavez Pass "are believed to have been named after an old Spaniard who was killed in the pass by Apaches. Some think, however, that it was named after Lt. Col. J. Francisco Chavez, builder of Old Fort Wingate, who guided the first gubernatorial party to Arizona in 1863." See Chavez Pass, Coconino The Hopi name for this location is Chubwichalobi. Ref.: 331, p. 37

CHAVEZ PASS pro.: /šávez/

Coconino   T16N R11E   Elev. c. 6000'

Lt. Col. J. Francisco Chavez, a member of the New Mexico Cavalry Volunteers (1861-64), in 1863 commanded the military escort for the first gubernatorial party of the Territory of Arizona. Later Chaves (*sic*) located the Chaves Road from Camp Verde to the Little Colorado River near the present Winslow, for a shorter route to Prescott via Antelope Springs. The road went through the pass bearing his name. There was a way station in the pass. The spelling Chavez is an error and the spelling Jarvis Pass is a corruption. Briefly the location was called Snow Lake where the Cavalry fought with Indians on November 25, 1875. In 1927 the USGS officially eliminated errors in spelling and the corruption Jarvis Pass. Ref.: 163, p. xxxvi; Museum of Northern Arizona; Joseph Fish, "Scrap Book"

CHEDISKI MOUNTAIN pro.: /tsédezsˀay/

Apache = "long white rock"

Navajo   T9N R15E   Elev. 6589'

The Apache name describes the fact that there is a bed of white sandstone forming a cliff on the northeast face of this mountain. The former name for this location was Chediski Butte, now called Lost Tank Ridge. Ref.: 329; Davis; Uplegger

CHELLY, CANYON DE pro.: /dəšéy/

Navajo: *ɬsey'* = "among the cliffs"

Apache   T5N R28E   Elev. c. 6000'

On February 14, 1931 a Presidential proclamation created Canyon de Chelly National Monument. This extraordinarily beautiful location was first seen by Lt. James H. Simpson and his party in 1849. It was then a stronghold for Navajo Indians. Still earlier, in 1805, Lt. Antonio Narbona and his Spanish forces battled with Indians in this canyon. (See Muerto, Canyon del, Apache) The first written description was that by Capt. Alexander William Doniphan, who called the location Cañon de el Challe. Simpson, in conversation with Señor Donaciano Bigil, Secretary of the Province, learned the Navajo origin of the canyon name. Attempts to understand the Navajo pronunciation and render it in spelling resulted in several names as follows: Cañon of Cheille (Kern, Sept. 5, 1849); Cañon de Chille (Heitman); Cañon Chenelle (Macomb map 1860); Chelly Canyon, and Canyon Chennele. In 1932 the USGS eliminated the variant spellings for Canyon de Chelly. During the campaign against the Navajo, a temporary fort was maintained for Federal troops at the mouth of the canyon. In 1863-64 Col. Kit Carson and his men marched the entire length of the canyon and Capt. Albert Pfeiffer traversed Canyon del Muerto from east to west, while Capt. A. B. Carey marched his men from west to east through the main gorge. The result was the ultimate surrender of the Navajo nation.

The canyon contains two notable monoliths associated with Navajo mythology. One, higher than the Washington monument, is Spider Rock. Here Spider Woman retreats and devours unruly Navajo children. Their bleaching bones can be seen at the top of this rock. Ref.: 331, p. 108; 15, p. 287; 167, I, 242; 143, p. 42; 13, "Canyon de Chelly," p. 4; 326, p. 190; 292, p. 24; 5, pp. 415, 415; 159, p. 485; 141, pp. 18, 35, Note 2

CHELLY, RIO DE

Apache

This is the old name for the wash now called Chinle Wash, which runs through Canyon de Chelly.

CHEMEHUEVI POINT   pro.: /čémǝývi^/

Yuma = "Piute Indian"
Mohave   T14N R20W

On February 23, 1854 Lt. Amiel W. Whipple wrote about Chemehuevi Indians occupying this beautiful valley, noting that many swam the Colorado River to bring grain and vegetables to Whipple's party. This quiet little valley is now under the lake formed by Parker Dam. Ref.: Harris; 168, pp. 231; 232; 346, p. 232

CHEOPS PYRAMID

Coconino (Grand Canyon)   T32N R3E   Elev. 5392'

This geologic formation is named for the Pharoah who constructed the great pyramid with relays of one thousand men every three months. George Wharton James said that the pyramid at the Grand Canyon has "a peculiar shape as of some quaint and Oriental device of symbolic significance. Ref.: 178, pp. 30, 31

CHERIONI WASH

Pima   T14S R6W

Mexicans call the wild chinaberry tree *cherioni*. Such trees grow sparsely along this wash, hence the name. Ref.: 57, p. 44

CHERIONI WELL

Pima

Rube Daniels c. 1914 dug this well in the Ajo Valley because the cherioni tree at the location was popularly believed by Papago to be an indication of the presence of water. However, Bryan says the well never produced much water. Ref.: 58

CHERRY: Because of the presence of wild cherry trees, several locations in Arizona bear the designation *cherry*. Examples follow:

Cherry   Yavapai   T14N R3E   Elev. 5096'

Formerly there were many wild cherry trees in this locality and the name derives from that fact. By curious coincidence, several years after the naming of this location, the Norville Cherry family arrived from Texas. That fact has led to some confusion concerning the origin of the name.
P.O. est. March 3, 1884, Cecelia De Kuhn, p.m.; disc. March 15, 1943; Wells Fargo 1903
Ref.: Allan; Frier; Schnebly

Cherry Canyon	Coconino	T20N R8E	
Cherry Creek	Gila	T8N R14E	
Cherry Creek	Santa Cruz	T23S R18E	
Cherry Creek	Yavapai	(1) T14N R3E	(2) T10N R2W
Cherry Creek R.R. Stn.	Yavapai	T13N R1E	

This is the name of the station at Dewey. See Dewey, Yavapai

Cherry Flat Recreational Gila
Area

This is in the Pinal Mountains near Miami.

Cherry Lodge	Greenlee	T3S R29E	
Cherry Spring	Gila	T11N R13E	
Cherry Spring	Pinal	T10S R15E	
Cherry Spring	Yavapai	T10N R2W	
Cherry Spring Canyon	Cochise	T12S R19E	
Cherry Spring Peak	Cochise	T12S R20E	Elev. 5362'
Cherry Trap Spring	Yavapai	T10N R2W	
Cherry Valley	Pinal	T10S R15E	
Cherry Valley Wash	Pinal	T10S R15E	

CHERUM PEAK pro.: /šrʌm/

Mohave   T23N R17W   Elev. 6978'

This peak takes its name from that of a Hualapai leader whose name is sometimes spelled She-rum. With his tribe he surrendered at Beale's Springs on March 30, 1874. He and his people were sent to the Colorado River Agency, where they suffered intolerably. Their horses nearly all perished for lack of grass and the people were dying because, instead of having twenty-four beeves a week, only seven were being delivered. They had gone to the Agency with Capt. Thomas Byrne, ostensibly their friend in charge of rations, and matters speak for themselves. In the absence of Capt. Byrne in March 1875, Agent J. A. Tonner told the Hualapai that Byrne would no longer distribute any rations and that rations could be obtained only from the Agency headquarters forty-five miles to the north. He then issued short rations. The Indians set out for the northern point, but actually headed for their own native mountains. They never returned to the Colorado River Agency. Ref.: 335, pp. 97, 98, 113

CHEVELON BUTTE

Coconino   T15N R14E   Elev. 6935'

This butte was named for a trapper who in 1851 poisoned himself here by mistakenly eating wild parsnips. He was buried nearby. Ref.: Kern, *Diary* (Oct. 2, 1851)

CHEVELON CANYON

Coconino/Navajo   T18N R17E

Chevelon Creek, also called East Clear Creek, runs through this canyon. In 1851 Lt. Lorenzo Sitgreaves called the stream Big Dry Fork. Thereafter travellers often camped at Big Dry Fork Crossing. According to A. F. Banta, John Mass renamed Big Dry Fork to Clear Creek. An early name for the canyon was Big Dry Wash. The name gradually shifted to Chevelon Canyon (see Chevelon Butte, Coconino).

In July 1882 Al Sieber's scouts learned that Apaches planned to ambush the scouting party by rolling boulders on it while it was traversing the canyon. Instead, the scouts and soldiers under Capt. Adna Romanze crossed above the canyon and surrounded the Indians. The resultant battle lasted four hours as five cavalry troops fought about fifty Apaches. For that reason, the site of the fight is sometimes called Battleground Ridge. Ref.: 294, p. 7; 345, III, 587; 224, p. 117; AHS, Banta Clipbook; 5, p. 457

CHEVELON CANYON LAKE

Coconino   T13N R14E

Waters backed up by Chevelon Canyon Dam form this lake, whence the name. See Chevelon Creek, Coconino

CHEVELON CANYON RANCH WILD LIFE AREA

Navajo

This wild life area has 59,632 acres. See Chevelon Creek, Coconino Ref.: 9, p. 3

CHEVELON CANYON WILD LIFE AREA

Navajo

This wild life area has one hundred and twenty-two acres. See Chevelon Canyon, Coconino/Navajo Ref.: 9, p. 2

CHEVELON CREEK WATER FOWL AREA

Coconino

This area was established with six hundred and sixty-eight acres in 1964. See Chevelon Canyon, Coconino Ref.: 9, p. 2

CHEVELON CROSSING

Coconino   T13N R13E

The first name suggested for this place was Barts Crossing, to honor Barton Lesch, who in 1958 was the forest ranger in charge of timber management for the area. However, a Forest Service policy rejects naming locations after persons alive at the time. Therefore it was called Chevelon Crossing because of its location. Ref.: 329

CHEYAVA FALLS   pro.: /čeyávə/
Hopi = "intermittent"

Coconino (Grand Canyon)   T32N R4E   Elev. c. 7000'

These falls were pointed out to Emery C. and Ellsworth Kolb by William Beeson in May 1903 when Beeson said that he saw "a big sheet of ice." They are said to have named this falls because it exists only intermittently. However, it should be noted that the name Teyava is that of a Havasupai Indian whose name meant "uneven, lame; one leg is shorter than the other." On the other hand the Hopi word for "intermittent" is Cheyava. Ref.: "Cheyava Falls," *Grand Canyon Natural History Notes*, Bulletin 2 (Nov. 1935), pp. 10, 15; 303, p. 168

CHIAPUK   pro.: /čiəpʌk/
Papago = "spring"

Pinal   T10S R2E   Elev. c. 2500'

In June 1940 the USGS eliminated the name Copperosity for this location. The earlier name, also attached to the Copperosity Mine nearby, is said to come from the prospectors' custom of asking each other, "How is your copperosity sagatiating?" The replies varied, one being, "As wide as a boxcar and as long as a freight train." A post office called Copperopolis was in existence briefly to serve miners in the area. Although the older name has given way to the Papago name for their village, it persists in the name of the Copperosity Hills.

P.O. est. as Copperopolis, Oct. 17, 1884, Edward E. Hellings, p.m.; disc. Sept. 4, 1885 Ref.: 262, p. 16; 59, p. 37; 18a; 329; Lenon

CHIAVRIA POINT
Coconino (Grand Canyon)   T32N R5E   Elev. 6217'

The USGS suggested this name in 1931 to honor Juan Chiavria, a Maricopa leader present at the battle of Bloody Tanks (*q. v.*). Chiavria was a friend to settlers during the Apache wars. Ref.: 329

CHIAWULI TAK   pro.: /čiuwli tá^k/
Papago = "barrel cactus sits"

Pima   T17S R21E   Elev. c. 2800'

This is a Papago village where bisnaga cacti abound. Variant and incorrect spellings for this location are Jeowic, Geowic, and Tjeavolitak. Ref.: 262, p. 12; 329

CHICHILTICALLI
Graham

It should be noted that this name was applied to "a mountain range, a mountain pass, a seaport, and a geological area." However, Bolton applied it as meaning a "ruined house." Although it appears impossible to give a precise location, the reader is referred to Pueblo Viejo, Graham. Ref.: 92, p. 168

CHICO, ARROYO
Spanish = "short"

Pima   T14S R14E

The name is descriptive, as this is indeed a short arroyo cutting through Tucson.

CHICO SHUNIE WELL   pro.: /čiyko šúwni^/
Pima   T13S R6W   Elev. 1795'

This well was dug by a Papago Indian nicknamed "Chico." Francisco Shunie's descendants lived here for many years. Ref.: Ketchum

CHIHUAHUA HILL
Coconino   T23S R24E   Elev. 5896'

In the 1890s Mexicans from Chihuahua came from there to work in the mines at Bisbee. They lived on this hill and named it for their native state. Ref.: Burgess

CHIKAPANAGI POINT
Coconino (Grand Canyon)   T34N R3W   Elev. 4800'

This location was named for a Havasupai boy who had a "quizzical bat-like expression

puckering his countenance," hence his nickname, meaning "bat." The location was not named for a Havasupai family. According to the source cited, his name is spelled Chickapanyegi. The variant spelling Chikapangi is a corruption.
Ref.: 178, p. 286; 174, p. 111

CHILCHINBITO CANYON
Navajo T36N R21E
In December 1970 the USGS eliminated the following names for this canyon: Burro Spring, Chil-chi-vi-to Canyon, Sumac Spring. See Chilchinbito (Spring), Navajo

CHILCHINBITO (SPRING) pro.: /tsiyᵛščinbi:ʔtó/
Navajo: *tsiichinbii'to'* = "water in the sumacs"
Navajo T36N R21E Elev. 6000'
As is characteristic of Indian place names, this one is precisely descriptive of the locality. The spring is in Chilchinbito Wash, sometimes called Bamboo Wash (because of the growth). Sumac is used by Navajo women in basketry. Here Navajos ambushed Piutes who were pursuing a Navajo Indian. The Piute's bones are used in the Enemy Chant or the War or Squaw Dance. The location is sometimes called Bitter Weed Springs and Sumac Springs. A community surrounds the school, and a trading post exists here. Ref.: 331, p. 38; 141, p. 191; 329

CHILDS
Pima T11S R6W Elev. 1428'
Thomas Childs, Sr. (b. April 14, 1839, Mississippi; d. Jan. 19, 1902) joined the rush to California in 1856. He was thereafter stationed at various Overland Stage stations including Maricopa Wells, Gila, and Gila Bend. By 1890 with his son Tom Childs, Jr. (b. June 10, 1870, Yuma; d. Feb. 5, 1951), he was ranching in the Ajo area where they had arrived in 1884. Several place names bear the designation Childs.
Ref.: 62; *Ajo Copper News* (Oct. 21, 1954), p. 7; AHS, Chambers Collection, Box 12, and *Arizona Album* (April 11, 1955)

CHILDS
Yavapai T11N R6E
This was the location of an Arizona Power Company transformer plant. It was named for a rancher in the locality.
P.O. est. Aug. 15, 1912, Landon V. Woodmansee, p.m.; disc. April 15, 1915
Ref.: 242; 18a

CHILITO pro.: /čiylíto/
Spanish = "little peppers"
Gila T15S R4E Elev. 4000'
Chilito was the name of the post office for the London-Arizona Mining Company headquarters. Mexicans called its first postmaster "Chilito" because of his fiery temper, hence the name.
P.O. est. March 27, 1913, John B. Crittenden, p.m.; disc. July 15, 1918
Ref.: George Ketenbach (Patterson Notes); 242

CHIMINEA CANYON NATURAL AREA
Pima
These one hundred and sixty acres were set aside on February 26, 1931.
Ref.: 243, p. 22

CHIMINEA PEAK pro.: /čimənèyə/
Spanish = "chimney"
Santa Cruz T22S R18E Elev. 4918'
"Chimney" is a mining term used to describe a type of outcrop rock. Ref.: Lenon

CHIMNEY: The use of the word *chimney* in place names usually indicates the presence of an old chimney or of a rock formation which looks like a chimney or creates a draft like a chimney's. The following are examples of such use in Arizona place names:

Chimney Butte Navajo T27N R18E Elev. 6553'
See Dilkon, Navajo

Chimney Canyon	Navajo	T17N R18E
Chimney Canyon	Pima	(1) T21S R11E (2) T13S R18E
Chimney Canyon	Santa Cruz	T22S R11E
Chimney Creek	Pima	T13S R17E
Chimney Flat	Coconino	
Chimney Peak	Navajo	
Chimney Peak	Yuma	c. 20 mi. N. of Yuma (1871)
Chimney Rock	Mohave	T40N R8W
Chimney Rock	Pima	T13S R17E
Chimney Rock	Yavapai	T14N R7W
Chimney Rock Canyon	Greenlee	T3S R32E
Chimney Spring	Apache	T11N R27E
Chimney Spring	Coconino	T22N R7E
Chimney Spring	Pima	T12S R17E
Chimney Wash	Apache	T11N R27E

CHINAMAN'S CANYON
Coconino
A variant name for the location was China Canyon. This canyon at the north end of
Bonito Street in Flagstaff was about two blocks long. Many years ago a Chinaman had a
garden in the canyon, but he and the canyon are both long since gone. By 1955 it had
been filled with rubbish. Ref.: Conrad; Switzer

CHINA PEAK
Cochise   T18S R23E   Elev. 7118'
Because Chinese from California financed and worked this mine near this peak, the
name was a natural result. Ref.: 18a

CHINA PEAK
Graham   (1) T3S R23E   Elev. 4372'
                                (2) T9S R20E   Elev. 6592'
The presence of chinaberry trees results in the name for these peaks.

CHINA SPRING CREEK
Gila   T7N R14E
There are chinaberry trees along this creek, hence the name.
Ref.: Blumer (through Woody)

CHINDE MESA   pro.: /číndíy/
Navajo = "haunted"
Apache   T21N R24E   Elev. c. 6000'
Navajo Indians avoid hogans in which a death has occurred, because they believe such
places to be haunted. According to a local story, a geologist with a field-mapping crew
accidentally fell into water. He entered a deserted hogan, stripped, and was drying
himself in the doorway when Navajo Indians rode along. Seeing the white body in the
darkened doorway, the Indians rode off in a rush, shouting "Chinde! Chinde!" The
mapping crew called the mesa Chinde. Ref.: Branch

CHINESE WALL
Maricopa   T1S R3E
Why this natural dike is called Chinese Wall is not known to the editor, although there
may be a fancied resemblance to the Great Wall of China.

CHINLE pro.: /čʔinːliᴧ/ or /činliy:/
Navajo: *ch'inlih* = "water outlet" or "it flows from the canyon"
Apache   T41N R24E   Elev. 5506'
The Navajo name derives from the fact that this location is at the mouth of Canyon de Chelly. It is also near Chinle Wash (a.k.a. Rio de Chelly and Nazline Wash). Spanish war and trade extended to this location from New Mexico in the early 19th century. Troubles with Navajo Indians who robbed New Mexicans of sheep and other possessions culminated in a peace conference between Navajo Indians and Col. Kit Carson on the knoll near the present monument headquarters in 1864. It marked the official end of Navajo warfare with whites. The first trading post at Chinle was begun in a tent in 1882, followed by a small trading camp under new proprietors, constructed in 1885. Missionaries arrived in 1904 and a small government school was opened in 1910. It is today an extensive establishment.
P.O. est. as Chin Lee, March 2, 1903, Charles L. Day, p.m.; name changed to Chinle, March 13, 1941 Ref.: 242; Burcard; 141, p. 35; 331, p. 39; 329

CHINLE VALLEY
Apache   T34N R26E
In June 1971 the USGS eliminated the names Chinle River and Chinle Wash in connection with this valley. See Chinle, Apache

CHINO VALLEY (P.O.) pro.: /číyno/
Spanish: *chino* = "curly hair"
Yavapai   T16N R2W   Elev. c. 4000'
A variety of grass is called *chino* because it has a somewhat curly appearance. Lt. Amiel W. Whipple in January 1854 noted that this area had an abundant growth of grama grass, called by Mexicans "de china." From that came the name Val de China or Chino. Until at least September 1871 the name Chino Valley was reported in accounts of military activities. Gradually it came to be called Big Chino Valley and is so referred to in newspaper dispatches in 1897. Steele (USGS Archives) notes that Chino Valley was the first site of Fort Whipple, from December 20, 1863 until the following May.
P.O. est. as Chino, Oct. 6, 1879, Benjamin J. Wade, p.m.; disc. July 25, 1891; reest. as Big Chino Valley, Nov. 13, 1883, George W. Banghart, p.m. The postmistress at the time when it was changed from Jerome Junction was Mrs. Sydney T. Fritsche.
Ref.: 242; 329; 346, p. 118, Note 5; 345, p. 15

CHINO VALLEY
Yavapai   T16–18N R2–3W
Because of overlapping locations, the USGS has separated this former Chino Valley into the following: Big Chino Valley, 35°11'35" (Elev. 5020"); Little Chino Valley, 34°50'20"/34°41'0"; Lonesome Valley, 34°46'45"/34°38'50". See Chino Valley (P.O.), Yavapai Ref.: 329

CHIRICAHUA
Cochise   T20S R31E   Elev. 4671'
The post office in the railroad depot at this location was named for the Chiricahua Apache Indians. The location was a cattle shipping point which at one time supported a small settlement. See Chiricahua Indian Reservation, Cochise
P.O. est. July 1, 1907, Henrietta Powell, p.m.; disc. Jan. 31, 1921 Ref.: 242

CHIRICAHUA BUTTE
Gila   T3N R21E   Elev. 6814'
This butte, also called Natanes Butte, was named for a band of Chiricahua Apache Indians active in the vicinity. Ref.: 18a; 329

CHIRICAHUA INDIAN RESERVATION pro.: /čiyriykáwə/
Apache: *tsil* = "mountain," *kawa* = "great"
Cochise
The name is an old one, appearing on a map dated 1588 as "Tierra de Chiriguanas." Kino c. 1697 spelled it Chiguicagui. On an 1820 map the name cited is Chiricaguis.

Following the treaty made with the Chiricahua leader Cochise at Sulphur Springs (T16S/R25E), Gen. O. O. Howard established the Chiricahua Indian Reservation with Thomas Jeffords as agent. The Chiricahua band of Apaches lived in these mountains, an explanation of why the mountains were so named. These Apaches were probably the most widely known of all Apache bands because their forays took them many miles from their mountain strongholds into Mexico and north into Arizona Territory. Never wholly conquered, they submitted of their own free will. The first headquarters for their reservation was at Sulphur Springs. The headquarters was then moved to Cienega de San Simon. From there it was moved to Pinery Canyon (in the Chiricahua Mountains) and the last headquarters was at Apache Pass (Fort Bowie). Continuing troubles with Rogers and Spence, who sold whiskey at Sulphur Springs, kept the Chiricahuas at war from 1876 to 1882 when one hundred and forty were ordered removed to Hot Springs, New Mexico, and three hundred and twenty-five to the San Carlos Indian Reservation. An additional four hundred ran away before capture, to commit further depredations. The reservation was restored to the public domain on October 30, 1876.
Ref.: 116, p. 532; 107, VIII, 14, 15

CHIRICAHUA NATIONAL MONUMENT
Cochise   T16S R29E

This national monument is a seventeen-square-mile region of rhyolite pillars, balanced rocks, magnificent cliffs, and canyons. It was unknown to white men until late 1886 when an ex-army sergeant, Neil Erickson (a homesteader) came upon it while he was pursuing a horse stolen from Col. Hughes Stafford by an Apache named Massai. The Apache name for this area is *Yahdesut* (= "point of rocks"). Erickson trailed the man and horse until nightfall. While returning to his home, he came upon huge and fantastic rock formations which he found almost overwhelming. His son-in-law Ed Riggs and his wife (Lillian Riggs) explored the hundreds of acres of wild life and strange formations. Through the efforts of Riggs, the area was set aside as the Chiricahua National Monument by presidential proclamation in April 1924. Geologists believe that the land, once relatively level, experienced violent upheaval with molten lava burst-out to spread over the plains. Apparently there were many such eruptions interspersed by centuries of geological inactivity. The earth slowly lifted and tilted and erosion gradually created the fantastic forms. These bear many descriptive names, such as Chinaman's Head, The Bishop, The Ugly Duckling, The Boxing Glove. Riggs named Duck-on-a-Rock, Balanced Rock, Thor's Hammer, and The Totem Pole. Friends and guests visiting the Riggs Faraway Ranch named others.
Ref.: Riggs; 13, Dodge, "Refreshing Interlude," pp. 7, 8; 5, p. 375; *Douglas Dispatch*, "50th Anniversary Edition" (1952), Section 6, p. 7

CHIRICAHUA PEAK
Cochise   T18S R30E   Elev. 9796'

This location has borne various names, including Round Mountain, Turkey Mountain, and Snow Shed. See Chiricahua Indian Reservation, Cochise Ref.: 18a

CHIRICAHUA WILD AREA
Cochise

This area consists of eighteen thousand acres at the summit of the Chiricahua Mountains. The elevation ranges from 7,200' to 9,795'. With no trails or roads other than those for fire protection, the area maintains its natural wild state as a haven for black bear, mountain lion, wildcat, foxes, coyotes, and other wild life. Ref.: 76, p. 14

CHITTY CANYON
Greenlee   T2N R28E

Chitty Canyon and Chitty Creek, which runs through the canyon, are on a ranch owned the place prior to 1903 by Allan Chitty. Later Joe Slaughter (d. 1956) owned the place. Ref.: Simmons; Scott; Reilly

CHIULIKAM   pro.: /čiúləkəm/
Papago = "where the willows grow"
Maricopa   T10S R3W

The name Chiukikam is preferred over the following variants: Pozo Colorado, Tschiulikam, Saucida, and Sauceda Well. In all instances, the names mean "red well," or "willow place." The USGS records the traditional Papago name as Suwuki Vaya or Vokivaxia (= "red well"), whereas the Mexican name is Pozo Colorado (= "red well"). The name Sauceda (= "willow") may reflect the location being near the Sauceda Mountains. Bryan said the place was "a very old rancheria, inhabited by two to four families," which have since departed. The USGS notes may be somewhat in error, as Chiulikam (112°31'30"/32°34'30") is not the same place as Suwuki Vaya (111°49'30"/32°06'30"). Ref.: 58;208, p. 383; 262, pp. 8, 13; 329; 167, II, 201, 470

CHIULI SHAIK   pro.: /čⁱulə šay/

Papago = "willow thicket"

Pima	T18S R7E	Elev. 3200'

The name describes the location of this Papago village, the upper one of three in Fresnal Canyon. This name is preferred to the following: Fresnal, Tshiuliseik, Kohi Kug, and Koxikux. All but Fresnal are at a different location. See Kohi Kug, Pima Ref.: 262, p 1; 57, p. 407

CHIWETON

Papago: *chiwe* = "long"; *tun* = "hill"

Pima	T18S R2E

The name "long hill" refers to a ridge west of this location. Bryan notes that this place is a summer agricultural location for the Papago Indians. The name is also spelled Cheweeton (Irrigation Service Map 1915). Ref.: 58

CHLORIDE

Mohave	T23N R18W	Elev. 4009'

The name for this former mining community derived from the fact that the exposed ores carried heavy silver chloride. The community was the first Arizona mining village to come into being in the 1860s and it continues to survive. The first mines discovered included those at Silver Hill in 1863 where Hualapai Indians laid their hands on the settlers' guns and used them to kill four miners. One was shot and two others were killed by stones thrown down the mining shaft. It was a mining camp by 1864 and developed into a town so that by 1900 its population was two thousand.
P.O. est. March 27, 1873, Robert H. Choate, p.m.; Wells Fargo 1903
Ref.: 200, pp. 51, 52; 168, pp. 81, 82; Schroeder

CHOCOLATE MOUNTAINS

La Paz	T2S R20W	Elev. 2822'

Dr. John C. Newberry of Lt. Ives' Expedition in 1857 named this low, twenty-five-mile-long range because it is chocolate colored. Ref.: 355, p. 74; 245, p. 24

CHOLLA: pro.: /čoyə/   This is the Spanish name for *Opuntia effulgens*, a variety of cactus which has spines tipped with minute barbs so that it sticks swiftly and painfully to any passing animal or person brushing against it, hence its name "Jumping Cholla." Other varieties are called Teddy Bear and Staghorn cactus. Because cholla grows abundantly in Arizona, several places reflect that fact in their names, as follows:

Cholla (R.R. Stn.)	Cochise	T12S R27E	Elev. 3700'
Cholla Basin	Maricopa	T7N R3E	
Cholla Canyon	Gila		
See Cave Canyon, Gila			
Cholla Mountain	Maricopa	T6N R1W	Elev. 2936'
Cholla Mountain	Pinal	T4S R8E	
Cholla Mountain, La	La Paz	T3N R20W	Elev. 2259'
Cholla Pass	Pima	T17S R9W	
Cholla Spring	Maricopa	T7N R3E	
Cholla Tank	Maricopa	T2N R9E	
Cholla Tank	La Paz	T1N R15W	
Cholla Wash, La	La Paz	T3N R20W	

CHOT VAYA
Papago = "sand well"
Pima   T15S R5E   Elev. 2675'
This is a temporary village on the Papago Indian Reservation. The USGS prefers calling it Sand Wells. Ref.: 262, p. 6

CHOULIC   pro.: /čúʌlə/
Papago = "corner" or "hipbone"
Pima   T20S R5E   Elev. 2470'
The name of this Papago Indian village is also incorrectly spelled Tjuuli Choulik. Ref.: 262, p. 1; 58; 57, p. 408

CHRISTMAS
Gila   T4S R16E   Elev. 2725'
Dr. James Douglas with two prospectors discovered copper at this location in the early 1880s, but they were unable to maintain their claim because the land was on the San Carlos Indian Reservation. Several years later George B. Chittenden succeeded in having Congress pass a bill to change the reservation lines and open the property for re-location. He planned it so he would receive news via telegraph to Casa Grande and then by messengers on horseback in relay so that the news arrived in his hands on his birthday, Christmas 1902. He rode immediately to locate the property and named it Christmas. Another version is that Alex McKay (b. 1841, Scotland; d. 1936) with Al Weldon and Jimmy Lee located the mine and named it Christmas because they hoped that "Santa Claus would bring them a fine future." They also found the mine during the Christmas season. This is denied by Mrs. Anee Forbach. Says she, "I don't know who gave out this information about the Christmas Mine. Mr. George B. Chittenden was a personal friend of mine for years and I have heard him relate the story of the mine ... But he did not locate it; it had been located by a Mike O'Brien and Mr. Chittenden bought the property from him." She further notes that it was a thriving town and mine until after 1918. She believes that the school teacher named the post office. In any event, this location is due to have all traces of mining activity erased.
P.O. est. April 5, 1905, E. A. Spann, p.m.; disc. March 30, 1935
Ref.: AHS, Castillo Collection, Box 1; State Library Files, unidentified clipping; 242; Mrs. Ann Forbach, Letter (Nov. 30, 1973); Varney

CHRISTMAS PARK
Coconino
This was the name many years ago for the area on the edge of the Coconino National Forest near Flagstaff. "The resemblance of the trees to Christmas trees accounts for the name of the park." Ref.: 166, p. 124

CHRISTMAS TREE LAKE
Apache   T6N R24E   Elev. 8240'
Trees here resemble Christmas trees, hence the name.

CHRISTOPHER CREEK
Gila   T11N R12E   Elev. 5760'
This creek is named for Isadore Christopher, who located his CI Ranch on it. In July 1882 he killed a bear, skinned it, and hung the skin in one of his cabins. While he was away the next day, Apaches came and burned his two log houses. The next visitors were troops who arrived while the cabins were still afire. The story spread that the soldiers had solemnly buried the bearskin, thinking the Apaches had skinned "poor old Christopher." Ref.: Woody; Croxen; 18a

CHROMO BUTTE
Gila   T2N R16E   Elev. 5771'
Barnes says that there used to be a chromo mine near here. In any event, the word may be considered descriptive as the area has a great deal of mineral color in it. Ref.: 18a

CHRYSOTILE   pro.: /krisotayl/
Gila   T4N R17E   Elev. 4600'
Asbestos is the common name for chrysotile. Formerly it was mined at this location,

hence the name. The asbestos mines were found by Tom West in October 1911 and finally sold to the Johns-Manville Company. As Arizona asbestos is white because it is iron free, that company had first refused to buy it because its customers were used to brown asbestos from Canada. Occasionally the name of this place is misspelled Chrysolite. However, Chrysolite is a magnesium iron silicate. There is also a variety of chrysolite which is actually an olive green stone, usually called peridot. See Peridot, Gila

P.O. est. Oct. 20, 1916, Nels A. Nelson, p.m.; disc. Oct. 25, 1932 Ref.: Woody; 242

CHUAPO WASH
Papago: *ku* = "big"; *tjuupo* = "natural water tank in rocks"
Pima   T12S R4W
At one time there was probably a deep water hole here but at present there is a thirty-foot-deep dug well. Ref.: 58

CHUAR BUTTE
Coconino (Grand Canyon)   T32N R5E   Elev. 6250'
Maj. John Wesley Powell used this name to honor a young Kaibab Indian leader named Chuaroompek. He was a friend of Jacob Hamblin, Powell's guide. Formerly this place was called Hercules Hill. Oddly enough Dellenbaugh notes that the Indian was called Frank. Over this butte in 1956 two transcontinental planes collided at 21,000'. Parts of the wreckage fell onto Chuar Butte. Ref.: 329; 88, p. 250

CHUBWICHALOBI
Hopi = "antelope notch place"
Coconino   T16N R12E   Elev. c. 6000'
This location is also known as Chaves Pass Ruin. Ref.: 331, p. 37; 167, I, 293

CHUCK BOX LAKE
Navajo   T10N R16E   Elev. c. 6000'
Cowboys on roundup away from headquarters have a chuck wagon for their cook to prepare meals. The Waters Cattle Company grange foreman c. 1887 could not drive the chuck wagon through here and had to unpack and abandon the chuck box, hence the name. Another possible source of the name may be that Capt. George Nyce, first Indian Service Ranger on the Fort Apache Indian Reservation, kept a supply box here. Ref.: Davis

CHUICHU   pro.: /čúwčuw/
Pima = "many caves"
Pinal   T8S R5E   Elev. 1455'
According to Lumholtz, there are natural cavities in the ground at this village of Kohatk Pima Indians. To quote one informant, "As far as it being named for caves, I know of no caves in the vicinity and I have lived close to those mountains and climbed some of them many years." Bryan spells the name Tschúhutscho or Tjúitjo. The name has been misspelled Chuichuschu, and Chiu Chuschu, but the usual form is Chuichu. Whites tend to pronounce this "Choochoo." According to white informants, Indians could hear the train and called the train Chuchu, which finally evolved into the name of the village. Ref.: 242; 58; 57, p. 391; 59, p. 371; Mrs. Anne Forbach, Letter (Nov. 30, 1973)

CHUI VAYA WELL   pro.: /čⁱu wà'a/
Pima = "cave well"
Pima   T20S R6E   Elev. 3163'
This place is said to be a summer village of the Papago Indians.
Ref.: 262, p. 2; Jones

CHUKUT KUK   pro.: /čúkut ku/
Papago: *tjukut* = "owl"; *ko* = "cry"
Pima   T19S R2E   Elev. c. 1500'
This summer Papago village had one hundred and forty families in 1865, a year in which Hartley noted that the name of the village occurred in many Papago stories. Possibly Mexicans translated the Papago name into a word familiar to them, the Nahuatl *Tecolatl*

(= "ground owl"), for they called the village Tecolate. It is possible that the Pima word *Tco'-oltûk* (= "corner") may be related to this location.
Ref.: 167, II, 173; 57, p. 392; 58; 262, p. 3; 329

CHUPAN MOUNTAINS
Pima   T17S R2W   Elev. 3044'
In 1964 local Indians called this place Turtle Tail, which may be a translation. See Mamatotk Mountain, Pima, and Mesquite Mountains, Pima

CHURCH ROCK
Navajo   T39N R21E   Elev. 5862'
This igneous lava plug rises abruptly from the valley floor. It looks like a church steeple, hence the name. Ref.: 141, p. 37; 331, p. 121

CHUSKA MOUNTAINS pro.: /tšošga:y/
Navajo: *chosga'i'* = "white spruce" or "fir"
Apache/New Mexico   T35N R30E   Elev. 8808'
In November 1847 Capt. Alexander William Doniphan led an army expedition pursuing Navajo Indians into these mountains. Kern noted them on August 30, 1849, as the Tschuski Mountains. Lt. James Hervey Simpson on his 1851 map separated them into a northern portion (Sierra de Tunecha) and a southern (Sierra de Chusca). The USGS mapping crew in 1892 added a third division at the northern end, terming it Lukachukai (*q.v.*). In 1963 the USGS approved the name Chuska for the entire range. Other spellings for this range are as follows: Choiskai, Tunitcha, Tunechan Carrizo (Gregory), Tchensa, Boundary Mountains, and Zilditloi Mountain (Navajo: *dzil* = "mountain," *ditloi* = "wooded"). Doniphan Pass is in these mountains. See Tunicha Mountains, Apache Ref.: 141, pp. 18, 27, 191, 197; 186 (Aug. 30, 1849)

CHUTUM VAYA pro.: /čútum wà'ə/
Papago = "bear well"
Pima   T19S R7E   Elev. 3713'
Why this name was given to the location of this temporary village is not known to me.
Ref.: 262, p. 2

CIBECUE
Navajo   T8N R27E   Elev. 4940'
This is an Apache community about two and one-half miles north of the site of the battle on Cibecue Creek (*q.v.*).
P.O. est. June 1, 1908, Mrs. Berna Coleman, p.m.; disc. May 15, 1933; reest. April 28, 1936, Mrs. Anne Cooley, p.m.; disc. Jan. 1, 1960 ("when Cibecut became an independent station of Show Low"). Ref.: 242; *Directory of Post Offices* (1960)

CIBECUE CREEK pro.: /ciʌbisuw/
Apache = "reddish bottom land"
Gila/Navajo   T8N R16E   Elev. c. 5200'
In the summer of 1881 serious trouble began developing at Cibicu (*sic*) Creek, an old Apache villa;ge. A medicine man named Nokay Delklinne (also rendered Noc-e-ca-klin-ny) led Coyotero Apaches in increasingly frenzied ghost dances. He promised to raise the Apache leader Diablo from the dead. Following his resurrection, Diablo would then lead Apaches in victory against the white man. To quell rumors of an impending uprising, Col. Eugene Asa Carr with six officers, seventy-nine soldiers and twenty-three Indian scouts, arrested Nokay Delklinne at Cibecue on August 31, 1881. More than three hundred hysterically excited Indians stood by during the arrest. Later while Carr was making camp, his Indian scouts turned against him, opening fire, killing Capt. Edmund C. Hentig immediately. The troops hastily retreated downstream. Before the battle ended, ten soldiers had been killed. Forty-seven Apaches were taken prisoner. In his reports Carr uses the name Cibicu as the place of battle.

Three of the mutinying Indian scouts were hanged at Fort Grant on March 3, 1882, and two others were imprisoned at Alcatraz.

It is worth noting that in his annual report Maj. Gen. Irvin McDowell commented: "The fact of the troops finding the medicine man with his people in their homes

[150]

where they had been planting corn shows they were not then for war. I cannot concur, therefore, in denouncing their conduct as treacherous (excepting the military scouts)."
Ref.: Uplegger; Davis; 5, p. 465; 83, p. 111; 224, pp. 232, 233; 311, p. 125; 242

CIBOLA   pro.: /cibówlə/
La Paz   T1S R23W   Elev. 250'
This community on the Colorado River is a recreational center and boat landing. Prior to 1900 it served as the Cibola Boat Landing where river steamers unloaded freight and took on wood for their boilers. Formerly a ferry here crossed the Colorado River to Blythe, California. It is also the site of the old Rhodes Ranch (q.v.).

In 1957 farmers constructed a bridge to enable them to carry their produce across the river. Its construction did not come to public attention until small-boat owners complained that the bridge was too low to permit passage under it.

Why this community should be called Cibola is not known. There has been much speculation where the fabled Seven Cities of Cibola were, some conjecturing them to be the Hopi Villages, whereas Luxan names the Zuñi pueblo (Cibola or Granada) visited by Espejo in 1583. The name is borrowed from that used by Coronado (1540) and other Spanish explorers. Although Coues and Bancroft assert that the name means "buffalo," according to Russell Cushing, "Cibola equals the 'Chi-vo-la' of Fray Marcus of Nizza, (which) equals the Zuñi name for themselves, namely, Shivona, or Shinwina." Oñate notes that the Zuñis called their last pueblo Cibola or Granada.
P.O. est. Jan. 23, 1903, Louis W. Bishop, p.m.; disc. Sept. 15, 1933; (post office shifted location: In 1903 it was T1S/R24E, southwest section 13; and by 1946, T1S/R23E, northeast section quarter 30). Ref.: 242; *Blythe Chamber of Commerce Cruise Bulletin* (Oct. 10, 1954); 77, p. 403, Note 6; 46, pp. 184, 235; 15, p. 44, Note 20; 1, pp. 73, 75, 76; 281 (Smithsonian Institution), p. 24; *Congres International des Americanistes* (Session 1890), p. 155

CIBOLA LAKE
La Paz
This lake at the lower end of Cibola Valley was created by silting after the Imperial Dam was closed in 1938. It closed off the river and created this lake.

CIBOLA LAKE WATER FOWL AREA
La Paz
This area consists of twenty-three hundred acres of controlled water fowl habitat. It was established in 1954. Ref.: 9, "Wild Life Bulletin 5," p. 1

CIBOLA NATIONAL WILD LIFE REFUGE
La Paz   T1-2S R24W
On August 21, 1964 8,208 acres of Arizona land (with some additional in California) was established to "reserve and enhance water fowl wintering ground in this portion of the Pacific flyway." Additional land is being added to the total of 16,627 acres in both states. It exists along twenty miles of the lower Colorado River in the Cibola Valley of Arizona and the Palo Verde Valley in California, about twenty miles south of Blythe. Ref.: "Final Environmental Statement," A-2; U.S. Fish and Wild Life Service Cibola Brochure

CIENEGA: *Cienega* is a Spanish word meaning "marsh." Emory defines it as "A valley or depression in a plain, where the water collects and can only escape by an obstructed outlet. Such a place is usually miry and boggy." The word occurs in several Arizona place names, some examples of which are listed below: Ref.: 106, p. 66

Cienega, Camp   Pima
On June 21, 1862 one hundred forty cavalrymen under Lt. Col. Edward E. Eyre of the First California Volunteers camped at this location adjacent to Cienega State Station (q.v.). Ref.: 224, p. 164

Cienega, La   Pima
See Cienega Stage Station, Pima

Cienega Amarilla   Apache
See Michaels, St., Apache

[151]

Cienega Canyon	Coconino	
pro.: /sénəkiy/	See East Clear Creek, Coconino	

Cienega Canyon	Navajo	T27N R20E
Cienega Creek	Apache	T5N R29E
Cienega Creek	Gila	T5N R18E
Cienega Creek	Graham	T2S R26E
Cienega Creek	Greenlee	(1) T2S R31E (2) T4N R30E
Cienega Creek	Pima	T18S R17E
Cienega Creek	Pima/Santa Cruz	T21S R17E

This creek enters Pantano Wash at T17S/R18E.

Cienega Creek	Yavapai	T13N R3E

See Cienega Spring, Yavapai

CIENEGA DE LOS PIMOS

Pima

A picket post was established here in October 1858 on the stage route from Tucson to the Rio Grande. On a map made by Capt. Overman, the post seems to be in the pass between the end of the Rincons and the next range south. This would place it in the vicinity of the old Cienega Stage Station (*q. v.*). On GLO 1869 the name has been changed to Cienegas de las Pimas. According to Barnes, in 1880 this entire area was a series of cienegas. Erosion replaced them with a deep wash. Ref.: 339, p. 18; 18a

Cienega de Sauz	Cochise

See Simon, San, Cochise

Cienega Draw	Apache	T9N R27E
Cienega Draw	Cochise	T15S R27E
Cienega Draw	Coconino	T12N R9E
Cienega Larga Creek	Gila	

On a military route map drawn by Lt. Thomas Bingham in November 1883, this creek is near Chevlon's Peak.

Cienega Ranch	Yavapai	T13N R2E	Elev. 5550'
pro.: /séynəkiy/			

The ranch headquarters, an old stone house still in use, was a stopping place for travelers. It had a post office.

P.O. est. April 25, 1877, George W. Hance, p.m.; disc. Nov. 15, 1892

Ref.: Goddard; Schnebly; 18a

Cienega Ranch	Yavapai

See Cienega Spring, Yavapai, and Shipp Mountain, Yavapai

Cienega, Sierra	Coconino

See Francisco Peaks, San, Coconino

Cienega Spring	Cochise	(1) T17S R31E (2) T15S R27E
Cienega Spring	Gila	T6N R14E
Cienega Spring	Maricopa	T4N R10E

CIENEGA SPRING

Yavapai   T13N R3E

In 1868 T. J. Buckman, who had a permanent camp at Fort Rock, trailed and caught up here with Indians who had stolen his stock. When the Indians camped for the night, Buckman and his son waited nearby. At dawn the two white men attacked the Apaches, who were busily feasting on a Buckman horse. Following the ensuing fight, Buckman found a spring where more Apaches were feasting. He was thus probably the first white man to see this spring. Henry Mehrens filed a claim on it in 1870, the year when the cavalry briefly had a post here. Ref.: AHS, Cienega Spring File

| **Cienega Springs** | Pima | T16N R17E | Elev. c. 2800' |

See Cienega Stage Station, Pima

CIENEGA STAGE STATION
Pima   T16N R17E

In 1858 the Butterfield Overland stage established a station here known as Cienega Springs, or La Cienega. The water was reported to be sweet, cool, and wholly potable. When the stage line ceased operation, the station was abandoned. Some time between that date and 1862, the commodious adobe buildings were destroyed by fire. The ruins were described by Lt. Col. Edward E. Eyre, who camped with the California Volunteers nearby on June 21, 1862. Following the Civil War, the station again began operating. Apaches attacked often. In 1867 W. A. ("Shot Gun") Smith and three companions were attacked. Only Smith survived after killing or wounding about eight Indians. By 1870 the place was being run by a man named Miller. In September Apaches butchered the mail rider and Scott Young, and again destroyed the station.

This location is sometimes confused with the railroad station at Pantano. Cienega went out of existence when the tracks passed over it in 1880 and a new station was built at Pantano. Ref.: 73, II, 152, 153; 224, p. 164; 107, V, 289; *Weekly Arizona Miner* (Sept. 3, 1870), p. 2

| **Cienega Springs** | La Paz | T10N R19W |
| **Cienega Valley** | Pima | |

See Empire Valley, Pima

| **Cienega Wash** | Graham | |

See Stockton Pass, Graham

| **Cienega Wash** | Pima | |

See Cienega Creek, Pima

CIMARRON MOUNTAINS   pro.: /simeràn/
Pima/Pinal   T10S R2E   Elev. 2948'

Mexicans refer to mountain sheep as *cimarron*. Wild mountain sheep still live, or formerly did, at many places in Arizona. This name is an error for Castle Mountains, Pima (*q.v.*). Ref.: 18a

CIMARRON PEAK
Pima   T11S R1W   Elev. 4108'

Roskruge called this "El Cero Cimarron." See Cimarron Mountains, Pima Ref.: 329

CINCH HOOK BUTTE
Coconino   T12N R9E   Elev. 7255'

Because of its cinch hook shape, this butte was being called by its present name as early as 1880. Ref.: 18a

CINDER: The use of the word *cinder* in place names arises from the presence of lava aglomerate. Examples follow:

| **Cinder Basin** | Yavapai | T22N R5E | |
| **Cinder Basin Wash** | Yavapai | T20N R10W | |

This name was applied by the USGS in September 1972. Ref.: 329

Cinder Flat	Coconino	T22N R9E	
Cinder Hill	Cochise	T23S R30E	Elev. 4745'
Cinder Hills	Cochise	T22N R9E	

See Hogback Mountain, Coconino

Cinder Lake	Coconino	T22N R8E	
Cinder Mountain	Coconino	T21N R9E	
Cinder Mountain	Maricopa	T7S R7W	
Cinder Pit Mountain	Apache	T8N R26E	Elev. 9300'

CINNABAR MINE
La Paz   T2N R20W   Elev. c. 600'
This location was believed to contain red mercuric sulphide, hence the name.
Ref.: 18a; Lenon

CIPRIANO HILLS
Pima   T16S R7W   Elev. 2604'
Several place names in this vicinity are named for Cipriano Ortega, who had a well in
these hills.

CIPRIANO PASS
Pima   T17S R7W
This pass separates the Tinajas Altas Mountains from the Gila Mountains. It is in the
foothills of the Cipriano Hills (q.v.).

CIPRIANO WELL
Pima
This well dug by Cipriano Ortega was also known in 1915 as El Pozo de Cipriano. He
was a Mexican-Papago who lived here with his family. Ref.: 58

CIRCLE CITY
Maricopa   T6N R3W   Elev. 1865'
The name describes the plan of this commercially developed location.

CITADEL, THE
Coconino   T25N R9E   Elev. c. 5000'
The Citadel is a pueblo ruin in Wupatki National Monument. It consists of fifty or more
rooms on a small mesa. As it probably served as a fort in its commanding position, the
name is suitable. Ref.: 71, p. 28

CITRUS VALLEY
Maricopa   T4S R6W
Much citrus fruit is grown here, hence the name.

CITY CREEK
Gila   T10N R9E   Elev. c. 4000'
In late 1870 a Mormon colony called Mazatzal City was at the juncture of this creek and
the Verde River. When the Mormons moved to Pine c. 1882, the creek became known as
City Creek. Ref.: Croxon; 18a

CLACK
Mohave   T21N R17W   Elev. c. 5000'
O. P. Clack (b. 1842, Texas) and his brother had the Oro Plata Mine at this location and
named its post office for their families. The name is perpetuated in that of Clack Canyon.
P.O. est. June 23, 1898, John W. Babson, p.m.; disc. Aug. 26, 1899
Ref.: 242; 62; Babcock

CLAIRE SPRING, SAINT
Maricopa   T7N R6E
Although Barnes says this location was named for William St. Clair (sic), a miner and
cattleman, the *Arizona Republic* in 1931 said it was named for H. B. St. Claire. The
1870 Census lists H. S. St. Clair (b. 1847, Massachusetts) as a farmer and it may well be
that the place was named for him.
Ref.: 18a; *Arizona Republic* (April 15, 1931), n.p.; 62

CLAN ROCKS
Coconino
This Hopi shrine is near Tuba City at the beginning of the salt-gatherers trail to salt
caves in a canyon of the Little Colorado River near its juncture with the Colorado. Here
Hopis pray and inscribe their clan mark on the rocks. Ref.: Mildred Hooper

CLANTON HILLS

Yuma   T2S R12W   Elev. 1508'

Available information indicates that this location was probably named for J. E. Clanton, who had a well "one half mile northeast of the point where the road between Palomas and Harquahala passes through the gap between the Gila Mountains and the Clanton Hills." On the other hand, Phineas Joseph ("Finn") Clanton (b. 1845, Maine; d. 1906), lived either in or near Yuma until c. 1895 when he settled at Clanton's Ranch in Gila County. A third possibility is that it was named for Thomas Newton Clanton (b. Missouri), who arrived in Arizona in 1877. However, as he ranched at Bigbug and then moved to Phoenix in 1880 to run a butcher shop, his connection with this place is remote and tenuous, being based upon a one-year contract to build ten miles of the Buckeye Canal. He therefore moved to Buckeye. The only Clantons who are clearly eliminated are those associated with Tombstone. See also Gila Bend Mountains, Maricopa/Yuma
Ref.: 224, III; 279, pp. 23, 206; Woody; Mercer; 355, pp. 142, 144; 63

CLARA PEAK

La Paz   T10N R15W   Elev. 2395'

The peak takes its name from that of the Clara Mine located by Sterling Winters. Here E. S. Osborne created a well which he sold with the mine to T. J. Carrigan, a prospector. It came to be called Carrigan Peak. It was corrupted to Corrigan Peak. Add to that a further corruption of Klara Peak, Karrigan Peak, and Kerrigan Peak. The December 1966 USGS decision to settle on Clara Peak is a welcome one. Ref.: 329; 182

CLARK, CAMP

Yavapai   Elev. c. 4000'

The original "Fort Whipple" at this location was established in 1863. When Fort Whipple was removed to its permanent location (December 1863), Maj. Willis issued orders saying that the old location would henceforth be called Camp Clark for John H. Clark, Surveyor General, who visited in August 1863. It was a sub-post of Fort Whipple. See Whipple, Fort, Yavapai
Ref.: *Arizona Miner* (May 25, 1864), p. 2; 224, pp. 155, 166

CLARKDALE

Yavapai   T16N R3E   Elev. 3550'

Senator William A. Clark (Montana, 1901-1907) bought the United Verde mines property in 1884. He later proposed erecting a smelter, and suitable land was found on the Jordan Ranch where ground was broken in 1910. The town of Clarkdale was laid out in 1914. The first furnace began operating on May 26, 1915. Along with Jerome (*q.v.*), Clarkdale went out of existence with the closing of the mines. Several years later Earle P. Halliburton bought it, but sold out still later to produce cement. It is now largely a retirement community.
P.O. est. Nov. 4, 1912, LaMont Coleman, p.m. Ref.: *Jerome Reporter* (Dec. 28, 1899), p. 2; 261, p. 14; 5, p. 332; 242

CLARKE'S CAVES

Coconino   T22N R9E

These caves were named for J. C. Clarke, who found five of them on the west side of a cinder cone about a mile northwest of Turkey Tanks. Ref.: 70, p. 78

CLARK PEAK

Graham   T8S R23E   Elev. 9006'

This peak is in the Clark Mining District, from which fact it derives its name. Clark Wash and its forks are in the vicinity. Ref.: 18a; 329

CLARKSTOWN

Pima   T12S R6W

Because of opposition to the company-owned town of Ajo built by the New Cornelia Copper Company, Sam Clark (b. Jan. 15, 1871, England; d. Oct. 3, 1933) laid out a town site near the reduction works of the mining company. His place was called Clarkston or Clarkstown. The copper company would not sell water to residents of the

new community and they retaliated by deepening a test shaft of a possible mining location, to get water. By 1917 Clarkstown had about one thousand residents, but toward the end of that year it began to decline. Meanwhile residents had applied for a post office to be called Wilson because of the popularity of President Woodrow Wilson. They also suggested the name Woodrow, but both names were ruled out by the Post Office Department. To evade the ruling they changed the name to Rowood, a simple inversion of the syllables in Woodrow. A month after having that post office go into effect, the name was changed to Sam Clark, but the name did not stick. Fire almost completely destroyed the community in 1931 and the remaining residents moved to Ajo. The post office survived for several years. It was finally moved to Gibson, still retaining its name of Rowood. See Gibson, Pima, and Clarktown, Pima
P.O. est. as Rowood, Jan. 21, 1918, Kallulah H. Holcumb, p.m.; name changed to Samclark, Feb. 26, 1918, but resc.; disc. July 30, 1955 Ref.: Ketchum; *Ajo Copper News* (Oct. 21, 1954), p. 2; 57, pp. 358, 559

CLARK VALLEY
Coconino   T20N R8E
The valley is named for the settler here, John Clark (b. March 13, 1839, Maine). Clark emigrated to California in 1859 to raise sheep, but when the railroad spoiled the free range there, he moved his five thousand sheep to Arizona. He lost two thousand during the three-month trip to Williams in 1877. The next year he settled at Clark Valley and remained until 1883. This area is now called Lake Mary Valley. Ref.: 224, III

CLAUDE BIRDSEYE POINT
Coconino (Grand Canyon)   T32N R2E   Elev. 6975'
This peak in 1964 was named by the USGS to honor Claude Hale Birdseye (1879-1941), a geographer and cartographer who explored part of the Grand Canyon in 1923. Ref.: 329

CLAY PARK
Coconino   T17N R7E   Elev. 6367'
In the early 1880s Ben Clay settled at this point, which at that time was known as Jack's Ranch. It is also known as Powell Park for William Dempsey Powell, who arrived in Arizona in 1875. See Jack's Canyon, Yavapai Ref.: 18a; Schnebly; Frier

CLAYPOOL
Gila   T1N R15E   Elev. 3334'
This settlement was developed by and named for Senator W. D. Claypool (d. 1956). The post office application notes that it was also called Inspiration Townsite.
P.O. est. July 27, 1917, Frank E. Hall, p.m.; disc. Feb. 15, 1933 Ref.: 242; Woody

CLAY SPRINGS
Navajo   T11N R19E   Elev. 6312'
These springs emerge from a clay tank, hence the name. There is a Navajo community and day school here.
P.O. est. Nov. 7, 1916, Mrs. Dora Petersen, p.m. Ref.: 242

CLEAR CREEK
Coconino/Navajo   T18N R16E
In December 1966 this name was changed from East Clear Creek and Big Dry Fork to Clear Creek. Sitgreaves in 1851 called its upper portion Big Dry Fork, but in 1882 John Mass, general passenger and freight agent of the A. & P.R.R. "discovered" it and renamed it. According to one source, either through "ignorance" or "gall," he so proclaimed his great discovery that it earned him a membership in the Royal Geographical Society. See Chevelon Creek, and Badger Creek, Coconino/Navajo
Ref.: AHS, A. F. Banta File; *Prescott Courier* (Aug. 14, 1920); 329

CLEAR LAKE
La Paz   T4S R22W
This lake was created by a backwater from the Colorado River to which it is connected by a narrow channel. The water used to be clear, hence the name, but it is no longer so. Ref.: Monson

CLEARVIEW

Apache   T10N R24E

This was the first post office name suggested for Pineyon, Apache, on March 3, 1916. See Pineyon, Apache Ref.: 242

CLEARWATERS

Yavapai   T18N R3W

This small station on the Arizona and Prescott branch of the railroad was named for the Clearwaters family which lived here.

P.O. est. June 9, 1887, David W. Clearwaters, p.m.; disc. Nov. 14, 1887 Ref.: 18a

CLEATOR   pro.: /kliyter/

Yavapai   T10N R1E   Elev. 4000'

When this location was first occupied (among the earliest in Yavapai County), it was called Turkey Creek because numerous wild turkeys were in the area. In 1864 the Turkey Creek Mining District was organized and by 1869 the miners had petitioned for a post office. There was a stage station here around which a community developed. It really took shape in 1904 when the railroad, which was being constructed from Mayer to the Crown King Mine, reached the present townsite. In 1905 James P. Cleator (b. 1870, Isle of Man; d. 1959), came on the scene and went into partnership with the then-postmaster, Levett P. Nellis, at Turkey. At a later date Cleator traded his ranching interests for Nellis' interest in the town, plus $2500.00. By the 1930s the mines in the region had been mostly worked out, and the railroad was abandoned in 1933. In 1947 Cleator offered his town for sale. It is today a small ghost town.

P.O. est. as Turkey Creek, July 15, 1869, James A. Flannigan, p.m.; disc. Dec. 20, 1869; reest. as Turkey, Feb. 18, 1901, Levrett Pierce Nellis, p.m.; name changed to Cleator, May 1, 1925, James P. Cleator, p.m.; disc. July 15, 1954

Ref.: *Weekly Arizona Miner* (July 22, 1871), p. 3; *Weekly Arizona Democrat* (May 20, 1880), p. 2; 242; AHS Clipping File, James Cleator; Sharlot Hall Museum Clipping File; Varney; *Arizona Republic* (May 19, 1980), p. 2

CLEMENCEAU

Yavapai   T16N R6E   Elev. 3300'

The smelting works for the United Verde Extension Mining Company were constructed at this location in 1917. It was first called Verde. To eliminate that name and possible confusion with other Verde post offices, at the suggestion of George E. Tener, vice president of the mining company, the name Clemenceau was substituted to honor Georges Clemenceau, French Minister of War during World War I. In his will Clemenceau left the town a "vase designed by Chaplet in a light lilac color." There is a letter in the Clemenceau High School in Cottonwood celebrating the event, but the vase remained in France. The smelter closed permanently in January 1937.

P.O. est. Feb. 24, 1917 as Verde, Jesse M. Foster, Jr., p.m.; name changed to Clemenceau, April 21, 1920, Roger W. Warren, p.m.; disc. July 31 1954

Ref.: 242; James S. Douglas, "The Name of Clemenceau, Arizona," *Prescott Courier* (no date); State Library Files; Schnebly

CLEMENT POWELL BUTTE

Coconino (Grand Canyon)   T32N R3E   Elev. c. 5500'

In 1932 the USGS approved this name to honor the assistant photographer of Maj. John Wesley Powell's second Grand Canyon expedition 1871-72. Ref.: 329

CLEOPATRA MOUNTAIN

Yavapai   Site of Jerome

In 1882 the town of Jerome began taking permanent shape, "crawling up the face of Cleopatra Mountain." Ref.: 108, p. 116

CLIFF DWELLER SPRING

Coconino (Grand Canyon)   T32N R3E

There are remnants of cliff dwellings near this spring, hence the name.

CLIFFS

Coconino   T21N R8E   Elev. c. 5000'

Not cliffs, but cliff dwellings, give this location its name. It was a railroad station.
P.O. est. March 22, 1907, James W. Rose, p.m.; disc. Jan. 31, 1916 Ref.: 18a; 242

CLIFF: The use of the word *cliff* in place names indicates that a cliff is in the vicinity. The
following are examples:

Cliff Spring	Coconino	T32N R4E
Cliff Spring	Mohave	T25N R18W
Cliff Spring	Navajo	T32N R20E
Cliff Spring	Yavapai	T15N R2E
Cliff Springs	Coconino	T12N R13E
Cliff Spring Canyon	Navajo	T39N R15E
Cliff Spring Valley	Navajo	T33N R20E

CLIFTON

Greenlee   T4S R30E   Elev. 3464'

Lt. John W. Bourke says that he was with an army scouting expedition c. 1869 which
found rich ore in the vicinity of the later Clifton. The men took pieces of ore to Tucson,
but not until c. 1872 did prospectors and miners from Silver City, New Mexico, explore
the area and establish copper mine locations. Among them were Charles M. Shannon,
Charles Lezinsky, and Lezinsky's brother. The location of the developing community in
the midst of towering cliffs probably led to its descriptive name, a "shortening of cliff
town." A. F. Banta in 1909 said that Henry Clifton with four other prospectors in 1864
discovered copper ore in this vicinity and because Clifton was the "leading spirit," the
place was named after him. There is no evidence to support Banta's assertion. (He was
not noted for being factual.)

Clifton remains subject to serious flooding. The worst occurred on December 4, 1906
during a thirty-hour rain which gave people forewarning of what might happen. Most of
them found refuge on higher ground, but eighteen drowned.
P.O. est. March 1875, Charles Lezinsky, p.m.; Wells Fargo 1885; incorp. March 11,
1909; Clifton made County Seat of new Greenlee County Nov. 8, 1910
Ref.: 49, pp. 98, 99; Riley; Scanlon; *Arizona Daily Star* (June 1, 1909), p. 2; 257, pp.
21, 115, 116, 117, 119, 124

CLIFTON HOT SPRINGS

Greenlee   T4S R30E

Years ago a bath house and swimming pool in Clifton were maintained so people could
bathe in Clifton Hot Springs, but this building is now gone. The springs are in back of the
old post office building.

CLINE

Gila   T5N R11E

This settlement was named for Christian Cline, a pioneer cattleman, who settled here c.
1876. A settlement gradually developed but is now gone, although many Cline
descendants live in the vicinity.
P.O. est. Sept. 12, 1891, Mrs. Ella E. Webb, p.m.; disc. Aug. 15, 1912
Ref.: 242; Woody

CLINE CREEK

Gila/Maricopa   T5–7N R10–wE

This is not the same location as that of Cottonwood Creek (T7N/R4E). See Cline, Gila

CLINTS WELL

Coconino   T14N R10E

This creek takes its name from that of Clint Wingfield, killed by the bandit Black Jack
Ketcham c. 1880. See Black Jack Canyon, Coconino Ref.: Hart

CLIP

La Paz   Elev. c. 450'

Clip was the Colorado River shipping point for the Clip Silver Mine (at T3S/R23W) five miles north of Silent. The mine had a ten-stamp mill at Clip, which was eight miles northwest of the mine in 1883. The mine was discovered in the early 1880s and operated by Anthony G. Hubbard and a man named Bowers until April 1887. In that time it produced more than a million dollars in silver, but from 1887 to 1925 it was relatively inactive. Later operations have not been very successful.

P.O. est. Feb. 6, 1884, Anthony G. Hubbard, p.m.; disc. Oct. 13, 1888
Ref.: 355, pp. 52, 56

CLOSTERMEYER LAKE

Coconino   T25N R6E   Elev. c. 5000'

This lake was named for William Clostermeyer, a cattleman who settled here and built a dam. Ref.: 18a

CLOVER: The presence of *clover* has led to that designation in several Arizona place names, examples of which follow:

Clover Camp	Graham	T1N R24E
Clover Canyon	Coconino	T13N R9E
Clover Canyon	Gila	T8N R12E
Clover Creek	Coconino	T13N R9E
Clover Creek	Gila	T10N R7E
Clover Creek	Graham	T1N R24E
Clover Lake	Coconino	T14N R9E
Clover Spring	Coconino	(1) T21N R2E (2) T13N R9E
Clover Spring	Gila	(1) T11N R8E (2) T8N R12E
Clover Wash	Gila	T9N R10E

CLUFF PEAK

Graham   T6S R21E

This peak was named because it is on the old Benjamin Cluff Ranch. Both Orson and Benjamin Cluff were in this vicinity by 1881. Ref.: *Graham County News* (Sept. 16, 1882), p. 2

CLUFF RANCH WILD LIFE AREA

Graham   T7S R24E

These four hundred and forty acres in the flood plain of Ash Creek are controlled by the Arizona Game and Fish Department for a fishery, recreational use, and a water fowl area. Ref.: 9, p. 1

CLUFF RESERVOIR

Graham   T7S R24E

There are two reservoirs by this name at the location given. See Cluff Peak, Graham

CLY BUTTE

Apache   T41N R21N   Elev. 5789'

Cly (d. 1934) was a Navajo leader now buried at the foot of the butte carrying his name. As Navajo custom requires a man's possessions to be destroyed when he dies, Cly's horse, sheep goats, and cattle were destroyed and his saddle buried with him.
Ref.: 191, pp. 117, 118

COAL MINE CANYON

Coconino   T31N R12E

At one time coal was actively mined in this canyon, hence its name. It is also sometimes referred to as Coal Canyon and as Coal Creek. The canyon is noted for its variegated coloring. Sands from this canyon are used by Navajo medicine men. See Ha Ho No Geh Canyon, Coconino Ref.: 71, p. 47; 331, p. 42

COALSON CANYON

Greenlee   T2S R32E   Elev. c. 5000'
Coalson Canyon is on the Coalson Ranch, abandoned by Nick Coalson c. 1930. He raised stock and broke wild horses. Ref.: Reilly; Simmons; Fritz

COBRE RIDGE   pro.: /kowbrey/
Spanish = "copper"

Santa Cruz   T23S R10E
Prior to 1890 copper claims were on this ridge, hence the name.
Ref.: 329, Gilbert Sykes, Letter (Aug. 1, 1941)

COCHISE   pro.: /kowčíys/

Cochise   T15S R24E   Elev. 4225'
The spelling proposed on the post office application for a mail stop at this railroad point was Cachise. The railroad station, established in 1887, made the headlines on September 9, 1889 when a train was held up here. The robbery was executed by Matt Burts and Billie Stiles, carrying out plans made by Burt Alvord, constable of Willcox, and by William Downing, a cattleman. A crook named "Three-fingered Jack" did not participate but informed on the others. They were captured. See also Cochise Butte, Coconino (Grand Canyon)
P.O. est. Aug. 1, 1896, Charles Raymond Sims; Wells Fargo 1903 Ref.: 242; 5, p. 439

COCHISE BUTTE   pro.: /kowčíys/

Coconino (Grand Canyon)   T33N R8E   Elev. 4225'
In 1931 the USGS suggested and approved this name to memorialize the Indian leader of the Chiricahua Apaches, Cochise. Cochise (d. June 8, 1874) gave no trouble to Americans until 1861 when, under a flag of truce and accompanied by other leaders, he visited Lt. George Bascom in Apache Pass. They wished to deny any part in the abduction of a white child. The young and inexperienced lieutenant lost his temper because the Indians refused to confess, and captured them. Attempting to escape, one was killed and four were caught, but Cochise disappeared with three bullets in his body. At once he began an unremitting campaign of vengeance for his companions, all three of whom had been hanged immediately. In 1871 Cochise was captured but escaped when he was ordered transferred to New Mexico. Two hundred of his band went with him. They did not capitulate until the Chiricahua Reservation was established in 1872. Ref.: 167, I, 317

COCHISE COUNTY   pro.: /kowčíys/
Cochise County, carved from Pima County (one of the four original counties in Arizona Territory), was created on February 1, 1881 and named for the famous Chiricahua Apache leader. Until 1929 Tombstone served as county seat, but in that year Bisbee took over and remains today the county seat. The county area is 4,003,840 acres, equivalent to Connecticut and Rhode Island combined. The history of this county is one of the most interesting in the state, inasmuch as it was not only the scene of Indian disorders, but also because of its remoteness from law and order, which made it a haven for outlaws. In addition, Tombstone from 1879 and for the next several years was the mining mecca as well as the most cultivated and cultured city in the entire west or southwest. Today Cochise County is a leader in mining and the raising of livestock and other agricultural pursuits.

COCHISE HEAD

Cochise   T16S R30E   Elev. 8109'
The name of this formation in the Chiricahua National Monument derives from its strong resemblance to an Indian profile, in which a large pine tree serves as an eyelash. The "profile" is more than a mile long. It is also known as San Simon Head.
Ref.: 71, II, 132

COCHISE MEMORIAL PARK

Cochise   T18S R23E   Elev. 7512'

Legend says that when Cochise died he was buried in Stronghold Canyon. On the night of his death in 1874 his followers ran their horses up and down the canyon to erase all traces of his grave. According to McClintock, however, following Cochise's death of malarial fever, his followers carried his body and placed it in a cave at this stronghold. McClintock also says that the only white man who knew where his body lay was his blood brother, the Indian agent Thomas Jeffords. Ref.: 5, p. 440; 224, p. 217

COCHISE PEAK

Cochise   T18S R23E   Elev. 6760'

This peak is the site of Cochise Memorial Park. Prior to the establishment of the Chiricahua Indian Reservation in 1872, this location was one of those used by the Chiricahua Apaches as a stronghold. This particular stronghold at Cochise Peak was near the center of the Chiricahua Indian Reservation. In this canyon Capt. Gerald Russell, Troop K, Third Cavalry, was watering horses when Cochise and his band attacked, killing Bob Whitney, his guide. Ref.: 49, p. 174; 18a

COCHISE STRONGHOLD

Cochise   T17S R23E

Although this location is referred to as though it were *the* specific stronghold for Cochise and his Chiricahua Apaches, as a matter of fact these Indians had several such locations to which they could retreat and find safety from pursuit by the United States Cavalry. See Dragoon Mountains, Cochise

COCHRAN

Pinal   T4S R12E   Elev. 1640'

This location according to Barnes was named for its first postmaster. However, on the "new post office" form in the National Archives the name of the postmaster is given as Henness. Cochran was the second postmaster. Nothing remains at this location today except a well preserved coke oven.

P.O. est. Nov. 5, 1904, Julian H. Henness, p.m.; disc. Jan. 15, 1915
Ref.: 242; 18a; Varney

COCKLEBUR WASH

Pinal

In 1913 this was a variant name for "Quitoa Wash," probably Quijotoa Wash. Ref.: 242

COXCOMBS

Coconino   T34N R4E   Elev. c. 6800'

These elongated sharp hills look like a coxcomb. In April 1964 the USGS changed this name from singular to plural form because actually this is a series of hills. Ref.: 329

COCONINO

Coconino   T30N R2E

This is the name of a railroad station on the branch line eight miles from the Grand Canyon.

COCONINO COUNTY   pro.: /kowkəniynow/

Hopi: *Ko'nino* (or) *kohonino* = "people to the west"

On February 19, 1891 Coconino County was carved from Yavapai County. The name refers to tribes of Indians such as the Walapai and Havasupai, who live in the vicinity of the Grand Canyon. The Hopi word has been spelled variously as follows: Cochineaus (Emory 1848), Cochnichnos (Bartlett 1854), Cojnino (Sitgreaves 1853, with a notation that a Havasupai Indian by that name served the expedition), Cominos (Brown, *Apache Country*, 1869), Cosninas (Garcés 1776). Files at the Museum of Northern Arizona state that the name derives from "Cohonina — Hopi word for Havasupai and Yavapai."

In 1887 William H. Ashurst of Flagstaff (cf. Ashurst Run, Coconino) called on the 14th Legislative Assembly to create "Frisco County," but he was defeated. A bill was then introduced in 1889 by Frank Rogers (cf. Rogers Lake, Coconino). It was passed but vetoed by the territorial governor, an act which the House overrode, but the Senate failed to concur. Sentiment favored creating a new county, however, and in 1891 Coconino County came into being, with its name having been suggested by Dan M. Riordan (cf. Riordan, Coconino). Coconino County contains great contrasts geographically, from the magnificent Grand Canyon and wooded San Francisco Peaks to the colorfully arid escarpment of the Painted Desert. With its 11,886,720 acres, the county is the largest in Arizona. The county seat is at Flagstaff. The county is noted for its agriculture, lumbering, and livestock raising. Ref.: 167, p. 538; MNA; 124, p. 60; Alfred L. Whiting, "Ethnobotany of the Hopi," Museum of Northern Arizona, *Bulletin* #15 (1939), p. 68

COCONINO NATIONAL FOREST
Coconino/Gila   T16N R7E
On July 2, 1908 Coconino National Forest was created from parts of Black Mesa (est. August 17, 1898), Tonto, and Grand Canyon Forest Reserves (est. February 20, 1893), plus all of the San Francisco Mountain Forest Reserve (est. August 17, 1898). The term "reserve" implied the withdrawal of resources from public use. This resulted in misunderstanding the purpose of the forestry program and the term was dropped with "National Forest" being substituted. Ref.: Bade; Keeney; 243, pp. 30, 34, 35

COCONINO PLATEAU
Coconino   T31N R5W
In 1932 the USGS eliminated the name Colorado Plateau in favor of Coconino Plateau. Wheeler named the Colorado Plateau in 1868. That name continued to be used by Dutton (1882), but according to Barnes in 1892 C. Hart Merriam used the name Coconino Plateau for the same area. A general name for it, long in use, was the Arizona Plateau or Plateau of Arizona. See also Mogollon Plateau, Coconino/Navajo
Ref.: 89, pp. 169, 170; 100, p. 14; 345, I, 12, 23; 18a

COCONINO POINT
Coconino   T29N R8E   Elev. 6600'
The Navajo name for this location is *Dzit Łibáii* (= "gray mountain"), which accounts for its also being known to white Americans as Gray Mountain. Why or when the name changed to Coconino Point is not known to the writer. Ref.: 331, p. 42

COCONINO RIM
Coconino (Grand Canyon)   T30N R4E
The name describes the fact that this is on the canyon rim at the north edge of the Coconino Plateau.

COCONINO WASH
Coconino   T30N R1E
This wash is on the Coconino Plateau, hence the name.

COCOPAH INDIAN RESERVATION   pro.: /kówkopa/
Yuma/California   T9S R24W
This Indian reservation was created on March 3, 1865. It has 240,640 acres. The Cocopah Indians have lived near the mouth of the Colorado River since at least 1600 and later extended into the mountains of Baja California. Although Fr. Francisco Garcés in 1775 estimated there were three thousand Cocopahs, there are now fewer than five hundred in the valley of the Colorado River. Ref.: 167, p. 319; 5, p. 390

COCOPAH POINT
Coconino (Grand Canyon)   T31N R1E   Elev. c. 5800'
This is one of the locations at the Grand Canyon named for Arizona Indian tribes. See Cocopah Indian Reservation, Yuma

COFFEE CREEK
Yavapai   T17N R4E
It is possible that this name is the result of a corruption of the name Coffer and that it was named for John H. Coffer (b. 1819, Illinois), who may have lived here c. 1880.
Ref.: 63; 18a; Museum of Northern Arizona

COFFEE POT ROCK

Yavapai

This location northwest of Soldier Pass Road in Sedona, Oak Creek Canyon, is descriptively named because it is shaped like an old-fashioned coffee pot.

COGSWELL BUTTE

Coconino (Grand Canyon)   T35N R2W   Elev. 4537′

The USGS approved this name in 1965 to honor Raymond Austin Cogswell (1873-1964), a photographer with the Julius F. Stone boat expedition through the canyon in 1909. Ref.: 329

COHATE

Pinal

Hodge says that Fr. Sedelmayr visited this Maricopa location in 1744. See Kohatk, Pinal Ref.: 167, p. 321

COHENOUR SPRING

Mohave   T26N R14W

Jacob Cohenour was the postmaster at Peach Springs (T25N/R11W) in 1887. See Coyote Spring, Mohave

COLCORD CANYON   pro.: /kálkerd/

Coconino   T20N R4E

In 1886 Col. William C. (Bill) Colcord and his brother Harvey with their mother settled near Potato Butte, moving up under the Mogollon Rim c. 1887. They arrived in Gila County and owned a ranch on the Chamberlain Trail. Later they established a ranch in what is now Colcord Canyon. The Colcord Canyon in Coconino was the location of their first ranch. Ref.: Woody; Mrs. William C. Colcord

COLCORD MOUNTAIN

Gila   T10N R14E   Elev. 7513′

The Forestry Service extended the Colcord name to this mountain. See Colcord Canyon, Coconino

COLCORD SPRING

Coconino   T20N R4E

This is the location of Col. William C. Colcord's second ranch under the Mogollon Rim. See Colcord Canyon, Coconino Ref.: *Hoofs and Horns* (July 1886); Woody

COLD: Noticeably cool temperature (usually that of water) has led to the use of the word *cold* in certain place names, examples of which follow:

Cold Creek	Greenlee	T5S R30E	
This location is also known as Rustlers Canyon.			
Cold Spring	Apache	T8N R25E	
Cold Spring	Gila	T11N R11E	
Cold Spring	Graham	(1) T2S R26E	(2) T5S R20E
Cold Spring	Mohave	T34N R9W	
This location is also known as Cole Spring.			
Cold Spring	Yavapai	T15N R9W	
Cold Spring Canyon	Gila	T6N R14E	
Cold Spring Canyon	Graham	T6S R21E	
Cold Spring Mountain	Greenlee	T4S R31E	Elev. 7054′
Cold Springs	Coconino		
See Big Cove Canyon, Coconino			
Cold Springs	Graham	T5S R24E	

Cold Springs	Yavapai	T13N R3W
Cold Spring Wash	Apache	T1N R6W
Cold Spring Wash	Mohave	T31N R9W
Coldwater	Maricopa	
See Avondale, Maricopa		
Coldwater Creek	Yavapai	T11N R5E
Cold Water Spring	Greenlee	T4S R31E
Coldwater Spring	Maricopa	T4N R9E
Coldwater Spring	Yavapai	(1) T11N R5E (2) T16N R6W

COLEDON

Maricopa   T5S R4W

Barnes says that this location on the S.P.R.R. in 1909 was called Cole, for a railroad engineer. In 1921 the map carries it as Coledon, "a better word to telegraph." After 1921 it disappears from GLO maps. Ref.: 18a

COLEMAN CREEK

Apache/Greenlee   T5N R30E

This location takes its name from that of Evans P. Coleman (b. Feb. 12, 1874, Pioche, Nevada; d. Dec. 15, 1954), whose family moved to Alpine in 1880. He became a cowboy and trail cook. In 1909 he completed his work as a missionary for the Mormons in the southern states. His family had moved to Thatcher in 1899 and he joined them there. Ref.: AHS, Coleman Collection, Box 1

COLEMAN LAKE

Coconino   T21N R2E

The original name of this location was the McCollum Ranch, corrupted to Collins Ranch on some maps. The name "Collins" was also a corruption inasmuch as the early ranch belonged first to John Cundy. The ranch then belonged to Nehemiah McCollum, who settled there c. 1878. Another misspelling is McCullum Ranch. His neighbor was T. A. ("Dad") Coleman, who in 1875 left Visalia, California, with thousands of sheep. Despite very heavy losses en route, he still had four thousand left when he arrived and settled near McCollum on May 12, 1876. He built a dam to impound water and Coleman Lake resulted. Ref.: Fuchs, Letter (April 30, 1956); Benham; Mark Smith; 124, pp. 50 (Note 83), 53

COLFRED   pro.: /kalfréd/

Yuma   T8S R16W   Elev. 328'

"Col." Fred Crocker was treasurer of the S.P.R.R. in 1881 and this railroad station was named for him. Ref.: 18a

COLLEGE PEAK

Cochise   T23S R29E   Elev. 6385'

Until 1892 the local name for this location was The Nipples, descriptive of the appearance of these two peaks. The name was first used apparently by cavalry units camped at White Springs as late as 1880. On GLO 1883 it appears on maps for the first time under the name College Peak. One peak, logically enough, is called North College Peak, and the other, South College Peak. Another name is Saddle Mountain, descriptive of the area between the two peaks, which looks like a saddle. Ref.: Riggs; Macia

COLONNADE, THE

Coconino (Grand Canyon)   T32N R3E   Elev. 7296'

The Colonnade includes the five terraces named for early Spanish explorers: Marcos, de Vaca, Tovar, Alarçon, and Garcés. Ref.: 178, p. 82

COLORADO, CAMP

La Paz
                          T8N R20W

Camp Colorado was established on November 24, 1868 and abandoned in 1871. It is to be differentiated from the Camp Colorado established by Col. William Hoffman (see Mohave Fort, Mohave). The Department of Arizona Map Sheet No. 3 (1875) names this place as Old Camp Colorado, indicating it had by then been abandoned as a sub-post for Fort Yuma. Ref.: 159, p. 490; 224, p. 152; 145, p. 128

COLORADO, CERRO

Pima   T20S R10E   Elev. 4202'

Mexicans use the name *cerro* to describe a conical red hill. This one was the site of the Heintzelman Mine. In 1854 Charles Debrille Poston and Herman Ehrenberg visited this territory to investigate mining possibilities and spent some time near Tubac where they found abandoned mines worth reworking. Poston in 1855 went east to raise financing and by March 1856 had organized the Sonora Exploring and Mining Company. It later bought the old Arivaca Ranch (see Arivaca, Pima). Included in their purchases was the Cerro Colorado Mine. The Heintzelman Mine, named for Samuel P. Heintzelman, president of the company, was the most famous of the twenty-nine mines of the Cerro Colorado Mining District. Its superintendent was John Poston, Charles' brother. After Federal troops withdrew from the area in the summer of 1861, Apache attacks forced the owners to abandon their holdings. Charles left his brother in charge, but John executed the foreman for stealing bullion. The Mexican miners then stole all they could handle — about $70,000. worth. Mexican outlaws came to steal and killed John with two of the employees. The silver cache has never been found. By 1864 the buildings were in ruins, but following the Civil War miners began returning and by 1870, fifty-eight people were living at Cerro Colorado.

P.O. est. April 17, 1879, William S. Reed, p.m.; disc. (?); reest. Aug. 21, 1906, David J. Burrow, p.m.; disc. April 15, 1911 Ref.: 242; 269, p. 17; 163, pp. 221, 222; 56, pp. 264, 265, 267, 270; 206, p. 194; Varney

COLORADO CITY

Mohave   T42N R6W   Elev. 4980'

This Mormon community had its beginnings in 1909 when "Old Man" Colvin joined the Lauritzen family already in the area. The Mormon polygamous colony was on Short Creek, so named because it is a short creek, but the colony was called Millennial City at the outset because it was viewed as "First City of the Millenium," in a paper called *Truth*, which advocated plural marriage. When the Federal Government attempted to enforce laws against polygamy, several Lee's Ferry polygamists moved to Short Creek, the name the colony had by the time the post office was established in 1913. Because of notoriety following a raid by Arizona state forces which netted two hundred women and children (which the state had to let go as the case fizzled), the community elected to change its name to Colorado City in 1958.

P.O. est. as Short Creek, July 15, 1913, J. W. Lauritzen, p.m.; name changed to Colorado City, Dec. 31, 1960 Ref.: 242; *Cincinnati Enquirer* (July 27, 1975), p. 6

COLORADO RIVER   pro.: /kalorádow/ or /kowlorǽdow/ or /kalerédow/

Spanish = "red"

Coconino	T29N R10W	La Paz	T9N R24W
Mohave	T33N R4W	Yuma	T5S R20W

This great river traverses Arizona from the Utah boundary in the north central part of the state, then south and west through the Grand Canyon, thence south, forming the western boundary of Arizona, separating it from California. Because various Indian tribes had their names for it, it seems well to place such names first in this entry inasmuch as the Indians were first in this territory. It should be borne in mind that the following spellings are those given by white men who first encountered them. The Yuma Indians who lived near its mouth called it the *Javil* or *Hahweel*; the Coco-Maricopas, who formerly lived along this river, called it the *Gritetho* or "Great River." The Havasupai name was *Hakatai*. (These Indians of course live along a side canyon of the Grand Canyon itself). Farther east and on the north side of the canyon live the Piute Indians, whose name for this stream was *Pah-gaiv*, meaning "Mighty River". The Piutes also had their name for the part of the river crossing through the Grand Canyon: *Pa-ha-weap* ("water down deep in the earth"). In 1882 the Hopi name (untranslated) was cited as being *Pi-sish-bai-yu*. Fr. Sedelmayr reported that the Pima Indians called it *Buqui Aquimuri*, meaning "Red River." The Navajo tribe also had its name for the Colorado River: *Pocket-To* ("Red River").

The first white man known to have seen the mouth of the Colorado River was a member of Alarçon's supply ship group for the Coronado Expedition in 1540. He was Francisco de Ulloa. Not he, but Capt. Fernando Alarçon first applied a Spanish name to this stream: *El Rio de Buena Guia* (= "The River of Good Guidance"), representing a portion of the motto on the coat of arms of the Viceroy of Mexico, Mendoza. The river* did not give him very good guidance, however, as evidenced by the fact that the Colorado River lay many, many miles west of the route taken by the Coronado Expedition. In 1541 Capt. Melchior Diaz came upon this river while travelling overland. He was much taken by the fact that the Indians along the banks kept themselves warm by holding fire brands close to their abdomens. He therefore called the stream *Rio del Tizon* (= "Firebrand River"). Both names were lost in the ensuing years when no white man came near this stream. The next white to do so was very far from its mouth. In 1604 Juan de Oñate saw the Colorado River from the juncture with the present Bill Williams River and named it the *Rio Grande de Buena Esperanza* (= "The Great River of Good Hope"). The Indians were still observing the same warming custom when Fr. Eusebio Kino came along and saw them near its mouth. Kino gave it still another name, *Rio de los Martires* (= "River of the Martyrs"). Kino's lieutenant Juan Mateo Manje learned from the Indians that the river must be enormous and thereafter he called it the "True Rio del Norte of the Ancients ... the fertile Colorado River." In 1716 Velarde said, "The name of the Rio Grande del Corral (the Colorado River) is given to the Colorado at its mouth ... this name may either be due to the color of its sand or it may be that coral is found on its shores...." Every newcomer saw fit to assume usually that he was the first to see this great stream and also to have the privilege of naming it, for new names continued to be applied. The next of record was that given by Fr. Hernando Escalante, who called it *Rio Del Cosnina* (for local Indians then called Cosninos and later Coconinos. They were the forerunners of today's Havasupai people.) Escalante also appears to have referred to it in his correspondence as the River of Mystery. Another name of uncertain origin is *El Rio de los Balsas*, a name reflecting the fact that the Indians used a kind of floating basket to push goods and at a later date, emigrants across the waters from one bank to another. The list of new names had still not come to an end when James Ohio Pattie in the 1830s came upon it and trapper-wise called it quite bluntly the Red River. Some who were exploring its northern stretches called it the Grand River. On an 1846 map, possibly because of developments in California, it is called Rio Colorado of California. On the Parke map of 1851 it is termed *Rio Colorado del Poniente* (*Poniente* = "west"). It was also called *Rio Colorado del Oriente* elsewhere. Maj. John Wesley Powell and his group in 1869 called it the Colorado River of the West. To Fr. Francisco Garcés must be given the credit for calling it in 1776 the Rio Colorado, today's Colorado River. Ref.: 15, pp. 35, 39, 155, 182, 402, 574; 89, pp. 28, 29, 82, 272, 273; 178, p. 230; 259, p. 23; 146, p. 12; 347, I, 205; 256, p. 119; 45, p. 415; 287, p. 28; 77, p. 144 (Note 58), 431, 431 (Note 19); 43, II, 244; Velarde *ms.* (Huntington Library), p. 104; 46, pp. 272; 273; 313a

COLORADO RIVER INDIAN RESERVATION

La Paz   T8N R19W   Elev. c. 600'

The first Indian superintendent for Arizona Territory was Charles Debrille Poston (see Poston Butte, Pinal), who in 1864 selected land on the Colorado River bottom lands to be set aside as an Indian Reservation. It was established on March 3, 1865 for Yavapai, Hualapai, and Colorado River tribes under the phrase "Indians of said river (Colorado) and its tributaries."

By curious extension of the intent of the phrase "and its tributaries" it has been possible to resettle Navajo and Hopi Indians on the Colorado River Reservation since waters from both the Hopi and the Navajo reservations drain into the Colorado River. The Colorado River Tribal Council on February 3, 1945 authorized such re-settlement and on September 1, sixteen Hopi families arrived. Many hundreds have now been resettled in this region. The reservation has 265,858 acres with headquarters at Parker. Ref.: 167, II, 374; 361, p. 394

COLOSSAL CAVE

Pima   T16S R27E   Elev. c. 4200'

In 1879 a man named Ross discovered this cave, which is so large that it has never been fully explored. Evidence reveals that ancient Indians used the cave. Now a tourist attraction, Colossal Cave earned notoriety in 1884 when men who had robbed an S.P.R.R. train holed up in it. The posse believed they had cornered the men and sat awaiting their emergence. They escaped through a hole on the other side of the hill. In 1896 the cave was called Mountain Springs Cave, named for the adjacent Mountain Springs Ranch. Ref.: *Arizona Enterprise* (June 14, 1896), p. 1

COLTER

Apache   T7N R29E   Elev. c. 8000'
James G. H. Colter (b. 1844, Nova Scotia) left Wisconsin in 1871, trailing a reaper overland from Topeka at the end of the railroad. He settled at what is now Colter Creek. On May 15, 1913 his son Fred T. Colter applied for a post office for the ranch headquarters. In 1917 he sold this property plus other Colter property, four thousand cattle, and many horses. Colter Butte at the Grand Canyon is named for Sen. Fred Colter.
P.O. est. Sept. 5, 1913, Duge Colter, p.m.; disc. Sept. 15, 1922
Ref.: *Arizona Cattleman* (March 10, 1917), p. 6; 225, p. 185; 329; 242

COLTON CRATER

Coconino   T2N R7E   Elev. 6232'
The USGS named this crater for Harold S. Colton (d. 1970), founder of the Museum of Northern Arizona and author of many papers on the San Francisco Mountain volcanic field. This name replaces the former name Crater 160. Ref.: 329

COLUMBIA

Yavapai   T8N R1W   Elev. c. 3500'
Columbia was the name of the post office serving the Columbia Mine here. It was sometimes referred to as Humbug because it was situated on that creek. Miners called it "Humbug" because rumors about abundant gold were simply humbug.
P.O. est. Sept. 25, 1894, M. Joseph Nolan, p.m.; disc. July 31, 1915
Ref.: 242; Gardner; 18a; Varney

COLUMBIA COPPER CAMP

Santa Cruz   T23S R24E
The Columbia Copper Mine was among the group active in the mid-1880s in the Helvetia District. See Helvetia, Pima

COLUMBINE

Graham   T8S R24E   Elev. c. 9000'
Columbine flowers in the meadows led to this name for a forest ranger station.
Ref.: Jennings

COLUMBINE FALLS

Mohave (Lake Mead)   T31N R16W
Edward Schenk of the Bureau of Mines suggested this name on January 14, 1945 because of the luxuriant growth of "yellow columbine near the falls." The USGS accepted it in May 1948. The name replaced the local name of Emery Falls, so called by Emery Kolb for himself. Ref.: 329

COLUMBINE: The presence of *columbine* accounts for the following names:

Columbine Spring	Maricopa	T7N R5E
Columbine Spring	Navajo	T6N R23E
Columbine Spring	Yavapai	T16N R2E

COLUMBUS POINT

Coconino (Grand Canyon)   T31N R1E
George Wharton James noted the name of this point on the Boucher Trail. It is among others named for explorers. Ref.: 178, p. 46

COMA-A
Navajo   T20N R18E
It is probable that these springs at one time served a large population, as evidenced by prehistoric ruins. In the 1880s Hopi Indians at the insistence of their Indian agent said they would settle at this spring to prevent Navajo Indians from taking over the Hopi reservation. In retaliation, Navajos burned Hopi homes, ruins of which can still be seen. The name Komor Springs is a corruption. Gregory says they were sometimes called Kaibito (Springs). Ref.: Colton; 141, pp. 137, 153, 191

COMANCHE POINT pro.: /kəmǽnčiy/ or /komǽnčiy/
Coconino (Grand Canyon)   T31N R5E   Elev. 6831'
The first name for this location was Bissel Point, named by George Wharton James for an official of the A.T. & S.F.R.R. James also calls it Comanche Point. The USGS changed the name officially from Bissel Point in 1927. Ref.: 178, p. 70; 329

COMB RIDGE
Apache/Navajo   T40N R22E   Elev. c. 6000'
The serrated red peaks of this ridge make it resemble a coxcomb.
Ref.: 141, pp. 37, 38; 129, p. 15

COMET PEAK
Pinal   T2S R10E   Elev. 2691'
This peak took its name from that of the Comet Mine, in operation prior to 1890.
Ref.: 18a

COMMERCE
Apache   In Round Valley Area   Elev. c. 6300'
William B. Gardner applied for a post office to be called Commerce but failed to get it because: (1) He could not give a precise location except "upper end of Round Valley" and (2) he could not post bond.
P.O. est. March 19, 1887, William B. Gardner, p.m.; disc. April 18, 1887
Ref.: Wiltbank; 158, p. 10

COMMISSION
Santa Cruz   1 mi. S.E. of Mowry Mine   Elev. c. 4000'
F. Biertu, a French mining engineer, in 1864 noted fifteen houses at a village called Commission on Commission Creek. It was the smelter and center for workers at the old Mowry Mine about a mile away. The Mowry settlement had two locations, the other being at Mowry Wash. Ref.: Hayes; 236, pp. 74, 75

COMOBABI pro.: /còwmwáhi/
Papago: *kom* = "hackberry tree"; *vaxia* = "well"
Pima   T16S R5E   Elev. 3200'
This is one of the oldest of the Papago villages in the Comobabi Mountains. The name as rendered is a corruption of the Papago name. This name has also been rendered Comobave and Comohuabi. Associated names include Comobabi Mountains (also spelled Carobabi on Sykes 1908, and Comovajca Mountains on Irrigation Service map 1915); Pass (T15S/R5E), Wash, and North Comobabi Mountains (T15S/R5E, Elev. 4788') Ref.: 58; 57, pp. 45, 368; 262, p. 12

CON CANYON
Gila   T1–2N R15–16E
Con Cowley ran cattle in this canyon in the early 1900s, hence the name.
Ref.: Devore; Woody

CONCHO pro.: /kánčo/
Spanish = "shell"
Apache   T12N R26E   Elev. 5931'
The name derives from the fact that this locale is in a shell-like basin. The first residents, Mexicans, settled here in the late 1860s. Mormons arrived in 1869, including William J. Flake and Bateman H. Wilhelm, who had bought land from J. F. Chaves. In 1880 about

a mile to the west a Mormon ward was organized and named Erastus for Erastus Snow, later one of the twelve apostles of the Church of Jesus Christ of Latter-Day Saints. Snow supervised organizing the ward. The Mexican village continued to retain the name of Concho. In 1890 the Mormon settlement adopted the same name.

Associated names include the following: Concho Creek (T13N/R26); Concho Flat (T13N/R22E); Concho Flat Wash (T13N/R22E); Concho Lake; Concho Spring (T12N/R26E); Concho Spring Knoll (12N/R26E, Elev. 6717').

P.O. est. as Erastus, May 28, 1881, Sixtus E. Johnson, p.m.; name changed to Concho, March 21, 1890, Leandro Ortega, p.m. Ref.: *Weekly Arizona Miner* (July 23, 1879), p. 3; 224, p. 183; Wiltbank; Stemmer

CONCHO LAKE WILD LIFE AREA
Apache   T12N R26E
This wild life area has two hundred and nine acres, of which forty are the lake. See Concho, Apache Ref.: 9, p. 2

CONE BUTTE
Gila   T4N R21E
This cone-shape location is also known as Cone Mountain, and was so called by Lt. Michler. It also appears on a military map of 1883 as Cone Peak.
Ref.: 242; Davis; 105, p. 105

CONE WASH
Mohave   T18W R15W
The current name is Bull Canyon.

CONFUCIUS TEMPLE
Coconino (Grand Canyon)   T32N R2E   Elev. 7128'
This formation — like others at Grand Canyon — has a fancied resemblance to a temple associated with originators and leaders of world religions. Ref.: 178, p. 46

CONGRESS
Yavapai   T10N R6W   Elev. 3040'
This location, now frequently called Old Congress, was named by Dennis May (d. Oct. 13, 1907), who located and named the Congress Mine in 1883. The mining community housed about four hundred mine employees in an upper and lower town. Later Diamond Jim Reynolds (d. March 1891) owned the mine. As a result of mining activity here, Congress Junction developed on the railroad. When Congress was discontinued as a post office, its name was then moved to Congress Junction or New Congress, which is today a cattle shipping point.

P.O. est. as Congress, Jan. 19, 1889, Charles A. Randall, p.m.; disc. Aug. 31, 1938; P.O. est. at Congress Junction, March 23, 1906, Oliver L. Geer, p.m.; name changed to Congress, Nov. 1, 1938; Wells Fargo (at Congress Junction) 1904
Ref.: *Arizona Journal Miner* (Oct. 12, 1897), p. 1; *Arizona Sentinel* (Oct. 16, 1907), p. 2; Hayden; 242

CONLEY POINTS
Gila   T11N R9E   Elev. 5564'
In the early 1880s the Conley family settled near these small peaks. This may have been the family of James Conley (b. 1836, Ireland). On the other hand, John Conley was in the Safford Valley by 1874. The name "Indian Delia's Place" came from the fact that an Indian woman filed a homestead claim on this same flat. Ref.: 61; 18a; AHS

CONNEL GULCH
Yavapai   T16N R7W
George Connell arrived in this area in 1873 and established a cattle ranch which used the Pitchfork brand. Ref.: Rosenberger; 18a

CONNOR CANYON
Gila   T5N R13E
A rancher named Connor had holdings in this canyon. See Rose Creek, Gila

CONQUISTADOR ISLE

Coconino (Grand Canyon)   T33N R2W   Elev. c. 3000'

This section of the Inner Gorge traverses a chasm named to honor explorers of the South Rim, including Lt. Joseph Christmas Ives, Capt. George M. Wheeler, Lt. Edward Fitzgerald Beale, Dr. A. H. Thompson, and Dr. John Newberry, according to James. The name suggests rather that it was named to commemorate Spanish explorers.
Ref.: 178, p. 83; 244 (June 20, 1939)

CONSTELLATION

Yavapai   T8–9N R3W   Elev. 4000'

This post office for the Constellation Mining Company was the location of the Monte Cristo Mine, named for the island in the *Count of Monte Cristo* where Edmond Dantes found riches.
P.O. est. Feb. 26, 1901, William F. Roberts, p.m.; disc. Jan. 31, 1939
Ref.: 242; Gardner; Varney

CONTENTION

Cochise   T19S R21E   Elev. 3792'

Hank Williams, one among thousands of prospectors who flocked to Tombstone in 1879, camped close to Ed Schieffelin. While tracing a loose mule, Williams noticed that the halter chains had scraped metallic ore and he immediately staked a claim. Dirk Gird, Schieffelin's partner, hotly contested the claim. As a result of the argument, when Gird and Schieffelin bought out Williams, their mine was called the Contention. The nearest available water was on the San Pedro River and there Contention City was established. When water flooding the mines made them unworkable, Contention went out of existence.
P.O. est. April 5, 1880, John McDermott, p.m.; disc. Nov. 26, 1888; Wells Fargo 1885
Ref.: 116, p. 545; 60, pp. 20, 21; 206, pp. 208, 209; Larriau

CONTINENTAL

Pima   T18S R13E   Elev. 2860'

This station on the railroad was named for the Continental Rubber Company, which in 1914 bought part of the old Canoa Land Grant. For many years the company successfully grew guayule (which produces rubber). In 1949 the Continental Company sold out to the Farmers Investment Company. By 1980 the area was gradually shifting to being residential rather than agricultural.
P.O. est. Jan. 12, 1916, Stanley F. Morris, p.m.; disc. Feb. 5, 1929
Ref.: 242; Warren Culbertson

CONTINENTAL MOUNTAIN

Maricopa   T6N R4E   Elev. 4521'

The mountain borrows its name from that of the Continental Mine, discovered by Charles Fleming in the 1870s. His cabin was at Fleming Spring.

CONTINENTAL SPRING

Gila   T1N R13E

This spring was named for the mine which is in the same location. Ref.: Woody

CONTRACT CANYON

Gila   T11N R9E

This canyon is named because it contains the Contract Mine claim. The same name is applied to Contract Spring. Ref.: Pieper

CONTZEN PASS

Pima   T13S R12E   Elev. 2489'

This pass was named for Fritz Contzen (b. Feb. 27, 1831, Germany; d. May 2, 1909), who arrived in the United States with his brother Julius in 1848. After service with the Boundary Survey Commission in 1854, Contzen settled and began ranching at Punta del Agua. He later was a trader with the Papago Indians and a partner in mining ventures.
Ref.: AHS, Cosulich Collection, Box 8; *Arizona Star* (Nov. 24, 1940); 224, III

CONWAY SEEP

Gila   T8N R12E

E. C. Conway and his family settled in this vicinity, hence the name. Conway Spring is here. Ref.: Woody

COOLEY MOUNTAIN

Navajo   T8N R23E   Elev. 7727'

Corydon E. Cooley (d. March 18, 1917), a scout at Camp Apache in 1872, had a ranch which offered accommodations to travelers (see McNary, Apache). This mountain is named for Cooley. Ref.: 49, p. 178

COOLIDGE

Pinal   T5S R8E   Elev. 1430'

Coolidge came into existence when Coolidge Dam was constructed, that fact making water available for irrigation. Both it and the dam were named for President Calvin Coolidge. The name was suggested by Richard J. Jones because President Coolidge's signature in 1924 had made the dam possible.
P.O. est. Jan. 11, 1926, Mrs. Dora H. Nutt, p.m. Ref.: 242; 185, pp. 52, 53

COOLIDGE DAM

Pinal/Gila   T3S R18E   Elev. c. 2400'

Coolidge Dam was when constructed the largest egg-shape multiple-dome dam ever built. The top is two hundred and fifty feet above bedrock. To overcome objections by Apache Indians to disinterment of the Apache graveyard which the dam waters would cover, a concrete slap was laid over the principal burying ground.

On March 4, 1930 the dam was dedicated and named for President Calvin Coolidge. Among the guests was Will Rogers. The then-impounded waters were sufficient only to cause a luxuriant grass carpet. Rogers said, "If this was my lake, I'd mow it." Eventually the impounded waters created the present San Carlos Lake.
P.O. est. July 26, 1927, Robert L. Rupkey, p.m.; disc. Jan. 31, 1956
Ref.: 242; 5, p. 147

COON: The abbreviation for *raccoon* ("coon") occurs in several place names, indicating either the presence of or an incident concerning a raccoon. Unless otherwise noted, such instances are listed below:

Coon Butte	Gila	T5N R14E	
See Coon Creek, Gila			
Coon Canyon	Pima		
See Siovi Shuatak, Pima			
Coon Crater	Coconino		
See Meteor Crater, Coconino			
Coon Creek	Apache	(1) T8N R28E	(2) T16N R24E
Coon Creek	Gila	T5N R14E	

King S. Woolsey in 1864 called this Sycamore Creek. Lt. John G. Bourke called it Raccoon in reporting a brush settlers had with Apaches near a prehistoric ruin on the creek banks.
Ref.: Woody; 224, p. 222; 49, p. 186

Coon Creek	Mohave	T40N R16W	
Coon Mountain	Apache	T19N R25E	Elev. 8009'
Coon Mountain	Coconino	T19N R13E	
See Meteor Crater, Coconino			
Coon Spring	Apache	T8N R26E	
Coon Spring	Gila	T1N R13E	
See Coon Creek, Gila			

COOPER FORKS

Gila   T6N R15E

These forks are named for Andy Cooper, who had a ranch here in the 1880s.
Ref.: Woody

COOPER POCKETS

Mohave

Barnes says that these were water holes "at southern edge of Hurricane Ledge about
thirty miles northwest of Mount Trumbull." Cooper was a sheepman (1862-74).

COOPER RIDGE

Coconino   T39N R2E   Elev. 7827'

This ridge, known as Cooper Corral Ridge until the name was changed by the USGS in
April 1960, was named for one of the first settlers in this vicinity. Ref.: 329

COPE BUTTE

Coconino (Grand Canyon)   T31N R2E   Elev. 4538'

In the 1870s a noted paleontologist, Edward Drinker Cope (1840-1897), investigated
cretaceous and tertiary strata of the West. This butte is named to commemorate his
work. Cope Plateau is also here.

COPPER BASIN

Yavapai   T13N R3W

By 1864 copper mining claims had already been located in this basin, a fact mentioned
by Charles C. Genung, who here passed the grave of one Mellen, a partner with a man
named Leigh. Genung was following the Copper Basin Trail where a year later (1865)
Indians would shoot the old scout Pauline Weaver (d. 1866) (see Weaver, Yavapai).
He survived. The post office called Copper Basin served miners in the area. Copper
Basin (No. 2) is at T9N/R1W. The name is shared by the following: Copper Basin Red
Spring (T13N/R3W); Copper Basin Spring (T9N/R1W); Copper Basin Trail; Copper
Basin Wash (T13N/R4W).
P.O. est. Aug. 4, 1888, Duncan M. Martin, p.m. Office not confirmed, so disc. Jan. 18,
1890; reest. July 28, 1891, Charles O'Malley, p.m.; disc. May 3, 1893
Ref.: 107, III, 258, 259

COPPER BOTTOM PASS

La Paz   T3N R20W

This pass contains the Copper Bottom Mine, hence its name.

COPPER: The occurrence of *copper* ores throughout Arizona has led to the use of the
term in place names. Examples follow:

Copper Butte	Pima	T12S R8E	Elev. 3240'
Copper Butte	Pinal	T3S R13E	Elev. 3269'
Copper Butte Mine	Pinal	T3S R13E	
Copper Camp Creek	Maricopa	T7N R7E	
Copper Canyon	Cochise	T24S R20E	
Copper Canyon	Coconino (Grand Canyon)	T33N R1W	

A copper mine in this canyon has a tunnel about one hundred and twenty feet deep. Ref.: 329

Copper Canyon	Navajo	(1) East Fork: T41N R18E	
		(2) West Fork: T41N R18W	
Copper Canyon	Pima	T12S R7W	
Copper Canyon	Pinal	T3S R13E	
Copper Canyon	Santa Cruz	T20S R14E	
Copper Canyon	Yavapai	T13N R4E	

Copper Center   Cochise

A post office provided service for employees at a smelter here.
P.O. est. Nov. 14, 1901, Ringwald Blix, p.m.; disc. Ref.: 242; Larriau

Copper City   Gila   T1N R15E

This was the camp of the Copper City Mine. Ref.: Woody

Copper Creek   Graham   T8S R19E

Copper Creek   Mohave   T17N R16W

See also MacKenzie Creek, Mohave

Copper Creek   Pinal   T10S R13E

In 1863 the Yellow Bird claim was located here. It produced silver, but underlying veins were copper ores. The mines were dormant from 1917 through 1933 when the Arizona Molybdenum Corporation bought the claims.
P.O. est. Oct. 8, 1907, Belle E. Sibley, p.m.; disc. Aug. 31, 1942 Ref.: AHS, Mammoth File; 242

Copper Creek   Yavapai   (1) T13N R3W   (2) T15N R9W

See Bagdad, Yavapai   (3) T10N R4E

Copper Creek Mesa   Yavapai   T15N R9W

Copper Glance Mine   Cochise   T23S R19E

This claim, located in June 1895, was owned by Fred Snyder and Charles N. Shibell.

Copper Gulf   Cochise   T23S R19E

This claim, located in June 1895, was owned by Fred Snyder and Charles N. Shibell.

Copper Gulf   Gila   T1N R15E

COPPER HILL

Gila   T1N R15E

Not only is this the name of a hill, but it was used also for the mining camp of the Iron Cap, Arizona Commercial, Superior, and Boston Mines. The gulch on this hill was the site of the road leading to the camp, as well as the place where many early mining strikes occurred. The community was on the south side of the hill. Another called Copper City was on the north side of Black Peak in Big Johney Gulch.
P.O. est. July 3, 1907, Ruth Hayden, p.m.; disc. Feb. 15, 1933 Ref.: 242; Woody

Copper Hill Wash   Pinal   T10S R15E

Copper King Canyon   Cochise   T23S R24E

Copper King Hill   Cochise   T23S R24E   Elev. 5757'

The Copper King Mine was here, hence the name. It was owned by the New England Copper Company. Ref.: Simmons

Copper King Mountain   Greenlee   T3S R29E   Elev. 6826'

COPPER MINE

Navajo

Van Valkenburgh says that this location is "twenty-five miles north of the Gap in the sandy juniper-covered Kaibito Plateau" and that there was a trading post here as well as a copper mine owned by the Coconino Copper & Chemical Company. The ore had been located by Thomas Varker Keam (see Keam's Canyon, Navajo) and his associates in the 1880s. Ref.: 331, p. 44

Copper Mountain   Gila   T7N R12E   Elev. 6676'

Copper Mountain   Greenlee   T4S R29E   Elev. 5244'

This is the site of Morenci. The copper has long since been mined out. Ref.: Simmons

Copper Mountain   Santa Cruz   T22S R17E   Elev. 5200'

Copper Mountain   Yavapai   T12N R2E   Elev. 5013'

Copper Mountains   Yuma   T11S R17W   Elev. 2808'

Copperopolis See Chiapuk, Pinai	Pinal	T10S R2E
Copperopolis Creek See Chiapuk, Pinal	Yavapai	T8N R2W
Copperosity See Chiapuk, Pinal	Pinal	T10S R2W
Copperosity Hills See Chiapuk, Pinal	Pinal/Maricopa/ Gila	T10–11S R2W1E

Copperplate Gulch   Greenlee   T4S R28E   Elev. c. 4800'
Ambrose Burke owned the Copperplate claims here. Ref.: Simmons

Copper Queen Mine   Cochise   T23S R24E
The first name for this mine was the Mercey Mine. It was changed to the Copper Queen Mine in 1877. See Bisbee, Cochise

Copper (R.R. STN.)   Yavapai   T16N R2W
P.O. est. Aug. 2, 1902, Rose Roberts, p.m.; resc. March 2, 1905 (never in operation)

Copper Reef Mountain   Graham   T4S R19E   Elev. 5431'
The Copper Reef Mine is here.

Copper Springs	Pinal	T8S R18E
Copper Valley	Maricopa	T2S R10W
Copper Wash	Maricopa	T2S R10W
Copper Wash	Yavapai	T16N R3W

CORCORAQUE BUTTE
Pima   T14S R10E   Elev. 2750'
The butte probably took its name from the Corcoraque Ranch at its base, but the meaning or origin of the name is unknown. It is also spelled Cocoraque. Mexican cocks crow, "Cock-oh-rah-kay!" Ref.: Lenon

CORDES   pro.: /kórdes/
Yavapai   T11N R2E   Elev. 3771'
Prior to the coming of the railroad this location was called Antelope Station. The post office refused to accept the name Antelope when a post office was sought by the Cordes family. They then used their name. A small community called Cordes Junction (Elev. 3790') is nearby. Cordes Peak (Elev. 4233') is also here.
P.O. est. June 9, 1886, John H. Cordes, p.m.; disc. Nov. 15, 1944 Ref.: 18a; 242

CORDOVA
Gila   T15E R1N
This was the townsite for the present Miami (q.v.). On July 15, 1909 the Cordova Townsite Company incorporated, planning to use the name Cordova, but it was rejected. Ref.: 284, p. 52

CORDUROY CREEK
Navajo   T8N R20E
In 1880 Fort Apache troops made a road by placing logs along the edge of the creek, creating a corduroy road. This name occurs first on the military route map dated November 1883, made by Lt. Thomas Bingham. It is also known as Forestdale Creek. Ref.: 18a; 242

CORE RIDGE
Coconino   T23N R7E   Elev. 10,500'
This prominent ridge between Fremont Saddle (10,800') and Mount Humphrey (12,794'), has a core of rock which fills the vents through which lava and ashes once burst to create the higher peak. Ref.: 71, p. 61

CORGIAT WASH pro.: /kówrjət/

Maricopa   T1S R2W

In 1915 a one-armed French farmer named Corgiat was farming along this wash, hence its name. The spelling Corgett is a corruption. Ref.: Parkman

CORK

Graham   T5S R24E   Elev. 2765'

The post office application form states that locally this was called Redland. The branch railroad contractor for the Arizona Eastern R.R. was William Garland (b. Cork, Ireland), who named this location as well as two others for his homeland. The others are Limerick (see Emery, Graham), and, according to Barnes, Dublin. Only Cork appears to have approached being a settlement.

P.O. est. May 18, 1916, Emory Stapley, p.m.; disc. Nov. 30, 1918
Ref.: 242; 18a; Jennings

CORMORANT CLIFFS

Mohave (Lake Mead)   T32N R16W

Cormorants can usually be seen in this vicinity.

CORN: The following place names are so called because at these localities Hopi and Navajo Indians raise maize:

Corn Creek   Apache   T4N R24E

See Little Bonito Creek, Apache

Corn Creek   Apache/Navajo

See Polacca Wash, Apache/Navajo

Corn Creek   Coconino   T23N R14E

See Corn Creek Wash, Coconino

Corn Creek Plateau   Apache   T4N R24E

Corn Creek Wash   Coconino   T22–23N R14E

In September 1967 the USGS eliminated the named Corn Creek and Oraibi Wash for this wash. Ref.: 329

CORNELIA, ARROYA

Pima

The Arroya Cornelia or Cornel does not appear in sources prior to 1916. It was probably named for the New Cornelia Mine, named by Col. John Greenway (see Ajo, Pima). The name Rio Cornez which appears on some maps is unknown in the vicinity of Ajo. It is also called Tenmile Wash. Ref.: Ketchum

CORNSTALK FLAT

Yavapai   T10N R4E

A man named Bishop, who maintained the Four Mile House here, had a cornfield, hence the name. Ref.: Dugas; Mrs. C. H. Peskey

CORNVILLE

Yavapai   T15N R4E   Elev. 3300'

Around the Pitchner place a settlement gradually formed. One of the earliest settlers was Henry Mortimer Cone. Various explanations of the name all hinge on the post office department having misread the name submitted for the post office, returning it as Cornville. Among the names said to have been so submitted are Coneville, Coaneville, and Cohnville. However, examination of the original post office application in the National Archives reveals a clearly legible "Cornville" as the name requested.

P.O. est. July 9, 1885, George A. Kingston, p.m. Ref.: Schnebly; *Arizona Republic* (April 15, 1980); 242

CORONADO

Greenlee   T4S R28E

This mining community was on Coronado Mountain, hence its name. The mining company post office was at the top of the Coronado Incline. Ore from the mines was sent

sixteen hundred feet down the incline in ore cars. Workers rode the cars to and from their work. On August 15, 1913 sixteen were on board when, as the ore cars neared the top of the incline, a coupling broke. Seven miners jumped clear, but nine were killed.
P.O. est. Jan. 23, 1913, S. F. Langford, p.m.; disc. Nov. 30, 1919
Ref.: Simmons; 257, p. 109; 242

CORONADO BUTTE pro.: /kárənado/ or /kórənado/

Coconino (Grand Canyon)   T30N R4E   Elev. 7120'

Francisco Vasquez de Coronado in 1535 arrived in Mexico with Viceroy Mendoza. Almost four years later he was designated governor of New Galicia and there in late April of 1539 he entertained Fr. Marcos de Niza, who was en route north, seeking the Seven Cities of Cibola. When de Niza returned in mid-summer, he told Coronado fabulous tales about wealth in Cibola. Coronado accompanied the friar to Mexico City. There de Niza's tales led to forming an expedition, with Coronado in charge. On February 23, 1540 three hundred and thirty-six Spanish soldiers, some wives and children, and hundreds of Indians set out. With them were five Portuguese, two Italians, one Frenchman, one Scot, and one German. The expedition group had the pomp and trappings of courtly warfare. After many hardships they arrived at the Zuñi villages on July 7, 1540. There was no gold but only houses of stone and mud. After further explorations the bedraggled expedition returned to Mexico City with Coronado "very sad and very weary, completely worn out, and shame-faced."

This butte in the Grand Canyon was named to commemorate Coronado as the first major explorer of what is now Arizona. Ref.: 357, pp. 379, 381, 382, 389, 402; 41, pp. 68, 69

CORONADO MOUNTAIN pro.: /kárənado/ or /kórənado/

Greenlee   T3S R29E   Elev. 7503'

Because many believed that Francisco Vasquez de Coronado traveled through this vicinity in 1540, Dan J. Grant named the mountain for the explorer. It is the location of the Coronado Mine and the former community of Coronado. Ref.: Farnsworth; Scott; Simmons, Riley

CORONADO NATIONAL FOREST

Graham   T9S R19E
Santa Cruz   T20S R15E
Pima/Cochise (and New Mexico)

This national forest was named for Francisco Vasquez de Coronado, who in 1540 led an expedition from Mexico City and passed through parts of what is today this national forest. It took fourteen government land shifts to create the present forest area. The first was the establishment on April 11, 1902 of the Santa Rita Forest Reserve, followed in July by the establishment of the Santa Catalina Forest Reserve. Then on July 20 was added the Chiricahua Forest Reserve. On November 3, 1906 two more reserves were created: (1) Baboquivari Forest Reserve, and (2) The Huachuca Forest Reserve. The Tumacacori Forest Reserve was added on November 7, having been preceded on November 5 by the Peloncillo Forest Reserve. On May 25, 1907 the Dragoon National Forest was established.

The first consolidation of the seven original forest reserves occurred on July 2, 1908 when Garcés National Forest was formed from the Baboquivari, Huachuca, and Tumacacori Forest Reserves. Simultaneously the Coronado National Forest came into being, carved from the Santa Rita, Santa Catalina, and Dragoon Forest Reserves. A third consolidation occurred when the Chiricahua National Forest absorbed the Chiricahua and the Peloncillo Reserves. Garcés National Forest did not last long, as it was added to the Coronado National Forest on April 17, 1911. The Chiricahua National Forest joined the Coronado family on July 6, 1917. The last consolidation took place on July 1, 1953 with additions to Coronado National Forest from Santa Teresa, Galiuro, Mount Graham, and Winchester divisions of Crook National Forest.
Ref.: 243, p. 34

CORONADO NATIONAL MEMORIAL pro.: /kárənado/ or /kórənado/

Cochise   T24S R20E   Elev. 6827'

This international park on the Mexican-United States boundary was named for Francisco Vasquez de Coronado (see Coronado Butte, Coconino (Grand Canyon)). In

1940 his name was given to Coronado Peak (Elev. 6864'), which up to that time had been called Cochise Peak, in this international memorial area. It was part of the plan to commemorate the 400th anniversary of Coronado's 1540 expedition. Plans were made to set up a monument near where Coronado may have crossed into what is now Arizona. On July 9, 1952 presidential signature established the 2,745 acres of the Coronado National Monument. Ref.: *Bisbee Daily Review*, "Fort Huachuca," *Get-acquainted Edition* (July 31, 1951); Grace M. Sparks, Letter (March 7, 1956); 243, p. 33

CORONADO TRAIL
Pima/Graham/Greenlee/Apache
This beautiful road through very interesting country goes from Clifton to Springerville. It was completed in 1926, at that time simply being called the Clifton-Springerville highway. John D. Guthrie of Clifton was en route to Europe when he read about opening this trail and he wrote at once to Pete Riley suggesting that it be named Coronado Trail because, "It was built on the route that the Spaniard Coronado actually took when he was looking for the Seven Cities of Cibola." The name was immediately accepted, although historically there is no proof to demonstrate that Coronado followed this route. Ref.: Pete Riley

CORONA MOUNTAIN
La Paz   T8N R15W   Elev. 1675'
The mountain takes its name from the presence of the Corona Mine. Ref.: 18a

CORONATION PEAK
Yuma   T7S R20W
In 1852 this mountain was being called Pagoda Mountain, as it looks like a pagoda. Bartlett in 1852 used the term Pagoda. Browne called it Corunnacion Mountain. Browne said, "The peaks bear a strong resemblance to those of a mitred crown, and seen in the glow of the setting sun, would readily suggest the idea of that gilded emblem of royalty." In November 1900 DeLancey Gill, an artist with the Old Yuma Trail Exploration party, renamed it Klotho Temple. The peak does resemble a spindle such as used by Clotho to spin the thread of life. (She was, of course, one of the Three Fates.) The name is also spelled Clothos Temple and Clothopas Temple. Ref.: 56, p. 78; 355, p. 318; 20, p. 188; 72, p. 175; 163, p. 173; 227, p. 140

CORRAL: The presence of either natural or man-made stock pens has led to the use of the word *corral* in the following place names:

Corral Canyon	Graham	T9S R19E	
Corral Canyon	Mohave	T41N R7W	
Corral Canyon	Santa Cruz	T23S R16E	
Corral Creek	Gila	(1) T7N R9E	(2) T2N R16E
Corral Creek	Gila	T6N R10E	
Corral Lake	Coconino	T37N R1E	
Corral Mountain	Pinal	T4S R17E	Elev. 3880'
Corral Nueva Spring	Santa Cruz	T22S R11E	
Corral Spring	Apache	T9N R27E	
Corral Spring	Graham	T9S R20E	
Corral Spring	Mohave	T18N R17W	
Corral Spring Mountain	Gila		
See Carol Spring Mountain, Gila			
Corral Valley	Coconino	T40N R4E	
Corral Viejo	Santa Cruz		
See Patagonia, Santa Cruz, and Mowry Mine, Santa Cruz			

CORTA (R.R. STN.)
Spanish = "cut wood"

Cochise   T22S R24E   Elev. 5166'

Firewood used to be loaded at this station. Ref.: 18a

CORTARO   pro.: /kortǽro/ or /kortáro/
Pima   T12S R12E   Elev. 2156'

At one time a heavy growth of mesquite and ironwood supplied firewood for local use, hence the name from the Spanish *cortar* (= "to cut"). There is today a community where in 1905 there was only a railroad stop.

P.O. est. Feb. 18, 1920, Richard C. Hunter, p.m. Ref.: 242; 182; 5, p. 384

CORVA
Spanish = "ham shaped"

Coconino   T22N R1E

This section house on the railroad takes its name from that of Corva Hill nearby, which is shaped like a ham. Ref.: 18a

CORWIN
Pima   T17S R13E   Elev. c. 3000'

The origin of this name is not known to the editor. It was on the Twin Buttes road.

P.O. est. July 10, 1912, Archibald W. Roberts, p.m.; disc. Feb. 15, 1915 Ref.: 242

COSME DE TUCSON, SAN
Pima

On the Kino map of 1702 is named a *visita* called Cosma at the s. e. foot of "A" or Sentinel Mountain. In 1757 Fr. Bernard Middendorf raised it to the status of a mission called San Cosme de Tucson, and a map shows it on the west side of the Santa Cruz River, directly north of San Xavier del Bac. See Tucson, Pima Ref.: 167, II, 428; 287, pp. 1, 12; 58

COSNINO CAVES   pro.: /kazniyno/
Coconino   T21N R9E

These caves are associated with Turkey Tanks (T22N/R9E). In 1877 Stanley Sykes and Charley McLean owned the tanks. They used the Turkey Track brand. In 1853 Lt. Amiel W. Whipple visited the caves and the nearby natural water tanks, now called Turkey Tanks. He called the caves Cosnino after Indians then living nearby whom Hopi Indians called Casninos. On September 10, 1857 Lt. Edward Fitzgerald Beale called them the Cosnurio Caves. He described them as large and divided by walls into various apartments still being used by Indians. A few months later on February 10, 1858 Beale altered the spelling to Cosmino Caves. Still later c. 1873 Capt. George M. Wheeler referred to them as the Coconino Caves. Havasupai Indians descended from the Cosninos. Ref.: 23, pp. 48, 49; 347, p. 168; 347, p. 181; 71, p. 41; 345, III, 629; 167, I, 538; 166, pp. 64, 65

COSNINOS, SIERRA DE LOS
Coconino

On a roughly-drawn map dated 1846 this location could easily be the Mogollon escarpment. See Francisco Peaks, San, Coconino, and Mogollon Rim, Coconino

COSPER
Greenlee   T3N R31E   Elev. c. 5800'

Cosper was the post office in the Cosper Ranch headquarters. James G. Cosper left his home in Alabama with his wife and children in 1869, headed for Texas. There he stayed until moving on to Arizona in the early 1880s. The liberal hospitality at the Cosper Ranch and the courtliness of the head of the household became legend. Out on the range the sons would invite campers they came across to visit the ranch house for meat, as their father thought nothing of killing a heifer for anyone who was hungry. "Uncle Toles" (John H. Toles Cosper) kept a fiddler on the payroll to assure having music whenever there was time for a dance. When he shipped cattle, he took his entire family and his fiddler to El Paso where he rented a whole hotel floor for a continuous party. Eventually, a lawsuit took all his wealth.

P.O. est. Aug. 26, 1914, Lu Ella Cosper, p.m. (probably never in operation)

Ref.: Fred Fritz, Notes; Pete Riley; 242

COTTON CENTER

Maricopa   T4S R4W   Elev. 715'

There is an area where much cotton is raised and ginned, hence the name for this settlement.

COTTONWOOD: The presence of cottonwood trees has led to using that designation for several place names. Examples follow:

Cottonwood	Apache	T21N R23E	Elev. 7500'
Cottonwood	Pinal	T16N R3E	

P.O. est. Nov. 9, 1881, Charles D. Hency, p.m.; disc. Feb. 4, 1884

COTTONWOOD

Yavapai   T16N R3E   Elev. 3310'

In 1874 soldiers from Camp Verde were stationed at an adobe house, but at that time there was no name for the present Cottonwood (where the house existed). As settlers moved in and the community developed, it took its name from a circle of sixteen large cottonwoods growing about one-quarter of a mile away from the Verde River. The place was unhealthful. Malaria and dysentery were severe problems as mosquitoes rose in thick clouds from stagnant pools left by receding floods. Such quinine as was available sold at $4.00 per ounce and could be bought only when it was in surplus at Camp Verde. Nevertheless, by 1879 several families had settled there, including the Nichols, Van Deerens, Hawkins, and Strahans. It is a curious fact that each family had nine children. The adobe building formerly used by soldiers became a school house. Today Cottonwood is a thriving community.

P.O. est. March 6, 1879, William H. Michael, p.m.

Ref.: Willard; Stemmer; 261, pp. 41, 153

Cottonwood Basin	Gila	T7N R9E	
Cottonwood Basin	Maricopa	T5N R7E	
Cottonwood Basin	Mohave		

This basin on the Colorado River formed when Cottonwood Island (named descriptively by Lt. Joseph Christmas Ives in 1857) disappeared under waters impounded by Davis Dam.

Ref.: Burns; Harris; 163, p. xliv

Cottonwood Basin	Yavapai	T13N R6E	
Cottonwood Basin Spring	Gila	T12N R8E	

Also known as Cottonwood Spring, Gila

Cottonwood Camp	Coconino (Grand Canyon)	T34N R6W	
Cottonwood Canyon	Apache	(1) T11N R31E	(2) T5N R9E
Cottonwood Canyon	Cochise	(1) T18S R19E	(2) T19S R29E
Cottonwood Canyon	Gila	T10N R13E	

See Sycamore Spring, Gila

Cottonwood Canyon	Graham	(1) T6S R20E	(2) T5S R27E
Cottonwood Canyon	Graham/Greenlee	T2S R27E	
Cottonwood Canyon	Mohave (Grand Canyon)	T34N R6W	
Cottonwood Canyon	Navajo	T9N R21E	
Cottonwood Canyon	Pinal	T10S R12E	
Cottonwood Canyon	Santa Cruz	T20S R13E	

Cottonwood Canyon	Yavapai	(1) T12N R3E	(2) T15N R6W
Cottonwood Cliffs	Mohave	T22N R12W	Elev. 3800'

In 1923 this name was changed from White Cliffs (Mohave). See Cottonwood Creek (#1), Mohave Ref.: 346, p. 202

Cottonwood Cove	Coconino	T41N R4E	
Cottonwood Cove Spring	Pima	T11S R17E	
Cottonwood Creek	Cochise	(1) T19S R29E	(2) T15S R30E
Cottonwood Creek	Coconino (Grand Canyon)	T30N R4E	
Cottonwood Creek	Gila	(1) T10N R7E	(2) T6N R11E

This creek is also in part called Walnut Creek.

Cottonwood Creek	Graham		

See Cottonwood Wash, Graham

Cottonwood Creek	Greenlee	T5S R32E	
Cottonwood Creek	Maricopa	T7N R4E	
Cottonwood Creek	Mohave	(1) T22N R12W	(2) T41N R3W
		(3) T20N R13W	

Accurate surveying removed confusion about whether Cottonwood Creek (1) was the same as White Cliffs Creek (now Knight Creek). It is not (see Knight Creek, Mohave). Cottonwood Spring (on GLO 1879) at the head of this creek gave its name to the creek. Ref.: 329

Cottonwood Creek	Navajo	T7N R23E	
Cottonwood Creek	Pinal	T3S R11E	
Cottonwood Creek	Yavapai	(1) T13N R6E	(2) T14N R8W
		(3) T8N R1W	
Cottonwood Draw	Cochise	T23S R31E	

Cottonwood Fork is on the Macomb map of 1860. See Pueblitos, Rio de los

Cottonwood Hill	Pinal	T7S R13E	
Cottonwood Island	Mohave		

See Cottonwood Basin, Mohave

Cottonwood Mesa	Yavapai	T12N R4E	
Cottonwood Mountain	Gila	T8N R11E	Elev. 4502'
Cottonwood Mountain	Graham	T6S R21E	Elev. 7489'
Cottonwood Mountains	Mohave	T22N R12W	Elev. 6322'

See Grand Wash Mountains, Mohave

Cottonwood Pass	La Paz	T6N R13W	

This is also called Sycamore Pass, La Paz

Cottonwood Peak	Cochise	T18S R19E	Elev. 7105'
Cottonwood Point	Mohave	T41N R6W	Elev. 6322'
Cottonwood Reservoir	Mohave	T24N R20W	
Cottonwood Ridge	Navajo	T9N R21E	
Cottonwood Seep	Navajo	T10N R19E	
Cottonwood Spring	Apache	T7N R29E	
Cottonwood Spring	Cochise	T18S R29E	
Cottonwood Spring	Coconino	(1) T41N R4E	(2) T39N R6E
		(3) T36N R2W	
Cottonwood Spring	Gila	(1) T10N R13E	(2) T12N R8E
		(3) T7N R10E	

Also known as Cottonwood Basin Spring, Gila

Cottonwood Spring	Graham	(1) T2S R27E	(2) T3S R19E
(3) T5S R19E	(4) T5S R21E	(5) T4S R25E	(6) T5S R26E
			(7) T5S R27E

Cottonwood Spring	Greenlee	T2S R29E	

Cottonwood Spring	Maricopa	(1) T7N R4E	(2) T3N R11E
		(3) T6N R10W	

Cottonwood Spring	Mohave/ Grand Canyon	T34N R6W	

Cottonwood Spring	Mohave	(1) T42N R6W	(2) T41N R9W
(3) T38N R15W	(4) T27N R14W	(5) T30N R12W	(6) T25N R21W
(7) T25N R18W	(8) T19N R20W	(9) T22N R20W	(10) T18N R10W
			(11) T17N R15W

Cottonwood Spring	Navajo	T25N R20E	

The former Navajo name Teadepahto as used in 1906 was eliminated by the USGS in 1969.

Cottonwood Spring	Pinal	T10S R12E	

Cottonwood Spring	Santa Cruz	(1) T22S R17E	(2) T20S R16E
		(3) T22S R12E	

Cottonwood Spring	Yavapai	(1) T16N R6W	(2) T13N R6W
	(3) T15N R5W	(4) T11N R2W	(5) T8N R5E

Cottonwood Spring Canyon	Graham	T7S R21E	

Cottonwood Station	Mohave	T20N R12W	

At the outset this location was a stage station. It gave way to a cafe run by Jim Cashman where teams used to stop on their way to Searchlight, Nevada. This location is now covered by waters impounded by Davis Dam. Ref.: Harris

Cottonwood Tailings Pond	Gila	T1N R14E	

Cottonwood Valley	Mohave		

This broad, open basin at the south end of Black Canyon was named by Lt. Joseph Christmas Ives in 1857. Ref.: 245, pp. 77, 78

Cottonwood Wash	Apache	T31N R24E	

The name is a translation of the Navajo, *T'iis Bito*.

Cottonwood Wash	Gila	T4N R13E	

Cottonwood Wash	Graham	T6S R24E	

Cottonwood Wash	Mohave	T41N R6W	

Cottonwood Wash	Navajo	(1) T13N R21E	(2) T11N R19E
		(3) T23N R23E	

Many names have been applied to sections of #3, such as the following: Ganado, Greasewood, Lower Greasewood, Pueblo Colorado. Locally the lower part that empties into the Little Colorado River is called Cottonwood Wash. On May 14, 1974 the USGS threw up its official hands and named the whole thing Cottonwood Wash. Ref.: 329

Cottonwood Wash	Pinal	(1) T5S R12E	(2) T6N R14E

Cottonwood Wash	Yavapai	T16N R6W	

Cottonwood Wash Spring	Yavapai	T17N R5W	

COUGAR CANYON
Gila   T4N R14E

There was a mountain lion den in this canyon, hence the name. Ref.: Devore

COUGHRAN CANYON
Yavapai

The USGS corrected the name of this canyon from Cowghran Canyon, but the origin of the name has not been learned. Ref.: 329

COURT HOUSE: Formations named below look either like a court house or, in some instances, a cathedral:

Courthouse   Maricopa   T1N R10W   Elev. c. 700'
Also known as Cathedral Rock, Maricopa Ref.: 18a

Court House Butte   Yavapai   T16N R6E   Elev. 5451'
Bill James, a settler about 1876, named this location, also known as Cathedral Rock. Ref.: 18a; Colton

Court House Rock   La Paz   T2N R11W   Elev. 2874'
In December 1963 the USGS changed the name from Court House Butte.

Court House Well   Maricopa   T19N R11E
There was formerly a stage station at this watering place. It is now a stock watering location. Ref.: 279, p. 206

COURTLAND

Cochise   T19S R25E   Elev. 5080'
At or near this location the Great Western Mining Company operated several mines. It was established in 1909 by W. J. Young, brother of Courtland Young for whom this location is named. Since the closing of the mines, it has become a ghost town. Many buildings have been sold and removed.
P.O. est. April 23, 1909, Harry Locks, p.m.; disc. Sept. 30, 1942; Wells Fargo 1910
Ref.: AHS, Names File; 242; State Library Files

COVE

Apache   T36N R29E   Elev. 6336'
This location is in a red sandstone cove. Very remote, it is an old Navajo rendezvous in a "maze of blind and hidden canyons and coves." Ref.: 331, p. 45

COVERED WELLS

Pima   T14S R2E   Elev. 2521'
Covered Wells is so named because the wells were protected by wooden covers. This Papago village has houses in two main groups along an arroyo and each section has a separate name. The group of houses at the west wells is usually called Covered Wells, a translation of the Papago name.

In 1884 Covered Wells was a mining center for which its three wells furnished water. Although a townsite was laid out then by M. J. Walsh, J. M. Kinley, R. D. Ferguson, M. M. Rice and M. Redding, mining declined and the place returned to being an Indian village. Wheeler called this location Vavaho; the name is also spelled Maisk. It has also been called Pozo Tapado (1912 Lumholtz). See Quijotoa, Pima Ref.: 58; 262, p. 5; 57, p. 366; 308, p. 77

COWBELL LAKE

La Paz   T4S R24W   Elev. c. 240'
In 1956 a cow with a bell around her neck was pasturing around this lake, hence the name. Ref.: Monson

COWBOY: When the word *cowboy* appears in place names it usually indicates a location where cowboys congregate or where an incident concerning a cowboy has occurred. The following are examples:

Cowboy Butte   Coconino   T42N R2W   Elev. 5048'

Cowboy Butte   Gila
See Bull Butte, Gila

Cowboy Canyon   Cochise   T13S R26E

Cowboy Canyon   Navajo   T7N R18E

Cowboy Flats   Cochise   T23S R32E

Cowboy Peaks   Yavapai   T14N R9W   Elev. 4200'

Cowboy Tank	Yavapai	T15N R3W
Cowboy Wash	Yavapai	T14N R9W

COW: The use of the designation *cow* in place names usually indicates a location where cows congregate or take refuge. Cowboys do notable cussing about rough canyons where it is difficult to dislodge cows during a roundup. The following are instances of such locations:

Cow Butte	Apache	T4N R29E	
Cow Canyon	Coconino	T20N R13E	
Cow Canyon	Gila	T12N R10E	
Cow Canyon	Greenlee	(1) T2S R29E	(2) T3N R31E
Cow Canyon	Mohave	T37N R15W	

See Crow Canyon, Mohave The name "Cow" is a corruption.

Cow Canyon	Yavapai	T11N R4E	
Cow Creek	Mohave	T10N R16W	
Cow Creek	Navajo	T10N R15E	
Cow Creek	Yavapai	(1) T19N R10W	(2) T8N R1W
Cow Crossing Tank	Coconino	T22N R2W	
Cow Flat	Greenlee/ Yavapai	T3N R32E	
Cow Head Saddle	Pima	T14S R17E	
Cowhead Tank	Pima	(1) T15N R11E	(2) T18N R8E
Cow Tank	Pinal	T7S R15E	
Cow Tank	Santa Cruz	T23S R13E	
Cow Head Trail Spring	Pima	T15S R17E	
Cowhead Well	Pinal	T7S R15E	
Cow Hill	Coconino	T17N R10E	
Cow Hill Tank	Coconino	T17N R10E	
Cow Lake	Coconino	T17N R10E	
Cow Pasture Butte	Gila	T6N R19E	
Cow Peak	Cochise		

See Helen's Dome, Cochise

Cow Spring	Navajo	T26N R22E	
Cow Tank	Coconino	(1) T20N R1E	(2) T27N R2E
	(3) T25N R2E	(4) T17N R9E	(5) T17N R10E	(6) T25N R12E

COWLIC pro.: /kawlik/
Papago = "little hill"
Pima   T19S R3E   Elev. 2098'
The name describes the location of this Papago village. The name has also been spelled as follows: Kavolik, Kaawlic, Kowlick. Ref.: 262, p. 14

COX
Yavapai
Wheeler noted in 1883 that "this was a post office on the Hassayampa Creek." It was near Prescott. Other than that no information is available.
P.O. est. July 18, 1883, William Durbin, p.m.; disc. Dec. 17, 1883
Ref.: 345, I, 299, Note 1; 242

COYOTE: Coyotes are abundant in Arizona. It is not surprising that many place names attest that fact. Examples follow:

Coyote Basin	Coconino	T17N R9E	
Coyote Butte	Gila	T5N R18E	Elev. 5615'
Coyote Buttes	Coconino	T41N R4E	Elev. 5840'
Coyote Canyon	Cochise	T22S R19E	
Coyote Canyon	Gila	T5N R18E	
Coyote Canyon	Pima	T21S R7E	
Coyote Canyon	Yavapai	T16N R2E	
Coyote Creek	Apache	T7N R31E	

This location is also called both Mamie Creek and Morrison Creek. The name Coyote in this instance was supplied by St. George Creaghe, a stockman who caught coyotes here and hence named it. Miles of Indian ruins line both sides of this creek, an indication that water was formerly plentiful. Ref.: Wiltbank; Wentz; 18a

Coyote Field	Pima	T14S R7E	
Coyote Hills	Apache	T9N R29E	Elev. 7810'
Coyote Hills Spring	Mohave	T21N R17W	
Coyote Howls Park	Yuma		

In early 1971 the Bureau of Land Management closed an unauthorized camp called "Big Wash" on public land north of Organ Pipe National Monument. To serve public need, business men in Why leased public land, donated materials and time and created Coyote Howls Park. Ref.: *Progressive Agriculture in Arizona* (Nov.-Dec., 1974), p. 15

Coyote Knoll	Graham	T7S R24E	Elev. 3900'
Coyote Lake	Apache	T7N R31E	

This lake was also called Pratt Lake (*q.v.*).

Coyote Mountains	Pima	T17S R8E	Elev. 6530'
Coyote Pass	Pima	T21S R7E	
Coyote Peak	La Paz	T2N R14W	Elev. 2300'
Coyote Peak	Yuma	T10S R17W	
Coyote Ranch	Pima		

See Poso Bueno Ranch, Pima

Coyote Reservoir	Apache

See H-V Reservoir, Apache

Coyote Spring	Apache	T9N R30E	
Coyote Spring	Cochise	T18S R19E	
Coyote Spring	Coconino	(1) T41N R3E	(2) T12N R11E
Coyote Spring	Graham	(1) T23S R23E	(2) T5S R26E
Coyote Spring	Greenlee	T5S R32E	
Coyote Spring	Maricopa	T5N R9E	
Coyote Spring	Mohave	(1) T34N R13W	(2) T25N R21W
		(3) T18N R12W	(4) T26N R14W

Spring #4 is also called Kohinoor Spring or Cohenour Spring (Mohave).

Coyote Spring	Navajo	T23N R18E
Coyote Spring	Pima	

See Pan Tak, Pima

Coyote Springs	Apache	T6NR25E

See Maito, Apache

Coyote Springs	Maricopa	T6N R1W
Coyote Springs	Navajo	T23N R18E
Coyotes' Spring	Pima	

See Pan Tak, Pima

Coyote Tank	Apache	T5N R29E
Coyote Tank	Coconino	(1) T24N R1W (2) T24N R1E (3) T17N R9E (4) T14N R8E
Coyote Tank	Yavapai	(1) T16N R1E (2) T11N R1E
Coyote Valley	Coconino	T41N R3E
Coyote Wash	Apache	T4N R30E

Spaniards called this wash Rio Negro. Its Navajo name is *Txo'nilts'ili* (= "sparkling water").
Ref.: Van Valkenburgh, *Master Key* (May 1945), p. 89

Coyote Wash	Coconino/ Navajo	T21N R15E

In March 1968 the USGS eliminated as names for this wash Castle Butte, Corn Wash, and Whe-yol-da Sah Wash. Ref.: 329

Coyote Wash	Coconino	T41N R3E
Coyote Wash	Graham	(1) T2S R20E (2) T6S R25E
Coyote Wash	Greenlee	T10S R32E
Coyote Wash	Maricopa	T4N R6W
Coyote Wash	Navajo	T23N R19E

An earlier spelling for this wash is a phonetic rendering: Ki-Ote-Te.

Coyote Wash	Pima	(1) T15S R16E (2) T21S R7E

See Pan Tak, Pima

Coyote Wash	Yavapai	T15N R1E
Coyote Wash	Yuma	T10S R18W
Coyote Water	Apache	

See Maito, Apache

Coyote Water Well	Yuma	T12S R17W
Coyote Well	Maricopa	T4N R6W
Coyote Well	Mohave	T14N R14W
Coyote Well	La Paz	T2N R14W

See Vinegaron Well, La Paz

Coyote Wells	Cochise	T12S R29E

C P BUTTE

Yavapai   T9N R5E   Elev. c. 4000'

This butte was named for the C P Mine, which in turn was named for its owner, Col. C. P. Roundtree. Ref.: 18a

CRABTREE: The presence of *crabtrees* possibly led to the following place names:

Crabtree Butte	Maricopa	T6N R9E Elev. 4819'
Crabtree Creek	Greenlee	T2N R29E
Crabtree Park	Greenlee	T2N R29E
Crabtree Spring	Maricopa	(1) T6N R9E (2) T3N R11E
Crabtree Wash	Maricopa	T3N R11E

CRACKERJACK RIDGE
Gila　　　　　　　　　　　　　　T11N R9E
The presence of the Crackerjack Mine on this ridge led to the name.

CRAIG
Apache　　　　　　　　　　　　　T11N R28E
This location was named for Dr. (E.G.?) Craig, a physician and sheepman who maintained a summer came here. See also Tule, El, Apache
P.O. est. Oct. 26, 1910, Ellis W. Wiltbank, p.m.; disc. Sept. 30, 1912
Ref.: 242; 18a; 329

CRAIG
Yavapai　　　　　　　　　　　　　T11N R3W
The name of this post office is the first syllable in the surname of its first postmaster.
P.O. est. Aug. 13, 1894, George W. Craighead, p.m.; disc. May 13, 1903

CRAMM MOUNTAIN
Maricopa　　　　　　　　T7N R4E　　　　　　　　Elev. 3920'
A prospector and miner named Cramm lived at the foot of this mountain in 1882, hence the name. Ref.: 18a

CRATER, THE
Pima　　　　　　　　　　T10N R6W　　　　　　　Elev. c. 2000'
This is a basin formed by erosion in horizontal lava flow. It looks like a volcanic crater. Ref.: 58

CRATER LAKE
Coconino　　　　　　　　T24N R6E　　　　　　　Elev. 8466'
The name is descriptive of the location.

CRATER MOUNTAIN
Yavapai　　　　　　　　　T14N R3E　　　　　　　Elev. 6004'
The name comes from a volcanic flow-out at the mountain top. Ref.: Allan

CRATER RANGE
Maricopa　　　　　　　　T9S R7W　　　　　　　Elev. 1754'
This mountain range is bordered on the south by Childs Valley. These very striking volcanic remnants are also called Crater Mountains. Ref.: Netherlan; 329

CRATER TANK
Pima　　　　　　　　　　　　　　T10N R6W
This tank is in The Crater (*q.v.*), hence the name.

CREMATION CREEK
Coconino (Grand Canyon)　　　　　T31N R3E
This creek lies below what was formerly called Cremation Point, where Indians used to throw ashes of their cremated dead over the cliff. Ref.: Kolb

CRESCENT LAKE
Apache　　　　　　　　　T6N R28E　　　　　　　Elev. 9039'
The Civilian Conservation Corps built dams at Big Lake and at this point in May 1930. Ed Becker of Springerville named this lake because of its shape. Ref.: Becker

CRESCENT RIDGE
Coconino (Grand Canyon)　　　　　T34N R2E
The name is descriptive.

CRESWELL TANK
Coconino　　　　　　　　　　　　T14N R13E
Rufus Creswell and his sons Stephen and Homer came into this area originally as

cowboys working for the Hashknife Ranch c. 1880. This tank is named for them. Ref.: Hart

CRITTENDEN, FORT

Santa Cruz   T20S R17E   Elev. c. 3200'

An adobe house called Casa Blanca existed at T21S/R16E, Section 20, in 1876. It had been there a long time, as is evidenced by the fact that James (Paddy) Graydon maintained the "U.S. Boundary Hotel" here in 1859, which served as a post office in 1860. It is doubtful that the place was white as the name indicates, but more probably it was the home of a man named White.

Near this location one-half mile east and on higher ground, was old burned-out Fort Buchanan (q.v.). The establishment of the new fort came about as a result of a reorganization of the army on July 28, 1866. As a district of the Department of California, Arizona became part of the Division of the Pacific. Gen. Thomas Leonidas Crittenden assumed command of the South District of Arizona in 1867 and kept that position through 1868. He returned from California with three hundred troops and very soon recommended that a new post be built near the site of Old Fort Buchanan "where there are many adobes made before the war and which can be used in new buildings. When built, the post at Tubac will be discontinued." There were two reasons for naming the new post Crittenden, the second being that he was the son of the Hon. John J. Crittenden of Kentucky. The fort was established May 4, 1868 and was abandoned June 1, 1873 because it was an unhealthful location. On July 22, 1884 the military reservation was transferred to the Interior Department.

The Census of 1870 reported fifty-two residents in Casa Blanca. The post office, which earlier had barely lasted a year and a half, came back into existence under the name Crittenden because of its adjacency to the military post. Casa Blanca flourished temporarily in January 1886 when Mexicans made mescal there. Their venture did not last long. Their stock was stolen, a few of the men were killed, and the rest abandoned the place.

Much of the land was owned by Rollen R. Richardson. In the late 1880s he moved the trading post, the railroad station, and what there was of the town to what is now Patagonia (q.v.). The railroad station had been important while the Harshaw and Mowry Mines were in operation. There was a mill at this location in the late 1870s. P.O. est. as Casa Blanca, Jan. 12, 1860, Thomas Hughes, p.m.; disc. Oct. 9, 1861; reest. as Crittenden, June 11, 1872, Thomas Hughes, p.m.; name changed to Casa Blanco (sic), April 27, 1882; name changed to Crittenden July 26, 1882; disc. Jan. 23, 1901; Wells Fargo 1885 Ref.: Lenon; Seibold; Arizona Mining Index (May 31, 1883), p. 3; 107, IV, 130, 131, and V, 251, 261, 297, 298; 62; 156, p. 183; 121a, pp. 7, 8; 286, p. 239; 163; 163, p. 43

CROOK CITY

Yavapai

No location is known for this place other than that given in the weekly Arizona Miner in 1875: "on east branch of Hassayampa near Maple Gulch." In that year it consisted of about fourteen miners' cabins. The settlement was named for the Gen. Crook Mine, which in turn was named for Gen. George Crook. It may have been in Crook's Canyon. Ref.: Weekly Arizona Miner (April 30, 1875), p. 3

CROOKED: Place names bearing this designation follow out what it implies. Examples follow:

Crooked Creek	Apache	T5N R25E
See Little Bonito Creek, Apache		
Crooked Mountains	Pima	T13S R1W
Crooked Ridge	Coconino	T34N R9E
Crooked Ridge	Navajo	T11N R18E

CROOK NATIONAL FOREST

Graham/Gila/Maricopa/Pinal

This national forest includes the following mountains: Santa Teresa, Pinaleno, Galiuro, and Mount Graham. In 1908 Crook National Forest was set aside as a reserve named for Gen. George Crook (b. Sept. 23, 1829, Dayton, Ohio; d. March 21, 1890). Crook led a successful campaign against Apaches while in command of the Military Department of Arizona 1871-1875. He returned to Arizona from 1882-1886. Not only did Crook improve conditions for Indians, he also reorganized and relocated unhealthful or deficient army posts, among them Camp Grant, seeing to it that good water was available at such posts. He also established first-class roads between the posts for wagons and ambulances. Further, the military telegraph line which originated in San Diego and went through Yuma was brought to Maricopa Wells where it branched, with one line going to Fort Whipple and the other to Tucson and thence to San Carlos, all under the direction of Crook.

Crook National Forest was formed from the Mount Graham Forest Reserve created in part in 1902. In turn it was abolished in 1935 when it was sliced on July 1, to form parts of the following national forests: Tonto, Gila, and Coronado. See also Coronado National Forest, Pima/Cochise
Ref.: 49, p. 252; 81, p. 160; 177, p. 130

CROOKTON
Yavapai   T22N R4W
This location on the A.T. & S.F.R.R. was named for Gen. George Crook. See Crook National Forest Ref.: 18a

CROSBY PEAK
Yavapai   T14N R9W   Elev. 4378'
This location takes its name from the presence of the Crosby Mine (T13N/R9W).

CROSS CANYON
Apache   T27N R28E   Elev. c. 6000'
A Navajo trail crossed this canyon, hence the name. A trading post and a small settlement have developed here. Ref.: 141, p. 151; 18a

CROSS CANYON TRAIL
Apache
This Navajo trail crosses from the mesa between Canyon de Chelly and Canyon del Muerto to the west rim of Canyon del Muerto, or vice versa. Ref.: 331, p. 24

CROSS MOUNTAIN
Yavapai   T2N R9W   Elev. 6625'
In 1854 Lt. Amiel W. Whipple named this mountain because of its form.
Ref.: 347, p. 200; Rothwell

CROTON SPRINGS
Cochise   T15S R24E   Elev. 4137'
These springs were so named as early as 1849 because the water tasted like castor oil (croton oil). Here in 1881 Thomas and Lizzie Kirkland Steele had a home and stage station where, according to Fish, they had been since 1874. Ref.: AHS, Lizzie Steele File; 101, pp. 188, 189; 116, p. 586

CROUCH CREEK
Gila   T9N R14E
An old army captain named Crouch drove cattle into this area c. 1880, hence the name. Ref.: McKinney

CROW CANYON
Mohave   T17N R14W
The name for this canyon has been in use for many years, probably dating to c. 1870 when the Stephens brothers and their family settled here. Cow Canyon is a corruption. Ref.: 329

CROWLEY
Gila   T1N R14E
Con Crowley, a cattleman and miner, ran cattle at this location, hence its name.
P.O. est. Dec. 16, 1909, James Lightfoot, p.m.; disc. Feb. 14, 1911 Ref.: 242; Woody

CROWN KING

Yavapai   T10N R1W   Elev. 5760'

In the 1880s this was a very active mining camp with a post office which took its name from the first man in this vicinity. It is currently a summer community.

P.O. est. May 23, 1888, George Paterson Harrington, p.m.; disc. May 15, 1954; Wells Fargo 1904 Ref.: 242; Schnebly; Varney

CROWN POINT

Yavapai   T9N R3W   Elev. 4365'

The Crown Point Mine was between the Crown King Mine at the top of the mountain and the Goodwin Mine near its base. It was named by its locators after the Crownpoint Mine at Gold Hill, Nevada.

P.O. est. June 7, 1899, Robert Joseph Bignall, p.m.; disc. Dec. 22, 1903
Ref.: 242; Gardner; 18a

CROZIER

Mohave   T15N R14W   Elev. c. 4000'

Samuel Crozier (b. 1841, Ohio) established the first cattle ranch in Mohave County in the early 1870s near where the Crozier section house on the S.F.R.R. is situated. The Census of 1880 has him listed as living in the Truxton Spring area. It is said he sold Peach Springs to the A. & P.R.R. in 1882. It was a principal source of water for the Hualapai Indians and was on the Hualapai reservation. Ultimately this led to a lawsuit c. 1927 by the Hualapai Indians against the railroad, in which the Indians asserted that Crozier never lived anywhere near Peach Springs and so had no right to a homestead claim in that area.

A Hualapai Indian cowhand working for Crozier adopted his employer's surname to replace his Indian name of Haka. The resulting name was Kate Crozier, a scout under Gen. Crook, Miles, and Willcox. In 1927 Kate Crozier testified that Sam Crozier did not sell Peach Springs, but did sell Truxton Springs to the railroad, the latter water being on Crozier's ranch. Kate Crozier added that the spring sold was that which ran at the former Crozier R.R. station, which by 1927 was known as Truxton Canyon station.
Ref.: Grounds; Harris; 335, pp. 156, 256, 270; 63; Babcock

CROZIER PEAK

Pinal   T5S R14E   Elev. 4273'

The name was that of a miner and prospector who had claims on this peak.
Ref.: 18a

CRUICE (R.R. STN.)   pro.: /kruws/

Yavapai   T21N R2W   Elev. 5126'

This location on the Ashfork-Prescott branch of the A.T. & S.F.R.R. was named for the assistant general freight agent, S. P. Cruice, according to Barnes. Marshall says it was named for Fred P. Cruice. Ref.: 18a; 218, p. 354

CRUZ

Pima   T15S R15E   Elev. c. 2600'

The first name for this location on the S.P.R.R. was Papago, later changed to Esmond. In 1912 the name was changed again, to Cruz, simply by dropping *Santa* from the name of the Santa Cruz River. The change was made to save time in telegraphy. Ref.: 18a

CRUZ, SANTA: Except where otherwise noted, the following place names arise because they are either on or in the vicinity of the Santa Cruz River or are named for the Blessed Cross in a missionary association:

Cruz, Santa   Cochise   (a presidio)
See Quiburi Ruins, Cochise

Cruz, Santa   Cochise
See Fairbank, Cochise

Cruz, Santa   Pima
See Haivana Nakya, Pima

Cruz, Santa   Pima

See Kom Vo, Pima

Cruz, Santa   Pinal   T9S R E

A post office was established here in 1910 to serve about one hundred fifty residents.
P.O. est. Jan. 4, 1910, Scott White, p.m.; disc. Feb. 14, 1911 Ref.: 242

Cruz Canyon, Santa   Santa Cruz

See Peck Canyon, Santa Cruz

Cruz Cienega, Santa   Pinal

This location on the Santa Cruz River between Maricopa and Gila Crossing was called by Fr.
Francisco Garcés in 1775 Las Lagunas del Hospital. Ref.: 77, p. 400

Cruz County, Santa

An exception to this listing. See Santa Cruz County

Cruz de Gaybaniptea, Santa   Cochise

See Babocomari, Fort, Cochise

Cruz de Quiburi, Santa   Cochise

See Quiburi (Ruins), Santa Cruz

Cruz Flats, Santa   Pinal   T2S R2E

CRUZ RIVER, SANTA   pro.: /sántə cruwz/ or /sǽntə cruwz/

This long and now intermittent river finds its source in the San Rafael Valley in Santa Cruz
County, then dips south into Mexico, after which it returns to Arizona and traverses Santa
Cruz, Pima, Maricopa, and Pinal Counties to its juncture with the Gila River. The name of
this river is one of the oldest place names in Arizona, Fr. Eusebio Kino having so referred
to it in the late 1690s. Currently the Santa Cruz River diminishes and disappears, having
no real "mouth," that having been dispelled in the Santa Cruz Flats (*q.v.*). Prior to the
construction of the Greene Canal and Reservoir, the Santa Cruz River joined the Gila.
Since that time the diversion of the river has caused floods in the Picacho area around Eloy
and the formation of Picacho Lake east of Eloy. It passes by (1) the ruined mission (now a
national monument) at Tumacacori; (2) San Xavier del Bac; (3) Sentinel Mountain and
Tucson.

Other names for this river are as follows: Santa Maria del Pilar (Kino, Sept. 1692);
Sobaipuri-Pima River (Fr. Jacobo Sedelmayr, 1744); Sweet Creek, a name found on a
military map in the National Archives. Ref.: 242; 287, pp. 34, 50, Note 62; 43, II, 249;
163, pp. 183, 184, 328; Stanfield

Cruz, Sierra de la Santa   Santa Cruz

See Canelo, Santa Cruz

Cruz Valley, Santa   Pima   T15S R13E

Fr. Eusebio Kino called this the Santa Maria Valley in 1695. See Cruz River, Santa

Cruz Village, Santa   Pinal   T2S R2E

The Gila River Indian Reservation Council reports that Pima Indians approved this name on June 19,
1940.

Cruz Wash, Santa   Pinal   T9S R13E

There is also a north branch of this wash (T6S/R4E). Ref.: 329

CRYSTAL CAVE

Cochise   T17S R31E

This cave is in Cave Creek Canyon at the end of a steep foot trail. Just beyond the
entrance is Devil's Elbow, a treacherous and difficult passage. The author was with a
group which attempted to crawl through, only to find that its ceiling had recently
collapsed. A member of the party had gone through the passage a week before. Beyond is
King Solomon's Temple which sparkles with crystal deposits.
Ref.: 5, pp. 373, 374

CRYSTAL CAVE

Pinal   T6S R13E

In early 1929 Messrs. Logan and Rhodes discovered this cavern and named it because the walls and roof of its two rooms sparkle with gypsum interspersed with crystals. Ref.: AHS Mammoth File

CRYSTAL CREEK

Coconino (Grand Canyon)   T32N R2E

The name comes from the fact that the water here is extremely clear. The first pilot to fly a plane in the Grand Canyon did so in 1929 while looking for the honeymooning Hydes, who had attempted to boat through the Canyon. At a point on the Rim above this creek the plane dropped down into the canyon. No sign of the couple was ever found. Ref.: Kolb

CRYSTAL FOREST

Apache   T17N R24E

The name for this part of the Petrified Forest National Monument comes from the fact that crystal formations occur here. It is also known as Second Forest.

CRYSTAL HILL

La Paz   T2N R18W   Elev. 1872'

Rock crystals occur here, hence the name. Ref.: Monson

CRYSTAL PEAK

Graham   T5S R20E   Elev. 7120'

Silicon dioxide crystals in the rocks are the cause of the name for this mountain. Ref.: 18a

C T SPRINGS

Navajo   T8N R17E

These springs are on the C T Ranch, from which they take their name.

CUERDO DE LENA WASH

Spanish = "cord of wood"

Pima   Elev. 1634'

Mexicans en route from Sonita, Mexico, camped in this wash where there was a heavy growth of mesquite. There they cut wood, hauling it in wagons to Ajo. Ref.: Ketchum

CULLEN'S WELL

La Paz   T7N R11W

Charles C. Cullen (b. 1825, England; d. Aug. 1878) was a stage station keeper near La Paz in 1870. In late 1863 he established a stage station and dug a two hundred and fifty-foot well, from which he sold water at $0.25 per animal, with men being "watered" free. Mrs. Cullen earned a reputation for preparing excellent meals for travelers. Following Cullen's death, the station was placed in charge of Peter Doll. By 1896 when the post office was established, the spelling had apparently been lost and the place was referred to as Cullings. Later when Joe Drew (the first postmaster) was station keeper, he "grieved that several deaths from thirst had occurred only a few miles from the station ... After that he raised a lantern every night above the well frame and as a result one evening an almost spent lad — at the point of lying down to die, had seen in the distance a glimmer of light from the windows of the station house," and creeping onward, found water and safety at this location. A smiliar story is told about Baker Peak, Yuma. P.O. est. as Cullings, Oct. 17, 1896, Joseph S. Drew, p.m.; disc. March 6, 1902 Ref.: 62; 314, p. 154; 252, Part 3, p. 4; *Arizona Republic* (Jan. 28, 1951), section 2, p. 3; *Arizona Sentinel* (Aug. 10, 1878), p. 3, and (Sept. 21, 1878), p. 4; 279, pp. 39, 206

CULLUMBER'S STATION

Yavapai

On February 22, 1872, Apaches killed S. T. Cullumber at his stage station near Date Creek. Ref.: *Weekly Arizona Miner* (Feb. 24, 1872), p. 2

CUMARO: This Spanish word means *hackberry*, a variety of tree native to Arizona. Its presence is indicated in the following place names:

Cumaro Canyon   Pima   T15S R18E
This location is also known as Martinez Wash and as Cumero Canyon (a corruption).

Cumaro Spring   Pima   T15S R18E

Cumaro Wash   Pima   T17S R18E
Also known as Martinez Wash

Cumero Canyon   Pima   T16S R18E
This is a corruption of the Spanish word *cumaro*. Cumero (T22S/R9E) was a Papago village said to have been near the Sonora border in 1871. The name was also spelled Camaro and Cumaro. Ref.: 167, I, 371

Cumero Mountain   Pima   T22S R9E   Elev. 4697'

Cumero Spring   Pima   T15S R18E

CUMMINGS MESA
Coconino/Utah   T42N R9E
This mesa was named for Prof. Byron Cummings (d. May 21, 1954), an archeologist, who was with John Wetherill and Charles Bernheimer on a journey in 1924 to Rainbow Natural Bridge, Utah. Cummings is probably the first white man to see this huge arch. Ref.: 129, p. 237; 14, p. 7

CUNNINGHAM PASS
Yuma   T7S R12W
After having been a sailor, Charles Cunningham arrived in this area in the mid 1860s, where he became a miner. He was friendly with Indians, but despite that fact on May 3, 1871 he was ambushed in Bell's Canyon (*q.v.*), Yavapai. Discovering they had killed a friend, the Indians left without mutilating his body as they did those of his three companions. Ref.: *Arizona Miner* (May 3, 1871); AHS Names File

CUNNINGHAM TRACT WILD LIFE AREA
Yuma
This wild life area of one hundred and seventy-five acres was bought by the Arizona Game and Fish Department in 1952. Ref.: 9, p. 3

CURLEY SEEP
Coconino   T24N R6E
This was the nickname of a cowpuncher who worked on the A One Cattle Company range. Ref.: Sykes

CURRY'S CORNER
Maricopa   T4N R4E   Elev. 2569'
As often occurs, someone puts in a store and gradually a community develops. Phoenix has engulfed it.

CURTISS
Cochise   T18S R21E   Elev. 3680'
The first name for this railroad station on the El Paso and Southwestern Railroad was Kenard. It was changed to honor Curtiss James of the Phelps Dodge Corporation. It is the location of the Apache Powder Company. Ref.: 18a; 299, p. 27

CURTISS
Yavapai   T18S R21E   Elev. c. 4300'
The reason for this name has not been learned.
P.O. est. Nov. 27, 1891, Marvin A. Baldwin, p.m.; disc. March 23, 1895

CUTTER
Gila   T1S R16E   Elev. 3167'
This section station is at the foot of a steep grade where formerly extra engines were hitched on to haul heavy freight loads over the divide between the Salt and Gila River

watersheds. It was named to honor E. Al Cutter, on the Board of Directors of the construction company for the Gila Valley, Globe, and Northern Railroad in the 1890s. Ref.: Woody

CYCLOPIC
Mohave   T28N R18W   Elev. 4320'

Cyclopic was the name of the post office for the Cyclopic Mine, discovered in the early 1890s by Messrs. Robert Patterson, Sol Rowe, and Glenn. They leased it to a Seattle company c. 1896. Cyclopic Wash is nearby (T29N/R19W). The name Cycloptic is a corruption.
P.O. est. July 7, 1905, Robert Nickel, p.m.; resc. Oct. 10, 1905; reest. Sept. 19, 1914, Stanley C. Bagg, p.m.; disc. Feb. 15, 1917 Ref.: 242; 200, p. 124

CYGNUS MOUNTAIN
Mohave   Elev. c. 5000'

On January 25, 1854 Lt. Amiel W. Whipple said he named a snow-capped range by this designation. He does not so state, but it may be that the white-backed range reminded him of a swan. In 1857 Marcou dubbed this same mountain Whipple Mountain. Curiously, several have tried to honor Whipple by naming peaks and mountains in Arizona for him, but his name never has become permanently attached to any such location. For instance, in 1857 Lt. Joseph Christmas Ives appears to have called The Needles (q.v.) "Mount Whipple" and in 1858 Lt. Edward Fitzgerald Beale so named a peak south of the junction of the Puerco and Little Colorado Rivers. Whipple's name does not remain where so placed. Ref.: 345, IV, 48

CYOTE SPRING
Mohave

This is the way some enterprising cartographer with imagination rendered "coyote." Although impossible to locate under this name at this late date, it is too good not to be included here. Ref.: "Map of Route, Fort Mohave to Prescott (1866); 242

CYPRESS: The presence of these evergreens is indicated in the following place names:

Cypress Butte	Yavapai	T9N R7E	Elev. 5513'
Cypress Canyon	Gila	T11N R9E	
Cypress Creek	Yavapai	T16N R9W	
Cypress Hill	Gila	T6N R9E	Elev. 5952'
Now called Cypress Peak, Gila			
Cypress Mountain	Yavapai	T15N R7W	Elev. 6251'
Cypress Peak	Maricopa	T6N R9E	Elev. 5952'
Cypress Ridge	Maricopa	T8N R8E	
Cypress Ridge	Yavapai	T15N R8W	
Cypress Spring	Yavapai	T15N R7W	
Cypress Thicket	Gila	T10N R9E	
See Rye Creek, Gila			
Cypress Park Forest Camp	Cochise	T19S R30E	

D

DAGGER BASIN

Gila   T4N R15E

Spanish daggers (low lying cactus that really stabs if run against) grow thickly in this area, hence the name. The name is shared by Dagger Canyon, Peak (Elev. 3260'), and Spring. Ref.: Devore

DAIRY MOUNTAIN

Gila   c. T9N R14E

About 1882 in the vicinity of Pleasant Valley, a pioneer named Bushman and others went to a lake at the top of this mountain (which accounts for the location assigned this point s.e. of Pleasant Valley). It was possibly named after the Pleasant Valley Dairy nearby. Ref.: AHS, John Bushman Collection, p. 38

DANA BUTTE

Coconino (Grand Canyon)   T31N R2E   Elev. 5030'

George Wharton James named this butte for James Dwight Dana (1813-1895), an eminent geologist. The USGS accepted the name in March 1906. Ref.: 178, p. 39

DANDY WIRE SPRING

Yavapai   T11N R2W

This name was given to one Pine Spring by the U.S. Forest Service because another Pine Spring is in the same section of land. Ref.: 329

DANE CANYON

Coconino   T13N R11E   Elev. c. 6500'

A sheepman named Frank Dane had a cabin at Dane Spring in this canyon c. 1918. Dane Ridge is also here. Ref.: Hart

DANIEL GULCH

Yavapai   T12N R1E

Tom Daniel, a prospector, worked in this area for several years. He had some gold claims on forestry land and forest maps show it as Danial Spring, an error. Ref.: Woody

DARBY ARROYO

Pima   T12S R6W   Elev. 1979'

The arroyo takes its name from that of a rancher who had a well in this arroyo (Elev. 1802'). Ref.: 329

DARK CANYON

Greenlee   T4S R29E

Residents say that this canyon is so deep and dark that the sun never shines in it, hence its name. Ref.: Jennings; Patterson; Scott

DARTON DOME

Coconino (Grand Canyon)   T23N R8E   Elev. 8408'

This knob was named for Nelson Horatio Darton (1865-1948), who investigated the stratigraphy of northern Arizona. Ms. Katherine Laing, a Geoscience student at the University of Arizona in 1971, suggested the name to the USGS. It is also known as Turkey Ridge. Ref.: 329

DARWIN PLATEAU

Coconino (Grand Canyon)   T33N R1W

In 1908 the USGS proposed and approved this name to honor the evolutionist. Ref.: 329; 178, p. 81

DATE

Yavapai   T11N R6W   Elev. 3367'

This railroad station takes its name from that of nearby Date Creek. Ref.: 18a

DATE CREEK

Yavapai/La Paz   T10N R8W

In 1863 Charles C. Genung noted that his group immediately noticed the beauty of this stream. They apparently heard the Indian word *A-ha-ca-zon* and interpreted it as meaning "sinking waters" with reference to a sink about twenty miles from the earlier Camp Date Creek location, but another source (Farish) reports they heard Indians call it *Ah-ha-carsona* (= "pretty water"). His party did not name this stream, but later settlers called it Date Creek, from the Mexican word *datal* (= "fruit of the opuntia cactus"). The cactus bears great clusters of fruit like dates. Ref.: 107, IV, 36; AHS, A. F. Banta; *Prescott Courier* (July 21, 1917)

DATE CREEK

Yavapai   T11N R6W   Elev. 3382'

It is probable that the location is that of the last position of Camp Date Creek, which was abandoned in 1873.

P.O. est. March 1, 1872, George H. Kimball, p.m.; disc. Oct. 18, 1880; reest. Oct. 29, 1904; order resc. May 5, 1905; reest. as Haynes, April 4, 1908, John H. Roberts, p.m.; name changed to Date Creek, Dec. 13, 1921; disc. Nov. 30, 1927 Ref.: 242

DATE CREEK, CAMP

Yavapai   T7S R12W

Date Creek, according to one source, was established by the California Volunteers in 1864 and had a small detachment until 1866. Then the troops moved twenty-five miles to the north to protect settlers bedevilled by Indians in Skull Valley. The first recorded skirmish was an attack on a wagon train on March 2, 1867. Skull Valley encampment was called Camp McPherson, named for Brig. Gen. James Birdseye McPherson (d. July 22, 1864, Atlanta, Georgia). The troops were moved from Camp McPherson to the junction of the North and South Forks of the creek and the name changed on July 15, 1868 to Camp Date Creek, a change made official by Gen. H. W. Halleck on November 23 of that year. Indians continued to harass settlers and in 1871 Vincent Colyer established a temporary reservation at the camp. There about two hundred and twenty-five Indians were gathered. They were transferred to Camp Verde Reservation in May 1873, and by order of Gen. O. O. Howard, Camp Date Creek and the Indian Agency were abandoned. Ref.: 107, VIII, 10; Willson; 156, p. 183; 206, p. 94; 159, pp. 427, 493

DATELAND

Yuma   T7S R12W   Elev. 450'

In about 1930 Mrs. William Harrison built a large home and work buildings to harvest a large grove of date trees, from which the name derives. Today, there is a stopping place for travellers along the main highway here, but it is not the same place as that built by Mrs. Harrison, which has long since ceased to exist.

P.O. est. July 18, 1942; Mrs. Jeanne Mae Collins, p.m.
Ref.: Johnson; Hayden; 264; 242

DAVENPORT HILL
Coconino   T21N R3E   Elev. 7805'
Thomas Davenport (b. 1877; d. Nov. 30, 1947) terminated his ranch activities south of Williams in 1892, moving from there to live in Williams. His ranch included this hill. Davenport Lake, a wet weather lake, also bears his name. Ref.: Fuchs, Letter, quoting *Williams News* (Dec. 4, 1947); Kennedy; Benham

DAVENPORT PEAK
Yavapai   T8N R7E   Elev. 4010'
Jake Davenport (not James Davenport) lived in this region in the 1870ᶜ. Davenport Ranch was at the mouth of Davenport Wash. Ref.: 18a

DAVID, ST.
Cochise   T17S R21E   Elev. 3850'
The thriving community of St. David was founded in August 1877 about a mile away from its present location, but malaria proved to be so terrible on the San Pedro River that the Mormon colonists moved to the present location of the town. P. C. Merrill, his sons and others dissatisfied with life at Jonesville, left that colony and first worked for Tom Gardner (see Gardner Canyon, Cochise) and then joined four other families to found St. David. The town was named by Alexander F. Macdonald to honor David W. Patten, a martyr of the Church of Latter Day Saints, who had been killed by a militia mob on October 25, 1838, at Crooked River, Caldwell County, Missouri. Travellers who notice the ponds above the level of the road may be interested in the fact that the earthquake of 1887 opened up new sources of water and the settlers developed artesian wells, the first in Arizona.
P.O. est. July 12, 1882, Joseph McRae, p.m. Ref.: 116, p. 584; AHS, Philoman Merrill File; 225, p. 235; Charles Seller, Letter (March 11, 1973); 264

DAVIS CREEK
Apache   T7N R30E
On February 9, 1858 Lt. Edward Fitzgerald Beale named this creek after the wagon master for Beale's Expedition. Ref.: 23, p. 92

DAVIS DAM
Mohave   T21N R21W   Elev. c. 700'
Authorization to construct this dam came in 1941 and construction began a year later on the earth and rock-filled embankment with its concrete spillway, intake system, and power plant. It was originally known as Bullhead Dam from a rock formation at the site. In 1941 it was renamed for Arthur Powell Davis, Director of Reclamation (1914-1923), among those responsible for initiating Colorado River development. Interrupted by World War II, construction was not completed on time, but in January 1950 the gates were closed, and water began to rise behind the two-hundred-foot-high dam.
P.O. est. in Clark County, Nevada, but changed to Mohave, Dec. 1, 1950; disc. Aug. 31, 1954 Ref.: "Davis Dam Power Plant," U.S. Dept. of Interior, Bureau of Reclamation, Region Three, Boulder City (Feb. 1953); Hornbuckle; 264

DAVIS MESA
Pima   T11S R17E
William C. Davis (b. April 26, 1842, Pennsylvania; d. Aug. 11, 1902) arrived in Tucson from Pennsylvania in 1869. Davis Mesa on the northeast slope of the Catalina Mountains is probably named for him, as is Davis Spring. Ref.: AHS, Chambers Collection, Box 7-8, Env. 17

DAVIDSON CANYON
Pima   T17S R17E   Elev. c. 3800'
At Davidson Springs in 1865 O. Davidson was a special Indian agent for Arizona with his headquarters in Tubac. The spring is in Davidson Canyon, the scene of several Apache attacks on settlers and soldiers. Among the victims was Thomas Venable, slain while hauling lumber from the Santa Rita Mountains with his twelve-mule freight team in 1870. His body was found two days later by Corp. Black, the mail rider who, two years later, was also killed by Apaches who tied him to a dry tree and burned him to death. Ref.: *Arizona Miner* (Nov. 22, 1865); 49, p. 107; 163, p. 232; 242

[196]

DAVIS

Yavapai   T16N R1E   Elev. c. 4500'

This abandoned station on the United Verde & Pacific R.R. was named for a teamster who hauled lumber to it from the saw mill at the base of nearby Mingus Mountain. Ref.: 18a

DAVIS CANYON

Gila   T1N R14E

Davis Canyon was named for John Davis, who had a saloon in it. Ref.: 284, pp. 50, 51

DAVIS-MONTHAN AIR FORCE BASE

Pima   T14S R15E

The Davis portion of the name derives from the name of Lt. Howard Davis, killed in line of duty in 1919. The land was formerly owned by Guy Monthan. Ref.: AHS Names File

DAVIS, MOUNT

Mohave   T25N R22W   Elev. c. 2000

This projection is described as a "symmetrical and prominent peak," the most conspicuous landmark north of Day Mountain (Calif.). Barnes suggests it may have been named by Lt. Joseph Christmas Ives for Jefferson Davis, Secretary of War (1853-1857). Ref.: 18a; 245, p. 79

DAVIS, MOUNT

Yavapai   T12N R1W   Elev. c. 8000'

During the Civil War Mount Davis was named after Confederate President Jefferson Davis to counter northern sympathizers who had named an adjacent mount Union Peak. Ref.: 18a

DAVIS RUIN

Pima   T12S R18E

This Indian ruin is on the old Davis Ranch, hence its name. Davis Spring (T11S/R17E) was a part of the same property. Ref.: 9a, p. 6

DAVIS SPRINGS

Pima   T17S R17E

Farish refers to springs by this name, but probably in error for Davidson Springs (*q.v.*). Farish probably picked up the name from an article in the *Weekly Arizona Miner* (Sept. 3, 1870), referring to the Apache massacre of Thomas Venable, Peter Riggs, and a Mexican. Ref.: 107, III, 141

DAZE LAKE   pro.: /dá<ziʌ/

Coconino   T16N R11E

William Daze (d. c. 1938) ran sheep in this area in the 1880s, although he was primarily a railroad man, serving as an engineer, a road foreman, a master mechanic and finally again as a road foreman. Ref.: Slamon; Kelly

DEAD BOY POINT

Gila   T8N R11E   Elev. c. 4000'

When cattle and sheepmen were feuding, two boys named Wiley Berry and Juan Rafael were murdered on December 22, 1903 in John Berry's sheep camp at this point by Zack Booth, a disreputable cowboy. Booth was hanged. Ref.: 18a

DEAD MAN CANYON

Graham   T7S R27E

Graves of seven or eight men were found in this canyon c. 1870. Ref.: Jennings

DEAD MAN CREEK

Yavapai   T8N R7E   Elev. c. 3500'

Boyd Dougherty and Judge Reiley found an unidentified dead man in this area. Ref.: 18a

DEAD MAN FLAT

Coconino   T25N R8E   Elev. c. 6500'
A place with the name "dead man" leads to the telling of tall tales. One account in this instance says that Indians attacked men driving horses between California and Colorado, with one Indian being killed. Another discusses a foreigner, scarcely able to speak English, who wandered into Flagstaff for help for his sick companion, left alone on the trail. By the time the rescue party reached him, he had been murdered. A straight-forward account is that of W. H. Switzer of Flagstaff, who when fourteen knew a trapper who asked the young man to go with him on a trip, but the boy refused. The trapper set out with his pack horse for the flats where his horse got loose. The trapper's body was found propped against that of his dead horse. By following the tell-tale tracks, it was simple to reconstruct what had happened. Apparently, the trapper pursued his horse for miles. Unable to catch it, he finally shot the animal. Then he sat with his back against the horse and shot himself, hence the name of the flat. Ref.: 71, p. 25; 5, p. 285; Switzer; Anderson

DEAD MAN GAP

Maricopa   T10S R6W   Elev. c. 1500'
It is believed locally that about 1913 a man died of thirst in this gap while trying to catch his loose horses. His grave is in the gap. Ref.: 58; Stout

DEAD MAN'S CANYON

Gila   T8N R14E
A trapper, Presilino Monje (with Bourke's party), apparently caught pneumonia. His companions carried him for two days strapped to his saddle in a chair made of mescal stalks but on March 23, 1873 he died and was buried in this canyon. It was named by Bourke in his honor.
    Tewksbury and Jacobs, associated with the Pleasant Valley War, are also buried in this canyon. Ref.: 49, pp. 211, 212; McKinney

DEAD RIVER

Apache   T18N R24E   Elev. c. 6000'
The river was first mapped by Whipple in 1854 as the Rio de la Iara, a name revised in 1855 to Rio de la Xara. By 1859 Whipple was showing it as Carrizo Creek, which it remained on all maps to 1880, appearing as such for the last time in 1899.
    This place has shifted location, occurring on GLO 1883 adjacent to Carrizo Creek, and on GLO 1933 adjacent to Lithodendron Wash. A story is still told locally that old man Lynn and his two little girls lived in a wagon, roaming up and down this ten-mile river to its junction with the Puerco River. They were not very bright. One day the children wandered into Adamanna saying that they thought something was wrong with the old man. Something was. He had been dead for several days.
Ref.: Grigsby; 329

DEAN PEAK

Mohave   T20N R15W   Elev. 8013'
William (Bill) Dean located a mine near this peak in 1877. Ref.: 329; Harris

DEBEBEKID   pro.: /dibdbdʔekʔid/
Navajo = "sheep lake"

Navajo   T35N R20E   Elev. c. 6000'
This is a Navajo sheep-watering location, also known as *Te-ye-ba-a-kit*. See also Forest Lake, Navajo, and Big Water, Navajo (under BIG) Ref.: 141, p. 191

DECEPTION GULCH

Yavapai   T16N R2E
In 1899 a mining camp was established near Jerome in this gulch. It had four saloons and, judging by the name, did not pay out very well. Ref.: *Arizona Journal Miner* (May 11, 1899)

DECKER WASH

Navajo   T11N R18E   Elev. c. 6000'

Z. B. Decker, a Mormon, was a sheepman in this area in the 1880s. See Aripine, Navajo Ref.: 18a

DEEP CREEK

Gila   T5N R15E

The name comes from the fact that the creek lies deep in a canyon.
Ref.: Cone Webb

DEEP WELL

Yuma   T2S R17W

By 1923 this old well was caved in and abandoned, but it was supposed to have been eleven hundred eighty feet deep. A variant name is Los Posos. (see Posa Plain, La, Yuma) Ref.: 279, p. 207

DEER: Deer abound in many parts of Arizona, which accounts for the following names:

Deer Basin	Yavapai	T13N R7E	
Deer Canyon	Navajo	T17N R17E	
Deer Creek	Apache	T5N R28E	
Deer Creek	Cochise	(1) T14S R19E	(2) T20S R32E
Deer Creek	Coconino	T35N R2W	
Deer Creek	Gila	T8N R10E	
Deer Creek	Graham	(1) T5S R19E	(2) T9S R20E
Deer Creek	Pima	T14S R18E	
Deer Creek	Pinal	T4S R16E	

Finding coal here in the 1880s, speculators tried unsuccessfully to take over land belonging to the San Carlos Indian Reservation. Many deer here led to the names Deer Creek Basin and Deer Coal Basin. Ref.: 49, p. 441

Deer Creek Falls	Coconino	T35N R2W	
Deer Creek Falls	Pinal	T5S R18E	
Deer Flat	Maricopa	T7N R5E	
Deerhead Creek	Greenlee	T2S R28E	
Deerhead Spring	Greenlee	T2S R28E	
Deerhead Spring	Pima	T14S R18E	
Deer Hill	Maricopa	T3N R12E	Elev. 3831'
Deer Hollow	Pima	T17S R9W	
Deer Lake	Coconino	T12N R13E	

Frank Lius, who raised horses, often camped here, as did travellers along the Verde River. Pius named the lake. Ref.: 18a

Deer Lake Canyon	Coconino	T12N R15E	
Deer Lick Canyon	Navajo	T11N R19E	
Deer Mountain	Greenlee	T4N R31E	Elev. 6703'
Deer Mountain	Yavapai	T19N R7W	
Deer Spring	Cochise	(1) T18S R30E	(2) T22S R19E
Deer Spring	Coconino	(1) T35N R2W	(2) T39N R3E
Deer Spring	Graham	(1) T5S R20E	(2) T4S R26E
Deer Spring	Pinal	T1N R12E	
Deer Spring	Yavapai	(1) T12N R1W	(2) T11N R2W

Deer Spring Creek	Gila/Navajo	T7N R22E	
Deer Spring Mountain	Navajo	T7N R22E	Elev. 7441'
Deer Springs (Town)	Navajo	T10N R18E	Elev. 6920'
Deer Springs Canyon	Navajo	T10N R18E	
Deer Valley	Maricopa	T4N R2E	

DEFIANCE, FORT
Apache   T1N R6W   Elev. 6862'

The location is given on the Navajo Base Line, although Fort Defiance by Arizona measurement is north of T27N. Prior to annexation of New Mexico Territory, Navajo Indians were stealing cattle and sheep from Rio Grande Valley settlers. When New Mexico became U.S. territory, control of the Indians was sought. In 1849, Col. John Washington, Military Governor of New Mexico, led an expedition into the Canyon de Chelly region, pausing on his return in the lovely meadow of Cañoncito Bonito (see Bonite Canyon, Apache), an ideal point for a military post.

In April 1851 Col. Edwin Sumner, newly appointed Military Governor of New Mexico, broke up the dissolute post at Santa Fe and in August marched into Navajo country to construct Fort Defiance. Under Maj. Electus Backus, Fort Defiance was established as a full fledged post on September 18, 1851, the first permanent post in present Arizona. In defiance of the Navajo, the soldiers dubbed their log and adobe fortification Fort Defiance. The Indians were not easily subdued. In 1860 some two thousand attacked but were driven off.

Early military posts show Fort Defiance in New Mexico, Arizona Territory not being created until 1864. During the Civil War, troops were withdrawn on April 25, 1861, and sent to Fort Fauntleroy, New Mexico. In the summer of 1863 Col. Christopher (Kit) Carson was assigned to conquer the Navajo. He established Fort Canby as a base camp, but its location is not entirely clear. It was probably a few miles east of Fort Defiance. Carson's campaign of scorched-earth tactics ended with the complete subjugation of the Navajo Indians and Fort Canby was abandoned. When the final treaty was arranged in 1868 at Fort Sumner, New Mexico, old Fort Defiance became the new Navajo Indian Agency with Maj. Theodore Dodd as Agent. In 1870 missionaries established a school in an abandoned adobe house.

The post office at the original Fort Defiance had the distinction of being the first in what was to become Arizona Territory, preceding that at Fort Buchanan (see Buchanan, Fort, Santa Cruz) by a few months.

P.O. est. April 9, 1856, John Weber, p.m. Ref.: 107, I, 308, 309; 141, p. 33; 206, p. 58; 331, pp. 57, 58; 224, p. 149; 145, p. 131; 361, p. 128, Note 8

DEFIANCE PLATEAU
Apache   T25N R29E

The name derives from that of Fort Defiance (see Defiance, Fort, Apache). The Board on Geographic Names in 1915 decreed that the name would be Chuska Plateau. However, Gregory objected, as the plateau in question is nowhere near the Chuska Mountains. He suggested instead that it be called Hubbell Plateau, for the noted trader Juan Lorenzo Hubbell. The B.G.N. refused that name and Gregory then suggested Whipple, which was also refused. The final decision was to call it Defiance Plateau and in 1974 the area was redefined by the USGS.

DELAWARE SPRING
Mohave   Location dubious

Lt. Edward Fitzgerald Beale named this spring in Engels Pass between Truxton and White Rock Springs for Dick Braṽe on April 23, 1859. Dick was a Delaware Indian who showed the springs to the exploring parties. Ref.: H. Floyd *ms.* (1858), Huntington Library

DELLENBAUGH, MOUNT
Mohave   T31N R12W   Elev. 7072'

Maj. John Wesley Powell named this mountain for Frederick S. Dellenbaugh, a member of the Grand Canyon Expedition 1871-1872. Ref.: 89, p. 259

DeLONG PEAK

Pima   T14S R17E   Elev. c. 6000'

This peak in the Santa Catalina Mountains was named for Sidney R. DeLong (b. Dec. 28, 1827, New York; d. 1914), the first mayor of Tucson (1872). For many years he had a trading post at Fort Bowie. Ref.: 224, III, 54; 18a; 62

DEL RIO DAM

Yavapai   T17N R2W   Elev. 4384'

A dam now exists at the site of the former Del Rio Springs where federal troops were encamped prior to their removal to the newly established Fort Whipple in 1864. An officer of that detachment remained at the site of the springs. He was Robert Postle (pro.: /Powstal/) (b. 1837, England; d. April 18, 1871), dismissed from service on December 31, 1863. He filed claim to Postle's ranch on January 13, 1865, living a lonely life until in 1867 David Wesley Shivers' family (from Missouri) stopped at the springs. One of their five children, Hannah, although barely fourteen, remained with Postle. In the 1870 Census, she is listed as his housekeeper. He died when she was nineteen. She lived as a pioneer woman, proving up her homestead, raising her children, and living out her life at Del Rio Springs. Many travellers write of having stopped at her large adobe house on the site of the old military encampment. After the disastrous fire which nearly destroyed Prescott in 1900, that city bought Del Rio and piped water from the springs to the city. In 1910 the Santa Fe R.R. bought the three thousand five hundred twenty acre Del Rio ranch, using it as a dairy ranch for the Fred Harvey hotels. Mules from the Grand Canyon pastured there. Ref.: *Prescott Evening Courier* (Jan. 18, 1956); *Arizona Miner* (March 13, 1869); 233, pp. 1-4; 297, p. 131, p. xxxvii (Postle's Ranch)

DEL SHAY BASIN   pro.: /del šey/

Apache = "red ant"

Gila   T8N R11E   Elev. c. 5000'

This basin was named for an Apache chief (whose name has also been spelled Del Che), who roamed this territory from 1870 until his death in 1874. He had a reputation for ferocity. The Indian had reason to be vicious, as he was treated badly. While he was a prisoner at Camp McDowell, he was shot in the back, and on another occasion the post doctor tried to poison him. In return, he was responsible for the death of many whites. Del Shay made friends with Charles Douchet, a soldier at Fort Reno, and showed him a gold mine in the basin which now bears the Indian's name. Douchet and his partner, Al Sieber (who served as chief of scouts for the Department of Arizona) located the Del Shay gold mine and named the basin for the Indian.

Barnes says that Dr. Warren S. Day, post surgeon at Camp Verde, bribed Del Shay's brother by tossing Mexican dollars to him until his greed overcame his resistance to telling them where Del Shay was. Soldiers returned to Camp Verde with Del Shay's head on July 29, 1874. Ref.: Mrs. Laura Cliff Griffin; Woody; AHS, Charles M. Clark, Letter (May 25, 1935)

DEL SHAY SPRING

Gila   T8N R11E

This spring at the head of Del Shay Creek is named for the Indian chief Del Shay, who often camped here. See Del Shay Basin, Gila Ref.: Griffin

DELUGE WASH

Mohave   T17N R15W   Elev. c. 2500'

A prospector named Tom Burch, or possibly Diamond Joe Reynolds (whose name may have been Joe Diamond), had a camp in this wash. It was destroyed by a deluge in 1873, hence the name. Ref.: Harris; 18a; 200, p. 22

DEMARAY POINT

Coconino (Grand Canyon)   T31N R3E   Elev. 5200'

This point was named for Arthur Edward Demaray (1887-1958), Director of the National Park Service in 1951. The name was applied by the USGS on July 14, 1964. Ref.: 329

DE MOTTE PARK

Coconino   T35N R2W   Elev. c. 7500'

Every automobile visitor to the North Rim uses a road through this open glade on the Kaibab Plateau. Maj. John Wesley Powell in August 1872 named the natural park for Dr. Harvey C. De Motte, Professor of Mathematics at Wesleyan University, who traveled briefly with Powell's party. During the 1880s this glade was referred to as VT Park because Van Slack and Thompson raised cattle with the V T brand (which belonged to the Valley Tannery of Orderville, Utah, where the two men lived). The cattle range was abandoned in 1919 and the name De Motte Park was reestablished. V T Lake and V T Hill owe their names to the same two cattlemen. Ref.: 322, VII (L939), 9; Schellbach File (Grand Canyon); 89, pp. 318-319

DENNEHOTSO

Navajo = "where the green line ends"

Apache   T40N R24E   Elev. 5000'

The name of this village with its BIA boarding school refers to the grassy area ending at the sandstone outcrops. Ref.: 329; 331, p. 51

DENNEHOTSO CANYON

Apache   T40N R24E

This canyon derives its name in the same way as does Dennehotso (q.v.). In 1921 it was also called Sahotsoidbeazhe Canyon, interpreted as meaning "where the short grass comes out from the canyon." This name was set aside because the description applies to many areas in Navajo country. Ref.: 329

DENNISON

Coconino   T20N R14E   Elev. 5002'

William E. Dennison (b. 1833, Virginia), a farmer, is said to have lived close to this siding on the railroad, although Barnes says it may have been named for Denny, an assistant road master for the railroad. The name occurs on the 1883 USGS map. Marshall says it was named for a locating engineer. Ref.: 62; 18a; 218, p. 364

DE NOON

Pinal

This mining camp two miles from the Reymert mill was named for the mine owner, Judge James De Noon Reymert, who in 1888 was a well known newspaperman and lawyer. See also Reymert, Pinal Ref.: *Arizona Star* (May 26, 1889), p. 4; AHS; 264

DESERT FACADE

Coconino (Grand Canyon)   T33N R5E

This cliff is descriptively named, as it is indeed a facade of the desert.

DESERT PEAK

Pinal   T10S R11E   Elev. 2608'

Hinton describes this peak as standing out in lonely beauty in a "combination of colors, so vivid ... as to defy ... Turner himself...."
Ref.: 163, p. 269

DESERT SAGE

Maricopa   T1N R7E

This small community a few miles east of Mesa took its name from the growth in the surrounding desert. Briefly it had its own post office, but it was discontinued some time in late 1973 or 1974, becoming a branch post office of Mesa.
Ref.: *Directory of Post Offices* (1974)

DESERT STATION

Maricopa   c. T3S R2W

To provide a relay point for the Butterfield Overland Mail in 1858, Desert Station was put into operation half-way between Maricopa Wells and Tezotal. It was aptly named

because water had to be brought to it from twenty miles away.
Ref.: 73, II, 172; "Letter of Mr. Wallace, June 15, 1860," *Daily Alta Californian* (July 1, 1860)

DESERT STATION
La Paz   T4N R15W

According to Martha Summerhayes, Desert Station in 1875 was owned by Englishmen named Hunt and Dudley, and the place was clean and attractive, unusual for a stage station. For some years the stage station was abandoned, coming back into use after a well about one hundred twenty feet deep was dug c. 1880. The name today is Desert Well, referring to a place about five miles southwest of Vicksburg.
Ref.: 314, p. 156; 279, p. 207; 163, p. xxvii

DESERT VIEW POINT
Coconino (Grand Canyon)   T31N R5E   Elev. 7438'

The name for this viewpoint was Navajo Point from 1906 until it was changed to its present name in 1932. A fine view from the South Rim underlies the name for the location. The Navajo refer to it as *Yahéháhi* (= "standing tower"). Ref.: 329

DESERT WELLS
La Paz   T4N R15W

This small community at the site of the old Desert Station (*q.v.*) was originally a service station with one water well, but by 1970 it had additional wells and about six families lived in the vicinity. Ref.: 329

DETRITAL WASH
Mohave   T29N R21W

This location used to be called Death Valley Wash for the portion from the community of Chloride north to the Colorado River. The name derives from the detritus marking its course. Ref.: Housholder

DEUBENDORFF RAPIDS
Coconino (Grand Canyon)   T34N R2W   Elev. c. 2500'

In 1932 the USGS approved the name for the rapids. The name is that of a boatman on the 1909 Galloway-Stone Expedition, who capsized in this rapid. The expedition had four boats, running from Green River, Wyoming, to Needles, California for the fastest trip then on record (encompassing two months and one week). Ref.: 329; Kolb

DE VACA TERRACE
Coconino (Grand Canyon)   T33N R2W   Elev. 4750'

The name for this terrace was proposed by Francois E. Matthes to E. M. Douglas, geographer for the USGS in 1906, and the name was approved officially in October 1908, to honor Spanish explorer Alvar Nuñez Cabeza de Vaca, lost among the Indians on the Gulf of Mexico Coast, c. 1528-1536. Ref.: 244, III, No. 10 (June 30, 1929); Schellbach File (Grand Canyon); 329

DEVA TEMPLE
Coconino (Grand Canyon)   T32N R3E   Elev. 7339'

In accordance with the decision to name several buttes after deities of various mythologies, Deva Temple was suggested by Henry Gannett in April 1906 and was approved the next day. Ref.: 329; 178, p. 30

DEVIL DOG HILLS
Coconino   T21N R1E   Elev. c. 5000'

Locally it is asserted that the extremely rough nature of these hills may account for their name. Ref.: Benham

DEVIL'S CACHE
Santa Cruz   T21S R13E   Elev. 4600'

The mineral deposits in this mile-long ridge yielded the name Devil's Cache or Cash

Box, which may be a corruption of Devil's Cache, the name used by Rockfellow in 1879. Ref.: Lenon; 286, p. 185; 277, pp. 39-40

DEVIL'S CHAIR
Coconino   Near Flagstaff
This huge chair-like rock formation reportedly earned its name when several children fell from it to their deaths. Ref.: Colleen Simons (Informant); Pat Terry (Collector, 1968)

DEVIL'S CHASM
Gila   T5N R14E
The devil himself seems to have formed this narrow canyon with its single entrance and very steep three thousand feet high cliffs. Ref.: Devore

DEVIL'S CORKSCREW
Coconino (Grand Canyon)   T32N R3E
The Bright Angel Trail no longer contains the spectacular Devil's Corkscrew which aroused terror in many a traveller en route from the Rim to the bottom of the Grand Canyon. The trail derived its name from the way that it curved back and around on itself. Ref.: 5, p. 492; 178, p. 61

DEVIL'S PUMPKIN PATCH
Coconino   T31N R10E
Many of the stone formations here resemble petrified pumpkins. The place is near Dinosaur Tracks. Ref.: 5, p. 413

DEVIL'S SLIDE RAPIDS
Coconino (Grand Canyon)
Brown applied this descriptive name in 1935 to rapids at the head of lower Granite Gorge. Ref.: 329

DEVIL'S THRONE
Santa Cruz   T21S R13E
This formation near Devil's Cash Box resembles an over-stuffed chair with a horseshoe-shaped "back" of rolling land around a piece of flat ground which forms the seat. Ref.: Lenon

DEVIL'S WINDPIPE
Yavapai   T13N R7E   Elev. 3200'
This short canyon was named by Indians because of a rock formation in it that reminded them of the devil's own windpipe. Ref.: 329; Goddard

DEVINE, MOUNT
Pima   T15S R5E   Elev. 4788'
In 1893 Pima County surveyor George Roskruge named this peak for John J. Devine, father of K. C. Devine, who c. 1890 had silver mines nearby. Ref.: Kitt; 329

DEVINS BUTTE
Apache
On an 1869 military map, this place shows as near the head of the Cibicu Rio. At that time Brig. Gen. Thomas C. Devins was serving as commandant for the Arizona District. Ref.: 159; 242; *Weekly Arizona Miner* (June 5, 1869)

DEVINS JUMPOFF
Apache
This point was not near Devins Butte on the military maps examined at the National Archives, but appears to be at the head of Webber's Creek. (Webber was the cartographer). See also Devins Butte, Apache Ref.: 242

DEVORE WASH

Gila   T2N R14E   Elev. c. 4000'

David Devore (b. 1856, Kentucky) helped his uncle, John Kennedy, drive stock in this area in 1875. Devore was both a rancher and miner, settling in Prescott in 1873, thereafter moving to Globe in 1880. Devore Wash is part of the old stock trail through the Tonto Basin. Ref.: Woody; 224, III

DEWEY

Yavapai   T13N R1E   Elev. 4556'

In 1872 Darrel Duppa had a stage station called Agua Fria at this location. The post office established in May 1875 was called Agua Fria Valley, this name being changed to Aguafria in 1892. The P.O. was disc. in 1895 as the Postal Department had a rule that an old name could not be used when a post office was reopened. The name Dewey was given to it upon its reopening in 1898, in honor of Adm. George Dewey. The railroad station at this location was and continues to be Cherry Creek, but this name was also unacceptable for the post office (it was in use for another location). In 1922, the post office at Haynes was shifted to delivery at Dewey.

P.O. est. as Agua Fria Valley, May 15, 1875, Dennis J. Marr, p.m.; changed to Aguafria, July 22, 1893; disc. Jan. 11, 1895; reest. as Dewey, June 2, 1898, Robert De Lange, p.m. Nat'l. Arch. postal-sites records named De Lange as p.m. in 1892. However, by July 18, 1898, Fred Hiltenbrandt was p.m. at Dewey. Ref.: *Arizona Miner* (Jan. 20, 1872); 242; 329

DIABLITO MOUNTAIN   pro.: /diablito/

Spanish = "little devil"

Santa Cruz   T20S R12E   Elev. 4742'

Local lore says that many devils are in the vicinity. Ref.: Seibold

DIABLO, CANYON   pro.: /kænyən dáyblo/ /kænyən diablo/

Spanish = "Devil's Canyon"

Coconino   T20N R12E   Elev. 5429'

In 1853 Capt. Amiel W. Whipple, then with the Ives party, called this deep gorge Cañon Diablo, describing it as a deep chasm which could be bridged by a railroad, as the banks would furnish stone. However, in November 1881 railroad construction was delayed by the lack of bridge materials, specifically lumber. A post office was soon established and both a Wells Fargo station and a trading post were located here by Frederick W. Volz in the 1890s. As his building was white, Navajo Indians referred to it as *Kinigai* (= "White house"). Their name for the canyon was *Kinigai Boko* (= "White House Canyon"). When the National Old Trail Highway (Route 66) came into being, Canyon Lodge was built here (c. 1923). It had a post office. The first meteorites found in Arizona were located here by sheepherders in 1886, a forerunner of the discovery of Meteor Crater (*q.v.*). The upper ridges of this area — no longer canyon-like — are sometimes called Canyon Diablo Wash.

P.O. est. as Canyon Diablo, Nov. 15, 1886, Charles H. Algert, p.m.; apparently out of operation, as postal records show it reest. on March 30, 1903, with Frederick W. Volz, p.m.; disc. Feb. 28, 1918; reest. as Canyon Lodge, June 23, 1924, Earl M. Cundiff, p.m.; disc. May 14, 1926 Ref.: 346, p. 163 and Note 2; 23, p. 46; 242; 329

DIAMOND BUTTE

Gila   T9N R12E   Elev. 6316'

This butte is topped by a diamond-shaped mesa. Diamond Rim forms its edge. Ref.: McKinney; Woody

DIAMOND BUTTE

Mohave   T37N R10W   Elev. 6250'

Frederick Dellenbaugh, artist and topographer with the second Grand Canyon expedition, gave the name because the exploring party found here an ant hill covered with quartz crystals sparkling like diamonds. Ref.: 88, p. 192

DIAMOND CANYON
Mohave   T27N R10W
On April 5, 1858 Lt. Joseph Christmas Ives and Dr. John S. Newberry arrived at the western end of the Grand Canyon at Diamond Peak and gave it and Diamond Canyon their names. As a traveller in 1890 noted, "On comparing the mud color of the Colorado with the crystalline purity of this creek, one realizes to what the latter might owe its name." Early-day tourists to the Grand Canyon viewed it from this point, staying at the Diamond Creek Hotel, a wooden building which disappeared after its abandonment, as ranchers and Indians carried away the frame building piece by piece for their own use. Diamond Creek in 1776 was called Arroyo de San Alexo by Garcés. Diamond Peak is nearby. Ref.: 5, p. 323; 18a; *The Pacific Coast* (1890), p. 302

DIAMOND FIELDS: Location: supposedly south of Hopi villages near Little Colorado River. In 1872 men named Arnold and Slack alledgedly salted this area with rough diamonds and capitalized at ten million dollars a plan to "mine" diamonds here. Clarence King, a geologist, visited the place and termed the salting a fraud because the stones had come from thousands of miles away.

Although the place was called the "*Arizona* Diamond Swindle," actually the fields which had been salted were in northwestern Colorado, a fact that did not keep some map makers from noting diamond fields in the extreme central northwestern part of Arizona. Ref.: 15, I, 591, 592

DIAMOND JOE PEAK
Mohave   T17N R14W   Elev. 1821'
Diamond Joe Reynolds, whose name may have been Joe Diamond, located a mine here. He is said to have owned the Diamond Joe Mississippi River Steamboat Line and also the Congress Mine in Yavapai County. This location is now abandoned. See Deluge Wash, Mohave Ref.: Babcock; 18a

DIAMOND MOUNTAIN
Maricopa   T6N R8E   Elev. 5120'
In 1903 this mountain did not have a name. It came later when the area was under the control of the Diamond Cattle Company, employing a diamond brand on cattle. The name was made official in 1946. Ref.: 18a; 329

DIAMOND POINT
Gila   T11N R11E   Elev. 6384'
Rock crystals here are locally called "Arizona diamonds."
Ref.: 18a

DIANA TEMPLE
Coconino (Grand Canyon)   T31N R1E
Earlier referred to as No Man's Land, this narrow mesa received its name in June 1908 when several classic mythological names were applied by the USGS.Ref.: 329

DIAZ PEAK
Pima   T18S R4W   Elev. 3913'
In 1945 the Park Service suggested this name for a peak in the Organ Pipe Cactus National Monument to honor Melchior Diaz. Diaz, who served with Coronado's expedition in 1540, made a trip overland to the Colorado River mouth, thus becoming the first white man to travel through the current monument. On his return journey, a greyhound was harrying sheep used for food. To force it away, Diaz rode at it with his lance. The lance caught in the ground and ran through Diaz' kidney. He died in agony. Ref.: Hensen; 329; 357, p. 407

DIAZ SPIRE
Pima   T17S R4W   Elev. 3892'
This spire near Diaz Peak was named in 1945. See Diaz Peak, Pima Ref.: 329

DICK PILLAR

Coconino   T33N R1W

This rock pillar was named for Robert Dick, a Scotch geologist, who assisted Hugh Miller during the latter's studies of Old Red Sandstone in the Grand Canyon.
Ref.: 178, p. 82

DICK WILLIAMS CREEK

Gila   T11N R12E

Dick Williams was an early ranger with a rock cabin on the bank of this creek.
Ref.: McInturf

DIFFICULT CANYON

Mohave

In a report dated January 15, 1868, Col. William Redwood Price said he named this canyon because his troops had great difficulty entering it in pursuit of Indians. The canyon, according to the report is about twenty-five miles north of Beale Spring in the Cerbat Range. Col. Price also said that a variant name for the Canyon was Cherum's Canyon, a fact which probably places it adjacent to Cherum Peak (T23N/R17W).
Ref.: 335, pp. 49, 80

DIGGER WASH

Navajo   T20N R22E   Elev. c. 6000'

Wild horses formerly dug for water in this stream bed. Initially the horse bands consisted of about ten mares and a stallion. The horses multiplied so rapidly that they soon roamed in huge herds. In this wash they were observed teaching their offspring to dig for water (found eighteen inches below the surface). Emigrants, not knowing this fact, not infrequently died of thirst in this area. Ref.: Branch; Grigsby

DILKON

Navajo   T23N R19E   Elev. 5885'

The nearby solitary desert hill was first known as Castle Butte (q.v.), said to resemble a "ruined medieval stronghold, having a causeway flanked by towers, above which [loom] embattlements and casements." This place is now known as Dilkon Hill (elev. 6178'). J. Barnet (Barney) Stiles operated a trading post, causing the name of the community to change to Stiles. In 1914 McPherson C. Maddox opened a post office named for himself. The next owner was Justus W. Bush, who in 1919 applied for the name Dilcon (sic), a partial use of the Navajo name for the butte behind his store. The Navajo name is *tsezhiihdikooh* (= "smooth black rock"). A nearby hill is descriptively called Chimney Butte.
P.O. est. as Maddox Aug. 28, 1913, McPherson C. Maddox, p.m.; changed to Castle Butte, Sept. 25, 1916; changed to Dilkon, Dec. 17, 1920; disc. Jan. 13, 1943; reest. at unknown date; disc. Jan. 1, 1956 Ref.: Richards; Museum of Northern Arizona Files; 141, pp. 137, 140; 329; 79, p. 56; 242

DINNEBITO   pro.: /ḏinébitó/

Navajo: *dine* = "the people"; *bito* = "water, spring"
Navajo   T31N R16E

Here Lorenzo Hubbell established a trading post, which was a center for Navajo living along the streambed which they referred to as Dinnebito. The name applies to a one hundred-mile wash extending through Navajo and Coconino counties.

DINNEBITO SPRING

Coconino   T28N R13E

The name has been variously spelled Dena bet Spring, Tenebito and Tinebito. See Sand Springs, Coconino, and Dinnebeto, Navajo Ref.: 141, pp. 154, 191; 331, p. 50; 329

DINNEHOTSO   pro.: /ḏinéha>tsol/

Navajo: *dine* = "the people"; *hotso* = "upper end of meadow"
Apache   T40N R23E

The name describes the situation of the land. See Pipe Rocks, Navajo
Ref.: 331, p. 51

DINNE MESA   pro.: /diné/
Navajo: *dine* = "the people"

Apache   T41N R27E   Elev. 6627'

The current name Dinne Mesa was made official in 1955 although it was first applied in 1907 by Herbert Gregory. In 1915 it was called *Toh'atin* (Navajo = "no water") and also No Water Mesa. Gothic Mesa was another early name for it. The term "Gothic" referred to the appearance of eroded land formations.
Ref.: 141, pp. 31, 90 (Note 2), 191, 192; 329

DINNER CREEK
Gila   T8N R13E

This creek in Dinner Canyon was just far enough away from their starting points so that traders paused here to eat their midday meal. Ref.: Woody

DINOSAUR CANYON
Coconino   T31N R10E

Dozens of three-toed dinosaur prints were discovered on white sandstone here in 1928 by Hubert Richardson, hence the name. Ref.: 331, p. 51

DINOSAUR CITY
Mohave   Eight miles west of Aubrey Valley south of
                                highway 66

The post office at this point was discontinued between March 30, 1973 and July 1, 1974, mail thereafter coming to it as a branch of Peach Springs. Ref.: 264

DIONISIO, SAN
Yuma   T8S R22W

At the junction of Gila and Colorado Rivers in 1701 Fr. Kino arrived at the then-large community of Indians and held mass on San Dionisio Day, naming the community for that fact (St. Dennis). See also Yuma, Yuma Ref.: 279, p. 65

DIPPING VAT SPRING
Apache   T9N R24E

As it is necessary for ranchers to dip livestock against worm and insect infestation, vats are customary. The one here has been in use for over thirty years. It is also called Dipping Vat Spring. Ref.: 329

DIX CREEK
Greenlee   T3S R31E

This two-pronged creek takes its name from that of Dick Boyles, who owned the Dix Ranch (a corruption) at the mouth of the Blue River. The branches are called Left-Pronged Dix Creek and Right-Pronged Dix Creek. Ref.: Mrs. Fred Fritz, Sr.

DIXIE
Mohave   Elev. c. 2500'

Mormons from Utah called the area of the Arizona Strip along the Virgin River by this name because of its warm climate, which enabled them to raise grapes, apples and other fruit. Ref.: 88, pp. 163, 164

DIXIE CANYON
Cochise   T22S R24E   Elev. 5939'

Prior to 1902 a black called Nigger Dick lived in this canyon at the springs where he farmed and had cattle. As a result the canyon came to be known as Dick's Canyon and finally as Dixie Canyon. See also Sherer Canyon, Cochise Ref.: 329; 18a

DIXIE MINE
Maricopa   T4N R3E   Elev. c. 500'

The location of the mine gave the name to the stop called Dixie on the railroad in the Gila Bend Mountains. Ref.: 279, p. 33

DIXIE SPRING
Yuma   T5S R18W

The Fish and Wild Life Service c. 1952 developed this spring and named it for an old-time prospector. Ref.: Monson

DOAK
Gila   T2S R14E

The reason for the name of this small settlement has not been ascertained.
P.O. est. Nov. 6, 1918, Margaret L. Tanner, p.m.; disc. March 3, 1921 Ref.: 242

DOBBS STATION
Pima   T19S R8E

E. W. Dobbs, a stage driver and miner, in 1884 established a stage station known as Half-way House on the route from Tucson to Quijotoa below Dobbs Buttes. Passengers dined at the station. Ref.: AHS, Rollin C. Brown File; 308, p. 79; Malcolm W. Wilson, Letter (with photo), (Tucson)

DOC CARTER'S SPRING
Yuma   T5S R18W

This spring in the southwestern part of the Castle Dome Mountains is named for Dr. Carter, a prospector. Ref.: Monson

DOCK
Pima: *dahk* = "nose"
Pinal   T3S R6E   Elev. 1500'

Pima Indians on the reservation referred to this railroad point as *Amelican dahk* (= "American nose"), possibly after the shape of a nearby peak and their perception of American noses. Ref.: 18a; 283, p. 158

DODSON WASH
Navajo   T11N R20E

This wash takes its name from that of Rube Dodson, a Mormon cattleman and farmer who used this canyon in the 1880s. It is also sometimes referred to as Mortensen Wash or as Morterson Wash. Actually Mortenson Wash joins Colbath Wash to form Dodson Wash. Ref.: 18a; 329

DODSON WASH
Pinal   T6S R15E

There is a possibility that this wash is named for Joseph N. Dodson, who was the postmaster at Old Camp Grant.

DOLAN SPRINGS
Mohave   T25N R19W   Elev. 3360'

This community of about three hundred people is adjacent to Dolan Springs, hence the name, but why the springs are so named is not known.

DOME
Yuma   T8S R20W   Elev. 191'

Prior to the coming of the railroad, the present railroad stop known as Dome existed under the name Gila City, established in 1858 when gold placers were discovered by Jacob Snively and Henry Burch. His name led to identifying the place also as Snively's. Prospectors by the thousands soon swarmed to Gila City. Four or five adobe buildings and hundreds of tents sheltered them. J. Ross Browne described the bustle, "Enterprising men hurried to the spot with barrels of whiskey and billiard tables; Jews came with ready made clothing and fancy wares; traders crowded in with wagons of pork and beans; and gamblers came with cards and monte-tables. There was everything in Gila City within a few months but a church and a jail...." Although a flood nearly wiped out Gila City in 1862, miners still roamed the region, dry washing for gold, but by 1865 nearly all gold and the miners as well were gone. By 1872 Gila City had shrunk to a single house, monte tables and a corral. A stage station was run by A. Lang, who sold it in late 1877 to Josiah Brown. The place was nearly dormant until the completion of the Santa Fe R.R. in northern Arizona caused a cessation of steamboat shipping on the Colorado, at which time the railroad siding at Dome (named for the nearby Castle Dome Mountains) became the principal shipping point for southern Arizona miners. By 1890 Dome had enough residents to seek its own post office, although a post office existed two miles away at Monitor on the outskirts of old Gila City at the mouth of Monitor Gulch. at the mouth of Monitor Gulch.

P.O. est. as Gila City, Dec. 24, 1858, H. Busch, p.m.; disc. July 14, 1863; p.o. est. as Dome, Dec. 16, 1892, William S. Hodges, p.m.; name changed to Monitor, date?; name changed to Gila, May 9, 1904, John R. Lee, p.m.; (first name suggested was Monitorio); name changed to Dome, May 16, 1905; disc. June 30, 1928; reest. May 22, 1929; disc. July 10, 1940; reest. Oct. 1, 1948; disc. between July 1, 1961 and June 30, 1962 as sub-station for Yuma. It should be noted that a p.o. was est. at Monitor on Dec. 3, 1890, Albert S. Potter, p.m.; disc. March 3, 1904; Wells Fargo 1906

Ref.: 279, p. 10; 355, pp. 86, 208; Mercer, "Desert Scrap Book;" *Yuma Daily Sun* (Aug. 26, 1953), II, 3; 107, I, 296; Lenon; Theobald; 242; *Arizona Sentinel* (Dec. 8, 1877), p. 3

DOME MOUNTAIN

Maricopa   T2N R8E   Elev. 3050'

This highest portion of a ridge looks like a dome. The name has been used since c. 1900.
Ref.: 329

DOME ROCK MOUNTAINS

La Paz   T5N R20W   Elev. 2400'

This range should not be confused with the Castle Dome Mountains to the southeast. In 1854 Lt. N. Michler of the Boundary Survey Commission referred to this mountain as Avie Tok-a-va or Dome Mountain, also called Sierra de San Pedro, which he said resembled a solid rock cathedral dome, noting that an Indian guide was supposed to live in the range. Near it he noted a second peak which he called Broken Dome. An early name for the first was Dome Mountain. A military map for the Department of New Mexico (1859) names this range "Sierra or Dome Mountains." The range has also been referred to as La Paz Mountains, probably because of the former presence of La Paz community nearby. Ref.: 106, pp. 104, 105; 329

DOÑA ANA COUNTY

New Mexico and Arizona

This was the name of one of the four counties noted by Mowry on his 1860 map prior to the creation of Arizona Territory from the then-extensive Territory of New Mexico. Doña Ana County covered what are now Graham, Cochise, and Greenlee Counties. See Pima County Ref.: 18a

DONEY PARK   pro.: /dó wniᴬ/

Coconino   T22N R8E   Elev. c. 4800'

This park-like area was named for Ben Doney (b. 1841; d. Oct. 30, 1930). Doney referred to this area as Black Bill Park. Doney, a Civil War veteran, settled in Flagstaff in 1883 and, convinced that the nearby hills contained buried Spanish gold, excavated many holes in nearby red cinder cones. As a result, the four small craters northwest of Wupatki are sometimes called Doney Craters and also Doney's Cone (T25N/R9E). Actually they are not craters, but cinder-cone mountains. The Navajo called the cone *Dzi Łłichii* (= "Red Mountain"). Navajos customarily used eagle feathers from eagles nesting at this place. Originally the area was called Dead Man's Flat (not the same as the present Dead Man Flat, which is on the other side of the peaks). See also Townsend, Coconino

P.O. est. Sept. 29, 1921, Frank G. Smith, p.m.; disc. March 26, 1923

Ref.: Colton, "Tracing the Lost Mine," p. 27; 276, p. 35; 331, p. 51; Bartlett; 242; Museum of Northern Arizona; 329

DON LUIS   pro.: /Don Luwiys/
Cochise   T23S R24E   Elev. c. 4000'
The post office sub-station at this location on the railroad was named for Lewis
Williams, who with his brother Ben promoted developing mines near Bisbee, and for the
fact that Mexicans referred to him as Don Luis.
P.O. est. May 7, 1903, John James Mercer, p.m.; disc. Aug. 31, 1933; Wells Fargo
1904; apparently reest. as p.o. is currently a sub-station for Bisbee
Ref.: "50th Anniversary Edition," *Douglas Dispatch* (1952), Section 8, p. 7; 242

DONNELLY WASH
Pinal   T4S R11E   Elev. c. 2300'
In 1879 a pioneer named Donnelly was living in what was called Donnelly Canyon. He
established his ranch on the course of this wash at the side of a spring visited by Fr.
Eusebio Kino in 1697 and named by him San Gregorio.
Ref.: Mrs. Dudley Craig; 45, p. 368

DORADO, CAMP EL
Mohave
A military camp was established opposite El Dorado Canyon, California, on the
Colorado River on January 15, 1867 and abandoned on August 24, 1867, probably
named because of its location. Earlier a ferry was established on the Arizona side, taking
its name for the post office from the fact that it served the California side at El Dorado
Canyon. ·
P.O. est. Jan. 17, 1867, Frank S. Alling, p.m.; disc. Sept. 27, 1867
Ref.: 159, p. 497; 145, p. 132

DORADO CANYON, EL
Mohave
According to Mallach, this canyon runs from the top of the Black Mountain for ten miles
to Lake Mohave. It was also the name of the post office at Camp El Dorado (*q.v.*).
Ref.: 215, p. 118

DORAN'S DEFEAT CANYON
Yavapai   T12N R7E
This name has been in use since the early 1900s, the time when Charlie Callaway's run-
away mule "Doran" met his Waterloo in this canyon. There is also a spring in the
canyon. Ref.: 233, p. 91

DORSEY GULCH
Greenlee   T3S R30E   Elev. c. 5500'
Hank Dorsey, a prospector, was in Clifton prior to 1872 and established claims in the
gulch bearing his name. Ref.: Fitzgerald; Sweeting

DOS CABEZAS   pro.: /dos cabéysas/
Spanish = "two heads"
Cochise   T14S R24E   Elev. 5071'
The present small community is named for the nearby two bald summits. The town is
approximately one-half mile west of Dos Cabezas Spring or Ewell Station, also called in
1851 Ewell Springs. The springs were used by the Boundary Survey party in 1851, but
not by the Butterfield Overland Stage. However, the Birch Stage route did use the spring
in 1857 at a station owned by the San Antonio and San Diego Stage Line. The springs
are also the site of the first school built in Cochise County in 1878, the year in which new
mines caused the town to prosper. See Dos Cabezas Peaks, Cochise, and Wrightson,
Mount, Santa Cruz
P.O. est. as Dos Cabezos, April 8, 1879, F. Beebe, p.m.; changed to Dos Cabezas, Jan.
1, 1949; disc. c. 1959 as independent station, becoming sub-station for Willcox; Wells
Fargo 1885 Ref.: John J. Howard, Letter to Mrs. E. Macia (June 10, 1928); 73, II,
139; 242; Varney

DOS CABEZAS PEAKS   pro.: /dos cabéysas/
Spanish = "two heads"

Cochise   T14S R23E   Elev. 8363'

Near the northern end of the Dos Cabezas Mountains loom two solitary pinnacles of great uniformity, which lack significant growth. From a distance they look very much like giant heads, hence the name, in use as early as 1851. Ref.: 254, p. 23

DOS NARICES MOUNTAIN   pro.: /dos nariysəs/
Spanish = "two noses"

Pinal   Unknown

According to Bourke, these two adjacent peaks, which resemble noses, are probably about twelve miles northeast from Old Camp Grant. Ref.: 49, p. 31

DOSORIS

Yavapai   c. 12 miles S. of Prescott

The Friebergen 1883 map shows this small mining camp. The mine was discovered in 1880 by Townsend Cox, who named it for his mother's home town, Dosoris Island, New York. It may have been in Dosoris Canyon. Ref.: 18a

DOS PALMAS WELL   pro.: /dos pálməs/
Spanish = "two palms"

Maricopa   T14N R4W   Elev. c. 800'

Two large yucca palms near this well led to the name. By the early 1930s almost everything associated with the place had been washed away. Ref.: 18a

DOUBLE ADOBE

Cochise   T22S R26E   Elev. 4009'

This almost deserted little community takes its name from a two-room adobe building with eighteen-inch walls containing several gun openings. The Double Adobe Ranch existed here when Tucson flourished in the 1880s. Ref.: "50th Anniversary Edition," *Douglas Dispatch* (1952), Sec. 5, p. 8

DOUBLE CABIN PARK

Coconino   T16N R18E

This place took on the name Double Cabin because the Jim Hawkins family and the Fain family had a reunion in what was then known as the Fir Park. Each family built a cabin, hence the name. Ref.: 261, p. 132

DOUBLE CIRCLE RANCH

Greenlee   T1S R28E   Elev. c. 5000'

In the late 1870s George H. Stevens used this location as a sheep ranch. A former sergeant of the Fifth Cavalry, Stevens married a high-caste Apache named Molly and established this ranch on Eagle Creek. It was then known as Little Stevens Ranch or the Eagle Ranch. The Apache name was *Too-der-nas-sose* (= "water arises from one spring and spreads around"). Joe H. Hampson owned the place from 1884 to 1908. In 1909 with Tom Wilson and Maj. Drum he organized the Double Circle Ranch, using as a brand one circle within another. Hampson sold out to his partners in 1912.

The Double Circle Ranch, totally-self-sustaining, was typical of early ranches. Everything had to be packed in, including a piano Mexicans lugged over rough mountains. At one time the Double Circle Ranch contained some one thousand two hundred square miles but the Depression with its low beef prices reduced cattle raising. In 1936 the San Carlos Indians administered the final blow by refusing to renew the grazing lease for the Double Circle.

In 1924 a post office called Woolaroc was established on the ranch. The name was suggested by W. Ellis Wiltbank to honor the name of the airplane which had won the Dole Honolulu-to-San Francisco race. Further, the plane name came from that of Frank Phillips' estate, which had *woo*ds, *la*kes, and *ro*cks.

P.O. est. Jan. 5, 1921, Anna E. Hoffman, p.m.; resc. Feb. 2, 1921; est. as Woolaroc, May 24, 1924, Willard L. Mabra, p.m.; disc. June 14, 1930
Ref.: 5, p. 432; 257, pp. 174, 175, 176; Fred Fritz Notes; Shannon; 83, pp. 46, 47; 351 (Smithsonian)

DOUBLE KNOLLS
Maricopa   T1N R7E   Elev. 1655'
These two small knolls near Tempe were formerly called Gregg Buttes, for Dr. A. J. Gregg. Ref.: 18a

DOUBLE PEAKS
Pinal   T8S R4E
These peaks on either side of the Gila River are sometimes referred to as South Butte or South Peak (Elev. 2815') and North Butte or North Peak (Elev. 2283'). The name Double Peak is of course descriptive. Actually this location is a single mountain mass with twin summits.

DOUBLE SPRINGS
Coconino   T18N R8E
In the early 1900s Less Hart used twin springs at this location. The place is now a camp ground. Ref.: Hart

DOUBTFUL CANYON
Cochise   T12S R32E   Elev. 5200'
The pass and canyon were named because Indians were so troublesome here that it was doubtful whether emigrants or soldiers could safely pass through. Butterfield Overland mail route had its Doubtful Pass Station in Doubtful (Pass) Canyon, shortened to Doubtful Canyon. Ref.: 198, p. 31; Schroeder

DOUDSVILLE   pro.: /dáwdisvil/
Mohave   T18N R21W
In 1870 Milo F. Dows (sic) (b. 1840, Pennsylvania) was a prospector and laborer in Mohave City. He owned a ranch here. His name is also spelled Doude. Ref.: Harris; 62

DOUGLAS
Cochise   T24S R27-28E   Elev. 3980'
In 1878 the locale of the future Douglas was known as Black Water. It was a dirty water hole, in use because water was scarce. In 1901 when the Phelps Dodge Mining Company moved its smelters from Bisbee, the new smelting plant took shape at Black Water. Later a town was established. W. H. Brophy and M. J. Cunningham with a surveyor located the corners for the new townsite. The site was in conflict with a location made by Parke Whitney, Charles A. Overlocke, and J. A. Brock, but a compromise was achieved. The new town was named for Dr. James Stuart Douglas. Dr. Douglas arrived in Bisbee in 1899 as assayer for the Copper Queen Mining Company. On November 11, 1891 he married the daughter of Lewis Williams. (See Bisbee, Cochise). In 1900 he was superintendent of a Phelps Dodge Mine in Sonora and was later president of the corporation.
P.O. est. March 5, 1901, Charles A. Overlock, p.m.; Wells Fargo 1904
Ref.: AHS, H. A. Merrill File; "50th Anniversary Edition," *Douglas Dispatch* (1952), Sec. 4, p. 4 and Sec. 3, 1:5; "Arizona Days and Ways," *Arizona Republic* (Aug. 8, 1954), p. 26; Frank C. Brophy, letter (April 29, 1960)

DOVE SPRING
Coconino   T17N R10E   Elev. c. 7000'
Great flocks of white doves use this as a watering place. Ref.: 18a

DOVE SPRING
Navajo: *hasbidító* = "dove water"
Navajo   T27N R21E
The Navajo name describes the location. Ref.: 331, p. 37

DOWLING
Pima   T18S R5W   Elev. c. 2000'
Pat Dowling, a miner, had a camp here on the Mexican border and maintained an adobe custom house. By 1915 little was left of the building.
Ref.: 58; 59, p. 421; AHS Names File

DOWNING PASS

Cochise   T17S R30E   Elev. 6352'

This pass in the Chiricahua Mountains was named for a sawmill operator who supplied lumber for the construction of Fort Bowie. The name Dawings or Dawnings Pass is incorrect. Ref.: 18a

DOX CASTLE

Coconino (Grand Canyon)   T33N R1E   Elev. c. 4500'

Virginia Dox was an early visitor here. It was named by George Wharton James. Ref.: 18a

DOYLE SADDLE

Coconino   T22N R7E   Elev. 11,354'

This place was named for Alan Doyle (b. Detroit, Michigan, 1850; d. 1920), a guide who came west when he was seventeen. He worked in Wyoming until 1870, then in Santa Fe and finally at Camp Verde, where he raised cattle. After selling out in 1881, he was a guide in this region. Dr. Harold S. Colton in 1933 suggested the name for both Doyle Saddle and Doyle Peak. Doyle Spring is near the peak. Ref.: Slipher; 18a; 224, III, 28-29

DRAGON CREEK

Coconino (Grand Canyon)   T33N R2E

Dragon Creek takes its name from The Dragon, descriptive of a geologic formation. Both Dragon Head (T33N/R2E) and The Dragon were names approved by the USGS in March 1906. Ref.: 329; 5, p. 489

DRAGOON MOUNTAINS

Cochise   T17S R23E   Elev. 7519'

The presence of the Third U.S. Cavalry Dragoons in these mountains accounts for the name, which in turn came from the fact that they used heavy carbines rather than the usual saber and revolver associated with cavalry. These mountains were the scene of several encounters with Apache Indians from 1857 through at least 1881 when the last clash occurred in South Pass (T19S/R24E). These mountains as well as other ranges in this part of Arizona were used by the Chiricahua Apaches as places of concealment. Cochise Stronghold (T17S/R23E) is in these mountains and it is said that the chief of these Apaches, Cochise, died here at what is now Cochise Stronghold. His warriors buried his body, riding over the ground to eradicate any traces of where he lies.

The earliest place name in this region was Railroad Pass, suggested by Lt. John G. Parke during a survey in 1856 as a possible route for a railroad. This is the place which is now called Dragoon Pass (T16S/R22E), a name applied to where the Butterfield Overland Stage maintained a station at what was then called Dragoon Springs, possibly discovered by scouts with the first detachment of U.S. dragoons detailed in the early part of 1856 to establish posts. The earliest name applied to the mountains was Dragoon Springs Mountains. When Uncle Billy (William) Fourr arrived in 1865, the springs had already run dry.

The location of the Butterfield station was the site of much bloodshed, the first occurring in September 1858 when Butterfield agent Silas St. John, in charge of the construction crew for the station, was attacked by three Mexican laborers. Three Americans were killed. Despite his left arm having been severed by an axe blow and an axe wound in his hip, St. John fought off the attackers. Then for three days he defended himself and his dead or dying companions from coyotes and buzzards. At noon of the fourth day troops arrived. They sent for a surgeon from Fort Buchanan. The surgeon, Dr. B. J. Irwin, rapidly rode the one hundred and sixteen miles and saved St. John's life. In addition, during the time that Arizona was partially under confederage control, a Confederate garrison under Capt. Sherod Hunter was attacked by Apaches near Dragoon Spring and lost four men, thirty-five mules, and twenty horses.

When the railroad was constructed, a depot was established at the highest point and hence was called Dragoon Summit (T16S/R22E), the name on the 1881 railroad map. On the post office application made in 1881, the name Dragoon Summit is requested. It was not, however, approved, the name being shortened to Dragoon. At that time the community consisted of a mining camp of almost two hundred, called simply Summit. In South Pass, Robert Dial owned a ranch in 1882. His name was sometimes mispronounced and misspelled Dahl.

The present town of Dragoon is approximately one-half mile from the old Butterfield station.

P.O. est. May 13, 1881, Cassius M. Hooker, p.m.; disc. Sept. 18, 1884; reest. Nov. 14, 1884, William Fourr, p.m.; Wells Fargo 1885

Ref.: Nuttall; Macia; Larriau; 224, p. 272; 73, II, 140-142; 107, II, 5; 159, pp. 435, 436, 447; 242

DRAKE

Mohave   T19N R17W   Elev. 4607'

First known as Sacramento Siding, this section house on a branch of the main railroad is a major shipping point for flagstone. Barnes says the name was changed to Drake in 1905, whereas USGS records (and Barnes) give its name as Griffith, and say that the name Drake came into use c. 1883 to honor William A. Drake who helped construct the railroad line. Drake is the name which is in use on official Arizona State Highway Department maps, but the USGS records that the name was changed to Griffith on November 14, 1930, to honor a bridge gang foreman by that name. Griffith Wash is at T19N/R18W.

P.O. est. as Drake, Nov. 10, 1936, Frank Schiel, p.m.; disc. April 15, 1939

Ref.: 18a; 242; 329; Harris; Schnebly

DREW SPRINGS

Coconino   Near Flagstaff

Charles W. S. Drew (b. 1875, Montreal) was living in Pima County in 1880, later moving to the springs which now bear his name. Ref.: 63; Slipher

DREW STATION

Cochise

This stage station, owned by Harrison Drew in 1881, was on the Drew Ranch which probably included the present-day Drew Tank (T14S/R30E). At this station the infamous Dr. Holliday murdered Buck Philpot. Ref.: Lariau; 60, p. 166

DRIPPING SPRING

Coconino (Grand Canyon)   T31N R2E   Elev. 5493'

This name was suggested by Frank Gannett in 1906. It is descriptive of the fact that water drops from clumps of maiden hair fern in the roof of a white sandstone ledge into a pool below. Ref.: 329; 5, p. 494

DRIPPING SPRING

Gila   T12N R9E   Elev. c. 3000'

A cattle ranch with a stage station for the Florence to Globe line existed here, taking its name from the dripping spring issuing from a cliff about four miles east of the ranch headquarters.

P.O. est. Nov. 13, 1886, Mrs. Marty Strockey, p.m.; disc. Feb. 6, 1890 Ref.: 18a

DRIPPING SPRINGS MOUNTAINS

Gila/Pinal   T4S R14E

In 1903 F. L. Ransome noted that the name Dripping Springs Range was vaguely applied to the area now called Dripping Spring Mountains, Gila/Pinal.

DRIPPING SPRINGS

Pima   T16S R6W

First known as Pozo Blanco (= "white pond or well or spring") these springs, which are descriptively named, lie just beneath a white gap called Puerto Blanco (= "white pass"). Dripping Springs Ranch takes its name from the spring. Ref.: 58

DRIPPING SPRINGS

La Paz   T3N R18W

When Fr. Eusebio Kino was first at this location in 1698, he called these natural rock tanks Agua Escondida (Spanish = "hidden water"), but in 1699 apparently applied the name Tinajas Altas (Spanish: *tinajas* = "water pools"; *altas* = "high"). The Kino map of 1701 uses the name La Tinaoca.

In 1702 when he was again at this location his party endured a tremendous storm which sent water roaring down the canyon, filling these high natural rock tanks, a fact which led Kino to call them Aguaje de los Alquives (Spanish: *aguaje* = "rapid current of spring water"; *alquives*, meaning not known. Jacobo Sedelmayr may have been here on November 23, 1750, describing it as "a spot in which there were three tanks of high elevation." De Anza and Font in 1776 called them Tenejas de Candelaria. The next documented reference is that of Lt. N. Michler in 1854, who noted that local Mexicans called the tanks "Tinejas Altas." He said there were eight such *tinejas*. These tanks were much used by emigrants traveling along the infamous Camino del Diablo.

The range in which these high tanks are was known as Tinejas Altas Mountains and the route from Welton south to them has been called Smugglers' Trail because it was used by bootleggers during Prohibition.

Ref.: 43, pp. 253, 254 (Note); 45, pp. 412, 413; 287, p. 68; 167, II, 754; 106, p. 114; 355, pp. 177-178; 57, p. 414

DRIPPING SPRINGS CANYON

Mohave   T20N R12W   Elev. 4000'

The canyon has been known by this name since 1920. The name derives from the presence of dripping springs near the head of the canyon. Ref.: 329

DRIPPING SPRING WASH

Gila   T3S R14E   Elev. c. 2500'

Lt. William H. Emory called this Disappointment Creek because on November 5, 1846 the Apaches failed to bring promised fresh mules to relieve those exhausted by a survey party expedition through the mountainous territory. However, the presence of dripping springs has led to the application of that name rather than the one used by Emory. Ref.: 105, p. 76; Woody

DROMEDARY PEAK

Pinal   T2S R11E   Elev. 3016'

This peak resembles the hump of a dromedary. Ref.: 18a

DRUMMOND PLATEAU

Coconino (Grand Canyon)   T32N R1W

This plateau bears a name applied by the USGS in 1915 despite the protest that it did not fit in well with nearby place names referring to classical mythology. It was named for Henry Drummond. Ref.: 329

DRY: Place names having the word *dry* associated with them are, naturally indicative of the state of affairs at the locations so named, unless otherwise noted. The following are examples:

Dry Beaver Creek   Yavapai   T15N R5E

According to Barnes, the name of this intermittent stream was applied because this fork was often dry vs. Wet Beaver Creek, the adjacent fork which was never dry. See also Beaver Creek, Yavapai Ref.: 18a

Dry Canyon	Apache	T8N R29E	
Dry Canyon	Cochise	(1) T19S R19E	(2) T22S R24E
Dry Canyon	Graham	T6S R27E	
Dry Canyon	Navajo	T10N R18E	
Dry Canyon	Santa Cruz	T21S R16E	
Dry Creek	Apache	(1) T3N R26E	(2) T18N R24E

[216]

Dry Canyon Spring	Graham	T5S R27E	
Dry Creek	Gila	T10N R13E	
Dry Creek	Graham	T5S R27E	
Dry Creek	Navajo	T18N R23E	
Dry Creek	Yavapai	(1) T17N R5E	
Dry Creek	Yavapai	(2) T18N R24E	

The term *dry* applies to at least sixty-four place names in Arizona for the obvious reason that such locations seldom have natural running or standing water. However, this one is not really a dry creek as it is possible to dig and obtain water. Further, the creek runs heavily during the rainy season. Ref.: Branch; Grigsby

Dry Dam	Navajo	T25N R17E	
Dry Dude Creek	Gila	T12N R11E	

This is a branch of Dude Creek and is possibly one of the few which is not named because of its utter aridity.

Dry Lake	Coconino	(1) T21N R6E	
		(2) T24N R5E	Elev. 7020'

This shallow lake on top of Dry Lake Mountain contains water in the rainy season but is normally dry. Locally it is called Little Mount Elden, a misnomer as it is situated incorrectly for such a name. The Dry Lake Hills (T22N/R7E) associated with this area are five small volcanic cones lying between San Francisco and Elden Mountains. They were named by Prof. Robinson in 1912. This lake was also once called Blowout Tank, referring to a natural tank formed by a volcanic blowout. Ref.: Colton; 276, p. 70; Paten

Dry Lake	Graham	(1) T1S R24E	(2) T7S R26E
Dry Lake	Navajo	T14N R18E	Elev. 5829'
Dry Lakes	Apache	T8N R30E	
Dry Lake Wash	Graham	T7S R26E	
Dry Mesa	Apache	T40N R28E	
Dry Mountain	Graham	T8S R28E	Elev. 4380'
Dry Park	Coconino	T36N R1E	
Dry Park Lakes	Coconino	T35N R2E	
Dry Pocket Wash	Gila	T10N R11E	

This is simply a "big pocket without water." Ref.: Webb; Pieper

Dry Prong	Graham	T4S R25E	
Dry Prong Canyon	Greenlee	T2S R31E	
Dry Valley	Navajo	T8N R22E	
Dry Wash	Coconino	(1) T23N R2W	(2) T34N R7E
Dry Wash	Pinal	T1S R14E	

In 1775 Garcés referred to this as *arroyo sin agua* or *arroyo seco*, both expressions meaning "dry wash." Ref.: 77, p. 112, Note 17

Dry Wash	Yavapai	T7N R1E	

DUCKNEST LAKE

Coconino   T19N R9E

Les Hart had a pasture which he fenced here in 1905 and it had the name at that time. He says many water fowl used to nest at this location. Ref.: Hart

DUDE CREEK

Gila   T12N R11E   Elev. c. 4000'

Frank McClintock, who ranched along this creek, gave it the name, but for reasons not now known. Ref.: 18a

DUDLEYVILLE
Pinal   T6S R16E   Elev. 1949'
After a survey of this part of Arizona in 1877-1878, a strictly farming community was established in this vicinity with many settlers nearby. Among the settlers was Dudley Harrington (b. 1832, Ireland). Despite some sources to the contrary, Dudleyville is not the site of the present Winkelman, which is about a mile away.
Ref.: AHS Names File; 62; 238, p. 32

DUGAS
Yavapai   T11N R43E   Elev. 3957'
Fred Dugas arrived in this area and established the Dugas Ranch in 1879. He considered his place the geographical center of Arizona. Dugas cared so much for his cattle that he observed where they preferred to lie and planted trees as well as putting up log water troughs for them, the result being that his ranch developed to look like a park. With more settlers entering the area, the need for a post office arose and as was customary, one was established in the Dugas ranch house headquarters.
P.O. est. Aug. 4, 1925, Mrs. Gertrude H. Dugas, p.m.; disc. June 15, 1938
Ref.: Dugas; 242

DUKE'S PEAK
Graham   T5S R19E
At this railroad stop on the Apache Railroad south of Silver Creek post office, there was a sub-post office in 1922, of which the postmaster was A. K. Duke. Ref.: 242

DUNCAN
Greenlee   T8S R32E   Elev. 3759'
J. Duncan Smith and Sheriff Guthrie Smith, brothers, sold their property to the Arizona and New Mexico Railroad, which was built in 1883 to connect Clifton and the main railroad line. The railroad stop on their former property was named for Duncan Smith. Another version asserts that two brothers named Duncan who lived in this locality were killed by Apaches about 1885. Duncan was across the river from Purdy (q.v.). The Purdy post office was closed and moved to Duncan when the railroad stop was established. Severe floods in 1979 caused the relocation of most of the town of Duncan.
P.O. est. Oct. 11, 1883, Charles A. Boake, p.m.; Wells Fargo 1885
Ref.: 68, p. 78; Cosper; 242

DUNCAN MOUNTAIN
Greenlee
In 1885 the range south of Chase Creek, the location of the Longfellow and other mines, was named after J. Duncan Smith. Ref.: *Clifton Clarion* (April 22, 1885)

DUNCAN TANK
Mohave   T34N R10W
Tap Duncan, an old time cowman, bought this ranch from Wellington Starkey c. 1904, renaming it the Diamond Bar Ranch. Prior to that time, the place was known as Grass Springs, the location of the O.K. and Excelsior Mines of the 1880s. Ref.: Harris

DUNN BUTTE
Coconino   T31N R4E   Elev. 5714'
William H. Dunn was a member of the first Colorado River Expedition in 1869. He was killed along with the Howland brothers by Indians. The name was applied by Frank Bond c. 1906. See Howlands Butte, Coconino Ref.: 322, p. 54

DUNN SPRINGS
Cochise   T15S R30E   Elev. c. 4100'
Jack Dunn served as an army scout in the 1870s, taking time out for prospecting, later building a cabin at this spring. See Bisbee, Cochise Ref.: AHS, H.A. Merrill File

DUPPA BUTTE
Coconino (Grand Canyon)   T33N R5E   Elev. 6708'
This butte was named by Frank Bond c. 1906 for Bryan Philip Darrell Duppa (b. 1833, France, son of a British Consul; d. c. 1888), known as Darrell Duppa, who settled in

Arizona in 1863. A soldier of fortune and reputedly the younger son of a British family and hence a "remittance man," Duppa established a stage station on the Agua Fria River. The place was little more than an open ramada. He served as secretary of the Swilling Canal Company, which in 1867 dug the first irrigation ditch to tap the Salt River. Ref.: 18a; 329

DURHAM WASH

Pinal   T8S R10E   Elev. c. 2000'

The Durham Cattle Company headquarters was at the head of this wash. Ref.: 59, p. 421

DUSTY CANYON

Coconino   T21N R9E

This descriptive name is the translation of the Navajo name for the canyon, *Doohaajoo*. Dusty Tank is in the canyon.

DUTCH FLAT

Mohave   T15N R24E   Elev. 3000'

This plain from which the Dutch Flat Road takes its name, was the home area for several Dutch and German families, one of which had a mine nearby. They were in the area in the early 1900s. Ref.: Housholder; Harris

DUTCHWOMAN BUTTE

Gila   T5N R12E   Elev. 5021'

An 1890 map bears the name Dutchman Butte. The butte resembles a Dutch wooden shoe. *The Phoenix Herald* (July 21, 1888) noted that the butte looked like a Dutch woman sitting down. Another possible origin of the name is the story that Apaches captured a Dutch woman and on this butte soldiers rescued her in a fight in which one soldier was killed. The military report is said to have listed the location as Dutchwoman Butte. A highly unlikely story is that Indians named it because they thought it looked like a Dutch woman's bustle and part of it like a Dutch Woman's bonnet. Ref.: Woody; 329

DUTTON HILL

Coconino   T20N R5E   Elev. 7658'

As this was a station on the old logging railroad, it seems likely that it was named for a mill superintendent named Dutton. The hill is also called Sliker. See Sliker Tank, Coconino Ref.: Conrad

DUTTON POINT

Coconino (Grand Canyon)   T33N R1W   Elev. 7869'

George Wharton James named this point for Maj. Clarence E. Dutton, the geologist author of *Tertiary History of the Grand Canyon District* (1882). Dutton named many places in the Grand Canyon. Dutton Canyon (a.k.a. Dutch Canyon, a corruption) is below the point. Ref.: 178, p. 40

E

EADS WASH
Gila   T3N R14E
Charley Eads had a farm at the mouth of Eads Wash, named for him. His farm washed away. Ref.: Woody

EAGAR
Apache   T8N R29E   Elev. c. 7000'
John Thomas Eagar (b. Dec. 20, 1851; d. March 12, 1942) was a pioneer living at Fort Milligan. From there he moved with his brothers Joel and William and the Robertsons to the future town of Eagar. The homestead deed is dated 1878. The farming settlement of Omer (named for Omer, a descendant of Esau) was organized in 1882 as a ward of the Mormon Church. The Eagar brothers donated ground for Union, formed when Amity and Omer joined. Union gave way to Eagarville. In December 1892 the school district was named Eagar and the town name also changed. The area behind the Eagar cemetery is the site of an outlaw battle where nine men of the Snider gang were killed.
P.O. est. Oct. 21, 1897, Emma Udall, p.m. Ref.: Wiltbank; State Library Files, George H. Crosby, Jr., "Something about Names;" 158, pp. 7, 21; 225, p. 185; 242; 322, p. 143

EAGLE CREEK
Graham/Greenlee   T5S R29E   Elev. c. 6000'
This creek was named by army scouts c. 1880 because of several eagles' roosts along the rhyolite bluffs. Variant names include Middle Prong Creek, East Fork Eagle Creek, East Eagle Creek. See also Woolaroc, Greenlee Ref.: Farnsworth; 119, pp. 65, 69, 70

EAGLE EYE MOUNTAIN
Maricopa   T6N R9W   Elev. c. 2000'
A formation like an eagle's eye on the northwest side of the Harqua Hala foothills gave this location its name. Ref.: 329; McClintock, Letter (1917)

EAGLE LANDING
La Paz   Elev. c. 500'
The Planet Mine and others in the Cienega Mining District shipped from this point about six miles south of the mouth of Bill Williams River. Ref.: 18a; Kitt

EAGLE NEST MOUNTAIN
Coconino   T23N R2W   Elev. 6000'
After finding an eagle's nest on it, a cattleman named the mountain. Ref.: 18a

EAGLE NEST PEAK
Maricopa
This location on a map dated 1866 is north of the Vulture Mine. It is probably the same as today's Eagle Peak. Ref.: 242

EAGLE NEST POINT
Navajo   T23N R19E   Elev. 6392'
Descriptive.

EAGLE PASS
Graham

This pass at the end of Arivaipa Creek leads across the north end of Mount Graham. It may have been named by troops in 1869, when it was mapped. Ref.: 242

EAGLE ROCK
Apache   T19N R24E   Elev. c. 5500'

This thirty-foot pedestal in the First Forest of the Petrified Forest National Monument formerly held an eagle nest. Variant: Eagle Nest Rock Ref.: Branch; 5, p. 312

EAGLETAIL MOUNTAINS
La Paz/Maricopa   T1N R10W   Elev. 2874/3300'

In this range are three peaks resembling the tail feathers of an eagle. The name appears on the Wheeler map of 1873. Ref.: Parkman; Monson; 279, p. 22

EAGLE TANK
Yuma   T9S R10W

This watering place consists of one principal natural rock tank and several smaller ones on the east side of the Aguila (= "Eagle") Mountains. The location is also known as Jaeger's Tanks because it was used by Louis Jaeger, who freighted ore from the Gunsight Mine to Yuma. Ref.: Lenon; 58; Jordan

EAR OF THE WIND
Apache   T40N R21E

This location is named for a natural arch which resembles a huge ear.

EAST BENSON
Cochise

This small station on the New Mexico and Arizona R.R. was dismantled in 1898 and its buildings removed to Nogales. Ref.: *Oasis* (Oct. 15, 1898), p. 1

EAST BOULDER CANYON
Pinal   T1N R9E

The name "Boulder" derives from the presence of huge rocks. The canyon was named c. 1900. Ref.: 329

EAST CEDAR MOUNTAIN
Yavapai   T9N R6E   Elev. 5445'

Cedar trees nearly cover this mountain, hence the name. Ref.: Schnebly

EASTER
Maricopa   T1S R4E

In 1915 this small community was nearly new. The post office name reflected the fact that it served the Easter Mine, so named because it was located on an Easter Sunday. By 1921 the place was known as Hanson or Hanson Junction.
P.O. est. June 3, 1915, Della S. Miller, p.m.; disc. Aug. 13, 1917
Ref.: Parker; *Tucson Citizen* (July 15, 1915); 242

EAST FORK OF VERDE RIVER
Gila   T11N R8E

This stream was named by King S. Woolsey during his expedition in 1864. Ref.: 18a; 224, III, 260

EAST FORK PARASHANT WASH
Mohave   T33N R12W

The USGS named this wash in 1971. Ref.: 329

EAST LEONARD CANYON
Coconino   T13N R12E

This canyon was named for a sheepherder in 1948. It is also known as Leonard Canyon and as Leonard Creek. Ref.: 329

EAST PEAK
Cochise   T18S R19E
This peak is at the east end of the Whetstone Mountains, hence its name. Ref.: 18a

EAST PHOENIX
Maricopa
William B. Hillings had a flour mill on the stage road passing through this area of the
present Phoenix. It may also have been called Mill City.
P.O. est. Aug. 19, 1871, Edward K. Baker, p.m.; disc. July 11, 1875
Ref.: *Weekly Arizona Miner* (Feb. 3, 1872); *Citizen* (Jan. 27, 1872)

EAST POINT
Mohave (Lake Mead)   T32N R20W
This name was suggested in 1946 by Ben Thompson of the Bureau of Mines, for the most
easterly point along the south shore of Lake Mead, immediately east of Boulder Canyon.
Ref.: 329

EAST VERDE RIVER   pro.: /vérdiyʌ/
Spanish = "green"
Gila   T11N R7E
On August 28, 1864, King S. Woolsey called this stream the East Fork of the Verde. It is
now known as the East Verde River. Ref.: Woody

EAST VERDE SETTLEMENT
Gila   T10N R9E
In the late 1870s Mormons settled on the south side of the East Fork of the Verde where
City Creek enters the larger stream. In c. 1882 they moved to Pine. The old settlement
area has since become a ranch. Ref.: Croxen

EBERT MOUNTAIN
Coconino   T25N R4E   Elev. 7336'
J. Franklin Ebert (b. 1851; d. Sept. 21, 1907) arrived in Arizona in 1870. He was a
stockman in the area. Ebert Spring also has his name. Ref.: Fuchs; *Williams News*
(Sept. 21, 1907) and (May 9, 1908)

ECHO CANYON
Maricopa   T2N R3E   Elev. c. 1300'
In parts of this canyon on the north side of Camelback Mountain when one shouts there
is a noticeable echo. Echo Canyon Bowl, a natural amphitheater, is in the canyon.
Ref.: Theobald

ECHO CAVE
Navajo   T40N R21E   Elev. 6200'
This cave is the most southerly on the Monument Valley Loop road. A shouted word
echoes from eight to sixteen times. The cave is the site of extensive Indian ruins.
Ref.: 191, pp. 118-119

ECHO PARK
Cochise   T16S R30E
At the foot of Bonita Canyon at one place on the trail a good echo sounds. The location
was named either by J. J. P. Armstrong or Ed Riggs in 1924. Ref.: Riggs

ECHO PEAKS
Coconino   T40N R7E   Elev. 5538'
Dellenbaugh wrote that while with Maj. Powell here, he decided to shoot in Glen
Canyon. The sound was like a thousand thunder claps with a far away echo as "peal after
peal of the echoing shot came back to us." Naturally they named the place Echo Peaks.
The name was extended by A. H. Thompson to the Echo Cliffs.
Ref.: 89, pp. 292-293; 322, p. 10

ECHO WASH

Mohave (Lake Mead)   (Bonelli Quad.)
This name was approved by the Board on Geographic Names in May 1948, to replace
Bitter Springs Wash or Bitter Wash. The change was made because of there being
several others bearing the latter names. Ref.: 329

ECKS MOUNTAIN

Apache   T10N R24E   Elev. 7861'
Ecks Nicholls maintained a ranch near this mountain. Ref.: 18a

E.C.P. PEAK

La Paz   T8N R12W   Elev. c. 4000'
Because this peak is on the East side of Cunningham Pass, the peak took its name from
the initials. Ref.: Lenon

EDEN

Graham   T5S R24E   Elev. 2752'
In September 1881 Mormon settlers from Brigham City built a cottonwood stockade in
this area. Settlers included three Curtis brothers (Lehi, Moses, and Moses M.), after
whom the settlement was known as Curtis. The post office was established under the
name Eden for its namesake in Utah which, in turn, was named for the original Garden of
Eden.
P.O. est. Aug. 7, 1892, William T. Oliver, p.m.
Ref.: 242; 329; 322, p. 122; 116, p. 248; 225, p. 248; 353, p. 15

EDITH

Maricopa   T2N R4E
The Judson Mine post office and community were named for the wife of the postmaster.
P.O. est. July 6, 1888, Johnson S. Todd, p.m.; disc. Dec. 28, 1888 Ref.: 18a

EDWARDS PEAK

Gila   T6N R10E   Elev. 5782'
Charles Edwards (b. 1846, N.Y.) established a ranch in what was known as Edwards
Park, an open park-like area of about four hundred acres. Later Edwards was murdered
en route to his ranch from Globe. Ref.: 18a; Woody; 63

EGLOFFSTEIN BUTTE

Navajo   T25N R18E   Elev. 6669'
Frederick F. W. von Egloffstein served as a topographer with the Fremont Expedition in
1853. Ref.: 245, p. 21

EHRENBERG

La Paz   T3N R22W   Elev. 288'
Despite its importance as a ferrying point for travelers to the West Coast and as a
terminus for river steamers carrying freight en route to Prescott, the community of
Ehrenberg consisted of one "straggling street of adobe houses." Little remains of this
once important shipping point on the Colorado River. First called Mineral City, its town
plot was surveyed by Herman Christian Ehrenberg (b. 1821, Germany), a graduate of
Freiberg University. Ehrenberg was a soldier of fortune, a mining engineer who came to
Arizona with Charles Debrille Poston in 1854 to reopen mines near Tubac. Later
Apache raids caused Herman Ehrenberg to move from Tubac to a point six miles north
of La Paz on the Colorado. From there he moved to survey Mineral City in 1863.
Ehrenberg was killed at Dos Palmas in the Mohave Desert in the fall of 1866. His friend,
Michael Goldwater, suggested renaming Mineral City in his memory, which was done in
1869. See Olivia, Yuma
P.O. est. Sept. 20, 1869, Joseph Goldwater, p.m.; disc. Dec. 31, 1913; reest. June 28,
1958 Ref.: 206, p. 142; 310, pp. 1-6; *Arizona Miner* (Oct. 23, 1866); 163, pp. 250-
251; 62; 242; 320, p. 17

EHRENBERG POINT
Coconino (Grand Canyon)   T63N R4E

In 1932 Frank Bond proposed this name to honor Herman Ehrenberg. See Ehrenberg, La Paz

EHRENBERG WASH
La Paz   T2N R20W

This wash was named for the settlement of Ehrenberg at its mouth. It is also known as Cinnabar Wash because of the Cinnabar Mine in one of the canyon branches. Ref.: 329

EIGHT O'CLOCK BASIN
Yavapai   T2N R10W

In 1972, scientists named an area of a volcanic basin astrogeologically by using a central point and one coordinate to indicate "12:00 o'clock." It was then possible to make references from the central point, such as that for Eight O'Clock Basin. Ref.: 329

ELAINE CASTLE
Coconino (Grand Canyon)   T33N R1E

The name was proposed by Francois E. Matthes in 1908. See Galahad Point, Coconino (Grand Canyon) Ref.: 329; Grand Canyon Files

EL: Spanish = "the" Place names beginning with *El* will be found under the major name. For instance El Capitan is listed under Capitan, El.

ELDEN MOUNTAIN
Coconino   T22N R7E   Elev. 9000'

This mountain was named for a sheepman, John Elden, whose headquarters were at its base in the early 1880s. His cabin was at Elden Spring where, while Elden was in Prescott buying supplies, one of his two children died. Its mother buried it in the snow and maintained a vigil at night to keep coyotes away. By 1883 discouraged when a second child died, Elden and his family had left the area. According to one source, Elden Spring is the same as San Francisco Spring on the trail used by Major G. B. Willis in 1862 and it may also have been referred to as Babbitt Spring (see Babbitt Bill Tank, Coconino). Barnes says that Lt. Edward Fitzgerald Beale gave the name San Francisco Spring to what is now Elden Spring. Elden Mountain was also known as Elden Mesa and as Mount Elden, but the name was officially changed to Elden Mountain in 1932. Ref.: Anderson; Switzer; 18a; 166, p. 73

ELDEN PUEBLO
Coconino   T21N R7E

According to Fewkes (1927), this Indian pueblo is a remainder of Sinagua occupation about 1250 A.D. Little remains of it except a few walls. Ref.: 184, pp. 31, 39; 5, p. 317

ELEPHANT BACK MOUNTAIN
La Paz   T3N R18W   Elev. 2699'

The name describes the humped appearance of this mountain.

ELEPHANT BUTTE
Navajo   T23N R17E   Elev. 5978'

This is an outstanding lava plug which resembles an elephant, according to Herbert Gregory. Ref.: 18a

ELEPHANT FEET
Coconino   T34N R13E

These curious rocks on the Hopi Indian Reservation resemble elephant feet and legs. The location is also known as Elephant Legs. Ref.: 5, p. 422

ELEPHANT HILL

Mohave   T26N R22W

At the base of a conical hill in a bend of the Colorado River, Dr. John S. Newberry of the 1851 Ives Expedition found a petrified elephant's tooth of *Elephas primigenius*.
Ref.: 245, p. 38

ELEPHANT'S TOOTH

Mohave   T19N R20E   Elev. 3666'

This huge white rock plug is silhouetted against a darker background and looks like a huge elephant tooth. See White Elephant, Mohave Ref.: 359, p. 77

ELEVATOR MOUNTAIN

Graham   T2S R27E   Elev. 7113'

This mountain slopes gradually from the valley floor on one side, but on the other drops from its summit like an elevator. Ref.: Simmons

ELFRIDA   pro.: /élf raydə/

Cochise   T20S R26E   Elev. c. 4000'

The Danish name of G. I. Van Meter's mother is the origin of this name. He donated the railroad right-of-way across his land and the company named this station for his mother at his request.
P.O. est. Dec. 15, 1914, Marie Harr Leitch, p.m.
Ref.: AHS, Letter, G. I. Van Meter to John Curry (Jan. 10, 1937)

ELGIN

Santa Cruz   T20S R18E   Elev. 4710'

This community may have taken its name from the home town (Elgin, Illinois) of a local storekeeper.
P.O. est. Jan. 3, 1910, Ruben B. Collie, p.m. Ref.: Seibold

ELIAS DRAW

Santa Cruz   T20S R12E

Juan Elias (b. Tubac, 1838; d. Tucson, 1896) and his brother Jesus Maria Elias were Mexicans who gained U.S. citizenship automatically with the signing of the Gadsden Purchase Treaty. Juan Elias, owner of the Sopori Ranch who also owned holdings in Mexico, then moved to Tucson. His brother was a famous scout and tracker, who served as a deputy sheriff under Bob Leatherwood. Ref.: AHS, Chambers Collection

ELKHART

La Paz   T6N R6W   Elev. c. 600'

This temporary siding was named for the construction crew foreman on the tunnel here.
Ref.: 18a

ELLENDALE

Coconino   T22N R8E

This was the first name proposed for the Doney post office. See Doney, Coconino
Ref.: 242

ELLIOT, MOUNT

Yavapai   T13N R1W   Elev. 6993'

A. G. Elliot located the Accidental Mine in this vicinity in 1874. Ref.: 18a

ELLIOT SPRING

Coconino   T19N R10E

An Arizona pioneer, possibly James McCandles Elliot (b. 1826, Pennsylvania), located his cabin at this spring prior to 1905. Ref.: 62; Hart

ELLISON

Gila   T5N R15E   Elev. c. 4000'

Jesse W. Ellison (b. Sept. 22, 1841, Texas; d. Jan. 21, 1934) in 1885 arrived at Bowie Station by rail with eighteen hundred cattle. There was so little water that his cattle

[225]

stampeded, with many hurtling pell-mell into arroyos. His cattle having been rounded up, Ellison headed toward Gila County, going first to Big Green Valley where he registered his brand as *Q*. When his house burned later in 1885, Ellison started another ranch in Star Valley under the name Q Ranch and lived at the location until 1915 when he sold to Pecos McFadden. Ellison Creek, also known as Moore Creek (T12N/R11E) also bears his family name.
P.O. est. Oct. 5, 1896, Jessie W. Ellison, p.m.; disc. March 16, 1907
Ref.: 224, III, 39; Woody; 242

ELOY   pro.: /iyloy/
Pinal   T8S R8E   Elev. 1565'
Some time between 1905 and 1918 the railroad applied the name Eloy to a section house here. There was no community until W. L. Bernard, J. E. Myer, and John Alsdorf bought land to raise cotton, heavily in demand following W.W. I. The three subdivided their land and proposed to develop "Cotton City." They applied for a post office to be named "Cotton City," but the postal department elected instead to use the name of the railroad section house as that is where the mail would be dropped.
    As for the name Eloy, it is asserted locally that someone connected with the railroad took one look at the barren desert there and named the place "Eloi," supposedly the Spanish pronunciation for the Biblical "Eli, Lama Sabachthani?" meaning "My God, My God, why hast Thou forsaken me?"
P.O. est. April 10, 1918, George L. Stronach, p.m. Ref.: Alsdorf; 242

ELVES CHASM
Coconino (Grand Canyon)   T32N R2W   Elev. 3200'
Fantastic travertine formations are in this canyon, making it like a fairy land.
Ref.: Kolb

EMERALD POINT
Coconino (Grand Canyon)   T34N R1E   Elev. 7560'
In 1908 the USGS proposed and approved the use of names of jewels for places in the Grand Canyon. Emerald Point is an example. Ref.: 329

EMERY
Graham   T4S R23E   Elev. 2690'
In 1901 the Holyoke family, which had been in the vicinity at least as early as 1888, was joined by Mormons, who applied the name Emery for its namesake in Utah.
Ref.: Mrs. Virgie Holyoke, *Utah Historical Quarterly*, X, 124

EMERY PARK
Pima   T15S R13E   Elev. c. 2500'
The Emery family took up residence adjacent to a railroad station called "Aguirre" on the Nogales line. The name was changed to Emery Park when the post office was established.
P.O. est. Sept. 21, 1928. (The name of the railroad station changed March 5, 1928); Camilla Emery, p.m.; name changed to Butland, Jan. 2, 1931; resc. Dec. 24, 1931; disc. Sept. 30, 1952 Ref.: 18a; Hayden; 242

EMIGRANT CANYON
Cochise   T15S R29E   Elev. c. 4200'
Emigrants on the transcontinental trail used to recuperate from their travels in this canyon. Ref.: Riggs

EMIGRANT PASS
Cochise   T15S R29E
This pass between two peaks in the Chiricahua Mountains takes its name from that of Emigrant Canyon. One peak elevation is 6226' and the other 6279'.

EMIGRANT SPRINGS
Cochise   T21N R28E   Elev. c. 5800'
Westbound emigrants stopped here because of potable spring water. Ref.: 18a

EMIKA

Pima   T12S R1W

This small Papago Indian village is also sometimes called Emita. The name derives from Papago meaning "My Clearing" or perhaps from *E Me*, a man's name. Papago *KA* indicates a pile of brush cut in making a clearing. Therefore *E EM KA* means that the man had a small clearing. Ref.: 329

EMMA, MOUNT

Mohave   c. T33N R8W   Elev. 7698'

In 1882 Dutton noted that a mesa five miles south of Mount Logan contained a dozen basaltic cones. He named the highest cone Mount Emma, for the wife of Maj. John Wesley Powell. Ref.: 100, pp. 103-104

EMPIRE MINE

Santa Cruz   South of Mowry Mine

Sylvester Mowry owned the Empire Mine near the Mexican border in 1860. He sold it and, as the Montezuma Mine, it was owned by Thomas Gardner and Hopkins, who in turn sold it to a New York Company. It then became the New York Mine.
Ref.: 18a; 236, pp. 60, 79

EMPIRE RANCH

Pima   T19S R17E

Although it shares the name, this place is not the same as the Esperanza Ranch (*q.v.*). This ranch, in what was later called Empire Gulch, was at first called the Fish Ranch because E. N. Fish owned it. In August 1876 Walter L. Vail and H. R. Hislop bought the Fish Ranch. Vail, a native of New Jersey, called the new ranch the Empire Ranch because he planned "to found an empire." The ranch had a herd of five thousand cattle. In 1879 Jerry Dillon established claims on the nearby mountains, called the Empire Mountains after the ranch. He relinquished his claims to Vail.
P.O. est. as Empire Ranch, May 7, 1879, John N. Harvey, p.m.; disc. May 3, 1880; reest. as Empire, June 21, 1880, George C. Algier, p.m.; disc. April 19, 1881
Ref.: AHS Files; 103, p. 32; 164, p. xix; 264

EMPIRE VALLEY

Pima   T18S R17E

This was the name used c. 1882 for what is today called Cienega Creek (*q.v.*). The stream course extends through the valley from the old Empire Ranch (*q.v.*). It was called Stock Valley and Meadow Valley, both reflecting the area being used as a cattle pasture. Ref.: 102, p. 2

ENEBRO MOUNTAIN   pro.: /enéybro/

Spanish = "juniper tree"
Greenlee   T3S R29E   Elev. 7510'

Although the local Mexican term for juniper and cedar is *tasquite* or *tascala*, an abundance of juniper here probably led to its Spanish name. Ref.: Simmons

ENGESSER PASS

Yuma   T2S R15W

A miner named Engesser located his workings in Section 18 of this township and range. Ref.: Monson

ENGLAND GULCH

Coconino

C. England (b. 1856, Virginia) was in this part of Arizona in 1880. Possibly he had the ranch after which this gulch takes its name.
Ref.: *Arizona Journal Miner* (March 1911); 63

ENGLE WELL

Maricopa   T7N R8W

In 1918 Zagel Engle was working on this well, also used as a watering place by others. It is possible that he had the Engle Mine (T5S/R13W). Ref.: 279, p. 207

ENID
Pinal   T4S R2E   Elev. 1285'
The name for this railroad section house appears on a 1905 railroad map. Its origin, however, has not been learned.

ENNIS
Maricopa   T3N R1W   Elev. c. 1400'
Barnes says that a Mr. Ennis once owned land here.

ENREQUITA
Pima/Santa Cruz   c. T24S R10E   Elev. c. 4000'
The post office served the mining camp here in 1866.
P.O. est. May 7, 1866, Charles H. Lord, p.m.; disc. June 24, 1867 Ref.: 18a; 264

ENTERPRISE
Graham   T7S R6E   Elev. 3020'
Enterprise, formerly a Mormon settlement, is no longer in existence. The name is typical of those selected by Mormon settlers, reflecting their hopeful industriousness.
Ref.: 18a; Jennings

ENTRO (R.R. STN.)
Yavapai   T14N R1W   Elev. 5132'
The Entro station was at the entrance to a small canyon, hence the name. Ref.: 18a

ENZENBERG CANYON
Pima   T19S R15E   Elev. c. 5950'
Enzenberg had a ranch and mine in this canyon. Ref.: 286, pp. 154, 159

EPITAPH GULCH
Cochise
This gulch is in the Tombstone Hills approximately five miles south of Tombstone. There is a possibility that it takes its name from that of the Epitaph Mine.

EPLEY'S RUIN
Graham   T7S R26E
The prehistoric pueblo ruins here were named for the owner of the ranch on which they are located. Ref.: 167, p. 430

EQUATOR
Yavapai   Elev. c. 4000'
A post office was established to serve this mining camp, the location of which is given as "near head of Cherry Creek, east side of Black Hills."
P.O. est. Dec. 12, 1899, Arthur Woods, p.m.; disc. Sept. 22, 1903 Ref.: 18a; 264

ERASTUS
Apache   c. T12N R24E
Mormons established a small community here to separate their children from those in the Mexican school at Concho, applying for a post office in July 1883. They named their community in honor of Erastus Snow. The location of the Mormon community was west of the actual community of Concho, but on December 6, 1895 they adopted the name Concho (q.v.). Ref.: Wiltbank; 18a; Stemmer; 242

ERICKSON PEAK
Cochise   T19S R30E   Elev. 7983'
Erickson's father came to the United States years before his son Neil and was killed by Indians in Minnesota. The son vowed to kill Indians and later emigrated, remaining in Boston only long enough to learn English and then enlist to fight Indians. Neil Erickson (b. April 22, 1859; d. Oct. 19, 1937) served for five years with the U.S. Army before homesteading near Stein's Pass in New Mexico. Appointed a forest ranger in 1903, he established his home near the base of the peak bearing his name.
Ref.: Lillian Riggs (daughter)

ERICKSON RIDGE
Cochise   T16S R29E
The ridge was named for Mr. and Mrs. Neil Erickson in 1919. See Erickson Peak, Cochise

ERNIE PYLE ARCH
Navajo   T41N R21E
This formation in Monument Valley south of the Big Hogan formation was named for Pyle, a well known war correspondent of World War II.
Ref.: *Sunset Magazine* (April 1953), p. 52

ESCALA   pro.: /eskála/
Spanish = "ladder"
Graham   T11S R27E   Elev. 3734'
This railroad point was so named because it is at the summit of the hill on which the track was laid zig-zag fashion, somewhat like a ladder. Ref.: 18a

ESCALANTE CREEK   pro.: /eskǝlántey/
Coconino (Grand Canyon)   T31N R5E
Fr. Hernando de Escalante in 1776 journeyed from Santa Fé to what is now Salt Lake and then southward to the Zuñi villages and back to Santa Fé. In 1869 while exploring the Grand Canyon, Maj. John Wesley Powell named this creek to honor him, calling it the Escalante River, and the country which it drains, Escalante Basin. This is not the stream referred to by Delenbaugh (which is in Utah). Ref.: 266, p. 138; 88, p. 210

ESCALANTE TERRACE
Coconino (Grand Canyon)   T31N R5E
This name was suggested by Francois E. Matthes in 1915 and was placed on the Shinumo quadrangle issued by the USGS. See Escalante Creek, Coconino (Grand Canyon) Ref.: 329

ESCUDILLA MOUNTAIN   pro.: /eskuwdiyǝ/
Spanish = "a pot for mush" or "dark blue pot"
Apache   T7N R31E   Elev. 10,912'
The name, in use at least as early as 1872, reflects the fact that the mountain has a high rim and a crater-like bowl (although lacking volcanic crater structure). It also looks dark blue. The local name for a mush pot is *Esqudilla*. The name Eskadere is a misspelling. One source calls it Sierra Azul (see derivation).
Ref.: Noble; Wiltbank; 342, I, 67, and III, 529; 329; Becker

ESCUELA   pro.: /eskwéylǝ/
Spanish = "school"
Pima   T14S R13E   Elev. c. 2600'
The first name suggested for the post office at this place was Indian School, for which the post office substituted Escuela, upon completion here of the school for Papago Indians.
P.O. est. March 25, 1907, Haddington G. Brown, p.m.; disc. Oct. 31, 1942
Ref.: 18a; 242

ESKIMINZIN SPRING   pro.: /es-kim-in-zin/
Apache = "big mouth"
Pinal   T5S R16E
Es-kim-in-zin (1829-1896) was a chief of the Arivaipa and Pinal Apaches. His Apache name was Hackibanzin (= "angry men stand in line for him"). In 1869 to avoid trouble with federal troops, he led his band into Old Camp Grant, seeking asylum and a permanent peace between his people and the whites. Some merchants in Tucson enlisted the aid of Papago Indians, the traditional Apache enemies, to massacre the Eskiminzin band. On April 30, 1871, the Tucson group attacked the Apaches' newly established agricultural community. The ensuing massacre is a black stain on Arizona history. At least one hundred and eighteen old men, women and children were killed, among them

two wives and five children of the young chief. He helped bury his family and others and settled down peacefully despite the horrible affair.

Unfortunately, about a month later some White Mountain federal troops travelled into the Arivaipa Creek area and came unexpectedly upon a small Apache group. The frightened troops opened fire, killing many members of Es-kim-in-zin's family. He fled into the mountains with the remainder of his band. He was captured and held prisoner at Camp Grant until October 5, 1874, when he was sent to the San Carlos Apache Indian Reservation. There he spent the remainder of his life, until in 1894 he was sent briefly to Mt. Vernon Barracks in Alabama as a "prisoner of war." He died at San Carlos. Today the spring used by this band of Apaches is also known as Young's Spring.

Variant spellings are Eskimenzin and Eskimazene. Ref.: 329; 202, pp. 59, 68, 71

ESPEJO BUTTE   pro.: /espeýho/
Coconino (Grand Canyon)   T32N R6E   Elev. 5750'
The U.S. Geographic Board approved the use of this name in May 1932. On November 10, 1582 Antonio de Espejo with Fr. Bernardino Beltran led an expedition to visit tribes in northern Mexico, arriving ultimately at the Zuñi villages. Hearing about a great lake sixty days' journey distant, he traveled on, possibly visiting the region of the present-day Jerome (q.v.), thereafter returning to Mexico City.
Ref.: *Enciclopedia Universal Illustrada*; 21, pp. 22, 23; 329

ESPEJO SPRING
Coconino   T29N R9E
Although the USGS records that in January 1915 Herbert Gregory named this spring Janus for Stephen James (?) and that the name was changed in April at the suggestion of Frederick W. Hodge, Gregory does not mention the name Janus Spring in his reference to this location. However, the Arizona State Highway Department computer listing of places by township and range lists this place as Janus Spring. See Espejo Butte, Coconino (Grand Canyon) Ref.: 329; Arizona State Highway Dept. Computer Lists; 141, p. 191

ESPERANZA RANCH
Pima   T18S R12E   Elev. 3813'
This was the name given by Bullinger and Rockfellow c. 1880 to what was later part of the New York Ranch. Bullinger had named it for his sister, but the "N.Y." brand gave rise to the later name. Esperanza Wash shares the older name.
P.O. est. Feb. 26, 1884, Hiram W. Blaisdell, p.m.; disc. Oct. 9, 1884
Ref.: 277, p. 98; 242

ESPLANADE BENCH
Coconino/Mohave (Grand Canyon)   T32N R1W   Elev. c. 4500'
The name (given in 1882) describes this level bench or terrace in the walls of the Grand Canyon. The location is still used as a place to rest on travel between points in the upper half of the Grand Canyon wall. Ref.: 329

ESTHWAITE
Pinal   T1S R11E   Elev. c. 2400'
The origin of this name has not been learned.
P.O. est. June 23, 1919, Richard W. Mattison, p.m. Ref.: 242

ESTLER PEAK
Yavapai   T12N R3E   Elev. 4250'
Estler Monroe (d. c. 1895) ran cattle and lived near this peak.
Ref.: Dugas; West

ESTRELLA   pro.: /estréyǝ/
Spanish = "star"
Maricopa   T5S R2W
This railroad siding took its name from the nearby Estrella Mountains (q.v.). Although the siding was in existence in 1881, the post office was not established until 1919.
P.O. est. as Estrella Hill, Jan. 6, 1919, Roy Lee Crowley, p.m.; name changed to Estrella, Nov. 17, 1932; disc. July 15, 1954 Ref.: Hayden; 242

ESTRELLA MOUNTAINS

Maricopa   T13S R1W–2E   Elev. 4503'

Although this low range had long been known to Pima Indians by the name of Kâ'matûk, its first recorded Spanish name was used by Garcés in 1775 as Sierra de San Joseph de Cumars. *Cumars* means "broad" or "thick" in Pima. In 1904 the Pima name was Kâ'matûk. The anglicized form for Kamatuk is Komatka, now applied to a small village at the foot of the mountains. Font in 1775 called the pass or gap Puerto de los Cocomaricopas. See John, Saint, Maricopa, and Komatke, Maricopa
Ref.: 58; 281 (Smithsonian), p. 23; 4, pp. 165, 166, 119, 110, Note 14; 77, p. 113

ESTRELLA VALLEY

Maricopa   T14S R1W–2E

The emigrant road to the west lay along the base of the Estrella Mountains (*q.v.*) and gradually the name came to be applied to the valley between these and the Maricopa Mountains. This section of the journey west came to be known as *Jornado de las Estrellas* (Spanish = "The Journey of the Stars"). Later the military telegraph and Butterfield Overland Stage route also passed through this valley.
Ref.: 5, pp. 236, 399; 163, p.

ETOI KI

Pima   T17S R4E   Elev. 2661'

Pronunciation varies, but it is often given as /Iy-toy/ or /Ey-iy-toy/. Etoi is the name of the culture hero of Papago and Pima Indians and *ki* means "house." He appears when his people are in need or have erred in their ways and require admonishment and instruction.

EUCLID

Maricopa   Location not known

Name origin not known.
P. O. est. Dec. 18, 1895, Charles W. Prauge, p.m.; disc. June 18, 1896 Ref.: 264

EUGENE GULCH

Yavapai   T12N R1W   Elev. c. 5000'

Hinton lists a mine called Eugenia at this point on the railroad and it may be that the creek and railroad station took their name from that of the mine. However, Barnes says that a miner who worked in the gulch was called Eugene, but that he may have spelled it Eugenia. Ref.: 18a

EUREKA

La Paz   T4S R22W

The Eureka Mining District was formed c. 1858. Eureka in 1866 was on the Colorado River twenty-eight miles north of Arizona City in the Eureka Mining District. The name is a common one in mining, inasmuch as the translation of this Greek word means "I have found it!" Ref.: 107, II, 292

EUREKA CANYON

Graham   T8S R22E

The headquarters of the Eureka Ranch was in this canyon. The Leach brothers had the Eureka Cattle Company in 1880. See Eureka Springs, Graham
Ref.: Jennings; 18a; 163, p. xxxi

EUREKA SPRINGS

Graham   T12S R20E   Elev. 4900'

This was a stage station on the road from Tucson to Camp Goodwin, as well as being the headquarters for the Eureka Cattle Company. George H. Stevens bought the station in 1873, but later sold it to Charles Leitch who, with his brother, established a cattle ranch with headquarters here in 1880. Ref.: *Arizona Sentinel* (Nov. 22, 1973); Jennings; 163, p. xxxi; 18a; 61, p. 67

EVANS MOUNTAIN

Pima   T11S R17E

This was named for Dr. Evans, who conducted an excellent school nearby.

EVANS POINT

Greenlee   T4S R30E   Elev. 3541'

In 1899 a partner in the Evans Van Hecke Mining Company owned this point of land, hence the name. Like other mining companies, this one issued scrip in place of U.S. currency. Its money bore the name "Evans Point, Arizona."

P.O. est. as Evans, April 4, 1899; Mongo R. W. Parks, p.m.; David M. Evans appointed p.m., April 22, 1899 (neither commissioned); disc. April 13, 1900

Ref.: Sweeting; 242

EVERETT TANK

Coconino   T20N R5E

The name derives from that of the man who used it for cattle prior to 1900.

Ref.: Hart

EVOLUTION AMPHITHEATER

Coconino (Grand Canyon)   T33N R1W

This name was proposed by Francois E. Matthes and was approved by the USGS in June 1908. Ref.: 329

EWELL'S STATION   pro.: /iwwelz/

Cochise   Elev. c. 4500'

This relay station on the route between Apache Pass and Dragoon Springs, fifteen miles west of the pass, was established by Capt. Richard Stoddert Ewell of the First Dragoons in 1859. Water was hauled here from Dos Cabezas Springs, which were also known as Ewell Springs. Ref.: 72, II, 139-140; 320, p. 182

EXCALIBUR

Coconino (Grand Canyon)   T33N R1E

This sharp, thin blade of rock towers four hundred feet. In suggesting the name in 1908, Francois E. Matthes wrote, "... happily chosen and alone gives warranty in my opinion for the introduction of Arthur, Guinevere and the others." Ref.: 329

EXPLORER'S PASS

La Paz   Elev. c. 400'

At this point (a.k.a. Purple Hills Pass) on the Colorado River where the Chocolate Mountains are close to the river, Lt. Joseph Christmas Ives and his party in 1857 named a narrow canyon after the *U.S.S. Explorer*, the steamboat used by the party while exploring for the head of navigation on the river. It rammed a rock (hence Explorer's Rock) and sank. Ref.: 89, p. 164; 245, p. 47

EZEKIELVILLE

Santa Cruz

In 1882 this was fifteen miles from Harshaw on the New Mexico and Arizona R.R. near old Fort Buchanan. A canvas town, it did not last long. Ref.: *Citizen* (Jan. 1, 1882)

F

FACE MOUNTAIN
Maricopa   T3S R9W   Elev. 2041'
This mountain *faces* Montezuma Head at the northwest corner.

FACE ROCK
Apache   T5N R28E
In Canyon de Chelly is a five-hundred-foot rock pillar which in silhouette looks like a face. The Navajo name is *Tse Binii'i* (= "face rock"). Ref: 331, p. 21

FAGAN, MOUNT
Pima   T18S R16W   Elev. 6186'
In 1880 Michael Fagan, a prospector and cattleman, owned a ranch near here.
Ref.: AHS Files; 18a

FAIN MOUNTAIN
Coconino   T21N R21E   Elev. 7571'
Using the 16 brand, William Fain watered cattle at Fain Spring (at the foot of this mountain). Sixteen Spring (T15N/R11E) takes its name from the Fain Brand. Fain Spring (T17N/R21E) shares the name.   Ref.: 18a

FAIRBANK
Cochise   T20S R21E   Elev. 3862'
N.K. Fairbank organized the Grand Central Mining Company in Tombstone in the 1880s. He was a stockholder of the railroad from Benson to Mexico. The junction point to Nogales was named for him. An Indian village called Santa Cruz was on this site in 1870, and occasionally arrow heads, bones, and broken pottery are found.
P.O. est. May 16, 1983, John Dessart, p.m.; Wells Fargo 1885.   Ref.: 18a; Macia; Larriau; 5, pp. 391–392; AHS Names File

FAIRCHILD DRAW
Coconino   T13N R12E
This location was used by a sheepman, Fletcher Fairchild (b. 1851, Illinois; d. Oct. 1899), who came to northern Arizona in 1887.   Ref.: Frank Fairchild, Letter (son); Hart

FAIR OAKS
Yavapai   T16N R5W   Elev. 5100'
This substation was in a grove of live-oak trees.   Ref.: 18a

FAIRVIEW
Cochise   T24S R27E
In 1979 a Fairview postal substation was at T24S/R27E (the site given to the post office in 1915). The site mapped in 1913, however, was T21S/R21E. Ref.: 242

FAIR VIEW

Coconino   T21N R21E   Elev. c. 6000'

The railroad map of 1884 places this railroad section house east of Ash Fork. Construction engineers named it because of the fine view westward. Ref.: 18a

FALFA pro.: /fælfə/

Maricopa   T1S R5E

A contraction of *alfalfa*, this name reflects the fact that much alfalfa is raised in the area. The name Falva is a corruption.

FAN ISLAND

Coconino (Grand Canyon)   T33N R1W   Elev. 5085'

The name reflects the shape of this small flat-topped fan-shaped butte.

FARRAR GULCH

La Paz   T4N R24W

Juan Ferrar (b. 1830, Sonora, Mexico), a laborer in this vicinity, found gold in this gulch in February 1862, and the news led to a miners' stampede into the area. It lasted until 1864. After that time Ferrar was a laborer at La Paz. Ref.: 107, II, 293–294

FAIRVIEW POINT

Coconino (Grand Canyon)   Elev. 8300'

The view from here presents a panorama of the Painted Desert. Ref.: 5, p. 491

FAY LAKE

Coconino   T24N R4E

Fred Platten, while riding one day with his wife and Lil Fay, came upon this lake. Platten named it for his wife's friend. Ref.: Platten

FELTON MOUNTAIN

Gila   T8N R11E   Elev. 4195'

The Felton family has had a ranch here for many years, using Felton Spring at this same location. Ref.: Woody

FENNER

Cochise   T17S R21E

This railroad station is named for Dr. Hiram W. Fenner of Bisbee, for many years chief surgeon of the Tucson division of the S.P.R.R. Ref.: 18a; 203, p. 36

FERN GLEN CANYON

Mohave (Grand Canyon)   T33N R6W

In 1964 this name was made official, replacing Fern Canyon. Ref.: 329

FERN GLEN RAPIDS

Coconino/Mohave   T33N R6W

Ferns grow abundantly in the canyon of these rapids.

FERN MOUNTAIN

Coconino   T23N R7E

Otto Platten named the mountain because of bracken growing heavily on its slopes. Ref.: Colton

FERN SPRING

Coconino   T34N R2W

This location, also called Dripping Pool, is pictured in Plate V of the source used, with a caption that minerals in the water from the dripping spring had created a projection extending eight feet from the wall of the canyon and that it was covered with maiden hair fern, hence the name. Ref.: 345, I, 52

FIFE CANYON

Cochise   T17S R29E   Elev. 5500'

A polygamous Mormon named Fife lived in this canyon with two wives and intentions of marrying a third. A Mexican employee killed one of the wives as she was setting out food for him on the porch. Hours later the murderer was caught and taken to Riggs home ranch (Faraway Ranch) and then to Fife's place where he was forthwith lynched.

Five Creek or Five Mile Creek bears the latter name because it is five miles along the creek from the Faraway Ranch to the Fife Ranch, hence the name also of Five Mile Canyon. The creek is also known as Witch Creek.   Ref.: Riggs; AHS, Choate File

FIGUEREDO CREEK   pro.: /fiygeréydo/

Apache/New Mexico   Elev. 6000'

Only a small portion of this stream is in Arizona, most of it draining the Chusca Valley of New Mexico. It was named for Roque de Figueredo, a missionary to the Zuñi Indians in 1629.   Ref.: 141, p. 91

FILLIBUSTER CAMP

Yuma   T8S R18W   Elev. c. 500'

This was the starting point for an ill-fated filibuster into Mexico, led by Henry A. Crabb. In 1856 Crabb, while visiting his wife's family in Sonora, met and talked to Pesqueira, an ambitious man who sought to unseat the legally elected Sonoran governor, Gandera. Pesqueira urged Crabb to support the insurrection with one thousand Americans. However, while Crabb was getting his men together, Pesqueira drove out Gandera and so had no further use for Crabb's army. Treacherously, Pesqueira denied any complicity, actually leading an attack against Crabb at Caborca in which more than half of Crabb's advance group of one hundred was killed or wounded. Crabb surrendered and he and his men were butchered. In 1858 Filibuster Camp was one of the original Butterfield Overland stage stations but was abandoned in 1859 and the facilities moved to Antelope Peak.   Ref.: 163, pp. 36, 37; Lenon

FINAL, CAPE

Coconino (Grand Canyon)   T32N R5E   Elev. 7919'

Maj. Clarence E. Dutton named this viewpoint in 1882 after a five-mile ride which brought him to this final view of the head of Grand Canyon. Ref.: 100, pp. 176, 181

FINLEY AND ADAMS CANYON

Santa Cruz   T23S R16E

The Finleys, a pioneer family in this region, no longer live here, but their name remains attached to this canyon.

FIREBIRD LAKE

Maricopa   T2S R4E

Firebird Lake is the site of a former gravel pit which supplied material for Maricopa Road south of Phoenix and later was excavated to help fill the road bed for I-10. The largest lake in the world devoted exclusively to boat racing, Firebird Lake was created by Buck Weber, a well driller, in the barren northern part of the Gila River Indian Reservation, using water so heavily laced with natural minerals that it is otherwise unusable. Strictly a recreational lake, it opened on May 3, 1975. The Indian community benefits from proceeds earned at the lake.   Ref.: *Arizona Daily Star* (May 25, 1975), Sec. 1, p. 1

FIRE BOX CANYON

Navajo   T5N R23E

Capt. George Nyce, the first Indian Service ranger on the White River Apache Indian Reservation, kept fire fighting tools in this canyon.   Ref.: Davis

FIRE POINT

Coconino (Grand Canyon)   T34N R1W

The name for this point on the North Rim was proposed by the National Park Service in July 1930 and approved in May 1932.   Ref.: 329

FIRST HOLLOW

Navajo   T7N R22E

Cattlemen who herded cattle from the R-14 Ranch to McNary named hollows according to their location, hence also Second, Third, and Fourth Hollow.   Ref.: Davis

FIRST KNOLL

Navajo   T10N R22E   Elev. 6814'

This solitary knoll, the first encountered en route from Snowflake to Holbrook, was named by James Flake. He also named the Second and Third knolls, but their names apparently were never mapped.   Ref.: 18a

FIRST MESA

Navajo   T28N R18E   Elev. c. 6500'

The Hopi mesas jut like fingers of a hand from the "palm" of Black Mesa. First Mesa is the first encountered when traveling from New Mexico westward. Known to the Spaniards in 1540, it was first seen by an American in 1858 (Lt. Joseph Christmas Ives). See also Polacca, Navajo.   Ref.: 150, p. 6

FIRST MESA SPRING

Navajo   T28N R18W

This spring is at the base of First Mesa.   Ref.: 141, p. 155

FIRST WATER CANYON

Gila   T5N R13E

This is the first turn-out water in Rockinstraw Canyon, hence the name.   Ref.: Woody

FISHBACK

Mohave

This sharp ridge south of the road above Union Pass was named by Jonathan Draper Richardson (1856–1940).   Ref.: Ferra (daughter)

FISH CANYON

Pima   T19S R15E   Elev. 5600'

A map c. 1875 shows a Fish Ranch near this canyon. The canyon may have been named for Edward Nye Fish, who moved to Arizona from California in 1865 and is known to have used Calabasas as his mailing address before moving to Tucson.   Ref.: AHS, Chambers Collection

FISH CREEK

Apache   T8N R27E R26E

There are two possible origins for the name: (1) many fish were reported to be in the creek; (2) an early settler named Fish lived in the vicinity. This creek was formerly Twenty-Four Draw, a name applied by the Forest Service. The name was officially changed to Fish Creek by the USGS in 1971.   Ref.: 18a; 329

FISH CREEK

Greenlee   T3N R28E

According to nearby residents, this creek has good fishing.   Ref.: Scott

FISH CREEK

Maricopa   T2N R11E   Elev. c. 300'

Here in about 1881 Jack Frasier established a station, naming the creek because it had some rather remarkable small reddish fish in it.   Ref.: 329, (1) McCormick, (2) Steele File

FISH CREEK CANYON

Maricopa   T3N R10E

This location was formerly called Box Canyon and was said to be "an almost perfect box canyon." See Fish Creek, Maricopa.   Ref.: 5, p. 367

FISH CREEK PEAK
Maricopa   T2N R10E   Elev. 3910′
This peak is on Fish Creek Mountain. See Fish Creek, Maricopa

FISHER SPRING
Gila   T9N R10E
Walter Fisher had a ranch and used this spring near Rye Creek. Ref.: Griffen

FISHER TANK
Coconino   T20N R7E or T21N R6E
There are two Fisher tanks near each other. One of these was on the map of Grand Canyon made in 1892, and one was named for Jerry Fisher, an early Forest Ranger in the region. Ref.: *Arizona Enterprise* (Oct. 6, 1982)

FISHTAIL CANYON
Mohave (Grand Canyon)   T35N R2W   Elev. c. 3000′
The upper end of this canyon branches like a fish tail. Fishtail Point overlooks the canyon. Ref.: Kolb

FISHTAIL RAPIDS
Mohave (Grand Canyon)   T35N R3W
The National Park Service suggested this name in July 1930 and it was approved by the USGS in 1932. See Fishtail Canyon, Mohave (Grand Canyon) Ref.: 329

FISKE BUTTE
Coconino (Grand Canyon)   T33N R1W
This name was proposed by the USGS in 1908 in honor of John Fiske (1842–1901), a strong advocate of the works of Huxley and Darwin. Fiske was a proponent of the solar mythology theory. Ref.: 329

FIVE BUTTES
Navajo   T22N R21E   Elev. c. 6000′
There are five buttes here, hence the name. Ref.: 18a

FIVE HOUSES
Navajo   T28N R18E
Gregory reports that five wells were sunk at this Indian ruins site (consisting of five houses). Ref.: 141, p. 166

FIVE HOUSES BUTTE
Navajo   T27N R19E   Elev. 6342′
Although this name is not used locally, it was probably given to the butte because of five houses some four miles north. Ref.: 329

FIVEMILE CREEK
Cochise   T17S R27E
This creek takes its course through Fife Canyon *(q.v.)* also referred to as Five Mile Canyon.

FIVEMILE LAKE
Coconino   T12N R8E   Elev. c. 5000′
This lake is five miles from the Mogollon Rim. The name came into use after 1895. Ref.: 18a

FIVE POINT MOUNTAIN
Gila/Pinal   T1S R14E   Elev. 5491′
When travellers going west enter the side road leading to the Castle Dome Mine a few miles beyond Miami, ahead they can see five points or tips of this mountain. Ref.: Woody; Craig

FLAG, RIO DE

Coconino   T21N R7–9E

This intermittent stream terminates east of Flagstaff, from which it takes its name, in use about ninety-five years. Both Sitgreaves and Whipple (1854) called it Rio de San Francisco. Among residents of Flagstaff, the name Rio de Flag vies in popularity with "River de Flag." The origin of the local name in the opinion of many is sly humor, since the stream usually runs only after heavy rain or when snow is melting. However, since every city of importance is on a river, residents place Flagstaff on one. Ref.: 329; Bartlett; 346, p. 167

FLAGSTAFF

Coconino   T21N R7E   Elev. 6894'

The Navajo name *kin ł ani* (= "many houses") certainly describes this community. The origins of the name Flagstaff, though obscure, can be ascertained by considering the history of the area. No springs are named on early military maps for this area other than Leroux Spring and San Francisco Spring, but on GLO 1879 appears the name Antelope Spring. At this spring in 1876 F.F. McMillan constructed a corral and shack at the base of what is now Mars Hill. He was joined by a group of land scouts sent out from Boston by the Arizona Colonization Company. On July 4, 1876 this party stripped a lofty pine and pinned a rough handmade flag to it. (Al Doyle of Flagstaff says that the flag was actually raised in May 1876). The scouts moved on, leaving the stripped tree at the location. Four years later buildings were erected near it to provide services for the railroad construction crew. The new depot, however, was inconveniently west of Antelope Spring and its developing community, and the business men there moved to the depot area. Behind them they left what came to be known as Old Town, at Old Town Spring in 1883. The dead tree continued to stand at the spring, being noted by travellers in June 1887 as they approached Flagstaff. If it is the tree which Lt. Beale is supposed to have used to mark his route (and perhaps as a flag pole in 1859), then it had lasted a long time. Furthermore, according to Beale's records, he was at the north end at the base of Mount Elden, not where the landmark existed. The dead tree was cut down in 1888 to provide wood for a stove in a saloon owned by Sandy Donahue.

The name Flagstaff was not the first suggested for the new railroad depot. The first was Beachville, to honor Charles Washington Beach (b. 1838, New York) of Prescott, but the name did not stick. The name Flagstaff was too obvious a choice for the location. P.J. Brannen, whose letter housed the first post office, suggested the name, noting that Flagpole Spring (another name for Old Town Spring) had really been the beginning of the community. In the early 1900s because of its altitude and clear air, Flagstaff was called the "Skylight City."

Flagstaff became Coconino county seat in 1891. It was incorporated as a town on June 4, 1894, and as a city in 1928. As the city grew it began taking in other communities. Among these was Milltown, a sawmill settlement east of Flagstaff, named for the poet Milton but corrupted to Milltown. Michael J. Riordan named it. The Ayers Sawmill was at that location. The railroad station at Milltown was called Agassiz.

Flagstaff shares its name with Flagstaff Lake, Spring, and Wash.

P.O. est. Feb. 21, 1881, James McMillan, p.m.; Wells Fargo 1885   Ref.: 15, p. 189; 331, p. 55; 116, p. 578; 320, p. 6; *Arizona Journal Miner* (April 10, 1889), p. 4; *Arizona Gazette* (May 6, 1881), p. 3; (Beachville); Anderson; Slipher; Switzer; 166, pp. 65–66, 80' 329; Mrs. Velma Rudd Hoffman, letter (March 25, 1960); 62; 240, p. 133

FLAT ROCK   pro.: /tsénts eye/
Navajo = "broad rock"

Apache   T5N R27E   Elev. c. 5700'

Flat Rock is in Black Rock Canyon not far from Antelope House. The Navajo name describes this isolated sandstone pile, which was once used by Navajo to escape from raiding parties. It has not been in use since the 1864 Kit Carson campaign. Ref.: 331, p. 24

FLATROCK SPRING

Mohave   T25N R13W   Elev. c. 5500'

A large flat rock standing on its edge near the spring results in the name.   Ref.: 18a

FLAT TOP BUTTE
Navajo   T21N R19E   Elev. 6485'
The name describes this nearly circular, flat butte with a diameter of approximately one mile. It is also known as Smith Butte. Ref.: 329

FLAT TOP MOUNTAIN
Gila   T1N R14E
This *is* a flat top mountain.

FLAT TOP MOUNTAIN
Pinal   T6S R17E   Elev. 3666'
... and so is this.

FLATTOPS, THE (*sic*)
Apache   Elev. c. 6000'
This location is on the road from the Petrified Monument headquarters going toward U.S. Highway 40 about two miles from the Monument headquarters entrance. In 1953 the name was given to these adjacent flat mesas by members of the staff from the Museum of Northern Arizona, which found pit houses nearby.   Ref.: Branch

FLEMING PEAK
Cochise   T20S R27E
This peak took its name from J.W. Fleming, who prospected in the Swisshelm Mountains. See Swisshelm Mountains, Cochise

FLEMING SPRING
Maricopa   T4E R6N
Charles Fleming (d. c. 1903) a miner, settled here c. 1875 and stayed until he died, working claims on Continental Mountain.   Ref.: *Carefree Enterprise* (Jan. 1982), p. 9

FLINT CREEK
Coconino (Grand Canyon)   T33N R1E
This creek was named by the National Park Service in May 1932 because of the geological formation along the stream.

FLINT'S STATION
La Paz
In 1868 this was a stage station on the La Paz-Date Creek route, three miles west of McMullen Station (*q.v.*).   Ref.: *Weekly Arizona Miner* (Nov. 21, 1868), p. 3

FLITNER CANYON
Cochise   T29S R16E
Frank Flitner, an engineer for the Bureau of Public Roads, surveyed whether routes into the Chiricahua National Monument should go through Pinery or Bonito Canyon. Flitner decided on Bonito. He admired this side canyon which now bears his name. The Riggs family named it for him c. 1930.   Ref.: Riggs

FLORENCE
Pinal   T5S R9E   Elev. 1493'
Levi Ruggles (b. Ohio), who came to Arizona as an Indian agent in 1866, patented land from which he transferred title for the town of Florence on October 30, 1875. The first house had already been built in 1866 and the town was firmly established by 1869. Ruggles had three daughters, whose names were Cynthia, Flora, and Florence, and having deeded the land, he named the town to honor at least two of them. According to another story, Gov. Richard McCormick, asked to name the town, did so after his wife. Others believe that Anson Pacely Kileen Safford named it for his sister. In 1921 completion of the Ashurst-Hayden Diversion Dam made irrigation water available and the town developed into an agricultural center. Florence became Pinal County seat on February 1, 1875.
P.O. est. Aug. 19, 1869, Thomas R. Ewing, p.m.; Wells Fargo 1879   Ref.: 163, p. 43;

5, p. 293; *Weekly Arizona Miner* (Oct. 31, 1868), p. 2; AHS Files; *Arizona Republic* (March 31, 1924), cited in Baldwin's *The History of Florence, Arizona*

FLORENCE JUNCTION

Pinal   T2S R10E   Elev. 1883'

People from Florence journeyed to this point to board a train to travel east or west. P.O. est. Nov. 15, 1933, Mrs. Mildred E. Hoffman, p.m.   Ref.: 242

FLORES   pro.: /flores/

Mohave   c. T22 or 23N R18W   Elev. c.4000'

The Flores post office served a mining community settled by prospectors from Nevada in Flores Wash in 1871. The mine, abandoned because of Indian problems, re-opened c. 1876. Once called the Five Forks Mine, it was sold in 1888 to the Flores Mine Company of Philadelphia, which worked it until 1893. The ownership accounts for its name. P.O. est. July 6, 1889, John H. Campbell, p.m.   Ref.: 200, p. 96; 329, 242

FLORES

Yavapai   T8N R5W

Originally this spur on the A.T. & S.F.R.R. was called Las Flores because during the period of railroad construction the desert here was covered with flowers.   Ref.: 18a

FLORIDA VALLEY, LA

Graham

This valley on a map of 1847 lies between the present San Pedro and San Simon Rivers. See Graham, Mount, Graham

FLOWERPOT WELL

Maricopa   T4N R5W

The name of this well perpetuates the fact that the Flowerpot Ranch had its headquarters nearby. It was established in 1899 by C. Warren Peterson, who used a flower pot design for his brand.   Ref.: 18a

FLOWING WELLS

Pima   T13S R13E   Elev. c. 2800'

Emerson Oliver Stratton, who owned this land in 1885, planned to use it for farming. So many successful wells were dug that the area came to be known as Flowing Wells. The name describes the excellence of these wells.   Ref.: AHS, Emerson O. Stratton *ms.*

FLUTED ROCK

Navajo: *zildassáani* = "Mountain set upon itself" pro.: /dziᵛˢᵗdaˡsa?ani/

Apache   T2N 57W   Elev. 8304'

The Navajo name Silh-tusayan was officially changed to the American name in 1932. It has also been called Black Rock and Zildassaani. The American name is a translation of the Navajo, so named because the high mesa is faced with fluted columns. The mesa had a heliograph station during the campaign against the Indians (1863-1864). Fluted Rock Lake is at T3N/R7W.   Ref.: 141, pp. 34, 9; 331, p. 56; 329

FLUX CANYON

Santa Cruz   T22S R15E   Elev. c. 4800'

One of the oldest mines in Arizona, the Flux Mine, is in this canyon. The name is a mining term referring to the purification of metals or to their fusion. Ore from this mine was smelted as early as 1858. It produced silverlead said to have been used for ammunition during the Civil War.   Ref.: 286, pp. 258-259

FLY'S PEAK

Cochise   T18S R30E   Elev. 9579'

In the late 1870s Camillus S. Fly was a photographer in newly established Tombstone. His pictures of early days in Arizona and of Gen. George Crook on campaign are famous.   Ref.: 18a; Lenon

FOOL HOLLOW WILD LIFE AREA

Navajo   T9N R21E

This wildlife and recreational area of two hundred and forty-five acres was bought in 1955 by the Arizona Game and Fish Department, which controls it. See Fools Hollow, Apache   Ref.: 9, p. 1

FOOLS GULCH

Yavapai   T10N R5W   Elev. c. 4000'

Ore in this gulch was so poor that prospectors expecting to find gold there were deemed fools. The post office served the Planet-Saturn Mine.

P.O. est. Jan. 15, 1897, William A. Clark, p.m.; disc. Oct. 30, 1897   Ref.: 18a; 242

FOOLS HOLLOW

Navajo   T9N R21E   Elev. 6256'

The name, in use since c. 1900, refers to the fact that a man named Adair intended to farm here, but local people knew that the land was so poor they called it Fools Hollow. The USGS referred to this as Adair Wash and as Right-Hand Draw until April 1964 when it settled on Right-Hand Draw. Associated names include Fools Hollow Draw, Lake, and Ridge. See Adair, Navajo   Ref.: 329; 18a

FORDVILLE

Pinal   T8S R16E   Elev. c. 3000'

Fordville served as the post office for the Ford Mine.

P.O. est. March 15, 1880, William A. Cunningham; disc. June 7, 1880

FOREBACH KNOLL

Pinal   T6S R6E

The spelling is probably in error as it was named for Peter Forbach (b. 1832, Prussia) or for Victor Forbach (b. 1842, Germany). Both were in Adamsville in 1870.   Ref.: 62; 63

FOREMAN WASH

Pinal   T9S R12E

The wash was named for a cattle ranch run by S.W. Foreman, who made the first survey of Tucson. The headquarters for the ranch were at the head of Suffering Gulch.   Ref.: 57, p. 383; 59, p. 422

FOREPAUGH

Maricopa   T7N R8W

The name was that of an old-time miner deemed a "desert rat" by his neighbors. There is nothing here now except a decaying and ancient service station beside the fenced highway. Forepaugh Peak is at T6N/R17W.

P.O. est. April 2, 1910, Charles B. Genung, p.m.; disc. July 15, 1916   Ref.: 18a; 242

FORESTDALE

Navajo   T9N R21E   Elev. 6079'

Forestdale was in a valley in the forest on the Mogollon Rim. In the fall of 1877 Oscar Cluff found this valley and soon moved into it with his family. His brother Alfred also arrived and suggested the name Forest Dale. A Mormon settlement was started at Forest Dale on February 18, 1878. Because it was on the Apache Indian reservation, all but three families abandoned it by 1879. Gen. E. A. Carr of Fort Apache assured them that they were not intruding on Indian land and invited other Mormons to colonize there. More Mormons joined the three families in 1882. In May 1882 Indians arrived at their traditional farming land with the intention of planting corn. Mutual animosity developed. It was assuaged by a treaty granting Indians the use of thirty acres. All was well until Lt. Charles Gatewood arrived. He ordered the Mormon settlers to move out by the following spring and they did so. By mid-1883 only Indians remained at Forest Dale. Today there are summer accommodations at Forestdale along Forestdale Creek and in Forestdale Canyon.   Ref.: 225, pp. 170-173; 322, p. 127

FOREST-GLEN HOUSE
Navajo   T39N R17E
This is the name of Indian ruins in the Navajo National Monument, because of "the fine growth of trees at the base of a large cliff-house." Ref.: B.A.E. No. 50, p. 21

FOREST LAGOONS
Coconino   Elev. c. 7000'
Lt. Joseph Christmas Ives named this flooded area in the pine forest at his Camp Seventy-Four. Ref.: 245, p. 110

FOREST LAKE
Navajo   T34N R19E
This small lake is in the only place in the area which has large trees, hence its name. It is not the same place as nearby Debebekid Lake. Under the heading *Big*, see Big Water, Navajo Ref.: 329

FORREST
Cochise   T24S R26E/T23S R25E   Elev. 4591'
This railroad spur marks the place where Henry F. Forrest (b. July 11, 1842, Missouri; d. 1935) maintained a ranch in the 1880s. Forrest arrived in Arizona as a prospector in 1863. He bought both the Kenyon and Bourke stage stations and established a ranch at Oatman Flat (*q.v.*). He left there to move to Dragoon Pass in 1879, where he lived until his death. Here in 1886 Bill Daniels was killed by Geronimo's band during the last Apache raid in Arizona – ironic, because Daniels came west specifically to kill an Indian. Forrest maintained watering troughs for freighters' teams hauling big lumber from Turkey Creek to the Copper Queen Mine. See also Forrest, Yavapai
P.O. est. Jan. 14, 1914, Josie Clymer, p.m.; disc. Nov. 15, 1917   Ref.: Burgess; Nuttall; AHS, William Fourr File; *Arizona Sentinel* (June 28, 1879)

FORREST
Yavapai   T1W R12N   Elev. c. 5000'
Henry F. Forrest (see Forrest, Cochise) for a few months in 1882 owned a small cattle ranch with a post office here.
P.O. est. April 21, 1882, Henry A. Marsh, p.m.; disc. Sept. 5, 1882   Ref.: 18a; 242

FORSTER CANYON
Coconino (Grand Canyon)   T33N R2W
This canyon was named for W. J. Forster (d. c. 1925), who worked on the U.S. Geologic Survey of this part of the Colorado River. USGS approved the name in February 1925. Forster Rapids are in this canyon.   Ref.: 329

FORT: To find entries such as Fort Defiance, Apache, see entry under Defiance, Fort, Apache.

FORTIFICATION HILL
Mohave   T31N R22W   Elev. 3718'
This point, which should not be confused with Sentinel Island, Mohave (*q.v.*), is sometimes called Fortification Mountain, both names reflecting the fact that it looks like an inaccessible fortress. Wheeler referred to it by name in 1871.   Ref.: Housholder; 343, I, 159

FORTIFICATION ROCK
Mohave   Elev. c. 3500'
Although close to Fortification Hill (*q.v.*), this place should not be confused with it. In 1857 Lt. Joseph Christmas Ives climbed to the top of this rock, which he named. He was exploring for the head of navigation of the Colorado River, and this rock gave him an excellent view both up and down stream. He terminated his exploration here. Ref.: 245, p. 18

FORT ROCK
Yavapai   T20N R10W   Elev. 4900'
The stage route between Prescott and Hardyville included a stop at this point. Soldiers

customarily escorted the mail carrier, Poindexter, to protect him from Indian attack. In the fall of 1866 three soldiers and Poindexter arrived at this station, run by J. J. Buckman, whose son Thad had just that day near their cabin constructed a stone playhouse about a foot high. Early the next morning Indians attacked, catching Buckman and McAteer (a soldier) outside the stage station. The two men sought protection in the low-lying stone playhouse. Poindexter, Thad, and Ed May holed up in the cabin. Their guns proved defective, so Thad shot his while they loaded for him and lifted the small boy to a loop-hole to take aim. All day the small party held off more than a hundred Hualapai Indians and finally drove them off. The name Fort Rock was inevitable, soon replacing that of the first post office, Mount Hope.

P.O. est. as Mount Hope, June 22, 1876, E. S. Smith, p.m.; name changed to Fort Rock, May 7, 1879, S. L. Bacon, p.m.; disc. Nov. 12, 1879 Ref.: 107, IV, 133-134; 314, p. 71; 163, p. xxxviii; P. O. Records; *Arizona Miner* (Nov. 30, 1866)

FORTUNA
Yuma   T20S R20W   Elev. 775'

The La Fortuna Mine was discovered c. 1893 by Charles Thomas, William Holbert, and two others. The La Fortuna Gold Mining and Milling Company was organized in 1896 to complete a twenty-stamp mill. Between 1896 and 1904 over two and a half million dollars in gold was recovered. After 1904 the mine was worked intermittently until 1924 when it was abandoned. There is little left today at this small mining community.

P.O. est. Aug. 28, 1896, John Doan, p.m. Ref.: 355, pp. 189-190; 242

FORT VALLEY
Coconino   T22N R6E   Elev. 7400'

In 1877 John W. Young (a son of Brigham Young) with other Mormons settled at Leroux Spring (*q.v.*). In 1881 they contracted to make railroad ties, pitching their tents on what they called Leroux Prairie. Reports of Apache Indian attacks led them to use railroad ties to form one side of a roughly hundred-foot-square stockade and a large log house. Young named it Fort Moroni for the Angel Moroni of the *Book of Mormon*. Indians did not attack. Young then used the fort to house his six wives. Some referred to the place as Fort Misery. In 1883 he sold his Moroni Cattle Company to the Arizona Cattle Company, which used the A-1 brand. The new owners changed the name of the place to Fort Rickerson, for Charles L. Rickerson, the cattle company treasurer.

Another place name in this same location received its first American name as a result of the A-1 cattle outfit operations. It was named c. 1884 Mount Wainwright, for Ellis Wainwright, who had an interest in the company. That name gave way to Wing Mountain, so named for "Old Man" Wing, a partner in the cattle venture and owner of the Wing Cattle Company.

In this valley in August 1908 was established the first forest experimental station in the United States under the name Fort Valley Experimental Forest. At that time Professor J. G. Lemmon (see Lemmon, Mount, Pima) suggested the name be changed to De la Vergne Park, but the name was not accepted. De la Vergne was an owner in the Arizona Cattle Company. He arrived in Arizona c. 1885. In 1920 the old stockade was destroyed. Today the area is called Fort Valley.   Ref.: Slipher; 71, p. 49; 225, pp. 153, 154; Conrad; Dietzman; Sykes; 166, pp. 77-78; AHS, T. A. Riordan File

FOSSIL BAY
Coconino (Grand Canyon)   T34N R2W

This is a natural amphitheater. See Fossil Rapids, Coconino (Grand Canyon)

FOSSIL CREEK
Gila/Yavapai   T11N R6-7E   Elev. c. 5000'

Fossil remains are found in the creek bed. Lummis said that the creek is so heavily charged with minerals that objects dropping into it, such as twigs, are coated rapidly with travertine. This fact led to naming the stream.   Ref.: Woody; 210, p. 143; 18a

FOSSIL POINT
Yuma   T8S R20W

Here in October 1917 Kirk Bryan found fossil bones. See Ligurta, Yuma
Ref.: 279, p. 75

FOSSIL RAPIDS

Coconino (Grand Canyon)　　　　　T33N R2W

The series of names associated with *fossil* in the Grand Canyon was suggested both by the Forest Service and by the National Park Service because of fossils being found in the locale. The Forest Service named Fossil Canyon in 1936 and others were added throughout 1930, all being approved in May 1932 by the USGS. They include Fossil Bay and Canyon.　Ref.: 329

FOSTER RAPIDS

Coconino (Grand Canyon)

The name "Foster" is an error for Forster. See Forster Canyon, Coconino (Grand Canyon)

FOUR BAR MESA　($\stackrel{4}{-}$)

Greenlee　　　　　T1S R29E　　　　　Elev. c. 6000'

John Joseph Filleman (b. May 2, 1861, Texas; d. July 10, 1942) in 1912 acquired a ranch from the Battendorf brothers, who had established it. Filleman, who had originated the $\stackrel{4}{-}$ brand in Texas, transferred it to Arizona in 1886.　Ref.: Fred Fritz, Notes; Mrs. Harris Martin, Letter (May 11, 1956)

FOUR CORNERS

Apache　　　　　T41N R31E　　　　　Elev. 4880'

The name reflects the fact that Arizona, New Mexico, Colorado, and Utah join at this point. Here in 1910 Wilken and Whitcraft operated a trading post. Not until about 1970, however, did a community develop, taking its name from the nearby monument. The Navajo name for this location is variously spelled as follows: Tees Nos Pos; Teec Nos Pos; Tisnasbas; and in one case, Carrizo (Navajo = "cotton woods in a circle"). The name Carrizo may be attributed to the fact that a small Apache band known as "Carriso or Arrow-reed People" lives in the nearby Carrizo Mountains and an Indian school and mission village took shape as Carriso.

P.O. est. as Carriso, Jan. 20, 1915, Mrs. Nellie Van Alen Bell, p.m.; disc. Jan. 31, 1920; reest. as Tees To, June 18, 1930, James C. McGuckin, p.m.; disc. Feb. 28, 1934　Ref.: 331, p. 60; 143, p. 129; 329; 242; 345, pp. 152, 153 (note 6)

FOUR MILE CANYON

Gila　　　　　T9N R14E

This canyon is four miles long, hence the name. Ref.: McKinney

FOUR MILE PEAK

Graham　　　　　T8S R19E　　　　　Elev. 6250'

Its location four miles southeast of Biscuit Peak gives this peak its name, shared by Four Mile Creek and Fourmile Spring.　Ref.: 18a

FOURMILE SPRING

Coconino (Grand Canyon)　　　　　T31N R2E　　　　　Elev. 5600'

This usually dry spring is four miles from the head of Hermit Trail, hence its name. Ref.: Kolb; 329; J.H. Butchart, Letter (1961)

FOURMILE SPRING

Graham　　　　　T7S R19E

There are four springs in the right prong of Four Mile Canyon. See Fourmile Peak, Graham

FOUR O'CLOCK HILL

Yavapai　　　　　T20N R10W　　　　　Elev. c. 4300'

With Greater Pasture at twelve of the "clock," this hill lies southeast, hence its name.　Ref.: 329

FOUR PEAKS

Maricopa　　　　　T4N R10E　　　　　Elev. 7645'

These peaks in the Mazatzal Mountains witnessed many an army skirmish with Indians from 1867 through 1874, a fact which probably accounts for their being called the Four

Peaks of McDowell, as troops were ordered from Camp McDowell to pursue Apaches here. The four peaks are rugged but evenly shaped. They mark the boundary line between Gila and Maricopa counties. Four Peaks Springs are at T4N/R10E. Ref.: 163, p. 289; 159, pp. 428, 440; 242

FOUR PEAKS
La Paz   T6N R18W   Elev. 1785'
These four low but prominent peaks are not far from Four Peaks Dam, which was built by the Civilian Conservation Corps c. 1938. Ref.: Monson

FOURR CANYON   pro.: /fer/
Cochise   T17S R23E
William (Uncle Billy) Fourr (b. July 11, 1842, Missouri; d. 1935) arrived in Arizona in 1863 as a prospector. Later with Henry F. Forrest he bought out the Kenyon and Bourke Stage Stations (1872). He was raided by Apaches at Oatman Flat, following which he moved to California, only to return to Arizona about 1880 and establish his ranch in the canyon which now bears his name. Ref.: AHS, Chambers Collection; 107, VIII, 26; Bennett; *Arizona Sentinel* (June 28, 1879)

FOURTH OF JULY WASH
Maricopa   T2S R9W   Elev. c. 800'
In the 1890s people on a camping trip enjoyed a memorable July 4th party in this wash, and the name Fourth of July Wash promptly was applied. Ref.: Parkman

FOWLER
Maricopa   T1N R1E
The school and post office substation as well as railroad spur at this place take their name from that of the three Fowler brothers who ranched here prior to 1893. Ref.: Parkman

FOX GULCH
Gila   T4N R11E
This mile-long gulch heads at Fox Gulch Spring. The gulch and spring take their name from Fox Farm (T1 N/R11E), which belonged to a man named Weiser, who raised foxes here prior to 1931. During the Depression he harvested the pelts. When his wife died he quit the business, soon thereafter leaving the area. Ref.: Woody

FRAGUITA, MOUNT   pro.: /frawíytə/
Spanish = "little forge"
Santa Cruz   T22S R10E   Elev. 5325'
The first mapped name for this peak is that on the 1853 Boundary Survey sheet No. 38: Cerro de Jaralito. The next name to occur is Fragita Peak on GLO 1888 township plat map. A minor spur of this hill came to be known as Mount Roddick, for Thomas G. Roddick (b. 1836; d. June 1879), who arrived in Arizona in 1865 and lived near this place until late 1874. At the time of his death, two physicians had a row over the cause of his demise. After one doctor broke his cane over the head of the other, an autopsy was ordered. The coroner's report solved nothing, since Roddick's death was declared due to a "complication of diseases."

Roddick was long gone by 1893 when Roskruge surveyed what was then still Pima County and applied the name Yellow Jacket Hill to the location. The name "Roderick" is a corruption, as are also Freguila and Fraquita. The name Fraguita was restored by 1920 because of a local report that a small blacksmith's forge had been found at the base of the mountain and hence the old name should be retained. It therefore was, but there is still a Yellow Jacket Spring at the same location. Ref.: AHS, Thomas G. Roddick File; 329; 18a

FRANCISCO GRANDE
Pinal   T6S R5E   Elev. 1350'
A small community has formed around the Hotel Francisco Grande at this location. The hotel was built c. 1968.

FRANCISCO PEAKS, SAN
Coconino   T22–23N R7E

Sometimes referred to as the San Francisco Mountains, this group of three peaks dominates the landscape to such an extent that it is no wonder that nearly all early visitors applied names to them. Their mass forms part of an area covering some three thousand square miles, part of one of the great volcanic regions in the United States. The peaks are important in the religious beliefs of northern Arizona Indian tribes. For instance, the Hopi call the peaks *Nuva-t kia-ovi* (= "the place of snow on the very top,") and believe that Kachinas (beneficient spirits of Hopi religion) reside here during the winter months. The Havasupai name is rendered *Hue-han-a-patch* (= "mountains of the Virgin Snow"). Navajo Indians call the peaks *Maanez'ash* (= "turned mountain") and *dook'o'osɬid* (= "Abalone Shell Mountain"). Because the peaks were venerated by Indians, Franciscan missionaries at the Hopi village of Oraibi (1629-1680) named the peaks to honor their patron saint. It was customary to substitute a Christian over a native name to demonstrate that Christian beliefs have power stronger than natives' beliefs.

In 1598 Fanforan called them the Sierra Sinagua (= "without water"). An additional Spanish name is Sierra Cienega, possibly a corruption for Sinagua. When Fr. Garcés saw these peaks in 1776, he called them Sierra Napoc. However, Garcés elsewhere uses the term *Napao* (probably referring to the Navajo), and hence Sierra Napoc might mean the Navajo Mountains. Another name found on old Spanish maps is Sierra de los Cosninos, the name of Indians living in the region. In 1853 Whipple named one peak San Francisco Cone. Not until relatively recent times did the three peaks have separate names assigned. When Gen. William J. Palmer made his railway survey report in 1868, he changed the name of San Francisco Mountain to Mount Agassiz (Elev. 12,340') (see Agassiz Peak, Coconino). Humphrey's Peak (T23N/R7E; elev. 12,633') is the highest peak in Arizona (see Humphrey's Peak, Coconino). The third in the grouping is Fremont Peak (T23N/R7E; elev. 11,940'). See Fremont Peak, Coconino   Ref.: *Citizen* (June 29, 1872), p. 1:4; "San Francisco Peaks," p. 1; Van Valkenburgh, *Master Key*, p. 92; 77, pp. 353, 353 (Note 32); 331, p. 134; 89, p. 385; Andrew Natonabak (Navajo Medicine Man, 1975)

FRANCISCO RIVER, SAN
Greenlee/Apache/New Mexico   T25S R30–31E

Cartographers had their problems trying to accurately map this stream which enters Arizona (in T2S/R31E) and debouches into the Gila River (in T5S/R30E). Other rivers have been confused with it. Although, for instance, early explorers called the present Verde River the San Francisco River, the two should not be confused. In 1764 Fr. Figueroa inaccurately mapped a San Francisco River. Lt. Emory also mapped a San Francisco River, now the San Carlos River. The "true" San Francisco River was noted by James Ohio Pattie on January 1, 1825. In 1876 cartographers gave it an East Branch. On the 1879 Smith map the Los Plates River is the same as the Blue Creek (shown on GLO 1921) — all this despite the fact that the Francisco River was mapped accurately on the General Survey map of 1874.

The town of Clifton has used the stream as a principal source of water for mining and other activities. Locally the stream is called the Fresco or Frisco, but in August 1962 the USGS officially deleted the names Fresco or Frisco.   Ref.: 256, p. 90; *Arizona Citizen* (Nov. 8, 1873), p. 2; 329; Figueroa *ms.* (Huntington Library)

FRANCISCO SPRING, SAN
Coconino

This place was the McMillan sheep company headquarters. See Elden Mountain, Coconino, and Leroux Spring, Coconino

FRANCIS CREEK
Yavapai   T16N R10W   Elev. 3020'

This creek is named for John W. Francis, a sheepman who lived in Flagstaff c. 1900.   Ref.: 18a; Thompson

FRANCOIS MATTHES POINT
Coconino (Grand Canyon)   T32N R4E   Elev. 8020'

While superintendent of the Grand Canyon in the early 1900s, Francois E. Matthes was responsible for naming many places in the Grand Canyon.

FRANCONIA

Mohave   T16N R20W   Elev. 1101'

Only a sign now marks the location of a former section house on the A.T. & S.F.R.R.,
named by Frank Smith (b. 1857, California), son of F. W. Smith, a railroad general
superintendent. Franconia Wash shares the name (T16N/R19W).   Ref.: 18a; Babcock

FRANKENBURG

Maricopa   T1N R7E   Elev. c. 1200'

This station on the railroad east of Tempe was established about 1902 by a cattleman
and farmer named Frankenburg.   Ref.: 18a

FRANKLIN

Greenlee   T9S R32E   Elev. 3725'

Led by Thomas Nations, Utah Mormons migrated here in 1895. When officials of the
church visited the locality in 1898 and organized it as a ward, they named their
community for Franklin D. Richards, a deceased apostle of the L.D.S. church.
P.O. est. Feb. 10, 1905, Nephi Packer, p.m.; disc. March 7, 1958   Ref.: 242; 353, p.
48; 225, p. 250

FRANK MURRAY'S PEAK

Mohave   T19N R21W   Elev. c. 2000'

On October 14, 1857 Lt. Edward Fitzgerald Beale saw and named this single peak for a
member of his party. Beale wrote that the pass was too rough for use by emigrants unless
it was developed somewhat. He and his party followed it, however, and for the first time
met Mohave Indians whom he described as a"fine-looking, comfortable, fat and merry
set; naked except for a small piece of cotton cloth around the waist and though bare foot
[they] ran over the sharp rock as though shod with iron. Some had learned a few words
from trafficking with the military post, two hundred and fifty miles off and one of them
saluted me with: 'God damn my soul eyes! ' 'Howdy do!' 'Howdy do!'"   Ref.: 23, pp.
73-75

FRASER CANYON

Pinal   T1N R11E

This canyon takes its name from that of Jack Fraser, a cattleman here about
1917.   Ref.: 329

FRAZIER WELLS

Coconino   T28N R8W

These are two wells at an abandoned school and sawmill, now a summer Indian camp.
They take their name from that of Fred Frazier (b. 1835, France).   Ref.: 329; AHS

FRED HART CANYON

Coconino   T13N R11E

This canyon was named for the man who owned the land about 1902.   Ref.: Hart

FREDONIA   pro.: /friydoniə/

Coconino   T41N R2W   Elev. 4680'

Seeking freedom from efforts to suppress polygamy, several Mormon families left Utah
and settled here in 1885, calling their place Hardscrabble. Erastus Snow, a prominent
Mormon, suggested the name "Fredonia" because the families were seeking freedom
from Federal laws. Locally the name is said to imply that as the Spanish word for "wife"
(doña), men living three miles north in Utah sent their extra wives to Fredonia to escape
law enforcement, whence "Free-the-wife."
P.O. est. April 6, 1892, William S. Lewis, p.m. Incorporated March 5, 1956
Ref.: AHS Names File; 225, p. 99

FRED WINN FALLS

Cochise   T18S R30E

This falls near the head of Cave Creek was named by the USGS in 1954 for Fred Winn
(b. 1880; d. Jan. 19, 1945), who in 1904 began his long career with the National Forest

Service. He was supervisor of the Coronado National Forest from 1925 until his retirement in 1942. John Hands Dam is here, impounding John Hands Lake.   Ref.: 329

FREE'S WASH

Mohave   T21N R15W   Elev. c. 5000'

In 1875 when Gov. Anson Pacely Kileen Safford journeyed through Arizona Territory, he noted stopping between Mineral Park and Greenwood City at Free's Wash. There he met and talked with Cherum, the Hualapai Indian chief (see Cherum Peak, Mohave). Mistaking the sound of the name of the wash, some referred to it as Freeze Wash, although in actuality the name seems to have derived from that of John Free, a local prospector.

In 1889 American Indians began performing ghost dances based on their belief that their Messiah was due to rescue them from white men. The Hualapai held a ghost dance in Free's Wash in 1890. Expecting visions of their Messiah and to invoke his resurrection, Indians danced until they collapsed from exhaustion.   Ref.: Babcock; *Arizona Miner* (June 6, 1875), 1:4; 335, p. 172; Harris; 314, p. 68

FREEZEOUT CREEK

Graham   T2N R26E   Elev. c. 5000'

The name Freezeout Creek derives from an incident during a cattle roundup. Supplies for cowboys were customarily packed on mule trains, sometimes over one hundred mules. While cowboys of the Double Circle were out herding on the San Carlos Indian Reservation, the supply mules stampeded and scattered packs everywhere. The cowboys waited in vain for the supply train to arrive with supper and bedding. Just about dark the weather turned foul with rain and snow. During the night three cowboys quit, but the others stuck it out. Thereafter when cowboys made camp at the same location, they referred to it as "Freeze Out." Freezeout Mountain shares the name.   Ref.: C. A. Smith, Jr. (interviewed by Woody)

FREMONT PEAK

Coconino   T23N R7E   Elev. 11,940'

Beginning in 1842 with an overland route to the Pacific, John Charles Fremont (b. Jan. 21, 1813, Georgia; d. July 13, 1890) earned fame as the Path Finder of trails in the west. He was the first Commissioner of the U.S. Boundary Survey Commission, but gave up that position in 1846 when appointed governor of the Territory of California. From 1878 to 1882 he was governor of Arizona Territory, a fact barely worth mentioning. Fremont never saw the peak named in his honor. See also Francisco Peaks, San, Coconino Ref.: 71, p. 61; 5, p. 319

FREMONT SADDLE

Coconino   T19N R7E   Elev. 10,800'

The name for this saddle was submitted by Harold S. Colton and approved by the USGS in 1933. See Fremont Peak, Coconino   Ref.: 329

FRENCH BUTTE

Navajo   T22N R19E   Elev. c. 6488'

This butte was named for Franklin French, a stockman and miner. He married a widow of Mormon John D. Lee and lived at Hardy Station twenty-four miles west of Holbrook where he and his wife supervised the station. French later moved to Winslow, where he died.   Ref.: "Archaeology of the Hopi Buttes ..." p. 3; 141, p. 153; 18a

FRENCH SPRING

Navajo   T22N R18E

This spring is at French Butte. (*q.v.*).

FRENCH JOE CANYON

Cochise   T19S R19E   Elev. c. 6000'

French Joe, whose last name is not known, mined with his partner, using a ranch in this canyon (c. 1879) as headquarters. Indians killed French Joe's partner. French Joe never returned to the ranch, but moved at once to a safer place on Babocomari Creek. His name is also applied to French Joe Peak (Elev. 7684'), and French Joe Spring (in the canyon).   Ref.: Bennett

FRENCHMAN MOUNTAIN
Mohave (Lake Mead)

This mountain (the highest point on Frenchman Ridge) was named for a mine dug by a Frenchman on the west side. It is asserted that the Frenchman salted his mine and sold it, thereafter returning to France. The name, long in local use, was approved by the USGS in May 1948. Ref.: 329

FRENCHMAN'S TANK
Yuma   T3S R15W

This location is also known as Fox Tank. See Tank Mountains, Yuma   Ref.: Monson

FRENCHY SPRING
Coconino   T22N R3E

The spring is named for a Frenchman who lived here. He died of influenza in Williams in 1918. Ref.: Platten

FRESNAL   pro.: /freznæl/
Spanish = "ash grove"

Pima   T18S R7E   Elev. 3125'

Pumpelly used the name Fresnal when he visited this canyon in 1860. Charles Debrille Poston in his Indian Affairs Report in 1863 also used the name, and a year later J. Ross Browne spoke of Fresnal as "a small Mexican town containing some ramshackle adobe huts built in the past twenty-four months," probably because the place was convenient for reducing ores stolen from nearby mines. Actually the name Fresnal could be applied to any of three Papago villages in Fresnal Canyon. Bryan noted them as follows: *Kóxikux* (*Koxi* = "mulberry tree"; *Kux* = "where it stands") is the most northern; second, Tshiuliseik (*Tshiuli* = "willow"; *Seik* = "forest"); third, *Pitóikam* (*Pitoi* = "ash tree"), three miles southwest of Tshíuliseik. Although one source asserts that Kóxikux is also called Ventana, the two places are actually separate. The name Fresnal also applies to Fresnal Canyon, Cerro del Fresnal, Fresnal Creek, Wash, and Well.   Ref.: 167, I, 476; 369, p. 40; 56, p. 281; 59, p. 422; 58

FRESNAL WASH
Pima   T18S R7E

Fresnal Wash is identical with Fresnal Creek, the name given it in 1893 on the Roskruge map of Pima County. The USGS approved the term Fresnal Wash in 1941. See also Fresnal, Pima

The term "Fresno" (Spanish = "Arizona ash tree") has been applied to several locations where such trees grow. The name *Fresno* may be assumed descriptive of the locale.

FREYA CASTLE
Coconino (Grand Canyon)   T31N R5E

Among many names associated with gods and goddesses and applied to temple-like formations in the Grand Canyon is that of Freya Castle, approved by the USGS on July 3, 1906. In Norse mythology Freya is the goddess of love. Ref.: 329

FRIJOLE MINE   pro.: /friyhowliy/
Spanish = "bean"

Santa Cruz   c. T21S R14E

While prospecting on the west slope of the Santa Rita Mountains, John A. Rockfellow located and named this mine because he thought it might supply the beans for awhile. Beans (*frijoles*) were a staple in pioneer diet. Ref.: 277, p. 59

FRISCO
Mohave   T22N R20W   Elev. c. 800'

Known locally as Union Pass, this mining camp at the foot of the pass in the Black Mountains had a post office which served the Frisco Mine. Frisco Peak is here. P.O. est. May 5, 1913, Cornelius J. Falvey, p.m.; disc. March 31, 1915 Ref.: Householder; 242; 18a

FRISCO CANYON

Greenlee   T25S R30E   Elev. c. 5000-2500'
Frisco Canyon is the channel for the San Francisco River, hence its name.
Ref.: Shannon

FRITSCHE

Yavapai   T17N R3W   Elev. c. 4000'
Although Barnes says this place was named for H. W. Fritsche, a stockman, it is
probable that it took its name from that of its first postmistress. The post office was
probably at the Fritsche Ranch and served several ranches in the vicinity, a not
uncommon practice. Fritsche Tank is nearby (T18N/R5W).
P.O. est. Jan. 23, 1913, Mrs. Sydney Fritsche, p.m.; disc. April 15, 1918   Ref.: 242;
18a

FRITZ CANYON

Greenlee   T1S R31E   Elev. c. 4000'
In the spring of 1887 Fred Fritz, Sr. (d. 1916) brought sixty head of cattle to the place
where he established his ranch one mile below the canyon bearing his name (ranch:
T1S/R30E). Fritz had first seen the area while trapping for beaver in 1885.   Ref.: Mrs.
Fred Fritz, Sr.

FRY CANYON

Coconino   T19N R6E
The canyon takes its name from that of Freeley Fry, who owned a ranch and lived with
his family here c. 1920.   Ref.: Frier

FRYE CREEK

Graham   T8S R25E   Elev. c. 4000'
To supply his lumber yard near Safford, Albert A. Frye obtained lumber from a mill in
the canyon bearing his name. The sawmill was built about 1879. A dam in the canyon
helps provide water for Thatcher and Safford. Frye Mesa is also here.   Ref.: Jennings;
329

FULLER SEEP

Yavapai   T9N R8E
This is the possible location of a post office which was never in operation. The postal
station was then the ranch of the Fuller family, local cattlemen. See also Horse Camp
Seep, Yavapai
P.O. est. March 15, 1898 as Fuller, Oscar Townsend, p.m.; disc. Jan. 30, 1899
Ref.: 18a; 242

FULTON SPRING

Coconino   T17N R9E   Elev. c. 6500'
Michael J. and Timothy A. Riordan, Flagstaff lumbermen, constructed a logging
railroad on which Fulton was a station named for Harry Fulton, who in 1887 ran seven
thousand sheep on his ranch about thirty miles south of Flagstaff. The spring is also
called Lindberg Spring.   Ref.: Slipher; 18a; Sykes

G

GADDES CANYON
Yavapai   T15N R2E
A family by this name is said to have lived in the canyon.   Ref.: Allan

GADDIS SPRING   pro.: /gédəs/
Mohave   T2N R17W   Elev. c. 5000'
The spring was named after the owner of a cattle ranch, Oregon Dakota Montana
Gaddis, at one time postmaster of Kingman.   Ref.: Harris

GADSDEN
Yuma   T10S R25W   Elev. 95'
The town site of Gadsden was laid out in 1915 on land originally owned by Edwards in
approximately 1900. Whether the town was named for the Gadsden Purchase or for
James Gadsden, the Secretary of State under whom the purchase was made, is not
definitely known.
P.O. est. Feb. 17, 1915, William M. Davison, p.m.
Ref.: 242; M. Conseler (Yuma 1964)

GADSDEN PEAK
Pima   T17S R5W   Elev. 2600'
Formerly known as West Twin Peak, this peak in the Organ Pipe National Monument
was renamed to honor James Gadsden, Minister to Mexico and negotiator of the
Gadsden Purchase, in his centennary year 1953.   Ref.: Henson; 329

GAEL (R.R. STN.)
Yuma   T8S R17W   Elev. 3849'
This place was named for Robert Gael, in charge of pumping water for trains
here.   Ref.: 18a

GALAHAD POINT
Coconino (Grand Canyon)   T33N R1E
This headland on the North Rim was among those named at the suggestion of Francois
E. Matthes and approved by the USGS in Oct. 1905. Other names proposed but not
approved included Carnation Point and Shaler Pyramid. It was among a number of
names drawn from the Arthurian legend.   Ref.: 329

GALENA
Cochise   T23S R24E
The town site for this mining community took its name from the old railroad siding
nearby, which in turn is derived from a mineral term meaning "a lead bearing ore."   Ref.:
C. E. Mills, manager, Phelps Dodge Corp., Copper Queen Branch, Letter (1956)

GALEROS BUTTE
Coconino (Grand Canyon)   T33N R5E
Frank Bond suggested this name in 1929 for Juan Galeros, who in 1540 tried to descend
the canyon wall with Cardenas. The USGS approved the name in 1932.   Ref.: 329

GALEYVILLE

Cochise   T17S R28E   Elev. 5700'

The mining community of Galeyville (Galzville and Gayleyville are errors) was laid out in 1880. John H. Galey opened the Texas Mine and Smelter here in Nov. 1881. Mining activity zoomed and died like a sky-rocket. The lawless fire-works may have begun when in order to promote sale of the mine miners smelted Mexican money and said it was the output of the mine. Galeyville was extremely isolated and lay on a trail from Mexico into the United States which was used by cattle rustlers, bandits, and smugglers. Rustlers holed up in side canyons and gorges near Galeyville while waiting for the healing of altered brands on stolen cattle. It was a two-way deal, with cattle being stolen in Mexico and sold in the United States and vice versa. In 1888 the San Simon Cattle Company forced or bought out squatters and Galeyville rapidly vanished, partially as the result of fires and partially the result of structures being carried away piece by piece as settlers built new structures in nearby Paradise.

P.O. est. Jan. 6, 1881, Frank McCandless, p.m.; disc. May 31, 1882

Ref.: Macia; Larriau; 146, p. 32; 60, pp. 88, 89; 206, p. 282; "Bad Men March Through Arizona History," *Arizona Daily Star* (May 27, 1932); AHS Names File; *Gazette* (April 1, 1881), p. 2:2; Bill Sanders (Tucson, 1962)

GALIURO MOUNTAINS pro.: /Gəlérə/

Graham/Pinal/Cochise   T7–12S R18–21E Elev. c. 5000 and 7328

The contemporary name of these mountains is an interesting example of how names alter because of cartographic errors. The changes can be traced on maps, the first name found being *Salitre* (= "nitrate"). Lt. John Parks (1854) maps the name as both Calitre and as Calitro, noting an abundance of limestone in the range. He added that the name might be a corruption of *Calizo* (= "lime"). Cartographers altered the *t* to *u*, and thence the name appeared as Caliuro. On the Williamson 1869 map, it is Galiuno. The alteratin of the C to G yielded the present-day Galiuro Mountains. An Indian skirmish was recorded in the Sierra Galiuro Mountains on February 13, 1871. Variants include Galloria Mountains. Ref.: 254, p. 23; 345, III, 591; 4, p. 141; 242

GALLETA WELL pro.: /gayeyétə/

Spanish = "a species of wild grass on range land"

Maricopa   T1S R7W   Elev. c. 1500'

The Flower Pot Cattle Company used this well for watering cattle, naming it for grass on the range.   Ref.: 18a

GALLOWAY CANYON

Coconino (Grand Canyon)   T34N R1W

This name was suggested by the National Park Service on July 10, 1930 and approved by the USGS on May 4, 1932 to honor Nathan Galloway (b. 1860, Wisconsin; d.c. 1919, a Mormon trapper who made several trips through the Grand Canyon by boat, including one with Julius F. Stone. Ironically this adventuresome man died of an epileptic fit by falling over his wagon gate and choking to death.   Ref.: 193; 220; 192, pp. 238-239.

GANADO pro.: /Gənádo/

Navajo   T27N R26E   Elev. 6400'

Charles Crary had the first Indian trading post at Ganado Lake in 1871. Another was soon opened by "Old Man" William B. Leonard. The locale was known to Navajo as *Lok'an Ntiel* (= "white reeds") and others used Pueblo Colorado, the name of the stream on which it was located. Lorenzo Hubbel (b. Nov. 27, 1853, New Mexico; d. Nov. 12, 1930) bought the post in 1876. Hubbel named his trading post Ganado to honor his friend Ganado Mucho, the last peace chief of the Navajo and the twelfth to sign the peace treaty of 1868 (see Fort Defiance), who ran sheep and cattle along the Pueblo Colorado. A Presbyterian mission with a school and hospital was established in 1901. Associated names include Ganado Lake and Wash (Apache/Navajo). See also Hubbell Hill, Apache

P.O. est. July 10, 1883, Charles Hubbell, p.m. Ref.: 5, p. 409; 326, p. 139; 331, pp. 64, 65

GAP, THE
Coconino   T34N R9E
The name describes a gap here in the Cedar Ridge sandstone.   Ref.: 331, p. 65

GAP CREEK
Yavapai   T12N R5E
A large spring called Brown Spring lies in the gap of this creek, hence the name is descriptive.   Ref.: Dugas

GARCES   pro.: /garséys/
Cochise   T23S R20E   Elev. c. 4000'
The now-vanished mining camp was first known as Reef, after the Reef Mine, in turn named because of the presence of a conspicuous rock reef. The first name proposed for the post office was Exposed Reef. When Joseph S. Palmerlee owned the land, the post office was moved six miles south and the name was changed to Palmerlee, and still later to Garcés for reasons not yet known. See also Garces Mesas, Coconino, and Garcia, Cochise
P.O. est. as Reef, Nov. 16, 1900, Mark Walker, Jr., p.m.; name changed to Palmerlee, Dec. 7, 1904, Joseph S. Palmerlee, p.m.; name changed to Garcé, April 12, 1911, Richard M. Johnson, p.m.; disc. May 24, 1926
Ref.: Macia; AHS Names Files; Theobald; 242

GARCES MESAS
Coconino   T25N R14E
Herbert Gregory c. 1915 named these mesas for Fr. Francisco Garcés (b. April 12, 1738, Spain), who arrived in Mexico in 1763. When Jesuits were expelled from New Spain in 1767, Fr. Garcés requested assignment there, arriving at his new post at San Xavier del Bac on June 30, 1768. For the ensuing ten years, Garcés journeyed in Arizona and California. He was in the vicinity of these mesas in 1776. Garcés was killed by Indians near the present-day Yuma on July 17, 1781.   Ref.: 141, pp. 17, 38 (Note 3)

GARCES TERRACE
Coconino (Grand Canyon)   T33N R2W
The name was suggested by the USGS in June and approved on Oct. 7, 1908 to honor the Spanish explorer and missionary, Fr. Francisco Garcés. See Garcés Mesas, Coconino   Ref.: 329

GARCIA
Cochise   T23S R21E
Nothing more is known about this place than the fact that a post office was established here on July 14, 1933, John F. Ashworth, p.m. The location is so close to Garces that the spelling Garcia may be an error.   Ref.: 242

GARDEN CANYON
Cochise   T22S R20E
Originally this canyon was called Tanner Canyon (or Hayes and Tanner Canyon) because prior to 1880 Hayes and Tanner had a sawmill in it. The military station at nearby Fort Huachuca grew produce in the canyon and the name underwent its change to the present form.   Ref.: 329; Bennett

GARDEN CANYON (R.R. STN.)
Cochise   T21S R20E
This was a station on the railroad serving Fort Huachuca. The postal sub-station here used the same name. Records in the National Archives reveal that the Overton post office (est. May 15, 1917) was identical with that at Garden Canyon. It should not be confused with Overton *Canyon*, Cochise (*q.v.*). See Sierra Vista, Cochise
P.O. est. as Overton, Nov. 11, 1917, Jean Clark Wilder, p.m.; disc. May 31, 1918; name changed to Garden Canyon, Dec. 12, 1918, William Carmichael, p.m.; named changed to Fry, April 1, 1937   Ref.: Bennett; Macia; 242

GARDEN CREEK
Coconino (Grand Canyon)   T31N R3E   Elev. c. 4000'
Indians irrigated their garden with water from this creek, hence its name.
Ref.: Kolb; J.H. Butchart, Letter (1961)

GARDEN OF THE GODS
Yavapai
This well known recreational area near Prescott has spectacular vari-colored rocks.
Ref.: 5, p. 288

GARDEN SPRING
Coconino   T20N R6E
Sometimes referred to as Otey Spring because Judge Otey logged in the vicinity, this
place name reflects the garden-like quality of its surroundings; hence the name is
descriptive. Ref.: Slipher

GARDNER CANYON
Pima/Santa Cruz   T19–20S R17–16E
In 1877 Thomas Gardner (b. April 13, 1820, New York; d. March 26, 1909) lived in
this canyon with his family. He arrived in Arizona in 1859, and ran cattle near the
present Lochiel. After 1867 he moved his herd close to the present-day Patagonia,
remaining until 1872. Thereafter he established his Apache Spring Ranch in this
canyon, keeping it until 1896. Ref.: AHS, Thomas Gardner File, "Reminiscenses of
Mrs. Mary Gardner Kane"

GARFIELD GULCH
Greenlee   T3S R29E   Elev. 4813'
In this gulch there was formerly a small community called Garfield, but for what reason
is not known. Ref.: Scott; Reilly

GARFIELD PEAK
Cochise
This peak in the Chiracahua National Monument was named for a member of the 10th
Cavalry during the Civil War. Garfield died c. 1882. When several 10th Cavalry men
gathered at the Riggs ranch in 1886, they built a monument to his memory, inscribing
their own names on the stones. When the monument began to disintegrate, the Riggs
family moved it into their home, using it to face the fireplace. Ref. Riggs

GARLAND
Yavapai   T20N R5W
This station on the P. & A.C.R.R. (the first railroad to Prescott), and later removed, was
named for William Garland, a railroad conductor. Ref.: 329; AHS Names File; 18a

GARLAND PRAIRIE
Coconino   T21N R4E   Elev. c. 5000'
In the 1880s the name for this location was Snider Prairie, probably because of Snider's
Water Hole where Companies C & F of the 1st California Volunteers cached their stores
in the bitter winter of 1863. (It is possible the place corresponds to Volunteer Spring.)
Fred G. Hughes was detailed with ten men to remain with the stores while awaiting
relief, and the detachment named the spot Snider's Water Hole. With his partner Ross,
William Garland bought the area from Elias Pitman, including the L O Ranch, and ran
cattle at this open park among the pines about 1885 to 1895. The brand in turn gave its
name to L O Spring, L O Canyon and L O Spring Canyon. Garland Spring is at Garland
Prairie.
P.O. est. as Snyder's Hole, Feb. 24, 1881, S. M. Gray, p.m.; disc. May 16,
1881 Ref.: 124, pp. 159-160 (Note 7); 107, pp. 42, 111; Postal Records

GARNET CANYON
Coconino (Grand Canyon)   T33N R1W
William Bass, an early settler at the Grand Canyon, named this canyon. The USGS
approved the name in June 1908. Ref.: 329

GARNET RIDGE
Apache/Utah   T41N R24E

In 1915 Herbert Gregory reported that the ground on this ridge was "strewn with garnets in unbelievable quantities, the source of the Arizona rubies," hence the name. Ref.: 141, p. 37; 329

GASH MOUNTAIN
Coconino   T17N R8E

In the mid-1870s John Gash settled on the flat at the foot of this mountain and herded cattle. Later Walter (?) Van Deren settled in the location and then named both the flat and the mountain for Gash. The spring on Gash Flat (T17N/R9E) is called Van Deren Spring. Ref.: 18a; Slipher

GATAGAMA POINT   pro.: /gǽtəgámə/
Coconino (Grand Canyon)   T34N R3W   Elev. 6102'

Several Havasupai Indian families helped prepare for the tourist industry in the late 1880s and helped maintain facilities. Gatagama Point and Terrace are named for one of these families. Ref.: 329

GATES FOUNDATION
Gila   T8N R10E

Tom Gates between 1880 and 1890 ran horses in Tonto Basin. Typical of those who intended to stake out land claims, he laid a foundation of four oak logs. Apparently he never built a cabin but moved away because of local suspicions about the ownership of some of "his" horses. See also Gates Pass, Pima   Ref.: 18a; Woody

GATES PASS
Pima   T14S R12E   Elev. 3727'

Prior to his activities in the Tonto Basin (see Gates Foundation, Gila), Tom Gates (b. 1834) was in this area near Tucson at least as early as 1865. The pass is very striking, being an abrupt cut at the top of the ridge through the Tucson Mountains. Tom Gates was living in Tucson in 1880. Ref.: 63; 18a

GATEWOOD
Cochise

This location in the San Simon Valley was named by Lt. Charles Baehr Gatewood (b. April 6, 1853), 6th U.S. Cavalry, who in 1866 succeeded in convincing Geronimo that he should confer with Gen. Nelson A. Miles and surrender.
P.O. est. June 7, 1890, Joseph M. Hooker, p.m.; disc. Feb. 5, 1894 Ref.: 63; 18a

GAVALAN PEAK
Apache = "hawk"

Maricopa   T7N R2E   Elev. 2980'

Frank T. Alkire climbed this peak in 1870 and, according to his letter to G. E. P. Smith, the correct name is the Apache rather than the Spanish word for "hawk." Soldiers in the late 1870s chased and here defeated Tonto Apache Indians who had raided Charles Mullen's place on New River. Alkire learned the story from Mullen when he bought Mullen's place in 1886. Ref.: Frank T. Alkire, Letter to G. E. P. Smith (Dec. 21, 1937)

GAWAIN ABYSS
Coconino (Grand Canyon)   T33N R1E

The name, drawn from Arthurian legend, was suggested by Francois E. Matthes to the USGS geographer. It was approved in 1908.

GEESAMAN WASH
Pima   T11S R16–17E

This wash bears the name of Finley (a.k.a. Phineas) Geesaman (b. 1830), who in 1906 lived in the canyon which this wash drains. "Geesman" is an error. Ref.: AHS, Great Register; 329

GEIKIE PEAK

Coconino (Grand Canyon)   T32N R1E   Elev. 4750'

Sir Archibald Geikie (1835-1924) was a Scots geologist and a director-general of the Geological Survey for the United Kingdom. During his visits to the Grand Canyon, he found evidence to support his erosion theories. Ref.: 329

GEMINI PEAK

Yavapai   T17N R9W

Lt. Amiel W. Whipple named this peak in 1854. He described it as a "remarkable mountain rising about two thousand feet above its sides ... and in the centre cut as it were in two equal peaks; hence called the Gemini." Ref.: 346, p. 99; 345, p. 94

GENERAL'S SPRINGS

Coconino   T13N R11E

Gen. George Crook discovered these springs in General's Springs Canyon. Near here he narrowly escaped Apaches c. 1871. Ref.: 49, p. 145

GENTILE SPRING

Mohave   T20N R17W

Gentile Spring (which on the G L O map of 1892 is *Gentle*) may have been named because non-Mormons settled near it. In 1872 Capt. George M. Wheeler noted that Mormons referred to others than themselves as Gentiles and said that gentiles "generally made small settlements convenient to mine districts and establish ranches along routes of communication." This location was also sometimes referred to as Railroad Spring. Ref.: 344, p. 32

GENTRY SPRING

Coconino   T12N R12E

This spring served as headquarters for Old Man Gentry (b. Redding, California), who grazed sheep throughout this area. He arrived in Arizona in the early 1880s. Associated names include Gentry Canyon Creek (T9N/ R12E, elev. 6587'). Ref.: McKinney; Davis; 18a

GENUNG MOUNTAIN

Yavapai   T10N R5W   Elev. c. 4600'

Charles Baldwin Genung (b. July 22, 1839, New York; d. c. 1938) arrived in Arizona at Yuma in 1863. A successful prospector, he located several good mines near Prescott where he had his ranch. The mountain, locally sometimes referred to as Boulder Mountain, was named for Genung in 1939 at the suggestion of Mrs. Statler, a neighbor. Genung Spring is on the mountain (T11N/R4W). Ref.: AHS, Names File and Chambers Collection; 62

GERALD WASH

Gila   T2N R15E   Elev. c. 3500'

This wash crosses the ranch established by James F. Gerald (b. 1837, Massachusetts), who arrived in Arizona in 1877. For awhile he was a hotel man in Pioneer. He bought land for a cattle ranch which he worked until his retirement in 1911. Gerald Hills are adjacent to the Wash. Ref.: Woody; 224, III

GERMA

Mohave   c. T17N R21W

The location was first called Snowball, according to J. H. Knight, who lived at the community, for a black who discovered the claim. The name of this short-lived mining community derived from the first letters of the *German*-American Mining Company of Los Angeles. Insufficient water to run the mill on a double shift closed the mine in 1906. German American Wash is an associated name.

P.O. est. Jan. 20, 1903, Isaac D. Hilty, p.m.; disc. Feb. 27, 1906 Ref.: 200, p. 186; Harris; 215, p. 139

GERONIMO pro.: /jeránimo/ or /heránimo/

Graham   T4S R23E   Elev. 2716'

This point on the Arizona Eastern R.R. was named for Geronimo, whose Apache name was Goklyia. Because Apache warriors he led in fights against Mexicans knew that Mexicans feared him and called him Geronimo, the Indians would scream his name during their attacks. This place came into existence long after Geronimo had left Arizona Territory. See Goodwin, Camp, Graham, and Thomas, Fort, Graham
P.O. est. as Geronimo Station, Jan. 9, 1896, George Rayfield, p.m.; disc. May 31, 1956   Ref.: 65, p. 29; 311, pp. 130, 133-134

GERONIMO HEAD

Maricopa   T29N R9E   Elev. 3509'

This mountain rock profile was named by Aubrey Drury in the early 1930s. Although the name was not accepted by the USGS in 1933, it is in use and accepted by the State of Arizona.   Ref.: 329; State Highway Department, Arizona

GERONIMO PEAK

Cochise

This peak near the community of Warren is described as "a finger of hooked rock." It is named for the Apache leader. See Geronimo, Graham   Ref.: 5, p. 378

GERONIMO'S SEEP

Cochise   c. T21S R32E   Elev. 4700'

Near the Ross Sloan ranch house is a spring concealed in cliffs. There Apaches always found clear cold water. Among them was Geronimo's band, and Geronimo surrendered here. See Goodwin, Camp, Graham   Ref.: 60, p. 96

GERTRUDIS, ARROYO DE SANTA

Mohave   T38N R5W

Fr. Escalante named this location in 1776. Later it was the site of Canaan Dam. Ref.: 42, p. 65

GIANT LOGS

Navajo   T16N R23E

The name describes an abundance of petrified logs here. This portion of the Petrified National Monument is sometimes called Rainbow Forest because of the varicolored logs.   Ref.: 329

GIANT'S CHAIR

Navajo   T27N R17E   Elev. c. 6500'

This huge volcanic plug resembles an enormous straight-backed chair, hence the name. Hopi Indians call it Hoyepi (= "where the birds first fly" or "where the eagles nest"). Here Hopi used to capture eagles for feathers required in religious rituals.   Ref.: 71, p. 44; 331, p. 65; 329

GIBBON MOUNTAIN

Pima   T13S R16E   Elev. 5801'

This mountain is on property owned by the Gibbon Ranch. Gibbon's Springs are south of Bear Canyon.

GIBSON

Maricopa   T7N R2E

Shortly after his arrival in 1912, Matthew Ellsworth Gibson, Sr. laid out a town site near Gibson Arroyo on a group of mining claims just north of those held by the New Cornelia Copper Company. When Clarkstown was nearly burned out in 1931, the Rowood post office was moved to Gibson. It is now called North Ajo. See Clarkstown, Pima Ref.: Ketchum; 57, p. 358; *Ajo Copper News* (Oct. 21, 1954), p. 5:3

GIBSON MOUNTAIN

Pima   T13S R16E

This is a variant name for Biggon Mountain (*q.v.*).

GIBSON PEAK

Gila   T10N R11E   Elev. 5815'

In the early 1900s three Mormon brothers — Arthur, Wash and Joe Gibson — maintained a ranch near this peak. Gibson Creek is here also. Ref.: Pieper; 18a

GIGANTES, LOS pro.: /hiyhánteys/

Spanish = "the giants"
T36N R27E
Apache   T36N R27E   Elev. (w.) 6460'   Elev. (e.) 6490'

These twin buttes are named on the 1860 Macomb map. The name describes the way they jut from the surrounding country. The Navajo name *ceézdélzah* means "stone juts out." Ref.: 141, p. 152; 143, p. 187

GILA BEND pro.: /híylə/

Maricopa   T5S R4W   Elev. 735'

This community is named because it is at the point on the Gila River where the river made a sweeping ninety-degree bend to the west, as noted by many travellers, some of whom called it the Big Bend, or Rinconada. Today's small city is not precisely at the bend referred to. Fr. Eusebio Kino visited this locale in 1699. Here Fr. Francisco Garcés in 1774 encountered an Indian rancheria which he called Santos Apostoles San Simon y Judas (Spanish = "the Blessed Apostles St. Simon and Judas"). De Anza called the place Opasoitac, and Garcés is said to have also called it Uparsoytac or Upasoitac. The Papago name *Uhupat Oidak* is *tesota* in Spanish (= "cat claw field") (see below: Tezotal). In 1850 there were Indian settlements on the great bend of the Gila River. They were as follows: l. *Vinyi'lkwukyáva* (= "where the black mountains meet"), said to have been on the west bank of the present Gillespie Dam; 2. The following were temporary sites: *Kwŭtupára* (= "last," probably because it was the most westerly); 3. *Tŭnkuvátc* (= "the middle one"); 4. An easternmost temporary settlement which apparently had no name. As is customary with Indian place names, each name is a descriptive locative.

At the original location of Gila Bend the freighting and mail station was called Gila Ranch (T5S/R4W). The name for the ranch on the site of a Maricopa Indian village was noted in 1854 by Lt. Parke as being Tezotal, for the desert ironwood tree listed as *olneya tesota* in Dr. John Torrey's botanical report for the Boundary Commission.

At one time along the stream course there was a South Gila Bend and North Gila Bend, about twenty miles apart. Both were probably in existence to serve emigrants. Papago Indians called the vicinity Petato, their word for the familiar vegetable green called "Lamb's quarter," which grew abundantly in the region. In 1865 settlers drove out the Indians, dug an irrigation ditch and began raising grain for freighters. Before long a small community developed around the stage station named Gila Bend. In 1880 railroad tracks were completed and a station was built away from the river, although the steam engines drew water from the river until the railroad sank its own wells. When that happened, the small community began relocating near the railroad. The first settler at the new town site (laid out by Daniel Murphy, John H. Martin, and William H. Barnes) was Daniel Noonan. Noonan had been postmaster at the Gila Bend post office at the river freighting and stage station. By 1910 all that remained at the older location were eight Papago families at Uhupatoidak.

P.O. est. May 1, 1871, Albert Decker, p.m.; disc. May 26, 1879; reest. at new location Aug. 4, 1880, Daniel Noonan, p.m.; Wells Fargo 1885   Ref.: Logan; 224, III, 274; *Ancient Mines of Ajo*, p. 19; *Weekly Arizona Enterprise* (Sept. 12, 1891), p. 1:5; 73, II, 173; 254, p. 39

GILA BEND MOUNTAIN

Yuma/Maricopa   T5–2S R4–12W   Elev. 2428/3170'

This mountain overlooks the bend in the Gila River, hence the name. It extends into Yuma County only to the pass which separates it from the Clanton Hills. See also Gila River   Ref.: 355, p. 144; 329

GILA BUTTE

Pinal   T3S R5E   Elev. 1657'

This butte overlooks the bed of the Gila River.

GILA COUNTY pro.: /híylə/

Gila County was formed on Feb. 8, 1881 from parts of Maricopa and Pinal counties. In 1889 it was extended eastward to the San Carlos River. The county seat was established at what was then called Globe City, now Globe (*q.v.*). The county was named for the Gila River, which constitutes its southern boundary. Elevation varies from 2123' at Roosevelt Dam to 7153' at Mount Ord. The San Carlos Indian Reservation covers half of Gila County. The principal industries of this beautiful region have always been and continue to be mining and agriculture, principally livestock.

GILA MONSTER

Maricopa

While Aubrey Drury was selecting names on the S.P.R.R. wagon tourist excursion on what is now the Apache Trail, he gave this name to a stone figure at the end of a butte thirty-three and a half miles from Mesa. It was approved on Nov. 7, 1917, but on Feb. 1, 1933, the USGS vacated the name.   Ref.: 329

GILA MOUNTAINS

Yuma   T8S R21E   Elev. 3150'

The name used by Spanish missionaries for this range was San Albino Mountains, but for what reason is unknown. In 1854 Lt. N. Michler referred to them as the Sierra de la Gila. During the heyday of gold placering, they were called the Gila Mountains. On the 1881 Chain and Hardy map they are designated Gila Range. Their gradual exploration led to dividing the range in 1912 into a northern section called Sierra de San Albino and a southern area called Sierra de las Tinajas Altas (Lumholz, 1912). By 1914 there was no longer any disagreement about calling the entire range the Gila Mountains. In 1930 their western segment was mapped and referred to as Vopoki Ridge. Yuma residents sometimes call them the Fortune Range.   Ref.: 58; 115, p. 4 (Huntington Library); 106, I, 104; 355, pp. 181-183; Lenon

GILA PUEBLO pro.: /híylə pueblo/

Gila   T1S R15E   Elev. c. 4000'

Prior to 1930 Charles Healy explored in Six-shooter Canyon for Indian ruins and found the Gila Pueblo, site of a large pre-historic Indian village. He sold it to the Medallion Society c. 1930, which developed headquarters for the study of Indian ruins in the region. In 1956 the former Healy Terrace was headquarters for the Southwestern Monuments Park Service.   Ref.: Woody; 5, p. 39

GILA RIVER pro.: /híylə/

One of the great rivers of America, the Gila River enters Arizona about one hundred and thirteen miles from its New Mexico source (elevation 9993'). It slices for hundreds of miles across Arizona to its junction with the Colorado River (elevation 125'). Prior to the Gadsden Purchase the Gila River was the boundary between the United States and Mexico. Its location relative to the five counties it now crosses is as follows: (east to west): (1) Greenlee, T6S/R32E; (2) Gila, T4S/R16E; (3) Graham, T3S/R20E; (4) Maricopa, T5S/R10W; (5) Yuma, T6S/R11W.

The name *Gila* was not used in the New World until 1630, at that time being applied to a province of New Mexico as *Gila* or *Xila*. As for the meaning of the word, Mrs. Mary B. Aguirre said that there is a Spanish expression *de Gila*, which means "a steady going to or from a place," adding that the Gila always had water in it. The latter part of the statement no longer pertains, but at least as late as 1909 it was possible to canoe its entire length in Arizona, a feat performed by Stanley Sykes of Flagstaff. Dams since built along the river course do not completely control severe flooding, as evidenced by heavy floods in recent years.

Various names have been applied to this river, some descriptive of the importance of the river to those along its banks, others pertaining to the nature of the water, and still others reflecting the efforts of missionaries to convert Indians to Christianity. For instance, Pima Indians simply referred to the stream as *Akee-mull* (= "the river"). At its juncture with the Colorado River where the water is very alkaline, Yuma Indians call the mouth of the river *hŏmkwñȧvȧvȧ* (= "flowing water that is salt"). Another Yuma name is *Hah-quah-sa eel* (= "running salty water"), in use c. 1930. Its first non-Indian name was Brazo de Miraflores, applied to it in 1540 when Capt. Fernando Alarcon named it, according to the memoirs of Castillo. Encountering the same river closer to its source in 1604, Juan de

Oñate named it the Rio del Nombre de Jesus (= "river of the name of Jesus"). Oñate's party explored to its junction with the Colorado River. For generations thereafter, no white man seems to have seen this river. In 1697 Fr. Eusebio Kino with Lt. Cristobal Martin Bernal followed the course of the San Pedro River to its juncture with what Kino called the Gila, the first time that name was recorded. In 1701 Kino called it Rio Grande de Hyla. However, in 1701 he also named its upper reaches the Rio de los Santos Apostoles (= "river of the sainted Apostles"), because he had already suggested naming its four principal tributaries after the four major Apostles and the name applied to their joining in forming the larger stream. The name Rio de los Santos Apostoles was still in use on a map made by Capt. Clark and sent to President Thomas Jefferson on April 7, 1805. Others, noting that Indians crossed this river in wicker baskets, called it the Rio de las Balsas (= "river of the rafts"). The list of names for this river is still not complete, however, for Benavides called it Apache de Xila, as did Sansom. The latter used this name at the hearing of the Inquisitor, although prior to that time he referred to it as the Rio del Coral (= "red river"). Fr. Francisco Garcés in 1775 applied still another name, Rio Jaquesila. The name *Gila* has been rendered as follows: Chila; Hila; Helah; Helay; Hyla. Salvatierra called it Rio de Grande.   Ref.: 15, pp. 163 (Note 41), 348, 349, 355; 256, p. 85 (Note 51); 146 p. 12; 45, p. 422; 77, pp. 541, 544, 136 (Note 48); 279, pp. 65, 66; 89, pp. 80, 82; 5, p. 29; 46, p. 275; 43, I, 127, 171, 194-195; AHS, Mary B. Aguirre File; 203, p. 3; 329; McClintock, Letter (Jan. 17, 1930)

GILA RIVER INDIAN RESERVATION

Pima/Maricopa   T3–1S R4–1E   Elev. c. 1200'

On Feb. 28, 1859 a reservation was established for Pima and Maricopa Indians living near the Gila River. Land was added from time to time until a slight reduction in acreage was made on July 19, 1915, so that today the acreage is 37,200. The reservation is bisected by the Gila River. See Gila River   Ref.: 167, II, 374; "Annual Report of the Arizona Commission of Indian Affairs (1954-1956)", pp. 4-5

GILA RIVER WATERFOWL AREA

Maricopa   T2S R5W

This ninety-two hundred and sixteen acre tract includes Robbins Butte and the Arlington area.   Ref.: 9, p. 1

GILA VALLEY

Graham   T2S R19E

It is also sometimes referred to as Safford Valley.   Ref.: 329

GILBERT

Maricopa   T1S R6E   Elev. 1235'

Robert Gilbert donated land to the Arizona Eastern R.R. for a station at this point. P.O. est. July 22, 1912, D. H. Butler, p.m.   Ref.: 329, Steele File; 242

GILBERT

Yavapai   T9N R3W   Elev. 4370'

The post office for the King Solomon Mine was named for its postmaster. P.O. est. Aug. 21, 1899, William J. Gilbert, p.m.; disc. Oct. 31, 1903   Ref.: 242; 18a; 320, p. 173

GILLESPIE DAM

Maricopa   T2S R5W   Elev. c. 600'

Constructed of brush, earth and rocks, the Peoria Dam flooded away in 1900. Another was built in 1906 by owners of the Enterprise Ranch, who wished to divert Gila River waters into the Enterprise Canal (constructed in 1886). In 1921 Frank A. Gillespie of Oklahoma built a concrete dam here and thereafter development of agriculture was rapid. Today the Gillespie holdings cover thousands of acres. In 1956 H. C. McMullen, who had an option to buy the land for eight million dollars, suggested naming the new community Arizona City. P.O. est. Aug. 24, 1925, Edward F. Holland, p.m.; disc. Nov. 2, 1925   Ref.: 5, p. 463; 279, p. 70; *Arizona Star* (Jan. 26, 1956), p. 3; 242

GILLESPIE RANCH

Graham   T7S R29E   Elev. c. 4000'

There is still evidence of the old Gillespie house and corrals on the east side of Stockton Pass. The place served as a way station between Fort Grant and Safford, where horses were watered at ten cents per head. On the ranch are Gillespie Flat (T9N/R25E), Gillespie Mountain (T10S/R26E, elev. 5223'), and Gillespie Wash (T9S/R27E). Ref.: Jennings

GILLETT

Yavapai   T7N R2E

In 1878 a community here served the Tiptop Mine and its mill site. The community was named for D. B. Gillett, Jr., superintendent of the Tiptop Mine. It was on the left bank of the Agua Fria River and hence in Yavapai County rather than Maricopa, the creek being the dividing line between the two. The name was sometimes spelled Gillette, an error. P.O. est. Oct. 15, 1878, John J. Hill, p.m.; disc. Aug. 11, 1887   Ref.: *Arizona Sentinel* (Feb. 9, 1878), p. 1:3

GILLILAND GAP

Gila   T11N R11E

John Gilliland (b. 1859, Texas; d. Jan. 3, 1937) arrived in Arizona in 1879 and served as foreman for the Stinson outfit. During the Pleasant Valley feud, he was shot at the Tewksbury ranch by boys repairing a rifle. The spelling "Gilliand" is an error. Gilliland Spring is near the gap.   Ref.: McKinney; 329

GILSON WASH

Gila   T2S R16E

An early name for this creek was Aliso Creek (Spanish = "alder tree") because of large groves of alders along its course. Sam T. Gilson, a cattle rancher on the San Carlos Indian Reservation, worked for the Indian agency. He had Apaches dig Gilson Well (T1S/R17E), after which he sold them water. His ranch was also a stage stop on the wagon road from Willcox to Globe. Gilson Well today is an Indian reservation cattle loading station.   Ref.: Woody; *Arizona Miner* (May 11, 1864), p. 3:3; 329

GISELA   pro.: /gaysíylə/ or /gaysílyə/

Gila   T9S R10E   Elev. 2880'

David Gowan with two others arrived here in 1881, but soon sold to Mort and John Sanders what was locally called Tonto Settlement. On the application for a post office, the name Gisela is given for the new post office. It was suggested by Mrs. Stanton, the local school teacher and wife of the postmaster, for the heroine of *Countess Gisela*, a novel. Gisela Mountain shares the name.

P.O. est. April 9, 1894, Fred Stanton, p.m.; abandoned July 1, 1906; new application filed July 7, 1907; disc. Aug. 31, 1911   Ref.: 116, p. 595; 242

GLASSFORD HILL

Yavapai   T14N R1W   Elev. 5151'
                            T14N R1W   Elev. 6161'

This name was suggested by Will H. Barnes in 1932 to honor Col. William A. Glassford, who as a lieutenant in the early 1880s operated a heliograph station on this hill, sending messages to Baker Butte and thence eastward. During the 1880s it was also referred to as Malpais Mountain (Spanish = "bad country"). Because the hill was used for a heliograph station it also is called Mirror Mountain. In 1929 Glassford told Sharlot Hall that the peak used to be called by his name and he would like to see the name Bald Mountain or Bald Hill replaced.   Ref.: 329; 18a; Rufner

GLEED

Yavapai   T22N R2W   Elev. 5452'

This section house on the A.T. & S.F.R.R. was named for C. S. Gleed, a railroad director (1900-1920).   Ref.: 18a

GLEESON

Cochise   T19S R25E   Elev. 4923'

With his wife, John Gleeson (b. Nov. 1861, Ireland) lived at various places in the
southwest before grub-staking a crippled friend. The friend located old turquoise mines
on Turquoise Mountain c. 1890. Indians mined turquoise prior to the coming of white
men, but it took the discovery of a new mine to give life to the region. In 1897 Gleeson
found the Copper Bell Mine and the almost defunct community known as Turquoise took
on new life. Gleeson sold out by 1914. Little remains at the site.

P.O. est. as Turquoise, Oct. 22, 1890, James W. Lowry, p.m.; disc. Sept. 17, 1894;
reest. as Gleeson, June 19, 1900 (application signed by Will S. Thatcher), Frank R.
O'Brien, p.m.; disc. March 31, 1939; Wells Fargo 1910   Ref.: Macia; 5, p. 441; 224,
p. 840

GLENBAR

Graham   T6S R24E   Elev. 2798'

The first name for this small community was Matthews, probably for Joseph Matthews,
a name it retained until at least 1906. In early 1880 Joseph and David Matthews bought
land here from Mrs. Patterson. By 1887 a Wells Fargo station was established here
under the name Fairview. The second time the post office was established (in 1908) the
post office application bore a request for the name Nonsuch. A derogatory name used by
outsiders was Hogtown. Why a final name change was deemed necessary is unclear, but
in 1917 residents selected the name Glenbar because many of them were Scots and
preferred the name.

P.O. est. as Matthews, Feb. 9, 1897, Hulda Blair, p.m.; disc. May 1, 1906; reest. as
Fairview, Sept. 28, 1908, Ephraim Larson, p.m.; name changed to Glenbar, Jan. 1,
1918, Lehi Larson, Jr., p.m.; disc. May 31, 1956; Wells Fargo (Fairview) 1887
Ref.: 224; Jennings; 353, pp. 13, 48; 116, p. 247; 225, p. 247

GLEN CANYON

Coconino   T41N R8E   Elev. c. 3000'

On Aug. 3, 1869 Maj. John Wesley Powell wrote about passing through this deep gorge,
noting that it had "carved walls, royal arches, glens, alcove gulches, mounts and
monuments; from which of these features shall we select a name? We decide to call it
Glen Cañon." See also Glen Canyon Dam, Coconino   Ref.: 266, p. 72

GLEN CANYON DAM

Coconino   T41N R8E

Bids were opened on April 11, 1957 for the construction of this seven-hundred-foot-high
dam, which impounds twenty-eight million acre feet of water to form Lake Powell. The
lake extends up the Colorado River some one hundred and eighty miles as well as into the
San Juan River (N.M.). These waters conceal walls of the canyon where gold
prospectors worked from boats numbering in the hundreds from about 1897 to 1904.
This area (partially in Utah) continues to be under development by the National Park
Service.   Ref.: 176, p. 33

GLENCOE

Santa Cruz   c. T24S R31E   Elev. 4000'

No information has been found other than the post office existed at or near the Reppy
Ranch.

P.O. est. Jan. 12, 1889, Loretta A. Reppy, p.m.; disc. Sept. 13, 1890   Ref.: 242;
Lenon

GLENDALE

Maricopa   T2N R2E   Elev. 1154'

Originally this location was called the Glendale Temperance Colony. The site was
selected by B. A. Hadsell in December 1891 in what was at the time called Glendale
Valley.   Ref.: *Weekly Arizona Enterprise* (Dec. 19, 1891), p. 1:7; Stone

GLENN, MOUNT

Cochise   T17S R23E   Elev. 7519'

This highest point in the Dragoon Mountains was named for Calvin Glenn (d.c. 1918), manager for the Chiricahua Cattle Company (c. 1888 – c. 1905). He became an independent cattle rancher. Glenn (not Gleen) Spring (T18S/ R19E) is an associated name.   Ref.: AHS Names File; 18a; 329

GLOBE
Gila   T1N R15E   Elev. 4682'
Despite legends about the origin of the name Globe, it derives from that of the Globe Mine, recorded as the Globe Ledge on Sept. 19, 1873 by Ben Regan, Robert and David Anderson, Isaac Copeland, William Sampson, William Long, T. Irwin, William Folsom, P. King, M. Welch, and B. Edward. The settlement for the new mining district was at the Ramboz Mine (see Ramboz Peak). There the Globe Mining District was organized in November 1875 in the Globe Hills. By 1878 the Ramboz settlement moved to Globe City, a better distributing point with ample water.

As usual, legend is of more interest than fact. One relates that D. B. (Gip) Chilson and Henry Wagner were prospecting in the Apache Peaks and learned that Indians were using silver bullets. They found the silver source, a huge mine. One locater said it was as big as the globe and so they called it Globe. A second legend says that when the small settlement had barely begun, cavalry men riding near what became the Old Dominion Mine found a perfectly round boulder, from which fact the name Globe derived. A third story asserts that among first indications of silver was the finding of a ball of silver ("Munson's Chunk") with markings on it like the outline of the earth, hence the name Globe. The silver sphere, however, was found after the name Globe had been selected.

The town site had been laid out by Alex Pendleton. The *Arizona Silver Belt* (May 2, 1878) made an editorial suggestion that the word "city" be dropped from the name Globe City. In October 1880 Globe was incorporated as a village, a fact apparently forgotten as the town of Globe was again incorporated in 1905. Citizens deemed city government so expensive that they disbanded the incorporation within a year, only to re-incorporate as a city in 1907. Globe Peak is nearby.
P.O. est. Dec. 22, 1876, Edward M. Pearce, p.m.; Wells Fargo 1885   Ref.: *Maricopa Book of Mines*; Woody; *Arizona Record* (July 21, 1929), p. 1; 270, p. 116; 56, p. 263

GOAT CAMP CANYON
Greenlee   T7S R32E   Elev. c. 6000'
The Zorrilla family of Clifton maintained a goat ranch in this canyon at one time.   Ref.: Patterson; Reilly

GOAT HEAD PEAK
Yavapai   T10N R4E
This sandstone bluff at its south end resembles a goat head, from which it derives its name. There also used to be wild goats in the vicinity.   Ref.: Allan

GOAT RANCH
Greenlee   T2S R29E
There were formerly two goat ranches in this locality, one belonging to Justo Gonzales and the other to the Zorrilla family.   Ref.: Simmons; Reilley; Paterson

GOAT'S SPUR
Yuma   T6S R17W
On Nov. 19, 1846 Emory made the following notation about this location: "... a spur of mountains ... came in from the southeast, sharp as the edge of a case knife and shooting into pinnacles ... On this spur we killed a mountain sheep, one of a large flock from which we named it Goat's Spur ..."   Ref.: 105, p. 92

GOBBLER PEAK
Apache   T6N R29E   Elev. 8919'
There are two Gobbler Peaks where many wild turkeys formerly existed. The other peak is near Greer.   Ref.: Noble; Wentz

GOBBLER POINT
Greenlee   T3N R29E   Elev. 8778'
Wild turkeys live here. A very large gobbler was killed at the place so named.   Ref.: 18a

GOD'S POCKET

Mohave   T32N R15–16W

The name applies to a vale east of the escarpment known as Cockscomb since 1924. It describes the reaction of R. Esplin and his party when they first came upon it. Ref.: 329

GOLCONDA

Maricopa   T23N R17W   Elev. c. 3500'

This mining camp was named by John Boyle, Jr. for his Golconda Mine. The community and mining were wiped out by fire. The mine was inactive for many years and has been worked only intermittently since 1956.

P.O. est. Oct. 12, 1909, William Pound, p.m.; disc. Feb. 21, 1918   Ref.: Babcock; Harris; 18a; 242

GOLD: Finding gold – or searching for it – has led to the words *golden* or *gold* in several place names. Examples follow:

Gold Basin   Mohave

Minerals were discovered here in the early 1870s. The name Basin or Gold Basin was applied in the early 1900s to a district in the Hualapai Wash area extending from White Cap Hills to Lost Basin. The name Gold Basin was applied to a town serving a mining community and mill. Scarcity of fuel and water and the difficulty of obtaining supplies kept activities in this region at a low level.

P.O. est. as Gold Basin, Sept. 20, 1890, Michael Scanlon, p.m.; disc. Jan. 4, 1894; reest. as Basin, Jan. 21, 1904, Eugene Derwood Chandler, p.m.; disc. June 15, 1907   Ref.: 242; Harris; 200, pp. 16, 118-119; Mallach

Gold Cañon (See Oro, Cañada del, Pima)
Golden   Maricopa   T2N R10W   Elev. c. 1100'

This station on the Parker branch of the main railroad was named for a nearby mining camp in the Harquahala Mountains. Ref.: 18a

Golden Palisades   Pinal   T10S R3E

The origin of this name has not yet been learned.

P.O. est. April 7, 1915, Arthur Elliott, p.m.; disc. Feb. 6, 1918   Ref.: 242

Golden Spray City   Mohave   (See Watertown, Mohave)

Gold Field   (See Youngberg, Pinal)

Gold Field Mountains   Maricopa   T2N R7–8E   Elev. 3269'

In 1933 these mountains were sometimes called the Bulldog or Yellow Iron Mountains. However, the Gold Field Mine was more important than the Bulldog Mine and the USGS authorized the official name Gold Field Mountains. They were also known as Harosoma Ridge and as the Oronai Mountains. See Youngberg, Pinal   Ref.: 329

Goldflat   Mohave   T20N R17W   Elev. c. 2500'

This small post office on the Hancock railroad siding derives its descriptive name because it is on the flat lands east of Goldroad.

P.O. est. June 23, 1908, Jacob A. Hamme, p.m.; disc. July 15, 1910   Ref.: 242

Gold Gulch   Apache   T6N R23E
Gold Gulch   Cochise   T13S R26E
Gold Gulch   Coconino   T9N R12E
Gold Gulch   Greenlee   T4S R29E   Elev. c. 5000'
Gold Gulch   Maricopa   T1N R13E

Here in 1882 Apaches ambushed miners from Silver City, killing several. Capt. Frink escaped by hiding under a bush. The gulch is also known as Placer Gulch.   Ref.: Scott; Patterson; 68, p. 72; 224, p. 236

Gold Hill   Santa Cruz   (See Benedict, Mount, Santa Cruz)

GOLDROAD

Mohave   T19N R20W   Elev. 3680'

The fact that there were several mines in the Goldroad District apparently led to the naming of the Goldroad Mine and its community, which became the principal distribution point for the region during its heyday in the early 1900s. The first name for the community of Goldroad was Acme. Minerals were first found in the district in 1860 by John Moss and his party and ore from the mine was treated at the Moss mill seven miles to the west. Mining in the area ceased briefly during the 1880s when rich ore was found in the Cerbat Mountains. As the value of gold increased, however, the Goldroad Mines re-opened about 1902, the year in which the big strike was made. In that year Joe Jenerez, a Mexican prospector, was grub-staked by Henry Lovin of Kingman. While searching for his burro, Jenerez stopped to rest and chipped idly at a rock with his pick. The top of the rock came away, revealing an ore chute of gold. Lovin and Jenerez sold their location for twenty-five thousand dollars. Lovin established a store at the community which almost immediately sprang up, whereas Jenerez drank up his share.

Another story says that Jenerez (or Jerez) picked up a piece of quartz which showed pure gold and set up a monument to stake the claim. A third story asserts that Jerez and Lovin sold their claim for fifty thousand dollars. By 1906 a French syndicate had control, having paid half a million dollars for one-fourth of the stock. A year later, however, the low grade of the ore caused the closing of the mine. In 1949 the remains of the operations and the community were razed to save taxes. On the flat below are the remains of what was once called Mexican Town. Gold Road Pass lies east of the community.

P.O. est. as Acme, Feb. 12, 1903, H. P. Ewing, p.m.; name changed to Goldroad, March 24, 1906, Enos Norton, p.m.; disc. 1925; reest. Dec. 20, 1937, Newton S. Lanier, p.m.; disc. Oct. 15, 1942   Ref.: Babcock; 242; 200, pp. 16, 152, 154-155; 359, p. 74

Gold Road Gulch (See Goldroad, Mohave)

Gold Road Pass (See Goldroad, Mohave, and Sitgreaves Pass, Mohave)

GOLD TOOTH SMITH SPRING
Gila   T7N R9E

The name of this spring has been used since 1925. It was originally Big Spring but about 1905 a Mr. Edwards bought the land and lived near this spring while he mined his property. From 1905 to 1925 it was called Big or Edwards Spring, but after Edwards' death, Gold Tooth Smith moved in and began mining near the spring, whence the name. Ref.: 329

Gold Tree Mine Santa Cruz (See Alto, Santa Cruz)

GOLDWATER LAKES
Yavapai   T14N R2W

One of two artificial lakes here is Upper Goldwater Lake, constructed in 1933. Both are named for Morris Goldwater, who continued the business of his father (Michael Goldwater) carrying freight and supplies for the army at Fort McDowell. He was mayor of Prescott for twenty years and vice president of the State Constitutional Convention of 1910. Ref.: 176, p. 12

GONZALES PASS
Pinal   T2S R11E   Elev. 2650'

This pass was named for Juan Gonzalez, a freighter. It lies in Gonzalez Pass Canyon.

GOODWATER
Navajo   T18N R23E   Elev. 5250'

Most well water in this area is saline, but when Dick Grigsby's brother dug a well in 1912 he found potable water. A community has developed around the trading post. Ref.: Branch; Grigsby

GOODWIN
Yavapai   T12N R2W   Elev. 6800'

Goodwin has had several names. The first is a bibliographic ghost post office named "Max." Barnes lists "Max" as being "somewhere in Apache County." Actually "Max" was the nickname of Redden B. Allred, postmaster at Maxton in 1881. It operated for the benefit of the Senator Mine, in existence as early as 1878, at which time its ores assayed at $85.00 per ton in gold. The post office lasted under three months. In 1901 Maxton post office was set up in a store and the name of the postmaster—Morilla T.

Alwens — was close enough to "Max" Allred's name to confuse the analysis later made by Barnes. In 1915, the name was changed to Senator. (See Venezia, Yavapai)

Why a further change was made in 1915 is not clear. However, a post office at Venezia was established. The post office site location map places Venezia in R1W, a slightly different location from Senator (R2W). Barnes says a native of Venice, one F. Scopal, insisted on the new name. The application for the new post office notes that locally the place was known as Bolada rather than as Goodwin, the latter being a name favored by some.

Someone must have been stubborn about the matter, for in 1935 the name was changed to Goodwin. However, this editor believes that the new Goodwin post office was about four miles northwest of the old Venezia/Maxton location, for the simple reason that records in the National Archives say so. See Venezia, Yavapai

P.O. est. as Maxton, Feb. 24, 1881, Redden A. Allred, p.m.; disc. May 13, 1881; reest. July 6, 1901, Morilla T. Alwens, p.m.; p.o. est. as Senator ("on former site of Maxton"), June 9, 1915, Mrs. Mary Wills, p.m.; Senator disc. Oct. 22, 1918; name of Venezia changed to Goodwin, June 1, 1935   Ref.: 242; 18a; *Prescott Journal Miner* (Oct. 14, 1906), p. 4; *Arizona Journal Miner* (Nov. 16, 1897), p. 4

GOODWIN CITY

Yavapai   Near Prescott

While the government party from Washington, D.C. was en route to establish the new Territory of Arizona, miners on Granite Creek started a community called Goose Flat on a mesa. Following the death of Arizona's first governor, John Gurley (who never saw the Territory), John N. Goodwin (b. Oct. 18, 1824, Maine; d. April 29, 1887) was appoinged territorial governor on August 20, 1863. The miners then named their small community Goodwin in his honor. Goodwin served until 1865 when he was elected delegate to represent Arizona Territory in Congress. He went east and never returned.

Scarcely had Goodwin City been laid out when Prescott was selected as the site for the new capital. Thereafter Goodwin City was sneeringly referred to as Gimletville. It soon vanished. The contemporary Goodwin is not at the same location as the original Goodwin mining camp.   Ref.: *Arizona Miner* (April 6, 1864), p. 2; *Arizona Republic* (Dec. 12, 1889), p. 4; 107, III, 187-188

GOODWIN, CAMP (OLD)

Graham   c. T9S R23E   Elev. c. 2000'

To protect Americans living at the end of Gila Valley, a military post was established here on June 21, 1864. King S. Woolsey said it was on a stream called the Tulerosa, known today as Goudy Creek. The camp was named for John N. Goodwin, Arizona's first territorial governor. Camp Goodwin was ill-fated. Unscrupulous contractors charged an estimated $150,000. for a few miserable adobe houses. The site was extremely unhealthy. Soldiers by the dozens sickened from malaria, a fact which led to abandoning Old Camp Goodwin. In 1870 the commanding officer, Maj. John Greene, established Fort Apache (*q.v.*) as a temporary camp while finding a new site for a post. Old Camp Goodwin was permanently vacated on March 18, 1871 and a new post established. The name Camp Goodwin was transferred (see Thomas, Fort, Graham) in 1881. The original Camp Goodwin was then serving as a sub-agency of the San Carlos Apache Reservation with some three hundred seventy-five Apaches under Geronimo, Juh, Nana, and Loco.   Ref.: *Arizona Miner* (Sept. 21, 1864), p. 1; Jennings; 116, p. 405; 145, p. 135; 224, p. 185; 83, p. 31

GOODWIN CANYON

Cochise   T15S R28E   Elev. c. 4500'

John N. Goodwin (see Goodwin, Yavapai) reportedly stopped at this location some time between 1864 and 1865, hence its name. This canyon behind the old Apache Pass stage station was called Cochise Canyon when the stage lines were routed through Apache Pass. Here Apache chief Cochise camped with seven hundred of his tribe, hence the older name. Another Apache leader known as Old Jack camped with five hundred men in front of the stage station at Goodwin Springs. Both the spring and the canyon were so called by 1859.

GOODWIN CANYON
Graham   T5S R21E
This canyon took its name from the location of the second Camp Goodwin. See Thomas, Fort, Graham

GOODWIN WASH
Graham   T5S R21E
This wash includes the Middle Fork (T5S/R20E), the North Fork (T4S-R20E), and the South Fork (T5N/R20E). See Goodwin Canyon, Graham

GOODYEAR
Maricopa   T1N R1W   Elev. 963'
Included in other acreage acquired by the Goodyear Tire & Rubber Company in 1916 to produce Egyptian long-fiber cotton was one tract crossed by the Chandler branch of the Arizona Eastern R.R. It had a station called Casaba. The word *casaba* is Spanish for "melon," and many melons grew in the vicinity. The main town for the development, one and a half miles north, was briefly known as Egypt (because of the variety of cotton), but the name Goodyear was soon applied to both the community and the cotton ranch. In 1944 the Goodyear Tire & Rubber Company sold its property. The name Goodyear was transferred from the discontinued post office to the new town of Goodyear. See Litchfield Park, Maricopa
P.O. est. Jan. 8, 1918, G. Lindley Gallands, p.m.; disc. Feb. 15, 1941; reest. in new location Nov. 22, 1944   Ref.: K. B. McMicken, Vice President, Goodyear Farms, Letter (March 28, 1956)

GORDON
Gila   T10N R13E   Elev. c. 5800'
A man named Gordon had a ranch here about 1885 with headquarters in Gordon Canyon. A post office was established to serve the area.
P.O. est. Sept. 10, 1913, Katie L. Payne, p.m.; disc. Oct. 22, 1915   Ref.: 18a; 242

GOUDY CREEK   pro.: /gódiy/
Graham   T9S R23E
In 1864 King S. Woolsey called this Tulerosa Creek. Grant Goudy lived at this location in Goudy Canyon for several years.   Ref.: Jennings; 18a; *Arizona Miner* (Sept. 21, 1864), p. 1

GOVERNMENT CANYON
Yavapai   T18N R1E   Elev. 5750'
During territorial days the term "government" was customarily applied to places used by soldiers. Troops returning from scouting excursions to Fort Whipple traversed this canyon.   Ref.: Merritt

GOVERNMENT CAVE
Coconino   T22N R4E   Elev. c. 7000'
This cave borrows its name from that of nearby Government Prairie. Lumber men were responsible for the name. It is a lava tunnel about a mile long, nearly forty feet high, and in some places about fifty feet wide. For years it was a source of ice for households. Ref.: "Government Cave," p. 1; 5, p. 320; 71, p. 29

GOVERNMENT HILL
Gila   T4N R12E
This hill between Theodore Roosevelt Dam and the community of Roosevelt juts into Roosevelt Lake. It was so named because houses were occupied by government employees.   Ref.: Woody

GOVERNMENT HILL
Pinal   T1N R12E   Elev. 5445'
After a Federal surveying party placed a bench mark on this hill, cowboys and settlers called it Government Hill.   Ref.: 18a

GOVERNMENT PEAK
Cochise   T14S R28E   Elev. 7587'
During the campaign against the Apache leader Geronimo, the army maintained a
heliograph station on this mountain, hence the name.   Ref.: Riggs

GOVERNMENT PRAIRIE
Coconino   T22N R4E
The name derives from the fact that cavalry stationed at Fort Whipple pastured horses
here and on Government Mountain during the summer. It is also thought that the name
comes from the fact that the old government trail passed close to the mountain.
Government Hill (T23N/R4E, elev. 8490') overlooks it, as do also Government Knolls
(T23N/R5E, elev. 7953').   Ref.: Bartlett

GOVERNMENT SPRING
Pinal   T2S R14E
This name was in use at least as early as 1880 because of the spring being used by the
military.   Ref.: Woody

GOVERNMENT SPRING
Yavapai   T10N R2E
This spring was used by the military during Indian warfare. The name is mentioned in
military reports in the early 1860s. It extends to Government Spring Gulch (T13N/R3E).
Ref.: West; Schroeder

GRAHAM
Graham   T6S R25E   Elev. 2875'
In 1879 this location was owned by the notorious Powers brothers and a friend named
Snyder (see Kielberg Peak, Graham). It was known as Rustlers Ranch. In Nov. 1880
Jorganson, George W. Skinner, Andrew Anderson, and James Wilson bought a square
mile of this land and in Jan. 1881 settlers arrived. The community was included in Saint
Joseph Stake of the Mormons when it was formed in Feb. 1883. In 1884 the town site
was surveyed and a meeting house constructed of mesquite poles. It had a dirt roof and
walls of heavy unbleached muslin. The community soon went out of existence and has
vanished.
P.O. est. March 17, 1882, Thomas Weirs, p.m.; disc. Sept. 24, 1885   Ref.: 224, pp.
246-247; 5, p. 553; 353, p. 9, Note 13; *Gila Valley*, p. 14; 116, p. 592

GRAHAM COUNTY
On March 10, 1881 Graham County was formed from parts of Apache and Pima counties.
It is believed the county was named for its most prominent mountain, Mount Graham
(*q.v.*). The first county seat was at Safford. E. Solomon wanted the county government
headquarters to be at his sawmill. In 1883 he took all the records and moved them to his
mill, thus placing the county seat at Solomonsville. When Greenlee County was created in
1915, citizens agreed to permit its formation provided that the county seat of Graham be
moved to Safford. Safford remains the county seat. Graham County, consisting of
2,950,400 acres, is largely an agricultural area.

GRAHAM, MOUNT
Graham   T8S R24E   Elev. 10713'
Sierra Florida is the earliest known name for the entire range in which Mount Graham is.
According to both Manje and Alegre, that name was applied by Fr. Kino's party in 1696
to a place where the chiefs of the Janos and Pima Indians met. Despite the application of
the name Graham by Americans, the name Florida persisted, being in use as late as
1868 when the name Florida and also Graham were used for the entire range, today
called Pinaleno Mountains. The name was applied to a single peak in June 1857 in a
military report: "Mount Graham or Floridian." As for the name Graham, there are three
possibilities about its origin. (1) Lt. William H. Emory referred to it as Mount Graham
on Oct. 28, 1846, possibly honoring William A. Graham, who in 1850 was not only
Secretary of War, but was also acting Secretary for the Department of the Interior. (2)
The mountain was named for Maj. Lawrence Pike Graham, Second Dragoons, who in
1848 journeyed from Santa Cruz on the San Pedro River to San Diego. (3) The

mountain was named for Col. James Duncan Graham, principal astronomer and head of the scientific corps for the Boundary Survey Commission in 1851. His wagon broke down when this peak was certainly in sight. On the other hand, he and Commissioner Bartlett disliked each other, a fact which militates against the mountain having been named for Col. Graham. Mexicans ignored all such names, referring to the mountains as Sierra Bonita, a name borrowed by Henry Hooker for his ranch (q.v., Graham). Ref.: 131, pp. 6, 20, 44, 72, 76; *Santa Fe Weekly Gazette* (Oct. 31, 1857); 105, p. 67; 15, pp. 626-627 (Note 12); 49, p. 207

GRAMA POINT
Coconino (Grand Canyon)   T33N R2E

The region has a rich growth of buffalo or grama grass. It is excellent for forage. The point formerly was called Judith Point.

GRAND ARMY WASH
Mohave   T27N R20W

This wash bore the name as early as 1906, borrowing it from the Grand Army of the Republic Mine.   Ref.: 200, p. 130

GRAND CANYON
Coconino/Mohave

One of the spectacular wonders of the world lies entirely within Arizona, and its most beautiful part – one hundred and five miles long – in the Grand Canyon National Park. The canyon name is descriptive, for in its depths are spectacularly grand formations. The depth of the canyon varies from three thousand to six thousand feet, and its width from four to fifteen miles, with its North Rim being higher than the South Rim. Between the rims lie innumerable sculptured chasms, buttes, and terraced walls formed, according to Francois Matthes, by erosion occurring principally from the bottom up, each cliff being undercut by the removal of soft shale, the resulting overhang then spalling. Vertical fractures have caused slipping along fault lines, thus forming side canyons and amphitheaters. The "temples" do not have such faults and are formed of solid strata.

The first white man to see this vast chasm was Garcia Lopez de Cardenas of the Coronado Expedition in 1540. Pedro de Tobar had reported that the Indians said a large river lay to the west of the Hopi Villages. Cardenas was sent to investigate, but turned away from the sight with the opinion that the region was worthless. Thereafter it was largely ignored until much later explorations began. Lt. Amiel W. Whipple in 1854 followed the lower Colorado River to the mouth of what he called Big Canyon. In 1857 Lt. Joseph Christmas Ives, after finding the headwaters of navigation of the Colorado River, went overland and reached the edge of the main gorge. Dr. John S. Newberry, geologist and surgeon for the Ives Expedition, was the first to give a detailed description of the great canyon and to point out the significance of its geological formations.

The first to conduct an expedition (in 1869) through the entire length of the Grand Canyon, using boats, was Maj. John Wesley Powell, a one-armed Civil War veteran. He made a second and more thorough exploration of Big Canyon in 1871-72 and soon thereafter changed the name in his report on the Grand Canyon. He was the first of many who have investigated the vast chasm. Most have applied place names which are still in use. Among such men were Maj. Clarence E. Dutton, Charles E. Walcott (c. 1880), Francois E. Matthes and Richard Evans (1902). Place names in the Grand Canyon reflect Indian life, historical events, and names of explorers and pioneers significant in Arizona history.

GRAND CANYON NATIONAL GAME PRESERVE
Coconino   T38N R2W

On Nov. 28, 1906 all lands of the Grand Canyon Forest Reserve north and west of the Colorado River were set aside as the Grand Canyon National Game Preserve. This area was taken over as the Grand Canyon National Park upon its creation by Act of Congress on Feb. 26, 1918.   Ref.: Kaibab National Forest, Office Files (Williams); 303, p. 49

GRAND CANYON (TUWEEP UNIT)
This section was the Grand Canyon National Monument from 1932 to 1974. Its three hundred and ten square miles in January 1975 became the Tuweep Unit of the Grand Canyon.   Ref.: 176, p. 36

GRAND CANYON (VILLAGE)

Coconino (Grand Canyon)   T31N R2E   Elev. 6876'

This small community is comprised of visitor accomodations and information points and administrative offices for the Grand Canyon. This location up until the name change in 1902 was called Hance's Tank. See Hance Creek, Coconino

P.O. est. as Grandcanyon, Feb. 3, 1902, Martin Buggeln, p.m.; Wells Fargo 1904   Ref.: 242

GRANDEUR POINT

Coconino (Grand Canyon)   T33N R2W

This was the name suggested on July 10, 1930 by the National Park Service. It replaced that approved in 1908, Tovar Point.   Ref.: 329

GRAND FALLS

Coconino   T24N R11E   Elev. 5500'

In 1851 Lt. Lorenzo Sitgreaves discovered and descriptively named these falls because of their magnificent drop of one hundred eighty-five feet (higher than Niagara). Usually dry, these falls become a "chocolate Niagara" during the rainy season when their thundering waters raise a yellow mist rising in the gorge below. During the dry periods one can see where lava from Rodin's Cone erupted a fiery molten stream which plunged over the canyon rim into the channel of the Little Colorado River, thus forcing it into a new course around the end of the lava. The lava flow produced the cataract. A variant name for Grand Falls is the Cascades (1860).   Ref.: Holton, "Grand Falls," p. 1; 71, p. 41

GRAND REEF MOUNTAIN

Graham   T6S R20E   Elev. c. 4500'

The name Grand Reef is a corruption of Granite Reef. The mountain is named for its being the location of the Granite Reef Mine, a name which derives in turn from the fact that the ground is solid granite. The mine was abandoned c. 1918.   Ref.: Jennings

GRAND SCENIC DIVIDE

Coconino (Grand Canyon)   T33N R1W

The term Grand Scenic Divide is apt. A visitor here can look both east and west and notice that the granite of the Inner Gorge disappears and westward the scenery differs vastly. Eastward where the granite is evident are temples, buttes and other fascinating formations.   Ref.: 178, p. 81

GRAND VIEW (R.R. STN.)

Yavapai   T13N R5W

This station on the Ashfork-Prescott-Phoenix R.R. lies at the top of the divide on Yarnell Hill. There is a marvelous view of the surrounding desert from its vicinity.   Ref.: 18a

GRAND VIEW PEAK

Graham   T8S R23E   Elev. 9612'

This peak about a mile distant from Mount Graham affords a spectacular view, hence its name.

GRAND VIEW TRAIL

Coconino (Grand Canyon)   T30N R4E   Elev. 7400'

The name describes the view at Grand View Point. From here in 1882 Pete Berry (see Bright Angel Creek, Coconino), wishing access to his copper mines, constructed the Grand View Trail, completing it in February 1893. Originally the trail was called Berry Trail. It was an extremely rough one, consisting at some points only of logs anchored by chains to the canyon wall. Along this trail in 1897 the Grand View Caves (now Horse Shoe Mesa Caves) were discovered by the copper company mine cook, Joseph Gildner. There are two caves, both about one hundred feet long.

   In 1901 Berry sold his interests to the Canyon Copper Company. The copper mines proved relatively unproductive, but the tourist business increased each year. Consequently the first hotel at the Grand Canyon, the Grand View Hotel, was privately built in 1904. The Grand View Hotel ceased operations in 1908, and the hotel was subsequently destroyed by the Park Service. See Piute Point, Coconino (Grand Canyon), and Pivot Rock Canyon, Coconino

P.O. est. as Grandview, Nov. 27, 1903, Harry H. Smith, p.m.; disc. Nov. 13, 1908   Ref.: Theobald; 178, pp. 66-67, 68; 242

GRAND WASH CANYON
Mohave (Lake Mead)   T32N R16W
This name was approved by the USGS in May 1948 for a narrow portion of the eastern part of Lake Mead. See Grand Wash Cliffs, Mohave

GRAND WASH CLIFFS
Mohave   T34N R14W   Elev. 4891'
Lt. William Fitzgerald Beale referred to this area as the Yampai Cliffs, an attempt to spell *Yavapai*. This one hundred and ten mile escarpment is also referred to as Lower Grand Wash Cliffs or Lower Grand Wash Ledge. These cliffs are also called the Grand Cliffs Range. The cliffs take their name from the Grand Wash running through Grand Wash Canyon, the trough of which was formed by the "faulting and tilting of a large crust block." It extends to form Grand Wash Valley, marked by detritus consisting of broken rocks and sand. The edge of this great valley is bordered by the Grand Wash Cliffs rising like steps from the lowland to the high plateaus.   Ref.: 23, pp. 78-89; "Lake Mead" (U.S. Government Printing Office, 1955); 200, p. 13

GRANITE
Yavapai   T15R 3W
A post office to serve about forty customers was established here, taking its name from nearby Granite Mountain, named geologically.
P.O. est. March 12, 1903, Earle D. Wharton, p.m.; disc. Oct. 11, 1904   Ref.: 329; 242

GRANITE CAP PEAK
Yuma
This is a prominent peak north of the Fortuna Mine (T10S/R20W), named by Kirk Bryan because the top of the mountain is reddish granite in conspicuous contrast to the dark base of hornblend gneisses.   Ref.: 58

GRANITE CREEK
Yavapai   T17N R2W
In 1864 miners named both the mountain and the creek.   Ref.: 18a

GRANITE DELLS
Yavapai   T14N R2W
This name used to be given as Granite Dalles, said to be derived from the French word *dalle*, meaning "flagstone or slab." Early French hunters also are said to have called a chasm or gorge *dalle*, meaning "a trough."
An early name for this location was Point of Rocks, which describes the location where Granite Creek encompasses miniature hills, mountains, and valleys. It was a dangerous spot in the early days because it was a perfect place for Indians to attack passersby. In 1867 Point of Rocks was owned by Louis A. Stevens (d. 1878). Today Granite Dells is a recreational area having a clear stream, lakes with shade trees, and picnic areas. See Granite, Yavapai   Ref.: *Arizona Miner* (April 6, 1872), p. 1 and (Sept. 21, 1867); AHS Names Files; 49, p. 160

GRANITE GORGE
Coconino/Mohave   T34–28N R1–13W
                                          Lower Granite Gorge: 2800'
Masses of pink and white granite result in the descriptive name of this forty-mile gorge, which is so long that the USGS has split its name into three sections: Granite Gorge, Middle Granite Gorge (Coconino, T34N/R2W), and Lower Granite Gorge (Coconino, T28N/R10W; Mohave, T28N/ R13W). Granite Gorge extends ten miles above Middle Granite Gorge, which is four miles long. Lower Granite Gorge extends for fifty miles, only six of which are in Coconino County. In Granite Gorge is a fiercely flowing rapids called Granite Falls and also called Monument Rapid. A third name is Granite

Rapids (T31N/R2W). The rapids were created by boulders tumbled down from a side tributary called Monument Creek (hence the name of Monument Rapid). Ref.: 5, pp. 484, 492; 192, p. 225; 329

GRANITE MOUNTAIN
Yavapai   T15N R3W

In 1869 Clarence King said that this mountain was the northern terminus of the Sierra Prieta and described it as an "immense pile of granite." For a brief time this mountain was called Gurley Mountain to honor John A. Gurley, appointed first Territorial Governor of Arizona in March 1863. However, the new governor never saw Arizona Territory, dying before traveling west of the Mississippi. Today possibly the only Arizona place carrying his name is Gurley Street in Prescott. See Granite, Yavapai Ref.: *Arizona Miner* (Jan. 23, 1869), p. 1; 56, p. 301; 242

GRANITE NARROWS
Coconino (Grand Canyon)

See Granite Gorge, of which this is a portion. The name describes the fact that the lower walls of the Grand Canyon close in on the Colorado River, not that the river itself narrows at this point. The name was approved in May 1932 after having been suggested by the National Park Service in 1930.

GRANITE PARK
Coconino   T30N R8W

This name was changed from Granite Canyon by the USGS in 1941 to avoid confusion with Granite Gorge Canyon. Ref.: 329

GRANITE PASS TANK
Pima   T13S R10W

This pass was developed by the Fish and Wild Life Service in 1953. Ref.: Monson.

GRANITE RAPIDS
Coconino   T31N R2W

The name Grand Falls was deleted because it is not really a falls and hence was changed to Granite Rapids on July 10, 1930 and approved by the USGS on May 4, 1932. See Granite Gorge, Coconino (Grand Canyon)

GRANITE
The following are descriptively named because of the presence of granite.

Granite Peak	Cochise	(T19S/R19E)	Elev. 7413'
Granite Peak	Cochise	(T23S/R20E)	Elev. 8350'
Granite Peak	Gila	(T3N/R15E)	Elev. 4941'
Granite Peak	Mohave	(T16N/R15W)	Elev. 7069'
Granite Peak	Yavapai	(T10N/R4E)	Elev. 5680'

GRANITE REEF DAM
Maricopa   T2N R6E   Elev. c. 1700'

This one-thousand-foot long diversion dam below the junction of the Verde and Salt Rivers was completed in 1908. The name is descriptive. Ref.: Gertrude Hill, Museum of New Mexico, Letter (Aug. 6, 1955)

GRANITE SPUR
Yuma   T8S R20W

A granite quarry nearby produced ballast for the railroad and for rail beds. Beginning in 1931, it was shipped from this spur on the S.P.R.R. The Southern Pacific Company shipped about forty-five cars of ballast per day. Ref.: 355, p. 208; Lenon

GRANT CREEK
Graham   T9S R23E

This creek takes its name from Fort Grant. One section of it (in quarter 31) is known as

Grant Draw. The wide draw section is also referred to as South Taylor Wash. It is an error to apply that name to Grant Draw.   Ref.: 329

GRANT CREEK

Greenlee   T3N R30E   Elev. c. 7500'

This creek takes its name from that of William Grant, a Scotsman who arrived in Clifton c. 1881. While prospecting and mining, he also ranched here.   Ref.: Reilly; 68, p. 68

GRANT, FORT

Graham   T9S R23E

The Apache Indian name for Camp Grant was *sit-la-lar-te* (= "floating wood"). When old Camp Grant was closed (see Grant, Old Camp, Pinal), another taking its name was established, according to Hamersly, on Dec. 19, 1872. The site had been selected by Col. William B. Royall. Other dates given for its inauguration are Jan. 18, 1873 and March 31, 1873, which may be accounted for by the fact that additional troops were sent to the new camp from Camp Crittenden (*q.v.*, Santa Cruz). The troops enjoyed the town of Bonita (*q.v.*, Graham), which offered rough and tough recreation, while officers and their ladies had a more genteel time at the ranch of Col. Henry C. Hooker. On April 5, 1879 Camp Grant officially became Fort Grant, but already its importance was waning as Fort Huachuca was emerging as a key post for southern Arizona Territory.

New Fort Grant gradually lost troops, with the last of the garrison being withdrawn in 1898 to take part in the Spanish-American War. Fort Grant was officially abandoned on Oct. 4, 1905. The post office closed two days later. A single caretaker remained, to be joined in May 1908 by Col. William F. Stewart and his cook. Stewart, an army veteran of forty years' service, had refused to retire and so was sent to his new post duties at Fort Grant. In 1912 the Federal government turned over control of the military reservation to the new State of Arizona. The post office at old Camp Grant removed to new Camp Grant. Name changed to Fort Grant, June 23, 1879; disc. Oct. 6, 1905   Ref.: 163, p. 311; 311, pp. 101, 123, 152, 155-156; 224, p. 151; 351; 242

GRANT, OLD CAMP

Pinal   T6S R16E   Elev. 2000'

In late 1859 a small garrison set up a camp here. Because of its location at the junction of Arivaipa Creek and the San Pedro River it was first called Fort Arivaipa, also spelled Arivaypa. On May 8, 1860, it became an official military fort, the first name giving way on Aug. 6, 1861, to Fort Breckenridge, for the then-vice president of the United States. Later the same year the fort was burned when troops were withdrawn for service elsewhere during the Civil War. A few months later, on May 29, 1862, the California Column reestablished the old camp and called it Fort Stanford, for Leland Stanford, then governor of California. On Nov. 1, 1865 the name was changed to Fort Grant by order of Gen. O. O. Howard to honor Gen. Ulysses S. Grant. Until 1872 (when it was moved to a new location) it was still being called Camp Grant. Some evidence exists that between October 1863 and July 1865 the name reverted to Fort Breckenridge, as it was so called in some sources.

Life of the original Camp Grant was tenuous. In 1866 a flood destroyed twenty-four of its buildings. New ones were erected on a flat knoll about a half-mile from the old site. These were scarcely in existence before Gen. McDowell issued orders on Oct. 31, 1866 to remove the troops to Camp McDowell, and from there to establish temselves at some other point, specifically a new camp to be named Camp Reno. Camp Reno was established, but Camp Grant continued its existence. In 1869 it was large enough to warrant having a post office one mile from the post. Old Camp Grant was a pest hole with malaria rampant. It might have continued its existence despite flood and disaster had it not become the scene of the wanton massacre of eight men and ten peaceful Apache women and children who had sought official refuge in the camp. (See Eskiminzin, Pinal) The massacre was perpetrated by a party of Americans and Mexicans accompanied by Papago Indians. All returned to their homes in Tucson and San Xavier boasting of their deeds. On April 24, 1871 (the day following the massacre) Gen. Howard visited the scene. On the ensuing day he, Maj. Crittenden and Col. Jones began looking for a site for a new post so that the military would be totally withdrawn from the Indian reservation area. It was the beginning of the end for old Camp Grant, as it came to be known when new Camp Grant was established. National indignation about the Camp

Grant massacre was high, with President Grant threatening to impose martial law on Arizona Territory unless the killers were prosecuted. The leaders were indicted, tried and almost immediately acquitted.

P.O. est. Aug. 19, 1869, George Cox, p.m.; removed to new Camp Grant   Ref.: 15, I, 497, 559; 159, pp. 477, 482; 145, pp. 126, 154; 311, pp. 1-2, 15-16, 71, 101; AHS, Richard Lord File

GRANT WASH, CAMP
Pinal   T7S R15E

This was the name given to the wash across the San Pedro River from its juncture with Arivapai Creek. See Grant, Old Camp, Pinal, and Box O Wash, Pinal   Ref.: AHS Names File

GRANVILLE
Greenlee   T3S R29E   Elev. 7040'

This recreation area on the Coronado Trail north of Clifton was formerly a small community serving nearby mines. Here horse and mule teams were shod and timbers were cut for the mines at Metcalf. Granville was a pioneer prospector c. 1885. Ref.: Reilly; Farnsworth; Scott; 18a

GRAPE VINE CANYON
Coconino   T17N R9E

Wild grape vines grow along this canyon for its entire length from Grape Vine Spring. The canyon is very rugged, having only one place where cattle can be herded across, this point being called Mormon Crossing. It may have been used by wagons coming from the east and headed for Mormon Lake.   Ref.: Pollock

GRAPE VINE CANYON
Gila   T3N R15E

Wild grapes grow in this canyon, particularly at the upper and lower springs in it.   Ref.: Woody

GRAPE VINE RAPIDS
Coconino (Grand Canyon)   T31N R4E

These rapids at the end of Grape Vine Canyon are among the three largest in the Grand Canyon. The name has been used since the early 1900s.   Ref. Kolb

GRAPE VINE SPRING
Gila   c. T10N R12E   Elev. c. 2500'

King S. Woolsey found and named this spring descriptively on June 10, 1864. Ref.: Woody

GRAPE VINE WASH
Mohave (Lake Mead)   T23N R16W

In 1926 the name Grape Vine Creek was occasionally used for the course of this stream, but in 1948 the USGS approved the use of the name Grape Vine Wash because it was used locally almost entirely.   Ref.: 329; Harris

GRASS CANYON
Coconino (Grand Canyon)   T34N R9W

The name describes the growth here.   Ref.: 329

GRASSHOPPER
Navajo   T8N R16E   Elev. 5912'

This name, in existence c. 1880, refers to Naz-chug-gee, an Apache woman who suffered from a hip malady, the translation meaning "the home of the woman who hops like a grasshopper" or simply "grasshopper." A later explanation for the name is that a sheepman named Jaques built an adobe house here about 1918 and noted hordes of grasshoppers. Grasshopper Butte (elev. 6424') lies above it.   Ref.: Dr. William Longacre (Tucson 1970); 18a; Davis

GRASSHOPPER FLAT
Yavapai   T17N R5E
Grasshoppers used to be in this area "by the millions."   Ref.: Schnebly

GRASSY KNOLL TANK
Apache   T16N R26E Sec. 32
The name is descriptive. Actually there are three tanks here, sometimes referred to as
Pablo Tank. The latter name is incorrect as Pablo Tank is at T16N/R26E, Sec. 17.

GRASSY MOUNTAIN
Greenlee   T3S R32E   Elev. 6334'
Formerly this mountain and many others in its vicinity had abundant grass. This is no
longer true.   Ref.: Simmons

GRASSY MOUNTAIN
Mohave   T33N R11W   Elev. 6640'
When rainfall is adequate, this mountain is usually covered with good grass. The name
Grass Mountain is incorrect for this location. Ref.: 329; 18a

GRAVEYARD CANYON
Gila   T1N R15E   Elev. c. 6000'
During the Pleasant Valley feud, young Jacobs and John Tewksbury were ambushed
and murdered in sight of their house in this canyon. Their enemy refused to permit
anyone to bury the bodies, which range hogs tore badly. When it was finally possible to
bury the remains, they were placed in an Arbuckle wooden coffee case and buried in a
single grave, hence the name.   Ref.: McKinney

GRAVEYARD GULCH
Cochise   T21S R21E
This gulch takes its name from that of the Graveyard Mine, which is in this canyon. The
mine was so named because the prospectors (Ed Schieffelin, Richard Gird and Al
Schieffelin) said they buried their hopes here. They abandoned it c. 1878-79.
Ref.: 206, p. 25

GRAVIS GULCH
Maricopa   T7N R4E
This gulch was probably named for T. Gravis (b. 1836, Virginia), who was a miner at
Wickenburg in 1870.   Ref.: 62

GRAYBACK MOUNTAINS
Yavapai   T13N R9W
Formerly called Capitol Butte, this large red butte with a gray top takes its name
descriptively. Old timers called it Gray Mountain.   Ref.: Schnebly; 71, p. 116

GRAY HILLS
Navajo   T40N R20E   Elev. 6188/6050'
The name for these two hills is a translation of the Navajo name, *baavaats' oosi* (=
"gray hills").

GRAY MOUNTAIN
Coconino   T29N R7E   Elev. 5030'
This mountain has a gray color when viewed from the east. The Navajo Indian name is
Dzit-Łibai (= "gray mountain") although they use the name for the area rather than the
mountain. See Coconino Point, Coconino   Ref.: 329; 331, p. 42

GRAY TANK
Yuma   T3S R19W
This small natural tank is named descriptively because of the color of the rocks.
Ref.: Monson

GREASER WASH
Greenlee   T6S R31E
This wash is so named because several Mexican wood cutters lived near the mouth of the canyon. The name was approved in 1959 rather than the variant School House Canyon, a name attributed to the fact that a school house used to be at the mouth. However, the name School House was not known locally and hence ot considered usable.   Ref.: 329

GREASEWOOD
Navajo: *diwoźhii bii'tó* = "water in the greasewood"
Apache   T34N R29E   Elev. 5900'
The name of this small community and trading post is a translation of the Navajo. The settlement is near Greasewood Spring. Its Navajo name is Dino'zhoo Bic'To'. Both the spring and the community are on Grease-Wood Flat. There are several Greasewood Springs on the Navajo reservation, so named because of creosote bush growing at such locations.   Ref.: 143, p. 142; 141, p. 192; 331, p. 69

GREASEWOOD
Navajo   T25N R23E   Elev. 5900'
This Navajo community was named because of the creosote or greasewood growth.

GREASEWOOD MOUNTAIN
Graham   T11S R25E   Elev. 7092'
A dense stand of creosote (known as "greasewood") is notable here, hence the name.

GREAT COLORADO VALLEY
La Paz
The name describes this largest of the many basins through which the Colorado River flows from Aubrey Canyon to the Chocolate Mountains.   Ref.: 200, p. 45

GREATERVILLE
Pima   T19S R16E   Elev. 5200'
In 1873 this now almost vanished community was known as Santa Rita, but the discovery of placer gold here in 1874 caused a gold rush which resulted in the town of Greaterville, named for an early resident called Greater. To work the placers by rocker and long Tom, water was brought in canvas and goatskin bags from Gardner Canyon four miles distant. By 1881 the gold was nearly exhausted and in consequence also of Indian attacks, the area lost inhabitants. From 1886 to 1900 it was dead, but enjoyed a brief revival when a hydraulic plant was installed in nearby Kentucky Gulch. The route through Greaterville was known as Renegade's Route, because it was used by outlaws on their way from the Mexican border to Tucson or vice versa. This place is now privately owned.
P.O. est. Jan. 3, 1879, Thomas Steele, p.m.; disc. June 30, 1946   Ref.: 238, pp. 158-159; Seibold

GREAT MOHAVE WALL
Coconino (Grand Canyon)   T31N R2E
This precipice on the South Rim was named by the USGS in 1927 for the Mohave Indian tribe.   Ref.: 329

GREAT PLAIN, THE
Pima   31°45'/112°17'
The name describes the area northwest of the La Lesna Mountains and southeast of the Mesquite Mountains. It first appeared on the 1899 International Boundary sheet. Ref.: 329

GREAT THUMB MESA
Coconino (Grand Canyon)   T34N R2W   Elev. 6755'
The name was suggested by Frank Bond in July 1929 and approved by the USGS in 1932. It looks like a huge thumb. Great Thumb Point is part of it.   Ref.: 329

GREENBACK VALLEY

Gila   T6N R12E

This name first appears on a manuscript map dated Nov. 17, 1866, with a notation that here six Indians were killed and five prisoners taken. The first settler here was David Harer, a man who followed a dream. Having dreamed of finding a beautiful valley with a spring and running stream, the young man reported his dream to an army officer. The officer later came across this valley and told Harer about the discovery. Despite warning that unfriendly Apache Indians would attack, Harer laid plans to settle in the valley and in 1875 he moved in, built a cabin, and made friends with the Indians. Two years later he brought in his family. He employed Indians to help him clear his land, giving one of them a five dollar bill. The Apache knew nothing about money and therefore stuck the bill into the blaze of a tree. Later Harer found it and decided that a fitting name for the valley was Greenback. Lookout Mountain (1907) is now called Greenback Peak (elev. 6535'), and Greenback Creek (T5N/R11E) is here also. The latter was mapped in 1867. Ref.: Packard (interviewed by Woody); 242; 329

GREENBUSH DRAW

Coconino   T24S R23E

The name has been in use for almost a century. It derives from that of Green C. Bush, a pioneer. Ref.: Burgess; 329

GREENE'S PEAK

Apache   T8N R26E   Elev. 10,132'

In 1873 Wheeler noted that this peak was the highest in the Sierra Blanca. It was named for Col. John Green, First Cavalry, then in command at Camp Apache.   Ref.: 342, I, 300; 18a; Wiltbank

GREENES WASH

Pinal   T9S R6E

This wash takes its name from that of William Cornell Greene (b. 1852; d. 1911), a developer who was responsible for Greene's Reservoir (T7S/R5E) and Greene's Canal (now gone). Greene spent much money erecting an earth-work dam c. 1909 in an attempt to dam the Santa Cruz River. Frank Jordan, on inspecting the dam, told Greene that the dirt was on the wrong side and that animals would burrow in and weaken it. Nevertheless, plans to irrigate the area were continued, including the construction of a store at the dam site. The dam washed out and was never rebuilt. The remaining dikes have created the unfortunate effect of backing up flood waters, creating a very shallow and widespread pond referred to as Lake Eloy. The wash has also borne other names; Quajata Creek (1897); Quajote Wash (1923); Guijotoa Draw (1933).   Ref.: Jordan; Stanfield; AHS files; 329

GREENLAND POINT

Coconino   T33N R4E

In 1902 the name proposed for this place by Francois E. Matthes was Walhala Plateau. It was approved in 1906. However, the earliest known Mormon settlers who grazed cattle in the vicinity called it Greenland Point.   Ref.: 329; 220

GREENLAND SPRING

Coconino   T33N R4E

Francois E. Matthes in 1925 suggested that the official name for this spring and plateau be adopted, as Mormon cattlemen had used it before 1902. The name is descriptive of "rich herbage."   Ref.: 329

GREENLAW

Coconino   T20N R8E

In 1903 a post office to serve about one hundred and forty people was established at Greenlaw's Mill, a lumber operation run by Charles Greenlaw. The post office was soon abandoned. The lumbering operation continued until 1925.
P.O. est. July 19, 1903, James C. Brodie, p.m.; disc. Jan. 4, 1904   Ref.: 242; Conrad

GREENLEE COUNTY

The name of the county is actually a solution to a battle for different names, in which the Arizona Copper Company sought to name the county for Mr. Colquhoun, their president, whereas the Detroit Copper Company sought to name it Douglas County after their president, Mr. Douglas. Others preferred "Lincoln County." "Mase" Greenlee (b. 1835, Virginia; d. April 10, 1903) was scarcely an outstanding citizen, but the compromise was reached and the county named for him. He made the first location in the Greenlee Mining District. Greenlee arrived in the area in 1874 but Indians forced him out soon thereafter. He returned in 1879. Greenlee County was created from the eastern portion of Graham County by the Twentyfifth Territorial Legislature on March 10, 1909, but it was 1911 before the county became an active organized unit. The youngest county in Arizona, Greenlee is principally a mining and stock-raising area with 1,199,360 acres. The county seat is at Clifton.   Ref.: 257, p. 229; *Arizona Daily Star* (March 2, 1909), p. 3

GREEN VALLEY

Pima   T17S R13E   Elev. 2887'

In the early 1960s a retirement village was begun at this location and named descriptively because of its overlooking agriculture in the valley. By 1982 it had developed into a sizable retirees' community.   Ref.: *Arizona Star* (June 1, 1975), p. 1

GREENWAY

Pima   T13S R13E

In 1929 Isabella Greenway (King) was patron for a veterans' settlement at Pastime Park, now engulfed by Tucson. When a post office was established for their convenience, it was named for her.

P.O. est. Dec. 1, 1929, Allie Dickerman, p.m.   Ref.: 242

GREENWOOD

Mohave   T13N R12W   Elev. c. 2500'

This now vanished mining community of the mid-1870s was named because of the many palo verde trees here. Its ten-stamp mill was used to smelt ore from the Greenwood gold mine, but the ores were too poor to support the operation for long. The spelling Glenwood is an error. Associated names include Greenwood Peak (elev. 3966') and Spring (T12N/R12W, elev. 3000').   Ref.: *Arizona Miner* (March 26, 1875), p. 4; (June 4, 1875, p. 1; 168, p. 252; 116, p. 579; Malach, Letter (March 8, 1973)

GREER

Apache   T7N R27E   Elev. 8340'

The 1879 arrival of the Willard Lee family (see Lee's Ferry, Coconino) resulted in the name Lee Valley for this area. Other Mormons soon followed and a community developed. The post office department asked for a short name. Residents selected Greer to honor Americus Vespucius Greer (b. 1832, Alabama; d. April 1896), who had laid out the town plat for Amity (see Round Valley, Apache) before joining the colony at Lee Valley. Greer's twin brother was named Christopher Columbus Greer. The area is now a fishing and resort center. The spelling "Geser" is a typographical error. Greer Valley, the current name for Lee Valley, was settled by Thomas L. Greer in 1879.

P.O. est. Oct. 21, 1897, Gaston Baker, p.m.; activated March 12, 1898, Hanna M. Wiltbank, p.m.   Ref.: 225, p. 186; 158, p. 18; *Saint John's Herald* (April 9, 1898), p. 4; 242

GREGG BASIN

Mohave   T18N R17W

In June 1946 the USGS accepted this name rather than Upper Lake for the basin between Virgin Canyon and Iceberg Canyon. The name was approved in 1948. Gregg Basin is the easternmost of the three occupied by Lake Mead. See Gregg's Ferry, Mohave   Ref.: 329

GREGGS FERRY

Mohave   T31N R17W

The ferry service across the Colorado River here was operated by Mike Scanlon (1881). When he left, Tom Gregg took over the ferry and renamed it for himself. Some maps show two ferries (Gregg and Scanlon) as being two miles apart, but this is an error. Ref.: Harris; *Mead Geologic*, p. 17; Babcock

GREY PEAK
Greenlee   T2S R29E   Elev. 7077'
This peak may have been named for a prospector living near its foot or because it is a gray basaltic formation. Mexicans call it Pistola Peak because it looks like a pistol. Ref.: 329; Simmons; 18a

GRIEF HILL
Yavapai   T14N R4E
It was difficult to haul freight over this route in bad weather. Also, Indians frequently attacked along the route. Therefore the name Grief was understandable. In an attack on May 6, 1869, Indians ambushed two ox teams protected by nine soldiers, a battle in which Indians killed one and wounded five, and escaped with corn, cotton, blankets, ammunition, and a gun. Ordinarily the Grief Hill route was avoided by civilian wagon trains which instead used the Fossil Creek road where the present highway exists. Ten graves on this hill attest to civilians being slain, as soldiers' bodies would have been returned to Camp Lincoln. In 1954 the remains of wagons made in the 1860s were found on the hill and transported to Camp Verde. The old route followed Grief Hill Wash. Ref.: Goddard; 261, p. 7; 107, IV, 102; 252, Part 2

GRIFFIN FLAT
Gila   T4N R14E
This flat, now covered by Roosevelt Lake, was owned by C. C. (Cliff) Griffin (b. Virginia; d. 1940s). In the 1880s he used both the 76 and 44 brands on his cattle. Griffin Wash cuts through this flat. Ref.: Woody

GRIFFITH
Mohave   T19N R17W   Elev. 2620'
First known as Sacramento Siding, this section house on the railroad had its name changed c. 1883 to Drake in honor of the railroad chief engineer. The final change came on Nov. 14, 1930 to honor a bridge gang foreman named Griffith. Griffith Wash (T19N/R18W) borrows the name. Ref.: Harris; 18a; 329

GRIGGS' FERRY
Mohave   T30N R17W
This ferry in 1934 was owned by Mrs. Bessie Griggs. It is now covered by Lake Mead. It is not the same as Greggs Ferry. Ref.: AHS, Isabella Greenway King Files

GRIMES SPRING
Gila   T10N R9E
This developed spring on Marysville Hill was named for a Mr. Grimes who lived in a cabin here for many years. The spring was also called Silver Spray Spring. Ref.: 329

GRIPE
Graham   T7S R27E   Elev. 3019'
Inspectors at the Arizona State Agricultural inspection point here named their small building Gripe to indicate what they did much of the time. A community has developed nearby. Ref.: 5, p. 341

GROOM CREEK
Yavapai   T13N R2W   Elev. 6250'
Col. Robert William (Bob) Groom (b. Aug. 24, 1824, Kentucky; d. Jan. 21 1899), a prospector and miner, arrived in Arizona in 1862. He surveyed the town site of Prescott and served as a member of the First Arizona Territorial Legislature. By 1901 enough lived nearby to warrant a post office and the name Oakdale was selected because the community had a grove of oak trees. After six weeks, however, the name was changed to Groom Creek. Groom's Hill (T8N/R3W; elev. 4700') borrows the name.
P.O. est. as Oakdale, July 1, 1901, Clara B. Riley, p.m.; name changed to Groom Creek, Aug. 19, 1901; disc. Jan. 31, 1942   Ref.: 176; *Prescott Courier* (July 21, 1917); AHS, Robert Groom File; 62

GROOM PEAK

Mohave   T15N R13W   Elev. 5078'

Bob Groom held mining claims near this peak, hence the name. See Groom Creek, Yavapai   Ref.: 18a

GROSSMAN PEAK

Mohave   T14N R18W   Elev. c. 5000'

A. G. Grossman, publisher of *The Needle's Eye* in Needles, California, placer mined near this peak. The name Crossman is an error.   Ref.: 18a

GROSS WASH

Mohave   T21N R17W

The wash is named for the Gross Mine near Mineral Park.   Ref.: 215, p. 123

GROSVENOR PEAK

Santa Cruz   T21S R14E   Elev. 5298'

The peak takes its name from H. C. Grosvenor (b. 1820, Ohio; d. 1861), manager of the Santa Rita Mine, who was killed here by Apaches. The name does not appear on maps, but it seems to be the same location as the current Josephine Peak. The name Grosvenor survives in Grosvenor Hills in the vicinity.   Ref.: 163, p. 190

GROWLER MOUNTAIN

Pima/Maricopa   T14S R6-7W/T10S 9RW
                                     Elev. Maricopa: 2630'; Pima: 2380'

This range took its name from the nearby Growler Mine, discovered and claimed by Frederick Wall. The name Growler is that of a prospector, John Growler. Associated names include Growler Canyon (T14S/R7W), Pass (T14S/R6-7W, elev. 1487'), Peak (Maricopa/Pima, T10-12S/R10-9W), Wash (a.k.a. San Cristobal Wash), and Well. Ref.: 58; 329; 18a

GU ACHI   pro.: /gu áči/

Papago: *gu* = "big"; *achi* = "narrow ridge"

Pima   T13S R3E   Elev. 2180'

This Papago village was visited by Fr. Kino in 1698. He referred to it as "the great Rancheria of Adid," calling it San Francisco del Adid. Papagos called it *kiate mihk* (= "burnt seeds"). The following are variant names: Santa Rosa (1865), Kuatshi (1912), Kuarchi (1953), and Santa Rosa Well (1937). Indians prefer Gu Achi. Gu Achi Peak (T12S/R5E, elev. 4556') and Wash (T12S/R4E) are associated with it. Ref.: 329; 262, p. 5; 57, pp. 391-392; 45, p. 398; 93, p. 5

GUADALUPE   pro.: /wadəlúwpe/

Maricopa   T15S R4E   Elev. c. 1248'

Yaqui Indians fled from Mexico at the turn of the century to avoid persecution under Porfirio Diaz, who sought to exile them from northwestern Mexico to tropical Yucatan. Among other villages, the Yaqui established Guadalupe, named for the Virgin of Guadalupe, patroness saint of Mexico. See also Pascua Village, Pima   Ref.: 5, p. 352

GUADALUPE CANYON

Cochise   T24S R32E

In the late 1870s and early 1880s Mexican and American rustlers and smugglers traveled through this canyon frequently, some meeting death by Apache attack. The reason for the name is not known.   Ref.: 60, p. 355

GUAJOLOTE FLAT   pro.: /wahalówtey/

Mexican-Indian = "turkey"

Santa Cruz   T23S R16E   Elev. 5800'

The flat took its name from the Guajolote Mine, located in 1880. It was then called the Old Lode. Guajolote Wash drains it.   Ref.: Siebold; 286, p. 294; 301, p. 20

GUEVAVI pro.: /wevávi^/ or /gwéváve/

Santa Cruz   T24S R14E

The first Jesuit mission in what is today Arizona was that at Guevavi. Fr. Kino visited here in Jan. 1691. He founded Los Angeles de Guevavi. By April 24, 1700 the mission had eighty-four sheep and goats, a wheat field, maize and beans, and an adobe home for the priest. Fr. Juan de San Martin arrived in 1701 and founded *visitas* at Tumacacori and Bacoancos (today Buena Vista). Guevavi lasted many years. In 1763 Fr. Ignatius Pfefferkorn was its priest, with *visitas* at Sonoitac, Calabazas, Tumacacori, and Arivaca. Prior to 1784 when Tumacacori became the head mission for the area, Guevavi was abandoned. It later became a ranch. Here in 1856 Indians killed Rafael Saavedra, who was attempting to rescue a woman from them. Today nothing remains of the old Guevavi mission. The present owners are protecting the site as best they can. The old mission was also known by the following names: Gusubac (1763, Pima = "great water"); San Felipe de Jesus Guevavi; San Miguel de Jesus Guevavi (after 1782); San Rafael (Jesuit name); Santos Angeles (Franciscan name); San Luis Guevavi (Venegas, 1759); Huavabi Ranch; Huebaji (Fish); Quevavi (1701); Cuababi. Ref.: Jones; Lenon; Glannon; 45, pp. 265, 512; 206, p. 35; 287, pp. 18, 45; 77, p. 257, Note 1; 142, p. 110; 167, I, 511; 15, II, 384, 385; 107, IV, 131; 242

GUIJAS MOUNTAINS

Spanish = "conglomerate" or "quartz pebbles"

Pima   T20S R9E   Elev. 4664'

These mountains take their name from the Las Guijas Mine. The name dates to the late 1860s. Its name refers to conglomerate containing gold. In 1854 Lt. N. Michler mapped the name Sierra del Mal Paid (Spanish = "mountains of rough country") to these mountains. Las Guijas Wash is in them. Ref.: 57, p. 379; 106, I, 119, 56, p. 265

GUINIVERE CASTLE

Coconino (Grand Canyon)   T33N R1E   Elev. 7725'

This name for a formation in the Grand Canyon was proposed in 1906 by Francois E. Matthes. The USGS approved it in October. Ref.: 329

GU KOMELIK   pro.: /guw kówməli?/

Papago: *gu* = "big"; *kom* = "flats"

Pinal   T10S R4E   Elev. c. 1600'

Papago Indians established this village at the site of an American stockman's abandoned well and cultivated crops in the big fields, from which it takes its name. In 1978 the name was changed to North Komelik by the USGS. It is also spelled as follows: Kukomelik (1912); Kumelih (1931); Komelih (1933); Komalik (1937); Comely (1920 U.S. Corps of Engineers) Ref.: 262, p. 1; 57, p. 408; 329; 59, p. 324; 58

GUN CREEK

Gila   T9N R11E   Elev. c. 4000'

This name appears on a military map of 1869. An early settler is said to have found an old gun along its banks. Ref.: 18a; 242

GUNSIGHT RANCH

Pima   T14S R4W

Originally, a well was dug on the ranch by a man named Haynes, hence the name Haynes Well, but because goats were raised here for many years, it is also sometimes called Goat Ranch or Goat Well. Still another name came into existence c. 1925 when the owner of the ranch was named Blair. The Papago name for the location is *Schuchuli* (= "many chickens") or *Sisalatuk* (= "goat ranch"). See Gunsight, Pima Ref.: 58; 59, p. 337; 262, p. 8

GUNSIGHT (TOWN)

Pima   T15S R3W   Elev. 1980'

On Nov. 25, 1878 the Gunsight Mine was located by Myer and three companions and named because it was near a mountain having a striking resemblance to a gunsight with the "barrel" of the gun being formed by a ridge. The gunsight portion of the formation looks like a flat whiskey bottle lying on its side. John Bracket ("Pie") Allen (b. 1818, Maine; d. June 13, 1899) was the first merchant for the mining camp and hence it was referred to as Allen or Allen City. Allen, who was first in Arizona in 1857 and again with the California Column in 1862, settled near Yuma and thereafter had stores at various mining camps. He was famous for his pies, hence his nickname. He later moved to Tucson, then spent the latter part of his life at Florence. Gunsight today has practically vanished. The name applies also to Gunsight Hills (T15S/R3–4W, elev. 2622'), Mountains (T17S/R11E, elev. 4680'), Pass (T14S/R4W), Ranch, Valley (T15S/R2W), named c. 1925), and Well. Ref.: AHS, John Brackett Allen File, and Emerson O. Stratton *ms*, p. 21; Lenon; *Arizona Weekly Citizen* (Nov. 5, 1882), p. 4; Jordan; 329

GUNSIGHT BUTTE
Gila   T7N R15E   Elev. 6242'
The name of this butte is descriptive of its appearance. Ref.: McKinney

GUNTHER CASTLE
Coconino (Grand Canyon)   T33N R5W
This peak in the Grand Canyon was named at the suggestion of Francois E. Matthes in 1906. It is one of those named from the Arthurian cycle. Ref.: 329

GU OIDAK   pro.: /guw óyda/
Papago: *gu* = "big"; *oidak* = "field"
Pima   T17S R3E   Elev. c. 2044'
The name describes the location of this large Papago village, which Lumholtz (1912) spelled Kuoltak. Gu Oidak Valley contains the village, and Gu Oidak Wash is in the valley. Ref.: 262, p. 14; 329

GU OIDAK WASH
Pima
The name Valshni Wash (1938) is not correct for this location. See Gu Oidak, Pima Ref.: 329

GURLI PUT VO   pro.: /gúli putwó/
Papago: *guli* = "old man"; *put* = "dead"; *wo* = "water hole"
Pima   T14S R4E   Elev. 2500'
This small Papago village in 1935 was called Dead Old Man's Pond, the name tracing to 1912. Even then none could remember who the dead old man was, and no Indian would have named him aloud in any event. The name was unusual because such ponds customarily owned by the tribe, in this instance belonged to one person. Phonetic renderings of the name are as follows: Kolpiatvóoka (1912, Lumholtz); Kol-pat-vooka (1935). Ref.: 262, p. 5; 18a

GUS PEARSON NATURAL AREA
Coconino
This one hundred and fifty-four acre area was established temporarily in the Coconino National Forest on Aug. 17, 1950. Ref.: 243, p. 22

GUTHRIE (R.R. STN.)
Greenlee   T6S R30E   Elev. 3414'
This point on the Arizona and New Mexico R.R. was named for Guthrie Smith, who with J. Duncan Smith sold land in 1883 to the Arizona Copper Company, which built the railroad to its mines at Clifton. Guthrie Peak is above the railroad.
P.O. est. Jan. 15, 1901, Ellen J. Brown, p.m.; disc. Aug. 1, 1922; Wells Fargo, 1904 Ref.: Cosper; 68, p. 74; 242

GUTHRIE MOUNTAIN
Pima   T12S R17E   Elev. 6464'
This location was named for John D. Guthrie of the U.S. Forest Service. Ref.: 18a

GU VO   pro.: /gú wow/

Papago: *gu* = "big"; *vo* = "charco" or "pond"

Pima   T16S R3W   Elev. c. 2400'

The name comes from the fact that this Papago village has a large pond in a wide sweeping curve from fifteen to thirty feet wide and thirteen hundred feet long. Fr. Kino visited in 1701. Variant spellings are as follows: Cubo (1912); Kuvo, (1912); Kerwo (1917). The name applies also to Gu Vo Hills (T15S/R3W, elev. 2720'), Pass, and Wash (T16S/R2W).   Ref.: 58; 279, p. 35

GYPSUM CREEK

Navajo/Apache   T41N R21–22E   Elev. c. 6000'

According to Barnes there is a "huge bed of gypsum on this stream," but Gregory notes nothing about a gypsum bed, although he says the water is unpalatable.
Ref.: 18a; 141, p. 49

GYPSUM LEDGES

Mohave (Lake Mead)   T31N R20W

This name was selected in 1946 and approved in 1948 to describe a series of gypsiferous projections from the southern shore of Lake Mead.   Ref.: 329

GYPSUM WASH

Mohave

This name was proposed in 1936 by C. R. Longwell. See Gypsum Ledges, Mohave (Lake Mead)   Ref.: Geo. Soc. America, *Bull*, Vol. 47, No. 9

H

HACKBERRY

Mohave　　　　　　　　　　　T23N R14W　　　　　　　Elev. 3580′

In October 1874 W. B. Ridenour and Samuel Crozier located the Hackberry Mine. A mining community soon developed. By March 1875 Isaac Putnam and John Kite were living with the locaters in a stone house near Hackberry Spring, and according to the *Weekly Arizona Miner*, they named their mine and community for "this tree which in summer bears an abundance of fruit ... (and) they have named the beautiful mine with the hope that it may prove as prolific of bullion as the tree is of edible berries ..."

Hackberry Spring supplied water for boilers in a large mill constructed in November 1877. It is probable that Hackberry Spring is the same as Lt. Edward Fitzgerald Beale's Gardiner Spring.

P.O. est. July 9, 1878, Alonze E. Davis, p.m.; Wells Fargo 1885　Ref.: 242; *Weekly Arizona Miner* (March 5, 1875), p. 2; *Arizona Enterprise* (April 27, 1878), p. 2; 168, pp. 87, 146; 163, p. 252; 246, p. 216; 200, pp. 20, 78

HACKBERRY: The word *hackberry* occurs in many Arizona place names, probably because of the hackberry trees at the locations. They grow along water courses, in canyons, and on desert grass land at elevations from about twenty-five hundred to six thousand feet. The pulpy wood has no commercial use, but its berries are edible.

Hackberry Basin	Maricopa	T7N R11E	
Hackberry Basin	Gila	T7N R10E	
Hackberry Butte	Pinal	T1N R11E	Elev. 4230′
Hackberry Canyon	Cochise	T12S R21E	
Hackberry Canyon	Pinal	T1N R11E	
Hackberry Creek	Pinal	T2S R13E	
Hackberry Creek	Yavapai	T11N R2E	
Hackberry Draw	Graham	T2S R19E	

This location is not the same as that of Triplet Wash.　Ref.: 329

Hackberry Gulch	Greenlee	T3S R30E	.

This location is not the same as that for Ash Spring Canyon.　Ref.: 329

Hackberry Gulch	Yavapai	T11N R3E	

(See Hodgkins Gulch, Yavapai)

Hackberry Mesa	Yavapai	T14N R7W	
Hackberry Mountain	Gila	T4N R14E	
Hackberry Mountain	Yavapai	T12N R6E	Elev. 5839′
Hackberry Spring	Graham	T4S R24E	

This name sometimes occurs as Hackleberry Spring, a corruption.　Ref.: 329

Hackberry Spring	Mohave	(2) T18N R13W	Elev. 3400′

(See Hackberry, Mohave)

Hackberry Spring	Pinal	T1N R11E	

Hackberry Spring	Yavapai	T12N R6E
Hackberry Springs	Cochise	T13S R20E
Hackberry Wash	Mohave	T22N R13W

The USGS officially applied this name in 1968. It is not the same as Truxton Wash. Ref.: 329

| **Hackberry Wash** | Pinal | T5S R14E |
| **Hackberry Wash** | Yavapai | T14N R2E |

HACK CANYON
Mohave   T37N R5W

Philip Hack (b. 1847, Germany) owned the Hack Canyon Mine in this canyon. Ref.: 63

HAECKEL
Graham   T8S R26E   Elev. c. 3000'

This station was named for an Irishman named Haeckel, who owned the railroad from Bowie to Globe. Ref.: Jennings

HA HO NO GEH CANYON
Navajo = "too many washes or drains"
Coconino   T29–30N R13–14E

The name for this canyon has been in existence since c. 1858. It is also called Coal Canyon or Coal Mine Canyon, although those names are not used by Navajos. Ref.: 329

HAIGLER CREEK
Gila   T10N R13E

Bob Sixby c. 1880 sold a ranch on this creek to Joseph Haigler, who was killed by Indians in 1882. Haigler Creek has springs along its course.   Ref.: State Library Files; McKinney

HAINES FLAT
Gila/Pinal   T5S R15E

The USGS gave this name c. 1906 to what is known locally as The Flat, to honor a homesteader named Haines. Ref.: 329

HAIVANA NAKYA
Papago = "crow hangs"
Pima   T16S R6E   Elev. 2835'

This Papago village on a 1917 Corps of Engineers map was called Baboquerque and in 1936 was referred to by the Sells Indian Agency as San Ysidro. Since 1939 its official name has been as given above. Ref.: 329

HAIVAN VAYA
Papago = "cow well"
Pima   T21S R5E   Elev. 2800'

This is a temporary village on the Papago Indian Reservation. Ref.: 329

HAKATAI CANYON
Coconino (Grand Canyon)   T33N R1W   Elev. c. 3700'

The name Falls Canyon was suggested in June 1910 by James McCormick. Hakatai is the Havasupai name for the Colorado River. Hakatai Rapids are at the canyon mouth. Ref.: 329; 178, p. 230

HALF MOON VALLEY
Cochise   T21S R29E

William Lutley, who lived here in the early 1880s, named the place because of its crescent shape. Ref.: 18a

HALFWAY BEND
La Paz   T8N R19W   Elev. c. 300'

In 1857 Lt. Joseph Christmas Ives named this bend after the Half-way Mountains (in

California adjacent to the bend). In 1864 Charles Debrille Poston suggested an Indian Reservation be established here (Colorado River Reservation). It was established in 1865 with John C. Dunn and Herman Ehrenberg as agents. The chief engineer in locating the Reservation said the Indians call a slough here Mad-ku-Dap.
Ref.: 107, III, 169; 116, p. 525; AHS

HALF WAY TANK
Yuma   T12S R16W
This man-made watering place was developed in 1952 by the Fish and Wild Life Service, which named it because it is half way between Brick Mountain and Tule Tank.   Ref.: Monson

HALF WAY WASH
Maricopa   T6S R9W
This wash half way between Sentinel and Oatman Ranch was named early in 1886 by Frank Jordan.   Ref.: Jordan

HALI MURK   pro.: /haˡmək/
Papago = "squash burned"
Pima   T16S R1E   Elev. 1873'
This small Papago village was a summer rancheria, used while fields were being cultivated. The place is also referred to as Hardimuk (a corruption). It has also been called the following: Mesquit (1865-1880, all maps), Mesqual (GLO 1897), Harlemuheta (1917 Corps of Engineers). Bryan interpreted the name as "burnt pumpkin." Hali Murk Wash is here.   Ref.: 329; 262, p. 10; 58

HALL BUTTE
Coconino (Grand Canyon)   T31N R4E   Elev. 5530'
Andrew Hall in 1869 was a member of Maj. John Wesley Powell's first expedition through the Grand Canyon. Frank Bond suggested this name in July 1929.   Ref.: 329; 18a

HALL CREEK
Apache   T7N R28E
This creek was named for John Hall, who settled here.   Ref.: Wentz

HALL'S FALLS
Apache   c. T4N R27E
John Hall had a cattle station near here on Pacheto Creek. The nearly eighty-five foot falls on the creek are also called the "Falls of the Pachete."   Ref.: Wiltbank; Davis

HAMBLIN CREEK
Coconino   T34N R8E   Elev. c. 5000'
Jacob Hamlin (sic) (b. 1821, Wisconsin; d. Aug. 31, 1886) was both an explorer and a Mormon missionary. He conducted early colonization of Mormons along the Little Colorado River. Hamblin Creek is on this route. Later he served as a guide for the journey Maj. John Wesley Powell made over the Lee's Ferry route to the base of the Echo Cliffs in the early 1870s. Most sources spell his name Hamblin and some give his birth date as 1819, but the 1880 Census varies.   Ref.: 63; 141, p. 42, Note 2

HAMBURG
Cochise   T23S R20E
Henry Hamburg of St. Louis developed a mining camp at the head of Ramsey Canyon where Hamburg post office served about one hundred and twenty-five.
P.O. est. Aug. 22, 1906, L. de Vere Hamburg, p.m.; disc. Jan. 31, 1916; reest. May 29, 1928; disc. Aug. 15, 1929   Ref.: 242; *Bisbee Review* clipping, State Library Files

HAMIDRIK POINT
Coconino (Grand Canyon)   T34N R3W   Elev. 6215'
This point on the South Rim was named by the USGS for a local Havasupai Indian family in February 1921.   Ref.: 329

HANCE CREEK
Coconino (Grand Canyon)   T30N R4E

In 1950 the National Park Service suggested naming this creek after Hance Rapids, both being named for "Captain" John Hance (b. Sept. 7, 1851, Tennessee; d. Jan. 9, 1919), who homesteaded on the South Rim in 1884. He had the distinction of having served first as a Confederate soldier and when taken prisoner, switching to serving as a Union man. He hauled fodder for stock at Camp Verde prior to arriving at his homestead. There in 1885 he built a log cabin for tourists at Glendale Spring, and soon earned a reputation for his ready wit, quick tongue, and tall tales. Hoping to increase his tourist trade and also to work mines in the canyon, he widened an old Indian trail along which the first tourist made his way to the river bed from the South Rim. He was Edward E. Ayer (see Ayer Peak, Coconino). The Hance Trail followed Hance Creek. The trail no longer exists.

According to Hance, he dug the Grand Canyon, using the excavated rocks and dirt to make the San Francisco Peaks.   Ref.: Hart; 333, pp. 19-20-21; 297, p. 162; Caption for Hance photograph (Naturalist Headquarters, Grand Canyon)

HANCOCK BUTTE
Coconino (Grand Canyon)   T33N R4E   Elev. 7629'

The USGS named this butte in May 1932 for Capt. William Augustus Hancock (b. May 17, 1831, Massachusetts; d. March 24, 1902), who served as a private with the California Volunteers at Fort Yuma in 1864. In 1869-1870 he was a post trader at Camp Reno. In August 1870 Hancock surveyed the town site for Phoenix. He erected the first house there. He later served as sheriff for Maricopa County.   Ref.: AHS; 329

HANDS PASS
Cochise   T16S R30E   Elev. c. 7000'

Frank H. Hands (1862 – 1936) and his brother John were instrumental in having a road constructed from Pinery Canyon through this pass to Portal, hence the name. Ref.: Riggs

HANGING TANK
Yuma   T4S R18W

This natural semi-permanent water hole in the central point of the Castle Dome Mountains "hangs" on the side of a mountain, hence the name applied by the Fish and Wild Life Service in 1955.   Ref.: Monson

HANNAH SPRING CREEK
Greenlee   T1N R31E

The name, in use since c. 1913, is that of a local man. There are both hot and cold springs.   Ref.: Fritz; 329

HANNEGAN MEADOW
Greenlee   T3N R29E   Elev. 9040'

Robert Hannegan, a miner in Nevada in the 1870s, was in San Francisco until he went to New Mexico in the early 1890s. According to a man for whom he worked, Hannegan ran cattle in the meadows for only one summer. When he refused to pay twelve hundred dollars he owed, two men stopped a stage coach and chained Hannegan to a tree, holding him until his son sent the money. Hannegan left the area soon thereafter. One man said that Hannegan "came in with cattle, made a small fortune, and was chased from the county or possibly killed by hi-jackers." The spellings Hannagan and Hannigan are incorrect.   Ref.: Cosper; Hermion Lindauer, Letter (Oct. 8, 1949), Hannegan Meadow Lodge; 329 (1929)

HANSBROUGH POINT
Coconino (Grand Canyon)   T37N R6E

This point, squarely in the middle of the Hansbrough-Richards Rapid in Marble Canyon, bears the name of Peter M. Hansbrough cut on a marble shaft. Here on July 15, 1889 Hansbrough's boat capsized when he attempted to push it off an overhanging shelf. Both he and Henry C. Richards drowned. Richards' body was never found. Hansbrough's was found six months later on a beach below President Harding Rapid. Both men were members of the Robert Brewster Stanton Expedition. Stanton named the location for

Hansbrough. Stanton reports how his party stood around Hansbrough's grave and prayed and "left him with a shaft of pure marble for his head-stone." See Stanton Point, Coconino (Grand Canyon)
Ref.: 89, pp. 361, 355-356; Schellbach File, Grand Canyon; 329

HANSBROUGH-RICHARDS RAPIDS
Coconino (Grand Canyon)   T37N R6E
This location, until 1974 called Twenty-Five-Mile Rapid, was renamed at the suggestion of P. T. Reilly. See Hansbrough Point, Coconino Ref.: 329

HAPPY CAMP
Maricopa   T5S R2W   Elev. c. 900'
Conklin noted this stage watering place was sterile and gloomy and scarcely deserved the name Happy. At this location, fifteen miles east of Gila Bend on the Maricopa desert, in 1879 W. F. Thompson had a well and store. Thompson was a stage driver in 1876. In 1877 H. M. Thompson and R. W. Masters were hauling water from the Gila River to sell at twenty-five cents a head here. Ref.: *Arizona Sentinel* (June 9, 1977), p. 3; *Arizona Sentinel* (Jan. 18, 1879), p. 3; 72, p. 311; AHS, Crampton File

HAPPY JACK
Coconino   T16N R9E   Elev. 7595'
This location was formerly known as Long Valley Road and also as Yellow Jacket Spring. The latter came from wasps at a minor spring known only to a few sportsmen and to fire guards. Another name by which it was known was Saginaw Camp, for the Saginaw and Manistee Lumber Company which used it. Roland Rotty (Coconino National Forest supervisor and a former forest ranger in Tie City) suggested the name Happy Jack for the summer logging camp post office, transferring the name from that of a Wyoming stage coach robber in Tie City Pass.
P.O. est. Aug. 22, 1949, Grace Edmunds, p.m. Ref.: Cline; Roland Rotty, *History of Happy Jack, ms.*; 242

HAPPY JACK WASH
Mohave   T17N R18W
This wash was named in 1967 for Happy Jack Bowman, who lived about six miles south of the wash.

HAPPY VALLEY SADDLE
Pima   T14S R18E
The name of this saddle in the mountains is derived from the name of nearby Happy Valley, named in turn for the Happy Valley Ranch. In 1876 the ranch on the east side of the Rincon Mountains belonged to Charley Page. Ref.: 164, p. xviii; 330, *ms.*, p. 1

HARCUVAR pro.: /hárkuwovar/
Mohave = "sweet water" or *aha* = "water"; *coo-bar* = "there's very little"
La Paz   T5N R13W   Elev. 1925'
The name for a railroad station on the Parker branch of the A.T. & S.F.R.R. was borrowed from one which appears on an 1864 map as Harcuvar Water, also spelled Harcouver Water. The same name was later given to a mining district (Harcouver), which had a post office at the railroad stop.
P.O. est. May 8, 1890, Frank Nicholson; disc. Aug. 19, 1893 Ref.: 242; 200, p. 14; Willson; AHS

HARCUVAR MOUNTAINS
La Paz/Maricopa   T8-9N R10-12W
These mountains were first mapped as Huacavah. On the 1874 Public Survey map, the name is Harquar Mountains. Harcuvar (T7N/R13W; Elev. 4618') is its highest point. See Harcuvar, Yuma

HARDEN CIENEGA CREEK pro.: /hardn siyénəgə/
Greenlee   T3S R32E
The origin of this name is not known at present. The name dates to at least 1885 when Jerry Stockton emigrated here from Trinidad, Colorado. Ref.: Fritz

HARDIN

Maricopa   T3N R2E

The store post office was established to serve about one hundred. There was no village. The reason for the name has not been learned.

P.O. est. March 26, 1898, Frank Moody, p.m.; disc. Oct. 27, 1898   Ref.: 242

HARD SCRABBLE: Areas difficult to travel through were often called Hard Scrabble. Examples follow:

Hard Scrabble   Coconino

Hard Scrabble Canyon   Gila   T11½N R7E
This canyon was named by army troops c. 1878.

Hard Scrabble Creek   Gila   T11N R7E
See Hard Scrabble Mesa, Gila

Hard Scrabble Mesa   Gila   T11N R8E
During the Indian troubles of the 1870s, army patrols gave the name to the creek and the mesa. On September 23, 1873, troops had a skirmish with Indians on the creek. The trail from Tonto Basin to Camp Verde crossed the mesa.   Ref.: McKinney; Woody; 18a; 159, p. 439

Hard Scrabble Wash   Apache   T15N R28E   Elev. c. 6000'
The Wabash Cattle Company owned a seep-type spring in this wash where after drinking at the spring, cows had a hard time scrabbling to get out of the wash.   Ref.: Grigsby

HARDSHELL

Santa Cruz   T23S R16E   Elev. 5150'

In 1879 Jose Andrade and David Harshaw discovered the Hardshell Mine, selling it in 1880 to Rollin R. Richardson. The post office shared the mine name, as did Hardshell Gulch.

P.O. est. Jan. 21, 1901, John C. Smith, p.m.; disc. July 7, 1901   Ref.: 286, p. 265; 242

HARDY

Greenlee   T7S R30E   Elev. c. 4000'

The post office at Hardy was named for Joe Hardy, a miner in the vicinity of Duncan who operated the Ash Creek mining property here as late as 1938.

P.O. est. Jan. 10, 1938, Mrs. Lavada McEuen, p.m.; resc. Feb. 15, 1938
Ref.: Empie; 242

HARDYVILLE

Mohave   T20N R22W   Elev. 550'

Today nothing remains of the small community established in 1864 by Capt. William Harrison Hardy (b. 1823, New York; d. 1908). He discovered the Hardy Mine (T19N/R20W; elev. 3235') in 1860. Hardyville was at the head of navigation of the Colorado and became a distribution and shipping point for mines in the Cerbat Mountains. By 1870 about twenty people were living at Hardyville (or Hardy's Landing). In 1872 the community served briefly as county seat, but in November fire destroyed the community. It was rebuilt. In 1906 it was still considered an important mining camp.

P.O. est. Jan. 17, 1865, William H. Hardy; disc. Feb. 19, 1883   Ref.: AHS, Charles Metcalf, Letter (March 10, 1906); 15, II, 614, Note 5; *Weekly Arizona Miner* (Nov. 30, 1872), p. 2; *Arizona Miner* (Sept. 21, 1864), p. 3; 168, pp. 43, 252; Babcock; Harris; 200, pp. 153, 176-177, 179

HARPER

Mohave   T18N R22W

In 1872 Jesse Harper (b. 1831, Ohio), the first settler here, ran a ferry across the Colorado at this place.   Ref.: Harris; Housholder; 62

HARQUA

Mohave: *ah-ha-qua* = "water"

Maricopa   T2S R7W   Elev. 1150'

A post office was established at this point on the S.P.R.R. It is not the same as

Harquahala in Yuma County.
P.O. est. March 22, 1927, Mrs. Margaret E. Ward, p.m.; disc. Dec. 31, 1932
Ref.: 242

HARQUAHALA
Mohave: *ah-ha-qua-hale* = "water there is high up"
La Paz   T4N R13W
This was the site of a mining camp, now gone. Spaniards found gold in the Harquahala
Mountains in 1762 and Pima Indians reported gold there in 1869. By 1888 prospectors
had created a boom town, but by 1897 their claims were almost exhausted. Sporadic
mining continued until about 1932. In 1981 several ghost-town buildings remained. See
Harrisburg, Yuma
P.O. est. March 5, 1891, Horace E. Harris, p.m.; disc. Aug. 31, 1918   Ref.: *Weekly
Arizona Miner* (Jan. 23, 1869), p. 2; Varney

HARQUAHALA MOUNTAINS   pro.: /hárkwəhəylə/ or /hárkuwheylə/
Mohave = "running water" or *ah-ha-qua-hale* = "water there is high up"
La Paz/Maricopa   T5N R11W/T6N R10W
In 1865 these mountains were called the Penhatchapet, probably because there was a
Pen-Hatchi-pet Water (spring) on the south slope. By 1869 the spring was called Hoc-
qua-hala Springs, a name gradually applied to the mountains themselves. The attempts
of white men to wrap their tongues around the Indian name has resulted in various
spellings: Huacahella, Har-qua-halle, and Hacquehila. In 1955, the local name was
Tehachapi. These are the most massive mountains in central-western Arizona.
Harquahala Peak (T6N/R10W; elev. 5720') is here amd overlooks Harquahala Plains
(T3–2N/R12–8W), that name replacing the older Centennial Valley or Eagle Tail
Valley.   Ref.: 107, IV, 11; 200, p. 14; 279, p. 209; Willson; Lenon; *Weekly Arizona
Miner* (July 31, 1969), p. 1; 242; 329

HARRIS
Mohave   T20N R17W   Elev. c. 3500'
George W. Harris, an engineer on the A.T. & S.F.R.R., had this section house named
for him.   Ref.: Harris (no relation)

HARRISBURG
La Paz   T5N R12W   Elev. c. 1500'
In 1866 Capt. Charles Harris, a Canadian who served during the Civil War with federal
forces, helped his partner Frederick A. Tritle haul a five-stamp mill to this location to be
used by the Socorro Mine (see Socorro Peak) and other mines nearby. They used the site
of the old Centennial stage station, which on GLO 1892 shows as Harquahala.
Centennial was adjacent to Orville and appears to have been absorbed by it. Orville was
near Palomas on the Gila River at T3N/R18W. (See Plomosa, Yuma) Its name was
changed to Plomosa (Spanish = "lead-bearing"). Today all that remains is the cemetery
with its memorial to an 1849 emigrant massacre.
P.O. est. as Orville, Feb. 2, 1880, William B. Ready, p.m.; changed to Plomosa, April 8,
1880, J. Coleman, p.m.; changed to Centennial, July 13, 1881, George A. Ellsworth,
p.m.; disc. March 26, 1886; reest. as Harrisburg, Feb. 4, 1887, William Beard; disc.
Sept. 4, 1906   Ref.: 200, p. 11; 5, p. 361; *Prospect* (June 15, 1901), p. 8; 242

HARRIS CAVE
Apache   T9N R26E
While wrestling with his brother, Will M. Harris (b. 1866) found this cave in 1883. They
tumbled into a lake (now called Harris Lake). Then they walked a short distance, at
which point Will suggested they dry their clothes on a rock. While doing so, Will noticed
an opening in the flat ground, partially concealed by large rocks. The boys entered and
discovered two caves, one about eighteen hundred feet long and the other over eight
thousand feet. They found Indian artifacts, including over two hundred pots, a jar filled
with turquoise, and another with shell earrings. Will Harris filed a claim to the land. The
cave is also known as Pottery Cave.   Ref.: Will M. Harris

HARRIS MOUNTAIN
Cochise   T16S R31E   Elev. 5469'
The name commemorates the Apache massacre of an emigrant and his family in 1873. Despite warnings not to do so, Harris had left the emigrant party at San Simon Cienega because Apaches had told him about a short cut by way of this mountain. Not until years later when a daughter was rescued from her Apache captors and brought back from Mexico was the massacre revealed. Soldiers found the bones of Harris, his wife, and two children in Hunt Canyon. A soldier carved a crude head board, "Here lies the Harris family killed by Apaches 1873." Ref.: Macia

HARRY EDWARD'S MOUNTAIN
Mohave   T19N R20W   Elev. 2542'
On October 12, 1857, Lt. Edward Fitzgerald Beale wrote of seeing a rugged mountain to the south. He named it for a member of his party. Ref.: 23, p. 72

HARSHAW
Santa Cruz   T23S R16E   Elev. 4850'
In December 1873 Indian Agent Thomas J. Jeffords asked David Tecumseh Harshaw, a cattleman in the San Pedro Valley, to remove his cattle from the Chiricahua Indian range. Harshaw moved his stock into an area that Mexicans still call Durasno because of its peach trees. There Harshaw located and developed mines, and by 1880 a lively mining camp with several stores existed on Harshaw Creek at the community. By 1881 David Harshaw had left. Mining gradually died out and in 1909 only a few families remained. Hermosa (Spanish = "beautiful") Hill is here. It and Hermosa Canyon borrowed their names from the Hermosa Mine three quarters of a mile south of Harshaw. It was located in 1877 and sold a year later to the Hermosa Mining Company of New York.
P.O. est. April 29, 1880, Dan B. Gillette, Jr., p.m.; disc. Feb. 28, 1903 Ref.: Lenon; *Arizona Citizen* (Dec. 30, 1873), p. 3; 146, p. 32; 286, p. 246

HART CANYON
Coconino   T13N R13E
D. F. Hart ran cattle on the range in upper Oak Creek in 1887. Ref.: Less Hart (no relation); 18a

HART PRAIRIE
Coconino   T23N R7E
Frank Hart (d. c. 1888) settled here in July 1876. It was also referred to as Interior Valley. (See Humphreys Peak, Coconino) Hart's partner, John Clark, was the first to arrive on horseback from California to look over the land, but Clark returned to the West Coast. Hart brought in sheep and settled. He found springs (now named for him) on both sides of the prairie. The contemporary name for this location is The Snowbowl. Ref.: Anderson; 71, p. 63; 329; Robinson, USGS Provisional Paper No. 76

HARTT
Pima   T17S R14E
This station on the S.P.R.R. thirty miles south of Tucson was named for William Hartt (d. 1899), who arrived in Arizona in January 1878 from Rochester, New York, and established a ranch here. Ref.: 277, pp. 1, 199

HARWOOD
Yuma
This landing on the Colorado River about twenty-eight miles north of Yuma was named by Capt. Jack Mellon, a Colorado River steamboat captain, for Col. Harwood, a member of the Gila Canal Company. The landing was at the head of the Colorado and Gila Canals. Ref.: 18a

HASBIDITO   pro.: /hašbíd:tò/
Navajo: *hasbidi* = "turtle" or "mourning dove"; *to* = "spring"
This name, used by Herbert Gregory on January 19, 1915, applies to a spring, a stream, and the valley through which it runs. It is also sometimes called Hospitito. Ref.: 329; 141, p. 191

HASKELL SPRING
Yavapai　　　　　　　　　　　　　　T16N R22E

Lt. Harry Haskell, 12th U.S. Infantry, was in charge of removing Indians c. 1873 from this location to the San Carlos Indian Reservation. The name Hasket Spring is a corruption.　Ref.: 18a; Schnebly; 329

HASSAYAMPA　pro.: /hæsiyæmpə/
Maricopa　　　　　　　　　　　　T1S R5W　　　　　　　　　Elev. 540'

This is apparently not the same place as the short-lived Hassayampa (below). The first settlers arrived here in 1886, the first family in what is now Arlington Valley having been the Davis family which arrived in 1878. This small community is at the lower end of Buckeye. The community was named by Osie Bales because it is at the point where the Hassayampa River trends into the lower Gila region.　Ref.: Parkman

HASSAYAMPA　pro.: /hæsiyæmpə/
Maricopa

This place was described as being at Walker Gulch and the lower end of Hesiampa in 1864.

P.O. est. March 28, 1881, Mrs. Matilda E. Spence, p.m.; disc. Oct. 6, 1882
Ref.: *Arizona Miner* (March 9, 1864), p. 2; 242

HASSAYAMPA RIVER　pro.: /hæsiyæmpə/
Mohave: *ah* = "water"; *si-am* = "big rocks"; *pa* = "place of"
Yavapai/Maricopa　　　　　　　　T10N R3W/T5N R4W

This stream has a Mohave name which Charles Genung learned from them and told to others. In Arizona miner lore, this stream came to be associated with liars, more specifically, prospectors who evaded direct answers about their locations or those who bragged about how good their finds were. Such men explained their lies by saying they drank Hassayampa River water that rendered them unable to speak the truth. The name has also been spelled as follows: Haviamp, Aziamp, and Ah-ha Seyampa. According to Charles Genung, the name meant "gliding or smooth running water." The Hassayampa Reservoir (T12N/R2W) was constructed in 1934. Related names include Hassayampa Sink (Maricopa) and Hassayampa Wash (Yavapai).　Ref.: Sharlot Hall Museum, Genung File; 177, pp. 362-363; 5, p. 162; 107, IV, 44; 157, p. 13; Jackson

HATCHER
Gila　　　　　　　　　　　　　　c. T11N R9E

This post office, probably at a ranch, was named for its postmaster. It served sixty residents.
P.O. est. June 23, 1896, John F. Hatcher, p.m.; disc. ?　Ref.: 242

HATCHTON
Yuma　　　　　　　　　　　　　Location unknown
P.O. est. Nov. 30, 1921, Frank E. Black, p.m.; disc. ?　Ref.: 242

HAT CONE
Mohave　　　　　　　　　　　　T37N R7W

This steep volcanic ash cone has a sharp peak like a conical hat.　Ref.: 42, p. 62

HAT MOUNTAIN
Maricopa　　　　　　　　　　　T9S R5W　　　　　　　　　Elev. 3482'

This round flat-top mesa looks like a hat, hence the name. It is also called Tea Kettle Mountain.　Ref.: 57, p. 212; 58

HATTAN BUTTE
Coconino (Grand Canyon)　　　　T32N R3E　　　　　　　　Elev. 5954'

This butte was named by Frank Bond in 1929 for Andrew Hattan, a cook and trapper on the second Powell Expedition through the Grand Canyon. It is also called Hattan Temple.　Ref.: 329

HAUFER WASH
Gila   T7N R10E

This wash is named for the school teacher at the school house here c. 1905. He lived north of the school house in an adobe home. This wash is called locally School House Wash.   Ref.: Cooper

HAUNTED CANYON
Pinal   T1N R13E

Pete Gann camped here during a night storm which caused stones and boulders to rumble and roll. During darkness, he thought the place was haunted, hence the name.   Ref.: *Arizona Enterprise* (Aug. 8, 1891), p. 3; Craig

HAVASU CANYON   pro.: /hǽvǝsuw/
Havasu: *haha* = "water"; *vasu* = "blue"
Coconino   T33N R4W

The upper part of this canyon was formerly called Cataract Canyon. Fr. Francisco Garcés in 1776 was the first white man who went from the canyon rim into this canyon to visit Havasupai Indians. His names for the creek which runs through the canyon were Rio Jabesua de San Antonio and Rio Cabezua, both phonetically akin to the word *Havasu*. Havasu Creek (in 1881, Havasupai Creek) is the largest stream feeding from the south into the Colorado River. In 1870 Maj. John Wesley Powell called Havasu Creek, Coanini Creek, a variation of Cosnino. Dr. A. H. Thompson of Powell's party said he believed Coanini Creek and the one Lt. Joseph Christmas Ives called Catarack (*sic*) Creek were one and the same. At one time the canyon was called Lee's Canyon because John D. Lee (see Lee's Ferry, Coconino) hid here to avoid capture for his part in the Mountain Meadows Massacre.

Havasu Canyon (a.k.a. Havasupai Canyon) is one of the most beautiful in the United States. The trail which begins at Havasu Hilltop twists along the fourteen-mile narrow Topocoba Trail, descending in the first one-and-a-half miles over one thousand feet, during which the traveller encounters at least twenty-nine switchbacks. At the base of the first abrupt drop is Topocoba Spring, sometimes called Tope Kohe Spring, in Topocobya Canyon, a side canyon through which the trail descends and enters Havasu Canyon. The stream through the red-walled canyon with its pinnacles of red rock is lined with willows. According to one source, Havasupai Indians say the towering red pinnacles are gods and that when they tumble, the tribe will be doomed.

Five water falls are in Havasu Canyon. They are as follows: Fifty Foot Falls (the first in the series), created by a flash flood in 1932; Navajo Falls (second in the series); Bridal Veil Falls, with lacy streamers dropping one hundred and ten feet in a twenty-foot broad veil (also called Havasu Falls); Mooney Falls (fourth in the series), named for James Mooney, an ex-sailor and prospector who in 1880 attempted to descend the two-hundred-and-twenty foot falls by sitting in a loop of rope while Indians lowered him over the cliff. The rope caught in a crack and Mooney swung helpless for two days. On the third day he fell to his death. His remains four years later were still at the foot of the cliff, but were later recovered and buried at the top of the falls; Beaver Falls (fifth in the series), is named because many beaver used to live here (also sometimes said to be in Beaver Canyon). Associated names include Havasu Creek (T33N/R5W) and Havasu Springs (T33N/R4W).   Ref.: Schroeder; 322 (July 21, 1872); 225, pp. 69–70; 266, p. 197; 5, p. 488; 53, pp. 655–656, 659; J.H. Butchart, Letter (1961)

HAVASU, LAKE
Mohave/La Paz   T11–13N R18–20W   Elev. 450'

Formerly known as Parker Dam Reservoir, Havasu Lake was renamed in December 1963 for the Havasupai Indians. It is a mile wide by forty-five miles long and encompasses the Havasu Lake National Wild Life Refuge. In 1963 the USGS again altered the name to the present Lake Havasu. Associated names include Lake Havasu City (T13N/R20W, elev. 482'), and Havasu Lake National Wild Life Refuge (Mohave/Yuma; T16–11N/R21–18W). During a flood in 1940, back-up waters from Hoover and Parker Dams (before Davis Dam was constructed) covered about four thousand acres of the Fort Mojave Indian Reservation and created an extension of

Havasu Lake which on January 22, 1941 was established as a National Wild Life Refuge. At the outset it included all of Havasu Lake, but c. 1964 it was reduced to a wild life habitat of 41,500 acres, about one-fourth of which is in California.
Ref.: 194, p. 74, Note 18; "Havasu Brochure," U.S. Fish and Wild Life Service; 89, p. 382; 178, pp. 55, 174; 266, p. 197; 276, p. 12

HAVASUPAI INDIAN RESERVATION

Havasu: *haha* = "water"; *vasu* = "blue"; *pai* = "people"
Coconino/Mohave   T33N R4W

Hodge referred to the small Havasupai Indian tribe as "the blue or green water people", describing them as "a small isolated tribe of Yuman stock...." Hodge adds that Whipple said that in 1850 the Cosninos (forebearers of the Havasupai) roamed the territory from the San Francisco Mountains to the Mogollon Rim and the Little Colorado Valley. Maj. John Wesley Powell said that a Havasupai chief pointed out to him former homes in that area occupied by the Indians until war-like tribes forced them to leave and to find safety in Havasu Canyon. The "Supai" Reservation of five hundred eighteen acres was created on June 8, 1880, with later changes adding two thousand five hundred forty acres in Havasu Canyon. Ref.: 167, I, 537, and II, 374; "Annual Report of the Arizona Commission on Indian Affairs, 1954 – 1955 –1956," p. 16; 276, p. 12

HAVASUPAI POINT

Coconino (Grand Canyon)   T32N R1W

Originally called Bass Hotel Point or merely Hotel Point, this place was renamed in May 1932 for the Havasupai by the USGS. The name Yava Supai is an error. See Havasupai Indian Reservation, Coconino/Mohave   Ref.: W. W. Bass File (Wickenburg, Arizona); 329

HAVILAND

Mohave   T16N R18W   Elev. 1480'

It has been conjectured that this section house on the railroad was probably named derisively as it is located in a volcanic flat, but has nothing whatever to do with fine clay used in making china.   Ref.: G.E.P. Smith (1929); 329; Housholder

HAWKINS BUTTE

Coconino (Grand Canyon)   T31N R4E   Elev. 5250'

W. R. Hawkins was a hunter and cook for Maj. John Wesley Powell's first Grand Canyon Expedition in 1869. Frank Bond suggested the name for the butte in 1929.   Ref.: 329

HAWK PEAK

Graham   T8S R24E   Elev. 10,600'

There are three possible origins for this name. (1) Russell Hawk was an early fire guard on nearby Mount Graham. (2) A Hawk family is said to have moved into this area (but in fact it arrived later than the establishment of the name for this peak). (3) There are many hawks in the vicinity. Hawk Peak Spring shares the name and location. Ref.: 329

HAWLEY LAKE

Apache   T7N R24E   Elev. 8175'

By damming Trout Creek c. 1966, Apache Indians impounded water to form Hawley Lake, which they named for Albert M. Hawley, superintendent of the Fort Apache Indian Reservation. During dam construction, armed Indian guards protected the site against supporters of the Salt River Project, who asserted that impounding Trout Creek waters would decrease water available for Project reservoirs. Undeterred, the Apaches then constructed at least twenty-five other dams, thus creating twenty-six lakes on the reservation.   Ref.: *Phoenix Gazette* (July 13, 1972), p. 16

HAYDEN: Several place names reflect the prominence of pioneer Charles Trumbull Hayden (b. 1825, Connecticut; d. Feb. 1900). Hayden arrived aboard the first Butterfield Overland stage in 1858, stepping off in Tucson. There he became a contractor for supplies for the military. In c. 1870 he moved northward, but was stopped by the flooding Salt River, which he viewed from atop what came to be known as

Hayden's Butte, today known as Tempe Butte. At that point he established a ferry and mill in 1872, becoming a highly successful businessman. With his family, he lived at what was then called Butte City until his death in 1900. The following place names reflect his prominence: [Ref.: Woody; 107, II, 288–290; 242]

Hayden Gila T5S R15E Elev. 2051'
This community was named by the Hayden, Stone & Co. mine operators for Charles Trumbull Hayden.
P.O. est. April 29, 1910, John T. Heins, p.m.; incorp. 1956

Hayden Junction Pinal T5S R15E
The rail line from Hayden here joined the S.P. R.R.
P.O. est. Dec. 3, 1910, Joseph B. Boughton, p.m.; Wells Fargo 1910

Hayden Mountain Coconino (Grand Canyon) T33N R4E Elev. 8350'
In July 1929 Frank Bond honored Hayden by naming this place for him.

Hayden Peak Pinal T4S R6E

Hayden's Butte Maricopa T1N R4E

Hayden's Ferry Maricopa T1N R4E
Hayden had a ferry and mill here in 1872. Its first name was Butte City because it lay below Hayden's Butte. Ref.: 242; Woody; 18a; 163, pp. 259-260; 206, p. 143

HAYES MOUNTAIN
Gila T2S R17E Elev. c. 4000'
W. C. Hayes and his son Zee ran cattle on the San Carlos Indian Reservation near here in the 1890s until forced off because cattle leases were rescinded for all except Indian cattle. Ref.: Woody

HAYES WASH
Pinal T3S R2E
Pima Indians named this wash to honor Ira H. Hayes, a U.S. Marine from the Pima Reservation, who helped raise the flag at Iwo Jima. Ref.: 128, p. 16

HAY LAKE
Coconino T16N R11E Elev. c. 5000'
Several place names in Arizona derive their name because wild hay was raised in the field or on the flats and cut either for the use of military livestock or, as in the case of Hay Lake, for stage teams on the Santa Fe-Prescott and other stage routes. Ref.: 18a

HAYNES
Yavapai T11N R6W Elev. c. 4000'
This railroad shipping point was named for Lloyd C. Haynes, superintendent of the Big Stick Mine. The post office application reveals that locally it was called Date Creek (not the same as Date Creek, Camp). See Date Creek, Yavapai
P.O. est. May 27, 1908, John R. Roberts, p.m.; name changed to Date Creek, Jan. 7, 1922 Ref.: 18a; 242

HAYSTACK: Several Arizona places bear the name *haystack* because of their fancied resemblance to stacked hay. Examples follow:

Haystack Butte Gila T6N R11E Elev. 2766'

Haystack Butte Navajo T23N R19E Elev. 2652'

Haystack Creek Gila T4N R16E
This creek takes its name from nearby Haystack Butte. See Bronson Canyon, Gila Ref.: Woody

Haystack Peak Yavapai T5N R17W Elev. 2788'

Haystacks, The Apache T26N R31E
These mounds are in the west part of the Second Petrified Forest. Ref.: Branch

Haystacks, The Apache
The haystacks are a group of small rounded hillocks about one mile south of Window Rock.
Ref.: 331, p. 174; 5, p. 409

[295]

Haystack Valley   Pinal   T7S R13E

Because of its shape, this valley was also called Round Valley.

HEADGATE ROCK DAM

La Paz   T10N R19W

This diversion dam took its name from a rock at the northern point of the 1865 Mojave Indian Reservation, at which time it was called Corner Rock. By 1908 it was known as Headgate Rock. To Mojave Indians, this area north of Parker Dam was known as *Ah-Va-Kou-o-Tut* (= "ancient home of the Mojave"). Many unsuccessful channels were drilled through the rock before it was possible to channel water to reservation lands from Parker Dam. Ref.: 200, p. 47; Thomas, "Ah-Va-Kou-o-Tut," p. 14

HEARST MOUNTAIN

Coconino   T22N R1E   Elev. c. 7500'

William Randolph Hearst was a partner in the Hearst-Perrin cattle outfit near this mountain in 1887. The same outfit also had holdings in Santa Cruz County.
Ref.: 18a; Kitt

HEART TANK

Yuma   T13S R12W

Fr. Eusebio Kino stopped at this water hole in 1699, while exploring what is now southwestern Arizona. A natural pot hole, it fills with rain water run-off and is the principal tank in the Sierra Prieta. It was a death trap for animals when the water had almost totally evaporated, because they could not climb out. In 1940 the Fish and Wild Life Service put in a dam to deepen it and blasted a ram for animals to use. It is so named because until it was deepened it had a conventional heart shape, hence the Spanish name Tinaja de Corazon (*tinaja* = "natural water hole"; *corazon* = "heart"). Pinto Tank is also here. Ref.: *Yuma Daily Sun* (Dec. 11, 1960);355, p. 188; 59, p. 404

HEATON

Pinal

Prior to the coming of the railroad in 1879 this place was called Maricopa. On the map it was about four miles west of the Phoenix railroad junction. It was also referred to as Maricopaville, a name under which it was the center of an early real estate promotion: A special train was run from San Francisco, loaded with potential investors who were given a map showing Maricopaville at the center of a "spider web-like tracery of railroads that ran to every point of the compass." Temporarily Maricopaville had a population of several thousand, but in the summer of 1887 the railroad offices were removed, together with the name, to the present railroad junction. The name of this place then changed to Heaton. Ref.: 224, p. 291

HEBER   pro.: /híyber/

Navajo   T12N R16E   Elev. 6439'

In 1876 and 1877 two companies of Mormon emigrants from Arkansas were assigned to Little Colorado River settlements. John W. N. Scarlett, first sent to Allen's camp, withdrew in 1883 to found Heber where John Bushman had found water in 1882. The new community was named for Heber C. Kimball, Chief Justice of the State of Deseret or, according to a second source, for Heber J. Grant, President of the Mormon Church. P.O. est. Sept. 11, 1890, James E. Shelley, p.m. Ref.: AHS, Richards File; 225, p. 155; 341, p. 4; 116, p. 564

HECLA

Yavapai   T3N R2E

The post office to serve this mining community was named for the Hecla Mine. A large stone corral there also led to its being called locally Stone Corral.
P.O. est. March 3, 1893, John H. Hutchins, p.m.; disc. Oct. 3, 1894   Ref.: 18a

HEINTZELMAN MINE

Pima

The mine was named in 1858 by Maj. Samuel Peter Heintzelman, president of the Sonora Exploring and Mining Company. See Cerro Colorado, Pima Ref.: 320, pp. 8-9

[296]

HELEN'S DOME

Cochise   T15S R28E   Elev. 6377'
In the 1850s Cow Peak was the name of this mountain because when viewed from Apache Pass, a live oak tree on top looked like a cow. Old timers occasionally call this conical mountain Helen's Doom, a name by which it was known as early as 1875. However, according to the post trader at Fort Bowie (Sidney DeLong), it was named for Mrs. Helen Hackett, wife of Capt. Hackett (stationed at Fort Bowie). Accompanied by friends, she climbed the peak, which was then named for her.   Ref.: Riggs; 18a; 319, pp. 94-95

HELIOGRAPH PEAK

Graham   T9S R24E   Elev. 10,028'
Station No. 3 of General Nelson A. Miles' heliograph system was on this peak. The heliograph system was in use from May 1, 1886 to September 30, 1886, sending over two thousand messages. The U.S. Forest Service suggested the name in November 1932 and the USGS approved it in December 1932.   Ref.: Jennings; 18a; 116, p. 673

HELL CANYON

Yavapai   (1) T7N R1W (2) T18N R1E (3) T8N R6E
There are three Hell Canyons in Yavapai County. The name of one dates to a military skirmish of July 3, 1869. A military report of November 25, 1872 called it "Red Rocks or Hell Canyon." The name mirrors the fact that these extremely rough canyons are hell to make one's way through. It is probable that Hell Canyon (Yavapai/Coconino) borders on the old Beale trail into Chino Valley, used in the pioneer days.
Ref.: Benham; AHS Names File; 159, pp. 434, 438

HELL HOLES

Greenlee   T5S R32E   Elev. c. 5500'
The extremely rough nature of this area led to its name, for if cattle made their way in, "It was plain hell to get them out." Hells Hole Peak overlooks this area.   Ref.: Scott; Patterson; 18a

HELL'S GATE

Gila   T10N R12E   Elev. c. 4000'
Hells' Gate is so named because it is at the beginning of a rough and dangerous trail named the Hell's Gate Trail, running from Green Valley to the juncture of Tonto and Haigler creeks. Hell's Gate Ridge overlooks the canyon and trail.   Ref.: McKinney; McInturff

HELLS HOLE

Gila   T11N R7E
Part of Workman Creek runs through this canyon, locally referred to as Hells Hole, on the Herbert Wertman ranch. It is very difficult territory to traverse. "Workman" is a corruption.   Ref.: 18a; Woody

HELMET PEAK

Pima   T17S R12E   Elev. 4015'
The name describes the shape of this peak.

HELVETIA

Pima   T18S R15E   Elev. c. 4400'
Before the Civil War, mines were probably being located in what later became the Helvetia District, but not until the late 1870s did L. M. Grover lay claim to the Old Dick from whence Dicks Peak (Santa Cruz; T22S/R12E; elev. 5396'), Heavyweight (from whence Heavyweight Hill), and Tallyho mines. They were not developed until 1881. The first mine to be worked was the Old Frijole, owned by John Weigle and William Hart. In the 1890s the claims were bought by the Helvetia Copper Company of New Jersey and under its direction the community of Helvetia took shape. It existed until December 2, 1901. In November 1903 the Helvetia Copper Company of Arizona took over and operated the mines, continuing until 1911. The low price of copper closed down

the mines. Briefly during World War I, the community enjoyed renewed life. Today only the cemetery and a ruined adobe house and tailings identify the old location, but the mine is again being worked. Helvetia Spring and Wash are here.

P.O. est. Oct. 6, 1899, William S. George, p.m.; disc. Dec. 31, 1921
Ref.: 286, pp. 25, 96, 97; 146, p. 47; 242; 50, pp. 68-70; Varney

HENDERSHOT PLACE
Gila   T11N R10E   Elev. c. 6000'
In July 1882 Apaches led by Nan-tia-tish attacked the Meadows family here at their ranch, killing the father and wounding two sons. The Indians also attacked McMillan and the Middleton Ranch. See McMillanville, Gila   Ref.: 18a; Woody

HENNESY CANYON
Coconino   T18N R9E
This canyon was named for "Old Man" John Hennesy, who was still living at this location as late as 1958. Hennesy Tank is also known as Chavez Tank. See also Padre Canyon, Coconino   Ref.: Paten

HENNING
Mohave   T17N R18W
For a period during the early existence of the A.T. & S.F.R.R., a post office existed in Sacramento Valley east of Needles at what is today only a section house on the railroad. The place was named for A. E. Henning, in charge of general water service for the railroad between Needles and Albuquerque.
P.O. est. Feb. 28, 1884, John H. Mollering, p.m.; disc. Feb. 5, 1886   Ref.: 18a; 242

HERCULES
Pinal
This was the first name of the mill site for the Ray-Hercules Mining Company. See Belgravia, Pinal

HERDER MOUNTAIN
Maricopa   T5N R8E   Elev. 3693'
The herding of sheep along a mountain trail led to its name. Sheep are wintered in the warmer and lower levels and then herded along a trail between Tonto Basin and the White Mountain country where they spend the summer.   Ref.: AHS; 18a

HEREFORD   pro.: /hérferd/
Cochise   T23S R22E   Elev. 4190'
When a community developed around his smelter, William Herrin named the place for his friend Benjamin J. Hereford, a Tucson attorney in the 1870s and later. The smelter shut down. When fire later destroyed it, Hereford was deserted until c. 1892 when Col. William Greene started a cattle ranch here.
P.O. est. Jan. 19, 1904, Benjamin F. Sneed, p.m.; Wells Fargo 1904   Ref.: AHS Names File; 18a; 242

HERMIT BASIN
Coconino (Grand Canyon)   T31N R2E
At this location Louis Boucher, a French Canadian, established Hermit Camp (for tourists) on the trail to the Colorado River bed. The name for the basin was suggested by Henry Gannett in 1906. Associated names include Hermit Camp, Hermit Creek, Hermit Falls (since 1930 called Hermit Rapids), Hermit Rim (above the Basin), Hermit's Rest (Elev. 5700' on the Rim, a rest area), and Hermit Trail. The trail was constructed in 1909 by forester Arthur C. Ringland at the request of the S.F.R.R. and Fred Harvey system. It has been abandoned.   Ref.: Kolb; 329; Verkamp

HERMIT RAPIDS
Coconino (Grand Canyon)   T31N R2E
In April 1930 the name Hermit Falls was changed to Hermit Rapids. See Hermit Basin, Coconino (Grand Canyon)

[298]

HERMOSILLO pro.: /ermosiyo/

Pinal   T6E R6S

This was a developing community in 1891. Nothing else is known concerning it. Ref.: 18a

HESS CREEK

Gila   T4N R16E   Elev. c. 4000'

A cattleman named Hess settled here and ran livestock along the creek. The USGS named Hess Canyon in 1946. Hess Flat (T4N/R17E) is nearby. Ref.: 18a; 329

HEWITT CANYON

Pima   T1S R11E   Elev. c. 2500'

The Hewitt family maintained a ranch at the mouth of this canyon, hence its name. Hewitt Ridge is also here and Hewitt Station was nearby. Ref.: 18a; Craig

HIAWATHA CREEK

Yavapai

On the Grid Map of 1865 this creek is south of Peeple's Ranch and north of Walnut Grove at right angles to the toll road. See Minnehaha, Yavapai

HIBBERD (R.R. STN.)

Navajo   T21N R11E   Elev. c. 5000'

I. L. Hibberd was a superintendent and later a general manager for the S.F.R.R. Ref.: 18a

HICKEY MOUNTAIN

Yavapai   T15N R2E   Elev. 7619'

Dennis Hickey maintained a potato ranch nearby in the early 1880s on Mingus Mountain. The name Hickory is a corruption. Ref.: 18a; Stemmer

HICKIWAN pro.: /ʔigkiwan/
Papago = "zig zag"

Pima   T12S R2W   Elev. 2194'

It is possible that Fr. Kino gave the name San Geronimo to the location in 1699. In October 1781 Fages said the place was called Cerro de la Pirigua or Tachitoa. The Papago *hik* may mean "rough" and may refer to hair cut short in jagged fashion, leading to the possibility that there is a local story underlying the name of this village. According to a USGS Water Supply Paper, "Perigua seems to be of Mexican origin. The Papago name is HIKIBON (where there is a rough mountain) and this name also has a Spanish spelling, JUQUIBO." The name has also been rendered as follows: Pirigua; Hikivo; Hikuwan; Hikjovn. Associated names include Hickiwan Peak (Elev. 2560'), Valley, and Wash (Pima/Maricopa, T11–10S/R2–3W). Ref.: 58; 329; W. S. Paper, p. 405

HICKS WASH

Gila   T2N R14E

The Hicks Ranch lies opposite this wash, hence the name. Ref.: Woody

HIDDEN: Many places in Arizona are named *Hidden* because of their remoteness or inaccessibility or because they are difficult to find, being somewhat concealed until one practically stumbles over them. The following are examples:

Hidden Canyon	Mohave	T36N R13W
Hidden Canyon	Yuma	T1S R18W
Hidden Hollow	Coconino	T21N R6E
Hidden Lake	Apache	T25N R30E
Hidden Lake	Coconino/Navajo	T11N R14–15E
Hidden Pasture	Cochise	T15S R19E
Hidden Pasture	Yavapai	T20N R10W

Hidden Rim	Mohave	T37N R14W	
Hidden Spring	Apache	T11N R27E	
Hidden Spring	Navajo	T11N R17E	
Hidden Spring	Pima	T16S R18E	
Hidden Spring	Yavapai	(1) T14N R5W	(2) T10N R5E
Hidden Valley	Maricopa	T1S R3E	
Hidden Valley	Mohave	T19N R19W	
Hidden Valley	Pinal	T5S R2E	
Hidden Valley	La Paz	T2S R22W	
Hidden Valley Mountains	Yuma	c. T2S R19W	

Until 1941 these mountains had no name. At that time an old character, Hector Garven Gray, was prospecting and writing western stories while living in this truly hidden valley area. Tired of life, Gray placed himself in his coffin, screwed down the lid and took poison in January 1942. He left a note leaving all he owned to Sears Roebuck because he owed them a bill.   Ref.: Monson

Hidden Wash	Mohave	T35N R12W
Hidden Water Spring	Maricopa	T3N R9E

HIDE CREEK
Yavapai   T17N R6W

This creek was named for a settler called Hide about whom little is known. Hide Creek Mountain (Elev. 7272') shares the name.   Ref.: Dorothy Rosenberger, Letter (Dec. 20, 1955)

HIEROGLYPH: The presence of hieroglyphs or pictographs has led to using the name in several Arizona place names. Examples follow:

Hieroglyphic Canyon	Maricopa	T6N R4W
Hieroglyphic Hill	Maricopa	T6N R4W
Hieroglyphic Mountains	Maricopa	

Now called Painted Rock Mountains. See Painted Rocks, Maricopa

Hieroglyphic Spring	Pinal	T1N R9E
Hieroglyphic Tanks	Gila	T11N R7E

HI FULLER CANYON
Coconino   T13N R10E

Hi Fuller lived in this canyon in the Tonto Basin prior to moving to Moqui Ranch in Coconino County. The place is also known as Fuller Canyon. The USGS replaced the name Fuller Spring in 1956, calling it Hi Fuller Spring.   Ref.: Hart; 329

HIGGINS TANK
Navajo   T31N R5W

J. M. Higgins maintained a dirt tank here about 1888 to catch flood water for his horses.   Ref.: 18a

HIGHBALL SPRING
Yavapai   T11N R4E

This is the spring where flat country gives way to rising ground. Here truckers used to accelerate or "high ball" in order to get up and over the divide. It is also sometimes referred to as High Ball Water.   Ref.: Dugas

HIGH LONESOME CANYON
Cochise   T21S R29E

The homesteader named Glenn wanted a place "off by himself and he sure got it," whence the name, which was in use before 1906.   Ref.: Burrall

HIGH TANKS
Yuma

In 1940-41 the Fish and Wild Life Service developed springs and natural water holes at the following locations by number name:

No. 2: T1N R17W, Section 11   Yuma   No. 7: T1N R17W, Section 29   Yuma
No. 3: T1N R15W, Section 6   La Paz   No. 8: T1N R17W, Section 31   Yuma
No. 6: T1N R17W, Section 19   Yuma   No. 9: T1N R17W, Section 29   Yuma
There are no #4 and #5.   Ref.: Monson

HIGLEY
Maricopa   T1S R6E   Elev. 1298'

S. W. Higley assisted in the construction of the Phoenix & Eastern R.R. on which lies the town of Higley.

P.O. est. Sept. 28, 1909, L. H. Sorey, p.m.   Ref.: 18a; 242

HILLCAMP
Gila   T3N R19E   Elev. 6000'

For five months a post office existed at the site of the sawmill camp on the San Carlos Indian Reservation, taking its name from that of the postmistress, added to "camp." It was also called Hilltop.

P.O. est. May 9, 1927; Mrs. Zoma Lee Hill, p.m.; disc. Oct. 4, 1927   Ref.: Woody; 18a; 242

HILLER'S BUTTE
Grand Canyon (Coconino)   36°09'/112°05'

This butte three miles north of the suspension bridge and one mile west of Bright Angel was named at the suggestion of Frank Bond in 1929 for John K. Hillers, photographer with the second Powell Expedition 1871-72.   Ref.: Kolb; 329

HILLSIDE
Yavapai   T3N R6W   Elev. 3853'

The Hillside Mine was located by John Lawler and B. T. Riggs in 1887. It had a post office. It was moved from the mine to the railroad station on Date Creek where a community developed. The name suggested for the community was Lawler, but as he was a humble man, he suggested it be called Hillside. Hillside Rocks are in the vicinity (T15N/R9W).

P.O. est. July 31, 1881, John W. Archibald, p.m.; disc. Jan. 1, 1962; Wells Fargo 1904   Ref.: Helen Lawler, Letter (June 1973); C. A. Anderson *et al, Geology and Ore Deposits of the Bagdad Area*, 1955

HILLTOP
Cochise   T16S R30E   Elev. 5720'

Frank and John Hands (see Hands Pass, Cochise) established the Hilltop Mine, selling it to a developer in St. Louis. It was near the top of a hill, hence the name of Hilltop on the west side of the mountain. A tunnel was put through to the east side where an even larger town developed. When the mine became inactive, Hilltop became a summer colony. The post office site record in the National Archives notes that in 1928 the post office was at Painted Rock townsite.

P.O. est. Aug. 15, 1919, Raleigh O. Fife, p.m.; disc. June 30, 1945   Ref.: Riggs; 242

HINDU AMPHITHEATER
Coconino (Grand Canyon)   T32N R2E

In 1882 Maj. Clarence E. Dutton wrote that this place had "profusion and richness (which) suggests an oriental character." The first name was Hindoo Amphitheater, changed to Hindu in March 1906.   Ref.: 100, p. 169; 329

HITT WASH
Yavapai   T17N R5W

The wash takes its name from James Hitt, who settled in this area c. 1880.   Ref.: 329

HI VIEW POINT

Coconino   T12N R10E

This viewpoint on the Mogollon Rim takes its name from that of Hi Fuller. See Hi Fuller Springs, Coconino

HOA MURK

Papago = "basket burned"

Pima   T13S R4W

This small Papago village in 1917 was known as Romaine's Field. By 1941 it was being called by its Papago name as given here. Ref.: 57, p. 8; 329

HOBBLE MOUNTAIN

Coconino   T25N R4E   Elev. c. 7000'

A man named Kinsey gave the name to this mountain when he found stolen calves hobbled here years ago. Ref.: 18a

HOCHDERFFER HILLS

Coconino   T23N R6E

These hills are named for George Hochderffer, the name having been in use since earlier than 1887. Ref.: 166, p. 107

HODGKINS GULCH

Yavapai   T11N R2W

Although this place is sometimes called Hackberry Gulch, people in the area agree that it should be Hodgkins to honor a pioneer in the area, as the name has been thus known for almost a century. Ref.: 329

HOGANSAANI SPRING

Navajo = "The Lone Hogan" or "At the Hogan"

Apache   T40N R26E

Herbert E. Gregory noted this name in January 1915 and reported it was also called Ojo de Casa (Spanish = "house well"). Ref.: 329; 141, p. 369

HOG CANYON

Gila   T10N R13E

The Tewksbury family maintained hogs on the oak mast in this canyon, hence the name. Ref.: McKinney

HOGE LANDING

La Paz   T4S R23W

B. L. Hoge maintained a livestock ranch (including Percheron horses) until the river bed filled upon the completion of Laguna Dam. He then established a cable ferry at this point to take stock across the river. Ref.: Monson

HOGTRAIL CANYON

Greenlee   T1N R28E

This name probably came into use because of many wild hogs in the area. The name has been in use since the early 1900s. Ref.: Scott

HOLBROOK

Navajo   T17N R21E   Elev. 5075'

In 1881 John W. Young, a railroad contractor, set up headquarters two miles east of the future Holbrook, where a little community was already in existence. Juan Padilla had built the first house immediately east of Horsehead Crossing above the junction of the Puerco and Little Colorado River in 1871. Berado Frayde (or Freyes) was in charge of Padilla's saloon and the place came to be known as Berado Station, a main crossing for travellers en route south. Padilla, his boss, was at best a haphazard merchant, pricing all articles at fifty cents regardless of true value. In 1881 the first railroad tracks were laid at Berado and extended west. In 1882 Holbrook came into being and Berado began to vanish, with Berado himself moving to Albuquerque. Gradually Horsehead Crossing disappeared as Holbrook grew in importance. Young named it in honor of H. R. Holbrook. It became the county seat in 1895 and is today an important community serving numerous ranches and trading posts.

P.O. est. Sept. 18, 1882, James H. Wilson, p.m.; Wells Fargo 1885

Ref.: 225, p. 163; 331, p. 72; 163, p. 296; 5, p. 313; 71, p. 45; Richards; Grigsby; W. S. Hulet, p.m. (Holbrook), Letter (1956)

HOLCOMB
Navajo   T11N R17E

Although this name is sometimes rendered Hokum and the place was known as Phoenix Park until the name was changed in 1923, the correct name is Holcomb. It is that of an old timer called "Red" Holcomb who lived here and spent most of his life running red horses. He had fiery red hair.   Ref.: 329

HOLDEN LAKE
Coconino   T22N R1E

T. F. (Fred) Holden, an early Arizona territorial rancher, ran the TFH cattle brand in this vicinity.   Ref.: Benham; Kennedy

HOLDER
Gila   T11(or 12)N R10E

John T. Holder maintained a cabin on the Rim and served as a game warden c. 1908-1909. He raised sheep and goats until foresters removed them from the Tonto Forest Reserve. His post office served residents in the region.

P.O. est. Sept. 5, 1896, John T. H. Holder, p.m.; disc. Aug. 6, 1897

Ref.: Hart; 18a; 242

HOLE CANYON
Gila   T6N R17E

The word *hole* in Arizona place names often refers to a small valley, as in this instance.

HOLE IN THE GROUND
Gila   T10N R11E

This is a descriptive name for the natural sink occurring in this canyon. Crystals found in this hole are referred to as "Arizona diamonds."   Ref.: Packard

HOLE-IN-THE-ROCK
Maricopa   T1N R4E   Elev. 1450'

This easternmost of the Papago Buttes has indeed a hole-in-the-rock. The name was suggested in November 1917 by William H. Gill of the Forest Service. This was on the homestead filed by Charles Debrille Poston on April 13, 1892.   Ref.: 329

HOLLOWAY SPRING
Coconino   T20N R3E

This place is sometimes referred to as Hitt Spring, changed to Halloway in 1964 because according to older residents, a Mr. Holloway built his cabin here about 1900.

Ref.: 329

HOLLYWOOD
Graham   T7S R26E

The reason for the name of this small community is not known.

HOLMES CANYON
Yavapai   T9N R5E   Elev. c. 5000'

R. J. H. Holmes, Jr. (d. April 26, 1931) ran cattle in Bloody Basin for many years. The canyon is in the basin as is also Holmes Creek (T 9N/R4E).   Ref.: 18a

HOLT
Cochise   T13S R29E   Elev. c. 4000'

From 1887 to about 1892 Col. J. M. Holt of Montana shipped cattle from this railroad point.   Ref.: 18a

HOLY GRAIL TEMPLE
Coconino (Grand Canyon)   T33N R1E   Elev. 6710'
Originally known as Bass Tomb, this place endured a name change in October 1908 as part of the policy to give fine heroic names to places in the Grand Canyon. Ref.: 329; 178, p. 80

HOLY JOE PEAK
Pinal   Elev. 5415'
An old prospector prone to preaching sermons earned himself the nickname Holy Joe. He prospected in this vicinity. Holy Joe Canyon, Pasture (Elev. 4802'), Springs, and Wash share the name. Ref.: 18a

HOMOLOBI pro.: /howmowləouviʌ/
Hopi = "place of the breast-like elevation"
Navajo   Elev. c. 4000'
Hopi tribal history says that the name refers to the ruins of five abandoned towns on the north side of the river at Winslow, left deserted when irrigation waters brought alkali to the surface. Later Mormons had the same problem. Ref.: 167, p. 558; 224, pp. 6, 46

HONEY BUTTE
Gila   T4N R12E
The name was applied in 1926 because of the wild bees thriving in the "cavities in the cliffs on the slopes of the hill." Near the top of the butte quantities of honeycombs hang from the cliffs. Ref.: 329

HONEYMOON
Greenlee   T2N R28E
This name was applied after Johnny Wheatly, a young forest ranger, honeymooned at a ranger's cabin here. Ref.: Shannon; 18a; Fritz

HOOKER BUTTE
Graham   T11S R22E   Elev. 4892'
Henry Clay Hooker (b. 1828, New Hampshire; d. Dec. 5, 1907) in the 1880s owned the famed Sierra Bonita Ranch near here.

HOOKER'S HOT SPRINGS
Cochise   T21S R13E   Elev. 4008'
Dr. King discovered these steaming hot springs in 1881, and named them for Henry Clay Hooker, owner of nearby Sierra Bonita Ranch. King was killed by Indians in 1884. Ref.: 18a; AHS, H. C. Hooker File; 62

HOOPER
Yavapai   T10N R1W
The post office at this location served a mining camp on Towers Creek. It is not yet known why it was called Hooper, nor has any record been found that it was known as Forsythe (Barnes), although the second postmaster was John Forsythe. Hooper Saddle is also here.
P.O. est. July 20, 1899, Mrs. Jane Foresight, p.m.; disc. Jan. 31, 1916 Ref.: 18a; 242

HOOVER
Maricopa   T4N R2W
On the application to have a post office at this S.F.R.R. station, the postmaster noted it was to be "Hoover." Herbert Hoover's prominence during WW I may have led to the name.
P.O. est. May 4, 1914, H. E. Hursh, p.m.; disc. July 31, 1915 Ref.: 242

HOOVER DAM
Mohave   T30N R23W   Elev. 640' at river bed
By Act of Congress December 21, 1928, construction was authorized for a dam, planned originally to be in Boulder Canyon. Hence it was first known as Boulder Dam. On September 17, 1930 the Secretary of Interior ordered the name changed to honor

President Herbert Hoover. In 1934 when democrat Harold Ickes took office as Secretary of the Interior, he issued a regulation to again call it Boulder Dam. President Truman changed the name back to Hoover Dam, noting that Hoover rose above "partisanship to do a distinguished service for his country at the bidding of a democratic administration." The gates for the dam closed on February 1, 1935. The impounded waters formed Lake Mead. Hardin Ferry was at the place where Hoover Dam now stands. Ref.: 5, pp. 147, 337, 338; 200, pp. 15, 26, 37; 261, p. 168; "Hoover Dam," U.S. Dept. of Interior, Bureau of Reclamation, n.d.

HOOVEY CANYON
Cochise   T17S R29E

This canyon is named for a man who homesteaded here. In 1917 it was called Green Canyon, but by 1931 it had taken on the homesteader's name, misspelled Huvey. Ref.: 329

HOPE
La Paz   T4N R14W   Elev. 1531'

In 1909 the community of Johannesberg arose. It had a short existence because the main highway changed its route in 1920 to by-pass it. At that time merchants, who had already moved once, moved from Vicksburg to the new location, naming it "Hope" to reflect their hope for good business. Ref.: Lenon; *Arizona Gazette* (Nov. 4, 1909), p. 11

HOPE, MOUNT
Mohave   T18N R8W

In 1854 Lt. Whipple named this conical peak because his thirsty party saw smoke of Indian fires on it, a fact indicating to them that they would probably find water there. Therefore they called the peak Mount Hope. It was also called Hope Peak. Ref.: 347, pp. 187, 189; 163, p. 302

HOPE WINDOW
Apache   T6N R11W

In 1915 Herbert Gregory named this hole in a large rock for his student volunteer assistant, Edna Earl Hope. Ref.: 141, p. 192

HOPI BUTTES   pro.: /hówpiᴧ/
Hopi: *hopitu* = "peaceful ones"
Navajo   T23N R18E   Elev. c. 6000'

Herbert Gregory in 1915 asked that the name be accepted officially as Hopi Buttes. These buttes are so called because Hopi Indians live near them. Prior to 1857 Spaniards called them Moqui Buttes, a name unacceptable to Hopi Indians because of *moqui* meaning "dead." On September 7, 1857 Lt. Edward Fitzgerald Beale called the conical points of these buttes Rabbit Hills. They are also called Rabbit Ear Butte. Both are descriptive names. Mexicans called these peaks Cerritos Azules, translated as "Blue Peaks" on the 1860 Macomb map. Ref.: *Masterkey*, 19 (May 1945) 89-94; 23, p. 45; 79, p. 101; 141, p. 37, Note 1; 331, p. 101

HOPI INDIAN RESERVATION
Coconino/Navajo   T28N R14W

From 1869 to 1875 an Indian agency was maintained for the entire contemporary Navajo/Hopi area at Fort Defiance. On December 16, 1882 the Hopi Indian Reservation was established, being enlarged on January 8, 1900 to its present size. Hopi Indians reside mainly in seven major villages. The Hopi Indian Reservation is surrounded by the Navajo Indian Reservation. See Hopi Villages, Navajo
Ref.: *Hopi Constitution*; 15, II, 547; 167, II, 374; "Annual Report of the Arizona Commission of Indian Affairs, 1954, 1955, 1956," p. 9

HOPI POINT   pro.: /hówpiᴧ/
Hopi: *hopitu* = "peaceful ones"
Coconino (Grand Canyon)   T32N R4E   Elev. 7071'

This was first called Rowe's Point after Sanford Rowe, who held mining claims along the South Rim. In accordance with the plan to name some Grand Canyon locations after

Arizona Indian tribes, the name was changed in March 1906 to Hopi Point. It is near Hopi Wall (T31N/R2E). Ref.: Verkamp; 329

HOPI POINT TRAIL CANYON
Coconino   T29N R8E
This canyon is part of the long trail leading from the Hopi Villages to the Grand Canyon and to the Havasupai village. Ref.: 178, pp. 57, 153-156

HOPI VILLAGES
Navajo/Coconino
All but one (Moenkopi) of the following are in Navajo County. For information about individual villages, see main entry under village name of cross reference as listed in Appendix.

Village	Pronunciation	Village	Pronunciation
Awatobi	/awá?owbồᴬ/	Polacca	/pówlaᴬka/
Bakabi	/bá:kavʷiᴬ/	Shungopavi	/səmówəpaviᴬ/
Hotevila	/hówᴬtvʷelə/	Sichmovi	/sitówməoviᴬ/
Kawaioku	?	Sikyatki	/siᴬkiᴧpkiᴬ/
Kuchaptuvela	?	Sipaulovi	/šipówləviᴬ/ or
Mishongnovi	?		/sówlowᵊpaviᴬ/
Moenkopi	/mównəkapki/ or	Tewa	/téowᵛa/
	/mównkapi/	Walpi	/wál:əpiᴬ/
Oraibi	/owɽ̣áyviᴬ/		

The first "foreigners" known to have set foot in what is now Arizona were a barefoot friar, Marcos de Niza, and his Moorish companion, Estevan. In 1539 these two set out from Mexico with high hopes and very active imaginations. Along the route Estevan usually went ahead of the more timid friar. One day a messenger returned along to tell Marcos de Niza that according to Estevan to the northwest lay wondrous cities with houses several stories high. The Moor was, of course, referring to the Zuni villages of New Mexico, a drab reality which treasurer-seeking white men rapidly enveloped in the imagined gold of the Seven Cities of Cibola. To the west, said the Indians, lay the Hopi villages. Hastening to overtake his advance scout on May 9, 1539, the friar entered the "wilderness" near the present-day Fort Apache Indian Reservation. Here he learned that Indians had killed Estevan. The friar had only a few Indians attending him, and he feared advancing alone. However, determined to view these settlements where it was rumored the people used implements of gold, Marcos de Niza reportedly did so from the entrance of today's Jeddito Valley. Then he returned to Mexico City as fast as he could go. What he said about gold to the north caused a near stampede on the part of wealth seekers. They wanted to leave at once for the fabled Seven Cities of Cibola. Viceroy Mendoza organized an expedition, and on February 23, 1540, Francisco Vasquez de Coronado took his position at the head of a gala army determined to go north and seize the wealth. The adventurers had all the trappings of court — shining armor, vizored headpieces, footmen carrying harquebuses, tons of supplies borne by a thousand horses and mules; tents, servants and herds of sheep, swine and cattle to feed the army en route. Supplies dwindled rapidly and the heavy shining armor was soon abandoned to rust along the trail. On July 7, 1540 a bedraggled and discouraged band entered a Zuñi village. To their dismay, they realized it was merely a miserable assembly of stone and mud huts and was far from being the culmination of the treasure seekers' dream.

To investigate rumors about villages lying to the west, Coronado sent Don Pedro de Tobar. He found several villages. One source lists their names as Kawaiku, Awatobi, Sityatki, Kuchaptuvela (Old Walpi), old Shungopovy, old Mishongnovi, and Oraibi. None at that time was atop the mesas where some now are. From the Hopi Indians de Tobar learned that a great river (no doubt the Colorado River) lay several days' journey westward. He traveled to the great canyon rim and, disgusted, departed.

In 1583 Fr. Espejo called the region Mohoce, but mentioned only five villages. Late in 1598 came Juan de Oñate, who made vassals of the Indians. In 1629 a mission was established in the Province of Tusayan.

The transfer of entire villages from lowland to mesa top apparently began in 1680 concurrent with the Pueblo uprising when the Indians ousted the Spaniards from New Mexico in a bath of blood. Whether the Hopi feared Spanish retribution or attack by the invading Navajo is not entirely clear, but the new mesa-top villages provided effective defense against attack by either.

It is conjectured that the name Cibola derived from a word meaning "buffalo," that buffalo may have wandered as far west as the Zuñi towns, and that Mexicans possibly used the name for the region because it was the only locale in which they had seen buffalo. As for the Seven Cities portion, it derives from a legend that at the time of the Moorish invasion of Spain, a bishop escaped by sailing westward in a small fleet with an entire community of over fifteen hundred people and vast treasure. Rumors arose about his establishing a rich bishopric where gold was freely available. The legend led to dreams on the part of young adventurers. As for the name *Mohace*, Spaniards rendered it as *Moqui* or *Moki*, a name detestable to Hopi because in their own language it means "dead." Nevertheless the name Moki was applied until 1895 when the Smithsonian Institution adopted the name Hopi, derived from *hopitu*, the name used by the tribe for its own people. Ref.: Schellbach File (Grand Canyon); 1, p. 75; 15, pp. 47, 547; Bartlett, 21, p. 38, Note 1; 46, p. 185; 140, p. 16; 152, p. 20; 167, I, 560, 561; 347, p. 156, Note 12; 357, pp. 356, 357, 359, 361, 362, 377

HOPKINS, MOUNT
Santa Cruz   T20S R14E   Elev. 8572'
Gilbert W. Hopkins (b. New York, 1830; d. March 1, 1865) arrived in Arizona in 1859. He served in the Territorial Legislature and as Superintendent of the Maricopa Copper Mines before reporting as a mining engineer to the Santa Rita Mining Company. He was killed by Apaches in 1865, and this peak in the Santa Rita Mountains was named for him. The Smithsonian – University of Arizona Multiple Mirror Telescope (MMT) Observatory is on the peak. Ref.: 163, p. 190; AHS, Gilbert W. Hopkins File

HOP MOUNTAIN
Navajo   T9N R21E   Elev. 6882'
Wild hops grew abundantly on this mountain. Hop Canyon (T9N/R20E) is also here. Ref.: 18a

HORMIGUERO   pro.: /ormigéro/
Spanish = "ant hill"
Maricopa   "N. side of Salt R., 3 mi. from Mesa, 1902"
Hodge asserts that the name is probably a translation of Pima *Statannyik*, (= "many ants") and that it may have been identical with *Ormejea* because the two villages were apparently adjacent. Anglicizing the name resulted in Hermho, although some doubt exists whether the two are identical, as Hermho in Pima is said to mean "once." P.O. est. as Hermo, May 17, 1901, Lewis D. Nelson, p.m.; disc. Sept. 12, 1901 (never in operation) Ref.: 167, I, 569, and II, 149, 635; 281, p. 23

HORN
Yuma   T5S R12W
This section house on the S.P.R.R. may have been named for Tom Horn – or it may not. See Horn Creek, Coconino (Grand Canyon)
P.O. est. Aug. 1, 1954, Mrs. Erna M. Stewart, p.m.

HORN CREEK
Coconino (Grand Canyon)   T31N R2E
Henry Gannett in 1906 suggested the name for this creek for Tom Horn, an army scout who served under Gens. Willcox, Crook, and Miles. A swashbuckling adventurer, he worked as a cowboy, a deputy under three different sheriffs, a rancher, a soldier with the Rough Riders in the Spanish-American War, and as a cattle detective in Wyoming. After being convicted of murder, he died on a Wyoming gallows. Ref.: 329; AHS, Chambers Collection

HORN MOUNTAIN
Yavapai   T12N R4E   Elev. 5878'
Here an early settler named Horner built a rock cabin to make it more convenient to take care of his cattle and horses. On this peak Fred Dugas (see Dugas, Yavapai) discovered

the remains of the Craddlebaugh massacre on the rim above Gap Canyon. Dugas, who had chased an old steer for hours at an ambling pace, came up to the mesa top with the cow ambling just ahead. When the cow stumbled, Dugas threw himself off his horse and tried to tail down the steer. He made a good connection and was dragged into a mesquite circle where man and beast went around and around. When he realized that the circling dragged him by a heap of big mule heads piled together, Dugas let go to investigate and found the Craddlebaugh remains. Craddlebaugh, a lieutenant stationed at Camp Verde, was with a mule train of soldiers and supplies and was ambushed by Apaches, entirely wiping out the party. The piled mule bones indicated the Indians had a mule-meat feast. Ref.: Duggas; West

HORRELL CREEK
Maricopa/Gila/Pinal   T2N R13E   Elev. 3170'
Marion Horrell established a ranch on Pinto Creek. His son Earl had a ranch on the Apache Trail near Spring Creek. Both Louis Horrell (brother) and Ed (Marion's father) raised cattle in this vicinity. The family name was a natural for this creek. Ref.: Woody

HORSE CAMP
Gila   T11N R12E   Elev. 6408'
Bill "Horse" McFadden and his son Pecos ranged horses here on top of Horse Mountain for summer pasture and at Horse Camp Canyon (T6N/R15E). Horse Camp Creek is near Horse Camp. Related names include Horse Camp Seep and Horse Canyon (T7N/R15E, a.k.a. Rock House Canyon). Ref.: McKinney; McInturff

HORSE CANYON
Greenlee   T1S R31E   Elev. c. 6000'
Fred Fritz, Sr. used this small rough canyon to corral and pasture his horses. With the addition of only a few fences, the natural high walls of the canyon formed a fine corral. Ref.: Fred Fritz, Sr.

HORSEFALL CANYON
Cochise   T16–17S R29–30E   Elev. c. 4000'
In the early 1900s a forest ranger en route to fight a fire stumbled off the trail. Both he and the lead horse of the pack train were killed, hence the name. Ref.: Riggs

HORSE MESA
Maricopa   T3N R10E   Elev. c. 2000'
Before 1914 stock on Horse Mesa could escape only through one very narrow entrance, customarily blocked by stockmen. During the twice-yearly sheep trek, herds were sometimes confined near here. Herders also grazed saddle and pack horses on the mesa. Ref.: 329

HORSE MESA DAM
Maricopa   T3N R10E   Elev. 1920'
This subsidiary to Theodore Roosevelt Dam was completed in 1927. It impounded water to create Apache Lake. For the convenience of workers, a post office existed during the construction period. See also Apache Cave, Maricopa
P.O. est. as Horse Mesa, Dec. 20, 1926; Daniel J. Jones, p.m.; resc. Sept. 2, 1927 Ref.: 5, p. 367

HORSESHOE: The shape of various places has led to the descriptive use of the word *horseshoe*. Examples follow:

Horseshoe	Pima	See Quijotoa, Pima
Horseshoe Bend	Gila	T4N R15E
Horseshoe Bend	Pima	See Quijotoa, Pima
Horseshoe Bend	Yavapai	T21N R2W
Horseshoe Bend Wash	Gila	T2N R15E
Horseshoe Canyon	Cochise	T19S R31E

This was an Apache stronghold.

Horseshoe Cienega	Apache	T8N R25E	
Horseshoe Draw	Greenlee	T4S R28E	Elev. c. 4500'

The name was in use before 1880.

Horseshoe Hill	Coconino	T24N R6E	Elev. 8269'
Horseshoe Lake	Coconino	T12N R12E	Elev. c. 7500'

The shape of this lake in wet weather gives it its name (Barnes) but Hart says the lake was named for the One Horseshoe Ranch in existence before 1890.

Horse Shoe Mesa Caves Coconino (Grand Canyon) T30N R4E Elev. 5238'

On December 2, 1937 the USGS changed the name from Grand View Caves. See Grand View Trail, Coconino (Grand Canyon)

Horseshoe Rapids Coconino (Grand Canyon) Elev. c. 1000'

On September 24, 1871 Capt. George M. Wheeler gave his name to the bend in the Colorado River at the head of Black Canyon, noting that the canyon walls rose fully seventeen hundred feet. Ref.: 345, I, 159

HORSE TANKS
Yuma   T2S R19W

In pioneer days the main road from Yuma to Ehrenberg ran within two miles of this spot, where coach drivers watered horses. In 1878 Nick Gunther and a man named Farrar proposed running their horse freight line to take advantage of these water holes, cutting out Tyson Wells and Desert Station entirely. This series of natural rock tanks in the Castle Dome Mountains numbers about a dozen, with the higher ones accessible only after dangerous climbing. Only the middle tank is readily accessible. When full, it holds about seventy thousand gallons. Ref.: Monson; 58; *Arizona Sentinel* (Aug. 18, 1878), p. 2

HORSE TANK CANYON
Gila   T11N R12E

A series of natural pot holes makes it possible to water horses here, hence the name. See Horse Camp, Gila Ref.: McKinney

HORSETHIEF BASIN
Yavapai   T99N R1E   Elev. c. 5500'

This area earned its name because horse thieves used this small open area as a place to conceal stolen horses. Today there are summer homes in this area. Horsethief Lake lies behind a small dam on Horsethief Canyon. Ref.: 18a; Schnebly

HORSE THIEF PASS
Coconino   East of Walker Lake

The old stage road to Tuba City from Flagstaff passed on the east side of Walker Lake through what was called Horse Thief Pass because a log cabin at its entrance was used by Mormon horse thieves. Ref.: *Flagstaff Whoa!* p. 124

HORSE THIEF TANK
Coconino   T31N R2E

Horse thieves used this location at the head of Hermit Creek to water their stolen stock. Ref.: Kolb

HORSE WASH
Yavapai   T16N R4W

According to Barnes, "In pioneer days Wallapai Indians stole a number of horses from Camp Wallapai." Troops overtook the party in this wash, hence the name. Ref.: 18a

HORTON CREEK
Gila   T11N R12E

Willis B. Horton (b. 1850, Mississippi) in the early 1880s lived on this creek. It shares its name with Horton Canyon (T11N/R10E) and Horton Spring. Ref.: AHS

HORUS TEMPLE
Coconino (Grand Canyon)   T32N R2E   Elev. 6150'
This name is among those for gods and goddesses approved by the USGS in 1906. Ref.: 329

HOSFELT PEAK
Gila   T6N R10E   Elev. 5770'
This peak takes its name from the Hosfelt Ranch owned by Charles Hosfelt prior to . 1920. Ref.: 18a

HOSKININNI MESA   pro.: /háskəniyniy/
Navajo   T41N R18E   Elev. c. 6000'
Hoskininni (d. 1909), a Navajo leader, led his people and flocks to live here following the end of the Navajo campaign, hence the name. He was reported to have a rich silver mine. See Defiance, Fort, Apache Ref.: 5, p. 423; 141, p. 47; 129, p. 15

HOSPITAL FLAT
Graham   T9S R24E
A house was constructed to be used as a hospital here for soldiers from nearby Fort Grant. The soldiers shared it with their women and it was never used as a hospital. Ref.: Jennings

HOSPITAL GULCH
Cochise   T17S R31E
In this gulch at the mining community of Paradise the Chiricahua Development Company maintained its headquarters and hospital. Ref.: *Arizona Daily Star* (March 27, 1932); AHS, Bernice Cosulich File

HOTASON VO   pro.: /hodeyšownwow/
Papago = "foot-of-rock-hill charco"
Pima   T13S R3W   Elev. c. 2000'
This name describes the location of a small Papago village. In this case the charco (pond) is in rocks at the base of the hills, whence comes its name Charco de la Piedra (= "stone pond"). Ref.: 262, p. 8; 57, pp. 423-424; 329

HOTEVILA   pro.: /hówᐱtvʷələ/
Hopi = "scraped back"
Navajo   T29N R16E   Elev. 6320'
The name for this Hopi village is borrowed from that of Hotevila Spring where entering the low cave to obtain water often resulted in a skinned back. The spelling is that used in the Hopi Constitution. On the other hand, Elsie Clews Parsons interprets the word as "cedar slope." Gregory says the name is Navajo, meaning "springs at head of canyon," but actually the Navajo name is *T'ohchin To'* (= "wild onion spring"). Whatever the meaning, the community was settled in 1906 by Hopi who lost the tug of war at Oraibi. In the year following, part of the same group formed Bakabi. See Oraibi, Navajo, and Bakabi, Navajo
P.O. est. as Hotevilla, Sept. 10, 1916, Emory A. Marks, p.m.; disc. July 15, 1943; reest. Dec. 16, 1946 Ref.: *Hopi Constitution*; 331, p. 75; 71, p. 47; 141, p. 75; 242

HOTOUTA AMPHITHEATER
Coconino (Grand Canyon)   T33N R1E   Elev. 3150'
This amphitheater was named for a Havasupai Indian whose father, Tom, was a Navajo. Hotouta was the last great Havasupai leader. Ref.: 178, p. 78

HOUCK   pro.: /hawk/
Apache   T22N R30E   Elev. 6139'
James D. Houck, the first settler, established Houck's Tank here. In 1874 Houck carried mail from Prescott to Fort Wingate, New Mexico, and in 1877 set up a trading post at Houck's Tank. In 1885 Houck moved away, but not before a post office had been established under the name Houck at Houck's Tank. Navajo Indians knew the location

as Maitoe (= "coyote springs"). In the same period Allan Johnson, a construction worker with the A.T. & S.F.R.R. settled about a mile away to herd cattle. He established a shipping point on the railroad c. 1900 and a small community known as Allantown developed. Though often confused, the two communities were not identical. On the post office site record in the National Archives, the post office closest to Houck's Tank is noted in 1895 as being "Allantown, 5½ mi. easterly." Allantown was on the railroad whereas Houck (at Houck's Tank) was not, a fact which should be kept in mind while examining the post office history below.

P.O. est. as Houck's Tank, Dec. 16, 1884, James W. Bennett, p.m.; name changed to Houck, Nov. 23, 1895; Wells Fargo 1907. P.O. est. as Allantown, Oct. 14, 1924, Joseph A. Grubbs, p.m.; disc. June 20, 1930 (Allantown fell into disrepair and disappeared); name changed to Houck, July 1, 1930 Ref.: Grigsby; David H. Clark, Letter (May 11, 1956); 143, p. 159; 331, p. 76; 116, pp. 552, 609; 242

HOUDON MOUNTAIN   pro.: /huwdán/
Gila   T9N R12E   Elev. c. 6000'
Lewis Houdon, a Swiss prospector, mined this area with Bob Sixby until killed Apaches in July 1882 during the attack by Nan-tia-tish. See Haigler Creek, Gila   Ref.: 18a; Woody

HOUSE MOUNTAIN
Yavapai   T16N R5E
This mountain looks like a huge house, hence its name.   Ref.: 18a; Schnebly

HOUSE OF HANDS
Navajo   T40N R20E   Elev. c. 6000'
In 1949 the Valley of Mystery in Monument Valley was explored. One of the first ruins investigated had hundreds of white hands painted on the cliff wall. This ruin is also known as the House of Many Hands.   Ref.: 191, pp. 15-16

HOUSE ROCK
Coconino   T39N R2W   Elev. c. 5500'
The Mormon Road (a trail) from Utah Mormon settlements to the Hopi country offered sparse shelter. Some travellers used as a shelter two large rocks fallen together in an inverted vee. About 1871 some unknown person used charcoal from the night fires to write on the rocks, "Rock House Hotel." Others soon changed the name to its present form, applying the name to a nearby spring as well. House Rock Canyon and Valley share the name.   Ref.: 89, pp. 304, 305; 88, p. 160

HOUSE ROCK VALLEY
Coconino   T38-39N R3-4E
Since 1906 a buffalo herd has been maintained on vast grazing lands here. Originally, it was owned by Buffalo Jones and Uncle Jimmy Owens, who in 1926 offered to sell the herd to the State of Arizona for $10,000., the herd at that time consisting of about eighty head. The state finally set aside money for the purchase. The buffalo herd today is controlled by the Game and Fish Commission. The herd occupies a reserve established by the U.S. Forest Service in 1951. See House Rock, Coconino and also Uncle Jim Point [Coconino (Grand Canyon)]   Ref.: 71, p. 34; *Arizona Big Game Bulletin*, "Buffalo Number," p. 958; 124, p. 130, Note 92; 5, pp. 293-294

HOUSHOLDER PASS
Mohave   T28N R21W   Elev. c. 2000'
In the early 1930s engineers needed a road to Hoover Dam for transporting supplies. They called for help on Ross Housholder of Kingman, an engineer. Percy Jones, locating engineer for the Hoover Dam project, named the pass to honor Housholder's expert help.   Ref.: Housholder

HOUSTON MESA   pro.: /hyúwstən/
Gila   T11N R10E   Elev. c. 5000'
In the early 1880s the Houston family settled and grazed cattle here. A member of the family, Sam, died here when his stirrup, which was hooked over the saddle horn, accidentally hit his pistol in the saddle scabbard, discharging it. Shot in the leg, he bled to

death. Houston Pocket (T10N/ R11 E) was a winter horse range.   Ref.: Woody; Mrs. John Wentworth (née Katherine Houston)

HOWARD CANYON
Cochise   T14S R27E

A pioneering family by this name lived in the canyon for many years and worked mines nearby. The Howards have been gone since about 1940.   Ref.: Riggs

HOWARD LAKE
Coconino   T25N R1E   Elev. c. 5000'

Several place names in this vicinity take their name from that of Charles E. Howard (b. June 6, 1856; d. March 14, 1922), who arrived in Flagstaff in 1881. He set up the Howard Sheep Company in 1893, later settling its headquarters in Ashfork. The names include Howard Hill (T28N/R1E), Mesa, and Mountain (T19N/R7E), and Spring. Ref.: Fuchs, Letter (April 30, 1956), Quoting *Williams Notes* (March 24, 1922); Benham

HOWELL MESA
Navajo   T29N R14E

Herbert Gregory in 1915 named this mesa for Edward E. Howell, who made the "first geologic traverse" of the area for the 1873 Wheeler expedition. The area is also called Cedar Mesa.   Ref.: 14, p. 39, Note 2, and p. 191

HOWELL'S
Yavapai   T13N R1W

A smelter at this location bore the name of the man who built and ran it. The post office was also named for him.
P.O. est. Feb. 15, 1883, William Adams, Jr.; disc. Nov. 16, 1893   Ref.: 18a; 242

HOWLANDS BUTTE
Coconino (Grand Canyon)   T31N R4E   Elev. 5584'

In 1929 Frank Bond suggested that this butte be named for Seneca and W. R. Howland (brothers), who were with Maj. John Wesley Powell's first Grand Canyon expedition in 1869. Following several harrowing experiences, the Powell party arrived at dangerous rapids. The Howland brothers and William H. Dunn, believing their lives in extreme danger, refused to travel farther. Powell permitted them to leave and they climbed the canyon walls to their rim. Ironically, Indians mistook the three men for marauding whites and killed them on the Shivwits Plateau.   Ref.: 322, p. 54, Footnote

HOXWORTH SPRING
Coconino   T19N R8E

This spring was named for Harry H. Hoxworth in 1883, a pioneer merchant in the new town of Flagstaff.   Ref.: Slipper

HUACHUCA CANYON
Cochise   T21S R20E

In 1903 Heitman in his *Register of the United States Army* noted that this canyon was called Central Canyon (the site of Fort Huachuca). By 1918 it was being called Post Canyon, no doubt because of the location of the military post at its mouth. However, by the 1930s it was being referred to as Huachuca Canyon, a transfer name. See Huachuca, Fort, Cochise

HUACHUCA CITY
Cochise   T21S R20E

This small community at the north gate of Fort Huachuca was founded in 1958 as a local store and was soon surrounded by a few mobile homes. It is now a small community on the east side of the highway.

HUACHUCA, FORT   pro.: /wačúkə/
Pima: *huachuca* = "it rains here"
Cochise   T22S R19E   Elev. 4800'

Some confusion has existed about the meaning of the name for this military location. In actuality it is a transfer word, having been applied first to the most southerly of the Pima or Sobaipuri villages where Kino and his party arrived (today the site of the Babocomari Ranch). The Indian village was indeed at a place where it rained, resulting according to Bolton, in "a most fertile valley with *carrizales* or reed marches...." There is no evidence to support the conjecture that Apaches borrowed this word to indicate "thunder." It is interesting to note that on the Nicolas de Lafora map of 1771 the term *Guachuca* is applied to a small stream entering the San Pedro River from the west near the Mexican border in what is today Arizona. How the name came to be transferred to the Huachuca Mountains is not clear. They were called the Sierra Espuela (Spanish = "spur, rowel") on an 1868 military map on which they were also referred to as Huatchua Mountains.

Camp Huachuca, which lies below Huachuca Peak, succeeded Camp Wallen on March 3, 1877, being established at the mouth of Central Canyon and taking its name apparently from its position on the east side of the Huachuca Mountains. Apache marauding necessitated enlarging the post and on January 21, 1871 its status was changed from a temporary camp to a permanent fort. After Geronimo's surrender in 1876, the post was relatively inactive until the Madero revolution in Mexico in 1911. It then became headquarters for border troops, reaching maximum importance during World War II with a complement of twenty-two thousand soldiers and eight thousand civilians. In 1949 the fort was transferred to the State of Arizona for its National Guard and was soon abandoned as a military establishment. However, with the increasing importance of electronic warfare, the post was reactivated in the early 1950s. By 1980 it had increased tremendously in importance, having an impact on enlarging nearby communities. It shares its name with that of Huachuca City and Huachuca Terrace. P.O. est. Camp Huachuca, Feb. 17, 1879 (to serve about three hundred), Frederick L. Austin, p.m.; name changed to Fort Huachuca, April 28, 1891; Wells Fargo 1885   Ref.: 43, p. 248, Note 2 and p. 360; 143, p. 137; 159 ..., II, 510; 242; 5, p. 392; De Lafora map (Huntington Library); 278, p. 222

HUACHUCA TERRACE

Cochise

This is a small community developed by the Utah Construction Company beginning in 1955. See Huachuca, Fort, Cochise

P.O. est. as San Jose Branch, Bisbee, July 5, 1955

HUALAPAI BAY   pro.: /wálǝpay/

Mohave (Lake Mead)   T30N R17W

This bay takes its name from that of the Hualapai Indians. In 1960 the name of this location was changed from Hualpai to its current correct spelling. See Hualapai Indian Reservation, Mohave   Ref.: 329

HUALAPAI CANYON

Coconino (Grand Canyon)   T32N R4W

In 1960 the current name was applied to this canyon to replace the older Hualpai and Walapai, both misconceptions of the spelling of the name of this tribe. See Hualapai Indian Reservation, Mohave   Ref.: 329

HUALAPAI INDIAN RESERVATION   pro.: /wálǝpay/

Hualapai = "pine tree people"

Coconino/Mohave   T25–33N R6–15W

The Hualapai Indians, a relatively small tribe, were originally Yuman Indians who lived on the middle portion of the Colorado River above the area occupied by Mohave Indians. They also inhabited the Sacramento, Yavapai, and Hualapai valleys in the Cerbat and Aquarius Mountains. Later they moved to live in the interior mountains. The tribe endured prolonged and severe struggles with intruding white men, and finally agreed to move to a reservation on the Colorado River (see Cherum Peak, Mohave) where they did not prosper. On January 4, 1883 a reservation in their native mountains was established. Additional acreage was allotted to form the current 997,045 extent. Tribal headquarters are at Peach Springs, Mohave.

The name Hualapai is attached to the following:

Hualapai Falls   See Mooney Falls, Mohave

Hualapai Island   Mohave (Lake Mead) T31N R17W

The USGS applied the name in 1960.

Hualapai Mountains   Mohave   T16–20N R15–16W   Elev. 7000'

These mountains bore the name Cerbat Mountains on the King map (1866). In 1960 the USGS corrected the spelling of the name from Hualpai to the current correct spelling.

Hualapai Peak   Mohave   T20N R15W   Elev. 8628'

Hualapais Spring   Mohave

The King-Gardner map of 1869 shows this spring in the pass through the Hualapais (*sic*) Mountains.

Hualapai Valley   Mohave   T22–28N R17–15W

In 1966 this name was corrected from the former Hualpai by the USGS.

Hualapai Wash   Mohave   T27–30N R17W

By USGS edict, this name replaced the former Hualpai Wash in 1960.

Hualpai   Mohave   See Hualapai Bay, Mohave

HUALPAI, CAMP

Yavapai   T18N R15W   Elev. 6000'

Because the troublesome Hualapai were quiet, Col. William Redmond Price recommended establishing a temporary camp in this vicinity on May 9, 1869. Camp Toll Gate was set up in a pass of the Aztec Mountains on a level mesa overlooking Walnut Creek. It was on the toll road between Prescott and Hardyville, owned by Capt. William H. Hardy (see Hardyville, Mohave). The name was changed to Camp Hualpai on August 1, 1870. It was abandoned on August 27, 1873. However, a community apparently developed, because a post office enjoyed a brief life at this location. Martha Summerhayes referred to it as "old" Camp Hualpai, describing it as a pleasant pine grove. Name changed to Juniper (see Juniper, Yavapai).

P.O. est. Nov. 22, 1882, Charles A. Behn, p.m.; disc. April 2, 1883
Ref.: 156, p. 137; 314, p. 72

Hualpai Island   Mohave   See Hualapai Island, Mohave

HUATCHUH MOUNTAINS

Cochise

These mountains are apparently about eighteen miles north of Babocomari Creek on an 1879 manuscript map. They may be either the Huachuca Mountains or possibly the current Winchester Mountains. See Huachuca, Fort, Cochise   Ref.: Huntington Library, Manuscript Map

HUBBARD

Graham   T6S R25E   Elev. c. 2500'

This community was organized as a branch of the Pima Ward, LDS, May 14, 1899, and became a separate ward on June 27, 1900, being called Hubbard to honor Elisha Freeman Hubbard, Sr., bishop for the settlement. The location is sometimes referred to as Kimbal, the name for a Mormon dam which later burned.

P.O. est. March 7, 1902, John Hancock, p.m.; disc. March 31, 1912
Ref.: 322, p. 187; 242; Jennings

HUBBELL BUTTE

Coconino (Grand Canyon)   T32N R5E (west wall)   Elev. 6450'

Frank Bond suggested the name for this butte in July 1929 to honor Juan Lorenzo Hubbell (b. Nov. 27, 1853, New Mexico; d. Nov. 12, 1930). Hubbell arrived in Arizona in 1871 and established a trading post at Ganado on the Navajo Indian reservation. Not only was he an outstanding trader to the Navajo, but he served as Coconino County sheriff and also in both the territorial and state legislatures.

Just below Hubbell Hill is the trading post operated by Hubbell for many years, today a national historical site established on April 3, 1967. An interesting story exists concerning the establishment of the trading post. Although the first trading post was at Ganado Lake and was operated by Charles Crary in 1871, nothing existed at the spot where today the Hubbell hacienda stands. At this exact spot Hubbell was attacked by hostile Navajos, who decided to burn him at the stake. They tied him to a mesquite tree and piled fire wood at his feet. A second Navajo party appeared and one of these Indians slashed the rawhide thongs binding Hubbell to the tree. The Indian rescuer said, "You no kill him, he my brother." The marauders returned Hubbell's goods and the entire incident became the inception of Lorenzo Hubbell's friendship with all Navajo. He lies buried on Hubbell Hill overlooking Ganado between the graves of his wife and Chief Many Horses, his Indian brother.   Ref.: 329; 331, p. 65

HUDGIN MESA
Santa Cruz   T15E R15S
When Paylin Hudgin was courting, he and his fiancée used to land his plane here on the east side of the Santa Rita Mountains for a picnic.   Ref.: P. Hudgin

HUERFANO BUTTE   pro.: /wǽrfáno/
Spanish = "orphan"
Pima   T18S R15E   Elev. c. 3500'
This little butte stands like an orphan near the Santa Rita Mountains. Here Apaches lanced Mrs. Larcena Pennington Page and pushed her over a cliff. The Indians took and wore her shoes to make tracks which would deceive her would-be rescuers. She heard the rescue party go by, but was unable to call out and lay there for days in bitter cold weather. She recovered sufficiently to make her way home without food or shoes and with only snow-water to drink.   Ref.: 205, p. 150

HUETHAWALI, MOUNT   pro.: /hwəwaliy/
Coconino (Grand Canyon)   T33N R1W
This is the Indian name for what has been described as "an almost detached mountain, crowned with irregular cross-bedded layers of white sandstone," near the center of the Grand Canyon.   Ref.: 329; 178, p. 81

HUGGINS PEAK
Pinal   T4S R18E   Elev. 4356'
According to Barnes, this peak near Bud Ming's ranch was called Quartzite Peak until about 1910. Then Albert Crockett borrowed the name Huggins Peak from that of a mountain in New Mexico. In 1915 Ming supplied the name Huggins Peak to government surveyors. There is a Quartzite Mountain nearby, which may indicate an error on Barnes' part.   Ref.: 18a

HUGHES, MOUNT
Santa Cruz   T21S R16E   Elev. 5861'
In 1867 Thomas Hughes (b. 1845, Pennsylvania) established the Pennsylvania Ranch at the base of the highest ridge which today bears his name. Apaches during one attack in March 1874 killed twenty-two on the Hughes ranch, going so far as to seize the ranch itself. Hughes crept back at night and liberated about one hundred hogs. His ranch had several names, the first being Cuevacita (Spanish = "little cave") because several caves are near a spring on the property. It was so named by Sr. Apodaca, a Spanish-American ranch owner in partnership before 1870 with "Frenchie" Lazzard. Lazzard sold to Hughes. A second name may have arisen because Hughes had a mentally retarded man working for him and the cowboys jokingly said that Hughes had bought a monkey and was training him to be a cowboy. This may be the origin of the name Monkey Springs Ranch. Hughes sold his ranch to Ashburn and Vail, who used the spring when they bought the ranch. They changed the ranch name to Monkey Springs Ranch. However, a Monkey Springs is documented on the 1875 map in *Arizona as It Is*. No evidence has arisen to indicate that the name Monkey Springs is a corruption of the name of Juan Mateo Manje, Fr. Kino's lieutenant. When Rollin R. Richardson bought the ranch in 1883, he called it the Pennsylvania Ranch to honor his native state.   Ref.: 62; AHS, Mary Gardner Kane File; AHS, James Gardner File & Thomas Gardner File; AHS, Rollin R. Richardson; 224, p. 201; Lenon

HUITZIL POINT   pro.: /hwiytziyl/
Coconino (Grand Canyon)   T32N R1W   Elev. 6281'
This point on the southeast side of Aztec Amphitheater was named for a Mexican tribe in June 1908.   Ref.: 329

HULL HILL
Yavapai   T2E R17N   [?]
This hill was named for George Washington Hull (b. c. 1836), an early prospector in Yavapai County who at one time owned nearly all the mining property in the Verde District. Hull Spring is on the hill.   Ref.: *Jerome Reporter* (dec. 28, 1899), p. 3

HULL TANK
Coconino (Grand Canyon)   T30N R4E
This tank was constructed by Phillip Hull, Jr., and his brother near the Rim of the Grand Canyon, it being the first watering tank in the vicinity. Hull brought horses to Hull Prairie in 1876. The name applies also to Hull Mountain, Hull Spring, and Hull Wash.   Ref.: Schellbach File, Grand Canyon

HUMBOLDT
Yavapai   T13N R1E   Elev. 4581'
On November 7, 1905 the name of this location was changed from Valverde to honor Baron Alexander von Humboldt (1769-1859), who had predicted that "the riches of the world would be found" in the center of the Great Peck Mining Company area. Both gold and silver were smelted at Humboldt until 1928.
P.O. est. Oct. 18, 1899 as Val Verde, John L. Davis, p.m.; name changed to Humboldt, Nov. 7, 1905; Wells Fargo 1906   Ref.: Schnebly; 5, p. 305; 242; Huntington Library

HUMBUG CREEK
Yavapai
This creek took its name in 1878 from the Humbug Mining District through which it runs. Miners who had heard rumors about good prospects on this creek called the whole thing a *humbug*. See Columbia, Yavapai

HUMMING BIRD SPRING
Maricopa
This spring in the Bighorn Mountains seventeen miles from the Palo Verde Mine, was named for the Humming Bird Mines owned by E. R. Cartwright.   Ref.: 279, p. 210

HUMMING BIRD SPRINGS
Pinal
A military party pursuing Indians in December 1872 reported camping at these springs at the summit of the Pinal Mountains, and that it was called *El Ojo de Chuparosa* (= "Humming Bird Springs").   Ref.: 210, p. 392

HUMPHREYS PEAK
Coconino   T23N R7E   Elev. 12,670'
The highest peak in Arizona is Humphreys Peak, an extinct volcano. It is one of three forming a rough U-shaped valley called the Inner Basin or Interior Valley. It was named in 1873 by G. K. Gilbert for his superior officer, Brig. Gen. Andrew Atkinson Humphreys, who had served with the Ives Expedition as a captain in 1851. On early maps Humphreys Peak was called San Francisco Peak. Old timers referred to it as Fremont Peak as often as they called it Humphreys Peak.   Ref.: 5, pp. 9, 319; 345, I, 32; *San Francisco Peaks*, pp. 1-2

HUNDRED-AND-FIFTY-MILE CANYON
Mohave (Grand Canyon)   T34N R4–5W
This canyon was named by Maj. John Wesley Powell because his party encountered it one hundred-fifty miles from where the plane-table traverse started.   Ref.: 329

HUNT
Apache   T14N R26E   Elev. c. 5500'
After leaving the service at Fort Apache in June 1872, Col. James Clark Hunt (b. July 21, 1836; d. March 29, 1890) settled at this location. An agricultural settlement developed, which had a post office. At the time the post office application was made, the place was known locally as Rockwood.
P.O. est. July 12, 1902, John H. Greer, p.m.; disc. Sept. 30, 1927   Ref.: Wiltbank; 225, p. 184; 242

HUNT CANYON (NO. 1)

Cochise   In Chiricahua National Monument
Elev. c. 5500'

Gov. George Wylie Paul Hunt (b. Nov. 1, 1859, Missouri; d. Dec. 24, 1934) served as governor six times. He had arrived in Globe penniless in July 1881 and was its first mayor when the town incorporated. During a visit to the Wonderland of Rocks, William Riggs advised the Governor against riding a horse known for its weak knees. Costumed in white riding clothes despite the rainy weather, Hunt insisted on riding the horse. In this canyon its knees did buckle, and the Governor tumbled off. The sad effect on his white riding habit ended his journey into the Wonderland of Rocks, but he left his name and dignity in this canyon.   Ref.: Riggs

HUNT CANYON (NO. 2)

Cochise   T20S R29E

This canyon is named for a cowboy who in the early 1880s turned rustler and murderer. According to the 1880 U.S. Census, his name was Zuing Hunt (*sic*) (b. 1858, Texas; d. April 1882). He arrived in Tombstone as a law-abiding freighter and cowboy, but soon began rustling cattle, a crime for which he was indicted in late 1881. Hunt disappeared into Mexico, returning in March 1882. He was said to be present when a Mr. Peel was murdered at the Tombstone mill, and next reported at Chandler's Ranch where shooting left one dead and several wounded. Hunt was wounded, captured, and brought to the county hospital. From there he was taken quietly at night in a wagon and was not seen again. About a month later his brother Hugh Hunt led a party to the place where "Zwing" was buried. His body had not been mutilated in the usual Apache fashion, so Indians had not killed him. On a nearby tree trunk was carved his name and the date of his death, and from that fact came the name of Hunt Canyon. Legend says that Hunt may have buried his treasure from the Skeleton Canyon massacre in the canyon where he himself lies buried. See also Skeleton Canyon, Cochise   Ref.: 241, pp. 218-219; 219, pp. 154-155, 156-157, 159-160; 60, p. 120; 63

HUNTER'S POINT

Apache   T25N R30E   Elev. 6620'

This place was named for John G. Hunter, a Navajo agent at Leupp in 1927. Ref. 331, p. 77

HURON

Yavapai   T13S R1E

The post office was at or in the railroad station on the Prescott-Middleton branch of the A.T. & S.F.R.R. As Huron (Michigan) had mines, this may be a transfer name. P.O. est. Oct. 27, 1901, Harry M. Stamp, p.m.; disc. Nov. 10, 1928; Wells Fargo 1903   Ref.: 242

HURRICANE CREEK

Apache   c. T6N R26E

This creek derives its name from the fact that in the early 1880s a high wind blew down trees along both its banks.   Ref.: 18a

HURRICANE LEDGE

Mohave   T40N R10W

Maj. John W. Powell applied the name to this ledge by transfer from the name of Hurricane Hill, where Mormons exploring for a road were caught by a high wind storm, hence the name. The name applies also to Hurricane Cliffs and to Hurricane Creek.   Ref.: 329; 88, p. 190; 89, pp. 308-309

HUTCH MOUNTAIN

Coconino   T17N R9E   Elev. 8650'

"Hutch," a sheepman named Hutchinson, kept sheep on this mountain.   Ref.: 18a

HUTTMAN WELL

Maricopa   T7N R9W

Hugo Huttman owned wells here.   Ref.: 279, p. 210

HUTTON BUTTE

Coconino   T33N R5E   Elev. 5500'

Oscar Hutton (b. c. 1830, Virginia; d. 1873 Tucson) was reputed to have killed more Indians than any other man in Arizona. He arrived in Arizona in 1863 and served with the Arizona Volunteer Infantry at Calabasas as a Second Lt. (1865-66), moving to Camp Date Creek. He was discharged on November 3, 1866, and was a packer and interpreter. In 1871 he was a guide at Camp Grant. He died when a mule kicked his face. Associated names include Mount Hutton or Hutton Peak (Gila, T1S/R13E, Elev. 5615') (named in 1875). Ref.: 329; AHS, Oscar Hutton File

HUXLEY TERRACE

Coconino (Grand Canyon)   T3N R1W

This area at the lower end of Granite Gorge in 1901 was called Observation Plateau, but the name was changed in June 1908 to Huxley Terrace. It is the central of three plateaus named for evolutionary scientists (the others being Darwin and Wallace). Thomas Henry Huxley (1825-1895) was an English biologist and philosopher whose lectures and essays in support of Darwin's theory earned him the name "Darwin's Bulldog." Ref.: 329; 178, p. 82

H-V RESERVOIR

Apache   T8N R31E

This is a small reservoir for watering cattle. It is named for the H-V brand, in existence since the 1880s. It is also known as Coyote Reservoir. Ref.: 329

HYDER

Yuma   T5S R11W   Elev. 536'

This is a station established in 1927 on the Phoenix-Welton branch of the S.P.R.R. Although legend says the name is "an Egyptian derivative meaning 'warm springs,' " the name actually has no such meaning. Hyder is a misspelling of Hayter, the name of the man who developed nearby Le Sage. Hyder Valley borrowed the name c. 1950. See Le Sage, Yuma Ref.: Mahomet Radwan, University of Arizona; 18a; Mrs. Howard Johnson (Dateland); 329

I

IBEX PEAK
La Paz   T5N R17W   Elev. 2800'
Although people used to tell stories about ibex in this vicinity, actually the animals were
ewes of mountain sheep. A group of domestic goats gone wild also used to live on this
peak. Their horns, too, resembled those of ibex. Ref.: Mercer

ICEBERG CANYON
Mohave   T32N R16W   Elev. c. 2000'
Because of the shape of the north wall of this canyon, Capt. George M. Wheeler in 1871
reportedly named it, although another observer says that Iceberg Canyon cuts through
the base of a tilted block and this may have resulted in its resemblance to an iceberg,
hence the name. Ref.: 89, p. 298; 200, p. 19

ICE CAVE
Coconino   T23N R8E
A few feet below the earth's surface these volcanic caves contain ice the year around. In
the 1880s ice from here was used in Flagstaff saloons. Ref.: 18a

ICEHOUSE CANYON
Gila   T1S R15E   Elev. c. 5000'
August Pieper (d. 1931), who arrived in Globe in 1883 from Silver City, New Mexico,
dug tanks here. It was named Icehouse Canyon because during the winter the tanks froze
and people cut and stored the ice. Pieper hauled ice to Globe by ox team and sold it for
25¢ per pound, mainly to saloons. Ref.: Ernest Pieper (son)

ICE POND
Coconino   T21N R2E
Prior to 1907 this pond was created by damming waterholes. Ice was cut for local use.
Ref.: Benham; Terry

I D TANK
Apache   T3N R24E
This waterhole is used by Apache tribal herds on what is called the *I*nterior *D*epartment
Ranch, hence the term I D Tank. Ref.: Davis

ILGES, CAMP
Maricopa   T6N R5E
This camp, in existence in 1867, was named for Maj. Guido Ilges. In 1873 Maj. Ilges
was a member of the Seventh Infantry. In 1879 he was transferred to the Fifth Infantry.
Ref.: 159, pp. 511, 562; 156, p. 183

I M PEAK
Yavapai   T10N R5E   Elev. 5988'
I M was the brand used by Jim Morrell, who ranged cattle here. Ref.: Dugas

IMPERIAL CANAL

Yuma (Mexico)   T6S R21W

In 1912 Emory Kolb wrote that this abandoned canal had nearly been destroyed by a great flood which in "a single night cut an eighty foot channel in the unyielding soil, and what had once been the northern end of the California Gulf was turned into an inland sea, filled with turbid waters of the Colorado...." See Imperial Dam, Yuma/California Ref.: 192, p. 312

IMPERIAL DAM

Yuma/California   T6S R21W

Originally called Cocopah Dam Site No. 3, this dam took its name from that of Imperial Valley, California, the largest area irrigated by (the All-American Canal) lower Colorado River water. Ref.: William J. Williams, Letter, Bureau of Reclamation, Boulder City, Nevada (June 4, 1956)

IMPERIAL VALLEY WILD LIFE REFUGE

La Paz   T3S R23W

This refuge established on March 14, 1941, encompasses 27,675 acres where bighorn sheep, Canada geese, ducks, herons, egrets, and other wild life abound.
Ref.: "Official Environmental Statement," U.S. Fish and Wild Life *Imperial Brochure*

IMPERIAL, POINT

Coconino (Grand Canyon)   T33N R4E   Elev. 8801'

The term "Imperial" applies to the dominance of this highest point on either the North or South Rim.

IMPERIAL WELL

Yuma   T8S R21W   Elev. c. 1000'

Alberto Imperial owned this well. Ref.: 279, p. 210

INDEPENDENCE, CAMP

Yuma   Elev. c. 220'

Camp Independence was established June 8, 1851 on the east bank of the Colorado near its junction with the Gila River, under the command of Lt. Thomas W. Sweeny. The command had one non-commissioned officer and nine enlisted men. Concerning its name, Sweeny states, "As touching myself it is an appropriate name for though I am not Monarch of all I survey my orders there are none to dispute." Fort Yuma on the California side of the Colorado replaced the camp in December 1851.
Ref.: 315, pp. 52, 54, 55

INDIAN: Considering that fourteen Indian tribes call Arizona home, it is not surprising that well over one hundred and fifty place names begin with the word *Indian*. In the following listing it may be assumed, unless information is given to the contrary, that the places have been named because of one of the following: (1) signs of former Indian habitation; (2) Indians living at the place; (3) encounter with an Indian or Indians, peaceful or otherwise; (4) place used by Indians; (5) fancied resemblance to an Indian.

Indian Butte	Gila/Maricopa	T6N R16E	Elev. Gila: 4975' Maricopa: 3745'
Indian Butte	Pinal	T7S R3E	Elev. 23,114'
Indian Buttes	Maricopa	T5N R5W	Elev. 1918'
Indian Camp Wash	Pinal	T5S R14E	
Indian Cave Spring	Greenlee	T2S R31E	
Indian Canyon	Cochise	T21S R28E	
Indian Canyon	Greenlee	T2N R31E	
Indian Canyon	Mohave	T30N R10W	
Indian Canyon	Pinal	T4S R18E	
Indian Canyon	Navajo	T7N R18E	

Indian Canyon	Yuma	T13S R18W	
Indian Creek	Gila/Navajo	T4N R22E	

According to local residents, signs of Indian habitation extend along this twelve-mile creek across Indian Flat. Indian Creek is also known as Nash Creek. Ref.: 329; Woody

Indian Creek	Greenlee	T2S R31E	

See Apache Gulch, Greenlee

Indian Creek	Yavapai	T13N R2W	

See Weaver, Yavapai

Indian Creek	Yavapai	T11N R3E	
Indian Cure Springs	Yavapai	T11N R26E	
Indian Delia's Place	Gila		

See Conley Point, Gila

Indian Flat	Coconino	T24N R7E	
Indian Flat	Navajo	T4N R22E	

See Indian Creek, Gila/Navajo

Indian Gardens	Coconino	T18N R6E	Elev. c. 4500'

At this location in Oak Creek Canyon, Yavapai or possibly Apache Indians raised vegetables. Ref.: Bartlett; 5, p. 330

Indian Gardens	Coconino (Grand Canyon)	T31N R3E	Elev. 3876'

A Havasupai family cultivated a garden here on Bright Angel Plateau, a fact known as early as 1869. Today the location is a stop for people using Bright Angel Trail. Ref.: 178, p. 33

Indian Gardens	Gila	T11N R12E	

This was one of the numerous gardens where Apaches raised pumpkins, beans, corn, and other produce. They also had gardens at Rice, Wheatfields, and near the Inspiration Mine. Ref.: Woody; 18a

Indian Gardens	Mohave	T28N R13W	
Indian Garden Spring	Coconino (Grand Canyon)	T31N R3E	

The father of Arizona Sen. Henry Fountain Ashhurst located this spring in 1887. See Indian Gardens, Coconino (Grand Canyon) Ref.: Cameron, *The Bright Angel Trail*, p. 14

Indian Head Canyon	Pinal	T7S R17E	
Indian Head Mountain	Santa Cruz	T22S R16E	Elev. 5400'
Indian Hill	Yavapai	T18N R1W	
Indian Hill	Yavapai	T13N R2W	

The first name for Indian Hill was Alex's Decoy. The name memorialized Indians ambushing and killing William Alexander here in 1865. Ref.: Kitt

Indian Hollow	Coconino	T35N R2W	
Indian Hot Springs	Graham	T5S R24E	Elev. 2795'

Here Indians used four hot springs medicinally, hence the name. In 1899 the Alexander brothers bought what was then known as Holladay Hot Springs and built a resort hotel, changing the name to Indian Hot Springs. Three springs — Beauty, Iron, and Mud — (have temperatures from 116°F to 119°F) and Magnesium Springs is 81°F.
Ref.: Jennings; *Arizona Bulletin* (May 26, 1899), p. 3; 5, p. 343

Indian Knoll	Mohave	T40N R5W	Elev. 5977'
Indian Lake	Coconino	T35N R3E	
Indian Mesa	Yavapai	T7N R1E	
Indian Oasis	Pima		

See Sells, Pima

Indian Oasis Mountain	Pima	T18S R4E	
See Sells, Pima			
Indian Pass	Mohave	T31N R22W	
Indian Peak	Greenlee	(1) T4N R31E	Elev. 8787'
		(2) T3N R30E	Elev. 8560'
Indian Peak	Maricopa		
See Little Granite Mountain, Maricopa			
Indian Peak	Yavapai	T18N R5W	Elev. 5455'
Indian Peak Wash	Mohave	T13N R19W	
Indian Pine	Navajo	T8N R23E	Elev. 7150'
Indian Point	Coconino	T18N R6W	
Indian Point	Coconino (Grand Canyon)	T32N R4E	
See Obi Point, Coconino (Grand Canyon)			
Indian Point	Maricopa	T6N R8E	Elev. 3684'
See Little Granite Mountain, Maricopa			
Indian Rock	Navajo	T14N R19E	
Indian Rocks	Greenlee	T8S R31E	
Indian School	Pima		
See Escuela, Pima			
Indian Spring	Cochise	T12S R32E	
Indian Spring	Graham	(1) T1S R22E (2) T4S R21E (3) T7S R22E	
Indian Spring	Maricopa	(1) T6N R8E (2) T3N R10E (3) T6N R6E	
Indian Spring	Mohave		
See Peach Springs, Mohave			
Indian Spring	Mohave	(1) T19N R19W (2) T18N R11W	
Indian Spring	Navajo	T27N R20E	
Indian Spring	Pinal	T3S R13E	
Indian Spring	Yavapai	T10N R2W	
Indian Spring Canyon	Maricopa	T6N R8E	
Indian Spring Peak	Maricopa	T6N R8E	Elev. 4920'
Indian Spring Wash	Maricopa	T6N R6E	
Indian Springs	Cochise	T12S R32E	
Indian Springs	Yavapai	(1) T17N R5W (2) T10N R2W	
Indian Springs Canyon	Cochise	T12S R32E	
Indian Springs Creek	Yavapai	T10N R2W	
Indian Springs Wash	Yavapai	T17N R5W	
Indian Tank Hill	Apache	T8N R30E	
Indian Village	Maricopa		
See Kyrene, Maricopa			
Indian Well Spring	Navajo	T11N R19E	
Indian Well Wash	Pinal	T10S R13E	
Indian Wells	Navajo	T23N R21E	Elev. c. 5500'

On the route to Keams Canyon and Holbrook, Navajos here dug a well. Rev. William R. Johnson in

1912 began a mission to supplement the store and post office. The Navajo name for the location is *Tohahadleeh* (= "where water is looped out"). They also call it *Bidahoche* (= "many red streaks up its slope"), referring to the nearby butte.

P.O. est. Feb. 12, 1910, G. L. Hubbell, p.m.; disc. 1965 Ref.: Burcard; 242; 331, p. 77; 143, p. 166

INFERNO, THE
Coconino (Grand Canyon)   T31N R2E
This descriptive name was first used on the 1906 Bright Angel USGS quadrangle map.
Ref.: 329

INGALLS LAGOON
Yuma   T9S R24W   Elev. c. 250'
In 1883 Capt. Frank S. Ingall (b. 1851, Maine; d. 1927) reported to Yuma to supervise the territorial prison. In an effort to discover which produce would grow well in the area, he farmed at Ingalls Lagoon. Ref.: Mrs. Addie Ingall Kline (daughter)

INGLESIDE
Maricopa   T2N R4E   Elev. 1300'
Now a private school, this location in 1884 was first a resort community under the aegis of William J. Murphy, who was responsible for planting the first citrus in Salt River Valley. Ref.: 177, pp. 437, 438

INITIAL POINT
Maricopa   T1S R1E   Elev. c. 1000'
Congress on July 2, 1864 provided for surveying within Arizona Territory and surveys went forward from Initial Point. A. B. Gray, surveyor for the boundary survey of Arizona, c. 1853 set up this first triangulation station for the Gila River survey, hence the name Initial Point;. Ref.: Lenon; 107, IV, 303-304

INSCRIPTION HOUSE
Coconino   T39N R17E   Elev. c. 5000'
In 1909 John Wetherill studied the half-obliterated inscription on this Indian pueblo ruin, making out the letters *CHOS* and the date 1661, followed by the letters *A d n*, obviously placed there by Spaniards. Ref.: 129, p. 162; 13, Brewer, "Navajo National Monument," p. 6; 177, p. 61

INSPIRATION
Gila   T1N R15E   Elev. 4907'
Isaac Copeland and William Scanlon owned the mine. According to legend, they needed money and had an "inspiration" to borrow from a bank, using the money to establish a successful mine which they named after the event. A second legend relates that Copeland, a spiritualist, had a vision or dream about the mine and then discovered it. The post office for the Inspiration Mine was established at the Warrior siding on the Arizona Eastern R.R. The company-owned community includes Moonshine Hill and the remains of the former Mexican village, Los Adobes, which had to be abandoned when the undermined ground began caving in. See Claypool, Gila
P.O. est. Jan. 3 1917, Robert Bruce Whithane, p.m. Ref.: 5, p. 347; AHS; 242

INSPIRATION POINT
Gila   Elev. c. 3500'
At this location on the Apache Trail at Theodore Roosevelt Dam, visitors have their first view of the lake. Aubrey Drury in November 1917 suggested the name to the S.P.R.R., which erected a tourist lodge here, now gone. Ref.: 329; Woody

IRENE
Pima   T16S R7E
This location on the railroad served the Irene Mine, named for Irene Matas (b. Sept. 17, 1888, Los Angeles, California). Locally the place is called Three Bridges because here tracks go both under and over the old highway.
Ref.: Lenon; AHS, Chambers Collection, Box 7-8

IRENE SPRING
Gila   T1N R15E

W. A. ("Doc") Vail (d. 1882) located a mining claim here and named it for his wife. Apparently they agreed to disagree, for later in conversation he changed it to his own name, but never officially. Vail was killed during an Express robbery, a deed for which the criminals were lynched. Irene appears to have been a bit troublesome. She married Albert Young, who soon divorced her. A man whom she was nursing made a will in her favor, and soon thereafter she was sued for trying to poison him — but she was cleared of the charge. Ref.: Woody

IRETABA CITY
Mohave   298 mi. N. of Yuma

This Colorado River landing (1870s) was named for the Mojave leader.

IRETABA CREEK
Mohave   35°15'/113°

This creek on the King-Gardner report map of 1866 is an extension of Muddy Creek southeast of Cross Mountain. Iretaba was a Mohave Indian leader and friend to white men. He served as a guide for the 1854 Ives Exploring party. Ref.: 242

IRON DIKE
Gila   T7N R9E   Elev. 5027'

The name results from the geologic appearance of this location. Ref.: Woody

IRON KING
Yavapai   T13N R1E

The name for the post office and mine derived from the presence of an outcropping strong in iron. The post office opened under the name Blanchard, for H. W. Blanchard. The post office name change reflected the emerging importance of the mine. Its operation has been intermittent.

P.O. est. as Blanchard, July 7, 1903, Annie M. Williams, p.m.; changed to Iron King, June 11, 1907; disc. July 15, 1912 Ref.: Schnebly; 242; 329

IRON MOUNTAIN
Pinal   T1N R12E

Robert A. Irion, who brought cattle from Colorado in 1877, pronounced his name "Iron." He settled near this mountain, named for him. The location is now Pinal Ranch. (See Pinal, Camp, Pinal) Ref.: Craig (stepdaughter)

IRON SPRINGS
Cochise

At this springs in the Mule Mountains in 1877 a troop from Fort Bowie camped while chasing Apaches. The men named it Iron Springs because of its taste. Ref.: "Arizona Days and Ways," *Arizona Republic* (Aug. 8, 1954), p. 52

IRON SPRINGS
Navajo   T14N R3W

In 1887 Will C. Barnes named this spring because of its strong iron taste. His ranch headquarters were here. Ref.: 18a; 242

IRON SPRINGS
Yavapai   T14N R3W   Elev. 6400'

The name derives from the strong iron taste of the water, although analysis reveals no iron in it. Sand surrounding the springs does contain iron. The location was a pioneer stage stop. Bob Atkinson, the stage station operator, put in an iron pipe from the springs to a watering trough and some believe the name may have arisen from that fact. Yavapai and possibly Apache Indians roamed the area, including nearby Boulder Hill. With the creation of a stop of the A.T. & S.F.R.R. here, Atkinson's income stopped. In 1900 he accepted a cash settlement of about two thousand dollars from the Iron Springs Outing

Club, formed by Phoenix businessmen, who then had a summer community here. It now has year-round residents. Iron Springs Wash is here.

P.O. est. Ironsprings, May 31, 1900, Elmer Hawley, p.m.; named changed to Iron Springs, May 4, 1950; Wells Fargo 1903

Ref.: 5, p. 288; AHS, Frank Alkire Files; 242

IRONWOOD TANK
Pima   T16N R9E

There are ironwood trees here. Ironwood is so dense that cutting it will soon dull sharp instruments. Indians used the wood for arrow points and tool handles. They also roasted and ate the seeds or ground them into piñole.

ISHAM   pro.: /yšəm/
Coconino   T21N R3E

This spring was named c. 1905 by Charles Isham. Ref.: Hart

ISIS TEMPLE
Coconino (Grand Canyon)   T32N R3E   Elev. 7028'

George Wharton James noted this temple-like formation before which are two "great cloisters." It is named for the Egyptian sun goddess. The name was approved by the USGS in 1906. Isis Point is on it. Ref.: 178, p. 31; 329

ISLAND MESA
Yavapai   T18N R4E   Elev. c. 4000'

Because Sycamore Creek flows on both sides of this mesa, it seems like an island. Ref.: 18a

ITAK
Papago: *vav* = "mountain"; *mo* = "head"
Pima   T20S R3E   Elev. 2297'

This Papago mountain is also called Rocky Point (1917, Corps of Engineers, to 1939 aeronautical chart of Douglas) and Vávemo, the latter referring to a low ridge with a noticeable rock on its top. Ref.: 329; 58

I T DRAW
Cochise   T15S R26E

The name derives from a brand used by a rancher at the region. Ref.: Riggs

ITHACA PEAK
Mohave   T23N R17W

This peak may have taken its name from that of the Ithaca Mine located here by Charles Sherman. A Hualapai Indian named Quartermaster showed the source of turquoise to Sherman. Early Mexican miners used to build a hot fire into which they put ore-bearing rock, and threw water on it to split it away from the turquoise chunks. This peak has been completely removed by mining.

Ref.: 215, p. 124; Housholder; 200, p. 219; Varney

IVALON
Yuma   T8S R23W

When use of the railroad yards in Yuma exceeded their capacity, work was moved to this place, sometimes in error referred to as Avalon. Ref.: Lenon

IVANPATCH (SPRING)
Piute = "small spring coming out of white saline soil with grass growing all around the place"
Mohave   T14S R27E

The Piute name, as is usual with Indian place names, accurately describes the location. Ref.: 329; 18a

IVES MESA

Navajo   T19N R17E   Elev. c. 6000'

Herbert Gregory named this mesa in 1915 for Lt. Joseph Christmas Ives, who traversed it in 1858. Ref.: 141, p. 191

IVES PEAK

Yavapai   T11N R9W   Elev. 3856'

Mount Ives is on the 1872 military map southwest of Artillery Peak. The name Ives Peak appears first on the 1879 Smith map. Possibly it was named for Lt. Joseph Christmas Ives, who in 1853 was with Lt. Amiel W. Whipple's party. The fact that Eugene S. Ives (b. Nov. 11, 1859, Washington, D.C.) was barely thirteen years old when the name Ives first appeared on maps makes it dubious that the peak was named for him, although he was at the turn of the century a prominent Arizonan. Ref.: 242; 329; Willson;18a

IVES POINT

Coconino (Grand Canyon)   T33N R1W   Elev. 6600'

Lt. Joseph Christmas Ives surveyed across northern Arizona (1851) and subsequently explored the Colorado River to its navigable headwaters. To honor Ives, the name was suggested in 1908 by the USGS. Ref.: 329

L X L BASIN

Mohave   T22N R17W

"The width and open character of the middle part" of this short valley basin derives from the name of the L X L Mine. It was named in 1906. Ref.: 200, pp. 107-115

J

JACK-IN-THE-PULPIT
Maricopa   T8S R3W   Elev. 2638'
This pinnacle of volcanic rock with its base resting in lava is one of three irregular ridges caused by lava bed erosion. It looks like a Jack-in-the-Pulpit. Ref.: 57, p. 225

JACKMAN WASH
Mohave   T19N R14W
This wash (a.k.a. Jackson Wash) was named for a local resident. Ref.: 329

JACK POT SPRING
Mohave   T16N R20W
Contrary to the inference of this spelling, this spring takes its name from the Jack Potts Mine discovered by John Potts, a miner, prospector, and Mohave County sheriff. Ref.: Harris

JACK RABBIT
Pinal   T9S R5E   Elev. 1550'
In 1885 Emerson O. Stratton and Al Robard located the Jack Rabbit Mine, which produced silver for several years. Later the Jack Rabbit Well was dug four miles north. The name Jack Rabbit is a translation of the Papago name for the location, *Tat Momoli* (*tat* = "foot"; *mumeri* = "run"; *kut* = "where"), deriving from the fact that Kohatk Pima Indians held foot races here. See Tat Momoli, Pinal
Ref.: 58; 57, p. 391; 262, p. 16; 59, p. 271; AHS, Emerson O. Stratton *ms*

JACK'S CANYON
Coconino   T14–19N R10–16E
An early name for the former stream in this canyon was Salt Creek, in use c. 1900, but long gone because the stream dried up c. 1903. According to Barnes, from 1869 – 1871 the canyon was the site of a cabin owned and operated by Jack De Schradt (or Dischrat), known as "Jack Dishrag," from whence the name Jack's Canyon. Ref.: 329; 182

JACK'S CANYON
Yavapai   T9N R4E   Elev. c. 5000'
C. M. (Jack) Montgomery, Al Doyle, and John Marshall maintained a trail called Jack's Trail from Montgomery's Ranch (in this canyon a.k.a. Jack's Gulch) between 1882 and 1884. Clay Park is on the site of Jack's Ranch. Ref.: 18a; Schnebly

JACK SMITH SPRING
Coconino   T23N R7E
Two springs bear the name of their owner, an employee at a nearby lumber mill. Jack Smith Tank is at T23N/R8E. Ref.: Sykes; 70, p. 63

JACK'S MOUNTAIN
Gila   T6N R13E   Elev. 5681'
Bill Lewis owned a mule named Jack, which frequently ran away and was always found

on this mountain, hence the name, according to Barnes. On the other hand, a life-time resident says it was named for pioneer Jack Wertman. Jack's Springs is on the mountain. Ref.: 18a; McKinney

JACKSON BUTTE
Gila   T3N R16E   Elev. 6106'
William Jackson ran stock at this butte, hence the name. Ref.: 18a

JACKSON MOUNTAINS
Graham   T6S R22E   Elev. 8,925'
Bill Jackson, a wagon boss and ranch foreman for the Arizona Land and Cattle Company at Holbrook from 1890 to 1895, settled near the base of this mountain c. 1900 to ranch cattle. It is also called Jackson Butte. Ref.: 18a

JACOB LAKE
Coconino   T38N R2E   Elev. 7921'
The first name c. 1930 for this location was Jacob Lake Camp. The lake is a shallow flood-water pool, named for Jacob Hamblin, a Mormon explorer in the 1860-1870s. Hamblin (b. April 2, 1819, Ohio; d. Aug. 31, 1886) began missionary exploration in Arizona in 1858 and also scouted for settlement sites in Little Colorado River country. During the 1870s he blazed the Mormon Road Immigrant Trail from Utah to the new settlements. He is buried at Alpine. Today there is a small community and camp ground at Jacob Lake.
P.O. est. Sept. 18, 1931, Harold I. Bowman, p.m.; disc. June 30, 1955
Ref.: 5, pp. 105-488; 242; 329

JACOB'S POOLS
Coconino   T38N R5E
Jacob Hamblin, the first white man to camp here, found two water pools in 1879 on his route to the Hopi Indian region. See Jacob Lake, Coconino Ref.: 88, pp. 158-160

JACOBS WELL
Navajo: 'aah hoyoolls'il = "tank of water"; 'axoyolcil = "hollow pool"
Apache   T19N R29E   Elev. c. 6000'
The term "well" was a colloquialism applied to small lakes in early Arizona. In 1853 there was no name for the hole which Lt. Amiel Whipple called a spring and described as a conical pit about three hundred feet wide at the top and one hundred and twenty-five feet deep. On September 1, 1857 Lt. Edward Fitzgerald Beale and his camels were at this water hole, which he called by its present name of Jacobs Well. By that time all but one of the Indian trails Whipple had noted were gone. The changes continued and by 1938 eroding winds had deposited silt so that the water was a mere five feet deep.
Ref.: 331, p. 79; 143, p. 172; 163, pp. 381-382; 347, p. 150; 23, p. 39; 204, p. 18; 348, p. 72; Burcard

JADITO SPRING
Navajo   T27N R21E
The name as spelled today goes back to earlier spellings known since 1886, among them the following: Jetty-to, Jedito, Je Ho-to, Jeddito, and Jettco-To. See Jadito Wash, Navajo Ref.: 329

JADITO WASH   pro.: /jédito/
Navajo: jado = "antelope"; to = "water"
Apache   T27N R21E to T23N R15E
Jadito Wash is one of four which carry water from Black Mesa (Apache County) through Hopi Butte country to the Little Colorado River. In 1967 the USGS incorporated the following into Jadito Wash: Corn Creek, Jadito Canyon, North Fork Corn Creek, and Jeddito Canyon. It runs through Jadito Valley.
Don Pedro de Tobar in 1540 was the first white man to visit the Jadito Valley, but T. V. Keams (see Keams Canyon, Navajo) was apparently the first to explore the extensive archeological resources of the valley, probably in the late 1870s.
Ref.: 141, pp. 38, 155; 152, pp. 17, 18

JAEGER TANKS

Maricopa   T9S R10W

Louis J. F. Jaeger (b. Bucks County, Pennsylvania; d. June 30, 1892) freighted ore from the Gunsight Mine to Yuma and used these tanks to water his teams. Their location near the Eagle Mountains, possibly coupled with ignorance about Jaeger, gradually shifted the name to Eagle Tanks. Ref.: Jordan; 224, III

JAKE'S CORNER

Gila   T8N R10E   Elev. 2845'

In 1956 this was merely a small store for tourists. It has developed into a community.

JAMES CANYON

Coconino   T19N R6E

This canyon was named for Bill James, a settler found dead here in 1896 or 1897. Ref.: Hart

JAMIESON TANK

Pinal   T6S R9E

The Jamieson brothers c. 1915 owned sixty-seven thousand acres in this region and ran sheep with their partners Alex McKay and W. C. Davis.
Ref.: AHS, Castillo Collection, Box 1

JANUS CRATER

Coconino   T23N R9E   Elev. 8004'

This location, a volcano with a double crater, was once known as Double Crater but at the suggestion of Harold S. Colton its two-headed nature has led to its naming for the god Janus, "the guardian of portals and patron of beginnings and endings." USGS accepted the name in 1969. Janus Spring (T29N/R9E) is an associated name. Ref.: 329

JAP SLOUGH

Mohave   T17N R22W   Elev. c. 700'

Here an oriental gardener raised produce, hence the name. When the river was dammed this location disappeared under water. Ref.: Housholder

JAQUES MOUNTAIN

Navajo   T10N R23E   Elev. 7003'

This isolated butte was named for Sanford Jaques, a sheepman and early settler. See Show Low (reference to Jacques Lake) Ref.: 18a

JASPER FOREST

Apache   T17N R24E

This location in the Petrified Forest National Monument is also known as First Forest. Quantities of jasper here led to the name, adopted by the USGS in 1967. Ref.: 329

JASPER SPRING

La Paz   T2N R17W

Jasper found in this vicinity led to naming Jasper Spring. Ref.: Monson

JAYCOX MOUNTAIN

Coconino   T17N R11E   Elev. 7431'

This mountain was named for Henry H. Jaycox (b. 1833, New York; d. Jan. 20, 1884), a scout and guide for King S. Woolsey's second and third expeditions in 1864. Jaycox camped at Jaycox Tank, from which the mountain was named. Jaycox Tank is at R10E. Ref.: 62; McClintock; Willson; AHS, Henry H. Jaycox File

JAYNES

Pima   T13S R13E   Elev. c. 2300'

This railroad station was named before 1890, hence possibly not for Allan B. Jaynes, in 1916 editor of the *Tucson Citizen*.
P.O. est. March 22, 1922, Hubert E. Hunts; disc. May 17, 1924

J D DAM LAKE

Coconino   T20N R3D   Elev. 6458'

The lake was formed by the construction of the J D Dam by J. D. Douglas, who maintained headquarters near the dam. The dam was constructed in the early 1930s on J D Dam Wash. Ref.: Benham

JEDDITO

Navajo: *jado* = "antelope"; *to* = "water"

Navajo   T27N R20E

The first name suggested for this location was Antelope Spring, an anglicizing of the Navajo name for the place. See Jadito Wash, Navajo

P.O. est. Nov. 26, 1920, Alma G. Roberts, p.m. Ref.: 242

JEDDITO MESA

Navajo   T27N R2E

The Navajo name for this location is *Dini'dziil* (= "game mountains"), no doubt referring to the presence of antelope which grazed nearby at Jadito or Jeddito Spring. See Jadito Wash, Navajo

JEFFORDS POINT

Coconino (Grand Canyon)   T33N R5E   Elev. 6547'

In 1932 Frank Bond named this for Thomas J. Jeffords, a scout, trader, miner, and friend of the Apache leader Cochise. Thomas Jefferson Jeffords (b. 1832, New York; d. Feb. 19, 1914) arrived in Arizona in 1862. Ref.: AHS, Jeffords File; 329

JENSEN CANYON

Coconino   T37N R3W

This canyon is named for a Mormon family in Arizona since the early 1880s. Ref.: 63; Hart

JERKED BEEF BUTTE

Gila   T7N R13E   Elev. 5950'

Estevan Ochoa, a leading Tucson merchant in the 1870s and 1880s, went temporarily out of business when Apaches rustled all his draught oxen. The Indians drove the animals across the Salt River and stopped on the slope of a high mesa to kill and jerk the beef, hence the name. They customarily preserved in this manner (also at Jerky Butte [Pinal, T8S/R13E, Elev. 4537']). Ref.: 146, p. 77

JEROME

Yavapai   T16N R2E   Elev. 5435'

As early as 1582 when Fr. Espejo and Farfán were in this region, Indians were working copper mines, probably for pigment. In 1873 Capt. John D. Boyd and some prospectors located several claims. John Ruffner, who owned the property, later leased it to Gov. Frederick Tritle, who interested Eugene Jerome of New York. Jerome agreed to finance the project, provided the camp be named for him. In 1886 W. A. Clark of Montana bought the claim and installed a new smelter.

In September 1898 fire consumed the entire business district. Its end as a mining community began in 1925 with a dynamite blast of the Black Pit which caused the entire town to begin sliding downhill. The concrete jail slowly skidded three hundred feet across the highway and tumbled onto its side. Other buildings followed. The town survives as a tourist attraction.

P.O. est. Sept. 10, 1883, Fred F. Thomas, p.m. Ref.: Schnebly; 242; *Jerome Reporter* (Dec. 28, 1899), pp. 6-7; 22, pp. 22-23; 261, pp. 12, 14; 359, p. 104; *Jerome Mining Notes* (April 30, 1899), p. 1; 5, pp. 333-334

JEROME JUNCTION

Yavapai   T16N R2W

This was the junction point for the narrow gauge railroad from Ashfork to Jerome. The name was changed to Chino Valley in 1923. Jerome Canyon is at T15N/R3W.

P.O. est. as Junction, July 18, 1895, George C. West, p.m.; name changed to Jerome Junction, Dec. 23, 1914; name changed to Chino Valley, May 11, 1923; Wells Fargo 1903 Ref.: 242; Theobald; Schnebly

JERSEY

Yavapai T12N R2W Elev. 5772'

Here was the post office for the Jersey Lily Mine, whose owner was a great admirer of Lily Langtry, a famous actress.

P.O. est. March 6, 1895, William H. Ferguson, p.m.; disc. July 31, 1909 Ref.: 18a; 242

JERUSALEM MOUNTAINS

Pinal/Gila T4S R17E Elev. 5290'

Cowboys who ventured onto the Apache Reservation to round up strays, kept extra saddle horses here while members of their group scouted the area. The cowboys called the journey "going to Jerusalem," hence the name. Jerusalem Canyon is on the mountain (a.k.a. Jerusalem Peak). Ref.: 18a

JHU'S CANYON   pro.: /hos/

Cochise T17S R30E Elev. 7000'

Jhu, an Apache leader, conducted Chiricahua Apaches from the San Carlos Indian Reservation on destructive raids throughout southeastern Arizona in the 1880s. Ref.: Burrall

JICARILLA POINT   pro.: /hikəriyə/

Coconino (Grand Canyon) T31N R1E

This location was named by the USGS in 1908 to honor the New Mexican Jicarilla Apache tribe.

JIM CAMP WASH

Apache T16N R23E

Three cowboys named Jim (Jim Donoghue, Jim Wagner, and Jim Bowen) used to camp here. The stone foundations for their shelter are still extant. Ref.: Grigsby

JIM SAM BUTTE

Gila T8N R13E Elev. 5323'

Jim Sam Haught (d. 1945) an early settler, moved from Payson to this butte c. 1918. Ref.: McKinney

J K MOUNTAIN

Gila T1N R13E Elev. 4490'

The name derives from the J K brand of John Kennedy (b. 1868, California), who arrived in this region in 1875 and ran cattle here. J K Spring is here. Ref.: Craig; Woody

JOE'S HILL

Yavapai T9N R3E Elev. 303'

This hill was named for Joe Mayer. See Mayer, Yavapai Ref.: 203, p. 49

JOE'S (sic) SPRING, SAINT

Coconino T11N R14E

This spring was located by Will and Parley Richards of Saint Joseph, who lived here in the 1880s. They named it for their home town. It is near Saint Joe Ridge and Saint Joe Canyon (T12N/R15E). Ref.: 18a; 171, pp. 41-42

JOHN LONG CANYON

Cochise T19S R29E

John Long lived in this canyon c. 1918. Ref.: Riggs

JOHNNY LYON HILLS

Cochise T15S R21E Elev. 5730'

John Lyon (b. 1856, Maryland), said he arrived at this location when "them hills was just little mounds." He lived in a dugout with a bunch of hounds complete with fleas. Lyon fell off a ledge and broke his hip, but managed to crawl to his dugout where he was found almost two weeks later. He recovered and sold out, living to be a typical old hermit. Ref.: Bennett

JOHNS, SAINT

Apache   T13N R28E   Elev. 5725'

Spanish explorers called the crossing of the Little Colorado River here El Vadito (= "The Little Crossing"). One legend says the name is that of the first woman resident, Señora Maria San Juan (= "Saint John") Baca de Padilla, and another says the name comes from the annual June 24th feast of San Juan, still celebrated by Spanish-Americans in the Southwest. William R. Milligan (See Round Valley, Apache) arrived here in 1866, followed in 1870 by Frank Walker, both settling near the present Saint Johns (See Meadows, The, Apache). A settlement began developing at the crossing of the Little Colorado River and by 1872 Spanish-Americans had agricultural communities. In 1874 Juan Sedilla built a stone cabin. In 1875 Solomon Barth sold his interests to Ammon M. Tenney, a Mormon who located on the G Bar or Sedro Ranch, thirty-five miles north of Saint Johns. Shortly thereafter arrived Wilford Woodruff, who on March 29, 1880 established a Mormon settlement about one mile north of Saint Johns. However, on September 19, 1880 Erastus Stone moved the settlement to high ground adjacent to the Mexican community and the name Salem was chosen for the new settlement. An application for a post office was denied because of hostility to Mormons.

Saint Johns became Apache County seat in 1879, briefly superseded by Springerville in 1880, as in 1882 Saint Johns again became the county seat. It retains that honor. P.O. est. as Saint John's, April 5, 1880, Sixtus E. Johnson, p.m.; name changed to Saint Johns, July 10, 1883 Ref.: Shreve; AHS, Evans Coleman File; Ammon Tenney File (Huntington Library); *Arizona Weekly Enterprise* (June 7, 1890); 331, p. 128; 225, pp. 165, 177, 178

JOHNS CREEK, SAINT

Gila   T10N R9E   Elev. c. 4000'

William O. St. Johns patented a ranch here, hence the name. The ranch was a general stopping place on the Globe-Payson road. Ref.: 18a

JOHNSON

Cochise   T15S R22E   Elev. 4985'

Before the railroad came through here in 1881, copper ores had been found. In 1883 the Peabody Company rejuvenated the old mine under a general manager named John M. Johnson and the community was named for him. The old hotel at Russellville was moved to the new town. The community and mine continue to be owned by the Coronado Copper & Zinc Company, which took them over in 1942. Johnson Peak (Elev. 6644') overlooks the location.

P.O. est. Oct. 31, 1899 (with first name suggested to be Johnsonville), W. de H. Washington, p.m.; disc. Nov. 29, 1929 Ref.: *Daily Republican* (March 9, 1883), p. 2; *Douglas Dispatch*, "50th Anniversary Edition," Section 4, p. 4; 242

JOHNSON CANYON

Coconino   T21N R1W

This canyon was named for Capt. George Johnson (d. before June 1885), who had a sheep ranch here in the late 1870s. Ref.: Kennedy; 124, p. 44, Footnote

JOHNSON CANYON

Greenlee   T3N R31E

In 1886 "Stuttering Charlie" Johnson settled in this canyon, hence its name. He was a Texas Ranger before arriving in Silver City, New Mexico, from where he moved to Greenlee County. In Arizona he used the LUE brand. See Big Lue Canyon, Greenlee Ref.: Fred Fritz

JOHNSON CANYON

Mohave   Near King Mine

Named for John (Jack) Henry Johnson, who homesteaded here. He located the C.O.D. Mine in 1878. Ref.: Mallach

JOHNSON CREEK

Coconino (Grand Canyon)   T42N R2W   Elev. c. 5000'

W. D. Johnson was a photographer for Maj. John Wesley Powell's second Grand

Canyon Expedition in 1871-1872. He may be the same Johnson who settled on this creek some ten miles from Kanab in 1871 with his four brothers. Ref.: 18a

JOHNSON CREEK
Yavapai   T21N R2W
This creek (a.k.a. Ash Creek, Ash Fork Draw, and Partridge Creek) was named for Capt. George Johnson (d. c. June 1885), who had a sheep ranch here in the late 1870s and early 1880s. He also had a ranch about nine miles west of Williams.
Ref.: Kennedy; 124, p. 44, Note

JOHNSON MOUNTAIN
Yavapai   Elev. 5752'
This mountain was named for Lester Johnson, who lived here.
Ref.: Rosenberger

JOHNSON POINT
Coconino (Grand Canyon)   T32N R3E   Elev. 5295'
On April 30, 1930 M. R. Tillotson, Grand Canyon National Park superintendent, suggested this name to honor Fred Johnson, a Park Ranger who drowned near here in 1929.
Ref.: 329

JOHNSON POINT
Coconino   T40N R7E
P. T. Rielly in 1969 proposed naming this point for Warren Marshall Johnson (d. 1902), who operated a ranch and Lee's Ferry (1876-1896). Ref.: 329

JOHNSON'S HOLE (Well)
Navajo   T8S R1W
This location is a narrow gateway pass to the top of No Name Mesa, discovered by Ezekial Johnson, who with John Wetherill served as a guide for the Charles L. Bernheimer Expedition to Navajo Mountain in 1922.

JOHNSON SPRING
Mohave   T21N R17W   Elev. c. 4000'
John (Jack) Henry Johnson, in this locale in 1882, discovered the C.O.D. Mine, and the spring is named for him. Johnson had a house, an orchard and "a nice layout."
Ref.: Harris

JOHNSON WASH
Yavapai   T13N R3E
In the 1890s Barry Johnson maintained wild horses here, training them on Racetrack Ridge above this wash. Ref.: Allan

JOKAKI   pro.: /jokákiy/
Hopi = "mud house"
Maricopa   T2N R4E   Elev. c. 1400'
This winter resort on Camelback Road in Scottsdale was built of adobes. A Hopi worker suggested the name.
P.O. est. Nov. 19, 1935, Robert T. Evans, p.m.; disc. Aug. 31, 1954 Ref.: 18a; 242

JONES
Cochise   T24S R28E
This post office, first called Military, was a branch of Douglas post office. Named to honor Harry J. Jones, killed in action on the border in 1915, it served Camp Harry J. Jones personnel.
P.O. est. as Military, May 27, 1915; name changed to Jones, May 18, 1921
Ref.: 242

JONES, CAMP HARRY J.
Cochise
This camp on the Mexican border at the edge of Douglas was active from 1910 to 1931. It was named for Harry J. Jones (b. Aug. 7, 1891, Illinois; d. Nov. 2, 1915), an enlisted

man shot while guarding the customs house in Douglas. In February 1916 the commanding officer of the 6th Brigade asked that the camp be named in his honor. Ref.: AHS, Cochran Collection, pp. 1-2

JONES PEAK

Cochise   T19S R30E   Elev. 8415'

A seventeen-year old boy — Lawrence Jones of Coolidge, Arizona — lost his life here in 1923 while on his way to join a forest fire crew. The U.S. Forest Service suggested the name in 1932. Ref.: 329

JONES POINT

Coconino (Grand Canyon)   T32N R3E   Elev. 5300'

Frank Bond in 1929 named this point for S. V. Jones, a member of the second Powell Grand Canyon Expedition (1871-72). Ref.: 329

JONES SPRING

Coconino   T16N R8E

In about 1876 Isaac Jones homesteaded here to raise cattle. He was called "Bar D" because of his brand. Ref.: 108, pp. 74-75; Hart

JONES WATER SPRING

Gila   T1N R13E

This site of a recreation area in the Crook National Forest is now part of Tonto Forest. It was named for a cattleman named Jones, who raised livestock here. Ref.: Woody

JOPS LANDING

Mohave   T14N R20W

Jops Landing (or Harbor) was named for people who lived here where farmers forded across the Colorado River. The landing is gone. Ref.: 329; Housholder

JOSE DEL TUCSON, SAN

Pima

The ruins of this *visita* of San Xavier were still in evidence until the City of Tucson tractored it out of existence in favor of a dump. This mission, built by Fr. Garcés in 1775, was on Mission Road near the base of Sentinel Peak ("A" Mountain). Ref.: 5, p. 396

JOSE DE SONOITA LAND GRANT, SAN

Santa Cruz   T22S R14E

The United States Congress confirmed seven thousand five hundred ninety two acres of this land grant. See Sonoita, Santa Cruz Ref.: 116, p. 428

JOSEPH CITY

Navajo   T18N R19E   Elev. 5083'

On March 24, 1876 Mormon emigrants arrived in this locale. They established three settlements. William Coleman Allen (b. Feb. 14, 1843; d. March 17, 1926) set up Allen's Camp, which soon bore the name Cumorah (from the hill where the gold plates of the *Book of Mormon* were found in Palmira, New York). One name suggested was Ramah City, but both this and Cumorah gave way on May 26, 1876 to Allen's Camp or Allen's City. Here the colonists constructed a cottonwood log fort. It was the start of the oldest Mormon colony in Arizona. On January 21, 1878 the name was changed to St. Joseph (for Mormon prophet Joseph Smith), but in 1923 railroad officials asked them to change the name to Joseph City to avoid confusion with St. Joseph, Missouri. Determination and sheer grit kept Joseph City in existence. By 1897 seven dams had been built and washed out by the flooding Little Colorado River. A Mormon leader said it was the "leading community in pain, determination and unflinching courage in dealing with the elements around them." In 1939 a dam was built which withstood the devastating torrents of the rampaging river. Joseph City Wash shares the name; its name was changed from St. Joseph Wash in 1923.

P.O. est. as St. Joseph, Feb. 21, 1878, John McLaws, p.m.; changed to Joseph, Oct. 31,

1898; changed to Joseph City, Dec. 19, 1923 Ref.: *Holbrook Argus* (Sept. 17, 1898), p. 5; Richards; Wiltbank; 71, p. 46; 225, pp. 139, 140; 331, p. 82; 341, pp. 4, 11, 18, 41; 5, p. 314

JOSEPHINE CANYON
Santa Cruz   T20S R14E

This canyon was named c. 1865 for Jim Pennington's youngest daughter. Josephine and her sister Larcena remained in Arizona when other members of the Pennington family departed for California. See Josephine Peak, Santa Cruz. Ref.: R. H. Forbes Letter to James McClintock (April 5, 1920), State Library Files

JOSEPHINE PEAK
Santa Cruz   T20S R15E   Elev. 8435'

In 1893 George Roskruge named this peak for Josephine Pennington, one of four daughters of Jim Pennington. Jim arrived with his father Elias Green Pennington and eleven brothers and sisters at old Fort Buchanan in June 1857. Penniless and completely exhausted and Larcena seriously ill, the family here dropped out of an emigrant train. The father and two sons (Jim and Jack) earned money by delivering wild hay to the fort while Larcena recovered. In December 1858 she married John Hempstead Page (see Madera Canyon, Pima/Santa Cruz). The Pennington family moved rather frequently. In 1869 it was at Tubac. Apaches killed Jim and his son Green Pennington, and the family then moved to Tucson. The older Pennington decided to move on to California but en route at Point of Mountain another daughter came down with pneumonia and died shortly thereafter. Josephine Peak was also called Grosvenor Peak (1861).
Ref.: R. H. Forbes, Letter to James McClintock (April 5, 1920), State Library Files; 117, pp. 3, 10, 12, 31

JOSE, SAN   pro.: /san howzey/ or /sæn hozey/
Graham   T7S R27E   Elev. c. 3500'

In 1873 Mexicans arrived at this location and by 1879 an old adobe fort known as Pueblo Viejo was here, surrounded by about twenty-five small adobe huts. William Munson opened a store, the result being that the place was called Munsonville. He sold his store to I. E. Solomon in 1874. Nearby was a pre-historic canal system which Mormons reactivated, calling it the Montezuma Canal. It supplied water to Lehi. Possibly because of this, there is one newspaper reference calling the community Montezuma.
P.O. est. as San Jose, Dec. 12, 1877, Jules Griego, p.m.; disc. Aug. 1, 1878; reest. March 30, 1904, Abelino Mejia, Jr.; disc. July 16, 1904 Ref.: AHS, Lilly Kirkland File; 168, p. 587; 353, p. 9; 225, pp. 213, 214; 116, p. 587; *Tucson Citizen* (July 5, 1873), p. 2; 242

JOSH, MOUNT
Yavapai   T15N R4W   Elev. 5956'

Edward and Clint Draper settled on the D-1 ranch c. 1875 southwest of this mountain. They named it for their father, Joshua Draper. Josh Spring shares the name.
Ref.: 18a

JOSHUA TREE FOREST
Yavapai   T10N R8W

The forest has an abundance of Joshua trees, a species of yucca cactus, hence the name.
Ref.: 5, p. 290

JOURNIGAN SPRING
Gila   T5N R12E

Jules Journigan, a pioneer rancher here, gave his name to this spring. Ref.: Gillette

JOY VALLEY
Graham   T11S R30E

This valley was named for Capt. Joy, a pioneer miner and settler. Ref.: 18a

JUAN DE LAS BOQUILLAS Y NOGALES LAND GRANT, SAN
Cochise   T20S R21E
United States Courts confirmed the grant acreage at seven thousand three hundred fifty-five acres. Ref.: 116, p. 428

JUAN MILLER CREEK   pro.: /wanmiler/
Greenlee   T2S R29E   Elev. c. 6000'
An old German, Von Müellar, lived here for many years. The spelling of the camp site and creek is a corruption. Ref.: Mrs. Fred Fritz, Sr.

JUAN SPRING, SAN   pro.: /sān hwān/
Spanish = "Saint John"
Pima   T17S R7E   Elev. 3635'
This spring is at a winter residence of Papago Indians. San Juan Wash is also here. Ref.: 58; 262, p. 426

JUMP-OFF CANYON
Gila   T4N R15E   Elev. c. 4000'
On this spot on the trail from the Mogollon Rim to the valley, the drop is so abrupt and steep, wagons had to first be unloaded, tied to a tree, and then lowered by rope, hand over hand, hence its name. The place is on an old military road between fort Apache and Fort Whipple. Ref.: Woody; Palmer *ms.*, III, 5 (U. of A.)

JUMPOFF CRATER
Coconino   T22N R10E   Elev. 6954'
This location is also called Cochrane Hill (for a former rancher who lived on the flat about one and a half miles southwest). Harold S. Colton in 1968 applied the name Jumpoff Crater to an area where family groups could "jump off the road ... on picnics...." Ref.: 329

JUNIPER HILL
Yavapai   T13N R4E   Elev. 5408'
Junipers grow thickly here.

JUNIPER MOUNTAIN
Gila   T7N R12E   Elev. 5888'
This mountain has three small tops and is sometimes called Bear Head Mountain. It is covered with juniper. The name is an old one, going back to at least 1866. In 1920 there was an open flat at the base of this mountain with a scattering of big juniper trees. By the mid-1950s, however, oak and pine underbrush was so thick that one could not see across the flat area. Juniper Canyon (a.k.a. MacDonald Canyon in 1946) is here. So is Juniper Spring. Ref.: McKinney; McInturff

JUNIPER MOUNTAIN
Yavapai   T21N R8W   Elev. 6750'
The hills are black with juniper.

JUNO POINT
Coconino (Grand Canyon)   T32N R5E
This name was approved in 1906, but about 1945 the name was deleted as an "unamerican misfit." Something went amiss, for the place is now mapped as Juno Temple. Ref.: 329

KABBA WASH

Mohave   T20N R14W

This wash took its name from the Kabba Mine in the wash. Ref.: 329

KACHINA POINT   pro.: /kəčiynə/

Apache   T20N R24E

This observation point was the site of the original headquarters for the Petrified Forest National Monument. It was named for sacred spirits of the Hopi Indians. Ref.: 329

KAIBAB DAM LAKE

Coconino   T22N R2E

Because of the shortage of water in the town of Williams, plans for Kaibab Dam were drawn up in 1949. The construction of the dam resulted in the formation of Kaibab Dam Lake. Ref.: 124, p. 139, Note 19

KAIBAB PLATEAU   pro.: /kaybæb/

Piute: *kaiuw* = "mountain"; *a-bwi* = "lying down"

Coconino (Grand Canyon)   T33N R3E   Elev. 8200'

In his April 30, 1874 report, Maj. John Wesley Powell wrote that Indians living on the great plateau north of the Grand Canyon call it *Kai-vav wi* (= "mountains lying down"), rendered phonetically in English as *Kaibab*. However, Kaibab was actually the Indians' name for themselves, as their name for the plateau was *Bucksin (sic)* (Piute = "deer"). The early white settlers misunderstood the name and altered it to Buckskin, a word which they knew. This fact accounts for the name Buckskin Mountains. As for the great forests here, the Kaibab Piute Indians call them the Kaibabits.
Ref.: AHS, Lyman S. Hamblin, Letter (Feb. 27, 1922); Schellbach File (Grand Canyon); 178, p. 25

KAIBAB INDIAN RESERVATION   pro.: /kaybæb/

Piute: *kaib* or *kaiba* = "mountain"; *ab* or *ba* = "on"

Mohave   T40–42N R25W

The name of this reservation is that of the Kaibab Piute Indians, whose name reflects the fact that they live on the great mountainous plateau of the Kaibab. A reservation of 121,000 acres was established on October 16, 1907, being completed on July 17, 1917. The tribal offices are at Moccasin. See Kaibab Plateau, Coconino
Ref.: 167, p. 641; "Annual Report of the Arizona Commission of Indian Affairs, 1954, 1955, 1956," p. 17

KAIBAB TRAIL

Coconino (Grand Canyon)

This trail goes from the North Rim to the Kaibab suspension bridge across the Colorado River. It was officially named by the USGS in 1937. Ref.: *Grand Canyon Nature Notes*, IV (June 30, 1930); 329

KAIBITO

Navajo: *kai bi to* = "willow spring" or "water in the willows"

Coconino   T37N R12E   Elev. 6070'

The name of this trading post and Navajo boarding school settlement comes from that of nearby Kaibito Spring. The name is also spelled Kaibeto. It applies to Kaibito Creek (or Wash) and to Kaibito Spring (named by 1915).

KAIBITO PLATEAU   pro.: /kʔa ybiyᵛ:to/ or /kabiyto/

Navajo = "willow spring"

Coconino   T39N R9E   Elev. 6830'

The name of this plateau is also spelled Kabito and Kaipeto. The name, which comes from that of Kaibito Spring, was applied to the plateau by Herbert Gregory in 1916 and changed to its current spelling by the USGS in 1932. Ref.: 141, p. 41; 329

KAIHON KUG

Papago = *kaihon* (from Spanish *cajon* = "box") "box stands"

Pima   T16S R3E   Elev. 2003'

This small Papago village is sometimes referred to as Old Quijotoa Well. Ref.: 57, p. 14

KAKA   pro.: /kagk/

Pima: *ka* = "pile of brush" (cut in making a clearing); *kaka* = "many such piles or a large clearing"

Maricopa   T10W R1W   Elev. 2255'

Fr. Kino in 1698 visited this Pima Indian village, calling it El Gaga. Others have spelled the name as follows: Cacate; Gaaka; Cacca; Caca Chimer; Cazlon (Wheeler survey). One source refers to Cacca in terms of "containing eight hundred and ten square miles more or less and being the land owned and occupied by said Pueblo of Cacca." From the location cited in this reference, it would appear to be the Gila Indian Reservation of today, although several sources refer to the village as being Papago. Ref.: 43, p. 399; 58; 167, I, 178; 262, p. 8; 57, p. 11

KANA-A VALLEY

Coconino   T23N R8E

In 1923 Harold Colton named this valley for the Hopi Kachinas, said to make their homes in Sunset Crater. Kana-a Creek and Wash are nearby. Ref.: 329

KANAB CANYON   pro.: /kənab/ or /kənæb/

Piute: *kanab* = "willows"

Coconino (Grand Canyon)   T34N R2E

Many willows grow here, hence the name. Kanab Creek runs in part through the Canyon. Ref.: 100, p. 124; 88, p. 241; AHS Names File

KANAB PLATEAU

Coconino/Mohave   T35N R5W   Elev. 5000'

Kanab Plateau (a.k.a. Kanab Mountain) was named by Maj. John Wesley Powell, whereas in 1882 Maj. Clarence E. Dutton named the area drained by the creek, Kanab Desert. Other associated names are Kanab Point (Mohave [Grand Canyon], T35N/R3W, Elev. 5737'), Kanab Rapids below the point, and Kanab Spring.

KANE SPRINGS

Pinal   T4S R14E   Elev. c. 4000'

This name, in use since 1900, probably comes from the name of the Kane Springs. They are in Kane (or Cane) Spring Canyon. Kane Spring Mountain borrows its name from Kane Ranch. At these springs Pearl Hart (b. 1881, Ontario, Canada) and Joe Boot robbed a stage coach. Pearl, a mining camp cook who had done mining, is said to have been trying to get money for her sick mother. The pair escaped but were overtaken about twenty miles from Benson. Boot was sentenced to thirty years. Pearl made friends with a jail trustee, who cut a convenient hole in the light plaster jail wall and pulled Pearl through to freedom. They fled to Lordsburg, where she was arrested and then sent to prison at Yuma. Because the Yuma prison was not equipped to take care of women, she was released when she promised to leave Arizona. She was next heard from in Kansas where she was charged with pickpocketing. She then departed from the scene. Kane Springs Mountain (Graham, T10S/R25E, Elev. 6908') may be an associated name. Ref.: *Cosmopolitan Magazine* (Oct. 1899) (Woody Files); *Coconino Sun* (Nov. 25, 1899)

KANGAROO HEADLAND
Coconino (Grand Canyon)   T34N R3W   Elev. 5889'
Frank Bond named this location in 1932 because in outline it resembles that animal. Ref.: 329

KANSAS SETTLEMENT
Cochise   T16S R25E   Elev. 4215'
In 1910 homesteaders from Kansas settled here and named it for their home state. Ref.: Riggs

KARRO (R.R. STN.)
Cochise   T13S R30E   Elev. 3593'
This location was named for Carr, a grading contractor. Ref.: 18a

KASTER
Mohave   T19N R16W   Elev. 5018'
This section house on the S.F.R.R. was named in the 1880s for a Dr. Kaster. Ref.: 18a; Harris

KATHERINE
Mohave   T21N R21W   Elev. 750'
A town has developed at Katherine Landing in this same locale on the Colorado River. Both the Katherine Mine and later the community of Katherine Beach derived their names from that of the sister of J. S. Bagg of Kingman, who discovered the mine c. 1920. Mining activity continued through 1942, although not at full capacity after 1929. P.O. est. Aug. 15, 1921, Alva C. Lambert, p.m.; disc. June 5, 1929
Ref.: Housholder; Burns; Hornbuckle; 242; "Davis Dam and Power Plant, U.S. Dept. of the Interior, Bureau of Reclamation, Region 3" (Boulder City, Nevada, Jan. 1, 1954)

KATHERINE WASH (OLD)
Mohave   T21N R21W
This place is also called Telephone Wash because here the A.T.T. line goes under the Colorado River. New Katherine Wash is at Katherine.

KAUFMAN SPRING
Coconino   T22N R4E
Jake Kaufman had cattle prior to 1930 and watered them at this spring. Ref.: Hart

KAWAIKA-A
Navajo   T27N R20E   Elev. 6400'
This important Hopi ruin on the rim of Antelope Mesa was attacked in 1540 by Don Pedro de Tobar, who destroyed the village. It was reoccupied prior to Luxan's visit in 1582, but finally abandoned before 1598. Kawaiokee and Kawaioku are variants. Kawaika Spring is here. Ref.: 21, p. 38, Note 5; 153, p. 81; 167, I, 564

KAYENTA   pro.: /káyəntə/
Navajo: *teh'nideek* = "a natural game-pit"
Navajo   T39N R19E   Elev. 5750'
The Navajo word from which the name Kayenta derives refers to a deep spring about three miles from the trading post established in 1910 by John and Louisa Wade Wetherill. The spring creates a bog hole where animals mired when they came for water. The first name for the trading post was Oljeto.
P.O. est. as Oljato, March 16, 1907, John Wetherill, p.m.; name changed to Oljeto, Jan. 31, 1911; name changed to Kayenta, March 21, 1911 Ref.: Barnes Notes; Burcard; 191, p. 48; 129, p. 191; 331, p. 83; 242

KAYENTA CREEK
Navajo
In December 1970 the USGS changed the name to Laguna Creek (*q.v.*).

KAYLER BUTTE
Gila   T7N R10E   Elev. 2916'
Kaler (*sic*) was a rancher here in the early 1900s. Kayler Spring is nearby.
Ref.: Woody

KEAMS CANYON
Hopi: *Pongsikvi* = "government town"
Navajo   T28N R20E   Elev. 6800'
This is the canyon in which the community of Keams Canyon lies. The first English
name for this location was Peach Orchard Spring, where in the early 1860s Billy Dodd,
brother of the agent for the Navajo, maintained a trading store. On June 4, 1872 the
name was changed to its present form with the arrival of Varker Keams (b. 1843,
England; d. Nov. 30, 1904). Keams had served with Kit Carson in the Navajo campaign
and later as an interpreter, moving then into Hopi country where he was made agent of
the Navajo on June 4, 1872 and started the first permanent white settlement. In 1886
twenty Hopi leaders requested the government to establish a school for Hopi children
and a year later the school commenced in Keams Canyon. In 1899 a separate Hopi
agency was established. It moved to its present site in 1902 from the trading post two
miles down the canyon.
P.O. est. March 28, 1903, Charles E. Burton, p.m. Ref.: 5, p. 126; 79, pp. 210-211;
141, p. 192; 331, p. 83; 242

KEARNY
Pinal   T4S R14E   Elev. 1850'
This town was included in construction of a special precipitation-flotation installation
by the Ray Mines Division of the Kennecott Company in 1958, with a community to
house plant workers and their families. The town is named for Gen. John Stephen Watts
Kearny, who crossed Arizona and passed near this spot in November 1846. The Parke
1851 map shows his route.
P.O. est. March 16, 1959, Mrs. Lena Johnson, p.m. Ref.: "Arizona Days and Ways,"
Arizona Republic (Nov. 9, 1958); p. 242

KEET SEEL RUINS
Navajo: (1) *kuts'uli* = "broken pottery"
        (2) *kin yits'iil* = "empty houses"
Navajo   T39N R17E
The extensive ruins in Keet Seel Canyon (Navajo National Monument) cover some
three hundred and sixty acres. The name was spelled Kietz Seel or Kiits'uli or Kits-il
until 1932 when it was changed to Kit Siel. The current preferred spelling is as given
above. Keet Seel Spring is near these ruins. Ref.: 141, pp. 44, 157; 331, p. 140

KELLEY'S BUTTE
Gila   T5N R21E
The Webber map of 1869 shows a trail for Maj. Kelley north from Sombrero Butte.
Kelley's presence may account for the name. Ref.: 242

KELLOGG MOUNTAIN
Pima   T12S R16E   Elev. 8385'
This mountain shows as Mount Lee on the Roskruge map of 1893. The name Kellogg
derives from that of William Kellogg, who owned a ranch on the northeast slope c. 1900,
or from the name of his brother Alexander, who worked on the north slope of the Santa
Catalina Mountains, rounding up wild horses. Ref.: AHS, G.E.P. Smith

KELLY
Yavapai   Loc. unknown
Charles I. Kelly had a mine and ranch and wanted to have a post office. The name was

entered officially, but Kelly was not commissioned and the post office was abandoned.
P.O. est. Nov. 12, 1888, Charles I. Kelly, p.m.; disc. Jan. 30, 1889 Ref.: 18a; 242

KELLY BUTTE
Gila   T5N R21E   Elev. 6130'
Sgt. Kelly was stationed at Fort Apache in the 1890s, having been there for several
years. No record exists of his being killed by Apaches. The butte is said to bear a
resemblance to Kelly's notable nose, hence the name. This butte is not the same as
Kelley's Butte. Ref.: Davis; Patterson

KELLY TANK
Coconino   T19N R12E
This is a stock pond on the Raymond Buffalo Ranch, owned and operated by the Arizona
Game and Fish Department. This tank was named for old Charley Kelly, who was found
dead in the water in 1897. See Yaeger Canyon, Coconino Ref.: Harris; 329

KELSEY CANYON
Cochise   T14S R20E
Old Man Kelsey had a bad time with Indians who "burned him out a time or two." He
left the area, but after many years came back and finally sold his holdings. Ref.: Bennett

KELTON
Cochise   T19S R25E   Elev. c. 3500'
Capt. C. B. Kelton homesteaded where the S.P.R.R. right-of-way to Mexico was to run,
and the railroad location is on his former property. The place was constructed in 1909.
In 1878 Capt. Kelton was living in Tucson.
P.O. est. Nov. 17, 1914, Bailey A. Taylor, p.m.; disc. Jan. 31, 1928
Ref.: AHS, Robert Alpheus Lewis File; *Bisbee Review* N.D., N.P.) (State Library); 242

KELVIN
Pinal   T4S R14E   Elev. 1840'
On the site of present-day Kelvin the Riverside State Station was inaugurated in 1877.
The town of Kelvin, established by the Ray Mining Company, was named by Lord
Gordon for Kelvin Grove, Scotland. Since it is the junction point which connects the
main railroad line with the branch to Ray, this place was also known in the early days as
Ray Junction.
P.O. est. as Riverside, Oct. 17, 1877, Charles D. Putnam, p.m.; changed to Kelvin, Feb.
1, 1900, Clifford E. McKee, p.m.; disc. Jan. 31, 1956; Wells Fargo 1904
Ref.: 242; *Florence Tribune* (Oct. 21, 1899), p. 3 (State Library Files); 276, p. 58; 346,
p. 175, Note 16; 159, I, 592; 315, p. 239

KENDALL
Maricopa   T1N R4E
This location on the Phoenix and Eastern R.R. was named for Frank Kendall, treasurer
of the Phoenix and Maricopa R.R. c. 1883. Ref.: 18a

KENDRICK PEAK
Coconino   T15N R2E   Elev. 10,418'
Lt. Amiel Whipple named this peak for Maj. H. L. Kendrick (d. 1891), in charge of the
Sitgreaves military escort in 1851 and later commandant of Fort Defiance. This peak
was created by four separate lava flows. Originally the peak was about forty-eight
hundred feet high, but erosion lowered the cone about a thousand feet, creating three
canyons in the process. Kendrick Park is in the area, as is Kendrick Spring.
Ref.: 276, p. 58; 346, p. 175, Note 16; 159, I, 592; 315, p. 239

KENILWORTH
Pinal   T5S R8E   Elev. c. 1400'
Judge Richard E. Sloan with Thomas Davis filed for a homestead with plans to develop
irrigation water. Davis, who had been born within a few miles of the castle which Sir
Walter Scott made famous, named the ranch Kenilworth. (Scott spelled the name of the

castle Kennilworth.) Their plans for irrigating were hounded by continuous drought and they were forced to abandon their project c. 1894.

P.O. est. Sept. 21, 1891, Thomas C. Graham, p.m.; disc. Jan. 11, 1895

Ref.: 297, pp. 65, 69, 70

KENNEDY DAM

Coconino   T19N R4E

This dam was named for William Kennedy, who lived nearby for sixty-five years beginning in the late nineteenth century. See also Antelope Lake, Coconino

Ref.: Sykes

KENNEDY PEAK

Graham   T9S R20E   Elev. 7540'

Hiram Kennedy maintained a well southeast of Camp Grant in the early 1870s and this peak was named for him. There was a stage station at this location between Grant and Old Camp Goodwin in 1873. Ref.: 242; *Arizona Courier* (March 8, 1973)

KENTUCK MOUNTAIN

Maricopa   T7N R6E   Elev. 5013'

This place was named for Jim Kentuck, a cattleman here prior to 1900. Although Barnes suggests that the name came from the nickname of Marcus Herring, it seems unlikely, as Herring was not associated with this area, but rather with the Bisbee locale. The name Kentucky Mountain is a variant. See Kentuck, Cochise Ref.: 18a; *Arizona Weekly Star* (Sept. 30, 1880), p. 3; Kitt

KENTUCK

Cochise   T14S R22E

Newspapers of the time did little to clarify who held the nickname "Kentuck" — Marcus Herring (b. Sept. 23, 1823, Kentucky; d. May 22, 1910) or Ray "Kentuck" Elderman, whose name was sometimes confused with that of George H. Eddleman. George Warren located the Copper Queen Mine, which Herring, Eddleman, Elderman, and others later sold. An article in the *Arizona Citizen* in 1875 referred to "Kentuck" Elderman as "an old guide and Indian fighter," a statement reiterated by the *Arizona Daily Star* in 1911. In any event, "Kentuck" — whoever he actually was — had a stage station at this location "a few miles east of Tres Alamos," in 1873. Ref.: AHS, Marcus Herring File; *Tombstone Epitaph* (April 14, 1888), p. 1; *Arizona Weekly Star* (Sept. 30, 1880), p. 3; *Arizona Daily Star* (Nov. 26, 1911), p. 1

KENTUCKY GULCH

Pima

This gulch was named for the Kentucky Mine, one of the most productive gold mines c. 1875. See Greaterville, Pima Ref.: AHS, Castillo Collection

KENYON STATION

Maricopa   T4S R7W

The first name for this stage station on the Butterfield Overland route was Murderer's Grave because here in 1857 a young man travelling under charge of his guardian murdered him and was immediately executed and buried. With the establishment of the Butterfield Overland route, the name was changed to honor Marcus L. Kinyon, in 1858 in charge of this division of the Butterfield line. McClintock says that Charles H. Kenyon (b. Feb. 1885, New York; d. 1906) operated the stage station before settling in Globe permanently in 1879. However, McClintock also notes that Kenyon bought the old Maricopa Wells Station, which he sold in 1878. The *Arizona Sentinel* of 1878 lists a man named Hudson as proprietor of Kenyon Station. There is a possibility that Charles Kenyon operated the station at its outset and that his name early became attached to the place. Whatever the facts, the stage station was the scene of another murder on August 18, 1873, when two Mexicans stabbed Ed Lumley and tortured him, trying to make him tell where he hid his money. All station keepers feared such attacks, because there were no banks and they had no alternative to hiding money. The fact that money was so

secreted led not only to robbery and murder, but also to current legends of buried treasure.
Ref.: 73, II, 174; AHS, Charles H. Kenyon File; 224, III; 225, p. 274; *Arizona Sentinel* (Oct. 12, 1878), p. 3

KERLIN'S WELL
Coconino   T22N R5W   Elev. c. 5000'
On July 13, 1859 this watering place was found and named for F. C. Kerlin, clerk with the exploring party of Lt. Edward Fitzgerald Beale. In June 1881 Coues found the name "Kerlin" scratched on rocks at this spring, which is also called Cullen's Well, an error. It was also mapped as Collins Well (1879-1883).

KEYHOLE NATURAL BRIDGE
Coconino   T34N R3W   Elev. 4543'
On April 16, 1956 while flying in the area, P. T. Reilly photographed this natural bridge. It is descriptively named.   Ref.: 329

KEYSTONE MINE
Mohave   T23N R18W   Elev. c. 4500'
The mill for Keystone No. 1 and No. 2 mines, the first and second constructed in 1870, began operating in 1876 and continued until 1882. The railroad station nearby (for shipping ore) was named for the mine. Ref.: Babcock; 200, p. 80

KEYSTONE RIDGE
Gila   T7N R15E   Elev. 5514'
This ridge borrows its name from that of the Keystone Mine, c. 1880. Keystone Mine shaft was on the ridge.

K 4 DRAW
Coconino   T22N R1E
This location is on the K 4 Ranch, hence its name.

KIBBEY BUTTE
Coconino (Grand Canyon)   T33N R4E   Elev. 7500'
Joseph Henry Kibbey (b. 1853, Indiana; died 1924) arrived in Arizona in 1887. He became an authority on water laws and a distinguished jurist. In 1889 he was appointed to the Arizona Supreme Court, but resigned when appointed Territorial Governor by President Theodore Roosevelt. He served 1905-1909. The name for this butte was suggested by Frank Bond in 1929. Ref.: 329

KIDDE CANYON
Gila/Graham   T2N R21E
This large canyon is named for an Indian family long resident in the area. It is misspelled Kidd Canyon. Ref.: 329

KIELBERG CANYON   pro.: /kiylberg/
Graham/Pinal   T10S R20–18E
Emil Kielberg, a Danish prospector, lived and prospected in this area from 1875 to 1920. The spelling "Kilberg" is incorrect. Kielberg Creek is partially in this canyon. At Kielberg Peak the Powers brothers murdered the sheriff. A posse killed two brothers at their cabin in Rattlesnake Canyon on February 11, 1918, and two served long prison sentences. All were WW I draft evaders. Ref.: 329; Jennings; Lenon

KIM
Yuma   T8S R14E   Elev. c. 400'
Epes Randolph, president of the S.P.R.R. had a Chinese cook named Kim (or Kin) on his private railroad car, and the siding was named for the cook. Because Kim had never seen his "town", Randolph arranged to drop him off for a visit. Kim left the train at that point, making the population temporarily consist of one. The Randolph private car pulled away, leaving him and the railroad spur alone. However, Randolph had arranged

for the next train to pick up the Chinese cook. When asked how he liked his town, Kim said, "Fine! Fine! It still has lots of room to grow." Ref.: Lenon

KIMBALL GROVE
Cochise   T20S R21E
A rancher here prior to the discovery of the Tombstone mines sold out to a man named Kimball, hence the name. Later when the railroad in 18181 put in a spur from Tombstone to Fairbank, a juncture here with the road straight on to Nogales formed a "Y" and the location was known as The Y before Kimball's name became attached to it. Ref.: Larriau

KIMBALL, MOUNT
Pima   T12S R14E   Elev. 7255'
Although the 1893 Roskruge map shows this location as Cathedral Rock, that place is actually three miles northeast. The peak was named for Fred E. A. Kimball (b. Oct. 22, 1863, New Hampshire; d. Feb. 4, 1930), who came to Arizona in 1899 and worked as a reporter on the *Arizona Star*. Later he was a book and stationery dealer as well as a publisher, legislator, and conservationist. The name was suggested by the Tucson Natural History Society in 1931 because Kimball had spent much of his time in endless exploration of this section of the Santa Catalina Mountains. Ref.: 329

KIMBALL'S LAKE
Cochise   Near Fairbank
The 1887 earthquake caused the overnight disappearance of this lake. Ref.: *Tombstone Epitaph* (May 4, 1887)

KINDER SPRING
Coconino   T13N R10E
Runyon C. Kinder was a sheepman in this area in the late 1880s. His name also applies to Kinder Crossing and to Kinder Draw. Ref.: 18a

KING ARTHUR CASTLE
Coconino (Grand Canyon)   T33N R1E   Elev. 7315'
The name for this peak was suggested by the USGS in October 1908 to carry out the policy of naming formations for characters in the Arthurian legend. It is described as a "castellated structure of red rock." Ref.: 329; 178, pp. 80-81

KING CANYON
Yavapai   T17N R1W
Thomas R. King (d. Feb. 2, 1832) established a horse ranch in this vicinity c. 1883. Later his nephews joined him and managed his ranch. King Peak (T14N/R9W; Elev. 4100') and King Spring (T18N/R1E), also bear his name. Ref.: 18a

KING CREST
Coconino (Grand Canyon)   T33N R1W
This location was named by the USGS for Clarence King, who in 1867 began surveying a potential route for a transcontinental railroad through the Grand Canyon. He was the first director of the USGS. Ref.: 329

KING GULCH
Greenlee   T4S R29E
The gulch (or canyon) was named because of the location of the King Mine at Metcalf. It also applies to King Canyon and King Creek. Ref.: Simmons

KINGMAN
Mohave   T21N R17W   Elev. 3325'
Kingman, the county seat of Mohave in 1887, was named for Lewis Kingman (1845-1912), chief engineer of the Western Division of the A. & P. R.R. He was the locating engineer and named this place for himself.
P.O. est. March 22, 1883, Edward F. Thompson, p.m.; Wells Fargo 1885; incorporated Jan. 21, 1925 Ref.: Patey

KINGMAN WASH

Mohave   T31N R23W

Until 1948 this wash was called Deadman Wash, but the name was officially changed in that year. See Kingman, Mohave Ref.: 329

KING'S CROWN PEAK

Pinal   T1S R13E   Elev. 5541'

This mountain, rounded at the top, took its name from the Silver King Mine, the miners deeming that the Silver King deserved a crown, hence the name. Ref.: Craig

KING VALLEY

Yuma   T2S R17W

This valley takes its name from the King of Arizona Mine. Although the name Kofa Plain was proposed for it, it was not adopted. Ref.: 329

KINISHBA   pro.: /kinisbà/

Navajo = "brown house"

Gila   T5N R22E   Elev. 5000'

Because of its location just southwest of Fort Apache, this extensive ruin used to be called Fort Apache Ruins. On flat ground at the end of a deep wash, it consists of buildings two and three stories high, with open courts and passageways. From 1935 through 1942 it was partially restored under the direction of Bryan Cummings of the University of Arizona. The structures, probably built between 1232 and 1328 A.D., have been occupied by at least three main cultural groups.
Ref.: 5, p. 444; *Scenic Guide to Arizona*, p. 22

KINLICHEE   pro.: /kin:azini'/

Navajo: *Kin Dah ichii'* = "red house in the distance" or "place of the red spot house"

Navajo   T27N R27E   Elev. c. 7100'

This location took its name from that of Pueblo Colorado, which the Navajo refer to as Kin Dah ichii'. During the Navajo war of 1863-64, Camp Florilla, an outpost of Fort Defiance, used a large spring here. Ref.: Farmer; 331, p. 84; 143, p. 175; Burcard

KINNEY MOUNTAIN

Navajo   T9N R23E   Elev. 7636'

J. P. Kinney was the first chairman of the Forestry Branch for the Indian Service and is deemed father of forestry law in the United States. Ref.: Davis

KINNIKINIC LAKE/   pro.: /kinəkinik/

Coconino   T18N R10E   Elev. c. 7000'

An old-time stockman, Less Hart of the Hart Cattle Company, in 1902 put a ditch into an old dry lake bed. He named the lake after nearby Kinnikinic Spring, which in turn took its name from the abundance of the shiny leafed *arctostaphloc* or bear berry, called *kinnik-kinnik* by Indians, who use its inner bark as tobacco. The name also applies to Kinnickinic Camp and Pueblo, and also to a wild life lake area of one hundred thirty-five acres. Kinnikinic Spring is at T18N/R11E. Ref.: Hart; 282a, pp. 34, 116

KINNIKINICK PUEBLO

Coconino   T17N R11E

This Sinagua Pueblo was built c. 1269 A.D. See Kinnickinic Lake, Coconino Ref.: 70, p. 123

KINO PEAK   pro.: /kiyno/

Pima   T15S R7W   Elev. 3197'

William Supernaugh, superintendent of the Organ Pipe Cactus National Monument, applied this name in 1945 to honor Fr. Eusebio Francisco Kino, who as a "padre on horse-back" was a tireless missionary from 1694 until his death in 1711. Ref.: Henson

KIRBY

Gila   T3N R13E

The first name suggested for the post office here was "Livingstone or Kirby (*sic*)
Station," in the home of a former forest supervisor named Lee Kirby, whose mother was
the first postmistress. The family arrived with Mormon settlers in the area about 1882.
On the post office application form, the name is quite clearly written "Amelia Kerby."
P.O. est. Sept. 21, 1914, Mrs. Amelia Kerby, p.m.; disc. May 7, 1917
Ref.: Woody; 242

KIRBY

Yavapai   T9N R3W

In 1883 Wheeler noted that this was a post office o Hassayampa Creek. Barnes says it
was near the Tip Top Mine. The reason for the name has not been established.
P.O. est. May 23, 1883, William C. Dawes, p.m.; disc. April 28, 1884
Ref.: 18a; 345, I, 299, Note 242

KIRKLAND

Yavapai   T13N R4W   Elev. 3927'

This location takes its name from that of William H. Kirkland (b. July 12, 1832,
Virginia; d. Jan. 1, 1899), who came to Arizona to live in 1856. He raised the first
American flag in Tucson when the Mormon Battalion went through it in 1846. In 1863
Kirkland, his wife, and two children moved to the valley which today bears his name,
where by 1864 the Kirkland family had built a stage station. In 1868 the Kirklands
moved to Phoenix. By 1869 at least twenty-five hundred acres of land had been
homesteaded in Kirkland Valley and a post office was established to serve the area. In
1894 the railroad laid rails through the valley and named the small railroad station after
the original settler, William Kirkland. The name also applies to other nearby locations.
Associated names include Lower Kirkland Valley (T13N/R5W), Kirkland Creek,
Junction (T12N/R4W, Elev. 4100'), and Valley.
P.O. est. as Kirkland Station (T12N/R4W), Dec. 19, 1899, Charley R. Bates, p.m.;
Wells Fargo 1903 Ref.: 242; 76, p. 292; 206, p. 143; 5, p. 289; 233, pp. 73-74-77;
Arizona Journal Miner (Jan. 10, 1899), p. 4; *Weekly Arizona Miner* (Feb. 13, 1869),
p. 2

KITCHEN RANCH, PETE

Santa Cruz   T23S R14E   Elev. 4250'

Pete Kitchen (b. 1819, Kentucky; d. Aug. 5, 1895) was a wagon master during the war
with Mexico, being mustered out in Oregon. There he joined the rush to the California
gold fields. In 1854 he began ranching at the Canoa Ranch in southern Arizona, but was
wiped out by Apache Indians during the early years of the American Civil War. He then
went to Sonora to search for gold, but returned empty-handed after 1864 to the Santa
Cruz Valley to find it in a state of desolation. Thereafter he settled at his El Potrero
Ranch on Potrero Creek, remaining there from 1869 to about 1876. Having been wiped
out once by Apaches, he was determined to avoid repetition, and built a small fort for his
ranch house. A sentinel was constantly patrolling the roof parapet. Men in the fields
carried rifles at the ready, swinging from plow handles. All carried revolvers. Despite the
war-like aspect of the ranch, travellers found it a busy and hospitable place, with the
sounds of blacksmiths and wagon makers at work. Apaches raided often, stealing stock
and studding pigs with arrows. On June 8, 1871 they caught Kitchen's stepson and killed
him. Nevertheless, Kitchen remained for many years. Despite his early relative
prosperity, Pete Kitchen lived in poverty in his later years. He died in Tucson. A post
office was established on the Kitchen Ranch with Kitchen serving as p.m.
P.O. est. as Monument, June 11, 1873, Peter Kitchen, p.m.; name changed to
Calabazas, April 26, 1880 Ref.: 49, p. 78; AHS, Pete Kitchen Files; *Arizona Daily
Star* (Feb. 24, 1955), p. 9; 297, p. 84; AHS, "Letter from Secretary of Interior
transmitting certain papers regarding the Sopori Land Grant"; Lenon

KITCHEN SPRING

Apache   T9N R26E   Elev. 7780'

Barnes quotes A. F. Potter as saying that Pete Kitchen was reported to have camped at
this spot, hence its name.

KITT PEAK

Pima   T17S R7E   Elev. 6875'

George Roskruge had in his Pima County surveying party an Indian named Kit, who served as cook and general roustabout. In his 1893 map this point is Kit's Peak, possibly indicating the location was named for the Indian. However, it may have been named either for Roskruge's sister, Mrs. William F. Kitt, or for his nephews, as the spelling of the name varies. On GLO 1896 it is Kitt's Peak, but reappears on GLO 1909 through 1921 as Kit's Peak. In 1958 the location became the site for a National Observatory. Ref.: Mrs. George F. Kitt; 329

KLAGETOH   pro.: /sˢey:itoʔ/

Navajo: *teeghi'to'* = "water going in the ground"

Apache   T24N R27E   Elev. 6420'

This school and Navajo community are west of Klagetoh Wash where there is a 12th century Indian ruin. The name describes running water vanishing in the bed of the wash. P.O. est. Nov. 14, 1933, William K. Rush, p.m.; disc. April 15, 1944 Ref.: 242; 331, p. 84

KLONDYKE

Graham   T7S R20E   Elev. 3467'

Prospectors returning from Alaska settled here and named it to commemorate their experiences in the Klondike. The name also applies to Klondyke Butte, Mountain, and Wash. P.O. est. Jan. 10, 1907, John F. Greenwood, p.m.; disc. Aug. 31, 1955 Ref.: 18a; 242

KLONDYKE MILL

Mohave   T25N R21W   Elev. 1200'

The Klondyke Mine was located in Oct. 1898 by William and George Cooke and Dick Blythe, who sold it in November. They built a mill with two batteries of five stamps installed in 1899. Indians sold them driftwood at $5.00 per cord to be used as fuel. By 1905 the Klondyke Mine was nearly exhausted, the price of its ore being assayed at $8.00 per ton vs. an earlier $38.00 per ton. Waters from Davis Dam now cover the mine and mill. Ref.: Housholder; Babcock; Harris

KLOTHO'S TEMPLE

Yuma   T8S R20W   Elev. 1666'

De Lancey Gill, an artist, was with the Old Yuma Trail party of W. J. McGee in November 1900 and named this peak, but his reason for so doing is not known at this time. See also Coronation Peak, Yuma Ref.: 227, p. 140

KNIGHT CREEK

Mohave   T20–18N R13W   Elev. 3800'

Accuracy in surveying led to the realization that Cottonwood Creek (#1, Mohave, *q.v.*) was north of the old White Cliffs Creek named by Lt. Amiel W. Whipple in 1854. Hence in 1933 the USGS gave the name Knight to the former White Cliffs Creek and removed the designation Cottonwood for this location. In 1854 Lt. Amiel W. Whipple wrote, "The northern ridge which bounds the valley is broken into white cliffs of fantastic shapes; hence the stream is called White Cliff Creek." The 1879 Willcox map of Arizona Territory carries the name White Cliffs Creek. On GLO 1912 the name has become Cottonwood Creek (#1, at T22N/R13W). On the 1933 GLO, Cottonwood Creek has shifted one stream farther north and the former White Cliff Creek is now named Knight Creek. The name was changed in 1923 to Knight Creek by the USGS (T20N/R12W, Elev. 3800'). The same spring is represented on GLO 1883. See Aquarius Mountains, Mohave, and Cottonwood Cliffs, Mohave Ref.: 347, pp. 96, 202, Note 7

KNOB HILL

Coconino   T23S R23E   Elev. 6040'

The name describes the appearance of this location.

KNOB MOUNTAIN
Gila   T9N R8E   Elev. 6255'
The name describes the appearance of the mountain.

KNOLL LAKE
Coconino   T12N R12E
There is a campground at this location. The name derives from that of a man who built
the first logging trail along Knoll Ridge, which is also named for him. Coincidentally it is
adjacent to a small rocky knoll at the northern end of Knoll Ridge. The name applies to
the seventy-seven acre Knoll Lake Wild Life Area and to Knoll or Knoll's Ridge.
Ref.: 329

KOFA   pro.: /kowfə/
Yuma   T6S R14W   Elev. c. 1700'
In 1896 Charles E. Eichelberger located the King of Arizona Mine, which he developed
with H. B. Gleason and Epes Randolph as partners. Between that date and July 1910,
the mine produced over $3,500,000. in ore. Eichelberger sold out in 1909 to Col.
Eugene S. Ives. The railroad station was named Kofa because the King of Arizona Mine
Company had a "branding iron" used to mark company property which read "K of A."
Lewis A. Alexander spotted the branding iron and named the railroad station post office
for the mining community. The name applies also to Kofa Butte, sometimes called Mud
Mountain because the butte looks like an old tailings dump and tailings are referred to as
"mud."
P.O. est. Jan. 17, 1900, Lewis W. Alexander, p.m.; disc. Aug. 27, 1928
Ref.: 355, pp. 109-110; Lenon; 242; Monson

KOFA DAM
Yuma   T2S R16W
The dam was built to impound water for the mining community at Kofa, but it leaked
through its face and was not much use. See Kofa, Yuma Ref.: Monson

KOFA GAME RANGE
Yuma   T1S R16W
This game refuge was established on Jan. 25, 1939 to encompass 660,000 acres
primarily fore big horn sheep. Ref.: Kofa Brochure "Final Environmental Statement,"
U.S. Fish and Wild Life Service

KOFA MOUNTAINS
Yuma/La Paz   T1-2S R16-17W   Elev. 1800'
This variant name for the S H Mountains was officially substituted on October 2, 1963
by the USGS with the notation that "Kofa Game Range would like to 'fumigate' the
original name." See S H Mountains, Yuma, and Kofa, Yuma Ref.: 329

KOFA QUEEN MINE
Yuma   T1S R17W
Every king must have his queen and hence the Kofa Queen Mine is the partner of the
King of Arizona Mine. These small workings are now abandoned. The name applies to a
canyon also. See Kofa, Yuma

KOFA WELL
Yuma   T2S R17W
A tremendous pile of ironwood ashes at this location is a reminder that the operation of
the Kofa Mine and Mill stripped the valley of all wood to fuel the mill operation. See
Kofa, Yuma Ref.: Monson

KOHATK   pro.: /gᵏowhat/
Pima = "where a hollow has been made"
Pinal   T10S R3E   Elev. 1639'
This Pima Indian village exists in a basin-like location, hence the name. Fr. Kino and
Capt. Diego Carrasco passed through this village in September 1698 and called it San
Bonifacio del Coati y del Sibuoidag (actually two villages). At the time Kino was

searching for a quicksilver mine reported to him by Sobaipuri Indians. On the Hartley 1865 map the place shows as Cojeta and on GLO 1879 as Cojela. Both names, as well as the spelling *Quajote* and *Quojote*, are corruptions. Browne spelled it *Cohota*. In June 1941 the name of Kohatk Valley was officially changed to its present form from Quajote Valley and Santa Rosa Wash. Ref.: 58; 57, pp. 9, 391; 167, I, 322; 262, p. 16; 329

KOHI KUG   pro.: /kowᵛhiᴧkù/

Papago: *koxi* = "mulberry tree"; *kux* = "where it stands"

Pima   T18S R7E   Elev. 3262'

In 1893 Roskruge incorrectly labelled this village Ventana, as Ventana is actually a different village called Chiuli Shaik (*q.v.*). In 1912 Lumholtz labelled it Koxikux, a corruption of the name. Another corrupt name sometimes used is Juit Vaya. The small Papago community is one of three on branches of Fresnal Wash. Any and all three are sometimes called Fresnal. Ref.: 262, p. 1; 329

KOHINOOR SPRING

Mohave   T26N R14W   Elev. c. 4000'

This spring, sometimes called Kayote Spring, was named because of the former presence of a man who spelled his name Cohenour. See Cohenour Spring, Mohave, and Coyote Spring, Mohave

KOHL'S RANCH

Gila   T11N R12E   Elev. 5350'

The post office at this location was established to serve residents and visiting sportsmen. P.O. est. Jan. 3, 1939, Mrs. Laura B. Kohl, p.m.; disc. 1974   Ref.: 242

KOKOPYNAME

Hopi: "house of the Firewood People"

Navajo   T28N R21E   Elev. 6440'

This large pueblo ruin is said by the Hopi to belong to the Kokop (Firewood) clan, originally a Jemez people. The clan is said to have moved and founded the pueblo of Sikyatki. Ref.: 152, p. 20; 167, I, 723

KOLB NATURAL BRIDGE

Coconino (Grand Canyon)   T33N R4E   Elev. 5420'
2500' below Point Imperial

John Brown and Joe Hamblin saw this natural bridge in 1871 while on the Powell Grand Canyon Expedition, according to Jack Roak, who in 1920 talked to John Brown about the matter. For many years the bridge was forgotten until Sen. Barry Goldwater flew over the arch in December 1952 and noticed the one hundred and forty-seven-foot-high span. In October 1954 Goldwater visited the bridge by helicopter to establish its definite location. The project was named for Emery C. Kolb (b. 1881, Pensylvania; d. 1976), who with his brother Ellsworth (1876-1960) lived on the South Rim of the Grand Canyon beginning in 1903. There Emery was known as a photographer to thousands of visitors. The Kolb brothers made two trips through the Grand Canyon and several hundred explorations within its walls. The location is sometimes called Kolb Arch. Ref.: Letter (copy), Jesse L. Nusbaum, Sr. to Otis T. Marsten (Sept. 6, 1955), Grand Canyon Files; *Chicago Tribune* (Nov. 30, 1954), n.p.; Emery Kolb; 121, pp. 30-31; J.H. Butchart, Letter (1961)

KOMATKE

Pima: *kamatuk wutca* = "below or at the foot of"; *kamatuk* (the Pima name for the Estrella Mts.)

Maricopa   T2S R2E

As is customary, the Pima Indians have named this village loction according to a nearby landmark, in this case the Estrella Mountains. The village is sometimes referred to as St. Johns, although actually St. Johns' Mission (or Chapel) is a half mile west of the village. When a post office was proposed for this location, the first name suggested was Gila

Crossing. However, the name Komatke was assigned by the Post Office Department. P.O. est. Sept. 9, 1915, Herman P. Alis, p.m.; disc. May 31, 1944
Ref.: 58; 57, p. 398; 242

KOMO POINT

Coconino (Grand Canyon)   T32N R4E   Elev. 8000'
This location, formerly known as Fafner Point, now bears the name of an Indian family and also the name of a plant used in making a pink dye. Ref.: 329

KOM VO   pro.: /kowmwow/

Papago: *cumaro* = "hackberry tree"; *vo* = "grows"
Pima   T17S R1W   Elev. c. 1500'
Some waterholes are referred to as *charcos* (= "ponds") and at the waterhole here hackberry trees grow abundantly. The name applies to a small Papago village with its white adobe church. Other names applied to this location are as follows: 1. Santa Cruz, because it is the name of the church; 2. Comeva, a corruption; 3. Comovo, a corruption; 4. Komuo, a corruption; 5. Pato (Spanish = "duck") because according to Bryan, Pato was the name of the principal Papago Indian at the village. Kom Vo Valley (a.k.a. Bajio Comovo, or "Lower Komvo," a corruption) also bears the name.
Ref.: 58; 57, p. 369; 262, pp. 10, 17; 329

KOTS KUG

Papago = "cross stands"
Pima   T18S R2E   Elev. 1900'
This small Papago village was formerly referred to as Stanford Ranch and as Toro's Ranch, both names deriving from the name of a rancher, Sanford Toro (*sic*). In 1941 the USGS officially adopted the Papago name for the location. Ref.: 329

KO VAYA   pro.: /kəʔwahə/

Papago = "badger well"
Pima   T16S R4E   Elev. c. 2400'
Prior to the creation of modern transportation systems on the Papago Reservation, some Papago villages were used mainly in winter, the people migrating temporarily in summer to agricultural areas on the reservation. Ko Vaya was such a winter village. Apparently it took strangers a long time learning how to pronounce the name of this location, much less how to render it in writing, as witness the following attempts: Cups (Lt. Juan Mateo Manje (Kupk [*q.v.*] is at T17S/R2E); Cahuabi (Pumpelly, 1863); Kavvaxlak (Lumholtz, 1912); Cababi (Hartley, 1865); Covajea (U.S. Corps of Engineers, 1917).
   Hinton noted a mine on the mountain near the village, which he called Cabibi (*sic*) Mine, saying it was as famous as the Ajo Mine. The mining community had a post office. The mountain name was also spelled Cababi.
P.O. est. as Cababi, March 12, 1883, Robert H. Choat, p.m.; disc. June 4, 1884
Ref.: 163, p. 227; 369, p. 38; 262, p. 5; 58; 57, p. 365; 329; 242

KRISHNA SHRINE

Coconino (Grand Canyon)   T31N R4E
This peak was named by the USGS in 1906 in accordance with the then existing policy to use the names of deities in various mythologies for outstanding temple-like formations in the Grand Canyon.

KUAKATCH   pro.: /kúəkəᶜ/

Papago = "end of mountain"
Pima   T3N R19W   Elev. c. 2400'
Frederick Wall, an American miner, discovered and named the Growler Mine and dug a well in connection with the mine. From that fact arose the names Wall's Well and Pozo de Frederico (*Pozo* = "well"). It was in use when Lumholtz visited in 1912. When mining ceased, Papago Indians used the well and started a community which is also a favorite camping spot while the Papago are harvesting saguaro cactus fruit, usually in May. Kuakatch has been called the "most beautiful and comfortable spot between Tucson and Sonoyta." The old well was fringed with mesquite, palo verde, and desert

willow trees. This place is near the peak which is known both as Gunsight and as Montezuma's Head. Kuakatch Pass shares the name. "Kookatsh" is a corruption. Ref.: Netherlan; Hensen; 58; 262, p. 7; 171, p. 74

KUI TATK
Papago: *kui* = "mesquite;" *tatk* = "root"
Pima   T16S R3E   Elev. 2043'
This was the original Papago village at what is now known as Vainom Kug or Vainom Kux (= "iron stands" or Pumphouse village.)   Ref.: 329; 58

KUPK
Papago: *kupk* = "dam"
Pima   T17S R2E   Elev. 1845'
In 1917 the U.S. Corps of Engineers referred to this Papago village as Copeka, a corruption. Ref.: 57, p. 10; 329

KUPK HILLS
Pima   T17S R1E   Elev. 2990'
The 1857 Boundary Survey Sheet No. 40 shows these low hills as Cerros del Tecolote. The U.S. Corps of Engineers in 1917 called them the Copeka Mountains. See Kupk, Pima
Ref.: 329

KWAGUNT CANYON
Coconino (Grand Canyon)   T33N R5E   Elev. 5000'
This canyon was named by Maj. John Wesley Powell for Quagunt, a Piute Indian who said his father owned the valley and canyon and used to live there and had given it to him. He also said the Indians killed deer on a butte, which later (1906) was named for him by Francois E. Matthes. Kwagunt Valley (a.k.a. Kwagunt Hollow) was named by Powell in 1869. Kwagunt Rapids runs through the canyon, as does also Kwagunt Creek. Ref.: 89, p. 326; 322, p. 102

L

LA BARGE CANYON
Maricopa/Pinal   T1N R10E   Elev. c. 3000'
With a cattleman named Charlebois, John LeBarge (*sic*) (b. 1856, Canada, naturalized 1876, Massachusetts) maintained herds in this canyon, hence its name. In 1890 LeBarge was prospecting in this area. La Barge Spring and Creek (a.k.a. Boulder Creek) are here. La Barge Mountain (Pinal) is at T1N/R11E (Elev. 5077'). Ref.: AHS Files

LADDER TANKS
Yuma   T4S R19W
These natural water tanks are at the bases of a series of small waterfalls. They look like a ladder. Ref.: Monson; 279, p. 211

LADYBUG PEAK
Graham   T9S R25E   Elev. 8773'
This peak is a breeding ground for ladybugs, present in such quantities that farmers scoop buckets of the insects at Lady Bug Saddle. Ref.: 329; Jennings

LAGUNA
Pima
In 1854 this stage station was said to be ten miles from "Teuson." Because the station was in fact nine miles from Tucson, it was also known as the Nine Mile Waterhole. It had over eighty residents in 1869. Ref.: *Weekly Arizonan* (May 22, 1869), p. 3; 26, p. 54; AHS Files

LAGUNA, LA pro.: /laguwnə/
Spanish = "pond"
Yuma   T7S R22W   Elev. c. 200'
Two ponds used to be here (just below present Laguna Dam), known as First and Second Lagunes. In 1862 when placer gold was discovered nearby on the California side of the river, there was already a small settlement here. There was an immediate increase in population, which dwindled almost as rapidly because the placers failed in 1864. Only a small community persisted. In 1902 the Reclamation Act provided for constructing Laguna Dam and a post office was established to serve the construction community. Its construction was interrupted by workers deserting to search for gold exposed by blasting in the quarry. By 1907 water was being impounded behind the forty-foot-high dam.
P.O. est. as Lagune, July 10, 1909, Robert G. Weatherstone, p.m.; disc. Dec. 20, 1928
Ref.: Mercer; 5, p. 273; AHS Names File; *Arizona Miner* (May 11, 1864), p. 3; 355, p. 217; 107, II, 294; Lenon; 242

LAGUNA CREEK
Navajo/Apache   T39N R22E
This stream is also known as Tyende Creek, To wan-on-cheo Creek (1906), and as Laguna Canyon. See Tsegi Canyon, Navajo Ref.: 329

LAGUNA MOUNTAINS   pro.: /laguwnə/

Spanish = "pond"

Yuma   T7S R21W   Elev. 1081'

These mountains derive their name from Lagunas or swamps along the Colorado River. See also Laguna, La, Yuma Ref.: 355, p. 211

LAGUNA, SIERRA DE

Spanish: *laguna* = "pond or swamp"; *sierra de* = "mountains of"

Pima   Elev. c. 4800'

Lt. N. Michler in 1854 called the southern and eastern portions of the Ajo Mountains by this name. Ref.: 105, I, 72; 58

LAKE: When *lake* is used as a generic, with a few exceptions which follow, the place name will be entered under the identifying name. For example, for Lake Mead, see Mead, Lake, Mohave.

Lake Montezuma   Yavapai   T14N R5E

This is a developing community. See Montezuma, Lake, Yavapai

Lake No. 1   Coconino   T19N R7E

In 1873 troops building the Crook Road encountered so many lakes that they used numbers to identify them consecutively to the east. Except for this and Lake No. 4, the numbers have since given way to other names. Crook Road or Crook Trail, also known as the Verde Road, extended from Fort Verde to Fort Apache along the Mogollon Rim, ending at Corydon E. Cooley's ranch. See McNary, Apache Ref.: 18a

Lakeside   Navajo   T9N R22E   Elev. 6718'

The first name for the Mormon settlement begun here in the early 1880s was Fairview. The damming of Showlow Creek created a lake and the name was changed to Lakeside, there already being two smaller lakes in the vicinity. The settlement was also called Woodland although maps place Woodland in R23E. Apparently the name of Woodland was changed in 1890 to Lakeside. P.O. est. June 7, 1906, John L. Fish, p.m. Ref.: 5, p. 450; 225, p. 168; 242

LAMBLY STATION

Maricopa   Elev. c. 2500'

In 1872 a Mr. Lambly kept a stage station about ten miles south of Wickenburg on the east side of the Hassayampa River. Ref.: *Weekly Arizona Miner* (Dec. 7, ;1872), p. 2

LANCELOT POINT

Coconino (Grand Canyon)   T34N R1E

This name was proposed by Francois E. Matthes and adopted in 1908 in accordance with the USGS policy of naming places for characters in the Arthurian cycle. Ref.: 329

LAND

Cochise   T18S R21E   Elev. 3656'

William C. Land (b. c. 1838, Texas) drove cattle across Arizona to California in the 1850s. In 1880 with a partner named Hay, he bought the Babocomari Land Grant and ran about forty thousand cattle. The drought of 1890-1892 put them out of business. The post office was established at the railroad stop fifty yards east of the small settlement and named for Land. P.O. est. June 15, 1911, Lou C. Woolery, p.m.; disc. Nov. 30, 1913 Ref.: AHS, Edward W. Land File; 242

LANDERS

Yavapai   T15N R6E

This location was apparently a ranch post office belonging to a man named Lander. There is today a Lander Spring noted at this location. P.O. est. Nov. 24, 1896, Dayton F. Crofut; disc. Jan. 16, 1897 Ref.: 242

LANDING FLAT

Gila   T11N R10E

This location took its name from the fact that airplanes landed here. Ref.: Woody

LANDON SPRING

Coconino   T20N R6E

Landon and his family lived in this location in 1905, with Landon earning his living as a general handy-man. Ref.: Hart

LANE MOUNTAIN

Yavapai   T9N R1W   Elev. 7150'

James Madison Lane, a miner, was in this region in 1876. Ref.: 18a

LANG CREEK

Apache   T8N R27E   Elev. c. 8000'

Tommy Lang settled here in 1879 on this now dry creek. Ref.: Wentz

LANPHIER CANYON

Greenlee   T3N R31E

This canyon was named for the Lanphier family, which lived here c. 1925. Ref.: 329

LA PAZ COUNTY

On Nov. 2, 1982, by majority vote the fifteenth county in Arizona came into existence, becoming a political entity on January 1, 1983. La Paz County is comprised of land separated from its parent county, Yuma, lying mostly north of the Gila and Salt River Base Line between townships north and south. See maps.

It takes its name from that of the first county seat for Yuma County, La Paz, which relinquished that honor to Yuma (then known as Arizona City) in 1870. The town of Parker is county seat for La Paz County.

LAPHAM TANK

Maricopa   T7N R10W

Frank C. Lapham owned three wells in this vicinity. Ref.: 279, p. 211

LARAMITA   pro.: /larəmiytə/

Cochise   Elev. c. 4000'

This is the name of the point of entry from Mexico used c. 1894 until Naco came into existence, at which time the entry office moved to Naco. Ref.: Burgess

LAUB

Cochise   18 mi. E. of Bowie (?)

The origin of this name is not known. It was said to be a section house on the S.P.R.R., which briefly had a post office. It has not been found on maps.
P.O. est. Oct. 19, 1900, Earl Silas Peet, p.m.; disc. Feb. 16, 1901 Ref.: 242

LAUFFER MOUNTAIN

Gila   T7N R13E   Elev. c. 5000'

Jacob B. (Jake) Lauffer (b. 1853, Michigan; d. 1888) prospected and ran cattle in this vicinity in the 1880s. He was wounded by outlaws at the mountain bearing his name on Aug. 3, 1888. See Buck Peak, Gila Ref.: 18a; *Great Register of Gila County*, 1886

LAVA: Because of former volcanic activity in Arizona, many place names use the term *lava* descriptively.

Lava Bed	Mohave	T34N R16W
Lava Butte	Coconino (Grand Canyon)	T32N R5E
See Black Knob, Coconino		
Lava Canyon	Coconino (Grand Canyon)	T32N R5E
Lava Canyon Rapids	Coconino (Grand Canyon)	T32N R5E

Lava Caves	Coconino	Between Kendrick Peak and Flagstaff

Ice from here was used by Flagstaff residents before they had artificial refrigeration. Ref.: Schnebly

Lava Cliff	Mohave	T28N R13W

Lava Creek	Coconino (Grand Canyon)	T32N R5E

Despite the fact that in 1930 this creek was known locally as Silver Creek, the USGS named it Lava Creek. It was also formerly called Chuar Creek. Ref.: 329, M. R. Tillotson, Letter (April 18, 1930) to Director, Grand Canyon National Park

Lava Cliff Rapid	Coconino (Grand Canyon)	6 mi. below Separation Rapid and 20 mi. below Diamond Creek

This location was named by Claude Birdseye in 1924 because of a "lava cliff on the right bank just above the rapids ..." Ref.: 36, p. 195

Lava Falls	Mohave (Grand Canyon)	T32N R7W	Elev. 4000'

This name was applied by members of Maj. John Wesley Powell's Grand Canyon Expedition, August 25, 1871. Dellenbaugh says it appears to have once been filled with lava to a depth of one hundred feet. Maj. Clarence E. Dutton in 1882 said that lava had burst from both sides of the canyon and dammed the river, but the river broke through again, creating both the canyon and Lava Falls Rapids. This is probably the place Thompson on March 31, 1872 called Lava Ridge. Ref.: 322, p. 73; 88, p. 192; 89, p. 224; 100, Plate XIX

Lava Falls Rapids	Mohave/Coconino (Grand Canyon)	T32N R7W

This rapid, up-canyon from the rapids, was named for a large lava pinnacle by Birdseye in 1924. Ref.: 36, p. 192

Lava Point	Coconino	T27N R8E

Lava Ridge	Coconino

See Lava Falls, Mohave (Grand Canyon)

Lava River Cave	Coconino	T23N R5E
Lava Spring	Maricopa	T1S R6W
Lava Spring	Navajo	T24N R21E
Lava Wash	Coconino	T27N R7E

LAVEEN

Maricopa	T1S R2E	Elev. 1030'

This small settlement takes its name from that of the first postmaster.
P.O. est. May 27, 1913, Miss Ferieda Laveen, p.m. Ref.: 242

LAVENDER PIT

Cochise	T23S R24E

The mine pit with the poetic name was named for Harrison Morton Lavender (b. Oct. 31, 1890, South Dakota; d. March 21, 1952), who began his career as a miner for the Calumet and Arizona Mining Company. When that company merged with Phelps Dodge Corporation in 1931, he was named mine superintendent for the Copper Queen at Bisbee. He was appointed general manager in 1937. So extensive is the pit that entire residential areas and businesses were relocated, as was the main highway. Now exhausted, it is one of the eyesores of America. Ref.: 197, p. 59; "*Arizona Days and Ways,*" *Arizona Republic* (Aug. 8, 1954), p. 2

LAWLER PEAK

Yavapai	T15N R9W	Elev. 4800'

John F. Lawler located claims here in 1880 and was one of the organizers of the Eureka Mining District, formed August 16, 1884. Lawler Creek (T12N/R7W) is an associated name. Ref.: 3a, p. 43; Mrs. John Lawler, Letter (June 30, 1973)

LAWRENCE CREEK

Gila   T4N R15E

This sand wash was named for a rancher who lived here. Ref.: Woody

LAWS SPRING

Coconino   T24N R3E

Lt. Beale named this spring for Maj. W. L. Laws. Ref.: 18a

LAYTON

Graham   T4S R21E   Elev. c. 2500'

Hyrum H. Tippets (or Charles Tippets (?)) a Mormon, arrived here on January 13, 1883 from Brigham City, Utah, and bought land from John Penfold. He was followed in 1884 by John Walker, Adam Walker, Benjamin Peel, and Charles Warner. They named their community for Christopher Layton (b. March 8, 1821, England; d. Aug. 7, 1898), who was sent from Utah to be the first president of the St. Joseph Stake of Zion in Arizona. This community is now a part of Safford. Ref.: 225, pp. 249-250; 116, p. 592; 15, p. 533; Jennings; 322, p. 37; 353, p. 16

LEACH'S ROAD

In 1857 to provide a route across the west to the Pacific coast, among others planned was Leach's Road from El Paso to Fort Yuma, named for James D. Leach, construction superintendent. It followed Cooke's route except it missed Tucson by turning north at the future site of Benson, following the San Pedro River to the Gila River. Leach was called to task for doing so, but defended his action by saying that the road cut off forty miles of travel. However, the stage lines did not use Leach's Road. Ref.: 5, pp. 104-105; 73, II, 130-131

LEBANON

Graham   T8S R25E

The first artesian well was located here in 1890. For many years it has been called Cactus Flat locally, but it was never known as Algodon (which was at another location). The community was named for the mountains of Lebanon in Syria. See Algodon, Graham

P.O. est. July 18, 1907, George A. Tanner, p.m.; resc. Dec. 20, 1907
Ref.: 353, pp. 48-56; Jennings; 322, p. 37

LE BARRON HILL

Coconino   T20N R6E

This hill was named for Oscar Le Barron. Several members of this family were in the vicinity. Ref.: Hart

LECHUGUILLA DESERT   pro.: /lečuwgiˆyə/

Spanish: *lechuguilla* = "frill; ruff"

Yuma   T11S R18W   Elev. c. 600'

Many century plants grow on this desert area. The spinate slender leaves form a kind of ruff around the center stalk. This area covers the valley between the Gila Mountains and the Cabeza Prieta and other mountains to the east. An associated name is Lechuguilla Mountains (or Sierra de la Lechugilla, T13S/R17W). Ref.: Monson; Mercer

LECHUGUILLA PEAK

Cochise   T14S R19E   Elev. 5009'

Century plants abound here. See Lechuguilla Desert, Yuma

LE CONTE PLATEAU

Coconino (Grand Canyon) T32N R1E

In 1908 the USGS proposed this name as submitted by Dr. Arnold Guyot to honor Professor Joseph Le Conte, a geologist who took observations with a stationary barometer for Guyot while exploring this locality. Ref.: 329

LEE CANYON

Coconino   T19N R3E

This tributary to Sycamore Canyon was named for John D. Lee, who lived for three years with the Havasupai Indians while hiding out after the Mountain Meadows Massacre of 1857. Lee Butte is at T17N/R8E. See also Lee's Ferry, Coconino, and Havasu Canyon, Coconino Ref.: 53, p. 655

LEE, MOUNT

Pima   T17N R6E

James (Jimmie) Lee (b. March 17, 1833, Ireland; d. Nov. 11, 1884) mined in the Santa Catalina Mountains and ran a flour mill. He was with Alexander McKay and Al Weldon when they discovered the Christmas Mine near Lee Mountain, Pinal (T4S/R16E, Elev. 3786'). Ref.: AHS, Chambers Collection, Box 12

LEE'S FERRY

Coconino   T40N R8E   Elev. 3170'

In 1860 Jacob Hamblin, a Mormon missionary, was unsuccessful in trying to cross the Paria River, but finally managed to do so on a raft in 1864 and soon thereafter established a minor Mormon settlement. Later the ferry was established about three miles above the present bridge across the Colorado River.

The Navajo name for this location is an introduction to its history, for it is *Tsina'ee Dahsa'ash* (= "where the boat sits") as indeed it did, for Maj. John Wesley Powell gave one of his boats to John Doyle Lee about 1873 and that was the beginning of Lee's ferry operations. The boat Powell gave to Lee was the "Nellie Powell," which Maj. Powell did not need because his exploring crew was short of men. The reason why Lee was at this location is also interesting: In 1857 a group of men reportedly disguised as Indians attacked a train of Arkansas and Missouri emigrants at Mountain Meadows (Utah) and killed one hundred and fifteen. Lee was accused of leading the attackers. He spent many years trying to escape the law (see also Lee Canyon, Coconino). He felt his loneliness apparently, for his name for this place was Lonely Dell, although it could not have been too lonely, for he was a polygamist. One wife was alone there frequently and perhaps she named it. In 1874 Lee disappeared again, but the law finally did capture him. He was shot standing in his coffin while protesting his innocence. His widow Emma ran the ferry under the name Little Colorado Station (because it was on the route to the Little Colorado Mormon settlements) until the Mormon church bought it in 1877, after which Warren M. Johnson operated it. In 1909 the ferry was sold to a cattle company and in 1916 Coconino County took it over, using it until Navajo Bridge was opened in 1929. Only a cemetery remains at the site of the original settlement.
P.O. est. Jan. 31, 1895, Warren M. Johnson, p.m.; disc. March 2, 1923
Ref.: 242; 225, pp. 90-91; 88, p. 211; 5, pp. 284-285; 71, p. 34; 329; *Weekly Arizona Miner* (June 18, 1875), p. 3

LEE'S FERRY ROAD

Coconino

This was the route established by Jacob Hamblin from the ferry to the Little Colorado River Mormon colonies.

LEE'S LOOKOUT

Coconino   T40N R8E   Elev. 3170'

This three-hundred-foot mound on the left bank of the Paria River is directly opposite Lee's Ferry and ranch and is said to have been used by Lee, who was in constant dread of being seized by U.S. marshals. See Lee's Ferry, Coconino Ref.: 192, pp. 181-182

LEE VALLEY WILD LIFE AREA

Apache

This one hundred and fourteen acre wild life area came into existence in 1960 and is managed by the Arizona Game & Fish Dept. See Greer, Apache Ref.: 9, p. 3

LEFEVRE CANYON

Coconino   T40N R1W   Elev. c. 7000'

The Lefevre family raised sheep in this canyon and on Lefevre Ridge. Ref.: 18a

LEHI pro.: /liyhay/
Maricopa   T1N R5E   Elev. 1230'
Under the presidency of Daniel W. Jones, nine Mormon families in March 1877 began settlements in the Salt River Valley. The settlers were unsuccessful, going into debt while building an irrigation ditch. They became so dissatisfied that most of them left under the leadership of Philomen C. Merrill (see David, St., Cochise). Those who stayed called their place Camp Utah. They soon laid out a village called Utahville, which also failed because one family refused to cooperate and closed off the streets on its land. Jones then laid out a small community on his own land and in 1880 the name Jonesville was voted for the place. The *Phoenix Herald* scornfully called it Bottom City because it was too near the Salt River. The post office refused to accept the names Jonesville, and Brigham Young, Jr. suggested the name Lehi to honor a prophet in the *Book of Mormon*.
P.O. est. May 26, 1884, James L. Patterson, p.m.; disc. March 5, 1904
Ref.: Daniel W. Jones, "Letter," *Phoenix Herald* (July 27, 1880), p. 1; 170, pp. 2-3, 88

LELAND BUTTE
Mohave   T19N R20W   Elev. 2973'
This butte takes its name from that of the Leland Mine in the upper part of this butte. It was located prior to 1900. Ref.: 200, p. 183

LEMMON, MOUNT
Pima   T11S R16E   Elev. 9,150'
To honor Dr. and Mrs. J. G. Lemmon of the Lemmon Herbarium, Oakland, California, Emerson Oliver Stratton named this peak in June 1880 while the Lemmons were there on a honeymoon. The community at this peak has developed into a thriving summer colony with a few winter residents. The first name suggested for the post office is also the name of one colonized section, Summerhaven.
P.O. est. Sept. 28, 1943, F. H. Zimmerman, p.m. Ref.: AHS, Emerson O. Stratton *ms.*, p. 63; 242; AHS, Allan B. James File

LEONARD CANYON
Coconino   T13–14N R12E   Elev. c. 5000'
This canyon is named for W. B. Leonard, a sheepherder here in the mid-1870s who had a trading post at Ganado. His home for his last years was near Navajo Springs. Associated names include Leonard Creek, Crossing, and Point. Ref.: 329; Schnebly; 18a

LEROUX SPRINGS pro.: /lərúw/
Coconino   T22N R6E   Elev. c. 7000'
In 1853 Lt. Amiel W. Whipple stopped at this spring, which he named to honor Sitgreaves' guide, Antoine Leroux (b. c. 1801, St. Louis, Missouri; d. 1898). Leroux was a trapper during the 1830s and in 1846 was a guide with the Mormon Battalion, thereafter serving with the U.S. Boundary Survey Commission from 1846 to 1848, and from 1849-1851 for Lt. Lorenzo Sitgreaves' expedition. Because this place was used by many travellers and military detachments, it came to be known by various names. For instance, Gen. G. T. Palmer refers to it as Christmas Spring, and Ammon Tenney said that Mormons along the Little Colorado River called it San Francisco Spring. It is also called Little Leroux Spring. Its spelling was almost as varied. For instance, Udell in his "Journal" in 1858 refers to it as Le Reax Springs. Another variant is Le Rous. Associated names include Le Roux Crossing, Prairie, Valley, and Wash. Whipple named the valley the Pueblo Colorado Valley. He called the Wash Leroux Forks.
Ref.: 346, pp. 11, 13, 156, 166; 23, p. 18; 225, pp. 152, 154; *Arizona Journal Miner* (Nov. 20, 1869), n.p. (State Library Files); Velma Rudd Hoffman, Letter (March 25, 1960); 141, pp. 34, 193

LEROY WASH
Pinal   T9S R3E
In 1890 this place was being referred to as a new town, being surveyed by Leroy O. Chilson for the Great Eastern Mining Company. Ref.: *Arizona Enterprise* (June 28, 1890), p. 4; Kitt; AHS Names File

[358]

LE SAGE

Yuma   T7S R12W   Elev. c. 700'

The Le Sage Development Company, approximately one mile east of the present Dateland, was at the Musina stop on the railroad where a post office for the private development existed. It consisted of little more than a building with some agricultural work nearby. It went out of existence when it burned c. 1931. The developer was named Hayter.

P.O. est. April 18, 1928, L. H. Jansen, p.m.; disc. Oct. 31, 1931
Ref.: Mrs. Howard Johnson (Letter); 242

LESLIE CREEK

Cochise   T21S R26E   Elev. c. 3500'

Both the canyon and creek take their name from that of Franklin Nashville Leslie (b. c. 1843, Galveston, Texas), known as "Buckskin Frank" because he was a dandy and a ladies' man. For a time he was an army scout with Gen. George Crook and with Gen. Nelson A. Miles, but by 1882 he was a bartender in Tombstone. Leslie was a quick man with a gun, an act made easier because welded to his weapon was a stud which fit into a groove on a silver plate fastened to his belt. He used his gun to kill at least three people, among them Olley Bradshaw at the Birdcage in Tombstone. He was living with her and she was playing fast and loose with a man named Neal, whom Buckskin Frank also shot. Leslie was imprisoned in Yuma. As one informant expressed it, "Some rich woman came along, got stuck on him, and it weren't long before she had him out." Leslie married her and left the country, leaving his name on a creek and canyon.

Ref.: Bennett; AHS, Frank Leslie File; *Arizona Daily Star* (May 4, 1897), p. 1; 241, p. 95

LESNA PEAK, LA

Spanish: *lesna* = "awl" or "arrowhead"

Pima   T19S R2E   Elev. 5384'

Both this peak and that known simply as Lesna Peak are in the Lesna Mountains. The names are descriptive of their arrowhead-like appearance. Another name for these peaks is Cerritos de los Linderos. Ref.: 329; 58; 262, p. 33; 105, I, 122

LEUPP   pro.: /luwp/

Coconino   T22N R13E

Francis E. Leupp (b. Jan. 2, 1849, New York City; d. Nov. 19, 1918) was Commissioner of Indian Affairs 1904-1909. A sub-agency for Navajo Indians established in 1908 was named for Leupp. The sub-agency has been consolidated with the Navajo headquarters at Window Rock. The Navajo name for Leupp is *Tsiizizi* (= "scalps"), referring to a story about a fight between Navajo and Hualapai Indians in which the Navajo took three scalps. Another legend states that the Navajo name refers to a former agent named Maxwell, who wore a wig. Leupp Corner is at T19N/R14E.

P.O. est. Aug. 5, 1905, John G. Walker, p.m. Ref.: A. McF. Greenwood, Asst. Commissioner Bureau of Indian Affairs, Letter (April 10, 1956); C. E. Lamson, Chief, Branch of Personnel, U.S. Dept. Int. Letter (April 26, 1956); 331, p. 87; 242

LEWIS & PRANTY CREEK

Maricopa   T2N R10E   Elev. c. 2500'

John Lewis and Fred Pranty settled on the creek and ranged cattle. Pranty began prospecting and mining in the Tonto Basin about 1900 and disappeared twenty-five years later, leaving his cabin and belongings undisturbed. Ref.: 329; 18a

LEWIS, CAMP

Yavapai

This camp shows on a map dated 1866, about forty-eight miles southeast of Montezuma Well and forty miles northeast of Fort McDowell. It was probably named for Col. Charles W. Lewis (b. 1825, Virginia; d. 1871, San Diego, California), who in 1865 was relieved of commanding troops at Calabasas to serve as colonel in the 7th Regiment of California Volunteers. He returned to his home in San Diego in March 1869.

Ref.: AHS, Charles W. Lewis File

LEWIS SPRINGS

Cochise   T21S R22E   Elev. c. 4000'
Because Fritz Hoffman located at these springs on June 6, 1878, they were first known as Fritz Springs. In 1889 the name was changed to Lewis Springs because Robert Alpheus Lewis (b. 1858, Kentucky; d. Feb. 15, 1900) had settled there and named the place for his father. Lewis had come from San Francisco in November 1878 to investigate assertions made by one A. C. Smith that rich silver could be found near what is now Bisbee. Lewis soon learned Smith had never been in Arizona, but liking both the man and the country, Lewis remained in the territory and kept Smith with him. On a trip to Huachuca for tobacco in April 1878, Lewis heard about rich ore in the Tombstone District. He was the fifteenth man to arrive, later settling at what is now Lewis Springs. He remained until 1884. He was killed in a bob-sledding accident in Oregon.
P.O. est. Nov. 15, 1904, on E.P. & S.R.R. at Lewis Spring Station, Virginia Poitevenl Clark, p.m.; disc. Sept. 30, 1933; Wells Fargo 1904
Ref.: AHS, Robert A. Lewis File; 242

LIBERTY

Maricopa   T1S R3W   Elev. 875'
The first post office was at the Toothaker Place. Altamount was the name of property owned by the Toothaker family (T1S/R2W). The post office at the Toothaker Place was not convenient for residents, so the Altamount post office was moved and its name changed to Liberty.
P.O. est. as Altamount, July 16, 1895, Harriet Toothaker, p.m.; disc. May 28, 1898; reest. Jan. 19, 1901, James Phillips, p.m.; disc. June 30, 1942 Ref.: Parkman; 242

LIGHT

Cochise   T17S R27E   Elev. c. 4200'
Between 1902 and 1910 homesteaders from Kansas, California, and Texas established the now-vanished community of Light, named for John W. Light (b. New York). The first name suggested for the community was Lightfield, but the post office turned down the name, using that of its first postmaster instead.
P.O. est. April 13, 1910, John W. Light; disc. Sept. 30, 1927
Ref.: Riggs; 242; AHS Names File

LIGHTHOUSE ROCK

La Paz   T3S R24W   Elev. 250'
Dr. John S. Newberry of the Ives' Expedition in 1857 noted that this conical rock looked like a lighthouse, hence the name. The rock pinnacle was at the center of the Colorado River, forcing river steam boats to go around it. Since the construction of dams, the Arizona channel has silted so that the rock now stands entirely on Arizona soil.
Ref.: 245, p. 24; Mercer; 200, p. 49; Blythe Chamber of Commerce, "Cruise Bulletin (Oct. 10, 1954)"

LIGHTNING MESA

Greenlee   T3S R31E   Elev. c. 5000'
The name derives from the fact that lightning strikes here more often than elsewhere in the area.

LIGURTA   pro.: /ligertə/

Yuma   T8S R20W   Elev. 230'
The name Ligurta may derive from anglicizing the Spanish word *lagarto* (= "lizard"). Lizards are abundant here. The name Fossil Point has also been used as fossils were found along the Gila River on October 13, 1917. Ref.: Willson; 279, p. 75

LIME: Several place names reflect the presence of lime. Examples follow:

Lime Creek	Gila	T6N R14E	
Lime Creek	Maricopa/Yavapai	T8N R6E	
Lime Hill	Pima	T14S R6W	Elev. 1840'
Lime Hills	Mohave	T41N R13W	

Lime Mountain	Maricopa	T2N R11E	Elev. 3999'
Lime Mountain Spring	Maricopa	T2N R11E	
Lime Mountain Spring	Navajo	T20N R23E	
Lime Peak	Cochise	T15S R22E	Elev. 6729'
Lime Peak	Yavapai	T2N R11E	Elev. 3801
Lime Spring	Navajo	T5N R25E	
Lime Spring	Yavapai	T11N R5E	

LIME KILN CANYON
Mohave   T38N R16W
This canyon derives its name from that of the Lime Kiln Mine (T37N/R16W) where
there was a lime kiln.

LIME KILN WASH
La Paz   T3N R22W
There was a lime kiln here.

LIMESTONE: The following places have limestone, hence the names:
Limestone Canyon	Coconino	T13N R12E	
Limestone Canyon	Gila	T11N R9E	
Limestone Canyon	Navajo	T9N R19E	
Limestone Canyon	Yavapai	T19N R2W	

This canyon supplies both limestone and flagstone, much being shipped to San Francisco following
the great fire in 1906.

Limestone Creek	Coconino	T13N R12E	
Limestone Gulch	Greenlee	T4S R30E	
Limestone Hills	Gila	T11N R7E	Elev. 5200'
Limestone Mountain	Cochise	T20S R29E	Elev. 7120'
Limestone Mountain	Graham	T4S R20E	Elev. 6687'
Limestone Mountains	Cochise	T15–16S R21–22E	

See Little Dragoon Mountains, Cochise

Limestone Pasture	Coconino	T13N R12E	
Limestone Peak	Yavapai	T18N R5W	Elev. 5464'
Limestone Pocket	Coconino	T19N R3E	

A ridge with a gently rounded summit forms a pocket or natural corral for herding livestock
here. Ref.: 329

Limestone Reservoir	Mohave	T36N R10W	
Limestone Ridge	Coconino	T36N R7E	
Limestone Ridge	Navajo	T8N R20E	
Limestone Spring	Coconino	T13N R12E	
Limestone Spring	Mohave	T23N R11W	
Limestone Spring	Navajo	T9N R20E	
Limestone Tanks	Coconino	(1) T13N R12W	(2) T21N/R7W
		(3) T25N/R10W	

LINCOLN, CAMP
Yavapai
Camp Lincoln, named for the recently assassinated president of the United States, was
an outpost of Fort Whipple in 1864, but was not officially Fort Lincoln until January

1866, when troops arrived on January 16th. It was "on the wrong side of the Verde River" on a mesa too small for buildings. By 1870 malaria had reduced the troops to five enlisted men and their commanding officer, Capt. H. S. Washburn. The site was replaced by Camp Verde five miles north. See Verde, Camp, Yavapai
Ref.: Huntington Library *ms*. 197 H, Arizona Volume; 107, IV, 109; 159, p. 547

LINCOLNIA
Mohave   T18N R22W   Elev. c. 500'
Edmund Lincoln operated a store at the construction camp of the Cottonia Land & Cotton Company. The first name for the post office reflected the name of the company, Cottonia, but the owner soon changed it.
P.O. est. Cottonia, May 12, 1910, Edmund Lincoln, p.m.; changed to Lincolnia, June 6, 1910; disc. Oct. 31, 1912 Ref.: Harris; 242

LINCON
Pima   T15S R4E
This Papago village name is a corruption of the Spanish *rincon* (= "corner"). It is in an angle or elbow made by mountains. Ref.: 57, p. 15

LINDBERG SPRING
Coconino   T2N R6E
Lindberg was a contractor for the Oak Creek Canyon road. Lindberg Spring was found during construction and was diverted to make two small ponds so that the road could go through. Ref.: Sykes

LINDEN
Navajo   T10N R20E   Elev. 6290'
In 1878 a Mormon settlement called Juniper began here. In 1893 the name was changed to Linden because of the many long-leaf cottonwoods on nearby Linden Wash. Linden Creek (Greenlee, T5S/R31E) shares the same origin.
P.O. est. Aug. 18, 1891, David E. Adams, p.m.; disc. May 31, 1958 Ref.: 242

LINDEN DRAW
Navajo   T10N R21E
This location, which is also known variously as Linden Wash or Reidhead Wash, was so named because of the long-leaf cottonwoods along its banks. See also Thistle Hollow, Navajo Ref.: 329; 18a

LINDSEY
Graham   T8S R21E
This canyon takes its name from the presence of lindsey groves at the head of the canyon.

LINO, VALLE DE
Spanish = "flax valley"
Apache
Fr. Francisco Garcés applied this name to the valley of the Little Colorado River on July 18, 1776, noting "much wild flax ... there."

LINSKEY (R.R. STN.)
La Paz   T7N R18W   Elev. 718'
This place on a branch line of the A.T. & S.F.R.R. was named for a track foreman, Pat Linskey (of the Arizona & Chloride R.R.). Ref.: AHS Names File; 18a

LION CANYON
Yavapai   T10N R4W
This canyon (a.k.a. Weaver Creek) was so named because several cougars were killed here years ago. Ref.: 329

LION RIDGE
Yavapai   T20N R10W
There are mountain lions here. Ref.: 329

LIPAN POINT pro.: /lipan/ or /lipən/

Coconino (Grand Canyon)   T31N R5E   Elev. 7400'

The first name for this place was Lincoln Point, for President Abraham Lincoln. In 1902 Francois E. Matthes suggested changing the name to conform with the policy of using Indian tribe names on South Rim locations. Lipan Indians, first mentioned in 1699 as allies of the Comanches, during the 18th century occupied that part of Texas drained by the San Saba and Colorado Rivers. Phonetically their name has been spelled as follows: Lee Pawnee, Seepan, Sinapan, and Gipanes. Ref.: Schellbach File (Grand Canyon); 77, p. 460, Note 14

LISCUM

Maricopa   T7N R4W   Elev. c. 3500'

This post office for the mine was named by the Phoenix Mine manager, Sam Hunnington, for Col. Emerson H. Liscum, who served in Arizona 1880-84.
P.O. est. March 16, 1901, Sam H. Hersell, p.m.; disc. Dec. 30, 1902 Ref.: 18a; 242

LITCHFIELD PARK

Maricopa   T2N R1W

To grow Egyptian cotton (see Goodyear, Maricopa), the Goodyear Tire & Rubber Co. in 1916 bought land west of the Agua Fria River. This place was briefly called Agua Fria Ranch, but the name was changed to Litchfield in honor of Paul W. Litchfield, company vice president. The first name proposed for the post office was Litchfield, but the post office department shortened it to Lichton.
P.O. est. Lichton, June 13, 1918, William West Burkie, p.m.; name changed to Litchfield Park, Aug. 26, 1926 Ref.: K. B. McMicken, Vice Pres., Goodyear Farms, Letter (Mar. 28, 1956); 242

LITHODENDRON WASH

Apache/Navajo   T21N R25E   Elev. c. 5800'

In 1853 when he encountered fossilized trees along this stream bed, Lt. Amiel W. Whipple named it Lithodendron Creek (= "stone trees"). Sections of this stream have had an assortment of names. For instance, part of it was known as Carrizo Creek (a.k.a. Dead River). Carrizo, as Gregory noted in 1915, was the name of the railroad siding but was not in local use for the wash except at its extreme lower end. In 1939 the USGS altered all names to Lithodendron Wash. Ref.: 242; 346, p. 153; 141, p. 34, Note 2, and p. 193; 329

LITTLE ASH CREEK

Pinal   T4S R16E

Ash trees grow along this stream bed.

LITTLE ASH CREEK

Yavapai   T11N R3E

Ash trees grow along this stream bed.

LITTLE BLACK HILLS

Pinal   T10S R18E

Since about 1950 this name has been used informally by ranchers and geologists to distinguish these hills from the larger hill mass to the north, known as Black Hills, near Mammoth. Ref.: 329

LITTLE BLACK SPOT MOUNTAIN

Navajo   T31N R19E   Elev. 7001'

This small, flat-topped peak is descriptively named. It has had various names as follows, all dropped by the USGS in June 1968: Amusove Mesa, Dzilth-dazzni, Zillesa Peak, Zillesa Mesa. In Navajo, Zillesa = "mountain surrounded by bare soil," a name Herbert Gregory translated in 1915. Ref.: 329; 141, p. 197

LITTLE BRUSHY MOUNTAIN

Apache   T5N R24E   Elev. 7550'

This mountain is said to be "so covered with brush that a rabbit would have to get on his hands and knees to crawl through it." Ref.: Davis

LITTLE BUTTE

Gila   T4N R16E   Elev. 4442'
Descriptive.

LITTLE BUTTE

La Paz   T7N R17W

Although the name of this butte is descriptive, the name Little Butte was first applied to the mine east of it. Ref.: *Geology of North Plomosa*, Figure 2

LITTLE CAPITAN VALLEY

Navajo   T39N R20E

The name of this valley derives from its being near Agathla Peak, earlier known as El Capitan.

LITTLE CHINO VALLEY

Yavapai

The north end of this valley lies at the south end of Big Chino Valley. See Big Chino Valley, Yavapai Ref.: 329

LITTLE COLORADO RIVER

Apache/Navajo/Coconino   T10–15N R28–22E

The current name, which was made official by the USGS in 1932, is a translation of *Colorado Chiquito* (Spanish = "Little Colorado or Little Red River"). It flows roughly northwest to join the Colorado River (T7N/R27E) at a point called by Garcés, Puerto de Bucareli. Since it was first encountered by Lt. Garcia Lopez de Cardenas of the Coronado Expedition in 1540, it has had a number of names, the first being Rio Vermejo (= "Red River"), and also Rio del Lino (= "Flax River") because of the wild flax along its banks. Juan Mateo de Oñate in 1604 called it *Colorado* (= "Red") and when Fr. Francisco Garcés encountered this stream on June 28, 1776, he called it Rio Jaquesila and also Rio San Pedro, curiously enough on July 18 calling its valley, Valle del Lino (= "Wild Flax Valley"). Farfan called it Rio de la Alameda. In 1854 Lt. Amiel W. Whipple noted that it was called the Flax River, "lately known as the Colorado Chiquito." The translation of the last name is that which it carries today. The Hopi name for this stream in 1882 was recorded as Ba-yu. Associated names include those of its gorge and forks, and the temporary name Little Colorado Station for Lee's Ferry (*q.v.*). Ref.: 77, pp. 354, 355, Note 36, p. 410; 345, I, 149, 178; 156, II, 26 (Note); 15, pp. 88, Note 21, and pp. 154-155; 41, p. 113; 89, p. 93; 46, p. 269; 242; 313a

LITTLE DE MOTTE PARK

Coconino

In 1882 Dutton named and described this location south of De Motte Park (*q.v.*). Ref.: 100, p. 138

LITTLE DIAMOND RIM

Gila   T12N R10E
Quartz crystals exist in this area. Ref.: Gillette

LITTLE DRAGON

Coconino (Grand Canyon)   T33N R2E

The name is descriptive of the appearance of this short spur. The name was made official in March 1906. Ref.: 329

LITTLE DRAGOON MOUNTAINS

Cochise   T15S R21E   Elev. 6729'

This range in 1879 was called Limestone Mountains, but the name was changed about 1900. See Dragoon Mountains, Cochise Ref.: 329

LITTLE DRY LAKE

Coconino
Descriptive.

LITTLEFIELD
Mohave   T40N R15W   Elev. 1858'
The first white man here was Daniel Bonelli, who settled on Beaver Dam Creek but was
washed out by floods in 1863. (See Bonelli's Crossing, Mohave) In 1865 a colony of
Mormons settled here at what was called Beaver Dams. Among the founders was Henry
W. Miller, hence it was also known as Millersburg. In 1867 the Virgin River again
flooded, forcing colonists to leave. In 1875 and 1878 more Mormon settlers arrived and
the thriving agricultural community of Littlefield began to take shape. Among the
settlers was Henry Frehner. According to Hulda R. Frehner, postmistress in 1923,
"The first ones that settled this place had it named Littlefield because their fields were
small but later on there was more land taken up, but it has always went by that name."
P.O. est. May 8, 1896, Matilda Frehner, p.m. Ref.: 242; 329; 225, pp. 117-118

LITTLE GIANT
Gila   Elev. c. 3500'
Mapped on GLO 1879, on north side of Mustang Mountains in S.W. portion of San
Carlos Indian Reservation, this place bears the nickname of George H. Stevens, an
active politician in the 1880s, who was married to an Indian woman. Their descendants
are today among highly respected leaders of the San Carlos Apache Indians. See
Stevens Ranch, Greenlee
P.O. est. April 1, 1879, Samuel A. Lowe, p.m.; disc. April 28, 1882 Ref.: Woody; 18a

LITTLE GILA RIVER   pro.: /hiylə/
Pinal   T4S R7E   Elev. c. 1500'
This branch of the Gila River used to fill when the larger river flooded. The name is
descriptive. Ref.: 18a

LITTLE GRANITE MOUNTAIN
Yavapai   T14N R3W   Elev. 7100'
The name is descriptive in contrast to nearby Granite Mountain.

LITTLE GREEN VALLEY
Gila   T11N R11E   Elev. c. 5000'
In 1876 when William Burch and John Hood settled in this locality, the two valleys
north of Payson were luxuriant meadows surrounded by timbered hills. The larger was
called Big Green Valley and the smaller, of course, Little Green Valley. Ref.: 18a

LITTLE HORN MOUNTAINS
Yuma   T1S R13W   Elev. 2881'
These mountains are named because of their relative size in association with the nearby
Big Horn Mountains. Both harbor bighorn mountain sheep. Ref.: 355, p. 131

LITTLE LITHODENDRON WASH
Navajo   T18N R22E
A railroad engineer named this Little Carrizo Wash in 1878 for a member of the
surveying crew. Earlier Lt. Sitgreaves in the 1850s called it Little Lithodendron
Wash. See Lithodendron Wash, Navajo

LITTLE MEADOWS
Mohave   T19N R19W
The name describes the location. A pumping station for the Gold Road Mine used to be
here and freighters used to stop overnight. Nearby residents had produce gardens here.
Ref.: Housholder

LITTLE MORMON LAKE
Navajo   T10N R22E
This small lake was so called to differentiate it from Mormon Lake. Ref.: 329

LITTLE PINE FLAT
Maricopa   T5N R9E
This flat, descriptively named, lies at the head of Pine Creek.

LITTLE RAINBOW VALLEY
Maricopa   T2S R3W
This valley lies between the Gila River and Rainbow Valley, hence its name. It is sometimes Rainbow Valley on maps, but never so called by residents, who sometimes refer to it as Hall Valley. Ref.: 329

LITTLE ROUND MOUNTAIN
Yavapai   T18N R5E   Elev. 6948'
The name describes this place, also known as Round Top Mountain or simply Round Mountain. Ref.: 329

LITTLES, CAMP STEPHEN D.
Santa Cruz   T24S/R14E
The 12th Infantry under Col. William H. Sage arrived in Nogales on April 27, 1914. During the Pancho Villa disturbances more than thirteen thousand troops were in this area. About five battles took place within Nogales itself. This military camp which was in the Via Coronado area of Nogales was named on December 18, 1915 for Pvt. Stephen D. Littles (b. Jan. 2, 1894, South Carolina), who was shot through the head by followers of Pancho Villa on November 26, 1915 on the border at Douglas. The camp was abandoned in 1931. Ref.: Jones, *Outguard*, I, 8; AHS, Cochran Collection

LITTLE SAN DOMINGO WASH
Maricopa   T7N R4W
Named for the Little San Domingo Mine (T7N/R3W).

LITTLESHOT, CAMP LOUIS
Pima   T20S R14E   Elev. 6650'
In 1909 this principal mining camp in Madera Canyon was near its head at the west base of Old Baldy. It was named for Littleshot, a miner. The name should not be spelled "Little Shot." Ref.: 286, pp. 167, 176

LITTLE SOMBRERO PEAK
Gila   T6N R15E   Elev. 5720'
The name describes the appearance of this peak.

LITTLE SPRING
Coconino   T23N R6E
The name is descriptive. The spring is on the homestead of a pioneer named Milligan, who settled here in 1887. Through error, it has appeared in print as Libble Spring. It is also known as Stokes Spring. Ref.: 166, p. 82

LITTLE DOUBLE TOP
Pinal   T8S R2E   Elev. 3100'
Descriptive.

LITTLETOWN
Pima   T15S R14E   Elev. 2715'
This small community on the highway east of Tucson was built c. 1950 by Lowman B. Lyon. It is a little town. Ref.: *Arizona Sunday Star* (June 1, 1975)

LITTLE TROUGH CREEK
Gila   T4N R19E   Elev. c. 4000'
This creek heads at Little Trough Spring and extends past Big Trough Spring. The Indian service put watering troughs in the canyon c. 1935, hence the name. Ref.: 329

LITTLE TURKEY CREEK
Gila   T7N R13E
This place is said to be "always a good spot for wild turkeys." Little Turkey Creek Spring is at its head. Ref.: McKinney

LITTLE VALLEY SPRING

Apache   T7N R28E
The name refers to the location. Ref.: 329; 242

LITTLE WALNUT CANYON

Gila   T9N R13E
Many walnut trees are in the canyon, hence the name. Ref.: McKinney

LITTLE WHITE HOUSE CANYON

Apache   T4N R27E
The Little White House Ruins lend their name to the canyon. Ref.: 331, p. 88

LITTLE WHITE TANKS

Yuma   T3S R18W
The rocks here are pale in color, hence the name. Ref.: Monson

LITTLE YAEGER CANYON

Yavapai   T15N R2E
This canyon may have been named for Charles Yager (*sic*) (b. 1848, Prussia), who was living in Williamson Valley in 1870. Ref.: 62

LIVEOAK

Gila   T1N R14E   Elev. c. 4000'
Live oak trees yielded the name for this location.
P.O. est. Nov. 3, 1905, Rey A. Hascal, p.m.; resc. Feb. 10, 1906 Ref.: 18a

LIVERPOOL LANDING

Mohave   c. T12N R18W   Elev. c. 500'
Landings along the Colorado River were used to ship ores and handle incoming supplies. Many were named for cities to which ores were being sent for smelting. No proof has been found that this was the case for Liverpool. Ref.: Housholder.

LIVINGSTON

Gila   T4N R13E   Elev. c. 3500'
In the late 1870s Charles Livingston ran the Flying V Ranch. His brand was in conflict with a Flying V brand owned by Jerry Vosburg in Yavapai County and when Gila County annexed part of Yavapai, Livingston relinquished his brand. In 1888 he homesteaded at the mouth of Pinto Creek. A small community arose. The name Cornutt was proposed for its post office as that was the name of the first postmaster, but Livingston was selected instead. Livingston was noted for its exciting horse races. With the completion of Theodore Roosevelt Dam, Livingston was abandoned as water began collecting in Roosevelt Lake. The former community is now covered by willow and mesquite trees.
P.O. est. June 6, 1896, James H. Cornutt, p.m.; disc. June 20, 1907
Ref.: 242; Cooper; Woody; 18a

LLANO DE LOS FLORES   pro.: /yano de las floras/

Spanish = "plain of the flowers"
Pima
This was the name used by Mexicans for the plain which they crossed in journeying from Cerro Colorado to Fresnal. It is on the Gird Map of 1865.
Ref.: 163, p. 227; 242

LOCHIEL

Spanish: *noria* = "well-water lifting device"
Santa Cruz   T24S R17E   Elev. 4200'
The border community of Lochiel was split in half when the Boundary Survey of 1890 was run. The Sonora portion continues to be called La Noria, a name which reflects the fact that several shallow wells were dug here (without hitting water). On the American

side the place was called Lenora Water Hole. Colin Cameron and his brother Brewster renamed it Lochiel for their ancestral home in Scotland. The Cameron brothers owned the San Rafael Land Grant, from which came another name for the post office. During the period of Indian raids, Lochiel was prosperous, a fact attributable to goods being smuggled across the border.

P.O. est. as La Noria, July 24, 1882, Robert Harrison, p.m.; disc. 1883; reest. as Lochiel (1.5 mi. north-northeast), Oct. 6, 1884, Abner B. Elden, p.m.; name changed to San Rafael, March 1, 1888; disc. Oct. 4, 1883; reest. as La Noria, Dec. 17, 1909; disc. Sept. 30, 1911 Ref.: AHS, Mary Harrison Chalmers *ms.*; Lenon; Glannon; 242; 116, p. 625

LOCKETT DRAW
Yavapai   T21N R3W
This draw is also called Tom Lockett Draw, as he once lived nearby. Although it has been mapped as Partridge Canyon, the name is not known locally. Ref.: 329

LOCKETT TANK
Coconino   T27N R7E
Formerly known as Jack's Tank, this location is a natural tank made by water pouring over a bluff, knocking out a huge basin. At one time here an old man had a rock house as a hangout for horse thieves. It is near Lockett Lake (T30N/R4E) so named for its owner, Henry Lockett, a sheep rancher. See Lockett Lake, Coconino Ref.: Mercer; 329

LOCKWOOD SPRING
Coconino   T19N R5E   Elev. c. 6800'
This spring may have been named for Lt. D. W. Lockwood of the Wheeler Surveying party (1871) or for a stockman murdered about fifty years ago.
Ref.: 124, p. 159, Note 5; AHS Names File

LOCOMOTIVE ROCK
Pima   T13S R6W   Elev. 2107'
When viewed from the north this rock looks like the front of a railroad steam engine. The place is also called Locomotive Butte and Locomotive Peaks. Ref.: 58; 57, p. 210

LOCUST CANYON
Coconino   (1) T21N R11E   (2) T35S R1E
Locust trees grow at both locations.

LOGAN
Pima   T15S R2E   Elev. c. 2500'
In 1872 George Roskruge laid out the site for a town to be called Brooklyn. It developed with the location of mining claims in the area, among those of John B. ("Apple Pie") Allen (b. 1819, Scotland; d. 1896), and others. In 1883 J. T. and W. R. Logan, brothers, dug a well, hitting water on April 8, 1884. Soon nearly two hundred adobe houses were here and in New Virginia, adjacent to it. By 1885 Logan City was a mining center for the Quijotoa Mining District and supplied water for neighboring mines. Logan is today abandoned. See also Gunsight, Pima, and Quijotoa, Pima
Ref.: 308, pp. 63, 65, 66, 67; 262, p. 5; *Weekly Arizonan* (May 23, 1885), p. 3; AHS, John B. Allen File and Chambers Collection

LOGAN MINE
Yavapai   T14N R3E   Elev. 5019'
In 1875 Charles E. Hitchcock located the Isabella Mine named for his youngest daughter. A man named Logan took it over and changed its name.
Ref.: *Weekly Arizona Miner* (May 28, 1875), p. 3

LOHALI POINT
Navajo: *thlo hali* = "fish spring"
Apache   T32N R23E
This mountain point is also known as Trout Spring. Variant spellings are as follows: Hlohale (1909), Hlohah le (1913), Lohali (Gregory, 1915).
Ref.: 141, p. 152; 329

LOKASKAL (SPRING)   pro.: /lók'a:ʰsika:d/
Navajo = "place where reeds grow"

Navajo   T32N R20E   Elev. c. 6000'
Gregory reported this name for a group of springs in 1915. The following are variant spellings: Lokasakal, Lucacsaca, Lucasaka, Lukasakad, Lokasakad. In 1932 the USGS set aside all in favor of the contemporary spelling.
Ref.: 329; 141, pp. 112, 153, 155, 193

LOLAMAI POINT
Hopi = "good"

Navajo   T37N R18E   Elev. 8022'
According to John Wetherill, Lolamai was the name of an Oraibi leader. Contemporary Hopi say the name should be spelled Loloma. With other Hopi leaders Loloma attended a Washington conference in 1882 to discuss Navajo encroachment on Hopi lands. He made an agreement with the U.S. Government which led to dissension among the Hopi, many being opposed to cooperating. Ref.: 223, pp. 51-52; 141, p. 193

LOMPOC
Graham   T11S R23E   Elev. c. 3500'
This stage station was established early in the twentieth century by people from Lompoc, California, hence the transfer name. The place has been gone for over half a century.
P.O. est. March 13, 1913, Sheldon S. Hardenbrook; disc. June 15, 1915 Ref.: 18a; 242

LONDON BRIDGE
Mohave   T13N R20W
London Bridge was moved from London, England, and was reconstructed on the Colorado River as a tourist attraction.

LONE: The descriptive terms *lone* and *lonely* apply to the following:

Lone Butte	Maricopa	T2S R3E	Elev. 1258'
Lone Butte	Mohave	T41N R5W	Elev. 6191'
Lone Hill	Pima	T12S R17E	Elev. 4080'
Lone Mountain	Cochise	T23S R19E	Elev. 6379'
Lone Mountain	Maricopa	(1) T2N R7E	Elev. 2800'
		(2) T5N R8E	Elev. 3222'
		(3) T6N R5E	Elev. 3372'
Lone Mountain	Pima	T17E R12S	
Lone Mountain	La Paz	T3N R12W	Elev. 1919'

A variant name is Lonesome Peak.

Lone Peak   Maricopa
See Tonopah, Maricopa

LONE PINE DAM
Navajo   T11N R21E   Elev. 6000'
At the time this dam was built, a single pine tree was near it. In 1940 the dam was the largest all-earth dam in Arizona and stored water to irrigate seventeen hundred acres. Wild ducks find refuge here. Ref.: 5, p. 449

LONESOME POCKET
Coconino   T19N R3E
This natural pocket is "a lonesome place to be in a snow storm." Ref.: Terry

LONESOME VALLEY
Yavapai   T14N R1E   Elev. 5017'
In 1879 stockmen named this place because "not a living creature was seen upon its many thousand acres." Ref.: *Arizona Sentinel* (May 24, 1879), p. 1; 329

LONE STAR

Graham   T7S R27E   Elev. 2951'

This railroad siding takes its name from that of the Lone Star Mine (T6S/R27E) on Lone Star Mountain (Elev. 5440'). The mine was reopened in 1950. Lone Star Wash is on the mountain (T6S/R26E). Ref.: Jennings

LONE TREE

Cochise   T14S R21E

Currently a triangulation station has this name. As Rockfellow describes it, "In a stretch of eight miles, there was an almost level mesa entirely timberless, with the exception of a single tree at the half-way point. This was a landmark and was called the 'Lone Tree.' " Rockfellow relates how a two-horse team escaped from its driver and took off across country with a reliable old horse and a foolish young one galloping together. The driver (a foreman) returned to the home ranch. The next morning as there was still no sign of the horses, he saddled up, took up their trail, and found them at Lone Tree. "They had run these several miles bearing away to the left of the ranch establishment and had run into the only tree in two townships. The foolish young horse had hit the tree with such a jolt that his neck was broken, and this in good daylight." Ref.: 277, pp. 139-140

LONETREE CANYON

Coconino (Grand Canyon)   T31N R3E

Two lone cottonwoods were at a small spring here. Ref.: Kolb

LONG: The descriptive word *long* applies to the following:

Long Canyon	(1) Apache	T6N R30E	
	(2) Cochise	(a) T14S R28E;	(b) T13S R23E
	(3) Coconino	(a) T14N R8E;	(b) T31N R3E
	(4) Maricopa	(a) T4N R10E;	(b) T8N R4E
	(5) Navajo	T39N R17E	
	(6) Yavapai	(a) T17N R7W	(b) T18N R5E;
		(c) T15N R3W;	(d) T9N R5E

Long Creek   Coconino (Grand Canyon)   T13N R14E

See Boucher Creek, Coconino (Grand Canyon)

Long Draw   Coconino (Grand Canyon)   T13N R14E

See Boucher Creek, Coconino (Grand Canyon)

Long Flat Wash   Apache   T36N R22E

This is said to be a translation of the Navajo name, which is descriptive. Ref.: 329

Long Fort   Coconino   T24N R11E

This site, according to Colton, might have been built by Spanish or American soldiers. It is eighty-eight feet long and fourteen wide. Ref.: 70, p. 70

Long Gulch   Gila   T5N R12E

This very long canyon enters Medicine Creek at Gleason Flat. There is also a possibility it was named for William Long, a miner in this area in 1873. Ref.: Devore

Long House Ruins   Navajo   T37N R17E   Elev. 6400'

These ruins consist of a surface pueblo on top of a large bald rock ridge in Long House Valley. They were probably occupied from 1000-1300 A.D. It is probably synonymous with Moqui Rock as noted by Richard Wetherill in 1897. Ref.: 87, p. 636

Long Jim Canyon   Coconino   T30N R3E
                          (Grand Canyon)

Long Jim was a well known sheepherder in the early days who "used to wander here with his sheep." Ref.: 178, p. 66

Long Lake   Coconino   T19N R10E

Long Lake   Navajo   T10N R22E   Elev. c. 9000'

Navajo: *be'ek'id honeez* = "long lake"

This lake is both long and narrow. Ref.: 143, p. 186

Long Log Draw   Navajo/Apache   T16N R23E

Petrified logs at this location in the Petrified Forest National Park are long, hence the name. Ref.: 329

Long Mesa   Coconino   T32N R4W
        (Grand Canyon)

This mesa is five miles long. The name has been in use since about 1920. Ref.: 329

Long Mountain   Mohave   T32N R10W

This name, in use for about seventy-five years, describes the fact that the mountain in the Hualapai Valley looks long. It is also known as Lone Mountain. Ref.: 329

Long Tom Canyon   Coconino   T12N R14E   Elev. c. 8000'

A sheepherder and hunter named Woolf c. 1882 camped here and named the location. Here in 1885 Will C. Barnes built a cabin, later used by forest rangers. See also Woolf Crossing, Coconino, and Larson Canyon, Coconino Ref.: 18a

Long Valley   Coconino   T14N R10E   Elev. 7000'

Long Valley Experimental Coconino   T14N R9E
Range & Forest

This location was established on March 31, 1936. It contains two thousand five hundred thirty-six acres. Ref.: 243, p. 22

Long Valley Road   Coconino

See Happy Jack, Coconino

LONGFELLOW INCLINE

Greenlee   T4S R29E   Elev. c. 5000'

The Longfellow Mine was among the earliest near Clifton. According to Wheeler (1873), its copper-bearing outcrops indicated a vast supply of ore. All that miners uncovered, however, was the fact that the mountain was practically pure copper. Ultimately it became an open-pit mine with the Longfellow Incline being used to haul groceries to the mercantile store in Morenci. Ref.: 68, p. 54; 163, pp. 82-83; Scott

LONGFELLOW RIDGE

Yavapai   T12N R1W   Elev. 6791'

Hinton in 1877 listed the Longfellow Mine for which this ridge is named. Longfellow Ridge Spring is here. Ref.: 18a

LOOKOUT: The commanding view at some places leads to using the term *lookout* as follows:

Lookout Mountain   Gila   T6N R12W   Elev. 6505'

This mountain is not to be confused with Baker Mountain (T6N/R14E). See Greenback Peak, Gila

Look-out Mountain   Pinal   T7S R16E

This conical hill guarding the entrance to Aravaipa Canyon was named in 1867. Ref.: 27, p. 301

Lookout Point   Coconino   T31N R2E   Elev. 4560'
        (Grand Canyon)

Lookout Point   Coconino   T19N R6E

Lookout Point   Gila   T7N R13E   Elev. 5953'

LOPEANT

Mohave

When the Mormon residents of this small community applied for a post office, they suggested the name Arizantelope, noting that the local name was Antelope. A compromise was reached by inverting the name Antelope: Lope/Ant. Variant names include Topeat and Topeant.

P.O. est. Jan. 28, 1921, Mattie Woodbury Ruesch, p.m.; disc. June 14, 1922 Ref.: 242

LORD, MOUNT

Pima   T12S R9E   Elev. 3825'

On his 1892 map of Pima County, George H. Roskruge named this peak for his neighbor, Charles H. Lord (b. 1833, New York; d. Mexico City, March 29, 1884). Lord was a surgeon with the army (1863-64) and at the Cerro Colorado Mine in 1866, where he was also postmaster. He became a successful merchant in Tucson. The firm of Lord and Williams failed in 1882, but by that time Lord had a sheep ranch in Sasabe Valley near this mountain with about sixteen thousand sheep. He was indicted for perjury and fled to Mexico. Ref.: AHS, Names File; 62

L O SPRING

Coconino   T20N R4E

The L O Ranch owned by the L O Cattle Company used this and Little L O Spring in L O Pocket at the head of Sycamore Canyon. Little L O Canyon (a.k.a. Little L O Spring Canyon) took its name from the smaller spring, now gone. L O Draw (Coconino; T23N/R1E) and L O Flat are similarly named. Ref.: 329

LOST: A number of place names beginning with *lost* suggests either that the locations were (or are) far away from civilization or the people were extraordinarily careless, for at least sixty such *Lost* locations exist in Arizona. Among them are three canyons, three lakes, five springs, ten tanks, four cabins, two camps, and a variety of objects such as arrowheads, basins, cows, dogs, guns, horses, mules, and a man named Wilson. A certain nostalgia exists in the place named Lost Eden Tank (Coconino; T14N/R10E). Examples follow:

Lost Basin   Mohave   T22N R20W   Elev. c. 4000'

In the early 1880s rumors spread about gold and silver in Lost Basin, but where "Lost Basin" was, no one seemed to know. Then in March 1885, the *Arizona Miner* printed stories about a "lost shaft" and old mine workings having been found somewhere in the region. Fred Nobman found the shaft and cleaned it out. As for the basin, it is described as "just a little basin all by itself, pretty well lost in the little hills around it." In 1906 it was listed as an important mining camp. See Scanlon's Ferry, Mohave, and Gold Basin, Mohave

P.O. est. July 11, 1882, Michael Scanlon, p.m.; disc. Jan. 13, 1891

Ref.: Harris; Babcock; Mallach; 200, p. 16

Lost Cabin Mine   Mohave   T24N R21W

In 1911 W. D. Grannis found this old mine, which still had part of a dugout cabin and old mine workings, hence the name. Ref.: 215, p. 111

Lost Cabin Spring   Mohave   T24N R21W

Lost Cabin Wash   Mohave   T24N R21W

Lost Camp Canyon   Gila   T10N R12E

Lost Camp Mountain   Gila   T10N R12E   Elev. 5631'

Lost Canyon   Cochise   T16S R29E

This little canyon is so concealed that it is also known as Hidden Canyon and as Surprise Canyon, the latter name denoting one's reaction on coming upon it. Ref.: Riggs

Lost Canyon   Coconino   T21N R2E

Lost Cienega   Greenlee   T3N R29E

Lost Creek   Mohave   T28N R13W

Lost Dog Canyon   Santa Cruz   T22S R12E

Lost Dutch Canyon   Maricopa   T2N R11E

Lost Dutchman Mine   Pinal

See Superstition Mountains, Pinal, and Weaver's Needle, Pinal

Lost Gulch   Gila   T1N R14E

Lost Gun Point   Navajo   T25N R17E

Lost Horse Peak   Maricopa   T7S R1W   Elev. 2175'

Lost Lake See Beasley's Tank, Coconino	Coconino	T19N R5E
Lost Lake	Greenlee	(1) T3N R28E (2) T10S R31E
Lost Man Creek	Mohave	T27N R11W
Lost Mountain	Yavapai	T18N R4E
Lost Mule Creek	Gila	T3N R21E
Lost Point	Coconino	T36N R1E
Lost Spring	Apache	T5N R27E
Lost Spring	Coconino	T24N R5E
Lost Spring	Mohave	(1) T41N R7W (2) T40N R14W (3) T32N R10W
Lost Spring Gap	Coconino	T42N R2W
Lost Spring Mountain	Mohave	T41N R8W
Lost Spring Wash	Coconino	T41N R2W
Lost Tank Canyon	Navajo	T9N R15E
Lost Tank Creek	Gila	T9N R15E
Lost Tank Ridge	Navajo	T9N R15E

Although the local name in use is Chediski Butte, the USGS has named this ridge for Lost Tank, "the only hydro-graphic feature found on the ridge." See Chediski Mountain, Navajo Ref.: 329

Lost Wilson Mountain	Coconino	T18N R6E

LOUDERMILK WASH
Maricopa   T2S R9W   Elev. c. 1300-1550'
This wash was named for a supplier named Loudermilk, who owned a well reportedly dug by men working on the state highway. Ref.: Parkman

LOUISE
Mohave   T21N R16W   Elev. 3500'
This railroad section house, now vanished, was named for the daughter of A. G. Wells, general manager and vice president of the railroad. Ref.: Babcock; 18a

LOUIS GULCH, ST.
Santa Cruz   T21S R15E   Elev. 5495'
This gulch takes its name from that of the St. Louis Mine, which was located in 1874 on the Empress of India lode and was developed in 1886 with a seventy-five foot shaft and drifts (side tunnels from the main shaft). Ref.: 286, pp. 155-156

LOUISIANA GULCH
Pima   T19S R16E   Elev. c. 5500'
This gulch takes its name from that of the Louisiana Mine, a productive gold mine from about 1875. It has been called Greaterville Gulch, but although it heads near Greaterville, it is not synonymous with that location.
Ref.: 329; 286, p. 163; AHS, Castillo Collection

LOUSY GULCH
Gila   T10N R10E   Elev. c. 5000'
Ben Cole and his sons Elmer and Link mined here during the winter in the 1880s. All picked up lice, hence the name. Ref.: 18a

LOVE
La Paz   T6N R12W
This station on the Parker branch of the S.P.R.R. was called Lockhart until the formal USGS name was changed to Love in 1921, to honor Ernest Love, a soldier who died in World War I. His father was a railroad engineer. Ref.: 18a; Lenon

LOWELL

Cochise   T23S R24E   Elev. 5250'

In 1901 the Lowell Mine was owned by a New England merchant. Further, the canyon of Bisbee was becoming congested and there was need to expand the residential area. The result was the establishment of two separate communities, Warren and Lowell, the latter being named by transfer from Lowell, Massachusetts.

P.O. est. Aug. 1, 1904, Edward F. Kelsey, p.m.; disc. June 17, 1907, but reest.; disc. Jan. 1, 1974; Wells Fargo 1909

Ref.: Burgess; 5, p. 172; Directory of Post Offices (1974)

LOWELL, FORT

Pima   T14S R14E   Elev. 2530'

On May 20, 1862, in pursuit of the Texas Rifles (Confederate troops under Capt. Sherod Hunter), Col. West led the California Volunteers into Tucson. West and his men camped on the southeast edge of Tucson at what is today Scott and 14th Street, adjacent to Armory Park (formerly called Military Park). Their encampment was known simply as The Post at Tucson. The camp was abandoned on Sept. 15, 1864 after the troops were called upon to serve in New Mexico during the Civil War. The old encampment was reoccupied in May 1865 and designated a permanent post on August 29, 1866. It was named to honor Brig. Gen. Charles R. Lowell, Sixth U.S. Cavalry (d. Oct. 20, 1864, Cedar Ridge, Virginia).

Because the Santa Cruz River no longer had enough water to serve the needs of the fort, a new site was found on the Rillito several miles east-northeast of the old Camp Lowell. Its abundant water made it possible to grow hay for the horses and to supply the requirements of the troops. The move to the new location of Camp Lowell was made on March 18, 1873. Lowell soon became an important community with two weekly newspapers, a public school, a church and the usual increment of places to entertain soldiers. The new post provided permanent quarters, a relief to the military, which had been housed in brush shelters and tents. Officers' quarters were large roomed and high-ceilinged adobe houses with wide porches. Visitors were extravagantly entertained.

On April 5, 1879 the name of the post was changed to Fort Lowell. Visitors to the ruins today are usually unaware that by Presidential Proclamation on May 15, 1866 Fort Lowell boundaries were extended to include 51,631.36 acres. The order came a little late, for Apache troubles were nearing an end and so was Fort Lowell as an active military post. On January 8, 1891 all troops at Fort Lowell were ordered to report to Fort Wingate, New Mexico, and on February 14, 1891 Fort Lowell fell into silence. The long rows of shade trees died from lack of attention and the buildings gradually fell into ruins. A small nearby community managed to survive. It has long since merged with an expanding Tucson. Today Fort Lowell is being restored and has an interesting museum.

P.O. est. as Fort Lowell, July 6, 1911, Egnazio Mulé, p.m.; disc. March 5, 1912

Ref.: 145, p. 142; 163, pp. 270, 312; 73, II, 60; 5, p. 297; 121a, p. 10; 339, pp. 24, 96-97, 118; *Arizona Citizen* (March 2, 1872), p. 3; 242

LOWELL OBSERVATORY

Coconino   T21N R7E   Elev. c. 7500'

On returning home from Japan in 1893, Dr. Percival Lowell (1855-1916) determined to carry on the work of Schiaparelli, an Italian expert about Mars, by equipping and putting into use an observatory to chart the approach of that planet to earth in 1894, at which time it would be closer than at any time again until 1956. Lowell selected Flagstaff as the best site and appropriately called the hill on which it was to be located Mars Hill. He endowed and directed the activities of the Lowell Observatory over the ensuing twenty-two years. Mars Hill may have at first been called Observatory Hill as it is a part of Observatory Mesa. Ref.: 139, pp. 358-359-360; 297, p. 170; 276, p. 69; Slipher

LOWER CORRAL CANYON

Gila   T14N R15E

Al Devore maintained a lower corral here. Ref.: Woody

LOWER GOLDWATER LAKE
Yavapai   T13N R2W

A dam was built behind the original dam forming Goldwater Lake, creating therefrom two bodies of water. The upper one was not named and hence the name Lower Goldwater Lake now applies to the lower part and Upper Goldwater Lake naturally to that portion. Ref.: 329

LOWER GRANITE GORGE
Coconino   T28N R13–10W   Elev. 2800'

According to Francois E. Matthes, "The second granite might be designated as Lower Granite Gorge." In 1915 when he made the suggestion, it was adopted for this fifty-mile long passage of the Colorado River. Ref.: 329

LOWER LAKE MARY
Coconino   T20N R8E   Elev. 6850'

Sink holes in the area made the erection of a dam essential, as water was needed to supply the nearby sawmill. The dam was built in 1903. Timothy A. Riordan, president of the lumber company, named the new lake for his eldest daughter, Mary. It was in Little Valley. When the mill went out of business, the owners gave the lake to Coconino County as a recreational area, but later the City of Flagstaff acquired it and rebuilt the dam in 1907. In 1941 upper Lake Mary was created and became a source of water for Flagstaff. The place has also been called Mary Lake and Mary's Lake. In the 1890s, it was called Little Valley. At the east end of the lower dam are ice caves from which ice used to be shipped to Flagstaff. However, a butcher got lost in it and although he lived, the cave was sealed to prevent a recurrence of this incident.
Ref.: Sykes; 76, p. 55; 5, p. 451; 329

LOWER LAKE MEAD
Mohave

In June 1946 Edward Schenk of the Bureau of Mines at Boulder City and Elzada U. Clover proposed this name for "that body of water between Boulder Dam and Boulder Canyon." The name, however, was not accepted. The Board on Geographic names in 1948 approved instead Boulder Basin (*q.v.*). Ref.: 329

LOWER RACETRACK MESA
Gila/Yavapai   T10N R6E

This location is the top of a ridge about a mile long by fifteen hundred feet wide. See Racetrack Mesa, Gila

LOW MOUNTAINS
La Paz   T7N R12W   Elev. 3548'

These mountains are low in their appearance, hence the name is descriptive.

LOWREY SPRING
Coconino   T40N R7E

This spring was named for David Crockett Lowrey, who homesteaded here in the 1920s and developed it. His patent was granted March 2, 1933. His name has been misspelled on some maps as Lowery. Ref.: 329

LOY BUTTE
Yavapai   T18N R4E   Elev. 5718'

This location, named for a ranger, is the site of Honennanki Ruins and is in addition a mythological Hopi town. It is near Loy Canyon (T19N/R5E), a.k.a. Hartley Canyon. Ref.: Colton; 329

LUCIFER POINT
Coconino (Grand Canyon)   T32N R5E

This name has been replaced and the location is now known as Natchi Point. See Uncle Jim Point, Coconino (Grand Canyon)

LUCKY CUSS MINE
Cochise   T20S R22E   Elev. c. 4000'
Al and Ed Schieffelin, brothers, found nothing in their initial search for precious metals in the future Tombstone. On his way to hunt deer one day, Al disdained ore which Ed showed him. Later he returned with a fat buck to find Ed raising a location monument. Ed shouted he had struck it rich. Al responded, "You are a lucky cuss," hence the name.
Ref.: 60, pp. 19-20

LUHRS
Maricopa   T1N R3E
A post office was established here in 1924. By 1947 the location was known as the Jefferson Street post office station.
P.O. est. March 3, 1924, S. J. Michelson, p.m. Ref.: 242

LUIS MARIA BACA LAND GRANT
Santa Cruz   T22S R14E
This land grant, also known as Baca Float No. 3, was one of five such tracts of about one hundred thousand acres each. They were made by the Mexican government in 1821 to heirs of Luis Maria Cabeza de Baca, authorized to choose land in New Mexico. However, as the heirs could not obtain what they wanted because of legal conflicts, in June 1860 the United States Congress authorized the heirs to select equal acreage in five bodies of land available in New Mexico (part of which later became Arizona). Float No. 2 in Yavapai County contained 92,160 acres and the Santa Cruz float over two hundred thousand. All grants were validated by the United States Supreme Court in 1914.

LUIS MARIA BACA LAND GRANT
Yavapai   (1) T10–11N R7–8W or (2) T18N R8W
The two locations cited reflect the recording in the National Archives, which places the grant in Yuma County and a contemporary location. See Luis Maria Baca Land Grant, Santa Cruz Ref.: 242

LUIS, SAN pro.: /San Luwis/
Spanish = "St. Louis"
Yuma   T11S R25W   Elev. 136'
This port of entry to Mexico is a thriving community. Papagos call it Gege who Kihm ("wildcat village"). The reason for the name has not been learned.
P.O. est. Nov. 30, 1928, O.L. Verdugo, p.m. Ref.: 242; 283, p. 12

LUIS MOUNTAINS, SAN pro.: /San Luwis/
Spanish = "St. Louis"
Pima   T22S R9E   Elev. 4668'
These mountains were named for the San Luis Mine (T21S/R9E), now abandoned.
Ref.: 18a

LUKACHUKAI pro.: /lok'ajuwga:y/
Navajo: *lok-ach-agai* = "reeds coming out into pass"
Apache   T35N R29E   Elev. 6421'
This Navajo trading post was established by George N. Barker in 1892, and Fr. Berard Haile built a mission school in 1916. The school was taken over by the government in 1933. The name is Navajo and refers to the patch of reeds in a cove at the western base of Lukachukai Pass. Although the name Lukachukai is now applied to this post, the name for the site of the post is *Checailyaa* (= "under the oaks") also spelled Chech'iyaa. See also Chuska Mountains, Apache
P.O. est. April 3, 1916, Sidney Boardman, p.m. Ref.: 242; 331, p. 88

LUKACHUKAI MOUNTAINS
Apache   T36N R29E   Elev. 9460'
These mountains are sometimes called the White Reed Mountains. See Lukachukai, Apache Ref.: 129, p. 76

LUKE AIR FORCE BASE

Maricopa   T2N R1W

This base was named for World War I pilot Frank Luke, Jr. (b. 1897; d. 1918), known as "Baloon Buster," killed in action while flying over German lines in 1918. In his thirty-nine days of combat, Luke was credited with twenty-one official victories.
Ref.: 5, p. 229

LUKEVILLE

Pima   T18S R5W   Elev. 1400'

Charles Luke of Phoenix established this small village on sixty-seven acres on the international border.
P.O. est. Jan. 1, 1949, Charles Luke, p.m.
Ref.: 242; *Phoenix Gazette* (July 5, 1949), n.p.

LULULONGTURKWI

Hopi = "Bullsnake point"

Navajo   Elev. 6000'

In 1901 this medium-sized pueblo ruin was excavated in the Jadito Valley across from Kokopke. Locally it used to be called the Peacock Ruin. A variant spelling of the name is Lululongturqui. Ref.: Museum of Northern Arizona; 152, p. 20; 167, p. 778

LURTY'S RANCH

Yavapai

Early in 1871 Moore K. Lurty (b. 1848, Kentucky) sold his Confederate Crossroads Ranch on the Prescott and Camp Verde Road between Grief Hill Road and Beaver Creek. The ranch served as a way station for travellers, freighters, and the military. The name was sometimes spelled Lerty's. Ref.: 62; *Weekly Arizona Miner* (Dec. 12, 1868) and (Feb. 18, 1871)

LUSK

Cochise

In 1908 when a post office was being proposed, this name was submitted first for what was later called Apache. See Apache, Cochise Ref.: 242

LUTTRELL

Santa Cruz   T24S R16E   Elev. 5300'

In 1880 Henry Holland sold a mining claim in Duquesne Gulch to Dr. J. M. Luttrell, a member of a party of Californians who then developed the Holland Company Smelting Works, of which J. K. Luttrell (b. 1847, Tennessee) was superintendent.
P.O. est. Aug. 23, 1880, Harrison Fuller, p.m.; disc. Jan. 19, 1883

LYDA CREEK

Greenlee   T5S R31E   Elev. c. 6000'

Lyda was the name of an old cheese-maker who made his home at this location and used Black Jack Canyon-Sawmill Road to bring his products into Clifton. The name has also been incorrectly spelled Lida Creek. Lyda Springs are on the Lyda Ranch.
Ref.: Mrs. Fred Fritz, Sr.

LYELL BUTTE

Coconino (Grand Canyon)   T31N R3E   Elev. 5368'

This butte was named for Sir Charles Lyell (1798-1875), a British geologist who wrote *Principles of Geology*, published in 1830 and 1832, a direct forerunner of Darwin's theory of evolution.

LYLE CANYON

Cochise/Santa Cruz   T22S R19–18E

This canyon was named for Ambrose Lyle (b. 1822, North Carolina; d. June 27, 1886), a cattle rancher well known throughout Cochise County. Lyle Peak (Elev. 7825') shares the name. Ref.: *Arizona Star* (June 27, 1886), p. 4

LYMAN LAKE

Apache   T11N R28E   Elev. 5978'

Following a controversy about the use of Little Colorado River water, Mormons were allotted the use of three-fifths of such water and in 1886 built a dam here. Because it drained Salado Spring, it was first called Salado Reservoir. This name soon gave way to Slough Reservoir. In 1903 a flood washed away the original dam. Another was immediately constructed and the name changed to Lyman, for Francis M. Lyman, a Mormon bishop. In 1915 it disappeared under flood waters. With state aid a third and enduring dam was constructed. The waters impounded by the dam are called Lyman Lake, a name which replaced the earlier name of Lyman Reservoir. The lake is now used for recreation. Ref.: Wiltbank; 5, pp. 428-429

LYNX CREEK

Yavapai   T13N R1W   Elev. 6225'

Five members of Capt. Joseph Walker's expedition were on Oolkilsipava (or Oolke-se-pave) River and while four hunted, Sam Miller panned for and accidentally found gold. The main body of the expedition immediately joined the group and on May 10, 1863 the Pioneer Mining District was formed. Between that date and September 1863, the name of the creek changed to Lynx Creek. The story was that Sam Miller found a lynx and when he leaned to pick it up, it sprang at him and wounded his arm. He kicked it to death. Lynx were not uncommon in this vicinity in 1863. Lynx Lake shares the name. It encompasses the fifty-five acre Lynx Lake Wild Life Area.
Ref.: 168, pp. 4, 8; *Weekly Alta Californian* (Sept. 26, 1863); Unidentified clipping, Sharlot Hall Museum, Prescott; 9, p. 4

LYONSVILLE

Mohave   Elev. c. 2500'

Residents of Virginia City said that the proposed community of Lyonsville, one-half mile away and close to Oatman, consisted of "one house to be built and the skeleton of a corral." The origin of the name is not known.
Ref.: 163, p. 252

M

MAC DONALD

Cochise   T19N R21E

MacDonald was named in 1882 for Alexander F. MacDonald, president of the Maricopa Stake of the Church of Latter-Day Saints. The settlement, a southern extension of St. David, was made by Henry J. Horne, Jonathan Hoopes, and others.
Ref.: 225, p. 286

MAC DONALD

Yavapai

This post office was ten miles southeast of Jerome and five miles southwest of Cottonwood. The origin of the name is not known.
P.O. est. Feb. 4, 1904, Fred H. Gorham, p.m.; disc. Aug. 15, 1905 Ref.: 242

MADERA CANYON   pro.: /məderə/

Spanish = "lumber"

Pima/Santa Cruz   T20–19S R14E   Elev. c. 6000'

In 1820 this canyon was known as Madera Canyon, being mentioned in the Canoa Land Grant as the point from which measurements were made. An 1856 map shows Puerto de los Muchachos (= "Boys' Pass) in this area, termed Sierra de la Madera. The name *Madera* is deserved, for from the first arrival of white men, this canyon has been noted for its fine timber. John Hempstead Page with his partner, Capt. Reynolds, whipsawed lumber here in 1858. His wife, Larcena Pennington Page, in 1860 persuaded her husband to take her to the lumber camp for her health. In this canyon she was captured and dragged off by Apaches (see Huerfano Butte).

At an elevation of 5260' where the canyon emerges into the plain, Theodore Welish built a white house in the 1880s. He also owned a store in Tucson called The White House. This caused many to refer to the canyon as White House Canyon. In March 1929 the U.S. Forest Service eliminated the name White House Canyon. The local name Box Canyon remains somewhat in use. Currently there is a small recreational community at the head of the canyon.
P.O. est. March 18, 1929, Catherine M. Dusenberry, p.m.
Ref.: 242; *Book of Records of Pima County*, 1820-1873, AHS; 117, p. 12; 286, p. 175

MAGMA

Pinal   T3S R8E   Elev. 1520'

A station called Webster was at the junction for the branch line to the Magma Mine on the Arizona Eastern Railroad. When the Magma Copper Company built the branch line c. 1915, the name of the railroad juncture was changed to Magma, and the name of the mine — which had been the Silver Queen (see Silver Queen) — was also changed, to Magma Mine. The word *magma* indicates a type of molten rock turned into igneous rock, much of which existed here. Webster was the first name proposed for the post office but Magma was finally selected. Magma Dam is nearby.
P.O. est. Jan. 7, 1915, George H. Parker, p.m.; disc. April 30, 1928
Ref.: 242; Woody; Craig; 359, p. 84

MAHAN MOUNTAIN
Yavapai   T16N R9E
"Long" Charley Mahan maintained a camp on the north slope of this mountain in the 1900s, hence the name. It is the center of the old 150,000 acre ranch west of Baca Float No. 5. Ref.: 261, pp. 118, 119; Mattie Mahan Hansen (daughter); 289, p. 10

MAHONE PEAK
Yavapai   T18N R10W   Elev. 7499'
Jim Mahone, a Hualapai Indian, was a scout and guide for Gen. George Crook. His home was near this peak, hence the name. About Geronimo, he said, "That man did a lot of killing of U.S. Army white men, etc. like that," and that Crook called on him to help clean up the trouble. When he was known to be about 95 or possibly 100 years old in 1931, the Indian was still drawing a government pension. The name Mohan Mountain is in error for this location. Ref.: 335, pp. 247-248

MAIDEN'S BREAST
Coconino (Grand Canyon)   T31N R2E   Elev. 5450'
The name is a translation of the Havasupai name for this place at the end of Maricopa Point. George Wharton James noted that the formation was crowned "with a small nipple in red sandstone." James adds that it was "quite a height for an earthly maiden." Ref.: 178, p. 32

MAISH
Pima   T16S R8E
Frederick Maish (b. 1835, Pennsylvania) arrived in Tucson in 1869 and soon had a ranch in what is now Avra Valley where he ran several thousand head of stock in partnership with Driscoll. The name has occasionally been misspelled Marsh. Ref.: 62; *Arizona Enterprise* (June 27, 1891), p. 3

MAITO
Navajo: *mai* = "coyote"; *to* = "water"
Apache   T6N R25E
As the name *Maito* infers that it is a spring, there is no need to add that generic to the name. Coyotes drink at this location, which is also known by the following names: Maitio Spring, Mayeto, Mailto Spring, Coyote Springs, Coyote Water. In March 1971 the USGS authorized Maito as the official name. Ref.: 329; 141, pp. 152, 193

MAKGUM HAVOKA
Papago: *vo* = "pond"; "caterpillar pond"
Pima   T13S R4E   Elev. 1860'
In August yellow black striped caterpillars appear locally in great numbers. Papagos boil and eat them. The location has also been called Makumvooka (Lumholtz, 1912). Ref.: 57, p. 5; 329

MALEY CORRAL   pro.: /meyley/
Greenlee   T3N R28E
James H. Maley or Mahley was registered in Cochise County in 1880. By 1884 the Maley brothers had a ranch where the corral is located north of and between Honeymoon Ranger station and Black River near Maylay Creek. See also Willcox, Cochise Ref.: *Cochise County Great Register, 1880;* Scott

MALLERY GROTTO
Coconino (Grand Canyon)   Elev. c. 5000'
This cave lies under the South Rim at the extreme west of the El Tovar amphitheater. Inside this 150 foot long grotto are Indian pictographs, and the location is named for Garrick Mallery, "the great authority on the pictographs of the North American Indians." Ref.: 178, pp. 23, 24

MALAPAIS: Locations have the word *malapais* or *malpais* (Spanish = "bad land"; pro.: mælpay) usually are rocky, volcanic or otherwise "bad" lands.

Malapais Hills	Pinal	T3S R7E	
Mal Pai	Apache		

P.O. est. June 7, 1890, John W. Phipps, p.m.; disc. Aug. 4, 1890 Ref.: 242

Malpais	Pima/Yuma (and Mexico)	

See Camino del Diablo, Pima/Yuma

Mal Pais	Pima

See Guijas Mountains, Las, Pima

Mal-Pais Butte	Apache

See Black Pinnacle Butte, Apache

Malpais Canyon	Maricopa	T4N R7E	
Malpais Hill	Pima	T11S R8E	Elev. 2682'
Malpais Hill	Yavapai	T9N R1E	Elev. 5632'
Malpais Hills	Pinal	T6S R16E	Elev. 2491'

See Santan Mountains, Pinal

Malpais Mountain	Greenlee	T3S R29E	Elev. c. 6000'
Malpais Mountain	Yavapai		

See Glassford Hill, Yavapai

Malpais Point	Apache

See Sezhine Butte, Apache

Mal Pais, Sierra del	Pima

See Guijas Mountains, Pima

Mal Pais Spring	Apache	T12N R26E	
Malpais Spring	Greenlee	T2S R30E	
Malpais Tank	Cochise	T21S R31E	Elev. 4515'

MAMATOTK MOUNTAIN
Pima   T18N R2W
This mountain is in the Mesquite Mountains, Pima. It is also called Chupan Mountain. See Mesquite Mountains, Pima

MAMMOTH
Pinal   T8S R17E   Elev. 2353'
Frank Shultz located the first mine in the Mammoth district and as early as December 27, 1872, the Mammoth Mine (T8S/R16E) was being worked by E. M. Pearce, C. O. Brown, and members of Tully Ochoa Company. This mine, sometimes referred to as the Old Mammoth Mine, was at a place referred to as Shultz after its locator, or sometimes as Mammoth Camp. Because ores could not be milled at the site, a stamp mill was constructed on the San Pedro River where the community of Mammoth is today. Ores were sent down from the mine to the town in buckets suspended on a wire cable and the returned buckets were filled with water for the mining camp. The Mammoth Mine was so named because it was said to contain huge ore veins. The name also applies to Mammoth Wash. See also Shultz, Pinal
P.O. est. as Mammoth, June 23, 1887, Louis Ezekiels, p.m.; name changed to Shultz, July 12, 1894, Mrs. Lizzie Schneider, p.m.; disc. April 21, 1902; reest. March 28, 1903 as Mammoth, E. E. Putnam, p.m. Ref.: AHS, Mammoth Files; 242; *Tucson Citizen* (Dec. 27, 1873), p. 3; 238, p. 47; 5, p. 89

MANAKACHA POINT
Coconino (Grand Canyon)   T33N R4W   Elev. 5811'
This location on the South Rim was named for a Havasupai Indian family. Ref.: 329

MANGAS MOUNTAIN
Gila   T6N R12E
There is a possibility that this mountain was named for Mangas Colorado ("Red Sleeves"), a prominent Apache leader. See Three Sisters Mountain, Gila

MANILA
Navajo   T18N R18E   Elev. c. 5000'
Lt. Amiel W. Whipple had his Camp 79 near here. The location later became a station on the S.F.R.R. It was named during the Spanish-American War after the chief city and capital of the Philippines. The name applies also to Manila Wash.
P.O. est. June 21, 1912, Clarence G. Wallace, p.m.; disc. June 15, 1918
Ref.: 346, p. 157, Note 13; 242; 18a

MANLEYVILLE
Pinal   T8S R14E   Elev. 4000'
With his sons in 1880 Joseph Chamberlan established the Willow Spring ranch in the valley of Camp Grant Wash. One of the sons, Manley R. Chamberlan, established a post office and called it after himself. A pony carried the mail from here between Tucson and the Riverside Stage Station before a four-horse coach began running the route and Manley became a stage station.
P.O. est. March 18, 1881, Manley R. Chamberlain (sic), p.m.; disc. July 5, 1886
Ref.: 238, pp. 40-41

MANSFIELD, CAMP
Apache   Elev. c. 7000'
Camp Mansfield, which Heitman locates seven miles south of Fort Defiance, may have been named for Maj. Gen. Joseph King Fenno Mansfield, who wrote the report about Fort Defiance in 1854 when he was an army inspector. He was appointed a Maj. Gen. on July 18, 1862. He was killed in the battle of Antietam, Virginia, shortly before Camp Mansfield was established. Ref.: 159, p. 522

MANSFIELD CANYON
Santa Cruz   T21S R15E   Elev. 4700'
In 1879 Jack Mansfield with Con Ryan discovered a mine in this canyon (or Gulch), hence the name. Ref.: 286, p. 226

MANUEL, SAN   pro.: /sæn mænuwel/
Pinal   T9S R17E   Elev. 3500'
San Manuel is a company-owned copper mining town established c. 1953 and given the name for its parent company.
P.O. est. April 1, 1954, Joseph Cittadini, p.m.

MANU TEMPLE
Coconino (Grand Canyon)   T32N R3E   Elev. 7181'
Following the policy of naming formations in the Grand Canyon for deities and great leaders of various religions, this name was given. Manu (Sanskrit = "man") is one of the fourteen demiurgic beings and the great law giver of the Hindu.
Ref.: 178, p. 30; 329

MANY FARMS   pro.: /da'akeyhalani/
Navajo: da'ak'chalani = "many farms"
Apache   T34N R25E   Elev. 5300'
The American name, a translation of the Navajo, refers to nearly seven hundred acres under cultivation by Navajos; hence the name is descriptive.
Ref.: 331, p. 92; 143, p. 189; Burcard

MANY GREASEWOOD VALLEY
Navajo   T34N R19E
Descriptive.

MANZANITA: (pro.: /manzaniytǝ/ or /mænzǝntǝ/ Spanish = "little apple") Place names having the word *manzanita* usually indicate local growth of the shrub *Arctostaphylos* or "manzanita," which is common in Arizona

Manzanita Creek	Coconino (Grand Canyon)	T32N R4E	
Manzanita Creek	Yavapai	T11N R4W	
Manzanita Mountain	Santa Cruz	T23S R11E	Elev. 4817'

The mountain derives its name from the presence of Manzanita Spring, which takes its name from a profuse growth of manzanita on the south side of the mountain. The name has been corrupted to Manzana.

| Manzanita Point | Coconino (Grand Canyon) | T32N R4E | Elev. c. 5000' |

In the 1920s Col. John White lived at the Grand Canyon. Late one season he hiked across to the North Rim and while ascending Bright Angel Creek noticed a large manzanita. He left a piece of wood inscribed "Manzanita Point." The point named by White is approximately opposite the mouth of The Transept. See also Manzanita Ref.: Stephen Jones, Letter (Feb. 7, 1930) (Grand Canyon Files)

| Manzanita Spring | Graham | T8S R23E | |
| Manzanita Spring | Santa Cruz | T23S R11E | |

MANZORA pro.: /mansorǝ/ or /mænsorǝ/
Cochise   T16S R23E   Elev. c. 4000'
On the Middlemarch post office location map of 1898, Manzora is indicated as a bend in the road. However, with the establishment of the Golden Rule Mine on the northeast slope of the Dragoon Mountains, a siding was established for shipping ores from that place and the name Manzora was applied to it. Why it is called Manzora has not been learned.
P.O. est. July 21, 1915, Harry O. Miller, p.m.; disc. March 30, 1918 Ref.: 242; Bennett

MAPLE CANYON
Greenlee   T1S R31E   Elev. c. 5000'
The name comes from the fact that there is a large grove of mountain maple here. Settlers used to tap these trees for maple sap to be boiled to sugar. Some tree trunks still have old plugs in them. Ref.: Mrs. Fred Fritz, Sr.

MAPLE CREEK
Yavapai   T12N R2W
In 1915 this creek was on a map which indicated it was two hundred feet west of Senator (Maxton). It appears to now be called Ash Creek.

MARANA pro.: /maranǝ/ or /mærænǝ/
Spanish = "tangle;" "impassable because of briers and brambles"
Pima   T11S R11E   Elev. 1900'
Although it is today in an agricultural region, the name reflects the fact that at one time the locality was noted for its extraordinarily thick stand of mesquite and other desert growth. The local name for the area was transferred to a flag station established here in 1890. There was no agriculture near until a Mr. Post instituted a project to install pumps in the 1920s, and the local name changed to Postvale, a community separate from the railroad station of Marana. Later, the community expanded to include the station.
P.O. est. as Postvale, March 5, 1920, Ophelia Knudsen, p.m.; Marana P.O., May 17, 1924, Jessie M. Dills, p.m.; Postvale consolidated with Marana Feb. 1, 1925
Ref.: 242; AHS Names File and Castillo Collection

MARBLE CANYON
Cochise   T15S R29E
There is a marble quarry at the canyon end, hence the name.

MARBLE CANYON
Coconino   T33N R5E

In 1869 Maj. John Wesley Powell applied the name Marble Canyon to this location. He noted that the boats passed between cliffs of what he mistook for marble, with a great number of caves, eroded on a grand scale with the walls towering hundreds of feet and rising at least 3500' at the canyon's lower end. The distance from the mouth of the Little Colorado to the head of the Grand Canyon at Lee's Ferry, through which the gorge extends, is nearly sixty-one miles. The exploring party had to make four portages, using ropes because of the extremely swift currents, whirlpools, and rapids. In 1961 the USGS officially changed the name to Marble Canyon, reversing the 1925 decision to call it Marble Gorge. Marble Viewpoint overlooks the gorge. On January 20, 1969, President Lyndon B. Johnson's signature established Marble Canyon National Monument (T35N/R5E).
Ref.: 322 (Aug. 22, 1872), p. 94; 266, pp. 76, 77, 79; 89, pp. 317, 318, 325

MARBLE CANYON (TOWN)
Coconino   T39N R7E   Elev. 3560'

This name is borrowed from that of Marble Canyon.
P.O. est. Oct. 14, 1927, Florence Lowrey, p.m.; disc. Feb. 28, 1935; re-est. Feb. 12, 1957; disc. Jan. 1, 1966

MARBLE HILL
Coconino   T23N R6E

The name Marble Hill derives from the fact that the summit of the central hill is a coarse-grain white marble. Ref.: 276, p. 71

MARCOS TERRACE
Coconino (Grand Canyon)   T33N R1W   Elev. 5000'

The name for this terrace was suggested by Francois E. Matthes in 1915, and it was adopted as being consonant with the policy of naming geographic features for noted explorers. Fr. Marcos de Niza (b. Nice, France), was the first Caucasian to enter what is now Arizona in 1539. He was ostensibly on a missionizing trip but was in fact more interested in finding the fabled Seven Cities of Cibola. Accompanying him was the dark-skinned Estevan, whom Marcos constantly used as an advance agent. Esteven took the step too far when he arrived at the Zuñi villages where the natives stoned him to death. Word came back to de Niza about the loss of his companion and he hastily returned to Mexico. There he spread rumors of golden cities which he had never seen but was sure were there. His tall tales led rapidly to the forming of the Coronado Expedition in 1540.
Ref.: 357, pp. 346, 361, 381, 382; 329

MARCOU MESA
Navajo   T19N R20E   Elev. 7000'

Lt. James Fitzgerald Beale in 1857 called this Rabbit Hills. In 1858 the name was changed to Marcou Mesa to honor the geologist who served with the Wheeler expedition. Marcou Crater is also named for him. Ref.: 141, p. 193

MARGARITA TANK
Santa Cruz   T23S R11E

This tank has borrowed its name from that of the Santa Margarita Mine, which in 1857 was one of the twenty-five mines on the Arabaca range. Santa Margarita Wash is also named from the mine.

MARGS DRAW
Coconino   T17N R6E

This draw was named for a twenty-five year old horse which pastured here. The place is also called Mortgage Draw. Ref.: 329

MARIA DEL PILAR, SANTA
Santa Cruz

This was the name applied by Kino in 1695 to the present Santa Cruz River. See Cruz River, Santa, Santa Cruz

[384]

MARIA RIVER, SANTA   pro.: /sántə mariyə/ or /sǽntə mariyə/
Yuma/Mohave/Yavapai   T11N R10W

New Mexico Governor Juan de Oñate encountered this river in 1604 and called it the
Rio de San Andres, possibly because he may have arrived at it on November 30, which is
Saint Andrew's Day. The name was applied not only to the present Santa Maria River,
but also to Bill Williams River. However, the Spanish name was forgotten until Jacobo
Sedelmayr c. 1747 called it the Rio Azul, which he did not see but had heard of.
According to Coues, Fr. Garcés reapplied the name Santa Maria to the entire river. The
Wheeler report notes picking up the name from early Spanish maps, but Wheeler applied
it only to the present Santa Maria River. Ref.: 345, p. 103; 77, p. 420 (Note 5), and p.
422

MARIA RIVER, SANTA (TOWN)
Mohave   T11N R12W

From 1897 to late 1901, this was a lively settlement around a stage station for a line
which ran from here to Congress Junction twenty-seven miles away. See Klondyke,
Mohave Ref.: *Arizona Journal Miner* (Oct. 13, 1897) and (Nov. 22, 1901)

MARIA GRANT, SANTISIMA DEL CARMEN
Santa Cruz

The name cited is that given on the Homestead Act of 1909. See Buena Vista Land
Grant, Santa Cruz Ref.: 242

MARIA SPRING, SANTA
Coconino (Grand Canyon)   T31N R2E   Elev. 6250'

Mary Jane Colter, architect, designed the Indian buildings near the El Tovar Hotel, and
named this spring, about twenty-one hundred feet down Hermit Trail. Ref.: Kolb

MARICOPA   pro.: /mærikópə/
Pinal   T4S R3E   Elev. 1175'

The first name for this point was Maricopa Junction because here the main transcontinental railroad joined a branch line to Phoenix. Placing the junction at Maricopa put
the old Maricopa Station (see Heaton, Pinal) out of existence. In 1887 the word
Junction was dropped. The post office at old Maricopa Station was moved to Maricopa
in the same year. Ref.: Kitt; *Phoenix Herald* (July 7, 1887), p. 2; *Arizona Sentinel*
(May 24, 1879), pp. 1,4

MARICOPA COUNTY   pro.: /mærikópə/

Originally Arizona Territory consisted of four counties: Pima, Yuma, Mohave, and
Yavapai. Maricopa, created on February 12, 1871, was named for the Maricopa Indians
(see Maricopa [Ak Chin] Indian Reservation, Pinal). Phoenix is the county seat as well as
the state capital. The county is a rich agricultural district and important industrially. Its
area is 5,904,640 acres.

MARICOPA (AK CHIN) INDIAN RESERVATION   pro: /mærikópə akčin/
Pinal   T4S R4E   Elev. 1225'

The Maricopa Indians are an important Yuman tribe which formerly lived in the Gulf of
California region but moved gradually to its present location. As early as 1775 they were
living with, but south of, the Pima Indians, who called them *Maricopa*, although they
referred to themselves as *Pipatsje* (= "of the people"). Garcés referred to them as *Opa*.
By 1826 they had moved to the mouth of the Gila River where Col. Kit Carson
encountered them. On February 28, 1859 a reservation was established for the
Maricopa and Pima Indians on the Gila River. It is separate from the one referred to in
this entry. The Maricopa (Ak Chin) Reservation was established on May 28, 1912 for
the Maricopa band of Papago Indians. It consists of 21,840 acres with tribal
headquarters at Ak Chin. Ref.: 167, p. 805; "Annual Report of the Arizona Commission of Indian Affairs, 1954, 1955, 1956," p. 7

MARICOPA MOUNTAINS
Pinal   T4S R3W   Elev. 3272'

In 1775 Fr. Francisco Garcés called this low range the Sierra Maricopa, naming the gap

through it the Puerto de los Cocomaricopas. This is the same range which Font spoke of as the Sierra de Comars. Another name applied to this widely scattered range of low lying hills is Maricopa Range (Lumholtz, 1915). The Maricopa name applied in 1883 was *We-al-hus*, the meaning of which is not known.
Ref.: 77, p. 113 (Note 18); 167, p. 805; *Phoenix Gazette* (Aug. 1, 1883), p. 3

MARICOPA VILLAGES
Pinal   T1N R1E
Emigrants crossing what is today this part of Arizona encountered several Maricopa Indian villages listed by Russell as follows: *Hi'nama, Hina Head* (*hina* = "a kind of fish"), *Tco'utcik*, and *Wutcik* (a Pima Village). Ref.: 281, *passim*

MARICOPA WELLS   pro.: /mæriko'pə/
Pinal   T3S R3E   Elev. 1500'
In his entry for November 3, 1775, Fr. Garcés notes he and Fr. Font "arrived at some pools of bad water, where some of our party were made sick, and for that they were called Las Luganas del Hospital...." This location, apparently later known as Maricopa Wells, was destined to become an important stop for emigrants and the Overland Stage route. This may have been the same spot which Fr. Kino in 1694 called San Andrew Coata. Here the Mormon Battalion under Col. Phillip St. George Cooke camped in December 1846 and dug out several pools or wells. The location gained importance with the coming of California-bound travellers, as it was the last water available prior to crossing the rugged country forty miles west to the first stop at Tezotal (see Gila Range, Maricopa). In 1857 the San Antonio and San Diego mail coaches made Maricopa Wells an intermediate station where eastbound coaches met west-bound and exchanged mail and passengers, who found only a shelter and a brush corral to receive them. In 1858 the Butterfield Overland stage constructed adobe buildings and a larger corral and reported that water in the six to eight wells was good. Pima Indians enlarged the population and a trading post was established where the Indians made a good living supplying emigrant trains with forage to cross the dreaded Forty-Mile Desert. A detachment of soldiers was attached to Maricopa Wells and the place was lively from dawn to dawn with often three to four wagons with teams of from eight to twenty mules and the people to use and drive them. Added to this were emigrant trains, their members bartering for supplies from the Indians and in turn the Indians bartered with the trading-post keeper. By 1870 sixty-eight people lived at Maricopa Wells and the station was run by James A. Moore, who in 1869 sold half of his holdings to Larkin W. Carr. A military telegraph line was strung through here in 1873. The coming of the railroad, however, was the end of Maricopa Wells as an important stop. For origin of name see Maricopa (Ak Chin) Indian Reservation.
P.O. est. as Maricopa, April 13, 1858, Francis J. Mullin; disc. March 18, 1859; re-est. as Maricopa Wells, Nov. 21, 1865, Luke D. Chadwick, p.m.; name changed to Maricopa and P.O. transferred to Maricopa Junction. Ref.: 77, p. 110 (Note 13), and p. 109; 73, II, 169-170; 56, pp. 102-103; 106, p. 117; AHS, Kirkland *ms.* and Emerson O. Stratton *ms.*; 224, III, 275; 165, p. 43; 167, II, 423

MARIJILDA CANYON   pro.: /mærəhÁldə/
Graham   T8S R25E   Elev. c. 5000'
The canyon was named for Marijilda Grijalva (sometimes spelled Merijilda). As a small boy, he was captured by some of Cochise's raiders at his birth place in Sonora and was a captive for seven years. He served as an interpreter for John P. Clum, agent at San Carlos Indian Reservation, and later as a scout for Gen. George Crook. He became a rancher in the Gila Valley. Marijilda Creek and Wash are also named for him. In the canyon are the Marijilda Ruins, having more than fifty rooms.
Ref.: AHS, Chambers Collection, Box 11

MARION
Yavapai   T10N R2W   Elev. 5449'
In 1871 this was described as "an infant town" named for John H. Marion (b. 1835, Louisiana; d. 1891). After arriving in Arizona in 1865, he prospected for about two years until hostile Indians discouraged his further efforts. There is no record of his

having done more than visit the "town" bearing his name, as by 1871 he was editor and part owner of the *Prescott Miner*.   Ref.: *Weekly Arizona Miner* (June 17, 1871), p. 3 and (July 1, 1871), p. 2; 107, V, 347, 350

MARKEEN MOUNTAIN
Greenlee   T4S R29E   Elev. 6373'
The mountain was so named because the Markeen Copper Company had a camp on it. Ref.: Sweeting

MARQUITTA PASS
La Paz   T4N R20W   Elev. 1623'
This pass derives its name from that of the Marquitta Mine. Ref.: 329

MARSHALL BUTTE
Apache   T5N R25E   Elev. 8840'
Robert P. Marshall served as chief of Fort Apache Indian Reservation Forestry Service from 1934–1937. He is known as the Father of the Wilderness areas established on Indian reservations, two of which are on the Fort Apache Indian Reservation. Marshall Flat (T9N/R25E) is also named for him, as is Marshall Mountain (T9N/R24E). Ref.: Davis

MARSHALL LAKE
Coconino   T20N R8E   Elev. 7133'
In 1892 John Marshall homesteaded here, later patenting the land. He was among the incorporators of the first bank in Flagstaff. Ref.: Frier; Slipher

MARSH BUTTE
Coconino (Grand Canyon)   T32N R1E   Elev. 4730'
The first name applied to this location was Endymion Dome. The name was changed at the suggestion by George Wharton James that it be renamed to honor the American paleontologist Othniel Charles Marsh (1831-99), who investigated fossils of the western United States. For many years Marsh directed the work of the division of vertebrate paleontology for the USGS. Ref.: 329; 178, p. 40

MARSH CREEK
Gila   T10N R13E   Elev. c. 5000'
This westerly flowing creek became a marsh because of beaver dams built along it and it remained so until the beavers were destroyed. Ref.: McKinney

MARSH PASS
Navajo   T38N R18E   Elev. 6750'
The Mexican name for this pass describes it well, La Puerta Limita (= "limited opening"). Along this pass as late as 1907 were many swamps and lakes, from which derives the name Marsh Pass. Since that time a deep arroyo caused by erosion from overgrazing and the cutting of deep wagon ruts, has drained the wet spots and the name Marsh is no longer descriptive. Ref.: MNA; 341, p. 93; 141, p. 36

MARTINEZ HILL   pro.: /martiynez/
Pima   T15S R13E   Elev. 2854'
When the San Xavier Indian Reservation was established in the early 1880s this small hill opposite the San Xavier Mission was owned by the Martinez family. All families except the Martinez family were made to leave the reservation, but Martinez remained, retaining about fifteen acres across the valley to the hill from the Santa Cruz River, which at that time passed on the west side of the hill. His daughter, Maria, married a Tucson jeweler named Berger. In 1891 the Berger house (consisting of three units) was in section 27, whereas Martinez Hill occupied sections 22, 23, 26, and 27. When Martinez died, the property passed to his daughter and gradually the name Berger Hill came into use, although residents of Tucson referred to the place as Sahuarito Butte. After promising to sell his land to the Indian service, Berger was appointed Indian Agent

on the reservation. In 1941 the USGS established Martinez Hill as the official name for the location.

The Martinez Hill Ruin is at the foot of this hill.

Ref.: 242; 329; AHS, G.E.P. Smith Report on Place Names, Nov. 15, 1941; 262, p. 40; *Hohokam Culture Dev.*, p. 111

MARTINEZ LAKE
Yuma   T5S R22W   Elev. 199'

The lake takes its name from a cattle rancher at this location, Gabriel Martinez (b. 1878). The lake waters now cover his ranch headquarters, hence the name. His ranch headquarters were at Martinez Well (T4N/R21W). Ref.: Monson

MARTINEZ WASH
Pima   T16S R18E

This location in 1958 was also called Happy Valley. See Cumero Wash, Pima
Ref.: 329

MARTIN MOUNTAIN
Yavapai   T14N R5W   Elev. 6433'

This mountain was named for John C. Martin, who became a resident of Prescott in 1892. He was owner/publisher of the *Arizona Journal Miner* for many years. Martin Spring (T10N/R3W) is also named for him. Ref.: 18a

MARTIN PEAK
Yuma   T4N R13W   Elev. 2333'

The peak was named for John B. Martin (b. 1842, Ireland), who was a miner in this area for many years, after having been at the Vulture Mine in 1870. Ref.: 18a; 62

MARTINSVILLE
Graham   T5S R24E   Elev. c. 4000'

William Garfield Martin, after being discharged from the 10th U.S. Cavalry, established a cattle ranch at Mud Springs and used the brand WGM on horses. Other discharged black soldiers and their families settled nearby, forming Martinsville. Many of their descendants still live in this vicinity. Ref.: Jennings

MARYSVILLE
Coconino   T10N R9E   Elev. 4600'

Marysville, a mining camp, was named for its first woman settler, Mrs. Mary Pyeatt. Established in March 1880, the settlement lasted about three years. It was on Marysville Hill. Ref.: 18a; Woody

MARYVILLE
Maricopa   T2N R5E   Elev. 1230'

Here in 1868 William Rowe maintained a Salt River crossing called Rowe's Station. He was not the first, for in 1865 Charles Whitlow had settled with his family to be near the newly established Camp McDowell (see McDowell, Fort, Maricopa). Whitlow, who supplied the post with forage, kept a general store. In 1874 he moved to Florence. Meanwhile a small community had developed. When a post office was established, Whitlow named the place Maryville to honor his daughter, Mary Elizabeth Whitlow (b. 1853, Kentucky). In 1877 Utah Mormons crossed the Salt River at this location to reach Lehi. Their use of the names Maysville and Marysville is a corruption.

P.O. est. April 25, 1873, Charles Whitlow, p.m.; disc. Jan. 4, 1874
Ref.: AHS, Mary E. Bailey File; *Arizona Miner* (Jan. 22, 1875), p. 2; 225, pp. 281-282

MASCOT
Cochise   T14S R27E

In 1915 the Mascot Copper Company was formed to exploit the Mascot Mine discovered by Charles Roberts. Mascot Canyon leads from the mine. The mine changed hands many times, and under various names stock was sold to many people, creating a speculator's paradise. The post office was established at the Mascot railroad stop.

P.O. est. July 31, 1915, Lily A. C. Hauser, p.m.; disc. Oct. 15, 1918
Ref.: 242; AHS Names File; *Bisbee Review*, State Library Clipping File; Riggs

MASIPA SPRING   pro.: /masíᵘpa/
Hopi = "gray spring"

Navajo	T23N R18E	Elev. c. 5000'

In 1932 Harold Colton wrote to Frank Bond of the USGS advising that Masipa should
be the official name for this spring, inasmuch as there are many springs called by the
Navajo name *Shanto* (= "sandy spring"). Shanto Spring was a variant name and
different location than Masipa Spring. A still earlier name for Shanto Spring was
Shungopa Spring, which supplied Shungopavi (a Hopi village) with water. Its flow failed
following a minor earthquake in 1870. Since that time Masipa has fulfilled that function.
Curiously, the USGS in March 1972 changed the name of Masipa Spring to Shonto
Spring to replace several others as well: Shato; Shan-to; Sunside Spring.
Ref.: Colton; 331, p. 146; 329

MASON HILL

Cochise	T23S R24E

In 1904 this location was owned by E. B. Mason, hence the name. Ref.: Bledsoe

MASONIC TEMPLE

Coconino (Grand Canyon)	T33N R1W	Elev. 6200'

In 1900 many geologic formations were named for prophets or buildings associated with
various religions or beliefs. This is an example.

MASON'S VALLEY

Pinal	T3N R8E	Elev. c. 3500'

This valley was about two miles from old Camp Pinal. The fact that it is on an 1869 map
indicates it may have been named for Julius Wilmot Mason, a colonel in the 5th U.S.
Cavalry, then in this region. The name appears again near the head of Pinto Creek on the
Mallory military map of 1875. Ref.: 49, p. 41; Woody

MASSAI POINT   pro.: /mæsiy/

Cochise	T16S R30E	Elev. 6870'

When the conquered Chiricahua Apaches were shipped by train to Florida, one member
of Geronimo's band escaped. He was Big-foot Massai, who returned and roamed
through the Chiricahua Mountains. In 1892 a rancher named Stafford camped with his
wife to barbecue beef for lunch. The place was very close to where Massai Point is today.
Massai was in the vicinity to steal a horse and planned to waylay and kill the rancher.
Mr. Stafford's keen eyes noted where the Indian had stepped across the road and the
rancher wisely back-tracked to where the Indian had come from rather than following
where he was heading. Massai meanwhile stole a horse. When Stafford and Riggs (see
Chiricahua National Monument) trailed the Indian, they found the growth impene-
trable, although Massai had been able to get through. Stafford retrieved his horse several
months later, but Massai was never seen again. Mr. Riggs suggested naming the point for
the big-foot Indian. The fact that the name is pronounced "mass*ie*" led to misspelling the
name of this location. Apaches called it *Yahdesut* (= "Point of Rocks").
Ref.: Riggs; *Douglas Dispatch*, "Fiftieth Anniversary Edition" (1952), sec. 6, p. 7

MASSICKS

Yavapai	T14N R1W

Massicks was the name of the post office, probably in the ranch house of the first
proposed postmaster. The place was said to be "nine mi. northwest of Dewey" when
Thomas Massicks applied for a post office in 1892, but it appears no office was
established until 1895. Thomas G. B. Massicks was its second postmaster.
P.O. est. March 6, 1895, Peter Meade, p.m.; disc. March 6, 1899 Ref.: 242

MATHER POINT

Coconino (Grand Canyon)	T31N R3E

Dr. Harold C. Bryant named this point c. 1953 for the first director of the National Park
Service, Stephen P. Mather. Ref.: Schellbach Files (Grand Canyon)

MATKATAMIBA   pro.: /mætkætəmiybə/

Mohave/Coconino (Grand Canyon)   T34N R4W   Elev. 3750'

In 1925 the USGS named this location for a Hualapai Indian family. The Mohave County portion of this canyon debouches into the Colorado River. Ref.: 329

MATKATAMIBA MESA

Coconino (Grand Canyon)   T34N R4W   Elev. 4267'

In 1925 the USGS altered this name, which had also been Marble Flats, to Marion Point. See Marion, Yavapai

MATTHES POINT

Coconino (Grand Canyon)   c. T32N R6E   Elev. 7864'

While supervising preparation of a topographic map of the Grand Canyon, Francois E. Matthes in 1902 named many locations for mythological deities and also for Indian tribes. The name for Matthes Point was suggested by Harold C. Bryant, a former supervisor at the Grand Canyon. Ref.: Harold C. Bryant, Letter (April 9, 1956) (Grand Canyon)

MATTHEWS (sic) MOUNTAIN, SAINT

Yavapai   T12N R1E   Elev. 6310'

According to Marion Alexander Perkins (see Perkinsville), a young woman who climbed this mountain left a card at the top asking that it be called St. Matthew, and Perkins began using the name. The spelling of this name as Mathews is an error. Ref.: 18a

MATTHEWS PEAK

Apache   T34N R6W   Elev. 9512'

This peak in the Tunitcha Mountains was named by Herbert Gregory to honor Washington Matthews, ethnologist-author of Navajo legends and ethnology. Ref.: 141, p. 193

MATTHEWS WASH

Graham   T7S R23E

This wash was named for a family of pioneer settlers who were in this area in the 1870s. Variant names which are incorrect are Matthewson Wash and Matthewsville Wash. See Glenbar, Graham

MATTHIE

Maricopa   T8N R5W

This stop on the Ashfork-Phoenix branch of the S.F.R.R. was named for a railroad superintendent who lost his life here in the 1920s in a motor car accident. Ref.: 18a

MAULDIN

Pinal   T9S R7E

The reason for the name of this post office has not been learned.
P.O. est. Oct. 9, 1940, Katherine M. Gordon, p.m.; disc. Sept. 30, 1943 Ref.: 242

MAVERICK   pro.: /mǽvəriyk/

Apache   T4N R26E   Elev. 7800'

The post office at this location was established in 1948 to serve a logging camp of the Southwest Lumber Company. The camp was near a small mud lake called Maverick Lake, which gave its name to the logging unit. The place was named by Platt Cline, public relations man for the lumber company. At the opening of this camp, for publicity a member of the Maverick family came for the dedication, together with the governor and other personages. An Apache Indian selected to drive the last railroad branch-line spike took advantage of the opportunity to harangue the audience in Apache, while an embarrassed interpreter attempted to cover up. The Indian finally refused to drive the spike. The company town was in existence for twenty years. The location was often

reported as the coldest place in the United States. In 1952 the thermometer plunged to -25°.
P.O. est. Jan. 10, 1948, H. R. Henderson, p.m.; disc. Jan. 1, 1968
Ref.: 242; Davis; *Arizona Republic* (March 31, 1976), p. B-1

MAVERICK BUTTE
Maricopa   T7N R5E   Elev. 4870'
J. M. Cartwright, a cattle rancher, and his associates found mavericks (unbranded) cattle in this locale years ago and branded the animals immediately. They named the mountain for the event. Ref.: 18a

MAVERICK HILL
Greenlee   T5S R32E
On this hill is Maverick Basin, a rock-strewn and brushy place where cattle hid and reproduced so that it was a fine place for "mavericks," hence the name. Ref.: 18a

MAVERICK MOUNTAIN
Apache   T3N R25E   Elev. 8086'
Unbranded cattle (mavericks) hid on this rough and wild mountain and as a result cattlemen named the location Maverick Mountain. Ref.: Wiltbank

MAXEY
Graham   T4S R23E   Elev. c. 2400'
Maxey, the civil adjunct of Fort Thomas, came into being with the relocation of Camp Goodwin at Fort Thomas. Maxey was named by James B. Collins, who had served under Maj. Gen. Samuel B. Maxey in the Confederate forces. Maxey was a thoroughly disreputable location, consisting largely of saloons and houses of prostitution and famed as a spot where government supplies could be bought by anyone.
P.O. est. as Camp Thomas, March 2, 1887, Frank Staples, p.m.; name changed to Fort Thomas, Feb. 28, 1883; name changed to Maxey, June 21, 1886, William Hibberd, p.m.; name changed to Fort Thomas, Feb. 8, 1887 Ref.: Jennings; 49, p. 441; 242; 18a

MAXWELL LAKE
Maricopa   T2N R7E
This location was named for George Hebert Maxwell to honor his work as a water conservationist. Ref.: 329

MAXWELL PARK
Coconino   T14N R9E
In Arizona open park-like spaces are frequently called parks. This one was owned by Len Maxwell, who had a ranch and a few cattle in the area from 1880 to at least 1908. Ref.: Hart

MAYER
Yavapai   T12S R1E   Elev. 4401'
Joe Mayer located at this place in 1882, building a store with accomodations for travellers. It was soon serving as a stage station and rapidly developed into a trading center and community serving the surrounding agricultural and mining area.
P.O. est. Jan. 11, 1884, Sarah V. May, p.m.; Wells Fargo 1903
Ref.: 242; *Arizona Journal Miner* (Jan. 4, 1888), p. 4; AHS; 5, p. 305

MAYSWELL
Mohave   T22N R17W
When mines were first being located in this area in the mid-1860s, Garland May (b. 1839, Virginia) dug a well in this canyon, hence the name. He had a mine which he discovered at the location in 1863 and named it the 63 Mine. He later sold it and entered the cattle business. Mayswell Peak overlooks the canyon. Ref.: 63; Harris

MAYTANK POCKET
Coconino   T19N R2E
The term "pocket" refers to a ridge with a gently rounded top and an abrupt dropoff to

flat land below. The flat area can be used as a pasture, as the "pocket" forms a natural corral. This location is also known as Lonesome Pocket, Limestone Pocket, Dead Man Pocket, and Lake Pocket. Maytank Canyon borrowed its name in 1949 from May Tank (T15N/R9E) near the head of its principal fork. Ref.: 329

MAZATZAL CITY   pro.: /mǽtæzəl/
Gila   T10N R9E
Mormon colonizers settled in this location in the late 1870s. It was described as a "very prosperous little Mormon settlement" in September 1889. Apparently it took its name from that of the Mazatzal Mountains. See also City Creek, Gila
Ref.: 225, p. 174; Woody

MAZATZAL MOUNTAINS   pro.: /mǽtæzəl/
Apache = "bleak, barren"
Yavapai/Gila/Maricopa   T9N R7E   Elev. Gila: 7128′;
                                                    Maricopa: 7637′
This range extends from the canyon of the East Verde River to the Salt River Valley, forming much of the boundary between Gila and Maricopa counties. These mountains are also referred to as the Mazatzal Range. They include the Mazatzal Wilderness. Ref.: 159, p. 428; 18a; 5, p. 484; 329

MAZONA
Mohave   T19N R20W
This was a community adjacent to Oatman in the early 1900s. Its name was also spelled Masona. Ref.: 215, p. 97

McALISTER
Cochise   T12S R24E   Elev. c. 4000′
This post office was established to serve about fifty-six families, mostly farmers in this area. It was named for its postmistress.
P.O. est. Jan. 5, 1911, Mary F. McAlister, p.m.; disc. Nov. 30, 1920
Ref.: 242; AHS, Names File; State Library Files, *Bisbee Review* (no date, no page)

McCABE
Yavapai   T13N R1E   Elev. 5237′
John H. Marion located a mine here, but was driven out by Indians. The mine remained idle until 1883 when Frank McCabe relocated it. In 1893 he sold half interest to Judge E. W. Wells and J. H. Packer. By 1898 a flourishing mining town had developed. It is now a ghost town. See Marion, Yavapai
P.O. est. July 23, 1897, Mrs. Marion C. Behn, p.m.; disc. but reest. June 18, 1917; disc. Oct. 31, 1917 Ref.: 242; "McCabe Mine, Its Early History," *Arizona Prospector* (May 4, 1901), p. 1; *Arizona Journal Miner* (Jan. 10, 1898), p. 4; 233, p. 63; Platten

M C CANYON
Coconino   T19N R1E
M C was the brand used by Nehemiah McCullum, who settled in this region in 1878. He ran about five thousand cattle. It is also called Grindstone Wash.
Ref.: *Prescott Weekly Courier* (May 11, 1893); 329

McCARTY CANYON
Coconino   T13N R10E
Joseph McCarty (b. 1833, Iowa) was a trapper and farmer in this region c. 1902. He died in the canyon, hence the name. It is also called McCarty Draw, a name which in 1966 officially replaced the names Miller Creek and Clear Creek. Another associated name is McCarty Ridge. Ref.: Hart; 63; 329

McCLEARY CAMP
Pima   T18S R16E
In 1909 the principal mining settlement in this region was McCleary Camp in the lower part of Stone Cabin Canyon (or McCleary Canyon). William B. McCleary had

established a ranch c. 1879 in the area. McCleary Peak (T19S/R15E; Elev. 8320') was so named in 1930. See Rosemont, Pima Ref.: 286, p. 167

McCLELLAN FLATS
Pinal   T8–6S R8E   Elev. 1450'
A pioneer family named McClellan settled here. McClellan Wash is also named for them. Ref.: 18a

McCLELLAN TANKS
Coconino   T35N R8E
This watering spot on the old Mormon trail was established by John McClellan (b. 1844, New York), a stockman at this location. Ref.: AHS, Names File; 62

McCLINTOCK RIDGE
Coconino   T12N R11E   Elev. c. 7000'
A cattleman, W. W. McClintock, homesteaded in 1904 at this ridge. Nearby are McClintock Canyon (or Draw), and McClintock Spring (T13N/R11E). Ref.: 18a

McCLOUD MOUNTAINS
Yavapai   T13N R7W   Elev. 4775'
These mountains may take their name either from that of William McCloud (b. 1848, Ohio), or his father, Robert McCloud (b. 1807, Ohio), both of whom were living in this vicinity in 1870. The name St. Cloud is an error. Ref.: 62

McCLURE, LAKE
Coconino   T14N R10E
Old McClure used to have stock at this location prior to 1900. Ref.: Hart

McCONNICO
Mohave   T20N R17W   Elev. 2930'
This community was named for S. B. McConnico, vice president and general manager of the Arizona and Utah R.R. in 1901. The railroad was built in Detrital Wash to serve mines in the Cerbat area. Ref.: David Myrick, letter (Sept. 23, 1959); Babcock

McCOY BRIDGE
Apache   T7N R25E   Elev. 7767'
This little logging camp bridge was named for the contractor of what was then the Cady Lumber Company. Ref.: Wiltbank

McCRACKIN MINE
Mohave   T13N R15W   Elev. c. 3400'
On August 17, 1874, Jackson McCrackin (b. 1821, South Carolina; d. Dec. 14, 1904) discovered the mine which bears his name. It was destined to be one of the most famous mines of its time. In its single huge vein the mine contained silver ore assaying at from $60.00 to $600.00 per ton. Within three years it was the best equipped mine in Arizona, with its ores being handled at nearby Greenwood. By 1880 over $6,000,000. had been earned by the mine. Somewhere along the years the *i* in McCrackin's name was replaced by an *e* so that the *Arizona Sentinel* noted that everything about the mine was well known except the correct spelling of its name. This is reflected in the name of the McCracken Mountains and of McCracken Peak (Elev. 3529').
P.O. est. Feb. 21, 1908, John L. Whitney, p.m.; disc. ?
Ref.: *Arizona Sentinel* (July 6, 1878), p. 1; 163, p. 162; 206, p. 199; 89, p. 199; 242

McCULLUM RANCH
Coconino   T19N R1E   Elev. c. 5500'
Nehemiah McCullum (b. 1841, Canada) established a cattle ranch in 1878 or 1879. He sold his holdings to the Perrin Land & Cattle Company in 1886. The 1870 Census spells his name McCallum.
P.O. est. Feb. 24, 1881, Robert McCallum, p.m.; disc. May 16, 1881
Ref.: 124, p. 53; 62

McDANIEL'S WELL

Yuma   T8S R20W

This well was developed by Eli W. McDaniel (b. 1827, Tennessee), but the water is too saline to drink. Ref.: 63; 279, p. 213

McDONALD, FORT

Gila   T9N R11E   Elev. c. 4800'

In the late 1870s Mort McDonald arrived in eastern Arizona with a string of saddle horses. For mutual security during the raids by Nan-tia-tish, the Apache leader, residents of Payson and Marysville used the butte where he settled, in 1881 and 1882, hence the name Fort McDonald. It was on McDonald Mountain.

    McDonald wintered his horses in a natural corral called McDonald Pocket. Ref.: Gillette; Woody; 18a

McDOUGAL SPRING

Coconino   T20N R3E

McDougal was a homesteader here c. 1900. Ref.: 329

McDOWELL

Maricopa   T4N R7E   Elev. 1450'

The location noted for this post office was that filed with the application in 1900, but a relocation notice in 1905 gave the coordinates as T3N/R7E. Apparently the post office shifted somewhat and in 1905, Mary K. Gill, the postmaster, proposed the name McDowell "because it is a historical name." She also suggested as alternate names Mead or Gates, but McDowell was accepted by the Post Office Department. By 1949 this same post office was located at 1350 E. McDowell Road, Phoenix. See McDowell, Fort, Maricopa

P.O. est. July 9, 1900, John W. Miller, p.m.; relocated Jan. 16, 1905, Mary K. Gill, p.m. It should be noted that a "new post office" was listed at the same second location; est. July 11, 1923 as Fort McDowell, Wilson Walker, p.m.; disc. June 30, 1928 Ref.: 242

McDOWELL CANYON

Maricopa   T4N R7E

In 1875 this was the name being used for the canyon leading to Fort McDowell. Ref.: 314, p. 224

McDOWELL, FORT

Maricopa   T4N R7E   Elev. 1500'

On August 19, 1865, five companies of California Volunteers established what at the outset was called Camp Verde because of its location on the west bank of the Verde River. The name was changed, however, on Sept. 7, 1865 to Camp McDowell to honor Maj. Gen. Irvin McDowell, at that time commanding officer for the Dept. of California and New Mexico. Because of its location adjacent to several Indian trails, the military establishment was very important inasmuch as it made it possible for troops to pursue marauding Indians with no loss of time. Despite its military importance, the post remained a very rough camp and although on April 12, 1867 its name was changed to Fort McDowell, it never was developed and equipped adequately. By 1874 its military importance had diminished considerably, but Fort McDowell was not abandoned until April 10, 1881. See also McDowell Indian Reservation, Fort, Maricopa

P.O. est. McDowell, Aug. 9, 1869, James A. Moore, p.m.; disc. when fort abandoned. Re-est. as Mead, Jan. 1, 1904, Charles Dickens, p.m.; rescinded April 5, 1904 (See McDowell) Ref.: AHS, Stanton D. Kirkham File; 224, p. 153; 163, p. a313; 242; 121a, p. 11

McDOWELL INDIAN RESERVATION, FORT

Maricopa   T4N R7E

A reservation for Yavapai, Mojave and Apache Indians was established by Executive Order on Sept. 15, 1903, and amended on April 21, 1904 to include 24,971 acres. It was established at abandoned Fort McDowell. Ref.: 167, II, 374

McDOWELL MOUNTAINS
Maricopa   T3N R5E   Elev. 4022'
These mountains derive their name from that of Fort McDowell to the east. See McDowell, Fort, Maricopa Ref.: 329

McDOWELL PEAK
Maricopa   T4N R5E   Elev. 4022'
McDowell Peak is also known as Sheldon Mountain. There is a second McDowell Mountain near the junction of the Salt and Verde Rivers (elev. 2828'). See McDowell, Fort, Maricopa

McFADDEN CREEK
Gila   T6N R13E
The old Circle Ranch owned by Bill McFadden is in the canyon through which the creek runs. His brand was a simple circle. Ref.: McKinney

McFADDEN HORSE MOUNTAIN
Gila   T6N R14E   Elev. 7523'
With his red-headed wife Nancy (d. 1930), Bill McFadden (d. Jan. 7, 1929) settled on McFadden Creek to the south of McFadden Peak. As they raised horses, they used McFadden Horse Mountain top for pasturage. Ref.: McKinney; Woody

McFARLAND CANYON
Maricopa   T7N R8E
This canyon is so named because William McFarland (b. 1838, Ohio) had a cabin here. He was a blacksmith in Casa Blanca in 1870. Ref.: 62

McGEE MOUNTAIN
Gila   T4N R15E   Elev. 3490'
An old prospector named McGee had a mine here which he claimed was an old Mexican location. Ref.: Woody

McGUIREVILLE
Yavapai   T14N R5E   Elev. 3300'
Prior to homesteading at this location, Eugene McGuire (d. 1944), served as a county employee. Ref.: Ralph Hall (McGuireville); Goddard

McHEFFY BUTTE
Mohave   T18N R20W
Harry McHeffy prospected here c. 1880. Ref.: 200, p. 62

McKAY'S PEAK
Apache   T7N R24E   Elev. 9171'
Alex McKay was a supervisor of Sitgreaves National Forest and later became a prominent cattleman. Ref.: 18a

McKEE, CAMP
Santa Cruz   T22S R13E   Elev. 3500'
When the United States as a result of the Gadsden Purchase of 1853 took possession of territory south of the Gila River, there was a Mexican fort near Calabasas. In June 1856 Dragoons under Maj. Enoch Steen marched from Tucson and occupied the old fort. Within a few months these troops were removed to Fort Buchanan. It was formally occupied by U.S. troops a second time with Union troops recruited near Santa Barbara, CA, led by Capt. Thomas Young. This First Batallion of Native Cavalry moved into the old fort on Aug. 21, 1865, and named it Fort Mason for Gen. John S. Mason of the California Volunteers, military commander of Arizona 1865-1866. These men had been stationed at Tubac, but the drenching rains "soon engendered fevers" and the move was made to Fort Mason. The name was changed to Camp McKee on Sept. 6, 1866. Continuing illness among the soldiers caused this camp to be abandoned on Oct. 1, 1866, when the troops were shifted to old Fort Buchanan.
Ref.: 159, p. 421; 145, p. 143; 206, p. 98; 224, pp. 168, 169; 107, IV, 99-195

McKENZIE PEAK
Cochise   T12S R31E   Elev. 4680'
This peak was named for a ranch owned here by J. M. McKenzie in 1917.
Ref.: *Arizona Cattleman* (Dec. 24, 1917), p. 5

McKENZIE WASH
Mohave   T18N R16W
John Kennedy McKenzie (b. 1846, Scotland) located and owned the Copper World
Mine at the head of this wash in 1888. He was a "mining man who made worlds of money
at the Cupel Mine." Ref.: Harris; 62

McKINNEY DAM
Pinal   T8S R16E
This dam takes its name from that of B. J. McKinney, who had a cattle ranch on the east
slope of the Santa Catalina Mountains in 1918.
Ref.: *Arizona Cattleman* (May 6, 1918), p. 2

McKITRICK CANYON
Greenlee   T2N R30E   Elev. 7000'
This canyon was named for an old timer whose name was spelled McKitricks. In 1890
he drowned in a few inches of water in the Blue River. He was found with his feet caught
up in the dashboard of his buckboard wagon, his head barely in the water. He was known
to be a heavy drinker. Ref.: Mrs. Fred Fritz, Sr.

McMILLAN SPRING
Coconino   T22N R7E
This headquarters for the McMillan Shipping Company was first called San Francisco
Spring. Originally McMillan's cabin was east of the spring. See Elden Mountain,
Coconino Ref.: 166, p. 75

McMILLANVILLE
Gila   T1N R16E
At one time McMillanville was larger than its neighbor, Globe. The community
developed after the discovery by Charles McMillan (b. 1846, New York) and Theodore
Harris of the McMillan Mine on March 6, 1876. Facts do not support the legend that on
the day prior to the discovery McMillan drank far too much in the roaring saloons of
Globe and that the next day he and Harris were prospecting and that McMillan took time
out to sleep it off. His partner waited and poked around into some soft sticky ore. Legend
says he woke McMillan, who was not too hung over to note that the find was a rich one.
By 1879 a five stamp mill had been constructed and by 1880 fifteen hundred were living
at this place. To celebrate Christmas, the prosperous miners decorated a tree with
"cigars, tobacco, dynamite fuses, grub, and bottles of whiskey." These two men also
owned the Stonewall Jackson Mine tunnel. In July 1882, when Nan-tia-tish and other
Apaches attacked McMillanville, the villagers took refuge in the tunnel. The Apaches
were finally overtaken at Big Dry Wash.
  By 1885 the ores were running weak and McMillanville began to fade. By 1890 it had
a single inhabitant. What little rubble remains of the development is a half mile south and
east of the highway.
P.O. est. McMillanville, Dec. 18, 1877, Charles T. Martin, p.m.; changed to McMillan,
Oct. 11, 1878; disc. Oct. 12, 1882 Ref.: Woody; 62; 163, p. 464; 270, p. 115; 359, p.
89; 5, p. 468

McMULLEN VALLEY
Maricopa/La Paz   T7N R12W   Elev. 2200'
In 1864 this valley was called Big Valley. It contained McMullen Wells, mapped in
1864. By 1869 the place was being mapped as McMullen's Valley. James McMullen (b.
1826, Tennessee) operated a stage station in 1872 on the Prescott-Ehrenberg route on
which he was also a stage driver. He later turned prospector in this valley. Occasionally
it is referred to as Grace Valley, for Grace Salome Pratt, whose husband (H. B. Pratt)
attempted to establish an agricultural colony in the Salome portion of the valley.

McMullen Wells were here also. Ref.: *Weekly Arizona Miner* (April 20, 1872), p. 3; 62; Lenon

McNARY
Apache   T8N R24E   Elev. 7316'

This location was first known as Cluff Cienega, named for Oscar and Alfred Cluff, who from 1879 to 1880 settled with their families at Forestdale and cut wild hay for livestock at Fort Apache. Shortly thereafter it was also known as Cooley or Cooley Ranch after Corydon E. Cooley (d. March 18, 1917), who had been a scout for Gen. George Crook. His ranch was a haven for travellers (at what is now Show Low). Capt. George M. Wheeler mentioned stopping at this location in 1871 near Cooley's Park. In 1924 a company sawmill town bought the location and named the property after itself, the McNary Lumber Company (James G. McNary).

P.O. est. Jan. 7, 1919, James C. Webster, p.m.; changed to McNary, Jan. 11, 1924 Ref.: Wiltbank; 225, p. 169; 49, pp. 178-179; 314, p. 123

McNEAL
Cochise   T21S R26E   Elev. 4164'

The first name for this location was Truitt, derived from the name of a pioneer cattleman who settled here. Among the first settlers was Judge Miles McNeal, who came to this area from Missouri and homesteaded c. 1908.

P.O. est. as Truitt, Jan. 9, 1909, J. H. Latimer, p.m.; name changed to McNeal, Oct. 1, 1909, Josephine A. Lane, p.m. Ref.: *Bisbee Review* (N.D.N.P.), State Library; "50th Anniversary Issue," *Douglas Dispatch* (1952), Sec. 8, p. 3; 242

McQUEEN
Maricopa   T1N R5E   Elev. 1225'

This stop on the Phoenix & Eastern R.R. in 1911 was mapped about two miles south of Mesa. It was named for A. C. McQueen, a livestock agent for the A.T. & S.F.R.R. in the 1890s. Ref.: 18a

McVAY
La Paz   T5N R15W   Elev. c. 1500'

This location on the railroad, used occasionally for loading ores or possibly granite, was named for McVay, who was said to be the first to drill a well for the railroad here. Ref.: 18a

McWHARTER
Yavapai   T14N R3E

Seth and Tildie McWharter ran cattle and owned a mine here in the early 1900s. Ref.: Allan

MEAD, LAKE
Mohave   T33N R16W   Max. water elev. 1229'

On Feb. 1, 1936, the water impounded by Hoover Dam (which had been called Lake Powell for Maj. John Wesley Powell, Grand Canyon explorer) was renamed to honor Dr. Ellwood Mead (b. Jan. 16, 1857, Indiana; d. Jan. 26, 1936). Dr. Mead was Commissioner of Reclamation from 1924 until his death and supervised the building of Hoover Dam. By volume Lake Mead is the world's largest man-made reservoir with five hundred and fifty miles of shore line, one hundred and twenty-five of which border Mohave County. The lake extends fifteen miles upstream. Beneath it are all old ferry landings along this part of the Colorado River. In 1948 to avoid confusion, the name Lake Mead was made official, taking precedence over Mead Lake or Mead Lakes. See Hoover Dam, Mohave Ref.: "Hoover Dam," U.S. Dept. of the Interior, Bureau of Reclamation (N.D.); 5, p. 338

MEAD NATIONAL RECREATION AREA, LAKE
Mohave   T33N R16W

This area includes the Colorado River, the nearby mountains, plateaus, and canyons, and also Lake Mead and Lake Mohave from Davis Dam sixty-seven miles downstream. See Mead, Lake, Mohave Ref.: 176, p. 12

MEADOW CREEK

Mohave T19N R19W Elev. c. 2500'

Fr. Francisco Garcés named this creek Aguage de San Pacifico. In 1857 Lt. Joseph Christmas Ives called it Meadow Creek because, after an arduous climb over the Black Mountains, he and his men found "a snug meadow carpeted with grass and fringed on one side with a growth of willows ..." The weary men and half-starved animals stayed here two days. This same creek in 1906 supplied water for the mining mill of the Gold Road mining district. Ref.: 335, p. 5, Note 5; 77, p. 316; 200, pp. 152, 156, 157

MEADOWS, THE

Apache T1N R6E Elev. c. 6200'

Frank Walker, an express carrier between Fort Wingate (New Mexico) and Fort Apache, built a shack at this location in 1870. Here the route crossed the Little Colorado River. Late in 1879 Mormon missionaries (Ira Hatch, Thomas Brookbank, E. C. Richardson, and J. B. Wakefield) built a house. A small settlement developed but was soon abandoned. See Johns, Saint, Apache Ref.: 116, p. 576; 225, p. 184; 331, p. 128

MEADOW VALLEY

Gila

Although Barnes reports a military outpost here in 1866 for Fort McDowell, no record exists concerning it other than a military manuscript map dated Sept. 27 – Oct. 6, 1866, and labelled "Trail of Mounted Scout from Fort McDowell, Arizona Territory," which shows this valley about twenty miles northeast of Fort McDowell. A skirmish with Indians occurred here between E Troop, First Cavalry, and the hostiles on Feb. 28, 1867. Ref.: 159, p. 427; 242

MEATH (R.R. STN.)

Yavapai T20N R2W Elev. c. 4800'

The Rev. Meany of Prescott suggested this name to railroad officials. Meath Dam borrowed the name, as did Meath Wash. Ref.: 18a

MEDICINE CAVE

Coconino T23N R8E Elev. 8000'

Research workers from the Museum of Northern Arizona in 1929 excavated this cave and found a medicine man's kit, hence the name. It is also called Medicine Fort. Medicine Valley is a transfer name. Ref.: Colton; Bartlett

MEDLAR SPRING

Yavapai T14N R2E

Louise Medlar taught school in Gila County in the 1880s – 90s and raised her family near this spring. Medlar Wash also bears her name. Ref.: Woody

MEESVILLE

Yavapai T10N R1W Elev. c. 6000'

In 1880 James Mees operated a mine at this location and ran a small post office.
P.O. est. Nov. 28, 1881, James Mees; disc. Sept. 2, 1885
Ref.: 18a; 345, I, 299 (Note ≠); 242

MELENDREZ PASS

Pima T19S R15E Elev. 5220'

A Mexican named Melendrez had constructed a stone and adobe home here at least as early as 1900. The name "Melendreth" appearing on GLO 1909 map is a corruption. Ref.: 18a

MERIDIAN

Maricopa T:0 R:0 Elev. 975'

The settlement was near the crossing of the Gila and Salt River meridian and the Gila and Salt River base line, hence its name.
P.O. est. Aug. 13, 1894, Edward K. Buker; disc. July 11, 1895 Ref.: 18a; 242

MERIDIAN BUTTE

Apache   T41N R22E   Elev. 6430'

Herbert Gregory named this butte because it is on the 110th Meridian. In December 1960, the alternate name Rooster Butte was eliminated. Rooster Butte was named for a formation called Rooster Rock (elev. 5984'). A second Meridian Butte in Apache County is adjacent (T40N/R22E, elev. 6221'). Ref.: 141, p. 193; 329

MERIJILDA, CAMP

Cochise

This fort in Apache Pass preceded that at Camp Bowie, which was erected on a nearby hill. See Marijilda Canyon, Graham

MERIWITICA CANYON   pro.: /mӕrowitikə/ or /mӕtowitikə/

Hualapai: *mulh-wide* = "hard ground"

Mohave   T28N R13W   Elev. 5500'

In 1872-1873 some sixty Hualapai Indians enlisted as scouts to fight Apaches. These men later resisted the order to remove the Hualapai tribe from Mohave County to the Colorado River bottoms, and half of them deserted to go with their tribe to what was then called Mut-a-witt-a-ka Canyon. They were starved by siege until they agreed to go to the Colorado River Indian Reservation about Feb. 2, 1874. The Indian name derives from a deposit of travertine on the canyon floor. The canyon in the plateau is a gash with five hundred foot cliff walls. Other names for this canyon include Matawidita Canyon and Matawidika Canyon. Ref.: Dobyns; 5, p. 323; 335, p. 211

MERLIN ABYSS

Coconino (Grand Canyon)   T34N R1E

This place name is another of those drawn from the Arthurian legend in the early 1900s by Francois E. Matthes.

MERRIAM CRATER

Coconino   T23N R10E   Elev. 6651'

The name for this crater was proposed on Nov. 19, 1928 by Harold S. Colton to honor Dr. Clinton Hart Merriam (1855-1942), author and naturalist, who made a biological survey of this region in 1889. The crater is a.k.a. Merriam Mountain. Ref.: 329

MERRICK BUTTE

Navajo   T41N R21E   Elev. 6193'

Two soldiers named Merrick and Mitchell were part of the military escort for the Navajo on their trek from this area to Fort Sumner, New Mexico, in 1864. En route they noted magnificent silver worn by the Navajo and decided to return to the area of Monument Valley where they thought the Indians mined the ore. They returned and found the silver, but not until 1879 did they find someone to finance their mining operations. Despite Piute warnings to stay away, Merrick and Mitchell went to the silver mine. As Mitchell emerged with ore samples, Indians shot him. Merrick sprang on his horse and galloped away. He was caught and killed at the foot of the butte which has his name today. Another version says that Mitchell escaped and was later shot. See Mitchell Butte, Navajo Ref.: 129, p. 96; 191, pp. 27, 30

MERRILL CRATER

Coconino   T21N R10–11E   Elev. 6560'

Dr. George P. Merrill (1854-1929) worked at Meteor Crater and was curator of geology at the Smithsonian. He was the first scientist to write a report on Meteor Mountain. Merrill Crater is on Merrill Mountain. Ref.: 329

MERRILL PEAK

Graham   T8S R23E   Elev. 9285'

Gerald Merrill, Jr. was a forest ranger on the Mount Graham Forest Reserve prior to 1908, but this peak is named for his family, as is also Merrill Creek. Merrill's father settled in the Gila Valley c. 1870 and established a temporary home in the Pinaleno Mountains. Ref.: E. E. Carter, Forest Supervisor, Letter (Nov. 23, 1949); 329

MERRITT CABIN

Coconino   T12N R11E

Johnny Merritt, who came to Arizona to work as a cowboy for the Hashknife outfit, ran a few cattle here at Merritt Spring in Merritt Draw c. 1890. Ref.: Hart

MERRITT PASS

Yavapai   T9N R7W

This pass was named for a highway engineer, George Merritt. Ref.: 329

MESA: This word is used to indicate table land. When it is so used, see entry by main identifying word, e.g.: Vaca, Mesa la.

MESA pro.: /meysə/

Maricopa   T1N R5E   Elev. 1240'

The first Mormon settlers in this area stayed for some time in Lehi, which was on the bluff above the Salt River, an area they called "the mesa." In May 1878, T. C. Sirrine located and deeded a section of land for an unnamed Mormon community under trustees C. R. Robison, G. W. Sirrine, and F. M. Pomeroy. Mail came via Hayden's Ferry until the new community had its own post office. The Post Office Department refused to accept the name Mesa for it because there was then a Mesaville in Pinal County. Therefore, to honor Charles Trumbull Hayden (see Tempe, Maricopa), the settlers named their community Hayden. Although Hayden Ferry had meanwhile changed its name to Tempe, then, as now, it was easy to confuse the post office. Mail service between the new Hayden and the old Hayden's Ferry was so snarled that in 1886 Hayden became Zenos (a prophet in the *Book of Mormon*). When Mesaville (Pinal County) ceased to exist as a post office in 1888, the name Zenos was rapidly changed to Mesa. The location was also known as Mesa City and, according to an 1880 newspaper article, as Bottom City.

P.O. est. Hayden, June 27, 1881, Fanny V. McDonald, p.m.; name changed to Zenos, May 15, 1886; name changed to Mesa, June 19, 1889; Wells Fargo 1903; incorporated July 15, 1883 Ref.: 170, p. 21; *Phoenix Herald* (Jan. 23, 1880), p. 1; 225, pp. 216, 217; 15, p. 532

MESA BUTTE

Coconino   T26N R6E   Elev. 7152'
Descriptive.

MESA BUTTE

Yavapai   T10N R4E   Elev. 5088'
Descriptive.

MESA COVE

Mohave   T31N R18W
Descriptive.

MESAVILLE

Pinal   c. T9S R17E   Elev. c. 2000'

This small settlement five miles south of Dudleyville was at or near the site of Old Camp Grant. Joseph N. Dodson arrived at this location in 1878. Originally this place was to be called Dodson's, but the Post Office Department did not accept that name. The petitioners had asked that Mesaville be named Dodsons for its first postmaster.

Dodson left the area in 1887, moving to Mammoth where he started a store.
P.O. est. June 6, 1878, Joseph H. Dodson, p.m.; disc. March 13, 1888
Ref.: 18a; AHS, Stratton *ms*. p. 24; 238, pp. 30, 31

MESCAL: Mescalero Apaches derived their name from their use of mescal (from agave cacti) as a food, prepared by removing cactus leaves and baking their white bases. Distilled alcohol (*mescal* and *tequila*) and industrial alcohol are also made from the central stems

and bases of the leaves. Many place names in Arizona reflect the fact that this cactus grows in the vicinity. Examples follow:

Mescal   Cochise   T16S R19E   Elev. 4058'
pro.: /meskæl/   Spanish = "century cactus" or "agave"
This name on the railroad was in existence at least as early as 1905. Mescal cactus is abundant in the area, as it is throughout the southwest. It is of great use to Indians and Mexicans.
P.O. est. March 3, 1915, Frank E. Black, p.m.; disc. Aug. 26, 1931 Ref.: 242

Mescal Arroyo   Pima   T17S R18E

Mescal Canyon   Cochise   T14S R26E

Mescal Canyon   Yavapai
See Mescal Gulch, Yavapai

Mescal Creek   Cochise   T19S R19E
See Mescal, Cochise

Mescal Creek   Gila   T3S R16E

Mescal   Pima   T17S R17E

Mescal Gulch   Yavapai   T16N R3E
A forest of century or mescal cactus grows here and Apache Indians have dug many mescal pits along this gulch to bake the cactus. According to Charley Yavapai, a two-day fight between Hualapais and Yavapais occurred in this canyon. It ended with nearly all the Hualapais dead. Six or seven temporarily escaped but were overtaken in Chino Valley. Because Indians customarily avoid places where death has occurred, no Indians will go into this canyon or near Mingus Mountain (in which the canyon lies). Ref.: Schnebly; 261, p. 124

Mescalero Point   Coconino   T31N R1E   Elev. 6635'
                                (Grand Canyon)
This point on the South Rim is named for the Mescalero Apache Indians.

Mescal Mountains   Gila   T3S R16E   Elev. 6564'
Lt. William H. Emory in 1864 called this range the Sierra Carlos Range, and in 1873 Gilbert in the Wheeler report called it the Gila Range. Ref.: 18a; 345, III, 513

Mescal Mountains   Pinal   T4S R18E

Mescal Peak   Graham   T8S R19E   Elev. 5648'

Mescal Spring   Cochise   T19S R19E

Mescal Warm Spring   Gila   T3S R17E
See Mescal Mountains, Gila

Mesqual   Pima   T16S R1E
See Hali Murk, Pima

MESQUITE: Mesquite trees, a variety of locust, grow along water courses throughout the southwest, attaining a height of from thirty to forty feet, and a diameter usually less than two feet. These trees figured importantly in pioneer days as trunks were used for building corrals, shelters, bridges, and as fence posts. Thousands of mesquite supplied fuel for mine smelters. Indians ate mesquite bean, or ground it to make flour, as did pioneers also. Livestock grow fat on mesquite beans. The following are examples of places where mesquite trees led to using the name:

Mesquit   Pima   T16S R1E
See Hali Murk, Pima

Mesquital   Maricopa/Yuma   T9S R10–11W
pro.: /meskiytál/   Spanish = "an area characterized by mesquite trees"
This location is covered by thickets of both living and dead mesquites. Ref.: 58

Mesquite, El   Pima
See Mesquite Charcos, Pima

Mesquite Charcos   Pima   T18S R2W
pro.: /meskiyt čarko/   Spanish: *charco* = "pond"
Mesquite grows abundantly at this location which also bears the Papago name Kuichituak (= "mesquite"), or Vatjeki (Papago = "small water hole" made by digging with a basket). Mesquite here were so thick that they so concealed the large water hole that it could not be seen from the road. Bryan reports that the charcos or water holes here were made by digging with a basket, which was also used to collect the water. The largest charco was from six to fifteen feet wide by about one thousand feet long. At one time the Papago Indians maintained a community here which Mexicans called El Mesquite. Today nothing remains of the community or the agricultural fields used by the Papagos. Ref.: 58; 163, p. 847; 57, p. 410

Mesquite Creek   Maricopa   T2N R10E

Mesquite Flat   Greenlee   T3S R31E

Mesquite Flat   Maricopa   T2N R9E

Mesquite Jim Well   Yuma   T5S R15W   Elev. 564'
"Mesquite Jim" Renner c. 1925 ran a garage at Mohawk. This well belonged to him. Ref.: Lenon

Mesquite Mountains   Pima   T17S R2W   Elev. 3789'
This range has three sections. Toward the south are tilted lava beds of relatively low ridges. At their extreme end is a large flat-topped mountain called Mamatotk by Papago Indians. North are irregular hills and conical peaks, the most northerly being called Chupan Mountains. The extreme northern part has two ridges resembling a fish tail. Ref.: 57, p. 369

Mesquite Spring   Yavapai   T13N R5E

Mesquite Springs   Gila   Elev. c. 4000'
Gen. George Crook's men visited this location in the early 1870s, at which time Archie McIntosh was a scout for Crook. McIntosh located his ranch here following the end of Apache troubles. Ref.: 49, p. 43; 18a

Mesquite Wash   Maricopa   T4N R8E

Mesquite Well   Maricopa   T7S R2W

Mesquite Wells   La Paz   T5N R13W   Elev. 2500'
In 1875 Martha Summerhayes noted that this location was a stage station and stopping point for travellers, who could water their stock here. At that time the place was kept by a Mexican who "worked the machinery with the aid of a mule ... with no living being except his mule for company...." Ref.: 314, p. 155; 246, pp. 214, 215; 279, p. 213

METATE RUIN   pro.: /mətatiy/
Spanish: *metate* = "milling stone"
Apache   T17N R23E
This pueblo ruin in the Petrified National Forest derives its name from the presence of many stone milling troughs (*metates*).

METCALF
Greenlee   T4S R29E   Elev. 4415'
In 1870 Capt. Chase with Bob Metcalf and his brother Jim pursued Apaches. They camped near the future Clifton while Bob Metcalf scouted and found rich copper deposits. He later staked the Metcalf claims. In 1889 the Shannon Copper Company was organized and bought claims near those held by Metcalf. Before 1900 a community named Metcalf developed. By 1910 it had nearly five thousand residents. By 1915 ores in the Metcalf area began diminishing. In 1918 the Arizona Copper Company bought the holdings and Metcalf began dying. All that remains today is an old concrete bank vault.
P.O. est. May 1, 1899, Sophie E. Shirley, p.m.; disc. May 15, 1936
Ref.: Scott; Peterson; Reilly; Shannon; Farnsworth; Simmons; 242; 257, pp. 13, 14, 77, 78, 79

METEOR CRATER
Coconino   T19N R13E   Elev. 5123'
Of the world's eleven major craters and clusters of craters, Meteor Crater is the second

largest. It was known to white men in 1871 merely as a great pockmark, holding no particular interest until 1886 when sheepherders found the first recognized meteorites near Canyon Diablo. In 1891 a U.S. Geological Survey party ruled out a volcanic origin for the crater, but its meteorite origin was not guessed at until 1903. In that year Daniel Moreau Barringer (1860 – 1929) was so certain that a meteorite had formed the crater that he filed a mining claim to the site. Drilling samples were 75% mineral. The extreme hardness of the metals and the quality of drill bits then available resulted in failure after failure in attempts to drill and market the metal. The stock market crash of 1929 ended mining attempts. Scientific interest in the crater, however, has maintained a high level. A 1951 survey with a Worden Gravimeter by Princeton University scholars revealed that the meteor six hundred feet under the crater surface must weigh at least 1,700,000 tons. A further study by the Carnegie Institute of Technology established at impact the mass probably weighed between 2,600,000 and 7,800,000 tons, most of which exploded and scattered to form the present crater rim. The rim is over one hundred feet above the original ground level. Even following thousands of years of silt accumulating in the crater bowl, the crater depth is nearly six hundred feet. It is about one mile in diameter. Prehistoric pit houses sit along the inside of the crater rim. Over the years the crater has had various names as follows: Barringer Crater; Great Arizona Crater; Crater Mound; Meteor Mountain; Coon Butte; Sunshine Crater; Franklin's Hole. Characteristically the Navajo name is fully descriptive: *!Adahoshani* (= "mass of cactus growing on the side of a bowl-shaped depression in the earth"). The name Sunshine Crater derived from the fact that the location is just south of the small railroad stop named Sunshine. As for Franklin's Hole, that can be attributed to A. Franklin Banta's assertion that he discovered the crater in 1873 and fired a gun to measure its diameter. He was at that time a guide with the Wheeler Expedition and the name of the crater appears on its records as Franklin's Hole.

P.O. est. as Sunshine, March 14, 1906, Samuel J. Holsinger, p.m.; disc. April 15, 1912; name changed to Crater, Sept. 10, 1920, Dorothy E. Hogue, p.m.; disc. July 15, 1921; Wells Fargo 1907 Ref.: 121, pp. 14, 18, 19, 23, 25; AHS, *Prescott Courier* (Aug. 14, 1920), and A. F. Banta File; 331, p. 97; 167, VIII, 32; 242

METHODIST CANYON
Gila   T5N R12E   Elev. c. 3500'
According to Barnes, Will Vineyard came upon a wild bee colony in a tree on this creek c. 1890. When he robbed the honeycomb, he said the bees went after him in a way that "would make a Methodist preacher swear." However, Vineyard's sister said a Methodist minister lost his way and spent the night there. According to her, the minister returned to the Greenback Ranch for directions. Thereafter the creek name commemorated the incident. It is also reflected in the name of the Creek and the Mountain. Ref.: 18a; Vineyard's sister, as related to Woody

METTLER CANYON
Cochise
Forest Ranger E. G. Mettler, a ranger in the Dragoon Mountains, had a cabin in this canyon. Ref.: Riggs

METZ FLAT
Greenlee   T4S R30E
Metz Flat was a section of what is now south Clifton. In 1900 Chinese raised vegetables on it. Henry Hill, who owned the flat, had a livery stable there. He subdivided and by 1905 it was Clifton's choice residential section. It is not known where the name Metz comes from. Ref.: 257, p. 102

MEXICAN HAT MOUNTAIN
Cochise   T19S R25E   Elev. 5200'
This mountain looks like a Mexican sombrero.

MEXICAN TRAIL
Apache   T5N R27E
This is the trail down which a division of Lt. Chacon's men rode in 1805 when they

attacked Massacre Cave. The Navajo name for this location is *Naakaii Adaani* (= "where the Mexicans came down"). Ref.: 331, p. 26

MEXICAN WATER

Navajo: *Naakaii to badayuznili* = "Mexicans dug shallow wells"

Apache   T41N R26E   Elev. 4840'

The American name is a translation of the Navajo. Gregory notes that the lower middle portion of Walker Creek was sometimes called Mexican Water and that the name was still retained for the trading store at the point where in 1879 Mormons crossed the creek. The present crossing, about three miles west of the trading post, was created with the completion of a steel bridge on July 1, 1939. Mexican Water is also known as Nokai or Nokaito, a name also used for Nokaito Bench (named in 1962 by the U.S.G.S.), and Nokaito Canyon. Ref.: 141, pp. 31, 91, 194; 331, p. 99

MIAMI pro.: /mayæmə/

Gila   T1N R14E   Elev. 3438'

The Mima Mine was located by Black Jack Newman, who named it for his fiancée Mima Tune. It was east of the Old Dominion Globe Mine in Big Johney Gulch. Contemporaneously James F. Gerald constructed a custom mill for a group of men from Miami, Ohio, in what was then called the west branch of Pinal Creek, but later known as Miami Wash. The flat in front of the mill was called Miami Flat for the Miami Copper Company, which owned both the mill and the mine. Gradually the names Mima and Miami blended so that the original intention to call the new community Mima was forgotten. The town of Miami sprang into existence in 1907, its growth insured by the Inspiration Mine Company, which began construction of a huge reduction plant in 1909. Miami is sometimes called "the Concentrator City."

P.O. est. July 30, 1908, Gilbert E. Hull, p.m. Ref.: Woody (quoting Mrs. Gerry Copland, friend of the Newman's); 242; 5, pp. 204, 225

MICA MOUNTAIN

Pima   T14S R16E   Elev. 8666'

Descriptive, because of large mica outcroppings. Ref.: 18a

MICHAELS, SAINT

Apache   T26N R30E   Elev. c. 7000'

The first historical mention of this location was made by Lt. James Hervey Simpson in 1850 when he called it Sieneguilla de Maria. At this location in the early 1850s, Mexicans accompanied by a Navajo named Tall Syphilis (*sic*) planned to hide a cannon and fire it at some ambushed Navajos. Syphilis, however, betrayed their plan to his fellow tribesmen, whom he rejoined and later became their chief under the name Delgadito. He signed the last treaty for the Navajo nation. The Franciscan Mission at Saint Michaels was begun in 1896, using funds supplied by Rev. Mother Katherine Drexel, founder of the Sisters of the Blessed Sacrament. On Oct. 11, 1897, two priests, Juvenal Schnorbus and Anselm Weber, arrived to take over the work. At that time the Navajo name for the location was *tso hotso* (= "yellow meadow"). Both names derive from the fact that at the end of summer the meadows are yellow with flowers and the grass also turns yellow in the summer heat. The two priests changed the name to Saint Michaels.

P.O. est. May 22, 1901, George V. Manning, p.m. Ref.: 242; 141, pp. 3;3, p. 33 (Note 2); 143, p. 283; 331, p. 129; 167, II, 412

MIDDLEMARCH

Cochise   T18S R24E   Elev. c. 4000'

Middlemarch is in the middle pass of the Dragoon Mountains. The half-way point on the military road from the Sulphur Springs Valley to Tombstone, it was named c. 1897 by M. M. O'Gorman, Vice President and General Manager of the Middlemarch Copper Company, who drew the name from George Elliot's novel *Middlemarch*. Middlemarch Canyon also has the name.

P.O. est. Feb. 15, 1898, Charles M. Laurence, p.m.; disc. Dec. 31, 1919

Ref.: Larriau; Macia; 242; State Library Files

MIDDLE POINT

Mohave   T31N R20W

This name was proposed by Ray Payser in 1940 because by nautical reading this location on the south shore of Lake Mead is the exact center of Virgin Basin. Ref.: 329

MIDDLETON

Yavapai   T11N R1E   Elev. c. 4000'

This post office was named for the Middleton family. It was at the end of the branch railroad to the Bradshaw Mountain mines. As the signature on the post office records in the Nat'l. Arch. reads "Middleton," the spelling Middelton is incorrect. Eugene Middleton (b. 1861, California) arrived in Arizona in 1873, joining his father, who located first at Tempe as a blacksmith, later living near Globe, and still later as a stockman in Pleasant Valley. Eugene stayed with his parents until 1888, after which he was a stage driver between Florence and Globe. He sold out in 1895. Middleton Creek is named for him. See Ocotillo, Yavapai

P.O. est. March 17, 1903, George Wallace Middleton, p.m.; disc. Jan. 8, 1908; Wells Fargo 1904 Ref.: 242; 224, III

MIDDLE WELL

Yuma   T4S R16W   Elev. c. 500'

This well is half-way between the railroad and the Kofa Mine. It is now dry and abandoned, but was originally developed to supply water for the King of Arizona Mine. Abel Figueroa used it for his stock after the mine closed. Ref.: Lenon; Monson

MIDGLEY CANYON

Coconino   T17N R6E

"Major" Midgley ran cattle in the 1890s. The spelling "Migley" is incorrect. Ref.: Hart

MIDLAND CITY

Gila   T1N R15E

The name continues in existence, attached to the Midland City Airport on the road between Globe and Miami. See Midmont, Gila Ref.: 284, p. 184

MIDMONT

Gila   T1N R15E

The first name proposed for this post office was Midland City, but the Post Office Department would not accept the name. See also Midland City, Gila

P.O. est. July 17, 1918, Louise Osborne, p.m.; disc. May 15, 1920 Ref.: 242

MIDNIGHT MESA

Yavapai   T9N R8E   Elev. 5000'

The name reflects the presence of black volcanic rock here.

MIDWAY

Cochise   T14S R27E

Established in 1909, Midway was half-way between Pearce and Kelton on the Arizona Eastern R.R. It was abandoned in 1926. Midway Canyon is a transfer name, as is also Midway Peak. Ref.: 18a

MIDWAY

Maricopa

This railroad siding on the Tucson, Cornelia and Gila Bend R.R. was half-way between Ajo and Gila Bend. Ref.: Lenon

MIDWAY

La Paz   T9N R16W   Elev. 2556'

This point on the abandoned Arizona & Swansea R.R. lay half-way between Bouse and Swansea. Prospectors frequently camped here. Ref.: 279, p. 215

MIGUEL, SAN pro.: /san migeyəl/
Spanish = "Saint Michael"

Pima   T21S R5E   Elev. 2477'
Papago Indians established this village c. 1914. In 1915 it had both Catholic and Presbyterian missions.P.O. est. June 15, 1917, Elizabeth T. Wolfe, p.m.; disc. May 22, 1918 Ref.: 58; 262, p. 3; 242

MILE 232.4 RAPID
Mohave (Grand Canyon)   T27N R11W
The name describes the location of this rapid, which is of interest because near here is where a bride and groom disappeared in 1928. The couple had a specially built raft which was found anchored with their Thanksgiving dinner on the table but no one on board. Ref.: 329

MILITARY
Cochise   T24S R28E
This branch post office eighty-six hundred feet west of the Douglas post office was established on May 27, 1915. The name was changed to Jones on May 18, 1921.

MILITARY HILL
Cochise   T20S R22E   Elev. 5313'
At this location troops were camped during the difficulties with Pancho Villa.

MILK CREEK
Coconino (Grand Canyon)   T33N R2E
In 1882 Dutton wrote that "the water ... has a faint whitish cast, like that which would be produced by putting a drop or two of milk into a bucket of pure water. I presume it is caused by a precipitation of lime. We call it the 'Milk Spring'...."
Ref.: 100, p. 139

MILK RANCH POINT
Coconino   T12N R9E   Elev. 7332'
A Mormon family had a small dairy at a spring here and sold dairy products to construction crews on the railroad. Ref.: Hart

MILKWEED SPRING
Mohave   T26N R13W
In early 1881 Charles Spencer claimed and possibly named Milkweed Spring as he was the first white man to live in this area. The name derives from the fact that milkweed grows abundantly along Milkweed Creek. See Spencer Canyon, Mohave
Ref.: 335, p. 135

MILKY WASH
Apache   T15N R24E   Elev. c. 6000'
Limestone and bentonite clay washed from the floor and walls of the canyon give a milky color to runoff water here. Milky Wash Ruin has largely disappeared by crumbling over the bluffs into the wash below. The small prehistoric pueblo houses featured stone fire altars. Ref.: Branch; 167, I, 863

MILL CREEK
Gila   T1S R15E
This creek derives its name from a now vanished small sawmill on the upper creek. The name has been in use since the early 1900s, although the location is also referred to as Mineral Creek. Ref.: 329

MILLER, CAMP
Yavapai
On an 1869 military manuscript map this place shows as thirteen miles northeast in a direct line from Fort McDowell. Ref.: 242

MILLER CANYON

Cochise   T23S R20E

In 1927 this name was changed from Mill Canyon. It takes its name from that of John J. Miller (d. c. 1916), who raised and sold produce. Ref.: Burgess

MILLER CANYON

Coconino   T13N R10E

This canyon was formerly called Grenego Canyon, Cracker Box Canyon and/or McCarty Draw, but the name was officially recognized as Miller Canyon in December 1966. It was McCarty Canyon or Draw because that was the name of a tracker found dead in it c. 1902. The name was changed to Miller when P. C. Miller built a cabin in the canyon to raise cattle. Ref.: 329; 18a; Hart

MILLER VALLEY

Yavapai   T14N R2W   Elev. 5438'

Samuel C. Miller (b. Nov. 4, 1840, Peoria, Illinois; d. Oct. 12, 1909) arrived in Arizona in 1861 as a prospector (see Lynx Creek, Yavapai), and then became a freighter. Brig. Gen. Thomas C. Devin reported in April 1869 that in 1866 Miller "treacherously and causelessly killed" Wauba Yuma, a Hualapai chief, and thus precipitated hostilities between the Indians and whites. Not until late 1869 was the Indian uprising quelled. Miller continued freighting until the railroad line was completed. Just before that time he sold his freighting interest and located Miller's Ranch, also called Burnt Ranch, in what is now Miller Valley. Ref.: 107, I, 261-262; 335, p. 91; AHS

MILLET POINT

Coconino (Grand Canyon)   T35N R1W   Elev. c. 6000'

Barnes associates with this location the name of Francis David Millet (1846-1912), an American artist who drowned when the *Titanic* sank. Ref.: 18a

MILLIGAN CREEK

Apache   T7N R29E

This location was named for Anthony Milligan. See Round Valley, Apache

MILLIGAN KNOLL

Apache   T8N R29E   Elev. 8000'

This location is also known as Saffel Knoll. See Milligan Creek, Apache, and Round Valley, Apache

MILLIGAN PEAK

Greenlee   T4N R31E   Elev. 8132'

This peak and Milligan Lake were named for an "old mysterious man" who had a grist mill and sold corn meal from his ranch on the Upper Blue River c. 1900. He had nothing to do with strangers. Only when he recognized someone who was riding to his house or barn would he come out from behind his buildings. Ref.: Fritz

MILLIGAN VALLEY

Apache   T7N R29E   Elev. 8050'

Milligan had his holdings here as early as 1875. See Milligan Creek, Apache, and Round Valley, Apache Ref.: *Arizona Miner* (Oct. 1, 1875), p. 3

MILLIONAIRE CAMP

Apache   T3N R24E

A group of asbestos mines claims at this location belonged to George England and two cow-puncher partners. England spoke so extravagantly about the possibilities of the mine that the Cross Camp S cowboys called it Millionaire Camp. Ref.: 5, p. 466

MILLION DOLLAR STOPE

Cochise   Elev. 4539'

A great gaping hole in Tombstone is named for the fact that nearly $1,000,000.00 in ore was mined from the tunnels of the Great Central Mine. In 1908 the shaft gave in just as a horse pulling an ice wagon was crossing the place and, of course, fell in. Aside from astonishment, the horse was untouched although the wagon was in splinters. The horse was led out of the hole by way of a tunnel to an old mouth of the mine one-quarter of a mile away. Ref.: 60, p. 381

MILLS CANYON
Gila   T4N R11E
Mills Flipper had a ranch at this location. He fell from a horse and broke his neck in the 1880s. Ref.: Griffen

MILLTOWN
Mohave   T18N R21W   Elev. 840'
In 1903 the Mohawk Gold Mining Company bought the Leland Mine and began developments, including a forty-stamp mill eleven miles to the southeast, to which the name Milltown was applied. Water came from a pumping plant on the Colorado River two miles below Needles. A narrow gauge railroad from Milltown to Needles was connected by a ferry with the S.F.R.R. Open range cattle necessitated placing a gate across the track, which meant that on every trip the engineer had to stop the train, open the gate, move the train through, close the gate, and then proceed. A severe Colorado flood washed out all but two miles of this track. Ref.: Housholder; 200, p. 183

MILLVILLE
Cochise   T21S R21E
Millville was northeast across the San Pedro River from the Charleston Mill and hence took the name Millville. See Charleston Mill, Cochise
P.O. est. May 26, 1879, John B. Allen, p.m.; disc. May 3, 1880 Ref.: 242

MILLVILLE
Coconino   T18N R8E
Mormons established a sawmill here in 1879, hence the name, although it was at Pine Springs. See Mormon Mountain, Coconino
P.O. est. as Pine Springs, May 20, 1879, Hugh Marshall, p.m.; disc. July 27, 1882

MILOS BUTTE   pro.: /maylows/
Coconino   T18N R8E   Elev. 7525'
An old-timer named Milos was in this area, but had his quarters at Flagstaff. Ref.: Corey

MILTON
Yuma   Location unknown
P.O. est. Dec. 20, 1887, Charles J. Taylor, p.m.; disc. May 22, 1891; reinstated July 1, 1944 Ref.: 242

MIMBREÑO   pro.: /mimbréynyo)
Spanish = "willow twigs"
Coconino (Grand Canyon)   T31N R1E   Elev. 6605'
This location is named for a southwestern Indian tribe, the Mimbreño Apache, who live in southwestern New Mexico.

MINERAL
Mohave
This location on the railroad spur below Mineral Park was created to unload mining materials and ship ores. See Mineral Park, Mohave
P.O. est. Sept. 28, 1908, John R. Sears, p.m. (dec.); resc. Dec. 17, 1908

MINERAL CREEK
Apache   T9N R26E   Elev. c. 7500'
This creek was named because of abundant alkali in it. Ref.: Wiltbank

MINERAL CREEK

Pinal/Gila   T1S R13E   Elev. c. 3500'

In November 1846 Maj. William H. Emory, who was with Gen. Stephen Watts Kearny and the Army of the West, camped at the mouth of a dry creek which had a spring flowing from the sand where two washes joined. Here Emory noted "many indications of gold and copper ores," hence he named the stream Mineral Creek. It is also called Hill Creek. Ref.: 105, p. 78; Lenon

MINERAL HILL

Pima   T16S R12E   Elev. 3650'

This location was a mining camp with a store and post office in 1920. At that time the road from Tucson to Nogales went through this community, but it went out of existence when the new road to Nogales was built. The post office was a branch. The hill is descriptively named. Ref.: 59, p. 351; 57, p. 374

MINERAL PARK

Mohave   T23N R18W   Elev. 4299'

Mineral Park was so named because of the rich abundance of various metals in the locality. In 1870 the first mine was located in this district with others following soon, including the Keystone and a thriving community developed. It was in a beautiful basin-like park between mountains rich in minerals. Briefly in 1873 Mineral Park was the seat of Mohave County. As mining production dwindled after 1880, Mineral Park became inactive. It came briefly back to life c. 1906. It is now the site of the open-pit copper mine at Ithaca Peak.

P.O. est. Dec. 13, 1872, Alder Randall; disc., but reest. Feb. 5, 1900, Isaac Conkey, p.m.; disc. June 15, 1912 Ref.: 200, pp. 16, 80; Babcock; 242; Lenon

MINESHAFT SPRING

Graham   T6S R20E

This spring was named because of the presence of a prospect tunnel about one thousand feet to the southeast. The name Minesha Point Spring is a corruption or typographical error. Ref.: 329

MING

Yuma   T8S R17W   Elev. c. 500'

Frank Ming served as mayor of Yuma c. 1920. The name Ming Spur appears on GLO 1933, but no earlier so that the location was probably named for Frank Ming, rather than for Dan Ming, a Graham County cattleman in the 1880s, who never lived in Yuma County. Ref.: Kline; Lenon

MINGUS MOUNTAIN

Yavapai   T15N R2E   Elev. 7720'

William Ming (b. c. 1851; d. Nov. 1911) died in his camp near Prescott where his body was found. He was a well known mine owner and miner on the mountain bearing his name. It was also known as Bee Mountain to the Yavapai Indians, none of whom would approach it because they feared those who had died in Mescal Gulch (see that entry, Yavapai). Ref.: *Prescott Courier* (Nov. 25, 1911), p. 8; 261, p. 124; Willard

MINGVILLE

Graham   T6S R19E   Elev. c. 4000'

Dan H. Ming (b. 1841; d. Nov. 1925), a cattleman, maintained a post office at this location on his ranch, hence the name. He was called "Big Dan" and he certainly was — 6'4". During the severe drought in 1885, cattlemen made a suggestion that, like the Hopi Indians, the gathering should pray for rain. Dan responded with the following: "Oh Lord, I'm about to round you up for a good plain talking. Now, Lord, I ain't like these fellows who come bothering you every day. This is the first time I ever tackled you for anything, and if you will only grant this, I promise never to bother you again. We want rain, Good Lord, and we want it bad; we ask you to send us some. But if you can't or don't

want to send us some, then for Christ's sake don't make it rain up around Hooker's or Leitch's ranges, but treat us all alike. Amen."
P.O. est. Jan. 26, 1881, Thomas I. Hunter; disc. Dec. 16, 1881
Ref.: AHS, Daniel H. Ming File

MINNEHAHA
Yavapai   T10N R2W   Elev. 5449'
Charles Taylor (b. c. 1824, New York; d. June 6, 1891) arrived in Arizona in 1863. He prospected and recorded several mines by May 21, 1875. He was living at his own ranch on Minnehaha Creek, the name of which came from a mine by that name. The creek at Minnehaha Spring was in Minnehaha Flat.
P.O. est. June 21, 1880, Charles Taylor, p.m.; disc. Dec. 31, 1910 Ref.: AHS, Charles Taylor File

MINNEHAHA SPRING
Yavapai   T10N R1W
This location is also known as Rabbit Spring. See Minnehaha, Yavapai Ref.: 329

MINT SPRING
Coconino   T17N R8E
Much mint grows at this spring. Ref.: Hart

MINT VALLEY
Yavapai   T15N R3W   Elev. c. 5000'
In the late 1860s a man named McKee settled in this region, but a three-year drought and Indian trouble forced him to leave. He liked the mint growing along the stream in the valley, hence his name for the area. Ref.: *Arizona Miner* (Jan. 20, 1872), p. 2

MIRAGE, EL
Maricopa   T3N R1W   Elev. c. 1800'
When residents applied for a post office here they noted that locally the place was called Agua Fria. The name El Mirage is not Spanish, but a coined name for what the residents viewed as an ephemeral settlement.
P.O. est. Jan. 20, 1947, Charles E. Reed, p.m.

MIRAMONTE   pro.: /mirəmantey/
Spanish = "mountain view"
Cochise   T17S R19E   Elev. 4000'
The name describes the location. People from St. David settled here and named it in 1913.
P.O. est. Jan. 1, 1918, Rebecca Lofgren, p.m.; disc. July 31, 1919
Ref.: 225, p. 236; 242

MISERY, FORT
Yavapai   Elev. 5355'
This was the name given to the first house built in Prescott, to provide quarters for Gov. John N. Goodwin and his party upon their arrival in 1865 in newly created Arizona Territory. It was a two-room log cabin built by Manuel Yersera, a member of the military escort, who stopped his loaded teams where Granite Street now turns to cross Granite Creek. One legend asserts that the building was called Fort Misery because of the manner in which its second occupant, Judge Howard, meted justice. A second legend says that the building was converted to a boardinghouse and the quality of the food was the cause of the name. An American dubbed "Virgin Mary" cooked meals for fifty men here. Her nickname is said to have derived from her many charities. Her real name may have been Mary Brown. The Arizona 1864 census notes her as having been born in Texas and lived in Arizona for the preceding eight years. She died at Lynx Creek in 1880.
Fort Misery No. 2, constructed in the early 1870s, was called Happy Valley possibly because it witnessed many happy times. It was probably where the Sharlot Hall Museum is today. Ref.: Garrett; AHS, Virgin Mary File; *Weekly Arizona Miner* (Dec. 19, 1868), p. 3, and (Nov. 26, 1875), p. 3; 224, III, 205-206

MISHONGNOVI

Hopi = "the other of two sandstone columns remains standing"

Navajo   T28N R17E   Elev. 6200'

The descriptive name refers to two irregular sandstone columns, one of which has fallen. The original pueblo was west of the present village. It was one of the old Tusayan (Hopi villages) colonies, but was abandoned prior to 1680 and the present town was then built. The Franciscans had a *visita* called San Buenaventura at the old site from 1629 to 1680. This location has the following variant names: Buenaventura (Vargas, 1692); Manzana (Schoolcraft); Masagnebe (Garcés, 1776); Masagniovi.

Ref.: *Hopi Constitution*; 5, p. 412; 71, p. 44; 331, p. 193; 167, I, 564, 871

MISSION CAMP

Yuma   T9S R19W   Elev. c. 600'

This location may have been named because it was the site of ancient mission ruins or, according to Charles Debrille Poston, from the fact that the U.S. Boundary Survey Commission camped here and their "mission" gave the place its name. John Killbride (b. 1820; d. 1870) constructed a stage station here on the Butterfield Stage route. He sold out to Peter Reed in December 1880. Reed had scarcely taken over when on December 24, three renegade Mexicans murdered James Lytle (a stage drive), Thomas Oliver (the cook), and Charles Reed (station manager). One newspaper reported that Mrs. Reed was also murdered. The murderers stole everything in sight and fled.

Ref.: AHS, Fr. Figueroa, Letter (Mar. 11, 1936); *Weekly Arizona Miner* (Jan. 7, 1870), p. 2; AHS, John Killbride File; 264a, p. 116

MISSOURI BILL HILL

Coconino   T25N R6E   Elev. 7240'

"Missouri Bill" ran sheep at this location c. 1900, hence the name. Ref.: Hart

MISTAKE PEAK

Gila   T7N R12E   Elev. 5930'

Because this peak looks vastly different when viewed from the Tonto Basin where it looks to be part of the main range, as opposed to viewing it from the other side where it looks like a separate peak, it has been called Mistake Peak. Ref.: 18a

MITCHELL BUTTE

Navajo   T41N R20E   Elev. 6382'

Mitchell, a twenty-one year old prospector, was killed by Piute Indians with his partner Merrick, according to Hoskinini Begay, a Navajo leader. The Indians deliberately picked a quarrel with the two men at the entrance to a rich silver mine in Monument Valley. According to Navajos who knew the story, the prospectors used water belonging to the Piutes. Merrick was immediately killed, but Mitchell escaped to this butte where he was found and killed. See also Merrick Butte, Navajo

Ref.: 5, p. 423; 129, p. 95; 191, pp. 31, 33

MITCHELL PEAK

Greenlee   T2S R29E   Elev. 7947'

Mitchell, a justice of the peace in Metcalf c. 1899 and superintendent of the Metcalf Mine, had an argument with a Mexican who owed him money. The Mexican left the store where the argument took place, got a pistol, and shot Mitchell as he came out. This peak is near where the murder occurred, hence the name. Ref.: Simmons; Farnsworth

MITTEN PEAK

Navajo   T41N R21E   Elev. 6210'

This formation, which stands approximately eight hundred feet above the surrounding valley, is named because from a distance it looks like a pair of mittens. Navajo Indians call it Big Hands and say that these once powerful but now still hands may some day return to rule over Monument Valley. See also Pilot Rock, Navajo

Ref.: 5, pp. 423-424; 141, p. 193; 191, p. 117

MITTRY LAKE
Yuma   T7S R22W

This shallow and largely stagnant lake was named for the contractor on the All American Canal. It is the site of the Mittry Lake Water Fowl Area, which consists of three thousand five hundred seventy-five acres, seven hundred of which are the lake itself. Ref.: Lenon; 9, p. 3

MOBILE
Maricopa   T4S R1E   Elev. 1327'

Forty blacks from Mobile, Alabama, homesteaded here and formed a community named for their native city. At the S.P.R.R. stop of that name, they established a post office. The area is known as Mobile Valley.
P.O. est. Feb. 6, 1925, Mrs. Elsie R. Luny, p.m.; disc. Jan. 1, 1964
Ref.: 242; 5, p. 387

MOCCASIN SPRINGS
Mohave   T41N R4W   Elev. 5080'

William B. Maxwell located at the springs before 1864, but was forced out in 1866 by Indian troubles. The place was infrequently used by Mormon pioneers and travellers. It is said that moccasin tracks in the sand near the springs led to the name. The Piute name was *Pa-it-spick-ine* (= "bubbling spring"). When the Kaibab Piute Indian Reservation was established with a day school and headquarters at this location, the post office was begun.
P.O. est. as Moccasin, March 30, 1909, Charles C. Heaton, p.m.; disc. Jan. 1, 1964
Ref.: 242; 5, p. 282; 225, p. 97

MOCKINGBIRD (MINE)
Mohave   T26N R21W

It is conjectured that the mine took its name from the presence of mockingbirds. The mining operation required a post office.
P.O. est. Feb. 8, 1907, William F. Ward, p.m.; resc. March 25, 1907 Ref.: 242

MOCKINGBIRD HILL
Maricopa   T7N R4W

In 1965 Mrs. Ida Smith Wickenburg requested that this name be used to "conform to a street name in Wickenburg." Ref.: 329

MOCKINGBIRD PASS
Yavapai   T10N R5E

This pass is so low and rough and has such a poor trail that "either there were a lot of mocking birds there or only a mocking bird could get through." Ref.: Dugas

MODEL CREEK
Yavapai   T11N R5W

This creek took its name from that of the Model Mine in this locality in 1879.
Ref.: Eckhoff map (1880)

MODOC MOUNTAIN
Greenlee   T4S R29E   Elev. 5226'

Modoc limestone composes most of this mountain. Ref.: Simmons

MODRED ABYSS
Coconino (Grand Canyon)   T33N R1E

This name was another of those drawn from the Arthurian legend in the early 1900s.

MOENAVE   pro.: /mównaviᴧ/
Coconino   T32N R10E   Elev. 5000'

In 1776 Fr. Francisco Garcés was the first white man to visit Havasupai Indians here. In 1871 Jacob Hamblin founded a Mormon colony in the oasis at Moe Ave Springs, but by 1900 only three families remained. In 1903 the Bureau of Indian Affairs bought the place. The springs as well as the settlement have disappeared. See also Moenkopi, Coconino Ref.: 141, pp. 144, 193; 331, p. 100; 225, p. 158

MOENKOPI   pro.: /mównkapiᴧ/
Hopi = "place of running water"

Coconino	T32N R11E	Elev. 4800'

This Hopi village took its name from that of springs here, hence the name. The Hopi village was begun by a leader of Old Oraibi named TIvi = ("Toobi" or "Tuba") in the 1870s. It had been occupied before, as it was probably the location which Juan de Oñate in 1604 called Ranchera de los Gandules, and in 1776 Fr. Francisco Garcés called it Concave, possibly an attempt to render the then-current name in Spanish. In 1879 TIvi permitted the Mormons to establish a colony here and John W. Young, a son of Brigham Young, built a woolen mill where the Indians were to work, but the project was soon abandoned. On a map dated 1891 is the following notation: "Tennehleto Spring, known now as Muencovi." Because the Mormons could not establish clear claim to the land in 1903, they sold their holdings to the Bureau of Indian Affairs.
Ref.: 331, p. 100; 225, p. 161; 167, I, 919; 242

MOENKOPI WASH

Coconino	T32N R15E

This wash has been known by various names, among them the following: Cosninas (Escalante); Biko hodo klizg; Bukudotklish; Dot klish. In September 1968 the USGS abrogated all names in favor of Moenkopi Wash. See Moenkopi, Coconino

MOGOLLON MOUNTAINS
Apache/Navajo/Coconino
These mountains were noted by Whipple as including the volcanic San Francisco peaks. See Mogollon Rim, Coconino/Navajo/Apache/Greenlee/Gila

MOGOLLON PLATEAU
This plateau was also known as the following: Colorado Plateau, Little Colorado Plateau, Coconino Plateau, Mogollon Mesa, Plateau of Arizona. See Mogollon Rim, Coconino/Navajo/Apache/Yavapai/Gila

MOGOLLON RIM   pro.: /mᴧgiyówn/

Coconino	T12N R8E
Navajo	T10N R20E
Apache	T8N R24E
Greenlee	T2N R30E
Gila	T11N R13E

The Mogollon Rim rises abruptly above the valleys and lower mountains so that it gives the appearance of a distinct rim and indeed in places one can look down from it as if standing on a cliff. Its name may derive from that of Juan Ignacio Flores Mogollon, Governor of New Mexico (1712-15), or from local infestation with such parasitical plants as mistletoe (Spanish: *mogollon* = "parasite"). The more than two-hundred-mile, two-thousand-feet escarpment is commonly referred to as "The Rim" and in one section as the "Tonto Rim." It was formed by geologic faulting from southeast to northwest. The top gradually leveled to form the Mogollon Plateau, on which waters run north while below The Rim drainage is southerly.

It has taken considerable time for geographers to determine exactly what to name which in connection with "Mogollon." Garcés on November 28, 1775 called the range of mountains Sierra del Mogollon. The 1851 Parke map of the Territory of New Mexico shows it in two sections as Sierra Mogoyone and Sierra Blanco. By the time Whipple commented on the mountains above The Rim in 1853, the spelling of the name had settled down to that of the governor and Whipple noted that "old Spanish maps included the 'continuous Mogollon chain...' called Sierra de los Cosninos, the name of a tribe of Indians inhabiting this region." Whipple noted that by his time a division existed between the two ranges. Curiously enough, Whipple earlier in his same manuscript spoke about a pass through the Mogoyon Mountains.

Further, the name Black Mesa which in 1879 "appears in smallish type as though limited to an area south of Flagstaff" had expanded to cover a very large area. To add to the confusion geographically the White Mountains (Sierra Blanca) are actually an extension of the Mogollon Rim.

Dellenbaugh, who apparently had more ability to write than to see, described the Mogollon Buttes as "swimming like ocean birds in the blue of the pure Arizona atmosphere and towering 10,000′ or more into the air." Another name applied to the plateau above the edge of the rim is Mogollon Mesa (Coconino/Yavapai: T13N/R11–7E).

The Board on Geographic Names was considerably puzzled by the confusion and noted that Mogollon Mesa and Mogollon Mountains appeared to refer to what is actually Mogollon Plateau which, in turn, was called Mogollon Rim on the 1939 Forest Service map of Tonto National Forest. It is further noted that the name Mogollon Range applied to T1N and T1–2S/R17–18W. It may be well to consider that The Rim itself is too extensive, too rough, too great a barrier to travel, to enable early geographers to explore thoroughly and know what they were talking about. Suffice that the name Black Mesa has gone out of use and other names have been absorbed into the general term Mogollon Rim.

Cowboys casually call The Rim by a name which might well apply to this entire entry: Muggy yawn. Ref.: AHS, G.E.P. Smith, Letters to Board on Geologic Names (Jan. 14 and 22, 1942); Schnebly; 345, pp. 15, 80; 77, p. 137; 167, I, 919; 177, p. 366; 89, p. 134; Lenon

MOHAVE COUNTY   pro.: /mowháv^/

The name *Mojave* is an attempt to spell the tribal name: *Aha macave* (= "people who live along the water"). Although the name of this county is officially written Mohave, it is named for the Mojave Indians, and perhaps the spelling should follow that preferred by the tribe. The county was created on November 8, 1864 with the official birth of the Territory of Arizona. The Mojave Indians, a tribe related to the Yuman, live along the Colorado River in the southwestern part of Mohave County. Originally Mohave County encompassed the entire northwestern part of Arizona, with the county seat at Callville. When the State of Nevada was created in 1865, Mohave County west of the Colorado River (including Callville) was ceded to the new state (over protests by the Arizona legislature). At that time Mohave County seat was relocated in Mohave City and then briefly in Hardyville. It was shifted to the mining center of Cerbat in 1871 where it remained until its removal to Mineral Park in 1873. When the railroad was completed through Kingman, the county seat was moved there in 1887, where it has remained. Mohave County contains 8,486,400 acres, making it the second largest county in Arizona. Mining and ranching are its principal industries. The county is very mountainous with many isolated areas, including that north of the Grand Canyon referred to as the Arizona Strip (partially in Coconino County). Both the Fort Mojave and Hualapai Indian Reservations are in Mohave County. Ref.: 15, pp. 522, 525, 527; Lawe, "Discover Beautiful Mohave County" (Mohave County Chamber of Commerce, Kingman); *Arizona Miner* (April 13, 1872), p. 4; 200, p. 43, Note A; 200, p. 8

MOHAVE, FORT   pro.: /mohav^/

Mohave: *aha* = "water"; *macave* = "along" or "beside"

Mohave   T19N R22W   Elev. 541′

The location given is for the ruins of this once-important military post. In March 1972 the USGS officially changed its former names to the one given above. Frederick W. Hodge in his *Hand-book of the American Indians North of Mexico* said that the name referred to *Hamock avi*, meaning "three mountains," or "The Needles." Apparently no one thought to ask Mojave Indians what their name meant, for in 1961 the tribal council was astonished to learn Hodges' explanation. The Mojave leaders explained their name as *Aha macave*, meaning "people who live along the water" (Colorado River). Tribal members are tolerant of the white man's attempts to pronounce their name. More than fifty variations exist, among them Jamajabs (Garcés); *a-mac-há vès (Whipple); Mohawa (Pattie, Personal Narrative)*; and Mohawe (Mollhausen, *Journal to the Pacific*). The spelling change from Mohave to Mojave was done at the request of tribal members.

In January 1859 Col. William Hoffman was assigned to campaign against the Mojave Indians, a handsome, well-built and at one time extremely war-like branch of the Yuman Indian tribes. Hoffman was instructed to establish a fort on the Mohave River or at the ford known as Beale's Crossing on the Colorado River. As the Mohave River or Wash was dry, Hoffman selected a crossing and established Camp Colorado where on April 26 Maj. Lewis Addison Armistead was placed in charge. A week later Armistead renamed the location Fort Mohave. Because of the Civil War, the post was abandoned in 1861, but was reestablished in 1863 as Camp Mohave. In 1890 the old fort was turned over for use as an Indian school. Ref.: 290, pp. 8, 71; *Weekly Alta California* (May 28, 1859); 163, pp. 313, 314; 17, pp. 247, 277 (Note); 224, p. 152

MOHAVE INDIAN RESERVATION, FORT
Mohave   T18W R10N

About three-quarters of the Fort Mojave Indian tribe live in the Mohave Valley, with the majority in Mojave Village, built in 1947 to house families whose homes were wiped out by a Colorado River flood. The village is on the California side of the river. In 1864 Charles Debrille Poston selected reservation land on the Colorado River bottom land, which was set apart by Congressional Act of 1865 for all the river tribes. Only the Chemehuevis and about one-half of the Mojave Indians occupied it, as both tribes had signed a treaty in 1867. On March 30, 1870 a reservation of five thousand five hundred and seventy-two acres was declared at the site of old Fort Mohave. The Act was made official by Executive Order on September 19, 1880, with additional land being added until acreage is now thirty-eight thousand three hundred eighty-two. See Mohave, Fort, Mohave Ref.: 163, p. 314; "Annual Report of the Arizona Commission of Indian Affairs, 1954, 1955, 1956," p. 14; 290, p. 11; 15, p. 545

MOHAVE, LAKE
Mohave   T24N R22W

The first name associated with this location was Bullhead Project, which during construction was changed to Davis Dam. The lake is formed by its impounded waters. Ref.: Hornbuckle

MOHAVE MOUNTAINS
Mohave   T15N R20W   Elev. 5100'

In December 1964 the USGS established this as the official name. Formerly these mountains had also been known by the following: Bill Williams Mountains; Chemehueve Mountains (for that Indian tribe); Sierra de San Ildefonso (Garcés); Mohave Range Ref.: 329

MOHAVE VALLEY
Mohave   T18N R22W

This valley is a large basin extending from Davis Dam about thirty-five miles southward to The Needles.

MOHAVE WALL
Coconino (Grand Canyon)

This location is a sheer three-thousand-feet-high wall, which is to the left of the point cut by Hermit Rapids. Ref.: 5, p. 484

MOHAWK
Yuma   T7S R15W   Elev. 545'

The original Mohawk stage station was twelve miles west of Texas Hill and was in existence by August 1857, at which time it was known as Peterman's, after the station keeper. The men who created the Butterfield Overland Stage route came from New York State and brought names from there to Arizona. By the latter part of 1860, they had changed the name of Peterman's to Mohawk. The stage station had several managers, among them John Kilbride (b. 1814, England; d. 1871), who committed suicide by taking poison and then jumping in the well at the stage station. Shortly thereafter the leaders of a six-horse coach team fell in the same well. The demise of the stage station soon followed. However, the name Mohawk was transferred to several nearby locations. Among them was Mohawk Gap (now called Mohawk Pass) between Texas Hill on the east and Antelope Hill on the west. By 1878 the nearby mountains bordering the western side of the valley were being called Mohawk Range, although in early days they had been called the Big Horn Mountains. The highest point in the range is Mohawk Mountain or Mohawk Peak. Today, only the north part (in T12S) retains the name Mohawk

Mountains, and the south portion is called the Bryan Mountains. With the completion of the railroad across southern Arizona, the old stage station was totally deserted. The present Mohawk or Mohawk Summit railroad location was established in the 1880s. The stage station and the railroad section house are not at the same location.

P.O. est. July 11, 1889, George William Norton, p.m.; Chrystoval p.o. (twelve miles distant) changed to Mohawk, Sept. 30, 1905; disc. Jan. 1, 1959; Wells Fargo (called Summit) 1903 Ref.: 242; 73, II, 184; AHS Names File; AHS, John Kilbride File; 224, p. 273

MOHAWK MOUNTAINS

Yuma   T10S R13W   Elev. 2400'

Only the north half of T12S is called Mohawk Mountains, the southern portion being called Bryan Mountains for Kirk Bryan. These mountains were also called by Antisell in 1857 the Big Horn or Goat Mountains, because of the presence of mountain goats. In 1881 the Chain and Hardy Map shows this range as Lomas Negras. See Mohawk, Yuma Ref.: 58; 355, p. 148; 329

MOIVAVI   pro.: /moy vʷáha/

Papago: *moi* = "many"; *vaxia* = "well, waterhole"

Maricopa   c. T10S R2W   Elev. c. 1000'

This is a small winter rancheria which has a well thirty-two feet deep. The location is also referred to as Mayvaxi and Mueykava (Wheeler). Ref.: 58; 57, p. 397

MOLINA BASIN

Pima   T13S R16E

This basin, one of a series on the south front of the Santa Catalina Mountains, is named for a pioneer family in the area.

MOLLIE'S MOUNTAIN

La Paz   South end of Granite Wash Mountains c. six mi. west of Salome

This mountain was named for a Mormon's daughter.

Ref.: 329; Schellbach File (Grand Canyon)

MOLLIE'S NIPPLE

Mohave   T31N R10W   Elev. 5551'

This location, also called White Cone, describes the appearance of the location. Who Mollie was is a mystery.

MONK DRAW

Graham/Cochise   T12S R26E   Elev. 4490'

This location, also known as Wood Canyon, was named for the Munk (*sic*) Ranch owned by Judge E. R. Munk in the early 1920s. See Wood Canyon, Graham/Cochise Ref.: 329; 240, p. 28

MONRIEAL WELL

Yuma   T12S R11W

Angel Monrieal drilled this well in 1952. Ref.: Monson

MONROE CANYON

Yavapai   T10N R5E

This location is also known as Little Red Creek. See Castle Creek, Yavapai

MONTANA RIDGE

Santa Cruz   T23S R11E

This name was accepted in 1941 and earlier for what is now referred to as Mule Ridge. Ref.: Gilbert Sykes, Report to Coronado National Forest Supervisor (Aug. 1, 1941)

MONTAZONA PASS

Pima   T11S R2E   Elev. c. 2500'

The *Montana-Arizona* Mining Company figured in a stock swindle c. 1933. The pass is near the Montazona Mine (T11S/R3E). Ref.: 262, p. 21

MONTE CRISTO
Pima   T11S R2E   Elev. c. 2500'
A post office here served the Monte Cristo Mine (T8N/R3E).
P.O. est. Nov. 10, 1921, Mattie Louisa Megason, p.m.; disc. Oct. 8, 1923 Ref.: 242

MONTE VISTA PEAK   pro.: /mántevistə/ or /mánteviystə/
Spanish = "mountain view"
Cochise   T18S R30E   Elev. 9373'
There is indeed a good view from this peak.

MONTEZUMA CASTLE NATIONAL MONUMENT
Yavapai   T14N R5E   Elev. 3200'
This five hundred and fifty-one acre tract contains ruins of an ancient cliff dwelling five
stories high, protected by a large natural cave. The location was established as a national
monument on December 8, 1906. The name derives from the popularly held belief that it
may once have been occupied by Aztecs, although there is no proof for the theory. The
inhabitants of these ruins are believed to have lived from the 11th century to about 1400
A.D. in numerous caves and erosion pockets lining Wet Beaver Creek. The first white
visitor is believed to have been Antoine Leroux in 1854. By 1895 vandals had placed
Montezuma Castle in a state of near-collapse. The Arizona Antiquarian Association
repaired the ruins. Lake Montezuma takes its name from being near the monument.
Ref.: 167, pp. 935, 936; Cook (Superintendent of Monument); 5, pp. 39, 331; 111, p.
530

MONTEZUMA HEAD
Maricopa   T3S R9W   Elev. 1800'
In 1872 John H. Marion wrote that this location "... is very much like the face and head
of an Indian, and which the Indians say is a profile...." It is also called Face Mountain,
but Montezuma Head is not exactly in the same location as Face Mountain.
Ref.: *Arizona Miner* (Jan. 20, 1872), p. 2; 57, p. 221

MONTEZUMA HEAD
Pima   T15S R4W   Elev. 3634'
This location looks not unlike the head and shoulders of a man. See Gunsight, Pima
Ref.: 58; Hensen

MONTEZUMA HEAD
Pinal   T3S R2E   Elev. 2420'
This looks like an Indian head, particularly as viewed from the east. Ref.: 18a

MONTEZUMA PASS
Cochise   T24S R20E
This pass is at the top of Montezuma Peak, Cochise.

MONTEZUMA PEAK
Cochise   T24S R20E
This name has been in use since the early 1900s, although it is sometimes referred to as
Ash Peak. Ref.: 329

MONTEZUMA PEAK
Pinal   T3S R2E   Elev. 4159'
This peak shares this name in common with other place names where popular fancy
deems Aztecs have been.

MONTEZUMA POINT
Coconino (Grand Canyon)   T32N R1W
This headland on the South Rim was named by the USGS in 1908. George Wharton
James had suggested Walapai Point.

MONTEZUMA'S CHAIR

Navajo   T24N R17E   Elev. 5710'
This enormous rock is shaped like a chair. Ref.: 18a

MONTEZUMA SLEEPING

Maricopa   T2S R1E   Elev. 3680'
This mountain looks like a recumbent person.

MONTEZUMA WELL NATIONAL MONUMENT

Yavapai   T15N R6E
This location is a detached portion of Montezuma Castle National Monument. Beaver
Creek has eroded the hill in which this natural well or small lake lies so that one side is a
cliff. One must climb the crater-like mound to see the well. A circular lake lying about
eighty feet below, it is four hundred and seventy feet across. Its depth is over fifty-five
feet. About a dozen Indian cliff dwellings are adjacent. On the flat, settlers built an adobe
fort with an interior well to enable them to withstand Indian attacks. Around it developed
a settlement called Montezuma City c. 1864. It was the site of the Wales Arnold ranch,
built from stones taken from the Indian ruins. A new owner destroyed the remains of the
fort in 1952.
P.O. est. Oct. 20, 1892, Amanda Mehrens, p.m.; disc. July 19, 1893
Ref.: Dugas; *Arizona Miner* (Oct. 26, 1864), p. 1; 210, pp. 127, 128; 5, p. 330; 163, pp.
382, 383

MONTGOMERY

Maricopa   T3N R3E   Elev. c. 900'
This post office was named for John Britt Montgomery (b. Jan. 4, 1839, Illinois; d. Dec.
24, 1916), who arrived in Wickenburg in December 1864. He was noted as being the
only person there who could whipsaw lumber. Later he established the Montgomery
Addition, now part of Phoenix, and still later raised cattle near the mouth of the
Hassayampa River. He used a flower pot design for a brand.
P.O. est. June 16, 1913, A. Arminda J. Montgomery, p.m.; disc. Jan. 31, 1920
Ref.: AHS, John Britt Montgomery File; 242

MONTOSO, CERRO   pro.: /cero montowso/

Spanish: *cerro* = "hill"; *montoso* = "hilly" or "mountainous," also "brushy"
Apache   T10N R26E   Elev. 8348'
The name describes the appearance of this hilly area. Mexicans say the name means
"brushy mountain." In July 1971 the USGS deleted the names Sierra Montosa and
Sierra Montrosa for these hills. Ref.: Wiltbank

MONUMENT (P.O.)

Santa Cruz   T23S R13E
This was the name of the post office on the Kitchen Ranch. The Monument post office
was briefly at the Benedict Ranch. See Kitchen Ranch, Pete, Santa Cruz
Ref.: 277, p. 26

MONUMENT CANYON

Apache   T41N R29E   Elev. c. 6000'
This canyon is named because of two huge rock columns at its juncture with Canyon de
Chelly. Spider Rock (about nine hundred feet high) in Navajo legend is the home of
Spider Woman. When Navajo childlren misbehave, their parents tell the woman on
Speaking Rock (over eight hundred feet high) across the canyon and she in turn informs
the spider, which descends, seizes the children, takes them to the top of the forty-foot
square column, and devours them. It is said that bleaching bones give the white color to
the top of Spider Rock. A name used by whites in 1931 was The Captains. Other spires
or monuments of red sandstone are in Monument Canyon, hence its name.
Ref.: 5, pp. 418-420; 13, Wyatt, "Canyon de Chelly"; "Canyon de Chelly National
Monument" (U.S. Dept. of Interior), pp. 2-3

MONUMENT CREEK

Coconino (Grand Canyon)   T31N R2E   Elev. c. 3000'

The name comes from the presence of a single one-hundred-foot high shaft visible from the Rim. Ref.: Kolb

MONUMENT MOUNTAIN

Coconino   T25N R14E

A stone government marker at the top of this mountain results in its name.

MONUMENT MOUNTAINS

La Paz

In 1857 Lt. Joseph Christmas Ives named this location (five miles from the mouth of Bill Williams Fork) because at that point "the river went around the base of a massive rock ... (and) the regular slopes gradually gave place to rough and confused masses of rock and the scenery at every instant became wilder and more romantic."
Ref.: 245, p. 57

MONUMENT PASS

Navajo   T41N R22E   Elev. 529'

This name has been in use since 1883. The pass is lined with a variety of monuments with such descriptive names as Castle Rock and Setting Hen. To the east are the Emperor with his pronged "crown," the Stage Coach, and the Bear and the Rabbit facing each other. Ref.: 5, p. 424; 141, p. 193

MONUMENT PEAK

La Paz   T10N R19W   Elev. 2446'
Descriptive.

MONUMENT POINT

Coconino (Grand Canyon)   T35N R1W

This name describes a prominent point of sandstone visible from the river. It was named by Maj. John Wesley Powell in 1883.

MONUMENT RAPIDS

Coconino (Grand Canyon)

This place is also known as Granite Falls. See Granite Gorge, Coconino (Grand Canyon) Ref.: Kolb

MONUMENT VALLEY

Apache/Navajo   T41N R22E   Elev. 4800-5200'

Conspicuous monumental mesas, spires, and buttes dot the floor of this spectacular valley, hence the name. The Navajo name is *Tsé bii ndisgaii* (= "valley in the rocks"). The valley is part of the old Piute Strip. By Executive Order in 1884, the western and northern sections were annexed to the Navajo Reservation, part later being restored to public domain, but returned to the Navajo Reservation by Congress in 1934.
Ref.: 141, p. 48; 331, p. 101

MOONEY FALLS

Coconino (Grand Canyon)   T33N R4W

Richard Evans named these falls for a sailor turned prospector, James Mooney, who in 1880 made a rope ladder with cottonwood limbs for rungs to cross a precipice formed by the falls. One rung broke and Mooney fell. He hung suspended for two days while would-be rescuers tried to reach him by tunneling through the soft travertine. On the third day he fell to his death on the rocks. His body remained there for four years. It was perfectly preserved by the chemicals in the travertine-laden spray and is now buried at the top of the falls. In 1925 it was proposed to change the name of this location to Hualapai Falls, but the change was not approved. Ref.: 329; 182; 37, p. 98; 5, p. 488

MOONEY MOUNTAIN

Coconino   T20N R5E   Elev. 7666'

Although a pioneer stockman is said to have camped at the base of this mountain, it has been suggested that the name derived from that of the prospector associated with Mooney Falls. See Mooney Falls, Coconino (Grand Canyon) Ref.: 18a

MOONLIGHT CREEK
Navajo: *olja* = "moon"; *to* = "water"
Navajo   T40N R18E
The name used today is a translation of the Navajo name, which is spelled variantly Oljato, Olja, Oljeto. In 1926 all these names were dropped in favor of Moonlight Creek. Ref.: 18a

MOORE CREEK
Gila   T12N R11E   Elev. c. 6800'
Rance Moore ran cattle at the Moore ranch here in 1886. See also Ellison Creek, Gila Ref.: Woody; 18a

MOORE GULCH
Maricopa   T8N R3E   Elev. c. 3000'
William Moore (b. 1841, New York) maintained a mining camp called Moore Camp five miles east of Gillette in 1877. See Gillette, Maricopa Ref.: 62; 18a

MOORE'S SPUR
Cochise   T21S R31E   Elev. 4600'
Peter L. Moore, who had a contract to haul six thousand cords of green oak from the Mule Mountains for use by the Copper Queen Mining Company, used oxen to bring the wood to Moore's Spur. Moore was the first owner of the Rafter X Ranch.
P.O. est. July 21, 1913, James Riley Phillips, p.m.; disc. Feb. 28, 1914
Ref.: Mrs. L. E. Moore, Jr., Letter (Jan. 31, 1980); 242

MOQUI SPRING   pro.: /mówkiʌ/
Coconino   T14N R11E   Elev. c. 6000'
This spring is in Moqui Draw. E. P. Carr, manager of the Waters Cattle Company c. 1884, named this spring for the Hopi Indians. It was also known as Pozo de Moqui and was a favored camping place because of its abundant flow. The term "moqui" was offensive to Hopi Indians as (used by early Spaniards to refer to Hopi Indians) the word actually was Navajo: *mogi*, meaning "dead." Navajo used it contemptuously with reference to the peaceful Hopi. Hopi called themselves *Hopitu* (= "the peaceful ones"). Ref.: 18a; 181a, p. 141 (Note 12)

MOQUITCH CANYON
Coconino   T37N R1E
Moquitch is the Piute corruption of *Moqui* (see Moqui Spring, Coconino). This canyon is presumed to have been named because of some evidence of prehistoric ruins here, as the Piute corruption means "dead people," a reference to the vanished tribe. Moquitch Point and Moquitch Spring are also here. Ref.: 181a, p. 141 (Note 12)

MORAN POINT
Coconino (Grand Canyon)   T30N R4E   Elev. 7157'
In 1873 Thomas Moran, a noted artist, visited the North Rim with Maj. John Wesley Powell. Moran's painting of the Grand Canyon on display in the capitol at Washington, D. C., is largely responsible for making the American public aware of the beauty of the Grand Canyon. The location was also known as Ute Point. Ref.: 88, p. 219

MORAS WASH, LAS   pro.: /las mórəs/
Spanish = "mulberries"
Pima   T20S R7E   Elev. c. 4000'
The wash borrows its name from that of the Las Moras Ranch, so named because it had many mulberry trees. Las Moras Well is on the ranch. Ref.: 57, p. 377

MORENA MOUNTAIN   pro.: /moréynə/
Spanish: *morena* = "black"
Pima   T21S R5E   Elev. 4346'
The 1857 Boundary Survey called this double-peaked mountain on the U.S.–Mexico

boundary Sierra de la Union. By 1899 it carried the name Sierra de la Morena, or Moreno, a name which may derive from the presence as early as 1873 of the Morena Mine. Locally, it has been called Horse Mountain. By decision of the USGS, the name is now Morena Mountain. Ref.: 329; 18a; 58

MORENCI   pro.: /morénsi/
Greenlee   T4S R29E   Elev. 4838'
The first name of this location was Joy's Camp, named for John A. ("Slim") Joy c. 1871. The location remained undeveloped until 1881 when William Joy sought a loan of $50,000. from the Phelps Dodge Corp. in New York City and offered his copper mine and smelter in Morenci as security. The Detroit Mining Co. formed with William (*sic*) Joy as president and general manager. Joy is said to have named the location for his home town in Michigan. In 1887 Joy sold his interest to Phelps Dodge. Open pit operations began here in 1937. They closed down in 1982.

The name applies also to Morenci Gulch and to Morenci Hot Springs (T5S/R29E). P.O. est. Feb. 16, 1884, George W. Davidson, p.m. Ref.: 242; 257, pp. 74, 75; 18a

MORENO FLAT
Pima
This flat is between Morena Mountain and the Pozo Verde Mountains, taking its name from the former. Ref.: 58

MORGAN CITY WASH
Yavapai/Maricopa   T7N R2W
This wash was named because the Morgan City Mine was here. See Morgan Mountain, Maricopa

MORGAN MOUNTAIN
Maricopa   T7N R1W
This location was named for Pat Morgan, an old prospector who uncovered rich ore in this region. Ref.: *Arizona Citizen* (April 4, 1874), p. 3, and (April 11, 1874), p. 2

MORGAN MOUNTAIN
Navajo   T9N R23E   Elev. 7627'
In the 1880s William Morgan herded sheep here. Ref.: 18a

MORGAN'S FERRY
Pinal   Elev. c. 1400'
Henry A. Morgan (b. 1841, Wisconsin; d. Oct. 15, 1908) arrived in Arizona on March 18, 1864. Briefly, he was an engineer at Maricopa Wells, but soon established a trading post and ferry on the Gila River just north of Maricopa Wells (T3S/R3E). In 1881 a severe flood washed away his ferry and trading post and Morgan, who also knew several Indian languages, became an interpreter. Ref.: AHS, Henry Morgan File; AHS, Emerson O. Stratton *ms.*, p. 9; *Weekly Arizona Miner* (Feb. 2, 1875), p. 4

MORI MESA
Coconino   T32N R10E
This mesa was named for Hosteen Mori, a Navajo medicine man. Ref.: 329

MORITZ LAKE   pro.: /morts/
Coconino   T24N R4E   Elev. c. 6500'
Joe Moritz, a stockman, created an artificial lake here c. 1910. In 1932 the USGS eliminated the following misspellings sometimes applied to this location: Mortiz Lake and Mortz Lake.

The name Moritz Hill (T23N/R4E) was changed to Moritz Ridge in December 1967. Ref.: Benham; Terry; McKinney; 329

MORMON CROSSING
Coconino   T14N R15E   Elev. c. 6000'
In 1879 Mormon settlers graded a road into Chevelon Canyon and established a settlement known as Mormon Crossing. As Chevelon Creek provided insufficient water,

the Valley of Agalon, as the Mormons called the place, failed to develop. See Grape Vine Canyon, Coconino Ref.: 18a

MORMON FLAT DAM

Maricopa   T3N R9E   Elev. 1547'

Most of Mormon Flat now lies under waters impounded by Mormon Flat Dam. In the 1880s Mormons living in the Salt River Valley occasionally grazed stock on the flat at the junction of the Salt River and La Barge Creek. There is no evidence that Indians and Mormons had trouble here, but stage drivers on the Apache Trail delighted passengers with stories of a harrowing Apache massacre of Mormons here.

Mormon Flat Dam was begun in 1923 as a subsidiary to Theodore Roosevelt Dam. It was completed in 1925. The water impounded formed Canyon Lake, a descriptive name. Ref.: G.E.P. Smith; 329; 5, p. 368; 18a

MORMON LAKE (TOWN)

Coconino   T18N R9E   Elev. 7180'

The first name for this community was Ashurst Run because the Ashurst family settled at Ashurst Spring near this valley and ran stock in the valley. The first name suggested for the post office was Lakeview.

P.O. est. Dec. 24, 1924, I. N. Swisher, p.m. Ref.: 242; 329

MORMON LAKE (VALLEY)

Coconino   T18N R9E

In 1876 the first Mormon settlers arrived in what they called Pleasant Valley. It offered excellent grazing land for cattle, but underground channels gradually filled with sediment so that by 1900 a lake had begun to replace the valley. Because of the presence of Mormon settlers, it was called Mormon Lake, a name submitted in April 1917 by the editor of the *Coconino Sun*. However, the lake is very shallow and in periods of drought again becomes pasture land. Ref.: 329; 5, p. 451; 166, p. 77

MORMON MOUNTAIN

Coconino   T18N R8E   Elev. 8440'

Mormon Mountain, the smallest volcanic mountain in the Flagstaff area, rises about fifteen hundred feet above Mormon Lake. In September 1878 Mormon colonists under Lot Smith established a dairy at Mormon Dairy Spring at the foot of Mormon Mountain on the west side of what was then known as Mormon Dairy Park or Pleasant Valley, now under the waters of Mormon Lake. There forty-eight men and forty-one women cared for one hundred and fifteen cows, producing butter and cheese.

Evidence that this location had been a lake earlier than 1878 shows up in the name Carleton Lake on a military map of 1864 (named for Gen. James Henry Carleton (d. Jan. 7, 1873), at that time in command of troops in the Territory of New Mexico). The name does not appear on subsequent military maps.

On the GLO map of 1892, Mormon Mountain is designated Mount Longfellow. The name derived from a station on the Central Arizona R.R. near the foot of the mountain, and was so named by Michael J. and Timothy A. Riordan of Flagstaff to honor the New England poet. Ref.: 276, p. 15; 341, pp. 18-19; 71, p. 55; 5, p. 451

MORMON RIDGE

Coconino   T36N R11E   Elev. c. 6200'

This ridge is on the Mormon Road on that part extending from Lee's Ferry to Moencopie, hence its name. It is the same ridge which Mormons called Lee's Backbone.

MORRISTOWN

Maricopa   T6N R4W   Elev. 1986'

Originally the railroad siding at this location was called Vulture Siding, as it was used by the Vulture Mine. By 1897 the siding was serving as a junction where passengers disembarked to take a stage to Castle Hot Springs, and in 1897 the name was changed to Hot Springs Junction. Still later it was changed again to reflect the name of George Morris, the first inhabitant of the location and the discoverer of the Mack Morris Mine. P.O. est. Dec. 7, 1897, Lee H. Landis, p.m.; Wells Fargo (Hot Springs Junction), 1903 Ref.: 242; *Arizona Journal Miner* (Nov. 4, 1897), p. 4; 242; 5, p. 356

MORSE CANYON
Cochise   T18S R29E

In 1882 Morse's mill was a voting place in Cochise County, with a population of ninety-four in the region. The canyon was named for the mill. See Turkey Creek, Cochise, and Ward Canyon, Cochise

MORTENSEN WASH
Navajo   T10N R20E

This wash was named for the Nels Mortensen family, which resided at Pinedale c. 1880. The name Mortersen is a misspelling and Mortenson is a corruption of the correct name. See Pinedale, Navajo Ref.: 329; 182

MORTGAGE SPRING
Coconino   T19N R6E

The name Mortgage Spring is a corruption. See Margs Draw, Coconino

MOSS HILLS
Mohave   T19N R14W   Elev. c. 2500'

Capt. John Moss (b. 1823; d. April 1880) was a prospector and an agent to the Mohave Indians. The Mohave leader Iretaba, grateful to Moss for his friendship, showed the miner gold diggings and Moss noted visible gold outcroppings. In 1863 or 1864 Moss located the Moss Mine in Moss Wash (T20N/R20W) about one and a half miles distant from the Moss Hills, which take their name from that of the mine. From a hole ten feet in diameter and depth, Moss is said to have taken out one quarter of a million dollars in gold. Despite his temporary wealth, he died in poverty.

Ref.: *Arizona Weekly Enterprise* (April 18, 1891), p. 1; 56, p. 7; 200, pp. 153, 170

MOUNTAIN DISTRICT
This division of the so-called Basin Range of southern Arizona lies between the Arizona Plateau and the Plains. It is a region of twenty-seven thousand square miles where range upon range of mountains cuts across the land, whereas the Plains contain both mountains and desert.

MOUNTAIN SHEEP SPRING
Mohave   T40N R14W

Signs of mountain sheep using this spring led to the name. At one time mountain sheep were quite common throughout what is now Arizona, but today they are becoming scarce. The spring is in Mountain Sheep Wash.

MOUNTAIN VIEW
Pima   T16S R16E   Elev. 3440'

At Mountain Springs a stage station with accomodations for travelers later became a resort hotel for visitors to Colossal Cave (then called Mountain Springs Cave). When the place burned, the name Posta Quemada gradually took over. It later became headquarters for a cattle ranch. Posta Quemada means "Burnt Post." See Colossal Cave, Pima Ref.: 136, pp. 20, 21, 24-25

MOUNT LEMMON SKI VALLEY
Pima   T11S R15E   Elev. c. 9000'

Ski runs at this location result in the name. The name "Sky Valley" is an error.

MOWRY HEIGHTS
Santa Cruz   T23S R16E

This is the top of the mountain where the old Mowry Mine is located, hence the name. See Mowry Mine, Santa Cruz Ref.: Lenon

MOWRY MINE
Santa Cruz   T23S R16E   Elev. c. 5500'

Why the original mine was called Patagonia is unknown, as there is no resemblance to Patagonia at the tip of South America nor are Indians in southern Arizona noted as a group for having big feet, as is sometimes alleged. In 1857 the Patagonia Mine was discovered by a Mexican herder who sold it for a pony and a few other articles to Capt. R. S. Ewell and "Col." J. W. Douglass. Thereafter Mexicans called it the Corral Viego Mine. Lt. Sylvester Mowry (b. Rhode Island; d. Oct. 25, 1871) graduated in 1852 from West Point but resigned as a first lieutenant on July 31, 1858 while stationed at Fort Crittenden. Mowry then bought the mine from Capt. Richard S. Ewell, Lt. I. N. Moore (see Fort Buchanan), Lt. Richard M. Lord, Col. James W. Douglass and others and changed its name. Mowry employed over one hundred men and shipped out $1,500,000. in ore. In June 1862 Mowry was seized and imprisoned as a Southern sympathizer. At the end of six months he was released, the court saying, "There is no evidence against him," although Mowry had drawn a map showing how Arizona was to be partitioned by the Confederacy. Meanwhile the government receiver for Mowry's mine had deliberately damaged its equipment. In 1864 Mowry was still attempting to get the Federal Government to turn his property back to him. The mine gradually fell into disuse. It was acquired by relocation in the early 1880s by Fish and Silverberg of Tucson, who then sold it to Steinfeld and Swain, Tucson merchants. They in turn in 1904 sold the mine and there was renewed activity briefly, but that too vanished.

Mowry was an indefatigible promoter of Arizona and twice was elected to Congress, but Congress refused to seat him, as Arizona was not yet a territory.

P.O. est. as Patagonia, May 7, 1866, Charles E. Mowry, p.m.; disc. June 24, 1867; reest. May 24, 1880, J. W. Davis, p.m.; disc. Nov. 22, 1880; reest. as Mowry, June 23, 1901, Violet Van Nostrand, p.m. (dec.); Dorette D. Davis, p.m.; disc. July 31, 1913; Wells Fargo 1903

Ref.: 205, p. 10, 110; 242; 206, p. 196; 286, pp. 296, 297, 305, 306

MUAV CANYON   pro.: /múwæb/
Piute = "divide"; "pass"
Coconino (Grand Canyon)   T34N R1W   Elev. c. 5000'
This canyon is near the Muav Saddle (Elev. 7050'), a pass in the Grand Canyon Rim at the top of the north wall. Maj. John Wesley Powell named it in 1869.
Ref.: Barnes' Notes; 100, p. 265

MUAV CAVES
Mohave (Lake Mead)
These caves are near Columbine Falls in the Muav formation, hence the name. The name, in local use since 1936, was approved by the USGS in 1948. Ref.: 329

MUCHOS CAÑONES   pro.: /muwčos kanyównes/
Spanish = "many canyons"
Yavapai   Near head of Santa Maria River   Elev. c. 5000'
Five canyons come together at this point, hence the name. Here on September 25, 1872 Companies B, C, and K of the Fifth Cavalry under Col. Julius Wilmot Mason battled Hualapai Indians who had tried to murder Gen. George Crook during a conference at Date Creek. More than forty Indians were killed.
Ref.: 159, p. 438; 224, III, 220; 49, p. 170

MUDDY CANYON
Yavapai   T20N R8W   Elev. c. 6000'
The road up the canyon to the stage station by this name was soft and muddy in the spring rains. Hinton noted that an old government camping ground was three miles beyond the location near the muddy canyon. An army skirmish occurred in the canyon on March 22, 1866. Ref.: 18a; 163, xxiv; 242

MUD LAKE
Coconino   T37N R1E
The name is descriptive. Cattle bogged down on the banks of this lake.   Ref.: Hart

MUD SPRING
Coconino   T18N R8E
According to an informant, "This is not really a muddy place; the spring just oozes out of the mud." Ref.: Hart

MUD SPRINGS

Cochise   T12S R22E   Elev. 4660'

The name describes a series of springs at the entrance of Mud Springs Canyon. Because the area is low in the valley, during the rainy season when cattle graze, it is easily stirred into a muddy mess. Ref.: Macia; Burgess

MUD SPRINGS CANYON

Greenlee   T2S R31E   Elev. c. 5000'

There are muddy springs in this canyon, hence the name. Ref.: Scott

MUD SPRINGS MESA

Graham   T16S R21E

The mesa takes its name from the presence of a mud spring nearby. Ref.: 329

MUD SPRINGS WASH

Gila   T3N R15E

This wash is near Muddy Springs, hence the name. Ref.: Woody

MUERTO, CANYON DEL

Apache   T5N R27E   Elev. c. 6000'

Early one morning in 1805 Lt. Antonio Narbona led Spanish soldiers into Canyon de Chelly to subdue Navajo Indians. Concealed high in the walls of the canyon, the wily Indians watched silently as the soldiers threaded by below. One old Indian woman had been a Spanish slave, and the temptation to scream insults was more than she could resist. Her high nasal curses revealed that the Indians were in a cave. Unable to shoot directly, the soldiers ricocheted bullets from the cave roof and slaughter followed. It follows that the name of the canyon would be Del Muerto (= "canyon of death"). Its variant name is Cañon Trigo (= "calamity canyon").

On January 25, Narbona reported killing ninety men, twenty-five women and children, and capturing thirty women, thirty horses, and thirty sheep. The bones of the dead remained in the cave. In 1886 James Stevenson, an archaeologist, found the bones and named Massacre Cave. The Navajo name is typically descriptive, being 'an-e'etseghi (= "back of in-between the rocks"), because its stream is a tributary to Chinle Wash in Canyon de Chelly. Ref.: 5, p. 421; Van Valkenburgh and Walker, *Master Key* (May 1945), pp. 89, 94; 326, p. 116; 15, p. 285, Note, and p. 7; 141, p. 35

MUERTOS, LOS   pro.: /los muértos/

Spanish = "the dead"

Maricopa   T1S R4E   Elev. c. 1500'

In 1887 Frank Hamilton Cushing excavated Indian ruins at this location and gave it its name. Ref.: 224, p. 11

MUGGINS MOUNTAIN

Yuma   T8S R19W   Elev. 1908'

A prospector who owned a burro called Muggins is said to have named these mountains for the animal. Ref.: Lenon; 355, p. 218

MULBERRY CANYON

Cochise   T21S R30E   Elev. 5728'

Wild mulberries growing in the canyon led to its name. Ref.: Riggs

MULDOON CANYON

Yavapai   T10N R1W   Elev. c. 4000'

Farrell Teirnen, a soldier at Camp Verde, was known as "Muldoon." His nickname came from that of "Muldoon, the Solid Man," a New York man widely noted for his strength and endurance. After his discharge Teirnen ran cattle in the canyon bearing his nickname. The spelling Mulden is an error. Associated names include Muldoon Spring. Ref.: 18a; Lenon

MULDOON GULCH

Yavapai   T10N R1W

This gulch is named for Bill Muldoon, who was in it looking for dry wood. According to the informant, "It took him twenty years to get it." Ref.: Dewey Born (Prescott, 1968)

MULE GULCH

Cochise   T23S R24E

See Mule Mountains, from which the gulch takes its name. At one time the gulch was called Mule Pass Gulch, but mining destroyed Sacramento Hill, creating such a break in the canyon that the word *pass* is no longer appropriate.

MULE HOOF BEND

Gila   T5N R18E   Elev. c. 3900'

This bend on the Salt River is shaped like a mule hoof, hence the name. It is in Mule Hoof Canyon.

MULE MOUNTAINS

Cochise   T22S R24E   Elev. 6870'

The Parke map of 1851 has the following notation on this range: "Coyetero Trail for plundered mules." The pass through these mountains is a translation of *La Puerta de las Mulas* (= "mule pass"), at the head of Mule Pass Gulch. The name Mule Mountains has become firmly attached, displacing the name on the range of mountains which Smith called Sierra de San Jose. See Mule Gulch, Cochise Ref.: 242; 241, p. 14; 5, p. 380

MULE SHOE BEND

Coconino   T29N R6E

The name is descriptive. Ref.: 18a

MULGULLO POINT

Coconino (Grand Canyon)   T33N R3W   Elev. 5040'

This point was named for a Havasupai family by the USGS.

MULLEN MESA

Yavapai   T8N R6E

This mesa was named for Charles Pleasant Mullen and his brother John, who lived here and raised cattle in 1900. Mullen Wash is on this mesa. Ref.: AHS, Frank Alkire File

MULLEN WELLS

Maricopa   T1S R7W   Elev. c. 800'

John Mullen owned these wells in the late 1800s. Ref.: 18a

MULLICAN CANYON

Yavapai   T15–16N R7E

Mullican Ranch was in this canyon c. 1890, hence the name. The name Mulligan is a corruption. Ref.: 329

MULLIGAN PEAK

Greenlee   T4S R30D   Elev. 5612'

Morris Mulligan, a prospector, worked in this area. Ref.: Patton

MUMMY CAVE RUINS

Apache   T6N R28E   Elev. c. 6200'

In January 1960 the USGS officially changed the name Mummy House to Mummy Cave. These ruins, the largest and most spectacular in Canyon del Muerto, consist of two large caves joined by a narrow three-hundred-foot-long ledge. The ruins have ninety rooms and three kivas, with low buildings, and a tower on the connecting ledge. Scientific evidence demonstrates that occupancy by basketmakers began here at least as early as 348 A.D. and lasted until about 1284 A.D. Basketmakers were known as dart throwers rather than using bows and arrows and had woven sandals and baskets. Later, Pueblo Indians constructed their homes over the centuries-old circular pit houses. Ref.: 5, pp. 420, 421; 331, p. 25; "Canyon de Chelly National Monument" (U.S. Dept. of Interior, n.d.), p. 3

MUNDS DRAW

Yavapai   T17N R2E

The draw is named for a stockman, John L. Munds, who served twice as sheriff of

Yavapai County about 1900. Munds was a station on the Chloride branch of the A.T. & S.F.R.R. Ref.: 18a

MUNDS PARK

Coconino   T18N R7E   Elev. 6812'

The designation "park" in the west usually refers to a natural clearing with a park-like aspect. Munds Park on Munds Mountain takes its name from that of James T. Munds (b. Roseburg, Oregon), who arrived in Arizona in 1875 with his parents. In 1883 he homesteaded at Munds Park. He cleared a trail to run cattle from the Mogollon Rim into Oak Creek Canyon. Ref.: 261, p. 129

MUNN

Pinal   T4S R11E   Elev. 1575'

This loading station on the Pacific & Eastern R.R. was named for the man supervising construction of the branch in 1903. Ref.: 18a

MUNSON CIENEGA

Graham

This location was probably the site of the Munson Ranch c. 1875. See Jose, San, Graham Ref.: AHS, Henry Proctor File

MURRAY WASH

Gila   T2N R14E

This area was owned by Jim J. K. Murray, who sold out to the Inspiration Mining Company. Ref.: Hicks

MUSHROOM REEF

Mohave (Lake Mead)   T31N R19W

This low sandy reef is near a large mushroom-shaped rock, hence the name, approved by the USGS in 1948. Ref.: 329

MUSIC MOUNTAINS

Mohave   T26N R15W   Elev. 6697'

In 1854 Lt. Joseph Christmas Ives named these mountains because the exposed strata looked like a huge sheet of music or a musical staff. Although identified on the Ives map, the inconspicuous landmark was overlooked by pioneers and later the same name was misapplied to a more conspicuous peak ten miles west. It is the latter Music Mountain to which Capt. George M. Wheeler refers in his 1870 expedition report.
Ref.: 163, p. 50; 345, III, 47 (Note 199)

MUSTANG MOUNTAINS

Cochise/Santa Cruz   T20S R19E   Elev. Cochise 5412'
                                                                 Santa Cruz 6469'

In 1694 Fr. Kino found that Indians in this region were riding horses (and their offspring) abandoned years earlier by ranchers run off by Indian raids. According to Bolton "... several stock ranchers near the Pima border had been abandoned, some of the stock was left unclaimed and soon became Mesteña or, in English, Mustang." Some of these wild horses still roamed in the Mustang Mountains in the early years of the 20th century. Mustang Peak (T20S/R18E) is 6317'. See also Whetstone Mountains, Cochise Ref.: 43, p. 358

MYRTLE

Gila   T11N R11E   Elev. c. 7200'

Mr. and Mrs. E. F. Pyle named their ranch for their daughter Myrtle, who died there and is buried near Bonito Creek. Other places with her name include Myrtle Lake (T12N/R11E), Myrtle Point, and Myrtle Trail. Ref.: Pieper; 242

MYSTERY, VALLEY OF

Navajo   T40N R20E   Elev. c. 6200'

This name, in use at least as early as 1949, refers to the valley from Kayenta to Goulding's trading post (Utah) west of Monument Valley. The Valley of Mystery, first entered by white men in 1949, is the site of well preserved prehistoric ruins.
Ref.: 191, pp. 15, 16

N

NA AH TEE CANYON pro.: /ná adiᴧ:h/
Navajo = "loco weed"
Navajo   T24N R21E   Elev. 6500'
Livestock which eats loco weed goes crazy. It grows abundantly in this vicinity. John
Wetherell said the name should be spelled Na-ettee, but this is dubious.
P.O. est. July 8, 1916, Harry W. Wetsel, p.m.; disc. Aug. 31, 1932
Ref.: 242; 203, p. 62

NACHES (R.R. STN.) pro.: /næčez/
Graham   T2S R20E   Elev. c. 2500'
Naches, son of Cochise, became leader of the Chiricahua Apaches after his father's
death. His name was also spelled Natchi. Ref.: 18a; 167; I, 317

NACO pro.: /nákow/
Cochise   T24S R24E   Elev. 4590'
The community of Naco was named because it is the border city on the railroad built to
serve mines at Nacosari, Mexico. The railroad was constructed in the early 1890's, at
which time the port of entry was transferred to the developing community from
Laramita (q.v.). Naco Hills are at T23S/R23E, Elev. 5760'
P.O. est. July 27, 1899, Kenneth C. Hicks, p.m.; Wells Fargo 1904
Ref.: 242; *The Oasis* (June 11, 1898), p. 2

NAEGLIN CREEK pro.: /néyglən/ or /níyglən/
Gila   T10N R14E   Elev. c. 5500'
This stream flows through Naeglin Canyon (or Naeglin Spring Canyon). It and the
canyon were named for Louis and Henry Naeglin, who settled here c. 1886. Louis, who
was present when Al Rose was shot in the Pleasant Valley feud, reported the killing.
Both Louis and Henry helped bury many killed during the feud. Naeglin Rim, where
Louis ran cattle, is above the creek. Ref.: Woody; McInturff

NAIL CANYON
Coconino   T37N R1W   Elev. c. 6000'
Alvin and Casper, sons of an early settler named Nagel, anglicized their name to *Nail*. It
applies to this canyon and to Nail Crossing (T40N/R3W). Ref.: 18a

NALAKIHU RUIN
Hopi = "house standing alone"
Coconino   T25N R9E
These ruins in Wupatki National Monument reflect Sinagua occupation from 1130 to
1150 A.D. The ruins stand off by themselves at the foot of a hill near the Citadel ruin.
Ref.: 13, Jones, "Red Ruins in the Black Cinder," p. 7; 5, p. 38

NANKOWEAP BUTTE pro.: /nænkowiyp/
Piute = "place where Indians had (a) fight"
Coconino (Grand Canyon)   T33N R5E   Elev. 5430'
A Piute Indian named Johnny said Indians fought at Big Saddle at the head of
Nancoweap (*sic*). Maj. John Wesley Powell heard the same name for the place on his

1871-1872 expedition. In 1927 the USGS officially adopted the spelling Nankoweap as proposed by the National Park Service. Associated names include Nankoweap Canyon (T34N/R5E, Elev. 5400') called Red Shales Valley by Thompson in 1872, Creek, Mesa (C. D. Walcott in 1927 gave the name to a small hill on the divide one mile west of the butte); Rapids, Trail (see also Tanner Trail, Coconino), and Nan Ko-Weep Valley (A. H. Thompson, October 19, 1872). Nankoweep is a variant spelling. Little Nankoweap and Little Nankoweap Creek are at T34N/R5E.
Ref.: 89, p. 326; Grand Canyon Files; 329; 322, p. 95

NARIZ, SIERRA DE LA   pro.: /naríys/
Spanish = "mountains of the nose"
Pima   T19S R3W   Elev. 2688'
These mountains, which extend into Mexico, were noted as having this name when Lt. Michler crossed them in 1854. There was a Papago village called Nariz nearby in 1863. Nariz Flats are at the base of these mountains. Ref.: 106, p. 122

NASH CREEK
Gila/Navajo   T4N R22E   Elev. c. 2600'
Lafayette P. Nash (b. Nov. 19, 1846, Ohio; d. March 13, 1914) arrived in Arizona in 1867. He worked first for Michael Goldwater at Ehrenberg, later freighting for Goldwater between Ehrenberg, La Paz, and Prescott. After being at the McCrackin Mine, he moved with his bride to Tonto Basin, staying for three years and then in 1881 established his ranch in Strawberry Valley. Under government contract, he supplied beef to Fort Apache in 1892. Attacked by an Apache with a large butcher knife, Nash with one blow of a meat cleaver killed him. He was tried, but the case was dismissed. His family moved to Phoenix and opened a store, and in 1910 he was appointed first Justice of the Peace in Miami, an office he served until he died.
Ref.: W. B. Nash, Jr., Letter (Nov. 1956)

NASH POINT
Coconino   T12N R8E   Elev. 6546'
This location was named for Buzz Nash. Ref.: Hart

NATANES PLATEAU   pro.: /nətǽneys/ or /nətǽnəs/
Apache: natan = "corn"
Graham/Gila   T3N R20E   Elev. 6000'
On an 1875 District of Arizona military map are noted the names Sierra del Natanes, Natanes Butte, and Milpa de Natanes (milpa = "corn field"). In the 1873 Wheeler expedition report, the area is referred to as Natanes Plateau. In 1865 the broad term Aztec Valley was applied to the whole area north of the Gila to the Mogollon Mountains. The name for the plateau has also been spelled Nantec, Nantack, Naches, and Mache, all such names being changed to the current spelling. An old form is perpetuated in the name Nantac Rim (Graham; T1S/R24). With references to Natanes Mountains (T1N/R23E, Elev. 7520'), a variant is Nantes. Natanes Peak is here.
Ref.: 329; 345; III, 527

NATCHI CANYON
Coconino (Grand Canyon)   T32N R5E
It was named for the son of Cochise (the Chiricahua leader), Naches. In 1921 the name of this canyon was officially changed to eliminate the names Naches and Mache. Ref.: 329

NATIONAL CANYON
Coconino (Grand Canyon)   T31N R6W
This name was in use for about sixty years. (It is a variant for Cataract Canyon.) Why the name National was used is not known. Ref.: 329

NATIONAL GEOGRAPHIC ARCH
Coconino   T41N R6E
This natural arch (250' wide by 165' high) is twelve and one-half miles north of Lee's Ferry. Its name was suggested in 1963 by Boyce K. Knight, who discovered it while flying c. 1957. The USGS refused to approve the name because of the policy to

disapprove commemorating "living persons," asserting that the status of organizations like the National Geographic Society is not greatly dissimilar from the status of living persons. Further, the Board on Geographic Names says it is "impossible to make subjective judgments of the worthiness of other organizations that might be similarly proposed." Ref.: 329

NATURAL BRIDGE
Apache   T27N R30E
The name derives from the fact that a seventy-five-foot-long petrified log spans a small canyon here in the Petrified National Forest.

NATURAL BRIDGE
Gila   T11N R9E   Elev. 4533'
David Gowen (d. Dec. 1929), a Scotch prospector who homesteaded here discovered this huge natural bridge in 1880. The arch opening averages 140' wide by approximately 400' long and the arch from the top of the bridge to the creek bed is about 128' on the north end and 150' at the south end. It is roughly five times the span of the famous Virginia Natural Bridge and is at least twelve times wider. Gowen planted an orchard of about twenty-five acres on top of the arch. This natural bridge is one of the wonders of the world, but a journey to its base is not to be undertaken lightly, for at the bottom lies a wild gorge with huge boulders. Gowen reported being lost for three days in caves within one hundred yards of his own house. Beneath the arch is the Great Basin, described as a "solid rock bowl some seventy-five feet in diameter and nine feet in depth; and so transparent that a white stone rolled down the natural trough (over one hundred feet long) in the side of the basin can be seen in all its bubbling course to the bottom of that chilly pool." The pool fills with water plunging over a white falls about thirty feet high. The natural bridge is also called Tonto Natural Bridge.
Ref.: 116, p. 58; 18a

NATURAL CORRAL CREEK
Gila   T1-2N R18E   Elev. c. 3800'
Apache cattlemen use a natural corral here, hence the name. It is also sometimes called Oak Creek. Ref.: 329

NATURAL TANK
Yavapai/Coconino
The word "tank" in the southwest indicates a nature-created place which can hold water sufficient for livestock and wild life, hence usually fairly large. There are at least three such natural tanks in Yavapai County: (T17N/R5E), (T16N/R6E), (T12N/R7E), and six in Coconino: (T30N/R7W), T16N/R8E), (T15N/R11E), (T16N/R11E), and (T15N/R11E). Other counties also have natural tanks.

NAVAJO
Apache   T20N R26E   Elev. 5676'
Here the A.T. & S.F.R.R. had a railroad station called Navajo Springs for nearby springs, but when the post office was established, the name was shortened to Navajo. By 1935 the post office site location map records the town name as Nee-al-neeng. It should be noted that when the post office was established at Window Rock on May 20, 1935, the name of the town was changed from Nee-al-neeny (Ni"anii'gi), a possible connection. Lewis Lynch had the trading post.
P. O. est. July 3, 1883, J.A. Smith, p.m.; disc. Feb. 14, 1884; reest. Sept. 27, 1884, Lewis Lynch, p.m.; Wells Fargo 1885. Ref.: 242; 18a

NAVAJO BRIDGE
Coconino   T40N R7E   Elev. c. 3500'
Prior to settling on a permanent name, this bridge was called Marble Canyon Bridge, Grand Canyon Bridge, and Lee's Ferry Bridge. It was dedicated on June 14, 1929. Names suggested by Pres. Heber J. Grant of the Mormon church were Hamblin (for Jacob Hamblin) and Has'te'le (for a "famous Navajo leader"). The Navajo name *Na'ni'ahstsoh* = "big span") did not endure. Ref.: 331, p. 103; 5, p. 285; 329

NAVAJO COUNTY pro.: /nævəho/

Navajo was carved from Apache County on March 21, 1895. It consisted of 6,343,040 acres. The county area is laid off in a fifty-mile-wide strip two hundred twenty-five miles long. Holbrook is the county seat. Passage of the bill creating it followed a two month fight in the state legislature, complete with a filibuster, and the bill passed within moments of adjournment. Will C. Barnes, its author, held out for the name Navajo rather than Colorado County. The name is fitting: thousands of Navajo live on the Navajo reservation partially within this county. The principal industries are agriculture, livestock, Indian products, lumber, and tourism.

The name Navajo has been variously interpreted. It is thought the word derives from *nava* (= "field") and *ajo*, a Spanish diminutive. Thus *navajo* may mean "a somewhat worthless field." Early-day Spaniards along the Rio Grande were familiar with the term *Apachu* (= "strangers") and *de Navahu* (= "of the cultivated fields"). Hewett investigated a Pueblo ruin of the pre-Spanish period, called by the Tewa Indians "nanahu," and conjectured that the term *Apachu de Navahu* referred to a band which had invaded the Tewa here, hence the name.
Ref.: 77, p. 161, Note 14; 326, p. 91; 15, I, 168, 171

NAVAJO CREEK
Navajo   T40N R12E
Powell's exploring party named this location. Ref.: 88, p. 149

NAVAJO FALLS
Coconino   T33N R4W
The falls were named for Chief Navajo (d. 1898). See Havasu Canyon, Coconino
Ref.: 337, p. 14; 53, p. 659

NAVAJO INDIAN RESERVATION
Apache/Navajo/Coconino
The Navajo Indian tribe occupies the largest Indian reservation, which includes much of northern Arizona as well as parts of New Mexico and Utah, and is comprised largely of barren land. A treaty ended almost two decades of trouble with the Navajo and an Executive Order of June 1, 1868 established a Navajo reservation. (see Defiance, Fort, and Chelly, Canyon de). Several amendments have increased the original acreage, the last occurring on January 28, 1908, when 82,500 acres were added. The reservation occupies 10,185,802 acres in Arizona with an additional 4,324,594 acres in Utah and New Mexico. Ref.: 167, II, 374; 224, p. 27; 71, p. 18; 5, p. 104

NAVAJO MESA
This is the name given on the Macomb map of 1860 for the area west and southwest of Sierra Carisso.

NAVAJO MOUNTAIN pro.: / nævəho/
Coconino/Utah   T42N R14E   Elev. 10,416'
                                          (Peak is in Utah)
The mass of Navajo Mountain rises solitarily above nearby Lake Powell. It is known to the Piutes as *Tucane* (= "high peak") and to Hopi as *Toko'nabi* or *Dokot'navi* (="high place"). The mountain is sacred to Navajo Indians, who call it *Naatsis'san* (= "head of sacred female pollen range" or "enemy hiding place"). When Maj. John Wesley Powell and his party explored Glen Canyon in 1872, they found carved on a rock the names of Seneca Howland, his brother O. G. Howland, and William Dunn, who had left Powell's 1869 expedition and had been killed by Indians nearby. Climbing out of the canyon, Powell viewed the massive mountain and named it Mount Seneca Howland. However, pioneers were then calling it Navajo Mountain. On the Macomb-Newberry map of 1869, it is designated Sierra Panoche (Spanish: *pinocha* = "pine leaf"), according to one source, although the word *panoche* refers to unrefined solidified brown sugar in large loaves which resemble the form of Navajo Mountain. One source identifies the mountain as Sierra Azul, but without citing the source (Jett). The name Sierra Azul was first used in 1662, but with no specific location. Espinosa says, "On the Sanchez (1752) and Pfefferkorn maps (late 1800) Sierra Azul appears in the center of a range of mountains in central Arizona. Kiepert's map (1852) shows a

Sierra Azul in southern Utah." Ref.: Burcard; 14, p. 7; 88, p. 141; 141, p. 45; 100, Note 1; 331, p. 105; Stephen C. Jett, "An Analysis of Navajo Place Names," pp. 176-177; Jose Manuel Espinosa, "The Legend of Sierra Azul," *New Mexico Historical Review,* IX (April 1934), 113-158

NAVAJO NATIONAL MONUMENT
Coconino   T38N R15E
On March 20, 1909 Presidential Proclamation set aside a tract of forty acres to preserve "... cliff dwellings new to science and wholly unexplored...." Later, the tract was expanded to three hundred sixty acres to include three exceptionally large and well preserved cave pueblos: Betatakin, Keet Seel, and Inscription House.
Ref.: Nail; 5, p. 38

NAVAJO SPRINGS
Apache   T20N R27E
The place name applies to a number of small springs about three miles southeast of Navajo railroad station (see Navajo, Apache). Edward Fitzgerald Beale called them Mud Springs. In a diary written by Floyd, a member of the Beale party, is the following: "The mud is very deep – a camel was mired in one over his hump and had to be drawn out with ropes." At these same springs on December 29, 1863 the government of Arizona Territory was formally inaugurated, the springs being the first point where the arriving government party was sure they were truly within the limits of the new territory (where their commission required them to take the oath of office). Richard C. McCormick, Secretary of Arizona Territory, raised the flag after having administered the oath of office to Governor John N. Goodwin and other officials.
Ref.: Floyd *ms.*, *Diary* (March 31, 1859), Huntington Library; 163, p. 42; 107, III, 69-70

NAWT VAYA
Papago: *nawt* = "sacation grass"; *vaxia* = "well, water hole, spring"
Pima   T16S R8E
This is a small Papago village where sacaton flourishes. The location has had several other names: Agua la Vara (Roskruge, 1893); Agua Lavaria (Corps of Engineers); Alamo (GLO 1921); Notvaya (Soil Conservation Service, 1938). All earlier names were set aside by USGS decision in April 1941. The name Agua la Vara refers to a spring near Nawt Vaya Pass. In 1917 Alamo was described as being a new village "at a well dug by American prospectors: one-half mile south of Agua Lavaria." Nawt Vaya Pass (T16S/R9E) shares the name.
Ref.: 58; 329; 262, pp. 12, 21; 57, pp. 163-350

NAZLINI   pro.: /kinssəga<ʌ:y/
Navajo: *názlini* = "flows in crescent shape"
Apache   T2N R27E   Elev. 6240'
Here Nazlini Creek or Wash curves through Nazlini Canyon along a deep gorge. The trading post takes its name from that of the creek. Many Indian ruins and old Nazlini camp sites are in the canyon where erosion long ago forced Navajos out. The name is also spelled Nashlini, Nashline, and Naskline. Ref.: 331, p. 107; 141, pp. 90, 194

NEAL MOUNTAIN
Gila   T9N R11E   Elev. 5432'
This mountain borrowed its name from Neal Spring (T9N/R10E), named for the man who developed it. Ref.: 329

NEAL SPRING
Coconino (Grand Canyon)   T33N R4E   Elev. 8175'
In 1932 this name was formally adopted for the spring at the head of Bright Angel Canyon. It was named for a cowpuncher. Ref.: Kolb; 329

NEEDLES EYE
Greenlee   T4S R32E
A hole in a needle-like rock formation gives the name to this location, a.k.a. The Needle. Ref.: 329

NEEDLES EYE
Pinal   T3S R17E   Elev. c. 2200'

The Needles Eye is a narrow section of this canyon of the Gila River where Coolidge Dam was constructed. Ref.: 18a

NEEDLES, THE
Mohave   T15N R21W   Elev. c. 650'

Three sharp peaks south of Topock at the eastern end of the Mohave Mountain range were given their descriptive name by Lt. Amiel W. Whipple in 1854. The Mohave Indian name for this group is *Huqueamp avi* (= "where the battle took place"), also rendered Hamookavi. The reference to a battle is one in which the god-sun Mastamho killed the sea serpent of Mohave mythology. See Topock, Mohave
Ref.: 290, pp. 7; 83; 200, p. 27; 346, p. 234 (Note 4)

NEGRO FLAT
Maricopa   T4S R1E

There is a tank here now called Negro Flat Tank, but formerly called North Tank. Railroad work gangs, predominately black, were housed around Mobile. Because of the presence of blacks, people began calling the area Negro Flat. Ref.: 329

NEGRO WASH
Gila   T2N R15E

The USGS altered the old name Nigger Wash to its current form. A black named Riley had a cabin and horse camp here.
Ref.: Riggs; 329

NELSON
Yavapai   T24N R10W   Elev. 5110'

Fred Nelson, a conductor on the construction train for the Santa Fe R.R., was living with his family in a "boarding car" of the train in 1883 when it arrived here. Nelson noticed the availability of good lime and other construction materials and started several quarries as well as a lime kiln. The community and Nelson Mesa (T15N/R9W) are named for him. P. O. est. Jan. 14, 1904, William Carey, p.m.; disc. July 15, 1965; Wells Fargo 1906   Ref.: Kelley; 335, pp. 214, 216; 242

NELSON RESERVOIR
Apache   T8N R30E   Elev. 7412'

The first settler to use the waters of Nutrioso Creek was Edmund Nelson in 1891. There is a reservoir here.
Ref.: C.H.W. Smith, engineer, Water Service Division, State of Arizona, Letter (April 26, 1956)

NEPHI   pro.: /niÿfay/
Maricopa   T1N R5E   Elev. c. 1250'

This community was engulfed by Tempe. This location was first called Johnsonville, named for Benjamin F. Johnson, who owned the land. In August 1887 Mormons living about two miles away in Tempe moved to this location and changed the name to Nephi. The name derives from that of the Mormon prophet Nephi, who recorded the *Book of Mormon* on plates of gold (see Cumora, Apache). The father of Nephi was Lehi, and the community of Lehi was near that of Nephi.
P.O. est. Feb. 19, 1889, Frank C. Johnson, p.m.; disc. Aug. 11, 1892
Ref.: AHS Names File; 225, p. 220

NESTOR, MOUNT
Coconino   T18N R8E   Elev. 7713'

The freighters' trail to Camp Verde and Fort Whipple had a stopping place at an overnight boarding place here. The mountain is named for the keeper of the station.
Ref.: Sykes

NESUFTANGA
Navajo   T28N R21E   Elev. 6460'

The ancient ruined pueblo at this location was described, but not named, in 1885. It was named and partially excavated by Dr. Walter Hough in 1901. He also called it Nesheptanga. Ref.: 167, II, 57

NEVIN (R.R. STN.)
Coconino   T21N R5E   Elev. c. 7000'
A. G. Nevin was a general manager for the S.F.R.R. Ref.: 18a

NEWBERRY MESA
Coconino (Grand Canyon)   T24N R13E   Elev. 5104'
Dr. John Strong Newberry (b. 1822; d. 1892), a surgeon and geologist on the Ives expedition in 1857-58, was the first to study and report observations of the lower Grand Canyon. Newberry described the mesa which carries his name. The name was applied in 1906. This place has also been called Wotan's Throne and Newberry Terrace. Newberry Point is here. It was named in 1908. Newberry Butte (T31N/R4E, Elev. 5104') was named in 1906. Wotan's Throne is near, but *not* identical.
Ref.: 141, pp. 38-38 (Note 2); Photo caption, Naturalist's Headquarters (Grand Canyon); 178, p. 37

NEW GREENWOOD
Mohave   T13N R12W
This was the name of a place four and five-tenths miles south of Greenwood, where a ten-stamp mill was built to serve the McCrackin and Signal mines.
Ref.: *Arizona Sentinel* (July 21, 1877), p. 2

NEW LONDON
Mohave   T22N R19W   Elev. 3800'
Only abandoned mine shafts remain to indicate where this small mining camp lay in 1880. The mine was closed in 1893. Ref.: Harris; 200, p. 185

NEWMAN CANYON
Coconino   T19N R8E
This canyon takes its name from that of Zeke and Lee Newman, cattlemen who arrived in Flagstaff in 1879. Ref.: Hart

NEWMAN PEAK
Pinal   T8S R9E   Elev. 4508'
This highest peak in the Picacho Mountains was named for a Federal soldier killed in the only Civil War battle in Arizona.
Ref.: Plaque at Site

NEW PHILIPPINES
In May 1704 Fr. Eusebio Kino proposed the name New Philippines for the region in which he was establishing missions in southern Arizona. Barring that name, he suggested to King Philip V, "unless your Royal Majesty prefers . . . that these new conquests . . . should be decorated with the name of the NEW KINGDOM OF NEW NAVARRE . . . . "   Ref.: 43, pp. 572, 573

NEW RIVER
Maricopa   T6N R2E   Elev. c.2400'
This stage station was operating on the banks of New River as early as 1868, but why it was called New River is not known. It was owned by Darrel Duppa and was referred to as Duppa Station by Lt. John G. Bourke. New River Mesa (T7N/R4E) and Mountains (T7N/R3E, Elev. 4722') share the name.
P. O. est. as Newriver, May 9, 1898, Ephraim Tomkinson, p.m. (dec.); post office never in operation   Ref.: 56, p. 308; 49, p. 172

NEWSPAPER ROCK
Apache   T18N R24E   Elev. c. 5500'
It is supposition that Indians conveyed news via picture writing, but that notion is the origin of the white man's name for petroglyphs in the Petrified National Forest. The petroglyphs are near an ancient pueblo of about one hundred and twenty-five rooms close to a cave which may have been used as a birthing room. That idea has led to the

assumption that picture writing was a form of doodling by restless fathers-to-be. The cave is called the Origin-of-Life cave.   Ref.: Branch; 5, p. 312

NEWTON BUTTE
Coconino (Grand Canyon)   T31N R3E   Elev. 5912'
This butte was named in 1906 for Sir Isaac Newton, whose theory of the power of gravity could enjoy a whale of a test by dropping an apple from here. Ref.: 329

NEWTON CANYON
Cochise   T16S R29E
A pioneer named Newton lived here c. 1880. Ref.: Riggs

NEW VIRGINIA
Mohave   T13N R13W   Elev. 1600'
In 1877 about six hundred and fifty people here depended for employment on the nearby McCrackin Mine, with a mill in New Virginia. After the Civil War many left the South for the West and brought with them place names from their native states, hence, possibly, this place name.
Ref.: *Arizona Sentinel* (July 6, 1878), p. 1; 163, pp. 251, 252; 116, p. 579

NEW WATER PASS
La Paz   T2N R16W   Elev. 2530'
This pass borrowed its name from that of New Water Well, a very old one which in turn probably was so named because it was developed while new mines were being located in the region. In the 1950s the Fish and Wild Life Service was calling it Livingston Pass, because a man by that name then lived here.   Ref.: Monson; 279, p. 215

NEW YEAR'S SPRING
Coconino   c. T22N R4E   Elev. c. 7500'
Lt. Amiel W. Whipple visited this spring on New Year's Day 1854. He described it as a two-foot-deep pool nearly twelve feet across with a layer of ice under the water. The name appears only on the Willcox (Smith) Military map of 1879.
Ref.: Fuchs, Letter (April 30, 1956); 346, p. 177; 348, II, 47

NIGGERHEAD MOUNTAIN
Cochise   4 mi. east of Douglas
Cattlemen from Texas who settled close to this location noted the resemblance of the volcanic formation to the descriptive name they applied c. 1903. Ref.: Burgess

NIGGER HEAD
Mohave   c. T22N R18W   Elev. c. 4200'
According to the informant, "This is a big mountain, black as coal," hence the name. Ref.: Harris

NIGGER WELLS
Maricopa
A single well here (north of White Tank Mountain about twelve miles from Wickenburg) was dug by a part-black Portuguese who c. 1866 had a bakery at Wickenburg. He believed it would pay to dig a well on the route between the Salt and Hassayampa Rivers, so he saved his money and began digging. Passersby noticed that the digging had stopped. On investigation they found the camp robbed and the well caved in. Its owner was killed by the cave-in. From that time the place was called Nigger Wells. According to one story, "Nigger Wells had a hard reputation and deserves it . . . it was started by a man who killed a man in self-defense, we think. In sinking it a nigger was caved in on and killed. Gus Swain was taking supplies to it and Indians killed him. Recent crimes committed near it are too well known to need mention." Three Mexicans held up a Chinese here.
    Another legend is that the well resulted when a freighter transporting twenty-six hundred pounds of dynamite stopped here. "Frenchy" de Baud noticed coyotes smelling around the canvas covering the dynamite. He took a potshot at the coyotes, but

hit the dynamite instead. It wiped out the varmints, creating what he called "one damn beeg hole."
Ref.: 107, II, 69; *Arizona Star* (Sept. 26, 1889), p. 4; *Arizona Weekly Enterprise* (April 21, 1888), p. 3

NIL
Maricopa   T1N R1E
A post office at this location must have been *nil*, as no other information has been found.
P.O. est. June 12, 1894, Edward K. Buker, p.m.; disc. (?)
Ref.: 242

NINE MILE CREEK
Cochise   T14S R28E   Elev. 4065'
The Nine Mile Ranch is on this creek nine miles out of Bowie, hence the name.
Ref.: Riggs

NINE MILE DESERT
Pinal/Pima   Elev. c. 1500-2300'
This is a nine-mile stretch of barren land which emigrants followed between Maricopa Wells and Point of Mountain northwest of Tucson. Ref.: 56, p. 131

NINE MILE PEAK
Pima   T14S R3W   Elev. 2560'
This prominent lava butte is nine miles east of the old Gunsight Mine, hence the name.
Ref.: 58

NINE MILE STAGE STATION
Yuma   Elev. c. 500'
This location, also called Nine-Mile Water, was nine miles east of Yuma on the road to Tucson. Ref.: 163, p. xxx

NINE MILE VALLEY
Coconino/Mohave   T35N R3W   Elev. c. 4500'
This valley extends for nine miles south from Fredonia, hence the name, or it may have been named for the nine mile base line established by A.H. Thompson of the Powell survey in 1872. Ref.: 18a; Schellbach File (Grand Canyon)

NIPPLE BUTTE
Navajo   T25N R18E   Elev. 6557'
The name describes the appearance of this location, which is also known as Barrel Butte. Ref.: 329

NITSI CANYON
Navajo = "antelope drive" (also spelled Nitsie)
Navajo   T3N R17E   Elev. c. 5000'
According to a Navajo informant, the name refers to the resemblance of the canyon to an antelope drive (or trap) structure. It was so called in 1909. Inscription House is in this canyon. Nitsin (*sic*) Canyon is here. Ref.: BAE Report No. 50, p. 4, Note *e*

N O BAR MESA
Greenlee   T2S R29E   Elev. c. 6000'
The N O– brand was registered by Cap Smith and his brother Bill, who sold out to the Battendorf brothers. However, the N O Bar Ranch (T2S/R29E) was homesteaded by Ed Laney. Ref.: Fred Fritz; Patterson

NOBLE MOUNTAIN
Apache   T6N R30E   Elev. c. 8000'
Edward A. Noble (d. Nov. 1909) homesteaded at the base of this mountain in 1881. He was a farmer and cattleman. The Forest Service gave his name to the mountain. It is shared by Noble Draw. Ref.: Noble (son)

NOBMAN CANYON

Mohave   T24N R17W   Elev. c. 3500'

On January 13, 1877 Fred Nobman with others signed a petition to Gen. August V. Kautz to force the Hualapai to stop killing cattle. Nobman with others had rediscovered the Lost Basin near Pearce Ferry on the Colorado River. The spelling Nodman is an error. Ref.: 335, p.115; Malach, Letter (March 14, 1973)

N–O CANYON (N BAR O)

Cochise   T12S R21E

The Canyon is named for the N–O Spring at T13S/R21E.

NOGALES   pro.: /nogæləs/ or /nogaliys/

Spanish = "walnuts"

Santa Cruz   T24S R14E   Elev. 3689'

The name Nogales predates the arrival of the Gadsden Purchase Boundary Survey party. In his report Lt. N. Michler speaks of visiting the commissioner in the "pretty little valley of Los Nogales," saying that the camp was near Los Nogales itself. On July 21, 1855 newspapers reported that the American and Mexican Boundary Commissions were encamped permanently in Los Nogales, eight miles from Calabasas on the road to Magdalena, Mexico. The official name for the camp was Monument. To eliminate any further doubt about this location, the *Weekly Arizonan* (April 21, 1859) may be quoted, "Monument or Nogales Rancho." Nogales Ranch was in Nogales Pass through which the railroad would later lay rails beside Nogales Wash. The ranch was a stage station and livestock center. On the Williamson-Robert map of 1868 it was called Dos Nogales and lies on the border adjoining the route from Tubac south into Mexico. On GLO 1869 the name is given as Nugales. In the late 1870s, plans were completed for the railroad to be built northward from Guaymas to the border and southward in the United States with the two to meet in Nogales Pass. A rush started as people tried to be part of what was expected to be a border boom town. At first Calabasas was so envisioned. (See Calabasas, Santa Cruz) Many went there but a few others went a little farther south. Among them was Jacob Isaacson (b. Dec. 9, 1853, Gulding, Russia; d. Dec. 29, 1928), an itinerant peddler who for the preceding five years had moved around in Arizona. He constructed a small store and warehouse straddling the international boundary line. A small settlement of tents, rude shacks and adobe rose around his store. The budding settlement was called Isaactown. Two years after Isaacson arrived, he helped as the final silver spike for the railroad was driven home.

Meanwhile an adjacent community known as Line City was developing on the international boundary and on the railroad line. Mexicans called the location Villa Riva. Apparently no one believed that Line City should be a permanent name, for the citizens were asked to select a name. As the railroad station was called Nogales, the citizens petitioned to have the post office name changed from Isaactown to Nogales. With the railroad work completed, a business lull fell on the small border community and Isaacson, a business man to his marrow, moved on to Mexico City. He died in Detroit.

Arizonans refer to the twin cities of Nogales (Nogales, Arizona, and Nogales, Sonora) as Los dos Nogales ("the two Nogales"). From its beginnings as a box car railroad station and a community of one or two stores, tents and a few mud huts, Los dos Nogales have grown into large, prosperous and attractive cities. Nogales, Arizona, is the county seat of Santa Cruz County.

P.O. est. as Isaactown, May 31, 1882, Jacob Isaacson, p.m.; name changed to Nogales, June 4, 1883, James Breeden, p.m.; Wells Fargo 1885; incorporated July 22, 1893

Ref.: 242; AHS, Jacob Isaacson File; 105, pp. 118, 176; *Sacramento Union* (July 21, 1885), p. 3; *Weekly Arizonan* (April 21, 1859), p. 3; *Yuma Sentinel* (Nov. 18, 1882), p. 1; 5, p. 210; *Arizona Sentinel* (Nov. 8, 1873), p.3; *Phoenix Herald* (Oct. 4, 1882), p. 3; Glannon; Jones

NOGALES SPRING

Pima   T18S R18E

A variety of walnut or butternut trees called *nogales* grows in many places in Arizona.

NOIPA KAM
Papago: *Nykokakam'* = "interpreter"
Pima   T13S R2E   Elev. 2107'
This is a small Papago community and farming area. The name is a Spanish corruption
of the Papago name. It is sometimes called Nyokikam or Noipa Kem. Noipa Kam Hills
are here. Ref.: 262, p. 6; 58

NOKAI CANYON
Navajo: *No-kai* = "Mexican person"
Navajo   T40N R17E   Elev. c. 5300'
In 1959 the USGS officially changed this name from Naki to its present spelling. It is
also referred to as Noki Creek or Canyon. Associated names include Nokai Mesa
(T41N/R17E). Ref.: 14, p. 11; 141, p. 194

NOLIC   pro.: /nowəliy/
Papago: "bend in wash"
Pima   T16S R5E   Elev. 2374'
In 1879 in this area Desert Well (or Wells) was the only watering place for livestock at
$0.25 per head. It had a post office. The Papago name came to be recognized gradually.
Bryan says the traditional Papago name used to be Vipenak (= "where vipenoi . . . is
growing"; i.e. strawberry cactus). However, residents preferred Nolia, a corruption of
Noria (Spanish = "well with a wheel and rope for raising buckets"). The place has been
recorded as Desert Well (1893, Roskruge), Noolik (Bryan Notes), Noolick (1912,
Luumis), Noli (1917, U.S. Corps of Engineers), and Nolic (USGS Water Supply
Paper #490 D).
P.O. est. as Desert, May 10, 1880, Charles H. Labarie, p.m.; disc. Sept. 2, 1885
Ref.: 58; 323; 256, p. 14; 271, pp. 28-29; 329; 262, p. 14

NO NAME MESA
Coconino/Utah   T42N R14E
Only a small portion of this mesa lies in Arizona. The remainder is in Utah. It was
known as No Name Mesa in 1922, and consequently calling it No Name Mesa
indicates it does have a name. The whole matter reflects a truism in place names:
Where no name exists, one will be applied, even though it may result in No Name.

NOONVILLE
Santa Cruz   T24S R13E   Elev. 4159'
Capt. John N. Noon, an Irishman, discovered the Noon Mine in 1879 and moved to the
location in 1887. The place was also called Noon Camp.
P.O. est. Oct. 31, 1888, Alonzo E. Noon, p.m.; disc. July 21, 1890
Ref.: 15, p. 628, Note 13; 18a

NORRIS TANK
Coconino   T20N R5E
The tanks at this location were named for Tom G. Norris, a lawyer c. 1900, who later
left this region and moved first to Prescott and then to Phoenix. Ref.: Slipher

NORTH CANYON
Coconino   T35N R3E   Elev. c. 5000'
Two canyons head near each other, their creek courses thereafter running nearly
parallel, hence their respective names of North and South Canyon. Ref.: 18a

NORTH FORK WHITE RIVER
Apache/Navajo   T5N R22E
The name is an old one. Other names used for it – Shake Creek, Snake Creek, and
White River – are misapplied. Ref.: 329

NORTH KOMELIK
Pinal   T10S R4E   Elev. 1600'
This Papago town name has been variously rendered, a fact which may be attributed to
the white man's inability to pronounce guttural elements in the Papago dialects. For

instance, it is also known as Gukomelik, Komalik, Komelih, Komlih, and Kukomalik. See Komelik, Pinal. Ref.: 329

NORTH MOUNTAIN
Maricopa   T3N R3E   Elev. 2104'
In use since c. 1880, the name derives from the location of this mountain at the north portion of the Phoenix Mountains. It is also known as Shaw Butte and as Sunnyslope Mountain. Ref.: 329

NORTH PEAK
Cochise   T14S R27E
This is the northernmost of the two peaks comprising Dos Cabezas Peaks, hence the name. Ref.: 329

NORTH PEAK
Gila   T9N R9E   Elev. 7449'
It is so named because it is the last mountain north in the Mazatzal range. Ref.: 329; Ransom (1917)

NORTH PINTA TANK
Yuma   T12S R13W
The Fish and Wild Life Service named this developed tank in 1952, naming it because of its location in the north part of the Sierra Pinta. Ref.: Monson

NORTH RIM
Coconino (Grand Canyon)   T40N R4W   Elev. 8200'
The term North Rim is applied to the Grand Canyon north of the Colorado River. The first tourist accommodations were called Wylie Way Camp, then Bright Angel Point, then Grand Canyon Lodge. North Rim is also the name of the summer post office and resort community at Bright Angel Point. To serve tourists the post office was established under the name Kaibab Forest at a site recorded as T33N/R3E. It operated for five days under the name North Run-Off Rim (T38N/R2E). In 1947 the name was changed to North Rim to accord with the name change by the National Park Service. See also Grand Canyon, Coconino/Mohave
P.O. est. as Kaibab, June 16, 1926, Woodruff Rust, p.m.; resc. Oct. 12, 1926; name changed to Kaibab Forest, June 16, 1926, William Rogers, p.m.; name changed to North Run-Off Rim, June 6, 1947; name changed to North Rim, June 11, 1947, Willson C. Fritz, p.m.; disc. Aug.31, 1955 Ref.: 242

NORTON LANDING
La Paz   T4S R23W   Elev. c. 250'
This landing on the Colorado River, used to unload supplies for the Red Cloud Mine, was named for George William Norton (b. Aug. 9, 1843, Indiana), an engineer. He arrived in Arizona in 1877 to supervise the building of the first railroad bridge across the Colorado River. Norton's Landing was in existence by late 1878. He then became a mining man, later farming and entering politics.
P.O. est. June 4, 1853, Jacob D. Dettlebach p.m.; disc. March 13, 1894
Ref.: Mercer; Willson; AHS Names File; Blythe Chamber of Commerce, "Cruise Bulletin" (Oct. 10, 1954); 224, III; *Arizona Sentinel* (Feb. 8, 1879), p. 3; 355, p. 52

NORTON TANK
Yuma   T7S R16W   Elev. 312'
First appears on 1912 maps. On the post office application form, the name suggested for the location was Lysleton, but someone at the Post Office Department crossed out that name and wrote in "Norton." It was the identical location of Mohawk where George William Norton was postmaster in 1889. (See Mohawk, Yuma and Norton Landing, Yuma). Charles G. Norton, the engineer who put in the first irrigation canal at Wellton, served as second postmaster at Norton in 1916.
P.O. est. Oct. 31, 1913, Robert Lee Wallace, p.m.; disc. May 20, 1925
Ref.: 242; Mercer

NOTTBUSCH BUTTE

Yuma   T1S R11W   Elev. 2187'

This cone-shaped mountain was named for J. Fred Nottbusch, who had a hotel, a store, and an apiary. He owned the small community of Palomas adjacent to this butte. Nottbusch owned about three hundred acres of land and also the Nottbusch or Silver Prince Mine (T4S/R15W), from which much ore was taken in 1912. The mine was sold c. 1940 and little by little vandals carried off or destroyed the entire community. The name is erroneously spelled Nottbush. Associated and variant names include Nottbusch Valley (T1S/R12W) and Nottbusch Wash (Maricopa, T5S/R10W).
Ref.: Lenon; Mercer; 355, p. 128

NOVINGER BUTTE

Coconino (Grand Canyon)   T33N R4E   Elev. c. 5800'

Frank Bond suggested that the butte name be changed from Ninety-four Mile Creek to Novinger Butte. The USGS approved in May 1932. Simon Horrvja (b. 1832, Pennyslvania; d. Jan. 24, 1904), who anglicized his name to Novinger, moved to Arizona from California in 1871. He settled one and a half miles away from the only two buildings in what was to become Phoenix. Ref. 329

NUGENT'S PASS

Cochise   T14S R22E   Elev. 4000'

In 1849 this pass was named for John Nugent, a member of Col. Hay's party.
Ref.: 101, p. vii

NUGGET CANYON

Pinal   T10S R16E

Nuggets were found on the surface here, hence the name. In the early 1950s, a nugget of pure silver weighing sixty-four ounces was found in this canyon.
Ref.: Woody

NUGGET GULCH

Pinal   T10S R17E

Emerson O. Stratton named this gulch or canyon in the 1880s.
Ref.: Kitt; AHS, Emerson O. Stratton, *ms.*, p. 51

NUGGET (MINE)

Gila   T8S R5E   Elev. c. 5200'

The Nugget Mine was located in 1879. A post office was established for the convenience of miners.
P.O. est. as Nugget, Jan. 7, 1881, George Fantan, p.m.; disc. March 10, 1884
Ref.: Woody; 270, p. 115; 321

NUÑEZ (R.R. STN.)   pro.: /núwnyez/

Pinal   T6S R5E   Elev. 1335'
Nuñez is said to have been named for Ventura Nuñez, who murdered G.R. Whistler at Burke's Station on July 7, 1874. See Burke's Station, Maricopa   Ref.: 18a

NUTRIOSO   pro.: /núwtri owso/

Apache   T7N R30E   Elev. 7700'
The name for this community derives from that of Rio Nutrioso, on the Military Department of New Mexico map of 1876. It is now Nutrioso Creek. According to legend, the first settlers killed a beaver (*nutria*) and a bear (*oso*), which hardly seems likely in view of the fact that the name dates back to at least 1867, when there were no settlers near here. The first settler was James G.H. Colter, who arrived in Round Valley in July 1875. In 1879 he sold his farm on Colter Creek (which empties into Nutrioso Creek) to William J. Flake. The Mormon settlers built a fort and by 1883 Hinton map calls the stream Neute Rosa, a corruption.
P.O. est. April 12, 1883, John W. Clark, p.m.
Ref.: 225, pp. 185, 186; Butler; Wentz

NUTT, MOUNT

Mohave   T20N R19W   Elev. 5216'

It is curious how even the simplest names can be corrupted. For instance, although this name had been mapped repeatedly since GLO 1887, on GLO 1921 the name is given as Mount McNutt, and on GLO 1933, as Mount Nut. Why it should be called Nut or McNutt is not known, as Nutt is its name.
Ref.: 200, p. 23

NUTTALL CANYON

Graham   T7-8S R23E

In the early 1900s the Nuttall family operated a sawmill here. The names Nuttle and Nut Fall Canyon are both corruptions. Ref.: 329

NYCE LAKE

Navajo   T10N R16E

George Nyce, a ranger on the White River Apache Reservation, had a cabin near this lake, which is named for him. Ref.: Davis

O

OAK:
A variety of oak and scrub oak are found in Arizona, leading to the designation *oak* in place names. Examples follow:

Oak Canyon   Gila   T6N R11E
In 1866 Capt. George B. Sanford found a well protected, old Indian rancheria in this canyon. He wrote, "A little stream issued from the rocks, and flowed through the canyon and some fine oak trees grew along the banks. From this circumstance, I call the place Oak Canyon." Ref.: 107, V, 199, 200

Oak Creek   Coconino/Yavapai   T15N R5E
This creek was named at least as early as 1914. Ref.: 329; Jesse Bushness (Forest Ranger, 1917)

Oak Creek   Gila   T6N R11E

Oak Creek   Graham   T10S R22E
The postmaster at Sunset named this place in 1917, but in 1921 on the post office location site map for the Sunset post office, he changed the name to High Creek. Ref.: 242

Oak Creek Canyon   Coconino/Yavapai   T19N R6E
On older maps this location shows under the name Wild Oak Creek Canyon. A traveller entering the canyon from the Coconino Plateau will do so via a steep, winding road which drops from seven thousand feet to two thousand five hundred feet. The present highway has existed since 1929. Oak Creek Canyon, one of the most spectacular in Arizona, is red rock country with massive buttes and spires carved by erosion. A nine hundred and forty acres was established on October 15, 1931 as Oak Creek Canyon Natural area. See also Sedona, Yavapai Ref.: 5, pp. 327-328; Sykes; 243, p. 22

Oak Creek Canyon Natural Area
See Oak Creek Canyon, Coconino/Yavapai

Oak Grove   Cochise   T12S R23E   Elev. 4447'
While searching in 1872 for cattle which departed at night, Henry C. Hooker found the spring where he established a stage station. Here he camped during 1872 with cattle "left over" after completing a government contract. Hinton described Oak Grove as a stage station and growing settlement. See Sierra Bonita Ranch, Graham Ref.: 159, p. 433; 206, p. 231; 163, p. 237

Oak Grove Canyon   Cochise
See Oak Grove, Cochise

Oak House
See Oak Springs, Apache

Oaks and Willows   Yavapai   c. T21N R5W
The Gardner 1866 map of the route from Fort Mohave to Prescott names this stage station. Later it was headquarters camp for the Perrin Livestock Company of Williams.
P.O. est. Feb. 12, 1880, Edwin Imey, p.m.; disc. June 10, 1880 Ref.: 242; 18a

Oak House (Ruin)   Apache
See Oak Springs, Apache

Oak Spring   Coconino   T22N R8E
Gov. John N. Goodwin in February 1864 named this spring.
Ref.: *Arizona Miner* (May 25, 1864), p. 4

Oak Spring   Gila
See Goldtooth Smith Spring, Gila

Oak Spring	Graham	(1) T4S/R20E
	(2 & 3)	T5S/R19E (two springs within
	(4) T9S/R20E	one section of land)

Oak Spring   Mohave   T40N R13W

This spring was named by Maj. John Wesley Powell's party c. 1869. Ref.: 88, pp. 191, 192

Oak Spring Canyon   Gila   T11N R11E

This canyon is also known as Oak Spring Draw (1939). Ref.: 329

Oak Spring Draw   Gila   T11N R11E

See Oak Spring Canyon, Gila

Oak Springs   Apache   T24N R3E

On the McComb map (1860) this location is called Willow Springs. Both oaks and willows grow here. In the nearby basin is a twelfth century Indian ruin called Oak House, a translation of the Navajo *check'ilbii-kin*. The Navajo name for the location is *tee Łch'initi'* (= "tule extending out" or "cattail outline"). Ref.: 331, p. 108; 143, p. 209

OAKLEY SPRINGS
Coconino   T32N R9E

See Willow Springs, Coconino

OATMAN
Mohave   T19N R20W   Elev. 2720'

The town of Oatman had enough residents to establish a post office in 1904. The name proposed for it was Fremont. Its first official name was Vivian, because it was adjacent to the Vivian Mine (about one-quarter mile away). The mine was discovered in 1902 by a half-breed Mohave Indian, Ben Taddock, who while riding along the trail saw free gold glittering and immediately located his claim. Taddock sold it in 1903 to Judge E.M. Ross and Col. Thomas Eqing, who in 1905 sold it to the Vivian Mining Company. Between 1904 and 1907 the mine yielded over $3,000,000. The location then briefly fell upon hard times, to be relieved by the discovery of the extremely rich Tom Reed Mine in 1910 by Ely Hilty, Joe Anderson, and Daniel Tooker, who called their claim Oatman. By 1916 the area that had been the Tom Reed-Gold Road District was being called the Oatman District. At that time Oatman Camp extended from the Tom Reed buildings in Section 14 (location of first post office) southerly through portions of Sections 22 and 23 to the "Lexington town site in Section 27." The name of the post office was changed to Oatman in 1909. Although legend says that Oatman was named for the massacre of the Oatman family, it seems more likely it was named for her son John Oatman, a wealthy one-half Mohave Indian miner. Olive Oatman was rescued at Ollie Oatman Spring, one-half mile north of the present town of Oatman.

P.O. est. as Vivian, March 1, 1904, James H. Knight, p.m.; name changed to Oatman, June 24, 1909 Ref.: 359, pp. 77, 78; 5, p. 236; 242; *Mohave County Miner* (July 20, 1919), I, p. 10; 200, pp. 180, 195; 215, p. 131

OATMAN FLAT
Maricopa   T5S R9W   Elev. 560'

In 1851 the Oatman family was en route with an emigrant train. Some left the group at Tucson and others paused at Pima Villages to rest. As Oatman was nearing the end of his resources, Royse Oatman, his wife, and seven children separated from the train. Without incident they reached what is now Oatman Flat and pitched camp for the night. There some Indians, friendly at first, slaughtered all except a son, Mary Ann and Olive, who were taken captive and later sold as slaves to Mohave Indians. The Indians threw Lorenzo Oatman, twelve years old, over the edge of the flat into a small ravine. Oatman Mountain (T4S/R9W; elev. 1732') overlooks it. Another name for the flat is Oatman Grove.

    Lorenzo was not dead. Slowly and painfully he made his way to safety. The bodies of the Oatman family were found where they were massacred. They are buried in a common grave below the flat near where Lorenzo had been thrown. Believing his sisters were alive, the boy refused to abandon his search. Mary Ann died in captivity and Olive was finally rescued in 1856.

    In 1862 Capt. Joseph Walker's expedition made its way across this same area from Sacaton Stage Station, just east of the Oatman grave. The station was owned by William

Fourr, who built his home here in 1862, hence its name of Fourr's Stage Station (in addition to its being called Sacaton Stage Station). Several Fourr children are buried near the remains of the old stage station. Fourr left when railroad trains began running nearby in 1879. In 1886 Thomas O. Jordan (b. 1838, Alabama; d. 1914), homesteaded at Fourr's old place. He had arrived in Arizona in 1885. See also Oatman, Mohave, and Aritoac, Maricopa Ref.: Jordan (son); 107, II, 244; 73, II, 176, 177

OATMAN MOUNTAIN

Maricopa   T4S R9W   Elev. 1732'
This low mountain is adjacent to Oatman Flat (q.v.), hence its name.

OATMAN'S

Maricopa   T5S R5W
This station was established at Painted Rocks (q.v.) several miles east of Oatman Flat. Here the road from Yuma branched to Phoenix or Tucson. It is not to be confused with the stage station constructed by William Fourr at Oatman Flat. Ref.: AHS Names File

O B DRAW

Cochise   T15S R26E
The O B brand, a very old one, is applied to this draw on the ranch using this brand. Ref.: Riggs

OBED

Navajo   T18N R19E   Elev. 5020'
Four separate colonies were established by Mormons who on March 24, 1876 arrived at the Little Colorado River. One was led by George Lake, and its first name was Lake's Camp, soon changed to Obed (a personage in the *Book of Mormon*). Lake's site was selected against the best advice of others, as it was swampy, subject to floods, and a source of malaria. Within a year the residents of Obed departed and Obed was no more. Their strongly built fort remained for years, being used as a cattle corral by the Aztec Cattle Company until the building was destroyed in 1895. Obed Meadow and Spring are here. Ref.: Richards; 225, p. 147; 347, pp. 2,4

OBI POINT   pro.: /obiy/
Piute = "pine nut tree" (piñon)
Coconino (Grand Canyon)   T32N R4E   Elev. 7928'
In 1906 the USGS eliminated three names for this point: Indian Point, Observation Point, and Baldur Point. The present name was applied because of a dense growth of piñon trees here. They grow throughout the area. Obi Canyon is also here. Ref.: 329; 178, p. 62

O'BRIEN GULCH

Yavapai   T9N R3W
It is possible that this location takes its name from that of Jacob O'Brien (b. 1820, Georgia), who was a farmer in this area in 1870. Ref.: 62

OBSERVATION POINT

Cochise   T23S R24E
From this parking vista on the main road above Bisbee, there is an excellent view of the town, hence the name.

OBSERVATORY MESA

Coconino   T21N R7E
This mesa extends from Fort Valley to near where the Lowell Astronomical Laboratory is at its south end, hence the name. The mesa consists of lava which erupted from Crater Hill (near its north end) and from a smaller volcanic hill to the east. Ref.: 276, p. 69

OCAPOS

Maricopa   T5W R2W   Elev. c. 1200'
This location on the *Southern Pacific Company* R.R. was established c. 1890, using reversed letters of the company name. Ref.: 18a

OCHOA (R.R. STN.)   pro.: /očóə/

Cochise   T24S R21E   Elev. 4333'
This station was named for Esteban Ochoa, who had a store here while the railroad was
under construction. See Ochoa Point, Coconino (Grand Canyon)

OCHOA POINT   pro.: /očóə/

Coconino (Grand Canyon)   T31N R5E   Elev. c. 4500'
This point, originally known as Ninety-Four Mile Rapid Point, had its name changed to
honor Esteban Ochoa (b. 1831, Mexico). Ochoa was a well known retail merchant in
partnership with Pinckney Randolph Tully in Tucson. He was also a partner of Pedro
Aguirre (see Aguirre, Pima). By 1870 Ochoa was freighting materials for the military
from Tucson to Camp Ord. He served as Tucson mayor in 1875. In addition, Ochoa was
a prominent rancher. To provide room for his tremendous sheep herds, Ochoa
established a ranch with its own settlement, called Ochoaville (see Ochoa, Santa Cruz).
Ref.: Lennon; AHS, Esteban Ochoa File; 329; 62

OCHOAVILLE

Santa Cruz
This settlement on the Elias Land Grant one-half mile from the international boundary
and two miles from Camp Huachuca, was begun by Esteban Ochoa, who had a large
sheep herd. The settlement in 1879 consisted of six dwellings and one store.
P.O. est. Nov. 11, 1879, Esteban Ochoa, p.m.; disc. Sept. 4, 1885
Ref.: *Arizona Daily Star* (Sept. 11, 1879), p. 3

OCOTILLO   pro.: /ókətíyə/

Spanish = "coachwhip shrub"
Pinal   T2S R5E   Elev. 1202'
The spelling Ocatilo is a corruption. This small town on the S.P.R.R. probably derives
its name from the presence of ocotillo, which is not a cactus, but a succulent. During
most of the year its long (sometimes more than six feet), thumb-size, thorny,
"coachwhip" branches have no leaves, but following sufficient rain, every branch
sprouts bright green leaves. The branches blossom with veritable tips of flame red
flowers. As ocotillo may be broken off and will root easily, it is used for fenced
enclosures. It is also used in roofs of *ramadas* (sun shelters).

OCOTILLO   pro.: /ókətíyə/

Spanish = "coachwhip shrub"
La Paz   T1N R17W   Elev. c. 1000'
This was the name of a mining camp which remained in existence as a ghost town for
many years, but is now almost completely eradicated. See Ocotillo, Pinal. Ref.: Mercer

OCOTILLO   pro.: /ókətíyə/

Spanish = "coachwhip shrub"
Yavapai   T2S R5E   Elev. c. 4000'
Ocotillo grows abundantly in this vicinity. Locally it was known as Middleton, which
was the name of the railroad station when the post office application was made. The
name Ocotillo was given to the post office by government officials. See Ocotillo, Pinal
P.O. est. June 21, 1915, Mrs. Hattie Langworth, p.m.; disc. May 30, 1925   Ref.: 242

OCTAVE

Yavapai   T9N R4W   Elev. 3300'
In 1863 a placer was claimed by eight men who laid out their camp here. Their Octave
Mine closed at the end of World War I and the camp was demolished to reduce taxes.
Although post office records report Octave and Weaver as being identical locations,
they were actually adjacent (see Weaver, Yavapai). The location of Octave on the post
office applications and site locations in 1900 was given as T10N/R4W.
P.O. est. Octave ("late Weaver"), May 11, 1900, David D. Jones, p.m.
Ref.: 359, p. 69; 242

ODART CIENEGA

Apache T4N R26E Elev. c. 6000'

Both this cienega and Odart Mountain (elev. 8524') were named because the area was used for summer range by a New Mexico cattle outfit using the O-dart brand (O→).

ODELL LAKE

Coconino T18N R7E

In 1896 Charlie Odell started a sheep outfit in the upper part of Munds Park, hence the name. Ref.: AHS

OHNESORGEN STAGE STATION

Cochise T16S R20E Elev. 4300'

This location on the east bank of the San Pedro River initially took the river's name for its own: San Pedro River Station. In 1852 the San Pedro River had a shallow bed nearly level with the surrounding ground, but the river was subject to flooding and erosion. In 1859 a bridge was built at this former fording place. The bridge was used by the First California Volunteers on June 23, 1862, at which time they noted that the old station had burned. In 1871 the station was back in operation as an overland stage stop, with eight soldiers to guard it and settlers. The stage station was a hollow square with thick adobe walls having port holes for guns in case of Indian attack. At that time William Ohnesorgen (b. 1849, Germany; d. c. 1930) owned it. He was brought to America in 1853, and his family settled in Texas. In 1867 he was in Mesilla, New Mexico, and in 1868, in Tucson as a clerk for Charles Lesinsky. With his brother he owned the old Duncan, Renshaw and Fowler Stage Station on the San Pedro about a mile north of the present Benson. In 1878-79 Ohnesorgen constructed a toll bridge here. It began to pay for itself in 1880 when mining supplies for Fairbank, Contention, and Charleston had to be shipped through here. Meanwhile, he had started a stage line from Tucson to Tombstone. He sold the line in 1880. The old stage station in 1883 washed away in a flood. Ref.: AHS, William Ohnesorgen File; 73, II, 149

OIT IHUK

Papago = "devil's claw field"

Pima T13S R1E Elev. c. 1800'

This small Papago village probably derives its name from the presence of the gourd vine known as devil's claw. Its gourds dry, shrinking into black two-pronged forms which resemble curled claws. Papago Indians use them in their basketry to produce black-brown designs. Ref.: 262, p. 6

OK NOTCH

Cochise T19S R24E

This notch is on the OK Ranch (T19S/R28E; elev. 5980'), hence its name.

OK WASH

Mohave T34N R10W

In the 1880s the OK Mine was located at Grass Springs, now called Duncan Tank (*q.v.*), by prospectors named Patterson, Rowe, and Fox. They hauled some of the ore to a four stamp mill at Grass Springs. Ref.: 200, p. 121

OLBERG

Pinal T4S R7E

Col. C. R. Olberg was chief engineer for the construction of the San Carlos Reservoir dams. He built diversion dams to the Indian lands in 1903, building and naming the town of Olberg after himself. In 1927 a railroad stop was authorized here and borrowed Olberg's name for it.

P.O. est. Jan. 6, 1927, Joseph O. Willett, p.m.; disc. Aug. 31, 1938

Ref.: 242; Hayden; Prather; *Tempe News* (Nov. 27, 1903), p. 4

OLD BERTRAM CANYON

Santa Cruz T24S R12E

This canyon takes its name from that of the nearby Old Bertram Mine.

Ref.: *Geology of Peña Blanca*, Plate 1, p. 5

OLD CAMP PINAL

Pinal

The 1883 Rand McNally Arizona Territory map shows this camp as Pinal Post Office, five miles west of its original location. See Pinal, Camp, Pinal Ref.: 242

OLD CAVES CRATER

Coconino   T22N R8E   Elev. 7183'

In September 1967 the USGS made the name Old Caves Crater official, deleting the following: Doney Hill (in Doney Park); Sheep Hill (location actually is T21S/R8E, Section 5); Cave Hill (name preferred by old timers). The generic *hill* is a misnomer as this is actually a crater and not really a hill. Indians once lived here in the caves. See Doney Park, Coconino Ref.: 329; 71, p. 27

OLD DOMINION MINE

Gila   T1N R15E   Elev. c. 3500'

This mine was named by Mrs. Rosa Barclay Pendleton (b. 1850, Virginia; d. 1933) to honor her native state of Virginia. The nearby smelter was moved to Globe. The Old Dominion Company in May 1844 bought the Globe Mine. After 1884 the former Globe Mine was generally referred to as the Old Dominion, but the mine originally so called has been abandoned. Ref.: Woody; 107, pp. 134, 117, 116 (Note "a"); AHS, Clipping File, Mrs. Rosa B. Pendleton, "obit" (Dec. 12, 1933)

OLD GLORY

Santa Cruz   T23S R11E

This post office for the mining camp of the American Flag Mine was established in 1893 as Oldglory, despite the desire of residents to call the place American Flag. The Post Office Department rejected the name American Flag because a post office by that name already existed in Pinal County. The name continued as Oldglory for some thirteen years, when petitioners were successful in separating it to Old Glory. Nothing remains here. Old Glory Canyon keeps the name alive.

P.O. est. June 15, 1896, John Houston Alexander, p.m.; name changed to Old Glory, Nov. 23, 1909; disc. Sept. 30, 1911, but re-est. Feb. 5, 1914; disc. Aug. 14, 1915 Ref.: Lenon; 242

OLD MAN MOUNTAIN

Mohave   N. side of Union Pass   Elev. c. 2500'

Jonathan Draper Richardson named this location c. 1885. It is a rock column with a single "eye," resembling an old man. Ref.: Ferra

OLD STAGE ROAD BUTTE

Yavapai   T20N R10W   Elev. over 5030'

The USGS gave the butte this name in 1972 because an old stage road exists nearby. Ref.: 329

OLD TRAILS

Mohave   T19N R20W   Elev. 2388'

The National Old Trails Association cooperated with the Daughters of the American Revolution in marking famous old trails which linked communities or districts in the expanding United States. One of them was Old Trails;, the route followed by both Lt. Edward Fitzgerald Beale (1858) and Capt. Lorenzo Sitgreaves (1854). The community of Old Trails took the name because it came into existence at the time the commemoration was receiving much publicity.

P.O. est. Oldtrails, Nov. 20, 1915; Ernle Sylvester Statton, p.m.; disc. July 21, 1925 Ref.: 242; Becker

OLD TUCSON

Pima   T14S R12E   Elev. 2644'

Originally constructed as a set for the motion picture "Arizona" in 1940, this highly commercialized location is supposedly a replica of Tucson of the 1860s. No communities existed on the west side of the mountains in the 1860s, and early Tucson had not the remotest resemblance to its "replica."

O'LEARY PEAK
Coconino   T23N R8E   Elev. 8916'
This peak was named for Daniel O'Leary (b. 1847, Ireland), a soldier at Apache Pass in 1870. He became a famous scout who saved Gen. George Crook from Indian attack at Date Creek in 1872. In 1879 he enlisted a company of Hualapai Indians to pursue Chiricahua Apaches. Ref.: 62; AHS, Daniel O'Leary File

OLIVE
Santa Cruz   T23S R16E   Elev. 4805'
Olive Camp, a mining community, was named for Olive Stephenson Brown (b. July 24, 1858), who married James Kilroy Brown and arrived in Arizona December 24, 1879. They first lived at Casa Grande, then moved to Tucson in July 1880, and later to Olive Camp. The mine, owned by S. D. Conway of Boston, was sold in the late 1880s. P.O. est. as Olive, March 4, 1887, Owen J. Doyle, p.m.; disc. May 23, 1892 Ref.: AHS, Olive Brown File

OLIVE CITY
La Paz   Elev. c. 500'
Olive City was on the Colorado River one mile north of Ehrenberg. Despite one reference which asserts it was the same location as Olivia, apparently that was not the case. (See Olivia, La Paz) Olive City was named by William D. and Isaac Bradshaw, who in 1863 maintained a Colorado River ferry here. Consequently the place was also known as Bradshaw's Ferry. Charles C. Genung wrote, "He was a hard-looking horse ... the city consisted of one house about twelve feet by ten feet by ten feet high covered with brush and sided up with willow poles stuck in the ground ... without any chinking." Quite naturally all signs of this so-called city have long since disappeared.
Ref.: Mercer, "Desert Scrap Book," *Yuma Daily Sun*, LXII (Oct. 30, 1954), II, 2; 107, IV, 34

OLIVIA
La Paz
Olivia was six miles below La Paz on the Colorado River. It was named by Myron Angel for Olive Oatman. See Oatman Flat, Maricopa Ref.: *Quarterly of California History*, XII (March 1933), 16

OLJETO WASH   pro.: /o:lje:to/
Navajo: *olja* = "moon"; *to* = "water"
Navajo   T41N R19E   Elev. c. 5100'
In January 1960 the USGS changed the following names to the present Oljeto Wash: Olgato, Olja, Olgeto, Oljeto Creek, Moonlight Creek. The name Moonlight Creek, or Moonlight Water, is simply a translation from the Navajo.
Ref.: 331, p. 110; 329; 14, p. 14

OLO CANYON
Havasupai: *olo* = "horse"
Coconino (Grand Canyon)   T34N R3W
This name was made official in 1925. Havasupai Indian horses range here. Ref.: 329

O'NEAL SPRING
Coconino   T21N R7E
Jim O'Neal, who homesteaded at this spring in March 1888, raised sheep. He later sold the spring to Michael J. and Timothy A. Riordan, and a pipe line was run from it to their lumber mill near Flagstaff. O'Neil Hill (or O'Neal Crater) has New Caves Acropolis at its top, an Indian ruin with numerous cave dwellings and a wall about one thousand feet long. There is a reservoir in the crater. Ref.: Wilson; Slipher; 71, p. 39

104 MILE CANYON
Coconino (Grand Canyon)   T34N R2W   Elev. 2250'
Several canyons on the Colorado River were named by the Powell expeditions according to the distance of the canyons from the exploring party's entering the Grand Canyon. Ref.: 267 (scattered references)

ONEIDA

Pinal

This stage station on the Butterfield route where it turned west near Sacaton Mountains was established c. 1858 or early 1859. As workers from upper New York State helped construct the stage line, this place was probably named for the home town of one. Ref.: 73, II, 165

O'NEIL BUTTE

Coconino (Grand Canyon)   T31N R3E   Elev. c. 6072'

In March 1906 this location was named for William O. (Bucky) O'Neil (b. 1860; d. 1898), who arrived in Prescott in 1879 and became a court reporter. His nickname "Bucky" came from the fact that he was fond of "bucking the tiger" or playing faro. He established the livestock magazine *Hoofs and Horns*. At the Grand Canyon he promoted copper mines as well as the establishment of a railroad to the Grand Canyon. O'Neil was mayor of Prescott when he organized a company of Rough Riders for the Spanish-American War. He was killed on San Juan Hill. Ref.: 329; Schellbach File (Grand Canyon); 62; 178, p. 36; 336, p. 136

O'NEIL CRATER

Coconino   T21N R9E

Colton says Red Peak is sometimes called O'Neill Crater for "Bucky" O'Neil. See O'Neil Butte, Coconino Ref.: 70, p. 66

O'NEILL PASS

Yuma   T15S R11W   Elev. c. 500'

Dave O'Neill was an old prospector who died of exposure and over-exertion c. 1916 in the pass in the O'Neill Hills where he is buried and which bears his name. His burros walked to Papago Well. People living there investigated and found his body. Ref.: Monson; 58; 57, p. 419

O'NEILL SPRING

Coconino (Grand Canyon)   T20N R7E

This spring was named for Jim O'Neill (b. 1844, Ireland), a scout for Gen. George Crook. Ref.: AHS Files; 63; 261, p. 159

ONION SADDLE

Cochise   T17S R30E   Elev. 7600'

Onion Creek headed close to where the road through Pinery Canyon tops the mountain, but the creek is now gone. Originally this place was called Onion Creek Saddle, descriptive of the wild onions which grew along the creek. Ref.: Riggs

ORACLE

Pinal   T9S R15E   Elev. 4514'

This name derives from that of a ship, *The Oracle*, on which Albert Weldon travelled around the Horn in 1875. Weldon built a brush camp while making assessments for the Oracle Mine. In 1880 he and Alexander McKay built a one-room adobe home near the mine. With McKay, he located the Christmas Mine in 1881. The town did not develop until after Apache Camp took shape for the Apache Mine. By January 1882 eight dwellings were at what was called Summit Spring or Oracle Camp. The future Oracle was half-way between Apache Camp and Tucson. J. C. Waterman and his family moved there from Mammoth because of malaria at their former home. They were followed by Mr. and Mrs. Edwin S. Dodge, who started a lodging house at the Arcadia Ranch, so named because the Watermans had come from Nova Scotia (= Arcadia). The Dodges applied for a post office to be called Arcadia Ranch, but the Post Office Department required single-named offices and turned it down. Weldon then suggested the name Oracle.

Associated names include Oracle Hill (T10S/R15E, elev. 5290'), Oracle Ridge (T11S/R16E), and Oracle Junction (*q.v.*).
P.O. est. Dec. 28, 1880, James Branson, p.m. Ref.: AHS; Emerson O. Stratton *ms.*, p. 54; *Weekly Arizona Enterprise* (Jan. 14, 1882), p. 3

ORACLE JUNCTION

Pinal   T10S R13E   Elev. 3312'

The name of this community c. 1885 was Represso, at which time it was a stop for changing horses for the freight and mail line from Tucson to the Mammoth Mine. William Neal, a black, held the contract for the line. The name Oracle Junction took over because this community lies where the road branches to Oracle or to Florence. Ref.: 238, p. 64

ORAIBI pro.: /owržžyviʌ/

Hopi: *Sip-oraibi* = "something that has been solidified" (in Hopi mythology, place where the earth was made solid)

Navajo   T29N R16E   Elev. 5675'

Oraibi vies with Acoma, New Mexico, for the honor of being the oldest continuously inhabited town in the United States. Sherds indicate occupancy since c. 1150 A.D. Old Oraibi is on top of a mesa (elev. 6040') and the newer town is at its foot. Luxan (Espejo Expedition) documented the name of the older town on April 24, 1583, when his party arrived at "Olalla," which he said was the largest of the Hopi towns. Luxan's attempt at spelling is not too far fetched, considering there are at least forty-nine variant spellings of the name of Oraibi. The population, once numbering in the thousands, was decimated by smallpox, drought, and the creation of new towns at Hotevilla and Bakavi (*q.v.*). Near Oraibi on the Hotevilla Trail is a line cut in rock to commemorate a tug of war between conservative and liberal Hopi about the education of Oraibi children. The losers moved away. Lower (New) Oraibi, settled before the tug of war, is also called Kai-Kocho-movi or Kiquchmovi because a spring by that name supplies water to the community. Old Oraibi is now practically a ruin. Oraibi Butte is here (T28N/R15E, elev. 6561') and Oraibi Wash passes by (Apache: T34N/R22E; Navajo: T29N/R15E; Coconino: T24N/R14E)

P.O. est. July 14, 1900, Herman Kampmeier, p.m. Ref.: 71, p. 43; 242; 182; 153, pp. 1, 4, 8; 331, p. 110

ORANGE BUTTE

Cochise   T12S R30E   Elev. 5257'

This name is noted on a map dated 1854. The butte is said to be descriptively named because of its shape and color. Because one side of the peak looks like iron, a variant name for it is Iron Butte. It has also been called Orange Peak (1869). Ref.: 18a

ORD, MOUNT

Apache   T6N R26E   Elev. 11,470'

This third highest peak in Arizona and the highest in the White Mountains was named for Maj. Gen. Edward Otho Cresap Ord, in charge of the Department of California during the Indian problems in Arizona. He was noted for his uncompromising attitude as an Apache exterminator. Ord Creek is on this mountain. See Apache, Fort, Navajo Ref.: 107, VIII, 22

ORD, MOUNT

Gila/Maricopa   T7N R9E   Elev. 7155'

Troops in Arizona in 1869 were commanded by Gen. Edward Otho Cresap Ord. At that time Camp Rio was at the foot of the mountain bearing the general's name, and a heliograph station was later located in 1886 at its top. See Ord, Mount, Apache Ref.: 18a; Woody

ORDERVILLE CANYON

Coconino   T39N R2E

The first Mormon settlers in the Little Colorado Valley in 1878 were members of a newly formed group called "The United Order," a cooperative in which all property was communal. One settlement was named Orderville. The United Order did not endure long, and the settlement vanished, but the name remains attached to this canyon. Ref.: Richards

OREJANO CANYON   pro.: /oreyháno/
Spanish: *orejano* = "maverick"
Greenlee   T15N R6W   Elev. c. 5000'
In this canyon cowboys branded cattle (mavericks = unbranded cattle). The name may
indicate particular attention being given here to identifying ear-slash brands (Spanish: *oreja* = "ear"). Ref.: Simmons

ORGAN PIPE CACTUS NATIONAL MONUMENT
Pima   T16S R7W   Elev. c. 1400'
This location was named because of the abundance of organ pipe cacti which resemble
organ pipes in the way the individual arms cluster from a central ground point. The
Monument set aside in 1937 measures 330,687 acres of desert, mountains, and plains,
and contains a magnificent reserve of virgin desert growth.
Ref.: 13, Natt N. Dodge, "Godfather of the Organ Pipes," pp. 1-3

ORGANIZATION RIDGE
Pima   T12S R16E
Many organizations maintain summer camps in the vicinity, hence the name.

ORIZABA
Pinal   T9S R4E   Elev. 1628'
The Orizaba Mine is reportedly named for a Papago Indian working in the area in 1903.
The mining camp had a post office.
P.O. est. Sept. 25, 1888, John Reiss, p.m.; disc. Aug. 11, 1893 Ref.: 18a

ORO   pro.: /oro/
Spanish = "gold"
Yavapai   T10N R1W   Elev. c. 4000'
This was the name of the post office established to serve the Oro Belle Mine owned by
George F. Harrington, who renamed the post office for himself.
P.O. est. Feb. 8, 1904, Benjamin Heller, p.m.; name changed to Harrington, March 4,
1904, Robert George Scherer, p.m.; disc. March 6, 1907; re-est. as Harrington (date
unknown); disc. Aug. 31, 1918
Ref.: 242; G.E.P. Smith; Willson

ORO BLANCO   pro.: /oro blanko/
Spanish = "white gold"
Santa Cruz   T22S R10E   Elev. 3970'
Placers worked at the original site ("Old" Oro Blanco) contained so much silver mixed
with the gold that the name for the location was an attempt to mirror that fact. The
workings were owned by Messrs. Handy, Hewitt, Leatherwood, Hopkins, Brown,
Ferguson, and "Yank" Bartlett. The placers on Oro Blanco Creek were so close to the
international boundary that a survey line was run to be certain they lay in Arizona. There
was no such doubt about the "New" Oro Blanco, which lay about nine miles north of the
placers. At the new location in 1873 (owned by Charles O. Brown, E. M. Pearce, J. W.
Hopkins, and Gov. John Safford), it was said that the location had been worked so long
ago that in some places large oak trees had grown at the site of obviously old mining
activity. Oro Blanco Mountain shares the name, as does Oro Blanco Peak (T24S/
R12E), and Oro Blanco Wash (Pima/Santa Cruz; T22S/R10E).
P.O. est. Oct. 2, 1879, William J. Ross, p.m.; disc. April 30, 1915
Ref.: *Arizona Citizen* (Dec. 27, 1873), p. 3, and (May 16, 1874), p. 2, and (May 30,
1874), p. 4; Lenon; 242

ORO, CAÑADA DEL   pro.: /kanyáda del oro/
Spanish: *cañada* = "dale" or "sheep walk"; *oro* = "gold"
Pinal/Pima   T10S R14E   Elev. c. 3000'
This fairly broad wash took its name from the existence of "extensive and rich placer

gold deposits" reputedly "worked 100 years or more since by the Jesuits...." It is now called Canyon del Oro.
Ref.: AHS, William Whelan Log; 168, p. 66; 49, p. 53; 224, p. 166

ORO, CAÑADA DEL (MINE)
Pima

Henry Aphold and his family owned this mine on the north slope of the Santa Catalina Mountains in 1881. A post office was established for the convenience of workers. It was named because of its location near Cañada del Oro.
P.O. est. March 28, 1881, Jose de Camacho, p.m.; disc. Oct. 12, 1882
Ref.: AHS, Chambers Collection, Envelope 15, Pockets 7 – 8

ORO VALLEY
Pima   T12S R14E   Elev. c. 3000'
This community, established by private interests c. 1970, was named because it is adjacent to Cañada del Oro. The town was incorporated in April 1974.
Ref.: Glendis Parker

OROVILLE
Greenlee   T4N R30E   Elev. c. 4200'
In the late 1870s George Wells started Wells Ranch across the river from where the Oroville post office would be established. Chinese living here raised produce for Clifton residents. By 1886 Charley Wing was farming at the old Wells Ranch. Unfortunately, local Mexican-Americans knew that the Chinese hoarded money to pay their passage to China, and in January 1904, a dynamite blast forced the Chinese to leave their homes, which were then subject to looting. About four Chinese were killed as they fled. As for the name Oroville, it is said to derive from gold having been discovered in the vicinity. It is interesting to note that on old records the name of the main street in Clifton is Oro Street.
P.O. est. as Oro, Oct. 19, 1880, Joseph T. Yankie, p.m.; disc. June 12, 1882
Ref.: Patterson; 18a; Patton

ORTEGA LAKE   pro.: /ortéygǝ/
Apache   T11N R25E   Elev. c. 7000'
Mormons at Concho bought a ranch here owned by Leandro Ortega. The area was used for lambing in the 1880s. Associated names include Ortega Draw (T10N/R24E), Mountain (T11N/R23E, elev. 7007') Sink (T11N/R26E), and Spring (T12N/R26E).
Ref.: 18a; Wiltbank

OSA, LA   pro.: /la osǝ/
Spanish = "bear" (female)
Pima   T22S R8E   Elev. c. 3500'
The name of Rancho de la Osa on La Osa Wash is said to have come from the fact that a Mexican cowboy roped and killed a silver-tipped bear and her cub. The place was also called Sturges' Ranch as Sturges bought it in 1885 and made it the headquarters for the La Osa Cattle Company. The headquarters actually were referred to as Las Moras. On his letterhead Sturges had a bear and three cubs. The ranch has changed hands many times both as a working cattle and as a guest ranch. Although there may be no connection, the De La Ossa family has been prominent for generations in Santa Cruz County and Sonora. The post office at La Osa has changed name, but not location, several times. It changed location once when Buenos Ayres handled the postal service. Also see Buenos Ayres, Pima; Sasabe, Pima, and Fernando, San, Pima
P.O. est. as La Osa, March 26, 1890, Paul Nathan Roth, p.m.; disc. Dec. 7, 1899, papers sent to Buenos Ayres. La Osa resumed operation Feb. 24, 1903; name changed to Sasabe, Aug. 24, 1905; name changed to San Fernando, April 21, 1919
Ref.: Lenon; Escalante; 18a; 242

OSA, MESA DE LA
Spanish = "bear's mesa"
Pima   T14S R7E
This mesa, which covers less than a square mile, is also known as Mesa del Oso and Mesa la Oso. Both names are misspellings. Ref.: 329

OSBORNE SPRING

Yavapai   T13N R2E

This spring was named for John Preston Osborne (b. March 26, 1815, Tennessee; d. Jan. 20, 1900). He arrived at Prescott in July 1864 and built one of the first hotels. His son credited him with sowing the first wheat at Del Rio, north of Prescott. In 1943 this spring was developed into Osborne Well. Osborne Spring Wash shares the name.
Ref.: AHS, John Preston Osborne Files; 62; 329

OSIRIS TEMPLE

Coconino (Grand Canyon)   T33N R2E   Elev. 6637′

In 1906 the USGS approved this name from among many of deities of various religions and mythologies, suggested by Francois E. Matthes. Osiris was the father of Horus. To quote James: " It is a gracefully domed temple in the cross-bedded sandstone and clearly reveals its 500′ superior height over Horus." Ref.: 178, p. 32; 329

OTERO CREEK   pro.: /otéro/

Maricopa   T5N R8E

Jesus Otero raised cattle at Otero Spring in Otero Canyon from 1884 to 1890. The location is also called Picadilla Creek. Ref.: 18a; 329

OTERO LAND GRANT

Santa Cruz   T21S R13E

This is the name of a pioneer family. The old Otero Ranch is now called Linda Agua. Otero R.R. station was at T22S/R13E.

OTIS

Pinal   Near Casa Grande

This location may have been named for Elwell Stephen Otis, military commander for Arizona Territory (May 24, 1897 – January 6, 1898). No proof, however, has been found to support this possibility.
P.O. est. Jan. 13, 1893, Thomas C. Carey, p.m.; disc. Aug. 19, 1893 Ref.: 242

OTTOMAN AMPHITHEATER

Coconino (Grand Canyon)   T32N R4E

In 1882 Dutton used this name. According to him, "It is notable for its magnificent display of buttes ... Perhaps the butte-work has its climax here...." The Turkish or Ottoman empire was noted for opulent magnificence. Ref.: 100, p. 175

OTTO TANK

Graham   T7S R22E

This earth-dam stock tank named for an old prospector is also called Auto Tank, an obvious corruption. Ref.: 329

OURY, MOUNT   pro.: /yúwriy/

Pima   T15S R18E   Elev. c. 6000′

Among early prominent residents of Tucson were three brothers, all born in Abingdon, Virginia. The oldest, William Sanders (b. Aug. 13, 1816; d. March 31, 1887) took part in the Mexican War, went to California during the gold rush, and arrived in Arizona in 1857 as the first agent for the Butterfield Overland Stage. Marcus (b. Feb. 3, 1821; d. 1865), whose name may have been Marius, was killed by Apaches near Tucson, a fact which may have led his brother William to hate Apaches. William was a leader in the Camp Grant Massacre. (See Grant, Old Camp, Pinal). Granville Henderson (b. March 12, 1825; d. Jan. 11, 1891) also went to California in 1849. Grant, as he was called, arrived in Arizona in 1859 and by 1860 was Chief Justice of the Supreme Court for the Provisional Government of Arizona. He resigned the same year. He achieved eminence as a lawyer and politician. In 1857 Grant led the party that went to the relief of the Crabb Expedition. See Filibuster, Yuma Ref.: AHS, Chambers Collection, Box 5-6, Envelope 12; AHS, William S. Oury File; 62

OUTLAW MOUNTAIN

Cochise   T22S R32E   Elev. 6240'

Outlaw Mountain was named because many outlaws, including the Clanton gang, hid out here at Outlaw Springs (T15S/R30E). Ref.: AHS Files; 18a

OVERGAARD

Navajo   T12N R17E   Elev. 6600'

This location was named for the Overgaard family. Christ Overgaard served as postmaster in 1939.
P.O. est. Oct. 14, 1938, William T. Shockley, p.m.; disc. Dec. 31, 1943; re-est. April 16, 1952 Ref.: 242

OVERNIGHT POINT

Mohave   T34N R12W

This stock tank was constructed by Wayne Gardner and Roland Esplin in the early 1950s. It earned its name because it was constructed in one day. In 1953 Gardner was stranded here and froze to death. The location is also called Gardner Reservoir. Ref.: 329

OVERTON

Maricopa   Said to be near Cave   Elev. c. 2800'
                            Creek 30 mi. N. of Phoenix

This stage station was maintained by C. L. Hall in 1881. Location not precisely known.
P.O. est. Oct. 6, 1880, Josiah Woods; disc. Oct. 3, 1881 Ref.: 242

OVERTON CANYON

Cochise   T16S R30E

This location took its name from that of the Overton post office. Capt. Gilbert E. Overton, 6th U.S. Cavalry, is said to have camped here in 1886. Overton Canyon is not the site of the Overton post office. See Garden Canyon, Cochise Ref.: 18a; 242

OWEN

Mohave   T35N R19W   Elev. c. 2400'

This location is the site of a now-abandoned mining camp named for either "Chloride Jack" or John Wren Owen (b. 1824, Illinois; d. Nov. 4, 1877), who came to Arizona with the California Column in 1864. In 1870 he was serving at Camp Crittenden. After his release from service, he served as Deputy Collector of Customs at Maricopa Wells, and at the time he died he was Treasurer of Maricopa County. A question remains whether "Chloride Jack" Owen is the same person as John Wren Owen, as no evidence links the latter with the Owen mining camp and district. "Chloride Jack" is an apt nickname for a miner, which John Wren Owen never was.

When the application for a post office was made, the first name suggested was Big Sandy because of its location on the Big Sandy River. However, post office authorities would not accept reuse of the name of the first post office here and Owens was substituted. Owens Peak is east of the Hualapai Mountains. See also Big Sandy, Mohave
P.O. est. as Big Sandy, June 7, 1890, Thomas H. Hunt, p.m.; disc. Nov. 21, 1890; re-est. as Owens, Jan. 28, 1899, Mrs. Nellie C. Cornwall, p.m.; disc. July 21, 1914
Ref.: 242; AHS, John W. Owen File; Babcock; 200, p. 24

OWL HEAD DAM

La Paz   T1N R16W

This dam was developed by the Division of Grazing about 1938 and named for a rock formation which looks like two owl heads. Ref.: Monson

OWL ROCK

Navajo   T40N R19E   Elev. 6547'

This formation is a slender sandstone pinnacle. Narrow at the base, it bulges at the center into two great over-hanging stone "wings," tipped by a small owl-like "head," hence its name. Ref.: 37, p. 245

OWLS' HEADS

Pinal   T8S R12E   Elev. c. 3600'

In 1879 William H. Merrit and E. Walker set up a mining camp here. The name describes the appearance of two nearby buttes.

P.O. est. as Owlhead, March 5, 1930, Mrs. Josie Marie Guss, p.m.; disc. Aug. 3, 1933 Ref.: AHS, Emerson O. Stratton *ms.*, p. 44; 242

OXBOW HILL

Gila   T10N R10E   Elev. 5050'

This location is named because in June 1871 Charles B. Genung was traveling with troops which came upon several ox yokes here. Apparently Apaches had run off oxen still under yoke, removing the yokes at this place. Genung named it Ox Yoke Mountain. Here Genung experienced first hand the wiliness of Apaches. The Mexican guide warned the military party that Indians on the south side might set the brush afire, and all rushed horses down trail. Despite the fact that the trail lay along the north side and that brush and grass do not burn readily, an on-rushing fire cut off nearly all the soldiers. They had to abandon the trail and make their way as best they could.

The Oxbow Mine developed a few years after the incident and a post office called Oxbow was established. Associated names include Oxbow Yoke Hill or Mountain and another Oxbow Mountain (Gila, T10N/R13E, elev. 6448').

P.O. est. as Oxbow, Aug. 21, 1894, Mrs. Elizabeth H. St. John, p.m.; disc. June 23, 1908 Ref.: Dugas; 107, VIII, 174, 175

OZA BUTTE

Coconino (Grand Canyon)   T32N R3E   Elev. 8065'

In 1906 the USGS adopted this name, said to mean a "bottle-neck basket" at the "end of a sort of neck." Ref.: 329

OZBORN

Maricopa

As there is no information in the National Archives, no available written record, and no sign whatever of this "location," the time has come to give Barnes' bibliographic ghost a decent burial. R. I. P.

P

PABLO, SAN   pro.: /san páblo/ or /sæn pǽblo/
Maricopa   Elev. c. 1150′
In 1873 residents of Tempe (*q.v.*) laid out a town next to Hayden's Ferry to house the
Mexican population. William Kirkland (see Kirkland Valley, Yavapai) gave seventy
acres of land for the Mexican village. Ref.: *Tucson Citizen* (May 31, 1873), p. 1 and p.
4; Barnes, quoting *Arizona Sentinel* (May 3, 1873)

PACIFIC CITY
Yuma   c. T3S R23W   Elev. c. 500′
Pacific City, a stage stop on the Yuma-Ehrenberg run in the 1880s, was probably named
for the nearby Pacific Mine.
P.O. est. as Pacific, Nov. 30, 1880, Paul Rizzilled, p.m.; disc. Dec. 20, 1880
Ref.: Preston Mercer, "Desert Scrapbook," *Yuma Daily Sun*, LXXII (Oct. 30, 1954)
I: 3; 242

PACKARD SPRING
Gila   T6N R10E
Amanda Packard, an early rancher, settled here and later had a store on Tonto Creek.
The ranch was on Packard Mesa. Ref.: Woody

PACK SADDLE MOUNTAIN
Cochise   T21S R29E   Elev. 6298′
The top of this mountain resembles the curve of a pack saddle. Ref.: 18a

PADDY CREEK
Apache   T3N R26E   Elev. c. 5800′
This location was named for Paddy Creaghe, killed by Apaches in the early 1880s.
Ref.: 18a

PADDY CREEK
Apache   Between Eagar and Alpine
Paddy O'Dell was an early settler here. Ref.: Wiltbank

PADILLA MESA   pro.: ./padiyə/
Coconino   T27N R14E   Elev. 6200′
In 1540 when Coronado sent a party to investigate the country west of the Seven Cities
of Cibola (see Hopi Villages, Navajo) Fr. Juan de Padilla accompanied Don Pedro de
Tobar. Padilla was killed by Hopi Indians. Herbert Gregory named this mesa in 1915.
Ref.: 141, p. 39, Note 1

PADRE, CANYON   pro.: /pádrey/ or pǽdrey/
Coconino   T20N R10E   Elev. c. 6000′
This canyon's name first appears on a blueprint map dated February 1872 (Jacob
Blickenderfer). Local opinion, however, holds that the name goes back to an expedition
by Spanish Fathers. It is said the name came from the fact that there was already a
Canyon Diablo (*q.v.*), and that a "good" name should balance it, hence Canyon Padre."

At one time Canyon Padre was called Hennessey Canyon for one John Hennessey, who lived in it. Ref.: Colton; Sykes; Hart; Slipher; 242

PADRES MESA   pro.: /pádreyz/
Spanish = "Fathers"
Apache   T22N R26E   Elev. c. 6000'
In 1915 Herbert Gregory named this location for the "Spanish Padres," the first white men to settle among Arizona Indians. Several padres lost their lives to defend their Christian faith. Ref.: 141, p. 194

PAGE
Coconino   T41N R8E   Elev. 4380'
The former construction community at Glen Canyon Dam has become a thriving recreational and business center. It was named for John Chatfield Page (b. Oct. 12, 1887; d. March 23, 1955), Commissioner of Reclamation 1937-1943. Commissioner Page spent years developing the upper Colorado River. See also Glen Canyon, Coconino P.O. est. Oct. 12, 1957, Mrs. Catherine A. Pulsifer, p.m.

PAGE SPRINGS
Yavapai   T16N R4E
In 1931 Jim Page owned these springs and a fish hatchery. It is now the Page Springs Fish Cultural Station. Ref.: *Yavapai Magazine*, XXI (May 9, 1931), 10, 11; 9, p. 1

PAGUEKWASH POINT
Piute = "fish tail"
Mohave (Grand Canyon)   T34N R3W   Elev. 5655'
This name was applied by the USGS in 1925 to a butte on the North Rim of the Grand Canyon. According to USGS records, "The name changes from Fish Tail to an Indian equivalent ... descriptive name." It does not, then, appear to be the name of an Indian family. At one time this location was also called Mohave Point. Ref.: 329

PAHKOON SPRINGS
Piute: *pah* = "water"; *koon* = "bubbling as though boiling"
Mohave   T36N R16W   Elev. c. 2500'
The Piute name describes the boiling as this spring bubbles. Attempts to anglicize the word have resulted in the following spellings: Pah-guhn Springs; Pa-a-coon Springs; Pah coon Springs; Pa-Koon. Ref.: 322, XI, 170

PAH UTE COUNTY
This area, which is now extreme southeastern Nevada, was formerly an Arizona Territory county. Congress on May 5, 1866 made it and a portion of Mohave County a part of Nevada. The name derived from that of the Piute Indians.

PAINTED CANYON
Mohave   T25N R22W   Elev. c. 600'
In February 1857 Lt. Joseph Christmas Ives was struck by the colors in this canyon and named it Painted Canyon. He said, "Various and vivid tints of blue, brown, white, purple, and crimson were blended with exquisite shading upon the gateways and inner walls, producing effects so novel and surprising as to make the cañon, in some respects, the most picturesque and striking of any of these wonderful mountain passes." It is on the Colorado River below Mount Davis. Ref.: 245, p. 79

PAINTED CLIFFS
Maricopa   T3N R10E   Elev. 3400'
R. F. Wilson gave these cliffs the name in 1915. The cliff face has rock in various shades of green tinted with gold. Ref.: 329; 5, p. 367

PAINTED DESERT
Navajo: *Halchiitah* = "amid the colors"
Apache/Navajo/Coconino   T20–34N R6–23E   Elev. from c. 4500' – 6500'
Spaniards first applied the term *El Desierto Pintado* in 1540. Quite independently, Dr.

Newberry of the Ives Expedition in 1858 called the same region the Painted Desert. Its name describes this vast area of brilliantly colored sand and stone which includes the Painted Desert within the Petrified Forest National Monument.
Ref.: 71, p. 4; 331, p. 311; Schellbach File (Grand Canyon)

PAINTED ROCK DAM

Maricopa   T4S R7W

The completion in 1965 of this dam by the U.S. Corps of Engineers caused the removal of Sil Murk. There is no reservoir behind the dam, which exists for flood control, not storage. Ref.: *Papago Bulletin* (Sept. 1965), p. 1; 329

PAINTED ROCK MOUNTAINS

Maricopa   T5S R8W   Elev. 1515'

These mountains received their name because of hieroglyphics. According to one source, the paintings consist of an acre of rocks (forty to fifty feet in height) covered with crude painted and carved pictures of men, insects, snakes, birds, and various other figures. The first white men to see them were the Spaniards, who are said to have named the Sierra Pintada in 1540, although this is dubious. Fr. Kino in 1699 called them the Sierra Pinta and somewhat later, on October 26, 1754, Fr. Jacobo Sedelmayr noted the petroglyphs, but called the mountains the Sierra Sivupuc (meaning not known). One hundred years later Emory on the Gadsden Purchase Boundary Survey map simply dubbed them Picture Rocks. Still another name, but not dated, is Piedras Pintadas (Spanish = "painted rocks"). In 1870, a guide called them Sounding Rocks.
Ref.: 43, p. 420; 77, p. 117, Note 24; 224, p. 17; 101, p. 218; 287 (Oct. 26); 64, p. 542

PAINTED ROCK (R.R. STN.)

Maricopa   T5S R8W

In 1905 this station existed between Theba and Tartron. It has since vanished.
Ref.: 242

PAINTED ROCK WILD LIFE AREA

Maricopa   T5S R8W

This area has 5,164 acres. See Painted Rock Mountains, Maricopa Ref.: 9, p. 3

PAINT POTS

Mohave   T31N R23W

In 1946 the Bureau of Mines suggested this name for a highly colored and dissected slope on the shore of Lake Mead. Ref.: 329

PAIR O'DICE CIENEGA

Apache   T4N R27E   Elev. 7320'

According to USGS files, this location was named by an early rancher who in winter "played cards." It seems obvious that the writer of that notation was not a gambler. It was also the name of the ranch from which it is likely the Cienega (= "swampy place") took its name. Ref.: 329

PAJARITO   pro.: /pahariᴧto/
Spanish = "small bird"

Santa Cruz   Elev. c. 4800'

A post office here was established to serve the Pajarito Mining District in the center of Peña Blanca and Walker Canyon area. See Pajarito Mountains, Santa Cruz
P.O. est. Jan. 3, 1880, John M. McArthur, p.m.; disc. April 9, 1883
Ref.: 264; *Geology of Peña Blanca*, p. 1

PAJARITO MOUNTAINS   pro.: /pahariᴧto/
Spanish = "small bird"

Santa Cruz   T24S R12E   Elev. 5236'

On the Mexican side of the boundary this range is called Sierra de los Pajaritos, a name in use when the Boundary Survey Commission mapped this section in 1853. Maj. William H. Emory noted that the mountains were part of the Arizone (*sic*) Mountains. On the Gadsden Purchase map the name is Pajarito or Arizona Mountains. The former probably derives from a butte called Pajarito Peak (elev. 4490'), which resembles a bird sitting on the mountain. Cowmen called it Pajarito. When mining recommenced at the Oro Blanco Mine, these mountains were naturally referred to as the Oro Blanco Mountains and the peak as Oro Blanco Peak. They were also sometimes called the Bird Mountains. Because of their location, another name for them was Bear Valley Mountains. Ref.: 106, pp. 60, 120; Lenon; 242; 165, p. 317; 18a; 163, p. 225

PALACE STATION
Yavapai   T12N R1W   Elev. 5856'
The stage station at this location was at Spence Spring on the Senator Trail from Prescott to Phoenix. It was owned by the Spence family. One of the latest structures built by pioneer white men, this station was abandoned about 1910. This station was in a home built by A. B. Spence in 1874. The Forest Service still uses the original cabin. Ref.: Theobald; Willson; Varney

PALISADE CANYON
Pima   T12S R16E
This canyon used to be called Pine Canyon. The upper ridge of this canyon is now called Spencer Canyon. The name Palisade is borrowed from that of Palisade Rock in the canyon, where it heads. The canyon was unnamed in 1905. Ref.: 329

PALISADES
Yavapai
In the early 1870s this was a station on the Central Pacific R.R. in Humboldt Canyon. From here ores from the Eureka District were shipped. Ref.: *Citizen* (July 18, 1874), p. 4

PALISADES CREEK
Coconino (Grand Canyon)   T32N R6E
This location was officially named in 1932 because it rises on the canyon wall near the south end of The Palisades of the Desert.

PALISADES OF THE DESERT
Coconino (Grand Canyon)   T31N R5E   Elev. c. 5000'
In 1902 Francois E. Matthes proposed this name as being descriptive of the bold cliffs which rise "in rhythmically spaced recesses and alternating humps and hollows which ... produce a striking resemblance to a palisade." Ref.: Matthes, *Unpublished ms.*, p. 2; 329

PALMA, LA   pro.: /la palmə/
Spanish = "the palm"
Pinal   T6S R8E   Elev. 1469'
The town site for this location was laid out in 1927. Ref.: *Arizona Daily Star* (May 1, 1927), p. 6

PALM CANYON
Yuma   T1S R18W   Elev. 2120'
This small community has developed near Palm Canyon, Yuma (*q.v.*).

PALM CANYON
Yuma   T1S R18W   Elev. 2500'
This side gorge of a wide canyon contains palms native to Arizona. The canyon, a bare thirty feet wide, contains a rare species of fan palm known as *Washingtonia Arizonica*. The narrowness of the canyon helps store heat which promotes growth of these trees. The former name of this canyon was Fish Tail Canyon because of a fish-tail fork at the canyon head, or (according to Lenon) because Fish Tail is a nearby peak. There are also palms in Four Palms Canyon on the north side of Signal Peak. Another canyon called Old Palm Canyon lies south and east of Palm Canyon, and in it the palms are not at the sides, but at the bottom of the canyon. Ref.: Monson; 31, p. 60

PALMERLEE
Cochise   T23S R20E

When both the site and name of the Reef post office were changed, the new location took the name of its first postmaster. Palmerlee was in existence in August 1906, but a post office was not established until 1907. See also Reef, Cochise, and Garces, Cochise
P.O. est. Nov. 11, 1907, Joseph Stephen Palmerlee, p.m. Ref.: 242

PALO ALTO   pro.: /pǽlo ǽlto/
Spanish = "tall tree"
Pima   T17S R9E   Elev. c. 2500'
In 1907 a very tall mesquite stood before the house of the Palo Alto Ranch, hence the name. The ranch loaned its name to Palo Alto Valley.
P.O. est. April 22, 1925, Walter A. Jost, p.m.; disc. March 1, 1928 Ref.: 242; Willson

PALOMAS   pro.: /palómǝs/
Spanish = "doves"
Yuma   T6S R12W   Elev. c. 600'
This location was first called Doanville for John Doan, a pioneer. Whitewing doves abound here in the summer, hence the name Palomas, which is now applied to Palomas Valley (T16S/R13W). The town was founded by J. Fred Nottbusch. See also Nottbusch Butte, Yuma
P.O. est. as Doanville, Nov. 22, 1889, Frank S. Schultz, p.m.; name changed to Palomas, April 18, 1891; disc. Aug. 31, 1938 Ref.: 242; Johnson; 18a; 279, p. 216

PALOMINAS   pro.: /palomiynǝs/
Cochise   T23S R22E   Elev. 4137'
This small community was a supply town for nearby mines. Ref.: Larriau

PALO VERDE   pro.: /palo vérdi/ or /pǽlo vérdi/
Spanish: *palo* = "stick" or "tree"; *verde* = "green"
Maricopa   T1N R7W   Elev. 2172'
This location borrows its name from that of the Palo Verde Mine, La Paz (T2N/R8W). See also Palo Verde Mountains, Pinal

PALO VERDE MOUNTAINS   pro.: /palo vérdi/ or /pǽlo vérdi/
Pinal   T5S R2E   Elev. 2029'
Many palo verde trees are in these mountains. Palo verde bark and twigs remain green the year around, except on old trees which develop brownish scaling on portions of the trees.

PAMELA
Yavapai (near Prescott)   Elev. c. 6000'
The reason for the name and the exact location are unknown.
P.O. est. Nov. 28, 1881, Fernando Nellis, p.m.; disc. April 27, 1883 Ref.: 242

PANAMITO POINT
Coconino (Grand Canyon)   T34N R3W
This location on the South Rim was named by the USGS in February 1925 for a Havasupai Indian. Ref.: 329

PANAMITO TERRACE
Coconino (Grand Canyon)   Elev. c. 4000'
Named by the USGS in May 1932. See Panamito Point, Coconino (Grand Canyon)

PANOCHE CREEK   pro.: /panóčey/
Coconino (Utah?)   Location imprecise
This name appears on the Hartley map. The word *panoche* for Mexicans means "solid cake of brown sugar," made by boiling and solidifying cane juices. See Navajo Mountain, Coconino

PAN TAK   pro.: /bᴾan tak/
Papago: *pan tak* = "coyote sits"

Pima   T16S R8E   Elev. 3416'

The name Coyotes Spring was in use in 1864 for this location, and on GLO 1879 it is called Cajote Spring. Another name, which appears on the 1875 War Dept. ms. map, is Ojo de los Coyotes ("Coyotes Spring": *ojo* = "eye" or "spring"). Lumholtz applied the Papago name Pantak in 1912. Associated names include Pan Tak Mountains (a.k.a. Coyote Mountains *q.v.*), Pan Tak Pass (T17S/R8E) and Pan Tak Wash.
Ref.: 329; 256, p. 12; 56, pp. 284, 285

PAN TAK PASS
Pima   T17S R8E

This pass lies between the Quinlan and Coyote Mountains at the head of Pantak Wash. It has also been called Alisa Pass (1865 Hartley), Aliz Pass (1869 Pumpelly); and Aliso Pass (1867 Mallory and Ward). It occurs on the 1884 A.T. & S.F.R.R. map as Allison Pass (a corruption). All such names derive from the presence of Aliso Spring in the pass itself. See Pan Tak, Pima Ref.: 329; 256, p. 21; 157, p. 226

PANTANO   pro.: /pæntænow/
Spanish: *pantano* = "swamp or body of water at head of a valley"

Pima   T16S R17E   Elev. 3561'

With the coming of the railroad in the early 1880s, tracks across the old stage station at Cienega (*q.v.*) destroyed it. For the convenience of residents, a new station was established at Pantano about one and a half miles east of the vanished Cienega. It is probable that the name Pantano was applied because its meaning is close to that of *cienega*.
P.O. est. July 2, 1880, Lyman W. Wakefield, p.m.; disc. April 30, 1950; Wells Fargo 1885 Ref.: Kitt; Lenon; AHS, Castillo File

PANYA POINT
Coconino (Grand Canyon)   T32N R4W   Elev. c. 4200'

This point was named by the USGS in February 1925 for either a Havasupai or Huala-pai Indian family. Ref.: 329

PAPAGO
Maricopa   T4S R9W

This location, now merely a site on the railroad, was formerly an Indian community supported by Mormons.

PAPAGO CREEK
Coconino (Grand Canyon)   T31N R5E

This creek rises southwest of Papago Point, from which it borrows its name. It was named in May 1932. See also Papago Indian Reservation, Pima Ref.: 329

PAPAGO INDIAN RESERVATION   pro.: /pæpəgo/
Pima: *pa'pat* = "bad" or "ugly"; *o'otam* = "people"

Pima/Pinal   T12–17S R1–5 and 11,1617E   Elev. c. 2400 – 1100'

The name which this tribe bears is not what they call themselves. Each of several regional groups of Papagos has its own name. According to a Papago informant, the name used by English speaking people is that used by Pima Indians. Although the Papago Indians had been friendly with the Americans since the 1850s, their reservation was the last permanent one, authorized in 1916 with the establishment of agency headquarters at Sells. The reservation was a long time becoming an actuality, for land was first set aside for these Indians on July 1, 1874, at San Xavier. Thereafter, additional acreage was added to form the Gila Bend (*q.v.*)–Pinal section as well as rounding out other areas to form the present 2,774,536 acres of the reservation. It is the second largest in the United States. The last allotment was made on June 13, 1939.
Ref.: Van Valkenburgh, "Tom Childs of 10-Mile Wash," p. 5; 167, II, 200, 374; "Annual Report of the Arizona Commission of Indian Affairs, 1954, 1955, 1956," pp. 11, 12

PAPAGO MEADOWS

Pima   T15S R13E

In 1879 this was the name for the now-cleared fields immediately south of the Mission of San Xavier. At that time it was covered with a thick forest of mesquite, some trees being two or three feet in diameter. Ref.: 277, p. 33

PAPAGO MOUNTAIN

Pima   T17S R10W   Elev. 2120'

This mountain borrows its name from that of the Papago Mine (T17S/R10W). See Papago Indian Reservation, Pima/Pinal

PAPAGO POINT   pro.: /pǽpǝgo/

Coconino   T31N R5E   Elev. c. 7000'

This location was named for the Papago Indians of southern Arizona and northern Sonora. It was named in July 1906. See Papago Indian Reservation, Pima/Pinal

PAPAGO (STATE) PARK

Maricopa   T1N R4E   Elev. 1450'

On April 13, 1892 Charles Debrille Poston filed a homestead for what he called Hole-in-the-Rock. The name comes from a large hole in the red rock hill which is now the site of a 2050 acre recreational and picnic area set aside in 1914 as the original national monument. On March 15, 1915 this park was created under the name Papago Saguaro National Monument, the name being suggested by O. A. Turney. The national monument cited was recalled on August 7, 1930. The presence of a State Rifle Range of 320 acres on the north has created the associated name of Phoenix Military Reservation. Because the location of the park is adjacent to the community of Tempe, it has also been called Tempe Park. In 1957 the large original area was divided into three units which include Papago State Park, Tempe Park, and Phoenix Military Reservation. Ref.: 329; 18a; Theobald; 133

PAPAGO VILLAGES

Maricopa

A series of Papago villages or rancherias existed in the flood plain of the Gila River below Gila Bend. They included Pelon, Pesota, Unpatoitak, and Siilimok. In 1699 Fr. Kino visited perhaps two villages, which he called San Felipe y Santiago del Oyadoibuise, and in 1700 he visited El Tutto west of that community. Ref.: 57, p. 400

PAPAGO WASH

Yuma   T15S R10W

This location derived its name from the presence of Papago Well just over the line in Pima County. See Papago Indian Reservation, Pima/Pinal

PAPAGUERIA

This is the name the Spanish gave on their maps to the region occupied by the Papago Indians. Pumpelly spelled it Papaqueria. See Papago Indian Reservation, Pima/Pinal Ref.: 369, p. 227

PAPALOTE WASH   pro.: /papalótey/

Spanish = "windmill"

Pima   T21S R11E   Elev. c. 3500'

This wash takes its name from being located on the Papalote Ranch, named for its windmill. Ref.: Seibold; 57, p. 379

PARADISE

Cochise   T17S R31E   Elev. 5500'

When one of the Reed daughters (see Cave Creek, Cochise) married George A. Walker, the young couple moved to an isolated place which they named Paradise because of their happiness. In 1901 the Chiricahua Development Company found ore here. Paradise was no longer in isolation, being replaced by a town which was a paradise for roisterers. It is now a ghost town.

P.O. est. Nov. 26, 1900, George A. Walker, p.m.; disc. Sept. 30, 1943

Ref.: Riggs; *Arizona Daily Star*, "Bad Men March through Arizona's History" (March 27, 1932); 242

PARADISE VALLEY

Maricopa   T4N R4E   Elev. c. 1350'

When Frank Conkey in 1899 was managing the Rio Verde Canal Company, the project promoters first saw this valley while it was covered with spring flowers and palo verde in bloom, hence the name. The name now applies to the town in the valley. Ref.: 18a

PARADISE VALLEY

Yuma   T3S R24W   Elev. c. 600'

This valley was named because a Mr. Bertkin, a pioneer, built a pumping plant here and dreamed of a ranch on the Colorado River which would be a true paradise. His dreams failed to develop into fact. Ref.: *Blythe Chamber of Commerce Cruise Bulletin* (Oct. 10, 1954)

PARALLEL CANYON

Gila   T10N R15E

This canyon runs parallel to Cherry Creek, hence its name. Ref.: Devore

PARASHANT CANYON

Mohave (Grand Canyon)   T32N R10W   Elev. c. 4500'

This location takes its name from the Piute name for a spring at the head of Parashant Wash, which becomes Parashant Canyon at Poverty Mountain. It was named about 1900. A local name for it is Mule Canyon.

PARASHANT WASH

Mohave (Grand Canyon)   T34N R12W

Another name for it is West Fork. See Parashant Canyon, Mohave (Grand Canyon), and Salt House Draw, Mohave Ref.: 329

PARIA RIVER   pro.: /payriyə/

Piute: *pah* = "water"; *rea* = "elk"

Coconino (Grand Canyon)/Utah   T41N R5E   Elev. c. 4500'

Fr. Escalante called this stream the Rio Santa Teresa. According to his diary, A. H. Thompson named this river, spelling it Pahreah. Before the coming of white men the Paria Valley supported herds of elk which, however, had almost disappeared by the mid-1850s. In 1872 Capt. George M. Wheeler noted that a "rude wagon-road" led to the mouth of this river. It was the Mormon Road (see Jacob Lake). The earlier spelling of Pahreah was eliminated in favor of Paria by the USGS in 1932.

Ref.: Jensen; *Utah Historical Quarterly*, p. 9; 122, p. 39; 345 ..., I, 54, 55; 140, p. 37

PARISSAWAMPITTS SPRING

Piute: *parush* = "flowing water"

Coconino   T35N R1E   Elev. c. 7000'

According to Dutton (1882), this location was called Parusi-wompats. He also notes that the last part of the word appears to have no meaning, but probably is associated with Indian mythology. Ref.: 100, p. 157

PARK, THE

Coconino   T14N R10E

In 1873 Capt. George M. Wheeler described the open areas which are frequently called "park" in the southwest: "We ... reached a most beautiful open park ... a rolling, natural park-like country, more beautiful than any artificial or cultivated park could be, and the most attractive landscape ever encountered by me ... the march was continued a little more than five miles to a prominence named Park Butte, it being surrounded by the most beautiful natural parks." Ref.: 322; 395, I, 65

PARKER

La Paz   T2N R19W   Elev. 420'

The establishment of the Colorado River Indian Agency (see Colorado River Indian Reservation) created the necessity for a post office. The name for it was selected to honor Gen. Eli Parker, then Commissioner of Indian Affairs (1871). The location is not identical with that for the town of Parker, not in existence until several years after the establishment of the original Parker. (See Parker [Town], Yuma)

P.O. est. Jan. 6, 1871, John H. Salt, p.m. Ref.: *Weekly Arizona Miner* (April 29, 1871), p. 1; *Arizona Sentinel* (Nov. 8, 1873), p. 3; 335, p. 294; 242

PARKER (TOWN)

La Paz   T9N R20W   Elev. 420'

A.T. & S.F.R.R. laid its rails through this area in 1903 and the old Parker post office was removed. Curiously, the locating engineer was Earl H. Parker. According to a newspaper account, the first stake for the new town was driven on June 6, 1906, by James Haddock, Otis E. Young, and C. W. McKee. Earl Parker reported that William A. Drake, General Superintendent and Chief Engineer for the railroad, said that the town had a double reason for being named Parker — after Parker himself and after the older Indian town called Parker. Both are in Parker Valley. In Nov. 1982 voters created La Paz County, of which Parker became the county seat.

P.O. est. Oct. 10, 1903; Louis W. Sinclair, p.m.; Wells Fargo 1908
Ref.: 242; 18a; *Arizona Star* (Jan. 13, 1909), p. 3

PARKER CANYON

Cochise/Santa Cruz   T23S R19E   Elev. 5525'

While making his way to California during the gold rush, William Parker (b. Aug. 9, 1824, Tennessee; d. 1923) and his party lost the main road and as a result Parker first saw the place where he would later return to settle — Parker Canyon. He was successful in California, returned to Missouri for his family and c. 1870 took them to Phoenix. In 1881 the family moved to Parker Canyon to avoid the "congestion" in Phoenix. Parker is buried in the canyon carrying his name. The name now also applies to Parker Canyon Lake and to Parker Canyon Wild Life Area (Santa Cruz).

P.O. est. as Parker Canzon, Feb. 8, 1912, Louis K. McIntyre, p.m.; name changed to Parker Canyon, Jan. 1, 1928; disc. Jan. 18, 1929
Ref.: Mrs. Emily Parker Gray (granddaughter), Letter (March 18, 1956); 242; 9, p. 4

PARKER CANYON CREEK

Santa Cruz   T24S R18E

According to post office records, the post office in 1912 was on Parker Canyon Creek. See Parker Canyon, Cochise/Santa Cruz Ref.: 242

PARKER DAM

La Paz   T11N R18W   Elev. c. 450'

This dam, which is three hundred and twenty feet high and eight hundred and fifty-six feet long, is a desilting basin for the Colorado River Aquaduct and also aids in flood control. It is at the confluence of the Colorado River with Bill Williams River. Construction began on July 29, 1927, and was completed September 1, 1938. Power began being generated on December 13, 1942, with the United States paying for half of the power plant. Workmen excavated two hundred and thirty-five feet for the concrete foundation but only eighty-five feet of the dam lies above the Colorado River bed. Above this foundation is a superstructure of sixty-three feet with a roadway across the top. Havasu Lake backs up behind the dam for forty-five miles. It takes its name from that of the community of Parker seventeen miles down river. Ref.: "Parker Dam and Power Plant" (Jan. 1, 1954), Bulletin (Boulder City, Nevada)

PARKER PEAK

Pinal   T3S R13E   Elev. c. 3500'

This peak, also called Parker's Peak, was probably named for Tom Parker, a prospector with claims in this area. The name appears on a ms. map of White Mountain Indian Reservation (April 27, 1876). Ref.: 242; 18a

PARKS

Coconino   T22N R4E   Elev. 7000'

This location has borne several names, the first being Rhoades, which name was suggested to the Post Office Department for the location in 1898. According to Mr. Sykes, who had a sawmill at Rhoades, a box car was used as a depot. It should be noted that the sawmill post office application at the National Archives shows the name Rhoades crossed off and the name "Maine" written in red and that the date of application is March 28, 1898, something over a month after the sinking of the *U.S.S Maine* on February 15, 1898. It seems fairly clear that locally the word did not get through, for mail was still being handled at the sawmill and not at the box-car depot. When a railroad depot replaced the box-car office, the name *Maine* was attached to it. shortly after the sinking of the *U.S.S. Maine*.

In 1907 the name of the post office of Rhoades was finally changed officially to Maine and the sawmill mail ostensibly was distributed at the depot post office. Still another slow change was to occur because Post Office Department employees had difficulty, then as now, keeping things straight and there was another station named Maine. That necessitated changing the name of Maine, Arizona, to Parks, Arizona. The original Rhoades was discontinued on June 11, 1910, which simplified the change. It remains Parks. There is no evidence from the post office site locations at the National Archives that there was ever a shift in location. However the "original" location in 1955 was being called Old Maine.

A store was also built at the location a few years later. When a school district developed, it took on the name *Maine*, and was still called the Maine Consolidated School in 1955, although in that year only two teachers were employed. When the highway was shifted, a new store was built by people named Parks and locally their name came to be applied to the post office and entire location of the community.

P.O. est. as Rhoades, March 28, 1898, William S. Bliss, p.m. (Post Office Department crossed out name and wrote in "Maine"). Name changed to Maine, Oct. 3, 1907, John T. Dennis, p.m.; disc. June 11, 1910; reest. (same location) July 23, 1914 (name submitted as Maine). P.O. Dept. crossed it out and inserted Parks, James W. Evans, p.m. Ref.: 242; Sykes; Best; 18a; Benham

PARKS LAKE

Graham   T10S R30E

This place is named for Jim B. Parks. It used to be called Whitlock Sink or Cienega (1864). The lake covers three hundred and twenty acres and serves as a water fowl habitat. It includes the Parks Lake Water Fowl Area. Ref.: Jennings; 9, p. 5

PARSONS PEAK

Graham   T8S R30E   Elev. c. 6000'

In 1871 Alexander Graves, a minister (parson), established a small dairy ranch in Parson Canyon, and both the peak and canyon derives their name from that fact. Ref.: 18a

PARTRIDGE CITY

Yavapai   T10N R5W   Elev. c. 4000'

William Partridge (b. 1825, England; d. Sept. 12, 1899) had a store and stage station at Antelope, which he called Partridge City. Partridge arrived in Arizona in 1864 and was a miner in 1870. He built his stage station in 1877. In the fall of that year Partridge was feuding with G. H. Wilson (see Antelope Peak and Antelope Valley, Yavapai) and was sent to Yuma prison. He was pardoned in 1880 and returned to Stanton. Ref.: 62; AHS, William Partridge File

PARTRIDGE CREEK

Coconino/Yavapai   T20N R3W   Elev. c. 5000'

On April 21, 1857 Lt. Joseph Christmas Ives made camp in what he called Partridge Ravine, but as he places Mount Floyd south of this location, it may not be the same as that named by Lt. Amiel W. Whipple (1854) on his map. In his diary, Möllhausen, a member of the Ives expedition, noted that many partridges lived along the creek. Whipple also noted great numbers of partridges. Ref.: 335, pp. 31, 33; 344, p. 35; 347, pp. 181, Note 25, and 185, Note 2; 348, p. 88

PASADERA HILL pro.: /pazədéyrə/
Spanish = "stepping stone"
Gila   T2S R15E
This name was suggested by F. L. Ransome in June 1911, because of "three small rocky points on the crest of the mountain" which resemble stepping stones.

PASCUA VILLAGE pro.: /páskwə/
Spanish: *Pascua* = "Easter"
Pima   Elev. 2400'
The Yaqui villages in the United States and elsewhere are noted for their religious festivals, particularly those at Easter. This largest Yaqui Indian village in Arizona used to be (and a portion still was in 1979) south of West Grant Road near the Freeway, but because of pressure to give over their land there, many of these Indians moved to an area south of Tucson near San Xavier Mission. Both locations carry the same name. The Yaqui Indians, whose native home is on the Yaqui River in Sonora, Mexico, came to Arizona to escape being sent into exile by the Mexican government. That government wished to move them from their native home to tropical regions in central Mexico. The Yaqui Indians arrived in the late 1890s and early 1900s and do not have reservation land.
Ref.: 5, pp. 297, 298

PASTIME PARK
Pima   T13S R19E
In 1929 this was the name of a railroad stop on the outskirts of Tucson. It has now been absorbed by the city. The location was a tent camp for veterans with respiratory problems. See Greenway, Pima Ref.: 242

PASTORA PEAK pro.: /pæstorə/
Apache   T39N R30E   Elev. 9412'
This name is sometimes spelled Pasture, probably because in 1875 W. H. Holmes used its good pasturage. Ref.: 18a

PASTURE CANYON
Coconino   T38N R3E
Good pasturage exists here. In August 1964 the USGS changed it to this name from Hagatagvitch Canyon, in turn changed to Pasture Wash in 1908. The name also applies to Pasture Canyon Lake (T32N/R11E). Ref.: 329

PATAGONIA pro.: /pætəgowninə/
Spanish: *patagon* = "big paw"
Santa Cruz   T22S R16E   Elev. 4057'
Bob Lenon conjectures that Emory of the Boundary Survey in 1855 reported killing a grizzly bear near Nogales and that seeing its huge paw print may have led to the name Patagonia. This location is not to be confused with that of the Mowry Mine and its Patagonia post office in 1866. Contemporary Patagonia is connected with the history of Crittenden (*q.v.*). A review of its history is necessary to understand the history of Patagonia. Rollen Richardson (b. July 10, 1846, Shippenville, Pennsylvania; d. February 6, 1923) in 1883 bought the Monkey Springs Ranch as well as squatters' rights at old Crittenden (on the railroad) and called the entire area Pennsylvania Ranch. In 1890 with his partners L. V. Gormley and Alex Harrison, he was running twelve thousand cattle, but a three-year drought forced them out of business. He sold in 1901 to Vail, Gates, and Ashburn, but reserved five hundred acres of land where Patagonia now is. In 1896 he had decided to move the community at Crittenden to the then-marshy area of Patagonia and proposed calling his new town Rollentown or Rollen after himself. The residents, who had no choice about moving, balked at the name and chose Patagonia after the name of the nearby mountain. As they had to sign the post office petition, Patagonia it was whether Richardson like it or not. See also Mowry Mine, Santa Cruz P.O. est. Dec. 15, 1899, Mrs. Mamie A. Chalpin, p.m.; Wells Fargo 1903; incorporated 1948 Ref.: 242; AHS, Rollen Richardson File; Lenon; *Tucson Citizen* (Nov. 11, 1896), p. 1

PATAGONIA LAKE

Santa Cruz   T22S R15E

E. H. Blue donated one hundred and ninety acres of his Sonoita Creek Ranch and in 1967 a dam was begun to impound waters of Sonoita Creek. It was completed in 1968 and Patagonia Lake opened on September 3, 1970. It is named after nearby Patagonia Mountain. Ref.: AHS, Lakes File

PAT CREEK

Greenlee   T2S R30E   Elev. c. 4000'

Pat Slaughter settled on this creek c. 1895, hence the name, which also applies to Pat Mesa and to Pat Mountain. Ref.: Shannon

PAT HILLS

Cochise   T16S R27E   Elev. 5007'

In 1878 Pat Burns (or Bierne) located at Pat Burns Cienega, a small spring, where he ran cattle for several years before moving on to Colorado. Ref.: 18a

PATIO   pro.: /pátio/

Yuma   Elev. c. 250'

The Spanish name *Patio* was given to the railroad yard at 4th and Madison Avenue in Yuma because the name was considered more euphonius than "yard." Railroad engineers also signed their log, "arrived Patio at such and such an hour," thus never actually officially arriving in Yuma. Ref.: Lenon

PAT KNOLLS

Apache   T7N R29E   Elev. 9651'

Pat Trainor ran cattle on these smooth hills in the 1880s. Whether the cattle were his or not is not known, but he was tried thirteen times for rustling — never convicted. Ref.: Becker

PAT MULLEN MOUNTAIN

Navajo   T9N R23E   Elev. 7612'

Pat Mullen was a pioneer stockman before 1900 at this place, hence the name. Pat Mullen Peak and Spring are here. Ref.: 18a

PATTIE BUTTE

Coconino (Grand Canyon)   T31N R3E   Elev. 5306'

Sylvester Pattie and his son James Ohio Pattie trapped beaver along the Gila River in 1825. They were the first American citizens to visit the Grand Canyon. The USGS named this butte in 1932. Ref.: 329

PAULDEN

Yavapai   T17N R2W   Elev. 4407'

Paul Pownall (son of the first postmaster here) according to Barnes was accidentally killed and his father named the post office for the boy. The application for a post office on file in the National Archives bears the name Spring Valley, not accepted by the Post Office Department. In 1926 the name was changed to Paulden from Midway Grocery. P.O. est. as Midway Grocery, April 21, 1925, Orville Titus Pownall, p.m.; name changed to Paulden, 1929 Ref.: 18a; 242

PAUL SPUR

Cochise   T24S R26E   Elev. 4220'

A lime plant and small community are at this place on the railroad, which also has a section house. It was named for Alfred Paul, Sr. (b. 1878, Germany). Paul arrived in Arizona in 1885 and helped lay out the site for Douglas. Because the Calumet and Arizona Mining Company there was using floatation to extract copper, Paul established a lime kiln at this location as lime was needed to neutralize acid in the ore. P.O. est. July 24, 1930, Bert Whitehead, p.m.; disc. May 2, 1958 Ref.: *Douglas Dispatch*, "50th Anniversary Edition" (1952), section 9, p. 2; 224, III

PAVO KUG WASH

Papago = "rock stands"

Pima   T16S R16E   Elev. c. 1800'

The wash takes its name from that of a nearby Papago village.
Ref.: 262, pp. 12, 27

PAYA POINT

Coconino (Grand Canyon)   T34N R3W   Elev. 5990'

This point was named for Lemuel Paya, a Supai Indian. Ref.: 329

PAYMASTER WASH

Graham   T3S R24E

This short wash or canyon has borne its name since about 1880. It was named for a
camping site on the route used by the paymaster coming from Fort Thomas to the San
Carlos Indian Reservation. Ref.: 329

PAYROLL GULCH

Mohave   T23N R18W   Elev. 5200'

This gulch was named for the Payroll Mine, in operation in 1906. The mine, located in
1867 by J. W. Murphy, was near the head of the gulch. Ref.: 200, p. 62

PAYSON

Gila   T10N R10E   Elev. 4887'

In 1882 Payson was founded as Union Park. Locally it was called Green Valley. John
and Frank C. Hise began a store in the little settlement. Their father visited them from
Chicago and then wrote to Senator Louis Edward Payson, Chairman of the Congressional Committee on Post Offices, to help establish a post office. The post office was
named for the senator.
P.O. est. March 3, 1884, Frank C. Hise, p.m. Ref.: 329; 5, p. 453

PAZ, CAMP LA

La Paz

A single company of soldiers was detached for duty at this location in January 1869. By
January 1874 this was recognized as a new military station with a notation that Camp
Beale Springs was no longer being used by the military. There may be an error in the
statement, inasmuch as the dates given by Hammersley for the existence of this military
camp are 1868 – 1871. Called Camp Lincoln, it served as a Fort Yuma Sub-post.
According to one source, Camp Lincoln was in existence in 1864.
Ref.: *Weekly Arizona Miner* (Jan. 9, 1869), p. 1, and (Jan. 22, 1875), p. 2; 224, p. 152;
159, p. 516

PAZ, LA   pro.: /la páz/

Spanish = "peace"

La Paz   T4N R21W   Elev. c. 500'

Pauline Weaver with a party of prospectors found gold in the Arroyo de la Tenaja on
January 12, 1862. It was the day of the Feast of Our Lady of Peace, and the name was
changed to La Paz. A boom mining town quickly developed with over five thousand
residents. In 1862 La Paz became the seat of Yuma County, but lost that honor in 1870
when the county records went down the Colorado River aboard the steamer *Nina Tilden*
to Arizona City (see Yuma, Yuma). The end was more than already in sight for La Paz,
however, for in 1869 the Colorado River changed its course and left La Paz high and dry.
By 1872 the community was fast on its way to becoming a ghost town. It has completely
disappeared.
P.O. est. Jan. 17, 1865, Charles A. Phillips, p.m.; disc. March 25, 1875; Wells Fargo
1870   Ref.: 168, p. 63; 107, I, 297; 206, p. 333; 224, p. 106; PrestonMercer, "Desert
Scrapbook," *Yuma Daily Sun* (April 12, 1954), p. 11; AHS, Figueroa *ms.; Weekly
Arizona Miner* (April 6, 1872), p. 2; 163, pp. 250, 251

P BAR LAKE

Greenlee   T3N R30E

This lake is named for the P Bar Ranch (Yavapai).

P B CREEK

Gila   T7N R14E

This creek takes its name from the brand of the P B Ranch owned by Alec Pendleton and his brother in the 1880s and early 1890s. (P B = Pendleton brothers). Ref.: McKinney

PEACH FLAT

Gila   T6N R15E   Elev. 5501'

According to an informant on the White River Apache Reservation, this location was named for an Apache scout who had peach-colored cheeks. However, another informant says that there was a peach orchard about ten miles on the trail below the home ranch. Ref.: Dale; Blumer; 49, p. 453

PEACH ORCHARD

Pinal   T1S R12E   Elev. 1877'

A miner planted several peach trees where he had a mining camp consisting of a few rock houses, hence the name. In the early fall of 1875 it was called Peachville. Actually, according to Mrs. Ann Forbach, Mr. Forbach "planted the peach seeds one time as he came to Sacaton from Illinois some time near 1870." Ref.: 163, p. xlvii; *Weekly Arizona Miner* (Sept. 3, 1875), p. 2; Mrs. Anne Forbach, Letter (Nov. 30, 1973)

PEACH ORCHARD SPRING

Gila   T10N R10E   Elev. 4800'

This is a developed spring just southwest of Payson. Guy Barkdoll in the 1920s had enterprises in Payson and until 1936 this spring was known by his name. However, the name Peach Orchard became attached to it because a peach orchard existed here at one time. Ref.: Woody; 329

PEACH SPRINGS

Mohave   T25N R11W   Elev. 4791'

Apparently the first foreigner to visit this location was Fr. Garcés, who on June 15, 1775 called it Pozos de San Basilio ("Saint Basil's Wells"). The next white visitor was Lt. Edward Fitzgerald Beale. On September 17, 1858 he stopped at what he called Indian Spring encampment. Beale also refers to Hemphell's Spring. The coordinates he cites (35°22'18"/113°16'57") are approximately at T23N/R10W, which suggests that it may be in actuality Peach Springs (T25N/R11W). In 1859 Floyd in his *Diary* (April 23) spells the name Hemphel and also Hemple. In the same year the Udell party camped here at what it called Hemphill Camping Ground. None of the visitors mentions peach trees.

In 1930 it was reported that there were three springs or groups of springs in Peach Springs Canyon, but all were unusable because they were filled in. Hualapai Indians formerly watered stock at the upper group. The central springs supplied water for railroad steam engines. Indians, who called these springs Pabroach, sued the railroad for using water belonging to the Hualapai tribe (see Crozier, Mohave). A community developed at the railroad depot where in 1883 ten saloons supplied abundant liquids so that one person said, "If a man can live on suction or drink, he can get fat...." but solids were scarce.

P.O. est. July 12, 1887, Jacob Cohenour, p.m.; Wells Fargo 1885

Ref.: 335, pp. 8, 9, 235, 8, Note 12; 5, pp. 322, 323; 325, pp. 53, 72; 163, p. xlvii, xlvi; Floyd, *Diary* (Huntington Library); 23, p. 78; 358, p. 52

PEACOCK SPRING

Mohave   T22N R14W   Elev. c. 4500'

March 31, 1857 was an extremely hot day and the mules being used by Lt. Joseph Christmas Ives, which had not had sufficient water for four days, were in great distress. G. H. Peacock, in charge of the mule train, "was riding in advance, discovered a large spring of clear, sweet water in a ravine ... There were no signs of the place having been used as a camp and even Ireteba did not appear to have known previously of its existence." The spring is named for its discoverer as are other nearby locations. The location of Peacock Spring on GLO 1869 is identical with the location of Truxton Spring on GLO 1883. Ref.: 335, p. 18; 245, p. 6

PEARCE

Cochise   T17S R25E   Elev. 4420'
John and William Pearce arrived with their father James in Tombstone in the early 1880s. Their father and mother were employed respectively as a miner and a boarding housekeeper. The two sons later began a ranch in the Sulphur Springs Valley. While riding the range, James Pearce was resting on top of Six Mile Hill and discovered rich gold ore in 1894. His Commonwealth Mine in the next eight years produced $30,000,000. in gold ore. In 1904 a cave-in shut down the mine, but in 1905 the construction of a cyanide plant to recover gold from the tailings put the place back into operation. Pearce sold his interest in the mine to a syndicate for about $250,000. At the time when the town of Pearce was developing, George H. Fitts (b. 1856, Massachusetts) established an addition, just west of the location, which was called Fittsburg, the first name suggested for the post office on the post office application. The location today is inactive.
P.O. est. March 6, 1896, Thomas Chattam, p.m.; Wells Fargo 1885
Ref.: 242; 63; AHS Clipping File, James Pearce; 18a; 5, pp. 440, 441

PEARCE FERRY

Mohave   T32N R16W   Elev. c. 1200'
In December 1876 Harrison Pearce (b. 1818) was sent by the Mormon church to operate a ferry at a crossing Jacob Hamblin located in March 1862. The place was then called Colorado Crossing. Although many maps give the name as Pierce, it is a misspelling. Pearce and his son James erected a stone building known as Fort Pearce, used by Mormons in defense against Shivwits and Uinkarets Indians. To that fact can be attributed the name Fort Pearce Wash (T41N/R10W). The ferry location many years ago disappeared under the waters of Lake Mead. Ref.: P. T. Reilly, Letter (March 23, 1969); 225, p. 96; 88, p. 191; Babcock

PEARCE MOUNTAIN

Apache   T9N R25E   Elev. c. 8000'
James Pearce, son of Harrison Pearce, who established Pearce Ferry in Mohave County, was the first Mormon settler at nearby Taylor. The spelling Pierce for this mountain is an error. Ref.: 329

PEARLY CREEK

Gila   T12N R11E
This location was named for Pearl Ellison, the oldest son of Jessie Ellison, a pioneer. The spelling of Pearly is incorrect.   Ref.: McKinney

PEA SOUP CREEK

Apache   T6N R26E
This location takes its name from the nickname of "Pea Soup" Larzelere (d. April 1937), a Frenchman who married a White River Apache and settled at this location. He had served at Fort Apache as a sergeant and remained upon his retirement from service. Ref.: Davis

PECK CANYON

Pima/Santa Cruz   T22S R11E   Elev. 3760'
Prior to 1886 this canyon was called Agua Fria Canyon. In this canyon A. L. Peck lived with his wife and children. The name of the canyon changed abruptly on April 27, 1886, when Apaches killed Peck's wife and baby and took a second child (a niece) captive. Peck, who was out on the range, was also captured. He was turned loose when he acted as though insane. The child was later recovered and Peck immediately left the area with it. The next resident was a Polish miner, Joseph Piskorski. A corruption based on Piskorski's being Polish led to the name Polaco, sometimes spelled erroneously Palaco. As Piskorski Canyon was also used, the whole matter was very confusing, but was resolved when the USGS officially on June 24, 1930 selected the name Peck. Peck Pass is at the head of the canyon. Ref.: Lenon; Kitt; 329

PECK MINE

Yavapai   T10N R1E   Elev. c. 3500'

Edmund George Peck (b. Dec. 28, 1830, Canada; d. Dec. 13, 1910) arrived in Arizona in 1863 and served as a scout and guide for troops at Fort Whipple. After retiring from the army, he was shown silver ore and immediately recognized having seen something similar. In company with T. M. Alexander, C. O. Bean, and William Cole, he located several claims in the Bradshaw Mountains and called the major one Peck Mine. Fish says that the first three men were prospecting while Peck hunted and he found a very heavy rock which proved out to be silver ore. In any event, by 1875 the Peck Mine was the most important in Arizona Territory and in the next three years it produced $1,200,000. in silver. A lawsuit instituted in 1878 dragged on and Peck died in poverty. From 1879 to 1910 he prospected unsuccessfully· in the vicinity of the mine.
Ref.: 107, II, 263, 264; 116, p. 539; 146, p. 58; 62

PECK'S LAKE

Yavapai   T16N R3E   Elev. 3332'

This lake may have been named for Edmund George Peck. (See Peck Mine, Yavapai.) The Yavapai name is *Hatalacva* = ("crooked water") because of the shape of the lake. According to an unidentified clipping at the Sharlot Hall Museum, this lake was formed when workmen removed hundreds of tons of earth to turn the Verde River from its natural channel. Ref.: 18a; Peck (no relation), Tuzigoot National Museum; Sharlot Hall Museum

PEDRICKS

Yuma   30 mi. down river from Yuma

John Pedricks (b. 1799) maintained a wood supply station for steamers on the Colorado River at this location. He sold out to Capt. Merrill, California Volunteers, in 1868.
Ref.: 62; Huntington Library, Johnson, "History of the Territory of Arizona," p. 1-E

PEDRO, SAN   pro.: /san peydro/ or /sæn pédrow/

Cochise   T19S R22E   Elev. c. 2500'

This location on the transcontinental railroad came into existence in 1879 when it was staked out on the right of way of the S.P.R.R. Ref.: *Arizona Star* (Nov. 7, 1879); AHS

PEDRO, SAN

Pima   T15S R8E   Elev. 2686'

The Papago name for this place is Viopuli (= "wild tobacco"; pro. /wiyowpʌl/), a variety of tobacco growing here. In 1912 Lumhoz called the village San Pedro, a name preferred by the USGS. Viopuli Wash (T14S/R8E) shares the name. Ref.: 58; 262, p. 12

PEDRO PRESIDIO, SAN

This military fortification in 1869 is mapped six miles south of the mouth of Babocomari Creek and in 1879 at the mouth of Bronco (*sic*) Creek on the San Pedro River. By the latter date it was in total ruins. It was first garrisoned c. 1835 to take action against Apache marauding. In 1856 Gray had noticed the ruins of the hacienda at this location, saying that the old ranches destroyed by the Apaches had been among the wealthiest in horses, cattle, sheep, etc. The hacienda and presidio were said to have been at the center of a large land grant ceded to Simon Elias. According to Barnes, Fitz Jefferson later established a ranch on this site. Ref.: *Arizona Star* (Nov. 7, 1878), p. 3; 138, p. 51; 18a

PEDRO RIVER, SAN   pro.: /san peydro/ or sænpédrow/

Pinal	T6S R16E	Elev. 4500 – 2000'
Cochise	T23S R22E	
Pima	T11S R18E	
Gila	T5S R15E	

Coues believes that this river is the same as that called the Rio Nexpa by the 1540 Coronado Expedition. Fr. Eusebio Kino in September 1692 clearly records the name as Rio de San Joseph de Terrenate. In Sonora, Mexico, the river flowed by the Terrenate Ranch. The river was also called de Quiburi. He also referred to it as Rio Santa Cruz, reflecting the name of the military unit stationed at Quiburi. In 1763, because Sobaipuri Indians lived along its banks, the river was called Sobahipuris (*sic*). The earliest date noted for naming it "Rio SN Pedro" was found on a map dated 1805. The name, however, was not known to Lt. Col. Phillip St. George Cooke, who in 1846 called it the Jose Pedro River. It should also be noted that in 1853 the Boundary Survey cartographer marked a place called Casas de San Jose just south of the international border then being surveyed. The same man noted mountains — Sierra de San Jose [Jose Pedro?] — nearby, a name found also on an undated 5th Military District Map. That portion of the river in Mexico is dubbed by the survey cartographer Rio Terrenate, whereas the same river north of the border is called Rio San Pedro. An oddity is the fact that three years earlier (1850), Col. Graham used the name Rio Puerco (Spanish = "dirty river"). Additionally, the Smith map (1879) notes a Mexican village called El Terrente and a San Pedro Presidio on the Arizona part of the river. Ref.: 43, I, 23, and II, 248; 46, p. 447; 142, pp. 13, 14; 77, p. 482, Note 29

PEELEY, MOUNT
Gila   T8N R8E   Elev. 7030'
This location was named by David Gowan, who was living nearby on Deer Creek in 1906 when Pele erupted in Hawaii. Ref.: 329

PEEPLES RANCH
Yavapai   T11N R4W   Elev. 4500'
Abraham Harlow Peeples (b. June 4, 1822, North Carolina; d. Jan. 29, 1892) arrived at Yuma in 1863 and with Pauline Weaver as guide, organized a prospecting expedition. (See Rich Hill, Yavapai) In 1865 he established a ranch in the valley bearing his name, but in 1870 moved to Wickenburg where he became a saloon keeper. Charles C. Genung bought his ranch and established a post office there. The spelling *People's* is incorrect.
P.O. est. Oct. 18, 1875, Charles C. Genung, p.m. Ref.: 5, p. 290; AHS Names File; *Arizona Miner* (June 10, 1871), p. 3

PEDRO SPRING, SAN
Cochise
This is the same as the location of San Pedro on GLO 1879. It is on the east bank of the San Pedro River southeast of the older San Pedro (Ohnesorgen). The springs were named by Gray in 1851. Ref.: 138 p. 50

PEDRO VALLEY, SAN
Cochise   T15S R20E   Elev. c. 3500'
This location was called Playa de los Pimas by Gray in 1851. In 1771 on a map by Nicola Delafora it was called Valle de los Sobaipurio, no doubt because it was the tribal home for the Sobaipuro Indians. The first settlers in this valley were Mexicans who had several fine large ranches, among them the one discussed under Pedro Presidio, San, Cochise. By 1874 Apaches had driven out all settlers and only the ruins of former ranches and settlements existed. However, this long and fertile valley (125 mi. long by 20 wide) began to be resettled in 1877. It takes its name from that of the river which runs through it. See Pedro River, San, Cochise Ref.: 238, p. 23; 138, p. 48

PEEPSTEM CANYON
Graham   T8S R19E
The name "Peepstem" is as used by ranch hands in the area. Ref.: 329

PELONCILLO, EL   pro.: /pelǝnsiyo/ Spanish = "little baldies"
Cochise   T1S R32E   Elev. 6401'
Greenlee   T10S R31E   Elev. 6571'
Graham   T7S R29E   Elev. 6211'
These three peaks, also called Sugar Loaf, are indeed little baldies. On the Parke map of 1851 they are called Black Mountains. These mountains are called the Peloncillo on the Boundary Survey map of 1854. The spelling may have been an error for Piloncillo (Spanish: *pilon* = "big pile," as in raw sugar canes, but *pelo* = "hair," or in vernacular, = "bald"). Ref.: Scott; 20, I, 363, 364, 367; 4, 152; Lenon

PEMBROKE

Yuma　　　　　　　　　　　　T8S R16W　　　　　　　　Elev. c. 500'

This railroad siding was in existence in 1911. In 1919 the S.P.R.R. dug a well to supply water for its steam engines here. Why it is so called is not known. Ref.: 280, p. 78

PEÑA BLANCA CANYON

pro.: /péynyə blánkə/　Spanish = "white rock"

Santa Cruz　　　　　　　　　T24S R12E　　　　　　　　Elev. c. 3500'

A white rock at the head of the canyon (at Peña Blanca Spring) is the explanation for the names of several places in this area. This canyon was called Atascoso Cañon in 1893 (Roskruge) and in 1919 Piño Blanco Canyon (U.S. Engineers). In late 1957 an earth dam was completed at T23S/R12E. Peña Blanca Lake behind Peña Blanca Dam has become a popular fishing and recreation area. The forty-seven acre lake serves as a wild life area. Ref.: Lenon; 329; *Arizona Star* (Feb. 24, 1955), p. 3; 9, p. 4

PEÑA BLANCA CREEK

Apache　　　　　　　　　　　T35N R5W

On September 5, 1849 Kern and Col. Washington camped at the Rio de Los Peñascos Blancos. It is probably identical with Peña Blanca Creek. For meaning, see Peña Blanca Canyon, Santa Cruz　Ref.: Huntington Library

PEÑASCO DAM

Santa Cruz　　　　　　　　　T23S R11E

This dam is in the section of land adjacent to Peña Blanca Dam (T23S/R12E). The name Peñascos is the Mexican name generally used for isolated pillars and monuments formed by lava flows and their dissection. Such formations occur in Peñasco Canyon. Ref.: 57, p. 93

PEÑASCO PEAK

Pima　　　　　　　　　　　　T12S R6W　　　　　　　　Elev. 3008'

This is the most northerly of four sharp peaks in the Little Ajo Mountains. See Peñasco Canyon, Pima　Ref.: 57, p. 208; 58

PENDLETON MESA

Gila　　　　　　　　　　　　T7N R14E

This mesa near P B Creek was named for brothers: Alec and George Allan Pemberton. Alec, a civil engineer, did much pioneer surveying in this area and in the early 1900s helped lay out the Apache Trail below Theodore Roosevelt Dam. Ref.: Woody

PEN POCKET

Mohave　　　　　　　　　　　T31N R11W　　　　　　　Elev. 6000'

The name describes the fact that this is a natural water pocket or reservoir where, before 1900, settlers built a pen to trap wild horses. It is also for the same reason called Ambush Water Pocket. The name "Ambush," however, may also be attributed to the fact that here William H. Dunn and the Howland Brothers (W. H. and Seneca) clambered out of the Grand Canyon after leaving the Powell Expedition party in 1869, traveling north and arriving at this large water pocket where Ute Indians were camped. The Indians received them well and fed them, but that night other Indians arrived with tales of miners' outrages and the band of Utes concluded that the three explorers were really miners and the next morning when the men came to fill their canteens, the Indians ambushed them. As a result Dellenbaugh gave the name Ambush Water Pocket to the location. Ref.: 89, pp. 228, 230; 329

PENZANCE

Navajo　　　　　　　　　　　T17N R20E　　　　　　　　Elev. c. 5500'

The railroad for many years used a rock quarry near here for riprap. Locally it is said that the place was named for Penzance in southwest England where there is also a quarry. The S.F.R.R. named this location in 1888. Ref.: John L. Westover (Joseph City), Letter (Dec. 23, 1955)

PEORIA

Maricopa   T3N R1E   Elev. 1140'

Before this location had a name, it had a dam which washed out and the discouraged white residents departed. (See Gillespie Dam). Their land was then turned over to two men named Murphy and Christy. They in turn sold it to Chauncey Clark, who arrived from Peoria, Illinois, c. 1887. Other owners with Mr. Clark included Mr. and Mrs. Albert J. Straw, Mr. and Mrs. James McMillan, W. T. Hanna, and Mr. and Mrs. Jack Copes. D. S. Brown and J. B. Greenhut (also from Peoria) planned the town site.
P.O. est. Aug. 4, 1888, James McMillan, p.m.; Wells Fargo 1903
Ref.: AHS, Robert J. Straw *ms*.

PEPCHILTK

Pima = "concave"

Pinal   Northeast of Casa Blanca

A family of Pima Indians with concave noses lived here. In 1872 the location was called Pepchalk. The place was still in existence in 1902, but has now completely vanished.
Ref.: 167, II, 22

PEPPERSAUCE WASH

Pinal   T10S R17E   Elev. c. 4400 – 2600'

While following the well travelled trail between Oracle and Apache Mine Camp, Louis Depew paused for lunch. He was very fond of peppersauce, always had a bottle with him, but when he took up his trail again, he left the sauce behind. His comrades at Apache Mine Camp joshed him about the loss and named the wash.

There is no evidence that Alex McKay or Al Welden were ever in this area. According to one informant, McKay was "never interested beyond Oracle."
Ref.: AHS, Emerson O. Stratton *ms*., p. 62

PERALTAS HILL   pro.: /per)'ltəs/

Pinal   T1N R10E

In 1956 this name was proposed for a hill north-northeast of Weaver's Needle. Don De Greg, who was seventy-four at the time and had spent a life-time in the region, said that Pedro Peralta was the original finder of the Lost Dutchman Gold Mine and that Peralta had walked from the original mine to the top of this hill (Elev. 2285') and there carved a symbol. Ref.: 329

PERIDOT   pro.: /peýradat/ or /peýrədat/

Gila   T1S R18E   Elev. 2600'

The name derives from the presence of smoky topaz and peridot, semi-precious stones. The headquarters of the Lutheran Mission for the San Carlos Indian Reservation is at this location.
P.O. est. Nov. 28, 1942, Leonard T. Malone, p.m.
Ref.: 242; Jennings; Mrs. Harvey C. Osborne, Letter (April 19, 1956)

PERIDOT CREEK

Apache   T3N R5W (Outlet)

This stream, which flows east out of Buell Park, was named "because of the preponderance of peridot olivine crystals in its bed." Garnets, called "Arizona rubies," are also found here. The name has been used since the early 1900s and is applied to Peridot Hill and to Peridot Ridge (T2N/R5W). Ref.: 97, p. 27

PERILLA MOUNTAINS   pro.: /periyə/

Spanish = "saddle horn" or "pommel"

Cochise   T23S R29E   Elev. 5919'

The name Peria Mountains appears on the War Dept. map of 1879, a corruption of the Spanish word *perilla*. The name describes the appearance of the top of this ridge, which may be identical with the Little Chiricahuas. The name has also been spelled Peria and Peri. Ref.: 329; Riggs

PERKINSVILLE

Yavapai   T18N R2E   Elev. 3847'

The first white settler here was James M. Baker (b. 1840, Missouri). Formerly a Montana prospector, he began raising cattle on the Verde River c. 1876, later entering partnership with John G. Campbell, using the 76 brand.

In 1899 Marion Alexander Perkins (d. June 20, 1927) sold his Texas stock and ranch holdings and set out for Arizona. In 1900 he bought out Baker and Campbell and drove stock to the 76 ranch, arriving on November 1. In 1912 the S.F.R.R. constructed a line from Drake to Clarkdale. It crosses the Perkins property and a station there was named Perkinsville. By 1929 the local name for this place was Dale or Story, for reasons unknown.

P.O. est. April 14, 1925, Annie Perkins, p.m.; disc. Aug. 1, 1939
Ref.: Robert E. Perkins, Letter (Dec. 16, 1955); 63; 242; 233, pp. 42, 45, 47, 49, 50

PERLITE SPRING

Pinal   T1S R11E

This location is named for the Perlite Mine (T2S/R12E).

PEROXIDE WELL

Maricopa   T1N R5W   Elev. c. 1350'

The Flower Pot Cattle Company in 1910 dug a stock well here. The water taste led to cowboys calling the location Peroxide Well. Ref.: 18a

PERRYVILLE

Maricopa   T1N R2W   Elev. 978'

Perry L. Carmean in the early 1920s started this community, but by curious coincidence its most prominent residents are members of the Perry family which moved there in 1929 after Carmean had left the area. In 1875 William H. Perry (b. 1846, Massachusetts; d. 1929) with his partner George Helm drove sheep from California to the vicinity of Williams. After selling his sheep in 1880, Perry brought in cattle from Utah through the Agua Fria River east of Cordes. In 1929 his family moved to Perryville.
Ref.: Perry (son)

PESHLAKAI POINT

Coconino (Grand Canyon)   T32N R6E

This location was named for a Navajo leader, Peshlakai Atsidi ("Silversmith") (1850 – 1939), who was "noted for his profound understanding of his fellow tribesmen and their problems." Ref.: 329

PESQUEIRA CANYON

Santa Cruz   T24S R13E   Elev. 4500'

In 1865 Capt. M. H. Calderwood of the California Volunteers was in command at Calabasas. While on the parade grounds one evening, he greeted a Mexican who rode up and asked permission to camp. It was granted. The next morning Calderwood was astonished to see, not the single camper, but the entire army of Gov. Ignacio Pesqueira of Sonora, including servants and much personal property. The Mexican general had fled with Emperor Maximilian's French troops scorching his heels in pursuit. Soon thereafter the French troops were withdrawn from Sonora and Pesqueira returned to assume control of Mexico. While in Arizona, he was the guest of Col. Charles W. Lewis, commandant at Tubac, a fact that came close to costing Lewis his commission for harboring foreign forces on American soil. Ref.: Lenon; AHS, Charles W. Lewis File; 107, IV, 190, 191

PESQUEIRA WASH

Pima/Santa Cruz   T20S R10E

This canyon takes its name from a pioneer family which has been in the area since prior to 1900. Ref.: Lenon

PETE MOUNTAIN

Santa Cruz   T20S R14E   Elev. 5640'

In the 1860s this was called Pecacho (*sic*). This location was named for Peter Gabriel

(b. 1838, Prussia; d. July 29, 1898), who by July 1878 was a prospector in Prescott. He moved from there to southern Arizona where he worked near the mountain which memorializes his name. It is also sometimes called Old Pete Mountain. From there he moved to Pinal County and served for three terms as sheriff. There in June 1888 he engaged in a gun fight in a Florence saloon with Joseph Phy, in which Phy was hit four times and Pete twice. Gabriel lived for ten more years and died at his Monitor Mine in Pinal County.

Those driving on the highway from Tucson to Nogales will see to the left of the road a section of Pete Mountain which is a towering bare rock resembling an elephant head, hence its name Elephant Head. Indians took captives to this point and tossed them. Hinton called it Sentinel Peak. In the early 1900s, it was also called Waldeck Peak, possibly because surveyor Phil Contzen (whose family came from Waldeck, Prussia) referred to it thus in a 1906 survey. Another name was Diablo Mountain ("Devil Mountain"), but for what reason is not known.

Near Elephant Head was the Elephant Head Mine, which for a brief time had a post office.

P.O. est. as Elephant Head, July 10, 1914, Henry W. Williams, p.m.; disc.?
Ref.: Lenon; AHS, J. Peter Gabriel File; Siebold; Jones; 163, p. 189; 242; 56, p. 225

PETER'S MOUNTAIN
Gila   T4N R11E   Elev. 3314'
Dave Peters in the early 20th century ran the 3– (3 bar) brand in this area, hence the name. Ref.: 18a

PETRIFIED FOREST NATIONAL MONUMENT
Apache/Navajo   T16N R23E
In 1851 Lt. Lorenzo Sitgreaves reported the presence of petrified trees in the northern part of the future Arizona, and in 1853 Lt. Amiel W. Whipple wrote about coming upon them in the Painted Desert on a vast nearly treeless plateau. He called the place Lithodendron Park. The Navajo call it *Sahdii Bisi* (= "chunks of earth sticking up alone"). They also refer to it as *tsénástánii* (= "stone logs"). Prior to 1906 the petrified colorful giants of the forest were being taken by train loads to make table tops, fireplaces, and indeed — because of their extreme hardness — to be ground up to make abrasive wheels. To stop vandalism this monument was created on December 8, 1906.

According to geologists, about 150,000,000 years ago water covered this area and fallen trees became water-logged, then gradually covered by sand and gravel. Their original wood was replaced by minerals from the water to form great columns of agate and carnelian. As the surface of the earth shoved slowly upward, erosion exposed the petrified logs. In the deep washes, such logs have been found three hundred feet below the surface. Areas within the National Monument are called First, Second, Third, and Fourth Forest, named consecutively from north to south. In addition Rainbow Forest lies northwest of Third Forest about two miles. The First Forest was so named because it was the first visited by tourists in days prior to the existence of automobiles when people rode in horse-drawn coaches. Many formations within the monument are named descriptively. Ref.: Branch; Grigsby; 177, pp. 113, 114; 242; 331, p. 112; 5, pp. 311, 312; 13, p. 1

PETROGLYPH
Maricopa   T7N R6E
Paintings and incised symbols on large rocks are common throughout Arizona. Hence the name "Petroglyph" associated with a location indicates the presence of such markings, made by prehistoric Indians for the most part.

PHANTOM CANYON
Coconino (Grand Canyon)   T32N R23E
The USGS named this canyon in 1906 because of tall tales about the supernatural related in connection with the place. Part of it is called Haunted Canyon. Phantom Creek, which runs through it, before 1906 was called first, West Fork, and then Bright Angel Creek. Ref.: 329

PHANTOM RANCH

Coconino (Grand Canyon)   T31N R3E   Elev. 2500'

In 1903 David Rust set up a permanent camp at this location for hunting parties and the venturesome who made their way to the bottom of the Grand Canyon. He called it, logically, Rust Camp. In 1907 as a further convenience Rust constructed a tramway sixty feet above the Colorado River, and for the first time travelers could make their way safely in a cage across the turbulent river. Theodore Roosevelt visited in 1913 and the name was promptly changed to Roosevelt's Camp. The Fred Harvey Company in 1921 began construction of the present resort, which was named Phantom Ranch by Mary Jane Colter, architect for some of the Fred Harvey establishments at the Grand Canyon. In 1937 a suspension bridge replaced the old cable car.
Ref.: Kolb; Emory C. Kolb, "Cheyeva Falls," *Natural History Notes* (Bulletin No. 2), p. 11; 331, p. 75; 192, pp. 174, 215

PHELPS BOTANICAL AREA

Apache   T6N R27E   Elev. 8500'

When the Apache National Forest was established in 1898 a reserve for botanical students was created on Phelps' homestead. Ref.: Phillips

PHILIPS RANCH

Greenlee   T5S R30E

"Gooseneck" Philips owned this ranch from 1910 to about 1924. He had a very skinny neck. Ref.: Shannon

PHILLIPS CANYON

Gila   T5N R17E

This canyon took its name from the presence of the Phillips Mine (T5N/R17E).

PHOENIX

Maricopa   T1N R2E   Elev. 1092'

A contractor, J. Y. T. ("Yours Truly") Smith, established a hay supply station about four miles from the center of the present downtown Phoenix, on the road to Camp McDowell. In September 1867 Jack Swilling (see Gillette) visited Smith and noticed that the Salt River was a potentially great source for irrigation waters. Swilling then organized the Swilling Irrigation Canal Company, with Henry Wickenburg and "Lord" Darrell Duppa. The new company began operations near the present Tempe, but soon moved to Smith's Station, as they needed a specific address to help speed supply deliveries. Swilling put in the first irrigation ditch about five miles above the present Phoenix and there raised pumpkins and jack rabbits, with the name Pumpkinville being applied to the site. Others in the area also raised pumpkins and the name spread to what was later Phoenix. Swilling, a southerner, suggested Stonewall, and someone else suggested Salina because the company planned to use Salt River water. Both were vetoed, the latter because the name implied the area might be a salt marsh. Duppa, noting signs of canals and villages of a vanished civilization, proposed the name Phoenix because a new city could be expected to rise upon the ashes of an old, as the legendary Phoenix which, consumed by fire, rose from its own ashes. Irrigation in the Salt River Valley soon attracted settlers and the future Phoenix began to rise. On October 15, 1870 residents selected and named the official town site and on December 23 lots were sold.

In early 1871 William B. Helling constructed a flour mill three miles east. The small community with the mill as its nucleus was called Hellings Mill or Mill City. As it was adjacent to Phoenix, it soon became East Phoenix. Ultimately it was engulfed by the larger community. In 1889 the state capital was moved from Prescott to Phoenix and there it remains. In 1891 there was danger that Phoenix would be consumed, not by fire, but by water when the Salt River rose and swept through the entire south end of the city, deep enough to cover office desks. The danger from such floods is still not entirely past but it is reduced by Bartlett Dam (*q.v.*) and dams on the Salt River.
P.O. est. at East Phoenix, Aug. 19, 1871, Edward K. Baker, p.m.; disc. July 11, 1876; p.o. est. June 15, 1869, J. W. Swilling, p.m.; Wells Fargo 1879; incorporated Jan. 3, 1881
Ref.: 116, pp. 443, 597; 15, p. 623; 5, pp. 217, 219, 221; 163, pp. 259, 260; *Weekly Arizona Miner* (Aug. 27, 1870), p. 1 and (Jan. 7, 1871), p. 1, and (Jan. 14, 1871), p. 3,

and (Feb. 3, 1872), p. 2; *Tucson Citizen* (April 20, 1872), p. 4, and (Oct. 29, 1870), p. 4, and (Jan. 7, 1871), p. 4; AHS, William Fourr Collection, p. 8

PHOENIX MOUNTAINS
Maricopa   T3N R3E   Elev. 2400'
Camelback is at the southern point of this group of hills, named for nearby Phoenix.

PHOENIX PARK CANYON
Navajo   T10N R17E   Elev. c. 6800'
James Stinson, a cattleman here in 1873, had lived in Phoenix and called his ranch, at the head of Phoenix Park Wash, after his former home. When Stinson sold to Daniel Boone Holcomb, this name gave way to Hokum or Holcomb, according to Barnes. However, the name has reverted to Phoenix Park Canyon. Ref.: 18a

PHOENIX SOUTH MOUNTAIN PARK
Maricopa   T1S R2E
The name describes the location of this fifteen thousand acre area in the Salt River Mountains. It lies south of Phoenix at South Mountain. Ref.: 5, p. 353

PIA OIK   pro.: /piyóy⁹/
Papago = "no fields" or "no one farms"
Pima   T17S R3W   Elev. 1957'
Despite the translation of the name, this Papago community is a permanent village in the agricultural area of the reservation. The name applies also to Pia Oik Pass, Valley, and Wash. Ref.: 262, p. 7

PIATO VAYA
Papago = "offal well"
Pima   T16S R2E   Elev. 2286'
This is a Papago village on the reservation. It is not known why it bears the awful name it does. It is at the north end of Piato Vaya Pass. Ref.: 262, p. 11

PICA (R.R. STN.)   pro.: /píykə/
Yavapai   T24N R8W   Elev. 5247'
This A.T. & S.F.R.R. station was first called Picacho, but as there was already a station by that name on the S.P.R.R., one had to be changed to avoid confusion. Representatives of the two railroads flipped coins to see which name would be changed and the A.T. & S.F. lost. It shortened the name to Pica. Ref.: 18a

PICACHO (TOWN)   pro.: /pikáčow/
Spanish = "peak"; "point"
Pinal   T8S R8E   Elev. 3382'
This entry refers to the community only. See Picacho Pass
P.O. est. July 10, 1907, O. W. Allison, p.m.; disc. Nov. 15, 1928; reest. Feb. 21, 1929 (local name Picacho City) Ref.: 242

PICACHO BUTTE   pro.: /pikáčow/
Spanish = "peak"; "point"
Yavapai   T21N R4W   Elev. 7250'
In 1854 Lt. Amiel Whipple passed south of this location and crossed the trail left by Lt. Lorenzo Sitgreaves. From that location Whipple moved on to Picacho Spring, which is so named on his map, as is this butte. Ref.: 347, pp. 178, 189, 190; 345, II, 32

PICACHO COLORADO   pro.: /pikáčow/
Spanish: *picacho* = "peak"; *colorado* = "red"
Gila   T5N R16E   Elev. 4777'
The name describes this red peak. Ref.: 18a

PICACHO MOUNTAINS   pro.: /pikáčow/
Spanish = "peak"; "point"
Pinal   T6S R10E
These mountains should not be confused with Picacho Peak (T9S/R9E), although

Bryan refers to them as the Picacho Peaks. He notes that the Pima Indians call them Mount Tacca or Ttacca and also Taceo. Another Pima name, recorded by F. Russell, is *ta-atukam*. Bryan adds that the Indian village which Fr. Kino called Santa Catalina de Cuitiobagum, and others, Quitoac or Bajioaquituno, has disappeared. The name of the location is, of course, descriptive. Ref.: 57, p. 388; 58

PICACHO PASS   pro.: /pikáčow/
Spanish = "peak"; "point"
Pinal   T9S R9E

This pass, about forty-five miles from the Gila River and the same distance from the civic center of Tucson, was an important place for travelers in the early days inasmuch as *tinajas* (natural rock tanks) here were filled with water at times when other tanks were bone dry. Furthermore, the peak above the pass was visible for many miles. The mail road passed through here, as did the Butterfield Overland route. The Mormon Batallion camped in this pass on December 17, 1846. The first Picacho Station was also in the pass, as might be expected, for it was the place where emigrants and other travelers could change horses, rest, and water stock.

In this pass on April 15, 1862 occurred the only Civil War battle in Arizona. Sixteen Confederates under Lt. Jack Swilling were returning from the Pima country after confiscating provisions intended for Union troops at Fort Yuma. Coming from the opposite direction, unknown to the Swilling party, was a company under Capt. William P. Caloway of the First California Infantry. From that group Lt. James Barrett with a detachment of cavalry detoured and struck Swilling's men on the flank in Picacho Pass. Lt. Barrett, Private George Johnson and Private William S. Leonard were killed, two Confederates were wounded, as were three Union men, and three Confederates were taken prisoner.

Picacho Peak (Elev. 3382') was sometimes called the Great Pocatcho. As the word *picacho* means "peak," the name Picacho Peak if translated would read Peak Peak.

The present town of Picacho is not at the same location as the old Picacho Station. Picacho Lake borrows its name from the pass. Ref.: Monument in Picacho Pass; 73, II, 163, 164; 106, pp. 117, 118; 56, p. 130; 224, p. 163; 116, II, 88; 26, p. 300

PICK-EM-UP
Cochise   Near Tombstone   Elev. c. 4000'

In 1890 the First Chance Saloon earned its name because it was the first chance for a drink after leaving Charleston en route to Tombstone. Around this location a small settlement arose called Brady House. In the saloon a tinhorn gambler called Johnny-Behind-the-Deuce (real name, Johnny O'Rourke) earned his name by consistently backing deuces. In a petulant fit of temper in Charleston, Johnny-Behind-the-Deuce shot Henry Schneider, a mining engineer and was promptly arrested. At that precise moment the mining mill whistle blew. The miners poured into the streets where the blood still ran. Their immediate response was a surge to lynch the murderer, thwarted when the constable and his prisoner set out on a horse-drawn wagon hell-bent for leather. Not to be dissuaded, miners mounted any available horse, climbed into buggies, clambered onto wagons, and lit out after the escaping pair. Two miles out of Tombstone at Jack McCann's First Chance Saloon stood a racing mare which McCann was preparing for a race at the Watervale track nearby. The constable shouted to McCann that he was trying to save Johnny-Behind-the-Deuce from the lynch mob. He yelled to the saloon keeper, "Pick-em-up!" McCann reached for Johnny and off they went on the mare, with the mob close behind. McCann and the gambler made it to Tombstone where with a shotgun the sheriff faced off the would-be lynchers. They dispersed and Johnny-Behind-the-Deuce was safe. Ref.: Larriau; 60, pp. 62, 63; *Tombstone Epitaph* (Aug. 9, 1890), p. 3

PICKET CANYON
Cochise   T16S R29E   Elev. 5200'

When the Riggs family began improving their ranch, they cut cypress in this canyon for pickets around their yard, hence the name. Picket Park (T16S/R20E) at the south end of the canyon is a natural park. Ref.: Riggs

PICKET POST MOUNTAIN
Pinal   T2S R12E   Elev. 4375'

Prior to the establishment of a military camp on this mountain in 1870, it was called

Tordillo Peak. A heliograph station was used on this mountain during the days of the Indian campaigns. Ref.: 5, p. 349

PICKHANDLE HILLS

Cochise   T23S R32E   Elev. 5344'

This group of hills was known locally to residents by this name. The name became official in 1966 at the suggestion of Richard Kelly, a graduate geology student. Ref.: 184a, p. 1; 329

PICTURE CANYON

Coconino   T21N R8E

The name derives from petroglyphs by the dozens on the basalt canyon walls. Ref.: 70, p. 51

PICTURE MOUNTAIN

Gila   T6N R21E   Elev. 6451'

This name, which has been in use since c. 1900, applies because it is possible to point out many "pictures" while looking at this mountain. It is also called Rock Mountain by the Forest Service. Ref.: 329

PICTURE ROCKS

Pima   T13S R11–12E   Elev. c. 5500'

Throughout Arizona one can see pictures painted by prehistoric Indians on rock surfaces, as in the case with this location.

PIEDMONT (R.R. STN.)

Yavapai   T10N R6W   Elev. 3345'

Barnes says this location was named because of the variety of colors on the nearby mountains.

PIEDRA   pro.: /piˣédrə/

Spanish = "stone"

Maricopa   T6S R6W   Elev. c. 700'

Volcanic rocks or "bombs" litter the ground around this railroad station. Because this location is the next west to Theba, it seems likely that it is identical with the former station called Painted Rocks (q.v.).

PIGEON CANYON

Mohave   T33N R14W   Elev. c. 4000'

The first Mormons here found large flocks of wild pigeons. Ref.: 18a

PIGEON CREEK

Gila   T8N R11E

The oak mast here provides food for clouds of pigeons. Pigeon Spring (T4N/R10E) serves as a feeding place for blue pigeons. Ref.: McKinney; Pieper

PIGEON CREEK

Greenlee   T2S R29E   Elev. c. 5000

In the 1880s wild pigeons abounded on this little stream, according to early settlers. Ref.: Scott; Fred Fritz Notes

PIG SPRING

Pinal/Gila   T10S R15E

Although various people have tried to dignify this by changing the name to Pigg, it is not a family name but derives from wild pigs existing and drinking here. Ref.: Woody

PILGRIM WASH

Mohave   T17N R14W

Pilgrim Wash about 1875 took its name from Pilgrim Spring nearby. By 1962 this wash had a variant name, Algrim Wash. Ref.: 329

PILOT ROCK
Mohave   T12N R19W   Elev. c. 1500'
Travelers and steamboat captains used this point as a navigational aid. Ref.: 18a

PIMA pro.: /piymə/
Graham   T6S R25E   Elev. 2848'
In February 1879 some Mormons, including W. R. Teeples, John William Tanner, Lem
Pierce, and Hyrum Weech, found a location in the Gila Valley where they planned to
place a canal. They named the location Smithville to honor Jesse N. Smith (b. c. 1834),
a Mormon leader who arrived in Arizona in September 1878 with Erastus Snow. By
April the village had been laid out in sixteen blocks of four lots each. Lawless men and
malaria beset these settlers. Nevertheless, they persevered. On the post office
application in the National Archives, it is noted that the place was called Smithville, but
the name Pima was requested for the post office in 1894.
P.O. est. Aug. 23, 1880, William R. Teeples, p.m.; name changed to Pima, Nov. 25,
1894, Henry G. Boyle, p.m.; Wells Fargo 1903 Ref.: 242; 225, p. 245; 116, p. 590; 15,
II, 593; 353, p. 11; AHS, J. Morris Richards Clipping Book

PIMA BUTTE
Pinal   T3S R3E   Elev. 1640'
This butte is on the Gila River Indian Reservation of the Pima Indians, hence its name.

PIMA CANYON
Maricopa   T1S R4E
Water in this canyon comes in part from a spring used by the Pima Indians, hence its
name.

PIMA COUNTY pro.: /piymə/
Prior to its being recognized as a political entity, the present Pima County was part of a
large area called Pimeria Alta (Spanish = "Upper Pima Land"). After many years of
missionizing in the region, Fr. Eusebio Kino in May 1704 suggested the name New
Philippines for it, but the name was not accepted. In 1716 Fr. Luis Velarde noted that the
name *Pima* probably derived from the fact that the Indians constantly repeated in negation
the word *pim*. Many years later Col. J. H. McClintock noted that "... there is a Pima word,
'Pima-tche', which means, 'I do not understand' and Pima may be a contraction. It is
plausible to assume that the Spanish discoverers might have asked, 'Who are you?' and the
reply had been quite naturally 'pima-tche, I do not understand.' " When the United States
annexed the region (then part of Mexico), southern Arizona was included in Doña Ana
County, which extended from the Colorado River to the present New Mexico border.
During the Civil War, Sylvester Mowry placed the name Ewell County on his 1860 map of
Arizona, including an extensive area to be named for Capt. Richard S. Ewell (see
Buchanan, Fort, Santa Cruz). In 1863 Arizona Territory was separated from the Territory
of New Mexico. Pima County was among the original four counties established by the
First Territorial Arizona Legislature on November 8, 1864. The name was given because
the region was the home of the Pima Indians, a peaceful agricultural tribe. The county
included all land south of the Gila River and east of Yuma to the Mexican border
(established by the Gadsden Purchase) and also Cochise County, which was formed later.
In fact, Pima County became much smaller, losing ground to Maricopa, Pinal, and
Cochise as well as to Graham County. Pima County today has 5,914,240 acres. The
county seat has always been Tucson. Ref.: Velarde *ms.*, Huntington Library; 163, pp.
522, 523; Clipping File, State Library Files

PIMA POINT
Coconino (Grand Canyon)   T31N R2E   Elev. 6750'
Until May 2, 1906 this location was called Seri Point. The Seri Indians live on the coast
of the Gulf of California in Sonora, Mexico. The name was changed to that of an Arizona
tribe. Ref.: 329; 5, p. 484

PIMA VILLAGES
Pinal/Maricopa   Elev. c. 1200'
The Pima or, as they were sometimes called, Pimo Villages, were a number of Indian

communities extending S.W. from Casa Blanca on both sides of the Gila River in the same area today known as the Gila River Indian Reservation. Some of the principal towns continue to exist, such as Sacaton, Snaketown, and Santan, but they did not have their current names in earlier days. Fortunately in 1904 Russell, agent for the villages, noted the following concerning them:

Petâ'íkuk": "Where the *petais* stands"

Tcupatäk: "Mortar stone"

Tcu'wutukawutûk: "Earth Hill"

Os Kâ'kûmûktco'tcikäm: "Arrow-bush standing"

Kó-okûpvan'sík: "Medicine paraphernalia"

Kâmít: "back"

Tco'ûtíkwútcík: "charcoal lying"

Akûtcíny: "Creek mouth" 15 mi. W. of Picacho.

Skâ'kâík: "Many rattlesnakes" On N. side of Gila River opposite Rso'tûk

Rsâ'nûk: "Beginning" About one mi. E. of Sacaton Station on Maricopa & Phoenix R.R.

Ka'woltûk'wutca: "Hill below" W. of R.R.

Hi'atam': "Sea-sand place," from Hi'akatcik, where the people of this village formerly lived. Hi'atam was just N. of Maricopa Station

Ka'mâtuk Wu'tcâ, Ka'mâtûk:"Below Gila Crossing" Ka'matuk is the Pima name of the Sierra Estrella

Herm'ho: "Once" or A'mû

Â'kimûlt: "Salt River," known by last name. Settlement on N. side of river, 3 mi. from Mesa

Os kuk: "Tree standing," or "black water"

We'tcu(r)t: "Opposite black water" (N. black water)

Harsanykuk: "Saguaro standing" or Sacaton Flats

S'a'opuk: "Many trees"; "the cottonwoods"

Tat'sítûk: "Place of freight," the settlement above Cruz Store

Kú-u Ki: "Big house," Sacaton

ꟿo'pohiûm: "Santan"

Hu'tcílttcík: "Round clearing," a village below Santan on the north bank of the Gila River

Vá-aki: "Ruin" or "Ancient House," Casa Blanca

Stâ'tânnyík: "Many ants," a village between the last two preceding named, on south bank of Gila

Pe-ep'tcílt ᒃ : "Concave" (from a family with noses of that shape), N.E. of Casa Blanca

Rsótûk :"Water standing," N.W. of Casa Blanca

The Pima Villages were an important stopping place on the early southern transcontinental route, for at them travelers could obtain forage and water for crossing the desolate desert between those points and California. Ammi White established a flour mill at Casa Blanca and served as an Indian trader in the villages. On March 3, 1862 the Texas Confederates under Capt. Sherod Hunter arrested White and confiscated fifteen hundred sacks of wheat. While so engaged, Hunter's men encountered Capt. McCleave and nine Union soldiers of the First California Cavalry, all of whom were captured with White and sent to the Rio Grande as Confederate captives.

P.O. est. as Pimo Village, June 21, 1851, Silas St. John, p.m.; disc. Dec. 6, 1871

Ref.: 281, pp. 22, 23; 101, p. 207, Note 14; 272, p. 228; 224, pp. 162, 273; 167, II, 397

PIMERIA ALTA

In Fr. Eusebio Kino's time, this area included northwestern Sonora and what is now southern Arizona, although no such boundary existed at the time. The land was occupied by the Upper Pima Indians and it was called Pimeria Alta to distinguish it from Pimeria Baja occupied by the Lower Pima Indians. See Pima County

PIMERIA WELL

Yuma   T8S R13W

This deep well was drilled by the Pimeria Land Company in about the center of San Cristobal Valley. Contrary to an opinion held by some, this well was not named for a man named Pimeria. Ref.: 57, p. 361

PINACATE VALLEY pro.: /pínəkáte/
Spanish: Corruption of Aztec *pinacatl* = "small ground beetle"
Yuma   T15S R12W   Elev. c. 200'
Most of this valley (a.k.a. Pinacate Plain) lies across the border in Mexico. In the valley black beetles (*Eleodes ornatus*) exist in myriads. The beetle responds to irritation by standing on its head. Ref.: 57, p. 420

PINAL pro.: /pinǽl/
Pinal   T2S R12E   Elev. 2529'
By 1875 the Silver King Mine required a smelter and as a result a mining camp four miles from the mine was established at the base of a high butte called Picket Post. (See Pinal, Camp) The developing community was also called Picket Post. As the camp expanded and had permanent stone and adobe buildings by March 1878, it became an important stage station on the road to Globe. In 1879 the name of the community was changed to Pinal, also referred to as Pinal City. The place was abandoned almost overnight when the Silver King Mine closed down in 1888. The location today is the site of the Thompson Southwest Aboretum founded by William Boice Thompson as an experimental station for plant research.
P.O. est. as Picket Post, April 10, 1878, William W. Benson, p.m.; name changed to Pinal, June 27, 1879; disc. Nov. 28, 1891; Wells Fargo 1875
Ref.: *Arizona Sentinel* (Oct. 6, 1877), p. 2, and (March 2, 1878), p. 3, and (July 5, 1879), p. 2; AHS, Emerson O. Stratton *ms.*; 56, p. 263; 206, p. 343

PINAL, CAMP pro.: /pinǽl/
Pinal   T3S R12E   Elev. 4500'
On November 28, 1870 a detachment of soldiers and an officer established a picket post in the Pinal Mountains under the name Infantry Camp (because only infantry were engaged). The camp was on top of a butte now known as Picket Post Butte at the head waters of Mineral and Pinto Creeks. On April 4, 1871, the name was changed to Camp Pinal, said to be in Mason's Valley. Under Gen. George Stoneman, U.S. troops began constructing the Stoneman Grade in 1870 on what was then called Picket Post Creek at the site of Infantry Camp. The trail was of huge importance to residents of Globe although it was never more than five miles long and travelers made their way west beyond it as best they could. Stoneman had planned to make Camp Pinal a permanent post, but he was relieved of his command, and under Gen. George Crook the post was abandoned in August 1871. No permanent location or settlement was made in the vicinity until 1877 when Robert A. Irion established his ranch headquarters at the site of old Camp Pinal. Since then the place has been called Pinal Ranch, formerly an important stopping point for travelers. Ref.: Craig (Irion's step-daughter); 145, p. 148; *Citizen* (Nov. 19, 1870, p. 1 and (Dec. 24, 1870), p. 4, and (July 15, 1871), p. 2

PINAL COUNTY pro.: /pinǽl/
Pinal
On February 1, 1875 Pinal County was formed from parts of Maricopa and Pima counties. The *Arizona Magazine* (Aug. 18, 1899) notes the county was named because of its pine-clad mountains. It was the home of the Pinal Apaches. In 1877 the county underwent slight modification to correct boundary error, and it also lost the Globe District to southern Gila County in 1881. The present county area is 3,441,920 acres and it includes parts of the Gila River (a portion of its boundary) and part of the San Carlos Indian Reservation. The county seat is Florence. Ref.: 15, p. 264; *Arizona Magazine* (Aug. 18, 1899), p. 38

PINAL CREEK pro.: /pinǽl/
Gila   T1N R15E   Elev. c. 4500'
This creek has its head waters at the east end of the Pinal Mountains, hence its name. Formerly holding water, it is now dry, its water having leaked into the shafts of the Old Dominion Mine. On June 13, 1864 the King S. Woolsey expedition named this stream, having the night before pitched camp next to it. As they reported in the morning, they were in a "beautiful valley" covered with corn and wheat fields.
Ref.: Woody; *Arizona Miner* (Sept. 7, 1864), p. 3

PINALENO MOUNTAINS pro.: /pinəléyno/

Apache: *pinal* = "deer";　　　　　　　Spanish: *pinal* = "pine"(?)　*llano* = "plain"
Graham/Cochise　　　　　　T12–8S R26–23E　　　　　　Elev. 8685'

In 1846 Lt. William H. Emory talked with Indians who said they were members of the "Piñon Lanos" tribe and he therefore applied the name to the mountains where they lived. This is the range which has Mount Graham as its highest point. The report of the Boundary Survey in 1852 corrects the spelling to Pinal Llano, a name used on the 1851 Sitgreaves map. In the same period this range was called the Sierra Florida or Florida Mountains, and they were also called the Sierra Bonita (see Graham Mountain, Graham). The name *Pinal Llano* means "pine plain," according to Gray (1856). G.E.P. Smith interprets the name *Pinal* as an Apache word meaning "deer." In any event, the Spanish pronunciation gradually became anglicized to the present pronunciation. Many refer to this range as the Graham Mountains.
Ref.: 242; 105, pp. 71, 73; G.E.P. Smith, Letter to *Star* (June 23, 1950); 138, p. 46

PINALENO SPRING

Graham　　　　　　　　　　T12S R26E
In 1884 Joseph Munk and his brother discovered and named this spring.
Ref.: 240, p. 28

PINAL MOUNTAINS pro.: /pinǽl/

Pinal　　　　　　　　　　T1S R14E　　　　　　　　Elev. 7850'
The earliest written spelling for the name for these mountains was Penal in 1789. Despite the fact that *pinal* is said to mean "deer" in Apache, the Apache Indian name for these mountains is Zil-In-dil-che-deig-e-la. The name Pinal Mountains was in use at least as early as 1864 when the Woolsey expedition passed through them (see Pinal Creek, Pinal). They were the home of the Pinal Coyotero Apache, often referred to as the Pinalenos. Ref.: 351; *Arizona Miner* (Sept. 7, 1864), p. 3

PINAL PEAK

Gila　　　　　　　　　　T2S R15E　　　　　　　　Elev. 7850'
King S. Woolsey with his expedition climbed it on July 4, 1864, and named it. See Pinal Creek, Gila Ref.: 18a

PINAL PEAK

Greenlee　　　　　　　　T3S R29E　　　　　　　　Elev. 7242'
This location is also called Pinal Point. See Pinal Mountains, Pinal

PINAL POINT

Coconino (Grand Canyon)　　T31N R5E
This location was named to honor Pinal County on June 3, 1906 according to the USGS. However, in this period other tribal names were also applied. Ref.: 329

PINAL (R.R. STN.)

Gila　　　　　　　　　　T1N R15E
This location takes its name from the nearby Pinal Mountains. See Pinal Mountains, Pinal

PINE:
The presence of pine trees has resulted in using the word *pine* in many place names. Examples follow:

Pine　　　　　　　Gila　　　　　T12N R8–9E　　　　Elev. 9359'
In 1879 Riel Allen settled with a group of Mormons and named the location because it was in pine timber country.
P.O. est. Jan 2, 1884, Mrs. Mary D. Fuller, p.m. Ref.: 242; 225, p. 174

Pine Butte　　　　　Gila/Maricopa　　　T8N R9E
Also known as Pine Mountain. The name Pine Butte came into use in 1928 after the establishment of the Pine Mountain Company here. Ref.: 329

Pine Canyon　　　　Cochise　　　　T17S R29E

Pine Creek　　　　　Cochise　　　　T16S R28E

Pine Creek Maricopa T3N R12E

As late as 1932 there was a large clump of pines at the head of the creek, practically the only pine timber in that section. The name had been in use since at least 1900. Ref.: 329

PINEDALE

Navajo T11N R20E Elev. 6454'

In 1879 Niels Mortenson settled here and the place came to be known by his last name. It was also referred to as Percheron because of a Percheron stallion Mortenson and the Petersons had brought to this location. By 1888, however, the settlement was being called Pinedale, reflecting the fact that it exists in an opening or dale in a pine forest. P.O. est. April 18, 1888, Lydia C. Bryan, p.m. Ref.: 225, pp. 168, 169; 322, p. 173

Pinedale Ridge	Navajo	T10N R19E	
Pinedale Wash	Navajo	T10N R19E	
Pine Flat	Coconino	T19N R2E	
Pine Flat See Wood, Camp, Yavapai	Yavapai	T11N R5E	
Pine Flat Spring See Wood, Camp, Yavapai	Yavapai	T14N R2E	
Pine Hill	Coconino	(1) T21N R3E (2) T18N R10E	Elev. 7332'
Pine Hollow	Coconino	T37N R2W	Elev. 6560'
Pine Hollow Canyon	Coconino	T41N R3E	
Pine Lake	Apache	T11N R24E	
Pine Lake	Coconino	T18N R10E	
Pine Lake	Navajo	T8N R23E	
Pine Mountain	Coconino	T16N R10E	Elev. 7996'
Pine Peak	Mohave	T17N R15W	Elev. 7225'
Pine Ridge	Cochise	T12S R21E	Elev. 5527'
Pine Ridge	Coconino	T19N R2E	Elev. 6720'

The descriptive English name is a translation of the Navajo *Ndishii' Deesk'id* or "pine ridge."

Pine Ridge Maricopa T5N R10E

This ridge formerly had an isolated batch of pines on the north slope, near the summit, hence the name.

PINE SPRINGS

Apache T23N R29E Elev. 6950'

The Navajo trading post and school are at this spring in the midst of juniper and piñon, trees which give the community its name. The Navajo here are noted for particularly fine weaving. The location in 1860 was called Agua Vibora. Ref.: 331, p. 113; 143, p. 221

PINE SPRINGS

Coconino T21N R1E Elev. 6367'

A sawmill was established here in 1876 by Mormons, who sold it in 1882 and moved to Pinedale. See Millville, Coconino
P.O. est. March 20, 1879, Hugh Marshall, p.m.; disc. July 27, 1882 Ref.: 242

Pine Springs Coconino T28N R8W

This is the place which Fr. Francisco Garcés called Pozo de la Rosa (Spanish = "rose well"), on June 19, 1775. Ref.: 77, p. 335, Note 19

PINERY CANYON

Cochise T17S R30E Elev. c. 4800'

The military cut trees here for use at Fort Bowie, hence the name. At one time the agency for the Chiricahua Apaches was in this canyon. Pinery Creek is in the canyon, and Pinery Peak is at its head. Ref.: Riggs; 107, VIII, 15

PINETOP

Navajo   T8N R23E   Elev. 6960'

A bachelor named Johnny Phipps (d. 1890) ran a saloon for the colored soldiers from Fort Apache. William L. Penrod (b. 1831; d. Aug. 21, 1916), and his family moved near Show Low in 1878, arriving from Utah and settling in Phipps' house. Initially the place was called Penrod. When Phipps died, Walt Rigney took over and soldiers began calling the place Pinetop, their nickname for Rigney. The location is in pines near the top of the Mogollon Rim. The Post Office Dept. abandoned the name Penrod and accepted the name Pinetop. Until 1906 the residents were thirteen Penrod children.
P.O. est. as Pinetop, Jan. 31, 1895, Edward E. Bradshaw, p.m.
Ref.: 242; Rollin Fish (quoting from 1905 Penrod Letter); 5, p. 450

PINEVETA   pro.: /páyn viytə/

Yavapai   T22N R3W   Elev. 7446'

On the Gardner map of 1866 this location shows as "Pinevela or Mt. Floyd." A military ms. map dated 1877 gives the spelling as Pineveta Mt. On October 4, 1857, Lt. Edward Fitzgerald Beale wrote that he had named the location Floyd's Peak. Whether he named it for Dr. Floyd, a member of the expedition, as was Beale's custom, or for John B. Floyd (then Secretary of War) is not certain. Secretary Floyd on May 10, 1858 transmitted Beale's report to the Speaker of the House. Floyd had been responsible for the organization of the Ives expedition also. Ref.: 242; 23, p. 66; 107, II, 17

PINEVETA PEAK

Yavapai

On a map dated 1905 this shows as the next peak northwest of Floyd Peak. See Pineveta, Yavapai

PINEYON   pro.: /pinyówn/

Spanish: *piñon* = "a conifer bearing edible nuts"

Apache   T10N R24E   Elev. c. 7000'

When the post office was established at this location, the residents asked for the name Clearview, but the name Pineyon was granted instead. It results from anglicizing the Spanish word *piñon*. The name is descriptive, as the settlement is surrounded by piñon trees.
P.O. est. March 3, 1916, Mrs. Mary A. Calaway; disc. Aug. 15, 1929
organization of the Ives expedition also. Ref.: 242; 23, p. 66; 107, II, 17

PINK CLIFFS

Navajo   T15N R18E

These cliffs are stained with red oxide of iron, hence their name.

PINKLEY PEAK

Pima   T16S R6W   Elev. 3145'

The National Park Service in 1931 named this most prominent peak of the Puerto Blanco Mountains for Frank Pinkley (b. 1881, Ohio; d. Feb. 14, 1940), superintendent of the Southwestern National Monuments (1924–1940). Ref.: 329

PINNACLE PEAK

Maricopa   T5N R5E   Elev. 3170'

This small granite mountain, named c. 1900, has a thirty-five foot pinnacle on its top. Ref.: 329

PINNACLE RIDGE

Graham   T6S R21E   Elev. 7275'

This ridge is marked by a series of pinnacles, hence the name.

PIÑON pro.: /pinyówn/

Spanish = "a conifer bearing edible nuts"

Navajo   T31N R20E   Elev. 6350'

In 1858 Capt. John G. Walker and his Mounted Rifles were the first Americans to cross this area, which Walker described as a broken, inaccessible region, largely uninhabited. In 1912 Lorenzo Hubbell built a trading post here at a time when the crop of piñon nuts was very large, hence the name.

P.O. est. Nov. 1, 1952, Fletcher Corrigan, p.m. Ref.: 31, p. 113; Thomas F. Corrigan (son), Letter (Nov. 1955)

PIÑON LLANO

This name appears on the Park 1851 map between Mount Graham and Mount Turnbull just south of the range. See Pinaleno Mountains, Graham/Cochise

PINTA, SIERRA pro.: /siyerə pintə/

Spanish: *sierra* = "mountains"; *pinta* = "painted"

Yuma   T16S R12W   Elev. 2950'

This range, which in 1912 was being called the Pinto Range and Pinta Mountains, has a painted appearance which results from the gneisses at the southern end (blackish) and the grayish-white granite at the northern end. Ref.: Mercer; 355, pp. 157, 158

PINTO pro.: /pinto/

Spanish = "painted" or "piebald" (with reference to a horse)

Apache   T19N R25E   Elev. c. 6000'

Now only a railroad stop, this location in the heart of the Painted Desert formerly had a post office. Its name may come from its location in the Painted Desert or possibly from some association with a pinto horse.

P.O. est. Feb. 27, 1902, Celia F. Henning, p.m.; disc. May 23, 1922

PINTO CREEK

Gila   T1S R14E

The varigated coloring of the stream banks and the hills along the creek course resulted in the name, in existence as early as June 1869 when it was referred to as Rio Pinto. Ref.: 159, p. 433

PINTO MESA pro.: /pinto/

Spanish = "painted" (with reference to a horse)

Yavapai   T13N R4E   Elev. 5408'

A pinto horse or cow roamed on this mesa, hence the name, which also applies to Pinto Mesa Spring.

PINTO TANK

Yuma   T13S R12W

This tank was named for the nearby Pinto Mountains. See Heart Tank, Yuma Ref.: Monson

PINYON MOUNTAIN

Maricopa   T3N R12E   Elev. 5268'

According to Barnes, pioneers named this mountain because a few piñon trees grew along its north slope.

PIONEER

Gila   T25S R15E   Elev. c. 4000'

In 1876 George Scott and John Brannan located the Pioneer Mine on the west side of the Pinal Mountains above Silver Creek. The Pioneer Mining District took its name from the mine, which was soon sold to an eastern company, the Howard Mining Company. It became very active and had a post office. The mining camp was rough and ready. For instance, on Christmas night 1882 a twenty-two year old man named Hartnett was challenged by Tom Kerr (both smaller and older) to try pinning down the latter's shoulders. Hartnett pinned him not only once, but twice, and Kerr became so furious that he shot his opponent four times and beat his head to a pulp for good measure. Kerr claimed self-defense, but his flagrant lie did not keep him from being immediately lynched. The name Pioneer also applies to the following: Pioneer Basin, Pioneer Mountain (Elev. 5982'), and Pioneer Pass.

P.O. est. April 24, 1882, Thomas A. Lonergan, p.m.; disc. Sept. 4, 1885
Ref.: Woody; 270, p. 116

PIONEER
Maricopa   T6N R2E

This location is a five hundred and fifty acre non-profit "living history" museum which depicts life in the late nineteenth century. Many pioneer buildings were moved to this site, which also has miners' and other cabins.

PIONEER STAGE STATION
Gila

This place was below the old Pioneer Mine and Camp on the road over Pioneer Pass between Globe and Dripping Springs Canyon. See Pioneer, Gila

PIPE CREEK
Coconino (Grand Canyon)   T31N R3E   Elev. c. 3500'

This creek was named in 1894 when Ralph Cameron found a meerschaum pipe while he, Peter H. Berry, and James McClure were prospecting. As a joke he scratched a date *1794* on it and placed it where others in his party would find it, which they did, and hence the name. Ref.: Emory C. Kolb; *Grand Canyon Nature Notes*, VIII (June 1933)

PIPE SPRING
Mohave   T40N R4W   Elev. 4952'

In 1852 Jacob Hamblin and other Mormon missionaries stopped here where they found the only water available in a sixty-mile radius. The men wagered with William ("Gunlock Bill") Hamblin that he could not shoot a hole through a handkerchief at fifty paces. He tried, but the cloth merely gave way to the impact of the bullet. Gunlock Bill then bet he could shoot the bottom out of Dudley Leavitt's pipe. Being a sensible man, Leavitt placed his pipe on a rock. Hamblin shot out its bottom. From this event came the name Pipe Spring. The party moved on, and not until 1863 did anyone settle here. Then Dr. James M. Whitmore came with his brother-in-law Robert McIntyre to raise cattle. They lived in a dugout on the east side of a small hill near the spring, but were killed by Indians on Jan. 8, 1866. B. P. Winsor, acting for Mormons, bought the property in April 1870 from Mrs. Whitmore, and in 1873 the Mormons formed a cooperative livestock association called the Winsor Castle Livestock Growers Association. The fort constructed at the location was called Winsor Castle. The building was constructed over the springs so that Indians could not poison the water supply. The structure housed the first telegraph office in Arizona, established in 1871. Over-grazing and drought devastated the area. The fort sometimes housed those who practiced polygamy as they sought refuge when word would come down the line that Federal law enforcement officers were seeking out such people. On May 31, 1923 the Pipe Spring National Monument of forty acres was set aside to preserve this outstanding example of how pioneers lived. Among Piute Indians, the springs were called Yellow Rock Water or Yellow Rock Spring. Pipe Valley Wash includes this area. Ref.: 13, "Pipe Spring...," pp. 1, 3, 4; 225, p. 98; 88, pp. 169, 185, 186; 5, p. 283

PIPESTEM CREEK
Greenlee   T1S R30E

The name describes the fact that the creek follows a course like the stem of a meerschaum pipe. Pipestem Mountains (T15S/R29E, Elev. 7121') are above the creek. Ref.: Simmons

PIPYAK
Papago = "columbine"
Pima   T13S R5E   Elev. 1905'

This is a small temporary village in the Pipyak Valley on the Papago Indian Reservation. It was noted by Sedelmayr in 1744 as being a Maricopa rancheria called Pipiaca. Ref.: 167, II, 260; 262, p.a 13

PIRTLEVILLE

Cochise   T24S R27E   Elev. 3955'

Elmo R. Pirtle (b. May 5, 1868, Tennessee; d. Aug. 1920) arrived in Douglas in 1901 where he became a real estate man. The post office at this location was named for him because he owned the property and established a settlement.

P.O. est. as Pirtle, Feb. 8, 1908, Cassius C. Hockett, p.m.; changed to Pirtleville, March 30, 1910, Jefferson J. Langford, p.m. Ref.: 224, III; AHS Names File

PISINIMO   pro.: /pəsúynmow/

Papago = "brown bear head"

Pima   T16S R1W   Elev. 1895'

The name for this small Papago village has been variously spelled Pacinimo, Perinimo, Pisineme, and Pisin Mo. In 1763 it was reported that the Opata Indians called the brown bear *Pisini*. The village is on Pisinimo Wash in Pisinimo Valley.

P.O. est. Aug. 7, 1939; resc. Oct. 19, 1939 Ref.: 167, II, 201; 142, p. 29

PISTOLA PEAK

Greenlee

This peak looks like a pistol. See Gray's Peak, Greenlee Ref.: Simmons

PITAHAYA CANYON   pro.: /pitəhayə/

Pima   T15S R5W   Elev. c. 2000'

Pitahaya is an old name for the saguaro cactus, which grows in abundance in this small canyon. It was named by A. A. Nichol c. 1930 while he was collecting botanical items. The canyon is sometimes erroneously called Grass Canyon. Grass grows luxuriantly during the rainy season. Ref.: Henson; William Supernaugh, Letter (March 5, 1956)

PITAHAYA REGION

This name was used by travelers in territorial Arizona and referred to the entire portion of southern Arizona where saguaro cactus continues to grow abundantly.

PITCHFORK CANYON

Graham   T10S R24E

This canyon takes its name from that of the Pitchfork Ranch.

PITMAN VALLEY

Coconino   T22N R3E   Elev. c. 6500'

Elias E. Pitman (b. 1826, Tennessee; d. 1888) traveled around the Horn to California in 1858, going from there to Arizona in 1862 where he established a cattle ranch in the valley now bearing his name, at what is now Chalender. He sold out to William Garland (see Garland Prairie, Coconino) in 1884 and returned to California.

Ref.: Fuchs, Letter (April 30, 1955); Mrs. Guy Pitman Taylor (daughter), Letter (April 4, 1956); 124, pp. 53, 54

PITOIKAM   pro.: /pitwikəm/

Papago = "sycamore place"

Pima   T19S R6E   Elev. c. 3600'

This is one of three villages in Fresnal Canyon. See Fresnal, Pima Ref.: 262, p. 1

PITTSBERG

Coconino   T23N R3W

This is a cinder cone which takes its name from Pitt Station on the A.T. & S.F.R.R. Grand Canyon branch. See Pitt Tank, Coconino Ref.: Museum of Northern Arizona

PITTSBURGH

Cochise   NE of Paradise six mi.   Elev. c. 5000'

The Cochise Consolidated Copper Company in 1905 petitioned for a post office by this name at a proposed town site which had been under development since 1903. Pittsburgh, Pennsylvania, was the home office for the company.

P.O. est. June 18, 1906, Harry Alexander, p.m.; resc. Oct. 9, 1906

Ref.: *Arizona Silver Belt* (Oct. 26, 1905), p. 4; 242

PITTSBURG LANDING

Mohave   T13N R20W   Elev. 440'

This now-vanished landing on the Colorado River was a trans-shipment point for freight and ores, the latter to be taken to smelting centers such as Liverpool or Pittsburgh. Ref.: Housholder

PITTS HOMESTEAD TANK

Coconino   T23N R3W

This location is also referred to as Homestead Tank. See Pitt Tank, Coconino

PITT TANK

Coconino   T23N R2W   Elev. c. 5000'

Prior to 1935 William Pitt, a sheepman, used this tank and Pitt Spring and maintained a livestock loading platform on the railroad. Ref.: 18a

PIUS DRAW

Coconino   T13N R12E

This location, also called Pius Farm Draw, was the location of a farm run by a pioneer named Pius.

PIUTE CANYON   pro.: /páyuwt/

Navajo   T41N R15E

This canyon is in territory traversed by Piute Indians. Maj. John Wesley Powell said that their name signified "True Ute" (*Pai* = "true"), a name which strictly belonged to the Corn Creek tribe in southwestern Utah, but applied more widely to other Piute Indians. In 1906 the name appeared on maps as Pah Ute. It is also spelled Paiute. It applies also to Piute Creek and Piute Mesa (T41N/R16E, Elev. c. 7100'). Ref.: 77, p. 405, Note 12; 141, p. 194

PIUTE POINT

Coconino (Grand Canyon)   T32N R1E   Elev. 6632'

The first name for this location was Grandview Point, the name being changed in 1927 by the USGS. See Grandview Trail, Coconino (Grand Canyon), and Piute Canyon, Navajo

PIVOT ROCK CANYON

Coconino   T13N R9E   Elev. 6901'

This canyon borrows its name from that of Pivot Rock, descriptively named, which is in the canyon. Ref.: Schnebly; 18a

PLACERITA   pro.: /plæceriytə/

Spanish = "little placer"

Yavapai   T11N R4W   Elev. 5300'

The presence of placer mines in this region probably resulted in the name of the post office and of the gulch. Mexicans found gold here in Placerita Gulch in 1868-69. Placerita Creek runs through the gulch.

P.O. est. Feb. 1, 1896, Louis H. Herron; disc. Aug. 15, 1910

Ref.: *Arizona Journal Miner* (March 10, 1891), p. 1; Platten; 242; 163, p. 101

PLAINS

This term is used to refer to a 27,000 square-mile region in southern Arizona, which comprises part of what is bordered by the Basin Range.

PLAINVIEW PEAK

Graham   T8S R24E

From this high bald peak or point there is a plain view of both the Gila and San Simon valleys. The name was approved in 1932. Ref.: 329

PLANET

Mohave   T11N R18W   Elev. c. 1200'

The Planet Mine was discovered in April 1864 by Richard Ryland. A small community arose near the mine and took its name. The community became a way station for travelers, called Colorado Station in 1877. Planet Peak (T10N/R17W, Elev. 3141') is nearby.

P.O. est. Jan. 16, 1902, Edward Henry Webb; disc. March 31, 1921

Ref.: 242; *Arizona Sentinel* (June 15, 1878), p. 2; 163, p. 157; AHS Names File

PLANTSITE

Greenlee   T4S R29E   Elev. 4240'

This is a "town" adjacent to Morenci, hence its name. It is the site of the main plant.

PLATA (R.R. STN.)

Pima   T12S R12E   Elev. c. 3500'

This station took its name from that of the Plata Mine nearby. Ref.: 163, p. 211

PLATTEN SPRINGS

Coconino   T23N R3E   Elev. c. 7000'

These springs were named for Fred Platten (b. 1849; d. March 2, 1939), who was a forest ranger in this region for many years. He held the Congressional Medal of Honor for gallantry in action against Sioux Indians on April 23, 1875.

Ref.: Mrs. Mary Ford Platten (widow)

PLATTSVILLE

Coconino

Nothing is known about this place except the post office information.

P.O. est. April 7, 1900, Eliel S. Sharpnack, p.m.; resc. Feb. 8, 1901

PLAYAS, LAS   pro.: /las pláyəs/

Spanish = "flat area"

Yuma   T15S R12W   Elev. c. 1000'

In 1854 Lt. N. Michler of the Boundary Survey group noted a low mesquite flat and called it Las Playas. He said it had water holes or *charcos* which filled during the rainy season. A *playa* may be exemplified by a flat lake bed which may temporarily be flooded. Ref.: 105, I, 115; 57, p. 106

PLEASANT VALLEY

Gila   T9N R14E   Elev. c. 6000'

This beautiful little valley was so named as early as 1869, when its name occurred on a ms. map. However, not the scenery, but a fierce and bitter feud between the Grahams and Tewksburys made the valley unpleasant. The feud was far bloodier than that of Harlan County, Kentucky.

Al Rose, a Dane, constructed a small stockade in the valley in 1877 and all was peaceful until John Tewksbury arrived in Globe in 1879 and, after gathering his son and livestock in California, settled in Pleasant Valley. The Grahams arrived from Texas about three years later. The Tewksburys helped protect sheep being driven through this region. Cattlemen reacted violently so that the battle was soon joined. Literally dozens were killed. In 1892 the feud ended abruptly when the last of the Grahams was slain in Tempe. Pleasant Valley, almost deserted during the hostilities, was slowly resettled.

Ref.: Woody; 116, p. 595; 5, p. 456

PLENTY

Apache   T11N R25E   Elev. 6000'

On the application for a post office in the National Archives, the local name for this community is given as Springlake, although the name Floy was requested for the post office. The name Floy is said to be that of a young woman in the community, Floy Greer. To avoid confusion with the post office at Eloy (Pinal County), the name of Floy was changed to Plenty on April 1, 1933, at which time Mrs. Floy D. Dickinson was postmaster.

P.O. est. Nov. 28, 1919, Rosa Despain, p.m.; name changed to Plenty, April 1, 1933

Ref.: 242; Noble; Wiltbank

PLOMOSA   pro.: /plomówsə/
Spanish = "lead-colored"

La Paz   T3N R18W   Elev. c. 1200'

As early as 1862 placer gold was being mined in the Plomosa District, which derives its
name from the coloring in the location. On the 1880 Eckhoff map the name is given as
Plomas. It was also sometimes spelled Plumas. See Harrisburg, La Paz Ref.: 146, p.
75

PLOMOSA MOUNTAINS   pro.: /plomówsə/
Spanish = "lead-bearing"

La Paz   T5N R18W   Elev. 3400'

According to a note on file at the USGS, "certain placers have evidently been called the
Plomosa placer diggings on account of containing lumps of lead ore." The name was in
use as early as 1869. In 1879 the name was also spelled Plumosa. Ref.: 329

POACHIE RANGE

Mohave   T13N R11W   Elev. 3700'

Isadoro Olea, a native Indian in the region, called these mountains the Pochi Mountains. The meaning has not been ascertained, but it may be the name of an Indian family.
It is also spelled Pochi. Ref.: Dobyns

POCKET CREEK

Gila   T5N R14E

The word *pocket* in Arizona refers to small rounded openings, not exactly canyons, in
the mountains. This place describes the location of a small creek. The term also applies
to Pocket Hill (Mohave, T41N/R13W), Pocket Lake (Coconino, T19N/R3E), and
Pocket Point (Coconino [Grand Canyon], T33N/R5W). Ref.: Blumer; Woody

POINT OF MOUNTAIN

Pima   Elev. c. 1900'

This stage station at a crossing of the Santa Cruz River about seventeen miles north of
Tucson was at the point of the mountains extending into the valley, hence the name.
Established by the Butterfield Overland Mail, it was partly destroyed by Confederate
forces in 1862. It was abandoned in 1871. Ref.: 73, II, 161, 162; 56, p. 131; *Arizona
Citizen* (Feb. 4, 1871), p. 3

POINT OF PINES (RUINS)

Graham   T1S R25E   Elev. c. 4500'

In 1945 Dr. Emil Haury and E. B. Sayles of the University of Arizona catalogued two
hundred ruins at this location and later established archeological diggings here. During
excavations, it was established that people were living here as early as 2000 B.C. The
ruins, which have at least eight hundred rooms on the ground floor alone, are of buildings
constructed c. 1100 A.D. Ref.: Emil Haury, "Operation; Pick'n Shovel," *Arizona
Alumnus* (Jan.-Feb. 1957), pp. 10-11

POINT OF THE MOUNTAIN

Apache   T8N R28E   Elev. 8860'

The name describes the location. Point of the Mountain Spring is also here.

POISON SPRING

Gila   T12N R10E

The water in this spring sickens stock, hence the name. Ref.: McInturff

POKER MOUNTAIN

Apache   T2N R25E   Elev. c. 7800'

In the mid-1880s several cattle outfits wintered in the gap between two mountains where
in camp cowpokes played poker endlessly, hence the names Poker Mountain and Poker
Gap. They called the nearby stream Freeze Out Creek. Ref.: 18a

POLACCA   pro.: /powlaˆkaka/

Hopi = "butterfly"

Navajo   T28N R18E   Elev. 5788'

In 1890 Tom Polacca, a Tewa Indian from Hano, moved down from the mesa to its base and established the village which bears his name.

P.O. est. Jan. 20, 1901, Richard James Barnes, p.m. Ref.: 242; Edward P. Dozier, "The Hopi and Tewa," *Scientific American* (June 1957), pp. 126, 136; 331, p. 116

POLACCA WASH

Apache/Navajo/Coconino   T32, 25–24N R22, 16–14E

In September 1968 under the name Polacca Wash the USGS consolidated the following: Burnt Corn Wash, Corn Creek, First Mesa Wash, Oraibi Wash, and Tachito Wash. See Polacca, Navajo Ref.: 329

POLAND

Yavapai   T12N R1W   Elev. c. 5500'

Davis Robert Poland (b. 1834, Tennessee; d. Feb. 23, 1882) arrived in Arizona in 1864. By 1871 he had built a cabin in the Bradshaw Mountains. In 1865 he had located the Poland Mine and a community developed. A post office was later established. The community of Poland Junction was five miles from the mine. Poland is now called Breezy Pines, a summer community. Poland Creek is nearby.

P.O. est. Nov. 1, 1901, James Rockwell Sias, p.m. (deceased); Frank Lecklider appointed Jan. 6, 1902; disc. Feb. 15, 1913; Wells Fargo 1903

Ref.: 242; AHS, Davis Robert Poland File

POLARIS

Yuma   T1S R17W   Elev. c. 1500'

The post office for the North Star Mine, said to have been discovered by reference to the Pole Star in 1909, derives its name from that fact. Also, it was found by Felix Mayhew due north of the Kofa Mine.

P.O. est. March 16, 1909, William R. Wardner, p.m.; disc. July 31, 1914

Ref.: Monson; Lenon; 242

POLARIS MOUNTAIN

Yuma   T1S R17W   Elev. 3624'

In April 1964 the USGS eliminated the name Summit Peak and substituted Polaris Mountain for this location. The North Star Mine is at the foot of the mountain. See Polaris, Yuma Ref.: 329; Monson

POLE BRIDGE CANYON

Cochise   T18S R30E

The Pole Bridge Canyon Natural Area lies within this region. It contains a rare species of southern Arizona pine, hence the name *Pole*. The name also applies to the three hundred and twenty acre Pole Bridge Canyon Natural Area, established February 26, 1931, and to Pole Camp Canyon. Ref.: 243, p. 22

POLE KNOLL

Apache   T8N R27E   Elev. 9793'

This knoll, which is burned over, was formerly covered with aspen trees which settlers used for poles. Ref.: Wentz

POLHAMUS

Mohave   c. 10 mi. N. of Hardyville

Capt. Isaac Polhamus, Jr. (b. April 7, 1828, New York; d. Jan. 16, 1922) stored goods awaiting shipment at a landing named for him. In 1870 he was superintendent of the Colorado Steam Navigation Co., for which he also served as a river pilot. His landing has long since disappeared. Ref.: 62; *Arizona Sentinel* (May 9, 1891), p. 1; Lenon

[493]

POLLES MESA   pro.: /pówliys/
Gila   T11N R8E
This location was named for Pohles Chilson, a rancher in this region.
Ref.: Pieper; Gillette

POLLUX TEMPLE
Coconino (Grand Canyon)   T32N R1E   Elev. 3649'
This location, named for one of the mythological twins (Castor and Pollux), was
officially named by the USGS in December 1937.

POLVO (R.R. STN.)   pro.: /pálvo/
Spanish = "dust"
Pima   T14S R14E   Elev. c. 2500'
The area in which this station was located was dry and dusty, hence the name.
Ref.: 18a

POLYGAMY CREEK
Apache   T7NR27E
In 1891 Jacob Noah Butler settled here with his two wives and twenty-two children,
hence the name. The creek, now dry, is in Butler Canyon. Ref.: Wentz

POMERENE
Cochise   T16S R20E   Elev. 3520'
Several names were suggested for this post office before the name Pomerene was
selected. In 1915 the application for the post office stated it was known locally as
Fairview, but the location was given as T21S/R21E. The first name suggested for the
post office was Robinson. Another name requested (on February 2, 1913) was Bueno.
Postal officials are said to have applied the name Pomerene for Senator Pomerene of
Ohio.
P.O. est. July 8, 1915, H. A. Kimmell, p.m. Ref.: 242

POOL KNOLL
Apache   T7N R28E   Elev. 9464'
The name "pool" in this instance derives from the fact that in the early 1880s cattlemen,
who pooled their forces during roundup, used the corral on this knoll to separate cattle
according to brands. Ref.: Wiltbank

POOL'S
Cochise   T17S R31E   Elev. c. 3800'
This location may have been named either for its first postmaster or for Dr. Josiah Pool
(b. Nov. 10, 1820; d. Sept. 21, 1902). The latter arrived in Arizona in 1882. He served
as a camp cook, cowpuncher, bookkeeper, and rancher. His first ranch was on the Santa
Cruz River south of Tucson. In 1883 he located his ranch north of Benson, but by 1894
he was at Mammoth, still later at Winkelman, and finally at Phoenix.
P.O. est. Nov. 19, 1901, John M. Pool, p.m.; disc. July 15, 1913
Ref.: 242; AHS, Frank M. Pool File

POORMAN'S WASH
La Paz   T4N R18W
This wash took its name from the nearby Poorman Mine (T3N/R17W).

PORPHYRY
Gila   T1N R14E   Elev. 4800'
This mountain took its name from that of the Porphyry Mine in Porphyry Canyon west of
the present Miami. Indians used ore from the canyon to make jewelry and when
prospectors saw pieces of the ore, they soon located the Porphyry Mine.
Ref.: Woody; 284, p. 15

PORRAS DIKES
Navajo   T39N R20E   Elev. 5685'
Herbert Gregory named these geological dikes for Fr. Francisco de Porras, a

Franciscan missionary to the Hopi from 1629 until his death at the hands of Indians in 1633. The place is also known as Colville, for C. C. Colville. Ref.: 141, p. 194; 329

PORTAL pro.: /pórtəl/

Cochise   T17S R31E   Elev. 4773'

This community is at the entrance, or portal, to Cave Creek Canyon. The name is English, not Spanish. Portal was founded by Otto Duffener and his brother c. 1900. In 1955 the Southwestern Research Station was established here. Portal Peak is nearby. P.O. est. April 10, 1905, Edward F. Epley, p.m.; disc. Jan. 1, 1965
Ref.: 242; Riggs; "The Southwestern Research Station of the American Museum of Natural History" (1955)

PORTER CREEK

Navajo   T9N R22E   Elev. c. 6000'

James Porter was a pioneer sheepman at this location, hence the name. His name also applies to a canyon, a lake, a mountain, and a spring, all in the vicinity. Ref.: 18a

PORTER SPRING

Gila   (1) T3N R12E   (2) T4N R12E

These springs were named for the Thaddeus T. Porter family, who drove cattle from Oregon to these springs in 1876-79. Ref.: *Republican* (March 10, 1942)

PORTER TANK DRAW

Navajo   T17N R20E   Elev. c. 6000'

This draw was named for Jack Porter, a sheepman who located rock tanks here c. 1887. Ref.: 18a

PORTLAND WASH

Mohave   T23N R21W

This wash, also known as Granite Wash, was named for the Portland Mine. Ref.: 329; Ranger Robert Burns (Katherine Boat Landing)

POSA PLAIN, LA pro.: /la pózə/
Spanish: *posa* = "well"

Yuma   T6S R19W   Elev. c. 500'

Two wells called Los Posos, which appear on the GLO 1867 due east of La Paz, probably led to the name of this plain. Over the years the name shifted from the wells to the valley and back again, appearing for the first time on both the wells and the valley on GLO 1892 as Posas Valley and Los Posos. The wells are also called Deep Wells because they are twelve hundred feet deep. Ref.: Monson; Willson

POSO, EL

Pima? Yuma?

There is a remote possibility that the county was misnamed, in which case the location might refer to Los Posos, Yuma County.
P.O. est. June 19, 1879, Damacio Garcia, p.m.; disc. Oct. 18, 1880

POSO BUENO pro.: /pozo bwéyno/
Spanish: *poso* = "well"; *bueno* = "good"

Pima   T18S R9E   Elev. c. 3000'

This post office was on the Poso Buenos Ranch owned by Hubbard W. Larabee and A. Hemme. The name derived from there being two productive wells on the ranch. P.O. est. Nov. 11, 1890, Hubbard W. Larabee, p.m.; disc. Nov. 11, 1895
Ref.: *Arizona Enterprise* (June 27, 1891), p. 3

POSO NUEVO pro.: /pozo nuwéyvo/
Spanish: *poso* = "well"; *nuevo* = "new"

Pima   T16S R7W

In 1891 a new well was sunk in the valley east of the Baboquivari Mountains, possibly on the Poso Bueno Ranch, hence the name. Ref.: *Arizona Enterprise* (June 27, 1891), p. 3

POSOS, LOS
Spanish: *posos* = "water pockets" or "wells"
Yuma
Elev. c. 500'
Los Posos, about four miles east of Tyson's stage statio, was used by travelers. Water pockets or wells were extremely important to travelers in desert country. A Yuma rancheria existed here in 1776, evidence the *poso* was also used by Indians. The name was sometimes spelled Los Pozos. See Posa Plain, La, Yuma Ref.: 167, II, 288

POSO SALADO   pro.: /pozo saládow/
Spanish: *pozo* = "well"; *salado* = "salt"
Pima   T12S R7W
The name, sometimes spelled Pozo Salado, indicates that the water here is brackish.

POSO VERDE   pro.: /pózo vérdiy/
Spanish: *pozo* = "well"; *verde* = "green"
Pima   T22S R7E   Elev. c. 4500'
In 1699 Fr. Kino called this location Guvo Verde (Papago: *guvo* = "well") because of its green color. The shift to the Spanish was complete by 1854 when Lt. N. Michler of the Boundary Survey party wrote about following the old trail around the southern base of the Sierra del Pozo Verde to the Agua del Pozo Verde. In 1863 a village with about three hundred and fifty Papago Indians existed here. The native name for it was Chutukwahia or Chulukwahia (= "green spring"). According to Papago legend there is a cave in the vicinity formerly occupied by an ogress called Haw-auk-aux (Cruel Old Woman), who appeased her voracious appetite by eating all the wild animals and then people. The Papago Indians consulted their Spirit of Goodness (the culture hero EE-EE-toi) and followed his advice to invite her to a big dance. She danced until she fell into an exhausted sleep and EE-EE-toi threw her over his shoulder and deposited her in the cave. The Indians then piled the cave entrance high with wood and set a fire. The evil ogress died. It is said that the foot prints of the Spirit of Goodness are visible near the cave.

The Pozo Verde Mountains (T22S/R7E) (or Sierra Verde) borrowed the name from that of the Indian settlement and well. They extend across the border into Mexico. The name Sierra Verde was in use in 1869. Ref.: 58; 45, pp. 281, 408, 409, 410; 106, p. 121; 57, p. 10; 167, II, 288; 242

POSTA QUEMADA CANYON   pro.: /postə keymádə/
Spanish: *posta* = "post"; *quemada* = "burnt"
Pima   T16S R17E   Elev. c. 3800'
The stage road from Tres Alamos to Tucson followed the canyon in which the Mountain Springs stage station and inn burned, causing a change to Posta Quemada ("burned post or inn"). The name dates prior to 1875. In 1904 the canyon was being referred to as Mountain Spring Canyon, but a private ranch retained the name of the former stage station. The ranch was sold c. 1980.
Ref.: AHS Names File; 329; 136, p. 25

POST CREEK
Graham   T9S R24E   Elev. c. 6500'
This creek was so named because it runs through the grounds of the army post, Fort Grant.
Ref.: 329

POST OFFICE HILL
Navajo   T7N R23E
The ridge bearing this name was so called at least as early as 1878. During bad weather when the roads were almost impassable, mail from Fort Apache was hauled by mule teams to a shack in Post Office Canyon halfway to Show Low and was left there to be picked up by a team coming from the opposite direction. From this fact came the name of both the canyon and hill. Ref.: Davis

POSTON pro.: /pówstən/
La Paz   T8N R21W   Elev. 330'
During World War II, Poston was established as an internment camp for twenty thousand Japanese-Americans. It was named for Charles Debrille Poston (see Poston Butte, Pinal), first Superintendent for Indian Affairs in Arizona. Poston was largely responsible for the creation of the Colorado River Reservation on which this place is located.
P.O. est. March 15, 1947, Esther L. Anderson, p.m. (to replace a branch post office est. March 1942); disc. Jan. 1, 1967 Ref.: 242; Savilla

POSTON BUTTE
Coconino (Grand Canyon)   T32N R5E   Elev. c. 5500'
The first name for this location was Plateau Point. The name was changed in 1932 to honor the "Father of Arizona," Charles Debrille Poston. See Poston Butte, Pinal

POSTON BUTTE pro.: /pówstən/
Pinal   T4S R9E   Elev. 1748'
This prominent point near Florence has borne several names, among them Stiles Hill (for the father of the notorious robber Billy Stiles), Primrose Hill (a name used by Poston himself in his *Journal* in 1877), and Parsee Hill. The Parsee were sun worshippers from whom Poston derived ideas concerning his own tomb. Charles Debrille Poston (b. April 20, 1825, Kentucky; d. June 24, 1902) settled in Tubac in 1853 with the Sonora Mining Company. Interested in having an Arizona Territory created, he worked hard, and as a result of his efforts he is sometimes called the "Father of Arizona." His *Journal* relates how he offered political plums for votes needed to pass a bill in Congress. When the "plums" had been distributed, Poston realized that he had forgotten to take one for himself. He was thereupon appointed the first Superintendent of Indian Affairs (see Colorado River Indian Reservation, La Paz/Mohave). In 1877 he was appointed to the U.S. Land Office in Florence. He had traveled and, much struck by sun worship, he noted that Primrose Hill looked like the pyramids of Egypt. He began preparing his own sun tomb on the hill by constructing a road to the top and sinking a shaft about thirty feet. When he died in near poverty in Phoenix, his wish to be buried on Primrose or Parsee Hill was ignored. A few years later the State Legislature voted $100. for a tombstone to mark his grave. However, Poston had been buried in a paupers' field and efforts failed to find his grave. In 1925 "his" remains were reburied under a monument atop Poston Butte, a long overdue honor for the first Arizona Territorial delegate to Congress.
Ref.: Preston Mercer, "Desert Scrapbook," *Yuma Daily Sun* (Aug. 8, 1954), III, 2; AHS, Emerson O. Stratton *ms.*; 133, 205, pp. 77, 78

POTATO BUTTE
Gila   T9N R13E   Elev. 6180'
This butte looks like a potato standing on end. Ref.: 18a

POTATO CANYON
Coconino   T38N R14E
The name is a translation of the Navajo name for it, Numasitso Canyon. Indians used to grow potatoes in the canyon bottomland. Ref.: 329

POTATO WASH
Navajo   T14N R16E   Elev. c. 5700'
This wash was named by Will C. Barnes, who raised potatoes here (1888-95).

POT HOLES
Coconino   T29N R7E
This location has several crater-like holes which fill with rain water and waters from melting snow. Ref.: 182

POTHOLES
Yuma   T6S R21W
There are "eroded sinks" in a rocky stretch of the Colorado River at this location, hence

the name. The actual holes where gold was found are on the California side. See Imperial Dam, Yuma Ref.: 320, p. 9

POT HOLES CANYON
Cochise   T19S R31E

The presence of pot holes in this canyon results in the name. Pot Hole Peak (Elev. 6880′) also bears the name.

POTRERO CANYON
Santa Cruz   T24S R13E   Elev. c. 3800′

According to one source, a *potrero* is a canyon flanked by high narrow mesa points. In this instance, however, as Potrero Creek emerges from the canyon it flows through a narrow area bounded by "low bluffs marking the edge of hilly country." Hinton applied the name *Potrero* to this portion of land traversed by the Santa Cruz River on both sides of the international boundary. See also Kitchen Ranch, Pete, Santa Cruz
Ref.: 286, p. 42; 163, p. 183

POTTER MESA
Apache   T16N R25E   Elev. 5802′

On this mesa Albert F. Potter developed Potter's Well, hence the name. Originally William Garland located here in 1885. Potter's Place Draw (T17N/R26E) is an associated place name. Ref.: Paul F. Roberts, Letter (March 25, 1957)

POTTER MOUNTAIN
Cochise   T22S R24E   Elev. 6525′

A highly respected pioneer, Tuck Potter (d. c. 1950), had this mountain named for him. He supported the development of Bisbee. Ref.: Burgess

POTTERY POINT
Gila   T5N R15E

This high point is the site of a prehistoric community where bits of pottery exist by the hundreds. Ref.: McKinney

POTTS MOUNTAIN
Mohave   T12N R14W   Elev. 3378′

John Coyle Potts (b. 1838, Pennsylvania) was a pioneer in the Prescott area prior to 1863. He later moved to Mohave County and became sheriff c. 1893. Potts Tank is on the mountain. Ref.: Harris; 62

POQUETTE HILL
Coconino   T22N R3E

This hill was named for the Poquette Homestead (T21N/R3E).

POVERTY KNOLL
Mohave   T35N R11W   Elev. 6347′

On GLO 1879 this place is named descriptively Solitaire Butte. Frederick S. Dellenbaugh named it Solitaire Butte because of its lonely, dark and forbidding appearance. The name was changed in 1923 to Poverty Knoll for reasons unknown. The name is applied to adjacent Poverty Mountain (Elev. 6791′) and to Poverty Spring.
Ref.: 89, p. 310

POWELL, LAKE
Coconino/Utah   T41N R9E

Waters impounded by Glen Canyon Dam form this lake. By resolution of the Utah Tourist and Publicity Council on June 20, 1959, the lake was named to honor Maj. John Wesley Powell, noted explorer of the Grand Canyon.

POWELL LAKE RESERVOIR
Mohave   T16N R21W

This reservoir covers two hundred and thirty-four acres and has a capacity of seven hundred acre feet. See Needles, The, Mohave

POWELL PEAK

Mohave   T16N R20W   Elev. 2353'

This peak overlooks Powell Lake Reservoir (T16N/R21W). See Needles, The, Mohave

POWELL PLATEAU

Coconino (Grand Canyon)   T33N R1W   Elev. 7680'

Although the name for the plateau was not officially adopted until 1932, it was so named by Maj. Clarence E. Dutton in 1882 to honor Maj. John Wesley Powell (1834-1902). Powell in 1869 led the first successful floating expedition through the canyon. He then named the Grand Canyon. He led a second expedition in 1871-72 to make scientific records. From 1870-79 Powell served as Chief of the Rocky Mountain Region Survey, and in 1879 was appointed first Director of the Bureau of American Ethnology. From 1881-94 he served as Director of the USGS. Ref.: 100, p. 164; 178, p. 79; 329

POWELL POINT

Coconino (Grand Canyon)   T31N R2E   Elev. 7050'

Until this location was officially named Powell Point by the USGS in December 1937 (because of its being the location of the Powell Monument) it was known as Sentinel Point, and then as Maricopa Point. See also Powell Plateau, Coconino (Grand Canyon) Ref.: Schellbach File (Grand Canyon)

POWELL SPRING

Yavapai   T14N R3E

This location was named for William Dempsey Powell (b. Jan. 1, 1846; d. 1936), who lived at this location from 1875 on. A miner, he later became a prominent stockman. Ref.: Mrs. Frier (daughter)

POWERS BUTTE

Maricopa   T1S R4W   Elev. c. 1000'

Col. J. C. Powers (b. Mississippi) was in the Arlington Valley area in the 1880s. An assiduous canal creator, he placed one at the west end of the butte bearing his name. Ref.: Parkman

POWERS HILL

Graham   T8S R20E   Elev. 5250'

This location was named for the Powers brothers c. 1917. They had a mine nearby (T10S/R20E). Ref.: 329

PRAIRIE TANK

Yavapai   T20N R22W   Elev. 5136'

The country here is flat, hence the name. The name applies also to Prairie Wash (Coconino [Grand Canyon], T31N/R2W), for a similar reason. There was once a railroad siding here. Ref.: 18a

PRATT (R.R. SIDING)

Maricopa   T6N R1E   Elev. c. 1400'

William B. Pratt owned a mine for which this was a mail and supply station. The small community was near a natural tank which was home for many very large frogs, hence the old name Frog Tanks. The first name suggested for the post office was Frog Tanks, but postal officials substituted the name Pratt. See Carl Pleasant, Lake, Maricopa
P.O. est. March 24, 1890, J.C.M. Copes, p.m.; disc. Aug. 25, 1896
Ref.: 242; *Arizona Daily Gazette* (May 9, 1894), p. 1

PRATT LAKE

Apache   T7N R31E   Elev. 7990'

This place, which was named for an early settler, was known locally as Coyote Lake. Ref.: 329

PRAYING WOMAN
Maricopa   T2N R3E
This formation on the north side of Camelback Mountain is also called the Monk. Both names are descriptive.

PREACHER CANYON
Gila   T11N R11E
In the 1880s during the Pleasant Valley feud, a preacher lived here, hence the name. He always carried a double-barrelled shotgun. He sang to warn that he was approaching. Ref.: McKinney

PRESCOTT
Yavapai   T13–14N R2W   Elev. 5354'
Prescott resulted from the establishment of the Territory of Arizona. On December 29, 1863 the territorial governing party arrived at Navajo Springs (see that entry, Apache). Gov. John N. Goodwin proclaimed that the seat of government would be near Fort Whipple, which had been established in November. On January 22, 1864, the party arrived at Fort Whipple and in May the site of the future Prescott was selected. The Indian name for the location was *In-dil-chin-ar* (= "pine woods"). Prescott was named in 1864 to honor William Hickling Prescott (1796 – 1859), a prominent historian. The name was preferred over others because of the "Aztec memorials everywhere existing in this region and confirming the conclusions of the great American historian." The growing community had local names, such as Goodwin City (for Gov. John Goodwin), Granite (it was on Granite Creek), Gimletville, and Fleuryville (for Judge Henry W. Fleury [d. 1896], who had his headquarters on the west side of Granite Creek.)
   Among the first settlers was Joseph Ehle (b. March 13, 1813, New York; d. Nov. 1912), who arrived from Colorado with his family on July 28, 1864. In 1865 he established a government road station at his ranch in Skull Valley, but returned in 1868 to Prescott. Prescott has the honor of having held the first rodeo in 1888, now an annual event held on July 4th.
   In 1867 Tucson became the territorial capital, but Prescott again became the territorial capital in 1877, retaining that honor until 1889 when the capital was moved to Phoenix. Prescott is seat of Yavapai County.
P.O. est. Aug. 25, 1863, Hiram W. Reid, p.m.; Wells Fargo 1879
Ref.: 351; *Arizona Journal Miner* (July 20, 1864), p. 3; 163, pp. 252, 253; 116, p. 568; 15, pp. 522, 536; 107, IV, 19; 233, pp. 136, 137

PRESCOTT NATIONAL FOREST
Yavapai   T14N R1W
On May 10, 1898 the Prescott Forest Reserve was created. On Dec. 30, 1907 Verde Forest Reserve was established. They were consolidated under the name Prescott National Forest on July 2, 1908, with additional acreage being added on October 22, 1934 from the Tusayan National Forest. Total acreage is 1,456,313. Ref.: 243, p. 35

PRESCOTT VALLEY
Yavapai   Elev. 5100'
This small community, founded in 1966, is on US 69, eight miles from Prescott. The name describes the location. See Prescott, Yavapai

PRESIDENT CANYON
Graham   T8S R22E
This dry canyon, also known as K H Canyon, is named for the President Mine (T8S/R22E).

PRESIDENT HARDING RAPIDS
Coconino (Grand Canyon)
This location was named for President Warren G. Harding. In this rapids Hansbrough's body was found. See Hansbrough Rapids, Coconino (Grand Canyon)

PRESTON MESA
Coconino   T34N R11E   Elev. c. 6000'
This location was named for Sam Preston, a Navajo trader. Ref.: 18a

PRESUMIDO PASS   pro.: /presuwmiydo/
Spanish = "show off, presumptuous"
Pima   T21S R7E   Elev. c. 4775'
The Spanish name describes the fact that this pass looks formidable, but actually is not. The name has been spelled as follows: Prescimuda, Prescimide, Prescimido, and Preciendo. Ref.: 329; 262, p. 21

PRICE (R.R. SIDING)
Pinal   T4S R11E   Elev. 1574'
There are two possible origins for the name of the community: (1) William Price was a merchant in Florence, who supplied contractors during the building of the railroad in 1903; (2) in the same year B. S. Price worked with the general railroad line contractor, George Tisdale.
P.O. est. Sept. 16, 1908, Henry Zeuner, p.m.; disc. March 15, 1923 Ref.: 18a; 242

PRICE, CAMP
Cochise   T20S R29E
In 1881 Camp Price, a military outpost, was also known as Camp Supply. It was at the head of Tex Canyon. A military telegraph station existed here. It may have been named for Lt. Col. William Redwood Price (d. Dec. 30, 1881), 6th Cavalry, active in the campaign against the Hualapai Indians. Price Camp (T19S/R30E) also shares the name, as does Price Spring. Ref.: 159, I, 807; 49, pp. 444, 445; AHS Names File (John Rockfellow)

PRICE CANYON
Mohave   T30N R11W
This canyon takes its name from that of Price's Spring, which is in the canyon. The spring was named on January 14, 1868, for Lt. Col. William Redwood Price, who was to receive his colonelcy on December 10, 1868 for service against the Hualapai Indians. It was named by 1st Lt. J. D. Stevenson. Price Pocket also carries the name. Ref.: 335, p. 55

PRIDHAM CANYON
Cochise   T19S R29E
In about 1906 George Pridham (b. 1841, New York) homesteaded here to raise grapes. He built a concrete dam for irrigation purposes on Pridham Creek and dug open wells, but the venture proved impracticable. Ref.: Riggs; 63

PRIETA, PRIETO: Place names with the designation *prieta* or *prieto* usually have a black appearance (Spanish: *prieta* = "black"; pro.: /priyetə/). The following are examples:

Prieta Peak   Pinal   T10S R5E   Elev. 3332'
The older name Prieto was corrected by the USGS to Prieta in 1941.

Prieta, Sierra   Yavapai   T13N R3W
Densely growing juniper gave these mountains their black appearance. Gilbert, of Wheeler's survey party, called them the San Prioeto, noting that little lava showed near Prescott. However, he added that the range became "eruptive in character near Postal's Ranch. See Granite, Yavapai
Ref.: 345, III, 125; 163, p. 301; King *ms*. (1854), (Huntington Library)

Prieto, Cerro ("black hill") Pima   T20S R8E   Elev. 4665'

Prieto, Cerro   Pinal   T10S R9E   Elev. 2688'

Prieto Plateau   Greenlee   T2S R29E

Prieto Wash, Cerro   Pima   T18S R10E

PRIME LAKE

Coconino   T20N R8E

This small lake used to be called Horse Lake (1908), but in 1964 the name was officially changed to Prime Lake. It was named for John Prime, who with John Marshall had a meat market in Flagstaff in the early 1880s. Ref.: 329

PRINGLE WASH

Gila   T5N R15E   Elev. c. 3200'

This wash crosses the Pringle Ranch owned by the three Pringle brothers, who arrived here in the early 1880s. Robert Pringle (b. 1848, Scotland) emigrated to the U.S. in 1868 and arrived in Arizona in 1882. His brothers were named John and Andrew. Andrew was killed in an argument over a saddle blanket. Ref.: Woody; 224, III

PROCTOR SPRING

Pima   T19S R15E

This spring is on Proctor's Ranch, hence the name. Proctor Wash (Pima/Santa Cruz) shares the name.

PROMONTORY BUTTE

Coconino (Grand Canyon)   T11N R13E   Elev. 8078'

This promontory on the Mogollon Rim overlooks the Tonto Basin. See also Hunter Creek, Gila

PROMONTORY BUTTE

Mohave (Lake Mead)   T25N R21W

This prominent viewpoint forms the north wall of the mouth of Black Canyon. The name, approved by the USGS in 1948, is descriptive.

PROSPECT

Cochise   T13S R19E   Elev. c. 4000'

This location, still in existence in 1903, had prospect holes dug near a mining camp. Fr. Kino probably visited near here in 1697 at a rancheria of the Sobaipuri, which he called Rosaria and also Jiaspi. Ref.: 167, I, 631; Burrell

PROSPECT CANYON

Coconino (Grand Canyon)   T33N R7W   Elev. c. 5200'

While working in the area, John Conners and Franklin French, prospectors from Holbrook, named this canyon so they could identify it. Prospect Point (T30N/R8W), Valley, and Ridge share the name.

PROTO CANYON

Santa Cruz   T24S R15E

The Proto family has lived here for several generations.

PROVIDENCE

Yavapai   T12N R1W   Elev. 5500'

The name may be that of a mine in the area which the post office served. P.O. est. March 4, 1899, Bradford Mott Crawford, p.m.; disc. Oct. 25, 1904; Wells Fargo 1903 Ref.: 242

P S KNOLL

Apache   T4N R27E   Elev. 8045'

This knoll is on the P S Ranch. It applies also to the quarter-section area of the P S Ranch Wild Life Area. Ref.: 9, p. 2

PUEBLO CANYON   pro.: /pwéblo/

Spanish: *pueblo* = "town"

Gila   T6N R14E   Elev. c. 4000'

A partially explored group of cliff dwellings in this canyon led to the name, which also applies to the Pueblo Mine, an asbestos mine. Ref.: 224, p. 14

PUEBLO COLORADO VALLEY

Apache   T25N R24E
Navajo   T21N R20E

The name Pueblo Colorado is said to derive from the Navajo *Kin Li Chee* (= "red village"). This area was named by Lt. Joseph Christmas Ives and Dr. John Newberry in 1858. Originally the name Pueblo Colorado (Spanish = "red town") Valley was applied only to the portion north of Ganado. Also called Pueblo Colorado Wash, it encompasses the following: Ganado Wash (upper part); Cornfields Wash, Twin Buttes Wash, and Pueblo Colorado River. See Kin Li Chee, Navajo Ref.: 141, p. 194

PUEBLO GRANDE (RUINS)   pro.: /pwéblo grandiy/

Spanish: *pueblo* = "town"; *grande* = "big"
Maricopa   T1N R4E

This ruin within the old Phoenix downtown central area was named because of its exceptionally large size.

PUEBLO VIEJO   pro.: /pwéblo viyeho/

Spanish: *pueblo* = "town"; *viejo* = "old"
Graham   T7S R27E   Elev. c. 2500'

Fifteen Mexicans were the first settlers in the Gila River Valley. They located in 1872 at Solomonville, calling their settlement Pueblo Viejo, according to Fish "probably on account of the many ruins found in the valley." In 1873 Indian ruins reportedly covering a tract one mile long by two miles wide were found here. Hodge conjectured that the ruins, which he called Buena Vista (Spanish = "pleasant view"), were the reason for the name Pueblo Viejo Valley. Some surmise that the ruins are possibly those called Chichilticalli (Nahuatl: *chichilti* = "red"; *calli* = "house") in the 1540 Coronado Expedition reports. The Pueblo Viejo Valley is sometimes called Upper Gila Valley. Ref.: 224, I, 168, 169; AHS, Lizzie Steele File; *Arizona Citizen* (March 8, 1873), p. 2; 168, pp. 45, 186; 116, p. 587

PUERCO RIVER   pro.: /perko/ or /pwerko/

Spanish = "dirty"
Apache/Navajo/New Mexico   T14–18N R20–24E

At flood stage the stream has a dirty color and carries much trash, hence its name. In 1848 Lt. James William Abert (with Beale's expedition) noted that for almost two-thirds of its one-hundred-and-forty-mile length, this stream was deep with sand and had vertical banks, often thirty feet high. Erosion reveals what torrents flood through the stream channels at certain seasons. Locally called the "Perky," it has borne a number of names. Whipple in 1853 called it the Rio Puerco of the West, to distinguish it from the Rio Puerco to the east in New Mexico. The name Puerco del Oriente or Puerco del Ouest both mean "Puerco of the West." Ref.: 1, p. 59; 345, II, 28

PUERCO RIVER (RUINS)

Apache

These ruins in the Petrified Forest National Monument contained one hundred and twenty-five rooms. See Puerco River, Apache/Navajo/New Mexico
Ref.: 13, Jepson, "Trees, of Stone," p. 4

PUERTA, LA

Cochise   T12S R32E

This location at the west entrance of Doubtful Pass was also called La Puerta Grande (= "big door" or "pass"). The name *La Puerta* was given to it by Gray, one of whose mule drivers exclaimed, "La Grande Puerta!" when the party came upon it. According to Gray, "I named it La Puerta — the door. None of the party but myself had previously been in this section of the country and there were no traces of anyone having passed through it until now...." See Simon Valley, San, Cochise Ref.: 138, p. 45

PUERTO BLANCO MOUNTAINS   pro.: /pwérto blánko/

Spanish: *puerto* = "door"; "pass"; *blanco* = "white"
Pima   T16S R12E   Elev. 3145'

This range is also called Bates Well Mountains and Dripping Spring Mountains

(Bryan). They are also called the Puerto Blanco Mountains because the old Spanish trail crossed the International Boundary and headed northward through a pass descriptively known as Puerto Blanco (= "white pass"). The name Puerto Blanco may derive from the fact that there are two white rocks at either side of the pass over these low mountains. The name Dripping Spring comes from the fact that Puerto Blanco Pass is at a spring called Dripping Spring, also descriptively named. Ref.: Hensen; Ketchum; Dodge; 13, pp. 2, 5; 59, p. 410; 58

PULCIFER CREEK

Apache   T9N R25E

The name Pulcifer has been in use since 1915. In 1939 nearby residents said that Pulcifer Creek was known to them as Supolvre and not as Sepulveda. Pulcifer Spring is an associated name. Ref.: 329

PULPIT ROCK

Cochise   T21S R20E

This name was applied as early as 1880 to a rock at Camp Huachuca. The name is descriptive. It is near the entrance to Echo Canyon and is a "huge mass of devil's cheese-ring type" balanced on a pedestal rock. It is more than sixty feet high.
Ref.: *Eleven Eaglets*, p. 296 (1905)

PUMP HOUSE WASH

Coconino   T19N R6E   Elev. 5000'

Water for the lumber mill at Flagstaff was pumped through the wash to the A. & P. R.R. from a spring where a concrete bridge crosses Oak Creek. The name Pump House Wash derives from the presence of the old pump house, a landmark since the late 1890s.

PUMPKIN KNOLL

Coconino   T24N R4E   Elev. 7490'

This knoll has the same location as Pumpkin Center, Coconino. Pumpkins grow readily in the desert.

PUNKIN CENTER

Gila   T6N R10E   Elev. 2350'

Before 1900, pumpkins grew profusely in this area. This location, also known as Tonto Basin, was formerly called Packard's Store. The store belonged to Amanda Packard, a cattleman who settled at the spring here. A small village has since developed at this location.
P.O. est. as Tontobasin *and* Punkin Center, May 8, 1929, Lillian L. Colcord, p.m.; name changed to Tonto Basin, May 2, 1930 Ref.: Cooper; Woody; 329

PUNTA DEL AGUA   pro.: /pánta del ágwa/

Spanish: *punta* = "point"; *agua* = "water"
Pima   T17S R12E   Elev. 2450'

Water in the Santa Cruz River used to resurface here after having been underground for some miles, and therefore the name was descriptive. Both the water and the resurfacing location have long since disappeared, but formerly the location was a stopping place for travelers. It was owned by a German (Fritz Contzen). His station was noted for solid old-fashioned meals. Years earlier (1859) the location was referred to as a "hacienda of the San Xavier Mining Company." Ref.: *Weekly Arizonian* (April 21, 1859), p. 3; 51, p. 326

PUNTENNEY

Yavapai   T18N R1W   Elev. 3840'

In 1879 George Puntenney arrived in Arizona. He built the first lime kiln here. The Puntenney Lime Company was sold to John T. Sheffield and Alfred Paul in 1929.
P.O. est. as Puntney, May 20, 1892, George Puntenney, p.m.; name changed to Puntenney (date unknown); disc. Sept. 30, 1932 Ref.: AHS, Eli Puntenney File; Garrett; *Builder and Contractor* (Oct. 30, 1929)

PUSCH RIDGE

Pima   T12S R14E   Elev. 5360'

A cattleman, George Pusch (b. June 24, 1847, Germany) arrived in Tucson on May 24, 1876, and soon established the Steampump Ranch near the ridge bearing his name. The ranch name came from a steam pump used to raise well water. Pusch Peak overlooks the ridge. Ref.: Pusch (son); *Pima County Court Register* (1894); 224, III

PUTEOSI CANYON

Coconino (Grand Canyon)   T33N R3W   Elev. c. 5000'

Puteosi is a Havasupai family name meaning "coyote." The USGS approved the name for this canyon in 1925. Ref.: 329

PUTMAN SPRING   pro.: /púwtmən/

Mohave   T24N R18W

This spring was named for John Putman, who prospected and mined in this region c. 1883. Putman Wash (T24N/R19W) also has his name. Ref.: Harris

PUTNAM WASH

Pinal   T7S R14E

This wash was named after the Putnam brothers, who created the road from Florence to Globe. Ref.: *Arizona Sentinel* (Oct. 6, 1877), p. 3

PYEATT CAVE

Cochise   T22S R19E

This cave is on the Pyeatt Ranch, hence the name.

PYMN CANYON

Mohave   T33N R10W

This canyon was named for a settler in this area prior to 1900. It applies also to Pymn Canyon Pond (T33N/R11W), a stock tank. Ref.: 329

PYRAMID

Mohave   T21N R22W   Elev. c. 600'

The post office at this location was initially called Sheeptrail because it provided mail services for miners at the Sheeptrail Mine. The name of this office was changed to Pyramid because of its location near Pyramid Rock. See Pyramid Canyon, Mohave P.O. est. as Sheeptrail, Oct. 29, 1898, John C. Dexter, p.m.; name changed to Pyramid, June 30, 1899, Louis K. Mace, p.m.; disc. Oct. 2, 1901 Ref.: 200, p. 39

PYRAMID BUTTE

Navajo   T23N R18E   Elev. 6263'

This butte looks like a pyramid, hence the name. It is also called Pyramid Mountain Ref.: 141, p. 136

PYRAMID CANYON

Mohave (Lake Mead)   T21N R22W   Elev. c. 600'

Lt. Joseph Christmas Ives named this canyon in 1857 because near the rapids there was a natural pyramid nearly thirty feet tall. The formation was known as Pyramid Rock, which now lies under water. Ref.: 245, p. 75

PYRAMID PEAK

Maricopa   T6N R3E   Elev. 2614'

This peak looks like a pyramid, hence the name.

PYRAMID PEAK

La Paz   T4N R14W   Elev. 2140'

This location was named for its fancied resemblance to an Egyptian pyramid. The name has been in use at least since the 1880s. Ref.: 329

Q

QUAIL: Because the attractive *Gambel's quail* occur in great numbers in many places in Arizona, the name is frequently associated with places within the state. Instances occur below:

Quail Canyon	Mohave	T41N R11W
Quail Draw	Mohave	T41N R11W
Quail Spring	Graham	T3S R19E

This spring on the San Carlos Indian Reservation is called Warm Spring by older Indians.

Quail Spring	Greenlee	T3S R30E
Quail Spring	Maricopa	T7N R3E
Quail Spring	Mohave	(1) T40N R12W (2) T24N R19W
Quail Spring	Pinal	T1S R11E
Quail Spring	Yavapai	(1) T12N R6E (2) T12N R2E
Quail Spring Canyon	Gila	T3N R13E
Quail Springs Wash	Gila	T3N R13E
Quail Springs Wash	Mohave (Lake Mead)	

QUAKING ASPEN CANYON
Coconino   T35N R1E

This canyon is named for quaking aspen trees which grow abundantly in this region. Formerly a stage station existed near Schell Spring in this canyon. Aspen trees grow also at Quaking Aspen Spring, Mohave (T39N/R14W). Ref.: Kinney

QUAKING ASPEN TRAIL
Coconino (Grand Canyon)

The USGS recommended changing the name of this trail to Swamp Point Trail. Ref.: 329

QUARTERMASTER CANYON
Mohave   T30N R14W   Elev. c. 3500'

This canyon derives its name from that of a Hualapai Indian called "Quartermaster," who lived here from the early 1900s to about 1930. His name applies also to Quartermaster Falls, named in 1935.   Ref.: Euler (M.N.A.)

QUARTZ HILL
Graham   T7S R20E   Elev. 5732'

The hill is so named because of the presence of quartz here.

QUARTZITE BUTTE
Santa Cruz

This butte in the Santa Rita Mountains about thirty miles south of Tucson was first known as Hart Butte for William Hart (d. 1899). He came to Arizona in January 1878 from Rochester, New York, with John A. Rockfellow and established a ranch adjacent to the railroad tracks. The name gradually fell into disuse and was replaced by the present name because of geologic formations. Ref.: 277, p. 199; 286, Plate IV

QUARTZITE CANYON
Apache   T1N R7W   Elev. c. 6000'
By decision of the USGS in 1932 this geologically descriptive name replaced the names Blue Canyon, Quarzo Canyon, and Paquette Canyon. The name Paquette was that of a local resident, Peter Paquette. Ref.: 141, pp. 89, 194; 329

QUARTZITE CANYON
Gila   T1N R15E
This canyon was named because of the geological formation here.

QUARTZITE MOUNTAIN
Pinal   T5S R18E   Elev. 4869'
In August 1963 the name was changed from Red Rooster Mountain to Quartzite Mountain because of such ore being found in the mine at this location. Ref. 329

QUARTZITE WASH
Apache   T2N R6W
Quartzite Wash Reservoir is at this location. See Quartzsite Canyon, Gila

QUARTZ KING
Yuma   T1N R18W   Elev. 500'
A post office was established here for workers at the Quartz King Mine. P.O. est. July 2, 1907, Willard William McCume, p.m.; disc. June 15, 1910 Ref.: 242

QUARTZ LEDGE
Gila   T7N R10E
Contrary to its name, this is simply a white ledge. Ref.: Packard

QUARTZ MOUNTAIN
Yavapai   T12N R3W   Elev. 5572'
This was named for the presence of quartz in the locale.

QUARTZSITE
La Paz   T4N R19W   Elev. 875'
The town of Quartzsite is in Tyson Wash about nine miles east of old Fort Tyson. The fort was privately owned, having been built in 1856 by Charles Tyson for protection against Indians. Tyson Wells (1868 called Hawk Springs) soon became a stage station on the road from Ehrenberg to Prescott. In 1875 Martha Summerhayes wrote that it was the most melancholy and uninviting place she had seen saying, "It reeks of everything unclean, morally, and physically . . . ."

When the stage line stopped running, Tyson's Well was abandoned However, in 1897 mining caused a local boom and a community developed, but not actually at Tyson's Wells. Therefore a different name was suitable so when the post office was reestablished, a new name was selected. George Ingersoll suggested the name Quartzite, although that metamorphic rock does not exist locally. The application for a post office suggests the name Quartz Valley, but the post office substituted Quartzsite (*sic*). The town contains the grave of Hadji Ali (b. 1829, Syria; d. Dec. 16, 1902), a camel driver for Lt. Edward Fitzgerald Beale. Hadji Ali, simplified to "Hi Jolly," was known to his neighbors as Phillip Tedro. When camels were abandoned for transportation in the American West, he kept several, using them to haul freight. In 1868 he turned the animals loose near Gila Bend and for years there were reports that camels roamed mountains of southwestern Arizona.

P.O. est. as Tyson, June 6, 1893, Michael Welz, p.m.; disc. Sept. 21, 1895; reest. as Quartzsite, April 30, 1896, George U. Ingersoll, p.m.
Ref.: 5, p. 361; 314, p. 157; *Arizona Sentinel* (June 19, 1897), p.2; 163, xxxvii; Preston Mercer, "Desert Scrap Book," *Yuma Daily Sun* (Oct. 7, 1953), II; 2, and (Oct. 5, 1953), p. 10; 242; Lenon

QUAYLE
Coconino   T15N R12E   Elev. c. 5800'
The Quayle family operated this post office for several years.
P.O. est. Nov. 11, 1914, Selma H. Quayle, p.m.; disc. Oct. 31, 1916 Ref.: 242

QUEEN
Pinal   T1S R11E
This post office was so named because of its location at the mouth of Queen Creek
Canyon.
P.O. est. April 21, 1881, Charles H. Miller, p.m.; disc. Sept. 5, 1881

QUEEN CREEK
Maricopa   T2S R7E   Elev. 1450'
According to the post office location form on file in the National Archives, this place
was known locally as Rittenhouse. Queen Creek was a railroad stop which developed
into a community. See Queen Creek (Pinal/Maricopa)
P.O. est. Jan. 27, 1913, Frank E. Ross, p.m. Ref.: 242

QUEEN CREEK
Pinal/Maricopa   T2S R8E
At first called Picket Post Creek, the name of this creek derived from that of the Silver
Queen Mine. The creek bed runs through Queen Canyon (or Queen Creek Canyon).
Ref.: Craig; Woody; 10, p. 21

QUEENS WELL
Pima   T13S R7E   Elev. 2025'
This Papago village had ten families in 1965. The reason for the name is now known.
Ref.: *Papago Bulletin* (1965)

QUERINO CANYON
Apache   T22N R29E   Elev. c. 5800'
This is the same location as that given for Helena Canyon. The name first appears as
Quirino on the Smith 1879 map as Quirino, and in the year following a small railroad
station is named Querino on the Rand McNally map (between Allantown and
Sanders), possibly indicating a construction station where the crew picked up the name
from that of the nearby canyon. The name Querino may possibly be a corruption of
Carino (see Pine Springs, Apache). The Spanish meaning of "tenderness" sheds no
light on the origin of the name. On GLO maps beginning in 1883, the name changed to
Helena Canyon, but for what reason is not known.

QUIBURI (RUINS)
Cochise   T19S R21E   Elev. 3792'
This place name derives partially from the plural of *ki* (Nevome = "houses"). In
November 1697 Fr. Eusebio Kino established the mission of Santa Cruz de Quiburi at
a Sobaipuri Indian village of about five hundred people. A Spanish presidio called
Santa Cruz was established. The following are variant spellings: Giburi, Kiburi,
Quiburio, San Ignacio Guibore, San Pablo de Quiburi, San Juan Quiburi, and
Quibury. Ref.: 167, II, 339; 15, p. 355; 45, p. 269; 44, p. 70

QUIEN SABE CREEK   pro.: /ki^en sábe/
Spanish: *quien* = "who"; *sabe* = "knows"
Maricopa   T7N R5E   Elev. c. 4000'
Someone named the creek and other locations nearby, but why, who knows?
Ref.: 18a

QUIJOTOA   pro.: /kiyhowtow?ə/
Papago: *kia hoa toak* = "carrying-basket mountain"
Pima   T14S R2E   Elev. 2800'
According to a newspaper article (1885), Papago Indians called mescal cactus and its
fibers *quijo*, a name also applied to baskets made of mescal fibers. Papago cone-shaped
burden baskets were carried like a back pack. The crest of nearby Ben Nevis Mountain

looks like such a basket and hence was called Quijotoa by Indians and prospectors alike. The name is shared by the Quijotoa Mountains or Range (T16S/R2E, Elev. 3925') and by Quijotoa Pass (T14S/R1E, Elev. 2775'), and Quijotoa Valley and Wash (T13S/R4E).

Mining occurred in this vicinity as early as 1774. When significant copper mining began c. 1879, the name Quijotoa was applied to the mines, the mining district, and – when an even richer deposit was found in 1883 by Alexander McKay, who called the find the Quijotoa Mine: to the developing mining camp. Charles H. Beckwith and George L. Rognon laid out a town site called Quijotoa City. Other town sites arose: New Viginia and Logan. On the post office application is a notation that locally the area was known as Covered Wells. However, by 1885 the ores were exhausted and the miners departed. The Indians remained in their own village. Various spellings for Quijotoa follow: Kihatoak (Pima name, 1908); Quejotoa (Poston, 1863); Tnijotobar (Bailey report, 1858); Quijotia (Pumpelly, 1870); Quyotia (Ms. map 1866, Huntington Library). In 1912 there was a placer gold mine and store called Horseshoe or Horseshoe Bend here, known to Papago Indians as *Komaktjivurt* (= "gray soil" or "caliche").

P.O. est. as Quijotoa, Nov. 19, 1883, S.J. Lord, p.m.; disc. Aug. 31, 1942
Ref.: 242; *Phoenix Herald* (Aug. 3, 1885), p. 2; *Arizona Sentinel* (Nov. 4, 1903), p. 1; 5, p. 399; 308, pp. 17, 18, 24; 58; 167; II, 340; AHS, Chambers Collection, Box 7-8

QUIJOTOA VALLEY
Pima   T14S R1W
This is also known as Pisinimo Valley (Pisinimo Village is in the valley). It is also sometimes called San Simon Valley because it is drained by San Simon Wash. See Quijotoa, Pima   Ref.: 329

QUINLIN MOUNTAINS
Pima   T17S R7E   Elev. 6875'
James Quinlin (b. 1839, Maine; d. 1892) arrived in Tucson in 1865. By 1884 he had a stage station at this location on the route from Tucon to Quijotoa. He was known then an "an old-time freighter," but was also a miner. As the stage station was at the northern base of the mountains when Roskruge surveyed Pima County in 1893, he named the mountains nearby for Quinlin. The station, called Quinlin, was at T13S/R7E.
Ref.: 308, p. 79; *Arizona Enterprise* (June 27, 1891), p. 3; AHS Names File; 62

QUITOBAQUITO SPRINGS   pro.: /kíyto bakíyto/
Papago = "house ring spring"
Pima   T17S R7W   Elev. 1844'
This is a pond today about sixty yards north of the International Boundary where the old springs once existed. It was an important watering place for Diaz, Kino, Garcés, de Anza, and others. The name *ki-to-bac* means a "watering place," to which was joined a designation (now lost) indicating "the first ring of thatch in a circular Papago house," thus "house-ring spring." The settlement by the same name was in Mexico. A larger town called Quito Bac farther south in Mexico may have led to the addition of the diminutive *quito* for the smaller settlement. Others theorize that the *bac* portion derives from the Papago *vapk* (= "water reeds"; "spring") plus the Spanish diminutive to result in "little spring," to which in turn a further diminutive might have been added to yield *quito bac quito*. The name refers also to hills and mountains (T17S/R8W). Lumholtz noted that the Papago name was *alivaipai*, also meaning "small springs." As for the pond, it is notable because in it are Percy minnows, a rare desert fish found at only one other place in Arizona. Variant spellings include Quitovac and Quitovaquita.
Ref.: Hensen; 13, Dodge, "Organ Pipe . . . ," p. 5; 227, p. 105, Note; 57, pp. 2, 426, 427; 77, p. 487, Note 33; 106, p. 115

QUIVERO (R.R. STN.)
Coconino   T25N R4E
According to the reports of the Coronado Expedition, Quivero must have been far east of Arizona, but this point on the Grand Canyon branch of the A.T. & S.F. R.R. was given the name.

R

RA, TOWER OF
Coconino (Grand Canyon)   T32N R2E   Elev. 6079'
In 1906 many place names culled from mythologies and religions were applied to places
in the Grand Canyon. This is one. Ra was the Egyptian sun god.

RABBIT
Pinal   T9S R5E   Elev. 3600'
The post office was on the Rabbit Ranch, hence the name.
P.O. est. Jan. 13, 1893, Andrew J. Dorin, p.m.; disc. June 21, 1905

RABBIT HILLS
Navajo
Lt. Edward Fitzgerald Beale knew these hills as Rabbit Hills. See also Marcou Mesa,
Navajo, and Hopi Buttes, Navajo   Ref.: Floyd *ms* (April 7, 1859), Huntington
Library

RABBIT SPRING
Navajo: *Gash to* = "rabbit spring"
Navajo   T25N R21E
The name is a translation of the Navajo name.

RACETRACK KNOLL
Coconino   T36N R3W
A favorite pioneer recreation was racing horses. Several place names reflect that fact.
This is an example.

RADIUM HOT SPRINGS
Yuma   T8S R18W   Elev. 380'
In 1930 C.A. Eaton of Yuma owned these thermal springs. He intended to develop them
as a health resort, using the word radium.   Ref.: 5, p. 389; 355, p. 220

RAFAEL, SAN
Pima   T18S R9E
This is the name of a Papago village, but who so named is not currently known.
Ref.: 262, p. 3

RAFAEL, SAN (P.O.)
Santa Cruz   T23S R17E
The San Rafael Ranch was owned by cattlemen Collin and Brewster Cameron c. 1889.
It consisted in part of the former San Rafael de la Zanja Land Grant. The Mexican
Government made it in May 1825 to Manuel Bustillo. Having been authorized to lay out
"four square leagues," Bustillo stretched hemp cord and measured four leagues square
(= sixteen square leagues), apparently misunderstanding what was meant. The acreage
confirmed by the United States Congress was seventeen thousand three hundred fifty-
three. Headquarters for the ranch were at Lochiel. See Lochiel, Santa Cruz
P.O. est. as San Rafael, Dec. 20, 1910, R.N. Keaton, p.m.; disc. May 31, 1917
Ref.: 242; *Weekly Arizona Enterprise* (Jan. 31, 1891), p. 1; Lenon

RAFAEL DEL VALLE LAND GRANT, SAN   pro.: /rafáyəl del váye/
Spanish= "Saint Rafael of the Valley"
Cochise   T22S R22E
Prior to its division this grant consisted of twenty thousand thirty-four acres. The United
States Congress confirmed fourteen thousand four hundred seventy-four acres. The
portion in Mexico was vested in the Camou brothers.   Ref.: 116, p. 428; 182

RAGGED TOP
Gila   T11S R8E   Elev. 3907'
The top of this place looks ragged, hence the name.

RAILROAD CANYON
Yavapai   T21N R6W
The Santa Fe R.R. planned to lay pipe to a reservoir in this canyon in 1898.
Ref.: *Oasis* (July 9, 1898), p. 1

RAILROAD PASS
Cochise   T16S R22E   Elev. 4291'
While exploring in 1856 for a feasible railroad route across the southwest, Lt. John G.
Parke noted this location between the Valle de Sauz (San Simon Valley) and the Valle de
las Playas (Sulphur Springs Valley). He suggested calling it Railroad Pass. It is also
called Dragoon Pass. However, the latter is not at the same place.   Ref.: 254, p. 20

RAILROAD PASS
Mohave   c. T21N R17W   Elev. c. 3300'
Fr. Francisco Garcés camped here in the mid-1770s as did Amiel W. Whipple in 1854.
The location seems identical with that Lt. Edward Fitzgerald Beale called Engle's Pass
on October 8, 1857. In 1857 Lt. Joseph Christmas Ives said his party named this
location Railroad Pass, recommending that it be used for the future railroad route. The
railroad tracks are now in it.   Ref.: Babcock; 335, pp. 5 (Note 5), 17

RAINBOW PLATEAU
Navajo/Coconino   T40-34N R15-1E   Elev. c. 6000'
This colorful area was named by Herbert Gregory in 1915. Lying partly in Utah, the
plateau is among the least known and most inaccessible parts of the Navajo Reservation.
It has innumerable red rock canyons varying from two hundred to two thousand feet
deep.   Ref.: 141, p. 44

RAINBOW SPRING
Navajo   T25N R20E
The name is a translation of the Navajo *naadziilii bii'to* (= "spring inside a rainbow").

RAINBOW VALLEY
Maricopa   T2S R2W   Elev. 1000'
The name applies to the post office and also to what is sometimes called Little Rainbow
Valley. The reason for the name has not been learned.
P.O. ext. Nov. 18, 1930, Allen Robbins, p.m.; disc. Oct. 9, 1933   Ref.: 242; 329

RAIN TANK
Coconino   T30N R2E   Elev. c. 6000'
This stock watering catchment for rain water is at the foot of Rain Tank Wash. Rain
Tank Flat (T33N/R5E) and Wash (T29N/R2E) borrow the name.   Ref.: Terry

RAINVILLE WASH
Greenlee   T9S R31E
This wash takes its name from that of the Rainville Ranch, through which it runs.

RAMO SHRINE
Coconino (Grand Canyon)   T31N R4E   Elev. 6411'
This name first appears in 1906, among others drawn from mythologies and religions.

RAMBOZ PEAK pro.: /ræmboz/
Gila   T1N R15E   Elev. 5050'
In 1875 Henry Ramboz (b. 1840, France; d. c. 1930) was working the Ramboz Mine at
Ramboz Spring where he lived with his partner, J.E. Wilson. His name has been
misspelled Rambo. The 1880 Census lists it as Ramboy. The small settlement at
Ramboz Camp was short lived, for water was scarce. Ref.: Woody; 116, p. 594; 63

RAMBOZ WASH
Gila   T1N R16E
The Wheeler expedition in 1870 called this Aliso Creek. It has also appeared on maps as
Rambo Wash. See Ramboz Peak, Gila

RAMER RANCH pro.: /réymer/
Gila   T10N R15E   Elev. c. 6000'
H.J. Ramer (b. 1850) bought the Cooper Ranch c. 1887 from Andy Cooper, a
participant in the Pleasant Valley War. Ref.: Woody

RAMONOTE PEAK pro.: /ramanowtey/
Spanish: *Ramonote* = "Big Ramon"
Santa Cruz   T23S R12E   Elev. 6047'
The suffix *ote* means "large or grand." A Mexican named Ramon is said to have been a
herder in early territorial days. Reputedly his eyes could not recognize ownership of
stock straying near his camp. The spelling Ramanote is incorrect. Ramonote Canyon
lies below the peak. Ref.: 18a

RAMPART CAVE
Mohave (Lake Mead)   T30N R16W
Because of its location this cave has had this name since at least 1936.   Ref.: 329

RAMSEY CANYON
Cochise   T23S R20E   Elev. 5000'
The canyon was named prior to 1880 for Frank Ramsey, who worked with his father for
a local cattle company. Ramsey Peak (Elev. 8725') overlooks the canyon and below it
was a small town called Turnerville. By 1915 it was being called Ramsey Canyon. See
also Sembrich, Cochise. Ref.: 242; AHS, Coat File; Larriau

RAMSGATE (R.R. SIDING)
Yavapai   T14N R3W   Elev. 5092'
Between this location and Iron Springs the railroad follows a crooked course, hence the
name Ramsgate because its twisting is reminscent of a ram's horn. Ramsgate Spring is a
transfer name. Ref.: Garrett; 18a

RANCH CREEK
Gila   T1S R16E
This creek, also known as Gilson Wash, derived its name from the fact that several
ranches lie along this creek. In September 1965 the USGS changed the name to Tulapai
Creek, although the name Ranch Creek had been in existence since c. 1905. Tulapai is
the name of a fermented Indian drink. Ref.: 329

RANDOLPH
Pinal   T6S R8E   Elev. 1440'
The railroad station was named for Col. Epes Randolph, vice president and general
manager of the S.P.R.R., and as the community developed, it took the same name.
P.O. est. Feb. 27, 1925, Eugene D. Chandler, p.m.
Ref.: 242; 185, pp. 33, 34; 5, p. 402

RANEGAS PLAIN
Hualapai: *hanagas* = "good"
Yuma   T5N R15W   Elev. c. 1500'
It seems likely that the current name is a corruption of the Hualapai word for "good,"

hanagas. The name first appears on an 1875 military map as Hanegras Plain. It then disappears until GLO 1877 on which it is spelled Ranegras. The current spelling is Ranegas. Ref.: 174, p. 83

RASO (R.R. STN.)

Cochise   T12S R25E   Elev. 4120′

Because of its location in Railroad Pass, the first name for this place was Railroad Pass. Barnes says that in 1903 it was shortened to Glade to expedite telegraphy. It was again changed in 1910 to Raso. Ref.: 18a

RASPBERRY CREEK

Greenlee   T2N R30E

Contrary to what one might expect, this location was actually named for a man whose surname was Raspberry. He was killed c. 1888 in the first Apache raid on Blue River. The creek extends through Raspberry Basin. Raspberry Peak (T3N/R30E, Elev. 8318′) is nearby. Ref.: Fritz

RATTLESNAKE: The presence of a variety of rattlesnakes throughout Arizona has often led to place names. Instances follow:

Rattlesnake Basin	Greenlee	T2N R29E	Elev. c. 7000′

A cattleman, John H. Toles Cosper, said that while he and a companion camped here c. 1925 they killed between sixty and seventy rattlesnakes in one week. Ref.: 18a

Rattlesnake Basin	Pinal	T5S R17E			
Rattlesnake Canyon	Cochise	T13S R21E			
Rattlesnake Canyon	Coconino (Grand Canyon)	T32N R3W			
Rattlesnake Canyon	Coconino/Yavapai	T16-17N R6-8E			
Rattlesnake Canyon	Graham	T8S R20E			
Rattlesnake Canyon	Greenlee	T5S R30E			
Rattlesnake Canyon	Pima	T13S R15E			
Rattlesnake Canyon	Pinal	T5S R17E			
Rattlesnake Canyon	Santa Cruz	T20S R14E			
Rattlesnake Canyon	Yavapai	(1) T13N R2E	(2) T9N R1E		
Rattlesnake Crater	Coconino	T21N R10E			
Rattlesnake Creek	Graham	T9S R19E			
Rattlesnake Dam	Santa Cruz	T22S R18E			
Rattlesnake Draw	Navajo	T11N R20E			
Rattlesnake Gap	Greenlee	T4S R13E			

This name was changed to Stray Horse Gap because its original name made visitors fearful of camping here. Ref.: Simmons

Rattlesnake Lake	Greenlee	T2N R29E		
Rattlesnake Mesa	Coconino	T19N R5E		
Rattlesnake Pass	Pima	T12S R12E		
Rattlesnake Peak	Cochise	(1) T17S R30E	Elev. 8640′	
		(2) T23S R19E	Elev. 7200′	
Rattlesnake Peak	Pima	T12S R15E	Elev. 6635′	
Rattlesnake Point	Apache	T4N R27E		
Rattlesnake Point	Cochise	T15S R30E	Elev. 5160′	
Rattlesnake Point	La Paz	c. 183 mi. N. of Yuma		

This was a steamer landing in the 1870s.

Rattlesnake Point	Maricopa	Near Fort McDowell
Rattlesnake Point	Navajo	T11N R19E
Rattlesnake Spring	Graham	T2S R22E
Rattlesnake Spring	Greenlee	T4S R31E
Rattlesnake Spring	Mohave (Lake Mead)	T28N R16W
Rattlesnake Spring	Yavapai	T13N R1W
Rattlesnake Tank	Coconino	T20N R1E
Rattlesnake Tank	Yavapai	T16N R7E	Elev. 4000'

In 1875 this watering place was called Updykes Tanks, according to Martha Summerhayes. Records in the Camp Verde store have an entry for George Opdyke (b. 1850, New Jersey; d. 1891). The 1880 Census spells his name Opdycke. The name was changed in 1885 from Updyke to Rattlesnake Tanks. Ref.: Gardner; C.C. Bean, *Journal of Accounts of Camp Verde* (*ms.*); AHS, John H. Marion File; 314, p. 139; 63

Rattlesnake Wash   Coconino/Yavapai   T19N R1E

RAVEN BUTTE
Yuma   T12S R18W   Elev. 1773'
Hornaday reported that tame and trusting ravens were here in abundance.   Ref.: 18a

RAVEN PARK
Cochise   T18S R30E   Elev. c. 8000'
Harry D. Burrall named this peak in 1906 because ravens nested here.   Ref.: Burrall

RAWHIDE MOUNTAIN
Graham/Pinal   T4S R19E   Elev. 5560'
This location is known to have had three names. The first was Hobson Mountain for a naval officer who served in the Spanish-American War. The second was Spion Kop, for its fancied resemblance to a hill so named in South Africa; and the third, Rawhide Mountain because in 1922 a Mexican goat herder who lived here patched his clothes with rawhide   Ref.: 329

RAWHIDE MOUNTAINS
Mohave   T11N R13W   Elev. 2400'
These mountains bore their current name prior to 1878. The name derived from the rough and ragged terrain. Bill Hearst opened the Rawhide Mine (T11N/R13W, Elev. 1100') in 1879. Rawhide Wash (Elev. 1750') borrows the name. Ref.: 18a; Mallach; 329

RAWLINS, CAMP
Yavapai   T17N R4W
This sub-post of Whipple Barracks was established in Williamson's Valley in February 1870. It was abandoned in September 1870. The camp probably was named for John Aaron Rawlins, Secretary of War (March 11, 1869 until his death on September 6, 1869)   Ref.: 145, p. 50; 159, p. 537

RAY (SITE)
Pinal   T3S R13E   Elev. 2024'
In 1882 the Ray Copper Company was organized and the town of Ray was established shortly after 1884. According to an *Arizona Star* article, the mining company moved its headquarters from Riverside to near the Ray Mine and planned to name the town Thurber, for H.K. Thurber, president of the company. The name was soon changed to Ray, after the Ray Mill which lay above the town. According to the post office application in 1899, the proposed office was to serve about four hundred people. Large scale operations did not begin until later, and the community remained small until 1909 when the town of Ray was constructed by the Arizona Hercules Copper Company on property belonging to the Hercules Townsite Company. Open-pit operations began in 1947. Ray Hill and Ray Junction (T4S/R13E) also shared the name.

P.O. est. Jan. 3, 1899, Charles R. Clauberg, p.m.; disc. Jan. 1, 1968
Ref.: 242; *Arizona Gazette* (Aug. 10, 1909), p. 2; 10, p. 91; *Arizona Star* (July 23, 1884), p. 4

RAYMOND RANCH
Coconino   T24N R6E   Elev. c. 5500'
At this location is a buffalo preserve of fifteen thousand three hundred and forty square acresmanaged by the Arizona Game and Fish Department. The herd was first placed on the ranch in 1945. Ref.: *Arizona Highways* (June 1964), p. 33

REALES, LOS   pro.: /los reyáləs/
Spanish = "a Mexican coin"
Pima   Elev. c. 2800'
Two locations had this name, both south of Tucson on the Santa Cruz River. In existence c. 1865, they first served as a foundry for a mine operated by S.R. Domingo. He paid workmen in Mexican coins called *reales*, two of which were worth about 25¢. Domingo would leave the foundry when it was time to pay his workmen and would return with money, a fact which led people to think he had buried his wealth somewhere nearby. People in the community near the foundry saw workmen carrying a box to a grave. It was not a coffin, but presumably contained Domingo's body. It was, according to accounts, even dripping blood and people assumed Domingo had been murdered for his money. A second Los Reales grew up on the east bank of the river. It had a blacksmith shop, two stores, and a cemetery. Ref.: AHS, A.W. Bourk's Scrap Book, and Cosulich Clipping Book; *Arizona Star* (June 27, 1937)

REAVIS CREEK
Pinal/Maricopa   T1N R11E
This creek is also known as Pine Creek, but the name was changed to Reavis in 1968 by the USGS. See Reavis Ranch, Maricopa

REAVIS RANCH   pro.: /révəs/
Maricopa   T2N R12E   Elev. c. 5500'
Elisha M. Reavis (b. 1830, Illinois; d. 1896) settled here c. 1875. He lived like a hermit and always carried a long rifle. He was last seen alive on April 20, 1896. On May 5, 1896 his badly decomposed and partially devoured body was found. By 1935 the location was called Pine Air. It was also known as Fraser's Ranch. By USGS decision in 1978, the name was officially designated Reavis Ranch. It applies also to Reavis Saddle Spring (T1N/R11E) Ref.: 329; 62

RED: Many place names in Arizona carry the simple descriptive word *red*, an indication of the appearance of the locations so named. Examples follow:

Red Basin	Pinal	T6S R17E	
Red Basin Springs	Yavapai	T12N R5E	
Red Bird Hills	Cochise	T15S R23E	
Named for the Red Bird Mine.			
Red Blanket Cave	Mohave	T36N R6W	
Red Bluff Mountain	Yuma	T7S R18W	Elev. 1905'
Red Bluff Spring	Yavapai	T12N R5E	
Red Bluffs Dam	Santa Cruz	T22S R11E	
Red Boy Peak	Pima	T18S R11E	Elev. 6026'
Red Bull Canyon	Greenlee	T2N R31E	
Red Butte	Coconino	(1) T40N R5E	Elev. 7324'
		(2) T30N R7E	Elev. 5316'
		(3) T28N R3E	

No. 3 is also called *Hue-ga-da-wi-za* (= "red butte"), and according to Barnes, until 1927 was called Mount Thorburn.

Red Butte	Maricopa	T2N R4E	

See Papago Butte, Maricopa

Red Butte	Pima	T15S R12E	Elev. 3004'
Red Butte	Yavapai	T18N R1E	
Red Canyon	Coconino (Grand Canyon)	T30N R4E	
Red Canyon	Gila	T6N R20E	
Red Canyon	Greenlee	T4S R30E	
Red Canyon Rapids	Coconino (Grand Canyon)		

See Hance Creek, Coconino (Grand Canyon)

Red Canyon Spring	Mohave	T17N R12W	
Red Canyon Trail	Coconino (Grand Canyon)		

See Hance Trail, Coconino (Grand Canyon)

Red Cheek Butte	Navajo	T7N R18E	
Red Clay Dam	Navajo	T25N R17E	Elev. 6495'
Red Clay Spring	Coconino	T29N R15E	
Red Cliff	Maricopa	T6N R4W	Elev. 2091'
Red Cloud Wash	Maricopa	T6N R6W	
Red Cloud Wash	La Paz	T4S R23W	

Before 1881 the Red Cloud Mining Company of New York bought a mine (Red Cloud Mine) in this wash, hence the name. Ref.: 355, p. 65

Red Cornfield Mesa	Apache	T7N R7W		
Red Creek	Yavapai	(1) T8N R1W	(2) T9N R6E	
Red Crossing	Mohave			

See Needles, The, Mohave, and Topock, Mohave

Red Flat	Yavapai	T17N R2E		
Red Hill	Coconino	(1) T24N R4E		Elev. 7750'
(2) T26N R3E	(3) T34N R8E	(4) T29N R7E	(5) T25N R7E	
		(6) T15N R13E	(7) T20N R5E	
Red Hill	Greenlee	T4S R30E		Elev. 4680'
Red Hill	La Paz	T3S R21W		Elev. 1507'
Red Hill	Navajo	T16N R15E		
Red Hill	Pima	T11S R9E		Elev. 2368'
Red Hill	Pinal	T8S R16E		Elev. 3452'
Red Hill	Santa Cruz	T23S R16E		Elev. 5800'
Red Hill	Yavapai	(1) T14N R7E		Elev. 6181'
		(2) T16N R7E		Elev. 6338'
Red Hills	Gila	T9N R11E		Elev. 5000'
Red Hills	Graham	T4S R24E		Elev. 4964'
Red Hills	Greenlee	T4N R31E		Elev. 8000'
Red Hills	Maricopa	T2N R9E		Elev. 2769'
Red Hills	Navajo	T17N R17E		Elev. 5397'
Red Hills	Pima	T13S R11E		Elev. 3150'
Red Hills	Pinal	T3S R13E		

Red Hills	Yavapai	T9N R7E	
Red Hills	La Paz	T4N R11W	Elev. 1800'
Red Knoll	Coconino	T20N R3E	
Red Knoll	Gila	T7N R20E	Elev. 6054'
Red Knoll	Navajo	T13N R17E	Elev. 6548'
Red Knolls	Coconino	T40N R5E	
Red Knolls Amphitheatre	Graham	T6S R23E	
Red Knolls	Graham	T6S R23E	
Red Knoll Canyon	Graham	T5S R27E	
Red Knoll Flat	Navajo	T13N R17E	
Red Knolls Amphitheatre	Graham	T5S R23E	
Red Lake	Apache	T3N R5W	
Red Lake	Coconino	T26N R5W	
Red Lake	Coconino	(1) T33N R13E (2) T16N R11E (3) T23N R2E	Elev. 5600' Elev. 6000' Elev. 5700'

All three are small communities adjacent to Red Lake, hence their name. At #3 is the Red Lake Trading Post and Red Lake R.R. siding. The temporary depot had a post office.

Red Lake	Mohave	T26N R17W	

P.O. est. June 16, 1888, Adah F. Stone, p.m.; disc. Sept. 3, 1888   Ref.: Benham; 242

Red Lake	Yavapai	T21N R8W	
Red Lake (R.R. Siding)	Coconino		

See Red Lake, Coconino

Red Lake Trading Post   Coconino

See Red Lake, Coconino

Red Lake Valley	Coconino	T23N R2E	

See Red Lake, Coconino

Red Lake Wash	Coconino	T23N R2E	

See Red Lake, Coconino

Red Mesa	Apache	T41N R28E	Elev. 5820'
Red Mesa	Coconino	(1) T23N R6W (2) T38N R8E	
Red Mesa Trading Post	Apache	T41N R28E	
Red Mountain	Cochise	(1) T23S R23E (2) T15S R29E	Elev. 5520' Elev. 6228'
Red Mountain	Coconino	T25N R5E	Elev. 7965'
Red Mountain	Greenlee	(1) T3S R28E (2) T1N R30E	Elev. 6491' Elev. 8154'
Red Mountain	Maricopa	(1) T5N R8E (2) T8N R3E	Elev. 3448' Elev. 4722'

For #1, see McDowell, Mount, Maricopa

Red Mountain	Santa Cruz	T22S R16E	Elev. 5847'

Locally, Mexican-Americans call it Sleeping Woman because it resembles a reclining woman. Ref.: Lenon

Red Mountain	Yavapai	T17N R5W	Elev. 5300'
Red Needle	Navajo	T27N R18E	Elev. 5664'
Red Peak	Apache	T35N R22E	
Red Peak	Coconino	T21N R9E	

See O'Neil Crater, Coconino

Red Peak	Greenlee		

See Rose Peak, Greenlee

Red Pocket	Coconino	T40N R4E	
Red Point	Apache	T39N R22E	Elev. 5591'
Red Point	Coconino	(1) T37N R2E	(2) T38N R7E
Red Point	Maricopa	T10S R10W	Elev. 1183'
Red Point	Navajo	T34N R21E	
Red Pond	Mohave	T34N R12W	
Red Reservoir	Coconino	T33N R6E	
Red River			

See Colorado River

Red Ridge	Pima	T11S R15E	
Red Rock	Apache	T37N R31E	Elev. 6371'

The name is translation of the Navajo: *tse ichii'dah'az kani* (= "red rock mesa"), referring to a three hundred and eighty-six foot high red sandstone peak. While surveying for water in 1892 in this region, Lt. W.C. Brown found many springs. A trading post was established here in 1906 and the town of Red Rock has developed nearby.   Ref.: Burcard; 143, p. 242; 331, p. 122

Red Rock	Gila	T7N R9E	Elev. 4991'
Red Rock	Mohave	T12N R19W	

See Topock, Mohave

Red Rock	Pinal	T10S R10E	Elev. 1867'

A small community developed here where the old railroad left the main line to service the Silver Bell smelter. A small conical red peak is the reason for the descriptive name.
P.O. est. as Red Rock, June 14, 1887, Joseph W. Haskin, p.m.; name changed to Redrock, Nov. 30, 1895; changed to Red Rock, June 1, 1950; Wells Fargo 1890   Ref.: Jordan; 242

Red Rock	Yavapai		

See Big Bug, Yavapai

Red Rock Canyon	Cochise	T19S R30E	
Red Rock Cliffs	Coconino	T27N R12 E	Elev. 5188'
Red Rock Country	Coconino/Yavapai	T17N R5-6E	

Military parties scouting for Indians called it Red Rock Country as early as 1869. Outcroppings in lower Oak Creek Canyon comprise wild and rugged country which cowboys call Hell's Hollow.   Ref.: 177, p. 57; 276, pp. 22, 23

Red Rock Gulch	Yavapai	T11N R3E	
Red Rock Hill	Navajo	T39N R19E	
Red Rock Reservoir	La Paz	T1N R19W	
Red Rock Spring	Gila	T11N R9E	
Red Rock Spring	Maricopa	T2N R13E	
Red Rock Spring	Mohave	(1) T36N R16W	(2) T22N R20W
Red Rock Spring	Navajo	T10N R19E	
Red Rock Valley	Apache	T37N R30E	
Red Rock Wash	Apache	T38N R31E	

Red Rock (R.R. Stn.)	Pinal		
See Red Rock, Pinal			
Red Rock Trading Post	Apache	T37N R31E	
Red Rocks Canyon	Yavapai		
See Hell Canyon, Yavapai			
Red Sands	Mohave	T41N R2W	
Red Seep Spring	Graham	T2S R25E	
Red Seep Spring	Yavapai	T16N R2E	
Red Shales Valley	Coconino (Grand Canyon)		
See Nankoweap Canyon, Coconino (Grand Canyon)			
Red Slide Peak	Navajo	T34N R19E	Elev. 6841'
Red Slide Peak Wash	Navajo	T34N R18E	
Red Spring	Coconino	T31N R7W	
Red Spring	Santa Cruz	T21S R12E	
Red Spring Pass	Santa Cruz	T21S R12E	
Red Tank Canyon	Greenlee	T3S R31E	
Red Tank Canyon	Pinal	T1N R11E	
Red Tank Draw	Yavapai	T15N R6E	
Red Tanks Divide	Pinal	T1N R11E	
Red Tanks Spring	Graham	T5S R28E	
Red Top Mountain	Navajo	T9N R20E	Elev. 6882'
Red Top Peak	Yuma	T10S R10W	
Red Valley	Apache	T7N R9E	

In 1960 the USGS changed the older name Black Creek Valley, in use as early as 1916, to Red Valley. Ref.: 329

Red Wash	Apache	T36N R31E	
Red Water	Apache	T35N R26E	

REDFIELD CANYON
Graham/Pima   T11S R19E

This name was in use prior to 1880. The location was named for the Redfield brothers. See Redington, Pima

REDFIELD CREEK
Pima

On a 1936 post office location inquiry reply form, this creek is listed as the nearest one to the Redington post office. The creek was named for the Redfield brothers. See Redington, Pima.   Ref.: 242

RED HORSE WASH
Coconino   T28N R2E   Elev. c. 6000'

Fr. Francisco Garcés camped at this location in July 1776 and called the pond (or well) Pozo de Santa Isabel. In 1927 the USGS officially changed the name to Red Horse Wash, naming it for a now-vanished stock tank called Red Horse Tank. Ordinarily this wash is dry, but on July 29, 1915, a flood here washed out the railroad bridge on the line to the Grand Canyon. That night the train from the Canyon was wrecked and Fred Terry, the fireman, drowned.   Ref.: Hart; Terry (no relation); 18a (quoting Coues)

REDINGTON
Pima   T12S R19E   Elev. 2890'

Henry and Lem Redfield in 1875 set up a post office at their ranch headquarters, using the name Redington because the Post Office Department refused to use their surname.

They settled approximately six miles south of the present community of Redington. Outlaws customarily hid out in the vicinity. In 1883 they robbed a stage about one and a half miles north of the old Riverside State Station. Frank Carpetner was caught. Lawmen tracked Joe Tuttle to the Redfield Ranch. In prison at Florence, Tuttle confessed that he and Charlie Hensley during the holdup committed murder. He and Lem Redfield were to be cut in on the loot. Redfield denied the accusation. Mob fury was high. To escort Lem to Phoenix for safety's sake, Henry Redfield joined seven men and a deputy U.S. Marshall and headed for the county jail at Florence. Thoroughly aroused, the people at Florence immediately lynched Lem and Joe Tuttle. Lem Redfield was a respected business man and citizen and there was much doubt that he actually had any part in the crime, but the reputation of the ranch and town remained dubious for years. P.O. est. Oct. 7, 1879, Henry F. Redfield, p.m.; disc. Dec. 31, 1940 Ref.: AHS, William Whelan File; 238, pp. 27, 28

REDMAN MESA
Gila   T7N R12E   Elev. c. 6000'
Joseph Redman, who ran a meat market in Globe, ranched in this area, hence the name. Redman Flat, Redman Crossing (on the Salt River), and Redman Mountain (T3N/R15E, Elev. 4680') are also named for him. Ref.: Webb

REDMAN MOUNTAIN
Gila   T3N R15E   Elev. 4680'
The spelling "Redmond" for this location is an error. See Redman Mesa, Gila

REDONDO, MESA
Spanish: *mesa* ="tableland"; *redondo* = "round"
Apache   T12N R24E   Elev. 6824'
The name is descriptive. In March 1966 the USGS eliminated the erroneous spelling *Redonda*.

RED ROOSTER MOUNTAIN
Pinal T5S R18E   Elev. 4878'
This high, red-colored mountain takes its name from that of Red Rooster Spring. In 1918 the mountain was also known as Quartzite Mountain. Ref.: 329

REED GULCH
Gila   T8N R10E
Reeds grow abundantly in this gulch, hence the name.
Ref.: Woody

REESE PARK
Coconino   T23N R7E   Elev. 11,474'
Both the peak and the canyon (T27N/R7E) were named for an early settler, possibly L.R. Reese (b. 1850, Ohio). Ref.: 329; 63

REEVE (RUIN)
Pima   T12S R18E
In 1956 Mr. and Mrs. Richard Reeve reported locating this stone walled prehistoric pueblo site on their ranch. It was named in their honor. Ref.: 92, p. 6

REGAL CANYON
Gila   T5N R17E
This canyon and creek take their name from that of the Regal Mine, which had a camp in this canyon. The mine in turn was named for its former owner and operator, Sol Regalmann of New York City. Ref.: Woody

REIDHEAD CROSSING
Navajo   T12N R18E   Elev. c. 6300'
Because a single yellow pine grew at the location, an early name for it was Lone Pine Crossing. Herman Woolf (see also Woolf Crossing, Coconino) maintained the crossing for awhile, selling it in 1878 to John Reidhead (d. 1916), a Mormon, who remained here

until 1883. Because of beaver along this stretch of Show Low Creek, it was sometimes known as Beaver Branch. A small settlement called Reidhead developed during Reidhead's occupation. On June 1, 1882, Apaches shot Nathan Robinson and settlers promptly left the vicinity. Ref.: 116, p. 573; 225, p. 169

REILLY PEAK
Cochise   T12S R22E   Elev. 7631'
James R. Reilly (b. Oct. 1830, Ireland; d. 1906) served as a soldier in Arizona 1857-1859. After his discharge, he became a freighter from Fort Buchanan to Magdalena, Sonora (1861-62), but when Indians stole his assets, he moved to Sonora, later killing a Mexican, for which he was exiled to La Paz, Baha California. In 1866 he went to Yuma and had a store and hotel. He studied law, and by 1878 he was in Phoenix, publishing a newspaper. By 1880 this peripatetic jack of all trades was a justice of the peace in Tombstone, soon thereafter establishing a ranch and stage station near the peak which has his name. The name Reiley is incorrect. Indians called his station Zill-Tarts-on-ar. Ref.: AHS, James Reilly File; Smithsonian

REIMER PEAK
Yavapai   T2N R3E   Elev. 5038'
Gus Reimer grazed his sheep in this area. Reimer Draw and Spring (T12N/R4E) share the name. Ref.: Dugas

RELIABLE
Yavapai   T8S R18E   Elev. 4300'
This was the post office for the Old Reliable Mine, hence the name.
P.O. est. May 13, 1890, Mrs. Margaret C. Liston, p.m.; disc. April 20, 1895
Ref.: 18a; 264

RENO, CAMP
Gila   T6N R9E
In July 1868 this sub-station of Fort McDowell was established in what was known as Green Valley. The camp was named for Brig. Gen. Marcus Albert Reno, formerly of the 12th Pennsylvania Cavalry. By September 22 at this poorly located post five companies were stationed to hold Apaches in check in Tonto Valley. Fully exposed, the camp was on an open mesa with two deep canyons containing water and brush on either side. There raiding Indians could hide. The camp was abandoned c. 1870.
After the withdrawal of troops, a small settlement may have developed. Ten years later a post office called Reno was opened here. Associated names are Reno Canyon (T6N/R10E), Mount Reno (a.k.a. Parker Butte after a Texan who settled there c. 1884), and Reno Creek.
P.O. est. Oct. 20, 1880, Isaac R. Prather, p.m.; disc. July 24, 1894
Ref.: 242; 206, p. 98; 107, V, 253, 262, 307, and VIII, 70, 71; 159, p. 431; *Arizona Miner* (Jan. 9, 1969), p. 1; (March 5, 1870), p. 3; (May 7, 1870), p. 2; *Phoenix Republican* (Sept. 30, 1891), p. 1

RENO PASS
Maricopa   T6N R9E   Elev. 4722'
The military road through this pass was constructed c. 1868 and named for Camp Reno to which it gave access. So rough and steep was the grade that at least two teams were used to pull a loaded wagon through. It took exceptional braking power to get wagons safely down grade. See Reno, Camp, Gila Ref.: Woody

REPPY (R.R. STN.)
Gila   T1S R30E   Elev. c. 4000'
This location was named for Charles D. Reppy (b. 1846, Illinois; d. 1946), who began his Arizona career as editor of the *Arizona Bullion* in Harshaw. In 1885 he bought the *Florence Tribune*. He remained in Florence until 1909. Ref.: 63; 211

RESERVATION CREEK
Apache   T5N R27E   Elev. c. 5000'
In 1864 this creek was called Rio Nutrioso. Its current name derives from its being on the

Fort Apache Indian Reservation. The same reason underlies the following place names: Reservation Flat (T8N/R24E); Reservation Lake (Elev. c. 9500'), and Reservation Spring (T9N/R24E).   Ref.: Davis

RETREAT, POINT
Coconino   Elev. c. 3000' in Marble Canyon
Frank Stanton named this location in 1889 because here the Stanton party left the Colorado River after an upset in which two members of the Brown party drowned. Ref.: Schellbach File (Grand Canyon)

REVENTON RANCH
Spanish: *reventon* = "a chore, drudgery"
Santa Cruz   T28S R13E   Elev. c. 4000'
On May 28, 1859, the *Weekly Alta Californian* reported that this location was owned by Mercer and Dodson. In that same year Elias Brevoort, former postmaster at Fort Buchanan, took over its ownership. It was a fortified ranch, often used as headquarters by the military. That the ranch was an old one is attested to by the fact that in 1864 the oldest Mexicans and Indians could not remember its beginnings. Apparently Browne confused this location with that of the Kitchen Ranch, for he reported that Elias Brevoort took off for Mexico and the place in 1864 was a ruin when as a matter of fact Brevoort was still living there for several years thereafter. At one time, however, Kitchen lived there. On the 1859 military map it shows as El Riverton, a corruption retained on the 1877 Rand McNally map. The spelling Revanton and Raventon are errors.
Ref.: *Arizona Miner* (July 6, 1864), p. 3; 121b, p. 327; 369, p. 45; 163, p. 224; 206, pp. 223, 224; 56, p. 259; Lenon; 242

REYMERT (SITE)   pro.: /ráymert/
Pinal   T2S R11E   Elev. 3160'
James de Noon Reymert established a smelting mill here. It had a post office. The community has been totally dismantled. The name applies to Reymert Wash.
P.O. est. May 19, 1890, Mrs. Elizabeth Reymert, p.m.; disc. May 27, 1898
Ref.: 242; Varney; AHS

REYNOLDS CREEK
Gila   T6N R13E
The first house on this creek was built by Glenn Reynolds, hence the name. In 1888 he was elected sheriff of Gila County. While he was escorting Apache prisoners to the railroad on November 2, 1899, Apache Kid killed him.   Ref.: McKinney; Woody

R-14 RANCH
Gila   T5N R21E   Elev. c. 4500'
Indians frequently used soldiers' surnames plus their own army numbers. Apache scouts serving as soldiers were assigned numbers. R-14 was a very prosperous cattleman and rancher. His Apache family name was Altaha.   Ref.: Davis

RHODES RANCH
La Paz   T1S R23W   Elev. c. 450'
After William B. Rhodes (also spelled Roods and Rodes) left what is now Santa Cruz County, he established a ranch on the Colorado River. While attempting to cross the Colorado during a rising flood on April 29, 1870, he drowned when his boat struck a snag and capsized. His Yuma ranch was eventually destroyed by treasure seekers. The location is today Cibola.   Ref.: *Arizona Miner* (May 7, 1870), p. 2; Blythe Chamber of Commerce "Cruise Bulletin" (Oct. 10, 1954)

RHODES RANCH
Santa Cruz   On Santa Cruz River south of Canoa Ranch   Elev. c. 3800'
In 1861 William (Bill) Rhodes (or Roods) was living here. Like other ranchers, he was in danger of Apache attack because of the withdrawal of Federal troops. Rhodes and a Mexican helper, while searching north and east for stray horses, stopped briefly at the Canoa Ranch, then serving as an inn. Later when Rhodes and the Mexican returned, they found three Americans and a Papago dead from an Apache attack. The Apaches returned to attack again. The Mexican escaped but Rhodes' horse gave out. Rhodes ran

to a thicket and hid in a dry water hole. He spread his revolver cartridges on the rim of the hole. When the Indians again attacked Rhodes calmly picked them off one by one, reloading after each shot. The Apaches tried again with the same results. As the Indians admired courage and strength, they retreated. Rhodes soon left the Santa Cruz Valley. See Rhodes Ranch, Yuma.   Ref.: Lenon; 34, p. 37

RHYOLITE CANYON
Cochise   T16S R29E   Elev. c. 5500'
Mr. and Mrs. Riggs named the canyon for the rocks in it.   Ref.: Riggs

RIBBON FALLS
Coconino (Grand Canyon)   T32N R3E   Elev. 3750'
About one-third of the way up the trail to the North Rim is this single falls in a cut through an overhang. It was so named by Francois E. Matthes in 1906 because the falls looks like a ribbon. Because of a note made then that travertine deposits at its base resemble a huge altar, the USGS in 1923 suggested the name be changed to Altar Falls. The change, however, was not made.   Ref.: 329; Kolb; 178, p. 27

RICE
Apache   T19N R24E   Elev. c. 6000'
Formerly there was a small community here called Old Stage Coach Tavern. The tavern had been formerly a stage station on the Star Route. The reason for the name Rice has not been learned.   Ref.: Grigsby

RICE PEAK
Pima   T11S R16E   Elev. 7584'
This highest peak on the spur called Oracle Ridge was named in 1881 for Gen. Elliott Warren Rice, "one of the original prospectors of the mountain."
Ref.: *Arizona Weekly Star* (April 28, 1881)

RICE PEAK   pro.: /ráysiʌ/ or /rays/
Yavapai   T11N R4E   Elev. 5333'
This peak was named for Willard Rice (d. Jan. 2, 1899), a miner who arrived in Arizona in 1864. He was employed on January 1, 1965 as a guide for Lt. Charles A. Curtis. In 1867, while serving as a scout for Lt. A. Beyta with New Mexico Volunteers, he helped battle Apaches here. The Indians gave them a sound defeat. Erroneously, Rice was reported killed at this battle. He later served as a guide for Capt. George M. Wheeler. His name applies also to Rice Canyon or Gulch (T12N/R4E) and to Rice Spring. Ref.: Dugas; 107, III, 329; Sharlot Hall Museum File

RICHARDS LAKE
Navajo   T15N T16N R17E
To provide water for his cattle, J.W. Richards ("Billie St. Joe") c. 1902 diverted waters from the Black Canyon into this crater.   Ref.: Richards; 18a

RICHINBAR
Yavapai   T10N R2E   Elev. 3000'
The locator of a gold mine in Agua Fria Canyon (a man named Zika) hoped that this place would yield bars of gold.
P.O. est. June 10, 1896, John A. Webb, p.m.; disc. March 15, 1912
Ref.: 242; *Prescott Courier* (July 21, 1917); 18a

RICHMOND BASIN
Gila   T2N R15E   Elev. c. 5600'
Mack Morris (b. 1833, Ireland) located his Richmond Mine here in 1876, hence the name of the basin. Nuggets of pure silver lay in the natural basin, and women made pin money by collecting them. Morris later lost his life in Tucson when his horses stampeded. Richmond's name is shared by Richmond Mountain (T2N/R16E, Elev. 5836').   Ref.: Mrs. Dudley Craig; 146, p. 64; 270, p. 115; 63

[523]

RICHVILLE

Apache   T10N R28E

Because of walnut trees here, the community was originally known as Walnut Grove. In 1883 a post office called Nero was established for a small colony of Mormons (T11N/R28E). By 1892 the location was being called Richey, for Joseph B. Richey, who settled here. In the same year the name of the post office was changed to Richville. In 1901 the location for the post office was switched to T10N/R28E, a fact which may or may not indicate an actual physical relocation, as it could reflect more accurate surveying. By the mid-1950s any signs of a community had disappeared, although some families still were living along this stretch of the Little Colorado River. Today the name applies to Richville Valley which once contained the community.

P.O. est. as Nero, Feb. 15, 1883, James W. Wilkins, p.m.; disc. May 5, 1883; reest. as Richville, April 26, 1892, William H. Sherwood, p.m.; disc. May 24, 1907
Ref.: 242; Wiltbank; Becker; Wentz; Noble; MNA

RIGGS, CAMP

Graham   c. T8S R23E

Lt. Col. Edwin A. Riggs chose the location for this post in May 1865. The camp was named for him. By transfer, the name now applies to Riggs Flat Wild Life Area (Cochise/Graham), which has an eleven acre lake, and to Riggs Mesa (T7S/R25E).
Ref.: 116, p. 405; *Citizen* (July 3, 1875), p. 4; 9, p. 4

RIGGS CANYON

Cochise   T16S R29E   Elev. c. 5000'

Ed Riggs named this canyon for his father. Ed came to Arizona with his parents in 1877.
See Ed Riggs Mountain, Cochise   Ref.: 116, p. 586

RIGHT HAND DRAW

Navajo   T10N R21E

In 1924 this location was called Fools Hollow. In 1964 the USGS changed the name to Right Hand Draw. See Adair, Navajo   Ref.: 329

RILLITO   pro.: /riyíyʌto/

Pima   T12S R12E   Elev. 2055'

The post office name was for a brief time Langhorne, the name of the postmistress at the time. See Rillito Creek, Pima

P.O. est. as Rillito, April 17, 1905, Catherine Elizabeth Langhorne, p.m.; changed to Langhorne, Sept. 11, 1908; changed to Rillito, Jan. 12, 1916   Ref.: 242

RILLITO CREEK   pro.: /riyíyʌto/

Spanish: *rio* = "river; *ito* = "little"
Pima   T13-14S R13-15E   Elev. 2500'

This normally dry wash is not exactly little when in flood. Its usual size, however, justifies its being called "little stream." The name first occurs on an 1875 military map, but it had the name when Fort Lowell was established on it in 1872 because it had sufficient water to raise hay.   Ref.: 49, p. 5

RIMMY JIMS

Coconino   T20N R12E   Elev. c. 6000'

The store here was established c. 1910 by a retired cowhand. When he arrived, local cowboys noted that instead of having a double-rigged saddle (cinch belt fastened to the saddle front and back), his was a single cinch belt attached to the center of the saddle skirt. This reminded them of rim-firing and led to his store being called Rimmy Jims. The name is shared by Rimmy Jims Tank (T27N/R9E).   Ref.: Store owner, 1958

RIMROCK

Yavapai   T15N R6E   Elev. 3639'

On the post office application is noted "no village." This location was a post office in a ranch headquarters and took its name from the rim rock formation on the bank of Beaver Creek.

P.O. est. July 11, 1928, Mrs. Ella Laudermilk, p.m.   Ref.: 242; Schnebly

RINCON MOUNTAINS pro.: /rinkán/
Spanish = "inside corner" or "nook"
Pima   T15S R16E   Elev. 6354'

In 1876 Joaquin Tellez and his wife owned the Rincon Ranch on the west side of these mountains. The name of the ranch probably came from the fact that the bend in this range forms an inside corner like the inside of a bent elbow. Rincon Peak (T15S/R18E, Elev. 8482') is the highest in this range. Associated names include the following: Rincon Range, Sierra el Rincon, Rincon Valley and Sierra del Ringon.   Ref.: 164, p. xviii; 190

RIO: When *rio* (Spanish = "river") is ued as a generic, see the first major name following the generic; i.e. for Rio Colorado, see Colorado, Rio.

RIORDAN pro.: /riyrdn/
Coconino   T21N R6E   Elev. c. 7000'

Timothy A. Riordan (b. Jan. 1, 1858, Chicago) arrived in Flagstaff in 1884 to be with his brother Dan (b. Chicago). Dan was Indian Agent at Fort Defiance 1880-84. They were joined by Michael James Riordan (b. 1865; d. Oct. 7, 1930). The brothers sold their lumber interest in 1897 and the settlement at Riordan was named for Dan after the brothers had left the area.
P.O. est. June 18, 1917, Howard V. Haeberlin (declined); p.o. est. March 26, 1918 at Riordan R.R. Stn., Veronica McGonigle, p.m.; disc. Sept. 25, 1925   Ref.: 242; AHS, Timothy A. Riordan File; Anderson; 224, III

RIPSEY HILL
Pinal   T5S R14E   Elev. 3570'

The Ripsey family maintained a ranch and ran cattle here at least as early as 1889. It may have been named for that fact or for the presence of the Ripsey Mine (T5S/R13E). Ripsey Peak (T5S/R13E), named by 1922, was so named because it is adjacent to the mine. Ripsey Spring is in Ripsey Wash (T4S/R13E).   Ref.: 329

RITA EXPERIMENTAL RANGE AND WILD LIFE AREA, SANTA
Pima   T18S R14E   Elev. c. 3000'

This area, set aside in 1903, was so named because it is on the western slope of the Santa Rita Mountains. Experiments cover deer management and rangeland management and improvement.   Ref.: 76, p. 9

RITA MOUNTAINS, SANTA
                                           Pima Elev. 9453'
Pima/Santa Cruz   T20S R15E   Santa Cruz Elev. 6186'

The earliest name recorded was Sierra de Santa Rita (Nicolas de La Fora, 1771). According to Hinton, almost a century later it was also being called Sierra Madre, possibly a corruption of Sierra de la Madera, a range in which Velasco (1850) noted a pass called Puerto de las Muchachos. Velasco's name was still in use in 1863. The Boundary Survey Commission in 1851 referred to these lofty mountains as the Santa Rita Mountains. Possibly the mountains were so named for the Santa Rita Mines in the foothills about ten miles east of Tubac. They were then worked by the Santa Rita Mining Company until Apaches forced their closing in 1861.
Ref: 242; 163, pp. 188, 189, 199; 236, p. 168; 20, I

RITTENHOUSE (R.R. STN.)
Maricopa   T2N R7E   Elev. c. 1800'

In 1919 C.H. Rittenhouse formed the Queen Creek Farms Company. A railroad station was constructed to ship produce.   Ref.: 309, p. 122

RITTER BUTTE
Coconino   T19N R6E   Elev. 6988'

Prior to 1950 the Ritter family had a ranch in this vicinity, hence the name. Ritter Mountain is a variant name. Ritter Spring is on the butte.

RIVERS
Pinal   "5 mi. W. of Sacaton and 50 from Phoenix"
The post office was established to serve Japanese "evacuees" on June 22, 1942. Neither

a postmaster nor an exact location was recorded and information was marked "classified."
P.O. est. June 22, 1942   Ref.: 242

RIVIERA
Mohave   T20N R23W   Elev. 600'
This community with a population of three thousand in 1970 was named for being on the Colorado River.

ROADRUNNER RAPIDS
Coconino/Mohave (Grand Canyon)   T29N R9W   Elev. c. 1400'
These rapids were named in 1974 for the bird native to the Southwest. The Park Service thus named it to replace the names Canyon Rapids and 217 Mile Rapids.   Ref.: 329

ROARING RAPIDS
Mohave   T29N R22W
Lt. Joseph Christmas Ives named this location descriptively in 1857.   Ref.: 245, p. 86

ROARING SPRINGS
Coconino (Grand Canyon)   T32N R4E   Elev. c. 5500'
At the head of Bright Angel Creek these springs gush from the canyon wall with a noticeable roar. In 1930 M.R. Tillotson, Grand Canyon Superintendent, extended the name to Roaring Springs Canyon.   Ref.: Kolb; 329

ROBBERS' ROOST
Coconino (Grand Canyon)   T17N R7E   Elev. c. 6000'
For years cattle rustlers and outlaws used this place on the North Rim. The best known was Butch Cassidy, a pseudonym for George LeRoy Parker. Asa ("Ace") Harris tracked Jim Parker, a train robber, here after Parker robbed the train at Peach Springs. In the ensuing gun battle Parker escaped.   Ref.: Harris; 323, p. 19

ROBBINS BUTTE
Maricopa   T1S R4W   Elev. 1162'
On January 1, 1886, G.A. Roberts homesteaded two miles west of this butte. Despite Barnes' saying that the correct name for the butte is Roberts, it was mapped before Roberts' arrival as Robbins Butte.   Ref.: Parkman

ROBERTS CIENEGA
Cochise   c. T17S R25E   Elev. c. 4000'
In the early 1880s at about six miles from the mouth of West Turkey Creek in Sulphur Springs Valley, the military maintained a temporary camp during the campaign against Vitorio. It was named for Lt. Col. Joseph Roberts, an aide to Gen. George Crook (1870-1873).   Ref. 18a; Barnes' Notes

ROBERTS MESA
Gila   T11N R11E   Elev. 6669'
In the 1880s Jim Roberts supervised the Pendleton brothers' ranch here. He departed without patenting his claim, which was later patented by Elam Bales.
Ref. Woody; McKinney; 18a

ROBINSON MOUNTAIN
Coconino   T23N R8E   Elev. 7911'
This location, sometimes called Robinson Crater, was named for Henry H. Robinson (1873-1925), author of the *San Franciscan Volcanic Field*, who surveyed this area for the U.S. Government. Robinson Crater (Elev. 7341') was named in 1931.

ROBLAS BUTTE   pro.: /róbləs/
Pinal   T1S R11E   Elev. 3110'
A Mexican named Roblas or Robles had a ranch on the eastern slope of this butte in the early 1900s, hence the name. Robles Canyon (Pinal) also has his name.   Ref. 18a

[526]

ROBLES JUNCTION

Pima   T14S R13E   Elev. 2650'

In 1884 Bernabe Robles (b. 1826) operated a stage line from Tucson to Quijotoa and one to Gunsight. He maintained a station on his ranch, which others called Spanish Ranch or Robles Ranch. He sold out in 1917. Where the road from Tucson split formerly with branches to Sasabe or to Sells, was Robles Junction, also called Three Points because of the formerly three-pronged road. Robles Pass (Elev. 2650') is nearby.   Ref. 308, pp. 69, 78; 62: *Arizona Cattleman* (March 10, 1917), p. 2

ROBLES WASH, LOS   pro.: /robleys/

Spanish = "oak trees"
Pima/Pinal   T11S R10E

There are oak trees in this wash, hence the name.

ROCHE, CHARCO DE

Pima

On a military map of 1859 this *charco* (pond) was noted southwest of Roche. The name was also given as Charco de Roth. It was twenty-five miles southwest of the Quijotoa Mountains. Nothing more is known at present.   Ref. 242

ROCK: Many place names in Arizona descriptively use the word *rock*.
Examples follow:

Rock Basin Spring	Greenlee	T2S R31E	
Rock Basin Tank	Mohave	T33N R10W	
Rock Butte	Yavapai	T19N R2W	Elev. 5435'
Rock Canyon	Cochise	T18S R30E	
Rock Canyon	Coconino	T39N R2W	
Rock Canyon	Gila	T6N R16E	
Rock Canyon	Mohave	T41N R9W	
Rock Canyon Point	Coconino	T39N R3W	
Rock Corral Canyon	Santa Cruz	T21S R12E	

This canyon takes its name from that of the Rock Corral Ranch at its base. Ranchers used materials at hand – whether mesquite, rocks, or natural pens easily closed off by blocking the entrance – as corrals.

Rock Corral Peak	Santa Cruz		

See Tumacacori Peak, Santa Cruz

Rock Corral Spring	Mohave	T18N R16W	
Rock Creek	Apache	T5N R24E	Elev. 6000'
Rock Creek	Cochise	T18S R28E	
Rock Creek	Gila	T9N R15E	
Rock Creek	Maricopa	T5N R9E	

A variant name is Ballantyne Canyon.

Rock Creek	Mohave	T18N R18W	
Rock Creek	Navajo	T8N R15E	
Rock Creek	Pinal	T1N R12E	
Rock Creek	Yavapai	T9N R2E	
Rock Creek Spring	Mohave	T18N R16W	
Rock, Fort	Yavapai	T20N R10W	Elev. 4900'

See Fort Rock, Yavapai

Rock Gap	Navajo	T37N R20E	Elev. 7388'

Rock Gap Valley	Navajo	T34N R20E	
Rock Hill	Yavapai	T9N R1W	Elev. 4255'
Rock Horse Canyon	Gila		

See Rock House Canyon, Gila

Rock House	Gila	T7N R15E	
Rock House Butte	Gila	T6N R17E	Elev. 5826'
Rockhouse Canyon	Cochise	T12S R21E	
Rock House Canyon	Gila	T7N R15E	

The name derives from the presence of a small rock house on the Flying V Ranch. The name Rock Horse Canyon is a corruption.

Rockhouse Canyon	Pinal	T3S R18E	
Rock Island	Maricopa	T4N R12E	
Rock Knob	Maricopa	T4N R6E	Elev. 2800'
Rock Mesa	Apache	T2N R9W	
Rock Mountain	Pinal	T3S R18E	
Rock Peak	Pinal	T3S R7E	
Rock Point	Apache	T35N R27E	Elev. 4000'

See Round Rock, Apache

The name is a translation of the Navajo *tsé ntsaa deez'áhí.*
P.O. est. Jan. 18, 1926, Raymond C. Dunn, p.m.; location changed Oct. 17, 1928 to Round Rock Village (17 mi. s.e.); disc. June 4, 1930   Ref. 242; 331, p. 124

Rock Point	Coconino	T36N R5E		Elev. 5480'
Rock Spring	Coconino	T38N R3W		
Rock Spring	Gila	(1) T5N R14E	(2) T2N R13E	
Rock Spring	Maricopa	T5N R7E		
Rock Spring	Mohave	T27N R19W		
Rock Spring	Yavapai	(1) T17N R5W	(2) T11N R6W	
		(3) T16N R4W		
Rock Spring Canyon	Cochise	T22S R19E		
Rock Spring Draw	Yavapai	T11N R4E		
Rock Springs	Yavapai	T8N R2E		Elev. 2000'

Ben Warner named this location in 1928 because the spring emerges from rocks.
P.O. est. Feb. 1, 1938, Ben Warner, p.m.; disc. May 31, 1955
Ref. Ben Warner, Letter (March 1, 1956); 242

Rock Springs (P.O.)
See Black Canyon, Yavapai

Rock Tank	Cochise	T20S R24E	
Rock Tank	Coconino	(1) T31N R1W	(2) T21N R1W
(3) T22N R4E	(4) T25N R3E	(5) T25N R6E	
	(6) T18N R6E	(7) T14N R8E	
Rock Tank	Graham	(1) T9S R28E	(2) T5S R27E
Rock Tank	Maricopa	(1) T5N R9E	(2) T5N R3E
		(3) T5N R5E	
Rock Tank	Pima	T12S R17E	
Rock Tank	Santa Cruz	T23S R13E	
Rock Tank	Yavapai	T13N R7E	
Rock Tank	Yuma	T9S R11W	

Rock Tank Canyon	Gila	T7N R15E

This is a variant name for Rock House Canyon, Gila

Rock Tank Canyon	Greenlee	T1S R31E
Rock Tank Canyon	Yavapai	T15N R8W
Rock Tank Dam	Navajo	T10N R23E

ROCKFELLOW DOME
Cochise   T17S R23E   Elev. 6638'

John Alexander Rockfellow (b. Jan. 30, 1858, New York; d. May 17, 1947) was first at Signal, moving in 1878 to Tombstone. He became a stockman (1883-1890). From 1898 to 1929 he served in the civil engineering office of Cochise County.
Ref. AHS, Chambers Collection; 277, p. 199

ROCKINSTRAW MOUNTAIN   pro.: /rógəntrə/
Gila   T3N R15E   Elev. 5385'

This is a corruption of the name of George Randolph Roggenstroh (b. 1856, Germany), who became an American citizen in Globe on September 18, 1882. In 1891 he assigned a mining deed at what is now known as Rockinstraw Mountain. The mountain is at the south end of the Apache Mountains, so called by 1870 when an army skirmish was recorded there. These mountains are also sometimes called the Sierra Apache.
Ref. Woody; *Gila County Great Register* (1886); 159, p. 435

RODEN SPRING   pro.: /rówdn̦/
Coconino   T23N R10E   Elev. c. 6000'

In 1884 the William D. Roden, Sr. family drove two hundred cattle from Texas to Arizona, wintering at Grand Falls on the Little Colorado River. The following spring three Hopi Indians passed by Roden Camp but did not stop for water, a fact which made Roden curious. Following them, he came upon an Indian sign made with stones near a bush. Crawling under, he felt moist ground. He dug the next day and found enough water to warrant his moving to this place. Roden Crater lies above the spring. A variant name is Rodin's Cone.   Ref. Switzer

RODOLFO WASH
Pima   T16S R12E

The name derives from a local name for a rock formation. It was applied by J.R. Cooper of the mapping crew in 1960. The name has no meaning, but seemed to be "in keeping with . . . early history."   Ref. 329

ROGERS LAKE
Coconino   T20N R6E   Elev. 7244'

Charles Thomas Rogers (b. 1892, Maine) arrived in Arizona in 1864. From May 1878 until early 1879 he had a cattle ranch near the lake bearing his name. Thereafter, using the 111 brand, he and his son Frank ran cattle near what is now Williams until the 1890s. He dammed rain waters to form this lake, now completely dry and bisected by the main highway. See Williams, Coconino   Ref. 62; Benham; Sykes; 124, p. 54; AHS, Charles Thomas Rogers File

ROGERS TANK
Yavapai   T17N R3E

Also known as Rodgers Tank, this location was named for Benton C. Rogers, a long-time employee of the U.S. Forest Service.
Ref. 329

ROK (R.R. STN.)
Yavapai   T19N R1W   Elev. C. 4800'

For celerity in telegraphy this place near Rock Butte was designated Rok.   Ref.: 18a

ROLL
Yuma   T8S R17W   Elev. 722'

John W. Roll homesteaded in this area in the early 1920's. He established its post office.

Roll Valley is a local name for Mohave Valley.
P.O. est. March 8, 1926, John W. Roll, p.m.   Ref. 242; Mercer

ROOF BUTTE

Navajo: *ádáádik'á* = "roof-shaped mountain on the run"

Apache   T35N R30E   Elev. 9835'

The name roughly translates the Navajo meaning. It is the highest place in the Lukachukai Mountains.
Ref.: Young; 331, p. 127

ROOSEVELT

Gila   T4N R12E   Elev. c. 2200'

This location was initially the post office for the construction crew of the Theodore Roosevelt Dam, from which it took its name. The original settlement at the crossing is now under waters impounded by the dam.
P.O. est. Dec. 18, 1903, William A. Thompson, p.m.   Ref. 5, p. 366; Woody; 242

ROSA GULCH, SANTA

Greenlee   T3S R29E   Elev. c. 4000'

The Santa Rosa Mine on Santa Rosa Mountain in a gulch at the base of this mountain, hence its name. The gulch is filled with mine waste.   Ref. Patton; Simmons

ROSA MOUNTAINS, SANTA

Pima/Pinal   T12S R5E   Elev. 4556'

Papago parishoners of the Gu Achi church honor Santa Rosa, hence the name. These mountains are also called the Gu Achi Mountains. In 1896 this group of mountains was mapped as Sierra de la Nariz. North of Gusano Pass it is also known as part of the Ajo Range. Associated names include Sierra de Santa Rosa, Santa Rosa Valley, Santa Rosa Ranch, and Santa Rosa Wash
(T10S/R4E).   Ref. 262, p. 36; 329, 58

ROSEBUD FLAT

Coconino   T22N R4E

Stanley Sykes (d. 1956) while sawmill foreman here named it because of its blanket of wild roses.   Ref. Sykes

ROSE CANYON LAKE WILD LIFE AREA

Pima   T12S R16E   Elev. c. 8000'

This seven-acre wild life area takes its name from nearby Rose Peak. This is also a recreational area. Rose Canyon runs through it and Rose Canyon Lake resulted from having dammed the creek. All are named for L.J. Rose (d.c. 1915), a miner. See also Rosemont, Pima

ROSE CREEK

Gila   T6N R13E   Elev. 5800'

This location in the early 1880s was called Connor Creek for Sam Connor, first to locate in the vicinity. Both Al and Ed Rose were early settlers in the region. A member of the Graham faction in the Pleasant Valley War, Al was rounding up cattle when he was killed in the feud in October 1887.   Ref.: Woody; 18a

ROSEMONT

Pima   T18S R16E   Elev. c. 4200'

The first name for this location was McCleary Camp, for William B. McCleary, who located mining claims here in 1894 and sold them to L.J. Rose (d. c. 1915). The Rosemont Mining and Smelting Company was sold in 1896 to the Lewisohn brothers of New York City.
P.O. est. Sept. 27, 1894, William B. McCleary, p.m.; disc. May 31, 1910
Ref.: 286, pp. 4, 25, 125; AHS Names File

ROSE PEAK

Greenlee   T1N R29E   Elev. 8776'

The name may be attributed to one of three things: (1) an abundance of wild roses; (2) the color of the iron-stained porphyry, hence the variant name Red Peak; (3) Rose being the name of a prospector here. The last is the most likely origin. See Rousensock Creek, Greenlee   Ref.: Scott; 329; Mrs. Fred Fritz, Sr.

ROSE WELLS
Coconino   T27N R6W

One of two wells here had potable water. They were dug by Banjo Joe, described as an "immense tall fellow with black whiskers, always smiling and laughing, played the banjo a lot." Rose Wells Ranch for many years had the only available water in the vicinity.   Ref.: Morse

ROSKRUGE MOUNTAINS   pro.: /raskruwj/
Pima   T14S R9E   Elev. 3738'

George J. Roskruge (b. April 10, 1845, England; d. July 27, 1928) named these mountains for himself when he surveyed Pima County in 1893. He arrived in Prescott in 1872, serving as cook and chainman to Omar H. Case, Deputy U.S. Surveyor for Arizona and New Mexico. He lived for forty-five years in Tucson.
Ref.: 58; 116, p. 457, Note 5; 224, III

ROSS SPRING
Coconino   T21N R3E   Elev. c. 6000'

Tom Ross and William Garland were cattle ranch partners from c. 1888 to 1895.
Ref.: Benham; 18a

ROUGH ROCK
Navajo: *cécîžî'* = "rough rock"
Apache   T35N R23E   Elev. 6300'
P.O. est. [?]; disc. Jan. 1, 1970   Ref.: 143, p. 250; 37, p. 250

ROUND: The term *round* is used descriptively when applied to many locations in Arizona, some of which follow:

Round Butte	Maricopa	T5N R7E	Elev. 2506'
Round Hill	Yavapai	T13N R1E	Elev. 5900'
Round Knob	Yuma	T10S R15W	Elev. c. 2500'
Round Mountain	Apache	T8N R29E	Elev. 8044'
Round Mountain	Cochise	T18S R30E	
See Chiricahua Peak, Cochise			
Round Mountain	Coconino	T24N R4W	Elev. 7214'
Round Mountain	Gila	T10N R14E	Elev. 6572'
Round Mountain	Greenlee	T10S R32E	Elev. 4494'
Round Mountain	Yavapai	T15N R7E	Elev. 6321'
Round Mountain Draw	Greenlee	T10S R31E	
Round Park	Cochise	T18S R30E	
Round Peak	Apache	T9N R10W	Elev. 6020'

ROUND ROCK (TOWN)
pro.: /tsénikà^ni/
Navajo: *tsé nikàni* = "round flat topped rock"
or *tsé ntsaa deez'a'hí* = "big rock extends"
Apache   T36N R27E   Elev. 6625'

Above the site of the town is a large flat rock – actually a mesa with two sections. At the base of one is the Round Rock Trading Post, the American name being a rough translation of the Navajo. In 1932 the name was changed from Tsenakaahn to the Americanized form. Another name is Round Rock Butte, a.k.a. Round Peak.
Ref.: 329; 331, p. 127; 141, pp. 29, 34

Round Top Butte	Maricopa		

See Round Butte, Maricopa

Roundtop Cone	Navajo	T24N R17E	
Round Top Mountain	Gila/Navajo	T16N R22E	Elev. 7189'
Round Top Mountain	Yavapai	T18N R5E	Elev. 6522'

This location is also called Little Round Mountain.

Round Valley	Cochise	T17S R31E	
Round Valley	Gila	T10N R10E	
Round Valley	Maricopa	T5N R8E	
Round Valley	Mohave	(1) T20N R13W (2) T16N R15W	
Round Valley	Pinal		

See Haystack Valley, Pinal

ROUND VALLEY (SITE)

Apache   T8N R29E   Elev. c. 6500'

This location bears a descriptive name (from its earlier Spanish name: *Valle Redondo* = "Round Valley"). In the winter of 1869 eight men (Dionicio, Eulalio, and Juan Baca; Gabriel Silva, Tony Long, William R. (Tony) Milligan, Marion Clark and Johnny Mc Cullough) constructed the first house here. Milligan and Long soon built additional houses, hence the name Fort Milligan. By 1872 Mexicans had begun their own colony, Valle Redondo, at the north end of the valley. Julius Becker arrived in 1875, followed by his brother Gustav in 1876, the year in which Julius established a store (the third oldest in Arizona). By that time outlaws were also using the valley. Mormons began homesteading in 1879. They included Americus V. Greer, Harris Phelps, William J. Flake, John Bourk, and Adam Greenwood. They established Alma Ward, which in 1882 was divided into Omer Ward (including the community of Omer) and Amity Ward (site of Fort Amity: T8N/R28E). "Omer" is a section in the *Book of Mormon*. To help settle differences, Union Ward was formed by 1885 from Amity and Omer. Omer developed into Springerville. The town of Eagar also arose. See Eagar, Apache, and Springerville, Apache   Ref.: Wiltbank; State Library Files, George H. Crosby, Jr., "Something about Names"; Becker, "75th Anniversary Number," *Apache County Independence News* (Aug. 31, 1951), p.2; 24, pp. 3, 4, 6, 7, 8; 225, p. 185

Round Valley Creek	Cochise	T17S R31E
Round Valley Spring	Yavapai	T17N R5W
Round Valley Wash	Yavapai	T17N R5W

ROUNDTREE CANYON

Yavapai   T9N R5E

This canyon was named for Col. C.P. Roundtree. Round Tree Spring by rights should be Roundtree. Ref. 329

ROUNDUP: Area customarily used to herd range cattle for branding and castrating sometimes carry the term *roundup*. Examples follow:

Roundup Basin	Yavapai	T14N R7E
Roundup Park	Coconino	T17N R8E
Roundup Grounds Canyon	Graham	T5S R21E
Roundup Park Springs	Coconino	T17N R9E

ROUNDY CREEK

Coconino   T38N R6E

This location was named for Lorenzo W. Roundy, a Mormon bishop who on May 28, 1876 drowned while attempting to cross the Little Colorado River at Lee's Ferry. A more recent name for this location is Tanner Wash. Roundy Crossing is an associated name.   Ref.: 141, p. 42, Note 1; 329

ROUSENSOCK CREEK pro.: /ráwzənsak/
Greenlee   T1N R29E   Elev. c. 6000'
This location on Rose Peak was named for a German prospector called Rousensauc
(*sic*). He and his partner Rose staked out claims on this peak. See Rose Peak,
Greenlee   Ref.: Mrs. Fred Fritz, Sr.; Simmons

ROVER PEAK
Yavapai   T8N R5E   Elev. 5285'
The Red Rover Mine, worked first in 1880, was at the base of this peak, hence the name.
A variant name is Rover Mountain.   Ref.: 18a

ROWE'S WELL pro.: /raws/
Coconino (Grand Canyon)   T31N R2E   Elev. 6681'
Stanford Rowe (b. Oklahoma; d. Oct. 1929), a pioneer stockman and guide, talked with
Capt. John Hance in June 1890 about locating water on the Rim of the Grand Canyon.
Hance told him there was probably water in a wash near the present Rowe Well or Hopi
Point. There Rowe noted that dirt held firm deer tracks, thus indicating moisture. He dug
down eighteen feet and hit solid rock. As he had already used up his homestead right, to
establish his claim he placed a mining monument at his well. Later he developed the
location into an auto camp for tourists, in operation until shortly before his death.
Ref.: 178, p. 13; 124, p. 74, Note 80; Naturalist H.Q. "History File" (Grand Canyon)

ROYAL, CAPE
Coconino (Grand Canyon)   T32N R4E   Elev. 7876'
Maj. Clarence E. Dutton named this point in 1882 because, he said, it is a "congregation
of wonderful structures, countless and vast, and of profound lateral chasms."
Ref.: 100, p. 176

ROYAL ARCH CREEK
Coconino (Grand Canyon)   T32N R2W
This name was proposed by the USGS in 1908 because of being near the Royal Arches,
a striking formation (T35N/R5E).   Ref.: 329

ROY TANK
Coconino   T20N R1E
This watering place was named for Roy Wolf, in this area in the early 1900s.
Ref.: Kelly

RUBY
Santa Cruz   T23S R11E   Elev. 4219'
Here the Montana Mine had a community called Montana Camp. Julius F. Andrews (b.
April 10, 1853; Ohio; d. c. 1921) arrived in January 1895 to run the store. Mining
activities increased markedly c. 1909. Soon thereafter Andrews sought a post office.
Records in the National Archives list the post office as Powmott. What happened to that
application is unknown, but within ten days Andrews renamed the post office to honor
his wife (née Lillie B. Ruby). In 1913 having run the store for eighteen years, Andrews
sold out and moved to Tucson.
   The Frazier brothers, Canadians, then operated the store. In 1914 renegades crossed
the International Boundary and murdered the Fraziers. A couple named Pearson
operating the store in 1921 were also killed by Mexican bandits. The renegades tried to
murder the Pearson's child, but an aunt grabbed the three-year old and hid in a canyon.
Caught and convicted, the murderers were en route to Florence when they killed the
sheriff and escaped. A posse from Nogales caught up with them.
   The Montana Mine at this location has enjoyed an on-again-off-again existence. The
mill was dismantled c. 1940. Associated names include Ruby Creek (two hundred yards
east of the store), Ruby Peak (Elev. 5050'), and Ruby Trail Dam (T23/R11E).
P.O. est. as Powmott, April 2, 1912, name changed to Ruby, April 11, 1912, Julius S.
Andrews, p.m.; disc. May 31, 1941   Ref.: G.E.P. Smith; Lenon; Mrs. Hugh Miller;
AHS Names File; 242

RUCKER CANYON (P.O.)

Cochise   T19S R28E   Elev. c. 6000'

The first name for this military location was Camp Supply, established April 29, 1878. Its name was changed to Camp J.A. Rucker to honor an officer who lost his life while trying to save the life of a fellow officer. On July 11, 1878, Lt. John A. Rucker, Lt. Austin Henely, and John Rope (an Apache scout) waited for a hard rain to abate. They were in a saloon on the left fork of the creek on which the post was located. The rain over, men mounted their mules and swam the flooded river. The officers followed, but made the fatal error of riding side by side in the swift current. It knocked one against the other, throwing them off their horses. From the banks, men threw ropes to the struggling officers. Lt. John A. Rucker, instead of saving himself, tried to save Lt. Henely. Rucker Canyon, called White River Canyon in the 1880s, was the site of the drowning. Indian scouts worked all night in water up to their arm pits, trying to find the bodies. On April 29, 1879 to honor Rucker, the name of Camp Supply was changed to Camp J.A. Rucker. During the early 1880s' pursuit of Geronimo, Camp Rucker was an important military station used for heliograph signals. By 1880 the area was being called Gray's Ranch or "Old Camp Rucker." Later a pioneer family named Powers took over the place. They set up a post office at their ranch headquarters, and called it Powers, the name of the postmistress. In 1891 the name was changed to Rucker. Although it is reported as being discontinued in 1906, it was called Rucker Canyon post office in 1917. Rucker Lake (T19S/R30E) resulted from damming the stream in the canyon.

P.O. est. as Powers, Dec. 1, 1887, James M. Powers, p.m.; changed to Rucker, June 20, 1891; by May 16, 1917 being called Rucker Canyon; disc. Aug. 15, 1929 (all post offices at the same location)   Ref.: 242; *Arizona Sentinel* (July 27, 1878), p. 1; *Salt River Herald* (Jan. 1, 1879), p. 2; *Arizona Historical Review* (Jan. 1936), pp. 44, 46; 145, p. 151; 159, p. 549

RUDD CREEK

Apache   T7N R29E   Elev. c. 7800'

A man of many talents, Dr. Rudd began his working career as a tanner, studied medicine and practiced for ten years following the Civil War. In 1876 while en route to Arizona from Arkansas Dr. William Mann Rudd (b. Sept. 27, 1827, Tennessee; d. Feb. 1915) met a man named Springer (see Springerville, Apache), who said that Springerville was a good place for settlers. Rudd bought a ranch and raised cattle along a creek which either he or his wife named after themselves. He was the first district attorney for Apache County. Rudd Knoll, Rudd Knoll Spring, and Rudd's Reservoir are associated names.   Ref.: Noble; Velma Rudd Hoffman (grand-daughter), Letter (July 10, 1957)

RUSSELL (R.R. SIDING)

Yavapai   T16N R1E   Elev. 5491'

According to Barnes, a man named Russell was superintendent for the Jerome narrow-gauge rail line to the Jerome mines. Russell Spring also carries his name.   Ref.: 18a

RUSSELL TANK

Coconino   T29N R5E

David Russell (b. 1836, Illinois?) used this stock tank for his cattle. Russell Tank is on Russell Wash.   Ref.: Hart; 63

RUSSELLVILLE

Cochise   T16S R22E

Russellville was short lived because the establishment of Johnson sounded its death knell. Here in 1882 a smelter was being erected and George J. Roskruge laid out a town site. It was also called variously Russell, Russell Camp, and Russell City. An associated name is that of Russellville Peak (T15S/R22E, Elev. 6616'), proposed in 1965 by Mrs. Larry Devner. There may be some connection between the name and the fact tht Capt. George Briggs Russell in April 1871 battled Cochise and one hundred and fifty Apaches near what later became Benson. Russell's command consisted of about eighteen men. The Indians retreated from the open plains to the mountains and there entrenched. Russell sent for reinforcements.   Ref.: Lenon; Macia; AHS, Russellville File and Johnson File; 107, VIII, 108; 277, p. 130

RUSSETT HILLS
Gila   c. T10N R9E
The name refers to the brown color of these hills.   Ref.: Woody

RUSTLER PARK
Cochise   T17S R30E   Elev. 8784'
This mountain-top level area with its good grass and fine springs was used by rustlers in the 1870s and 1880s. They rested stolen cattle here until new hair grew out over altered brands. Today this location is a recreation area. It includes Rustler Canyon (T20S/ R29E).   Ref.: Riggs; 76, p. 13

RUSTLER PARK
Graham   T4S R20E
In 1879 this area was called Rustler's Ranch (T6S/R24E) because it was used by cowboys reputed to be rustlers. They included the Powers brothers. Rustler Park Canyon runs through the area.   Ref.: 353, p. 9, Note 13

RUTHERFORD
Yavapai   T13N R5E   Elev. 2400'
The Hopper family named this location for O.H. Rutherford, a close friend who lived in Jerome.
P.O. est. Sept. 14, 1907, Elizabeth Hopper, p.m.; disc. May 25, 1911
Ref.: 242; Barnes' Notes

RYAN
Coconino   T38N R1W   Elev. c. 7800'
According to Barnes, this location was first called Coconino, so named by Aguilla Nebeker, who with his partner Ryan worked mines here c. 1900. Barnes also says that when Nebeker sold to Ryan, the name was changed from Coconino to the form now in use. However, it should be noted that in its brief existence, the post office was known solely as Ryan and on the application form the name of the proposed postmaster was Roy Nebeker Davidson. The name now extends to Ryan Station Water Fowl Area.
P.O. est. Feb. 6, 1902, Cass Lewis, p.m.; disc. July 18, 1902
Ref.: 18a; 242; Arizona Game and Fish, p. 1

RYE
Gila   T9N R10E   Elev. 3135'
Formerly the election precinct in this district was known as Wild Rye because of the wild rye growing along the banks of Rye Creek. The population was widely scattered. The small settlement at Rye lay at a crossing on the creek. During the Pleasant Valley feud it provided a natural refuge for all. See Gilliland Gap, Gila
P.O. est. Oct. 14, 1884, Mary E. Boardman, p.m.; disc. Oct. 9, 1907
Ref.: Woody; 5, p. 453; 242

RYE CREEK
Gila   T9-10N R9-10E
This creek heads in the center of Cypress Thicket at c. 4000'. The thicket is descriptively named. See Rye Creek, Gila

S

SABINO CANYON   pro.: /sabíyno/
Pima   T12S R15E   Elev. c. 2700-3700′

According to a man born and raised in this canyon, the name is attributable to a desert
shrub called *sabino* or *savino*, which grows abundantly here.   Ref.: Juan Figueroa

SABINO CANYON
Pima   T18S R8E

This canyon was named because of the presence here of the Sabino Otero Ranch. The
Sabino Otero Land Grant claim (T20S/R13E) was disallowed by the U.S. Land Claims
Court. From 1885 to 1891 there was a dam at the head of this canyon, but it washed
away. Sabino Wash is an associated name.   Ref.: 242; *Arizona Enterprise* (June 27,
1891), p. 3

SACATE   pro.: /zakátey/
Nahuatl: *cacatl*; Spanish: *sacate* = "forage grass"
Pinal   T3S R4E   Elev. 1128′

In 1775 Fr. Francisco Garcés described *Sacate* where this Indian village is today. Its
name does not appear on maps until GLO 1892 (Sacaton Station). To avoid confusion
with the town of Sacaton, a stage station on the Butterfield Overland Stage route and
now a village on the Pima Reservation, the name of this location was changed to
Sacate.   Ref.: 77, p. 87, Note 24

SACATON   pro.: /sakətówn/ or /sǽkətow^{n}n/
Spanish = "tall, rank herbage, unfit for forage"
Pinal   T4S R6E   Elev. 1274′

Despite the meaning of the name, in this section of Arizona sacaton (*Sporobulus
wrightii*) is a forage. The word is also said to refer to broad, flat land rather than to a kind
of growth. The Pima Indian name was *Uturituc* (= "the corner") because here new and
old branches of the Gila River came together. Prior to and in 1904 the Pima name was
Ku'-u-Ki (= "big house"). Fr. Eusebio Kino first visited here in 1697 and recorded its
name as Tusinimo, but as he arrived on the first Sunday of Advent, he renamed it to La
Encarción. Lt. Juan Mateo Manje wrote, "Tusonimo . . . is so named from a great heap
of horns, from the wild or sylvan sheep, which appears like a hill; and . . . they make the
common subsistence of the inhabitants." The latter name has also been rendered
Sudacson and Sutacuison. Kino also interpreted the Indian name as Sudason and
Soacson, the latter gradually altering to Sacaton. In 1775 Fr. Francisco Garcés called it
both Vturituc and San Juan Capistrano. Fr. Oblasser in 1935 noted the Papago spelling
was rendered as Chusoni Mo.

In 1857 Sacaton Station on the Butterfield Overland stage route was one and a quarter
miles east of the present-day community. The route followed a pass between Thin
Mountain (elev. 1750′) and the Sacaton Mountains. The community has long been
headquarters for the Pima Indian Reservation, for a brief period having a post office
called Pima Agency. (See also Sacate, Pinal). Associated names include Sacaton Butte
(elev. 1280′), Sacaton Crossing, Sacaton Flats (Pinal/Maricopa; T3S/R8E), which
Pima Indians c. 1904 called Harsanykuk; Sacaton Peak (T5S/R7E; elev. 2755′), and
Sierra Sacatones.

P.O. est. as Sacaton, Jan. 6, 1871, Peter Forbach, p.m.; disc. March 11, 1873; reest. as

Pima Agency, Feb. 1, 1875, Howard C. Christ, p.m.; changed to Sacaton, Jan. 3, 1876; name changed to Sacaton Indian Reservation, August 8, 1883, Frank Cummins, p.m.   Ref.: 246, p. 199; 77, p. 88, Note 28; 43, pp. 284, 372, Note 3; 73, II, 165, 166; Mrs. Annie E. Forbach Letter (Nov. 30, 1973); 281, p. 23; 167, II, 647, 877-878; 116, pp. 255-256; 242

SACATON BRANCH
Pinal

This location was also known as Sacaton Crossing. It was on the road from Oracle to Reddington on the San Pedro River. Barnes reported it had a post office, but official records do not substantiate the statement.
P.O. est. Sept. 23, 1895, Nannie B. Young, p.m.   Ref.: 50, p. 177; 18a

SACATON WASH
Cochise   (1) T12S R24E   (2) T19S R20E
In this instance the name *Sacaton* indicates the presence of plants such as reeds, which cannot be used for forage. See Sacate, Pinal

SACRAMENTO PIT
Cochise   T23S R24E
Sacramento Hill or Mountain had an elevation of 5656'. Stripping began in 1918 and the hill gradually disappeared as copper ores were removed, and Sacramento or Lavender Pit resulted. See Lavender Pit, Cochise   Ref.: 197, pp. 58, 59

SACRAMENTO VALLEY
Mohave   T20N R18W   Elev. c. 3000'
According to Fish, prospectors from Sacramento, California, were at the site of Chloride c. 1857 where good rains had produced high grass and field flowers which reminded them of their home, hence the name. On the other hand, Alonzo Davis wrote that in 1864 soldiers of Company I, 4th California Volunteers, prospected in the Hualapai Mountains next to the San Francisco Mining District. They organized their own mining district which, Davis said, "We thought it appropriate to name . . . 'Sacramento' Mining District, which we accordingly did . . . , and so the valley separating the two ranges of mountains became known as the Sacramento Valley."

The place is sometimes called the Detrital – Sacramento Valley or simply Detrital. The latter name refers to geologic debris in the valley. Sacramento Wash (T23N/R18W) is in the valley.   Ref.: 116, p. 346; Davis *ms.*, (Huntington Library); Babcock; Housholder; 146, p. 66

SADDLE BUTTE
Coconino   T24N R18E   Elev. 6449'
This butte dips to connect Navajo Mountain with No Name Mesa, forming a "saddle." It was named by Charles L. Bernheimer in 1922.

SADDLE MOUNTAIN
Coconino (Grand Canyon)   T34N R4E   Elev. 8420'
The name describes the appearance of this mountain. It is applied to Saddle Canyon (T34N/R1W) also.   Ref.: Bureau of Am. Ethnology, *Bulletin* (1926), p. 133

SADDLE MOUNTAIN
Maricopa   T1N R8W   Elev. 3037'
The highest elevation in a mass of low mountains and hills resembles a saddle. It is also called Saddleback Mountain.   Ref.: 18a; 329

SADDLE MOUNTAIN
Maricopa   T7N R8E   Elev. 6535'
This mountain lowers between two peaks, forming a saddle, hence its name.

SADDLE MOUNTAIN
Pinal   (1) T5S R16E   Elev. 4240'
                                   (2) T1L S R21E   Elev. 4233'
Wheeler descriptively named the first. Antisell on November 4, 1846, named the

[537]

second. Although it is now sometimes called Tilted Peak, the accepted name for the second is as given above.   Ref.: (1) 345, III, 509; (2) 4, p. 75

SAEVEDRA SPRINGS
Mohave   T21N R18W
On Oct. 7, 1857 Lt. Edward Fitzgerald Beale was so disgusted with his Mexican guide Saavedra that he wrote the guide was "an old wretch and a constant source of trouble to everyone, and his entire and incredible ignorance of the country renders him totally unfit for any service." On October 12 Beale noted that Saavedra had located a spring, a fact which pleased Beale because it was the first thing old Saavedra had found that "he had started to look for since our departure from Albuquerque."
Ref.: 23, pp. 27, 67; 325, p. 41

SAFFELL KNOLL
Apache   T8N R29E   Elev. 7794'
The USGS records that this was named for a pioneer family in the Springerville area. The name is applied also to Saffell Canyon.

SAFFORD
Graham   T7S R26E   Elev. 2920'
In 1874, weary with having their ranches at Gila Bend washed out by the flooding Gila River, some farmers settled at this place, naming it for Gov. Anson Pacely Killen Safford (b. Feb. 14, 1840, Vermont; d. Feb. 15, 1891), who was then visiting in the valley. On Jan. 28, 1874 C.M. Ritter established the townsite and Joshua E. Bailey opened the first store and the post office in the settlement. The community was the county seat until 1883 when that function was moved to Solomonville. The county seat returned to Safford in 1915. Associated names include Safford Peak (Pima, T12S/R12E, elev. 3565'), and Safford Valley.
P.O. est. March 15, 1875, Joshua E. Bailey, p.m.; Wells Fargo 1903
Ref.: AHS, Joshua E. Bailey File; 62; 116, p. 588; 225, pp. 242. 547

SAFFRON VALLEY
Coconino (Grand Canyon)   T34N R1E
The name for this valley was proposed by the USGS in 1908.   Ref.: 329

SAGEBRUSH: This descriptive term applies to some place names in Arizona.
Examples follow:

Sagebrush Canyon	Apache	T33N R23E	
Sage Brush Point	Coconino (Grand Canyon)	T32N R3W	
Sagebrush Spring	Coconino	Upper Moencopi Wash area	
Sagebrush Wash	Navajo	T35N R18E	Elev. 6430'

SAGE PEAK
Cochise   T19S R30E   Elev. 8400'
This peak was named for Harley H. Sage, a forest ranger who entered the Forest Service on Sept. 26, 1916. He died of Spanish influenza on Nov. 13, 1918. A copper shield on the mountain commemorates his death in the service of his country. The peak was named in 1932. Ref.: 329

SAGINAW
Pima   T23S R24E
The townsite of this location was named by the Saginaw Development Company c. 1905 for the Saginaw Shaft located nearby. The company had its principal office in Saginaw, Michigan.   Ref.: C.E. Mills, Letter (Feb. 14, 1956)

SAGUARO
Pima   T11S R8E   Elev. 2519'
This place with a notation that it was a "town" was so named by the USGS, which said that it should not be spelled Sahuaro, Sahuara, nor Sahuaro. The USGS withdrew the decision on Feb. 27, 1961. Ref.: 329

SAGUARO GAP   pro.: /səwåro/
Pima   T13S R10W
Multiple saguaro cacti are here, hence the name.

SAGUARO LAKE
Maricopa   T8N R8E   Elev. 1535'
This lake was created by the Stewart Mountain Dam on the Salt River. Completed in 1930, it is two hundred and twelve feet high. The lake, about ten miles long, has a capacity of 69,765 acre feet. It was named for the Arizona State cactus flower. Ref.: 5, p. 350; 329

SAGUARO NATIONAL MONUMENT   pro.: /səwåro/
Pima   East: T15S R16E   Elev. 2660'-8666'
                               West: T13S R11E   Elev. 3273'
The eastern National Monument was established on March 1, 1933 to preserve approximately ninety-nine square miles of saguaro cacti. The second section, west of Tucson, was established in 1961.   Ref.: 329; 13, Dodge, "Wilderness of Unreality," p. 3

SAHUARITA   pro.: /sawaríytə/
Spanish = *"little saguaro"*
Pima   T17S R14E   Elev. 2702'
In 1879 James Kilroy Brown established the Sahuarita Ranch south of Tucson, naming it because there were many saguaro in the vicinity. It was mapped that year as Saurita. Pedro Aguirre used the ranch headquarters as a stage station on the route between Tucson, Arivaca, and Quijotoa. The developing community was called Sahuarito, after the ranch. Brown gave the railroad the right of way with the provision that the railroad station be named Sahuarito, but the name came through as Saurita on an 1884 railroad map. When Geronimo was active in the region, Brown moved his family to Olive Camp where he was associated with the Olive Mining Company. He sold his ranch c. 1886 and the area fell into a decline, with the post office being discontinued. Hinton referred to this place as Columbus for reasons unknown. As activities gradually increased and a community re-developed here, the post office was re-established. Sahuarita Butte (T15S/R13E, elev. 2850') and Wash (Pima/Pinal, T11S/R13E) also have many giant cacti.
P.O. est. Sept. 4, 1882, James K. Brown, p.m.; disc. July 11, 1886; reest. as Sahuarita, Oct. 15, 1911, Thomasa G. Dumont, p.m.   Ref.: AHS, Mrs. J.K. Brown *ms.*, and Castillo Collection, Box 1; 163, pp. xxxiii, xxiv

SAHUARO GAP
Yuma   T13S R10W
In 1952 the deep well at this location was drilled inadvertently by a private citizen on government land. It takes its name from the gap and presence of saguaro cacti.

SAINT: For place names beginning with the term *St.*, or *Saint* see entry by first major word thereafter. Example: for Saint Johns see Johns, Saint.

SALERO MOUNTAIN   pro.: /səléro/
Spanish = "salt cellar"
Santa Cruz   T21S R14E   Elev. 5507'
An offshoot of the Sonora Mining Company under the name Santa Rita Mining Company began reworking an old mine here in 1858. The mines included the Salero Mine about a third of the way up the face of what J. Ross Browne called Salero Hill, today known as Salero Mountain. No evidence has been found to substantiate that Jesuits worked the mine in the 17th century, but it was worked by Mexicans from about 1828 to 1830. Another source says that the name of the mining company was the Salero Mining Company, organized by John W. and William Wrightson with their brother John as manager, with headquarters at Tubac. Others in the venture included H.C. Grosvenor, Gilbert W. Hopkins, and Rafael Pumpelly, a geologist. Only Pumpelly escaped death at the hands of the Apaches. He also escaped having any place in Arizona named for him. (See Wrightson, Mount; Grosvenor Peak; Hopkins, Mount). Because of problems with Apaches, after a fierce battle the Hacienda de Santa Rita was abandoned

on June 15, 1861. In 1865 the company went out of business and because of problems with Baca Float No. 3 land titles, the mine was inoperative until c. 1876. John E. McGee tried to reopen it and operate the old hacienda, and a small community called Toltec came into existence. However, land title difficulties continued, McGee departed, and mining was sporadic thereafter.

George Clark operated it from 1884 to 1890.

P.O. est. as Salero, Aug. 13, 1884, Lizzie Durand, p.m.; disc. April 17, 1890 Ref.: Lenon; *Arizona Sentinel* (June 29, 1878); 56, p. 230; 286, pp. 194, 195; 224, p. 105; 163, pp. 202, 203

SALIDA GULCH pro.: /səláydə/
Yavapai   T13S R1W

This gulch was named for a big mining company called Salida (in Colorado). Salida Spring is in the Gulch. Ref.: Gardner

SALINA
Navajo: *tselani* = "rocks standing up"
Apache   T30N R23E   Elev. 6600'

The name of this settlement on the Navajo Indian Reservation is a corruption of the Navajo name. It was changed officially to Salina by the USGS in Dec. 1960. Salina Spring is nearby.   Ref.: 331, p. 129; 329

SALLY MAY WASH
Yavapai   T12N R6E

The name is also spelled Salome. The USGS files carry the surprising notation, "name for a lady." The name has been in use since c. 1880. It applies also to Sally May Spring.

SALMON LAKE
Coconino   T13N R8E   Elev. c. 6000'

In 1880 a practical joker named "Old Man" Williams, a butcher at Camp Verde, told men going on a turkey hunt they would not need to take much grub because he had hidden canned salmon in a tree near a small lake. The men found neither turkeys nor salmon and nearly starved. Thereafter, the lake was called Salmon Lake. It is in Salmon Lake Basin below Salmon Lake Butte. Ref.: 18a

SALOME pro.: /səlówmiᴧ/ or /səlówm/
La Paz   T5N R13W   Elev. 1876'

In 1904, speculating that the railroad would lay tracks through the area, Charles H. Pratt with the help of Ernest and Dick Wick Hall laid out a town plat here. Dick Wick Hall, a noted humorist, said the town was named because Mrs. Grace Salome Pratt took off her shoes and the hot sand burned her feet, hence the slogan, "Salome where she danced."

The railroad missed the town by a mile and the community had to be moved. Hall had so much trouble getting Post Office Department permission to move the mail service that his final application reads as follows: "One and a half miles closer to defeat," making the word defeat look like *depot* (which he wrote quite clearly a few lines further down on the form). Salome Peak (T6N/R14W, elev. 3991') and Wash have associated names.

P.O. est. Feb. 21, 1905, Charles H. Pratt or Dick Wick Hall, p.m.; location changed Feb. 21, 1906; Wells Fargo 1906   Ref.: *Prescott Journal Miner* (Aug. 21, 1906), p. 5; *Arizona Sentinel* (Aug. 29, 1906), p. 3; *Phoenix Enterprise* (Jan. 12, 1905), p. 3; 242

SALOME CREEK pro.: /séləméy/ or /sǽliᴧmey/
Gila   T4N R12E   Elev. c. 4000'

The Spanish pronunciation for the creek name as spelled above was altered by the first American settlers to Sally May, and the legend arose that a pioneer with two wives settled here and named it for both wives. Another version says he had two daughters, hence the name. Probate records do not substantiate either story. According to USGS records in 1964, the nearby mountain was "named after an Indian in the 1880s and still in use." They failed to say whether the mountain or the Indian is in use. The spelling Salume is a variant. Salome Mountain (T4N/R11E, elev. c. 5426') is an associated name.   Ref.: Place Names Committee, Arizona Pioneers Historical Society, *Third Annual Report*, (Dec. 29, 1937); 49, p. 451; 329

SALT CREEK
Coconino (Grand Canyon)   T31N R2E
This creek was named by Henry Gannett in 1906. The water tastes salty.   Ref.: 329

SALT CREEK
Coconino/Navajo   T17N R13E
Springs along this creek are alkaline, hence the name. See Jack's Canyon, Coconino/Navajo. Ref.: 18a

SALT CREEK
Gila   T1S R21E   Elev. c. 3500'
A large salt spring on this stream results in this name, which is also a translation of the Navajo *todoknozh bikoo* (= "salt water canyon"). Salt Mountain (T2S/R20E) overlooks it.   Ref.: 18a; 331, p. 26

SALT HOUSE DRAW
Mohave   T32N R13W
This draw was named because it had a building where salt was stored for cattle. Ref.: 329

SALT RIVER
Gila/Maricopa   T4N R16E   Elev. c. 4000-1000'
This largest tributary to the Gila River flows over two hundred miles in a southwesterly direction to join the Gila River near Phoenix. It passes through an area in which it picks up salts which give its waters a brackish taste. In 1698 Fr. Eusebio Kino called it the Rio Salado, also saying he had named it for the Evangelist Matthew. In 1736 or 1737 Fr. Ignacio Xavier Keller apparantly named the junction of the Verde and Salado Rivers the Rio de la Asuncion, the name also used in 1744 by Fr. Jacobo Sedelmayr. This same section of the river in 1766 was called Rio Compuesto (= "Put-together River"). On Nov. 3, 1775 Fr. Francisco Garcés noted that it was called Rio de la Asumpcion, a variant. In 1851 Lt. Parke mapped it as Rio Salines. By 1852 it was called the Salado, Salinas, or Salines River. Its upper portion was referred to as the Black River. Capt. George M. Wheeler in 1873 used two names: Prieto (= "black"), and also Salt River. The Pima Indian name in 1903 was *a'kimùlt* (= "salt river").

Much of the brackishness in the river comes from Salt River Draw. King S. Woolsey operated a salt mine in the draw from 1876-1879, and the military map for 1879 records a salt works at extensive Salt Banks. Until 1908 the history of the Salt River was one of prosperity wiped out by floods, as far as farmers were concerned. The Salt River Project has caused the construction of several dams (Theodore Roosevelt, Horse Mesa, Mormon Flat, and Stewart Mountain), to control the river and to provide irrigation and electricity. The Salt River Mountains (Gila, T3N/R14E) are adjacent to it. Associated also are the Salt River National Wild Life Refuge (Gila, T4N/R12E) on Roosevelt Lake; Salt River Peak (Gila, T2N/R14E; elev. 4857'), Salt River Range, and Salt River Valley (a.k.a. The Valley of the Sun, with Phoenix at its approximate center).
Ref.: Woody; 163, p. 75; 168, p. 235; 279, p. 64; 281, p. 23; 15, p. 357; 287, pp. 5, 20, 46; 20, p. 240; 27, p. 110, Note 15; 242; 256, p. 130, Note 63; 342, I, 63; 5, pp. 350, 351

SALT RIVER (P.O.)
Maricopa   T2N R5E   Elev. c. 1300'
Taking its name because of its adjacency to the Salt River, this post office was at the S.P.R.R. crossing on the Scottsdale-Mesa Road. Because of occasional flooding of the river, the mail used to come from Mesa rather than Scottsdale.
P.O. est. Aug. 21, 1912, Effie C. Coe, p.m.; disc. Oct. 15, 1916   Ref.: 242

SALT RIVER CANYON
Gila   T5N R17E   Elev. 3000'
Several engagements of the military with Apaches took place in this canyon, the first on Aug. 28, 1866. See Salt River, Gila/Maricopa   Ref.: 159, p. 426

SALT RIVER DRAW
Navajo/Gila   T7N R16E
This location is also called the Salt Banks. In 1879 military maps show a salt works at

the junction of the two streams. It was operated by King Woolsey from 1876 until Woolsey died in 1879. Indians continue to obtain salt from this location. Water flowing over the lip of the cliff leaves salt on the cliff face and gives a brackish taste to the stream. See Salt River, Gila/Maricopa   Ref.: Woody

SALT RIVER INDIAN RESERVATION
Maricopa   T2N R6E   Elev. c. 1500'
Pima Indians from Pima Butte settled at *S-a'al-kuig* (= "little mesquite trees"), which on June 4, 1879 was established as the Salt River Indian Reservation for Pima and Maricopa Indians. The name comes from the fact that it is on the Salt River. Currently it consists of 47,007 acres.   Ref.: 167, II, 374; "Annual Report of the Arizona Commission of Indian Affairs 1954, 1955, 1956," p. 6

SALT SEEPS WASH
Navajo   T20N R20E
The name describes the character of this water course. It was also known in 1942 as Sears Wash. The name Cottonwood Wash should be applied only to the wash into which it drains. Ref.: 329

SALT SPRINGS
Navajo   T19N R17E
These springs are on Cottonwood Wash near where it enters the Little Colorado River. In 1853 it was used by Lt. A.W. Whipple as a stopping place and was later important on the road between old Fort Wingate (New Mexico), and Fort Whipple, Arizona. Ref.: 331, p. 130

SALT SPRINGS WASH
Mohave   T30N R19W
The name comes from the fact that this wash heads at salt springs.   Ref.: 18a

SALT TRAIL CANYON
Coconino   T32N R7E
The name is a translation of the Navajo name for the trail through this canyon. *A'shi'i Na'stiin.*

SAMANIEGO PEAK   pro.: /səmaniyéygo/
Pima   (1) T17S R11E   Elev. 5591'
                                  (2) T11S R15E   Elev. 7715'
George Roskruge named No. 1 peak on his 1893 Pima County map. Mariano G. Samaniego (b. July 26, 1844, Mexico; d.c. 1887) was made a citizen under the terms of the Gadsden Purchase. He lived in New Mexico until arriving in the Tucson area in 1869 where he owned the Canჳada del Oro Ranch near Oracle as well as Rillito Ranch northeast of Tucson. A freighter and stage line operator between Tucson and Oro Blanco, he sold his contracts in 1881 to enter the cattle business. Associated names include Samaniego Hills (Pinal, T10S/R9E); Samaniego Ridge (Pima/Pinal; T11S/R10E), and Samaniego Spring (Pima, T11S/R15E)   Ref.: Kitt; 224, III

SAMANIEGO RIDGE
Pima/Pinal   T11S R10E
This ridge is part of peak No. 2. See Samaniego Peak, Pima

SAMANIEGO SPRING
This spring was on the Cañada del Oro Ranch. See Samaniego Peak, Pima

SAM HILL DRAW
Gila   T19N R10E
Sam Hill, a pioneer prospector, had a cabin here. Ref.: 18a

SAM HUGHES BUTTE
Pima
Samuel Hughes (b. 1829) was a prominent Tucson citizen in the 1880s.   Ref.: 62; 18a

SAMPLE

Cochise   Elev. 3538'

The post office at the Sample Mine was named for Comer W. Sample, a rustler who was hanged as a participant in the so-called Bisbee Massacre of Dec. 8, 1883.
P.O. est. July 28, 1886, Pablo Rebeil, p.m.; disc. Oct. 31, 1887   Ref.: 18a

SAMPLE WASH

Pinal   T5S R15E

This was was named because the Sample Mine was in it.

SAN: For place names beginning with the designation *San*, see entry by first major work thereafter (e.g., for San Cosme, See Cosme, San).

SANCHEZ   pro.: / sánčez/ or /sænčez/

Graham   T6S R27E   Elev. 3100'

In February 1889 Lorenzo Sanchez settled here with his twelve children. In 1891 he established a school, all the pupils being his children. Since practically everyone in town was called Sanchez, it was an obvious name for the post office.
P.O. est. July 30, 1901, Hignio Costales, p.m.; disc. Nov. 9, 1903
Ref.: 242; 18a; Jennings

SANDAL TRAIL

Navajo   T38N R17E

The National Park Service in the Navajo National Monument made this trail. Visitors follow footprints painted on rocks.   Ref.: 13, Brewer, "Navajo..., p. 4

SAND: This word is used descriptively in many Arizona place names, as follows:

Sana Draw	Coconino	T14N R14E	
Sand Dunes	Maricopa	T5S R6W	
Sand Dunes	Yuma	T12S R21W	
Sand Flat	Yavapai	T18N R2E	
Sand Hollow	Mohave	T40N R16W	
Sand Hollow Wash	Mohave (Nevada)	T40N R16W	
Sand Springs	Coconino	T27N R13E	Elev. 5213'

This village and springs are on the east bank of Dinnebito Wash.

Sand Springs	Navajo	T41N R20E	
Sand Tank	La Paz	T2N R19W	
Sand Tank Mountains	Maricopa	T6S R3W	Elev. 4084'

This name was given to the mountains c. 1920 by Kirk Byran.

Sand Tank Wash	Maricopa	T6S R4W	
Sandtrap Wash	Mohave	T11N R13W	

The USGS changed this name from Maggie Wash in 1967.

Sand Wash	Graham	T6S R19W	
Sand Wash	Greenlee	T7-8S R32-31E	
Sandwash Spring	Gila	T9N R10E	
Sand Wells	Pima		

Formerly Chot Vaya.

Sandy Point	Mohave (Lake Mead)	T31N R17W	

SANDERS

Apache   T21N R28E   Elev. 5800'

Although Barnes says this place was named for C.W. Sanders, office engineer of the

A.T. & S.F.R.R., on GLO 1889 it is spelled Saunders and therefore may derive from that of Art Saunders, operator of the trading post. It is also worth noting that the community was named Sanders, but there was already a station by that name on the railroad, and hence the railroad depot was called Cheto.

P.O. est. Nov. 24, 1896, Dayton T. Crowfut, p.m.; reest. Sept. 1, 1932, Orville L. Hathorn, p.m.   Ref.: Richards; 18a; 331, p. 131; 242

SANDERS MESA
Yavapai   T14N R9W
This mesa was named for Thomas Sanders, who kept a stage station in the vicinity in the 1880s.   Ref.: 262, p. 40

SANDY
Mohave   T17N R13W
This location was named because it was on Sandy Creek.
P.O. est. June 8, 1892, Mrs. Nellie C. Hunt, p.m.; disc. Jan. 31, 1900   Ref.: 242

SANDY BOB CANYON
Cochise   T22S R23E   Elev. 5700'
Sandy Bob maintained a stage station in the mid-1880s at the north end of the route through the Mule Mountains to Bisbee, hence the name of this canyon.
Ref.: Spencer Map 1886; 242; *Oasis* (Jan. 4, 1899), p. 6

SANENEHECK ROCK
Navajo: *enee* = "thief"; *tse* = "rock"; *sa* = "an equivalent of *tse*"; (remainder of name not analyzed in records searched)
Navajo   T36N R16E   Elev. 6656'
In 1932 the USGS changed the spelling Ja-ne-heck to the current spelling. The reason for the name of this isolated rock peak is not known. Ref.: 331, p. 194; 329; 141, p. 194

SANFORD BUTTE
Santa Cruz   T22S R15E   Elev. 4695'
Denton G. Sanford (b. March 7, 1833, New York; d. Jan. 23, 1885) homesteaded a ranch in 1862. On Nov. 14, 1878 he bought what is now the Circle Z Ranch, obtaining a patent to the land on April 30, 1879. The ranch was not known by that name until after his death of malaria.   Ref.: AHS, Denton G. Sanford File; Lenon

SANFORD CANYON
Pima   T18S R17E
This canyon was named for Don G. Sanford, a rancher here in the early 1880s. He sold to Walter Vail.   Ref.: Kitt

SANTA: For entries beginning with the word *Santa*, see entry by first major word thereafter. For example, for Santa Rosa Gulch, see Rosa Gulch, Santa. Exception: Santa Claus, Mohave, and Santa Cruz County.

SANTA CLAUS
Mohave   T23N R18W   Elev. 3384'
This place, which was projected as a subdivision, never developed, but is nationally known because its imaginative "Christmas" architecture has attracted many visitors. It was the dream child of Mrs. Nina Talbot of Los Angeles. She weighed three hundred pounds and advertised she was the biggest real estate agent in California. She and her husband Ed moved to Kingman and from there to Santa Claus where Ed designed the building. Mrs. Talbot added to the fame of their location by sending Christmas cards to visitors. The location was for sale in January 1983.   Ref.: Housholder

SANTA CRUZ COUNTY   pro.: /santə cruwz/ or /sæntə cruwz/
On March 15, 1899 the smallest of Arizona counties was created from parts of Pima and Cochise counties. Nogales is the county seat. The county was named for the Santa Cruz River. Other names proposed for it were Papago County and Grant County. Historically Santa Cruz County is perhaps the most interesting in Arizona, for it includes explorations by Americans seeking a way to wealth in the California gold rush in 1848.

New roads followed ancient Indian trails. Apache warfare and battles with Mexicans during insurrections in that country add to the historic luster of this county, and some of the oldest mines in Arizona are in it. Santa Cruz County now counts agriculture, mining, and international trade among its major industries. As for the beauty of Santa Cruz County, its 797,240 acres hold wooded mountains and desert valleys, running streams and dry arroyos, all with notable flora and fauna.

SANTAN   pro.: /santan/
Pinal   T3S R5E   Elev. 1250'
The Pima name for this location prior to 1904 was *à-àt'kăm va-aki* ("sandy ancient house"). According to Pima calendar sticks, the Indian settlement was in existence in 1857. Papago call the location Santa Ana, the normal pronounciation of which is *sántanə*, corrupted into Santan because the final syllable is seldom sounded. The Santan Mountains (T3S/R6E, elev. 3093') share the name, although sometimes called Malpais Hills.
P.O. est. April 27, 1921, Mrs. Jeanie M. Tucker, p.m.; disc. Feb. 29, 1932
Ref.: 281, p. 24; Lenon; 242; 18a

SANUP PLATEAU
Mohave   T29N R12W   Elev. 4800'
According to Barnes, the eastern Indian word *sannup* indicates a word used in Massachusetts for a "married Indian man." How or why it was appled to this plateau and to Sanup Peak is not known.   Ref.: 18a; Lenon

SAPANA VAYA
Papago = "odor-of-coyote well"
Pima   T21S R7E
This is the name of a Papago village and well.   Ref.: 262, p. 4

SAPPHIRE CANYON
Coconino (Grand Canyon)   T32N R1E   Elev. c. 4000'
Although Barnes says that this canyon was named by Maj. John Wesley Powell because of its coloring, the USGS records say that the name was proposed by that office in June 1908.   Ref.: 18a; 329

SARAH DEMING CANYON
Cochise   T16S R30E   Elev. c. 6000'
In 1923 Ed Riggs escorted the first party to see Balanced Rock in what is now Chiricahua National Monument. Sarah Deming was the only non-Arizonan woman in the party. She slipped and tore a hole in the seat of her pants and Aunt Martha Riggs immediately concealed the rip with her own apron which Miss Deming hastily tied on backwards. A new place name came instantaneously into being. Sarah Deming Trail is in the canyon.   Ref.: Riggs

SARDINA PEAK
Santa Cruz   T21S R12E   Elev. 5606'
A Mexican named Sarvinia lived for years near this peak and his name, gradually anglicized to the more familiar Sardina, was applied to the peak. The name is shared by Sardina Canyon and Dam. Ref.: 18a

SARDINE CREEK
Greenlee   T3S R30E
The name is said to be descriptive of the steep and narrow character of the canyon through which this creek runs. Sardine Falls and Saddle share the name.   Ref.: Scott

SASABE   pro.: /sásəbey/ or /sæsəbiy/
Papago: *shashovuk* = "echo"
Pima   T22S R8E   Elev. 3566'
According to Bourne, "The hills around are hollow so when you shout you can hear your echo answer you." The meaning of the name was also reported earlier both by an Arizona newspaper in 1869 and by Kirk Bryan many years later. Bryan notes that

Sasabe was originally a Papago village called Shashovuk, a name shared by the Mexican and American custom houses. The Mexican custom house was about five miles south of the boundary, a fact in accord with the placing of Zazabe, also spelled Zasabe, about eight miles south of the border on the Smith map of 1879.

The name Sasabi Flat occurs on maps from 1869 on. It applied both to a small border community or stage station and to the valley north of the border (sometimes spoken of as the head of Altar Valley). In 1862 a newspaper discussed the proposed post office at Sasabe Flat, a place which consisted of a few Mexicans in a small hovel actually in Mexico. The newspaper was probably mistaken, for a post office and stage station were at Sasabe Flat. Possibly to avoid confusion about the Mexican and United States locations, the post office name was changed to Providence Wells in 1878. Under that name it was in operation a very few months, as the stage line was soon discontinued. Thereafter there was no post office on the border until La Osa post office was established. On GLO 1896 La Osa shows on the border four miles southwest of Sasabi Flat. In the same year Buenos Ayres (ranch) lies four miles northeast of Sasabi Flat, a fact which clearly separates the two post offices.

The La Osa post office went out of existence in 1899 and mail was handled by the Buenos Ayres post office. On February 24, 1903, the Buenos Ayres post office changed its name to La Osa. Confusion must have resulted, for that name in turn was changed to Sasabe on August 23, 1905. The Buenos Ayres/La Osa/Sasabe post office was discontinued on June 30, 1914.

Residents of Arizona were not confused by the locations. For instance, Kirk Bryan wrote in *Routes to Desert Watering Places* (1922) that "the left-hand road goes south to a gate, beyond which is San Fernando, a new village on the Rebeil Ranch with a post office, store, and custom house. This is now the usual port of entry from Mexico, replacing in large measure the older Sasabe. At the gate at San Fernando, a road from the west comes from La Osa and the Sasabe road goes east and southeast down the slope to Sasabe." He was, of course, referring to Sasabe, Mexico two miles southeast of La Osa.

As for San Fernando (today's Sasabe), it was a private development under hard-working Carlos Escalante, nephew of Don Fernando Serrano, who escaped from Mexico during the 1910 Madero Revolution and surveyed six hundred acres where he settled in 1913 as a cattleman on the old Rebeil Ranch. Carlos Escalante arrived in 1916. In that same year a new port of entry from Mexico was established here with the setting up of three tents. The change in location was necessary because water had given out at the old Sasabe. Young Escalante worked hard to build quarters for people moving in from old Sasabe. He named the new village San Fernando to honor his uncle. In December 1916 an application was made for a post office at the new location. On that application in the Nat'l. Arch. the name is proposed because "it had been there by that name since March 1890." Thus quite clearly San Fernando was either at or not far from the first La Osa post office, not to be confused with Buenos Ayres. However, the Post Office Department substituted the name San Fernande (*sic*). Inevitably the new post office was confused with San Fernando, California, and the name of San Fernande was changed to Sasabe in 1926. Associated or variant names in the area include Arroyo del Sasabe, Sasabe Flat Valley, and Sasabi Flat (or Sasaby Flat).

P.O. est. Sasabe Flat, Aug. 17, 1869, Juan Elias, p.m.; name changed to Providence Wells, July 30, 1878, Andalucia Aguirre, p.m.; disc. Oct. 21, 1878; reest. as La Osa, May 26, 1890, Paul M. Roth, p.m.; disc. Dec. 12, 1899 (mail to Buenos Ayres); reest. as San Fernande, Dec. 28, 1916, William Beckford Kibbey, Jr., p.m.; name changed to San Fernando, Nov. 15, 1923; name changed to Sasabe, Feb. 10, 1926.   Ref.: *Weekly Arizona* (Nov. 20, 1862), p. 2; *Arizona Sentinel* (Dec. 31, 1877), p. 3; 59, p. 378; *Arizonan* (Nov. 27, 1869); 50, p. 227; AHs, Castillo Collection, Box 1; Mrs. Carlos M. Escalante; 242; 107, VII, 139; 167, II, 468; 57, p. 378

SASCO (RUINS)

Pinal   T10S R9E   Elev. 1806'

A branch railroad spur formerly extended from Red Rock to the smelter for the Silver Bell Mine. The smelter was on a small but prominent hill. Its name came from the initials of the *S*outhern *A*rizona *S*melting *Co*mpany.

P.O. est. April 3, 1907, Charles O. Matthews, p.m.; disc. Sept. 15, 1919
Ref.: Jordan; 59, p. 367

SASETANHA MESA

Navajo = "long, narrow, standing rock"
Apache   T33N R22E   Elev. 7999'
The Navajo name reflects the fact that this mesa has narrow fingers extending from the main mass of Black Mesa. Rain Mountain, a peak on this mesa, was not so mapped prior to 1968. The mesa name is also spelled Sastanha, but Sasetanha has been in use since at least 1892. Ref.: 329

SAUCEDA MOUNTAINS   pro.: /séydə/

Spanish: *sauce* = "willow"; *its* = "little"
Pima/Maricopa   T10S R3W   Pima: Elev. 4118'
                                                        Maricopa: Elev. 3397'
Willow trees grow in this area, hence the name. Associated or variant names follow:

Sauceda See Chiulikam, Pima	Pima	
Sauceda Wash	Maricopa	T5S R5W
Sauceda Well See Chiulikam, Pima	Pima	
Saucedo Mountains See Sand Tank Mountains, Pima	Pima	T12S R1W
Saucida See Chiulikam, Pima	Pima	
Saucito See Chiulikam, Pima	Pima	
Saucito Canyon	Pima	T13S R18E
Saucito Mountain	Pima	T17S R8E
Saucito Wash	Pima/Santa Cruz	T20S R12E

SAUL POINT

Navajo   T11N R19E   Elev. c. 6000'
Lt. John Gatewood named this for an Apache Indian scout dubbed "Saul." The name was in use at least as early as 1882.   Ref.: 18a

SAWBUCK MOUNTAIN

Graham   T2N R26E   Elev. 6881'
This mountain resembles a pack saddle of the sawbuck type, hence the name.   Ref.: 18a

SAWED OFF MOUNTAIN

Greenlee   T3N R30E   Elev. 7440'
John H. Toles Cosper named this mountain in 1883 because one point looks as though its tip had been sawed off.   Ref.: Simmons

SAWIK MOUNTAIN

Pima: *sah* = "red"; *wick* = "mountain"
Maricopa   T2N R6E   Elev. 2135'
The name is that used descriptively by Pima Indians. It is also sometimes called Sheldon Mountain. Ref.: 329

SAW MILL: The name *saw mill* applies to several locations because a sawmill is now or once was in the vicinity. Examples follow:

Sawmill   Apache   T2N R6E   Elev. 7700'
The Navajo tribal council operates a sawmill here. There is also a trading post dating to 1907. The location used to be referred to as Nehiegee, an attempt to spell the Navajo word *nīʼiijihi* (= "sawmill").
P.O. est. as Niegehe, Sept. 6, 1941, Genus Alex Baird, p.m.; resc. Dec. 30, 1941; reest. as Sawmill, Nov. 3, 1952, Mrs. Myrtle B. Lee, p.m.; disc. May 22, 1964 Ref.: 331, p. 139; 141, p. 36

Sawmill	Cochise	T23S R19E	
Sawmill Canyon	Gila	T3N R18E	
Sawmill Canyon	Graham	T8S R22E	
Sawmill Canyon	Greenlee	T3N R31E	
Sawmill Canyon	Mohave	T21N R17W	
Saw Mill Canyon	Pima/Santa Cruz	T19S R15E	Elev. 3969'

By 1869 Sam Hughes and Henry Lazard (b. Oct. 30, 1831, France; d. March 11, 1895) constructed a sawmill, which burned in 1870. Roskruge in 1893 mapped it as Dowdle Canyon because David Dowdle owned a ranch nearby. Ref.: AHS, Henry Lazard File

Sawmill Creek	Gila	T4N R18E	Elev. c. 4000'
Sawmill Gulch	Yavapai	T13N R1W	
Sawmill Hills	Coconino	T17N R10E	Elev. 7661'
Sawmill Mountains	Mohave	T34N R8W	
Sawmill Point	Coconino (Grand Canyon)	T36N R1W	
Sawmill Spring	Apache	(1) T9N R26E	(2) T8N R28E
Sawmill Spring	Cochise	T23S R20E	
Sawmill Spring	Coconino	T22N R4E	
Sawmill Spring	Graham	T7S R22E	
Sawmill Spring	Greenlee	T3S R29E	
Sawmill Spring	Santa Cruz	T20S R15E	
Sawmill Wash	Coconino	T17N R10E	

SAWTOOTH: A ragged sawtooth appearance has resulted in the following names:

Sawtooth Mountain	Apache	T6N R23E	
Sawtooth Mountains	Pinal	T9S R6E	Elev. 2359'
Sawtooth Peak	Coconino	T21N R1W	Elev. 6185'
Sawtooth Peak	La Paz	T3N R21W	Elev. 2230'

This was formerly Farrar Peak. See Farrar Gulch, Yuma

Sawtooth Ridge	Pinal	T1N R12E

SAXE'S STATION
Pinal   At foot of Pinal Mountain
In the 1880s E.A. Saxe operated stage to the Silver King (Gila) and Quijotoa (Pima) Mines. He had a station here. Ref.: Craig, "A Pack Train," *ms.*, U. of Arizona; p. 222

SAXON DAIRY RANCH
Santa Cruz
In 1919 this location was owned by Harry J. Saxon, hence the name. See Kitchen Ranch, Santa Cruz Ref.: *Arizona Cattleman* (March 24, 1919), p. 5

SAYERS
Yavapai   T8N R3W
This ranch post office, named for its postmaster, served about fifty people.
P.O. est. Aug. 1, 1908, George Sayers, p.m.; disc. July 15, 1913 Ref.: 342

S B MOUNTAIN
Maricopa   T6N R8E   Elev. 3695'
This mountain was so named because it was a hard place ("a son of a bitch") on which to catch cattle.

S CANYON

Graham   T8S R25E

This canyon initially extends northwest but twists so much that it has an *S* appearance, hence the name. It was also sometimes called South Canyon. Ref.: 329

SCATTERVILLE

Mohave

In 1877 because new buildings were strung along over a three-mile stretch of the Sandy River the area was called Scatterville. It may have been what developed into the town of Signal. See Signal, Mohave   Ref.: *Arizona Miner* (Nov. 2, 1877), p. 1

SCHEELITE CANYON

Cochise   T23S R20E

This canyon was named because of varicolored crystal and calcium tungsite or Scheelite here. Scheelite Ridge is also here.

SCHELLBACH BUTTE

Coconino (Grand Canyon)

In 1975 the USGS selected this name to honor Louis Schellbach (1887-1971), Chief Grand Canyon National Park Naturalist, 1940-1956. The name was proposed by Joseph Hall. Ref.: 329

SCHELL GULCH

Gila   T4N R13E   Elev. 2500'

This canyon was named for Robert H. Schell (b. 1845, Canada), in 1886 a resident of Gila County. He may have lived on this gulch. Ref.: *Gila County Great Register* (1886)

SCHNEBLY HILL

Coconino   T18N R6E   Elev. 6530'

Theodore Carlton Schnebly (b. Dec. 29, 1868, Hagerstown, Maryland; d. March 13, 1954) came to Arizona from Gorin, Missouri, on Oct. 12, 1901. He bought land from Frank Owenby, first settler in the area, and in 1902 constructed the road over the hill which bears his name. Ref.: Schnebly (son)

SCHOOLHOUSE WASH

Gila   T3N R13E

There was formerly a school house in this wash area. See Haufer Wash, Gila

SCHUCK

Papago: *schuck* = "black things"

Pima   T15S R7E

The Roskruge map of 1893 records Santa Rosa Ranch, on GLO 1897 simply as Santa Rosa. Neither name was used locally, as residents designated the following as the name of their village: *Schuchk Ka Wuacho Awotam* (= "people who live under the black things"). The present name is of course an abbreviation. Ref.: 329; 262, p. 12

SCHULTZ PASS

Coconino   T22N R6E   Elev. 8000'

This pass was named for a sheepman, Charles H. Schultz. At the east end of the road through the pass is a spring, first called Schultz Spring, then Elden Spring, and later – when the Babbitt brothers raised foxes there – it was called Babbitt Spring. (See Babbitville Tank, Coconino)

Schultz Peak is a variant name for Schultz Mountains where c. 1922 the Lowell Observatory had a temporary observatory. Schultz Spring is here.

Ref.: Anderson; Slipher; Sykes

SCHULZE PASS

Gila

According to the step-granddaughter of Charles Schulze (who owned the Schulze Ranch and ran the post office), the ranch was three and one-half miles from Miami, "just on the

other end of Bloody Tanks." Schulze (b. 1841, Germany) moved with his wife and children from Kansas to Arizona in 1883, settling at a fine spring. They eventually had eleven children, seven of whom died: two of pneumonia, one of a heart attack, one of a leg gangrene, two of cancer, and one following years of paralysis caused by a tunnel cave-in. The ranch in 1980 was still owned by two of Schulze's children.
P.O. est. July 12, 1894, Mrs. Lizzie Schneider, p.m.; disc. April 21, 1902
Ref.: Woody; 63; Irma M. Nava, Letter (Feb. 7, 1980)

SCHUNYAK
Papago = "much corn"
Pima   T15S R7E
This is a small community on the Papago Reservation.   Ref.: 262, p. 13

SCORPION RIDGE
Coconino (Grand Canyon)   T32N R1E
This is a southwestern spur of Sagittarius Ridge. The name was proposed by the USGS in June 1908 when the fashion was to name locations in the Grand Canyon after constellations and mythological personages but its outline looks like a scorpion's body.

SCOTIA CANYON
Cochise   T23S R19E
A man from Nova Scotia formerly lived in the canyon.   Ref.: 329

SCOTT MOUNTAIN
Pinal   T3S R14E   Elev. 5115'
This mountain was probably named for George Scott (b. 1832, Alabama), in Nov. 1875 one of the organizers of the Globe Mining District.   Ref.: Woody

SCOTTSDALE
Maricopa   T2N R4E   Elev. 1262'
An Army chaplain, Maj. Winfield Scott (b. Feb. 26, 1837, Michigan; d. Oct. 16, 1910) first visited this area in 1881. Later he homesteaded, taking out a patent in 1891. Meanwhile he served at Fort Huachuca, leaving his brother George in charge of the homestead. Following his retirement, Scott promoted property near his home as a health and agricultural center. The name Scottsdale became official in 1896 with the establishment of a school district. It had seventy residents in 1897.
P.O. est. Jan. 21, 1897, James L. Davis, p.m.; incorp. June 25, 1951
Ref.: 135, n.p.; 242

SCOTT'S WELL
La Paz   T2N R17W
This watering spot was named for Ben Scott, a pioneer rancher.   Ref.: Monson

SCREWBEAN SPRING
Mohave   T13N R19W   Elev. c. 2500'
A lone screwbean tree here gave rise to the name for this spring.   Ref.: Harris

SCRIBNER GULCH
Santa Cruz   T23S R11E
This short ravine was named for a man who worked the Grubstake Mine.   Ref.: 329

SCYLLA BUTTE
Coconino (Grand Canyon)   Elev. 3555'
This butte is on the south wall of Granite Gorge at the mouth of Slate Creek. In June 1908 the USGS named it in accord with the policy of naming locations of mythological personages.

SEAL MOUNTAIN
Yavapai   T9N R3W   Elev. 5116'
This mountain was pictured as the background for the first Arizona Territory seal (used c. 1883-1890), hence its name. The seal included a miner with pick, shovel and

wheelbarrow, and the motto *ditat deus* (= "God enriches"). Only the motto was retained on the state seal after Arizona achieved statehood in 1912.   Ref.: 18a

SECO, ARROYO
Spanish: *seco* = "dry"
Pima   T19S R9E
The name reflects the normal state of most washes in Arizona.

SECRET MOUNTAIN
Yavapai   T18N R4E   Elev. 6560'
W.W. Van Deren named this mountain. It is a narrow, low hogback lying between Secret Canyon (T19N/R5E) and Low Canyon.   Ref.: 18a

SECRET PASS
Mohave   T21N R20W   Elev. c. 3400'
Marauding Indians used to "disappear" on Secret Hill. It took a long time for pursuers to find the pass through which they were escaping, hence the name for it and for Secret Pass Canyon (T20N/R20W) and for Secret Pass Wash (T20N/R18W). A post office provided mail service for the Secret Mine here, close to Secret Spring (a.k.a. Secret Pass Spring).
P.O. est. April 29, 1916, Mrs. Ada Webster, p.m.; disc. May 15, 1917
Ref.: 242; Harris; 329; 200, p. 23

SECUNDINO WELL   pro.: /sèkuwndíyno/
Pima   T20S R9E   Elev. c. 3000'
A Mexican named Secundino dug this well c. 1910. There is a spring here.
Ref.: 18a; 58

SEDONA   pro.: /siydównə/
Coconino   T17N R6E   Elev. 4240'
This thriving community in Oak Creek Canyon was named by Ellsworth Schnebly for his sister-in-law, Sedona N. Schnebly (b. Feb. 24, 1879; d. Nov. 13, 1950). See Schnebly Hill, Coconino
P.O. est. March 4, 1902, Theodore Carlton Schnebly, p.m.   Ref.: 242; Schnebly (son)

SEE CANYON
Gila   T11N R13E
This canyon was named for either Charley See or John See, father and son. The father settled here at See Spring c. 1900.   Ref.: McInturff; Woody

SEEPAGE MOUNTAIN
Yavapai   T16N R5W   Elev. 6230'
Considerable seepage on the south and east sides of this mountain result in the name, which is shared by Seepage Canyon.   Ref.: 18a

SEEP: The descriptive term *seep* occurs in the following place names:

Seep Spring	Coconino (Grand Canyon)	T32N R1W	
This location was named by the USGS in 1908.			
Seep Spring	Greenlee	T2S R31E	
Seep Spring	Maricopa	T6N R10W	
Seep Spring	Yavapai	(1) T15N R3W	(2) T12N R2W
Seep Spring Canyon	Greenlee	T4S R31E	
Seep Spring Mountain	Greenlee	T2S R31E	Elev. 6241'

SEGEKE BUTTE
Navajo = "square rock"
Navajo   Elev. c. 6000'
This butte is roughly square, hence the name. A variant spelling is Se-gi-ke Butte.
Ref.: 141, p. 194

SEKLAGAIDESA CANYON
Navajo = "prominent white cliffs"
Apache   T39N R28E
Gregory noted the name in 1915. It describes the location. Fr. Haile spells it *tse lazai dez-a* (= "white rock point").   Ref.: 329; 141, p. 195

SELIGMAN
Yavapai   T23N R6W   Elev. 5250'
The first name for this location was Prescott Junction. A small community developed when the railroad from Prescott to the main line was completed in 1886. With the completion of the Ashfork railroad branch, however, the older Prescott branch was abandoned. Prescott Junction thereafter gradually came to be called Seligman, after the Seligman brothers, New York bankers connected with the A. & P. R.R., who owned the Hashknife Cattle Company. In May 1897 the A. & P. R.R. reorganized, abandoning Williams as its western terminus, substituting Seligman. The Williams round house was moved to Seligman. In July the S.F.R.R. emerged from the reorganization. Seligman Canyon is at T16N/R9W.
P.O. est. Oct. 26, 1886, James Daly, p.m.; Wells Fargo 1887 (Prescott Junction).
Ref.: 242; *Prescott Weekly Courier* (Aug. 6, 1886), p. 3; 124, p. 66

SELLS
Pima   T17S R4E   Elev. 2360'
The Papago name for this location (headquarters for Papago Indian Agency) is *Kumkachutz wawasit* (= "turtle stuck"). That name was used for the location in 1941, but earlier referred to the adjacent town, Artesa. Artesa is at the north end of the Artesa Mountains, hence its name. The older Artesa was in existence in 1909, but by 1920 had moved within a mile of Indian Oasis (now Sells). Indian Oasis then consisted of a store owned and operated by Joseph and Louis Menager, who dug the first well in the area. In 1909 he established a post office for which Joseph was the first postmaster, serving until 1919. At that time the name of the post office and community was changed to Sells for Cato Sells, Commissioner of Indian Affairs, hence the name Sells Agency. The name applies also to Sells Valley (T18S/R4E) and Sells Wash (T17S/R3E).
P.O. est. as Indian Oasis, June 1, 1909, Joseph Menager, p.m.; name changed to Sells, May 19, 1919   Ref.: 242; 58; 329; 59, p. 393; 262, p. le

SELLS WASH
Pima   T17S R3E
This location in 1939 was known as Gu Oidak Wash in its lower course and also as Big Fields Wash, but by action of the Papago Tribal Council, the name Sells Wash is official. See Sells, Pima   Ref.: 329

SEMBRICH
Cochise   T23S R20E   Elev. c. 3800'
The post office application in the National Archives notes that locally this place was called Ramsey Canyon. The name Sembrich is that of a settler in the Huachuca Mountains c. 1879.
P.O. est. Sept. 22, 1915, John W. Noel, p.m.; disc. Oct. 27, 1916   Ref.: 242; 18a

SENATOR MOUNTAIN
Mohave   T28N R19W   Elev. 5127'
John Burnett discovered a mine here. He sold it to Senator Page of Los Angeles in 1892, hence the name.   Ref.: 200, p. 126

SENITA PASS   pro.: /səniytə/
Pima   T17S R6W   Elev. c. 3500'
This pass has several senita cacti in it, hence the name. Senita is popularly known as "old man" cactus because of its bearded appearance.   Ref.: Hensen

SENTINEL
Maricopa   T6S R9W   Elev. 689'
Nearby Sentinel Peak (Elev. 1077') lends its name to this location. The hill commands

the surrounding plain like a sentinel. It is near Sentinel Wash (T6S/R10W), on Sentinel Plain.
P.O. est. June 20, 1880, William H. Burke, p.m. (see Burke's Station); Wells Fargo 1880. Ref.: 242

SENTINEL BUTTE
Pima   T15S R17E   Elev. 3355'
Descriptive

SENTINEL ISLAND
Mohave (Lake Mead)   T29N R22W
Joseph Christmas Ives in 1861 called this island (in Lake Mead near the mouth of Black Canyon) Fortification Rock. The USGS in 1948 changed the name to Sentinel to avoid confusing it with Fortification Hill. Ref.: 329

SENTINEL PEAK
Cochise   T18S R30E   Elev. 8999'
The names Sentinel Peak and Square Peak are descriptive. Ref.: 5, p. 375

SENTINEL PEAK
Mohave   North of road in Union Pass
Jonathan Draper Richardson (b Nov. 23, 1856, Tennessee; d. May 19, 1940) named this huge stone pinnacle. Richardson, who was severely wounded while battling Indians in the Dakotas, moved to Arizona for his health. He rode shot-gun with the payroll for the Pine Shade Mine until it closed in 1897. He then moved to Union Pass. Ref.: Ferra (daughter)

SENTINEL PEAK
Pima   T14S R13E   Elev. 2897'
Often called A Mountain because of the huge *A* white-washed annually by University of Arizona students, this peak has had many names. The Spanish name for it was Picacho del Centinela. It was called Picket Post Butte (Eckhoff, 1880) and Sentinel Peak because "in early Tucson a sentinel station was erected and someone stationed there to give warning whenever enemies approached. It was used as a sentry station in the Civil War." A *ms.* in the Huntington Library (1897) notes it as "a dark colored hill covered with rocks thrown up in titanic heaps called the Picacho de Metates." Because Warner Mill was at its base, it was also sometimes called Warners Mountain. The Papago name for it is Chuk Shon, referring to the village formerly at its base. Ref.: Huntington Library; Eckhoff 1880 Map; *Arizona Weekly Star* (March 28, 1878), p. 3

SENTINEL PEAK
Santa Cruz   T23S R11E
This commanding peak used to be called Mount Bartlett (for "Yank" Bartlett) and its sister peak, Mount Jewett (both government packers employed on the Boundary Survey). The current name is descriptive. Ref.: 329; Gilbert Sykes, Letter to Coronado National Forest Supervisor (Aug. 1, 1941)

SENTINEL ROCK
Coconino   T41N R8E
This lone sandstone pinnacle is about three to four hundred feet high. It stands alone like a sentry, hence the name give it by Dellenbaugh on October 18, 1872. Ref.: 88, p. 149

SEPARATION RAPIDS
Mohave (Grand Canyon)   T28N R12W
In 1869 while on his exploration of the Grand Canyon, Maj. John Wesley Powell noted that this turbulent rapid was fraught with extreme danger, so much so that W.H. and Seneca Howland along with William Dunn refused to go through it. Separation Canyon shares its name. It was first called Catastrophe Rapid by A.H. Thompson of Powell's party, probably because of the death of Howland and Dunn. The Howlands and Dunn separated from Powell's party here, hence its name. See Howland Butte, Mohave (Grand Canyon) Ref.: Schellbach File (Grand Canyon)

SEPULVEDA CREEK
Apache   T9N R25E
This name, also sometimes spelled Supolvre, was given preference over Sepulveda Wash by the USGS in June 1940. Sepulveda Wash is here.

SERAFIN, SAN   pro.: /san særəfin/
Pima   T13S R4E
This small Papago Indian settlement is also known as Ak-chin, but is not to be confused with Ak-chin (Pinal County). In 1940 the Papago Tribal Council officially decided to use the name of the church (San Serafin) for the entire settlement. The village was dedicated to St. Francis of Assissi in 1939. San Serafin is his Spanish name.

In 1698 Fr. Eusebio Kino came to a Pima rancheria which he called San Rafael del Actum el Grande, the Indians' Ak-chin (= "arroyo's mouth"), or Great Ak-chin (so named to set it apart from the smaller Ak-chin). The name San Serafin de Actum appears in the Lt. Juan Mateo Manje 1700 report. In 1701 Manje spelled the name Guactum. De Anza and Fonte in 1780 called it San Serafino del Napcut. Over the years the settlement was gradually deserted until finally it was used only as a summer residence by one or two families. By 1901 they too had left, but by 1917 it was reoccupied (apparently since 1914). The Mexican name according to "Slim Joe" Manuel was Aketun, further corrupted to Kuituni, La Kuitini, and La Quituni.
Ref.: 329; 58; 57, pp. 9, 394; 43, p. 400, Noter 1; 262, p. 5; 167, II, 453

SERVOSS
Cochise   T16S R24E   Elev. c. 3500'
This station serving the New York Ranch was named for Walter Servoss (b. Rochester, New York; d. 1908), who visited Arizona with John Rockfellow in 1883. Servoss went on to South America but returned years later to be Rockfellow's and Hartt's partner.
P.O. est. Feb. 28, 1911, William A. Carr, p.m.; disc. April 15, 1920
Ref.: 242; 277, pp. 42, 199

SETSILTSO SPRINGS   pro.: /céc?iltso^h/
Navajo: *check'il tsho* = "big oak"
Apache   T38N R25E   Elev. c. 6000'
The name probably derived from the presence of a large oak tree. Various spellings follow: Saeltso; Salltso; Sueltso; Tsa-tsil-too.   Ref.: 329; 141, pp. 152, 195

SEVEN FALLS
Pima   T13S R15E
There are seven falls here. Seven Cataracts is their older name.

SEVEN MILE CANYON
Gila   T8N R13E   Elev. c. 4200'
This canyon is seven miles from Young on an old wagon road to Globe. Ref.: McKinney

SEVENMILE HILL
Navajo   T4N R23E   Elev. c. 6500'
Sevenmile Canyon heads on this hill. Sevenmile Rim (6441') is at T4N/R23E. The hill itself was at a point seven miles on the road to Fort Thomas from Fort Apache, hence its name. On Aug. 30, 1881 Apaches massacred and burned four Mormons at the top of the hill and that afternoon killed an army telegraph line repair crew near Black River. On the night of Sept. 2, Col. Carr left Fort Apache with Troop E and an Apache Scout (Cibicu Charley). Finding the massacred Mormons, the party felt fortunate to escape the Apaches.   Ref.: 83, pp. 127, 133

SEVEN-MILE MESQUITE
Graham   T3S R24E
This stage station was kept by a Mr. Adams on the road from the San Simon railroad station to Camp Thomas.   Ref.: Wister, p. 840

SEVENMILE WASH

Gila   T2N R16E

This location is also known as Sevenmile Creek, Sevenmile Canyon (#2), and Sevenmile Draw. Sevenmile Crossing was at the juncture of this stream with the Salt River. Sevenmile Mountain is at T3N/R17E.

SEVEN SPRINGS WASH

Apache   T16N R26E

A group of seven perennial springs was first noted in GLO surveys in the late 1890s. The wash originates here, hence its name.   Ref.: 329

SEVENTY-FIVE MILE RAPID

Coconino (Grand Canyon)   T31N R5E

This rapid at the mouth of Seventy-Five Mile creek was formerly called Nevills Rapids, for Norman Nevills (d. 1949), who made several boat trips in the Grand Canyon. In 1966 the USGS changed the name to Seventy-Five Mile Rapid because of its location in the series of Grand Canyon rapids.   Ref.: 329

SEVENTY-SIX GULCH

Cochise   T13S R26E

This is also called Little California Gulch, both names deriving from those of mines nearby.   Ref.: Mrs. Laura H. Griffin

SEVENTY-SIX RANCH

Gila   T8N R10E

The ranch was seventy-six miles from Globe, hence the name and brand used for many years by Cliff Griffin. See also Perkinsville, Yavapai   Ref.: Griffin

SEVERIN CANYON

                                        T13S R23E

This canyon was named c. 1900 for a pioneer in the area.   Ref.: 329

SHADOW MOUNTAIN

Coconino   T30N R9E   Elev. 5422'

What looks like a shadow on the Painted Desert is in reality a low, dark lava hill, hence the name.   Ref.: 5, pp. 482-483

SHALAKO

Navajo   T25N R16E   Elev. 5520'

This landmark rises like a plug above the landscape. It looks somewhat like a slender kachina called *shalako* by Hopi Indians who, after visiting Zuni Indians in New Mexico, brought back and began using the Zuni shalako ceremony.   Ref.: Tom Harlen, U. of A. Dendrologist (1981)

SHALER PLATEAU

Coconino (Grand Canyon)   T32N R1E

In 1929 the USGS officially accepted this name, which honors an American Geologist associated with Harvard University. It shares its name with Shaler Pyramid.

SHANNON BASIN

Mohave   T15N R13W   Elev. c. 1800'

This basin was named for the Shannon Mine (T11N/R14W).

SHANNON MOUNTAIN

Greenlee   T4S R29E   Elev. 5520'

Among the first miners in the Clifton area were Charles and Baylor Shannon, nephews of Robert and Jim Metcalf. Charles located claims on Chase Creek. At what was later Metcalf, he built the Shannon smelter for the Shannon Copper Company on this mountain, hence the name. It is also called Shannon Hill.   Ref.: Reilly; Shannon; Scott; 257, pp. 76, 77

SHANUB POINT
Piute = "dog"
Mohave (Grand Canyon)   T34N R4W   Elev. 5611'
At least as early as 1925 this point was named for a Piute Indian family. Ref.: 329

SHAW BUTTE

SHAW BUTTE
Maricopa   T3N R3E   Elev. 2149'
This butte was named for an early settler who at his request was buried at the base of this butte. Ref.: 329

SHAW PEAK
Cochise   T17S R30E   Elev. 7730'
This peak is on the Shaw Ranch, hence the name.

SHEBA TEMPLE
Coconino (Grand Canyon)   T31N R4E
In 1906 the USGS named this peak on the North Wall in line with its policy to name formations after personages in ancient literatures and mythologies.

SHEEHY CANYON
Santa Cruz   T20S R13E
This canyon was named for Edward T. Sheehy, who c. 1925 served with the United States Border Patrol. The location is also erroneously called Sheshe. Sheehy Spring (T24S/R17E) shares the name. Ref.: Seibold; 329

SHEEP: Many place names in Arizona reflect the fact that raising sheep is an important industry. The following are examples:

Sheep Basin	Cochise	T16S R22E	
Sheep Basin Mountain	Gila	T8N R11E	Elev. 6263'
Sheep Camp	Graham	T11S R19E	
Sheep Camp Springs	Yavapai	T15N R4W	
Sheep Camp Wash	Graham	T11S R19E	
Sheep Canyon	Cochise	T14S R28E	
Sheep Creek	Maricopa/Yavapai	T8N R8E	

SHEEP CROSSING
Apache   T7N R27E   Elev. c. 9000'
Raising sheep requires that the herds be shifted for summer grazing from low hot areas to cool mountains. An old established trail existed from Phoenix to the White Mountains. Moving flocks along it took three months. This important upper Sheep Crossing lay on the west fork of the Little Colorado River. Formerly numerous migrating sheep cropped growth so close that cattle were deprived of forage, a fact which caused severe trouble between sheepmen and cattlemen. Ref.: Becker

Sheep Dip Canyon	Apache	T6N R9W		
Sheep Dip Creek	Apache	T7N R8W		

There is a government-built sheep dipping vat used here by Navajo herders. The creek water is potable.

Sheep Dip Wash	Apache	T7N R10W		
Sheep Gulch	Yavapai	(1) T11N R3E	(2) T9N R2E	
Sheep Mesa	Maricopa	T4N R8E		

This is also called Black Mesa (An error; Black Mesa is one mile northeast).

Sheep Mountain	Coconino	T34N R7E	Elev. 6120'

Sheep Mountain	Maricopa	T8N R8E	Elev. 6976'
Sheep Mountain	Pima	T17S R9W	Elev. 1977'
Sheep Mountain	Yavapai	T8N R1W	
Sheep Mountain	Yuma	T10S R19W	Elev. c. 2000'

Mountain or bighorn sheep here led to the name.

Sheep Mountain Spring	Pinal	T1N R10E	
Sheep Peak	Pima	T12S R8W	Elev. 2217'
Sheep Pocket Trough	Mohave	T37N R9W	
Sheep Point Canyon	Apache	T6N R28E	
Sheep Ranch Canyon	Santa Cruz	T23S R17E	
Sheepshead Canyon	Yavapai	T16N R4E	

A sheep stock tank is near the head of this canyon.

Sheep Saddle	Greenlee	T2N R29E	
Sheepskin Spring	Navajo	T35N R16E	Elev. 6120'
Sheep Spring	Coconino	(1) T18N R8E	(2) T11N R14E
Sheep Spring	Navajo	T29N R18E	

This location is also called Kanelba Spring. Stephens says Kanelba derives from Hopi *Kane'lpabi* = "Sheep water place." Ref.: 307, p. 1156

Sheep Spring	Yavapai	(1) T18N R5W	(2) T13N R3E
(3) T15N R3W	(4) T9N R1E		
Sheep Spring Point	Coconino	T11N R14E	
Sheep Tank	Coconino	(1) T20N R2W	(2) T20N R4E
(3) T27N R2E	(4) T25N R4E	(5) T31N R1E	(6) T15N R9E
Sheep Tank	Pima	T11S R8W	

Named because of bighorn or mountain sheep in the vicinity. This location is also called Sheep Shit Tank.

Sheep Tank Draw	Coconino	T15N R9E	
Sheep Tank	Yuma	T1S R15W	

This is the location of the Sheep Tank Mine also.

Sheep Tank Peak	Pima	T11S R8W	

Also called Sheep Shit Peak (Bryan Notes)

Sheepskin Wash	Navajo	T14N R19E	
Sheep Wash	Cochise	T16S R21E	
Sheep Wash	Coconino	T34N R7E	
Sheep Wash	Gila	T5N R15E	
Sheep Wash	Graham	(1) T4S R26E	(2) T8S R21E
Sheep Wash	Greenlee	T1S R29E	

SHELDON
Greenlee   T7S R31E   Elev. 3600'
In 1884 this now vanished railroad station was named for a railroad man during the construction of the railway. The community once had a school house, but now little remains. Sheldon Canyon and Mountain (T7S/R30E, Elev. 5410') share the name. P.O. est. June 13, 1908, John F. Holder, p.m.; disc. Nov. 29, 1919 Ref.: 242; 329

SHELL MOUNTAIN
Gila   T9N R15E   Elev. 6383'
Fossil shells on this mountain resulted in the name. Ref.: McKinney

SHERIDAN MOUNTAIN
Yavapai   T15N R6W   Elev. 6190'
Thomas Sheridan (b. 1838, Ireland) was living in Williamson Valley in 1870, moving from there to the mountain that bears his name in 1877. He raised horses, watering them at Sheridan Lake.   Ref.: 62; 18a

SHERIDAN MOUNTAINS
Pima   T12S R3E   Elev. 3264'
This small range, also called Sheridan Hills, was named for Gen. Phillip Sheridan at least as early as 1910. Sometimes confused with the nearby Cimarron Mountains, they are south and separated from them by Montezuma Pass.
Ref. 262; p 34; 329

SHIBELL, MOUNT   pro.: /šaybél/
Santa Cruz   T22S R13E   Elev. 5146'
Charles A. Shibell (b. Aug. 14, 1841, St. Louis, Missouri; d. Oct. 21, 1908) arrived in Arizona in 1862 as a teamster for Gen. J.H. Carleton. Following his discharge in 1863, he went to Tucson. He was elected sheriff in 1874. He engaged in mining and ranching and was also a merchant and hotel operator.   Ref.: *Tucson Post* (Oct. 24, 1908); 224

SHINARUMP CLIFFS
Coconino/Mohave   T41N R3W   Elev. 5303'
Maj. John Wesley Powell learned the name from Piute Indians during his 1872 exploration of the Grand Canyon. The meaning of the name has not yet been ascertained. Shinarump Point (Coconino, T42N/R2W) borrows the name.
Ref.: 267, p. 13

SHINGLE MILL MOUNTAIN
Graham   T8S R24E   Elev. 6323'
There used to be a shingle mill on this mountain. Shingle Mill Canyon is on this mountain. Ref.: 329

SHINUMO ALTAR   pro.: /šinəmo/
Piute = "old people cliff dwellers"
Coconino(Grand Canyon)   T35N R1W   Elev. 6520'
On naming this location, Frederick Dellenbaugh said the towering formation "looked very much like a great altar," and also that Piute Indians called ancient inhabitants Shinumo. He applied the name to it and Shinumo Canyon (T33N/R1W) (replacing the older name, Snake Gulch) on a descriptive rather than on an archeological basis. In 1908 William Base renamed the canyon Serpentine because it snakes its way, and that name was later attached to Serpentine Rapids. Dr. A.H. Thompson rendered the name Sheno-mo. It has also been called Mesa Butte. Associated names include Shinumo Amphitheater and Creek (T33N/R1W). Shinumo Garden (T35N/R1W) was the site of Bass' cabin and garden. Here grew "excellent melons, canteloupes, radishes, onions, corn, squash, beans, with fair size peach and other trees," where prehistoric Indians had also grown produce. Shinumo Rapids are at T33N/R1W. Here too was Shinumo Trail, sometimes called Bass Trail as it extended from the Bass cable to Powell Plateau. Francois E. Matthes in 1906 deleted Bass' name. Shinumo Wash lies at T36N/R5E.
Ref.: 88, pp. 184, 310; Schellbach (G.C.); 178, p. 87; Francois E. Matthes to USGS geographer E.M. Douglas, Letter (9-13-06)

SHIPLEY
Mohave   T25N R10W   Elev. 4950'
The Shipley brothers, who drilled wells for the railroad, used a blind siding here to accommodate their equipment.   Ref.: 18a; Harris

SHIPOLOVI   pro.: /šowlówəpaviᴧ/ or /šowpáulaviᴧ/
Hopi: *shipaulavitu* = "place of mosquitoes"
Navajo   T28N R17E   Elev. 6200'
Shipolovi was founded c. 1750. The translation of the Hopi meaning is misleading, inasmuch as it really refers to a clan living there now (formerly at Homolobi). They

abandoned Homolobi because of hordes of mosquitoes. Shipolovi residents include people from Shongopovi. Attempts to spell the sound of Shipolovi have led to the following; Sha-pah-lah-wee (Macomb, 1860); Shipaulovi, Shipowlawe, Ci-pau-lo-vi, Shi-paui-i-luvi, Shipolia (Barnes, 1935), and Sipaulovi. The Zuñi name for this village is Ah-le-la. Ref.: Hopi Constitution (preferred spelling = Sipaulovi); 167, II, 551; 347, III, 13; 112, p. 32; 141, p. 44

SHIPP MOUNTAIN
Yavapai   T14N R7W   Elev. 5184'
Here Jeff Shipp, a cattleman c. 1880, had a ranch, but his headquarters were at the Cienega Ranch on the Santa Maria River. The location is also known as Big Shipp Mountain. Ref.: 18a

SHIVA TEMPLE
Coconino (Grand Canyon)   T32N R2E   Elev. 7650'
In 1880 Maj. Clarence E. Dutton named this location, describing it as "the grandest of all the buttes and the most majestic in aspect, though not the most ornate . . . it stands in the midst of a great throng of cluster-like buttes . . . in such a stupendous scene of wreck, it seems as if the fabled 'Destroyer' might find an adobe not wholly uncongenial." Shiva is the Destroyer of the Hindu triad. Ref.: 100, p. 130

SHIVWITS PLATEAU
Mohave   T34N R13W   Elev. 6300'
In 1875 the Shivwits Indians, a Piute tribe formerly in this area, (Shivwits = "people of the springs") numbered only one hundred and eighty-two. By 1909 only one hundred and eighteen were still in southwestern Utah. Maj. John Wesley Powell named the plateau for its former inhabitants. He spelled the name Sheavwitz. Others have rendered it as Shiwits, Shiwitz, and Shivivits. This location was also called Sanur Plateau. Ref.: 167, II, 552; 200, p. 30; 344, p. 37; 329

S H MOUNTAINS
Yuma   T1S R16W   Elev. 1800'
Gradually the name S H Mountains has been replaced by the name Kofa Mountains. The name S H Mountains is much older and until very recently was preferred locally. Arizona pioneer Charles B. Genung said that when the California Column entered Arizona via Ehrenberg, it passed north of this range. The soldiers noticed a series of large peaks, each with a smaller one behind and between it and the next large peak. The men were quick to catch a resemblance to outhouses, hence the name S H Mountains (not in the abbreviated form). That came into use as women asked what the men called the mountains. Old timers, delicate about such matters, invented the answer that the name meant Short Horn, so in the early 1900s these mountains were dubbed Short Hort Mountains. A second version varies only in substituting prospectors for soldiers. Darton is responsible for the third version; the name derived from the presence of a Stone House. No evidence has so far substantiated his statement. However, on GLO 1912 Stone Cabin Gap Wash (north of Palomas) ends in the S H Mountains. A stone cabin location is mapped on GLO 1921, but it is sixteen miles west. Ref.: State Library Files; 355, p. 106; 5, 470

SHONE'S CROSSING
Navajo   T12N R21E   Elev. c. 6200'
When discharged from the cavalry at Fort Apache c. 1879, John Shone started a cattle ranch here at the crossing for the stage line to Fort Apache. The name was also spelled Shoens Crossing. Ref.: 18a

SHONTO
Navajo = "spring"
Navajo   T37N R16E   Elev. 6450'
The name of this settlement and trading post on the Navajo Indian Reservation is also spelled Shanto and Shato. Many springs have the identical name. The Shonto Trading Post was begun in 1915 by Joe Lee and John Wetherill, who sold out to Harry Rorick. See Betatakin, Navajo Ref.: 141, pp. 43, 195

SHONTO (SPRING)
Coconino/Navajo   T36N R15E   Elev. 7049'
This location is also known as Sha-to (= "sun side spring"). The Navajo name is also spelled Shaantoh (= "spring on sun side of hill"). Herbert Gregory in 1915 first applied the name Shonto to this place. In 1972 the USGS settled on the "Shonto" spelling in an attempt to clear away various renderings of the word. It shares its name with Shonto Plateau, the settlement, and Shonto Wash. Ref.: 329; 331, p. 145

SHOPISHK   pro.: /šápic/
Papago = "pass"
Pinal   T8S R5E   Elev. 1490'
Earlier names for this location include Ko-opke (Papago = "place of the dam"), Kupk and Kopeka – all reflecting the fact that prior to 1915 Papago Indians built a dam here. In June 1941 these earlier names were eliminated and the present name made official. Shopishk Valley is also here. Ref.: 58; 262, p. 19

SHORT HILL
Yavapai   T20N R10W   Elev. 5254'
This hill was named in 1972 because it is "the smallest hill among the group around the dome" north of Crater Pasture. Ref.: 329

SHOSHONE POINT
Coconino (Grand Canyon)   T31N R3W
This location was formerly called Cremation Point because here Indians dropped ashes of their dead into the depths of the Grand Canyon. The name was changed to honor a Plains tribe. This scenic point is now closed to tourist traffic and preserved for a "locals only" picnic area.

SHOW LOW
Navajo   T10N R22E   Elev. 6331'
The first postmaster here was Corydon E. Cooley (d. March 18, 1917). A scout with Gen. George Crook (1872-73), Cooley married the daughter of Chief Pedro of the White Mountain Apaches. They had their home on the creek here in 1875 and it gained fame for comfort, a bountiful table, and cleanliness not often encountered by pioneer travelers. Cooley's partner in the venture was Marion Clark. Realizing the arrangement wouldn't work, the two men agreed to play seven-up to decide who should leave. When the last hand was dealt, Cooley needed a single point to win. Clark, running his hands over the cards, said, "If you can show low, you win." Cooley threw down his hand saying, "Show low it is." And Show Low became its name. Clark moved to a ranch near the present Pinetop. In 1881 Cooley sold half interest to Henry Huning of Las Lunas, New Mexico. They set up a store for travelers and also entered the cattle and lumber business. They too agreed to disagree (in 1890) and sold out as a unit to W.J. Flake, who wished to initiate a Mormon settlement. Cooley moved onto the White Mountain Apache Reservation. Today Show Low shares its name with Show Low Creek and Lake (T9N/R22E). In 1958 the lake was called Jacques Lake (named by the Phelps Dodge Corporation). The spelling probably should be Jaques, as Sanford Jaques ranched here (T10N/R23E). The lake holds water impounded by Show Low Dam, completed in 1953.
P.O. est. Aug. 19, 1890, Corydon E. Cooley, p.m.   Ref.: 5, p. 442; 225, p. 168; 329

SCHULTZ
Pinal   T8S R16E
The first name for this place was Mammoth Camp. Near here are both Mohawk Mine and Mammoth Mine, discovered by Frank Schultz (d. 1918), hence the name. On the post office application the names of both are suggested for the new post office, but the Post Office Department inserted Schultz' name in their place. Schultz Spring is also here.
P.O. est. Nov. 5, 1894, Lizzie Schneider, p.m.; disc. April 21, 1902
Ref.: 242; 238, p. 47

SHUMWAY

Navajo   T12N R22E   Elev. 5700'

A man named Wamsley settled in this place c. 1877, and in 1881 Charles Shumway constructed a flour mill nearby. Shumway was the first Mormon across the Mississippi. He was one of one hundred and forty-three Mormons who arrived in Salt Lake with Brigham Young. The name applies also to Shumway Butte (Elev. 6117') and Indian ruins.

P.O. est. Jan. 3, 1895, James Pearce, p.m.; disc. Oct. 11, 1956

Ref.: 242; 329; 225, p. 167, II, 560

SHUNGOPAVI   pro.: /šǝmówǝpaviᴧ/

Hopi = "a place of chumoa" (a kind of grass or reed)

Navajo   T28N R17E   Elev. 6562'

In 1629 missionizing Spaniards founded San Bartolome de Xongopavi near an old spring at an Indian settlement, today called Old Shongopovi. A new village arose, and there in 1680 Fr. Joseph de Truxillo was martyred and the mission destroyed. The new town of Shongopavi is atop the mesa rather than at the ancient spring. F. W. Hodge lists fifty-six variant spellings for this Second Mesa village, a few of which follow:

Comupavi (Onate 1958)

San Bartolome de Xongopavi (Betancourt 1694)

San Bernardo de Jongopabi (Vargas 1692)

Showmouth-pa (Domenech 1860)

Shu-muth-pa (Whipple 1877)

Shimopavi (Bandelier 1890)

Ci-mo-pavi (Fewkes 1892)

An associated name is that of Shungopovi Spring

P.O. est. as Chimopovy, Feb. 12, 1925, Marietta Euband; name changed to Shungopavy, May 1, 1934; disc. June 30, 1942   Ref.: 242; 167, II, 553, 554, 564; 331, p. 145; 111, p. 582

SHUTE SPRINGS

Gila   T3N R14E

This is the location where George Shute settled in the 1880s.   Ref.: Woody

SICHOMOVI   pro.: /sitóowᵛmǝoviᴧ/

Hopi = "place of the wild currant bush mound"

Navajo   T28N R18E   Elev. 6218'

In 1782 this community was spoken of as having been founded in recent years. It arose when Walpi became over-crowded. Wild currant bushes growing on a knoll resulted in the descriptive name. In 1875 the name appears on the Mallory map as See-cho-maw-wee. It has also been spelled Si-tcúm-o-vi, Si-chom-ivi, Sivuini, and Sichomivi

Ref.: 242; 141, p. 195; 167, II, 564; 150, p. 6; 112, p. 32

SIEBER POINT

Coconino (Grand Canyon)   T34N R4E

This point was named to honor Al Sieber (b. Feb. 29, 1844, Germany; d. Feb. 19, 1907). He was raised in Pennsylvania. After serving in the Civil War, Sieber arrived in Arizona in 1868. He was a guide and scout for the military. Apaches trusted him. Totally fearless, even in Indian camps he would reprimand Apaches crazy drunk on *tizwin* (= native beer). Sieber was permanently crippled by wounds received in Indian skirmishes. While he was helping build Theodore Roosevelt Dam, a boulder fell and killed him. Barnes suggested naming the point for Sieber.

Ref.: Woody; 5, pp. 454, 455; 18a

SIEGFRIED PYRE

Coconino (Grand Canyon)   T32N R5E

This peak on the North Wall was named by the USGS in 1906 in line with its policy to name formations for mythological personages.

SIERRA: Spanish = "mountains." Place names beginning with the word *Sierra* are listed according to the first main word following the designation *Sierra*. For example, for Sierra Ancha, see Ancha, Sierra. The single exception is Sierra Vista, Cochise, a city.

SIERRA VISTA

Cochise   T21S R20E   Elev. 4600'

This community is at the mouth of Garden Canyon. The first post office outside the fort came into existence when the commanding officer of the Fort discovered the post-mistress engaged in a profitable business bootlegging whiskey to soldiers. Her family was ordered to leave the military reservation at once. Her husband, however, was a feisty Civil War veteran who loudly asserted that the might of the Post Office Department was greater than that of the United States Army, and he'd be blasted if his family was going to move. Infuriated, the commanding officer sent wagons which hauled the family off with dispatch, depositing them at the north gate of the post. There they went back into business. In setting up a post office, authorities named it for Thomas J. Turner (arrived in Arizona, 1882), later sheriff of Cochise County (1901-1904). The railroad siding already had his name.

The community had an on-again-off-again existence according to the fortunes of the Fort itself. With the establishment of the old post as an electronic proving ground, the town snapped out of somnolence and in 1982 is a thriving city. The post office followed the fortunes of the Fort, enduring a series of name changes. The information is complicated by the existence of a railroad siding first called Turner, but in 1928, changed to Campstone (pronounced Campstun).

P.O. est. as Turner, July 15, 1897, Horace H. Temple, p.m.; disc. Dec. 31, 1919; est. as Overton (T22S/R20E), June 11, 1917, Mrs. Jean Clark Wilder, p.m.; disc. May 4, 1918; reest. as Garden Canyon, March 4, 1919, William Carmichael, p.m. (four miles east from Turner, on railroad); name changed to Fry, April 1, 1937 (for Oliver Fry. L.S. Fry was postmaster in 1937); incorporated as Sierra Vista by petition Aug. 9, 1955 Ref.: 242; Lenon; Macia; Larriau; Bennett

SIERRITA MOUNTAINS

Spanish: *Sierrita* = "little mountains"

Pima   T18S R11E   Elev. 6206'

These low lying hills have sierra-type topography, hence the redundant name: "Little Mountain Mountains." Ref.: 57, p. 252

SIF VAYA

Papago: *siv* = "bitter"; *vaxia* = "well"

Pinal   T9S R2E

The name Bitter Well is a translation of the Papago name for this place and applies in English to several locations. See Bitter Well entries.

SIGILLARIA GROVES (North Sigillaria Forest)

Apache

These groves and forest are north of Adamana. *Sigillaria* is a species of ancient tree which has calcified in dark adamant. Ref.: 209, pp. 109, 113

SIGNAL

Mohave   T13N R13W   Elev. 1500'

With the completion in 1877 of the mill for the Signal Mine, the community of Signal took shape. It was about nine miles from both the Signal and the McCrackin Mines. Like other typical early-day mining communities, Signal had stores, work shops, hotels, and saloons. Surveyed by Richard Gird, within eight months of its creation the town had two hundred buildings and a population of nearly eight hundred. According to a visitor in February 1878, it was extraordinarily isolated: "freight... at this time came by rail to the west side of the river at Yuma and thence by barge up the river to Aubrey Landing where it was loaded on wagons and hauled by long mule teams thirty-five miles upgrade to Signal. The merchants considered it necessary to send orders six months before the expected time of delivery... and up to this time the nearest post office was Ehrenberg on the Colorado River, fifty miles away." When Ed Schiefflin brought ores from Tombstone to Signal to run an assay, Richard Gird became interested in Tombstone, as did many other miners who flocked from Signal to Tombstone. See Scatterville, Mohave

P.O. est. Oct. 15, 1877, Thomas E. Walter, p.m.; disc. May 14, 1932
Ref.: Housholder; *Arizona Sentinel* (Oct. 13, 1877), p. 2 and (July 6, 1878), p. 1; 163, pp. 251, 252; 277, pp. 8, 9

SIGNAL: Many place names in Arizona bear the designation *Signal*. Whether such places were used for signaling by Indians or soldiers or were used because their prominence made it possible for people to determine where they were is often not known. Examples follow:

Signal Butte	Maricopa	T17N R7E	Elev. 1717'
Signal Butte	Yuma	T7S R16W	Elev. 614'
Signal Canyon	Mohave	T13N R13W	

See Signal, Mohave

Signal Hill	Cochise	T20S R24E	Elev. 5164
Signal Hill	Coconino (Grand Canyon)	T32N R1W	Elev. 6780'
Signal Hill	Coconino	T22N R1W	Elev. 7444'
Signal Hill	Pima	T13S R11E	Elev. 2425'
Signal Mountain	Maricopa		
Signal Mountain	Maricopa	T2S R7W	Elev. 2180'
Signal Mountain	Mohave	T13N R13W	Elev. 2351'
Signal Mountain	Pinal	T1S R13E	Elev. 4829'

A military heliograph station for old Camp Pinal was on this mountain, hence the name. Ref. Craig

Signal Mountain	Yuma	T1S R18W	Elev. 4877'

The highest point in the S H (or Kofa) Mountains was so named because of its strategic location for sending signals. It is said to have been a station on the old heliograph system.
Ref.: Monson; Lenon

Signal Peak	Gila	T2S R15E	Elev. 7875'

The name was in use at least as early as 1864. At one time there was a main relay station in the army heliograph system atop this peak. Ref.: 5, p. 347; Huntington Library

SIKORT CHUAPO pro.: /síkərt čiəpᴧ/

Papago: *sikort* = "round;" *tjuupo* = "rocky cavity with water"

Pima   T12S R3W   Elev. c. 2500'

The round spring at this location was dug out and improved by a man named Redondo. In 1910 Pozo Redondo (= "Redondo's Well") was at the east end of Redondo Canyon. Redondo overstocked and overgrazed the range and was forced to leave. Papago Indians who settled at the spring descriptively named it Sikort Chuapo. A variant is Sikort Juupo. The Sikort Mountains (Elev. 3603') are also called Pozo Redondo Mountains. Sikort Chuapo Pass is here. Sikort Chuapo Wash (T11S/R5W) is also called Rio Cornez or Childs Wash.   Ref.: Netherlan; 58; 262, p. 8; 57, p. 423

SIKUL HIMATK

Papago: *sikul* = "water going around"

Pima   T15S R3E   Elev. 2147'

The name refers to the fact that at the watershed here some flows north to the Gila River and some south toward the Altar River. This location is a small Papago village, occasionally uninhabited. Roskruge in 1893 called it Vaheja. In 1937 the Bureau of Public Roads called it Siclehema. It is at Sikul Himatk Wash.
Ref.: 329; 57, pp. 366, 392; 262, p. 5

SIKYATKI (RUIN)

pro: /siᴧkⁱᴧpkᴧ/

Hopi = "yellow house"

Navajo   c. T28N R18E   Elev. 6000'

This ten to fifteen acre ruined pueblo of the Fire Wood (Kokop) Hopi clan spreads over two knolls. Tradition says warriors from Walpi and perhaps other Hopi villages destroyed it. The reason for its name is not known.   Ref.: 155, p. 63; 167, II, 572

SILENT
La Paz   T4S R23W   Elev. c. 500'
Although Barnes says that this small community was probably named for Charles Silent, in 1880 an Associate Justice of the Territorial Supreme Court, no documentary evidence has been found to substantiate the statement. It appears rather to have been named for the Silent Mine in the Silver Mining District. In 1880 a small smelter was erected at Silent and operated intermittently for about three years. The Silver Mining District became active in 1879 when George Sills, Neils Johnson, George W. Norton, and Gus Crawford relocated many abandoned claims and organized the district.
P.O. est. Nov. 8, 1880, Charles T. Norton, p.m.; disc. March 13, 1884
Ref.: Willson; 355, p. 52

SIL MURK   pro.: /siẏəl muk/
Papago: *sil* (corruption of Spanish *silla*) = "saddle"; *mok* = "burned"
Maricopa   T4S R7W
The reason for the name is not known. C. 1892 fourteen Papago families moved here from Sauceda and established a village. The location was also called Siilimok. In 1965 because the village was on the flood plain of the lake backing up behind Painted Rock Dome, twenty families from this village were relocated elsewhere.   Ref.: 58; 253, p. 1

SIL NAKYA   pro.: /si^l nakhyə/
Sil: (corruption of Spanish *silla*) = "saddle"; *nakya* = "hanging"
Pima   T4S R5E   Elev. 2211'
This is a small Papago village, but the reason for the name is not known. Bolton says that this place may be where Manje visited with Fr. Kino in 1693, calling the place Cups. The following are other names: San Lorenzo (Lumholtz, 1912); Silinakik (1912); Silynarki (Barnes, 1935); Saranake (Sills Agency, 1936); and Seranake (USGS, 1936). Ref.: 58; 44, p. 281; 262, p. 12

SILVER: With the exception of three descriptively named locations which had a silvery appearance (see below), the following were named because of the presence of silver ore:

Silver Bear Gulch   Cochise   T23S R24E
The Silver Bear Mine was in this gulch.

Silverbell   Pima   T12S R8E   Elev. 2628'
Originally the Silverbell Mine camp was at T11S/R8E. It and the Gold Bell Mine were in the Silverbell Mining District. The company was first called Peltonville, for the president of the Huachuca Development Company.
P.O. est. Aug. 18, 1904, Roger W. Warren, p.m.; disc. Nov. 15, 1911; reest. June 1, 1953; Wells Fargo, 1906 Ref.: 242; 329, AHS, Castillo Collection, Box 1

Silverbell Mountains   Pima   T11S R8E

Silverbell Peak   Pima   T12S R8E   Elev. 4261'

Silverbell Valley   Pima   South of Silverbell Mts.

Silverbell Wash   Pima   T11S R8E

Silver Camp Canyon   Cochise   T14S R26E

Silver Clip Claim   La Paz
See Clip, La Paz

Silver Creek   Gila   T3S R15E

Silver Creek   Greenlee   T3S R30E

Silver Creek   Mohave   T19N R20W
In 1906 an important mining camp on the creek resulted in this name.   Ref.: AHS, Davis Collection, "Pioneer Days," p. 55; 201, 16

Silver Creek Spring	Mohave	T20N R20W	

See Silver Creek, Mohave

Silver Creek Wash	Mohave	T20N R21W	

See Silver Creek, Mohave

Silver Hill	Mohave	T23N R18W	Elev. 4123'

See Silver Creek, Mohave

Silver Hill	Pima	T20S R10E	

See Abbie Waterman Peak, Pima

Silver King	Pinal	T2N R10E	Elev. 3553'

Four farmers – Isaac Copeland, William Long, Charles Mason, and Ben Reagen – while en route to the two-year old Globe Mine, discovered the Silver King Mine. Mason had heard from a soldier named Sullivan about a curiously heavy and soft black rock the soldier found while working on Stoneman's Grace (see Pinal, Camp, Pinal). He told Mason near the foot of the grade, but when his enlistment expired, Sullivan left the region. While Mason had seen the rock, he did not look for its source. Apaches attacked him and his friends, killing a man named William Sampson. One mule sensibly left during the fight, and it was later found standing on an outcropping of chloride of silver, whence Sullivan's black rock. The men took Sampson's body with them – and it conceivably could be the one found in an old earthen oven at Camp Supply. The silver samples proved so rich that the four men believed they must have found the kind of silver mines, hence its name. An immediate stampede of miners seeking to cash in on the promised bonanza created the community of Silver King, which had stamp mills at Picket Post. By 1880 the boom was nearing extinction and today little remains at the site. A notable exception is a dog's grave with a marker: "King, a true pal, died 1940."

P.O. est. Dec. 21, 1877, S.B. Chapin, p.m.; disc. May 15, 1921
Ref.: 242; Woody; 168, pp. 118, 119; 359, pp. 85, 86, 93; Varney

Silver King Wash	Pinal	T1S R12E	

See Silver King, Pinal

Silver Mountains	Mohave	T22N R17W	Elev. 5410'
Silver Mountain	Yavapai	T9N R1W	Elev. 6120'
Silver Mountains	Yavapai		

See Bradshaw Mountains, Yavapai

Silver Peak	Cochise	T17S R31E	Elev. 7975'
Silver Queen Mine	Pinal	T6S R14E	

Locators recorded this mine on Dec. 4, 1871, and named it because they "knew it was not big enough to be the king." Ref.: Woody

Silver Range	Yavapai		

See Bradshaw Mountains, Yavapai

Silver Reef Mountains	Pinal	T8S R5E	Elev. 2471'

The now abandoned Silver Reef Mine was so named because it was on a reef-like ledge in these mountains. Silver Reef Pass lies between them and the Tat Momoli Mountains, and Silver Reef Valley is south of the mountains. Ref.: Stanfield

Silver Reef Pass	Pinal	T8S R5E	
Silver Reef Valley	Pinal	T9S R5E	
Silver Reef Wash	Pinal	T9S R5E	
Silverstrike Spring	Cochise	T14S R28E	

The now abandoned Silverstrike Mine was at this spring.

SILVER BUTTE

Gila		T6N R20E	Elev. 6131'

Young juniper trees at night here look as though tipped with silver. Ref.: Davis

SILVER CREEK

Navajo	T11N R22E

This sparkling creek, which extends about forty miles to join the Little Colorado River,

was named descriptively by early settlers. In 1875 Martha Summerhayes referred to the community on the creek which shared the name.
P.O. est. Sept. 9, 1905, Rafael Carillo, p.m.; disc. July 6, 1932
Ref.: 242, 18a; 314, p. 125

SILVER LAKE
Pima   T S R E
In 1880 this now vanished resort and lake was on the stage road from Tucson to San Xavier Mission. Damming the Santa Cruz River created the lake. A race track, pavillions, bath house, boats, and a hotel set in pleasant groves of trees attracted many visitors. The lake water irrigated farmland.   Ref.: 81, p. 238; *Arizona Star* (June 11, 1880); AHS, Castillo Collection, "Reminiscences of Rafael Ochoa"

SIMMONS
Yavapai   T17N R3W   Elev. 4551'
In the early 1860s several people named Simmons arrived in Williamson Valley or Simmons Valley, Thomas Wilson Simmons (b. 1837, Arkansas) among them. Simmons station, where stage lines stopped so that passengers could eat, was soon active, having a post office also. The post office with William John Simmons as post master was established under the name Wilson in Jan. 1871. It was named in honor of "the late Commissioner of the General Land Office." Although a newspaper article said that the name was changed from Wilson to Vitty, no such change is recorded in the postal records at the Nat'l. Arch. In 1873 the anme of Wilson was changed to Williamson Valley and the office operated under that name for almost a decade until the name was again changed, this time, to Simmons. Locally the place was called Crossroads, but that name too was officially abandoned in 1881.
P.O. est. as Wilson Jan. 20, 1871, William John Simmons, p.m.; changed to Williamson Valley Oct. 9, 1873, Mrs. Betsey Zimmerman, p.m.; name changed to Simmons July 5, 1881, Stephen Breon, p.m.; disc. April 21, 1931.
Ref.: *Arizona Miner* (April 29, 1871), p. 1; *Arizona Citizen* (Nov. 1, 1873), p. 2; *Prescott Weekly Courier* (Aug. 6, 1886), p. 3; Platten; 242; 62

SIMON, SAN
Cochise   T13S R31E   Elev. 3613'
In 1859 a Butterfield Overland stage station was established at this location as a team change station. Permanent water at the location on the San Simon Creek resulted in its becoming a steam railroad stop at a later date.

SIMON RIVER, SAN   pro.: /san si∧mówn/ or /sæn si∧mówn/
Spanish: "Saint Simon"
Cochise/Graham   T12S R30E
A notation on file at the USGS in Reston, Virginia, says, "Local people call it the longest wash in Arizona, so they class it as a river." It should be noted, however, that as late as 1900 the river ran with water its full length to where it joins the Gila River and the San Simon Valley was fertile and beautiful, but over-grazing and removing soil-holding brush timber hastened its deterioration into a largely dry wash with eroded gorges one hundred feet wide, and gulleys twenty fee across and thirty feet deep. It still runs its full length during periods of heavy rain. The earliest name for the course of this former stream is on a map dated 1700 where it appears as R. de Sonoca, which by 1849 was being mapped at the Rio de Suanca, with a settlement called Suanca not far from its headwaters. Another map (1847) gives the name as R. Suanuco. When Lt. Gray and his exploring party came over the pass into the Valle de Sauz (Spanish: "Valley of Willows"), they came through what they called La Grande Puerta or La Puerta ("The Great Pass"), as it was a pass or door to the Pacific waters, the first they had encountered. Maj. Emory of the Boundary Survey group noted that Mexicans called it San Domingo, Rio Suanca, or Rio Sauz. Its upper reaches were in a marshy area of permanent water called Cienega de Sauz (Spanish = "willow swamp"), also called the San Simon Cienega. Robert Eccleston and his emigrant party crossed the stream in 1849 and, finding no name for it on maps, called it Welcome Creek, but the name did not endure. The names for this location as mapped over the years are an interesting commentary on how this once living stream gradually became a dry wash. By 1879 Smith applied the name San Simon Cienega only to the portion near the Mexican border,

marking the remainder "Underground passage of Rio de Sauz." In that same year for the first time he used the name San Simon Valley. On GLO 1879 the name is San Simeon Valley and the river is called Sauz River. Doubtless the use of the names *Sauz* and *Salix* reflect the fact that desert willow trees grow abundantly along the course of the wash.

Related place names include Simon, San; Simon Cienega, San (T15S/R32E); Simon Creek, San; Simon Dam, San (T11S/R29E); Simon Head, San (T16S/R30E); Simon Peak, San (T11S/R31E, Elev. 5325'); Simon Valley, San (T13/7S, R31/27E); Simon Valley, San (T12/16S, R1E/2W; Elev. 1800-1945'); and Simon Wash, San Ref.: Huntington Library (maps); 138, p. 45; 224, p. 115; 106, p. 93; 101, p. 180; 73, II, 130; 20, I, 366, 371

SIMPSON CREEK
Apache   T4N R6E   Elev. c. 7500'
In 1915 Herbert Gregory named this location for Capt. James Hervey Simpson (d. March 2, 1883), who mapped the route and kept the journal of the crossing made by the first whites across the Lukachukai and Chusca Mountains in 1849-50.
Ref.: 141, pp. 71, 28 (Note 3), 91

SINAGUA VALLEY
Coconino   T24N R8E
Harold C. Colton applied the name Sinagua (*sin* = "without"; *agua* = "water") to the prehistoric remains east of the San Francisco Mountains established in the cinder fall zone of Sunset Crater. The Sinagua Indians lived in this valley about 800-1200 years ago. The name for the valley was suggested by Dr. Troy L. Pewe in 1971.
Ref.: 184, p. 23; 329

SINKING SHIP BUTTE
Coconino (Grand Canyon)   T30N R4E   Elev. 7344'
In 1930 M.R. Tillotson, Superintendent of the Grand Canyon National Park, suggested that the name of The Three Castles be changed to simply Sinking Ship "because of the dip or tilt of the strata." Locally it is still called The Battleship, referred to in the *National Geographic* (1914) incorrectly as "The Battleship Iowa."
Ref.: 329; Susie Verkamp

SINKS, THE
Navajo   T18N R5W   Elev. c. 6000'
A series of holes varying from twenty-five feet deep and a few feet across to others over nine hundred feet in diameter collect rain water which sinks rapidly, hence the name. Ref.: 5, pp. 448, 449

SINYELLA MOUNT
Coconino (Grand Canyon)   T34N R4W   Elev. 5445'
All place names listed as "Sinyala" are in the vicinity of this location which according to records on file at the USGS was named for Judge Sinyella, an Indian Chief (b. 1853), still living in 1923. The date of birth may be somewhat in error as Spier in 1928 noted that this Havasupai leader was about ten years old in 1855. His descendants, who continue to spell their name Sinyella, reside in Grand Canyon Village. The older Sinyella was a guide for George Wharton James, who deemed him "one of the most intelligent Indians of the whole tribe (Supai)." Ref.: 329; Susie Verkamp; 178, p. 154; 303, p. 358

SIOVI SHUATAK   pro.: /siowl šuətə/
Papago: "sweet water"
Pima   T17S R3W   Elev. 2094'
This small Papago village has been known by a number of names, some of which follow:

Coon's Can Well (1917, U.S. Corps of Engineers)

Cochibo (1921, GLO)

Shoivo (1925, USGS Water Supply Paper, 499)

Manuel's Well (1931, U.S. Indian Irrigation Service Paper)

Con Quien (1935, Barnes)

Sweetwater (1936, Sells Indian Agency Annual Report) (Now official name)

A Papago named Slim Joe Manuel owned this stock-watering place with two wells, hence the name Manuel's Well. The name Cochibo indicates it may have been used for pigs (Papago: *kochi* = "pig"; *vo* = "well").
Ref.: 329; 262, p. 7; 57, p. 412

SIPAPU CAVERN

Hopi: *sipapu* = "entrance to the underworld"
Coconino   T25N R8.5E

This cavern is actually two caves along the north-south fault line through the western part of Wupatki National Monument. These caverns are at least two hundred-and-ninety-feet deep.

SITE SIX

Mohave   T13N R20W   Elev. c. 400'

During World War II this place was an auxiliary airfield for Kingman AFB. Its name derives from its sequence in the series of auxiliary airfields. It is now used by fishermen.   Ref.: Heilinger; Housholder

SITGREAVES, MOUNT

Coconino   T23N R4E   Elev. 9000'

This location was named for Capt. Lorenzo Sitgreaves, who probably passed near here when his topographic expedition crossed northern Arizona in 1851. See Sitgreaves National Forest   Ref.: 347, p. 175, Note 16

SITGREAVES NATIONAL FOREST

Apache/Navajo/Coconino   T9-11-13N   R24-20-13E

On July 1, 1908 parts of Black Mesa Forest Reserve (est. Aug. 17, 1898) and Tonto National Forest (est. Oct. 3, 1905) were consolidated to form Sitgreaves National Forest, named for Lt. Lorenzo Sitgreaves (d. May 14, 1888), who made the first topographical military trip across northern Arizona in 1851. Gross acreage is 883,919.
Ref.: 243, p. 36

SITGREAVES PASS

Mohave   T19R 20W   Elev. 3610'

When Lt. Edward Fitzgerald Beale with his party went through this pass on October 15 and 16, 1857, he named it John Howell's Pass, for a member of his party. Lt. Joseph Christmas Ives with his group went through the same pass on March 25, 1858, naming it for Lt. Lorenzo Sitgreaves. (See Sitgreaves National Forest) Sitgreaves never used the pass, but went through Union Pass on November 5, 1851. Because Sitgreaves Pass is above the town of Oatman, it is sometimes called Oatman Pass.   Ref.: 5, p. 325; 23, pp. 77, 78; 335, p. 5, Note 5

SIX BAR RIDGE

Yavapai   T9N R4E

This ridge takes its name from being on the 6 Bar Ranch.

SIXTYMILE CREEK

Coconino (Grand Canyon)   T33N R5E   Elev. 4250'

The fact that this creek is about sixty miles down the Colorado River from Lee's Ferry led Francois E. Matthes, Richard F. Evans, and J.R. Evans to suggest its name. It applies also to Sixty Mile Canyon and Rapids.   Ref.: Letter rom Matthes and Evans (Nov. 27, 1926), to U.S.G.B. Chairman, Grand Canyon Files

SKELETON CANYON

Cochise   T21S R32E   Elev. 4985'

The isolated and rugged terrain on the Mexican boundary of southeastern Arizona provided a perfect route for smugglers. Here in 1881 five American bandits ambushed a Mexican smuggler pack train. Curly Bill and Old Man Clanton, both notorious bad men, made a rich haul at the cost of an estimated six to nineteen brutally murdered Mexican *vaqueros*, whose bodies were left where they fell. Coyotes and buzzards stripped the bodies to the bare bones, a fact which gave the name "Skeleton" to the canyon. The ambush point is called Devils Kitchen.

The Americans were said to have seized $75,000. in Mexican silver, although the *Tombstone Epitaph* (Aug. 5, 1881) set the treasure at $4,000. and the death list as four. It also reported that probably twenty Americans ambushed sixteen Mexicans. The few Mexicans who escaped vowed vengeance. They had it in Guadalupe Canyon where they ambushed Old Man Clanton and murdered him with four others.   Ref.: 116, p. 622; 241, p. 119; 60, pp. 283, 352

SKELETON RIDGE
Yavapai   T11N R6E   Elev. 5953'
The name derives from the appearance of this narrow sharp ridge with its rib-like branches. Ref.: 18a

SKINNER RIDGE
Coconino   T29N R3E
This ridge and Skinner Pasture Tank were named for Ben Skinner, who homesteaded at this location.   Ref.: Smith; Hart

SKULL VALLEY
Yavapai   T13N R4W   Elev. 4253'
It is said that the first white man entering this valley found piles of bleached Indian skulls. They were also seen by soldiers in Capt. Hargraves' Company of First California Volunteers escorting Coles Bashford to Tucson in March 1864. The bones remained from a bitter battle between Apaches (who had stolen stock from the Pima Village) and Maricopa, with the latter victorious.

On August 12, 1866 Mr. Freeman with five citizens and four soldiers battled more than one hundred Indians near here. The Indians had previously stopped the same party and forced them to return to the military encampment at the Skull Valley station (Camp McPherson). On their second encounter one white man returned to the post for help and Lt. Oscar Hutton arrived. An argument arose, with the Indians contending that all water and grass belonged to them and the whites must leave the valley. A fight began, and when it ended twenty-three Indians were dead on the field and several more were found some distance away. All were left where they fell. Associated names include Camp Skull Valley (later Camp McPherson and finally called Camp Date Creek, (*q. v.*), Skull Valley Station, Skull Valley Wash.
A post office was established at the Skull Valley stage station, at Ehle's Ranch.
P.O. est. April 26, 1869, John E. Dunn, p.m.; disc. Jan. 25, 1973; Wells Fargo 1903   Ref.: 242; *Arizona Miner* (Jan. 20, 1872), p. 2; 335, pp. 37, 39; 116, p. 381; *Arizona Citizen* (Jan. 25, 1973), p. 2

SKULLY CREEK
Greenlee   T5-6S R32-32E
The name probably derives from the "numerous skulls of animals on the course of the creek." Ref.: 329

SLADE RESERVOIR
Apache   T7N R28-29E   Elev. c. 9200'
This reservoir, on land patented by Henry Slade c. 1894, is also known as Cahon Reservoir and as New Reservoir. See also Atcheson Reservoir, Apache
Ref.: Wiltbank

SLATE CREEK
Coconino (Grand Canyon)   T32N R1E
Slate occurs along this creek.

SLATE CREEK
Gila   T7N R9E   Elev. 3500'
The name derives from the fact that slate occurs here.   Ref.: Cooper

SLATE MOUNTAIN
Coconino   T24N R5E   Elev. 8215'
This mountain, which rises about one thousand feet above the surrounding area, is noted for its erodable slate formations, hence the name. Associated names include Slate Lakes (T24N/R6E) and Slate Lakes Cave. Ref.: 276, p. 85

SLATE MOUNTAINS
Pinal/Pima   T10S R5E   Elev. 2003'
This range has a dark slate color. The range has also borne the following names: Sierrita Prieta (1893, Roskruge); Sierra Prieta (Spanish: *sierra* = "mountains," *prieta* = "black") (1909 GLO); Black Range (1912, Lumholtz). Ref.: 57, p. 243

SLAUGHTER DRAW
Greenlee   T3N R28E
Joe Slaughter had a ranch in this draw, having bought out three ranches c. 1930. His ranch headquarters were at T2S/R30E. Ref.: Shannon

SLAUGHTER HOUSE GULCH
Yavapai   T14N R2W
Several slaughter houses were in this gulch. Ref.: Merritt

SLAUGHTER MOUNTAIN
Graham   T3S R25E   Elev. 6556'
A cattleman, Pete Slaughter, grazed cattle on the San Carlos Indian Reservation in this area c. 1885. Ref.: 18a

SLEEPING BEAUTY PEAK
Gila   T1N R14E   Elev. 4890'
From the southeast this mountain looks like a reclining woman with long streaming hair. Sleeping Beauty Spring is on the mountain. Ref.: Woody

SLIDING ROCK RUINS
Apache   T5N R27E   Elev. c. 4500'
The name derives from the fact that the ancient walls are gradually sliding down into Canyon de Chelly. The ruins date to the 12th century. Ref.: 5, p. 419; 331, p. 19

SLIKER HILL   pro.: /sláykər/
Coconino   T20N R5E   Elev. 7575'
This hill was named for Gene Sliker (d. c. 1954), a long-time Flagstaff resident. Sliker Tank is on Dutton Hill. See Dutton Hill, Coconino

SLUMGULLION PASS
Yuma   T4S R17W
This pass is a low saddle in the southeastern part of the Castle Dome Mountains. It was named for a pass in southwestern Colorado. The name has been in use since at least the early 1950s. Ref.: Monson

SMALL BUTTE
Pima   T40N R11E   Elev. 5354'
It is, being just large enough to deserve the name.

SMALL POINT
Coconino   T40N R5E
This point is so mall that its name is apt.

SMELTER
Pinal   T2S R12E
This community, noted as a "town" on the Arizona State Highway computerized readout, is in or adjacent to the larger town of Superior.

SMELTER CANYON
Gila T14N R14E
The name states a fact, as it has a smelter in it. Ref.: Woody

SMITH BUTTE
Navajo T21N R19E Elev. c. 5800'
Bill Smith, a cattleman, maintained a cow camp at Smith Spring six miles east c. 1890.
See also Flat Top Butte, Navajo Ref.: 141, p. 153

SMITH CANYON
Greenlee T2S R29E
This canyon takes its name from that of Cap Smith and his brother Bill, who had a cabin
here in 1903. Both the cabin and the men are long gone. Ref.: Simmons

SMITH CANYON
Yavapai T15N R6W Elev. 3195'
John and William Smith, cattlemen, used the Dumbbell brand here in 1903. Smith Mesa
(T16N/R6W) is an associated name. Ref.: 18a

SMITH CIENEGA
Apache T6N R26E Elev. 10,040'
This cienega (= "swampy area") is at the head of Smith Creek. It is also the beginning of
the North Fork of the White River. See White River, Apache

SMITH PEAK
La Paz T8N R11W Elev. 4957'
This location, also known as Pete Smith Peak, took its name from that of a miner who
held a claim on the peak c. 1925. Ref.: 18a

SMITH'S MILL
Maricopa c. T6N R4W Elev. c. 2500'
W.C. Smith built a quartz mill for the Vulture Mine here in 1873.
P.O. est. June 27, 1874, Peter Taylor, p.m.; disc. May 1, 1877 Ref.: *Tucson Citizen*
(July 18, 1874), p. 4

SMITHVILLE
Yavapai
This mining community was named for A.M. Smith, superintendent of the Garden Era
Mining Company. It was on Cherry Creek, about thirty miles from Prescott.
Ref.: *Weekly Arizona Miner* (Sept. 19, 1879), p. 2

SMOKE SIGNAL
Navajo T30N R21E Elev. 6400'
The reason for the name of this small community has not yet been learned.

SMOKETREE WASH
Mohave T13N R20E
The lovely desert trees called smoketrees line this wash.

SMOKY HOLLOW
Gila T10N R12E
Cowboys who camped here noted that the smoke hung low, hence the name.
Ref.: McInturff; Blumer

SMOOT LAKE
Coconino T24N R3E Elev. c. 6000'
William H. Smoot (d. 1902), a cattleman, arrived here from Prescott c. 1881 and
remained until he died. Ref.: 124, p. 53, and Footnote

SMOOTH KNOLL

Apache   T11N R25E   Elev. 6961'
The name describes the appearance.

SMUGGLER CANYON

Greenlee   T5S R29E
The name derives from that of the Smuggler Mine in this canyon.

SNAKE GULCH

Coconino (Grand Canyon)   T38N R3W   Elev. c. 5000'
The name describes the way this narrow twisting canyon snakes its way through the
country. The name was in use in 1886. It has since been replaced by the name Shinumo
Canyon. See Shinumo Canyon, Coconino (Grand Canyon) Ref.: Schellbach File
(Grand Canyon)

SNAKETOWN

Pima: *ska-kaik* = "many rattlesnakes"
Pinal   T3S R4E   Elev. 1175'
This is a Pima village with many ancient mounds and an abundance of rattlesnakes.
Ref.: 59, p. 427

SNIVELY HOLES

Coconino
On an 1878 map, this location is seventeen and a half miles southwest of Leroux
Springs. See Gillette, Maricopa

SNOWFLAKE

Navajo   T13N R21E   Elev. 5580'
The Indian name for this location was *Todihi Biih'ili* (= "where it flows into the dark
water"). In 1875 Martha Summerhayes visited the ranch here, owned by James Stinson.
She wrote that many so-called ranches were adobe ruins, but remained on maps because
they were usually near a spring or creek and hence served as travelers' camp sites.
Stinson sold land in July 1878 to William Jordan Flake (b. July 3, 1839, North
Carolina). In the early fall Erastus Snow and a group of twelve destitute families arrived
from the settlement at Taylor, which had failed. A town site was surveyed on Flake's
property and the new community took the name Snowflake after its founders. Among
Mormons in the 1880s it was referred to as Snowflake Camp. When Apache County was
formed in 1879, Snowflake was the county seat, an honor it retained until 1881 when
Springerville was chosen, only to be replaced in 1882 by Saint Johns as county seat.
P.O. est. as Snow Flake, June 27, 1881, William D. Kartchner, p.m.; name changed to
Snowflake, Sept. 17, 1906 Ref.: 225, pp. 164, 165; 314, p. 125; 331, p. 148; AHS,
Consulich Collection, Box 4, "Snowflake Ward Booklet," p. 10; 242

SNOWSHED PEAK

Cochise   T18S R30E   Elev. 9600'
"The Snowshed" is actually a ridge of the Chiricahua Mountains. Snow collects on the
ridge, which becomes a snowshed when the whole mass breaks off in a small
avalanche. Ref.: Riggs

SNOWSLIDE SPRING

Coconino   T23N R7E
Snow remains in this ravine through the summer, partially because snowslides fill it to a
considerable depth. The spring here takes its name from that fact.

SNOWSTORM MOUNTAIN

Gila   T10N R9E   Elev. 5162'
The nearby Snowstorm Mine is said to have been located during a severe snow storm.
The mountain takes its name from that of the mine. Ref.: 18a

SNYDER HILL
Pima   T15S R12E   Elev. 2642'
This hill was named in the early 1900s because of the Snyder Mine (T19S/R15E), located by Douglas and Fred Snyder (who also spelled their name Schnyder).
Ref.: Kitt

SOAP CREEK (#1)
Coconino   T39N R6E
This stream was also known as Clear Creek and as Spring Creek. Although cited as Soap Creek, "Soap Creek #2"apparently is not identical with #1, but they are close neighbors. See Badger Creek, Coconino   Ref.: 88, p. 159

SOAP CREEK (#2)
Coconino   T39N R6E
In 1873 the water running in this creek was so poisonous that cattle died from drinking it. In appearance it was then "something like soap suds, but now it's tolerable fair water." Soap Creek Pasture is here also, and Soap Creek Rapids are at T38N/R6E
Ref.: Huntington Library, Mormon Collections (1873)

SOAP CREEK RAPIDS
Coconino (Grand Canyon)   T38N R6E
In these rapids Brown, the president of the railroad company trying to survey a route via the canyon, drowned in May 1889 during Stanton's first expedition. For origin of name, see Soap Creek (#2), Coconino   Ref.: 192, p. 210

SOCKDOLAGER RAPIDS
Coconino (Grand Canyon)   T31N R4E   Elev. 3250'
The rigors undergone by the Powell Grand Canyon expedition are well exemplified in their encounter with Sockdolager Rapids. Steering their fourteen-foot boats, they heard a sullen, increasingly thunderous roar ahead. Then the river suddenly seemed to drop out of sight. Dellenbaugh wrote, "The narrow river dropped suddenly and smoothly away and then, beaten to foam, plunged and boomed for one-third of a mile . . . the boats rolled and pitched like a ship in a tornado. As we flew along . . . I could look up under the canopies of foam pouring over gigantic black boulders, first on one side and then on the other . . . the boats . . . leaping at times almost one-half their length out of the water, to bear themselves quite as far on the next lunge." The term *sockdolager* was a slang term used to indicate a "heavy or knock-down blow," or "a finisher," and the party used it to name these rapids.   Ref.: 88, pp. 226-227; 89, p. 330; *Oxford English Dictionary*

SOCORRO PEAK   pro.: /səkóro/
Spanish: *socorro* = "help"
La Paz   T5N R12W   Elev. 5681'
The Socorro Mine was located here in the 1880s by people from Socorro, New Mexico, hence the name. This peak is the highest in the Harquahala Mountains.   Ref.: 18a

SODA SPRING
Yavapai   T15N R6E
This spring lends its name to a ranch owned in c. 1885 by Robert Finnie. The spring has a natural bouyancy and effervescence and a 60°F temperature the year around.
Ref.: 50, p. 45

SOLANO WASH
Pima   T17S R8W
So named because it is near the San Solano Mission at Topawa.

SOLDIER CAMP
Pima   T11S R16E
Because wild turkeys roosted thickly in the low-branching pines, this place in 1882 was known as Turkey Roost. In 1885 soldiers tracking Geronimo camped here, hence the

later name. It was in Soldier Canyon (T13S/R16E). The path they used is now called Soldier Trail. Ref.: AHS, Emerson O. Stratton *ms*, p. 70; AHS, "11th Annual Report," Place Name Committee (Nov. 17, 1945)

SOLDIER CAMP WASH
Gila   T6N R15E   Elev. c. 4500'
In the early 1870s soldiers pursuing Apaches used Soldier Hill as a camping spot as scouting parties ranged along this wash, hence the name.
Associated names include Soldier Camp Creek and Soldier Camp Mountain (T9N/R11E, elev. 5200'). Soldier Creek courses through the wash.   Ref.: McKinney; 18a

SOLDIER HOLES
Cochise   T20S R26E
In 1881 soldiers bivouacked and rested here while securing additional provisions to enable pursuing renegades. Later, artesian wells were developed and the place became a well known stop-over for teamsters hauling lumber from sawmills to Tombstone and Bisbee. The Soldier Hole Ranch headquarters sold whiskey and served meals. It was also called Descanso and Brophy Well. The artesian wells stopped flowing after the earthquake of 1887. See Brophy Well, Cochise   Ref.: 277, pp. 131, 133; 278, p. 41

SOLDIER LAKE
Coconino   T16N R11E   Elev. c. 5800'
Because it was on the regular route from Fort Whipple to New Mexico, this location was probably used by the military. Here Capt. Charles King and his men rested after a battle with Apaches in October 1874.   Ref.: 18a

SOLDIER SPRING
Apache   T4N R27E
At one time Apaches killed two soldiers here, hence the name.   Ref.: Davis

SOLITAIRE BUTTE
Mohave   T35N R11W   Elev. 6347'
Dellenbaugh gave this location the name Solitaire because it had "a dark, weird, forbidding look." It is now called Poverty Butte. See Poverty Knoll, Mohave
Ref.: 89, p. 310

SOLITUDE, CAPE
Coconino (Grand Canyon)   T32N R6E   Elev. 6157'
This butte stands alone at the juncture of the Little Colorado and Colorado Rivers, hence the name, which was in use at least as early as 1900.   Ref.: 178, p. 71

SOLOMON
Graham   T7S R27E   Elev. 3000'
This place was first called Munsonville because in 1873 William Munson built an adobe house and store here. Isador Elkan Solomon (b. 1844, Germany; d. Dec. 4, 1930) arrived in Arizona in 1876 with his wife and brother. He soon bought out Munson, plus several thousand acres in Pueblo Viejo Valley. Isador added to Munson's buildings, opening a larger store. He also produced mesquite charcoal for fueling the Clifton smelter. William Kirkland, the local mail carrier, suggested the name Solomonville for the proposed post office. In 1883 the small community became Graham County seat. For a while the name on post office records was Solomonsville, possibly because the postmaster inserted an *s* in the hand-made cancellation stamps.
P.O. est. as Solomonville, April 10, 1878, Isador E. Solomon, p.m.; name changed to Solomon, Dec. 14, 1950; Wells Fargo 1903   Ref.: AHS, Lizzie Steel File; 225, pp. 242, 244; 257, p. 18; 108, p. 16; Theobald; G.E.P. Smith

SOLOMON PASS
Graham   T6S R27E
This mountain pass at the southeast end of the Gila Mountains is eight miles south of the town of Solomon, hence the name. It is a.k.a. Solomonsville Pass.

SOLOMON TEMPLE
Coconino (Grand Canyon)   T31N R4E   Elev. 5070'
This location was named in 1906 in accordance with the USGS policy of naming features in the Grand Canyon for important personages of ancient literatures and mythology.

SOLS WASH
Yavapai/Maricopa   T8N R6W
This wash takes its name from that of Sol Francisco, a Yuman Indian, influential in obtaining the release of Olive Oatman from Indian captivity in 1856. Other Indians killed him c. 1858. Ref.: 18a

SOMBRERO BUTTE
Pinal   T8S R18E   Elev. 5690'
This butte is shaped much like a Mexican hat, hence the name. There was a settlement called Sombrero Butte at the base of this butte c. 1919. The post office application gives the local community name as Bunker Hill.
P.O. est. March 28, 1919, Mrs. Clara Johnson, p.m.; disc. May 31, 1935
Ref.: 242; 238, pp. 55, 56; 5, p. 341

SOMBRERO PEAK
Gila   T6N R15E   Elev. 6436'
This peak resembles a Mexican hat called a *sombrero*.

SOMERTON
Yuma   T9S R24W   Elev. 101'
In 1898 people in the agricultural area ten miles south of Yuma discussed founding a town to provide facilities for potential residents, and a site on the Algodones Land Grant was selected. It was named Somerton at the suggestion of Capt. A.D. Yocum, after his home town.
P.O. est. Oct. 12, 1898, Minne E. Case, p.m.   Ref.: 242; *Yuma Sun* (Sept. 30, 1898), p. 5; *Arizona Sentinel* (Jan. 24, 1900), p. 3

SONERATA
Maricopa   T1S R6E   Elev. 1237'
The State Highway Department designates this location as a town. It is just north of Gilbert. The origin of the name has not yet been ascertained.

SONOITA   pro.: /sonóytə/
Papago: *shonoidag* = "place where corn will grow"
Santa Cruz   T20S R17E   Elev. 4865'
A traveler in 1859 said that the entire Sonoita Valley was golden with grain, one field having one hundred and fifty acres of corn, hence the name ("place where corn will grow"). It is an old one, having been known to Fr. Eusebio Kino, who in 1698 visited the Sobaipuri chief Coro at a settlement called Los Reyes or Los Reyes de Sonoydag. Coro and his people had just moved about two or three miles southwest of present-day Patagonia as a result of their victory over Apaches, whose vengeance they feared. A half century later during the 1750 Pima Revolt ninety-one were living at what was called San Miguel of Sonoitac. In 1768 the community of Sonoita became a *visita* of Tubatama, Sonora. It was deserted by 1790. On May 15, 1825 Leon Henores bought a small Mexican land grant called San Jose de Sonoita, lying on both sides of Sonoita Creek. Following the Gadsden Purchase, the United States Land Court confirmed 7,592 acres of the grant. In 1856 Col. Gray called the stream running through the grant the Sonoita or Clover Creek.
   Hinton also visited this region where the corn was growing as lushly as ever and noted it did as well there as in Missouri bottomlands and that the Sonoita River surfaced several times withing twelve miles of Camp Crittenden. Because of increasing Apache harassment in the period 1861-1876, the Sonoita Valley was nearly uninhabited by white men.
   The present community of Sonoita came into existence in 1882 on the newly

constructed railroad line. The town, established east of the old Sobaipuri rancheria, had a post office.

Associated names include Sonoita Creek (T22S/R15E), Sonoita Land Grant, Sonoita River, and Sonoita Valley (T17S/R)

P.O. est. May 8, 1912, Clara L. Hummel, p.m. (A notation on the postal records in the National Archives said that there was a railroad station but no village.)

Ref.: 242; *Arizona Citizen* (June 1, 1872), p. 2; 45, pp. 385, 386; 167, II, 391, 616; 5, p. 26; 116, p. 428; 43, p. 233; 171, p. 86; 163, p. 214; 138, p. 51; Oblasser, Fr., Letter to Frank C. Lockwood (May 5, 1935); 136, p. 2

SONORA pro.: /sanorə/
Pinal   T3S R13E   Elev. 2250'

Mexicans working for the Ray Consolidated Copper Company established and named this settlement for the Mexican State of Sonora, adjacent to the Arizona boundary. The name *Sonora* is said to derive from the Opata Indian word *sonot* (a corruption of Spanish *señora*). The settlement on Sonora Hill (elev. 2637') was wiped out by open pit mining.

P.O. est. Oct. 4, 1911, Frank Abril, p.m.; disc. Jan. 1, 1966

Ref.: 242; AHS Names File

SONOYTA VALLEY
Pima

This valley shows on the 1893 Roskruge map. See Agua Dulce Mountains, Pima

SONSELA BUTTES pro.: /só?silà/
Navajo: *so's ila* = "stars lying down" or "stars set"

Apache   T5N R30E   Elev. 8887'

Gregory said that the name of these buttes meant "twin stars," but why these volcanic buttes are so called has not been learned. The name is also spelled Sonsala and Sonsola. "Sosile" is a corruption.   Ref.: Burcard; 331, p. 149; 141, pp. 34, 195

SOPORI RANCH
Santa Cruz   T19S R13E   Elev. 3250'

The name *sopori* is possibly a corruption of the name of the Sobaipuri Indians. (See Arivaipa Canyon, Pinal) Pima Indians long had a rancheria on the Altar road near this old ranch which, according to *Rudo Ensayo* (1763), was called Sepori. In 1751 it was abandoned because of the Pima Revolt. The location was taken over as a Mexican land grant by Joaquin Astiazaran following an auction held between 1830-1838 at Horcasitas (instead of at Tubac). The grant, one of those rejected by the U. S. Land Courts after the Gadsden Purchase, covered 142,721 acres. In 1854 Lt. N. Michler noted that its major spring, Ojo del Agua de Sopori, once irrigated the Sopori Valley and had a single peach tree at its source. Later the ranch was owned by James W. Douglass. Its owner was a member of the Sopori Land and Mining Company, which reported the Sopori Mine as very productive. Apache raids drove off the mine owners and workers and in 1861 Raphael Pumpelly noted the ranch was deserted. When Hinton visited, it was still deserted with little left other than adobe walls and collapsed roofs, but he said it had abundant promise as a cattle range and mining prospect. Associated names include Sopori Valley and Sopori Wash (Santa Cruz/Pima).   Ref.: 58; 167, II, 510; 369, p. 47; 272, pp. 192, 193; 163, p. 221; 106, p. 119; 236, p. 81; 56, p. 260; 33, p. 75

SORENSON
Yavapai   T11N R6W

Peter Sorenson (b. 1840) proposed himself for postmaster at a station to serve fifty in a mining community. He was so unsure where he was that he filed it for Mohave County. In the ensuing confusion, it was established, the orders rescinded, and then re-instated in another county – Yavapai. It so remained.

P.O. est. July 13, 1903, Benjamin F. Ferris, p.m.; resc. Dec. 16, 1903; est. Dec. 27, 1903, Peter V. Sorenson, p.m.; disc. June 6, 1904   Ref.: 242; 63

SOTO PEAK
Pima   T17S R11E   Elev. 4527'

This peak was named because it is on the Soto Ranch. Soto Wash is at T17S/R10E. See also Gunsight Mountain, Pima

SOUR WATER CANYON
Coconino (Grand Canyon)   T35N R13E

There used to be a spring in this wash, now dry, which had a bitter taste (perhaps from decayed vegetation), hence the name. See Sour Water Wash, Yavapai   Ref.: Woody

SOUTH BRUNO CANYON
Cochise   T20S R29E

A variant and incorrect corruption is Brunner Canyon. See Bruno Canyon, Cochise

SOUTH BUTTE
Pinal   T4S R11E   Elev. 2948'

This butte is on the south side of the Gila River bed and opposite its companion on the north side of the river, hence its name.

SOUTH CANYON
Coconino   T34N R3E

Parallel canyons head close together here and the name of this canyon derives from the obvious location of one relative to the other. South Canyon Spring is here also. Ref.: 18a

SOUTHERN BELLE CANYON
Pinal   T10S R16E

This canyon was named because the Southern Belle Mine was in it. A gold mine, it was developed in the 1880s. J.L. Clark maintained a store here. The mine closed in 1889.   Ref.: AHS, Castillo Collection, Box 1; 238, p. 26

SOUTHFIELD CANYON
Graham   T9S R19E

Also known as Field Canyon, so named because of an open field near the mouth of the canyon, but as it was also south, the name changed.   Ref.: 329

SOUTH KOMELIK
Pima   T20S R6E

In 1978 the USGS eliminated the following names for this location: Comely, Komalik, Komelik. See Komelik, Pima

SOUTH MOUNTAIN
Pima   T16S R2E   Elev. 4158'

The name derives from the location of this mountain at the southern end of the Quijotoa range. Its columns of purple-red sheets of lava rise abruptly above the landscape.

SOUTH MOUNTAINS
Maricopa   T1S R3E   Elev. 2600'

This mountain range has also been called the Salt River Mountains and the Salt River Range. Indians called the range *Mohatuk* (= "greasy mountain"), because the rocks look greasy when wet. Pima legend says that after the great flood, Elder Brother emerged as ruler and Coyote as his subordinate. Coyote was sent to free animals from a dark cave. There Rabbit had died and to prevent Coyote from getting him, the other animals decided to burn Rabbit. Coyote was sent to the Sun to get fire and when he looked back he saw smoke and returned at once to find the people already burning Rabbit. They formed a tight circle to shut out Coyote, who ran around trying to find an opening. He found his way in by leaping over two short men and immediately bit out Rabbitt's heart and ran away north across the Gila River. There he stopped and ate the heart and the grease fell from it among the stones of the mountains and the marks last to this day.   Ref.: Barnes, quoting Frank Russell (Smithsonian Institution), 1902

SOUTH TUCSON
Pima   T14S R13E   Elev. 2438'

This mile-square community has a government independent of that of its surrounding neighbor, Tucson. It derives its name because of the location relative to a time when Tucson did not enclose it.

SOWATS CANYON

Piute: *showap* = "tobacco"
Coconino (Grand Canyon)   T36N R3W

A plant called *showap* grows in this canyon. It is used in Piute religious rites. Sowats Point and Spring are at T36N/R2W.   Ref.: 329

SOZA MESA

Cochise   T12S R20E

This mesa overlooks the abandoned Soza Ranch (T12S/R19E), hence the name. Soza Wash is also here.

SPANISH RANCH

Yuma   T9S R19 (or 20) W

This location is on the Palfrey S.P.R.R. 1879 map, on the old stage road west of Texas Hill.   Ref.: 242

SPEAR'S LAKE

Mohave   T18N R22W

This was named for Augustus A. Spear (b. 1831, Rhode Island). It is near Powell R.R. Station (T16N/R20W) where Spear was postmaster in 1883. (His brother Banjamin S. (b. 1837, New York), was the first and only postmaster at Beale Springs 1873-1876). Gus was an Indian scout before he became a rancher.   Ref. Harris; 62; 200, p. 190

SPECTER CHASM

Coconino (Grand Canyon)   T34N R2W

The name was proposed by the USGS in June 1908 for this canyon in the South Rim. In 1932 it named the spur opposite it Specter Terrace, and added the name Specter Rapids as proposed by the National Park Service in 1927.   Ref.: 329

SPENCER CANYON

Mohave   T27N R13W   Elev. c. 2800'

Charles Spencer (b. 1840, New York) raised cattle in the Sacramento Valley, but when trouble with sheepmen developed there, he moved into the country behind Music Mountain. A close friend of the Hualapai Indians, he married a Hualapai woman, built a home in Meriwitica Canyon, and served as an interpretor for the Hualapai in government matters. He was a civilian packer at Camp Willow Grove c. 1868 and in the 1870s was a guide for Capt. George M. Wheeler. He was also a mining partner with another famous scout, Dan O'Leary. He carried mail from Camp Willow Grove to Hardyville and was attacked by Hualapai Indians on what is now Spencer Creek (T17N/R9W) on March 23, 1868. Spencer was wounded at least six times while serving as a guide and Indian scout. Unfortunately, Spencer took on as a partner a man named Cohan, with whom he quarrelled over livestock. Spencer threatened to kill Cohan if the latter ever came onto the Hualapai Reservation. They met in Truxton Canyon, quarrelled concerning an acre of ground, and Cohan killed Spencer. Sam Crozier was executor for Spencer's estate. See Crozier, Mohave
Ref.: AHS, Daniel O'Leary File; 62; 335, pp. 127, 156, 347, 348

SPENCER TERRACE

Coconino (Grand Canyon)   T33N R1W   Elev. 5450'

The plateau is one of those associated with others named for leading scientists. Until the early 1900s this location was known as Mystic Spring Plateau, but then the name was changed to honor evolutionist Herbert Spencer (1820-1903), a British philosopher who defended the great scientific movement of the second half of the 19th century.
Ref.: 178, p 82

SPIDER ROCK

Apache   T5N R28E   Elev. 6855'

The USGS in January 1960 eliminated the names Monument Rock, The Captains, and The Monuments. The name now used reflects a Navajo legend that Spider Woman lives atop this rock. Here she drags bad children and eats them. Their bleaching bones can be seen at the top of this column, taller than the Washington Monument. See Monument Canyon, Apache

SPINE, THE

Pinal   T3S R13E   Elev. 3160'

This sharp ridge resembles a spine, hence the name. It is probably the same location which Antisell in 1854 described as follows: "... the 'Spire' hills present an appearance alike fantastic and grand; from the warm tone of the flesh-colored felspar, the absence of vegetation, its extreme roughness in ascent from the huge masses of rock on its side and base, and the pointed pinnacles and turrets which its outline, sharply defined on a clear sky, presents, the observer is forcibly struck with the singularity of the landscape." Ref.: 4, p. 140

SPITZ HILL

Coconino   T22N R4E   Elev. 7700'

Joe Spitz lived at Spitz Spring in 1904 or 1905, hence the name.   Ref.: Kennedy

SPONSELLER LAKE

Apache   T10N R24E   Elev. 6952'

Joseph Sponseller grazed sheep here in 1883 on Sponseller Mountain (Elev. 7231'). There is a railroad stop at T9N/R23E.   Ref.: 18a

SPOONHEAD, MOUNT

Coconino (Grand Canyon)   T32N R3W   Elev. 5940'

Spoonhead was a Havasupai Indian with a "queer head which looked more than ever like the bowl of a spoon," hence his nickname. He carried mail in President McKinley's time. The place is a.k.a. Spoonhead Butte.   Ref.: 174, p. 168; Kolb

SPOTTED MOUNTAIN

Navajo   T7N R16E   Elev. 6289'

Timber clumps made "spots on this mountain," hence the name.   Ref.: 18a

SPRINGS: The presence of water is so important in desert country that the finding of a spring has led to the use of the designation in many Arizona place names, some of which follow:

Spring, The	Mohave	T13N R13W	Elev. 1550'
Spring Beach Spring	Coconino	T18N R9E	
Spring Branch	Pima	T15S R13E	
Spring Canyon a.k.a. Wild Cherry Canyon	Apache	T4N R27E	
Spring Canyon	Cochise	T23S R24E	
Spring Canyon	Graham	(1) T7S R20E	(2) T6S R28E
Spring Canyon	Greenlee	T2S R31E	
Spring Canyon	Mohave	(1) T30N R18W	(2) T30N R10W
Spring Cove	Mohave	T30N R18W	
Spring Creek	Cochise	T23S R23E	
Spring Creek	Gila	(1) T3N R13E	(2) T11N R12E
Spring Creek	Graham	T5S R24E	
Spring Creek	Navajo	T8N R16E	
Spring Creek (3) T14N R7E	Yavapai (4) T10N R23E	(1) T18N R4E (5) T9N R2W	(2) T12N R3E (6) T14N R9W
Spring Garden See Buford Hill, Graham	Graham		
Spring Gulch	Yavapai	T12N R4E	
Spring Mountain	Maricopa	T3S R6W	Elev. 2120'
Spring Mountain	Navajo	T9N R23E	Elev. 7203'

Spring Peak	Yavapai	T14N R9W	Elev. 4100'
Spring Ridge	Navajo	T8N R16E	
Spring Valley	Coconino	T23N R14E	
Spring Valley	Yavapai	T7N R1W	
Spring Valley Knolls	Coconino	T23N R4E	
Spring Valley Wash	Coconino	T26N R2E	
Spring Wash	Yavapai	T9N R6E	

SPRINGERVILLE

Apache · · · T9N R29E · · · Elev. 6856'

The first name for this area was Valle Redondo (Spanish = "round valley"). Here in 1871 William R. Milligan settled along with Marion Clark, Johnny McCullough, and Tony Long. Already in the valley were Dionicio, Elalio and Juan Baca, and Gabriel Silva, who lived in a separate settlement called Valle Redondo at the north end of the valley. The area was a haven for horse thieves, who had a regular round robin of stealing horses in southern Arizona, rebranding them in Round Valley, and selling the animals in northern Arizona. They followed the same procedure in the opposite direction. Settlement, particularly of Mormons, was steady (see Round Valley, Apache). Merchant Harry Springer arrived in 1875 to establish Springer's store west of the site of Omer across the Little Colorado River. He stupidly trusted outlaws with feed and seed on credit and soon went broke. In less than a year he left. When they had to name their post office, the joshing residents chose the name Springerville. For two years (1880-1882) Springerville served as county seat. In 1885 the original town name of Omer was changed to Springerville because the Mormons had moved from there to Eager.

Julius Becker (d. 1893) arrived on August 28, 1876 with his brother Gustav and established their first store. These men used ox trains to haul goods from New Mexico until about 1890 when they substituted horses and mules for the oxen. After 1895 a branch railroad spur to Magdalena, New Mexico, shortened the livestock haul. Trucks began to be used in 1918.

Julius W. Becker (Gustav's son) helped establish a transcontinental highway through Springerville. In 1910 A.L. Westgard drove a Pathfinder auto over the route, the first to make the transcontinental journey. On Sept. 29, 1928 the National Old Trails Association with the D.A.R. commemorated the pioneer trail across the United States by erecting twelve statues of the "Madonna of the Trail," and one was placed in Springerville. It was cast by sculptor August Lienback and made of algonitestone, a composite poured mass of great density and durability.

P.O. est. Oct. 29, 1879, Charles A. Franklin, p.m. (a.k.a. A.F. Banata)

Ref.: Becker; Wiltbank; 345, I, 70, 71; 24, pp. 3, 9; *Apache County Independence News* (Aug. 31, 1951), p. 2; 225, pp. 165, 184, 185; 213, p. 399; 206, p. 340; George H. Crosby, Jr., "Something about Names," State Library Files

SPRUCEDALE

Greenlee · · · T4N R29E · · · Elev. 7632'

E.H. Patterson had a dude ranch here with a post office called Espero (pro.: espéyro = "hope, waiting" or "expectation"). The ranch has since changed hands and is now known as Sprucedale.

P.O. est. Jan. 11, 1919, Sophia J. Taylor, p.m.; disc. Feb. 28, 1934

Ref.: Wiltbank; Reilly

SPRUCE MOUNTAIN

Yavapai · · · T13N R1W · · · Elev. 7693'

The name derives from the presence of trees referred to as spruce, which are in reality Douglas fir. Spruce Canyon is at T14N/R3W. The presence of spruce has also led to the name of a second Spruce Mountain (Apache, T6N/R26E, Elev. 10,346').

Ref.: Gardner

SPUD ROCK

Pima · · · T14S R18E · · · Elev. 8613'

William H. Barnett and Jim Miller, S.P.R.R. engineers c. 1900, raised potatoes and cabbage close to this very large rock, which looks like a potato. They named it for their major crop. There is a stone cabin and a permanently running spring at this location, both used by cattlemen who conduct an annual roundup for three ranches. It culminates at this location.   Ref.: 136, p. 42

SQUARE: The shape of some locations has led to using the term *square*. Examples follow:

Square Butte	Coconino	T3N R13N	Elev. 6920'
Square Butte	Greenlee	T4S R29E	Elev. 4880'
Square Mountain	Cochise	T13S R23E	Elev. 5692'
Square Peak	Cochise	T19S R30E	
Squaretop Hills	Cochise	T18S R27E	Elev. 5449'

SQUASH MOUNTAINS
Navajo/Apache   T32N R22E

This location probably coincides with the contemporary Black Mesa. The name Squash Mountains was used on the Smith map. The mountains are on the first standard north of the Hopi villages, according to a map dated 1885. Crane in 1929 used the name Squash Blossom Butte, lapsing into purple prose: "an inverted bloom that the storm of aeons had carved and a million rare sunsets tinted . . . Indians revere the squash blossom as a symbol of fruition . . . it is found in Navajo silver-work . . and when one goes into Hopi land, he finds it imitated in the drawing of their maids' hair. So they named this Altar." See Black Mesa, Navajo/Apache
Ref.: 79, p. 73; Huntington Library

SQUAW: Many place names in Arizona bear the designation *squaw*, but for what reason is not usually known. Whether someone actually encountered an Indian woman at such places or the locations resemble Indian women is anybody's guess. Where knowledge exists, it is cited below:

Squaw Butte	Gila	T3N R14E	
Squaw Butte	Yavapai	T10N R6E	Elev. 4333'
Squaw Canyon	Coconino	T35N R1E	
Squaw Coxcombs	Coconino	T24N R3E	
Squaw Creek	Apache	T5N R26E	

This is the English translation of the Navajo: *Adzani Diko* (= "Woman Canyon").

Squaw Creek	Graham	(1) T1N R24E (2) T7S R20E (3) T4S R20E	
Squaw Creek	Greenlee	T1N R30E	
Squaw Creek	Yavapai	T9N R3E	
Squaw Creek Mesa	Yavapai	T8N R2E	
Squaw Dance Valley	Navajo	T34N R20E	
Squaw Flat	Maricopa	T8N R8E	

This name, devised by Aubrey Drury, was not known locally c. 1918.

Squaw Flat Spring	Maricopa	T8N R8E	
Squaw Gulch	Santa Cruz	T21S R15E	
Squaw Mesa	Gila	T8N R14E	Elev. 1603'

This was a favorite lookout for Apache Indians.   Ref.: McKinney

Squaw Mesa	Yavapai	T7N R1W	
Squaw Mountain	Cochise	T20S R31E	Elev. 5280'
Squaw Mountain	Coconino	T24N R4E	
Squaw Mountain	Yavapai	T9N R3E	Elev. 5905'

| Squaw Peak | Gila | T3N R15E | Elev. 4786' |

Bourke called this location Turret Butte because its upper portion is a turret-shaped cliff above the sloping butte shoulders. Who changed the name to Squaw or why is not known. Middleton men called it Squaw Tit, but their women made them change it to Peak. See Turret Butte, Gila Ref.: Woody

| Squaw Peak | Maricopa | T2N R3E | Elev. 2608' |

The USGS named it Squaw because it "seemed hardly large enough for a full-sized buck mountain."

| Squaw Peak | Mohave | T29N R20E | |

| Squaw Peak | Yavapai | (1) T13N R5W | Elev. 4178' |
| | | (2) T13N R4E | Elev. 6525' |

Named by Dudley Brooks, military telegrapher at Camp Verde 1878-81, who had a ranch near here. Ref.: 18a

| Squaw Peak Canyon | Yavapai | T13N R5E | |

| Squaw Pocket Well | Mohave | T24N R21W | |

| Squaw Spring | Coconino | T35N R1E | |

| Squaw Spring | Graham | T4S R19E | |

Named by Clay Beauford, who once surprised an Indian woman here and through her captured a band of Apaches.

| Squaw Tank | Yuma | T1S R17W | |

| Squaw Tits | Maricopa | T9S R1W | Elev. 4021' |

| Squaw Tits Peak | Maricopa | T7S R2W | Elev. 2489' |

Named descriptively because of a "peculiarly shaped pinnacle of rock." Ref.: 57, p. 226

STACEY'S SPRING
Coconino   T21N R8E

Beale named this spring on San Francisco Peak for Col. May Humphreys Stacey (b. 1838, Pennsylvania), who was with Lt. Edward Fitzgerald Beale's expedition in 1857. They found this spring north-by-east seven miles from Leroux Spring. Stacey was a captain with the 12th U.S. Infantry at Mohave City in 1870. Ref.: 23, p. 51; 62

STAGECOACH
Yuma   T1S R18W

This pass between the west end of the S H or Kofa Mountains and the Hidden Valley Mountains is on the old stage road between the King of Arizona Mine and Ehrenberg, hence the name. Ref.: Monson

STANDARD
Navajo   T10N R20E   Elev. c. 6000'

This was a post office for the Standard Lumber Company sawmill, established in 1922. P.O. est. June 25, 1924, Mrs. Agnes Cheshire, p.m.; disc. Oct. 15, 1938 Ref.: 242; 18a

STANDING COW RUINS
Apache   T5N R27E

The name is a translation of the Navajo: *begoshii sizi'ni'* (= "standing cow"). The name derives from a pictograph in Canyon del Muerto. Ref.: 331, p. 24; 5, p. 420

STANFIELD
Pinal   T6S R4E   Elev. 1300'

Nixon W. Stanfield homesteaded here c. 1910. When a post office was established, it was called Summerland. In 1943 a store was built east of the present town and two years later another store was erected, known as Table Top, its name being derived from that of a nearby mesa. When residents applied for a post office, they suggested the name Tabletop, noting that locally it was called Stanfield, the name suggested by Mrs. Bess Prather, postmistress at Casa Grande.

P.O. est. as Summerland, Nov. 22, 1913, N.W. Stanfield, p.m.; disc. June 15, 1918; reest. as Stanfield, Feb. 9, 1948, Earle Ellenworth, p.m.
Ref.: 242; John D. Lannen (Ellsworth son-in-law); Prather

STANLEY
Graham   T4S R19E
A post office was established at this location to serve one hundred and fifty people in mining camps at Gordon Gulch. It borrowed its name from nearby Stanley Butte (T5S/R19E, Elev. 7029'), named for a Lt. Stanley stationed at Fort Grant in the 1880s.
P.O. est. Nov. 5, 1906, John Blake, p.m.; disc. Nov. 10, 1925   Ref.: 242; 18a

STANSHUATUK
Papago = "hot water"
Pima   T19S R1E
This small Papago village on the reservation is at the site of a deep well (450') drilled c. 1915 by the Serventi brothers, cattlemen, who could not clear their title to the land. It has been known by the following names: La Moralita (1912, Lumholtz); Cervanti's Well (1917, U.S. Corps of Engineers); Serventi Well (1919, USGS); Molonitos (1931, Indian Service); Molinton (1937, American Geo. Soc. Hisp. Am.) Ref.: 329; 262, p. 3

STANTON
Gila   c. T2N R15E
In 1880 Stanton was a stage station in Richmond Basin at the Mack Morris mill. For a time it was a small settlement and school district with ranches along the nearby creek. The Inspiration Copper Company bought out all water rights and now nothing remains.
P.O. est. May 14, 1880, Thomas L. Johnson, p.m.; disc. Nov. 1, 1882
Ref.: 18a; Woody

STANTON POINT
Coconino (Grand Canyon)   T34N R2W   Elev. 6315'
In 1890 Robert Brewster Stanton (1846-1922) superintended a Grand Canyon boat exploration for the Denver, Colorado Canyon, and Pacific R.R. to establish the feasibility of having rails run through the Grand Canyon. In 1925 the USGS named this point for him.

STANWIX
Maricopa   T6S R11W   Elev. 5544'
This Butterfield Overland station in 1858 was called the "Dutchman's," but two years later a traveler noted it was called Stanwix's Station, under the managership of Mr. Wash Jacobs, road agent. Conkling says that one Stanwix, early in the region, called the location Stanwix Ranch, Flap Jack, or Flat Creek. It was on Stanwix Flats. Capt. Sherod Hunter and his Confederate soldiers occupied Stanwix in April 1862, but withdrew when they heard the California Column was approaching. On GLO 1869 the name is Grinnel Station, after Henry Grinnel, who also worked for the Butterfield Overland stage. Earlier, he had a station by the same name at another location. By 1877 this location was again mapped as Stanwix.
Ref.: Lenon; *Weekly Arizona Miner* (Dec. 3, 1975), p. 4; "Letters from Notes of the Trip Overland," *Daily Alta Californian* (June 24, 1886); 73, II, 182

STARGO GULCH
Greenlee   T4S R29E   Elev. 4800'
This valley was named about 1934 for the housing area along it. In 1902 it was known as Apache Gulch. The mining company developed a housing area here, called Stargo (Elev. 4680').

STARK (R.R. STN)
Cochise   T24S R23E   Elev. 4380'
This place on the old El Paso and Southwestern R.R. was named for William Stark, who had a store and post office in the now-vanished depot. The Starks homesteaded here in the late 1870s.
P.O. est. July 18, 1913, Solomoń F. Pyle, p.m.; disc. Feb. 15, 1921   Ref.: Burgess; 242

STARR VALLEY
Gila   T10N R11E   Elev. 4554'
This valley takes its name from that of John Starr (b. 1833, Belgium), who was a miner in
this area in 1878. Andrew M. Houston and his brother Samuel named the location for
Starr.   Ref.: AHS Files; 62

STEAMBOAT
Apache   T27N R23E   Elev. 6200'
Gregory noted that this "erosion remnant is shaped like a boat," hence he gave it this
name in 1915. There is a Navajo settlement here. An earlier name shown on the
McComb map of 1860 was White Spring. The locality takes its Navajo name of *hóyéé*
(= "fear" or "water is scarce") from a spring about one-quarter mile north of the trading
post. Above the spring on the sandstone walls are inscriptions in English and one in
Spanish: *A 20 Abril Ano de 1666 p° de Montaya.* There are also Indian petroglyphs.
Steamboat Canyon and Wash are associated names.
Ref.: Burcard; 331, p. 151; 141, p. 195

STEAMBOAT MOUNTAIN
Coconino (Grand Canyon)   T34N R1W   Elev. 7429'
So named by George Wharton James because of its shape.   Ref.: 178, p. 5

STEAMBOAT MOUNTAIN
Pinal   T4S R15E   Elev. c. 3500'
Cowboys thought this mountain looked like a huge steamboat when seen from the Gila
River, hence the name.   Ref.: 18a

STEAMBOAT ROCK
Coconino   T18N R6E
This rock in Oak Creek Canyon is part of Wilson Mountain. It looks very much like an
old-fashioned river steamboat with a pilot house.   Ref.: Schnebly; Stemmer

STEAMBOAT ROCK
Gila   T4N R12E
Named in 1917 by Aubrey Drury because of its shape and also known as Submarine
Rock because "the level of water (Roosevelt Lake) may cover it at times."   Ref.: 329

STEAM PUMP RANCH
Pima   T12S R14E   Elev. c. 3000'
A steam pump was used to raise well water at this ranch owned by George Pusch. The
ranch was a stopping point for watering freight-hauling teams. See Pusch Ridge, Pima
Ref.: 238, p. 64

STEELE'S STATION
Cochise   T13S R24E   Elev. 4215'
Thomas Steele (b. Sept. 8, 1844, Missouri; d. Aug. 28, 1916) in 1873 constructed a
stage station at Croton Springs near what are now called Steele Hills (T14S/R23E,
Elev. 5270') on the road to Globe. In 1876 Tom Williams operated it. The springs were
renamed Steele Springs in 1877. By 1880 William Whalen (b. 1843, Canada; d. 1908)
was running it under the name Point of Mountain Stage Station. The coming of the
railroad put it out of business.
Ref.: AHS, William Whalen File, and Lizzie Steele *ms.*, and Thomas Steele File;
Arizona Citizen (Oct. 10, 1874), p. 4

STEHR LAKE
Yavapai   T12N R6E   Elev. c. 3728'
This artificial lake was named in 1908 for the treasurer of the Arizona Power Company,
Fredrick W. Stehr, former secretary of the Arizona Power Company. The company
constructed a power plant at Fossil Creek.   Ref.: Malcolm M. Bridgewater, Arizona
Public Service Co., letter (Sept. 13, 1965)

STEPHEN BUTTE

Navajo   T26N R20E   Elev. 6568'

This name was proposed by the USGS in October 1908 to honor A.M Stephen, an ethnologist who lived for many years at Keams Canyon and is buried at this location. Ref.: 141, p. 195; 182

STERLING SPRING

Coconino   T19N R6E

This spring is now under the highway in Oak Creek Canyon. Its most notable contribution to history is that a man named Sterling counterfeited money here. Ref.: Sykes

STEVEN CANYON

Santa Cruz   T21S R15E

This canyon takes its name from that of rancher Lou Steven, who was in the area c. 1930.   Ref.: Lenon

STEVENS GORGE CANYON

Gila   T1S R14E

This location was named for Hiram Sanford Stevens (b. 1832, Vermont), who arrived in Arizona in 1854. An astute trader and politician, Stevens was also a professional gambler. He was elected to the U.S. Congress in 1874 and again in 1876, selecting as "his shock troops in his hardest campaign 'the Knights of the Green Cloth.' " With the help of these professional gamblers, he won the election. Ref.: 62; 206, p. 142; 224, p. 52

STEVENS MOUNTAIN

Pima   T17S R10E   Elev. 4411'

The mountain takes its name from the nearby Stevens Ranch, noted for its excellent water coming from an artificial fifty-foot long tunnel cut in a hillside. Stevens Wash is also here.   Ref.: 57, p. 373; 59, p. 253

STEWARD POCKET

Gila   T10N R10E   Elev. 4875'

The first settler here was Ben Steward, hence the name. "Stewart" is a misspelling. Ref.: 18a; Gillette

STEWART CRATER

Coconino   T23N R9E   Elev. 7177'

Harold S. Colton originally named this location for Jules Marcou, who was in this area 1860-70. Why the name of this volcanic crater was changed from Marcou to Stewart is not known.   Ref.: 329

STEWART MOUNTAIN

Maricopa   T3N R8E   Elev. 2988'

Jack Stewart ran cattle from his ranch near this mountain 1880-1900. The Stewart Mountain Dam, a portion of the Salt River Valley Reclamation project, was named for this mountain.   Ref.: 18a, 5, p. 350

STEWART MOUNTAIN DAM

Maricopa   T3N R8E   Elev. 2800'

This dam, begun in 1928 as part of the Salt River Valley Reclamation project, was completed in 1930. The dam, which is two hundred and twelve feet high, created Saguaro Lake, also called Stewart Mountain Lake.   Ref.: 5, p. 350

STINKING SPRINGS

Apache   T14N R26E

The water in these springs, always warm, smells because in it are sulphur and other minerals. They are on Stinking Springs Mountain.   Ref.: Stemmer

STINSON MOUNTAIN

Yavapai   T16N R6W   Elev. 6411'

James Stinson (b. 1839; d. Jan. 8, 1932) settled near this mountain in 1872, but removed himself rather hurriedly to establish a ranch which later became Snowflake (*q. v.*). After leaving there in 1879, he located in Pleasant Valley in time to play a large part in the Pleasant Valley war. Before 1877 he had hired the Grahams and Tewksburys to work for him, but when they began gunning for each other, Stinson quickly got out of the way.   Ref.: Rosenberger; 5, p. 459; 18a

STINSON WASH

Navajo   T11N R18E

James Stinson from 1873-79 maintained a ranch on this wash and in Stinson Valley. See Snowflake, Navajo, and Stinson Mountain, Yavapai   Ref.: 18a

STOA PITK   pro.: /tówa pit/

Papago = "white clay"

Pima   T17S R1W   Elev. c. 2500'

White clay deposits near this Papago village give it its name. The name Towapit (Barnes 1935) is a corruption.   Ref.: 262, p. 8

STOA TONTK

Papago = "white mound"

Pima   T18S R1W   Elev. c. 2200'

There are white clay deposits near this permanent Papago village, hence the name. Ref.: 262, p. 3

STOA VAYA

Papago = "white well'

Pima   T14S R1E   Elev. 2440'

The site of this Papago village in Spanish is called Poso Blanco (1893, Roskruge), and Pozo Blanco (1912, Lumholtz), both names reflecting the presence of a "white well" or waterhole here. In the past it was also known as Komo Vaya or Koma Vaxia (*Kom* = "a kind of tree"; *vaxia* = "waterhole" or "spring").   Ref.: 262, p. 10; 58; 167, II, 288

STOCKHAM (R.R. STN.)

Pima   T13S R13E   Elev. 2700'

Tucson has now engulfed this siding named for John Stockham, Jr., who worked with a railroad bridge gang and owned land here c. 1904.   Ref.: Jordan; 18a

STOCKPEN CANYON

Greenlee   T5S R30E

There is a tank for stock in this natural pen, hence the name.

STOCKTON HILL

Cochise   T20S R24E   Elev. 5593'

Eugene Edmonds (b. 1834, New York) was nicknamed "Stockton" because he survived the Stockton, California, Indian massacre. He was a freighter in Tucson in 1870, later settling at the Stockton Ranch, a favorite stopping place for freighters and outlaws on the road from Tombstone to the Chiricahua Mountains. Stockton Draw is at T19S/R24E. Ref.: Macia; 62; 60, p. 115

STOCKTON HILL

Mohave   T22N R17W   Elev. 4800'

This location, also called Stockton, takes its name from that of Stockton Camp (T22N/R17W), named by Johnny McKinsey, a Scotsman. The Stockton Mine was located c. 1880. Although it was said to have produced ores as early as the 1860s, facts indicate otherwise, which eliminates the possibility that it was named by miners who came from California to Arizona in the 1860s. Miners in this area were either Arizonans or "Cousin Jacks," the latter being Cornishmen, called Cousin Jacks because to bring other Cornishmen to the United States and to evade immigration laws, they had no hesitation about designating previously unknown "relatives" as cousins. Refusing to let other miners work with them, they are reported to have had the nasty habit of permitting something lethal to fall on any miner with the temerity to try to work alongside a Cousin Jack.

P.O. est. as Stockton Hill, March 7, 1888, William H. Lake, p.m.; disc. July 11, 1892   Ref.: Harris; 200, p. 107; 146, p. 68; 163, pp. 160, 252

STOCKTON PASS
Graham   T9S R25E   Elev. c. 4500'
This location, sometimes referred to in early military reports as Stockton Gap, was named after Stockton, a cattleman. It has also been called Eagle Pass because it is near Eagle Rock Peak (T9N/R24E).
Associated names include Stockton Pass Dam and Wash (T8S/R26E) and Stockton Wash (*sic*) and Dam (T7S/R26E).   Ref.: 311, pp. 128-129

STODDARD
Yavapai   T12N R2E   Elev. 3906'
Isaac T. Stoddard owned the Stoddard-Binghamton Mine, which he named for himself and his native town in New York. He was Secretary of Arizona Territory (1901-07). The community which served the mine has now vanished. The name also applies to Stoddard Spring here.
P.O. est. Dec. 15, 1882, George N. Birdsall, p.m.; disc. Sept. 15, 1927
Ref.: Schnebly; AHS Names File; 329; 242

STONE AXE RUIN
Apache   T18N R24SE
Numerous stone axes found when this ruin was excavated in 1901 led to the name. The locale has been grossly vandalized, parts of the buildings being used to construct a dam.   Ref.: Branch; 167, II, 638

STONE CABIN
Yuma   T2S R19W   Elev. 1518'
Now in ruins, Stone Cabin was built as a way station on the old Dome-Quartzsite road.   Ref.: Lenon; 355, p. 77

STONE CABIN CANYON
Pima   T19S R15E
Nine mining claims in the northwest part of the Santa Rita Mountains probably were the cause for establishing a post office at this location, which is not precisely known. See Florida Canyon, Pima
P.O. est. Dec. 28, 1880, John P. Zimmerman, p.m.; disc, Feb. 16, 1881
Ref.: 286, p. 168

STONE FERRY
Mohave (Lake Mead)   T32N R20W
Stone or Stone's Ferry was a principal crossing for traffic between Utah and northwestern Arizona. Mail carried on horseback to Pioche, Nevada, in the 1870s used the ferry at the mouth of the Virgin River. It should not be confused with Bonelli's Crossing at the mouth of Detrital Wash about three miles away. It bore the nickname "The End of the Death Trail" because it was "on the far side of a desolate and deadly land which many of those in quest of California gold never succeeded in crossing." In 1877 the Hencoop Hotel offered shelter for travelers here. It was made of cottonwood poles and willows covered with mud and roofed with canvas and gravel, the whole thing chained to the ground to keep high winds from blowing it away. In that year it was run by a man called Pony Thompson, who also ran the ferry. The ferry is now covered by the waters of Lake Mead.   Ref.: 15, p. 338; Housholder; 116, p. 552; 225, p. 97; Huntington Library

STONEMAN LAKE
Coconino   T16N R8E   Elev. 6722'
In 1865 this body of water in the crater of a volcano was called Chavez Lake (see Chavez Pass, Navajo), changed by John F. Marion to Stoneman Lake for Gen. George Stoneman. Stoneman (1822-1894) was a lieutenant with Lt. Col. Phillip St. George

Cooke when the Mormon Batallion crossed Arizona in 1846. In 1869 Stoneman was assigned to command the newly formed Military Department of Southern California, with Arizona headquartrs at Fort Whipple. He assiduously established new posts, improved old ones unnecessarily, and was rigid in his punishment of Indians. He tried unsuccessfully to establish a road called Stoneman's Grade (see Pinal, Camp, Pinal). Despite his success in paving the way for truces with the Mohave, Hualapai, Yavapai, and the so-called Apache-Yumas, he was relieved of his command, being replaced by Gen. George Crook in June 1871. He served as governor of California 1883-1887.

Stoneman Lake was also called Owens Lake, but the name was officially changed by the USGS to Stoneman Lake in 1924. A summer colony existed here until World War II. P.O. est. April 22, 1924 at Morin Inn, Phillip J. Morin, p.m.; disc. Dec. 2, 1939   Ref.: 242; 107, VIII, 97, 104; 261, p. 7; 168, p. 238; pp. 451, 452, 558

STORM CANYON
Gila   T3N R15E   Elev. 3072'
While rounding up cattle in November 1898, Jack Knightson, Bob Sloan, and J.B. Henderson camped here and were caught in a severe snow storm. Stranded, they nearly starved. They lost their horses and had to struggle to McMillanville through snow at least seven feet deep and through drifts they estimated to be fifty feet deep, hence the name Storm Canyon.   Ref.: Woody; 18a

STORM RANCH
Yavapai   T18N R3W   Elev. 5163'
James P. Storm had a ranch post office called Storm. He later served as Yavapai County Treasurer.
P.O. est. June 20, 1894, James P. Storm, p.m.; disc. Jan. 23, 1901
Ref.: AHS Names File; 18a

STOTONIC
Papago = "many ants"
Pinal   T3S R5E   Elev. c. 2000'
In June 1940 the Pima-Maricopa tribal council adopted the name Stotonic for this village. The name has also been spelled Stontonyak and Stotonyak.
Ref.: 262, p. 10; 329

STOTT CANYON
Navajo   T11N R15E
This canyon traverses the Stott Ranch, in existence in 1904. It is the site of a prehistoric pueblo ruin called Stott Ranch Ruin.   Ref.: 167, II, 644

STOVAL
Yuma   T8S R13W   Elev. 776'
Stoval has undergone many name changes. Initially it was identical with Texas Hill (1860).

Texas Hill, the stage station was so named because Texas emigrants were said to have been killed there. Also, Texans kept cattle in the area in the early days (possibly in 1850s and early 1860s).

However, the first name which is mapped is Grinnel Station, so named for its stage station manager, Henry Grinnel. Grinnel Station was not identical with, but was near, Texas Hill Camp (1869). By 1875 Grinnel Station was out of existence and Texas Hill Camp is mapped southwest of Teamsters Camp. Stanwix is noted in the vicinity of old Grinnel, but is in Maricopa County. All were in what was called San Cristobal Valley, with the station at its center.

In April 1889 the *Arizona Star* noted that a new settlement named Crystoval had as residents about one hundred people from St. Louis, who planned to farm. A variant spelling was Chrystoval. The paper said Crystoval was north of Aztec Station on the S.P.R.R. Actually, Texas Hill R.R. Station was between Aztec and Mohawk. The newspaper story is somewhat at variance with a source which says Oscar F. Thornton began a farmer's garden at this location c. 1882, naming the place Christvale. Thornton was appointed postmaster at Texas Hill (R.R. Station) in 1888. (The name Chrystoval had been suggested for that new post office.) Note that the name Texas Hill was soon changed to Chrystoval.

P.O. est. as Texas Hill, June 19, 1888, Oscar F. Thornton, p.m.; name changed to Chrystoval, Sept. 25, 1888; name changed to Stoval, May 26, 1913; disc. March 31, 1916; Wells Fargo (Texas Hill) 1888 (Briefly, the mail was handled at Mohawk (*q.v.*).) Ref.: Mercer; 73, II, 183; 320, p. 17; *Phoenix Herald* (Oct. 18, 1888), I, 3; *Arizona Daily Star* (April 20, 1889), p. 4; 242

STOVE HILL
Gila   T7N R10E

This hill at the foot of Reno Mountain was a difficult route on a steep grade on the eastern portion of Reno Pass. It was given its name when a large army stove being hauled to Camp Reno fell off the pack animals. For years thereafter the oven door and its iron top were landmarks, in use until the 1880s.   Ref.: AHS, Frank Alkire Collection

STRATTON CAMP
Pima   T11S R16E   Elev. c. 6500'

Emerson Oliver Stratton (b. Nov. 1, 1846, Clyde, New York; d. Aug. 14, 1925) arrived in Arizona in 1875. After serving as a bookkeeper at the Maricopa Wells Stage Station, he became a rancher and in 1881 was associated with the Apache Camp Mine. He then developed the Stratton Mine at this location, later selling it to the Stratton Copper Company.   Ref.: AHS, Chambers Collection, *Arizona Album* (May 17, 1955)

STRATTON CANYON
Pima   T11S R16E

This canyon, also called Stratton Gulch, was named c. 1880 when Stratton owned the Pandora Ranch, which in 1885 was incorporated with the Inter-Ocean Cattle Company. Stratton Saddle is above the canyon. Stratton Wash (Pima/Pinal) is at T10-11S/R17E. See Stratton Camp, Pima   Ref.: AHS, Emerson O. Stratton *ms.*, 57, 70

STRAWBERRY
Gila   T12N R8E   Elev. 5813'

The first American name for this location and one by which it was known locally in 1886 was Strawberry Valley, because of the wild strawberries which grow profusely in the region. This is the area which in 1864 Henry Clifton, a member of King S. Woolsey's second expedition, said was called Wah-poo-eta because it was the home of a Tonto leader of that name. Prescott citizens called the man Big Rump. Associated names include Strawberry Canyon, Creek, Hollow, and Mountain (Elev. 6794').
P.O. est. Dec. 13, 1886, Lafayette P. Nash, p.m.; disc. Dec. 31, 1904
Ref.: Woody; 18a; 116, p. 596

STRAY HORSE CREEK
Greenlee   T2N R29E   Elev. c. 7000'

The name *Rattlesnake* was formerly applied to many places in this vicinity, because when the Cosper cattle were driven up the trail to Hanegan Meadow, cowboys paused along here and would usually stir up at rattlesnake at what is now Stray Horse Spring (T1N/R29E). A Forestry Service official traveling through here decided that the name Rattlesnake would scare tourists who would then not stop at the beautiful campsite and spring, so c. 1925 he renamed it Stray Horse. There was, however, no horse concerned. Associated names include Stray Horse Divide and Stray Horse Gap (T4N/R31E).
Ref.: Miller; Reilly

STRAY HORSE GAP
Greenlee   T4S R31E

The former name for this place was Rattlesnake Gap. See Stray Horse Creek, Greenlee   Ref.: Simmona

STRICKLAND SPRING
Yavapai   T16N R4W   Elev. 4800'

George Arnold Strickland settled here and operated the Simmons Stage Station in the late 1870s, after which he started a sheep ranch and built troughs here and in Strickland Wash.   Ref.: 18a

STRIP, THE
Coconino/Mohave

That northern part of Arizona which is cut off from the rest of the state by the Grand Canyon is called The Strip, a descriptive name.

STRONGHOLD CANYON
Cochise   T17S R23-21E   Elev. 7512'

This canyon derives its name because it heads at the so-called Cochise Stronghold, where according to tradition, Cochise was buried by members of his tribe. Signs of the grave were erased by his followers racing their horses up and down through this canyon.   Ref.: 5, p. 440

STURDEVANT POINT
Coconino (Grand Canyon)   T32N R3E   Elev. c. 5000'

Glen B. Sturdevant, Grand Canyon National Park naturalist, drowned just below this point while serving as a ranger in 1929. The USGS approved the name in 1932. Ref.: 329, M.R. Tillotson, Letter (April 30, 1930) to Director of National Park Service

SUBLIME, POINT
Coconino (Grand Canyon)   T32N R1E   Elev. 7465'

Dutton named this location in 1882 saying, "We named it *Point Sublime* . . . by far the most sublime of all earthly spectacles."   Ref.: 100, pp. 140, 141

SUCKER GULCH
Pima   T19S R16E

This gulch was named because of the Sucker Mine, which was producing gold c. 1875.   Ref.: AHS, Castillo Collection, Box 1, p. 3; 286, p. 163

SUGARLOAF: The term *sugarloaf* has been used descriptively where locations resemble mounds of unrefined sugar. The following are examples:

Sugarloaf	Coconino	T14N R8E	Elev. 6448'
Sugarloaf	Navajo	T14N R20E	Elev. 5728'
Sugarloaf	Yavapai	T15N R4E	
Sugarloaf	Yuma	T7S R22E	Elev. 668'
Sugar Loaf Hill	Cochise	T20S R25E	Elev. 5143'
Sugarloaf Hill See Sugarloaf Peak, Coconino	Coconino		
Sugarloaf Mountain a.k.a. Sugar Loaf	Cochise	T16S R29E	Elev. 7307'
Sugarloaf Mountain	Maricopa	(1) T4N R8E (2) T4N R8W (3) T7N R4E	Elev. 2884' Elev. 3418' Elev. 3879'
Sugarloaf Mountain	Mohave	(1) T30N R23W (2) T20N R25W	Elev. 1800' Elev. 1900'
Sugarloaf Mountain See Sentinel Peak, Pima	Pima		
Sugarloaf Mountain	Yavapai	(1) T18N R3W (2) T14N R3E	Elev. 5438' Elev. 6500'
Sugarloaf Peak	Coconino	T23N R7E	Elev. 9281'
Sugarloaf Peak	La Paz	T3N R20W	Elev. 675'

S U KNOLLS
Apache   T6N R28E   Elev. 9419'

The brand S U was used in the 1880s by Stevens, Upshur, and Burr, who maintained a summer camp for the S U Cattle Company here.   Ref.: 18a; Becker

SULLIVAN POINT
Coconino (Grand Canyon)   T33N R4E   Elev. 8324'
In 1932 Will C. Barnes named this location (a.k.a. Sullivan Peak) for Jeremiah William Sullivan (b. 1844, Canada), who arrived in Prescott on Dec. 2, 1868. He had a cattle ranch in Chino Valley. Other places having his name include Sullivan Butte (Yavapai, T17N/R3W), Sullivan Lake (Yavapai, T17N/R2W, Elev. 4348'), and Sullivan Tank (Yavapai, T20N/R7W). Ref.: 329, 18a

SULLIVAN SPRING
Yavapai   T9N R1W   Elev. 5758'
This spring was named for a miner, Matthew Sullivan, who had a claim nearby. Ref.: 18a

SULPHUR SPRINGS
Cochise   T16S R25E
The Wheeler report noted that this spring (in Sulphur Draw) had potable water but that when it stagnated, "a small trace of sulphuretted hydrogen is developed from the action of decaying vegetable matters." The presence of two springs at this location was important in the early days, as they supplied emigrant trains with the only water between Apache Pass and Dragoon Springs. The stage station was run by Rogers and Spence, who had located near the springs in 1868. When Gen. O.O. Howard established the Chiricahua Indian Reservation in 1872, the Indian agency was first at Sulphur Springs. Rogers had one hundred and sixty acres of land on the reservation, where he set up a trading post. Rogers and Spence were lawless, freely selling whiskey to the Indians. On April 6, 1876, in a "row over the sale of the liquor," described as "vile whiskey," the Indians killed Rogers and Spence at the Sulphur Springs Station.
    Associated names include Sulphur Hills (T17S/R26E, Elev. 5120'), Sulphur Peak (T18S/R31E, Elev. 8099'), and Sulphur Springs Valley (*q.v.*). Ref.: 345, III, 592; 65, pp. 178, 179; 116; p. 532; *Arizona Citizen* (Sept. 20, 1872), p.1, and (Oct. 19, 1872), p. 2

SULPHUR SPRINGS VALLEY
Cochise/Graham   T16S R25E
On a military map for 1859 this valley is designated Valle de Las Playas, derived from the Playa de las Pimas, the then-current name for the dry lake near Willcox. By 1875, however, because of the importance of Sulphur Springs, that name had come to be applied to the length of the entire broad valley. It averages more than twenty miles in width. It should be noted that there are several so-called Sulphur Springs in this valley. See Sulphur Springs, Cochise, and Willcox, Cochise

SULTAN
Yavapai   c. T13N R7W
The name for this post office was derived from that of a mine owned by a champagne salesman, Harry La Montague.
P.O. est. Feb 11, 1903, Harry La Montague, p.m.; disc. June 27, 1904
Ref.: 242; Gardner

SUMMER BUTTE
Coconino (Grand Canyon)   T32N R3E   Elev. 5160'
This location was named for John C. Summer, who was with Maj. Powell's 1869 Grand Canyon expedition. As it is not a point, the name *Sumner* Point should not be used, since it is also misspelled. Summer's Amphitheater is here. Ref.: 18a

SUMMERHAVEN
Pima   T11S R16E   Elev. 8000'
William Reed and a man named Carter homesteaded at this location in 1882, but failed to complete the requirements. They called their location Carter's Camp. Its current name, originally Summer Haven, was given by Gen. Frank A. Hitchcock, who was instrumental in getting the highway to Mount Lemmon constructed. Hitchcock said that such a road was needed so that residents of Tucson could get to a "summer haven" in the cool Santa Catalina Mountains. The highway to Mount Lemmon bears his name.

Frederick E.A. Kimball helped with the project. See Kimball Peak, Pima
P.O. est. May 26, 1924, Frederick E.A. Kimball, p.m.; disc. Oct. 14, 1929
Ref.: AHS, (1) Emerson O. Stratton, *ms.*, p. 63, (2) Frederick E.A. Kimball File; The
Catalina View (Tucson: Catalina Savings and Loan Assoc., 1978), n.p.

SUMMIT
Cochise   T17N R23E
This was the name used in 1882 as a place to register voters in Cochise County. At that
time it had a population of twelve voters. It is another name for Dragoon Summit Stage
Station.   Ref.: *Tombstone Epitaph* (July 15, 1882), p. 3; Larriau

SUMMIT
Yuma
This was at the top of the railroad grade, hence the name. See Mohawk, Yuma

SUMMIT CANYON
Gila   T11N R9W
This location was named because of the presence of the Summit Mine.

SUMMIT MOUNTAIN
Coconino   T20N R2E   Elev. 7797'
The nearly flat top of this mountain affords marvelous views from two raised points. The
name is descriptive. Summit Spring at its base borrows the name.

SUMMIT VALLEY
Coconino   T40N R2E
This curiously contradictory name is actually descriptive of the fact that the Powell
exploring party, according to Dellenbaugh, found it on top of a plateau. "As it was on top
of the mountain, Bishop recorded it in his notes as Summit Valley and so it ever after
remains."   Ref.: 89, p. 305

SUMNER POINT
Coconino (Grand Canyon)
This is a double corruption inasmuch as it is actually a butte and the man's name is
Summer. See Summer Butte, Coconino (Grand Canyon)

SUN CITY
Maricopa   T3N R1E   Elev. 1145'
This retirement community "is identical (including the name) to two other cities
developed by Webb: Sun City, Florida, and Sun City, California." The community
opened in April 1960.   Ref.: *Arizona Highways* (Nov. 1967), p. 6

SUNDAD
Maricopa   T3S R9W   Elev. 980'
The now-vanished community was once proposed as a desert sanatorium.
Ref.: Theobald

SUNE WELL   pro.: /šuniy/
Yuma   T13S R7W
This watering place was named for a Sand Papago leader, Chico Sune. Sune Village
used to be nearby.   Ref.: Monson

SUNFLOWER
Maricopa   T6N R9E   Elev. 3410'
On the post office application in the National Archives, the local name is given as
Diamond Ranch. The post office was established to serve employees of the Sunflower
Mine (T7N/R8E). Sunflowers grow profusely in this region.
P.O. est. April 28, 1943, Walter B. Davis, p.m.; disc. April 30, 1949   Ref.: 242

SUNFLOWER BUTTE
Navajo   T22N R20E   Elev. 6335'
This is a large volcanic butte. Sunflowers made of skin and wood by prehistoric Indians

were found in abundance here. The name Pumpkin Flower Butte is not known locally.   Ref.: 329; 18a (quoting "Report," p. 65, U.S. Bureau of Ethnology)

SUNFLOWER FLAT
Yavapai
Black-eyed Susans grow abundantly here.

SUNFLOWER MESA
Gila   T11N R10E
On the old road from Camp McDowell to Camp Reno there was a very difficult stretch which had two water stations, one of which was at Sunflower. Here in 1875, just off the Indian Reservation, some families were attempting settlement. While the men were out looking for ranch sites, the women remained in camp and were terrified when a horse wandered in shot full of arrows. A stranger advised the women to leave at once. One of settlers asserted that the horse had actually been shot by traders who did not want other whites settling in the area. The story was denied by Edward A. Clarke, who talked about an Indian raid in Sunflower Valley. The settlers had stopped on Sunflower Creek.
Ref.: *Weekly Arizona Miner* (Oct. 1, 1875), p. 2, and (Oct. 8, 1875), p. 2; 163, p. 281

SUN FLOWER MESA
Greenlee   T20S R30E   Elev. c. 4000'
Sunflowers grow abundantly here.   Ref.: Scott

SUNFLOWER VALLEY
Maricopa   T7N R8E
This location was named because of the masses of black-eyed Susans growing in it. The name dates to c. 1870. There is a possibility that the Sunflower Creek mentioned under Sunflower Mesa was actually in Sunflower Valley. See Sunflower Mesa, Gila
Ref.: 107, I, 197

SUNGLOW
Cochise   T18S R29E   Elev. c. 6000'
In 1920 Jeff P. Thomason, Sr., noted that the sun strikes this area in the early morning and envelopes it in a golden glow, and he therefore named it Sunglow. On the post office application form is noted the fact that it was called Wilgus, but that was stretching a point inasmuch as Wilgus was actually two miles away. Near Sunglow Johnny Ringgold ("Ringo"), a notorious bad man, was discovered propped in the fork of a tree with a bullet through his head. No one had heard shots. The coroner's jury brought a verdict of suicide, somewhat dubious considering that Ringo's revolver was fully loaded. Little remains of Sunglow today.
P.O. est. Aug. 27, 1921, Jefferson P. Thomason, p.m.; P.O. moved to Wilgus (two miles away), Sept. 30, 1928; disc. Dec. 30, 1933   Ref.: 242; Riggs; 203, p. 83

SUNIZONA
Cochise   T18S R26E   Elev. 4330'
This location, a land developer's project in the early 1970s, failed to develop more than a few residences. The name combines "sunny" with Arizona.

SUNNYSIDE
Cochise   T23S R19E   Elev. 5825'
This location was a religious community established in the 1880s by Sam Donnelly. Donnelly had been a leading patron of the tough San Francisco water-front bars, but began his regeneration when he overheard another patron suggest that Scotty commit a crime at a cost to the other drinkers of a shot of whiskey. Scotty as sober enough to give the men a tongue lashing. He then wandered out and stumbled into a Salvation Army meeting. He became a Salvation Army officer and street preacher. Gradually developing his own religious ideas, he moved on to Tombstone and ran into a man named Sinclair, locator of the Copper Glance Mine (sometimes incorrectly called The Glance). They developed plans for a religious community and c. 1888 The Donnellites (a name they did not use) moved to the location of the Lone Star Mine. The mine paid off and the community prospered. Brother Sam died in 1901. The mines gradually played out and closed down in 1933. Private owners took over the mine and the town. There are several

intact buildings at the location, which is now a ghost town under the supervision of caretakers.

P.O. est. Nov. 25, 1913, Lucy Langford, p.m.; disc. March 15, 1934

Ref.: 242; Varney; 277, pp. 150, 152

SUNNYSLOPE
Maricopa   T3N R3E   Elev. c. 1400'

The name describes the fact that this location is fully exposed to the sun. For many years it was a haven for people with respiratory diseases. Ref.: 5, p. 354

SUNRISE SPRINGS
Apache   T25N R25E

A white settlement existed here as early as 1907. In October 1928 the name of the post office was Cornfields. The substitute name was necessary when the post office was reestablished, because of the Post Office Department policy of not re-using an older name. The name Cornfields indicates that Navajo Indians raise corn in this vicinity.

P.O. est. as Sunrise Springs, April 12, 1913, Benjamin E. Harvey, p.m.; disc. Dec. 24, 1920; reest. as Cornfields, Aug. 4, 1922, William M. Black, p.m.; disc. March 15, 1934   Ref.: 242; 141, pp. 37, 137

SUNSET
Graham   T10S R21E   Elev. 4811'

This post office was established to service the mines on Sunset Peak, from which it takes its name.

P.O. est. Feb. 15, 1917, Mrs. Ella Nichols, p.m.; disc. Jan. 1, 1932   Ref.: 242

SUNSET
Navajo   Elev. c. 4000'

During the Mormon emigration of 1876 (see Joseph City, Navajo), Sunset was one of five Mormon colonies, the name deriving from that of Sunset Gap (see Sunset Crossing, Navajo). Settlers under the leadership of Lot Smith and Lorenzo Roundy initially were upstream two miles from this location, three miles north of Winslow on Little Colorado River, where they built a fort of drift cottonwood logs. Because of undependable irrigation and poor soil, the colonists abandoned Sunset by 1878, the last to leave being Lot Smith and his family. Only a graveyard remains as a reminder of this vanished settlement.

P.O. est. July 5, 1876, Alfred M. Derrick, p.m.; disc. Nov. 23, 1887

Ref.: 331, p. 153; 225, p. 142; 341, p. 1

SUNSET, CAMP
Navajo

During his Navajo campaigns, Col. Kit Carson "is said to have established a Camp Supply, a.k.a. Camp Sunset, on the Little Colorado River, about a mile or two from the present town of Holbrook." According to Hart, Sunset Camp was six miles east of Winslow c. 1858-62. See also Supply, Camp, Navajo   Ref.: 224, p. 157; 156, p. 183

SUNSET CRATER NATIONAL MONUMENT
Coconino   T23N R8E

Sunset Crater National Monument was created by presidential decree on May 26, 1930, setting aside its three thousand and forty acres, which contain the Bonita Lava Flow and the Ice Caves. The Navajo name for this location is *Dzil Bilstsh Litsoi* (= "yellow topped mountain"), a clue to the reason why in 1892 Maj. John Wesley Powell, then director of the USGS, named this volcanic cone Sunset Crater. The cinder colors at the top are bright yellow which shades down through oranges and reds and deep reds into black volcanic ash near its base. He called it Sunset Peak, but it is not a *peak* inasmuch as the cone rises one thousand feet above the surrounding country but has an interior pit about thirteen hundred feet in diameter and four hundred feet deep. A trail up the side of the cone leads to a view of the deep crater formed c. 1066 A.D. by volcanic eruption.

The Ice Caves were formed when the hot surface mass cooled, leaving a crust while the molten lava underneath flowed away. As lava is a poor heat conductor, it retains cold air. Such air settles in the cave and ice is a year-round phenomenon. In fact, in the 1880s ice from this and similar lava caves was supplied to homes and saloons in Flagstaff. Visitors also view an extraordinarily rough area of ridges and cones used by astronauts when they were training to land on the moon.   Ref.: 13, Dale King, "Sunset Crater," p. 2; 331, p. 153; 5, p. 286

SUNSET CROSSING
Navajo   T19N R16E   Elev. c. 3500'
On April 7, 1858 Lt. Edward Fitzgerald Beale used this crossing, as did also Capt. George M. Wheeler in the 1870s. Sunset Crossing was the only one with a rock bed. It is on a rocky ledge of the Little Colorado River on the route to Camp Verde and Fort Whipple which proceeded via Sunset Gap, a pass through the mountains to the southwest twenty miles from the current community of Winslow. Here William Blanchard and J.H. Breed operated a store while the railroad was being built 1878-1883. From that fact Sunset Crossing came to be known as Blanchard Crossing or as Breed Crossing. In December 1881, "Thick-lipped Joe" Waters and William Campbell murdered Blanchard. They were caught, jailed, and lynched at Saint Johns.
Ref.: Richards; 345, III, 638; 22, p. 24

SUNSET GAP MESA
Coconino   T17N R13E
This is the name used by Wheeler for "two mesas of three hundred to four hundred feet in height . . . the road to Prescott passes through the gap between them." See Sunset Crossing, Navajo, and Sunset Pass, Coconino   Ref.: 345, III, 638

SUNSET PASS
Coconino   T17N R13E   Elev. c. 6000'
The old Hopi trail, after crossing the Little Colorado River near Sunset Crossing, proceeded through this place, also known as Sunset Gap. The pass is between two lava-topped mesas called Table Mountain (descriptive) and Sunset Mountain. The trail then proceeded to Chavez Pass. In Sunset Pass Capt. Charles King battled Apaches in October 1874. The experience was the basis for his novel *Sunset Pass*. See also Jack's Canyon, Coconino   Ref.: 18a; 22, p. 24

SUNSET PEAK
Greenlee   T4S R30E   Elev. 6983'
This peak in a canyon is the last thing the setting sun strikes. The peak was used as a heliograph signal station in 1886 during Gen. Nelson A. Miles' campaign against Apaches.   Ref.: 18a; Scott

SUPAI
Coconino (Grand Canyon)   T33N R4W   Elev. 3195'
This is the Havasupai village in the Grand Canyon, which can be reached only on foot, mule back, or by helicopter. Severe floods have hit it occasionally. For instance, in 1911 a forty-foot wall of water swept away all buildings as Indians clung to the cliff sides to escape the raging torrent.
P.O. est. Oct. 6, 1903, W.T. Shelton, p.m.   Ref.: 53, p. 671; 242

SUPAI (R.R. STN.)
Coconino   T21N R1E   Elev. c. 6000'
This station on the A.T. & S.F.R.R. at the junction of the east and west bound tracks was named for the Havasupai Indian tribe, whose reservation is nearby. Trains pause here to test brakes before dropping downgrade to the west.
P.O. est. Sept. 5, 1896, Rufus C. Bauer, p.m.   Ref.: Terry

SUPAI TRAIL
Coconino (Grand Canyon)   T33N R4W
Until 1938 this fourteen-mile trail was called Topocoba Trail. The name was changed by the USGS. The trail drops from Havasu Hilltop into Havasu Canyon, descending over one thousand feet in the first mile and a half, during which the traveler encounters at least twenty-nine switchbacks. The trail was created about 1930 to replace the old wagon road formerly used by miners in the canyon.   Ref.: 53, pp. 655, 656; 178, p. 55

SUPERIOR

Pinal   T1S R12E   Elev. 2820'

In 1900 the name of this location as it appeared on a map of the Pioneer Mining District was Hastings, but the name changed in that year due to the work of George Lobb, who laid out a town site for a community to be called Superior because the existence of the town depended upon the operations of the Arizona and Lake Superior Mining Company. By 1904 Superior had many tents, several primitive board homes, a store, boarding house, blacksmith shop, and a post office with Lobb as postmaster. With the construction of a huge smelter in 1914 by the Magma Copper Company, the future of Superior in the roster of Arizona communities was secured to last as long as copper ores continued to be fed into the smelter. In 1981 the smelter closed down.

P.O. est. Nov. 19, 1902, George Lobb, p.m.   Ref.: *Arizona Blade* (April 2, 1904), p. 1; 5, p. 349; 242

SUPERSTITION MOUNTAINS

Pinal/Maricopa   T1N R9E   Elev. 5057'

A Pima Indian legend says that the foam of a great flood caused a broad white streak in the limestone, extending for several miles near the top of the face of the rough Superstition Mountains. This legend is reflected in the Spanish name for the mountains, *Sierra de la Espuma* (= "mountains of the foam"). Another story concerning the name is that valley-dwelling Indians considered the mountains bad medicine because anyone who entered them would never return. In the 1870s these mountains were also called the Salt Mountains. They are adjacent to the Salt River, hence the earlier name. According to Will Barnes, the mountains were "so called from stories told to early settlers and travelers by Indians . . . Apaches watched for stragglers from the top" and if the stragglers were either Papago or Pimas, Apaches would kill them. It should be noted that Indians hold strong beliefs about the spirits of the dead. On two occasions U.S. cavalrymen fought with Apaches in these mountains and emerged with few casualties. It should also be noted that the famous Lost Dutchman Mine is associated with these mountains. The highest point is Superstition Peak.   Ref.: 5, p. 350; *Tucson Citizen* (Dec. 24, 1870), p. 4; 329; 224, p. 22; 159, pp. 438, 440

SUPI OIDAK

Papago = "cold field"

Pima   T20S R6E

This is a small village on the Papago Indian Reservation.   Ref.: 262, p. 1

SUPPLY, CAMP

Navajo   1 mi. east of present Holbrook   Elev. 6000'

Col. Kit Carson had a temporary camp here in 1863 while on his expedition against the Navajo. Hart places it two miles east of Holbrook.

Ref.: 224, p. 157; 206, pp. 97, 98; 156, p. 184

SUPPLY, CAMP

Pinal   T2S R12E

This location, two miles south of the present town of Superior at the end of the Stoneman Grade, was a military supply point in 1870 for those building Stoneman's Grade. There are earthen ovens here. See also Silver King, Pinal   Ref.: Woody

SURPRISE

Maricopa   T3N R1W   Elev. 1178'

This small community has been in existence since c. 1949. According to an informant, the fact that it came into existence is the reason for the name.   Ref.: Anonymous

SURPRISE CANYON

Mohave   T29N R13W   Elev. c. 2100'

This canyon, also called Green Spring Canyon, in 1915 was described as having "a rather inconspicuous entrance obscuring the large canyon until viewer was directly before it," hence the name.   Ref.: 329

SURPRISE VALLEY
Apache   T15N R26E   Elev. c. 5000'
A small Mormon settlement once existed on Surprise Creek, which runs through the valley. The origin of the name is not known.   Ref.: 18a

SURPRISE VALLEY
Coconino (Grand Canyon)   T35N R2W
In 1882 Dutton wrote that this valley forms a *cul de sac* on the Tapeats Trail and that it was named by Beaman and Riley in 1872.
Ref.: 100, p. 160; Schellbach File, Grand Canyon

SURPRISE WELL
Maricopa   T1S R7W   Elev. 1500'
Most wells along Centennial Wash were sunk from one to three hundred feet to obtain water. As this one yielded good water at forty feet, it was quite a surprise, hence the name.   Ref.: 18a

SUTHERLAND PEAK
Cochise   T23S R20E   Elev. 7262'
Jim Sutherland had a ranch in Hayfield Canyon where he raised cattle. Barnes says he was proud of being called the homeliest man in Arizona. While digging a well, he fell to his death. The name *Southerland* is a misspelling.

SUTHERLAND WASH
Pima   T11S R14E
Sutherland Wash is on Sutherland's Ranch

SUWUKI CHUAPO
Papago = "red spring"
Maricopa   T16S R4E
This was a temporary Papago village used for summer farming.   Ref.: 262, p. 15

SUWUK TONTK
Papago = "red mountain"
Pima   T18S R5E   Elev. 3041'
According to a newspaper article, this was the Papago name for what in 1952 was called Nigger Toe Peak.   Ref.: AHS, Chambers Collection, Box 9 (June 6, 1952)

SWALLOW MOUNTAIN
Yavapai   T9N R3W
This mountain was named for the Swallow Mine (T8N/R2W).

SWALLOWS NEST RUIN
Navajo   T39N R17E
This cliff-dwelling ruin in a cliff niche looks like a swallow's nest, hence the name.   Ref.: Bureau of American Ethnology, *Bulletin No. 50*, p. 12

SWAMP CREEK MOUNTAIN
Navajo   T9N R15E   Elev. 6825'
The mountain is named for adjacent Swamp Creek (T10N/R15E), which is swampy.

SWAMP LAKE
Coconino (Grand Canyon)   T34N R1E   Elev. 7500'
This is a small intermittent lake on Rainbow Plateau which in 1908 was called Fen Lake by the USGS. In 1924 J.R. Eakin of the National Park Service learned from a local cowboy that the place was known as Swamp Lake and the name Fen Lake was then replaced. Both names are descriptive   Ref.: 329

SWAMP POINT
Coconino (Grand Canyon)   T34N R1W   Elev. 7522'
This point on the North Rim in 1908 was called Tulip Point by the USGS. However,

when M.R. Tillotson (Grand Canyon National Park Superintendent) on April 14, 1930 wrote to the Director of the National Park Service that the location had always been known as Swamp Point "presumably because of its proximity to Swamp Lake," and that Tillotson could not understand why the name was changed to Tulip, it was then changed in 1932 to Swamp Point by the USGS. The name Swampy Point, which occurred on some maps, was also removed.   Ref.: 329

SWANSEA
La Paz   T10N R15W   Elev. 1300'
Swansea was the community surrounding the smelter built to handle ores from nearby mines. Its first name was Signal. On March 26, 1872 the community was totally destroyed by an earthquake, the superintendent of the smelting works being the only fatality. The name Swansea derives from the fact that prior to the erection of the smelter, it had been necessary to ship ores great distances for smelting. The name Swansea is a borrowed name from that of Swansea, Wales, a smelting city. The community for several years had a post office, but today it is a ghost town. The smelter walls are still standing.
P.O. est. March 25, 1909, Mrs. Stella Siprell, p.m.; disc. June 28, 1904
Ref.: Lenon; *Arizona Sentinel* (April 6, 1872), p. 1; 279, p. 223; *Arizona Daily Star* (Jan. 15, 1909), p. 4; Varney

SWEENY
Mohave   T17N R22W
There is a possibility that this location was named for a man named Sweeney (Samuel?) (b. Dec. 23, 1820, Ireland; d. April 10, 1892), who lived in this area, according to a manuscript in the Huntington Library.
P.O. est. Dec. 18, 1905, James E. Bond, p.m. Bond refused the commission and the office never opened; disc. May 23, 1906   Ref.: Huntington Library; 242

SWEETWATER
Pima   T17S R3W   Elev. 2094'
The current name, selected by the Pima-Maricopa Indian Community Council in June 1949, is a translation of the Papago name, Siovi Shuatak (= "sweetwater'; pro. /siowl šuətə/). The Papago name in 1925 was rendered as Shiovo in USGS Water Supply Paper #499. It has also been known as Manuel's Well because a Papago named Slim Joe Manuel owned this two-well stock-watering place (1931). Earlier (1921 GLO) it was mapped as Cochibo, possibly indicating it was used for pigs (Papago: *kochi* = "pig"; *vo* = "well"). By 1927 the U.S. Corps of Engineers had mapped it as Coon's Can Well, and it is worth noting that the Cooncan Mine was close by. Barnes included it in 1935 as Con Quien, possibly a corruption aiming at an unauthentic Spanish origin. Among associated named are the following: Siovi Shuatak Pass and Wash, and Sweetwater Pass (see Agua Dulce, Pima).   Ref.: 262, p. 7; 57, p. 412; 329; 18a

SWEETWATER
Pinal   T3S R5E
In 1868 George F. Hooper and Company had a store and stage station here. In 1870 F.M. Larkin owned the stage station. The Pima Agency for Arizona Territory was across the road from it in 1879.   Ref.: *Weekly Arizona Miner* (Oct. 24, 1868), p. 4; 242, (Lt. R.H. Saugs, "Claims and Improvements, July 31, 1870")

SWICKERT SPRING
Mohave   T24N R18W   Elev. c. 4000'
A prospector named Swickert camped at this spring whenever en route to Chloride from his mine in Searchlight, Nevada. The name *Swicker* is a misspelling. Swickert was something of a character; he wore a sun helmet painted green and spoke with a "wangy old voice." He sold his mine for gold coin, a team of horses, and a buckboard, keeping the money from it in cans under his bed, but he said, "The old Piute squaws got most of it."   Ref.: Housholder

SWIFT TRAIL
Graham   T8S R25E
Theodore Swift (b. Dec. 20, 1871, Iowa; d. 1955), a Forest Service supervisor,

succeeded in having this road to the top of Mount Graham established, thereby opening up a new and very beautiful recreation area.   Ref.: 224; III; Jennings

SWIFT TRAIL JUNCTION
Graham   T8 S R26 E   Elev. 3231'
A small community has developed here to serve the needs of travelers and visitors to the recreation areas of Mount Graham.

SWILLING BUTTE
Coconino (Grand Canyon)   T33N R5 E   Elev. c. 6000'
John ("Jack") W. Swilling (b. 1830, South Carolina, d. Aug. 12, 1878) had this butte named in his honor by Frank Bond in 1932. See Gillette, Maricopa   Ref.: 329; 62

SWILLING GULCH
Yavapai   T8N R1 E   Elev. c. 4000'
This was no doubt named for Jack W. Swilling (see Gillette, Maricopa) as his ranch was on this gulch. This is also no doubt the ugliest place name in Arizona.

SWINGLE WASH
Pinal   T6S R15E
A rancher named Swingle had holdings on this wash in 1889.

SWISSHELM
Cochise   T21S R28E   Elev. 5200'
This post office was established to serve approximately one hundred who worked at a mine on this mountain. It took its name from its location in the Swisshelm Mountains. P.O. est. Dec. 12, 1907, Wilson R. Holland, p.m.; disc. April 9, 1908   Ref.: 242

SWISSHELM MOUNTAINS
Cochise   T19S R27E   Elev. 7185'
The Mountain Queen Mine was located on Sept. 5, 1878 by Henry Henson, J.W. Fleming, and John Swisshelm (d. c.1908). The name of the mountains at that time was descriptive: Pedrogosa Mountains (Spanish = "rocky" or "stony"). The three men renamed the mountain range and also its highest point, which they named Fleming Peak.   Rev.: 329; *Arizona Star* (Feb. 22, 1920), p. 5; Kitt

SWITZER MESA
Coconino   T21N R7E   Elev. c. 6800'
This mesa, which commands a view of Flagstaff on the east, was named for William Asa Switzer, who came to Flagstaff in 1884.   Ref.: Sykes (née Switzer)

SYCAMORE: At least seventy-four locations in Arizona bear the designation *Sycamore*. In the majority of instances the name indicates the presence of sycamore trees, the largest and possibly most beautiful of desert trees. Their white trunks and irregular branches form remarkable scenes. The following are instances of the use of *Sycamore:*

Sycamore (R.R. Stn.)   Yavapai   T17N R2E

Sycamore Basin   Yavapai   (1) T13N R17E
This valley in 1946 was called Doe Basin.   Rev.: USGS

Sycamore Canyon runs through this basin.   (2) T18N R3E

Sycamore Canyon   Yavapai   T11N R4E

Sycamore Canyon   Cochise   (1) T19S R29E   (2) T21S R19E
This was the name proposed for the site of a community now called White Horse Lake.

Sycamore Canyon   Coconino/Yavapai   T17-21N R3-4E
This canyon contains many cliff dwellings. In some places it is very wide and perhaps 2000' deep, leading to its nickname of the Miniature, or Little, Grand Canyon.

Sycamore Canyon Wilderness Area
See Sycamore Canyon, Coconino/Yavapai

Sycamore Canyon	Gila	(1) T10N R13W (2) T3N R15E

Also called Cottonwood Canyon.

Sycamore Canyon	Graham	(1) T3S R27E	(2) T6S R21E
		(3) T11S R25E	(4) T11S R20E

Sycamore Canyon	Maricopa	T8N R4E

Sycamore Canyon	Pima	(1) T19S R7E	(2) T17S R15E
		(3) T12S R16E	(4) T14S R18E

Sycamore Canyon	Santa Cruz	(1) T24S R15E (2) T23S R11E

Sycamore Canyon	Yavapai	T12N R6E

Sycamore Creek	Coconino	T19N R4E

Sycamore Creek	Gila	(1) T2N R18E

King S. Woosey named this Raccoon Creek in 1872 when a battle occurred here with Apaches.
(2) T6N R10E

It is also known as Cline Creek for George Cline, who had lived in the area since 1886. He said he never knew it by any name other than Sycamore Creek. Ref.: 329

Sycamore Creek	Graham	(1) T9S R20E	(2) T4N R17E

Sycamore Creek	Maricopa	T4N R8E

Sycamore Creek	Mohave	T15N R12E

Sycamore Creek	Yavapai	(1) T18N R3E	(2) T14N R7W
		(3) T9N R7E	(4) T11N R3E

Also called Dry Creek (1943). This was the location of the Sycamore Ranch.
P.O. est. April 15, 1911, Mrs. Ethelle Rosenberger, p.m.; disc. Sept. 30, 1912

Sycamore Gulch	Graham	T3S R20E

Sycamore Gulch	Greenlee	T3S R29E

Sycamore Mesa	Yavapai	(1) T11N R3E	(2) T15N R6W

Sycamore Pass	Yavapai	T18N R3E

Sycamore Pass	La Paz	T16N R14W

See Cottonwood Pass, La Paz

Sycamore Point	Coconino	T19N R4E

Sycamore Rim	Yavapai	T15N R6W

Sycamore Spring	Cochise	(1) T19S R29E	(2) T19S R23E

Sycamore Spring	Gila	(1) T6N R10E	(2) T3N R15E
		(3) T10N R13E	

In 1937 #3 was also called Cottonwood Spring, but by 1974 there were no cottonwoods.

Sycamore Spring	Graham	(1) T5S R19E	(2) T4S R20E
	(3) T6S R21E	(4) T5S R27E	(5) T11S R25E

Sycamore Spring	Maricopa	(1) T6N R8E	(2) T7N R5E

Sycamore Spring	Pinal	T1N R12E

Sycamore Spring	Yavapai	(1) T12N R4E	(2) T13N R6E
		(3) T15N R6W	

Sycamore Springs	Graham	T3S R27E

Sycamore Tank	Yavapai	(1) T18N R3E	(2) T12N R5E
		(3) T13N R6E	(4) T15N R5W

SYKES KNOB
Pima   T11S R16E
Named for forest ranger Gilbert Sykes. Ref.: Sykes

T

TABERNACLE, THE
Coconino (Grand Canyon)   T31N R5E
This peak in the Grand Canyon was named in June 1906 by the USGS.

TABLE: Some noticeably flat places in Arizona have the term *table* in their names. Instances are cited below:

Table, The   Gila   T10N R9E   Elev. 4145'
A flat-top mountain, this is a descriptive name.

Table Lands, The   Pinal   T5S R17E   Elev. 3487'

Table Mountain   Gila   T10N R9E   Elev. 4145'

Table Mountain   Graham/   (1) T4S R25E   Elev. 5315'
                                            Greenlee   (2) T2S R27E   Elev. 5644'

Table Mountain   Maricopa   T7N R2E   Elev. 1895'

Table Mountain   Mohave   T27N R19W   Elev. 5175'

Table Mountain   Pima   T12S R14E

Table Mountain   Pinal   T7S R18E   Elev. 5426'

Table Mountain   Yavapai   (1) T8N R8E   Elev. 5426'
(2) T15N R3W   Elev. 5567'   (3) T14N R4E
(4) T12N R5E   Elev. 5088'   (5) T9N R6E   Elev. 2944'
                                                            (6) T16N R7E   Elev. 6197'

Table Mountain Plateau   Mohave   T27N R19W   Elev. 5175'

Table Rock   Coconino   T38N R2W

Table Rock   Pinal   T7S R3E

Table Rock Canyon   Coconino   T38N R1W

Table Rock Spring   Coconino   T38N R2W

Table Top   Apache   T8N R29E

Table Top Mountain   Apache   T8N R29E   Elev. c. 9000'
Also called Flat Top Mountain.

Table Top Mountain   Gila   T10N R10E   Elev. 5260

Table Top Mountain   Greenlee   T2S R31E   Elev. 5104'

Table Top Mountain   Pinal   T8S R22E   Elev. 4373'
Formerly called Flat Top Mountain, its name was changed in 1941 by USGS.

Table Top Mountain   Yavapai   T17N R5E   Elev. 4800'

Table Top Mountain Mesa Greenlee   T3S R31E

Tabletop Mountains   Pinal   T8S R22E   Elev. 4373'

Tabletop Valley   Pinal   T9S R2E

TACNA pro.: /tǽknə/

Yuma   T8S R16W   Elev. 332'

The name *Tacna* has had an on-again-off-again existence. The first name applied to this place was Antelope Hill in 1859, a stage station (see Antelope Hill, Yuma). When the railroad station was constructed, the name was changed to Tacna, but it and its post office soon expired. When Max B. Noah arrived from Texas in the early 1920s, the local atmosphere underwent a change. Noah set up business under a tree with a barrel of gasoline and a hand pump. He was noted for his tall stories, one of which may have been that in the 17th century a Greek priest named Tachnapolis came from California to Arizona to spend his last days with the Indians, who abbreviated his name to Tachna or Tacna. Noah actually had picked up the name Tacna from an old railroad siding sign and used the name when he applied for a post office at the community he was busily establishing. He sometimes called it Tacna-by-the-Sea because it had so much sand. He did so well that he sold a complete town at public auction in 1941, along with his restaurant "Noah's Ark," known to thousands of travelers. A competitive restaurant four miles from Tacna was operated by Joe E. Ralph (d. c. 1934), who called his place Ralph's Mill. After the sale of Tacna, its post office was moved to Ralph's Mill – Tacna Post Office." The name on the old railroad siding was also relocated at Ralph's Mill and the older location was then referred to as Noah.

P.O. est. as Tacna, July 9, 1888, Edwin Mayes, p.m.; disc. July 22, 1898; reest. June 9, 1927, Max B. Noah, p.m.   Rev.: Kelland; 242; Lenon

TAH CHEE WASH

Navajo = "red water"

Apache   T33N R22E   Elev. c. 6000'

For many years this wash was the source of a red dye used by Navajo Indians, hence the name. Formerly it was known as Tahchito Creek, but in August 1968 the USGS changed the spelling to that given above.   Rev.: 329; 141, pp. 41, 195

TAHUTA POINT

Supai: *Tahota* = "something concealed"

Coconino (Grand Canyon)   T34N R2W   Elev. 6485'

This location was named in 1925 for Tahuta Jones, a venerable Havasupai woman. Rev.: 329; 303, p. 313

TALAHOGAN CANYON

Navajo = "house at the water"

Navajo   T27N R19E   Elev. c. 6500'

A Navajo home (*hogan*) in 1886 existed at Talahogan Spring, from which this canyon takes its name. Talahogan Wash, erroneously spelled Telehogan, runs through the canyon. The name is also spelled Talla-hogan.

TALIESEN WEST pro.: /tæliʌésən/

Welsh = "shining brow"

Maricopa   T3N R5E   Elev. c. 1800'

Taliesin (or Taliesin West) is the winter quarters of Frank Lloyd Wright's Taliesin Fellows, a group of architectural apprentices. Built in 1939 of native minerals, it is an embodiment of Wright's architectural principles. The name derives from that of a poet at King Arthur's Round Table, who sang of the glories of fine arts.

Rev.: 5, p. 146; Frank Lloyd Wright, Letter (July 3, 1957)

TALL MOUNTAIN

Navajo: *zilnez* = "tall mountain or tall mesa"

Navajo   T39N R16E   Elev. 7596'

This is a mesa. The name is a translation of the Navajo. It is also spelled Zilh-nez Mesa (1906); Zilner (1937); Dzilnez (1915, Gregory). See Zillnez Mesa, Navajo   Ref.: 329

TAM O'SHANTER PEAK

Gila   T4S R15E   Elev. 4639'

This peak has a crest like that of a tam o'shanter.   Ref.: 18a

TANGLE CREEK

Yavapai   T9N R5E   Elev. 3077'

Not only is the course of this creek crooked, but there is a great tangle of underbrush lining its banks, hence the name. Tangle Peak (T9N/R6E; Elev. 3542') is just above the creek. Ref.: 18a

TANK: The name *tank* is commonly employed to designate small and shallow reservoirs, which in Arizona may be man-made or natural. Mexicans call such locations either *represso* or *charco*. Such watering places are usually for livestock. The following are examples:

Tank Canyon	Mohave	T34N R15W
Tank Canyon	Pima	T18S R11E
Tank Canyon	Yavapai	T11N R5E
Tank Creek	Yavapai	(1) T14N R6W (2) T10N R3E
Tank Creek Mesa	Yavapai	T14N R6W
Tank Gulch	Gila	T11N R8E
Tank Hill	Cochise	T23S R24E

Before Tombstone came into existence, people lived at Watervale, laying foundations for tents. After they moved to Tombstone, taking the tents with them, in 1879 they put a huge tin water tank on top of the hill, hence the name. Ref.: Nuttall

Tank House Canyon   See Rock House Canyon, Gila

Tank in the Road	Coconino	T15N R12E
Tank Mountains	Yuma	T4S R14W Elev. 2207'

Several natural water tanks give rise to this name. The northwest half of the range is called Frenchman Mountains and the east half is sometimes called Puzzles Mountain. Ref.: 335, p. 123

Tank Pass	La Paz	T6N R14W
Tank Wash	Yavapai	T13N R7W

TANNER CANYON

Coconino (Grand Canyon)   T31N R5E   Elev. c. 4500'

Because rustlers used it, it was called also Horse Thief Trail. At its base in 1886, William Bass came on five rustlers with eighteen freshly-branded horses. In 1889 Seth B. Tanner with Franklin French and others developed the old trail from the South Rim of the Grand Canyon to the Colorado River where it joins Nankoweap Trail to the North Rim. Hence it was a.k.a. Tanner-French Trail. The trail followed what in 1906 was named Tanner Canyon. Ref.: 178, p. 55; 5, p. 483; 323, p. 19, 179, pp. 242, 245

TANNER CROSSING

Coconino   T29N R9E   Elev. c 5000'

This crossing in December 1905 was named by the USGS for Joseph Tanner. It was near Cameron and had the only rocky bottom available in the vicinity to permit pioneers to avoid treacherous quicksands while crossing the Little Colorado River. Ref.: 329

TANNER SPRINGS

Apache   T22N R25E   Elev. 5685'

This location in 1851 was called La Xara Springs, and in 1859 Ojo La Xara. By 1876 it was being called Jara Springs. When Seth B. Tanner (see Tanner Canyon, Coconino (Grand Canyon)) opened a trading post here, it carried his name. It was not always a peaceful place, for here in 1884 cowboys had a bloody fight with Navajo Indians, both groups wishing to use its water. Ref.: 331, p. 154

TANQUE   pro.: /tǽnkiy/

Spanish = "tank"

Graham   T9S R27E   Elev. 3259'

The Arizona & Eastern R.R. put in a water tank to service steam engines at this location, hence its name. Ref.: 18a

TANQUE VERDE

Pima   T13S R15E   Elev. 2600'

The present-day community is not the same as that on GLO 1892, which was close to Fort Lowell. See Tanque Verde Ranch, Pima

TANQUE VERDE RANCH   pro.: /tánkə vérdi/ or /tǽnki vérdi/

Spanish = "green tank"

Pima   T13S R17E

In 1862 or 1863 William Oury (see Oury, Mount, Pima) established the Tanque Verde Ranch for his blooded cattle, numbering about five hundred. (Ed.: This place had nothing to do with the extensive Juan Tellez property to the south in the Rincon Mountains Valley). On moonlit nights Apaches raided his herds, and to stop them Oury went to the ranch to live. One moonlit night he and his men hid and waited around the brush corral. The men were told not to shoot until the Indians had killed an animal and began skinning it. They heard an owl hoot, a usual Apache signal. The Indians came on to the corral, killed a steer, and started to skin it. Oury and his men fired, killing three Apaches. After that, Indians stayed away. Other settlers began moving in to run cattle on the same range. A small community developed, called Tanque Verde. The name Tanque Verde comes from the presence of some fairly large water holes containing green algae, at the base of Tanque Verde Ridge (T14S/R17E), a northwestern extension of the Rincon Mountains. The ridge should not be confused with the Agua Verde Range (Roskruge, 1893), which is actually a ridge extending west from the Southern end of the Rincon Mountains. Associated names include Tanque Verde Canyon (T13S/R17E), Creek (in the canyon), Falls, Mountains (a variant name for the Rincons), Peak (T14S/R17E, Elev. 7040'), and Wash. An early name is that of Tanque Verde Hot Springs. In 1881 these were known as Fuller's Springs and Resort, and also as Agua Caliente, names in use at least as early as 1872. Ref.: *Tucson Citizen* (April 13, 1872), p. 2; *Tucson Directory* (1881), p. 47; 81, p. 238

TANTO (*sic*) MOUNTAINS

Yavapai

This is the name which shows on Jan.-Feb.-March 1866 map by Clarence King and J.T. Gardner, northeast of Fort Whipple. The name is given as Tanto Mountains or Plateau and shows on the east side of the Prescott Plains. Ref.: 242

TAPCO (R.R. STN.)

Yavapai   T16N R3E   Elev. c. 3500'

This place name on the Drake and Clarksdale branch of the S.F.R.R. was derived by taking the first letters of the following: *The Arizona Power Company.* Ref.: 242

TAPEATS CREEK

Coconino (Grand Canyon)   T35N R1W

On September 6, 1872 Dr. A.H. Thompson wrote that Ta Pits was the name of this creek. Dellenbaugh spelled it Tapeets and said it was so called after a Piute Indian who owned it. Locally it was often called Thunder River because of the noise as it rushes through a rocky gorge where it is fed by Thunder Spring. Maj. Clarence E. Dutton notes that a trail, Tapeats Trail, T35N/R2W, was created on the north side of Tapeats Amphitheater in 1876 as a result of a rumored finding of placer gold in the Colorado River bed. Dutton's party used the disintegrating trail in 1880. Associated names include Thunder Cave, Thunder Spring, Trail, and also Tapeats Amphitheater, Cave, Rapids (T34N/R2W), Spring (T29N/R9), Terrace (T34N/R1W), and Trail.
Ref.: 88, p. 240; 322, 329, p. 98; Grand Canyon, Place Names File, Feb. 25, 1937; 100, p. 159; Dellenbaugh, Letter to Mrs. Rose Hamblin (Aug. 25, 1934)

TAPPAN SPRING

Coconino   T29N R9E

This spring takes its name from that of Joe B. Tappan, a sheepman (1887). It was also used by rustlers as their headquarters c. 1880 until cowboys caught up with them. Thereafter wandering cowboys or cattlemen during branding sessions occasionally stopped here. Associated names include Tappan Spring Canyon, and Tappan Wash (T29N/R6E), until 1964 called Cedar Wash.
Ref.: 166, p. 64; 119, p. 122; AHS Names File

TARTRON

Maricopa   T6S R8W   Elev. c. 900'

This was a steam engine water replenishment stop on the S.P.R.R. The reason for the name is not known.

TATAI TOAK

Papago: *tatai* = "road runner; *toak* = "mountain"

Pima   T12S R2W

This small settlement borrows its name from a nearby mountain called Road Runner Mountain (Elev. 2480') and the settlement has been called Road Runner (*WPA Guide Book*; 1953 Phoenix Aero Chart). It has been misspelled Tatria Toak and Tatia Toak. Ref.: 329; 58

TATK KAM VO

Papago = "root place charco" (pond)

Pima   T16S R4E

This is, or was, a small Papago village three and one-half miles southwest of Pisinimo. Ref.: 262, p. 10

TATKUM VO

Papago = "snorer's charco" (pond)

Pima   T16S R4E   Elev. 1220'

This small village on the Papago Reservation has also been known as Serape (1938 base map, Chukut Kuk District). Ref.: 262, p. 3

TAT MOMOLI

Pima: *tat* = "foot"; *mumeri* = "run"; *kut* = "wear"

Pinal   T9S R5E   Elev. 1550'

This village, which Bryan called Taht Mahmeli, was near the now-abandoned Jack Rabbit Mine. According to tradition, the Indian name reflects the fact that Kohatk Pima Indians held foot races. Indians are such fleet runners that they can catch rabbits by hand. A variant spelling for this location is Tatatamumerikut (1912, Lumholtz). The name is shared by the Tat Momoli Mountains (a.k.a. Silver Reef Mountains in one section), Pass (T9S/R4E), Valley (T9S/R5E), and Wash (Pinal/Pima; T9S/R5E), until 1941 spelled Tat Mahmeli Wash. Ref.: 58, p. 262; pp. 16, 19, 22, 28; 57, p. 391

TAWA POINT

Apache   T19N R24E

Should be spelled Tewa Point, for the Tewa Indians.

TAWAHPAH

Navajo = "the spring of the Sun"

Navajo   T28N R18E

This name has occasionally been spelled Tawaph, a corruption. Ref.: 79, p. 341

TAYLOR

Navajo   T12N R21E   Elev. 5630'

The first community called Taylor was on the Little Colorado River at T18N/R19E where John Kartchner and eight Mormon families from Utah started a community on January 22, 1878. Between that date and July, they built five dams, every one of which washed out. They then moved to Silver Creek where Daniel Bagley had already settled. Under John Kartchner they arrived here in January 1878 from the first Taylor. The settlers selected the name Walker for their post office, but the Post Office Department turned it down as there was already a Walker post office in Arizona Territory. The Mormons then selected Taylor to honor John Taylor, English-born president of the Church of Jesus Christ of Latter-Day Saints, wounded by the mob which killed Joseph Smith in 1844.

P.O. est. March 28, 1881, Jesse N. Perkins, p.m.

Ref.: 225, pp. 148, 166, 167; 116, p. 564

TAYLOR BUTTE

Cochise   T22S R27E   Elev. 4659'

This butte was named for the owner of its stone quarry. A very similar butte nearby has led to their being called Twin Buttes. Ref.: 18a

TAYLOR PASS

Graham   T8S R23E

This place was named for John Taylor, a Mormon, who maintained a small sawmill nearby. It was so named c. 1932. Ref.: 329

TAYLOR'S FERRY

La Paz   T1N R23W

This ferry was in existence in 1946, but the reason for the name other than the possibility Taylor was the owner can only be conjectured. Ref.: 242

TEAMSTERS CAMP

Yuma   T7S R13W   Elev. c. 500'

Teamsters' Camp Station was in operation in January 1872. The turn off on the old route to the Ajo Mining District was about four miles west of this station, and one may conjecture that perhaps freight wagon teamsters used this as a stopping point, hence the name. Ref.: *Weekly Arizona Miner* (Jan. 30, 1872), p. 2; *Arizona Sentinel* (Jan. 11, 1879), p. 3

TEAPOT MOUNTAIN

Coconino

This location in Oak Creek Canyon northeast of Sedona resembles a giant teapot with a distinctly separated spout.

TEAPOT MOUNTAIN

Pinal   T3S R13E   Elev. 3400'

This location is also called Tea Kettle Mountain. It has both names because it looks like a tea pot. Ref.: 10, p. 69

TEEC NOS POS TRADING POST

Apache   T41N R30E   Elev. 5368'

In 1961 several names were eliminated in favor of that given above. They are as follows: Carrizo; Teecenaspas; Tesnospas; Tisnasbas. Associated names include Tec Nos Pos Wash, Teec Nos Pos Canyon (also spelled Tisnasbas), and Teec Nos Pos Wash. Tees or Tes Nos Pos are variant spellings. Ref.: 329

TEEL CANYON

Pinal   T2S R12E

This name, in use since the early 1900s, is that of an early settler here. Ref.: 329

TEEPEES, THE

Apache   T18N R24E   Elev. c. 5600'

These eroded sandstone formations in the Petrified Forest National Monument strongly resemble Indian teepees. Ref.: 5, p. 312; Branch

TEES TO pro.: /tʔiyvsto/

Navajo: *tees* = "cottonwood trees"; *to* = "water"

Navajo   T24N R18E   Elev. 5745'

This name has also been spelled Teas Toh. In 1930 when the Cedar Springs Store and Trading Post was abandoned and its operation moved to Juan Lorenzo Hubbell's Trading Post (also at this location), the name Cedar Springs was dropped. Tees Toh Wash is also here (a.k.a. Seba Dalkai Wash, North Fork Corn Creek, and Corn Wash (1966)).

P.O. est. as Cedar Springs, April 1, 1910, Charles Hubbell, p.m.; name changed to Tees To, June 18, 1930; disc. Feb. 29, 1934 Ref.: 242; 18a

TELEGRAPH CANYON
Pinal   T2S R12E
The first telegraph line to serve Superior went through this canyon.   Ref.: Craig

TELEGRAPH PASS
Maricopa   T1S R3E   Elev. 1980'
The military telegraph line from San Diego reached Maricopa Wells in October 1873.
At that point it branched, one line running to Tucson and the other to Phoenix and
Prescott through this pass in the Salt River Mountains.
Ref.: Kitt; *Weekly Citizen* (Oct. 25, 1873), p. 3

TEMPE   pro.: /tempiy/
Maricopa   T1N R4E   Elev. 1159'
Charles Trumbull Hayden (b. April 4, 1825, Connecticut; d. Feb. 5, 1900) arrived in
Tucson in 1857 on the first Butterfield Overland Mail coach. In 1871 he established a
flour mill at the site of the future Tempe and also set up a ferry across the Salt River,
hence the name Hayden's Ferry. Because it was close to a butte, the location was
sometimes called Butte City, but the name gradually shifted by 1879 to Hayden's Butte
and much later, to Tempe Butte (Elev. 1495'). According to Hinton there were extensive
prehistoric Indian ruins and canals, and Bartlett of the Boundary Survey Commission
(1853) visited these ruins at what Hinton calls La Tempe. Darrell Duppa is credited
with giving the name Tempe to the area, borrowing it from a vale in Greece. The name
was applied to an area which was a plain. When Mormons arrived in 1875 and camped
on the north side of the river, they learned that "Tempe or Hayden's Mill" would be a
good place to stop for a few days. The Mormons prospered and on July 23, 1882 bought
Hayden's eighty acres of land between his ferry and the Mexican town of San Pablo, by
then bearing the name Tempe. The name of the post office had already been changed to
Tempe.
P.O. est. as Hayden's Ferry, April 25, 1872, John J. Hill, p.m.; changed to Tempe, May
5, 1879; Wells Fargo 1888; incorporated Nov. 26, 1894   Ref.: *Arizona Miner* (Nov.
9, 1872), p. 1; *Phoenix Herald* (Nov. 27, 1894), p. 1; 163, pp. 410, 411; 225, pp. 198,
219; 116, p. 465, Note 6

TEMPLE, THE
Mohave (Lake Mead)   c. T30N R19W
This location was named in the early 1870s by Daniel Bonelli. He called it the Mormon
Temple, but the name has since been shortened.   Ref.: 259, p. 36

TEMPLE BAR
Mohave   T30N R19W   Elev. 1250'
A resort community has arisen at the Temple Bar boat anchorage. In the 1880s a small
mining camp existed here or very close to it. The name is borrowed from that of The
Temple. An associated name is Temple Wash, until 1948 a.k.a. Temple Bar Wash. See
Bonelli's Crossing, Mohave, and The Temple, Mohave   Ref.: 329

TEMPLE BUTTE
Coconino (Grand Canyon)   T32N R5E
This name was applied in May 1932 by the USGS to this butte, which looks like a
temple. Ref. 329

TEMPLE ROAD
Mohave/Utah   T41-38N R9-10W
In the 1870s Mormons hauled timber from Mount Trumble to build St. George Temple,
Utah. The route was also called Temple Trail. According to Barnes, engaged couples
made the three hundred and fifty mile journey by wagon from Little Colorado
settlements and others in northern Arizona "across the Colorado on Lees Ferry and up
through Buckskin Mountains and down the Hurricane Ledge to St. George . . . as a
preliminary to marriage."   Ref.: 42, p. 58; 18a

TEMPLE TRAIL TANK
Mohave   T38N R9W   Elev. 5450'

This stock tank is on the road used by builders of the Mormon Temple at St. George, Utah, in the early 1870s to haul timber from Mount Trumbull to the temple site.   Ref.: 18a

TEN-MILE CAMP
Maricopa   T8S R10W

In 1857 this stage station on the San Diego mail route lay ten miles west of Gila Ranch, hence the name. It was on Tenmile Wash.   Ref.: 73, II, 173, 174

TENMILE WELL
La Paz   T8N R18W

This cattle well owned by Thomas W. Bales is ten miles southeast of Bouse and the same distance northwest of Desert Well, hence the name.   Ref.: 279, p. 223

TENNESSEE GULCH
Mohave   T23N R18W

This gulch takes its name from that of the Tennessee Mine owned by the Tennessee Mining Company in 1906. The mine has been in operation since c. 1890. It was a lead mine.   Ref.: 200, pp. 52, 55

TENNEY'S GULCH
Coconino   T35N R5W   Elev. c. 6000'

In 1870 Ammon Tenney, in company with Mormon guide Jacob Hamblin, explored this part of Arizona with Maj. John Wesley Powell. Tenney Spring is here.
Ref.: 18a; AHS Names File

TENNY FLAT
Navajo   T9N R23E

This is named for a settler whose name is spelled "Tenney" by Barnes and "Tenny" in the Arizona Historical Society Names File. It has been misspelled Tinny. See Woodruff, Navajo

TERESA MOUNTAINS, SANTA
Graham   T5S R20E   Elev. 8282'

This name, sometimes spelled Santa Theresa, appears on military maps of the early 1880s. The origin of the name has not been learned.   Ref.: 242

TERMINUS
This was a post office maintained aboard a railroad car which escorted the work crews for the laying of the railroad rails across Arizona. The post office originated at Yuma and went out of existence on the eastern boundary of the territory.
P.O. est. Jan. 27, 1879, Frank B. Wightman, p.m.; disc. April 11, 1881; Wells Fargo 1879

TEWA   pro.: /téowᵛa/
Navajo   T28N R18E   Elev. 6200'

In the 1680 Pueblo Rebellion against Spanish rule, four thousand Tewa Indians were reduced to one thousand. The Spaniards were ousted but returned in 1693 and enslaved most remaining Tewa. In 1696 two hundred men, women, and children escaped, going first to the Zuni villages. Peaceful Hopi, recognizing what astute warriors the Tewa were, invited the homeless people to settle among the Hopi, the idea being that the Tewa would fight battles for the Hopi tribe. They settled on First Mesa at Tewa Spring. The name Hano is a contraction of the Hopi word for this group, *anopi* (= "eastern people"). They remain a distinct group. Military maps occasionally show their location under the name Tegua.
P.O. est. Aug. 10, 1900, Sarah E. Abbott, p.m.; resc. Jan. 15, 1901
Ref.: 95, pp. 127, 130; 167, p. 531

TEXAS CANYON
Cochise   T16S R22E   Elev. c. 5400'
First mapped in 1869, this canyon was called Quercus Canyon. *Quercus* means "dwarf oak," which grows abundantly in this region, according to Antisell of the Boundary Survey Commission in 1854. The unusual name was susceptible to misspelling, and in 1864 it was altered to Querhus Canyon. The Gird map (1864) shows Dragoon Springs in what is called Querous Canyon. Still later the name was corrupted to Quihuis Canyon. Conkling in discussing the stage route calls it Cuercas Canyon. The high hopes of the David Adams family of Texas to reach the west coast were ruined in this canyon where Indians stole Adams' horses and left him and his family completely destitute. With his brothers Will and Wilbur, he settled on nearly level ground, calling it Adams Flat. Texas Canyon is named for their native state. The main highway across southern Arizona traverses this canyon, which has superb scenery. The road passes through a mass of jumbled rocks of incredible shapes, their color varying from pink to deepest amethyst.   Ref.: Nuttall; Bennett; 73, II, 140

TEXAS HILL WILD LIFE AREA
Yuma
This wild area contains one thousand two hundred ninety-two acres. It was established in 1961. See Stoval, Yuma   Ref.: 9, p. 1

TEX CANYON
Cochise   T20S R29E
This canyon at the southern end of the Chiricahua Mountains was named for Scott (Tex) Whaley, one of two whites who accompanied Lt. Charles B. Gatewood on his journey to see Geronimo in 1886. Tex homesteaded here.
Ref.: AHS, Neil Erickson, Letter (Nov. 17, 1926)

T-4 SPRINGS
Santa Cruz   T21S R18E
This series of springs in a small wash takes its name from a cattle brand used here in the 1880s.   Ref. 329

THATCHER
Graham   T7S R25E   Elev. 3929'
In July 1881 John M. Moody bought the Conley Ranch. In 1882 Moody was joined by four additional Mormon families. Christopher Layton selected the town site on May 13, 1883. He decided on another one a half mile south on higher land in 1885 and bought it on October 9. The name Thatcher was selected as the result of the Christmas visit by Mormon apostles Moses Thatcher and Erasmus Snow in 1882.
P.O. est. March 10, 1888, Mrs. Elizabeth Layton, p.m.; Wells Fargo 1903
Ref.: 353, pp. 15, 42; 225, p. 249

THEBA
Yuma   T6S R5W   Elev. c. 800'
The origin of this name is not known. It is today a railroad stop at the headquarters of Gillespie Farms.   Ref.: Stout

THEODORE ROOSEVELT DAM
Gila   T4N R12E   Elev. 2146'
The dam was erected at a ford used by Indians to cross the Salt River at the mouth of Tonto Creek. From at least 1882 ranchers and farmers called this place The Crossing. A settlement developed, which is today under waters impounded by the dam. The first stone for the future dam, at the time called Tonto Dam, was laid on September 20, 1906 and the structure completed on February 5, 1911. On April 15, 1915, water overflowed the dam. As this happened several more times, the spillways were raised c. 1936. The rising impounded waters caused the relocation of the settlement at the crossing and the town of Roosevelt was consequently moved. Commonly referred to as Roosevelt Dam, the dam name was officially changed by Congress in August 1959 to Theodore Roosevelt Dam.
P.O. est. Jan. 22, 1904, William A. Thompson, p.m.
Ref.: Woody; 5, pp. 366, 367; 83, pp. 159, 160; State Library Files

THEODORE ROOSEVELT LAKE
Gila/Maricopa   T4N R11E
Theodore Roosevelt Lake was created by waters impounded behind Theodore Roosevelt
Dam. The lake is twenty-three miles long. See Theodore Roosevelt Dam, Gila

THIMBLE MOUNTAIN
Mohave   T19N R19W   Elev. 4062'
This mountain looks like a thimble, hence the name. Originally it was known locally as
Squaw Tit, but in 1968 residents were willing to accept a substitute as the original name
might be "considered objectionable."   Ref.: 329

THIMBLE PEAK
Pima   T5S R7E   Elev. 1750'
This peak looks like a thimble on top of a rock point.   Ref.: 329

THIN MOUNTAIN
Pinal   T5S R7E   Elev. 1750'
The mountain is thin, hence the name. See Sacaton, Pinal

THIRD FOREST
Navajo
This is the last of three petrified-log forests encountered by visitors making the north-
south tour through the Petrified Forest National Monument. See Petrified Forest
National Monument.

THIRD MESA
Navajo   T29N R16E   Elev. c. 6500'
This mesa is west of Second Mesa, one of three occupied by Hopi villages. Oraibi and
Hotevilla are on Third Mesa. See Hopi Villages, Navajo

THIRTEEN MILE ROCK
Yavapai   T13N R6E   Elev. 5514'
The name derived from the fact that this prominent rock is thirteen miles east of Camp
Verde on the old military road.   Ref.: Goddard; 18a

THIRTEEN MILE TANK
Coconino   T13N R7E
This tank on the railroad was thirteen miles from Ashfork. The use of diesel engines has
made such water stops obsolete and this tank has almost disappeared, but the name
remains attached to Thirteen Mile Spring (T13N/R6E).   Ref.: Slamon

THOMAS CREEK
Greenlee   T1N R30E   Elev. c. 6000'
This creek was named for Charley Thomas, a cattleman who wintered his steers here c.
1940.   Ref.: Mrs. Fred Fritz, Sr.; Reilly

THOMAS, FORT
Graham   T4S R23E   Elev. 2713'
The location cited is that of the current community of Fort Thomas, now called
Geronimo. Because of unhealthful conditions, soldiers were moved from Camp
Goodwin to what was later known as Fort Apache. When a suitable spot was found and a
fort established there on August 12, 1876 by Capt. Clarence M. Bailey, there was
nothing to hinder applying the old name Camp Thomas to the post and this was done.
The name Camp Thomas derives from that of Brig. Gen. Lorenzo Thomas (d. March 2,
1875). It was six miles east of the old Camp Goodwin and three-quarters of a mile south
of the Gila River. The name was changed to Camp Apache in 1871. On May 18, 1877
the name was changed again to Fort Thomas.
    As old Camp Goodwin had proved an expensive fraud as far as the government was
concerned, the greatest caution was used in establishing Fort Thomas. Funds for the
new post were few. By 1879 Fort Thomas had only two adobe barracks, one two-room
adobe shack for the commanding officer and his family, a guard house, and an adjutant's

office. The soldiers built these structures themselves at no expense to the government. Only the post trader had decent quarters. When funds finally became available in 1884, a handsome post came in existence. It was a little late, for Geronimo surrendered in 1886 and that was the beginning of the end for Fort Thomas. It was abandoned on November 22, 1892.

Prior to the establishment of the military encampment, the Indians had a name for the location which they continued to use: *Ta-lar-che* (= "it belongs to the Indians"). The community still in existence bears the name of a leading Apache, Geronimo, whose capture caused the demise of the military encampment. Around old Fort Thomas a community took shape (see Maxey, Graham). The town of Geronimo was on the site of the Fort Thomas establishment in 1876 by Capt. Bailey.

Here in the summer of 1895 the railroad plans to lay lines across the Gila Valley were stopped in their tracks. The Apache Indians steadfastly refused to permit the line to cross their reservation. The dispute was resolved by agreeing to allow Apaches free train rides. There has been some confusion about the post offices at Maxey and at Ft. Thomas, which were adjacent to each other. The name changes are given below:
P.O. est. as Camp Goodwin (at old site), March 5, 1875, Thomas McWilliams, p.m.; transferred to new post and in existence until disc. Oct. 18, 1880; p.o. at Maxey est. as Camp Thomas, March 2, 1877, Frank Staples, p.m.; name changed to Fort Thomas, Feb. 28, 1883; Wells Fargo 1903
Ref.: 121a, p. 12; 145, p. 157; 83, p. 31; 224, p. 156; 353, p. 52; 351; Lenon

THOMPSON BAY
Mohave   T13N R20W
This bay was named for Ben Thompson, assistant superintendent of the Lake Mead Recreation Area National Park Service in 1947.

THOMPSON CANYON
Coconino (Grand Canyon)   T33N R3E   Elev. 8250'
Two cattlemen named Van Slack and Thompson (b. 1820, Tennessee) ran livestock, using the VT brand. See De Motte Park, Coconino Ref.: 18a; 62

THOMPSON PEAK
Yavapai   T13N R6W   Elev. 4704'
This location was named for an early homesteader on whose land it is. It was also known as Bismarck Mountain. Ref.: 329

THOMPSON POINT
Coconino (Grand Canyon)   T34N R1W   Elev. 6920'
This location was named for Dr. A.H. Thompson, with Maj. John Wesley Powell's second Grand Canyon Expedition 1871-72. He was Powell's brother-in-law. Ref.: 100, p. 171; 329

THOMPSON VALLEY
Yavapai   T13N R6W
In 1869 this location is given as Tompkins Valley where an army skirmish against Indians occurred on November 10. The valley was named for Maj. John Thompson of the First New Mexico Volunteers, who had several skirmishes with Indians in this area. See Yava, Yavapai Ref.: *Arizona Miner* (June 10, 1871), p. 3; *Weekly Arizona Miner* (March 12, 1870), p. 3

THORN PEAK
Coconino   T13N R9W   Elev. 3851'
This peak was named for the commander of a little-known military expedition, Lt. Thorn, the escort for a Mr. Collier to California in 1859. Ref.: 224, p. 117

THOR'S HAMMER
Coconino (Grand Canyon)   T30N R4E   Elev. 7400'
James named this feature because of its resemblance to a hammer huge enough to be used by the god Thor. Thor Temple is at T32N/R4E (Elev. 6719'). Ref.: 178, p. 56

THOUSAND CAVE MOUNTAIN

Apache   T13N R30E   Elev. c. 5500'

Numerous caves here result in the name. Many Indian relics have been found in the caves.   Ref.: 18a; Shreve

THOUSAND POCKETS

Coconino   T41N R7E   Elev. c. 6000'

Maj. John Wesley Powell called this area Thousand Wells because of its numerous water pockets.   Ref.: 266, p. 189

THREE BAR WILD LIFE AREA

T3N R10E

This area has 38,897 acres with livestock grazing excluded so that wild game can be maintained and water shed studies conducted.
Ref.: *Wild Life Research in Arizona*, 1969-70, p. 85

THREE BUTTES

Pinal   T9S R12E   Elev. 3379'

The name is descriptive.

THREE MILE LAKE

Coconino   T22N R2W   Elev. c. 6500'

Three Mile Lake lies that distance from Williams, hence its name. It is a wet weather lake.   Ref.: Benham; 18a

THREE POINTS

Pima   T15S R10E

The road from Tucson until c. 1980 had a junction forming a *Y* here with one branch going to Sells and the other to Sasabe, hence the name Three Points. It is also called Robles Junction.

THREE R CANYON

Santa Cruz   T22S R15E   Elev. 5400'

This canyon or gulch takes its name from the presence of the Three R Mine, in operation in the early 1900s. Three R Mountain shares the name.   Ref.: 286, p. 282

THREE SISTERS

Navajo   T41N R21E   Elev. 6313'

This is a descriptive name for a fantastic formation in Monument Valley.

THREE SISTERS BUTTES

Cochise   T16S R25E   Elev. 4827'

These buttes resemble each other. Their descriptive name has been in use since at least 1870.   Ref.: 163, p. 231

THREE SISTERS BUTTES

Mohave   T20N R10W

These buttes huddle together like closely allied sisters, hence the name.   Ref.: Harris

THREE SISTERS PEAKS

Coconino   T22N R1E   Elev. 7643'

They are close together and look alike.   Ref.: Fuchs

THREE TURKEY CANYON

Apache   T4N R9W

This is the location of Three Turkey House Ruins, so named because the cliff house has three red and white turkeys painted on the plastered walls of one of the cliff houses.   Ref.: 331, p. 157

THUMB BUTTE

Graham/Greenlee   T7S R29E   Elev. 5120'

Like other locations, this one is named because it looks like a thumb. The following are examples:

Thumb Butte	Mohave	T21N R20W	Elev. 3168'
Thumb Butte	Santa Cruz	T23S R12E	Elev. 5300'
Thumb Butte	Yavapai	T14N R3W	Elev. 6522'
Thumb Butte	Yuma	T5S R18W	Elev. 2120'

This one looks more like a mitten than a thumb.

Thumb Peak	Yuma	T4S R18W	Elev. 3407'

THURBER'S CAMP

Coconino   T25N R6E

When J.W. Thurber ran a stage line from Flagstaff to the Grand Canyon, he maintained a way station here at Sunset Point, the terminus of the stage line. He sold out to Martin Buggeln in June 1901. Ref.: Museum of Northern Arizona; 240, p. 142

TIDWELL WASH

Gila   T3N R17E

Silas Tidwell constructed a relatively unsuccessful ore mill here in the 1870s. Ref. 18a

TIGER

Pinal   T8S R16E   Elev. 3200'

This community was named for the Tiger Mine despite a local legend that residents chose the name for their post office because one of them had a tobacco pouch made from a tiger scrotum.

P.O. est. April 20, 1939, Thomas Leo Chapman, p.m.; disc. Nov. 26, 1954

TIGER

Yavapai   T10N R1W   Elev. 6500'

This community developed in 1880 around the Tiger Mine, which gave the name Tiger to the entire mining district, including Tiger Canyon (T9N/R1W) and Tiger Creek. It was one of the richest silver mines in Arizona Territory and the first silver mine of importance discovered in northern Arizona. Ref.: Theobald; 146, p. 50

TILLMAN DRAW

Coconino   T15N R13E

This may have been named for John Tillman (b. 1837, Russia), who was at Spencer's Ranch in the 1880s. Ref.: 63

TILTED MESA

Coconino (Grand Canyon)   T33N R5E   Elev. 5500'

George Wharton James gave this location the descriptive name Tilts. The name Tilted Mesa, suggested by Francois E. Matthes, describes the sloping tableland west of Marble Gorge. Ref.: 178, p. 71; 221

TIMBER CAMPS MOUNTAIN

Gila   T4N R17E   Elev. 6527'

The name derives from the presence of a sawmill (c. 1874), which cut timber for the mine shafts. The USGS name Three Camp Mountain was never used locally. Ref.: 10, p. 135; 329; 182

TINAJA PEAK   pro.: /tináha/

Spanish: *tinaja* = "tank or water hole"

Pima   T18S R12E   Elev. 4515'

According to Barnes this is a descriptive name. There are natural water holes here.

TINAJAS pro.: /tənáhas/
Spanish: *tinajas* = "water holes or tanks"
Yuma   At mouth of Gila River
Hodge believes that this former Yuma rancheria just southeast of the mouth of the Gila
River was named by Fr. Eusebio Kino in 1699. It has had a number of other names as
follows: La Tinaoca (1701, Kino); Tinajas de Candelaria (1776, de Anza and Font);
Tinaxa (1702, Kino); Candelaria (1777, Font).   Ref.: 167, II, 754

TINAJAS ALTAS pro.: /tənéyhas áltəs/
Spanish: *tinajas* = "water holes or tanks" *altas* = "high"
Yuma   T13S R17W   Elev. 2764'
As these tanks are on the old Camino del Diablo, they were much used by emigrants.
From eight to ten water holes in rock crevices are in the Tinajas Altas Mountains. Many
mortar holes are near these tanks, evidence that they were used by Indians long before
white men ever saw the watering places. These tanks are highly visible from the east.
They are probably not those visited in 1698 by Fr. Kino, as witness his name of Agua
Escondida (Spanish = "hidden water"). Jacobo Sedelmayr may have visited these
tanks on November 23, 1750, for he wrote "of a spot in which there were three tanks of
high elevation." He did not, however, apply a name. Lt. N. Michler of the Boundary
Survey Commission in 1854 wrote that Mexicans called these tanks "*tinejas altas . . .
natural wells formed in the gulleys . . . there are eight of these tinejas, one above the
other, the highest two extremely difficult to reach.*" The name used by Americans today
is Dripping Springs. (See Dripping Springs, Yuma) Variant and curious misspellings
include Tinajualto, Tinaxa, Tinechas, and Tinejas Altos. Ref.: 227, p. 138; 106, p.
114; 369, p. 59; 287, pp. 68, 74; 43, pp. 412, 441; 57, pp. 414; 422; 5, pp. 389-390;
Lenon

TINAJAS ALTAS MOUNTAINS
Yuma   T13S R17W   Elev. 2764'
Until 1921 these mountains were mapped as part of the Lechuguilla Mountains. The
Tinajas Altas Mountains are separated from the Gila Mountains by a small pass, but
some consider them part of the Gila Mountains. The route from Wellton to these
mountains is called Smugglers Trail, as it was used by liquor smugglers during
Prohibition days. See Tinajas Altas, Yuma   Ref.: 5, pp. 389, 390; 58; 57, p. 426

TINAJAS ALTAS PASS
Yuma   T1S R17W
This long canyon-like pass is so narrow that some do not believe that it truly separates
the Tinajas Altas Mountains from the Gila Mountains and that in reality the mountains
are one group. The name of this pass is also sometimes give as Cipriano Pass for
Cipriano Ortega, who owned a well in the area. See Tinajas Altas, Yuma

TINAOCA, LA
Yuma
The name Tinaoca was on the Kino map of 1701 for the rancheria just southeast of the
mouth of the Gila River. See Dripping Springs, Yuma and Tinajas, Yuma

TINTOWN
Cochise   Elev. c. 6000'
Mexicans working for the Bisbee mines c. 1904 built houses of flattened tin cans, oil
containers, and scraps of discarded lumber to form their own community. Tintown
homes often housed two or three families. This place has disappeared.
Ref.: 5, pp. 378, 379

TIPOFF, THE
Coconino (Grand Canyon)   T31N R3E
At this point on the South Kaibab Trail begins a series of switchbacks at which the mule
rider or hiker "tips off" down toward the bottom of the Grand Canyon. The canyon
section is a.k.a. Tip Over Canyon (T34N/R2E). Tip Over Spring is in the canyon.
Ref.: 5, p. 493

TIPTON, MOUNT
Mohave   T2N R18W   Elev. 7148'
In 1858 a Lt. Tipton served with the expedition of Lt. Joseph Christmas Ives. Ref.: 182

TIP TOP
Yavapai   T8N R1E   Elev. 2500'
The name of this mine, which was discovered in 1875, came from the fact that it was
considered a "tip top" prospect, partially because from the viewpoint of "chloriders"
(old-time miners), it was a good place from which to haul rock for reduction elsewhere.
The area attracted enough people so that in 1897 Tip Top had a school. It has now
almost completely disappeared except for its cemetery.
P.O. est. as Tip Top Mine, March 4, 1875, Winthrop A. Rowe, p.m.; disc. Nov. 18,
1879; reest. as Tip Top, Aug. 12, 1880, Edwin G. Wager, p.m.; disc. Feb. 14,
1895   Ref.: Schnebly; Theobald; *Daily Arizona Journal-Miner* (Nov. 16, 1897), p. 4;
146, p. 51

TITHUMIJI POINT
Coconino (Grand Canyon)   T33N R3W   Elev. 5811'
A 1925 USGS decision used the name of a Havasupai Indian family for this location on
the South Rim. Ref.: 329

TIYO POINT
Coconino (Grand Canyon)   T32N R3E   Elev. 7762'
In March 1906 the USGS replaced the name Jupiter Point with the name Tiyo Point, for
the Hopi snake hero. Tiyo Point Trail is here.   Ref.: 329

TODASTONI WASH
Apache   T41N R30E
Gillmore spells this name Todanestya. As with other Indian place names, the name is
accurately descriptive of the location. In translation it means "the place where water
comes like fingers out of a hill."   Ref.: 129, p. 15

TODD BASIN
Mohave   c. T23N R18W   Elev. 2200'
Samuel Todd (b. 1820, Indiana; d. 1879), one of the founders of Mohave County and its
first treasurer, may be the person for whom this basin is named, but Mallach says it was
named for the Todd brothers who were the first to arrive at the basin, a statement which
seems closer to fact, as the mining area came into prominence after Samuel Todd's
death. Harris, a pioneer in the county, says it was named for John Todd, a miner. It
remained active from at least 1883 through about 1910.
Ref.: Mallach; Kitt; Harris; 63; 200, p. 16

TOHADISTOA SPRING
Navajo   T32N R21E
This place name is rather interesting because, although Gregory listed it in 1915 and
others picked it up, nothing that it means "bubbling water is here," apparently the water
was here but the Navajos did not say so. Hence it was withdrawn as a place name by the
USGS in 1969 because it was "not known locally." It was also spelled To'hah'le'tess'ta.
Ref.: 18a; 141, pp. 155, 196; 329

TOH AH CHI
Navajo: *to hach'l* = "dipping for water"
Navajo   T31N R16E
The name is descriptive of what occurs at this spring. The name is also spelled
Tohatchi.   Ref.: 331, p. 158

TOH CHIN LINI CANYON
Navajo = "canyon mouth"
Apache   T39N R28E
In 1960 the USGS changed the name from Chinlini Canyon to that given above. Toh

Chin Lini Mesa is at T40N/R29E (Elev. 6760'). See Walker Creek, Apache
Ref.: 329; 141, pp. 91, 191

TOH DE COZ SPRING   pro.: /tódik?ow:z/
Navajo: *toh* = "water"; *dikóózh* = "bitter"
Navajo   T31N R21E   Elev. c. 6000'
This locative name is also spelled Todokozh. According to Gregory, the word is applied
to several springs on the reservation. The bitter taste may come either from suplphur or
salts.   Ref.: 141, pp. 152, 158, 196

TOLANI LAKES   pro.: /tós^{s}ani/
Navajo: *to* = "water"; *thalini* = "many bodies together" or "much"
Coconino   T24N R14E
This name, recorded by Gregory in 1915, is descriptive. Several fresh water lakes are
scattered in seven basins where the divide separate the following three washes: Jadito,
First Mesa, and Oraibi.   Ref.: 141, pp. 39, 117

TOLCHICO
Navajo: *toecheekoh* = "ford"
Coconino   T34N R8E   Elev. c. 5000'
The name, also spelled Tolchaco, indicates the place is on the banks of the Little
Colorado River at a ford, which flows with water colored by red clay. Its first American
name was Woolf's Crossing. Here Hermann Wolf, or Woolf (b. 1810, Germany; d.
Jan., 1899), built a sandstone trading post and had a ferry. He moved here from his ranch
in Navajo County (see Woolf's Crossing) after having spent his life as a mountain man
(with Kit Carson, among others). According to notes in the Museum of Northern
Arizona, his trading store was about two miles south of Tolchaco. The location was also
known later as Voltz Crossing for another early trader at Oraibi and Canyon Diablo.
Both men tracked beaver in the marshes and swamps formerly in this vicinity. In 1904 a
Methodist mission was established at the vanishing trading post. The now-abandoned
site has nearly dissolved back into the desert. Tolchico Gap is nearby.
P.P. est. as Tolchaco, March 3, 1903, Charles Robinson, p.m.; disc. Aug. 31,
1922   Ref.: 242; 331, p. 159; 141, pp. 39, 196; 119, p. 305; Museum of Northern
Arizona

TOLFREE
Coconino (Grand Canyon)   T30N R5E   Elev. c. 6800'
This place took its name from that of its only postmaster, who had a hotel at the Grand
Canyon at the top of Hance Trail.
P.O. est. Aug. 13, 1894, Lyman H. Tolfree, p.m.; disc. Feb. 2, 1896
Ref.: 242; AHS Names File

TOLLESON
Maricopa   T1N R1E   Elev. 1016'
This station on the railroad was named by W.G. Tolleson for his family in 1912.
P.O. est. April 28, 1913, Leon H. Tolleson, p.m.; incorporated 1929
Ref.: 242; State Library Clipping File

TOLL GATE
Yavapai
William H. Hardy constructed a toll road from Mohave to Prescott in 1871. He
maintained a toll gate, called Tollgate Camp. Pioneers who created such roads
customarily collected tolls from others using them. See Hualpai, Camp, Yavapai, and
Aztec Pass, Yavapai   Ref.: *Arizona Miner* (Nov. 25, 1871), p. 1

TOLLHOUSE CANYON
Greenlee/Graham   T6S R30E
This canyon is adjacent to Tollgate Canyon. An old toll road once followed this canyon
to a low pass over the Peloncillo Mountains.   Ref.: 329

TOLTEC   pro.: /tówltek/

Pinal   T7S R7E   Elev. 1505'

When Frank Hamilton Cushing studied prehistoric Indians in the Casa Grande area c. 1888, he classified them with those of Toltec Indians. Later investigations demonstrated that the Indians were not Toltecs. However, a post office was established at this location and took its name from that of the railroad station here. Associated names include Toltec Buttes. Toltec City is a variant and Totec is a misspelling.

P.O. est. June 24, 1892, Julia S. Fishback, p.m.; order resc. Aug. 24, 1892; reest. March 5, 1910, Charles Lazier, p.m.; disc. July 31, 1922; reest. as Toltec City; disc. Jan. 1, 1966   Ref.: 242; 297, pp. 51, 52

TOLTEC POINT

Coconino (Grand Canyon)   T32N R1W   Elev. 6470'

This location was named in 1908 in accordance with the USGS policy of naming locations at the Grand Canyon for Indian tribes. Prior to 1900 one archeological theory concerning Indians in Arizona asserted that Toltec Indians from Mexico lived as far north as the Gila River.

TOMBSTONE

Cochise   T20S R22E   Elev. 4563'

Ed Schieffelin (d. May 12, 1897) is responsible for the name of this community. He was at Signal (Mohave) when he learned he could travel with military men through Indian-infested southeastern Arizona. A miner differs from a prospector in that the miner takes over what the prospector locates, and prospectors have an insatiable love for the quest. Schieffelin was a prospector, so he packed his few belongings and off he went. He was at Camp Huachuca in the fall of 1877. It was in the heart of Apache land, and a bloody land it was. To prospector Schieffelin the bare, richly colored hills northeast looked promising. He disregarded warnings that if he were to go along in that direction, he would find his tombstone rather than a mine. Alone, he cautiously made his way, camping at night without fires and making no move without carefully inspecting the landscape for Apaches. He took care to camp, not beside water, but near it, crawling slowly to water at night, then creeping back again to shelter for sleep. In September 1879, he made his first strike. Recalling the dire warnings, he named it Tombstone and hastened northwest to Signal to have ore assayed by Richard Gird. He also wanted to enlist the aid of his brother Al. The ore was so rich that Al, Gird, and Ed left for the Tombstone location. There they settled down at a place which in 1879 was called Gird Camp. The boom was on. A tent community arose near what was later called Tank Hill about three miles west of present Tombstone. Lack of water there was a major problem, although there was a running stream. Near its base was the community of Watervale. The name Tank Hill came into existence as the miners moved away and a water tank was set up on the hill. Watervale (T22S/R19E) was temporary, for it lacked room for building permanent structures and the hordes of newcomers preferred a level place for their town.

The indefatigable John B. Allen (see Gunsight, Pima), whose stores arose as fast as mining communities died, in 1879 was called the "founder of Tombstone City" where he was in the van, building the first permanent home. By the end of 1879 Tombstone had about one hundred permanent residents plus at least a thousand others camped in tents on nearby hills. The Tombstone Town Association had been formed on March 5, 1879 because Richmond and the small community on the grounds of the west side mine could not contain the increasing population. Richmond was so named by Virginians who flocked to the region. Tombstone took its name from its first and most successful mine.

By late 1881 Tombstone had become one of the largest cities in the west. Badmen who whooped it up in Tombstone were peaceful, compared to the ruckus they created at nearby Charleston or across the valley in the mountains at Galeyville. Often overlooked is the fact that Tombstone was probably the most cultured city west of the Mississippi. At that time it had a population of fifteen thousand and was larger than San Francisco. At its opera house the best of the world's musicians and actors performed. Ironically, although water was scarce in the mines it drowned Tombstone's hopes and plans. As the mining shafts plunged ever deeper, moisture began seeping in. When the shafts reached five hundred feet, pumping had to be initiated, but it did little good. Furthermore, the surface pumps at the Grand Central and Contention Mine burned in 1886, and in 1887 the mining shafts they served filled rapidly with water. As the mines flooded, the town began to shrivel and by 1890 Tombstone was nearly dead. In 1901 a serious effort was made to pump out the mines. It achieved partial success but in 1909 the everlasting water overworked the pumps. They stopped, and again water flooded the mines. The town, however, took pride in calling itself the "town too tough to die." For years it led an anemic existence, barely tottering along. As the past receded, the town has become increasingly interesting and today the community flourishes as a tourist attraction.

Ed Schieffelin, ever the prospector, departed to seek wealth from the earth in the far away Yukon. His search came full circle when his body was brought years later for permanent burial at the place where he had crept at night to obtain water while waiting to make his strike at Tombstone. He was interred there at his own request. He once said that the two most glorious nights he had ever known were those during which he had slept on the hill where he is now buried on the outskirts of Tombstone.

As for Tombstone, it served as the seat for Cochise County from 1881 to 1929 when the county seat was moved to Bisbee. It shares its name with Tombstone Canyon (T23S/R24E), Gulch, Hills (Elev. 4974'), a.k.a. The Burros (to distinguish them from their larger neighbor, the Mule Mountains. Tombstone Canyon is a.k.a. Mule Gulch. P.O. est. Dec. 2, 1878, Richard Gird, p.m.; Wells Fargo 1885; incorporated Jan. 3, 1881 Ref.: Nuttal; Macia; *Bisbee Review;* State Library Clipping File; *Weekly Arizona Star* (March 13, 1879), p. 3, and (Sept. 18, 1879), n.p.; 146, p. 35; *Bisbee Daily Review* (Aug. 3, 1931); 241, pp. 14, 15

TOM KETCHUM CANYON
Cochise   T21S R29E
This canyon took its name from that of a prominent pioneer who had holdings here c. 1915.   Ref.: Riggs

TOM MIX WASH
Pinal   T7S R11E   Elev. c. 1800'
Tom Mix (b. Jan. 6, 1880; d. Oct. 12, 1940), possibly the most popular western star of the 1920s, was killed in this wash when his car went out of control and turned over. There is a rest stop dedicated to him nearby.

TOM'S CREEK
Coconino   T13N R9E   Elev. c. 6500'
Tom Maitell, known locally as "Greasy Tom," was the first settler and built his cabin on this creek.   Ref.: 18a

TOM THUMB BUTTE
Maricopa   T10S R3W
Tom Childs, a local rancher, probably gave the descriptive name for this butte. Ref.: Stout

TONALEA   pro.: /tóniˇhēlɪ̃ʌ/
Navajo: *to* = "water"; *neheelii* = "where it sinks in"
Coconino   T34N R13E   Elev. 5600'
The first name suggested for the post office here was Red Lake. Originally this location was an ephemeral sink, eliminated by an earth-dam storage lake. The community is on a small hill overlooking the site. Because the name Red Lake is so common in Navajo country, the present name was substituted as being more distinctive.
P.O. est. July 3, 1925, John Patrick O'Farrell, p.m.
Ref.: 242; 331, p. 160; 141, p. 107

TONOKA   pro.: /tənuykə/
Papago: *tohnk* = "dike, dam"
Pima   T16S R4W   Elev. c. 2000'
This is a Papago village on Tonoka Wash. The name is said to have a Spanish origin, although some assert that its name means *knee*. It has also been called Barajita.
Ref.: 262, p. 7; 58; 57, p. 412

TONOPAH
Maricopa   T2N R7W   Elev. 1119'
The post office application notes that the local name for this place was Lone Peak. Why

it was called Tonopah is not now known, but that name was in use here on the railroad in 1930. The adjacent area is called Tonopah Desert. See Wintersburg, Maricopa
P.O. est. June 16, 1934, John Harvey Beauchamp, p.m.   Ref: 242; 279, p. 227; 283, p. 43

TONTO   pro.: /tánto/
Spanish = "foot" or "stupid"
Gila   T7N R10E   Elev. 2488'
This post office was at a place called Howell's Ranch at the foot of a trail called The Jump-off. It served the Cross-7 Cattle Company.
P.O. est. Feb. 20, 1884, James B. Watkins; disc. June 6, 1902   Ref.: 18a

TONTO BASIN
Gila
Bourke best describes this area by noting that it is a basin only in the sense that "it is all lower than the ranges enclosing it." On the north it is bounded by the thousand-foot high cliffs of tthe Mogollon Rim, on the west by the Mazatzal Mountains, on the south and southeast by spurs of the Superstition Mountains and the Pinal Mountains. It contains a mountain range, the Sierra Ancha. There is little basin-like about the terrain, for it is very rugged, cut by canyons. Hodge noted that its vast area was for many years used as a secure hiding place by various Apache groups and by white renegades. Tonto Basin was the scene of the bloody Pleasant Valley feud in which thirty lost their lives. As time passed, the conception of what constituted Tonto Basin changed so that today it includes the area of Tonto and Rye creeks.
   Initially the name Tonto Apache was applied to nearly all Indians in Arizona Territory between the White Mountains and the Colorado River, including members of at least two linguistic families. That fact precludes saying that the Tonto Apache were a particular Apache group. However, in 1866 in a letter appeared the following statement: "Tontos, a Spanish word meaning foolish, this tribe is the least brave, smallest, and ugliest of the Apache tribes." It might be conjectured that outsiders considered that any Indian venturing into this area was foolish. Consequently the comment found in a report dated 1873-75: "Tontos are called by the whites 'coous' (or *kuhuss*), a Mexican name meaning 'foolish.' The Apache frequently called them *lo-co* (= "fools")." That statement would appear to indicate that Tonto Apaches were viewed by Apaches themselves as being separate from other Apache groups.
   According to Hodge, "Bands living in the Tonto Basin were so isolated that they had the characteristics of a distinct group, and they developed a dialectic difference not easily understood by the other Apache." Hodge adds that prior to 1865 they had always lived near the junction of the Verde and Salt Rivers, but that they moved into the Tonto Basin following the establishment of Fort McDowell. He adds, "They were low in the scale of humanity and relatively harmless." There is a possibility that the name *Tonto* is itself a corruption as a manuscript dated 1820 gives their name as Tantos.
   The Tonto Basin remains largely uninhabited to this day.   Ref.: 49, p. 145; 168, p. 236; 15, pp. 453, 454; 350; 167 . . . , II, 9; Huntington Library, "N.S. Higgins *ms* # 180, Apache," Smithsonian Institution, Letter from Higgins to Prof. Joseph Henry (April 21, 1866)   The name Tonto occurs in the following:

Tonto Creek   Gila   T10N R12E   Elev. c. 4000'
King S. Woolsey named this stream on June 8, 1864.   Ref.: 18a

Tonto Lake   Apache   T4N R26E   Elev. 7698'
This is a thirty-three acre man-made lake created in 1943 and named for Tonto Creek. See Tonto Basin, Gila

Tonto Mountain   Gila   T8N R8E

Tonto Mountain   Yavapai   T15N R4W   Elev. 5631'

Tonto National Forest Gila/Maricopa   T8N R11E
The Tonto Forest Reserve was created on October 3, 1905. It increased in size on October 22, 1934 with the addition of the Bloody Basin section from the Prescott National Forest and further increased in size on July 1, 1953 with the addition of the Globe Division of the Crook National Forest. It comprises approximately 2,812,060 acres. The purpose of this national forest is to protect the watershed of Theodore Roosevelt Reservoir. See also Sitgreaves National Forest, Apache   Ref.: 243, p. 36

Tonto
National Monument   Gila   T4N R12E   Elev. 2300'
The eleven hundred acres of this national monument were set aside in December 1907 to preserve an abandoned prehistoric Indian village with which the Apaches had no connection. Visitors customarily see only the lower room in a cave about forty feet deep by eighty-five feet long. The ruin was occupied by the Salado people c. 1200 A.D., who had arrived in the Tonto Basin and Roosevelt area about one hundred years earlier. Ref.: 13, Peavy, pp. 3, 6

Tonto Natural Bridge   Gila   T11N R9E

Tonto Pasture Spring   Yavapai   T15N R4W

Tonto Peak   Gila   T1S R15E   Elev. 7848'
This highest peak in the Pinal Mountains was named by the King S. Woolsey expedition, which used it in 1864 to make a sighting. It is now known as Pinal Peak.
Ref.: *Arizona Miner* (Sept. 21, 1864), p. 1

Tonto Rim   Apache   T3N R24E

Tonto Spring   Gila   T10N R12E

Tonto Spring Valley   Yavapai   T15N R4W
In 1870 five ranches were located on the Prescott to La Paz road about twenty miles west of Prescott, with William Cory and A.J. Shanks the first residents. By 1875 J.B. Rupley and H.T. Crum were operating Tonto Station, a way station for travelers midway between Mint and Skull Valleys. Ref.: *Weekly Arizona Miner* (March 5, 1870), p. 3; (April 16, 1875), p. 2, and (May 28, 1875), p. 2

Tonto Trail   Coconino   (Grand Canyon)
This name was proposed by the USGS in March 1906 for a trail on the South Rim near Granity Gorge, being named for the so-called Tonto Apache. See Tonto Basin, Gila Ref.: 329

Tonto Wash   Yavapai   T14N R4W

# TONUK VO
Papago = "ridge pond" or *ton* = "hill"; *vo* = "waterhole"
Pima   T17S R2E   Elev. c. 2000'
This small Papago community takes its name from having a pond adjacent to a long ridge which runs west from it. The location is also called Papatjuik. It may be the one Lumholtz termed Thiovi. See Cubo, Pima Ref.:57, p. 353; 58

TONY RANCH SPRINGS
Pinal   T1N R13E
As this is the location of the Tony Lopez Ranch, the name of the spring derives from that fact.

# TOPAWA   pro.: /tòwpáow/
Papago = "it is a bean"
Pima   T18S R5E   Elev. 2474'
Indian boys play a game here in which they use a red bean, hence the common name for this large Papago community. The game itself is called *Mawi*, and Mexicans sometimes called the place Mawi. The traditional name of the community was Goksamuk, which in Papago means "burnt dog," a name perpetuating the folk memory of a time when a dog was burned during a Papago gathering. The San Solano Mission is at Topawa. It has also been spelled in various ways, some of which follow: Topahua (1912, Lumholtz); Koksumok (1912, Lumholtz map); Topawo (1924, Arizona Bureau Mines.) Topahua and Topawo are variants. Topawa Hills are at T19S/R5E (Elev. 1775') and Topawa Wash is at T19S/R6E.
P.O. est. June 14, 1917, Thomas JS. Throssell; resc. Nov. 24, 1917; reest. Feb. 7, 1925, Bonaventure Oblasser, p.m. Ref.: AHS, Castillo Collection, Box 1; 262, p. 1; 57, p. 408; *Papago Bulletin* (1965)

TOPAZ CANYON
Coconino (Grand Canyon)   T31N R2E
Barnes says that Powell named this canyon because of its coloring. The name was approved by the USGS in 1908. Ref.: 18a; 329

TOPOCK pro.: /towpak/

Mohave   T15N R21W   Elev. 580'

The name Topock may have been transferred from the Mohave name cited by Kroeber as *Tohopau-'wave,* which was on the California side of the Colorado River "in Needles at the 1902 ice-house." Its meaning is not known to this editor. As for the location of the Arizona side of the river, a post office was established here in February 1883 under the name Needles, derived from its adjacency to the three nearby mountains called The Needles. Later in the same year the name was changed to Powell, a railroad stop (now a section house) about a mile distant (T16N/R20W). The post office was discontinued in 1886.

During the next several years a community grew across the river in California and took over the name of Needles. By 1890 the location was known as Red Rock and as Red Crossing, but a year later a newspaper noted that a new "city" was being established under the name of Mellon near The Needles at Red Rock. It was so named to honor John (Jack) Alexander Mellon (b. 1842, New Brunswick), a noted river captain so devoted to his piloting that he once spent eighty hours in the wheelhouse and worked fifteen years with only two weeks off. In 1903 Mellon opened a post office. It was discontinued in 1909. An application in 1915 to reopen the post office notes that the place was "called Mullen locally" (a corruption of the earlier name), but that the railroad stop was called Topock. As postal regulations would not permit again using the name Needles, Topock was selected for the post office name.

Topock shares its name with Topock Bay (T16N/R21W) Topock Marsh (Mohave/California: T16N/R21W) is part of Havasu Lake Refuge and is sometimes called Lake Powell. It and the bay form Topock Tract Water Fowl Area, a three hundred and twenty acre habitat bought in 1957 by the State Game and Fish Department.

P.O. est. as Needles, Feb. 15, 1883, Augustus A. Spear, p.m.; changed to Powell, Oct. 11, 1883; disc. July 9, 1886; reest. as Mellen (*sic*), March 26, 1903, Emilie O. Holstein, p.m.; disc. April 30, 1909; reest. as Topock, Dec. 28, 1915, Enos W. Norton, p.m.; Wells Fargo 1903   Ref.: 62; *Arizona Sentinel* (May 9, 1891), p. 3; 194, p. 168, Note 7; 200, p. 27; Huntington Library; 242; Housholder; 9, p. 3

TOPOCOBA HILLTOP

Havasupai: *topoco* = "hilltop; *ba* = "spring"

Coconino (Grand Canyon)   T33N R3W   Elev. 4075'

This area takes its name from the presence of Topocoba Spring, which James spells Topocobya. According to J.W. Fewkes (1908), in the Hopi language the ending *bya* refers to a river, whereas the ending *ba* refers to a spring. The Hilltop, as it is occasionally called, is at the head of the Supai Trail descending through Havasu Canyon. The spring is on the trail rather than on the Hilltop itself, as has sometimes been recorded; it "flows out of the base of the immense cliff down which one fork of the trail descends." A variant name for the spring and gorge is Tope Kobe.

Ref.: 329; Schellbach File, Grand Canyon; 178, pp. 55, 173, 174

TOREVA

Navajo   T28N R17E   Elev. 5940'

The site of this Hopi village is at the base of Second Mesa where there is a spring which "twists" from the earth. According to Hopi legend, Toreva Spring came into being following the Great Flood. As the flood receded and the land was drying up, the Hopi feared lacking water so they sent a runner to the sacred San Francisco Mountains, which they called Nuvatiki. He came back with water from the sacred fountain, which men of the Flute Society planted, creating this spring. A Baptist mission was opened here in the 1890s. On a post office location map in the National Archives is noted the fact that "the local name is Second Mesa."

P.O. est. Oct. 1, 1900, Frank D. Voorhees, p.m.; disc. July 24, 1937

Ref.: 331, p. 159; 119, p. 132; 242

TORNADO CANYON

Greenlee   T2N R30E

Cowboys named this canyon because during a very high wind the forest was blown down. Ref.: Fritz

TORNADO PEAK

Gila   T4S R15E   Elev. 4483'

The peak was named from the fact that the Tornado Mining Company made a gold strike near it in March 1927. The Mining Company in turn takes its name because in earlier years a tornado swept through this area. Ref.: 18a

TORO, CAÑADA DEL

Pima   T18S R2E

This was named because a man named Toro had a ranch here. Toro Spring and Wash are at T20S/R12E. See Kotskug, Pima

TOROWEAP CLIFFS

Hopi = "garden spot"

Mohave (Grand Canyon)   T34N R7W

In Powell's 1874 report this place was called To-ro-wip Cliffs. The variant name for this location is Mu-koon'-tu-weap. In Piute this name is said to mean "steep canyon." See Toroweap Valley, Mohave (Grand Canyon) Ref.: 267, p. 13

TOROWEAP VALLEY

Hopi = "garden spot"

Mohave (Grand Canyon)   T33N R7W

Maj. John Wesley Powell descended the old Toroweap Trail to this valley and the Colorado River. Although this is probably the shortest route down from Toroweap Point to the Colorado River from the Rim, it is unquestionably one of the roughest as it exists in a volcanic area which is difficult to traverse. Gregory notes that the valley was also called Tuweap Valley. One source notes that the Piutes do not pronounce the letter *R*, which may account for the difference in the two names. Another notes that the word is Piute, but there is some confusion what the name may mean in Piute: (1) a gulley or dry wash, or (2) greasewood. The Hopi name seems more appropriate than either of the Piute renditions. Interpretation of the Hopi meaning was that given by a Piute informant named Joedie. Whatever the meaning of the word, the valley is bounded on the east by an abrupt eight or nine hundred feet high wall called Toroweap Cliffs. The name of the valley was first applied as spelled at the heading of this entry by Dr. A.H. Thompson of Powell's party. The name Tornado as once applied by the U.S. was an inadvertent corruption. Toroweap Lake here is a dry lake.
Ref.: 322, p. 9; 88, p. 192; 266, pp. 186, 188; 140, p. 21; 329

TORRANCE WELL

Maricopa   T7N R8W

In 1879 this was known as Blank Tank. Later Clay Torrance owned this well, hence the name. Ref.: 279, p. 224

TORRION LAND GRANT

Santa Cruz

In 1836 the Mexican government granted land south of the Tubac presidio, extending to Tumacacori, to Jose Zosa. Ref.: 33, p. 74

TORTILLA FLAT   pro.: /tortíyə/

Spanish = "omelet" or "thin oven-cake"

Maricopa   T2N R9E   Elev. 1760'

The community here takes its name from masses of flat rocks resembling tortillas. Tortilla Campground is here and Tortilla Mountain is nearby (T2N/R10E, Elev. 4198').
P.O. est. Sept. 8, 1927, Mathis Johnson, p.m. Ref.: 5, p. 368; 242

TORTILLA FLAT   pro.: /tortíyə/

Spanish = "omelet" or "thin oven-cake"

Mohave   Elev. c. 1500'

In the early 1880s a Mexican settlement on the north side of New Virginia near Signal was called Tortilla Flat because Mexicans lived here. Others said that its "leading

industries" are . . . "raising watermelons, making adobes, and keeping bit saloons."
Ref.: 163, p. 252; Mallach

TORTILLA MOUNTAINS   pro.: /tortíyǝ/
Spanish = "omelet" or "thin oven-cake"
Pinal   T4S R13E   Elev. 4170'
Maj. William H. Emory named these mountains in 1853. They were described in 1872
by Arch R. Marvine of the Wheeler expeditions as low scattered hills having
"occasionally high table-top buttes." He called the highest Tortilla. A variant name is
Tortilato Mountains, or Tortilla Butte. Tortilla Pass is at T1N/R11E
Ref.: 345, III, 224

TORTOLITA MOUNTAINS   pro.: /tortǝlíytǝ/
Spanish = "little turtle dove"
Pima/Pinal   T10S R13E   Elev. c. 4127'
This is the same locality which Font in 1775 called Llano del Azotado (*llano* = "plain";
azotado = "a flogged man") because on the plain near these mountains a deserting
muleteer was caught and flogged. In 1880 they were called Bloodsucker Mountains. The
current name, as was noted in 1916, derives from the fact that there were multitudes of
small doves here prior to 1916. Lt. John Bourke reports that Cochise and his Apaches
attacked the Gatchell-Curtis wagon train here. Also when a military detachment was
ambushed, only one soldier escaped. The men sent to look for the lost soldier found his
tracks and those of a huge mountain lion; following the tracks, they found a place where
they read signs of a struggle and then of something having been dragged off.
    In 1932 the USGS eliminated the following names occasionally applied to these
mountains: Tortillita (Sierra), Tortolitas, and Tortollita.   Ref.: 329; 77, p. 82, Note
13; 49, pp. 39, 40; *Arizona Enterprise* (Dec. 29, 1892), p.5

TORTUGA BUTTE, LA
Pima   T14S R9E   Elev. 3027'
This butte is on the La Tortuga Ranch, hence the name.

TOTACON   pro.: /tóssika<ʌn/
Navajo: *Tótikan* = "sweet water"
Apache   T40N R27E   Elev. 5360'
There is a Navajo settlement and trading post here. In 1937 the USGS changed the
name to Sweetwater, but in 1963 went back to the original name, eliminating variant
spellings as follows: Talacon, Totlacon.   Ref.: Burcard; 329; 331, p. 154; 143, p. 289

TOTAL WRECK
Pima   T18S R17E   Elev. c. 4600'
In 1879 John T. Dillon found the silver mine here. (One source gives his name as
Dilden.) When Dillon (a cowboy) went to Walter Vail in 1881 to make out recording
papers and seek financing, he described the mineral formation as almost a total wreck,
and Vail immediately named the location. When the mine was sold for taxes in late
1882, Vail and his friend Gates bought it. By October 1883 a newspaper said that the
miners' town was in the condition designated by the name of the mine. The mine was
worked desultorily until about 1911.
P.O. est. Aug. 12, 1881, Nathan R. Vail, p.m.; disc. Nov. 1, 1890
Ref.: 164, p. xii; AHS, Jerry Dillon and Green File; 286, p. 142; *Arizona Sentinel*
(Oct. 13, 1883), p. 2

TOTEM POLE
Navajo   T41N R21E   Elev. 5617'
This large column in Monument Valley resembles a totem pole, hence the name. See
Yei-Bei-Chai, Navajo

TOTONTEAC
Navajo
This is the name of the Martinez and other Spanish Colonial maps assigned to the

general southwestern area of what is now Arizona. The name later was applied to the Hopi Villages region. See Hopi Villages, Navajo   Ref.: Huntington Library

TOTOPITK   pro.: /top't/
Papago = "crooked" or "lopsided"
Pima   T10S R1E   Elev. 2064'
This Indian village is usually occupied in summer. About eight families are reported living here each year near what is sometimes called Totobit Tanks, the tanks being pot holes worn in the black lava and conglomerate. The name has been variously spelled as follows: Totobitk (1912, Lumholtz); Tautabit (1915, Indian Service Map); and Totabit (1921 GLO). It is also possible that this is the location cited by Sedelmayr in 1744 and spelled Tuesapit.   Ref.: 58; 57, p. 96; 262, p. 16; 59, p. 378

TOURIST
Coconino (Grand Canyon)
This was the first post office at the Grand Canyon. See Hance Creek, Coconino (Grand Canyon)
P.O. est. May 10, 1897, John Hance, p.m.; disc. April 12, 1899   Ref.: Theobald

TOVAR TERRACE   pro.: /towvár/
Coconino (Grand Canyon)   T33N R2W   Elev. 50000'
Pedro de Tovar (or Tobar), son of the Keeper of the Arsenal in Mexico City, accompanied Coronado on the 1540 Expedition to find the fabled Seven Cities of Cibola. On his excursion to the Hopi Villages (see Tovar Mesa, Navajo), he heard about a great canyon and when he reported this to Coronado, Cardenas was sent to investigate (see Cardenas Butte, Coconino (Grand Canyon)). The area surrounding the El Tovar Hotel at the Grand Canyon has several place names bearing his surname. The hotel, for instance, is in the El Tovar Amphitheater. El Tovar Point (elev. 7050') is at the end of the Amphitheater. The name of this point has been changed to Grandeur Point because of its fine view of the hotel and the canyon.
   Associated names include Tovar Amphitheater (T31N/R2E); Tovar Hill (T31N/R3E); Tovar Mesa (Navajo; T25N/R16E), which was named by Herbert Gregory:
Ref.: 178, pp. 25, 38, 74; *Grand Canyon Nature Notes*, III (June 30, 1929); Schellbach File (Grand Canyon); 357, pp. 390, 477; 141, pp. 38, 151, 196

TOWAGO POINT
Coconino (Grand Canyon)   T33N R3W   Elev. 5958'
This point was named for a Havasupai family in February 1925.   Ref.: 329

TOWEL CREEK
Yavapai   T12N R6E
This creek earned its name c. 1900 when Charlie Wingfield, a cowboy, camped here with a group of cowboys taking part in a rodeo. Charlie lost a perfectly good bath towel and "never ceased mourning for it during the whole rodeo." It was years before the USGS realized that the western pronounciation of "Towel" should not be spelled "Taul" and in 1968 changed the official records from Taul Creek to Towel. Associated names include Towel Peak and Towel Spring.   Ref.: 261, p. 91; 329

TOWER BUTTE
Coconino   T41N R10E   Elev. 5285'
This butte looks like a tower, hence the name. Erosion cut canyons in the flat-topped mesa to form this butte.   Ref.: 141, p. 44

TOWER MOUNTAIN
Yavapai   T10N R1W   Elev. 7626'
In 1873 George W. Tower mined here and later on he established the Potato Ranch, sometimes called the Tower Ranch.   Ref.: 182a

TOWER OF RA
Coconino (Grand Canyon)   T32N R2E   Elev. 6076'
In 1906 the USGS named a number of locations in the Grand Canyon for deities of ancient mythology. Ra was the Egyptian god of the sun.

TOWER OF SET
Coconino (Grand Canyon)   T32N R2E   Elev. 6026'
In 1906 the USGS named a number of locations in the Grand Canyon after deities of ancient mythology. Set was the Egyptian god of war. This location was named by artist Thomas Moran c. 1879. Ref.: 178, p. 53

TOWNSEND
Coconino   T22N R8E   Elev. 6938'
This small community was called Doney for a Civil War veteran who lived here until he died in 1932. It was renamed in 1936 for John Townsend, a noted scout and Indian fighter. See Townsend Butte, Yavapai, and Doney Park, Coconino
P.O. est. as Doney, May 16, 1922, Frank J. Smith, p.m.; disc. May 31, 1924
Ref.: 5, p. 317

TOWNSEND BUTTE
Yavapai   T10N R1E   Elev. 3950'
When a boy, John Townsend survived an Indian raid during which members of his family were killed. Thereafter he was a relentless Indian fighter, often trailing Indians alone at night. In June 1871 he organized an expedition of twelve civilians and a small detachment of soldiers to pursue Apaches who had stolen one hundred thirty-seven head of cattle. They found the Apaches feasting on horse flesh and killed fifty-six Indians without suffering casualties. Indians later ambused and killed him, but respecting his bravery, left his body covered with a fine blanket. Ref.: 5, p. 305

TRAIL: Several places are called *Trail* because trails exist there. Examples follow:

Trail Canyon	Coconino	T39N R3E
Trail Canyon	Greenlee	T5S R29E
Trail Canyon	Mohave	T28N R10W
Trail Canyon	Navajo	T10N R18E
Trail Canyon	Pima	T19S R16E
Trail in the Crack	Apache	In Conyon de Chelly
Trail of Graves	Maricopa/La Paz	

This was the term for the pioneer road between Wickenburg and Ehrenberg because many died of thirst or at the hands of Mojave Indians. Ref.: 15, p. 358

Trail Rapids Bay	Mohave	T31N R19W
Trail Rapids Wash	Mohave	T30N R19W
Trail Where the Enemy Walked Up	Apache	

On the north side of Canyon de Chelly about two miles from its mouth is a horse trail crossing talus. It was used by Ute Indians who raided Navajos in the canyon and its branches in the 1840s. The Navajo name *('anaa'sinyilhaayàhi)* refers to the fact that the enemy (a Hopi woman) walked up this trail onto the mesa between Canyon de Chelly and Canyon del Muerto. Ref.: 141, p. 20

TRANSEPT, THE
Coconino (Grand Canyon)   T31N R3E   Elev. 4750'
This location was named by Maj. Clarence E. Dutton in 1882. He noted that near Vulcan's Throne were arms of a transept, the main chasm being regarded as the nave. Ref.: 100, pp. 92, 172

TRAVERTINE CANYON
Coconino (Grand Canyon)   T31N R2E   Elev. 3000'
Seepage has deposited travertine on this canyon wall, hence the name. Travertine is soft green stone, a deposit left by waters heavily charged with calcium carbonate. Travertine Creek is in the canyon. Travertine Falls (Mohave) are at T27N/R11W. Ref.: Kolb

TRES ALAMOS   pro.: /treys ǽləmos/
Spanish = "three cottonwood trees"
Cochise   T15S R21E   Elev. c. 2500'
In 1867 because of difficulties with Apaches, an army picket post was established here.
It consisted of a non-commissioned officer and ten soldiers, the detachment being
relieved at monthly intervals. Apparently they were ineffective because seven men were
murdered in a year's time in the vicinity, causing it to be abandoned. Bourke notes that
Apache attacks continued through 1871. Thomas Dunbar had a stage station here in
1877, hence the name Dunbar's. He hired a man named Montgomery to run the post
office, hence the name Montgomery sometimes on maps. Although referred to as a
settlement, actually small ranches lined the San Pedro River for some twelve miles.
Barnes notes that when he was a Tres Alamos in February 1880, the main house was
under huge cottonwoods, hence the name of the location. See also Benson, Cochise
P.O. est. Dec. 2, 1874, John Montgomery, p.m.; disc. Sept. 15, 1886; Wells Fargo
1879   Ref.: 224, p. 204; 339, p. 18; 49, p. 101; *Citizen* (June 6, 1875), p. 1; 116, p. 585

TRES BELLOTAS CANYON   pro.: /treys beyótəs/
Spanish: *tres* = "three"; *bellota* = "acorn" (local usage: refers to oak trees)
Santa Cruz   T23S R10E   Elev. c. 4000'
The name refers to two wells about a mile apart in this canyon where there are oak
trees.   Ref.: Glannon; 59, p. 428

TRIANGLE CANYON
Cochise   T15S R30E   Elev. 3500'
The canyon has two branches with a triangular point between, hence the name.

TRIGO MOUNTAINS   pro.: /triygo/
Spanish = "wheat"
La Paz   T1S R22W   Elev. 2600'
Locally these mountains were known as the Chocolate Mountains, except for the portion
north of Weaver Pass, which was called Trigo. Their name comes from the fact that a
variety of Indian wheat (*plantago ignota*) grows abundantly in the uplands. Cattle relish
the wheat. The name Chocolate Mountains derives from the color of a portion of the
range. North Trigo Peaks are at T2N/R21W (Elev. 2170'). Associated names include
Trigo Pass (T1N/R20E) and Wash (T1N/R21W).   Ref.: 355, pp. 18, 50

TRIPLE ALCOVES
Coconino (Grand Canyon)   T34N R5E
The name is descriptive.

TRIPLETS, THE
Gila   T1S R19E   Elev. 5376'
The name describes the appearance of these three small peaks. They have also been
called Triplet Mountains, Mount Triplet, Three Peaks, and Triplets Peaks.
Ref.: Uplegger

TRIPP AND UNDERWOOD WASH
Graham   T6S R24E
Tripp and Underwood were early settlers.   Ref.: 329

TRI-STATE VIEWPOINT
Mohave (Lake Mead)   T19N R20W   Elev. c. 1100'
From here three states – California, Nevada, and Arizona – are visible.

TRITLE, MOUNT   pro.: /tráytʌl/ or tráytļ/
Yavapai   T12N R2W   Elev. 7800'
This location was named for Frederick A. Tritle (b. Aug. 7, 1833, Pennsylvania; d. May
1906), who was sworn in as Arizona's seventh Territorial Governor (including Gurley,
who died on February 6, 1882 before taking office). He served until May 5, 1886. Tritle
had extensive mining interests, including some in this region. There is a Tritle Peak in
Coconino (Grand Canyon) at T33N/R4E, Elev. 6750'.   Ref.: Garrett; 116, p. 635

TROUT CREEK
Mohave   T18N R13W   Elev. c. 3500'

In 1871 Wheeler reported that this creek abounded with excellent trout. Lt. Amiel W. Whipple called it Bill Williams Fork (in error). This creek is one of the three largest which empty into the Big Sandy.   Ref.: 346, p. 212; 200, p. 50

TROY
Pinal   T3S R14E   Elev. 3644'

The first mining community here on Troy Mountain (Elev. 4970') was called Skinnerville, after a local resident. When the Troy Manhattan Company took over the mine, the name was changed to reflect the home town of one of the owners.
P.O. est. April 27, 1901, Mrs. C.T. Hutchings, p.m.; disc. Sept. 15, 1910
Ref.: 18a; 242

TRUITT
Cochise   T21S R27E

The Truitt Ranch was on the Arizona and Eastern R.R. north of McNeal. See McNeal, Cochise

TRUMBULL, MOUNT
Mohave   T35N R8W   Elev. 8029'

This name applies to a mountain and to a post office. Mount Trumbull is in the Northside Mountains, so named by Lt. Joseph Christmas Ives in 1858. Maj. John W. Powell during the 1871-72 exploration of the Grand Canyon named three major volcanic peaks in these mountains after individuals. This one he had named in the fall of 1870 for Lyman Trumbull, Senator for Illinois, 1854-1871. Powell's party called the entire group of volcanic peaks after the Indians who made their home here, the Uinkarets (*Uinkaret Kaib* = "pine mountains"). The Indians called them *oo-na-ga-re-chits*, which may be considered a form of the name Uinkarets. In 1961 the USGS eliminated the following names: High Mountains, Northside Mountains, and Pine Mountains. Powell named a second peak (T34N/R9W) for Gen. John A. Logan, calling it Mount Logan. Mount Ellen was also named by Powell. Dutton named the largest for Powell's wife, Emma.   Ref.: 322, p. 72, Footnote; 343, p. 62; 88, pp. 186, 187; 329; 266, pp. 131, 199, 200

TRUMBULL, MOUNT (TOWN)
Mohave   T35N R10W   Elev. 5329'

The post office application states that the local name is Bundyville. Members of the Bundy family have served as postmasters: James Bundy (1923) and Mrs. Genevieve Bundy (1942). Bundy Ponds (T37N/R6W) is an associated name. See Trumbull, Mount, Mohave
P.O. est. Dec. 23, 1919, Lillie B. Iverson, p.m.; disc. July 31, 1954   Ref.: 242

TRUXTON CANYON
Mohave   T25N R15W   Elev. c. 3500'

Coues believes that the location called Arroyo de San Bernabe by Francisco Garcés is identical with today's Truxton Canyon or Wash. Through this canyon runs a creek (or "river"), the Yampai, named by Lt. Lorenzo Sitgreaves, a name which he understood his guide, Antoine Leroux, had applied to Indians whom Sitgreaves' party met on October 28, 1851. Cliffs along the eastern edge of the stream were called Yampai also, but today they are called Grand Wash Cliffs.

Lt. Edward Fitzgerald Beale on October 8, 1857 described the progress of his surveying party through this canyon to what he named Truxton Springs. Noting that at the springs the canyon was about two hundred yards wide, he called that location Engle's Pass after Capt. Frederick Engle, U.S.N. Beale described the place as "a beautiful one; the water pouring over the rocks is received in a basin twenty feet in diameter and eight or ten feet deep . . . the spring and the first water on entering the first cañon, at its commencement, is three, or four, miles, above." The Beale party stayed here all day shoeing and resting their exhausted mules. Beale named the springs Truxtun, either for his brother Truxtun, or his mother, whose maiden name was Emily Truxtun. (His wife's maiden name was Mary Edwards.)

Several skirmishes with Indians took place at or near these springs, for the simple reason that Indians used it and objected strenously to sharing the water.

Lt. Ives left another place name temporarily in this area, possibly at the smaller of the two springs named by Beale. Ives called it Peacock Spring, but the name disappeared by 1880. In 1883 the A. & P.R.R. put in a large pump at Truxton Springs to service steam engines. That fact led to a suit with the Hualapai Indians (see Crozier, Mohave). Diesel engines eliminated the need for watering stops and only a section house remains at Truxton today. However, a new community of Truxton developed a mile west of Peach Springs beginning in October 1951, when D.J. Dilts, who arrived in Arizona in July 1942 as a supervisor for the S.F.R.R., established a restaurant and service station there. Dilts named his small settlement for Truxton railroad siding and Truxton Canyon. Associated names include Truxton Plateau, Valley (GLO 1883), Wash (T25N/R10W), and that of the Truxton Canyon Sub-Agency, established by Executive Order on December 22, 1898, which set aside six hundred and sixty acres for a Hualapai Indian school (see Valentine, Mohave). Ref.: 335, p. 216; Mrs. Velma Rudd Hoffman, Letter (March 25, 1960); 23, pp. 69, 78, 79; 77, p. 322, Footnote 6, and p. 7, Note 8; 294, p. 15; Dilts; Glaser

TSAILE (CREEK) pro.: /tsé:hyíli/
Navajo: *tséhili* = "where water enters a box canyon"
Apache   T33N R29W   Elev. c. 6200'
In 1968 the Navajo Tribal Council approved the spelling Tsaile for the stream which Gregory called Spruce Brook. He said it "dropped into the Canyon del Muerto at Sehili." His name of *Sehili* applied to a small settlement. The name Spruce Brook was first used in 1857 by Capt. Simpson because of many spruce trees lining it. A trading post was established at Tsehili in 1885, but was abandoned in 1890 when heavy snows forced Navajos to move their flocks of sheep into Chinle. The following are variants: Tse'a'lee, Tsali, Salee, Tsalee Creek, and Brook Creek. Associated names include Tsalee Butte, Creek, and Pinnacle.
Ref.: 141, pp. 90, 150, 195; Burcard; 329; 331, p. 161

TSAY BEGEH
Navajo = "valley within the rocks:"
Navajo   Elev. c. 6000'
This tiny valley in Monument Valley has a descriptive name.   Ref.: 191, p. 118

TSAY-YAH-KIN pro.: /tséya:kin/
Navajo = "house of many people"
Navajo   Elev. c. 6000'
This prehistoric ruin in Monument Valley was discovered late in 1949 in a large crevice at the head of a box canyon. The name refers to its former population.   Ref.: 191, p. 16

TESGI CANYON
Navajo = "in between the rocks"
Navajo   T38N R17E   Elev. c. 6200'
Tsegi Point is also here, as is the settlement of Tsegi. The Navajo word *tsegi* is applied generally to deep canyons with sheer walls. This location is an instance. This one was also called Laguna Canyon as late as 1918 because it contained a chain of lakes (since drained). In 1912 a flood washed out dams and initiated erosion resulting in canyon depths of over fifty feet.   Ref.: 13, Brewer, "Navajo National Monument," p. 6; 331, p. 140; 141, pp. 47 (Plate XIV), 192

TSEGI (MESAS) pro.: /tséyi?/
Navajo = "mesas trenched by canyons"
Navajo   T38N R17E   Elev. 8065'
This area is a series of mesas cut by canyons. One – Skeleton Mesa – has a skeletal look, as it is sliced by three canyons. Two other mesas – Azansosi and Hoskinini – lie a thousand feet lower so that the series looks like steps. Extensive cliff-dweller ruins attest to the mesas' having been a population center. A variant spelling is Segi.
Ref.: 141, pp. 36, 47, 38

TSEGIHATSOSO (CANYON)

Navajo: *tsegi* = "in between the rocks"; "slim canyon in the rocks"
Apache   T40N R18E   Elev. c. 6000'
The word *canyon* is redundant. In the National Archives postal records for March 20, 1909 is the spelling Tsagy-at-sosa Canyon at the location cited. The canyon name describes its narrow and deep location. The name is also spelled Segihatsosi, Sagyatsosi, Tsegihotsosi, and Tseyi-hatsosi.
Ref.: 242; 141, pp. 48, 195; 331, p. 141; 329

TSEGITOE (SPRING)   pro.: /tsiʌhyiʌˀtohi/

Navajo: *tsiyi't ohi* = "spring in the forest"
Apache   T2N R9W   Elev. c. 4100'
The word "spring" is redundant. The descriptive name is also spelled Segatoa and Segetoa.   Ref.: 141, pp. 151, 194

TSIN SIKAAD

Navajo = "tree setting up"
Apache   c. 15 miles n.e. of Chinle
Van Valkenburg says this historically important place is in "barren sandstone country and plains which slope west from the Navajo cordillera toward the Chinle Valley" where c. 1854 "the last Naachid or tribe assembly was held" and that Naachid, a type of dancing, was one of the most important and spectacular of Navajo ceremonials. Judging by the translation of the name, I dare conjecture that the ceremony may have been a seasonal one in which a tree was set up in a hole, a custom observed among Mexican Indians by Spaniards when the foreigners first arrived in the New World.
Ref.: 331, pp. 162-163

TUBAC   pro.: /tuwbǽk/ or /tuwbák/

Pima: *chuevak* or *tjiuvak* = "where something (bodies) rotted"
Papago: *tachi-o-wa'k* = "place of decay"
Santa Cruz   T21S R13E   Elev. 3200'
The name refers to an Indian legend about an attack and the odor of rotting bodies. Fr. Bonaventure Oblasser believes that the Spanish attempt to pronounce the Papago name *chuevak* is encompassed in *Tubac*. That there was a *visita* known as Tubac is evident from an entry in the baptismal records of the Guevavi Register, which records the baptism of a child from Tubac on November 12, 1741, when it was generally referred to as "Santa Gertrudis de Tubaca." This "mission," called San Gertrude, was plundered during the Pima Indian Revolt of 1750. To protect such settlements, a Spanish military post (or presidio) was established in 1752 on the west bank of the Santa Cruz River under the name San Ignacio. It was the first fort in Arizona to be garrisoned with Spanish soldiers. In 1764 Juan Bautista de Anza was given command, which he retained until 1776 when he led an expedition to what is now San Francisco, California. In the same year the garrison was moved from Tubac to the future Tucson. When petitions had no effect on having Spanish troops return to Tubac, the inhabitants established their own garrison of Pima Indians. In 1824, four years after Mexico had taken over the area from Spain, a Mexican garrison was stationed at Tubac presidio. In 1828 a silver mine was being worked nearby, a fact which was to have an effect on the future of Tubac. In the spring and summer of 1852, Tubac was the temporary home of Mormons who attempted to settle, but lack of rain forced them to leave. By 1854 it was described as a deserted village where the "wild Apache lords it over this region, and the timid husbandman dares not return to his home." In September 1856 the Sonora Mining and Exploring Company established its headquarters at Tubac. The population consisted of three hundred miners, mainly from Texas. This fact was one result of the Gadsden Purchase and the consequent protection offered by U.S. troops. These troops, however, were withdrawn in 1861 to take part in the Civil War. The result was a series of Apache depradations that depopulated, not only Tubac, but all of Santa Cruz Valley. In 1871 the *Arizona Miner* reported a single man living there. Before long the abandoned presidio (which had served as headquarters for the mining company) was in ruins. By 1908 almost all of what had comprised Tubac had disappeared. Gradually, however, a community again took hold. The American town site was laid out in c. 1878 by Solon M. Allis. It should be noted that the original location was partially in the extreme northwest corner of Baca Float No. 3,

whereas the current town is entirely outside the Float, part of it being "lost" when the Float was surveyed. Tubac was declared a national monument in 1976.

Associated names include Tubac Creek (T21S/R12E), and Tubac Range (= Atascosa Mountains, q.v.).

P.O. est. Feb. 21, 1859, Frederick Hulseman, p.m.; disc. July 14, 1863; reest. July 13, 1864; disc. Nov. 30, 1942   Ref.: Lenon; Fr. Bonaventure Oblasser, Letter to Frank C. Lockwood (May 5, 1935); Huntington Library; 57, p. 14; 168, p. 18; 77, p. 69, Note 2; 15, pp. 369, 383, 384; 142, p. 141; 106, p. 118; 236, p. 25; 133 (1856); 163, pp. 180, 184; 228, n.p.; 160, pp. 38, 39; *Weekly Arizona Miner* (Nov. 4, 1871), p. 1; 167, II, 830; 121a, p. 13; 293, p. 203; Henry F. Dobyns, "Tubac: Where Some Enemies Rotted," *Arizona Quarterly,* XIX (Autumn 1963), 229-232

TUBA CITY   pro.: /túwbə/

Coconino   T32N R11E   Elev. 4450'

This location was visited by Fr. Francisco Garcés in 1776. Here at Tuba Spring in 1875 Mormons under James S. Brown constructed a stone building near the site of the Indian village of Moencopie. Three years later Erastus Snow platted a for the town at Musha Springs two miles north of Moencopie. He named it for the Hopi leader responsible for establishing Moencopie (see Oraibi, Old, Coconino): His name was T Ivi, which Mormons pronounced both as Tocobi and also as Tuba. TIvi had gone with Jacob Hamblin to Utah in November 1870 and served as Hamblin's guide. Mormons set up their colony without realizing they were on land reserved for Indian use, and in 1903 this fact led to their having their holdings bought by the U.S. Government, after which the Mormons left.

P.O. est. July 31, 1884, Thomas W. Brookbank, p.m.; name changed to Tuba, April 23, 1894; name changed to Tuba City, March 26, 1903, F. Tanner, p.m.   Ref.: 242; 224, II, 453; 331, pp. 163, 164; 141, pp. 42, 143; 225, pp. 80, 158; 1, p. 30

TUCKER (R.R. STN.)

Yavapai   T16N R3W

This location on the railroad was named for Bill Tucker, an early day railroader on the old A. & P. line from Seligman to Prescott. He was also a horseman. Tucker Spring (T20N/R4W) is an associated name.   Ref.: Kelly

TUCKET CANYON

Mohave (Grand Canyon)   T34N R6W   Elev. c. 4000'

This canyon is in the Tucket Mining District, hence its name. The name Tuckup is a corruption. The place is also known as 164 Mile Canyon. It is possible that this canyon is what Lt. Edward Fitzgerald Beale called Tucker's Pass, naming it for the blacksmith on his 1857-58 expedition. Although the USGS in August 1964 adopted Tuckup Canyon as the official name for Tucket Canyon, the decision does not seem justifiable. Associated names include Tuck Up Point (a.k.a. Tuckup Rocky Point) and Tuckup Trail.   Ref.: Mrs. Velma Rudd Hoffman, Letter (March 1960); 23, p. 59

TUCSON   pro.: /tuwsán/ or /túwsan/ or /túk-san/

Papago: *chuk* = "black;" *shon* = "base," "bottom" or *Tˢ-îuk-shàn* = "black base" (Referring to mountain west of Santa Cruz River)

Pima   T14S R13E   Elev. 2389'

The name of the city of Tucson derives from that given to Sentinel Mountain by Papago Indians, Tˢ-iuk-shan, referring to the fact that the base of the mountain is darker than its summit. Hodge also says that Tu-uk-so-on means "black base." Kirk Bryan said that the black hill was Tumamoc Mountain rather than Sentinel Mountain. Indians customarily name locations for nearby landmarks, hence the name of the now-vanished Indian community at the base of Sentinel Mountain. Spanish pronounciation yielded Tuqui Son or the current Tucson. Apaches had their own name for the Anglo/Mexican town; *Sa-sits-go-lon-a* (= "many chimneys").

Evidence that the government buildings area of Tucson was once occupied by prehistoric Indians has been found twice, first in 1928 and again in December 1955 when the floor of a hohokam pit house dating to 900 A.D. was uncovered. Also revealed was a section of the former wall around the Old Pueblo. In 1697 Fr. Eusebio Kino referred to San Agustin de Oiaur, noting that it was on the banks of the Santa Cruz River and that between that place and San Xavier del Bac lay the most thickly populated and

[630]

fertile spot of the entire Santa Cruz Valley. Kino did not call it Tucson, but co-existent was Chuk Son near Sentinel Mountain. The supremacy of Jesuits vanished and Franciscans took their place in Arizona, and in 1751 the Indian settlement of Chuk Son became a *visita* of San Xavier del Bac. San Agustin de Tucson (on a ridge about two miles southeast of the old Jesuit location) by 1763 was large enough to be referred to as a little Spanish settlement. Fr. Francisco Garcés established what was designed to be a permanent Spanish settlement here in 1768. Almost immediately thereafter Apache raids forced abandonment of both San Agustin de Tucson and San Agustín de Oiaur, as well as of San Cosme and San Xavier, except for the Jesuit missioner at San Xavier, Fr. Alonzo Espinosa. Ultimately he was killed.

With the withdrawal of the Spanish troops from the presidio at Tubac, under the *Reglamento y Instrucciones para los Presidios* of 1772 the transfer of that garrison was ordered, but it did not take place until 1776. The site for the new presidio was the former settlement of San Agustin de Tucson, hence the name Presidio de San Agustin de Tucson. According to a reliable source, "There is nothing to indicate that San Agustin was defended by walls, as was Tucson in later years, but this is not surprising as the new post was no doubt more or less a replica of the old one at Tubac, which was a haphazard collection of buildings located on a slight elevation overlooking the river...."

The same source has an interesting comment on the erection of the wall about the presidio at a later date. According to the source, Garcés did indeed create a walled section, but it was "west of the river at the foot of Sentinel Peak. The wall about the presidio was not built by him. This is evident from Arricivita's 'Cronica Serafica' written in 1791." Further, the Reyes report of 1772 states that there was then neither a priest's house nor a church at Tucson. When a chapel was established for the presidio in 1776, it was called Nuestra Señora de Guadalupe.

Following the revolution against Spanish rule, along with the rest of the region the small community in 1820 became a part of Mexico, and it remained so until the Gadsden Purchase. To distinguish the nearby Indian village from the presidio, the latter was called San Agustin de Pueblito de Tucson. This same location in Reyes' report is San Jose de Tucson. It was hardly what could be called a thriving community when the Mormon batallion under Lt. Col. Phillip St. George Cooke marched through in 1846, seeking an emigrant road across the southwest to California. They paused long enough to raise the American flag over this purely Mexican community. Mexican troops withdrew before their arrival but repossessed the town after the Mormon batallion moved on.

In 1856 the United States took military possession of the Gadsden Purchase, taking over land south of the Gila River to the present Mexican border. The first troops stayed briefly in Tucson but by 1857 were at Fort Buchanan, Santa Cruz County. Browne, who visited Tucson village in 1860, described it as "the most wonderful scatteration of human habitations as I ever beheld – a city of mud-boxes, dingy and dilapidated, cracked and baked into a composite of dust and filth ... these are what the travelers see, and a great many things more but in vain he looks for a hotel or lodging-house. The best accommodations he can possibly accept are the dried mud walls of some unoccupied outhouse." It was a station on the Butterfield Overland stage route, but that fact had little civilizing effect. By the summer of 1861 there were sixty-eight American voters in the town, who assembled and voted to join the Confederacy in the War Between the States. In February 1862 their desire became a reality with the arrival of two hundred Confederates from Texas under the command of Capt. Sherod Hunter. The visit of these men was cut short by word that about eighteen hundred Union men in the California Column under command of Col. James H. Carleton, had every intention of retaking the Old Pueblo. On May 20 the Confederates withdrew from Tucson and Lt. Col. West soon raised the American flag once again over Tucson. The California Column left the village in pursuit of the Confederates, and Tucson retreated into itts usual somnolent state. It was disturbed briefly in May 1864 with the appointment of William S. Oury as mayor and the municipality of Tucson was established with the signature of the territorial governor.

By 1866 Company C, First U.S. Cavalry, camped in Tucson, the way being cleared by cutting shrubbery on Tucson Military Plaza. This company moved some weeks later to Old Camp Grant. By 1867 by a majority of one vote in the Territorial Legislature, Tucson became the territorial capitol and remained so until 1877 when the capitol was removed to Prescott. Tucson sagged once again, this time to be revived by the discovery of silver at Tombstone, a fact which caused Tucson to become a stopping point en route to the fabled riches of Tombstone. The town gradually became a departure point for many mining camps in southern Arizona and Sonora, Mexico. The growth of the community was slow but never dull, at least in the hours of darkness, when Tucson was reputed to be wide open, rough, and ready.

During World War II, Air Corps fields and other military camps acquainted many men and women with the desirability of living in Arizona. Prior to World War II, the population of Tucson numbered fewer than forty thousand, but immediately after the war it began to grow, sprawling across the desert and losing much of the western atmosphere which had endeared it to thousands. With other parts of the Southwest, the city underwent phenomenal growth beginning in about 1960.

It should be noted before closing this entry that the spelling of the community name has been rendered at least forty different ways, a few of which follow:

Styuk-son	**Stycson**	**Tuozon**
Tuqulson	**Stjockson**	**Fruscon**
Tugson	**Tuczon**	**Toison**
Tubson	**Tuvoon**	**Stjukshon**
Tuquisson	**Tuhso**	

Associated names include Tucson Mountains (*q.v.*) and Tucson Wash (T9S/R16E). P.O. est. July 13, 1865, Mark Aldrich, p.m.; Wells Fargo 1879; incorp. Feb. 7, 1877. (See Buchanan, Fort. Actually, the p.o. was not for the village of Tucson.)
Ref.: Fr. Bonaventure Oblasser, Letter to Frank C. Lockwood (May 5, 1935); 206, p. 323; 15, I, 369, 381, 182, 513; 5, pp. 255, 256; 56, pp. 131, 132; 73, II, 157 107, III, 71; 72; 351, pp. 73, 75; 277, p. 29; 224, p. 277, AHS, Christopher Layton File; 77, p. 78, Note 11; 45, pp. 376, 377; 105, p. 67; 49, p. 83; *Arizona Star* (Feb. 24, 1955), p. 4; 228, n.p.

TUCSON MOUNTAINS
Pima   T14S R12E   Elev. 4205'
In 1775 Fr. Francisco Garcés called these Sierra Frente Negra (Spanish = "black base" or "front"). These are the mountains directly west of Tucson. See Tucson, Pima   Ref.: 77, p. 81, Note 13

TUFA   pro.: /tuwfə/
Cochise   Elev. c. 4000'
A marble quarry here had a siding on the railroad out of Douglas, hence the name. Tufa is a form of water-deposited carbonate of lime.
P.O. est. Jan. 29, 1903, Katie Hines, p.m.; resc. Aug. 1, 1903

TULAPAI CREEK
Gila   T2S R16E
Indians use agave cactus to make a kind of beer called *tulapai*, for which they collect plants along this creek. See also Ranch Creek, Gila, and Gilson Wash, Gila
Ref. Woody; 329

TULE:
The presence of reeds, often of the cattail variety, led to the use of the word *tule* (pro.: *tuwli*) in many Arizona place names, some of which follow:

Tule (El)   Apache   T11N R28E   Elev. c. 6200'
El Tule, a small Mexican settlement, took its name from the fact that many reeds grow nearby. The post office location form notes that the place was also called Craig and Lyman Reservoir. The Post Office Department deleted *el* from the name.
P.O. est. July 15, 1898, Severo Chavez, p.m.; disc. Aug. 20, 1903   Ref. Wiltbank; 242; 329

Tule Basin	Coconino	T20N R1E	
Tule Butte	Coconino	T13N R8E	Elev. 6626'
Tule Canyon	Gila/Maricopa	T3N R12E	
Tule Canyon	Graham	T5S R20E	
Tule Canyon	Yavapai	T11N R5-4E	

This canyon is also known as Dry Creek, a misapplication as Dry Creek has a different location.

Tule Creek	Coconino	T19N R4E	
Tule Creek	Greenlee	T2S R28E	
Tule Creek	Yavapai	T8N R1E	
Tule Desert	Yuma	T13S R14W	

This long, open valley is east of the Cabeza Prieta Mountains.

Tule Lagoon	Yuma	T9S R24W	
Tule Mesa	Yavapai	T12N R5E	Elev. 6682'

According to Fred Dugas, "Tule Springs lies up there. More cattle have bogged down in the tules than you ever saw."

Tule Mountains	Yuma	T14S R14W	Elev. 2200'

The name of these mountains, also called Tuseral Mountains, probably comes from that of Tule Tank. There is a rank growth of tules around the spring at the tank. See Tule Tank, Yuma Ref. 329; 35, p. 160

Tule Spring	Graham	T5S R20E	
Tule Spring	Maricopa	T6N R1W	
Tule Spring	Mohave (Grand Canyon)	T33N R6W	
Tule Springs	Pinal	T10S R16E	
Tule Springs	Greenlee	T25S R28E	
Tule Springs	La Paz	T3N R20W	
Tule Tank	Coconino	T20N R1E	
Tule Tank	Yuma	T3S R16W	

This location was a camping place of the Sand Papago Indians, who called it *Otoxakan* (= "where there is bulrush or tule"). The tank is a plunge pool at the foot of the falls. Ordinarily water can be reached by digging in the sand that fills the pool. Lenon thinks this may be Kino's Agua Escondida (= "hidden water"). It is hard to locate. Ref. 57, p. 421; Lenon

Tule Tank	Yuma	T14S R15W	

This location is also called Tinajas de Tule (Emory, 1857).

Tule Tank Wash	Coconino	T19N R3E	
Tule Tubs	Graham	T1S R23E	

This is a ranch headquarters on the San Carlos Indian Reservation.

Tule Wash	Mohave	T17N R12W	
Tule Wash	Yuma	T14S R13W	
Tule Well	Yuma	T14S R14W	

Although this used to be a way station on the Camino del Diablo, it now has water polluted with insects, ground rodents, and adobe ruins. In 1942, however, the Fish and Wild Life Service once again improved this well, but the water was twenty feet underground. Bryan says that the original well was dug out by prospectors about 1907 and that in 1941 the old well existed nearby with steps leading down to the water. Ref. Monson; 57, pp. 416, 420

Tule Wells	Cochise	T12S R31E	
Tule Wells Canyon	Cochise	T12S R31E	

TULLY

Cochise		T17S R21E	Elev. c. 388'

This was the site of the Tully, Ochoa & Company store, whose headquarters were in Tucson. This location was also referred to as Tullyville. Pinckney Randolph Tully (b. 1824, Mississippi; d. Nov. 10, 1903) freighted merchandise to Tucson from Las Cruces, New Mexico. He moved to Tucson in 1868, serving as mayor twice and as Territorial Treasurer for four years. The fact that the post office was in business for just a few months suggests that the location may have been established to service the railroad construction gang.

According to an article in the *Star* in 1880, this location was formerly called La Cienega. It is not, however, identical as the name applied to the general vicinity was La

Cienega c. 1865. Also, Tully should not be confused with Pantano (T16S/R17E). All that remains at this location today is a railroad siding.

Tully Peak (T14S/R16E) is an associated name.

P.O. est. June 21, 1880, John O'Dougherty, p.m.; disc. Nov. 8, 1880

Ref. 62; AHS, Chambers Collection, Box 12; *Arizona Album* (May 7, 1953); *Arizona Star* (April 29 1880)

TUMACACORI MOUNTAINS

Santa Cruz   T20S R12E   Elev. 5642'

In 1870 Pumpelly ascribed the name Arizona Mountains to all mountains from Nogales to the Altar Valley south of Arivaca, hence including these mountains. Their eastern portion includes several well defined summits bearing their own names, among them Atascosa Mountain and Sardina and Diablito Mountains. The Chain and Hardy map of 1881 supplies the name Tumacavori Mountains. See Tumacacori National Monument, Santa Cruz   Ref. 58; 57, p. 251

TUMACACORI NATIONAL MONUMENT

pro.: /tuwməkǽkoriʌ/ or /tuwməkákoriʌ/

Papago: *chuuma gagri* or *tchookum kavolik* = "where caliche curves"

Pima: *tse-ma-ka-kork* ="curved peak" or "shelves or ledges"

Santa Cruz   T21S R13E   Elev. 3275'

The name describes the appearance of the nearby mountains, which appear to slant. Hodge says the area was the former home of the Sobaipuri Indians. Here Kino first visited a large Pima town, called Tumacacori, in 1691. He established a *visita* in 1696, calling it San Cayetano de Tumacacori, also spelled San Cayetano Tumapacori. The village was on the east bank of the Santa Cruz River. Font's map shows the place in existence in 1707. When Jesuits were expelled from all Spanish dominions in 1767, Franciscans took over the mission chain in northern Sonora, calling this location San Ignacio de Tumacacori. Because of Apache depredations, the mother mission at Guevavi was abandoned in 1773, with San Jose de Tumacacori taking over its function as headquarters mission.

Apaches marauded with increasing frequency in the Santa Cruz Valley. The effect on the mission at Tumacacori is attested to by the fact that in 1764 one hundred and ninety-nine Indian neophytes were at the mission, but by 1772 only thirty-nine remained. The church on the east bank by that time was almost in ruins. Some time prior to 1791 a new roof was put in place. A new church was under construction on the west bank of the river by 1800.

Although some assert that Apaches destroyed the new church in 1820, in fact the new church was not dedicated until 1822, as attested to by the following: When Fr. Carrillo died in 1795, he was buried in the old church at the foot of the altar. Fr. Gutierrez, his successor, served for the ensuing twenty-six years, dying on December 13, 1821. Exactly one year later, as part of the dedication of the *new* church, the bodies of both priests were reinterred before the altar of the new church. The new church underwent thorough Apache destruction, judging by extant ruins. However, a resident priest continued to serve until 1841, at which time the ruined church was abandoned. It has never been reoccupied.

Barnes says that the Tumacacori de las Calabasas y Guebavi Grant was made in 1806 to Juan Laguna, then governor of the Tumacacori Indian village; Laguna never assumed ownership and in 1844 the place was sold at auction by an act of the Mexican congress. Barnes adds that the U.S. Land Court rejected the entire 73,246 acres claimed under the Grant.

The first Americans to visit this location in the early 1850s noted the church and mission ruins. Only two or three Germans were then living in the vicinity. They too soon moved away.

There have long been rumors that missionaries concealed vast fortunes in gold and silver. Around the turn of the century the legend of Tumacacori treasure attracted people who ransacked the grounds and the church. In 1907 Will C. Barnes, then an assistant U.S. forester, suggested protecting the ruins by proclaiming them a national monument. To establish it, Carmen Mendez relinquished ten acres of Homestead No. 3035 and the Tumacacori National Monument was authorized by Theodore Roosevelt's signature on September 15, 1908.

The community of Tumacacori adjacent to the national monument maintains a post office.
P.O. est. July 14, 1905, Frank A. Edwards, p.m.; resc. Sept. 12, 1905; reest. March 19, 1947, Rauel Pyron Valenzuela, p.m.   Ref.: 167, II, 836, 837; 15, I, 385, 475; 106, pp. 95, 118; 163, p. 19; 329, Arthur Noon, Letter from Gilbert Sykes (Aug. 1, 1941); 242; 18a; "Tumacacori National Monument" (N.D.), pp. 1, 4; 43, p. 264; Fr. Bonaventure Oblasser, Letter to Frank Lockwood (May 5, 1935); Henry F.Dobyns, "Tubac: "Where Some Ememies Rotted," *Arizona Quarterly,* xix (Autumn 1963), 232

TUMACACORI PEAK
Santa Cruz   T21S R3E   Elev. 5151'
A variant name for this peak is Rock Corral Peak (1943 USGS). See Tumacacori National Monument, Santa Cruz

TUMAMOC HILL
Papago = "horned toad hill"
Pima   T14S R13E   Elev. 3100'
In 1902 a laboratory for desert botanical research was constructed here.
Ref.: 58; 177, p. 321

TUNA CREEK
Coconino (Grand Canyon)   T32N R2E
This creek is in the north wall of the Grand Canyon and was named because of abundant prickly pear cactus which bears a fruit called *tuna*. In 1764 Figueroa noted that "Opata Indians call the plant *nopal* and the fruit *nabu* until it was quite ripe, at which time it was called *naco*." The USGS changed the name from Border Creek to this name, but the date is not known.   Ref.: Figueroa *ms.* (Huntington Library); 329

TUNICHA MOUNTAINS   pro.: /tóntsa:/
Navajo: *tóntsaa* = "big water"
Apache   T35N R30E   Elev. 9575'
The area abounds in small lakes and ponds, hence the name. Lt. James Hervey Simpson in 1849 called these mountains Sierra de Tunecha, a name he picked up from a work called "Doniphan's Expedition." He said that he found no granite such as described in the work. The name of these mountains is also spelled Tunitcha and Tune-chah. Other spellings include Tunicha, Tyincha, and Tunintsa. See Chuska Mountains, Apache
Ref.: 141, pp. 27, 196; 292, pp. 47, 60, 62

TUNNEL, THE
Gila   T12N R10E   Elev. c. 7500'
The escarpment of the Mogollon Rim is so steep that only a few roads lead from the high plateau to land below the Rim. In 1885 the Arizona Mineral Belt Railroad planned to lay tracks to join Globe and Flagstaff, a plan that involved getting the rails from the low basin land up over the Rim. Believers in the project took their pay in grubstake and stock and used their own mules to help dig a tunnel for the railroad. In 1887 Alec Pendleton, the railroad surveyor, found what he considered a better route and the tunnel was abandoned after having been carved only some seventy-five feet.
The unfortunate stockholders lost their investment when the road was sold by the Yavapai County sheriff to the Riordan Lumber Company of Flagstaff. As late as 1920 piles of axe-hewn ties lay along the proposed right of way south of Mormon Lake. The gaping hole of the tunnel remains.   Ref.: Croxen, Letter (Aug. 10, 1955); Woody

TUNNEL MINE SPRING
Yuma   T1N R18W
There is a spring in an old mining tunnel dug years ago at this location, hence the name.   Ref.: Monson

TUNNEL RESERVOIR
Apache   T7N R27E   Elev. c. 8000'
To fill this reservoir a tunnel had to be drilled to a natural lake, hence the name. This six hundred and ninety-four feet reservoir was appropriated in 1887.
Ref.: Wiltbank; 24, p. 29

TUNNEL SPRINGS
Coconino T21N R7E Elev. c. 7500'
Someone apparently tunnelled at this early-day watering place and the name hence became attached to it. Ref.: Slipher

TUNNEL SPRINGS
La Paz T1N R17W
There is a cave at this spring which is described as "the best bighorn sheep watering hole on the entire Kofa Game refuge." Ref.: Monson

TURKEY A number of place names in Arizona have their origin in the fact that wild turkeys were or are abundant at such locations. In the list below where definite information is known, it will be given. Examples follow:

Turkey Yavapai

See Cleator, Yavapai

Turkey Butte Coconino T19N R5E Elev. 7374'

Turkey Canyon Yavapai T21N R6W

Turkey Creek Apache T5N R31E Elev. c. 8400'

Turkey Creek Cochise T18S R27E

On this creek from 1880 to 1884 a man named Morris maintained a sawmill to produce lumber for the Copper Queen Mine at Bisbee. It was the only place where timbers at least one foot in diameter could be obtained. Morris named this creek because of the wild turkeys here. Ref.: 18a; Burgess

Turkey Creek Coconino T12N R12E Elev. 7000'

See also Darton Dome, Coconino

Turkey Creek Gila (1) T8N R14E (2) T2N R21E
(3) T7S R19E (4) T1N R25E

Turkey Creek Greenlee (1) T1S R29E (2) T14N R32E

Turkey Creek Pima T14S R18E

Turkey Creek Santa Cruz T22S R18E

Turkey Creek Yavapai (1) T18N R6W (2) T11N R1E

Turkey Creek (#2) was organized as a mining district in 1864.
P.O. est. July 15, 1869, James A. Flanagan, p.m.; disc. Sept. 20, 1869
Ref.: *Weekly Arizona Democrat* (March 20, 1880), p. 2

Turkey Creek Canyon Cochise

Lillian Riggs said that this is the correct name for what is sometimes called Turkey Canyon, but that actually it should be called Masies Canyon. See Masies Canyon, Cochise

Turkey Creek Ridge Coconino T18S R26E

Turkey Flat Gila T8N R11E

Turkey Flat Graham T9S R25E Elev. 7404'

This summer colony on the Swift Trail is on Turkey Flat, hence the name.

Turkey Hill Navajo T10N R20E

This location was named by Stanley Sykes, who used to hunt wild turkey here. Ref.: Sykes

Turkey Hill Ruins Coconino T22N R8E

This prehistoric ruin at the foot of Turkey Hill is a long two-storied structure, probably built between 1203 A.D. and 1278 A.D. It takes its name from that of the hills. Ref.: 5, p. 317

Turkey Hills Coconino T21N R8E

Turkey Lake Navajo T11N R21E

Turkey Mountain Cochise T18S R30E

This is a variant name for Chiricahua Peak.

Turkey Mountain Coconino T15N R10E

Turkey Mountain	Gila	T10N R14E
Turkey Mountain	Graham	

See Turtle Mountain, Graham

Turkey Mountain	Greenlee	T1S R29E
Turkey Park	Cochise	T17S R30E
Turkey Park	Coconino	T22N R7E
Turkey Pen Canyon	Cochise	T18S R29E
Turkey Ridge	Gila	T11N R12E
Turkey Ridge	Coconino	T23N R8E

See Darton Dome, Coconino

Turkey Roost	Pima	T23N R8E

See Soldier Camp, Pima

Turkey Spring	Coconino	T12N R11E
Turkey Spring	Gila	T7N R13E
Turkey Spring	Navajo	T11N R16E

In May 1886 Will C. Barnes camped here with a trapper named Woolf (see Woolf's Crossing, Coconino), who found a clutch of wild turkey eggs, hence the name. Ref.: 18a

Turkey Tanks   Coconino   T22N R9E

These tanks were discovered by Whipple in 1853. He called them the Cosnino Caves. Ref.: 71, p. 41

Turkey Water   Navajo   T13N R16E

This name is a translation of the Navajo name *Taazhibito.*

TURNBULL, MOUNT

Graham   T4S R20E   Elev. 8282'

Apache Indians called the mountain *Zill-gish-clar-zhe* (= "high mountain"). At 3:00 p.m. on October 30, 1846 Lt. William H. Emory and his Boundary Survey party passed around the base of this mountain. Emory called it Mount Turnbull. However on the 1851 Sitgreaves map the name of this mountain is Pinʒon Llanos (= "pine plains"), a name which could have been applied to either the adjacent area or to the mountain range (see Pinalenos Mountains, Graham).

It has been conjectured that Mount Turnbull was named for Charles Nesbit Turnbull, said to have been a lieutenant with the Boundary Survey Commission 1854-1856. However, Turnbull was only fourteen at the time and it seems unlikely that the mountain was named for young Turnbull. It is further conjectured that it might have been named for his father, William Turnbull, an army engineer who designed the Washington Aquaduct Bridge (Francis Scott Key Bridge?), which was completed over the Potomac River in 1843. Ref.: AHS, F. Wadel Information; 105, p. 69; 351 (Smithsonian Institution)

TURNER

Pinal   Location unknown

P.O. est. Oct. 21, 1880, George Danforth, p.m.; disc. Dec. 7, 1880

TURQUOISE CANYON

Coconino (Grand Canyon)   T32N R1W   Elev. 3500'

Barnes says that Maj. John Wesley Powell named this canyon for its beautiful coloring. Ref.: 18a

TURQUOISE MOUNTAIN

Mohave   T23N R18W   Elev. 4402'

In 1906 turquoise was being actively taken from several mines in this vicinity. Ref.: 200, p. 218; Harris

TURRET BUTTE

Gila   T3N R15E

Bourke used this name in his account of the battle on October 27, 1872, at Apache Cave (T3N/R10E). Escaping Indians took refuge here. The circular mountain rises to a columnar peak. Soldiers crawled to its summit on their stomachs in darkness and unobserved, reaching the top at dawn. Charging into the Apache camp, they panicked the Indians, some of whom leaped from the cliff. To quote Gen. Crook, "These were mashed into a shapeless mass. Of the few women who survived, some told Maj. John Randall that their band had killed three white men on the Hassayampa, among them one named Taylor. He had been tortured by being stuck full of splinters which were then set afire."

Bourke named the place Turret Butte because it is shaped like a fort turret. It is known today as Squaw Peak, possibly because only women survived the attack. See also Apache Cave, Maricopa   Ref.: 49, p. 201; 82, p. 178; Woody

TURRET PEAK

Yavapai   T10N R5E   Elev. 5400'

This peak name derives from the turret-like appearance of the mountain summit.

TURTLEBACK MOUNTAIN

Yuma   T3S R11W   Elev. 1423'

From a distance this mountain looks not unlike a turtle. In 1923 the name was changed from Pass Mountain (because of the pass it contains) to that given above. Locally it is often referred to as Red Mountain because of its color.   Ref.: Mercer; 329

TURTLE MOUNTAIN

Cochise   T19S R29E   Elev. 8540'

Harry D. Currall, who built the trail to this peak c. 1906, named the peak because it resembles the head and body of a turtle. It is also called Ravens Peak.   Ref.: Burrall

TURTLE MOUNTAIN

Graham   T5W R28E   Elev. 6635'

The descriptive name for this location was suggested in a paper by L. A. Heindle and R. A. McCullough. Through a corruption in the name, it has also been represented on maps as Turkey Mountain.   Ref.: 158a; 329

TUSAYAN   pro.: /túwsayan/

Coconino   T30N R2E   Elev. 6000'

A post office was established here to service a lumber camp about seven miles south of Grand Canyon Village. The name was taken from the early Spanish name for Black Mesa, location of the Hopi Indian Villages.

P.O. est. June 16, 1933, J. Vincent Gallindo, p.m.; disc. Feb. 27, 1937   Ref.: 242

TUSAYAN

Navajo

Gregory says that the Spaniards, who used this name for Black Mesa (area of the Hopi Indian Villages), thus interpreted the Zuñi name for the region, meaning "people of Usaya." See Hopi Villages and Black Mesa, Navajo   Ref.: 141, pp. 16, 196

TUSAYAN NATIONAL FOREST

Coconino

Tusayan National Forest in July 1910 was carved from the western part of the Coconino National Forest. On August 4, 1934, its 1,141,259 acres were transferred to the Kaibab National Forest.

TUSAYAN RUINS

Coconino (Grand Canyon)   T30N R5E   Elev. 6800'

This small ruin back of the museum on the South Rim is one of more than fifteen hundred prehistoric ruins at the Grand Canyon. Pueblo dwellers lived here in probably 1200 AD and abandoned it c. 1400 AD. It was excavated and named by Harold S. Gladwin in 1930. Its name is that used by Spanish explorers for the region of the Hopi Villages.   Ref.: Schellbach File (Grand Canyon)

TUSCUMBIA MOUNTAINS
Yavapai   T11N R1W   Elev. 6672'
James Burd Wilson and James McLean located the Tuscumbia Mine c. 1883 on this
mountain. They named it both for the Tuscumbia River and town in Alabama, as they
were born there. Tuscumbia Creek shares the name.   Ref.: 18a

TUSERAL TANK   pro.: /tuwsural/
Yuma   T13S R15W
This tank is in the mountains bearing the same name. Nothing is known about why they
are so called.   Ref.: Monson

TUTHILL, FORT
Coconino   T21N R7E   Elev. 6970'
The Coconino County Park and Recreational Area is what remains of Camp Tuthill,
which came into being in 1928. It was named for Brig. Gen. Alexander MacKenzie
Tuthill, commander of the Arizona National Guard, which had used the camp as its
headquarters. It was made a county park and recreational area on April 11, 1955.
Ref.: 5, p. 328; Mrs. Corey; Sykes; Slipher

TUWEEP
Hopi = "garden spot"
Mohave   c. T33N R7W   Elev. 5000'
The post office at this location was established to serve ranchers in the area. The name
was also spelled Tuweap. See Toroweap Valley, Mohave
P.O. est. Sept. 9, 1929, Mabel K. Hoffpauir, p.m.; disc. Dec. 31, 1950, with order
modified Jan. 26, 1951   Ref.: 242; 140, p. 21

TUYE SPRING   pro.: /toye:?/
Navajo: *tóyéé* = "hazardous water"
Apache   T27N R23E   Elev. c. 6000'
Gregory notes that this is a common name for springs which lie at the heads of box
canyons. He also says that the word *tuye* = "echo of thunder." That interpretation,
coupled with that of Van Valkenburgh's "hazardous water" translation, gives credence
to the explanation made by Fr. Haile, who says that the Navajo use this name for
watering places which attract lightning. The word is also spelled as follows: Togay,
Togai, Tuyey.   Ref.: 331, p. 165; 141, p. 196

TUZIGOOT NATIONAL MONUMENT   pro.: /túwziʌguwt/
Apache = "crooked water"
Yavapai   T16N R3E   Elev. 3478'
On July 25, 1939 Tuzigoot was made a national monument. It consists of forty-two
acres which contain at least three pueblos with a total of more than one hundred and ten
rooms. Evidence of the high level of culture here from c. 1000-1400 AD is in the
museum at the monument. The name for this monument was selected by Apache
Indians, who translate it as meaning "crooked water," borrowing the name from theirs
for Peck's Lake (below the pueblo).   Ref.: 13, Cotter, "Tuzigoot National Monument," p. 4, 6; Peck; 5, pp. 38-39, 332

TWENTY-FOUR DRAW
Apache   T8N R27E   Elev. c. 8500'
Prior to 1900 the huge Twenty-Four Land and Cattle Company had a corral at this
location, hence the name. The outfit was the largest in its part of Apache County, in
1881 running fifteen thousand head of cattle north of Springerville. The company used
the 24 brand, which caused them trouble with the notorious Clantons, who ran the H
Bar V ranch across the state line in New Mexico, using the 24 brand. The Clantons
easily altered the brand to their own. See also Fish Creek, Apache
Ref.: Wiltbank; Becker

TWENTY-NINE MILE BUTTE
Coconino   T13N R8E   Elev. 7251'
It was customary to name locations by their distance from army posts. Such is the case

with this butte, which on the old Crook Road is that distance from Camp Verde.
Ref.: Goddard; 18a

TWENTY-SEVEN MILE LAKE
Coconino   T13N R8E
This lake is twenty-seven miles from Camp Verde. See Twenty-Nine Mile Butte,
Coconino

TWENTY-TWO MESA
Yavapai   T11N R4E
This mesa is named for the cattle brand developed by pioneers here. Fred Dugas said
that the place was called Lee's Mesa and the cattleman who had used a *2* for his brand.
When Wallace Lowe came in, he added another *2*, hence the *22* brand and the name of
the mesa. Ref.: Dugas

TWIN BUTTES: Several locations are descriptively named because of the adjacency
of buttes. Examples follow:

Twin Buttes	Apache	T14N R27E	
Twin Buttes	Cochise	T23S R25E	

See Baylor Butte, Cochise

Twin Buttes	Gila	(1) T11N R7E	Elev. 6016'
		(2) T5N R11E	Elev. 2574'
Twin Buttes	Maricopa	(1) T1N R4E	Elev. 1334'
		(2) T5N R1W	Elev. 2194'
Twin Buttes	Mohave	T6N R10W	Elev. 6055'
Twin Buttes	Navajo	T18N R23E	Elev. 5675'

In March 1971 the USGS eliminated the following names for this location: Twin Mesa, Zuni
Mesas, and Zuni Mountain.

Twin Buttes (Town)	Pima	T17S R13E	Elev. 3500'

A large mine was the cause for the now-vanished railroad spur and small community here. See
Marjorie Wash, Pima

Twin Buttes	Pinal	T4S R8E	Elev. 1848'
Twin Buttes	Yavapai	(1) T15N R5W	Elev. 4500'
		(2) T14N R7E	Elev. 6258'
Twin Butte Wash	Apache/Navajo		

See Pueblo Colorado Wash, Apache/Navajo

TWIN: The following place names derive from the fact that the two features so named
in each instance are enough alike to be termed twins.

Twin Coves	Mohave (Lake Mead)	T32N R16W	
Twin Creek Canyon	Mohave	T31N R12W	

This is the west fork of Twin Spring Canyon which it joins at T31N/R12W.

Twin Dam	Greenlee	T10S R32E	
Twin Domes	Pinal	T3S R13E	
Twin Falls	Apache	T40N R30E	Elev. 6360'
Twin Hills	Pima	T14S R16E	Elev. 3305'
Twin Knolls	Graham	T8S R29E	Elev. 4554'
Twin Lakes	Navajo	T10N R15E	Elev. c. 6000'
Twin Mesa	Navajo		

See Twin Buttes, Navajo

Twin Oak Canyon	Navajo	T9N R18E	
Twin Peaks	Apache	T12N R25E	Elev. 6048'

Twin Peaks	Greenlee	T6S R32E	
Twin Peaks	Maricopa	T7N R5W	Elev. 3382'
Twin Peaks	Pima	(1) T17S R5W	Elev. 2615'
(2) T12S R11E	Elev. 2767'	(3) T13S R7E	Elev. 2443'

The former Mexican name for these hills was Picacho de Calero (Spanish: *picacho* = "peak"; *calero* = "lime"). Limestone from this area is used in producing cement. Ref.: 10, p. 29

Twin Peaks	Yavapai	T10N R1E	Elev. 6378' and Elev. 6878'
Twin Peaks	La Paz	(1) T5N R12W	Elev. 3019'
		(2) T3N R16W	Elev. 2770'
Twin Point	Mohave (Lake Mead)	T30N R13W	
Twin Spires	Yuma	T1N R18W	Elev. 2360'
Twin Spires Canyon	Yuma	T1N R18W	
Twin Spring	Coconino	T21N R2E	

The early name for this location was Andrews Spring, for Tom Andrews, who in 1903 established his claim near this spring. The earlier name has been lost over the years. Ref.: Benham; Smith

Twin Springs   Mohave (Lake Mead)   (1) T31N R12W (2) T19N R19W

There is only one spring at this location, but there is a tendency to pluralize names and the word "springs" in this case is local usage, not fact. Ref.: 329

Twin Springs Canyon   Mohave   T30N R12W

See Twin Springs, Mohave

Twin Springs Wash   Mohave (Lake Mead)

See Twin Springs, Mohave

Twin Tank Draw Coconino (Grand Canyon)   T31N R4W

Twin Tanks Wash	Yuma	T8S R20W	
Twin Trail Canyon	Apache	T5N R28E	
Twin Tree Canyon	Navajo	T10N R18E	
Twin Wash	Navajo	T18N R22E	Elev. c. 5300'

TWO BAR CANYON
Maricopa/Gila   T3N R12E

This canyon is named for a brand on cattle which grazed here. The brand was used by Earl Bacon, in the 1880s a freighter to Pleasant Valley. Ref.: Cooper

2 BAR MOUNTAIN
Gila   T3N R12E

The name Cathedral Peak for this location is an error. See 2 Bar Canyon, Maricopa/Gila Ref.: Cooper

2 BAR RIDGE
Maricopa   T3N R12E

This ridge is on the northwest slope of 2 Bar Mountain. See 2 Bar Canyon, Maricopa/Gila

2/E WASH
Graham   T9S R21E

This location, as late as 1962 called Hansen Canyon, takes its name from a cattle brand used in the vicinity. Ref.: 329

TWO GUNS
Coconino   T20N R12E

This location is the site of a "town" and a store owned by "Two Gun" Miller, who named it after his nickname. Miller, who said he was an Apache, feuded with the man who owned a store opposite Miller's place and killed him. Miller was acquitted. The victim was buried in a grave marked "killed by Indian Miller," but the Indian late one night painted out the grave inscription. He was jailed for desecrating a grave. Miller, who lived in a large cave, had a quick temper which flared whenever archaeologists tried to enter his home.

P.O. est.: date not in Nat'l. Arch.; disc. Jan. 1, 1973   Ref.: Colton; 242; L.S.M. Curtin, "Reminiscences in Southwestern Archaeology, III," *The Kiva* (Dec. 1960), 3

TWO: In the following instances the use of the word *two* in place names is descriptive of the number of similar items at the location:

Two Peaks	Maricopa	T1S R3E
Two Red Peaks Valley	Navajo	T33N R20E
Twin Springs Ridge	Coconino (Grand Canyon)	T34N R1E
Two Troughs Canyon	Graham	T7S R22E
Two Weeks Spring Canyon	Cochise	T19S R31E

These springs are useful only two weeks during a year.   Ref.: Burrall

Two White Rocks Wash	Navajo	T35N R20E

TYENDE CREEK   pro.: /thye?nde:h/
Navajo = "where they fell into a pit" (i.e., where animals bog down)
Navajo   T37N R22E
This creek is named on a 1968 map as Bambo Wash, for whatever reason. Emerging from Laguna Canyon at Marsh Pass, it is the longest perennially flowing stream in the region. The name is also spelled as follows: Ta-enta Creek, Kayenta Creek, Laguna Creek. See Laguna Creek, Navajo   Ref.: 141, pp. 87, 196; 331, p. 166

TYENDE MESA
Navajo   T39N R18E   Elev. 6060'
In 1932 the following names were eliminated by the USGS in favor of that at the end of this entry: Kayenta, Ke-en-ta, Te-en-ta. See Tyende Creek, Navajo

TYENDE WASH
Navajo   T37N R22E
In December 1970 the USGS changed the name of this wash to Laguna Creek. See Laguna Creek, Navajo

TYNDALL DOME
Coconino (Grand Canyn)   T33N R1W
This location is one of those in the group named for 19th century scientists. John Tyndall (1820-1893) was a physicist.

TYRIA WASH
Yavapai   T20N R10W
This wash was named in 1972 for the site of a homestead formerly owned by the Tyria family.   Ref.: 329

TYRO WASH
Mohave   T22N R21W
This wash is named because of the presence of the Tyro Mine. (T21N/R20W).

U

UDALL DRAW
Apache   T8N R26E
The Udall family emigrated to this area at the behest of the Mormon church. The family
has had many jurists and legislators, as well as teachers, among its members. The name
is shared by Udall Draw Springs and Udall Park

UINKARET PLATEAU   pro.: /uwíyngֻkaerət/
Piute = "place of pines"
Mohave   T39N R4W   Elev. 5840'
This location is also known as Antelope Plains and as Wonsits Plateau. The Piute name
for antelope is *wonsits*. Antelope existed here in great herds in Powell's day. Another
name for it is Wonsits Tiravu. This plateau extends more than fifty miles and is bounded
on the south by the Grand Canyon, on the east by Kanab Plateau, on the west by
Hurricane Caves, and on the north by the Vermilion Cliffs. See Trumbull, Mount,
Mohave   Ref.: 140, p. 37; 329, 88, pp. 254, 255

UKWALLA POINT   pro.: /úkwalə/ or /ə́kwalə/
Coconino (Grand Canyon)   T33N R4W   Elev. 5840'
This location, named for an Indian family, for accuracy should be spelled Uquella as
that is the way the family (which lives at Grand Canyon Village) spells it.
Ref.: Verkamp

UNCLE JIM POINT
Coconino (Grand Canyon)   T33N R4E   Elev. 8250'
In 1906 Frank Bond recommended that this point be named Natchi or Naji Point (pro.)
/nȁčiy/ or /nȁji/ for Natchi, son of Cochise, the famed Chiracahua Apache leader. In
1876 Natchi succeeded his father, but was exiled to Florida in 1889. Prior to placing his
name on this landmark, the name had been Lucifer Point. The name was to undergo
another change, this time to Uncle Jim Point in honor of Uncle Jim Owen (d. 1939). He
pioneered in the Texas Panhandle in 1876, going from there to Indian Territory
(Oklahoma) and then to the Grand Canyon region (1885) where he served as game
warden of the Kaibab National Forest for twelve years. He once said he made as much
as $500. a day hunting mountain lions for cattlemen. In 1905 he had eight buffalo
shipped to Arizona and in 1926 sold a greatly increased herd to the State of Arizona.
Uncle Jim's Buffalo Pasture is adjacent to the point. See also House Rock Valley,
Coconino   Ref.: Kolb; Clipping from Amarillo, Texas, newspaper, Grand Canyon
Files; 329, M.R. Tillotson, Letter (1930)

UNCLE SAM HILL
Cochise   T20S R22E   Elev. 4767'
The presence of the Uncle Sam Mine (T23S/R24E) on this hill in the early 1900s led to
the naming of the location. Uncle Sam Gulch is at T23S/R24E.   Ref.: Macia; 18a

UNION
Maricopa   T1N R1E
The Union Mine owned in 1897 by Frank Alkire was near here, and the Union Hills

(T4N/R3E, Elev. 2383') share the name.
P.O. est. June 20, 1887, E.J. Elzy, p.m.; disc. Oct. 30, 1888
Ref.: AHS, Frank Alkire Collection, Box 5

UNION
Mohave   T21N R18W   Elev. c. 3500'
At this juncture the road to Union Pass met the station on the Arizona & Utah
R.R. Ref.: 18a

UNION BASIN
Mohave
This basin northeast of the old Cerbat Mine is one of three depressions collecting water
from Grand Wash. Ref.: 200, pp. 91, 98

UNION, MOUNT
Yavapai   T12N R1W   Elev. 7950'
This mountain was named in the early 1860s by Union sympathizers. See also Davis,
Mount, Yavapai Ref.: 242

UNION PASS
Mohave   T21N R20W   Elev. 3600'
The reason for this name has not yet been learned. It was in use at least as early as 1870,
the pass itself having been known since Nov. 5, 1851 when Capt. Lorenzo Sitgreaves
crossed the Black Mountain Range through it. The route through the pass was important,
used by miners who picked up supplies at Chloride and took them west to Nevada
through this pass and via a ferry across the Colorado River to Searchlight, Nevada. In
1871 the Union Pass Station was managed by U.E. Doolittle. See also Frisco,
Mohave Ref.: *Weekly Arizona Miner* (June 30, 1871), p. 2; *Walapai Papers*, p. 5,
Note 5; 200, p. 25

UNKAR CREEK
Piute = "red creek"
Coconino (Grand Canyon)   T31N R5E   Elev. c. 5000'
This creek is on the north wall of the Grand Canyon. The name is descriptive. Unkar
Creek Rapid shares the name.

UPPER GRAND WASH CLIFFS
Mohave   T33N R14W   Elev. c. 6500'
This is a series of cliffs about twenty-six miles long. See Grand Wash Cliffs, Mohave

UPPER HOLDING RAVINE
Pinal   T9S R14E
This is a natural area for corraling livestock

UPPER LAKE
Mohave (Lake Mead)
This name was proposed in June 1946, but was not accepted. See Gregg Basin, Mohave
(Lake Mead)

UPSET RAPIDS
Coconino/Mohave (Grand Canyon)   T34N R4W   Elev. 3250'
The first upset of a boat in the 1923 Birdseye expedition occurred at this previously
unnamed location. Ref.: 123, p. 524

USERY MOUNTAIN
Maricopa   T2N R7E   Elev. 2959'
King Usery maintained a ranch here c. 1879, hence the name. Ref.: 18a

USTER WELL
La Paz   T7N R9W
In the early 1900s Frank Uster owned this well. Ref.: 279, p. 224

UTEVAK

Papago = "bear grass"
Pima   T20S R6E   Elev. c. 1800'
This is a temporary or summer-use village on the Papago Indian Reservation. Papago
basket makers use bear grass to produce black or dark brown portions of the basket
designs.   Ref.: 262, p. 2

UTTING

La Paz   T6N R16W   Elev. c. 600'
This siding on the railroad was named for Charles Utting, a Spanish-American War
veteran who lived in Phoenix. Migrant workers' cabins can be seen from the highway at
this point.   Ref.: 18a

V

VACA HILLS
Spanish = "cow"
Pima   T13S R6E   Elev. 2920'
These hills are on the Papago Indian Reservation. The reason for the name is not known.   Ref.: 262, p. 37

VAIL
Pima   T16S R16E   Elev. 3220'
Sources prior to the early 1870s do not mention the Vail brothers (Walter L. and Edward L.). Walter (1852-1906) came from Virginia City, Nevada, to Tucson in November 1875. His brother Edward arrived in 1879. The Vails gave the railroad permission to lay tracks across their ranch property. The Vail station is between the Empire and Rita stations on old railroad maps. In 1883 a post office was established at Pantano (T16S/R17E), which was a mile east of Vail. Vail Trap Spring (T16S/R18E) shares the name. See also Pantano, Pima, and Total Wreck, Pima
P.O. est. Feb. 26, 1901, Harry A. Mann, p.m.; Wells Fargo 1903
Ref.: 242; 164, p. x; AHS, Chambers Collection, Box 3-4; Kitt

VAIL LAKE
Coconino   T20N R8E   Elev. 7161'
Sheepmen used this area for lambing; which led to its name of Lambing Lake, still in use in 1908. James ("Jim") A. Vail, a pioneer incorporator of the first Flagstaff bank, established a cow camp beside this lake c. 1910. Its name gradually reflected that fact. In April 1964 the USGS eliminated the name Lambing Lake.   Ref.: 18a; Slipher; 329

VAINOM KUG
Papago = "iron stands"
Pima   T16S R3E   Elev. 2060'
This Papago village is near an abandoned well and ruined steampump of the old Weldon Mining Company, to which the name "iron stands" or "iron pipe" may refer. In 1917 the Corps of Engineers called this place Steam Pump Village. The surrounding area is sometimes called Pumphouse. The Papago name of this village is also rendered as follows: Vainomkux, Kvitak; Kvitatk, Kui Tatk.   Ref.: 59, p. 372; 58; 262, p. 14; 329

VAIVO VO   pro.: /wàyva wów?/
Papago = "cocklebur charco" (= pond)
Pinal   T8S R4E   Elev. c. 1400'
The variant name for this village is its translation (Cocklebur or Cucklebur). It is possibly the place which Fr. Eusebio Kino called San Angelo del Botum. Another spelling is Votum. Vawa Hills are here.   Ref.: 58; 262, p. 16

VAKOMOK
Papago = "rusty"
Pima   T20S R3E
This is the site of a former Papago village which also bore the following names: Comoti, Comot, Rusty Shovel (1931 Indian Irrigation Service).   Ref.: 262, p. 3

VALENTINE

Mohave   T23N R12W   Elev. 3800'

The Truxton Canyon sub-agency for the Hualapai Indians is on federal land here, whereas the post office and store are now private land, although formerly on agency land. This location was made a sub-agency to the Colorado River Agency in 1951. According to locations, the Truxton railroad siding is about a mile away from the post office (at T24N/R12W) and at a somewhat higher elevation (4320'). On May 14, 1900, six hundred and sixty acres were set aside and an Indian school built. Because the post office as a result was on agency land, the first Indian agent was also postmaster when the Truxton Canyon post office was established. With the discontinuance of the Indian school, the post office was removed to its present location, necessitating a change in the name of the post office, which was then called Valentine to honor Robert G. Valentine, Commissioner of Indian Affairs (1908-1910).

P.O. est. as Truxton, Dec. 17, 1900, Henry P. Ewing, p.m.; name changed to Valentine, Feb. 24, 1910   Ref.: 242; Glaser; Harris; 335, p. 202; 5, p. 323

VALLE   pro.: /væliʌ/ (sic)

Spanish = "valley"; *prado* = "meadow"

Coconino   T26N R2E   Elev. c. 6000'

In the mid-1920s the old name of Valle was changed to Prado and applied to a railroad station here. However, there was already a Prado on the Prescott-Phoenix ("P-line") branch of the railroad so that the name reverted to Valle. The small open meadow here was the site of the Valle airport.   Ref.: Benham; Terry

VALLEY

Yavapai   T18N R22W   Elev. 4573'

The name comes from the fact that this railroad location lay at the head of Chino Valley. Ref.: 18a

VALLEY FARMS

Pinal   T5S R9E   Elev. 1485'

When the post office was established, it served a number of farms in the valley, hence its name.

P.O. est. June 9, 1942, Ruth E. Wright, p.m.   Ref.: 242

VALLEY HEIGHTS

Maricopa   T3N R2E   Elev. c. 1500'

This location is above the valley, hence the name.

P.O. est. Feb. 3, 1914, Thomas J. Crowe, p.m.; disc. Dec. 9, 1914   Ref.: 242

VALLEY VIEWPOINT

Navajo   T8N R17E

From here there is a fine view of the valley, hence the name.

VAMORI   pro.: /váməri/

Papago = "basin" or "swamp"

Pima   T20S R4E   Elev. 2248'

The name comes from the fact that this small Papago village lies in the basin. On an 1869 map the name is spelled Bamori Spring, a natural confusion of *b* and *v*. Vamori Wash (a.k.a. Gu Oidak Wash) runs through the basin.   Ref.: 58; 262, p. 3

VANAR

Cochise   T14S R32E   Elev. c. 3800'

Barnes says that the first name of this location was Vanarian, shortened to expedite telegraphy. Why this railroad location was so named is not known. Vanar Wash (T13S/R52E) shares the name.

P.O. est. Jan. 21, 1914, B. Imogene Rice, p.m.; disc. Oct. 14, 1916   Ref.: 18a; 242

VASEY'S PARADISE

Coconino (Grand Canyon)   T36N R5E   Elev. c. 5000'

George W. Vasey (1822-1893) was a botanish with the U.S. Department of Agriculture

1872-1893. On August 9, 1869 Maj. John W. Powell thus described this location:

> The river turns sharply to the east and seems enclosed by a wall, set with a million brilliant gems ... on coming nearer we found fountains bursting from the rock high overhead and the spray and the sunshine forms the gems which bedeck the wall. The rocks below the fountain are covered with mosses and ferns and many beautiful flowering plants. We named it Vasey's Paradise in honor of the botanist who traveled with us last year.

Not everyone viewed it the same way. Dr. A.H. Thompson said, "The Major says that the place is called 'Vasey's Paradise' but if it is, it is a Hell of a Paradise."
Ref.: 266, p. 76; 322, p. 93, Footnote; Schellbach File (Grand Canyon)

VAYA CHIN
Papago = "well's mouth"
Pima   T12S R1W   Elev. 2130'
This is a small Papago village which appears erroneously on a 1930 road map as South Well.   Ref.: 262, p. 8

VEKOL
Pima = "grandmother"
Pinal   T9S R2E   Elev. 3625'
A post office called Vekol provided mail service for employees of the Vekol Mine. In 1864 John D. Walker organized a company of Pima Indians to fight Apaches. Thereafter Walker remained as a trader with the Pimas, living near them, learning their language and becoming their close friend. The Indians told him about an old silver mine which they probably called *vekol*. In 1880 Walker told Peter R. Brady. This so displeased the Indians that they said they would refuse to show Walker the location if he were accompanied by anyone other than his own brother. With his brother (Lucien E.) and Indians, Walker went secretly at night to find the old mine. Brady followed, revealing himself almost at the moment that the Indians uncovered the mine. Walker admitted Brady to part ownship. The tree partners were offered over $150,000. for the mine but refused to sell. Today the name Vekol is shared by the Vekol Mountains (T10S/R2E, Elev. 3625') and by Vekol Wash (Maricopa/Pinal; T5S/R1E). The mountains until 1941 were a.k.a. Bitter Well Mountains.
P.O. est. Sept. 25, 1880, William T. Day, p.m.; disc. Oct. 30, 1909
Ref.: *Arizona Journal Miner* (Oct. 1, 1908), p. 3; 29'7, pp. 36, 37; 205, pp. 82, 83

VENEZIA
Yavapai   T12N R2W
Barnes lists "Max" as being "somewhere in Apache County." Considering the difficulty encountered in untangling references pertaining to this entry, his bewilderment is understandable. "Max" in reality was the nickname of Redden A. Allred, postmaster of the supposed "Max" post office. The name of the post office in 1881 was Maxton, not Max. The Maxton p.o. operated for the benefit of employees at the Senator Mine, in existence by 1878, at which time its ore assayed at $85.00 per ton in gold. (See Goodwin, Yavapai)

In 1901 the Maxton p.o. was in a store owned by John A. Twigg until at least 1906. The postmaster in 1901 was Morilla T. Alwens—a name close enough to "Max" Allred's name to confuse Barnes' analysis. Why in 1915 a further change occurred is not yet clear, but the name was then changed to Venezia, located on the post office site map as being in R1 W, which may be a clue to its being in a different location. Records in the National Archives states that the local name was Bolada, not Goodwin (a name favored by some residents). Barnes says a native of Venice—one F. Scopal—insisted on the name being Venezia.

Close study of maps reveals that the Goodwin post office was not the same as that at Venezia, but operated some five miles northwest of the older Maxton/Venezia location. Records in the National Archives back up map analysis.
P.O. est. as Maxton, Feb. 24, 1881, Redden A. Allred, p.m.; disc. May 13, 1881; reest. July 6, 1901, Morilla T. Alwens, p.m.; name changed to Venezia, Aug. 24, 1915, Don J. Tomlinson, p.m.; p.o. est. as Senator ("on former site of Maxton"), June 9, 1915, Mrs. Mary Wills, p.m.; Senator disc. Oct. 22, 1918; name of Venezia changed to Goodwin, June 1, 1935   Ref.: 242; *Prescott Journal Miner* (Oct. 14, 1906), p. 4; *Arizona Journal Miner* (Nov. 16, 1897), p. 4; 18a

VENTANA   pro: /ventánə/
Spanish = "window"
Pima   T11S R1E   Elev. 2234'
This is a Papago village for which the name White's Well is incorrect. See also Kohi
Kug, Pima, and Ventana Canyon, Pima   Ref.: 262, p. 8

VENTANA CANYON
Spanish = "window"
Pima   T13S R14E   Elev. c. 3500'
A formation of rocks near the head of this canyon looks like a window or hole. Another
Ventana Canyon (T13S/R15W) shares the name. Ventana Pass is at T12S/R1E.

VENTANA MESA
Spanish = "window"
Apache   T32N R25E   Elev. c. 6000'
Several natural rock windows on this mesa led to the name.   Ref.: 141, p. 196

VENUS TEMPLE
Coconino (Grand Canyon)   T32N R5E   Elev. 6285'
This location was named in accordance with the USGS decision c. 1905 to name
locations for deities of ancient religions and mythology.

VERDE, CAMP   pro.: /vérdi/
Spanish = "green"
Yavapai   T14N R5E   Elev. 3147'
The camp borrows its name from the river on which it is. In June 1865 J.N. Swetnam (b.
Nov. 11, 1842) left Prescott with nine men to explore the feasibility of establishing a
farming community in the Verde Valley. A small colony began taking shape at the
junction of the Verde and Clear Fork about three and one-half miles from the present
Camp Verde. In early 1866 the settlers constructed a small private fort which they
named Camp Lincoln. Regular troops soon occupied it, using the same name. Because of
confusing its name with that of Camp Lincoln in Dakota Territory, the name was
changed to Camp Verde on November 23, 1868. The site was unhealthful. Malaria was
rampant. In 1871 Gen. George Crook ordered the camp moved to a healthier place and
in 1871 it was relocated a mile south on higher ground. In the interim the Rio Verde
Reservation was temporarily established by Vincent Colyer. The name of Camp Verde
was changed in 1879 to Fort Verde. The post was abandoned on April 10, 1890. The
settlement of Camp Verde developed despite the withdrawal of troops. For that reason
the post office was reestablished.
P.O. est. as Camp Verde, March 14, 1873, George W. Hance, p.m.; reest. Aug. 8, 1898,
M.L. Head, p.m.   Ref.: Goddard; 242; 261, pp. 5, 6, 8, 106; 121a, p. 14; 145, p. 158;
Weekly Arizona Miner (Dec. 12, 1868), p. 2; 82, p. 166, Note 8; 206, p. 94; 107, VIII, 12

VERDE HOT SPRINGS
Yavapai   T11N R6E
Indians and settlers used these medicinal hot springs. A variant name is Indian Hot
Springs.

VERDE RIVER   pro.: /vérdi/
Spanish = "green"
Gila/Yavapai/Maricopa/Coconino   T10N R6E
Depending on what section of this river they encountered, various people have applied a
series of names. For instance on May 8, 1583, Don Antonio de Espejo, according to
Luxan, called it El Rio de los Reyes (= "Kings' River"). In 1604 Juan de Oñate, who
encountered this stream near its headwaters, called it Rio Sacramento. Sedelmayr in
1744 seems to be the first to call it Verde, that name reflecting the fact that Indians called
the river *green*. Indians said that the stream flowed past a mountain ridge ribbed with
rocks of green, purple, and other colors. When Lt. Amiel W. Whipple saw its
headwaters in 1853, he called it Bill Williams Fork. Whipple also noted that his guide
Antoine Leroux called it Rio San Francisco because its source was in the San Francisco

Mountains. Whipple also acknowledged that the early Spanish explorers and Indians called it Rio Verde. On a military map for the Dept. of New Mexico 1859/1867, is a notation "Rio Verde or San Fernando." Gen. Palmer in 1866 recorded that the river was sometimes called the San Francisco for the same reason. The need to identify where fights with Indians took place frequently made the military use the name Verde and the name gradually settled into being Verde River. The name is shared by places near the river.   Ref.: 22, p. 30; 15, pp. 346, 348; 287, p. 39; p. 178, Note 20; 252, Section 2, 1866; 345, p. 80; 242

VERDE ROAD
Yavapai/Coconino
This military road from Fort Verde to Fort Apache was created in 1873 to facilitate troop movements from the headquarters of Gen. George Crook at Prescott and Fort Apache. A string of wet-weather lakes along this road was numbered in sequence as they occurred, i.e. Lake No. 1, etc.   Ref.: 18a

VERDE VALLEY
Yavapai   T16N R3E
This is the valley of the Verde River, roughly from the juncture of the Verde River and Sycamore Creek southeast to near the junction of Verde River and Fossil Creek. In 1853 Lt. Amiel W. Whipple noted that the valley had "clear rivulets with fertile valleys and fine forrest trees. The wide belt of country . . . bears every indication of being able to support a large agricultural and pastoral population." It was, however, subject to multiple Indian attacks and hence was slow to be settled. A newspaper in late 1875 noted that a party of forty people with twelve wagons and two hundred and fifty head of stock were en route to the Verde settlement and that the "vacated Indian reservation is being thickly settled up." See also Verde, Camp, Yavapai
Ref.: 346, p. 195; *Weekly Arizona Miner* (Oct. 15, 1875), p. 2

VERMILION CLIFFS
Coconino   T41N R5W   Elev. 3775'
This small community consists of little more than a store catering to tourists. See Vermilion Cliffs, Coconino

VERMILION CLIFFS
Coconino   T39N R7E   Elev. 5360'
These cliffs were so called by Maj. John Wesley Powell, who wrote, "I look back and see the morning sun shining in splendor on their painted faces; the salient angles are on fire and the retreating angles are buried in shade, and I gaze on them until my vision dreams and the cliffs appear a long bank of purple cliffs plowed from the horizon high into the heavens." The section north of Third Creek is called Towers of Third Creek and also Tumurru (Piute = "a rock rover's land").   Ref.: 88, pp. 150-151, 158; 266, pp. 112, 113; 306, p. 210; Schellbach (Grand Canyon) File

VERNON
Apache   T10N R25E   Elev. 6960'
B.H. Wilhelm settled here and named it Vernon in 1894 for W.T. Vernon. It became an important sawmill town, but in 1954 that activity moved to the vicinity of Lakeside. Vernon Creek (T9N/R25E) shares the name.
P.O. est. April 25, 1910, Mrs. Fanny Northrup, p.m.   Ref.: Noble; 242

VESTA TEMPLE
Coconino (Grand Canyon)   T31N R1E   Elev. 5200'
In accordance with USGS policy c. 1905, this location was named like others in the Grand Canyon for a deity of an ancient religion and mythology.

VIASON CHIN
Papago = "mouth of erosion"
Pima   T16S R1E   Elev. 1900'
On a 1915 Indian Service map this small village is named Via Santee. The name is descriptive.   Ref.: 58; 262, p. 10

VICENTE WASH, SAN
Pima   T16S R7E
This wash passes by the old San Vicente Ranch, from which it takes its name.
Ref.: 262, pp. 13, 28

VICKSBURG
La Paz   T5N R14W   Elev. 1382'
Victor E. Satterdahl had a post office in his store. On the post office application he
suggested the name Victor, but when the post office turned down the name, Vicksburg
was selected in its place.
P.O. est. April 20, 1906, Victor E. Satterdahl, p.m.; Wells Fargo 1907
Ref.: 242; 5, p. 369

VICTORIA PASS
Pima   T17S R6W
This pass takes its name from that of the Victoria Mine, which was being worked for
silver in the early 1900s.   Ref.: Hensen; Supernaugh

VICTORINE CROSSING
Coconino   T14N R12E
There is a possibility that this location was named for Castillo Victorino (b. 1840,
Mexico).   Ref.: 63

VIEWPOINT
Apache   T36N R30E   Elev. 9114'
From this highest point in the Lukachukai Mountains, there is a view deep into Arizona
and New Mexico.   Ref.: 141, p. 29

VILLA BUENA RUIN   pro.: /víyə bwéynə/
Spanish = "good town"
Maricopa   T1N R1E   Elev. c. 800'
This location was named by Dr. O.A. Turney.   Ref.: 18a

VINEGARON WELL   pro.: /vínəgarown/
La Paz   T2N R13W   Elev. c. 500'
The well is an old one owned c. 1920 by the Thomas W. Bales Cattle Company. One
species of scorpion is called *vinegarroon* because when disturbed it gives off an odor like
that of vinegar. These scorpions occur throughout the Southwest, but are no more
abundant at this location than elsewhere. Vinegaroon Wash (or Vinegaron Wash) is at
T7S/R20W.   Ref.: Mercer; 279, p. 225

VINEYARD MOUNTAIN
Gila   T4N R11E   Elev. 3458'
Both this mountain and Vineyard Canyon were named for John Allan Vineyard, an early
settler on Tonto Creek.   Ref.: Agnes Ollsen (Vineyard's daughter)

VIOLET POINT
Coconino (Grand Canyon)   T33N R1E   Elev. 7530'
This head on the North Rim is at the south end of Rainbow Plateau. It is one of several in
the vicinity named for colors in the rainbow.

VIRGIN BASIN
Mohave (Lake Mead)   T32N R21W   Elev. c. 1000'
This location is the center one of three basins occupied by Lake Mead. In 1948 the

USGS dropped the following names in favor of Virgin Basin: Middle Basin, Middle Division, and Middle Lake. The basin drains the Virgin River.   Ref.: 329

VIRGIN BASIN
Yuma   T3S R18W   Elev. c. 800'
This name, in existence for many years, is descriptive of a location noted for its virgin vegetation. Virgin Peak (T1S/R13W, Elev. c. 2500') is an associated name.
Ref.: Monson

VIRGIN CANYON
Mohave   T30N R18W
Wheeler in 1871 named this boundary canyon between Nevada and Arizona because "this is our first cañon upon entirely new ground." Dellenbaugh objected to the statement because Wheeler was not the first to cross that portion of the United States. A variant spelling is Virgen Canyon.   Ref.: 343, I, 161; 89, pp. 297, 298

VIRGINIA CITY
Pima   T15S R2E   Elev. c. 3000'
This location was laid out in 1854 by W.J. Dougherty, W.R. Gleason, and L.D. Chilson. At the same time sites were laid out for communities called Brooklyn, Logan City, and New Virginia, to serve the Quijotoa Mining District.   Ref.: 308, pp. 70, 71

VIRGIN MOUNTAINS
Mohave   T39N R14W
The local name for these mountains in 1872 was Mingkard Mountains. In December 1962 the USGS changed the name of Bunkerville Mountains to the name given above, which had been in use for many years. Bunkerville was the name of a Mormon community. See Virgin River, Mohave   Ref.: 322, p. 74; 329

VIRGIN RIVER
Mohave/Nevada   T40N R16W   Elev. c. 2000'
The first name applied by other than Indians was Rio Virgen, by Fr. Escalante in 1776. The river has had various names, among them on a later map (showing Escalante's route) the river name is Rio Fulfureo de las Piramides. Still another name is Pilar, also attributed to Escalante. By sheer coincidence Jedediah Smith traveled along this river with Thomas Virgin in 1826, but Smith called it the Adams River. In 1857 Lt. Joseph Christmas Ives was not deterred from knowing it was the Virgen River. For unknown reasons, on the 1869 territorial map it is the Santa Clara River. Piute Indians continue to use their own descriptive name for this stream: *Pah-Roose* (= "very muddy stream"). In 1932 the USGS eliminated the spelling Virgen and the name Pilar River in favor of the current name Virgin River.
Ref.: 345, III, 109, 110; 259, p. 60; 306, p. 243; 245, p. 77

VISHNU TEMPLE
Coconino (Grand Canyon)   T33N R5E   Elev. 7529'
This location was named by Clarence Dutton in 1882, who said it looked like an oriental pagoda. James added that it is "without doubt the most stupendous mass of nature's carving in the known world."   Ref.: 100, p. 148; 178, p. 37

VISTA ENCANTADORA   pro.: /vistá enkántədorə/
Spanish = "enchanting view"
Coconino (Grand Canyon)   T33N R4E   Elev. 8500'
In 1941 Dr. Harold C. Bryant, Supervisor of Grand Canyon National Park, changed the name from Vista Encantada (= "enchanted view") to Vista Encantadora (= "enchanting view"), the latter being more suitable.   Ref.: Bryant, Letter (April 9, 1956)

VISTA POINT
Greenlee   T3N R29E
This is a view point, hence the name.

VIVIAN WASH
Mohave						T19N R20W

The principal mining camp and this wash took their name from that of the Vivian Mine, about one-quarter mile below Vivian and west of Vivian Wash. See Oatman, Mohave

VOCK CANYON   pro.: /vowk/
Mohave						T24N R17E						Elev. c. 3800'

Cris Vock, a cook for cowboys, developed Vock Spring (T23N/R17W) here and began raising cattle in the canyon, hence the name. The spellings Vogt and Vought are incorrect.   Ref.: Harris

VOLCANIC MOUNTAIN
Apache						T14N R27E						Elev. 5960'

The name describes the nature of this mountain.

VOLUNTEER SPRING
Coconino					T21N R5E

This name appears on a map in the National Archives dated 1881. In 1887 it belonged to Walter J. Hill, a sheepman. It may be the same location as New Year's Spring, but the 1881 map shows it east of New Year's Spring. The spring is on Volunteer Prairie. Barnes says that it was named by a detachment of the California Volunteer Regiment which came to Arizona and camped at this location in 1863. Associated names include Volunteer Canyon (T20N/R4E), Mountain (Elev. 8047'), and Wash (T20N/R4E). Ref.: 242; 18a

VOPOLO HAVOKA
Pima: *vopelo* = "burro"; *vo* = "pond"; *ha* = "there"
Pima						T19S R4E						Elev. 2211'

This small village on the Papago Indian Reservation was so noted in 1941 with a variant and incorrect name given as Vopelohavooka or Burro Pond Village. Ref.: 262, p. 14; 58

VOTA
Cochise						T22S R20E

The reason for this name is not known.
P.O. est. April 21, 1881, Ira J. Richards, p.m.; disc. Feb. 26, 1883   Ref.: 242

VULCAN'S THRONE
Mohave (Grand Canyon)			T33N R7W						Elev. 5108'

Maj. Clarence Dutton named this location in 1882. He was the first to apply names of deities from ancient religions and mythologies to features in the Grand Canyon. Vulcan's Throne is a volcanic cone towering six hundred feet high on the cap of the Inner Gorge. It is only one of one hundred and sixty-nine volcanoes in the immediate vicinity.   Ref.: 100, pp. 4, 92

VULTURE
Maricopa					T6N R5W						Elev. c. 2800'

In 1863 Henry Wickenburg (see Wickenburg, Maricopa) discovered the Vulture Mine, among the richest in Arizona history. One legend says he shot a vulture and on picking it up noticed nuggets lying around. A second legend says his burro ran away and the angered Wickenburg threw rocks, but paused when he noticed that the rocks contained gold. Still a third says that he saw buzzards hovering over the peak (Vulture Mountain or Peak) on the day he made his rich discovery. During the Civil War the Vulture Mine helped supply a great demand for gold. By the end of the war forty mills were operating at the mine and another four were built on the Hassayampa in 1865. In 1879 James Seymour, a New Yorker, bought the supposedly worked-out Vulture Mine. He built a new mill opposite the mine location at a community named for himself. The post office was always at Seymour. It was not the same location as the old Vulture City. Mine operations faded gradually and ceased in 1942. The Vulture Range (or Mountain) at T6N/R5W shared the name while the mine was in use. Vulture Siding served as a shipping point.
P.O. est. as Seymour, June 20, 1879, Isaac H. Levy, p.m.; changed to Vulture, Oct. 4, 1880; disc. April 24, 1897   Ref.: 5, p. 57, 358; 163, p. 260

W

WAGONER
Yavapai T10N R3W Elev. 3381'
Ed Wagoner founded the town named for him. The post office application says that the office would serve about fifty ranchmen and miners.
P.O. est. Jan. 24, 1893, M. A. Wagoner (*sic*); disc. Jan. 1, 1970
Ref.: *Arizona Journal Miner* (March 27, 1899), p. 4; 242

WAGON: Wagons played a significant part in pioneers' settling in Arizona. Reference to the word *wagon* occurs in several place names and it may be assumed that wagons or wagon parts were concerned. No definite information has been learned on most. Examples follow:

Wagon Box Draw	Coconino	T20N R12E	
Wagon Canyon	Apache	T40N R24E	
Wagon Canyon Spring	Mohave	T17N R11W	
Wagon Draw	Coconino	T13N R15E	
Wagon Tire Flat	Yavapai	T19N R1W	Elev. c. 4500'

The name derives from the fact that for years an old wagon tire was leaning against a tree here. Ref.: 18a

Wagon Tire Wash	Yavapai	T19N R1W	

See Wagon Tire Flat, Yavapai

Wagon Wheel Wash	Mohave	T18N R14W	
Wagon Wheel Trading Post	Yavapai	T10N R3W	Elev. 3381'
Wagon Wheel Canyon	Navajo	T10N R15E	

WAHAK HOTRONTK
Papago = "road goes down"
Pima 32°11'/112°22'
This Papago village is known to many as San Simon Indian Village. The Papago name is descriptive. Ref.: 262, p. 10; 329

WAHL KNOLL
Apache T7N R28E Elev. c. 7800'
In the early 1800s John C. Wahl ran cattle here, but lived in Springerville. Ref.: 18a

WAHWEAP BAY
Mohave (Lake Mead) T41N R8E
The reason for this name has not yet been learned. The Wahweap Marina (T42N/R8E) is headquarters for National Park Service operation in this area and also serves vacationers. Ref.: 317, pp. 29, 30

WAKEFIELD CANYON
Pima T17S R18E
This location was named for Lyman Wakefield (b. 1853; d. Oct. 1, 1910), in 1898

sheriff of Pima County, a member of the Wakefield Brothers firm. he was also a cattleman and store owner. His general store at Pantano in 1878 served as the post office. Wakefield Canyon was his location at Pantano and Wakefield Creek ran through it. Wakefield Spring was also here. His mine was at T23S/R20E.
Ref.: AHS, Chambers Collection, Box 9-10; 242

WALAPAI POINT
Coconino (Grand Canyon)   T32N R1W   Elev. 6714'
This name is in line with the USGS policy of naming places in the Grand Canyon for Indian tribes. Their name, however, is usually Hulapai.

WALCOTT TRAIL
Coconino (Grand Canyon)   T32N R5E
This trail down the North Rim follows Chuar Creek. It was named for Dr. Charles D. Walcott, Director of the USGS and Secretary of the Smithsonian Institution in the early 1880s, who was responsible for the first detailed stratigraphic work on the Grand Canyon. Ref.: 178, p. 58

WALDRON TRAIL
Coconino (Grand Canyon)   T31N R2E
A cattleman named Dan Hogan and one named Carruthers ranged stock in the Hermit Basin and built this trail for access. It was part of the old Boucher Trail. See Hermit Trail, Coconino (Grand Canyon) Ref.: Schellbach File (Grand Canyon)

WALKER
Yavapai   T13N R5W (1894)   T13N R1W (1932)   Elev. 6200'
Walker guided an expedition sent by Capt. Bonneville from Great Salt Lake to California and scouted for Col. Kit Carson. In 1861 he found gold in what was later Yavapai County, but put off further investigation. Capt. Joseph Reddeford Walker (b. 1798, Tenn.; d. 1876) conducted a gold prospecting expedition into this area in 1863. In May a man named Miller found more than $4000. worth of gold in a single panning from Lynx Creek. Walker then moved his main camp to the location, so rich that only butcher knives were needed to dig gold from the rock seams. The place was sometimes called Walker Diggings. Walker returned to California in 1867. Confusion arose in the years following about a second Joseph R. Walker also in the 1863 expedition. He was in fact Joseph Rutherford Walker, a nephew.
    Walker Gulch (T8N/R2W) and Walker Mountain (T14N/R6E, elev. 5925') have associated names.
P.O. est. Dec. 15, 1879, William L. Lewis, p.m.; disc. Sept. 30, 1940
Ref.: *Weekly Arizona Miner* (June 5, 1869), p. 3; *Arizona Miner* (Nov. 27, 1869), p. 2; 5, p. 4; 224, pp. 109, 110; 242

WALKER BASIN
Yavapai   T14N R7E
This location on a mountain takes its name from that of Joe Walker, a bachelor cattleman who was here c. 1875. Ref.: R. W. Wingfield, Letter (Feb. 11, 1956)

WALKER BUTTE
Pinal   T4S R8E   Elev. 1988'
The Pima Indian name for this butte was Cheene Peak, mapped as early as 1879. By 1907 the name Walker Butte was being used and the USGS officially changed the name. It was named, according to Barnes, for Lt. John D. Walker. See Vekol Mine, Pinal Ref.: 18a; 329

WALKER CANYON
Santa Cruz   Elev. 5700'
William Henry Walker (b. Jan. 16, 1859, Watsonville, California; d. Aug. 25, 1944) in 1886 arrived in Arizona and settled in the canyon bearing his name. Later he moved near Calabasas to a ranch involved in title difficulties connected with the Baca Float Land Grant. Ref.: Virgil Walker, Letter (March 1956)

WALKER CREEK

Apache   T41N R25E   Elev. c. 6200'

When Herbert Gregory discarded the name Gothic Wash for this location, he named it
for Capt. John George Walker (d. July 20, 1893), who was the first to cross this stream
while with the Macomb expedition in 1859. Gregory noted that Navajos called the upper
portion *Chinlini* (= "place where water comes out of a canyon"). The canyon it
traverses is Chinlini Canyon. Its lower middle section is Mexican Water. It also runs
through Walker Creek Valley. Ref.: 141, p. 90, Note 2, and p. 191

WALKER LAKE

Coconino   T23N R6E   Elev. 7910'

Walker Lake is a volcanic cup formation on top of Walker Mountain. The name
formerly used by cattlemen for this location was Blowout Tank. Some people refer to the
location simply as The Basin. As for the name Walker, one informant says that there was
a sign tacked to a tree with that name on it, but that the word *Lake* was not included.
Locally it was believed that two young Mormons attempted to settle and that one of them
was named Walker, possibly "Ace" Walker. Their cabin later burned. Whatever the
case, in 1910 Ace Walker was a bullwhacker helping to freight supplies to Lee's Ferry.
Walker Hill is nearby (T22N/R5E, elev. 7690'). Walker Tank is at T14N/R9E.
Ref.: Switzer; Slipher; *Arizona Enterprise* (Sept. 18, 1878); AHS, Daniel O'Leary File

WALLACE BUTTE

Coconino (Grand Canyon)   T33N R1W

This butte on the South Wall was named for Alfred Russell Wallace (1823-1913), an
English naturalist. The name Wallace Dome was suggested in September 1915 instead
of Tyndall Dome as "this would complete the set of noted evolutionists." It is on
Wallace Plateau. Ref.: 329, Francois Matthes, Letter to E.M. Douglas, geographer

WALLA VALLEY

Hopi: *wala* = "gap"

Coconino (Grand Canyon)   T33N R2E

According to Fewkes, the name means "the gap." This location was formerly known as
Tranquil Valley (in use since the early 1900s). Older names (Thurso and Pond Canyon)
have been discarded. Ref.: 112, p. 32; 329

WALL CREEK

Coconino (Grand Canyon)   T32N R4E   Elev. c. 5000'

The name Wall Creek was apparently applied by the National Park Service c. 1926. The
location had been known as Beaver Creek, a translation of the Piute name *Pounc-a-gunt*
(= "Beaver Creek"), as noted by A. H. Thompson in 1872 although he learned from the
Indians that the beaver had been long gone. In 1932 the Bureau of American Ethnology
reported that beaver were still to be found in the canyon.
Ref.: BAE Bulletin (1926), pp. 82, 137; Schellbach file (Grand Canyon); 322 (Oct. 22,
1872)

WALLEN, CAMP

Cochise   T20S R21E

Many years ago prior to the establishment of this post an Indian village called Huachuca
(or Guachuca) existed here under the leadership of Taravilla ("The Prattler"). On May
6, 1866 a camp was established on the old Babocomari Ranch (see Babocomari,
Cochise), using the old ranch buildings. It was first called New Post, but on May 9 the
name changed to Fort Wallen, for Lt. Col. H. D. Wallen, commander of the Northern
Arizona Military District (1866-67). The fact that the post was on privately owned land
caused problems and, following orders issued on June 30, 1869, the post was abandoned
on October 31, 1869. The old ranch was soon taken up by the Messr. McGary and seven
thousand sheep. Ref.: *Arizona Citizen* (Aug. 15, 1874), p. 1; *Weekly Arizona Miner*
(Jan. 9, 1869), p. 1; *Arizona Enterprise* (Jan. 18, 1890), p. 1; 145, p. 159; 45, p. 360;
163, pp. 234-235

WALNUT: The designation *walnut* in connection with place names usually indicates the presence of walnut trees. In the following list, except where specific information is given, it is assumed that such is the case:

Walnut	Coconino	T21N R9E	
See Winona, Coconino			
Walnut Canyon	Cochise	(1) T14S R27E	(2) T22S R29E
Walnut Canyon	Coconino	T21N R8E	
Walnut Canyon	Gila	T6N R10E	
Walnut Canyon	Greenlee	T6S R30E	
Walnut Canyon	Navajo	T10N R20E	
Walnut Canyon	Pinal	T3S R12E	
Walnut Canyon National Monument	Coconino	T21N R8E	Elev. 6500'

Lt. Edward Fitzgerald Beale on February 6, 1858 wrote that his party breakfasted at Walnut Creek where they spent the day exploring ancient ruins. Capt. Amiel Whipple called Walnut Creek Pueblo Creek because of the numerous Indian village ruins along it. Its contemporary name of Walnut Creek changes to San Francisco Wash at the juncture with the S.F.R.R. The ruins here are among the most interesting in Arizona, for a visitor comes upon them at the rim of a deep ravine and winds his way along the path from level to level downwards to the creek bed. The route edges along in front of walls built to create rooms from overhanging rock ledges. The dwellings here were first investigated in 1883 by James Stevenson. Unfortunately, he was followed by vandals who made the place a souvenir hunting ground. Extreme vandalism led to protective measures and the national monument was created on November 30, 1915.
Ref.: Sykes; Museum of Northern Arizona; 13, Dale S. King, "Monument to Vandalism," pp. 2, 5, 6; 23, p. 82; 347, p. 191, Note 8; 13

Walnut Creek	Coconino	T21N R8E

This name was used by Lt. Edward Fitzgerald Beale in 1859 when his party explored the ruins now in Walnut Canyon National Monument. Whipple called it Pueblo Creek.

Walnut Creek	Gila	T9N R13E

This location is also called Cottonwood Creek. See Cottonwood Creek, Gila

Walnut Creek	Mohave	T19N R17E
Walnut Creek	Navajo	T9N R23E
Walnut Creek	Yavapai	T18N R6W

This was also the name of a stage station on the Prescott-Mohave road.

Walnut Draw	Navajo	T12N R22E	
Walnut Flat	Gila	T11N R11E	
Walnut Gap	Cochise	T15S R23E	
Walnut Grove	Yavapai	T10N R3W	Elev. 3469'

Here a town was laid out and several buildings erected by Mormons in 1864. It may have borrowed its name from that of nearby Walnut Canyon, which has many walnut trees. There may also have been walnut trees in the community itself. In their attempts to control flooding of the Hassayampa River, the people constructed Walnut Grove Dam. It was known to be weak. In 1890 efforts were made to strengthen it, but too late. A violent rain storm raised fears for people in the lower valley and a rider mounted a swift horse to warn them. He stopped for one drink and had several. The flood broke the dam and washed away the saloon with him still in it. About eighty drowned.
P.O. est. June 24, 1874, Jane Oswald, p.m.; disc. April 30, 1915
Ref.: *Arizona Miner* (May 11, 1864), p. 3; 242; Kelly; 5, p. 357

Walnut Gulch	Cochise	(1) T13S R26E	(2) T20S R21E
Walnut Mountain	Greenlee	T7S R30E	Elev. 5120'
Walnut Spring	Cochise	T22S R29E	
Walnut Spring	Gila	T10N R15E	

Walnut Spring	Graham	(1) T8S R21E (2) T11S R25E
		(3) T11S R20E
Walnut Spring	Maricopa	(1) T6N R8E (2) T2N R12E
		(3) T7N R5E
Walnut Spring	Mohave	T24N R13W
Walnut Spring	Navajo	T9N R22E
Walnut Spring	Pinal	T3S R13E
Walnut Spring	Santa Cruz	T30S R14E
Walnut Spring	Yavapai	(1) T14N R2E (3) T11N R1W
		(2) T13N R5E (4) T9N R4E
Walnut Spring Canyon	Maricopa	T7N R5E
Walnut Springs	Cochise	T18S R24E
Walnut Springs	Graham	T5S R26E
Walnut Springs	Greenlee	T7S R30E
Walnut Wash	Cochise	T15S R23E

WALPI   pro.: /walːəpi˄/
Hopi: *wala* = "gap"; *opi* = "place of"

Navajo   T28N R18E   Elev. 6225'

The Hopi name for this mountain notch is Wala. Below the contemporary village on the mesa is Old Walpi, now a ruin. It was at first called Walpi, but later Kuchaptuvela (= "ash hill terrace"), which was still occupied when Fr. Antonio Espejo visited on April 21, 1583. When its inhabitants c. 1629 moved to Kisakobi (= "place of the ladder house"), Old Walpi was abandoned. The Spanish mission at Kisakobi was destroyed during the Pueblo uprising in 1680, thus ending efforts at that time to Christianize Hopi Indians. Kisakobi was abandoned and on First Mesa the present Walpi was constructed. Walpi Spring is at the base of First Mesa. Various attempts to render the name of the present town have resulted in the following variants:

Gaspe (1583, Luxan)
Gualpi (1782, Morfi)
Po. (Pozo) de una vida "moquis" gualpe (1851, Parke)
Hualpee (1875, Mallory)
Hualpi)
Gualpi) (1915, Gregory). See also Polacca, Navajo
Wolpi)

Ref.: 112, p. 32; 150, p. 5; 167, II, 901; 71, p. 44; 111, pp. 578, 579; 141, p. 197

WALTENBURG CANYON
Coconino (Grand Canyon)   T33N R1W   Elev. 3000'

John Waltenburg worked with William Bass as a helper-partner for about eighteen years. In 1917 he spent a month with Levi Noble of the USGS, checking data for the Shinumo Survey. Following that assignment, Waltenburg worked on Noble's farm in southern California until his death. The USGS in April 1964 changed the name from this correct spelling to Walthenberg, which is incorrect. An earlier rendering by the USGS was Waltenberg Canyon. Waltenburg Rapids are in the canyon. The spelling "Waltheburg" is an error. Ref.: Schellbach File (Grand Canyon); H. C. Bryant, *Memo*, March 15, 1950 (Grand Canyon); William W. Bass Materials (Wickenburg, Arizona); Grand Canyon History Files (Grand Canyon)

WARD CANYON
Greenlee   T4S R30E   Elev. c. 4000'

Here in the early 1900s Johnny Ward had a slaughter house, whence the name. It was the scene of an attack by Apaches on Mexicans in April 1880. The now vanished railroad from Clifton to Lordsburg went through this canyon. Ref.: Patterson; 68, p. 57

WARD POCKET
Yavapai   T15N R2E
This location and Ward Pocket Canyon were named for Bill and George Ward, who sporadically worked mines in the canyon. Ref.: Allan

WARD SPRING
Cochise   T12S R32E
L. H. Brooks, a cattlemen, in 1917 bought the Ward Ranch, from which this spring takes its name. Ref.: *Arizona Cattleman* (Nov. 19, 1917), p. 5

WARD TERRACE
Coconino   T29N R11E   Elev. c. 5400'
According to Herbert Gregory, who gave the name to this place, Lester F. Ward's work "in the Painted Desert region marked the beginning of detailed stratigraphic studies for the Navajo Reservation." The location is also called Ward Mesa.
Ref.: 141, p. 40, Note 1; 71, p. 36

WARM: A number of place names incorporate the designation *warm*, an indication of the water temperature. Examples follow:

Warm Creek	Gila	T4N R14E	
Warm Creek	Yavapai		
See Willow Grove, Camp, Yavapai			
Warm Spring	Coconino	T33N R8W	
Warm Spring	Gila	T4S R16E	
Warm Spring	Graham	T5S R19E	
Warm Spring	Mohave	T19N R19W	
Warm Spring	Yavapai	T15N R9W	
Warm Spring Canyon	Mohave	T19N R19W	
Warm Spring Creek	Yavapai	T15N R8W	
Warm Springs	Coconino	(1) T33N R8W	(2) T38N R1E
Warm Springs Creek	Gila	T2N R20E	
Warm Springs Lake	Coconino	T38N R1E	
Warm Springs Point	Coconino	T38N R1E	

WARREN
Cochise   T23S R24E
This town was named for George Warren (b. 1844, New York), who was grubstaked by John Dunn to work on a claim in Mule Gulch. Warren Hill is here.
P.O. est. May 11, 1907, Harry B. Hanscom, p.m.; Wells Fargo 1908
Ref.: 242; 5, p. 378; 63

WARSAW
Santa Cruz   T23S R11E
There was a temporary mining settlement at the now-abandoned Warsaw Mine in Warsaw Canyon. Ref.: 57, p. 151

WASHBOARD WASH
Navajo   T15N R20E   Elev. c. 5000'
This dry wash where it crossed the old stage road to Fort Apache was cut up with small arroyos "like a washboard." Ref.: 18a

WASHINGTON CAMP
Santa Cruz   T24S R16E   Elev. 5400'
The mining camps here and at Duquesne were so close together, both in location and

historically, that they can scarcely be treated separately. In the early 19th century Mexican miners built adobe smelters in this area. Although an important mine (the San Antonio) was located, in 1863 because of Apache harrassment, few miners moved in. A few hardy white pioneers lived in the region in the late 1860s or early 1870s, among them Thomas Gardner (see Gardner Canyon, Santa Cruz). One mine discovered was the Washington Mine. Mount Washington appears on GLO 1883. Four years later Washington Camp on Washington Gulch was noted on GLO 1887, with the mountain about a mile northwest of the camp. The Bonanza Mine was located by Thomas Shane, W.E. Hensley, and N. H. Chapin in the early 1880s. The Bonanza was sold to the Duquesne Company c. 1889, and an influx of miners followed. The mining camp at Duquesne was about three-quarters of a mile from Washington Camp. Both had ready access to at least eighty mining claims on sixteen hundred acres. A half dozen mines had their ores reduced at Duquesne Camp. The Duquesne Mining and Reduction Company (home office, Pittsburgh, Pennsylvania) gave the name Duquesne to its headquarters at Duquesne. The reducing plant was at Washington Camp, with several dwellings between the two communities. There is little activity in this area today.

P.O. est. as Washington, May 13, 1880, William B. Hopkins, p.m.; name changed to Duquesne, June 6, 1890; resc. Oct. 28, 1890; name changed to Duquesne, Aug. 17, 1904; disc. Feb. 14, 1920 Ref.: 242; 286, pp. 321, 322, 327; *Arizona Star* (Feb. 24, 1955), p. 5; 146, p. 43

WASSON PEAK

Pima   T13S R12E   Elev. 4677'

The name of this peak first appeared on the 1893 Roskruge map. It was named for J. A. Wasson (b. Aug. 20, 1833, Wayne County, Ohio; d. Jan. 16, 1909), who arrived in Arizona in 1869. During the formation of Arizona's public school system, Wasson was right-hand man to Gov. A.P.K. Safford. Wasson also founded the *Tucson Citizen*. The name of this peak was changed by Eldred D. Wilson and his partner Jenkins to Amole Peak (pro.: /əmówliy/; Spanish = "soap root") when a prospector said that was its name. In 1968 when the western section of the Saguaro National Monument was created, the name Wasson Peak was restored by the USGS. Wasson Peak (Yavapai, T10N/R1W) shares the name. Ref.: 10, p. 33; G.E.P. Smith, Letter (Nov. 3, 1939) to USGS; 116, p. 456

WATAHOMIGI POINT

Coconino (Grand Canyon)   T33N R4W   Elev. 5640'

This point was named for a Supai family which still lives in Grand Canyon Village. The spelling Watohomigi is incorrect. Ref.: Verkamp

WATER: The designation *water* in connection with place names emphasizes the importance of that liquid to people in Arizona. Unless otherwise noted, the presence of water in the following locations may be assumed:

Water Canyon   Apache   T8N R29E

The Eagar brothers irrigated with water from this canyon, which parallels waterless Dry Canyon, hence the name of both. See Eagar, Apache Ref.: Wiltbank

Water Canyon	Graham	T27S R21E
Water Canyon	Greenlee	T2S R28E
Water Canyon	Mohave	T36N R4W
Water Canyon	Navajo	T10N R20E
Water Canyon Creek Point	Mohave	T36N R4W
Water Canyon Reservoir	Apache	T6N R28E
Water Fall Canyon	Apache	T33N R23E
Water Fall Canyon	Graham	T6S R20E
Water Fall Spring	Apache	T33N R23E
Waterhole Canyon	Coconino	T31N R7E

WATERMAN MOUNTAINS

Pima   T12S R9E   Elev. 3433'

George Roskruge named this peak in 1893 for Abbie Waterman, after a mine named for her. J. C. Waterman named the mine for one of his two daughters. In 1880 the Abbie Waterman Mine was the leading producer in the Silver Bell District. Waterman Pass (T13S/R9E) and Peak (Elev. 3808') also have the same name origin.
Ref.: AHS, Emerson O. Stratton *ms.*; 146, p. 46

WATERMAN WASH

Maricopa   T2S R2W   Elev. c. 800'

A Col. Waterman (first name unknown) in the 1880s explored the Buckeye and Arlington region for canal locations. He is said to be buried in the wash which carries his name. Ref.: Parkman

WATERS DRAW

Coconino   T12N R13E

This location belonged to the Waters Cattle Company of St. Joseph, Missouri, which ran cattle here 1883-1897, hence its name, applied also to Waters Draw Spring.
Ref.: 18a

WATSON LAKE

Yavapai   T14N R2W   Elev. c. 5200'

This artificial lake was named for Senator James W. Watson (Republican, Indiana) in 1916. He was president of the Arizona Land and Irrigation Company. Ref.: Merritt

WATSON PEAK

Yavapai   T9N R1W   Elev. c. 6000'

This peak and Watson Spring (T12N/R1W) were named for Henry Watson, who mined here in 1882. Ref.: 18a

WAUBAYUMA PEAK

Mohave   T18N R16W   Elev. 7602'

This peak was named for Wauba Yuma, a Mohave leader.

W C PEAK

Yuma   T7N R13W   Elev. 3905'

*W*est side of *C*unningham Peak, hence the name. Ref.: Lenon

WEAVER PASS

Yuma   T2N R20W   Elev. 1306'

Named for Pauline Weaver. See Octave, Yavapai, and Antelope Peak, Yavapai

WEAVER PEAK

Yavapai   T11N R5W   Elev. 6572'

Named for Pauline Weaver. See Octave, Yavapai, and Antelope Peak, Yavapai

WEAVER'S NEEDLE

Pinal   T1N R10E   Elev. 4553'

This landmark may have been named for the scout Pauline Weaver or because it resembles a weaver's needle. This prominent rock spire is alleged to be a key landmark pointing the way to the Lost Dutchman Mine. The Gadsden Purchase in 1854 put the Lost Dutchman Mine within the United States' boundaries and hence it was no longer accessible to Mexicans. A Mexican is said to have given a map to the mine to a Dutchman, who relocated and used the gold source for many years, not greedily. He died without revealing its location. Many who attempted to follow the man to his mine died in the attempt. Ref.: 5, pp. 163, 164; Willson; 329

WEBB

Cochise   T20S R26E   Elev. 4190'

The first name requested for this post office was Tyler (by its first postmaster). The post office requested an even shorter name and Mr. Tyler suggested that it be called for J. D. Webb, his wife's father. This post office was at Caliente Station on the El Paso & Southwestern R.R.

P.O. est. Sept. 30, 1909, Robert M. Tyler, p.m.; disc. Aug. 5, 1938

Ref.: 242; AHS, A. S. Porter, Letter (Oct. 12, 1929)

WEBB
Yavapai

This post office near Prescott was named for its first postmaster, who was in office only a few months.

P.O. est. Jan. 8, 1892, John A. Webb, p.m.; disc. May 13, 1892 Ref.: 242

WEBBER CREEK
Gila   T12N R9E

The name of this creek first appears on a map made by C. H. Webber in 1868, on a scout conducted by Col. Nevin. Webber may have named it for himself. Ref.: 242

WEBBER PEAK
Graham   T5S R26E   Elev. 6100'

This peak takes its name from that of John Webber, an early Gila Valley settler, c. 1915. Barnes says originally it was called Casimiro Peak. "Weber" is a misspelling. Ref.: 329; 18a

WEBB MOUNTAIN
Maricopa   T2S R6W   Elev. 1879'

Samuel M. Webb (b. 1870, New Mexico) moved from Ramsey Canyon in the Huachucas where he lived as a child, to his ranch in Webb Valley at the head of Arlington Valley. In 1917 he dug the Webb Well here to supply water to the Arizona Gold Hill Mining Company. The mountain derives its name from that of the well. Ref.: 63; 279, pp. 71, 72, 226

WEBB PEAK
Graham   T8S R24E   Elev. 10,029'

According to a letter in the USGS archives, this peak was named for John Webb, "who in 1852 operated a sawmill in the canyon just under this peak."

Ref.: 329, J. F. Muller (Aug. 20, 1932)

WEBSTER
Pinal   T3S R8E

Webster was postmaster for an office in his home. See Magma, Pinal Ref.: 329

WEBSTER MOUNTAIN
Gila   T1S R14E   Elev. 7507'

John R. Webster (b. 1842, Wisconsin) was living in Globe in 1886 and this mountain was probably named for him, as were Webster Gulch and Spring.

Ref.: *Gila County Great Register* (1886)

WEBSTER SPRING
Greenlee   T1S R32E

This spring was located by Judd Webster, first supervisor of Greenlee County, who had his ranch here. Ref.: Cosper; Reilly; Scott

WEEPING CLIFFS
Mohave (Lake Mead)   T31N R16W   Elev. c. 1200'

This name was applied first in 1948 at the suggestion of Edward Schenk "because of the constant dripping of water over these cliffs." Ref.: 329

WELCH
Coconino   T21N R1W

This former section house on the S.F.R.R. was named for the Welch family, none of whom are now in the vicinity, nor have they been since at least c. 1940. Ref.: Slamon

WELDON

Pima   T16S R4E   Elev. 2616'

The mining community of Weldon, named for Albert Weldon, at one time had several thousand residents, all of whom moved away when the mine closed down. This location, now a small Papago community, is called San Antone.

P.O. est. Sept. 17, 1904, J. Wight Giddings, p.m.; disc. May 15, 1912
Ref.: 59, p. 324

WELL-THAT-JOHNNY-DUG

Maricopa   T10S R5W

One assumes that Johnny did, but who he was or when remains a question.

WELLTON

Yuma   T9N R18W   Elev. 354'

To supply steam engines with water, several deep wells were sunk here, hence the name Wellton. Just west of this thriving agricultural community on the Gila River was San Pedro, referred to by Fr. Eusebio Kino in 1699. The name Wellton applies also to Wellton Hills (T10S/R18W, elev. 1195') and Mesa (T8S/R17W).

P.O. est. June 29, 1904, Benjamin Massey Lee, p.m.; Wells Fargo 1909
Ref.: 242; 5, p. 389; 45, pp. 413, 414

WENDEN

Yuma   T6N R12W   Elev. 1869'

In the late 1890s Otis E. Young, who founded this community, wished to name it for his farm in Pennsylvania, called Wendendale. Post office officials shortened the name to Wenden.

P.O. est. June 21, 1905, Harry B. Hanna, p.m.; Wells Fargo 1907 Ref.: 242; 329

WEPO SPRING   pro.: /wiphowya/

Hopi = "onion"

Navajo   T29N R18E   Elev. 5790'

It is not known why this name was given this locality. The spring is important in Hopi ceremonials, particularly those associated with the snake dance. Wepo Wash (T27N R19E) and Valley share the name. The name has also been rendered as follows: Wipho (1891, Stephen); Weepo (1893, Donaldson); Wipo (1915, Gregory).
Ref.: 167, II, 963; 141, p. 197

WESCOGAME POINT

Coconino (Grand Canyon)   T33N R4W

This location on the South Rim was named for a Supai family which still lives in Grand Canyon Village. Ref.: Verkamp

WESTERN BEND

Coconino (Grand Canyon)

In 1882 Dutton said that the Colorado River makes its second "great detour to the south" and then turns northwest again. He called the location Western Bend.
Ref.: 100, p. 23

WESTERN CANYON

Santa Cruz   T22S R18E

On the 1948 USGS map, the canyon is called Government Tank Canyon, but because it is the most westerly of three canyons which join to form O'Donnell Canyon, its name was altered in 1960 to Western Canyon. Ref.: 329

WEST: The designation *west* in place names commonly designates the location relative to another in the vicinity. For information about place names in the following list, refer to the major entry: i.e., for West Fork Black River, see Black River. Most exceptions are noted.

West Branch of   Gila
Pinal Creek

See Bloody Tanks, Gila, and Miami, Gila

West Cedar Mountain   Yavapai   T9N R5E   Elev. 5489'

West Chandler   Maricopa   T1S R4E   Elev. 1165'

In 1896 the first name for this location — Kyrene — was changed to West Chandler. The name Kyrene may have been chosen to match the classical name of nearby Tempe, as Kyrene is a form of the name Cyrene (in ancient Carthagenia). Because the small community was not on the railroad, it was served by Peterson Switch, a siding and section house named for Nils Peterson (b. 1843, Denmark), who owned a cotton gin there. Ref.: 63; 18a; Theobald

West Chevelon Canyon   Coconino   T12N R13E

West Chevelon Creek   Coconino   T12N R13E

West Clear Creek   Coconino/Yavapai   T14N R7E   Elev. c. 6000'

Formerly referred to as Clear Creek, the name was changed to distinguish it from another Clear Creek, which in turn was altered to East Clear Creek. Ref.: 329

West Cottonwood Ridge   Navajo   T11N R18E

West Doubtful Canyon   Cochise   T13S R32E

West Elk Spring   Coconino   T23N R4E

West Fork   Mohave   T33N R12W

Formerly known as Parashant Wash, this place had its name changed because with its east fork it forms Parashant Wash. Ref.: 329

West Fork Black River   Apache

See Black River, Apache

West Fork, Little Colorado River   Apache

West Fork Pinto Creek   Pinal/Maricopa   T1N R12E

West Fork Sycamore Creek   Maricopa   T7N R9E

West Granite Mountain   Maricopa   T5N R8E   Elev. 4555'

West Hay Hollow Draw   Navajo   T14N R23E

West Indian Pine   Navajo   T8N R23E   Elev. 7160'

West Lake   Coconino   T36N R1W

West Lake Point   Coconino   T36N R1W

West Long Hollow   Navajo   T12N R18E

West Mesa   Apache   T37N R28E   Elev. 7693'

West Mesa   Mohave   T40N R11W

West Mesa   Yavapai   T18N R8W

West Mitten Butte   Navajo   T41N R21E   Elev. 6178'

West Mohave Wash   Mohave   T12N R17W

West Moonshine Draw   Coconino   T13N R11E

West Palomas Plain   Yuma

See King Valley, Yuma

West Park Draw   Navajo   T10N R17E

West Peak   Graham   T8S R23E   Elev. 8685'

West Point   Maricopa   T7N R3E   Elev. 3720'

West Poker Mountain   Apache   T2N R24E   Elev. 6755'

West Polecat Canyon   Cochise   T13S R26E

West Santa Cruz River   Pima   T15S R13E

West Silver Bell Mountains   Pima/Pinal   T11S R7E   Elev. 2760'

West Spring	Apache	T8N R25E	
West Spring	Pima	T13S R16E	
West Spring	Pinal	T1N R12E	
West Spruce Mountain	Yavapai	T13N R3W	Elev. 7150'
See White Spruce Mountain, Yavapai			
West Steep Hill Valley	Navajo	T33N R21E	
West Sunset Mountain	Coconino	T17N R13E	
West Turkey Creek	Apache/Navajo	T4N R22E	
West Twin Peak	Pima	T17S R5W	
West Twin Peak	Yuma		
See Gadsden Peak, Yuma			
West Wash	Yuma	T8S R20W	
West Water Canyon	Mohave	T26N R13W	
West Water Wash	Yavapai	T11N R8W	
West White Tail Creek	Cochise	T16S R29E	
West Wing Mountain	Maricopa	T5N R1E	Elev. 1930'

WET BEAVER CREEK
Coconino/Yavapai   T15N R7E   Elev. c. 6800'
Two adjacent creeks were called Beaver Creek and to distinguish them, one was termed Wet and the other – usually dry – earned the name Dry Beaver Creek. Ref.: 18a

WET BOTTOM CREEK
Gila   T10N R7E   Elev. c. 4000'
Only occasionally is the bed of this creek moist, whereas formerly it was almost continuously wet. The original name of this creek was Wet Ass Creek. Cowpokes usually "bogged down to their butts" while crossing cattle at this place and so named it. Wet Bottom Mesa (T10N/R6E) is above the creek.
Ref.: Harry Hancock, Letter (May 1960); Gilette

WETHERILL MESA
Navajo   T40N R20E   Elev. 6160'
This mesa was named for John Wetherill, trader to the Navajo. See Kayenta, Navajo
Ref.: Museum of North Arizona

WHEATFIELDS
Gila   T12N R15E
The name Wheatfields is applied to much of the valley below the confluence of Pinal Creek with its west branches. In August 1864 the King S. Woolsey expedition came across an extensive Indian wheat field here. Woolsey's men threshed, made the flour into *piñole*, and turned their horses loose to eat the remaining wheat in the field. They applied the name Wheatfield to the area. Despite the scourge of malaria present in this region, many ranches were established. There was a community of Wheatfields briefly in this valley. The ranches and farms were bought by the Inspiration Consolidated Copper Co. c. 1912, not only for water rights, but for safety in case the tailings dams should break.
P.O. est. Oct. 20, 1880, E. F. Killner, p.m.; disc. March 17, 1881
Ref.: Woody; 206, p. 141; 163, p. 264

WHEAT FIELD
Navajo   T7N R23E
Navajo raise wheat at this location, hence the name.

WHEATFIELD CREEK

Apache   T5N R30E   Elev. c. 7300'

This perennial stream was called by Simpson in 1849 Cieneguilla de Juanito (= "Juan's Swamp Land"), and is called by Navajo *Kodizis'* (= "water strung out"). The name Wheatfields reflects the fact that Navajo raise wheat in this area where in 1909 the United States Government set up an irrigation project. Wheatfield Lake is at T6N R30E (elev. 7281'). Ref.: 141, p. 35, Note 3; Van Valkenburgh, *Masterkey* (May 1945), p. 90

WHEELER POINT

Coconino (Grand Canyon)   T33N R1W   Elev. 6500'

James says this point was named for Capt. George M. Wheeler, who in 1871 surveyed across northern Arizona. Ref.: 178, p. 82

WHEELER WASH

Mohave   T20N R14W

During his surveying travel through northern Arizona, Lt. George M. Wheeler camped in this wash, hence the name. Miners in this area, who came in from San Francisco shortly thereafter, made the first mining location and named it the Wheeler Lode, a forerunning of the name of the wash itself. Ref.: 215, p. 109; 200, p. 139

WHETSTONE MOUNTAINS

Cochise/Pima   T18S R19E   Elev. 7354'

Prior to their being called the Whetstone Mountains, Mexicans called them Mestinjes (= "mustangs" or "wild horses") because a herd of wild ponies lived in these hills. When Lt. Bourke last saw the herd in 1870, the name of the range was already in transition because novaculite, an excellent whetstone mineral, was found in them. Whetstone Spring in 1864 was on the San Pedro Road. Ref.: Larriau; 49, p. 102

WHIPPLE

Yavapai   T14N R2W   Elev. c. 5000'

This location was named to honor Lt. Amiel W. Whipple. See Whipple, Fort, Yavapai P.O. est. Feb. 12, 1887, Charles H. Allaback, p.m.; disc. May 24, 1898

WHIPPLE, FORT

Yavapai   T14N R2W   Elev. 5000'

General Orders No. 27 dated October 23, 1863, Santa Fe, established a military detachment called the District of Northern Arizona, for the protection of miners. A small detachment under Maj. Edward B. Willis and Capts. Hargrave and Benson with two companies of California Volunteers established Camp Clark on December 23, 1863, twenty-five miles northeast of the future Prescott at Del Rio Springs on Postle's Ranch. It was named for Surveyor Gen. John A. Clark. With the arrival a few days later of Gov. John N. Goodwin and his party in Arizona Territory, Goodwin read a proclamation at Navajo Springs establishing the seat of the Territorial government in the vicinity of mines on Granite Creek. There is no question that Gov. Goodwin had designated that the location for the seat of government "will for the present be at or near Fort Whipple." The military party, after some preliminary scouting, on May 18, 1864 moved to the rapidly developing Whipple Barracks, also called Prescott Barracks.

In December 1864, according to an account in the *Arizona Miner* in 1868, Whipple Valley was the name used for the valley of the future Prescott area. See Whipple, Fort, Yavapai. (Ref.: *Arizona Miner* (Dec. 26,1 1868), p. 2

Whipple Barracks was named in honor of Brig. Gen. Amiel Weeks Whipple (b. 1818, Massachusetts; d. May 7, 1863), fatally wounded at the battle of Chancellorsville, Virginia. Whipple was closely associated with Arizona Territory, as he had been a second lieutenant with the group which in 1849 surveyed the boundary between the United States and Mexico. In October – December 1851 Whipple had surveyed the Gila River to its juncture with the Colorado River. Two years later he explored for a possible railroad route across northern Arizona to the Pacific (1853-56).

Its name remained Whipple Barracks from 1869 to 1884. It was officially established on April 15, 1870 under the Military Department of Arizona, which included also all of California south of a "line drawn eastward from Point Concepcion." In 1877 all such headquarters were moved to Los Angeles despite vigorous protests by Arizonans.

Meanwhile, under date of October 10, 1871, General Orders No. 19 changed the quartermaster's depot to a depot to be used for repairs and to be known as Whipple Depot. Thus in 1879 the post had two divisions, one known as Fort Whipple and the other as Prescott Barracks, but both were combined into Whipple Barracks. A general name for the establishment was Camp Whipple.

As for the post, it was fairly typical. Lt. John Bourke said that Fort Whipple was a "ramshackle tumble-down palisade of unbarked pine logs ... supposed to 'command' something, exactly what, I don't remember, as it was so delapidated that every time the wind rose, we were afraid that the palisade was doomed. The quarters for both officers and men were also log houses, with the exception of one single-roofed shanty ..., constructed of unseasoned, unpainted pine planks and there it served as Gen. Crook's headquarters...." Bourke referred to it as Fort Whipple, a name also used by an Arizona newspaper in 1864. The designation "fort" gradually went out of use.

Whipple Barracks became the social center for territorial residents. They battled valiantly to maintain its existence, but it was discontinued in 1898, and then, under public pressure, re-garrisoned in 1902. The barracks buildings were rejuvenated in 1904. Thus the inevitable was put off for a few years, but in 1912 border difficulties with Mexico caused its ultimate abandonment when its troops were sent to the Mexican border. In 1922 the old military reservation was transferred to the Secretary of the Treasury for use by the Public Health Service. Today old Whipple Barracks, or as it is again being called – Fort Whipple – is a veterans' hospital.

P.O. est. as Whipple, Feb. 12, 1887, Charles A. Allaback, p.m.; disc. May 24, 1898
Ref.: 242; 121a, pp. 14, 15; 159, p. 535; *Arizona Miner* (Nov. 4, 1871), p. 3 and (March 9, 1864), p. 3; 346, pp. 7, 9; 15, p. 522; 145, p. 160; 49, p. 160; 163, pp. 255, 256; 82, p. 173, Note 1; 224, pp. 155, 156

WHIPPLE LAKE
Navajo   T30N R21E
This lake was on the old ranch owned by Edson Whipple in the 1940s.   Ref.: 329

WHIPPLE'S CROSSING
Mohave
This location on the Colorado River shows on the military map of New Mexico 1859-67 as north of The Needles and south of Fort Mohave and Beale's Crossing.

WHIPSAU
Yavapai   T8N R3W   Elev. c. 3200'
The Whipsau Mine and several others were so named because timber was whipsawed at such places to provide shoring for shafts. The post office served the Whipsau Mine and others in the vicinity. Whipsau Creek is an associated name.
P.O. est. June 15, 1900, John B. Spangler, p.m.; disc. ?

WHISKEY CREEK
Navajo: *to diłxił* = "dark water"
Apache   T5N R30E   Elev. c. 6150'
The color of this water is like that of whiskey, attributable to an under-water plant. The name is a translation of the Navajo name.
Ref.: Young; Burcard; 141, p. 90; 143, p. 318

WHITE CANYON
Coconino (Grand Canyon)   T34N R1W
This canyon was actually named for a prospector, although there is a large white wedged rock in it. White Creek is in this canyon. Ref.: Kolb

WHITE CANYON
Pinal   T3S R12E
An early settler gave his name c. 1900 to this place. Its location is not the same as that of Walnut Canyon, which flows southwest and south about five miles to join Walnut Canyon. Ref.: 329

WHITE CAVE SPRING
Navajo   T30N R16E   Elev. c. 6000'
This spring emerges from a cave of light-colored rock, hence the name. Ref.: 18a

WHITE CLIFF VALLEY
Mohave
This is the valley through which White Cliffs Creek flows. See Cottonwood Creek #1,
Mohave Ref.: 346, p. 202

WHITE CONE
Navajo: *Hakaltizh* = "penis head"
Navajo   T26N R21E   Elev. 6094'
The White Cone Trading Post takes its name from a nearby peak of light sandstone
which the Navajo named descriptively. White Cone Spring is here.
Ref.: 143, p. 319; 331, p. 171

WHITE HILL
Coconino   T25N R4E   Elev. c. 6000'
Limestone here results in the descriptive name. Ref.: 18a

WHITE HILLS
Mohave   T27N R20W   Elev. 2800'
White Hills was the name of a mining community in the low, gentle White Hills. In 1892
Hualapai Jeff, an Indian, after showing Henry Shaffer rich silver ore, took him to its
source. It was a rich find, and by July 23, 1892 the community was booming with about
two hundred residents, four saloons, three restaurants, and fifty tents. Two years later
the White Hills Mining Company owned a town with fifteen hundred population. In
1895 the company was sold to an English firm, which promptly went so heavily in debt
that it could not make final payment and the company was offered at a sheriff's sale. One
of the original owners, a man named Root, bought it with the help of D. H. Moffat. The
ores were rapidly depleted and the community failed. A flash flood on August 5, 1899
flooded the mine shafts.
P.O. est. Oct. 20, 1892, William H. Taggart, p.m.; disc. Aug. 15, 1914
Ref.: *Arizona Sentinel* (July 23, 1892), p. 1; 359, pp. 79, 80; 200, p. 127

WHITE HORSE HILLS
Coconino   T23N R6E   Elev. 9065'
Robinson called the location Marble Hills but in 1932 the USGS eliminated that name.
According to George Hochderffer, the name was first applied to White Horse Mountain.
During the spring of 1888, Hochderffer's father bought some Indian ponies from an
Indian and put the ponies out for winter range on the mountain which now carries the
name. One of the ponies, "a pinto with about as much dun color as white," spent the
whole year on the south side of the mountain and did so for more than twenty years. She
died on the mountain and in consequence it bears the name given by the A-1 cowboys.
 Here in 1888 Mrs. George Hochderffer (née Mary Baker) discovered White Horse
Spring, for several years known as Mary's Spring. The name gradually shifted to White
Horse Spring. Ref.: 166, pp. 137, 138

WHITE HORSE LAKE
Coconino   T20N R4E   Elev. c. 6000'
In September 1934 plans were completed to create a community lake by damming a
tributary to Sycamore Canyon. The dam was finished in early 1935. It earned its name
because when people rode out to look at the proposed lake site, there was a white horse
standing in the middle of it. Simple as the name is, it has twice been corrupted, once into
White Lake (USGS, 1955) and another time into White House Lake (USGS, 1962).
 Run-off from heavy snows in 1936 nearly ruined the new dam, saved only by quick
action of Williams residents. In 1951 the dam was raised to double the capacity of White
Horse Lake. Ref.: 124, p. 147; Benham

WHITE HORSE PASS
Pinal   T8S R5E   Elev. c. 2000'
A white log which looked like a horse's head used to be near this pass, hence the name.
Ref.: 18a

WHITE HOUSE RUINS   pro.: /kiniʌ:ʔnaʔiga<ʔy/
Navajo: *knii'na'igai:* = "horizontal white streak in the middle of the house"
Apache   T5N R10W   Elev. c. 6600'
On September 8, 1849 Lt. James Hervey Simpson looked quietly down on the sleeping
ruins of Casa Blanca, known today as White House Ruins (in Canyon de Chelly
National Monument). In 1873 Capt. George M. Wheeler translated the Navajo name to
White House because of "a long wall in the upper part of the ruin ... plastered with white
clay." A study of annual growth rings in beams taken from this ruin reveal its early
construction as 1066 A.D. Ref.: Burcard; 345, I, 75; 13, Charles D. Wyatt, "Canyon
de Chelly," pp. 8, 9; 292, p. 75; 143, p. 319

WHITE LEDGES
Gila   T4N R15E
These ledges along the Salt River appear white, hence the name. Ref.: Woody

WHITE MESA
Coconino   T26N R9E   Elev. c. 6800'
Gregory said that this white wall sandstone mesa dominated the landscape.
Ref.: 141, p. 41

WHITE MESA ARCH
Coconino   T35N R13E
The natural arch at the southeast edge of the mesa is descriptively named. It is an arch
and a natural bridge spanning an erosion valley. Ref.: 329

WHITE MOUNTAIN LAKE
Navajo   T11N R2E   Elev. c. 5960'
The post office here serves a resort community. White Mountain Lake is a reservoir
created by an earth dam completed in 1911. It was then called Daggs Reservoir. The
name Baggs Reservoir is a corruption which occurred on some maps. Some older
ranchers call it Silver Lake. In 1964 when it was sold to a development company, the
name Daggs was changed to one they thought had more sales appeal. Ref.: 329

WHITE MOUNTAIN RESERVOIR
Apache   T7N R27E
This reservoir, named because it is in the White Mountains, dates to 1894 and has a
2391 acre-foot capacity, but has no dam to bring it to its capacity level.
Ref.: Wiltbank; 24, p. 19

WHITE MOUNTAINS
Apache/Navajo   T7N R24E   Elev. 10,000–12,000'
The Apache Indian name for these mountains is *Zil-clo-Ki-sa-on* (= "White Mountains"). The Spanish name Sierra Blanca (= "white mountains") was probably used
because the mountain summits are usually snow-capped seven months of the year. The
highest peaks are Mount Baldy and Mount Ord. The chain contains part of the largest
unbroken virgin ponderosa pine forest in the United States, extending from the Mogollon
Mountains in New Mexico to the San Francisco Peaks near Flagstaff, Arizona.
Ref.: Becker; 163, p. 309; 177, p. 134; 349

WHITE PICACHO
Yavapai   T7N R2W   Elev. 4283'
The name is descriptive of the location. Here Col. Jacob Snively was prospecting when
murdered by Apache Indians. Ref.: 224, p. 189

WHITERIVER

Navajo   T5N R22E   Elev. 5236'

This community is the headquarters for the White River Apache Indian Reservation on the North Fork of the White River. The first name suggested for the post office was Apache School, but the Post Office Department selected White River.
P.O. est. Sept. 8, 1898, Effie M. Russell, p.m. Ref.: 242; Davis

WHITE RIVER

Apache/Navajo/Gila   T6–5N R25–21E

Lt. John Bourke noted that "two branches of the Sierra Blanca River unite almost in front of Camp Apache," the name *Sierra Blanca* being the Spanish for "White Mountains." Bourke's name derives from the river's having its source in those mountains. Its two branches were called the North Fork and the East Fork. The local name for the stream was Sink Creek or Shake Creek, the latter a corruption. The USGS in 1971 altered both local names to North Fork White River. Smith Cienega is the long-pronged tributary of the North Fork. As further evidence supporting the origin of the name, it may be noted that in 1873 Wheeler called it White Mountain Creek.
Ref.: 49, p. 142; 345, I, 62; Wentz; Wiltbank; 329

WHITE ROCK: The designation *white rock* in place names may be assumed to be descriptive. Examples follow:

White Rock	Coconino	T37N R8E	
Whiterock Canyon	Coconino (Grand Canyon)	T32N R5W	
White Rock Canyon	Greenlee	T3S R31E	
White Rock Canyon	Mohave	T30N R23W	
Whiterock Mesa	Gila	T11N R8E	Elev. 4709'
White Rock Mesa	Navajo	T36N R22E	
White Rock Spring	Apache	T27N R23E	

(Ives: "beneath a projecting rock of white sandstone") Ref.: 245, p. 128, App. B

White Rock Spring	Cochise	T14S R28E
White Rock Spring	Pinal	T1N R10E
White Rock Spring	Yavapai	T14N R3W

WHITE SAGE FLAT

Coconino   T39N R1W

White sage is abundant here and in White Sage Wash.

WHITE'S BUTTE

Coconino (Grand Canyon)   T31N R2E

This location was named for a prospector. He was not James White, who claimed he had gone through the Grand Canyon on a raft in 1857, a discredited tale. Ref.: Kolb

WHITE SPRUCE MOUNTAIN

Yavapai   T14N R3W   Elev. 7690'

This name was applied when a dense grove of white spruce was here. The name West Spruce Mountain is a corruption. Ref.: 18a

WHITE TAIL CANYON

Cochise   T15S R31E

This location was named because of white tailed deer that used to be abundant here. White Tail Creek is in it and White Tail Pass (T16S/R29E) is above it. Ref.: Riggs

WHITE TANK MOUNTAINS

Maricopa   T3N R3W   Elev. 4083'

These mountains derive their name from the fact that there used to be a natural tank called White Tank. Rock surrounding the tank was whitish in color, hence the name.

[670]

Water pouring down fifteen feet dug out a hole as big as a house. Between 1898 and 1902 a cloudburst rolled tons of dirt and rocks into it and filled the hole.
Ref.: Parkman; 279, p. 227

WHITE TANKS
Pima   (1) T11S R17E   (2) T13S R17E
These are potholes in white rock, hence the name. Ref.: 58

WHITE TOP MESA
Apache   T36N R23E
Gregory noted that this location, which he called White Top Butte, had a white sand-stone cap over red. It includes Desaki Mesa. The USGS notes that *Desaki* seems to attempt to spell the Navajo word for "mesa," *dah azka*. Ref.: 141, p. 197; 329

WHITEWATER
Cochise   T20S R26E
The location was named for Whitewater Draw. This was the post office at the Whitewater Ranch. When established, the p.o. was in Section 14, but in 1906 it was in Section 22 (within a mile of the Elfrida railroad station). The post office application says that the post office was intended to serve one hundred in the village of Whitewater and fifty elsewhere.
P.O. est. Dec. 27, 1906, Elsworth A. Crawford, p.m.; disc. Aug. 16, 1918
Ref.: 242; *Bisbee Review* (in State Library Clipping File), n.d., n.p.; AHS Names File

WHITE WATER DRAW
Cochise   T19S R27E   Elev. c. 4000'
The creek running through this draw was heavily charged with alkali and left a white sediment along the bank, hence its name. Where this creek crosses the border into Mexico, Mexicans call it Agua Prieta (= "black water").
Ref.: *Bisbee Reviewe* (State Clipping File), n.d., n.p.; 329

WHITE WELL
Yuma   T10S R12W   Elev. c. 500'
Wesley White dug this well c. 1920, striking salt water at one hundred and ten feet.
Ref.: 18a

WHITFORD CANYON
Pinal   T1S R12E
This canyon is so named because it is on the Whitford Ranch.

WHITING
Coconino   T13N R13E
The name for this small post office probably derives from that of the family of the first postmaster. Whiting Knoll (T9N/R26E, Apache, Elev. 9348') shares the name.
P.O. est. Sept. 21, 1943, Mrs. Mabel Whiting Shumway, p.m.; resc. Oct. 21, 1944
Ref.: N. R. Abrams, Asst. P.M. General, Post Office Dept., Letter (March 28, 1956); 242

WHITLOCK CIENEGA
Graham   T10S R20E
In 1864 Gen. Carleton sent Capt. J. H. Whitlock to campaign against Apaches on the upper Gila River. A battle with Indians is said to have occurred here. It shows as Whitlock on GLO 1869. See Parks Lake, Graham Ref.: 249, p. 50

WHITLOCK SINK
Graham   T10S R30E
Now called Parks Lake (*q.v.*). Ref.: Jennings

WHITLOW CANYON
Pinal   T1S R10E
A cattleman named Charles Whitlow maintained a ranch and stage station at the head of this canyon. Ref.: Kitt; 18a

WHITMORE CANYON
Mohave   T34N R9–10W
This location was also known as Queantoweap Valley. See Whitmore Pools, Mohave
Ref.: 329

WHITMORE POOLS
Mohave   T32N R9W   Elev. c. 6000'
In 1863 Dr. James Whitmore (d. Jan. 8, 1866) settled at Pipe Springs (*q. v.* Mohave).
He used several waterholes throughout this region. Indians killed him. Associated
names include Whitmore Canyon (T34N/R10W), Point (T32N/R9W), Rapids (Coco-
nino/Mohave; T32N/R9W), Spring (a.k.a. Big Spring), and Wash (T33N/
R9W). Ref.: 141, p. 157; 18a

WHITNEY
Mohave   T16N R13W
Col. Buell surveyed in 1874 for a townsite which he named for a former California state
geologist. Ref.: *Arizona Citizen* (Sept. 26, 1874), p. 1

WHY
Pima   T13S R5W   Elev. 1784'
This small settlement began as a store at the junction of the Tucson-Ajo road with the
Organ Pipe Cactus National Monument road. According to Mrs. Peggy Kater, an
original settler, it earned its name in 1965 because tourists kept asking, "Why are you
living way out here?"

WICKENBURG
Maricopa   T7N R5W   Elev. 2908'
Henry Wickenburg (Heinrich Heintzel: b. 1820, Austria; d. 1905) arrived in Arizona in
1862. Years earlier he left Austria where police were after him for selling coal from his
father's property instead of turning it over to the state. In 1864 he discovered the Vulture
Mine, but sold it and became a rancher near what is now Wickenburg, a name first used
while James A. Moore was a guest there. In writing to Gov. John N. Goodwin, Moore
headed a letter "Wickenburg Ranch." Prior to that time the area was called Hassayampa Sink. As the Vulture Mine developed, so did the village at Wickenburg as a
supply point. By 1870 four hundred and seventy-four people lived in Wickenburg. The
place was plagued by Indian attacks. The most noted was the so-called Loring or
Wickenburg massacre in which Henry Loring, who was with the 1871 Wheeler Survey,
and his companions on a stage coach were brutally slain.
    While the village of Wickenburg prospered, Henry Wickenburg did not. He failed as a
rancher. Discouraged and tired, Wickenburg shot himself in 1905, fifty-one years to the
day after the first ore from the Vulture Mine had been crushed. The Wickenburg
Mountains (Yavapai/Maricopa: T7N/R4W, Elev. 2736') share the name.
P.O. est. June 19, 1865, B. T. Powell, p.m.; Wells Fargo 1903
Ref.: *Weekly Arizona Miner* (Dec. 26, 1868), p. 2, and (Nov. 18, 1871), p. 3; *Oasis*
(April 20, 1897), p. 2; 107, IV, 44; 163, p. 44; 49, pp. 166, 167

WIDE: The use of the word *wide* frequently designates the physical nature of the
location, of which the following are instances:

Wide Butte	Navajo	T23N R19E	Elev. 6482'
Wide Hollow	Graham	T5S R24E	
Wide Mesa	Apache	T34N R28E	
Wide Mouth Canyon	Graham	T7S R23E	

WIDE RUINS   pro.: /kinᵗʰyey:l/
Navajo: *tsn-tyel* or *Tse kteel* = "wide rock" or *kin* = "pueblo house"; *tyel* = "house"
Apache   T23N R27E   Elev. 6265'
This name of a Navajo community and trading post is a translation of the Navajo name,
sometimes referred to as *Kin tiel*. The Kintiel (or Wide Ruin) site covers about thirty
acres, thus warranting the name Wide Ruin. The pueblo was built between 1264 and

1285 .D. by ancestors of the Zuñi Indians. The prehistoric structures were built across Wide Ruin Wash in Wide Ruin Valley.
P.O. est. Oct. 16, 1933, Dora W. Balcomb, p.m.; disc. March 31, 1938
Ref.: 331, pp. 21, 172; 242; Burcard; 167, I, 698; 141, p. 35, Note 1

WIDFORSS POINT
Coconino (Grand Canyon)   T32N R3E   Elev. 7650'
On June 7, 1928 a note was found in a tin can at this location. It stated, "Point MacKinnon, Nov. 26, 1892, present, Colonel H. MacKinnon, Gren. Gds., London; Col. W. S. Cody (Buffalo Bill)...." and others. MacKinnon was here after shooting his first buck on Kaibab Plateau. To honor eminent Grand Canyon artist Gunnar Mauritz Widforss (b. Oct. 21, 1879, Sweden; d. at Grand Canyon, Nov. 30, 1944), the name of the point was changed on December 2, 1937 to its present form. Widforss became an American citizen so that he could spend his life living at and painting the Grand Canyon. Since 1937 MacKinnon Trail has been called Widforss Trail.
Ref.: Schellbach File (Grand Canyon); Kolb

WIKIEUP   pro.: /wiki^p/
Mohave   T16N R13W   Elev. c. 2500'
The term *Wickiup* is used for conical Indian brush shelters or mat-covered houses. The name Wikieup was chosen because an Indian brush shelter was at a spring near the proposed post office, but the application had as preferred names Owens and Neal, noting that residents called it Owens. The Owens Ranch lay about two miles south of Wikieup and presumably was there before 1879. Further, the mining district was called Owens. As for the proposed name of Neal, Mrs. Owens (who was living at the Owens Ranch) had a granddaughter named Mrs. John Neal.
    A fourth suggestion for a name was Sandy because the location is on the Big Sandy River. It was rejected because there was already a post office by that name.
    Wikieup Canyon (T16N/R5W) reflects the fact that Indians in the area had brush shelters. This location is misnamed Wake-up Wash on GLO 1909, an obvious corruption.
P.O. est. Oct. 20, 1920, William F. Buchanon, p.m. Ref.: Rosenberger, Letter (Feb. 1, 1956); 242; 167, II, 950

WILBUR CANYON
Yavapai   T15N R3E
This location was named for a resident in the early 1900s. His first name has not been learned.

WILD BAND POCKET
Mohave   T38N R6W   Elev. c. 4200'
Dutton said this shallow valley was named because wild horses gathered at rain pools here. This is apparently the place which Bolton refers to in connection with Fr. Escalante's 1776 visit, saying that the name came from the fact that wild horses watered at these pools. Bolton calls it Wild Horse Band Pools. Dellenbaugh saw at least twenty horses "spinning across the plain one behind the other like a train of railways cars, a huge stallion playing locomotive." Wild Band Spring (Coconino: T38N/R2W) and Valley share the name.
Ref.: 100, p. 80; 88, p. 251

WILD BUNCH CANYON
Greenlee   T1S R31E   Elev. c. 4000'
Cattle which escaped branding hid out in this rough canyon, hence the name.
Ref.: Mrs. Fred Fritz, Sr.

WILD CAT: The presence of wild cats may be assumed in connection with the following place names:

Wild Cat Canyon   Coconino   T40N R1W   Elev. c. 6000'
Robert (Bob) Casbeer named this canyon because here in a single night a wild cat killed several of Casbeer's sheep. In December 1962 the USGS made the name official by eliminating a second name for the canyon, Little Wild Cat Canyon. Ref.: 18a; 329

Wild Cat Canyon	Cochise	(1) T12S R20E (2) T22S R24E
Wild Cat Canyon	Gila	T3N R13E
Wild Cat Creek	Apache	T4N R27E
Wild Cat Draw	Yavapai	T18N R1E
Wild Cat Hill	Coconino	(1) T23N R3E
		(2) T21N R8E Elev. 7024'
Wild Cat Hill	Maricopa	T6N R5E Elev. 3257'
Wild Cat Peak	Cochise	T12S R20E Elev. 4876'
Wild Cat Peak	Coconino	T34N R12E Elev. 6805'

This name is a translation of the Navajo *Nishduitso* (= "mountain lion"). Ref.: 141, p. 41

Wild Cat Point	Apache	T4N R27E
Wild Cat Spring	Cochise	T12S R20E
Wild Cat Spring	Coconino	T12N R9E
Wild Cat Spring	Navajo	T11N R15E
Wild Cat Wash	Cochise	T23S R29E

WILD CHERRY CANYON

Apache   T4N R27E   Elev. c. 5600'

This name in Canyon de Chelly National Monument is a translation of the Navajo name, *didze sikaad* (= "wild cherry tree standing up"), with reference to a "spring by which a chokecherry tree stands." Because of this spring at the head of the canyon, a variant name is Spring Canyon, but in January 1960 the USGS eliminated the variant. Among trails down the canyon walls is the Sunshine Trail (Navajo: *Shaa'toho ha atiin*), so named because sunshine quickly melts snow here. Ref.: 331, p. 20; 329

WILD COW: Because unbranded or escaped cattle habitually are found in certain places where it is usually hard to handle them, some place names bear the designation *wild cow*. It is possible, of course, that a single incident with a wild and woolly maverick has led to place naming. The following are examples:

Wild Cow Canyon	Pima	T19S R18E
Wild Cow Ravine	Pinal	T9S R14E
Wild Cow Spring	Pima	(1) T11S R15E (2) T19S R18E
Wild Cow Wash	Apache	T16N R24E

WILDFLOWER GULCH

Yavapai   T11N R1W

This gulch is named for the Wildflower Mine (T10N/R1W).

WILD HOG CANYON

Santa Cruz   T23S R15E

This canyon is also called Jabalina (= *Javelina* or Wild Pig) Canyon.

WILD HORSE CANYON

Graham   T1S R21E   Elev. c. 3000'

About 1910 a band of wild horses in this canyon was rounded up and exterminated to prevent dourine among Indian ponies. Ref.: 18a

WILD HORSE CIENEGA

Apache   T8N R25E

In the early 1900s so many horses had run wild on the plains of northern Arizona that many had to be eradicated because they were ravaging the land of forage and creating serious erosion problems. Another name for this place is Wild Horse Spring. Ref.: Grigsby

WILD HORSE LAKE
Navajo   T10N R16E

To corral wild horses, Daniel Boone Holcomb in the early years of the century built a trap corral here. See Wild Horse Cienega, Apache Ref.: 18a

WILD HORSE SPRING
Coconino   T20N R2E

In 1964 this was a dry spring in Wild Horse Canyon.

WILFORD
Navajo   T11N R16E   Elev. c. 6000'

In 1883 Wilford was a small and prosperous settlement, established by John Bushman and other Mormons from St. Joseph. They named it to honor Wilford Woodruff, president of the Mormon church. Because of lack of water, this community went out of existence in 1885 when its residents moved to Heber. Ref.: 225, pp. 155, 156

WILGUS
Cochise   T18S R29E   Elev. c. 5000'

The post office at this location was established as Aztec, a year later changed to Wilgus by the postmaster, whose middle name was Wilgus. Indians killed him. His small dog was keeping vigil when his body was found under snow.
P.O. est. as Aztec, July 21, 1887, William Wilgus Smith, p.m.; name changed to Wilgus, Feb. 21, 1888; disc. Jan. 31, 1911
Ref.: Riggs; AHS, Miles Rutherford Choat File

WILHOIT
Yavapai   T13N R3W   Elev. 5022'

This small community exemplifies what can happen when someone starts a service station, which a man named Wilhoit did here prior to 1950. A community developed around it. Ref.: Sears; Gardner

WILLAHA
Supai = "watering place"
Coconino   T27N R1E   Elev. c. 6200'

Despite its name, the natural tanks here were normally dry. Water had to be hauled (for stock) from Williams on the Grand Canyon railroad. Ref.: Terry; 18a

WILLCOX
Cochise   T14S R25E   Elev. 4167'

The first name for this location was Maley (*sic*), because the railroad right-of-way extended through James H. Mahley's ranch. At the time, Mahley (b. 1850) was a resident of Dos Cabezas where he had moved in 1882. Simultaneously Gen. Orlando B. Willcox (1823–1907) was commander of the Military Department of Arizona (1877-1882), stationed at Fort Whipple. The town site for the future Willcox was laid out in 1874 by M. W. Stewart. The first child born there was the son of Anthony Powers, and Gen. Willcox sent a silver cup with his initials on it in "consideration that the boy be named Willcox Powers." Not only the boy received the name, but the name of Maley was changed to Wilcox (*sic*) in October 1880. An apocryphal story says that when the first train came through with Gen. Willcox aboard, he received an ovation. Just as Gen. Willcox appeared on the observation platform, railroad officials also aboard asked what the name of the new town was. A mighty shout from the crowd gave the ans-wer: "Willcox! Willcox!"

This important agricultural and cattle center is close to Willcox Playa (T15S/R24E), an enormous shallow dry lake which Antisell in 1854 called Playa de los Pimas, and by Mexicans, Playas (their term for a dry lake devoid of plant life). Sometimes it was mapped only as Dry Lake (Smith, 1879). Still another name for the dry lake is Lake Cochise (177, p. 9). It was also called Soda Lake (Hinton) or Alkali Flats (GLO 1883). On the original map of the Gadsden Purchase, it is noted as Willcox Dry Lake, a fact which may make all other stories about the origin of the name for the community simply apocryphal. The community name may be a borrowed name. When rain waters fill this lake, it looks as though it is fairly deep. During World War II U.S. Navy pilots flying a large amphibious aircraft could not resist the temptation of landing on a lake in the middle of the desert. The plane grounded and sat there for months.

The Willcox Water Fowl Area consists of four hundred and forty acres which the Arizona Game and Fish Department acquired in 1969. About sixty acres are ponds. P.O. est. Sept. 13, 1880, John F. Row, p.m.; name changed to Wilcox, Oct. 19, 1890; name changed to Willcox, Nov. 23, 1889; Wells Fargo 1885
Ref.: Kitt; *Arizona Range News* (Aug. 4, 1911), p. 6; 242; 60, pp. 371-372; 9, p. 3

WILLCOX
Mohave   Location unknown
P.O. est. Oct. 1, 1923, Harry O. Parks, p.m.; disc. (?) Ref.: 242

WILLIAMS
Coconino   T22N R2E   Elev. 6770'
This community at the base of Bill Williams Mountain borrows its name from the mountain. The first settlers here in 1876 were Sam Ball and John Vinton, but they sold their interest to Charles Thomas Rogers. Rogers established a post office at his ranch.

The coming of the railroad brought prosperity, interrupted by the Depression, but today Williams is an important lumbering and cattle center as well as being known as the "Gateway to the Grand Canyon."
P.O. est. June 14, 1881, Charles T. Rogers, p.m.; Wells Fargo 1885
Ref.: 116, p. 578

WILLIAMS CAMP
Gila   T1S R14E
This post office was named for Lillian Williams, first postmaster here.
P.O. est. May 28, 1927, Lillian Williams, p.m.; disc. June 1, 1928 Ref.: 242

WILLIAMSON, PORT
Yuma   45 mi. above Fort Yuma on Colorado River
In 1864 this location on the Colorado River was the chief supply point for the Eureka Mining District. It served briefly as a postal stop between La Paz and Arizona City. It may have been named by using the first name of its only postmaster.
P.O. est. Oct. 16, 1866, William Thompson, p.m.; disc. June 13, 1867
Ref.: 242; 236, p. 87

WILLIAMS SPRING
Mohave   T17N R11W
This spring took its name from Bill Williams River, now Big Sandy River.

WILLOW: The presence of lovely desert willow trees has led to the designation *willow* in several place names, some of which follow:

WILLOW BEACH
Mohave (Lake Mead)   T29N R22W   Elev. 720'
The first name for this location was Harrisville, derived from the fact that Sandy Harris worked placers here prior to 1880. Harris constructed a cabin of willow sticks. During the 1880s the location was taken over by C. M. Sharp, a Swiss, who also worked placers. The name then was Sharp's Bar. During the Depression, several people again worked the sand bars for placer gold and the name became Placerville. At the same time Al Jagerson had a store and a boat landing here. He later exchanged it for a house in Chloride owned by Benn and Anna Wright. It is interesting that Mrs. Wright's father was Sandy Harris. Gradually a small community and resort center developed, today called Willow Beach. Willow trees grow here today, as they did in Sandy Harris' time.
Ref.: Housholder; 215, p. 116; Harris (no relation); 329

Willow Canyon	Pima/Cochise	T18S R19E
Willow Canyon	Coconino	T38N R2W
Willow Canyon	Mohave (Grand Canyon)	T33N R6W

Willow Canyon	Pima	T12S R16E	
Willow Cienega	Apache	T4N R26E	
Willow Creek	Apache	T3N R24E	
Willow Creek	Coconino	T14N R13E	
Willow Creek	Coconino (Grand Canyon)		

This is on the Bright Angel Trail and may be now known as Garden Creek. Ref.: 178, p. 63

Willow Creek	Gila	T7N R15E	
Willow Creek	Graham	(1) T1N R25E	(2) T8S R20E
Willow Creek	Greenlee		

See Beaver Creek, Greenlee

Willow Creek	Greenlee	(1) T5S R31E	(2) T4N R29E
Willow Creek	Maricopa	T2N R9E	

This is now called First Water Creek on some maps.

Willow Creek	Mohave	T21N R12W	
Willow Creek	Navajo	T9N R15E	
Willow Creek	Yavapai	(1) T14N R3W	(2) T9N R1E
Willow Creek Canyon	Coconino	T13N R13E	
Willow Creek Park	Yavapai	T14N R2W	
Willow Creek Reservoir	Yavapai	T14N R2W	

WILLOW GROVE, CAMP

Mohave   T21N R12W

A military report dated July 29, 1867 notes an encounter here at "Willow Grove or Warm Creek." A camp was established on August 23, 1864 and discontinued June 30, 1869. At Willow Grove Springs in October 1864 (then Willow Spring), J. Hundredmark & Company set up a way station for travelers. Martha Summerhayes wrote that it had a small cluster of willow trees. The location was unhealthful for troops and livestock alike, and during the winter of 1868-69, thirty-five cattle starved to death. They had access to a haystack which according to report was more filled with dirt than hay. By 1871 the place was in ruins.

P.O. est. as Willow Ranch, Feb. 12, 1880, Edwin Imey, p.m.; disc. June 10, 1880

Ref.: 335, pp. 35, 89; *Arizona Miner* (July 24, 1869), p. 2; *Citizen* (Aug. 15, 1874), p. 1; 159, pg. 429; 314, pp. 70-71, Footnote 17; *Arizona Miner* (Nov. 23, 1864), p. 4

Willow Grove Springs	Mohave	T21N R11W	
Willow Gulch	Cochise	T15S R28E	Elev. 7817'
Willow Lake	Yavapai	T14N R3W	

This lake is named for Willow Creek. Ref.: Merritt

Willow Mountain	Graham	T1N R26E	Elev. 7817'
Willow Park	Maricopa	T1N R2E	
Willow Patch Draw	Navajo	T15N R18E	
Willows, The	Mohave		

See Willow Grove, Mohave

Willow Spring	Apache	(1) T3N R24E	(2) T24N R30E

See Oak Springs, Apache

Willow Spring	Coconino	(1) T38N R2W	(2) T20N R3E
	(3) T13N R10E	(4) T27N R12E	(5) T31N R14E
Willow Spring	Gila	(1) T6N R15E	(2) T9N R10E

Willow Spring	Graham	(1) T8S R19E		

This spring is also called Roy Spring because it was developed by Roy Martin.

		(2) T5S R21E	(3) T11S R25E	(4) T11S R25E
Willow Spring	Greenlee	T3N R29E		
Willow Spring	Mohave	(1) T34N R6W		

This spring is also called June Spring.

		(2) T11N R5E	(3) T15N R5W	(4) T11N R1W
		(5) T14N R6W	(6) T15N R6W	(7) T11N R2W
Willow Spring	Pinal	T8S R14E		
Willow Spring Basin	Yavapai	T9N R7E		
Willow Spring Canyon	Gila	(1) T11N R10E	(2) T6N R15E	
Willow Spring Canyon	Santa Cruz	T23S R16E		
Willowspring Gulch	Gila	T1N R14E		
Willow Spring Gulch	Yavapai	T11N R4E		
Willow Spring Mountain	Maricopa	T7N R6E	Elev. 4914'	
Willow Spring Ranch	Mohave			

See Willow Grove, Mohave

Willow Springs	Coconino	(1) T32N R9E		
		(2) T32N R9E (a community)	Elev. 4817'	
Willow Springs	Maricopa	T2N R9W		
Willow Springs	Yavapai	T12N R6E		

This shows as Oakley Springs on the 1879 Mallory map.

Willow Springs Canyon	Coconino	T11N R14E
Willow Springs Canyon	Greenlee	T11S R32E
Willow Springs Canyon	Maricopa	T1N R9E
Willow Springs Creek	Maricopa/Pinal	T2N R9E

This is also called First Water Creek.

Willow Springs Lake	Coconino	T11N R14E

This is also called Bear Canyon Lake.

Willow Springs Ranch	Pinal	

See Linda Vista, Pinal

Willow Spring Wash	Graham	T10S R27E
Willow Springs Wash	Maricopa	T6N R4E
Willow Tanks	Coconino	T41N R8E
Willow Tanks	Maricopa	T2N R8E
Willow Valley	Coconino	T15N R10E
Willow Valley Dam	Coconino	T15N R10E
Willow Wash	Cochise	T19S R22E
Willow Wash	Mohave (Lake Mead)	T35N R16W
Willow Wash	Navajo	T11N R18E

WILSON CANYON

Coconino   T18N R6E

A man named Wilson was killed in this canyon, hence the name. Wilson Mountain shares the name. Ref.: 18a

WILSON CREEK

Gila   T8N R14E

This location was the site of the Middleton Ranch, which was bought by George Wilson in the 1880s. See also Wilson Spring, Yavapai Ref.: Woody

WILSON PUEBLO

Coconino   T20N R12E   Elev. c. 6000'

The Museum of Northern Arizona excavated this Indian ruin (dated to c. 1050 A.D.), naming it for Ida G. Wilson, librarian at the then State College in Flagstaff. She was responsible for arousing the interest of the museum staff in excavating.
Ref.: Bartlett

WILSON SPRING

Yavapai   T13N R4E

This was the location of a travelers' way station built by George H. ("Yackey") Wilson on the road created by C. B. Genung from Wickenburg to Kirkland Valley.
Ref.: 107, VIII, 310, 311

WILSON WELL

Yuma   T7S R22W

This well was owned by John Wilson c. 1920. Ref.: 279, p. 227

WINCHESTER

Cochise

In 1882 this was a voting precinct serving fifty-one residents. See Winchester Mountains, Cochise Ref.: *Tombstone Epitaph* (July 15, 1882), p. 3

WINCHESTER MOUNTAINS

Cochise/Graham   T13S R23E   Elev. 7631'

These mountains were named for Henry D. Winchester in 1882.
Ref.: *Tombstone Epitaph* (April 3, 1882), p. 1

WINCHESTER PEAK

Graham/Greenlee   T11S R31E   Elev. 5127'

There is a probability that this peak was named for First Lt. Hiram F. Winchester, 6th Cavalry (d. May 29, 1881). Ref.: 159, p. 1049

WINCHESTER PEAK

La Paz   T5N R14W   Elev. 2766'

This peak takes its name from that of Josiah Winchester, a miner and prospector who owned the Desert Mine in this locality c. 1910. Ref.: 18a

WINDMILL GULCH

Mohave   T19N R13W

This gulch is named because it is the location of the Windmill Ranch.

WINDOW, THE

Pima   T1S R15E   Elev. 7395'

This is a natural rock opening at the head of Ventana Canyon in the Santa Catalina Mountains. The first to use the descriptive name was Emerson O. Stratton in the 1880s. Window Rock is here. *Ventana* is Spanish for "window."
Ref.: AHS, Emerson O. Stratton *ms.*

WINDOW MOUNTAIN

Pima   T12S R1E   Elev. 2961'

This mountain is an English translation of the former name of a Papago village three miles to the west of La Ventana (Spanish = "window"). Window Valley is adjacent (T13S/R2E).

WINDOW ROCK
Navajo: *tseghahoodzani* = "rock with a hole through it"
Apache   T26N R31E   Elev. 6880'
The American name for this location is a translation of the Navajo, so named because
there is a large natural rock window adjacent to the headquarters of the Bureau of Indian
Affairs and the Navajo Tribal Council buildings. The name the B.I.A. proposed to use
for the new community was *Ni''anii'gi* (Navajo = "Earth's Center"), a ceremonial
name which the Navajo found objectionable when used in a secular sense. On May 20,
1935 the name of the new community was changed from its initial name of Navajo
Central Agency to Ne'al'neeng, a faltering attempt to anglicize the Navajo ceremonial
name. Because it was objectionable to the Indians, the name was subsequently changed
to Window Rock on August 31, 1935.
P.O. est. as Navajo Agency, Jan. 30, 1936, William H. Daley, p.m.; name changed to
Window Rock, August 1, 1936 Ref.: 242; 331, pp. 20, 174; 326, pp. 243-244

WINDSOR SPRING
Gila   T8N R9E   Elev. 6500'
In the late 1880s Walter Windsor (d. March 14, 1947), established a ranch and mining
claim near this spring at Windsor Camp. See Winsor Camp, Gila Ref.: Goode

WINDSWEPT TERRACE
Hopi: *A-Ku-Hi-Evi* = "windswept terrace"
Navajo   T27N R18E   Elev. 6342'
The American name for this flat-topped summit is a translation of the Hopi name. The
American name has been used since c. 1930. The place has also been known as Badger
Butte. Ref.: 329

WIND or WINDY: The application of the words *wind* or *windy* usually indicates that
wind is particularly noticeable at the location so named. Examples follow:

Wind Whistle Canyon	Navajo	T29N R21E	
Windy Canyon	Graham	T4S R27E	
Windy Canyon	Mohave	T28N R27W	
Windy Hill	Gila	T4N R12E	Elev. 2460'
Windy Pass	Maricopa	T2N R11E	
Windy Point Vista	Pima	T12S R16E	
Windy Ridge	Yavapai	T16N R8W	
Windy Spring	Graham	T3S R27E	
Windy Valley	Apache	T34N R25E	

WINGFIELD MESA
Yavapai   T13N R5E
The Wingfield family were pioneers in Yavapai County, hence this name.

WINKELMAN
Pinal/Gila   T5S R15E   Elev. 1972'
In this general area at the mouth of the San Pedro River was Ojio, a Sobaipuri rancheria
visited by Fr. Eusebio Kino in 1697. The Spaniards also called it La Victoria because
Kino's party had come safely through a region believed to be inhabited by cannibals.
    According to the original post office application, this place was first called Dudleyville.
However, Dudleyville was not at the exact location where Winkelman is but was over a
mile away (T7S/R16E). In 1878 and 1879 a number of farmers settled in this region,
among them William Dudley Harrington, who established his ranch in 1879. For
supplies the settlers went to Florence or to Riverside, twenty miles away. For the
convenience of his neighbors and himself, Harrington established a post office at his
ranch, using his middle name (Dudley) for it. The settlers fully expected a branch of the
railroad (Phoenix & Eastern R.R.) to pass through Dudleyville and follow the course of
the San Pedro River to Benson. Railroad engineers decided otherwise, and Winkelman

took shape near the mouth of the San Pedro River. The railroad line ran near a ranch owned by Peter Winkelman (Pinal County) and the new community derived its name from that fact. The new community displaced the remaining few members of a tribe of Apache Indians which had lived at what is now Winkelman. They continued to live there until their leader Pachene died.

Meanwhile overgrazing left the land subject to erosion, and floods washed away land and broadened the San Pedro River. Several times the store at Dudleyville had to be moved. Apparently the post office at Dudleyville continued its existence, for its name was changed to Feldman in 1911, for Henry Feldman, as the post office was in the Feldman ranch house. He was manager of a cattle ranch owned by George Pusch (see Pusch Ridge, Pima).

P.O. established as Dudleyville, May 9, 1881, William Dudley Harrington, p.m.; name changed to Feldman, Nov. 22, 1911, Hugh H. Ballinger, p.m.; disc. Sept. 11, 1924. P.O. est. at Winkelman, Dec. 19, 1904, Ernest A. Spann, p.m.; Wells Fargo 1906 Ref.: 242; AHS Clipping File, Dixie Morgan Interview; *Arizona Republican* (April 15, 1931); 238, pp. 32, 57; 329; 43, pp. 366, 367; 167, II, 112

WINONA   pro.: /wáynównə/

Coconino   T21N R9E   Elev. 6000'
The first name for this location on the S.F.R.R. was Walnut, as it lay one mile east of Walnut Creek. Confusion arose because there was another railroad location called Walnut, so the railroad company changed it to Winona in 1886. The reason for selecting "Winona" is not known. A small community developed, kept alive by railroad work beginning about 1912. A school was built about 1915 on land donated by the Forestry Service. It was in session only in summer because heavy winter snows shut down just about everything. Possibly the first tourist camp in the United States was here, built by Billy Adams on the old Santa Fe Trail c. 1920. However, the highway was shifted and the settlement died.
P.O. est. Feb. 21, 1924, Myrtle Adams, p.m.; disc. Aug. 15, 1943
Ref.: Sproat; Mr. & Mrs. Billy Adams; 242

WINSLOW

Navajo   T19N R15E   Elev. 4856'
With the inauguration of service by the A. & P. R.R. (now the S.F.R.R.), the importance of Sunset Crossing diminished when the railroad established a terminal in 1881 at what is now Winslow. The first settler in the late 1880s was F. G. Demarest, who pitched a tent. The town may have been named for a prospector called Tom Winslow, who asserted in 1920 that it was named for him. It seems more likely that it was named for Gen. Edward Winslow, president of the old St. Louis & San Francisco R.R., associated with the new transcontinental line. As usual, the Navajo name for the locale is the most apt: *Beeshsinil* = "iron lying down."
P.O. est. Jan. 10, 1882, U. L. Taylor, p.m.; Wells Fargo 1885
Ref.: 331, pp. 174, 175; AHS, Richards Diary

WINSOR, CAMP

Gila   T9N R12E
Winsor Camp is a line camp with a cabin, corral, and windmill. The name is misspelled as it was owned c. 1890 by Walter Windsor (d. March 14, 1947). This one is used by grazing permit in Tonto National Forest. It is also called Upper Corral. "Winter Camp" is a corruption. Ref.: 329

WINTERSBURG

Maricopa   T1N R6W   Elev. 1008'
The first name suggested for this small community was Tonopah, but the post office crossed out that name to avoid confusion with Tonopah in Nevada. It was called Wintersburg because of its location at the Winters Well on a cattle ranch on Winters Wash (or Winters Well Wash) owned 1885–1925 by E. H. Winters (b. 1845, District of Columbia). The Wintersburg post office was adjacent to a railway base called Tonopah (T2N/R7W).
P.O. est. Sept. 10, 1930, Mace L. Kintch, p.m.; disc. July 17, 1941
Ref.: 242; 63; 279, p. 227

WISE MESA
Santa Cruz   T23S R12E
This is named for a family well known in the area. Ref.: Lenon

WISHBONE MOUNTAIN
Apache   T9N R25E   Elev. 8823'
This mountain looks like a big wishbone. Ref.: 18a

WITCH WATER POCKET
Piute: *Innupin* or *oonupin*: *Picabu* = "witch water pocket"
Mohave   T35N R7W   Elev. c. 6000'
An Indian named Chuar told Frederick Dellenbaugh that Indians believed this rocky pool was a "favourite haunt of witches. These were often troublesome and had to be driven away or they might hurt one." Dutton described it as weird, with "jagged masses of black lava still protruding through rusty decaying cinder ... The pool itself might well be deemed the abode of witches." Ref.: 100, p. 84; 88, p. 251

WITTMAN
Maricopa   T5N R3W   Elev. 1696'
The name Nada or Nadaburg (Spanish: *nada* = "nothing") was applied to the railroad location because there was nothing there. As a community gradually developed, the name was changed to Wittman for one of the men who financed rebuilding Walnut Grove Dam.
P.O. est. as Nada, Aug. 2, 1920, John P. Berry, p.m.; changed to Whittman, Feb. 1, 1929; changed to Wittman, March 1, 1934; order resc. March 4, 1935 Ref.: 242; 18a

WODO, MOUNT
Coconino (Grand Canyon)   T33N R3W   Elev. 5230'
In 1925 the USGS approved naming this butte for an Indian family.Ref.: 329

WOLF HOLE
Shivwits: *Shina-bitz-spits* = "coyote spring"
Mohave   T39N R12W   Elev. 4600'
Barnes says that in translating the Indian name, Maj. John Wesley Powell substituted the word *wolf* for *coyote* when naming the spring. Wolf Hole Lake, Mountain, and Spring are here. In 1921 the USGS eliminated the name Shina-bitz-spits for the spring.
P.O. est. April 10, 1918, Dexter Mitchell Parker, p.m.; disc. April 20, 1927
Ref.: 18a; 242; 329

WOLFLEY HILL
Pima   T21S R3E   Elev. 2665'
This location was named for Lewis Wolfley (b. Oct. 8, 1839, Philadelphia; d. Feb. 12, 1910), on March 28, 1889 sworn in as Arizona's 9th Territorial Governor (including John Gurley, who never assumed office). He was recalled in 1892.
Ref.: Parkman; AHS File

WOLF MOUNTAIN
Apache   T9N R25E   Elev. 8288'
In the early 1900s this location was called Tamar Mountain, derived from the fact that the Tamar Sheep Company maintained a summer camp here. The Forestry Service, not knowing the local name, substituted the current one. In 1926 the USGS eliminated the older name of Tamar Mountain. Ref.: 18a; 329

WOOD, CAMP
Yavapai   T16N R6W   Elev. 5700'
The first name for this location, Kymo, was given to it by Paul Wright of Kentucky. He married a Missouri woman c. 1880 and in honor of the occasion combined the abbreviations for the names of their states into Kymo.
In the early 1890s a cavalry captain named Wood camped here on a scouting expedition and gradually the place came to be known as Camp Wood. When the post office was reestablished in 1926, the name Camp Wood was used because postal regulations

forbade a second use of the name Kymo. In the post office location application for 1903, the postmaster wrote that the place was "sometimes called Camp Wood," but on the 1926 application for a new post office, the local name is given as Pine Flat. Camp Wood Mountain Seep Spring is here.
P.O. est. as Kymo, April 29, 1893, Robert H. Ferguson, p.m.; disc. July 26, 1907; reest. as Camp Wood, June 19, 1926, Harry S. Knight, p.m.; disc. Jan. 1, 1962
Ref.: Gardner, Rosenberger; 242; AHS Names File

WOODCHUTE MOUNTAIN
Yavapai   T16N R2E   Elev. 7834'
Fuel for the Jerome Mines came from Woodchute Mountain where the logs were cut and sent sliding down a chute. The logs were then used for open roasting to remove sulphur from ores. The resultant killing fumes and the unceasing demand for timber denuded the mountain. Ref.: Stemmer

WOOD: Except for a few instances given in individual entries, it can be safely assumed that the majority of locations with the designation *wood* simply underscores the importance of trees in a region which is mostly desert. On the other hand, the designation *Woods* probably usually indicates a person rather than a tree. The following are examples of the use of the word *wood* in place names:

Wood Camp Canyon	Pinal	T1S R12E	
Wood Canyon	Apache	T3S R29E	

This location is sometimes called Knight Creek, although it is actually a fork of that creek.

Wood Canyon	Cochise/Graham	T11S R25E

This canyon, also called Monk Draw in Cochise County, was named for Miles L. Wood (d. Nov. 30, 1930), a former butcher at Old Camp Grant, who maintained a hostelry called Hotel de Luna in this canyon c. 1885 near New Camp Grant. The name "Monk" should be spelled Munk.
Ref.: 311, p. 121; Kitt

Wood Canyon	Cochise	(1) T15S R28E	(2) T12S R32E
		(3) T16S R30E	(4) T23S R24E
Wood Canyon	Greenlee	T3S R28E	
Wood Canyon	Navajo	T11N R19E	
Wood Canyon	Pima	T18S R18E	
Wood Canyon	Pinal	T1N R13E	
Wood Canyon	Santa Cruz	T21S R16E	
Wood Canyon	Yavapai	T15N R5W	
Wood Canyon Park	Cochise	T16S R30E	
Wood Canyon Wash	Cochise	T12S R23E	
Woodchopper Wash	Maricopa	T5N R7W	
Wood Creek	Pinal	T1N R13E	
Wood Creek	Yavapai	T13N R5W	
Wood Creek Spring	Pinal	T1N R13E	
Woodcutters Canyon	Cochise	T22S R19E	
Wood Mountain	Cochise	T15S R29E	Elev. 7323'

See Wood Canyon, Cochise/Graham

WOODRUFF
Navajo   T16N R22E   Elev. 5240'
Luther Martin and Felix Scott settled two miles south of the present village c. 1870, and in 1876 Mormons from Allen's Camp (see Joseph City, Navajo) looked over the area with the thought of establishing a colony. They departed and in 1877 Ammon M. Tenney arrived. Lewis P. Cardon and a few other settlers also arrived, and for about a year the place was called Tenney's Camp. The name Woodruff was adopted in February

1878 to honor Wilford Woodruff, president of the Mormon church. The turbulent Little Colorado River washed out dams here seven times between 1880 and 1890. Woodruff Butte (Elev. 5671') and Lake are here also.
P.O. est. May 14, 1880, James Deans, p.m.
Ref.: Richards; 225, pp. 161, 162; 331, pp. 176, 177

WOODS CANYON
Coconino   T11N R14E
This canyon takes its name from that of J. X. (Jack) Woods (d. 1925), who grazed sheep in this canyon in the 1880s. Ref.: 329; 18a

WOODS CANYON
Yavapai/Coconino   T14N R7E
John Woods in 1875 located a ranch in this canyon (T17N/R7E). Ref.: 18a

WOOD SPRING
Gila   T2N R15E
When Mark Hicks developed this spring, he named it for Johnny Woods, who had lived here. Woods Spring Wash shares the name. Ref.: Woody

WOOD'S RANCH
Pima   T16S R15E   Elev. c. 3300'
John M. Wood, a rancher, established a post office for the convenience of residents nearby. He named it for himself.
P.O. est. as Wood, July 2, 1884, John M. Wood, p.m.; disc. Oct. 7, 1884
Ref.: 242

WOODY MOUNTAIN
Coconino   T20N R6E   Elev. 8054'
Old John Woody, who at one time served as Deputy Sheriff of Coconino County, established his ranch headquarters at Woody Spring on this mountain c. 1885. Woody Ridge and Spring are here also. Ref.: Keeley; AHS Names File

WOOLAROC
Greenlee   T1S R28E   Elev. 4800'
Despite the assumption that this post office at the Double Circle Ranch was named because the ranch is in a wild and woolly place filled with rocks, the fact is that the name was suggested by forest ranger W. Ellis Wiltbank when the post office refused to approve the name Eagle. That name had been proposed because the ranch is on Eagle Creek. The name *Woolaroc* is that of the plane which won the Dole San Francisco-to-Hawaii race, piloted by Arthur C. Goebel. Goebel wrote a letter to Will C. Barnes explaining that the name Woolaroc came from the "woods, lakes, and rocks ... on ... the game reserve" owned by Frank Phillips, president of Phillips Petroleum Company, which sponsored the plane in the race. See Double Circle Ranch, Greenlee
P.O. est. April 29, 1927, Willard L. Mabra, p.m.; disc. June 14, 1930
Ref.: 242; 329; Shannon

WOOLEY
Pinal   T4S R13E
This railroad siding was named for a man named Wooley, owner of the Wooley Mine about five miles southwest of Kelvin. Although records in the USGS say that the post office was in Wooley's home in 1925, no record of a post office there has been recovered from the National Archives. Ref.: 329; Structural Investigation ..., p. 4; 242

WOOLHOUSE MOUNTAIN
Navajo   T10N R23E   Elev. 6850'
In 1884 Manuel Candelaria constructed a warehouse on this mountain to store wool obtained during spring sheep shearing. The wool had to be stored because buyers were often delayed by bad roads or flood waters, and the storehouse here gave rise to the name. Ref.: 18a

WOOLSEY LAKE

Apache   T6N R24E

This lake was named for Theodore S. Woolsey, Jr., first supervisor of the Black Mesa Forest Reserve. See Sitgreaves National Forest

WOOLSEY PEAK

Maricopa   T3S R6W   Elev. 3170'

This highest peak in the Gila Bend Mountains was named for King S. Woolsey. See Woolsey Point, Coconino (Grand Canyon). Ref.: 5, p. 463

WOOLSEY POINT

Coconino (Grand Canyon)   T33N R4E   Elev. 7225'

This point (a.k.a. Woolsey Butte) was named to honor King S. Woolsey (b. 1832, Alabama; d. June 29, 1879), who arrived in Yuma in 1860 almost penniless. Within a few years he made his fortune in mining and ranching, and in milling flour. Woolsey's ranch near the present Prescott was called Agua Fria (Spanish = "cold water"). The first route established under authority of the First Territorial Legislature in 1864 originated at Prescott, passed by Woolsey's ranch, followed Black Canyon and ultimately reached the Pima Villages. It was called the Woolsey Trail, today's Black Canyon Highway. Woolsey moved to a new location which he called Agua Caliente (Spanish = "hot water"), in partnership with George Martin. Martin sold out to Woolsey c. 1868 and assumed charge of the stage station nearby (Burkes), which had been out of operation. Woolsey over the years led a number of expeditions through eastern Arizona, prospecting and searching for hostile Indians. He was a colonel in the First Arizona Volunteers. Associated names include Woolsey Tank and Woolsey Wash (Yavapai, T14N/R4W). Woolsey Peak (Maricopa, T3S/R6W, Elev. 3170') is also named for Woolsey. Ref.: 5, pp. 304, 305, 463; 107, III, 132

WOOLSEY TANK

Maricopa   T3S R7W

This natural rock tank is in Woolsey Wash. Close by is another tank which is actually the Perhaps Mine prospect hole, in existence since at least 1915. See Woolsey Point, Coconino (Grand Canyon) Ref.: 297, p. 229

WORKMAN CREEK

Gila   T6N R14E   Elev. c. 5400'

The name "Workman" is a corruption of the name of Herbert Wertman (b. Bald Knob, Michigan), who lived about four miles away from Workman Creek near Workman Creek Falls in the 1880s. Wertman was a packer for military pack trains at Fort Apache in 1880. Barnes describes Wertman as being over six feet tall and weighing about one hundred and forty pounds, with his long yellow hair occasionally tied with a blue ribbon. Ref.: 18a; Woody

WOTAN'S THRONE

Coconino (Grand Canyon)   T31N R4E   Elev. 7700'

This flat-topped peak was named c. 1906 in accordance with the policy of the USGS to name such locations for deities of ancient religions and mythologies. The first name for this location was Newberry Terrace, for John Newberry of the Ives Expedition (1857). Ref.: 178, p. 37

WRATHER ARCH

Coconino   T7E R41N   Elev. 5200'

This arch was seen by Royce Knight as he flew a plane over Paria River Canyon. It was named for Dr. Embry Wrather (b. 1883; d. Nov. 28, 1953), who rose from being a packer for the USGS in 1907 to being its director in 1943. He was said to be the world's foremost petroleum geologist, noted for his "brilliant application of micropaleontology to the search for oil." Ref.: 329

WRIGHTSON, MOUNT

Santa Cruz   T20S R15E   Elev. 9453'

This prominent peak in the Santa Rita Mountains has a number of names. J. Ross

Browne, in 1864 called its two main peaks The Teats. Browne was nearby in 1859 when William Wrightson, manager of the Salero Mining Company, was killed in a row with Mexicans. Hopkins, after whom the second of The Teats was named Mount Hopkins, was also killed at a later date. The peak is also well known as Old Baldy, which aptly describes its rocky top. Currently, the name applies to the USGS triangulation station. The name Old Baldy was the nickname of young Capt. Richard S. Ewell, stationed at Fort Buchanan 1857–1860. He was a great favorite with his men, who privately called him Baldy because of his shining pate. When he asked about it, his men said that they were talking about the mountain top, not his. Hinton calls it variously Mount Wrightson, Old Baldy, and Sentinel Peak. Because it is the most prominent in the range, it has often been called Santa Rita Peak. Ref.: AHS Names File; 56, p. 25; 205, pp. 179, 180; 163, pp. 183, 188; 224, p. 182; Lenon

WRIGHTSTOWN

Pima   T14S R15E   Elev. c. 2500'

Frederick C. Wright established a post office in his ranch home. This community has now been swallowed by Tucson.

P.O. est. as Wrightstown, Feb. 11, 1914, F. C. Wright, p.m.; disc. Sept. 21, 1921

WRONG MOUNTAIN

Pima   T15S R18E   Elev. 7786'

Government surveyors c. 1910 mistook this mountain for Rincon Peak. When they discovered their mistake, they named this location Wrong Mountain. Ref.: 18a

W S LAKE

Greenlee   T2N R32E

This location was used by an English cattle syndicate which had the W S brand. It ran about twenty-five thousand head of cattle until a terrible drought and low prices c. 1901 put it out of business. W S Mountain (Elev. 8430') shares the name.
Ref.: Mrs. Fred Fritz, Sr.

WUKOKI RUIN

Coconino   T25N R10E

This Indian ruin is considered a Hopi ancestral home and may have been inhabited by the Snake People. Ref.: 167, II, 564

WUKOPAKABI

Hope = "great reed or arrow house"

Apache   T27N R26E

This ruin and nearly vanished pueblo covers a small site at Ganado, locally called Pueblo Wukopakabi Ganado and Pueblo Colorado. It was inhabited by the Pakab or Reed People of the Hopi. See Ganado, Apache Ref.: 167, II, 976

WUPATKI NATIONAL MONUMENT   pro.: /wópatkiᴬ/

Hopi = "tall house"

Coconino   T25N R10E   Elev. c. 6200'

These ruins have more than eight hundred separate sites. In 1851 Lt. Lorenzo D. Sitgreaves' Expedition camped here. The principal major ruins at this national monument are Nalakihu Ruins (Hopi = "house alone"), restored in 1933 by the Museum of Northern Arizona; Teuwalanki Ruins (Hopi = "Citadel") and Wupatki (Hopi = "tall house"). They date to Sinagua occupation 1120–1225 A.D. The monument of over 35,865 acres was established in 1924 to preserve many unexcavated and unrestored ruins of red sandstone. Ref.: 5, pp. 285, 286; 13, David Jones, "Red Ruins in the Black Cinder," p. 7; 184, p. 37

WYMOLA

Pinal   T9S R9E   Elev. 1775'

This railroad siding on the S.P.R.R. was in existence in 1881. Why it was so named is not known. Barnes spells it Wynola, but railroad maps have Wymola.

X

XAVIER, SAN

Pima   T17S R12E   Elev. 2525'
This large permanent Papago community is at the sub-agency headquarters for the San
Xavier Indian Reservation. See Xavier del Bac Mission, San, Pima
P.O. est. Aug. 7, 1915, Forman M. Grant, p.m.; disc. May 31, 1917
Ref.: 262, p. 40; 242

XAVIER DEL BAC MISSION, SAN pro.: /san əfir del bak/

Spanish = "St. Francis Xavier"
Papago: *Bak* = "the river sink"
Pima: *Vaaka* = "adobe house"
Pima   T15S R13E   Elev. 2525'
The name of this mission exemplifies the custom of using a Christian name in
combination with a native one to designate a mission. In this instance, the saint's name
was applied by Fr. Eusebio Kino, who had vowed that he would devote his life to his
patron saint, San Francisco Xavier ("Apostle of the Indies") if God granted him
recovery from an illness Kino endured in 1663. Kino in 1665 entered the novitiate of the
Society of Jesus. He hoped to be sent to the Philippines, but was instead sent to what is
today southern Arizona and northern Sonora, Mexico. In 1692 he visited the Pima
village to which he gave his patron saint's name plus the Pima locative *del Bac*. On April
28, 1700 Kino wrote that he had brought in cattle and founded a ranch in January 1697,
and on April 28, 1700, ". . . we began the foundations of a very large and
spacious church and house, all the many people working with much pleasure and zeal,
some in excavating for the foundations, others in hauling many and very good stone of
tezontle from a little hill which was about one-quarter of a league away." The first
mission location was on a level flood plain about two miles north of the present mission.
It was closer to Martinez Hill than the present mission (the hill from which the *tezontle*
stones were obtained). The mission building was destroyed during the Pima Revolt of
1751. A year later, Franciscans replaced Jesuits and Fr. Francisco Garcés arrived. He
served for about ten years. The present mission, known as the "White Dove of the
Desert," was constructed between 1783-1797.   Ref.: 58; 167, II, 463; 45, pp. 33, 34,
265, 268, 498, 507; 43, I, 122, 235, 263; 15, pp. 379, 380; 160, p. 177; 163, p. 43

XAVIER INDIAN RESERVATION, SAN

Pima   T15S R12E   Elev. c. 2550'
This Papago Indian reservation was established by Executive Order on July 1, 1874.
While R. A. Wilbur was its Indian agent, several old Mexican families were on the land,
including members of the Elias, Grijalva, Carrillo, Cassias, Angulo, Ortega, Aguirre,
Viego, Herrera, Cruz, and Franco families, all still prominent in Tucson.   Ref.: 242

Y

YAEGER CANYON (#1)
Coconino   T18N R11E
This canyon is named for a sheep rancher, Harlow Yaeger (1900-1930). The spelling *Yeager* is incorrect, as is also the name Kelly Canyon. The latter is a current name, probably because the canyon is near Kelly Tank, a stock pond.   Ref.: 329

YAEGER CANYON (#2)
Coconino   T2N R11E
This was named for a German called Yaeger who took up claims here. A local informant says it was not named for Louis Yaeger (Barnes), who was born long after the name was applied. As Charles Yaeger (b. 1848, Prussia) was living in Williamson Valley in 1870, this place may have been named for him.   Ref.: Stemmer; 62; 18a

YAEGER SPRING
Yavapai   T15N R2E
Louis Yaeger (b. 1877; d. 1911) had a mine in Yaeger Canyon and used the spring to water sheep. When Yaeger attempted to separate his sheep from those of a Mexican sheepherder, he was fatally shot. The spring and canyon were named thereafter. Yaeger railroad siding is here also.   Ref.: 329; West; 18a

YAKI POINT   pro.: /yákiʌ/
Coconino (Grand Canyon)   T31N R3E   Elev. 3800'
George J. Wharton James named this place c. 1900 to honor the Indians "who are now making so valiant a struggle for the possession of their homes along the Yaki River in Mexico." They were struggling against being transported to a tropical climate in Yucatan. Many fled to the United States. See Guadalupe, Maricopa   Ref.: 178, p. 36

YALE POINT
Apache   T34N R23E   Elev. 8050'
Herbert Gregory named this headland for Yale University.   Ref.: 141, p. 197

YAMPAI
Yavapai   T24N R9W   Elev. 5200'
The post office application says that the name comes from the fact that this location is on the Yampa Divide. The name Yampai was first used by Lt. Edward Fitzgerald Beale. The railroad station was here.
P.O. est. May 15, 1901, Robert L. Barry, p.m.   Ref.: 242

YANKEE JOE CANYON
Gila   T3-4N R16E
This canyon was named for Joe Yankie, who c. 1874 with Jim Bullard located and operated several claims.   Ref.: 257, p. 14

YANKS CANYON
Santa Cruz   T23S R11E   Elev. c. 4000'
This canyon takes its name from that of Yank Bartlett, a freight teamster whose partner's

name was Hank Hewitt. Hank and Yank also supplied hay to Camp Grant.
Ref.: Lenon; Theobald; 107, II, 118; *Arizona Miner* (April 27, 1872), p. 1

YANKS SPRING
Santa Cruz   T23S R11E
In 1886 Yank Bartlett, who had been a packer for the Boundary Survey group and
thereafter a teamster, was wounded here by an Apache of Geronimo's band. At the time
Yank was trying to bring a wounded friend to safety. See also Bear Valley, Santa Cruz,
and Bartlett Mountain, Sant Cruz   Ref.: 329; Gilbert Sykes, Letter to Coronado
National Forest Supervisor (Aug. 1, 1941)

YAPONCHA CRATER
Coconino   T23N R8E
This location was given the name of the Hopi wind god because his home is in a crevice
here. The place is an indescribable jumble of lava from the Bonita Lava flow. Astronauts
did some training here for their moon landing. See Bonita Lava Flow, Coconino
Ref.: 13, p. 7

YAQUI TANKS   pro.: /yákiʌ/
Yuma   T1S R16W   Elev. c. 2300'
A Yaki Indian in the early 1900s lay in wait at this natural waterhole for mountain sheep
and deer, hence the name. He sold the meat to the cook at the Kofa Mine.   Ref.: Monson

YARBO MINE
Yavapai   T13N R2E
The presence of this mine led to the naming of Yarbo Wash, sometimes incorrectly
spelled Yarber. A stamp mill for gold existed in this wash prior to 1900. Yarbo Spring is
here.   Ref.: Woody; West

YARNELL
Yavapai   T10N R5W   Elev. 4840'
Harrison Yarnell (d. Aug. 11, 1916), located and worked the Yarnell Mine, which he
sold c. 1892. The Yarnell family was among the earliest to settle in this region. The first
post office, called Yarnell, was discontinued. When it was reestablished in 1928, postal
rules called for it to have a new name and it was called Peepless Valley. The reason
becomes clear when it is realized that the present Yarnell Hill was Antelope Hill, the
scene of a very rich gold discovery in the early years by Abraham Peeples and others.
However, because everyone locally referred to the place as Yarnell, the name was
changed to Yarnell. The name also refers to the hill itself and to a spring (T10N/R4W).
P.O. est. as Yarnell, Oct. 18, 1892, Frank McKean, p.m.; disc. April 30, 1911; reest. as
Peeples Valley, Aug. 6, 1928, Mrs. Susie McCrea, p.m.; name changed to Yarnell, Dec.
1, 1933   Ref.: 242; State Library Files; 18a; AHS Names File

YAVA   pro.: /yǽvǝ/
Yavapai   T13N R6W   Elev. 3500'
The post office application in the National Archives notes that locally this place was
called Thompson Valley. The postmaster coined the name Yava, using the first four
letters of the county name.
P.O. est. Jan. 15, 1916, William JW. Davis, p.m.; disc. Feb. 28, 1954
Ref.: Davis; 242; *Weekly Arizona Miner* (March 12, 1870), p. 3

YAVAPAI COUNTY   pro.: /yǽvǝpay/
Hodge says that the name derives from *enyaeva* (= "sun") and *pai* (= "people"). An
initial act of the First Arizona Territorial Legislature was the creation of four counties.
One was Yavapai County. As originally established, it reached from New Mexico on the
east to the middle of the Gila River on the south, north to the Utah boundary, and west to
the boundary it still shares with Mohave County. Later it lost acreage for the formation
of Gila, Maricopa, Coconino, and Apache counties. However, Yavapai County remains
larger than the state of New Jersey, with an acreage of 5,179,240. The county seat is at
Prescott, which also served twice as the Territorial capital (1864-67 and 1877-89). It is
the home of the Yavapai Indians, commonly called Apache-Mojaves in territorial days.

Yavapai County history is replete with stories about fabulous mines and placers, about Indian fights and pioneer settlements. It is notable for stock raising.
Ref.: 167, II, 994; 77, p. 325, Footnote; 224, IV, 15; 15, pp. 522, 523, 610, 611

YAVAPAI INDIAN RESERVATION pro.: /yǽvəpay/
Yavapai: *enyaeva* = "sun"; *pai* = "people"
Yavapai   T14N R2W
In the late 1880s Yavapai Indians were popularly called Apache Mojave Indians. They are a Yuman tribe, not Apache. See also Havasupai Indian Reservation, Coconino

YAVAPAI POINT pro.: /yǽvəpay/
Coconino (Grand Canyon)   T31N R3E   Elev. 6600'
This location was first called O'Neill's Point. The name was changed on the recommendation of Francois E. Matthes, with a notation that "O'Neill [was] a politician notorious for his gambling exploits." The location was renamed in accordance with the then-existing policy of the USGS to name places at the Grand Canyon for Arizona tribes. Ref.: 329

Y BAR BASIN
Gila   T8N R10E
This small basin-like location was named for a brand used by a pioneer cattle rancher in the region. It is also called Bar Basin. Ref.: 329

YEI BEI-CHAI (MESA)
Navajo   T41N R22E   Elev. 5200'
At the northern tip of this mesa is a series of rock formation which looks like Navajo dancers in a line as in the nine-day healing ceremony of the Yei-Bichei (= spirits representing the gods). At their right center is a formation called the Totem Pole. Ref.: 191, pp. 88, 119

YELLOW JACKET: The ferociousness of yellow jacket wasps has earned them a right to be remembered in place names which it may be assumed reflect their fierceness, unless otherwise noted below:

Yellow Jacket   Coconino
See Happy Jack, Coconino

Yellow Jacket Canyon   Coconino   T20N R11E
The American name is a translation. Navajo: *tsis'naltsooi'* (= "yellow jackets"). Navajos named this canyon because they were once pursued by Ute Indians whose horses ran into a yellow-jacket wasp nest in the canyon.

Yellowjacket Canyon   Graham   T2S R22E

Yellowjacket Canyon   Yavapai   T10N R5E

Yellow Jacket Cienega   Apache   T8N R25E

Yellow Jacket Creek   Yavapai   T12N R4-3S
Also known as Spring Creek

Yellow Jacket Draw   Coconino   T14N R10E

Yellowjacket Gulch   Yavapai   T12N R4E
Also called Rice Gulch

Yellowjacket Hill   Santa Cruz
See Fraguita Peak, Pima

Yellowjacket Mesa   Yavapai   T12N R4E

Yellow Jacket Mine   Santa Cruz   T22S R10E (abandoned)

Yellow Jacket Mountain Santa Cruz   T22S R10E   Elev. 4750'
This was named for the Yellow Jacket Mine located by Thomas G. Roddick (d. June 1879), who arrived in Arizona in 1865. When he died his doctors sued each other. In court one broke his cane over the head of the other. The judge ordered an autopsy of Roddick, and settled the matter by deeming the cause to a "complication of diseases." Ref.: AHS, James G. Roddick File

Yellowjacket Spring	Coconino	(1) T19N R10E (2) T16N R9E

See Happy Jack, Coconino

Yellowjacket Spring	Yavapai	T12N R4E
Yellowjacket Spring	Greenlee	T2S R29E
Yellowjacket Spring	Maricopa	T3N R12E
Yellow Jacket Spring	Navajo	T6N R22E
Yellow Jacket Spring	Pinal	T1N R12E
Yellow Jacket Spring	Santa Cruz	T22S R10E

This spring was named for the Yellow Jacket Mine. See Yellow Jacket Mountain, Santa Cruz

Yellow Jacket Spring	Yavapai	T12N R4E
Yellow Jacket Wash	Pima	T22S R10E
Yellowjacket Well	Graham	T2S R21E
Yellowjacket Well	Pinal	T7S R14E

YELLOWSTONE: In some places, the rock is noticeably yellow. The following are examples:

Yellowstone Canyon	Apache	T34N R27E
Yellowstone Canyon	Graham/Greenlee	T6S R29E
Yellowstone Canyon	Navajo	T9N R20E
Yellowstone Canyon	Pima	T18S R7E
Yellowstone Mesa	Mohave	T39N R5W
Yellowstone Spring	Mohave	(1) T39N R6W (2) T36N R13W
Yellowstone Wash	Mohave	T38N R6W

YORK
Greenlee   T6S R31E   Elev. 3500'

This location in York Valley on the railroad was named for the George R. York ranch (on the bend between Clifton and Duncan). On April 22, 1882 Apaches led by Loco attacked and killed Felix Knox and five others at the York station. According to Mrs. York, who witnessed the attack, there were about five hundred Apaches. Soon thereafter while trailing his stolen horses, George York was ambushed and killed. He is buried at the ranch site.

The post office was established in 1882 when the railroad came through and was discontinued eighteen months later. When it was reestablished, postal authorities did not permit using the old name. The names Coronado and Toledo were both suggested, but the name York (T7S/R30E) was finally re-approved.

P.O. est. as York, Jan. 16, 1882, Lou M. Butler, p.m.; disc. July 9, 1883; reest. as York, March 28, 1911, Mrs. Lottie Ruley, p.m.; disc. Feb. 28, 1920

Ref.: 242; Woody; 68, pp. 75, 76; 116, p. 617

YOUNG
Gila   T9N R14E   Elev. 5115'

After the bloody Pleasant Valley feud ended, settlers gradually returned to the valley, and by 1896 the need for a post office developed. Locally it was called Pleasant Valley. However, there was already a post office of that name near Flagstaff, so the post office here was named Young for Silas Young, who had a ranch in the valley. He was the father of the first postmistress, who homesteaded on the Graham place when Graham left with his cattle between 1887 and 1892.

P.O. est. June 25, 1890, Ola Young, p.m.   Ref.: McKinney

YOUNGBERG
Pinal   T1N R8E   Elev. 2029'

In 1893 when George U. Young arrived, Gold Field had twenty-nine houses with about fifteen people who mined for gold nearby. *Desert Magazine* said, "Rumors suggest that the gold field site may have furnished the Dutchman with his plethora of gold." Although the place was also referred to as Youngsberg after its founder, the name Gold Field was used in establishing the post office. By December 1897 the boom days were over and Gold Field was already a ghost town.

Some years later a small community developed. It was called Youngberg, to honor George U. Young (b. Feb. 10, 1867, Indiana), who served as Secretary for the Territory of Arizona (1909-1910). Mr. Young owned controlling interest in the Goldfield Mine. When a post office was reactivated, the old name Goldfield could not be used. The post office application suggested the name Young City, but Youngberg was used in its place. P.O. est. as Goldfield, Oct. 7, 1893, James L. Patterson, p.m. (deceased); office activated March 12, 1894, J.G. Patterson, p.m.; disc. Nov. 2, 1898; reest. March 15 1920 as Youngberg, Stiny Wilson, p.m., but office assumed by Rolla W. Walling; disc. Oct. 30, 1926 Ref.: 242; 224; III; 18a; "In the Shadow of a Legend, "*Desert Magazine* (April 1918), p. 30; "List of Ghost Towns,," Phoenix Chamber of Commerce (Nov. 26, 1948)

YOUNGTOWN
Maricopa   T3N R1 E   Elev. 1135'
The first name for this location was Marinette, named in 1912 by homesteaders for their home town in Wisconsin. In 1955 a real estate development began constructing a retirement community under the euphemistic name of Youngtown.
P.O. est. as Marinette, March 4, 1912, E.J. Helsley, p.m.; name changed to Youngtown, Jan. 1, 1958   Ref.: 242; 18a; "Days and Ways," *Arizona Republic* (Jan. 25, 1959)

YUCCA: The presence of yucca cactus with its striking candle-like white blossoms on a central stalk probably accounts for the following place names:

Yucca   Mohave   T17N R18W   Elev. 1817'
The settlement here is in area noted for its fine stand of Joshua tree yucca cacti, hence the name. During the early mining days in the White Hills of Gold Basin area, yucca wood was used for fuel to operate hoists.
P.O. est. June 3, 1905, Louis Janc, p.m.; Wells Fargo 1885   Ref.: 242; Harris

Yucca Flat   Navajo   T35N R19E   Elev. 6940'

Yucca Hill   Navajo   T35N R19E

Yucca Spring   Mohave   T27N R19W   Elev. 5175'

YUMA pro.: /yúwmə/
Yuma   T8S R23W   Elev. 141'
It seems likely that the name Yuma is derived from the Old Spanish word *Umo* = "smoke"), particularly as the earliest explorers wrote not only of seeing much smoke along the banks of the river, but also of how Indians carried warm coals clutched to themselves to stay warm on cold mornings. In fact the local name for Indians was *Umo*. It is interesting to note that the Indian name was spelled Jamas on an 1820 map, repeated on an 1849 map, a further indication that the name may be derived from their use of smoke as the *J* is pronounced like an *H* (not like a *Y*. Further, as late as the early 1900s, it is customary for young boys to carry pots of burning, smoking *buhach* (= "manure") and for a small fee to accompany walkers, thus discouraging hordes of mosquitoes.

The first white man to pass the site of the future Yuma was Hernando de Alarcɳon, who in 1540 sailed part way up the Colorado River in his unsuccessful attempt to deliver supplies to the Coronado Expedition. Over a century later (1691) Fr. Eusebio Kino was in this area searching for a route to California from Sonora, Mexico. In the fall of 1700 Kino followed the Gila River. He turned south on the Colorado River and reached the Yuma Indian rancheria opposite what was Fort Yuma many years later. He named the place San Dionisio because he had arrived on that saint's day. The name is spelled Doonsyio on his 1701 map. Three-quarters of a century later (on December 4, 1775) Fr. Francisco Garcés arrived at what he called the Pueblo de la Concepcion and established the Mission de la Purisima Concepcion (in California) on the strait between two low hills through which the Colorado River flowed south of its juncture with the Gila River. Authorities in Mexico City failed to follow through on promises Garcés made to the Yuman leader Palma, and here the Indians murdered Garcés on July 17, 1781. The Indian revolt left the mission in smoldering ruins.

The discovery of gold in California in 1848 changed the course of events for the future Yuma. Driving livestock, emigrants along the southern route made their way painfully across the rugged desert. Sometimes they made rafts to ship their goods down the Gila River. When they arrived at the Colorado River they had to have some means to cross. At first Indians helped by ferrying goods and people in small basket "boats" which swimming Indians pushed. Before long a group of white men saw the possibility of profit and in 1849 established a ferry. It was run by a scoundrel named John Gallantin, who with a Dr. Lincoln took advantage of the bounty then offered by Mexico for Indian scalps. These whites scalped innocent and friendly Indians, some Mexicans, and dark-haired emigrants. The Mexican government, which then owned the land, sought retaliation. Gallatin escaped to the eastern part of the Territory of New Mexico. There he gathered twenty-five hundred sheep by stealing or buying them and headed for California with the sheep and twenty-one Americans. Not only the Mexican government, but Indians wanted his scalp. At the Colorado River he lost it.

A ferry across the Colorado was a necessity, and on July 11, 1850, Louis J.F. Jaeger (b. 1824, Pennsylvania; d. June 30, 1892) arrived from California and started a legal ferrying service. The community that arose on the California side was called Jaegerville. In that same year, both for the protection of emigrants and to provide facilities for the coming Boundary Survey, a military encampment was established about a mile upriver from Jaeger's ferry. There on December 1, 1850, Lt. Thomas W. Sweeny and his nine-man detachment pitched tents. Sweeny wrote that the party "call our position Camp Yuma in honor of the tribe of Indians who inhabited the surrounding country. We subsequently moved to a hill about a mile farther up opposite the mouth of the Gila River, and this post we still retain." There on the California side of the river Fort Yuma was established. In June 1852 John Bartlett of the Boundary Survey Commission remarked that he observed "traces of the Old Spanish Mission buildings."

As far as the Arizona side of the river was concerned, nothing much happened until Charles Debrille Poston arrived after having fled from Apache depredations along the Santa Cruz River (see Tubac, Santa Cruz). Jaeger refused to take Poston and his companions across the river unless paid $25.00 a head, but the party had not a dime. Poston, always a promoter with ideas, set up his surveying instruments and he and his companions began busily surveying a "town site." The matter ended with Jaeger taking shares in the proposed "city" and ferrying the party across the river free. It is significant that on August 15, 1854 Poston certified the town plat in San Francisco, noting that the proposed community had "about nine hundred and thirty-six acres . . . which is to be laid off as a city called 'Colorado City'."

A post office was established in 1857. Its name was changed to Arizona in 1858, hence the designation Arizona, New Mexico Territory. In 1866 the name was changed to Yuma. That name lasted for three years, giving way to Arizona City. The county seat was moved from La Paz to Arizona City in 1870. By an act of the Legislature, Arizona City was incorporated on March 11, 1871. On February 3, 1873 the name of the town was changed for the last time, to Yuma. By 1870 more than eleven hundred people were living in Yuma, today a thriving city.

P.O. est. as Colorado City, Dec. 2, 1857, John B. Dow, p.m.; name changed to Arizona, March 17, 1858; disc. June 8, 1863; reest. as Yuma, Oct. 1, 1866, Francis Hinton, p.m.; name changed to Arizona City, Oct. 28, 1869, James M. Barney, p.m.; name changed to Yuma, April 14, 1873; Wells Fargo 1865 (oldest in Arizona Territory)   Ref.: Lenon; Dr. Bertha Bascom; Kline; 224, III; 315, pp. 50, 51; 133; 163, pp. 244, 245; AHS; *Weekly Alta Californian* (July 30, 1859); 369, p. 60; 15, pp. 489, 616; 77, p. 548; 45, pp. 438, 439; 106, p. 103; 206, p. 333; *Citizen* (Jan. 25, 1873), p. 1, and (Jan. 23, 1875), p. 1; 62

YUMA COUNTY   pro.: /yúwmə/

Prior to the formation of the Territory of Arizona, what is now Yuma County was part of Doña Ana County, Territory of New Mexico. The alleged Confederate sympathizer Sylvester Mowry (see Mowry, Mount, Santa Cruz) optimistically proposed a map of Arizona in 1860 in which this county was labeled Castle Dome County, the name coming from that of the famous Castle Dome Mining District. An initial action of the First Territorial Legislature on November 8, 1868 created the original four counties of Arizona, among them being Yuma County. Yuma County retains its original boundaries. However, in late May 1982 residents voted to split the county into a northern and a southern division, inasmuch as the two have distinctly different interests. At the time of preparing this volume, the matter had not been settled. It encompasses 6,390,400 acres. The first county seat at La Paz (*q. v.*) was moved in 1870 to Yuma where it has remained. From the outset mining has been important in Yuma County. Today agriculture is of prime importance. It shares its name with Yuma Mesa (T9S/R22W), Yuma Valley (T9S/R24W), and Yuma Wash (T2S/R22W).

No book about Arizona would be complete without including the story about the wicked soldier stationed at Fort Yuma who after his death returned from Hell to get his blankets.

YUMA INDIAN RESERVATION
Yuma/California   T16S R23W

This reservation was established on September 27, 1917 under the name Cocopah Reservation. It contains five hundred and eighty-seven acres. The Cocopah Indians are a branch of the Yuman family which in 1604-1605 lived near the mouth of the Colorado River, but later moved slightly north (still in Mexico). Maj. Samuel P. Heintzelman in 1856 reported seeing them near the Mexican boundary line.   Ref.: "Annual Report of the Arizona Commission of Indian Affairs, 1954, 1955, 1956," pp. 14, 18

YUMA HILLS
Yuma

In 1854 Lt. N. Michler reported that his camp was "opposite the military post on the left bank of the Colorado, between the Plutonic Ridge on the east, and a low range of sand and gravel hills, called the Yuma Hills on the west."   Ref.: 106, p. 103

YUMA POINT   pro.: /yúwmə/
Coconino (Grand Canyon)   T31N R2E   Elev. 6250'

In accordance with the policy extant in 1925, the USGS named this point for an Arizona Indian tribe, the Yuma Indians.

YUMA TRAIL
This name was in use in the early 1900s. See Camino Diablo

YUMTHESKA POINT
Coconino (Grand Canyon)   T33N R4W   Elev. 4290'

In 1925 the USGS placed this name on this location. It is the name of an Indian family. It applies also to Yumtheska Mesa.   Ref.: 329

YUNOSI POINT
Coconino (Grand Canyon)   T33N R5W   Elev. 5600'

Yunosi, the widow of a Supai Indian named Hotouta, had visions of his spirit. During such times she spoke, calling out, "Big Chief Tom!" She would then turn to others and inquire of them with a shriek, "You no see?" Her American name derived from that. In 1925 the USGS named this point for her, mistakenly assuming they were naming it for an Indian family. The spelling Yonosi is incorrect.   Ref.: 179, pp. 250, 255, 256; 329

Z

ZAZABE SPRING

Pima

In 1867 this location was described as being south of the southern end of Zazabe Valley and eleven miles from a Papago trail leading from Fresnal. See Sasabe, Pima
Ref.: 208, p. 341

ZELLWEGER

Pinal   T4S R13E   Elev. c. 2400'

This location on the old Arizona and Eastern R.R. was so named for John Zellwager, Sr., a cattleman in the vicinity. Ref.: 18a

ZENIFF

Navajo   T14N R18E   Elev. 6133'

The location for this post office is that given on the 1922 application in the Nat'l. Arch. Currently the location is listed as T13N/R19E, possibly the result of more accurate surveying. On the application it is noted that the local name is Dry Lake, and the name suggested for the post office is Heward. It was called Dry Lake because it was next to a basin, normally dry, which in the 1880s when filled with flood water was used by thousands of range stock. The name was still in use in 1930. It was also called Big Dry Lake. The Mormon farming community which developed took the name Zeniff for a character in the *Book of Mormon*. The area is today relatively deserted.
P.O. est. June 19, 1922, John Albert Bowler, p.m.; disc. July 15, 1933
Ref.: 242; Richards; 163, pp. 292-293

ZIEGLER MOUNTAIN

Apache   T10N R24E   Elev. 7721'

This location was named for an early settler, whose name is also spelled Zegler. The name Zegler Mountain was in use c. 1900. Zeglar Spring shares the name.
Ref.: 329

ZILBETOD PEAK

Navajo: *dzil* = "mountain"; *betod* = "bare or bald"
Apache   T39N R30E   Elev. 9284'

Gregory translated this name from the Navajo in 1915. Ref.: 141, p. 197

ZILNEZ (MESA)   pro.: /dzilšnne:z/

Navajo: *dzil* = "mountain"; *nez* = "long"
Navajo   T39N R16E

Considering the aptness of the Navajo descriptive name, the reason for the USGS changing it to Tall Mountain is unclear. The Navajo name has also been rendered Zilth Nez Mesa. The word *mesa* is redundant.
Ref.: 141, p. 197; 13, Brewer, "Navajo ...," p. 2

ZILTAHJINI MESA   pro.: /dziˡšdahžin/
Navajo = "standing cranes"

Navajo   T32N R17E   Elev. 7107'

Barnes says that Fr. Berard Haile renders this name as "Navajo — *delth-na-zina,'* — standing cranes."

ZONIA
Yavapai   T11N R4W

The post office at this location served employees of the Zonia Mine.
P.O. est. Feb. 9, 1900, John M. McCaffrey, p.m.; disc. Dec. 13, 1900

ZOROASTER TEMPLE
Coconino (Grand Canyon)   T32N R3E   Elev. 7136'

George Wharton James seems to have named this location, described as "a pillar of fire," which is struck by the first rays of sunrise and the last rays in the evening. The name is suitable because Zoroaster is associated with fire. The USGS approved the name in 1906. Ref.: 88, p. 30; 329

ZUÑI POINT   pro.: /zúwniʌ/ or /zúwnyiʌ/
Coconino (Grand Canyon)   T30N R5E   Elev. 7284'

This location was named c. 1925, in accordance with USGS policy, for the Zuñi Indians of New Mexico. They live along the central eastern border of Apache County, Arizona.

ZUÑI RIVER
Apache/New Mexico   T14N R28E

The name for this tributary of the Little Colorado River was in use at least as early as 1844 when it appears on a map by Josiah Gregg. According to Casteñada, the Coronado Expedition (1540) called this stream the Colorado because of its muddy red waters. In 1849 Lt. Simpson called it the Rio del Pescado, acknowledging it was also called the Rio de Zuñi. The Zuñi Indians live near it in New Mexico.
Ref.: 292, p. 89; 357, p. 482, Note 1

ZUÑI WASH
Apache   T15N R29E

This wash derives its name from the fact that it heads in the Zuñi Mountains of New Mexico. Ref.: Stemmer

ZUÑI WELL   pro.: /zúwnyiʌ/ or zúwniʌ/
Apache   T20N R24E   Elev. 5392'

While prospecting for oil c. 1917, the Zuni Oil Company drilled a well and at six hundred feet hit petrified wood so dense that no drill then available could pierce it. When an alternate well shaft was sunk, the company struck abundant salt water, which is used for sanitary facilities at the Petrified Forest National Monument. Ref.: Branch

Appendix

Many who use this volume will find the following section invaluable, for it contains hundreds of obscure and variant names which are cross referenced to major entries in the preceding text. The list is the result of having examined Arizona maps which date from the 1600s to the 20th century, noting place names and tracing the multitude of changes which have occurred with some. No locations will be noted unless they differ from that of the entry to which the name is cross indexed.

Aaivonam	See Ahe Vonam, Pima
Aakta	See Cajilon, Pima
Aaribac	See Arivaca, Pima
Aatci	See Achi, Pima
Â'ât kam va-alo	See Santan, Pinal
Abineau Canyon	See Aubineau Canyon, Coconino
Abra, La	See Avra Valley, Pima
Abray Landing	See Aubrey Landing, Mohave
Acadia Ranch	See Oracle, Pinal
Achie	See Achi, Pima
Acme	See Goldroad, Mohave
'Adahili'ni'	See Grand Falls, Coconino
!Adahosha'ni'	See Meteor Crater, Coconino
Adair Wash	See Adair Spring, Navajo
Adams Flat	(T4N/R7E) See Texas Canyon, Cochise
Adams Peak	(T16S/R22E; Elev. 5840') See Texas Canyon, Cochise
Adams River	See Virgin River, Mohave
Adid	See Gu Achi, Pima
Adobes, Los	See Inspiration, Gila
'Aedsani Nobitiin	See Woman's Trail, Apache
Agalon, Valley of	See Mormon Crossing, Coconino
Agathlan	See Agathla Needle, Navajo
Agatha Peak	See Agathla Needle, Navajo
Agua Caliente Creek	(T13S/R16E; Elev. c. 4000') See Tanque Verde Hot Springs, Pima
Agua Caliente Hill	(T13S/R16E; Elev. 5350') See Tanque Verde Hot Springs, Pima
Agua Caliente Mountains	(Elev. 1250') See Agua Caliente, Maricopa
Agua Caliente Ranch	See Tanque Verde Hot Springs, Pima
Agua Caliente, Santa Maria del	See Agua Caliente, Maricopa
Agua Caliente Wash	See Tanque Verde Hot Springs, Pima
Agua Cercada Spring	(1: T22S/R10E) (2: T23S/R12E) See Agua Cercada Canyon, Santa Cruz
Agua del Pozo Verde	See Pozo Verde, Pima
Agua Dulce, Sierra de	See Agua Dulce Mountains, Pima
Agua Escondida	See Tinajas Altas, Yuma, and Tule Tank, Yuma
Agua Fria	See Dewey, Yavapai
Agua Fria Canyon	See Peck Canyon, Pima/Santa Cruz
Agua Fria Valley	See Dewey, Yavapai
Aguage de San Pacifico	See Meadow Creek, Mohave
Aguaje de los Alquives	See Dripping Springs, La Paz

Aguajito	See Purcell, Pima
Aguajito Wash	See Aguajita Spring, Pima
Agua La Vara	See Nawt Vaya, Pima
Agua Lavaria	See Nawt Vaya, Pima
Aguato	See Awatobi, Navajo
Aguatove	See Awatobi, Navajo
Aguatuyba	See Awatobi, Navajo
Agua Verde Range	See Tanque Verde Ridge, Pima
Agua Verde Wash	See Agua Verde Creek, Pima
Agua Vibora	See Pine Springs, Apache
Aguila, Sierra de	See Aguila Mountains, Yuma
Aguirre Pass	See Aguirre Peak, Pima
Agustin de Oyaur, San	See Tucson, Pima
Agustin de Tucson, San	See Tucson, Pima
Aha'a Chi	See Antelope Spring, Mohave
A-Ha-Ca-zon	See Date Creek, Yavapai
Ah-Ah-Pook Creek	See Ahapook Creek, Mohave/Yavapai
Ah-Ha-Carsona	See Date Creek, Yavapai
Ahuato	See Awatobi, Navajo
AH-Va-Koo^u-O-Tut	See Headgate Rock Dam, La Paz
Ajo, Mount	(Elev. 4829') See Ajo, Pima
Ajo Mountains	See Ajo, Pima
Ajo, Valley of the	(T12S/R6W) See Ajo, Pima, and Ajo Peak, Pima (adjacent to the valley)
Aktjim	See Ak Chin, Pinal
A-Ku-Hi-Evi	See Windswept Terrace, Navajo
Akútcimy	See Pima Villages, Pinal/Maricopa
Alameda, Rio de La	See Little Colorado River
Alamo	See Nawt Vaya, Pima
Albino Mountains, San	See Gila Mountains
Alchesay Flat, Spring	(T6N/R23E; Navajo) See Alchesay Canyon, Maricopa
Alchesay National Fish Hatchery	(T6N/R23E; Navajo) See Alchesay Canyon, Maricopa
Al Cukson	See Ali Chukson, Pima
Aleh-Zon	See Arizona
Alexandria	See Alexandra, Yavapai
Alexo, Arroyo de San	See Diamond Creek, Mohave
Alex's Decoy	See Indian Hill, Yavapai
Algodones Land Grant	See Somerton, Yuma
Algrim Wash	See Pilgrim Wash, Mohave
Ali Chuk Valley	See Ali Chukson, Pima
Ali Chuk Wash	See Ali Chukson, Pima
Alimo	See Alamo, La Paz
Ali Molena Canyon	See Ali Molina, Pima
Ali Molina Canyon, Wash	See Ali Molina, Pima
Alisa Pass	See Pan Tak Pass, Pima
Aliso Creek	See Gilson Wash, Gila, and Ramboz Wash, Gila
Aliso Pass	See Pan Tak Pass, Pima
Alitjukson	See Ali Chukson, Pima
Alivaipai	See Quito Baquito Springs, Pima
Aliza Pass	See Pan Tak Pass, Pima
Aljibe	See Montezuma Head, Pinal
Allantown	See Houck, Apache
Allen	See Gunsight, Pima and Logan, Pima
Allen City	See Gunsight, Pima and Logan, Pima, or Joseph City, Navajo
Allen's Camp, City	See Joseph City, Navajo
Allentown	See Houck, Apache
Allison Pass	See Pan Tak Pass, Pima

Alma Ward	See Round Valley, Apache
Alpha	See Burke's Station, Maricopa
Altamount	See Liberty, Maricopa
Alta Pimeria	See Xavier del Bac, San, Pima
Altar Falls	See Ribbon Falls, Coconino (Grand Canyon)
Altar, El	See Altar Valley, Pima
Altar Wash	See Altar Valley, Pima
Alto Gulch, Hill	See Alto, Santa Cruz
Alum Gulch	See Alum Canyon, Santa Cruz
Alvarez Mountains	(Elev. 3248' and 2830') See Alvarez, Charco de, Pima
Amadoville	See Amado, Santa Cruz
Amberon Point	(T7N/R27E) See Amberon Flat, Apache
Ambush Water Pocket	See Pen Pockets, Mohave
American Flag	See American Mine, Mohave, or Old Glory, Santa Cruz
American Flag Spring	See American Flag, Pinal
Amity	See Round Valley, Apache
Amity, Fort	See Round Valley, Apache
'Anaa'sinyiłhaayáhi	See Trail: Trail where the Enemy Walked Up, Apache
Ana de Quibori, Santa	See Quiburi (Ruins), Cochise
Anagam	See Anegam, Pima
Anderson Gap, Mesa, Point	See Anderson Canyon, Coconino
Anderson Spring	See Anderson Canyon, Cochise, or Anderson Canyon, Coconino
Andres Coata, San	See Maricopa Wells, Pinal
Andres, Rio de San	See Big Sandy River, Mohave
Andrews Spring	See Twin Springs, Coconino
Andrus Draw	See Andrus Canyon, Mohave
Andrus Point	(T32N/R10W; Elev. 5245') See Andrus Canyon, Mohave
Andrus Spring	See Andrus Canyon, Mohave
'Ane'etseghi	See Muerto, Canyon del, Apache
Anegam Wash	See Anegam, Pima
Anekam	See Anegam, Pima
Angeles de Guevavi Mission, Los	See Guevavi, Santa Cruz
Angeles, Santos	See Guevavi, Santa Cruz
Angelo del Botum, San	See Vaiva Vo, Pima
Angel Plateau	See Indian Garden, Coconino (Grand Canyon)
Anicam	See Anegam, Pima
Annex Wash	See Annex Ridge, Yavapai
Antelope	See Lopeant, Mohave
Antone, San	See Weldon, Pima
Anuawooch	See Ahan Owuch, Pima
Anvil Rock Station	See Anvil Rock, Yavapai
A One Crater	See A One Mountain, Coconino
Aqua Caliente	See Agua Caliente, Maricopa
Aqua Fria	See Agua Fria, Maricopa, and Mirage, El, Maricopa
Aqua La Varia	See Nawt Vaya, Pima
Araby Valley	See Araby, Yuma
Aravaipa Creek	See Aravaipa Canyon, Pinal/Graham
Aravaipa Valley	(T7S/R20E; Graham) See Aravaipa Canyon, Pinal/Graham
Aravaypa, Fort	See Grant, Old Camp, Pinal, and Aravaipa, Camp, Pinal
Aravypa Canyon	See Aravaipa Canyon, Pinal/Graham
Arcadia Ranch	See Oracle, Pinal
Archi	See Achi, Pima
Aribac, La	See Arivaca, Pima
Aribaipai	See Aravaipa, Pinal
Aritutoc	See Aritoac, Maricopa
Arivaca Creek	See Arivaca, Pima
Arivaca Junction	(T19S/R12E; Elev. 3070') See Arivaca, Pima

Arivaca Lake	(T21S/R11E) See Arivaca, Pima
Arivaca Valley	See Arivaca, Pima
Arivaca Wash	(T21S/R9E) See Arivaca, Pima
Arivaipa, Camp	See Grant, Old Camp, Pinal
Arivaipa Canyon	See Aravaipa Canyon, Pinal/Graham
Arivaipa Creek	See Aravaipa Canyon, Pinal/Graham
Arivaypa, Fort	See Grant, Old Camp, Pinal
Arivaypa River	See Arivaypa Canyon, Pinal/Graham
Arizantelope	See Lopeant, Mohave
Arizola Mountains	See Casa Grande Mountains, Pinal, and Arizola, Pinal
Arlington Mesa	See Arlington, Maricopa
Arlington Valley	See Arlington, Maricopa
Armer and Tanner Winter Camp	See Armer, Gila
Armer Gulch	(T4N/R14E) See Armer, Gila
Armer Mountain	(T6N/R12E; Elev. 7310') See Armer, Gila
Armer Wash	See Armer, Gila
Armory Park	See Lowell, Fort, Pima
Arnett Canyon	See Arnett Creek, Pinal
Arnold Mesa	See Arnold Canyon, Yavapai
Arnold Place Spring	See Arnold Canyon, Yavapai
Artillery Park	See Artillery Mountains, Mohave
Aryvipai Springs	See Aravaipa, Camp, Pinal
Artutoc	See Oatman Flat, Maricopa
Ash Fork Draw	See Ash Fork, Yavapai
Ash Hill Terrace	See Walpi, Navajo
Ashurst Lake	(T19N/R9E) See Ashurst Run, Coconino; Mormon Lake, Coconino, and Horse Lake, Coconino
Ashurst Spring	(T19N/R10E) See Ashurst Run, Coconino
Asientic'häbi	See Needles, The, Mohave
Assamp River	See Hassayampa River, Yavapai
Asthonsosie Mesa	See Azansosi, Navajo
Atascosa Canyon	See Atascosa Mountains, Santa Cruz
Atascosa Peak	See Atascosa Mountains, Santa Cruz
Atascosa Spring	(T23S/R11E) See Atascosa Mountains, Santa Cruz
Atascoso Cañon	See Peña Blanca Canyon, Santa Cruz
Aubineau Peak	(Elev. 11,838') See Aubineau Canyon, Coconino
Aubineau Springs	See Aubineau Canyon, Coconino
Aubrey	See Aubrey Landing, Mohave
Aubrey City	See Aubrey Landing, Mohave
Aubrey Peak	(No. 1); (T12N/R15W; Elev. 2953') (No. 2); (T15N/R14W; Elev. 5078') See Aubrey Landing, Mohave
Aubrey Spring	(T28N/R8W; Coconino) See Aubrey Landing, Mohave
Aubrey Valley	(T24N/R7W) See Aubrey Cliffs, Coconino
Aubry	See Aubrey Landing, Mohave
Audley	See Aubrey Landing, Mohave
Augustin de Oaiur, San	See Augustin (Mission of), San, Pima, and Tucson, Pima
Augustin de Pueblicito de Tucson	See Augustí (Mission of), San, Pima, and Tucson, Pima
Aulick Range	See Aubrey Cliffs, Mohave
Avalon	See Ivalon, Yuma
Avansada, Mesa de La	See Bernardino Land Grant, San, Cochise
Avia Tok-A-Va	See Dome Rock Mountains, La Paz
Avra, La	See Avra Valley, Pima
A-Vuc-Hoo-Mar-Lish	See Casa Blanca, Pinal
Awatobi Mesa	See Awatobi, Navajo
Awatobi Springs	(T27N/R19E) See Awatobi, Navajo
Awatovi Creek	(T33N/R5E; Coconino [Grand Canyon]) See Awatobi, Navajo
Awatubi	(T33N/R5E; Coconino [Grand Canyon]) See Awatobi, Navajo
Awatubi Crest	(T33N/R5E; Coconino [Grand Canyon]) See Awatobi, Navajo

Aztec	See Wilgus, Cochise
Aztec Amphitheater	(T32N/R2W; Coconino [Grand Canyon]) See Aztec Peak, Gila
Aztec Gulch	(T22S/R16E; Santa Cruz) See Aztec, Santa Cruz, and Aztec Peak, Gila
Aztec Hills	(Elev. 1185') See Aztec, Yuma, and Aztec Peak, Gila
Aztec Mountain	See Ancha, Sierra, Gila, and Aztec Peak, Gila
Aztec Valley	See Natanes Plateau, Gila
Azul, Rio	See Bill Williams Mountains, Coconino
Azul, Rio	See Blue River, Greenlee, or Maria River, Santa, Yavapai
Azul, Sierra	See Blue Range, Apache, or Navajo Mountain, Coconino, or Blue River, Greenlee
Azure Ridge Draw	See Azure Ridge, Mohave (Lake Mead)
Baaki	See Casa Blanca, Pinal
Babacomari Land Grant	See Babocomari Land Grant, Cochise
Babaho	See Maish Vaya, Pima
Babbits	See Babbitt Spring, Coconino
Babbitt Lake	(T25N/R5E) See Babbitt Bill Tank, Coconino
Babbitt Tank	(1)(T28N/R4E); (2)(T16N/R12E); (3)(T22N/R1E); (4) (T15N/R14E); (5) (T21N/R11E); (6) (T17N/R17E); See Babbitt Bill Tank, Coconino
Babbitt Tank Canyon	(T17N/R17E) See Babbitt Bill Tank, Coconino
Babbitt Wash	(T21N/R11E) See Babbitt Bill Tank, Coconino
Babbitt Water	(T14N/R14E) See Babbitt Bill Tank, Coconino
Babiteioida	See Arivaipa Canyon, Pinal
Babocomari Creek	(T19S/R20E; Cochise/Santa Cruz); See Babocomari Land Grant, Cochise, and Wallen, Camp, Cochise
Baboquerque	See Haivana Nakya, Pima
Baboquivari Camp	(T19S/R7E) See Baboquivari Peak, Pima
Baboquivari Canyon	(T19S/R7E) See Baboquivari Peak, Pima
Baboquivari Forest Reserve	See Coronado National Forest, Pima, and Baboquivari Peak, Pima
Baboquivari Mountains	(T18S/R7E) See Baboquivari Peak, Pima
Baboquivari Plain, Valley	See Altar Valley, Pima, and Baboquivari Peak, Pima
Baboquivari Wash	(T19S/R7E) See Baboquivari Peak, Pima
Babuquiburi	See Baboquivari Peak, Pima
Babuquivera Plain	See Altar Valley, Pima
Baby Canyon Indian Ruins	See Baby Canyon, Yavapai
Baby Rocks Mesa	(Elev. 5542') See Baby Rocks, Navajo
Bacabi	See Bakabi, Navajo
Bacobi	See Bakabi, Navajo
Bacovi	See Bakabi, Navajo
Badger Butte	See Windswept Terrace, Navajo
Badger Canyon	See Badger Creek, Coconino
Badger Creek	See Clear Creek, Coconino/Navajo
Badger Din Well	See Badger Den Well, Graham
Badgers Well	See Cobabi, Pima
Baecker Butte	See Baker Butte, Coconino
Baggs Reservoir	See White Mountain Lake, Navajo
Bagley	See Taylor, Navajo
Bagnall Hollow	See Adair, Navajo
Bah Ki	See Casa Blanca, Pinal
Bailey Wash	(T21S/R8E) See Bailey Peak, Pima
Bajia Santa Rosa	See Santa Rosa Mountains, Pima
Bajio Aquituno	See Picacho Mountains, Pinal
Bajio Comovo	See Komvo Valley, Pima, and Kum Vo, Pima
Bakabi Springs	See Bakabi, Navajo

Bakavi Springs	See Bakabi Springs, Navajo
Baker Butte	See Baker Peaks, Yuma
Baker Lake	See Baker Butte, Coconino
Baker Pond	See Government Tank, Cochise
Baker Spring	See Baker Butte, Coconino
Bako-Shi-Gito	See Bagashibito Canyon, Navajo
Balakai Point	(T28N/R23E); Apache) See Balakai Mesa, Apache/Navajo
Balakai Wash	See Balakai Mesa, Apache/Navajo
Balanced Rock	See Chiricahua National Monument, Cochise
Baldur Point	See Obi Point, Coconino (Grand Canyon)
Ballantine Canyon	See Rock Creek, Maricopa
Ballantyne Canyon	See Rock Creek, Maricopa
Ballenger	See Brigham City, Navajo
Ballinger's Camp	See Brigham City, Navajo
Balsas, El Rio de Los	See Gila River
Balsas, Rio de Las	See Gila River
Balukai Mesa, Point, Wash	See Balakai Mesa, Apache/Navajo
Bambo Wash	See Chilchinbito Spring, Navajo, and Tyende Creek, Navajo
Bamori Spring	See Vamori, Pima
Banfield Mountain	(T14N/R8E) See Banfield Spring, Coconino
Banfield Tank	(T14N/R9E) See Banfield Spring, Coconino
Bangart	See Del Rio, Coconino
Banner Canyon	(T16N/R12W) See Boner Canyon, Mohave
Bannon Creek	See Banning Creek, Yavapai
Baragan's Well	(T4S/R12W) See Baragan Mountains, Yuma
Baragon Mountains	See Baragan Mountains, Yuma
Barajita	See Tonoka, Pima
Barajita Valley	See Tonoka, Pima
Barbershop Spring	(T12N/R11E) See Barbershop Canyon, Coconino
Barbocomeri	See Babocomari Land Grant, Santa Cruz
Bardgeman Wells	See Bardgeman Wash, Navajo
Bar Foot Park	See Bar Foot Peak, Cochise
Barkdol Spring	See Peach Orchard Spring, Gila
Bark's Station	See Burkes Station, Maricopa
Bar M Spring	See Bar M Canyon, Coconino
Barnes Spring, Wash	See Barnes Peak, Gila
Barney Knoll	See Barney Flat, Coconino
Barney Ridge	See Barney Pasture, Coconino
Barney Spring	(T19N/R6E) See Barney Pasture, Coconino
Barney Spring Canyon	(T19N/R6E) See Barney Pasture, Coconino
Barrel Butte	See Nipple Butte, Navajo
Barrie Islands	See Barrier Islands, La Paz
Barriers, The	See Barrier Islands, La Paz
Barringer Meteorite Crater	See Meteor Crater, Coconino
Barrio Libre, El	See Tucson, Pima
Bartlett Reservoir	See Bartlett Dam, Maricopa
Bartolome de Xongopovi, San	See Shungopavi, Navajo
Barts Crossing	See Chevelon Crossing, Coconino
Basalt Canyon	See Basalt Cliffs, Coconino (Grand Canyon)
Basalt Canyon Creek	See Basalt Cliffs, Coconino (Grand Canyon)
Basalt Creek	See Basalt Cliffs, Coconino (Grand Canyon)
Bascom Tank Canyon	See Baskin Tank Canyon, Gila
Basilio, Pozos de San	See Peach Springs, Mohave
Basin, The	See Walker Lake, Coconino, or Gold Basin, Mohave
Bass Cable Ferry Crossing	See Bass Canyon, Coconino (Grand Canyon)
Bass Camp	See Bass Canyon, Coconino (Grand Canyon)

Bass Hotel Point	See Havasupai Point, Coconino (Grand Canyon), and Bass Canyon, Coconino (Grand Canyon)
Bass Lake	See Peck Mine, Yavapai
Bass Rapids, Station, Tomb, Trail	See Bass Canyon, Coconino (Grand Canyon)
Batamote Tank	See Batamote Mountains, Pima
Batamote Wash	(1) (T11S/R11E); (2) (T19S/R11E) See Batamote Mountains, Pima
Batamote Well	(T11S/R6W) See Batamote Mountains, Pima
Bates Canyon	See Batesville, Pinal
Bates Mountains	(T15S/R7W; Elev. c. 2900') See Bates Well, Pima
Bates Well Mountains	See Bates Well, Pima, and Puerto Blanco Mountains, Pima
Bat House Ruin	See Chakpahu, Navajo
Bat Rock	See Bat Canyon, Apache
Battleground, The	See Cedar Springs, Graham
Battle Ridge	See Battleground Ridge, Coconino
Bat Trail	See Bat Canyon, Apache
Bawley, Bawley Wash	See Bowley, Pima
B Canyon	See Bee Canyon, Gila
Beachville	See Flagstaff, Coconino
Beale's Crossing	See Mojave, Fort, Mohave
Beargrass Flat	(T4S/R18E; Elev. 4000'; Pinal) See Beargrass Basin, Graham
Beauty Springs	See Indian Hot Springs, Graham
Beaverhead Flat	(T15N/R5E) See Beaverhead, Yavapai
Bed Rock Camp	See Bass Canyon, Coconino (Grand Canyon)
Bedrock Canyon	See Bedrock Rapids, Coconino (Grand Canyon)
Bee Mountain	See Mingus Mountain, Yavapai
Begashabito Canyon, Valley	See Begashibito Wash, Navajo
Bekihatso Wash	See Bekihatso Lake, Coconino
Beki'shibito	See Begashibito Canyon, Navajo
Bell Butte Springs	See Bell Butte, Navajo
Bellemont Flat, Prairie, R.R. Siding	See Bellemont, Coconino
Belle Spring	(T21N/R6E) See Bellemont, Coconino
Bellota Spring	(T12S/R17E; Pima) See Bellota Canyon, Santa Cruz
Bell Rock Spring	See Bell Rock, Yavapai
Belmont Mountain	(T4N/R7W; Elev. 2528') See Belmont Mountains, Maricopa
Benson Pass	See Benson, Cochise
Benton Creek	See Benton, Greenlee
Berados Station	See Holbrook, Navajo
Berkich Park	See Montezuma Peak, Cochise
Bergemeyer Wash	See Bergemeyer Cove, Mohave
Berger Butte	See Martinez Hill, Pima
Berk's Station	See Burke's Station, Maricopa
Bermejo, Rio	See Little Colorado River, Coconino
Bernabe, Arroyo de San	See Truxton Canyon, Mohave
Bernadina	See Bernadino, Cochise
Bernadino, San	See Agua Caliente, Maricopa, or Awatobi, Navajo
Bernadino del Agua Caliente, San	See Agua Caliente, Maricopa
Bernadino Land Grant, San	See Bernadino, Cochise
Bernadino Springs, San	See Bernadino, Cochise
Bernadino Valley, San	See Bernadino, Cochise
Bernardo, San	See Awatobi, Navajo
Bernardo de Jongopabi, San	See Shungopavi, Navajo
Berry Trail	See Grand View Point and Grand View Trail, Coconino (Grand Canyon)
Betatakin Canyon	See Betatakin, Navajo

Betatakin Overlook, Point	(Elev. 7140') See Betatakin, Navajo
Bichard's Store	See Casa Blanca, Pinal
Bidahochi Spring	See Bidahochi Butte, Navajo, and Indian Wells, Navajo
Biddahoochee	See Bidahochi Butte, Navajo
Biddehoche	See Bidahochi Butte, Navajo
Bieehsinil	See Winslow, Navajo
Big Bug Creek	(T11N/R2E) See Big Bug, Yavapai
Big Bug Mesa	See Big Bug, Yavapai
Big Carrizo Wash	(Navajo) See Carrizo, Apache
Bigelow Peak	See Bigelow, Mount, Pima
Big Eye Wash	(T7S/R17W) See Big Eye Mine, Yuma
Big Hope House	See Giant Chair, Navajo
Big Horn Peak	See Big Horn Mountains, Maricopa
Big Horn Spring	See White Cliff Creek, Mohave/Yavapai
Big Horn Well	(T2N/R8W) See Big Horn Mountains, Maricopa
Big Johnnie Canyon	See Big Johney Canyon, Gila
Big Jonnie Canyon, Big Johnnie Gulch	See Big Johney Canyon, Gila
Big Sandy	See Owens, Mohave, and Big Sandy River, Mohave
Big Shipp Mountain, Wash	See Shipp, Mount, Yavapai
Bilas	See Bylas, Graham
Bill Arp Spring	See Bill Arp Creek, Yavapai
Billings (R. R. Sta.)	See Billings Gap, Apache
Bill Williams Delta	See Havasu National Wild Life Refuge, Mohave/La Paz
Bill Williams Fork	See Trout Creek, Mohave; Bill Williams Mountain, Coconino, and Big Sandy River, Mohave/Yuma
Bill Williams Mountains	(T12N/R17W; Elev. 2700') See Mohave Mountains, Mohave
Bill Williams River	(T11N/R14W) See Big Sandy River, Mohave/Yuma
Billy Moore's Station	See Avondale, Maricopa
Bird Springs Wash	(T22N/R15E) See Bird Springs, Navajo
Biscuit Peak Spring	See Biscuit Peak, Graham
Bishop, The	See Chiracahua National Monument, Cochise
Bismarck Lake	(T23N/R6E) See Bismark Canyon, Coconino
Bismarck Mountain	(T13N/R7W) See Thompson Peak, Yavapai
Bita Hache	See Bidahochi Butte, Navajo
Bitahochee	See Bidahochi Butte, Navajo
Bitahotsi	See Bidahochi Butte, Navajo
Bittahochee	See Bidahochi Butte, Navajo
Black Diamond Peak	(Elev. 7114') See Black Diamond, Cochise
Blackhorse	See Black Horse Creek, Apache, and Tyende Creek, Navajo
Blackhorse Wash	See Tyende Creek, Navajo, and Blackhorse Creek, Apache
Black Jack Cave	(T4S/R31E) See Black Jack Canyon, Greenlee
Black Jack Mountain	(T4N/R16E; Elev. 4851'; Gila) See Black Jack Canyon, Greenlee
Blackjack Rim	See Big Lue Mountains, Greenlee
Black Jack Spring	See Black Jack Canyon, Greenlee
Black Water Chapel	See Blackwater, Pinal
Black Pit	See Jerome, Yavapai
Blair Ranch	See Gunsight, Pima
Blanca, Sierra	See White Mountains, Greenlee/Apache, or Mogollon Rim
Blanca Lake, Sierra	(T6N/R29E; Elev. 8435'; Apache) See White Mountains, Greenlee/Apache
Blanca River, Sierra	See White River, Apache
Blanchard Crossing	See Sunset Crossing, Navajo
Blank Tank	See Torrance Well, Maricopa
Bloodsucker Mountains	See Tortolita Mountains, Pinal
Blood Sucker Wash	(T8S/R14E) See Tortolita Mountains, Pinal

Bob Thompson Park	See Bob Thompson Peak, Cochise
Bodaway Mesa	See Bodoway Mesa, Coconino
Bog Butte	See Bog Creek, Apache
Bohner Canyon	See Boner Canyon, Mohave
Bolada	See Venezia, Yavapai
Bonche's Fork	See Bouche's Fork, Navajo
Bond Spring	(T23S/R20E; Cochise) See Bond Canyon, Santa Cruz
Bonelli Bay	See Bonelli's Crossing, Mohave
Bonelli Ferry	See Bonelli's Crossing, Mohave
Boo-Koo-Dot-Klish	See Blue Canyon, Navajo
Bootlegger Spring	(T18S/R18E; Pima); (T1N/R13E; Pinal); (T16N/R4W; Yavapai) See Bootlegger Spring, Gila
Bootlegger Trap Spring	(T1N/R13E; Pinal) See Bootlegger Spring, Gila
Boot Mountain	See Boot Peak, Yuma
Borianna Mine	See Boriana Canyon, Mohave
Boriena	See Boriana Canyon, Mohave
Born, Lake	See Boot Lake, Coconino
Borne Lake	See Boot Lake, Coconino
Bottom City	See Lehi, Maricopa, and Mesa, Maricopa
Boucher Rapids	(T32N/R2E) See Boucher Creek, Coconino (Grand Canyon)
Boundary Mountains	See Chuska Mountains, Apache
Bouse Hills	(T7N/R16W; Elev. 1924') See Bouse, La Paz
Bouse Wash	(T8N/R19W) See Bouse, La Paz
Bowers Ranch	See Agua Fria Ranch, Maricopa
Bowie Military Reservation, Fort	See Bowie, Fort, Cochise
Bowie National Historic Site, Fort	See Bowie, Fort, Cochise
Bowie Peak	See Bowie Mountain, Cochise, and Bowie, Fort, Cochise
Bowie Station	See Bowie, Cochise
Boxing Glove, The	See Chiracahua Mountains, Cochise
Boyce Camp	See Pine Flat, Coconino
Boyer Gap	See Bowyer Peak, Yuma
Bradshaw	See Bradshaw Mountains, Yavapai
Bradshaw Ferry	See Ehrenberg, Yuma, and Olive City, Yuma
Bradshaw Range	See Bradshaw Mountains, Yavapai
Bradshaw's Ferry	See Ehrenberg, Yuma, and Olive City, La Paz
Brady Canyon	See Brady Peak, Coconino (Grand Canyon)
Brady House	See Pick-Em-Up, Cochise
Brandenberg Wash	See Brandenberg Mountain, Pinal
Brannaman	See Branaman, Pinal
Brawley Wash	(T13S/R11E; Elev. 2217') See Bowley, Pima
Brawly Wash	See Bowley, Pima
Brayton	See Bouse, La Paz
Brazo de Miraflores	See Gila River
Breckenridge, Fort	See Grant, Camp Old, Pinal, and Stanford, Fort, Pinal
Breed's Crossing	See Sunset Crossing, Navajo
Breezy Pines	See Poland, Yavapai
Bridal Veil Falls	See Havasu Canyon, Coconino (Grand Canyon)
Bridge Canyon Rapids	See Bridge Canyon, Mohave
Bright Angel Amphitheater	See Bright Angel Creek, Coconino (Grand Canyon)
Bright Angel Canyon	See Bright Angel Creek, Coconino (Grand Canyon)
Bright Angel Point	(Elev. 8145') See Bright Angel Creek, Coconino (Grand Canyon), and North Rim, Coconino (Grand Canyon)
Bright Angel River, Spring	See Bright Angel Creek, Coconino (Grand Canyon)
Bright Angel Wash	(T31N/R2E) See Bright Angel Creek, Coconino (Grand Canyon)
Brill Ranch	See Allah, Maricopa
Broadway Mesa	See Bodoway Mesa, Coconino

Broken Dome	See Dome Rock Mountains, La Paz
Bronkow Mine	See Brunckow Mine, Cochise
Brookbank Point	(T11N/R15E; Elev. 7684') See Brookbank Canyon, Navajo
Brook Creek	See Tsaile, Apache
Brooklyn	(T15S/R2E) See Logan, Pima
Brownell Mountains	(T14S/R2E; Elev. 3573') See Brownell, Pima
Brownell Valley	(T14S/R2E; Elev. 2700') See Brownell, Pima
Brown Mountains	(T14S/R12E; Elev. 3112') See Brown Canyon, Pima
Brownsville	See Peach Orchard, Pinal
Brown Wash	(T18S/R8E) See Brown Canyon, Pima
Bruce Canyon	See Bruce, Mount, Santa Cruz
Bruce Knoll	(T7S/R23E; Elev. 3520') See Bryce, Graham
Bryce Mountain	(T5S/R26E; Elev. 7298') See Bryce, Graham
Bryce Peak	(T5S/R26E; Elev. 7298') See Bryce, Graham
Buckeye Hills	(T2S/R5W; Elev. 1782') See Buckeye, Maricopa
Buckeye Valley	(T1S/R4W) See Buckeye, Maricopa
Buck Farm Lake	See Buck Canyon, Coconino
Buckskin Mountain	(T41N/R2E) See Kaibab Plateau, Coconino/Utah
Buckskin Plateau	See Kaibab Plateau, Coconino/Utah
Buddha Cloister	See Buddha Temple, Coconino (Grand Canyon)
Buell Park, Wash	See Buell Mountain, Apache
Buena Ayres	See Aguirre Peak, Pima, and Buenos Ayres, Pima
Buena Guia, El Rio de	See Colorado River
Buena Ventura	See Betatakin, Navajo
Buenaventura, San	See Mishongnovi, Navajo
Bueno Vista	See Black River, Apache
Bueno Vista	See Pueblo Viejo, Graham
Buffalo Creek	See Black River, Apache
Buffalo Crossing	(T4N/R28E; Greenlee) See Black River, Apache
Buffalo Hill	(Elev. 4300') See Buffalo Gulch, Gila
Buffalo Ridge	(Elev. 4300') See Buffalo Gulch, Gila
Buford Canyon	(T7S/R20E) See Buford Hill, Graham
Buford, Mount	See Beauford Mountain, Gila
Bukodotklish	See Blue Canyon, Coconino/Navajo
Bule Park	See Buell Park, Apache
Bullard Canyon	(T2S/R32E) See Bullard Peak, Greenlee
Bullard Wash	(T9N/R10W) See Bullard Peak, Yavapai/La Paz
Bulldog Canyon	(T2N/R8E) See Bulldog Mine, Pinal
Bulldog Mountains, Range	See Gold Field Mountains, Maricopa
Bulldog Wash	T1N/R8E; Maricopa/Pinal) See Bulldog Mine, Pinal
Bullfrog Ridge	(T6N/R8E) See Bullfrog Canyon, Gila
Bullhead	See Bullhead Rock, Mohave
Bullhead Dam, Ridge	See Davis Dam, Mohave
Bullrush Canyon	(T39N/R4W) See Bullrush Wash, Mohave
Bulrush Point	(T37N/R3W) See Bullrush Wash, Mohave
Bully Bueno Mine	See Bueno, Yavapai
Bumble Bee Canyon	See Black Canyon, Yavapai
Bumblebee Creek	See Bumble Bee, Yavapai
Bundy Ponds	See Trumbull, Mount (Town), Mohave
Bundyville	See Trumbull, Mount (Town), Mohave
Bunker Hill Spring	See Bunker Hill, Coconino
Bunker Trail	See Bunker Hill, Coconino
Bunkerville Mountains	See Virgin Mountains, Mohave
Buqui Aquimuri	See Colorado River
Busac	See Aravaipa Canyon, Pinal
Bush, Fort	See Alpine, Apache
Bush Valley	See Alpine, Apache
Butland	See Emery Park, Pima

Butler Mountain	(T9N/R25E; Elev. 8367') See Butler Canyon, Apache
Butler Pass	(T8N/R15W) See Butler Valley, La Paz
Butte City	See Tempe, Maricopa, and Hayden's Ferry, Maricopa
Cababaos	See Calabasas, Santa Cruz
Cababi Mountain	See Ko Vaya, Pima
C A Bar Creek	See C A Bar Ranch, Greenlee
Cabeza del Gigante	(Spanish: *cabeza* = "head"; *del gigante* = "of the giant") See Castle Dome Peak, La Paz
Cabeza Prieta Game Range	See Cabeza Prieta, Yuma
Cabeza Prieta Mountains	(T14S/R11W) See Cabeza Prieta, Yuma
Cabeza Prieta Pass, Peak	See Cabeza Prieta, Yuma
Cabezua, Rio	See Havasu Canyon, Coconino (Grand Canyon)
Cabibi	See Ko Vaya, Pima
Cabin Tank	See Adams Tank, Coconino
Cabin Valley	See Antelope Valley, Mohave
Caca Chimir	See Kaka, Maricopa
Cacate	See Kaka, Maricopa
Cacca	See Kaka, Maricopa
Cachise	See Cochise, Cochise
Cahon Reservoir	See Atcheson Reservoir, Apache
Cahuabi	See Ko Vaya, Pima, and Guevavi, Santa Cruz
Caietano, San	See Calabasas, Santa Cruz
Cajon, Cerros del	See Castle Dome Mountains, La Paz
Cajote Spring	See Pan Tak, Pima
Calabasas Canyon	(T24S/R13E) See Calabasas, Santa Cruz
Calabazas	See Kitchen Ranch, Pete, Santa Cruz, and Calabasas, Santa Cruz
Calderwood Butte	See Calderwood Peak, Maricopa
Calera Wash	See Calera Canyon, Pima
Caliente, Ojo	See Agua Caliente, Maricopa
Caliente Station	See Webb, Cochise
Calitre	See Galiuro Mountains, Graham
Calitro	See Galiuro Mountains, Graham
Caliuro Mountains	See Galiuro Mountains, Graham
Callen's Well	See Cullen's Well, La Paz
Calloway Lake	See Calloway Butte, Coconino
Callville Basin	See Boulder Basin, Mohave (Lake Mead)
Callville Islands	See Beacon Rock, Mohave (Lake Mead)
Calumet Gulch	(T3S/R13E; Pinal) See Calumet, Gila
Calva Draw	(T3S/R20E) See Calva, Graham
Camel, The	See Camel Rock, Yavapai
Cameron Trail	See Bright Angel Trail, Coconino (Grand Canyon)
Campanile, The	See Napoleon's Tomb, Mohave (Lake Mead)
Campbell	See Cerbat, Mohave
Campbell Francis Wash	(T27N/R8E) See Campbell Draw, Coconino
Camp Grant Wash	(T7S/R15E) See Grant, Old Camp, Pinal
Campstone	See Turner, Cochise
Canao Ranch	See Canoa Ranch, Pima
Candelaria	See Tinajas, Yuma
Canelo Pass	See Canelo Hills, Santa Cruz
Canille	See Canelo, Santa Cruz, and Canelo Hills, Santa Cruz
Canille Mountains	See Canelo Hills, Santa Cruz
Canoa Canyon, Crossing	See Canoa, Pima
Canoa Land Grant	See Canoa, Pima
Canoa Ranch	See Canoa, Pima
Canoa Wash	(T22S/R9E) See Canoa, Pima
Canoe Crossing	See Canoa, Pima

Cañon	See Black Canyon, Yavapai
Cañoncito Bonito	See Bonita Canyon, Apache
Cañon Creek	See White Cliffs Creek, Mohave/Yavapai
Cañon Diablo	See Diablo, Canyon, Coconino
Canova Springs	See Cane Beds, Mohave
Canyon Bonito	See Bonito Canyon, Apache
Capital Butte	See Capitol Butte, Yavapai
Capital Flat, El	See Agathla Needle, Navajo
Capitan, El	See Agthla, Navajo
Capitan Canyon, El	(T4S/R15E) See Capitan, El, Gila
Capitan Flat, El	See Agathla Needle, Navajo
Capitan Mountain	See Capitan, El, Gila
Capitano Creek	See Capitan, El, Gila
Capitan Pass	See Capitan, El, Gila
Capitan Pass Spring	See Capitan, El, Gila
Capitan Peak	See Capitan, El, Gila
Capitan Trap Spring	See Capitan, El, Gila
Capitan Wash, El	See Agthla Needle, Navajo
Capitol Dome	See Castle Dome Mountains, La Paz
Cardenas Creek	See Cardenas Butte, Coconino (Grand Canyon)
Cariño Canyon	See Pine Springs, Apache
Carleton Lake	See Mormon Mountain, Coconino
Carlos Butte, San	See Butte, The, Pinal
Carlos, Old San	See Carlos, San, Gila, and Carlos Indian Reservation, San, Gila
Carlos Agency, San	See Carlos Indian Reservation, San, Gila
Carlos, Camp San	See Carlos, Fort San, Gila
Carlos Island, San	See Antelope, Coconino
Carlos Mountains, San	See Mescal Mountains, Gila
Carlos Picket, San	See Carlos, Fort San, Gila
Carlos Post, San	See Carlos, Fort San, Gila
Carlos Range, Sierra	See Mescal Mountains, Gila
Carlos, Rio de	See Carlos River, San, Gila
Carlos, Rio San	See Carlos River, San, Gila
Carl Pleasant Dam	See Carl Pleasant Lake, Maricopa
Carnation Point	See Galahad Point, Coconino (Grand Canyon)
Carnero Creek, Spring	See Carnero Lake, Apache
Carobabi Mountains	See Comobabi Mountains, Pima
Carpenter Ranch	See Boyles, Greenlee
Carrigan Peak	See Clara Peak, La Paz
Carrigan Well	See Clara Peak, La Paz
Carriso	See Four Corners, Apache
Carriso Creek	See Carrizo Creek, Apache
Carrizo	See Four Corners, Apache
Carr Lake Draw	(T16N/R22E) See Carr Lake, Navajo
Carr Mountain	(Elev. 7619') See Carr Peak, Gila
Carr Peak	(T23S/R20E; Elev. 9225') See Carr Canyon, Cochise
Carter's Camp	See Carter Canyon, Pima
Casaba	(T2N/R1W) See Goodyear, Maricopa
Casa Blanca	See White House, Apache
Casa Blanca	See Crittenden, Fort, Santa Cruz
Casa Blanca Canyon	(T19S/R14E) See Crittenden, Fort, Santa Cruz
Casa Blanca Creek	See Crittenden, Fort, Santa Cruz
Casa Blanco	See Crittenden, Fort, Santa Cruz
Casa Grande Mountains	(T7S/R6E; Elev. 2350') See Casa Grande National Monument, Pinal
Casa Grande Valley	(T5S/R4E) See Casa Grande National Monument, Pinal
Casa Montezuma	See Casa Grande National Monument, Pinal

Casas de San Pedro	See Pedro River, San, Cochise
Cascade Creek	See Cataract Canyon, Coconino
Cascades, The	See Grand Falls, Coconino
Cashner Cabin	See Casner Mountain, Yavapai
Casimiro Peak	See Webber Peak, Graham
Casimiro Spring	(T10N/R25E; Elev. 7180') See Webber Peak, Apache
Casner Butte	(T15N/R6E; Elev. 5131') See Casner Mountain, Yavapai
Casner Cabin Draw	(T19N/R5E) See Casner Mountain, Yavapai
Casner Canyon	(T16N/R6E) See Casner Mountain, Yavapai
Casper	See Cosper, Greenlee
Cassadore Creek	(T1N/R19E) See Cassadore Mesa, Gila
Cassadore Spring	(T2N/R18E) See Cassadore Mesa, Gila
Cassador Ranch	See Cassadore Mesa, Gila
Castle Dome Landing	(T5S/R21W; Elev. 160') See Castle Dome (Town), Yuma
Catalina Cuitchibaque, Santa	See Catalina Mountains, Santa, Pima
Catalina de Cuitiobagum, Santa	See Picacho Mountains, Pinal
Cataract Creek	See Cataract Canyon, Coconino (Grand Canyon), and Havasu Canyon, Coconino (Grand Canyon)
Catarina Mountains, Santa	See Catalina Mountains, Santa, Pima/Pinal
Catarina, Sierra de Santa	See Catalina Mountains, Santa, Pima/Pinal
Catastrophe Rapid	See Separation Rapid, Mohave (Grand Canyon)
Catback Mountain	See Cat Mountain, Pima
Cathey Spring	See Cassidy Spring, Graham
Cayetano, San	See Calabasas, Santa Cruz
Cayetano de Calabazas, San	See Calabasas, Santa Cruz
Cazadero Spring	See Cassadore Mountain, Gila, and Cassadore Mesa, Gila
Cazlon	See Kaka, Maricopa
CCC Canyon	(T16N/R1E; Yavapai) See CCC Canyon, Santa Cruz
CCC Spring	(T15S/R17E; Pima) See CCC Canyon, Santa Cruz
CCC Trail Reservoir	(T38N/R5W; Mohave) See CCC Canyon, Santa Cruz
Cebadilla Pass	See Cebadilla Mountain, Pima
Ceballeta Mountain	See Cebadilla Mountain, Pima
Cecelia, Cerro de Santa	See Antelope Hill, Yuma
Ce'ezde'lzah	See Gigantes, Los, Apache
Cemetery Hills	See Cemetery Ridge, Yuma
Cemetosa Wash	See Cementosa Wash, Yuma
Centennial	See Harrisburg, La Paz
Centennial Valley	See Harquahala Mountains, La Paz/Maricopa
Centinel	See Harrisburg, La Paz
Central Wash	(T7S/R25E) See Central, Graham
Cerbat Canyon	(T22N/R17W) See Cerbat, Mohave
Cerbat Peak	(Elev. 5204') See Cerbat, Mohave, and Cerbat Mountains, Mohave
Cerbat Range	See Cerbat Mountains, Mohave
Cerbat Wash	(T21N/R18W) See Cerbat, Mohave
Cerritos Azules	See Hopi Buttes, Navajo
Cerritos de Los Linderos	See Lesna Peak, Pima
Cervanti's Well	See Stan Shiatak, Pima
Cha-Ez-Kla Rock	See Chaistla Butte, Navajo
Chalender Lake	See Chalender, Coconino
Challe, Canyon de El	See Chelly, Canyon de, Apache
Challendar	See Chalender, Coconino
Chambers Draw	(T6N/R28E) See Chambers, Apache
Chambers Wash	See Chambers, Apache
Chandler Junction, Ranch	See Chandler, Maricopa
Chaol Creek	See Chaol Canyon, Coconino
Charcoal Gulch	(1: T13N/R1W; 2: T10N/R1W; Yavapai) See Charcoal Canyon, Mohave

Charcoal Spring	(T13N/R1W; Yavapai) See Charcoal Canyon, Mohave
Charcoal Tank	(T22N/R2W; Coconino) See Charcoal Canyon, Mohave
Charcoal Tank	(T11S/R29E; Graham) See Charcoal Canyon, Mohave
Charleau Gap	See Charouleau Gap, Pinal
Charleaux Gap	See Charouleau Gap, Pinal
Charolean Gap	See Charouleau Gap, Pinal
Charoleau Gap	See Charouleau Gap, Pinal
Chaves Crossing	(T17N/R6E) See Chavez Pass, Coconino
Chaves Spring, Pass	See Chavez Pass, Coconino
Chavez Mountain	(Elev. 6902') See Chavez Pass, Coconino
Chavez Spring	(T13N/R12E) See Chavez Pass, Coconino
Chavez Well	See Chavez Pass, Coconino
Chéch'ilyaa	See Lukachukai, Apache
Chediski Butte	See Lost Tank Ridge, Navajo
Chediski Peak	(T9N/R16E; Elev. 7460') See Chediski Mountain, Navajo
Chediski Ridge	See Chediski Mountain, and Lost Tank Ridge, Navajo
Cheene Peak	(T4S/R8E) See Walker Butte, Pinal, and Vekol Mine, Pinal
Chegui, Sierra de	See Carrizo Mountains, Apache
Chemehuebi Point	See Chemehuevi Point, Coconino (Grand Canyon)
Chemuehueva Valley	See Chemehuevi Valley, Mohave
Chemehuevi Mountains	See Mohave Mountains, Mohave
Chemehuevi Wash	(T13N/R19W) See Chemehuevi Valley, Mohave
Chennelle, Cañon	See Chelly, Canyon de, Apache
Cherum Canyon	See Difficult Canyon, Mohave
Cheto	See Sanders, Apache
Chevalon Butte	See Chevelon Butte, Coconino
Chevalon Creek, Fork	See Chevelon Canyon, Coconino
Chevelon Canyon Dam	(T13N/R14E) See Chevelon Canyon, Coconino
Chevelon Canyon, West	(T14N/R14E) See Chevelon Canyon, Coconino/Navajo
Chevelon Creek	(T14N/R14E) See Chevelon Canyon, Coconino
Chevelon Draw	(T13N/R14E) See Chevelon Canyon, Coconino
Chevelon Ridge	(T12N/R14E) See Chevelon Canyon, Coconino
Chevez Pass	See Chavez Pass, Coconino
Chevlon Creek	(Navajo) See Chevelon Canyon, Coconino
Chevlon's Butte	See Chevelon Butte, Coconino
Chico Shunie Arroyo	See Chico Shunie Well, Pima
Chico Shunie Hills	(T13S/R7W; Elev. 2144') See Chico Shunie Well, Pima
Chico Shunie (Town)	(T13S/R7W; Elev. 1740') See Chico Shunie Well, Pima
Chiguicagui	See Chiricahua Indian Reservation, Cochise
Chikapanagi Canyon	See Chikapanagi Point, Coconino (Grand Canyon)
Chikapanagi Mesa	(T31N/R3W) See Chikapanagi Point, Coconino (Grand Canyon)
Chikapanti Mesa	See Chikapanagi Point, Coconino (Grand Canyon)
Chila (River)	See Gila River
Chil-Chin-Be-To	See Chilchinbito (Spring), Navajo
Chilchinbito Creek, Wash	See Chilchinbito (Spring), Navajo
Childs Mountain	(T11S/R7W; Elev. Pima, 2862'; Maricopa, 1515') See Childs, Pima
Childs Valley	(T11S/R8W) See Childs, Pima
Childs Wash	See Childs, Pima, and Sikort Chuapo, Pima
Chilechinito	See Chilchinbito, Navajo
Chimihuevis Mountains	See Mohave Mountains, Mohave
Chiminea Canyon	(T14S/R17E; Pima) See Chiminea Peak, Santa Cruz
Chiminea Mountain	See Chiminea Peak, Santa Cruz
Chimopovi	See Shungopavi, Navajo
Chimopovy	See Shungopavi, Navajo
China Canyon	See Chinaman's Canyon, Coconino

Chinaman, The	See Chiricahua National Monument, Cochise
Chinaman's Head, The	See Chiricahua National Monument, Cochise
China Spring Canyon	(T7N/R14E; Gila) See China Peak, Graham
China, Val de	See Chino Valley, Yavapai
Chinde Point	(T20N/R24E) See Chinde Mesa, Apache
Chinle Creek	See Chinle, Apache
Chinle Wash	(T34N/R26E) See Chinle, Apache, and Chinle Valley, Apache
Chin Lee	See Chinle, Apache
Chinline Canyon	See Walker Creek, Apache, and Toh Chin Line Canyon, Apache
Chino	See Chino Valley, Yavapai
Chino Creek	See Chino Valley (P.O.), Yavapai
Chino Point	(T23N/R6W) See Chino Valley (P.O.), Yavapai
Chino (R. R. Siding)	See Chino Valley, Yavapai
Chino Wash	See Chino Valley (P.O.), Yavapai
Chiquito Colorado	See Little Colorado River
Chiricahua Forest Reserve	See Coronado National Forest, Pima/Cochise
Chiricahua Mountains	See Chiricahua Indian Reservation, Cochise, and Dos Cabezas Mountains, Cochise
Chitty Creek	See Chitty Canyon, Greenlee
Chiu Chuscha	See Chiuchu, Pinal
Chivano-Ki	See Casa Grande National Monument, Pinal
Chi-Vo-La	See Cibola, Apache
Chloride Flat	See Chloride, Mohave
Chocolate Canyon	See Chocolate Mountains, Yuma
Chowo	See Kohi Kug, Pima
Choiskai	See Chuska Mountains, Apache
Choulik	See Choulic, Pima
Christmas Spring	See Leroux Spring, Coconino
Christopher Mountain	(T11N/R13E; Elev. 6960') See Christopher Creek, Gila
Christvale	See Stoval, Yuma
Chrysolite	See Chrysotile, Gila
Chrystoval	See Stoval, Yuma
Chuar Creek	See Lava Creek, Coconino (Grand Canyon), and Chuar Butte, Coconino (Grand Canyon)
Chuar Lava Hill	(Elev. 3945') See Chuar Butte, Coconino (Grand Canyon)
Chuar Valley	See Chuar Butte, Coconino (Grand Canyon)
Chuevak	See Tubac, Santa Cruz
Chuili Shaik	See Sweetwater, Pima
Chukma'dk	See Blackwater, Pinal
Chuk Shon	See Sentinel Mountain, Pima, and Tucson, Pima
Chukubi	See Mishongnovi, Navajo
Chukuk Wash	(T19S/R1E) See Chukut Kuk, Pima
Chumatjuikson	See Ali Chukson, Pima
Chuparosa, El Ojo de	See Humming Bird Spring, Maricopa
Church Rock Valley	(T38N/R20E) See Church Rock, Navajo
Chusca	See Chuska Mountains, Apache
Chushoni Mo	See Sacaton, Pinal
Chusca, Sierra de	See Chuska Mountains, Apache
Chuskai Mountains	See Chuska Mountains, Apache
Chuska Plateau	See Defiance Plateau, Apache
Chuska Valley	See Chuska Mountains, Apache
Chutukivahia	See Pozo Verde, Pima
Chutum Vaya Pass	See Chutum Vaya, Pima
Chutum Vaya Wash	(T19S/R5E) See Chutum Vaya, Pima
Cibecue Canyon	(T7N/R18E) See Cibecue Creek, Gila/Navajo
Cibecue Peak	(T7N/R19E; Elev. 6507') See Cibecue Creek, Gila/Navajo

Cibecue Trading Post	(T8N/R17E; Navajo) See Cibecue Creek, Gila
Cibola, Seven Cities of	(New Mexico) See Cibola, Yuma, and Hopi Villages
Cibola Valley	(T1S/R24W) See Cibola, Yuma, and Cibola National Wild Life Refuge, Yuma
Cieneguilla Chiquita	See Black Creek, Apache
Cieneguilla de Juanito	See Wheatfields, Navajo
Cignus Peak	See Cyngus Peak, Mohave
Cimarron Saddle	(T12N/R6E; Yavapai) See Cimarron Mountains, Pima
Cimarron Spring	(T11N/R6E; Yavapai) See Cimarron Mountains, Pima
Cimeron Mountain	(T2N/R11E; Ele;v. 5570'; Maricopa) See Cimarron Mountains, Pima
Ci-Mo-Pavi	See Shungopavi, Navajo
Cinnabar Wash	(T3N/R22W) See Ehrenberg Wash, La Paz
Circle Prairie	See Point of Pines, Graham
Circle Z Mountain	See Bloxton, Santa Cruz
Circle Z Ranch	See Sanford, Santa Cruz, and Bloxton, Santa Cruz
Citrus Heights	(T2S/R7E) See Chandler Heights, Maricopa
Civano	See Casa Grande, Pinal
Clack Canyon	See Clack, Mohave
Claire Mountain, Saint	(Elev. 3219') See Claire Spring, Saint, Maricopa
Claire Peak, Saint	(Elev. 4220') See Claire Spring, Saint, Maricopa
Clanton Well	See Clanton Hills, Yuma
Clara River, Santa	See Virgin River, Mohave
Clara Well	See Clara Peak, La Paz, and Butler Valley, La Paz
Clark, Fort	See Clark, Camp, Yavapai
Clarkston	See Clarkstown, Pima
Clark Wash	(Pinal/Graham, South Fork, Graham: T8S/R19E; North and South Fork, Pinal: T8S/R18E) See Clark Peak, Graham
Clear Creek	See West Clear Creek, Yavapai
Clear Creek Canyon	See McCarty Draw, Coconino
Clifton Peak	(Elev. 4582') See Clifton, Greenlee
Cline Mesa	(T9N/R13E) See Cline, Gila
Cline Ranch	See Cline, Gila
Clip Wash	(T3S/R23W) See Clip, Yuma
Clothopas Temple	See Coronation Peak, Yuma
Clothos Temple	See Coronation Peak, Yuma
Cloud Mountains, St.	See McCloud Mountains, Yavapai
Clough Cienega	See McNary, Apache
Clover Creek	See Sonoita, Santa Cruz
Cluff Cienega	See McNary, Apache
Cluff Ranch	(T7S/R24E) See Cluff Peak, Graham
Cly Spring	(T40N/R21E; Navajo) See Cly Butte, Apache
Coal Canyon, Creek	See Coal Mine Canyon, Coconino
Coal Mine Mesa	(T30N/R12E; Elev. 6141') See Coal Mine Canyon, Coconino
Coal Mine Wash	(T34N/R15E; Navajo) See Coal Mine Canyon, Coconino
Coal Spring Canyon	(T34N/R15E) See Coal Mine Canyon, Navajo
Coanini Creek	See Havasu Canyon, Coconino
Coati, El	See Kohatk, Pinal
Cobabi	(T15S/R5E; Elev. 2700') See Ko Vaya, Pima
Cobabi Mountains	See Ko Vaya, Pima
Coches Canyon	See Turkey Creek, Cochise/Santa Cruz
Cochibo	See Sweetwater, Pima
Cochibo Well	See Sweetwater, Pima
Cochise Canyon	See Goodwin Canyon, Cochise
Cochise, Lake	See Willcox, Cochise
Cochivo	See Sweetwater, Pima

Cochrane Hill	See Jumpoff Crater, Coconino
Cocklebur	See Vaiva Vo, Pinal
Cockscomb Butte	(T22N/R19E; Elev. 5949'; Navajo) See Coxcombs, Coconino
Coconino Camp	See Ryan, Coconino
Coconino Caves	See Cosnino Caves, Coconino
Coconino Dam	(T19N/R9E) See Coconino County
Cocopah Dam Site No. 3	See Imperial Dam, Yuma
Cohnville	See Cornville, Yavapai
Cojate	See Kohatk, Pinal
Cojeta	See Kohatk, Pinal
Colcord Canyon	(T10N/R14E; Gila) See Colcord Canyon, Coconino
Cole	See Coledon, Maricopa
Coleman Knoll	See Coleman Lake, Coconino
Coleman Spring	(T16N/R27E) See Coleman Creek, Apache/Greenlee
Cole Spring	(T34N/R9W) See Cold Spring, Mohave
Collins Ranch	See Coleman Lake, Coconino
Collins Well	See Kerlin's Well, Coconino
Colorado, Camp	See Mohave, Fort, Mohave
Colorado Chiquito	See Little Colorado River
Colorado City	See Yuma, Yuma
Colorado County	See Navajo County
Colorado Crossing	See Pearce Ferry, Mohave
Colorado de Los Martires, Rio	See Colorado River
Colorado Mountains, Cerro	(T19S/R11E; Ele;v. 5319') See Colorado, Cerro, Pima
Colorado of California, Rio	See Colorado River
Colorado Plateau	See Colorado Plateau, Coconino, and Mogollon Plateau, Coconino
Colorado Range	See Black Mountains, Mohave
Colorado, Rio	See Little Colorado River
Colorado River of the West	See Colorado River
Colorado, Sierra	See Rincon Mountains, Pima
Colorado Station	See Planet, Mohave
Colorado Wash, Cerro	See Colorado, Cerro, Pima
Colter Butte	(T33N/R5E; Coconino [Grand Canyon]) See Colter, Apache
Colter Creek	See Colter, Apache
Colter Reservoir	(T6N/R27E) See Colter, Apache
Columbine Canyon	See Cave Canyon, Mohave
Columbus	See Sahuarita, Pima
Colville	See Porras Dikes, Navajo
Comanche Creek	(T32N/R5E) See Comanche Point, Coconino (Grand Canyon)
Comar Spring	See Coma-a Spring, Navajo
Comars, Sierra de	See Estrella Mountains, Maricopa, and Maricopa Mountains, Maricopa
Comate	See Camote, La, Pima
Comely	See Komelik, Pima
Comeva	See Kom Vo, Pima
Commission Creek	See Commission, Santa Cruz
Commonwealth Mine	See Pearce, Cochise
Comobabi Pass	(T15S/R5E) See Comobabi, Pima
Comobabi Wash	See Comobabi, Pima
Comobavi	See Comobabi, Pima
Comohuabi	See Comobabi, Pima
Comote	See Vakomok, Pima
Comoti	See Vakomok, Pima
Comovajca Mountains	See Comobabi, Pima

Comovo	See Kom Vo, Pima
Comovo Valley	See Kom Vo, Pima
Compuesto, Rio	See Gila River
Comupave	See Shungopavi, Navajo
Concabe	See Moenkopi, Coconino
Concentrator City	See Miami, Gila
Concho Creek, Flat, Flat Wash	(T13N/R26E) See Concho, Apache
Concho Lake, Spring	See Concho, Apache
Concho Spring Knoll	(Elev. 6717') See Concho, Apache
Congress Mine	See Congress, Yavapai
Connell Mountains	(T16N/R7W; Elev. 5750') See Connell Gulch, Yavapai
Connor Creek	See Connor Canyon, Gila, and Rose Creek, Gila
Con Quien	See Sweetwater, Pima
Contention City	See Contention, Cochise
Contract Spring	(T11N/R9E) See Contract Canyon, Gila
Conway Spring	See Conway Seep, Gila
Cooley	See McNary, Apache, and Forestdale, Apache
Cooley Knoll	(T11N/R22E; Elev. 6461') See Cooley Mountain, Navajo
Cooley's Ranch	See McNary, Apache, and Forestdale, Apache
Coolidge Lake	See Carlos Lake, San, Pinal/Gila/Graham
Coon Butte	See Meteor Crater, Coconino
Coon Can Mine	(T16S/R4E) See Sweetwater, Pima
Coon Can Well	See Sweetwater, Pima
Cooper Corral Ridge	See Cooper Ridge, Coconino
Cooper Gulch	(T1N/R15E) See Cooper Forks, Gila
Cooper Ranch	See Ramer Ranch, Gila
Copeka	See Kupk, Pima, and Shopishk, Pinal
Copeka Mountains	See Kupk, Pima
Cope Plateau	See Cope Butte, Coconino (Grand Canyon)
Cooper Basin (No. 2)	(T9N/R1W) See Copper Basin, Yavapai
Copper Basin Red Spring	(T13N/R3W) See Copper Basin, Yavapai
Copper Basin Spring	(T9N/R1W) See Copper Basin, Yavapai
Copper Basin Trail	See Copper Basin, Yavapai
Copper Basin Wash	(T13N/R4W) See Copper Basin, Yavapai
Coral, Rio del	See Gila River
Cordes Junction	(Elev. 3790') See Cordes, Yavapai
Cordes Peak	(Elev. 4233') See Cordes, Yavapai
Corgett Wash	See Corgiat Wash, Maricopa
Corino Canyon	See Pine Springs, Apache
Cornel Arroyo	See Cornelia, Arroya, Pima
Corner Rock	See Headgate Rock Dam, La Paz
Cornez, Rio	(T12S/R5W) See Cornelia, Arroya, Pima
Cornfields	(T26N/R25E; Elev. 6175') See Sunrise Spring, Apache
Cornfields Wash	See Pueblo Colorado Wash, Apache/Navajo
Corn Wash	See Tees Toh Wash, Navajo
Coronacion Mountain	See Coronation Peak, Yuma
Coronado Creek	See Coronado Mountain, Greenlee
Coronado Peak	(Elev. 6864') See Coronado National Memorial, Cochise
Coronado Plateau	See Marcos Terrace, Coconino (Grand Canyon)
Coronado Ridge	(T3S/R29E; Elev. c. 6500') See Coronado Mountain, Greenlee
Coronado Spring	See Coronado Mountain, Greenlee
Corrigan Peak	See Clara Peak, La Paz
Corrigan Well	See Cardigan, Pima
Cortes Peak	See Cordes, Yavapai
Corva Hill	See Corva, Coconino
Cosmas	See Tucson, Pima, and Cosme de Tucson, San, Pima
Cosmin Cave	See Cosnino Caves, Coconino
Cosninas	See Moencopie Wash, Coconino

Cosnina, Rio de	See Colorado River
Cosnino	See Cosnino Caves, Coconino
Cosnino (R. R. STA.)	See Cosnino Caves, Coconino
Cosnurio Caves	See Cosnino Caves, Coconino
Cotton City	See Eloy, Pinal
Cottonia	See Lincolnia, Mohave
Cotton Wash	See Cottonwood Wash, Graham
Covajea Mountains	See Ko Vaya, Pima
Cove Mesa	(T37N/R28E; Elev. 6960') See Cove, Apache
Cove Wash	(T37N/R29E) See Cove, Apache
Cowgrhan Canyon	See Coughran Canyon, Yavapai
Crater	(T20N/R12E) See Meteor Crater, Coconino
Crater	See Jump Off Crater, Coconino
Crater Hill	See A One Mountain, Coconino
Crater Mound, Mountain	See Meteor Crater, Coconino
Crater Mountains	(T9S/R8W; Ele;v. 1754') See Crater Range, Maricopa
Crater 160	See Colton Crater, Coconino
Cremation Point	See Shoshone Point, Coconino (Grand Canyon)
Cristobal Valley, San	See Stoval, Yuma
Cristobal Wash, San	See Growler Wash, Maricopa/Yuma
Crittenden	See Patagonia, Santa Cruz
Crook's Canyon	(T12N/R1W) See Crook City, Yavapai
Crook's Road, Trail	See Lake No. 1, Coconino
Crossing of the Fathers	See Lee's Ferry, Coconino
Crossing, The	See Theodore Roosevelt Dam, Gila
Crossman Peak	See Grossman Peak, Mohave
Cross Roads	See Simmons, Yavapai
Crouch Mesa	See Crouch Creek, Mesa
Crozier (R. R. Stn.)	(T24N/R13W) See Crozier, Mohave
Crozier Tank	(1) (T26N/R12W); (2) T15N/R14W) See Crozier, Mohave
Crozier Well	(T15N/R15W; Elev. 3700') See Crozier, Mohave
Crystal Rapids	(T32N/R1E) See Crystal Creek, Coconino (Grand Canyon)
Crystal Ridge	(T33N/R2E) See Crystal Creek, Coconino (Grand Canyon)
Crystal Spring	(T35N/R3E) See Crystal Creek, Coconino (Grand Canyon)
Crystoval	See Stoval, Yuma
Cuarzo Canyon	See Quartzite Canyon, Apache
Cubit Tubig	See Komelik, Pima
Cubo	See Gu Vo, Pima
Cubo Hills	See Gu Vo, Pima
Cucklebur	See Vaiva Vo, Pinal
Cuercas Canyon	See Texas Canyon, Cochise
Cuevacita	See Hughes Mountain, Santa Cruz
Cullen's	See Cullen's Well, La Paz
Cullen's Wash	See Cullen's Well, La Paz
Cullen's Well	See Kerlin's Well, Coconino
Cullin's Wash, Cullin's Well	See Cullen's Well, La Paz
Cumars, Sierra de San Joseph de	See Estrella Mountains, Maricopa
Cumopavi	See Shungopavi, Navajo
Cumorah	See Joseph City, Navajo
Cunejo de Los Pimas	See Cienega, Pima
Cunningham Mountain	See Cunningham Pass, Yuma
Cunningham Valley	See Butler Valley, La Paz
Cunningham Wash	(T9N/R13W) See Cunningham Pass, La Paz
Cups	See Ko Vaya, Pima, and Sil Nakya, Pima
Curley Seep Spring	See Curley Seep, Coconino
Curnutt	See Livingstone, Gila
Curtis	See Eden, Graham
Cutterville	See Cutter, Gila

Cuvo	See Gu Vo, Pima
Cyclopic Wash	(T29N/R19W) See Cyclopic, Mohave
Cycloptic	See Cyclopic, Mohave
D'Abineau Canyon, Peak, Springs	See Aubineau Canyon, Coconino
Dagger Canyon	See Dagger Basin, Gila
Dagger Peak	(Elev. 3260') See Dagger Basin, Gila
Dagger Spring	See Dagger Basin, Gila
Dahl	See Dragoon Mountains, Cochise
Dane Cabin, Ridge, Spring	See Dane Canyon, Coconino
Danial Spring	See Daniel Gulch, Yavapai
Daniel Arroyo	See Adobe Wash, Pima
Date Creek Indian Agency	See Date Creek, Yavapai, and Date Creek, Camp, Yavapai
Date Creek Mountains	(T10N/R6W; Elev. 3500') See Date Creek, Camp, Yavapai
Date Creek, North Fork	(T7S/R12W) See Date Creek, Camp, Yavapai
Davenport Lake	(T22N/R3E) See Davenport Hill, Coconino
Davenport Wash	See Davenport Peak, Yavapai
Davidson Spring	See Davidson Canyon, Pima
Davis Spring	(T11S/R17E) See Davis Ruin, Pima
Dawing Pass	See Downing Pass, Cochise
Day's Camp	See Horseshoe, Pima
Daze (R. R. Stn.)	(T22N/R1W) See Daze Lake, Coconino
Dead Man Wash	(T25N/R9E) See Dead Man Flat, Coconino
Dead Old Man's Pond	See Gurli Put Vo, Pima
Death Valley Wash	See Detrital Wash, Mohave
Deer Creek Basin	See Deer Creek, Pinal
Deer Creek Coal Basin	See Deer Creek, Pinal
Deer Lake Canyon	See Deer Lake, Coconino
Del Shay Creek	See Del Shay Basin, Gila
Denabet Spring	See Dinnebito, Navajo
Desaki Mesa	See White Top Mesa, Apache
Descanso	See Brophy Well, Cochise
Desert	See Desert Wells, Pima
Desert View	See Desert View Point, Coconino
Desert Well	See Nolic, Pima
Desierto Pintado, El	See Painted Desert, Apache
Detrital-Sacramento Valley	See Sacramento Valley, Mohave
Detrital Valley	See Sacramento Valley, Mohave
Devil Dog Tank	See Devil Dog Hills, Coconino
Devil's Elbow	See Crystal Cave, Cochise
Devil's Kitchen	See Skeleton Canyon, Cochise
Dewey	See Calva, Graham
Dewogibito	See Greasewood Spring, Apache
Diablito Springs	(T21S/R12E) See Diablito Mountain, Santa Cruz
Diablo, Canyon	See Lawton Canyon, Maricopa
Diablo Mountain	See Pete Mountain, Santa Cruz
Dial	See Dragoon Mountains, Cochise
Diamond Canyon	See Diamond Peak, Gila
Diamond Creek, Peak	See Diamond Canyon, Mohave
Diamond Ranch	See Sunflower, Maricopa
Diamond Rim	(T11N/R11E) See Diamond Butte, Gila
Dick Hart Draw	See Barber Shop Canyon, Coconino
Dick Hart Ridge	(T13N/R11E) See Barber Shop Canyon, Coconino
Dicks Canyon	See Dixie Canyon, Cochise
Dicks Peak	(T22S/R12E; Elev. 5396'; Santa Cruz) See Helvetia, Pima
Didze Sikaad	See Wild Cherry Canyon, Apache
Diego, Sierra de San	See Aubrey Cliffs, Coconino

Dinnebito Wash	(Navajo/Coconino) See Dinnebito, Navajo
Dinner Canyon	See Dinner Creek, Gila
Dionisio City	(T25S/R9W) See Dionisio, San, Yuma, and Yuma, Yuma
Disappointment Creek	See Dripping Springs Wash, Gila
Dino'zhii Bii'to'	(T35N/R29E) See Greasewood Creek, Apache
Dixie National Forest	See Coconino National Forest, Mohave/Coconino
Dix Mesa	See Dix Creek, Greenlee
Doanville	See Palomas, Yuma
Dobbs Buttes	(T15S/R9W; Elev. 3683') See Dobbs Station, Pima
Dobbs Wells	See Dobbs Station, Pima
Dobono Canyon	See Aubineau Canyon, Coconino
Dobono's Peak	See Aubineau Canyon, Coconino
Dobono Springs	See Aubineau Canyon, Coconino
Dodson's	See Mesaville, Pinal
Doe Basin	See Sycamore Basin, Yavapai
Dokot'navi	See Navajo Mountain, Coconino/Utah
Doll	See Alma, Pinal
Dome Mountain	See Dome Rock Mountain, La Paz
Domingo, Rio San	See Goodwin, Camp, Graham
Domingo, San	See Simon, San, Cochise
Doña Ana County	See Pima County
Donal W. Waddell Dam	See Carl Pleasant Lake, Maricopa
Doney	See Doney Park, Coconino
Doney Cone, Crater, Hill	See Doney Park, Coconino
Doney Mountain	(T25N/R9E; Elev. 5589') See Doney Park, Coconino
Donnelly Canyon, Ranch	See Donnelly Wash, Pinal
Donsill Canyon	See Andrus Canyon, Mohave
Dook'o'oslid	See Francisco Peaks, San, Coconino
Doonysio	See Yuma, Yuma
Doran's Defeat Spring	(T12N/R6E) See Doran's Defeat Canyon, Yavapai
Do-Sa-Pons	See Carlos, San, Gila
Dortch Canyon	See Chaol Canyon, Coconino
Dos Cabezas Mountains	(T14S/R28E) See Dos Cabezas Peaks, Cochise
Dosoris Canyon	(T12N/R2W) See Dosoris, Yavapai
Dosoris Spring	See Dosoris, Yavapai
Dot Klish Canyon	See Blue Canyon, Coconino/Navajo, and Moenkopi Wash, Coconino/Navajo
Double Buttes	See Double Knolls, Maricopa
Double Crater	See Janus Crater, Coconino
Doubtful Pass Station	See Doubtful Canyon, Cochise
Doyle Peak	(T23N/R7E; Elev. 11,460') See Doyle Saddle, Coconino
Doyle Spring	See Doyle Saddle, Coconino
Dragon, The	See Dragon Creek, Coconino
Dragon Head	See Dragon Creek, Coconino (Grand Canyon)
Dragon Head Butte	See Dragon Creek, Coconino (Grand Canyon)
Dragoon	(T16S/R23E; Elev. 4613') See Dragoon Mountains, Cochise
Dragoon, Camp	(T18S/R24E) See Dragoon Mountains, Cochise
Dragoon National Forest	See Coronado National Forest, Pima/Cochise
Dragoon Peak	(T16S/R23E; Elev. 6533') See Dragoon Mountains, Cochise
Dragoon Spring Mountains	See Dragoon Mountains, Cochise
Dragoon Spring (Butterfield Stn.)	See Dragoon Mountains, Cochise
Dragoon Summit	See Dragoon Mountains, Cochise, and Summit, Cochise
Dragoon Wash	(T16S/R22E) See Dragoon Mountains, Cochise
Drake Well	See Griffith, Mohave
Dripping Pool	See Fern Spring, Coconino (Grand Canyon)
Dripping Spring Amphitheater	See Dripping Springs, Coconino (Grand Canyon)

Dripping Spring Mountains	(T3S/R14E; Gila/Pinal) See Dripping Spring, Gila
Dripping Spring Mountains	See Puerto Blanco Mountains, Pima
Dripping Springs Trail	See Boucher Creek, Coconino (Grand Canyon); Hermit Trail, Coconino (Grand Canyon); and Dripping Springs, Coconino (Grand Canyon)
Dripping Springs Valley, Wash	(T3S/R14E) See Dripping Spring Mountains, Gila/Pinal
Dripping Vat Spring	See Dipping Vat Spring, Apache
Dry Lake	See Zeniff, Navajo
Dry Lake Hills, Mountain, Wash	See Dry Lake, Coconino
Dublin	See Cork, Graham
Duck on a Rock	See Chiricahua National Monument, Cochise
Dude Lake	See Dude Creek, Coconino
Dueztumac	See Agua Caliente, Maricopa
Dunbars	See Tres Alamos, Cochise
Dunlap	See Aravaipa, Graham
Dunn Springs Mountain	(T15S/R30E; Elev. 6503') See Dunn Springs, Cochise
Duppa Station	See New River, Maricopa, and Duppa Butte, Coconino (Grand Canyon)
Duquesne	(T24S/R16E) See Washington Camp, Santa Cruz
Duquesne Gulch	(T24S/R17E; Elev. c. 5500') See Washington Camp, Santa Cruz
Durasno	See Harshaw, Santa Cruz
Durazno Canyon	(T20S/R10E; Pima) See Washington Camp, Santa Cruz
Durham Hills	(T8S/R12E) See Durham Wash, Pinal
Dusty Tank	See Dusty Canyon, Coconino
Dutch Canyon	See Dutton Canyon, Coconino
Dutch Flat Road	See Dutch Flat, Mohave
Dutchman's, The	See Stanwix, Maricopa
Dutton Canyon	See Dutton Point, Coconino (Grand Canyon)
Dzilijini	See Black Mesa, Apache
Dzittichu	See Doney Park, Coconino
Eagle Eye Peak	See Eagle Eye Mountains, Maricopa
Eagle Nest Rock	See Eagle Rock, Apache
Eagle Peak	See Eagle Nest Peak, Maricopa
Eagle Ranch	See Double Circle Ranch, Greenlee
Eagletail Peak	Maricopa (T1N/R10W; Elev. 3300') See Eagletail Mountains, La Paz/Maricopa
Eagletail Valley	See Eagletail Mountains, Yuma/Maricopa
Eagle Tanks	See Jaeger Tanks, Maricopa
East Araby	See Araby, Yuma
East Clear Creek	See Clear Creek, Coconino/Yavapai, and Big Dry Fork, Coconino
East Eagle Creek	See Eagle Creek, Greenlee
East Fork Eagle Creek	See Eagle Creek, Graham/Greenlee
East Mitten Butte	(T41N/R21E; Elev. 6223') See Mitten Peak, Navajo
East Pinedale	See Pinedale, Navajo
Ebert Spring	See Ebert Mountain, Coconino
Echo Canyon	See Echo Park, Cochise
Echo Canyon Bowl	See Echo Canyon, Maricopa
Echo Cliffs	See Echo Peaks, Coconino, and Vermilion Cliffs, Coconino
Eden Spring	See Eden, Graham
Edmunds Lake	See Davy Lake (1887), Coconino
Ed Riggs Mountain	(T16S/R29E; Elev. 6153)' See Riggs Canyon, Cochise
Edwards Park	See Edwards Peak, Gila
Edwards Spring	See Gold Tooth Smith Spring, Gila
Egypt	See Goodyear, Maricopa, and Litchfield Park, Maricopa
Ehle's Ranch	See Skull Valley, Yavapai
Elden Mesa	See Elden Mountain, Coconino

Elden Spring	(T21N/R7E) See Elden Mountain, Coconino, and Babbitt Spring, Coconino
Elephant Head	See Pete Mountain, Santa Cruz
Elephant Head Mine	See Pete Mountain, Santa Cruz
Elephant Legs	See Elephant Feet, Coconino
Ellen, Mount	See Trumbull, Mount, Mohave
Ellison Creek	See Ellison, Gila
Eloy, Lake	See Greenes Wash, Pinal
Emery Falls	See Columbine Falls, Mohave
Emigrant Hills	(T15S/R29E; Elev. (1) 4396' (2) 4443') See Emigrant Canyon, Cochise
Emperor, The	See Monument Pass, Navajo
Empire Gulch	(T19S/R16E) See Empire Ranch, Pima
Empire Mountains	(T18S/R17E; Elev. 5378') See Empire Ranch, Pima
Encarnacion	See Sacaton, Pinal
End of the Death Trail, The	See Stone Ferry, Mohave
Endymion Dome	See March Butte, Coconino (Grand Canyon)
Engesser Mine	See Engesser Pass, Yuma
Engle's Pass	See Truxton Canyon, Mohave, and Railroad Pass, Mohave
Enid Mountains	See Estrella Mountains, Pinal
Escalante Basin, Butte, River	See Escalante Creek, Coconino
Escritas Piedras Pintadas, Sierra	See Painted Rocks, Maricopa
Escudilla Peak	See Four Peaks, Apache, and Escudilla Mountain, Apache
Escudillo, Sierra	See Escudilla Mountain, Apache
Eskadere Mountains	See Escudilla Mountain, Apache
Eskimazene Ranch Wash	See Eskiminzin Spring, Pinal
Eskimenzin Spring	See Eskiminzin Spring, Pinal
Eskiminzin Fort Rock	(T5S/R17E; Elev. 3274') See Eskiminzin Spring, Pinal
Eskiminzin Wash	(T6S/R16E) See Eskiminzin Spring, Pinal
Espejo	(T32N/R5E) See Espejo Butte, Coconino (Grand Canyon)
Esperanza, Sierra de	See Ajo, Pima
Esperanza Wash	See Esperanza Ranch, Pima
Espero	See Sprucedale, Greenlee
Espuela, Sierra	See Huachuca Mountains, Cochise
Espuma, Sierra de La	See Superstition Mountains, Pinal
Estrella Hill	See Estrella, Maricopa, and Estrella Mountains, Maricopa
Estrella, Sierra	See Estrella Mountains, Maricopa
Eureka Mountain	(T11S/R19E) See Eureka Canyon, Graham, and Eureka Springs, Graham
Eureka Ranch	(T9S/R21E) See Eureka Canyon, Graham, and Eureka Springs, Graham
Evans	See Evans Point, Greenlee
Ewee-Tha-Auaw-Ali	See Ancha, Sierra, Gila
Ewell County	See Pima County
Ewell's Pass	See Apache Pass, Cochise
Ewell's Springs	See Dos Cabezas, Cochise
Explorers Canyon	See Cardenas Terrace, Coconino (Grand Canyon)
Explorer's Column	See Chelly, Canyon de, Apache
Exposed Reef	(c. T23S/R20E) See Reef, Cochise
Ez-Kim-In-Zen Recreational Area	(T13S/R11E; Pima) See Eskiminzin Spring, Pinal
Fafner Point	See Komo Point, Coconino (Grand Canyon)
Fain Spring	(T17N/R21E) See Fain Mountain, Coconino
Fairview	See Glenbar, Graham or Lakeside, Navajo
Fairview Point	See Far View Point, Coconino (Grand Canyon)
Falls of the Pachete	See Halls's Falls, Apache
Falva	See Falfa, Maricopa
Faraway Ranch	See Fife Canyon, Cochise, and Chiricahua National Monument, Cochise

Farrar Peak	See Saw Tooth (Sawtooth Peak), La Paz, and Farrar Gulch, La Paz
Feldman	See Winkelman, Pinal
Felipe de San Jesus Guevavi, San	See Guebavi, Santa Cruz
Fen Lake	See Swamp Lake, Coconino
Fernando River, San	See Verde River, Yavapai
Fernando, San	See Sasabe, Pima, and Osa, La, Pima
Fern Canyon	See Fern Glen Rapids, Coconino/Mohave (Grand Canyon)
Fife Peak, Spring	See Fife Canyon, Cochise
Fifty-Foot Falls	See Havasu Canyon, Coconino
Fire Box Creek	(T5N/R24E; Apache) See Fire Box Canyon, Navajo
Fir Park	See Double Cabin Park, Coconino
First Forest	See Petrified National Forest, Apache/Navajo, and Jasper Forest, Apache
First Lagune (sic)	See Laguna, Yuma
First Mesa Wash	See Polacca Wash, Apache/Navajo
Fish Creek Mountain	(Elev. 4940') See Fish Creek, Maricopa
Fish Tail Canyon	See Palm Canyon, Yuma
Fishtail Point	(T35N/R3W) See Fishtail Canyon, Mohave (Grand Canyon), and Paguekwash Point, Mohave (Grand Canyon)
Fittsburg	See Pearce, Cochise
Fitz Jefferson's Ranch	See Pedro Presidio, San, Cochise
Fitz Ranch	See Pedro Presidio, San, Cochise
Five Mile Canyon	See Fife Canyon, Cochise
Five Mile Pass	See Fivemile Lake, Coconino
Five O'Clock Wash	See Sand Wash, Greenlee
Flagstaff Lake	See Horse Lake, Coconino
Flagstaff Spring	See Flagstaff, Coconino
Flagstaff Wash	See Flag, Rio de, Coconino
Flake	See Aripine, Navajo
Flat Mesa	See Gray Mesa, Navajo
Flat Top Mountain	See Table Top Mountain, Apache
Flax River	See Little Colorado River, Coconino
Fleming Spring	See Continental Mountain, Maricopa
Fleuryville	See Prescott, Yavapai
Flickner Canyon	See Flitner Canyon, Cochise
Flores Gulch, Wash	See Flores, Mohave
Florida, Mount	See Graham, Mount, Graham
Florida, Sierra La	See Graham, Mount, Graham
Florilla, Camp	See Kinlichee, Apache
Floy	See Plenty, Apache
Floyd, Mount	See Pineveta Peak, Coconino
Floyd's Peak	See Pineveta Peak, Coconino
Fluted Rock Lake	(T3N/R7W) See Fluted Rock, Apache
Flux Gulch	See Flux Canyon, Santa Cruz
Flying V Canyon	(T5N/R18E) See Livingston, Gila
Fools Canyon	(T9N/R4W) See Fools Gulch, Yavapai
Fools Hollow Draw	See Fools Hollow, Navajo
Fools Hollow Lake, Ridge	(T10N/R21E) See Fools Hollow, Navajo
Forepaugh Peak	(T6N/R17W) See Forepaugh, Maricopa
Forepaw	See Four Peaks, La Paz
Foresight	See Hooper, Yavapai
Forest	See Forrest, Cochise, or Forrest, Yavapai
Forestdale Canyon	See Forestdale, Navajo
Forestdale Creek	See Forestdale, Navajo, and Corduroy Creek, Navajo
Forster Rapids	See Forster Canyon, Coconino (Grand Canyon)
Fortification Mountain, Ridge	See Fortification Hill, Mohave
Fort Mojave Reservation	(T17N/R21W) See Mohave County
Fort Pearce Wash	(T41N/R10W) See Pearce Ferry, Mohave

Fortuna Station, Wash	(T8 S/R21 W) See Fortuna, Yuma
Fortune Range	See Gila Mountains, Yuma
Forty-Mile Desert	See Maricopa Wells, Maricopa, and Desert Station, Maricopa
Fossil Canyon	See Fossil Rapids, Coconino (Grand Canyon)
Fossil Mountain	(T32 N/R1 W) See Fossil Rapids, Coconino (Grand Canyon)
Fossil Springs	(T12 N/R7 E) See Fossil Creek, Gila/Yavapai
Four Mile Creek	(T7 S/R19 E) See Four Mile Peak, Graham
Four Palms	(T1 S/R18 W) See Palm Canyon, Yuma
Four Peaks Dam	(T6 N/R18 W) See Four Peaks, La Paz
Four Peaks Springs	See Four Peaks, Maricopa
Fourr Grave	(T5 S/R9 W) See Oatman Flat, Maricopa
Fourr's Stage Station	See Oatman Flat, Maricopa
Fourth Forest	See First Forest, Apache
Fourth Hollow	See First Hollow, Navajo
Fourth of July Butte	(T2 S/R8 W; Elev. 1626') See Fourth of July Wash, Maricopa
Fox Farm	(T10 N/R11 E) See Fox Gulch, Gila
Fox Gulch Spring	See Fox Gulch, Gila
Fox Tank	See Frenchman's Tank, Yuma
Fraguita Wash	(Pima/Santa Cruz) See Fraguita, Mount, Santa Cruz
Francisco Cone, San	See Francisco Peaks, San, Coconino
Francisco del Adid, San	See Anegam, Pima, and Gu Achi, Pima
Francisco Javier del Bac, San	See Xavier Del Bac, San, Pima
Francisco Mountain, San	(T23 N/R7 E; Elev. 12,600') See Francisco Peaks, San, Coconino
Francisco Mountain Forest Reserve, San	See Coconino National Forest, Coconino
Francisco Mountains, San	See Francisco Peaks, San, Coconino
Francisco, Rio de San	See Flag, Rio de, Coconino
Francisco River, San	See Verde River, Yavapai
Francisco Wash, San	(T22 N/R10 E) See Francisco Peaks, San, Coconino
Francisco Xavier de Bac, San	See Xavier, San, Pima
Franconia Wash	(T16 N/R19 W) See Franconia, Mohave
Franklin's Hole	See Meteor Crater, Coconino
Fraser's Ranch	See Reavis Ranch, Maricopa
Fraser's Station	See Fish Creek, Maricopa
Frasier	See Fish Creek, Maricopa
Frederico, Pozo de	See Kuakatch, Pima
Freezeout Creek	See Poker Mountain, Apache
Freezeout Mountain	(T3 N/R26 E; Elev. 7719') See Freezeout Creek, Graham
Freeze Wash	See Free's Wash, Mohave
Fremont	See Oatman, Mohave
French Joe Camp, Spring	See French Joe Canyon, Cochise
French Joe Peak	(Elev. 7684') See French Joe Canyon, Cochise
Frenchman Mountains	See Tank Mountains, Yuma
Frenchman Peak, Ridge	See Frenchman Mountain, Mohave (Lake Mead)
French Spring	See French Butte, Navajo
French Trail	See Tanner Trail, Coconino (Grand Canyon)
Frenchy Canyon, Hill	(T21 N/R3 E) See French Spring, Coconino
Frente Negra, Sierra	See Tucson Mountains, Pima
Fresco	See Alpine, Apache
Fresco River	See Francisco River, San, Greenlee
Fresnal Canyon	(T19 S/R7 E) See Fresnal, Pima
Fresnal, Cerro del	(T23 S/R9 E; Elev. 4500') See Fresnal, Pima
Fresnal Creek	See Fresnal, Pima, and Fresnal Wash, Pima
Fresnal Well	See Fresnal, Pima, and Pitoikam, Pima
Fresno Spring	(T21 S/R12 E; Santa Cruz) See Fresno Canyon, Pima

Fries Wash	See Free's Wash, Mohave
Frisco	See Alpine, Apache
Frisch County	See Coconino County
Frisco Peak	See Frisco, Mohave
Frisco River	See Francisco River, San, Greenlee
Fritsche Tank	(T18N/R5W) See Fritsche, Yavapai
Fritz Springs	See Lewis Springs, Cochise
Frog Tanks	See Carl Pleasant, Lake, Maricopa/Yavapai
Frog Tanks Dam	See Carl Pleasant, Lake, Maricopa/Yavapai
Fry	See Sierra Vista, Cochise
Frye Canyon	See Frye Creek, Graham
Frye Creek Dam	(T7S/R25E) See Frye Creek, Graham
Frye Mesa	See Frye Creek, Graham
Frye Mesa Reservoir	See Frye Creek, Graham
Fuller Canyon, Pass	See Tanque Verde Hot Springs, Pima
Fuller's Hot Springs	See Tanque Verde Hot Springs, Pima
Fuller's Springs	See Tanque Verde Hot Springs, Pima
Fulton Canyon	See Fulton Spring, Coconino
Gabriel de Guebavi, San	See Guebavi, Santa Cruz
Gaetan, San	See Calabasas, Santa Cruz
Gage, El	See Kaka, Pima
Gah-Kotkh	See Quijotoa, Pima
Galluno, Sierra	See Galiuro Mountains, Graham
Gallagher Peak	See Clara Peak, Yuma
Galloria Mountains	See Galiuro Mountains, Graham/Pinal/Cochise
Gaizville	See Gayleyville, Cochise
Ganado Lake	See Ganado, Apache
Ganado Wash	(Apache/Navajo) See Ganado, Navajo; Pueblo Colorado Wash, Navajo, and Cottonwood Wash, Navajo
Gandules, Rancho de Los	See Moenkopi, Coconino
Garces National Forest	See Coronado National Forest
Garden of Allah	See Allah, Maricopa
Garden of the Gods	See Castle Rocks, Mohave
Garden Ridge	(T22S/R20E) See Garden Canyon, Cochise
Gardiner Spring	See Hackberry, Mohave
Garland	(T21N/R24E) See Garland Prairie, Coconino
Gash Flat	(T17N/R9E) See Gash Mountain, Coconino
Gaspe	See Walpi, Navajo
Gatagama Terrace	See Gatagama Point, Coconino
Gates	See McDowell, Maricopa
Gato, El	See Cat Mountain, Pima
Gayleyville	See Galeyville, Cochise
Geesaman Spring	(T11S/R16E) See Geesaman Wash, Pima
Geesman Canyon, Wash	See Geesman Wash, Pima
General Hitchcock Point	(T12S/R16E) See Summerhaven, Pima
General's Springs Canyon	See General's Springs, Coconino
Gentle Spring	See Gentile Spring, Mohave
Gentry Canyon	See Gentry Spring, Coconino
Gentry Creek	(T9N/R12E; Gila) See Gentry Spring, Coconino
Gentry Mountain	(T9N/T15E; Elev. 6587'; Gila) See Gentry Spring, Coconino
Genung Springs	(T11N/R4W) See Genung Mountain, Yavapai
George Otey's Tombstone	See Capitol Butte, Yavapai
Geowic	See Chiawuli Tak, Pima
Gerald Hills	See Gerald Wash, Gila
German American Wash	See Germa, Mohave
Geronimo, Camp	See Goodwin, Camp, Graham

Geronimo Cave	(T5N/R23E; Navajo) See Geronimo, Graham
Geronimo, Mount	(T18N/R10E; Coconino) See Geronimo, Graham
Geronimo, San	See Hickiwan, Pima
Geronimo's Surrender	(T21S/R32E) See Geronimo's Seep, Cochise, and Goodwin, Camp, Graham
Gertrude, San	See Tubac, Santa Cruz
Gertrudis de Tubaca	See Tubac, Santa Cruz
Geser	See Greer, Apache
Gibbon's Springs	See Gibbon Mountain, Pima
Gibson Arroyo	See Gibson, Pima
Gibson Creek	See Gibson Peak, Gila
Gibson Tank	(T5N/R2E) See Gibson, Maricopa
Giburi	See Quiburi, Cochise
Gigante, Cabeza del	See Castle Dome, La Paz
Gila Bonita Creek	See Bonita Creek, Graham
Gila Center	See Blalock, Yuma
Gila City	See Dome, Yuma
Gila Crossing	See Kumatke, Maricopa
Gila Indian Reservation	(T5S/R5W) See Gila River Indian Reservation, Maricopa
Gila Peak	(T3S/R23E; Elev. 6629') See Gila Mountains, Graham
Gila Ranch	See Gila Bend, Maricopa
Gila Range	See Mescal Mountains, Gila, or Gila Mountains, Graham
Gila River Canyon	(T4S/R7W) See Gila River
Gila Station	See Gila Bend, Maricopa
Gillespie Flat	(T9N/R25E) See Gillespie Ranch, Graham
Gillespie Mountain	(T10S/R26E; Elev. 5223') See Gillespie Ranch, Graham
Gillespie Wash	(T9S/R27E) See Gillespie Ranch, Graham
Gillette	See Gillett, Yavapai
Gilliand Gap, Springs	See Gilliland Gap, Gila
Gilson Creek	See Gilson Wash, Gila
Gilson Well	(T1S/R17E) See Gibson Wash, Gila
Gimletville	See Goodwin City, Yavapai
Gird Camp	See Tombstone, Cochise
Gisela Mountain	See Gisela, Gila
Glance	See Sunnyside, Cochise
Gleen Springs	See Glenn Springs, Cochise
Glendale Temperance Colony	See Glendale, Maricopa
Glendale Valley	See Glendale, Maricopa
Glenn Spring	(T18S/R19E) See Glenn, Mount, Cochise
Glenwood	See Greenwood, Mohave
Globe City, Hills, Ledge, Peak	See Globe, Gila
Globe Mine	See Old Dominion Mine, Gila
Goat Mountains	(Maricopa/La Paz) See Big Horn Mountains, Maricopa/La Paz
Goat Ranch	See Gunsight Ranch, Pima
Goddard's	See Black Canyon, Yavapai
Goksamuk	See Topawa, Pima
Golden Spray City	See Watertown, Mohave
Gold Field	See Youngberg, Pinal
Gold Road Gulch	See Goldroad, Mohave
Gold Road Pass	See Goldroad, Mohave, and Sitgreaves Pass, Mohave
Gold Tree Mine	See Alto, Santa Cruz
Gonzalez Pass Canyon	See Gonzalez Pass, Pinal
Goodwin Spring	See Goodwin Canyon, Cochise
Goose Flat	See Goodwin City, Yavapai
Gordon Canyon	See Gordon, Gila
Gothic Mesas	See Dinne Mesa, Apache
Gothic Wash	See Walker Creek, Apache

Goudy Canyon	See Goudy Creek, Graham
Government Hill	(T23N/R4E; Elev. 8490') See Government Prairie, Coconino
Government Knolls	(T23N/R5E; Elev. 7953') See Government Pririe, Coconino
Government Spring Gulch	(T13N/R3E) See Government Spring, Yavapai
Government Tank Canyon	See Western Canyon, Santa Cruz
Government Wells	See Quartzsite, La Paz
Grace Valley	See McMullen Valley, La Paz
Grand Canyon Bridge	See Navajo Bridge, Coconino
Grand Canyon Forest Preserve	See Coconino National Forest, Coconino
Grand Canyon National Forest	See Coconino National Forest, Coconino
Grand Canyon National Monument	See Grand Canyon (Tuweep Unit)
Grand Cliffs Range	See Grand Wash Cliffs, Mohave
Grande de Buena Esperanza, Rio	See Maria River, Santa, Mohave
Grande de Hyla, Rio	See Gila River
Grande, Rio de	See Gila River
Grandview	See Grand View Trail, Coconino (Grand Canyon)
Grandview Caves	See Horse Shoe Mesa Caves, Coconino (Grand Canyon), and Grand View Trail, Coconino (Grand Canyon)
Grand Wash Bay	(T33N/R16W) See Grand Wash Cliffs, Mohave
Grand Wash Valley	See Grand Wash Cliffs, Mohave
Granite Basin	(T14S/R5W) See Granite, Yavapai
Granite Basin Lake	(T14N/R3W) See Granite, Yavapai
Granite Falls	See Granite Gorge, Coconino (Grand Canyon), and Mounument Rapids, Coconino (Grand Canyon)
Granite Mountains	(T13S/R10W) See Granite Pass Tank, Pima
Granite Range	See Prieta, Sierra, Yavapai
Granite Rapids	See Granite Gorge, Coconino (Grand Canyon)
Granite Reef Mountain	(T6S/R20E) See Grand Reef Mountain, Graham
Granite Reef Mountain	(T2N/R6E; Elev. 2135') See Sawik Mountain, Maricopa
Granite Spring	(T16S/R21E) See Granite Canyon, Cochise
Grant Draw	See Grant Creek, Graham
Grant Goudy Trail	See Goudy Creek, Graham
Grant Hill	(T9S/R24E; Elev. 9450') See Grant Creek, Graham
Grape Vine Canyon	See Magazine Canyon, Maricopa
Grape Vine Canyon	(T31N/R16W) See Mead, Lake, Mohave
Grapevine Creek	(T30N/R4W) See Hualpai Creek, Mohave
Grape Vine Mesa	(T30N/R16W) See Mead, Lake, Mohave
Grape Vine Spring	(T17N/R11E) See Grapevine Canyon, Coconino
Grape Vine Spring	(T34N/R16W) See Mead, Lake, Mohave
Grass Canyon	See Pitahaya Canyon, Pima
Grasshopper Butte	(Elev. 6424') See Grasshopper, Navajo
Grass Valley	See Arivaipa Valley, Graham or Gisela, Gila
Gravel Spring Canyon	See Grover Spring Canyon, Navajo
Graveyard Canyon	See Dead Man Canyon, Graham
Gray Mountain	See Capitol Butte, Yavapai
Greasewood Wash	See Cottonwood Wash, Navajo
GreatAkchin	See Serafin, San, Pima
Great Arizona Crater	See Meteor Crater, Coconino
Great Basin	See Natural Bridge, Gila
Greaterville Gulch	(T19S/R17E) See Greaterville, Pima, and Louisiana Gulch, Pima
Great Pocatcho	Se Picacho Peak, Pinal
Great Thumb Point	See Great Thumb Mesa, Coconino (Grand Canyon)
Greenback Creek	(T5N/R11E) See Greenback Valley, Gila
Greenback Peak	See Greenback Valley, Gila
Green Canyon	See Hoovey Canyon, Cochise

Greenes Canal	See Greenes Wash, Pinal
Greenes Resrvoir	(T7S/R5E) See Greenes Wash, Pinal
Greenhaw	See Greenlaw, Coconino
Greenland Lake	See Greenland Spring, Coconino
Green, Mount	See Green's Peak, Apache
Greenspot Draw	(T9N/R28E; Elev. 8900') See Carnero Lake, Apache
Green Valley	See Payson, Gila, and Reno, Camp, Gila
Green Valley Creek, Hills	See Payson, Gila
Greenwood Peak	(T12N/R12W; Elev. 3966') See Greenwood, Mohave
Greenwood Spring	(T12N/R12W; Elev. 3000') See Greenwood, Monave
Greer Valley	See Greer, Apache
Gregg Buttes	See Double Knolls, Maricopa
Gregorio Spring, San	See Donnelly Wash, Pinal
Grief Hill Wash	See Grief Hill, Yavapai
Griffin Wash	See Griffin Flat, Gila
Griffith Wash	(T19N/R18W) See Griffith, Mohave
Grinnells Station	See Stoval, Yuma
Gritetho	See Colorado River
Groom's Hill	(T8N/R3W; Elev. 4700') See Groom Creek, Yavapai
Groom Spring Wash	(T14N/R14W; Mohave) See Groom Creek, Yavapai, and Groom Peak, Mohave
Grosvenor Hills	See Grosvenor Peak, Santa Cruz
Grove of Robinson, The	See Catalpa, Gila
Growler	See Growler Mountains, Pima
Growler Canyon	(T14S/R7W) See Growler Mountains, Pima
Growler Creek	(T10S/R10W) See Growler Mountains, Pima
Growler Mine	See Growler Mountains, Pima
Growler Pass	(T14S/R6W; Elev. 1487') See Growler Mountains, Pima
Growler Peak	(T12S/R8W; Elev. 3029') See Growler Mountains, Pima
Growler Valley	(T11S/R9W; Maricopa/Pima) See Growler Mountains, Pima
Growler Wash	(T12S/R10W; T14S/R7W; Maricopa/Yuma See Growler Mountains, Pima
Growler Well	See Bates Well, Pima, and Growler Mountains, Pima
Gu Achi Mountains	See Rosa, Mountains, Santa, Pima, and Gu Achi, Pima
Gu Achi Peak	(T12S/R5E; Elev. 4556') See Gu Achi, Pima
Gu Achi Wash	(T12S/R4E) See Gu Achi, Pima
Guachapa Mountains	See Rita Mountains, Santa, Pima/Santa Cruz
Guachuca	See Huachuca, Fort, Cochise
Guactum	See Serafin, San, Pima
Guajolote Wash	See Guajolote Flat, Santa Cruz
Guebabi Canyon	(T23S/R14E) See Guevavi, Santa Cruz
Guijas Mine, Las	See Guijas Mountains, Pima
Guijas Wash, Las	See Guijas Mountains, Pima
Gunsight Hills	(T14S/R3W; Elev. 2622') See Gunsight, Pima
Gunsight Mountains	(T17S/R11E; Elev. 4680') See Gunsight, Pima, and Sikort Chuapo Mountains, Pima
Gunsight Pass	(T14S/R4W) See Gunsight, Pima
Gunsight Valley	(T15S/R2W) See Gunsight, Pima
Gunoka Valley	See Tonoka, Pima
Gunsight Wash	(T13S/R5W; Elev. 1600') See Gunsight, Pima
Gunsight Well	See Gunsight, Pima, and Gunsight Range, Pima
Gu Oidak Valley	See Gu Oidak, Pima
Gurley Mountain	See Granite Mountain, Yavapai
Gusubac	See Guebavi, Santa Cruz
Guthrie Peak	(Elev. 6571') See Guthrie, Greenlee
Gu Vo Hills	(T15S/R3W; Elev. 2720') See Gu Vo, Pima
Gu Vo Pass	(T15S/R3W) See Gu Vo, Pima
Guvo Verde	See Poso Verde, Pima

Gu Vo Wash	(T16S/R2W) See Gu Vo, Pima
Gypsum Reefs	See Gypsum Ledges, Mohave (Lake Mead)
Hacienda de Santa Rita	See Salero Hill, Santa Cruz
Hackatal Canyon	See Hakatai Canyon, Coconino
Hackleberry Spring	See Hackberry Spring, Graham
Hacquahalia Water	See Harquahala Mountains, La Paz
Hacquehila Mountains	See Harquahala Mountains, La Paz
Hah-Quah-Sa-Éel	See Gila River
Hah Weal	See Colorado River
Hakatai Rapids	See Hakatai Canyon, Coconino (Grand Canyon)
Ha Kitchi Kavo'o	See Aha Kitcha Kukavo, Mohave
Hak-Sag-Walliwa	See Ash Creek, Mohave
Halchiitah	See Painted Desert, Apache/Navajo
Half-Way House	See Dobbs Station, Pima, or Bower's Ranch, Yavapai
Hali Murk Wash	See Hali Murk, Pima
Hall of Montezuma	See Casa Grande National Monument, Pinal
Halloysite	See Chambers, Apache
Hamblin Bridge	See Navajo Bridge, Coconino, and Hamblin Creek, Coconino
Hamblin Ridge	(T33N/R9E) See Hamblin Creek, Coconino
Hance Canyon	See Hance Creek, Coconino (Grand Canyon)
Hance Rapids	(T31N/R4E) See Hance Creek, Coconino (Grand Canyon)
Hance Tank	See Hance Creek, Coconino (Grand Canyon and Grand Canyon (Village), Coconino (Grand Canyon)
Hance Trail	See Hance Creek, Coconino (Grand Canyon)
Hanecras Plain	See Ranegras Plain, La Paz
Hanegas Plain	See Ranegras Plain, La Paz
Hanegra Plain	See Ranegras Plain, La Paz
Hannagan Creek	See Hannegan Meadow, Greenlee
Hannigan Creek	See Hannegan Meadow, Greenlee
Hano	See Tewa, Navajo
Hansen	See Easter, Maricopa
Happy Hollow	See Peach Orchard, Pinal
Happy Valley	See Happy Valley Saddle, Pima, or Misery, Fort, Yavapai
Harcuvar Peak	(T7N/R13W; Elev. 4618'; La Paz/Maricopa) See Harcuvar Mountains, La Paz, and Harcuvar, La Paz
Harcuvar Water	See Harcuvar, La Paz
Harcouver District	See Harcuvar, La Paz, and Harcuvar Mountains, La Paz/Maricopa
Hardemui	See Hali Murk, Pima
Hardin Ferry	See Hoover Dam, Mohave
Hardshell Gulch	See Hardshell, Santa Cruz
Hardy	See Havre, Navajo
Hardys Landing	See Hardyville, Mohave
Hár-Hel-To-Per-E-Pár	See Carlos, San, Gila
Harlemuheta	See Hali Murk, Pima
Harosoma Mountains	(T2N/R7E) See Goldfield Mountains, Maricopa
Harosoma Ridge	See Goldfield Mountains, Maricopa
Harper Slough	See Harper, Mohave
Harquahala Peak	(T6N/R10W; Elev. 5720') See Harquahala Mountains, La Paz/Maricopa
Harquahala Plains	(T3N/R10W) See Harquahala Mountains, La Paz/Maricopa
Har-Qua-Halle	See Harquahala Mountains, La Paz/Maricopa
Harquar Mountains	See Harcuvar Mountains, La Paz/Maricopa
Harrahs Peak	See Boneyback Peak, Gila
Harrington	See Oro, Yavapai
Harrisburg Valley	See Harrisburg, La Paz

Harris Lake	See Harris Cave, Apache
Harrisville	See Willow Beach, Mohave (Lake Mead)
Ha'rsanykuk	See Pima Village, Pinal/Maricopa
Harshaw Creek	See Harshaw, Santa Cruz
Hart Butte	See Quartzite Butte, Santa Cruz
Hart Spring	See Hart Prairie, Coconino
Hasbidito Creek, Spring	See Hasbidito, Apache
Hasiamp River	See Hassayampa River
Hasket Spring	See Haskell Spring, Yavapai
Hassamp River	See Hassayampa River, Yavapai/Maricopa
Hassayampa Lake	See Hassayampa River, Yavapai/Maricopa
Hassayampa Plain	(T5N/R6W) See Hassayampa, Maricopa, and Hassayampa River, Yavapai/Maricopa
Hassayampa Sink, Wash	See Hassayampa River, Yavapai/Maricopa
Has-Te-Le Bridge	See Navajo Bridge, Coconino
Hastings	See Superior, Pinal
Hatalacva	See Peck Mine, Yavapai
Haunted Canyon	See Phantom Canyon, Coconino (Grand Canyon)
Havasu City, Lake	(Mohave T13N/R20W; Elev. 484') See Havasu, Lake, Mohave/La Paz
Havasu Creek, Falls	See Havasu Canyon, Coconino (Grand Canyon)
Havasupai Canyon, Creek	See Havasu Canyon, Coconino (Grand Canyon)
Havasupai Wash	(T14N/R20W; Mohave) See Havasupai Indian Reservation, Coconino/Mohave
Hawilhamook	See Harquahala Mountains, La Paz/Maricopa
Hawk Peak Spring	See Hawk Peak, Graham
Hawk Springs	See Quartzsite, La Paz
Hayes and Tanner Canyon	See Garden Canyon, Cochise
Hay Mountain	(T20S/R24E; Elev. 5306'; Cochise) See Hay Lake, Coconino
Haynes Well	See Gunsight, Pima
Heads at Seven Mile Hill	See Seven Mile Hill, Navajo
Healy Terrace	See Gila Pueblo, Gila
Heavyweight Hill, Mine	(Santa Cruz) See Helvetia, Pima
Heffner Canyon	See Bladder Canyon, Gila
Hela (River)	See Gila River
Helah (River)	See Gila River
Helay (River)	See Gila River
Helena Canyon	See Querino Canyon, Apache
Helen's Doom	See Helen's Dome, Cochise
Hell Canyon	See Lawton Canyon, Maricopa
Helling's Mill	See Phoenix, Maricopa
Hell's Gate Ridge, Trail	See Hell's Gate, Gila
Hells Hole Peak	See Hell Holes, Graham
Hell's Hollow	See Red Rock Country, Coconino
Helmet Mountain	See Benedict, Mount, Santa Cruz
Helvetia Mine	(T21S/R14E; Santa Cruz) See Helvetia, Pima
Helvetia Spring, Wash	See Helvetia, Pima
Hemphell's Spring	See Peach Spring, Mohave
Hemphill Campground Springs	See Peach Springs, Mohave
Hemphill's Spring	See Peach Springs, Mohave
Hemple Spring	See Peach Springs, Mohave
Hencoop Hotel	See Stone Ferry, Mohave
Hercules Hill	See Chuar Butte, Coconino (Grand Canyon)
Hermho	See Hormiguero, Pinal
Hermit Camp, Creek, Falls, Rim	See Hermit Basin, Coconino (Grand Canyon)
Hermit's Rest	See Hermit Basin, Coconino (Grand Canyon)
Hermo	See Hormiguero, Pinal

Hermosa Hill	See Harshaw, Santa Cruz
Hermoso Canyon	See Harshaw, Santa Cruz
Hesiampa	See Hassayampa River, Maricopa
Hess Canyon, Flat	See Hess Creek, Gila
Heuthawali, Mount	See Bass Camp, Coconino (Grand Canyon)
Heward	See Zeniff, Navajo
Hewitt Ridge, Station	See Hewitt Canyon, Pinal
Hi'atam	See Pima Villages, Pinal/Maricopa
Hiawatha	See Minnehaha, Yavapai
Hickiwan Peak	See Hickiwan, Pima
Hickiwan Valley	(T12S/R2W) See Hickiwan, Pima
Hickiwan Wash	(T11S/R3W; Pima/Maricopa) See Hickiwan, Pima
Hickory Mountain	See Hickey Mountain, Yavapai
Hide Creek Mountain	(Elev. 7272') See Hide Creek, Yavapai
Hi Fuller Spring	See Hi Fuller Canyon, Coconino
High Ball Water	See Highball Spring, Yavapai
High Creek	See Oak Creek, Graham
High Mountains	See Trumbull, Mount, Mohave
High Tanks	See Tinejas Altas, Yuma
High View Point	See Hi View Point, Coconino
Hikibo	See Hickiwan, Pima
Hikibon	See Hickiwan, Pima
Hikivo Perigua	See Hickiwan, Pima
Hikuwan	See Hickiwan, Pima
Hila, Rio de	See Gila River
Hill Creek	See Mineral Creek, Pinal/Gila
Hillside Rocks	(T15N/R9W) See Hillside, Yavapai
Hilltop	See Hillcamp, Gila
Hinson	See Avra, Pima
Hitt Spring	See Holloway Spring, Coconino
Hlohale	See Lohali Point, Apache
Hoc-Qua-Hala Springs	See Harquahala Mountains, La Paz/Maricopa
Hoganville	See Quartzsite, La Paz
Hogtown	See Glenbar, Graham
Ho-Ho-Qom (sic)	See Casa Blanca, Pinal
Hokum	See Holcomb, Navajo, and Phoenix Park Canyon, Navajo
Holladay Hot Springs	See Indian Hot Springs, Graham
Holmes Creek	(T9N/R4E) See Holmes Canyon, Yavapai
Holy Joe Canyon, Springs, Wash	See Holy Joe Peak, Pinal
Holy Joe Pasture	(Elev. 4802') See Holy Joe Peak, Pinal
Hömkwïtävävä	See Gila River
Hooper Saddle	See Hooper, Yavapai
Hop Canyon	(T9N/R20E) See Hop Mountain, Navajo
Hope, Mount	See Fort Rock, Yavapai
Hopi Mesas	See Hopi Villages, Navajo, and Black Mesa, Navajo
Hopi Wall	(T31N/R2E) See Hopi Point, Coconino (Grand Canyon)
Horner Gulch	See Homer Mountain, Yavapai
Horse Camp Canyon	(T6N/R15E) See Horse Camp, Gila
Horse Camp Creek, Seep	See Horse Camp, Gila
Horse Canyon	(T7N/R15E) See Horse Camp, Gila
Horse Creek	See Horse Mesa, Maricopa
Horsehead Crossing	See Holbrook, Navajo
Horse Mountain	See Horse Camp, Gila
Horse Mountain	See Morena Mountain, Pima
Horsethief Canyon, Lake	See Horsethief Basin, Yavapai
Horsethief Train	See Tanner Trail, Coconino (Grand Canyon)
Horton Canyon	(T11N/R10E) See Horton Creek, Gila
Horton Spring	See Horton Creek, Gila

Hospital Lagoons	See Maricopa Wells, Maricopa
Hospitito Spring	See Hasbidito (Creek), Apache
Hota Shonevo	See Hotason Vo, Pima
Hotauta Amphitheater	See Hotouta Amphiteater, Coconino (Grand Canyon)
Hotel Point	See Havasupai Point, Coconino (Grand Canyon)
Hotouta Canyon	See Hotouta Amphiteater, Coconino (Grand Canyon)
Hot Springs	See Tanque Verde Hot Springs, Pima
Hot Springs	(T7N/R1W) See Castle Hot Springs, Yavapai
Hot Springs Canyon, Creek	See Hooker's Hot Springs, Cochise
Hot Springs Junction	See Morristown, Maricopa
Houck's Tank	See Houck, Apache
Houden Mountain	See Houdon Mountain, Gila
House of Civano	See Casa Grande, Pinal
House of Many Hands	See House of Hands, Navajo
House Rock Canyon, Spring, Wash	See House Rock, Coconino
Houston Creek	(T11N/R6E; Yavapai/Gila) See Houston Mesa, Gila
Houston Pocket	(T10N/R11E) See Houston Mesa, Gila
Howard Hill	(T28N/R1E) See Howard Lake, Coconino
Howard Mesa	See Howard Lake, Coconino
Howard Mountain	(T19N/R7E) See Howard Lake, Coconino
Howard Peak	(Elev. 7531') See Howard Canyon, Cochise
Howard Point	See Green Howard Tank, Coconino
Howard Spring	See Howard Lake, Coconino
Howell's Ranch	See Tonto, Gila
Hoyape	See Giants Chair, Navajo
Hóyéé	See Steamboat, Apache
Huababi	See Guevabi, Santa Cruz
Huacava Mountains	See Harcuvar Mountains, La Paz/Maricopa
Huacavah	See Harcuvar Mountains, La Paz/Maricopa
Huachuca, Camp	See Huachua, Fort, Cochise
Huachuca Forest Reserve	(Cochise) See Coronado National Forest, Pima
Huachuca Mountains	See Huachuca, Fort, Cochise
Huachuca Peak	(T23S/R19E; Elev. 8406') See Huachuca, Fort, Cochise
Hualapai, Camp	See Hualpai, Camp, Yavapai
Hualpee	See Walpi, Navajo
Huatchua Mountain	See Huachuca, Fort, Cochise
Hubbell Hill	See Hubbell Butte, Coconino (Grand Canyon)
Hubbell Plateau	See Defiance Plateau, Apache
Hubbell Trading Post National Historic Site	(T27N/R26E; Elev. 6500'; Apache) See Hubbell Butte, Coconino (Grand Canyon)
Huebaji Mission	See Guevavi, Santa Cruz
Hue-Ga-Da-Wi-Za	(T28N/R3A) See Red Butte, Coconino
Hue-Ga-Woo-La	See Bill Williams Mountain, Coconino
Hue-Han-A-Patch-A	See Francisco Peaks, San, Coconino
Hull Mountain, Spring	See Hull Prairie, Coconino
Hull Tank, Wash	See Hull Prairie, Coconino
Humboldt Mountain	(T7N/R5E; Elev. 5239') See Beauford, Mount, Maricopa
Humbug	(T8N/R1W) See Columbia, Yavapai
Humphrey Mountain	See Core Ridge, Coconino
Hundred-And-Forty-Mile Canyon	See Hundred-and-Fifty-Mile Canyon, Mohave (Grand Canyon)
Hundred-And-Thirty-Five-Mile Rapids	See Hundred-and-Fifty-Mile Canyon, Mohave (Grand Canyon)
Hungo Pavie, Po De	See Shungopavi, Navajo
Hurey Canyon	See Hoovey Canyon, Cochise
Hurricane Cliffs, Hill	See Hurricane Ledge, Mohave
Hu'tcilttcik	(Pinal) See Pima Villages, Pinal/Maricopa

Hutton, Mount	(Gila) See Hutton Butte, Coconino
Hutton Peak	(T1S/R13E; Elev. 5615'; Gila) See Hutton Butte, Coconino
Huvey Canyon	See Hoovey Canyon, Cochise
Hyder Valley	(T5S/R11W; Yuma/Maricopa) See Hyder, Yuma
Hyla, Rio Grande de	See Gila River
Iara, Rio de La	See Dead River Wash, Apache
Iceberg Ridge	See Iceberg Canyon, Mohave
Ignacio de La Canoa, San	See Canoa, Pima
Ignacio del Babocomari, San	See Babocomari, San, Cochise
Ignacio Guibori, San	See Quiburi Ruins, Cochise
Ignacio, San	See Tubac, Santa Cruz
Ildefonso, Sierra de San	See Mohave Mountains, Mohave
Imperial Reservoir	See Imperial Dam, Yuma
In-Dil-Chin-Ar	See Prescott, Yavapai
Infantry Camp	See Pinal, Camp, Pinal
Inner Basin	See Humphreys Peak, Coconino
Innupin Picabu	See Witch Water Pocket, Mohave
Interior Valley	See Hart Prairie, Coconino, and Humphreys Peak, Coconino
Irene Gulch	See Irene Spring, Gila
Irion's Ranch	See Pinal Ranch, Pinal, and Iron Mountain, Pinal
Iron Butte	See Orange Butte, Cochise
Iron Canyon, Spring	(T1N/R13E) See Iron Mountain, Pinal
Iron Pipe	See Vainomkux, Pima
Iron Pipe Village	See Kui Tatk, Pima
Iron Spring	See Indian Hot Springs, Graham
Iron Springs Wash	See Iron Springs, Yavapai
Isaacson	See Nogales, Santa Cruz
Isis Point	See Isis Temple, Coconino (Grand Canyon)
Island Lake	See Arrastra Lake, Yuma
Ivanpah Spring	See Ivanpatch (Spring), Mohave
Ives Mountain	See Bill Williams Mountain, Coconino
Jabalina Canyon	See Wild Hog Canyon, Santa Cruz
Jabesua de San Antonio, Rio	See Havasu Canyon, Coconino (Grand Canyon)
Jack Rabbit Wash	(T2N/R5W) See Jack Rabbit, Pinal
Jackrabbit Well	See Jack Rabbit, Pinal, and Tat Momoli, Pinal
Jack's Gulch	See Jack's Canyon, Yavapai
Jack Smith Tank	(T23N/R8E) See Jack Smith Spring, Coconino
Jackson Butte	See Jackson Mountains, Graham
Jackson Wash	See Jackman Wash, Mohave
Jacks Springs	See Jacks Mountain, Gila
Jacks Tank	See Lockett Tank, Coconino
Jacks Trail	See Jack's Canyon, Yavapai
Jacob Canyon	See Jacob Lake, Coconino
Jacob Lake Camp	See Jacob Lake, Coconino
Jacques Lake	See Show Low Lake, Navajo
Jadito Valley	See Jadito Wash, Navajo
Jaeger's Ferry	See Yuma, Yuma
Jaegerville	See Yuma, Yuma
Jagway Valley	(T34N/R11W) See Agway Valley, Mohave
James Kennedy Lake	See Antelope Lake, Coconino
Janus Spring	(T29N/R9E) See Janus Crater, Coconino
Jaquesila de San Pedro, Rio	See Little Colorado River
Jaquesila, Rio	See Gila River
Jaquin Village	See Chagit Vo, Pima
Jaralito, Cerro de	See Fraguita Peak, Santa Cruz

Jara Spring	See Tanner Spring, Apache
Jaramillo, Rio	See Little Colorado River, Coconino, and Zuñi River, Apache
Jarilla Mine	See Alum, Santa Cruz
Jarosoma	See Goldfield Mountains, Maricopa
Jarvis Pass	See Chavez Pass, Coconino
Java	See Thompson Valley, Yuma
Javill	See Colorado River
Jaycox Tank	(T17N/R10E) See Jaycox Mountain, Coconino
J D Dam Wash	See J D Dam Lake, Coconino
Jeddito Spring	See Jeddito Mesa, Navajo, and Jadito Spring, Navajo
Jeddito Valley, Wash	See Jadito Spring, Jadito Wash, and Jeddito, Navajo
Je Ho-To Spring	See Jadito Spring, Navajo, and Jeddito, Navajo
Jeowic	See Chiawuli Tak, Pima
Jerky Butte	(T8S/R13E; Elev. 4537'; Pinal) See Jerked Beef Butte, Gila
Jerome Canyon	(T15N/R3W) See Jerome Junction, Yavapai
Jerusalem Canyon, Peak	See Jerusalem Mountain, Pinal
Jettco-To Spring	See Jadito Spring, Navajo
Jewell Park	See Buell Park, Apache
Jewett Mountain	See Century Peak, Santa Cruz
Jiaspi	See Prospect, Cochise
Jila, Rio	See Gila River
Jiquibo	See Hickiwan, Pima
J K Spring	See J K Mountain, Gila
Jok-Ha-We-Ha	See Bill Williams Mountain, Coconino
Joe Canyon, Saint	(T12N/R15E) See Joe's Spring, Saint, Coconino
Joe Ridge, Saint	See Joe's Spring, Saint, Coconino
Johannesberg	See Hope, Yuma
John Hands Dam, Lake	See Fred Winn Falls, Cochise, and Hands Pass, Cochise
John Howells Pass	See Sitgreaves Pass, Mohave
Johns, Saint	(T1S/R2E) See Komatke, Maricopa
Johnson Peak	(Elev. 6644') See Johnson, Cochise
Johnsonville	See Johnson, Cochise, or Nephi, Maricopa
Jones Ferry	See Hoover Dam, Mohave
Jonesville	See Lehi, Maricopa
Jongopabi	See Shungopavi, Navajo
Joppa	See Aripine, Navajo
Jordan Ranch	See Clarkdale, Yavapai
Jornada de Las Estrellas	(Pinal/Maricopa) See Estrella Mountains, Pinal
Jose de Tucson, San	See Tucson, Pima, and Jose del Tucson, San, Pima
Jose de Tumacacori, San	See Tumacacori National Monument, Santa Cruz
Jose Pedro River	See Pedro River, San, Cochise
Joseph de Cumars, Sierra de San	See Estrella Mountains, Maricopa
Josephine Creek	See Crittenden, Fort, Santa Cruz, and Josephine Peak, Santa Cruz
Joseph, Saint	See Joseph City, Navajo
Joseph Wash, St.	See Joseph City Wash, Navajo
Jose, Sierra de San	See Mule Mountains, Cochise
Josh Spring	See Josh, Mount, Yavapai
Josquin Village	See Chagit Vo, Pima
Joy's Camp	See Morenci, Greenlee
Juan Capistrano, San	See Sacaton, Pinal
Juan Quiburi, San	See Quiburi Ruins, San, Cochise
Juan, San	See Johns, Saint, Apache
Juan Wash, San	(T18S/R10E) See Juan Spring, San, Pima
Judge Otey's Tombstone	See Capitol Butte, Yavapai
Judith Point	See Grama Point, Coconino (Grand Canyon)
July 4 Butte	See Fourth of July Butte, Maricopa

Junction	See Jerome Junction, Yavapai, and Chino Valley, Yavapai
June Spring	See Willow Spring, Mohave
Juniper	See Linden, Navajo, or Hualpai, Camp (Old), Yavapai
Juniper Canyon	See Juniper Mountain, Gila
Juniper Flat	(T7N/R14E; Elev. 6112') See Juniper Canyon, Gila, and Juniper Mountain, Gila
Juniper Gulch	(T10N/R1E; Yavapai) See Charcoal Gulch, Yavapai, and Charcoal Canyon, Mohave
Juno Temple	See Juno Point, Coconino (Grand Canyon)
Jupiter Point, Temple	See Tiyo Point, Coconino (Grand Canyon)
Juquibo	See Hickiwan, Pima
Kaawlic	See Cowlic, Pima
Kabito Plateau, Spring	See Kaibito Plateau, Coconino
Kaibab, Kaibab Forest	See North Rim, Coconino (Grand Canyon)
Kaibabito	See Kaibab Plateau, Coconino (Grand Canyon)
Kaibab Mountains	See Kaibab Plateau, Coconino (Grand Canyon)
Kaibab National Forest	See Kaibab Plateau, Coconino (Grand Canyon), and Coconino National Forest, Coconino
Kaibab Trail Suspension Bridge	See Phantom Ranch, Coconino (Grand Canyon)
Kaibito Creek	See Kaibito, Coconino
Kaibito Spring	See Kaibito Plateau, Coconino, and Kaibito, Coconino
Kaipeto Plateau	See Kaibito Plateau, Coconino
Kaka Valley	(T10S/R1W; Maricopa, Pima) See Kaka, Maricopa
Kaka Wash	See Kaka, Maricopa
Kalven	See Kelvin, Pinal
Kâmatùk	See Estrella Mountains, Maricopa
Kâmatukwúcha	See Komatke, Pinal, and Pima Villages, Pinal/Maricopa
Kâmatuk Wútcâ Ka'matùk	See Pima Villages, Pinal/Maricopa
Kami't	See Pima Villages, Pinal/Maricopa
Kana-a Creek, Wash	See Kana-a Valley, Coconino
Kanab Creek	(T36N/R3W; Coconino/Mohave) See Kanab Canyon, Coconino (Grand Canyon)
Kanab Desert, Mountains	See Kanab Canyon, Coconino (Grand Canyon)
Kanab Point, Rapids, Spring	(T35N/R3W; Elev. 5735'; Mohave [Grand Canyon]) See Kanab Canyon, Coconino (Grand Canyon)
Kanelba Spring	See Sheep Spring, Navajo
Kane Spring Canyon	See Kane Springs, Pinal
Kane Spring Mountain	(T10S/R25E; Elev. 6908'; Graham) See Kane Springs, Pinal
Karrigan Peak	See Clara Peak, Yuma
Katherine Beach, Boat Landing, Wash	See Katherine, Mohave
Kavaviak	See Ko Vaya, Pima
Kavolik	See Cowlic, Pima
Kavvaxlak	See Ko Vaya, Pima
Kawaika Spring	See Kawaika-a, Navajo
Kawaiokee	See Kawaika-a, Navajo
Kawaioku	See Kawaika-a, Navajo
Ka'woltuk Wutca	See Pima Villages, Pinal/Maricopa
Kayler Spring	See Kayler Butte, Gila
Ke-En-Ta Creek	See Laguna Creek, Apache/Navajo
Ke-En-Ta Mesa	See Laguna Creek, Apache/Navajo, and Tyenda Mesa, Navajo
Keet Seel Canyon	(T38N/R17E) See Keet Seel Ruins, Navajo
Keet Seel Spring	See Keet Seel Ruins, Navajo
Kelly Canyon	(T20N/R7E) See Yaeger, Coconino
Kendrick Park	(T24N/R6E) See Kendrick Peak, Coconino

Kendrick, Mount	(T23N/R23E; Elev. 10,418') See Kendrick Peak, Coconino
Kendrick Spring	(T24N/R5E) See Kendrick Peak, Coconino
Kennard	See Curtiss, Cochise
Kennedy's Well	(T8S/R21E) See Kennedy Peak, Graham
Kentucky Mountain	See Kentuck Mountain, Maricopa
Kerrigan Peak	See Clara Peak, La Paz
Kerwo	See Gu Vo, Pima
Keystone	See Keystone Mine, Mohave
Kia Hoa Toak	See Quijotoa, Pima
Kia-Kocho-Movi	See Oraibi, Navajo
Kiburi	See Quiburi, Cochise
Kidd Canyon	See Kidde Canyon, Gila/Graham
Kielberg Creek	(T10S/R18E) See Kielberg Canyon, Graham
Kielberg Peak	(T10S/R19E; Elev. 6880') See Kielberg Canyon, Graham
Kiet Siel	See Keet Seel Ruins, Navajo
Kietzeel	See Keet Seel Ruins, Navajo
Kihàtoak	See Quijotoa, Pima
Kiits'iili	See Keet Seel Ruins, Navajo
Kilberg Canyon, Creek, Peak	See Kielberg Canyon, Graham/Pima
Kimball	(T6S/R25E; Elev. 2865') See Hubbard, Graham
Kimball Peak	See Kimball, Mount, Pima
Kinder Crossing	(T14N/R11E; Elev. 6779') See Kinder Spring, Coconino
Kinder Draw	See Kinder Spring, Coconino
King Canyon, Creek	See King Gulch, Greenlee
King of Arizona Mine	See Kofa, Yuma
King Peak	(T14N/R9W; Elev. 4100') See King Canyon, Yavapai
King Solomon's Temple	See Crystal Cave, Cochise, and Cave Creek, Cochise
King Spring	(T18N/R1E) See King Canyon, Yavapai
Kinigai Boko	See Diablo, Canyon, Coconino
Kin láń	See Flagstaff, Coconino, and Betatakin, Navajo
Kinnickinick Canyon	(T17N/R10E) See Kinnikinic Lake, Coconino
Kinnikinic Lake Wild Life Area	See Kinnikinic Lake, Coconino
Kinnikinic Spring	(T18N/R11E) See Kinnikinic Lake, Coconino
Kin Teel	See Wide Ruins, Apache
Kin Tiel	See Wide Ruins, Apache
Kintyel	See Wide Ruins, Apache
Kinyon Station	See Kenyon Station, Maricopa
Ki-Ote-Te Wash	See Oraibi, Navajo, and Coyote Wash, Navajo
Kiquchmove	See Oraibi, Navajo
Kirkland Creek	(T13N/R6W) See Kirkland, Yavapai
Kirkland Junction	(T12N/R4W; Elev. 4100') See Kirkland, Yavapai
Kirkland Valley	See Kirkland, Yavapai
Kirtak	See Kuy Tatk, Pima, and Vainomkux, Pima
Kisak-Ovi	See Walpi, Navajo
Kit Siel	See Keet Seel Ruins, Navajo
Kits-Il	See Keet Seel Ruins, Navajo
Kit Sil	See Keet Seel Ruins, Navajo
Kit Sil Wash	(T40N/R27E) See Keet Seel, Navajo
Kit's Peak	See Kitt Peak, Pima
Klagetoh Wash	See Klagetoh, Apache
Klara Peak	See Clara Peak, La Paz
Klondike	See Klondyke, Graham
Klondyke Butte	(T3N/R14E; Elev. 3040'; Gila) See Klondyke, Graham
Klondyke Mountain	(T3N/R14E; Elev. 3954'; Gila) See Klondyke, Graham
Klondyke Wash	See Klondyke, Graham
Klotho Peak	See Coronation Peak, Yuma
Knoll Lake Wild Life Area	See Knoll Lake, Coconino

Knoll Ridge	See Knoll Lake, Coconino
Kodizis'	See Wheatfields Creek, Apache
Kofa Butte	(T2S/R16W) See Kofa, Yuma
Kofa National Wild Life Refuge	(T1S/R17W) See Kofa, Yuma, and Kofa Game Range, Yuma
Kofa Plain	See King Valley, Yuma
Kofa Queen Canyon	(La Paz, T1N/R18W) See Kofa Queen Mine, Yuma, and Kofa, Yuma
Kofa Valley	See King Valley, Yuma, and Kofa, Yuma
Kohatk Valley	(T10S/R2; Pinal/Pima) See Kohatk, Pinal
Kohatk Wash	See Kohatk, Pinal
Kokopki	See Kokopnyma, Navajo
Koksumok	See Topawa, Pima
Kokuli	See Hickiwan, Pima
Kolb Arch	See Kolb Natural Bridge, Coconino (Grand Canyon)
Kolipatvawka	See Gurli Put Vo, Pima
Kol-Pat-Vooka	See Gurli Put Vo, Pima
Komaktjivurt	See Horseshoe, Pima, and Quijotoa, Pima
Komalik	(Pinal) See the following: North Komelik, Pima; South Komelik, Pima; Gu Komelik, Pima
Komelih	(Pinal) See Gu Komelik, Pima; North Komelik, Pima; and South Komelik, Pima
Komelik Mountain	(T11S/R4E; Elev. 1863') See Gu Komelik, Pima
Komelik Pass	(T11S/R5E) See Gu Komelik, Pima
Komertkewotche	See Estrella Mountains, Pinal
Komoktetuvávosit	See Artesa, Pima
Komo Vaya	See Stoa Vaya, Pima
Komuó	See Kom Vo, Pima
Kom Vo Valley	(T17S/R1W-1E) See Kom Vo, Pima
Kookatsh	See Kuakatch, Pima
Ko'-Okůp Van'sĭk	See Pima Villages, Pinal/Maricopa
Ko-Opke	See Shopishk, Pima
Ko Vaya Hills	See Ko Vaya, Pima
Ko Vaya Wash	(T15S/R4E) See Ko Vaya, Pima
Kowlick	See Cowlic, Pima
Koxikug	See Chiuli Shaik, Pima
Koxikux	See Chiuli Shaik, Pima
Kthil Kisov Gova	See Ash Fork Ridges, Coconino, and Ash Fork, Yavapai
Kuakatch Pass	(T15S/R5W) See Kuakatch, Pima
Kuakatch Wash	(T14S/R5W) See Kuakatch, Pima
Kuarchi	See Gu Archi, Pima
Kuat-Shi	See Gu Achi, Pima
Kuchaptuvela	See Walpi, Navajo
Kuck Son	See Tucson, Pima
Kuichituak	See Mesquite Charcos, Pima
Kuitak	See Vainomkux, Pima
Kuit Vaya	See Kohi Kug, Pima
Kukomalik	(Pinal) See Gu Komelik, Pima, and North Komelik, Pima
Kumelih	See Gu Komelik, Pima
Kumkachutz	See Sells, Pima
Kum Vo	See Kom Vo, Pima
Kuoltak	See Gu Oidak, Pima
Ku'-U Ki	(Pinal) See Pima Villages, Pinal/Maricopa
Kuvaipa	See Quitovaquita, Pima
Kuvo	See Gu Vo, Pima
Kvitatk	See Kui Tatk, Pima, and Vainomkux, Pima
Kwagunt Butte	See Kwagunt Canyon (Coconino [Grand Canyon])
Kwagunt Creek	See Kwagunt Canyon, Coconino (Grand Canyon)

Kwagunt Hollow	(T36N/R1W) See Kwagunt Canyon, Coconino (Grand Canyon)
Kwagunt Rapids	(T33N/R5E) See Kwagunt Canyon, Coconino (Grand Canyon)
Kymo	See Wood, Camp, Yavapai
Kyrene	(T1S/R4E; Elev. 1190') See West Chandler, Maricopa
La Barge Creek	See La Barge Canyon, Maricopa
La Barge Mountain	(T1N/R11E; Elev. 5077'; Pinal) See La Barge Canyon, Maricopa/Pinal
La Barge Spring	See La Barge Canyon, Maricopa/Pinal
Lady Bug Saddle	See Ladybug Peak, Graham
Laguna Canyon	See Tsegi Canyon, Navajo
Laguna Dam	See Laguna, La, Yuma
Laguna de La Esperanza, La	See Ajo, Pima
Laguna Negra	See Bonito Creek, Apache
Laguna Reservoir	See Laguna, La, Yuma
Lagunas del Hospital, Las	See Maricopa Wells, Pinal, and Cruz Cienega, Santa, Pinal
Lagune	See Laguna, La, Yuma
Lake Cochise	See Willcox, Cochise
Lake Havasu City	See Havasu, Lake, Mohave
Lake Mary	See Mary, Lake, Coconino, and Clark Valley, Coconino
Lake Mary Spring	See Mary, Lake, Coconino
Lake Mary Valley	See Lower Lake Mary, Coconino
Lake Mead Recreational Area	See Mead, Lake, Mohave
Lake Mohave Resort	See Katherine, Mohave
Lake No. 4	(T12N/R11E) See Lake No. 1, Coconino
Lake No. 2	See Carr Lake, Coconino
Lake Pleasant	See Carl Pleasant Dam, Maricopa
Lake's Camp	See Obed, Navajo
Lakes of Short Creek	(T41N/R6W) See Colorado City, Mohave
Lakeview	See Mormon Lake, Coconino
Lambing Lake	See Vail Lake, Coconino
Lana Negra	See Agathla Needle, Navajo
Lane Spring	See Lane Mountain, Yavapai
Langhorne	See Rillito, Pima
La Paz	See Paz, La, La Paz
Lawler	See Hillside, Yavapai, and Lawler Peak, Yavapai
Lechuguilla Mountains	(T13S/R17W) See Lechuguilla Desert, Yuma
Lechuguilla, Sierra de La	See Lechuguilla Desert, Yuma
Lee Butte	(T17N/R8E) See Lee Canyon, Coconino
Lee Mountain	(T17N/R8E) See Lee's Ferry, Coconino
Lee Mountain	(T4S/R16E; Elev. 3786'; Pinal) See Lee, Mount, Pima
Lee Park	See Bert Lee Park, Coconino
Lee Ranch	See American Ranch, Yavapai
Lee's Backbone	See Mormon Ridge, Coconino
Lee's Ferry Bridge	See Lee's Ferry, Coconino, and Navajo Bridge, Coconino
Lee's Mesa	See Twenty-two Mesa, Yavapai
Lee Spring	(T17N/R8E) See Lee's Ferry, Coconino
Lee Valley	See Greer, Apache
Lefevre Ridge	See Lefevre Canyon, Coconino
Leland Wash	See Leland Butte, Mohave
Lemmon Canyon	(T12S/R15E) See Lemmon, Mount, Pima
Lenora	See Lochiel, Santa Cruz
Leonard Camp, West	See Leonard Canyon, Coconino
Leonard Creek, Crossing, Point	See Leonard Canyon, Coconino
Le Reax Spring	See Leroux Springs, Coconino

Le Rous Spring	See Leroux Springs, Coconino
Le Roux Crossing	See Leroux Springs, Coconino
Le Roux Prairie	See Valley, Fort, Coconino, and Leroux Springs, Coconino
Le Roux's Fork	See Leroux Springs, Coconino
Leroux Valley	See Le Roux Springs, Coconino
Leroux Wash	(T18N/R20E; Navajo) See Le Roux Springs, Coconino
Lerty's Ranch	See Lurty's Ranch, Yavapai
Leslie Canyon	See Leslie Creek, Cochise
Lesna Mountains, La	See Lesna Peak, La, Pima
Leupp Corner	(T19N/R14E) See Leupp, Coconino
Lewis Mountain	See Kit Carson Mountain, Maricopa
Lewiston	See Bowie, Cochise
Lexington	See Oatman, Mohave
Libble Spring	See Little Spring, Coconino
Lichton	See Litchfield Park, Maricopa
Lida Creek	See Lyda Creek, Greenlee
Lightfield	See Light, Cochise
Lime Kiln Canyon	See Calera Canyon, Santa Cruz
Limerick	See Cork, Graham
Lincoln Camp	See Paz, La, La Paz
Lincoln Point	See Lipan Point, Coconino (Grand Canyon)
Linden Creek	(T5S/R31E; Greenlee) See Linden, Navajo
Linden Wash	See Linden Draw, Navajo
Linderos, Cerritos de Los	See Lesna Peak, La, Pima
Line City	See Nogales, Santa Cruz
Lino, Rio de	See Little Colorado River
Litchfield	See Avondale, Maricopa, and Litchfield Park, Maricopa
Litchton	See Litchfield Park, Maricopa
Lithodendron Creek	See Lithodendron Wash, Apache/Navajo
Lithodendron Park	See Petrified Forest National Monument, Apache
Little Blue Creek	See Blue Creek, Greenlee
Little Bog Creek	See Bog Creek, Apache
Little Bonito Creek	See Bonito Creek, Apache
Little California Gulch	See Seventy-Six Gulch, Cochise
Little Carrizo Wash	See Little Lithodendron Wash, Navajo, and Little Lithodendron Wash, Apache
Little Clayhole Valley	See Antelope Valley, Mohave
Little Colorado Plateau	See Mogollon Plateau, Coconino/Navajo
Little Colorado River Gorge	(T32N/R6E) See Little Colorado River, Coconino
Little Colorado River, East Fork	(T6N/R27E) See Little Colorado River, Apache
Little Colorado River, South Fork	(T7N/R28E) See Little Colorado River, Apache
Little Colorado River, West Fork	(T6N/R27E) See Little Colorado River, Apache
Little Colorado Station	See Lee's Ferry, Coconino
Little Doubful Canyon	See Doubtful Canyon, Cochise
Little Elden Mountain	See Elden Mountain, Coconino
Little Elden Spring	(T22N/R8E) See Elden Mountain, Coconino
Little Emigrant Canyon	See Emigrant Canyon, Cochise
Little Giant's Chair	See Giant's Chair, Navajo
Little Harquahala Mountains	(T4N/R13W; Elev. 2160') See Harquahala Mountains, La Paz
Little Hill	See Cowlic, Pima
Little Leroux Spring	See Leroux Spring, Coconino
Little L O Spring Canyon	(T20N/R4E) See L O Spring, Coconino
Little Mount Elden	See Dry Lake, Coconino
Little Mount Ord	(T7N/R9E; Elev. 6114') See Ord, Mount, Apache
Little Nankoweap	(T34N/R5E) See Nankoweap Butte, Coconino (Grand Canyon)
Little Nankoweap Creek	(T34N/R5E) See Nankoweap Butte, Coconino (Grand Canyon)

Little Oraibi	See Moenkopi, Coconino
Little Ortega Lake	(T11N/R25E) See Ortega Lake, Apache
Little L O Spring	See L O Spring, Coconino
Little Roden Wash	See Roden Crater, Coconino
Little Salt River Valley	See Catalpa, Gila
Little Shipp Mountain	(T14N/R7W; Elev. 4955') See Shipp Mountain, Yavapai
Little Shipp Wash	(T14N/R8W) See Shipp Mountain, Yavapai
Little Steve's Ranch	See Double Circle Ranch, Greenlee
Little Double Mountain	(Pinal) See Double Mountain, Coconino
Little Trough Spring	See Little Trough Creek, Gila
Little Tucson	See Ali Chukson, Pima
Little Turkey Creek Spring	See Little Turkey Creek, Gila
Little Valley	(T34N/R7E) See Lower Lake Mary, Coconino
Little Wing Mountain	(T22N/R6E; Elev. 7700') See Wing Mountain, Coconino
Liveoak Gulch	See Liveoak, Gila
Live Oak Mine	See Porphyry Mine, Gila
Livingston Pass	See New Water Pass, La Paz
Llano del Azotado	See Tortolita Mountains, Pima
Lockett Lake	(T30N/R4E) See Lockett Tank, Coconino
Lockett Meadow Spring	(T23N/R7E) See Lockett Lake, Coconino
Lockhart	See Love, Yuma
Locomotive Butte, Peaks	See Locomotive Rock, Pima
L O Draw	(T23N/R1E) See Garland Prairie, Coconino, and L O Spring, Coconino
L O Flat	See Garland Prairie, Coconino, and L O Spring, Coconino
Logan City	See Logan, Pima
Logan, Mount, Peak	See Trumbull, Mount, Mohave
Logan Wash	See Logan Mine, Yavapai
Lok'an Ntiel	See Ganado, Apache
Lokasakad (Spring)	See Lokaskal (Spring), Navajo
Lokasakal (Spring)	See Lokaskal (Spring), Navajo
Lomas de Canelo, La	See Canelo Hills, Santa Cruz
Lomas Negras	See Mohawk Mountains, Yuma
Lone Mountain	See Long Mountain, Mohave
Lone Peak	See Tonopah, Maricopa
Lone Pine	See Reidhead, Navajo
Lone Pine Crossing	(T12N/R18E) See Reidhead Crossing, Navajo
Lonesome Peak	See Lone Mountain, La Paz
Lone Star Mountain	(Elev. 5440') See Lone Star, Graham
Lone Star Wash	(T6S/R26E) See Lone Star, Graham
Longfellow, Mount	See Mormon Mountain, Coconino
Longfellow Ridge Spring	See Longfellow Ridge, Yavapai
Long Valley Road	See Happy Jack, Coconino
L O Pocket	(T20N/R4E) See L O Spring, Coconino
Lorenzo, San	See Sil Nakya, Pima
L O Spring	(T17N/R6W; Yavapai) See Garland Prairie, Coconino, and L O Spring, Coconino
Lowell, Camp	See Lowell, Fort, Pima
Lower Andrus Spring	See Andrus Canyon, Mohave
Lower Basin	See Boulder Basin, Mohave (Lake Mead)
Lower Camp Verde Indian Reservation	See Camp Verde Indian Reservation, Yavapai
Lower Chevelon Creek	See Chevelon Creek, Apache
Lower Crossing	See Pedro, San, Cochise, and Ohnesorgen Stage Station, Cochise
Lower Grand Wash Cliffs, Ledge	See Grand Wash Cliffs, Mohave
Lower Kirkland Valley	(T13N/R5W) See Kirkland, Yavapai
Lower Miami	(T1N/R15E; Elev. 3349'; Gila) See Miami, Gila
Lower Moss Wash	(T20N/R20W) See Moss Hills, Mohave

Lower Peach Springs	(T26N/R11W; 3950') See Peach Springs, Mohave
Lower Ruin	See Tonto Basin, Gila
Lower San Pedro	See Pedro River, San, Cochise
Lower Verde Indian Reservation	(T14N/R5E) See Verde, Camp, Yavapai
Lowery Spring	See Lowrey Spring, Coconino
Lowlander Lake, Park	See Beasley Lake, Coconino
Loy Canyon	(T18N/R5E) See Loy Butte, Yavapai
Lucacsaca	See Lokasakad, Navajo, and Lokaskal Spring, Navajo
Luis Guevavi, San	See Guevavi, Santa Cruz
Luis Wash, San	(T21S/R9E) See San Luis Mountains, Pima
Luka Chugai	See Lukachukai Mountains, Apache
Lukachukai Creek, Wash	(T36N/R27E) See Lukachukai, Apache
Lukasakad	See Lokaskal Spring, Navajo
Lukasalid	See Lokaskal Spring, Navajo
Luna Lake	See Luna Lake Water Fowl Area, Apache
Lyda Springs	See Lyda Creek, Greenlee
Lyle Peak	(Elev. 7825') See Lyle Canyon, Cochise
Lyman Dam	See Lyman Lake, Apache
Lynx Lake	See Lynx Creek, Yavapai
Lynx Lake Wild Life Area	See Lynx Creek, Yavapai
Lysleton	See Norton, Yuma
Mac Donald Canyon	See Juniper Canyon, Gila
Machi Canyon	See Natchi Canyon, Coconino
Mackinnon Point	See Widforss Point, Coconino (Grand Canyon)
Mack Morris Mill	See Stanton, Gila
Maddox	See Castle Butte, Navajo, and Dilcon, Navajo
Madera Canyon (Town)	(T20S/R14E) See Madera Canyon, Pima/Santa Cruz
Madre, Sierra	See Rita Mountains, Santa, Santa Cruz
Mad-Ku-Dap	See Halfway Bend, La Paz
Magma Dam	(T3S/R9E) See Magma, Pinal
Magnesium Springs	See Indian Hot Springs, Graham
Mai-I-Toh	See Maito, Apache
Mailto Spring	See Maito, Apache
Main	See Parks, Coconino
Maine	See Parks, Coconino
Maish-Vaxia	See Covered Wells, Pima
Maish Vaya	See Covered Wells, Pima
Maisk	See Covered Wells, Pima
Maispvaxia	See Covered Wells, Pima
Maitoe	See Houck, Apache
Makumvooka	See Makgum Havoka, Pima
Malay Creek	(T3N/R27E; Graham/Greenlee) See Willcox, Cochise, and Maley Corral, Greenlee
Malay Gap	(T3N/R27E; Elev. 8200') See Willcox, Cochise
Maley Gap	(T3N/R27E; Elev. 8200') See Willcox, Cochise
Maley Canyon	(T14S/R27E) See Willcox, Cochise
Mama Komt	See Mesquite Mountains, Pima
Mammoth Camp, Mine	See Mammoth, Pinal
Mammoth Wash	(T10S/R6E) See Mammoth, Pinal
Mamtotk Peak	See Mamatotk, Pima
Manachaka Point	See Manakacha Point, Coconino (Grand Canyon)
Manila Wash	See Manila, Navajo
Manje's House	See Casa Grande National Monument, Pinal
Manje Springs	See Hughes Mountain, Santa Cruz
Mansfield Gulch	See Mansfield Canyon, Santa Cruz
Manuel's Well	See Sweetwater, Pima
Many Farms Lake	See Many Farms, Apache
Manzana	See Mishongnovi, Navajo

Manzana Mountains	See Manzanita Mountains, Santa Cruz
Maple Peak	(T13N/R31E) See Maple Canyon, Greenlee
Marble Canyon Bridge	See Navajo Bridge, Coconino
Marble Canyon National Monument	See Marble Canyon, Coconino
Marble Flats	See Matkatamiba Mesa, Coconino (Grand Canyon)
Marble Gorge	See Marble Canyon, Coconino
Marble Hill	See White Horse Hills, Coconino
Marble Quarry	See Marble Canyon, Cochise
Marble Viewpoint	(T35N/R3E) See Marble Canyon, Coconino
March	See Maish, Pima
Marcou Crater	(T23N/R9E; Elev. 7177') See Marcou Mesa, Coconino
Margarita Wash, Santa	(T20S/R8E) See Margarita Tank, Pima
Maria del Agua Caliente, Santa	See Agua Caliente, Maricopa
Maria Mountain, Santa	See Bill Williams Mountain, Coconino
Maria Mountains, Santa	(T17N/R6W; Yavapai) See Maria River, Santa, La Paz/ Yavapai
Maria, Sieneguilla de	See Michaels, St., Apache
Maria Valley, Santa	See Cruz Valley, Santa, Santa Cruz
Maricopa Point	See Powell Memorial Point, Coconino (Grand Canyon)
Maricopa Station	See Maricopa, Pinal, and Heaton, Pinal
Maricopaville	See Heaton, Pinal
Maricopa Junction	See Maricopa, Pinal
Maricopa Lake	(T3N/R1E) See Maricopa (Ak Chin) Indian Reservation, Pinal
Maricopa Peak	(T8S/R1W; Elev. 4084') See Maricopa (Ak Chin) Indian Reservation, Pinal
Maricopa Range	See Maricopa Mountains, Pinal
Marijilda Creek	(T8S/R16E) See Marijilda Canyon, Graham
Marijilda Ruins	See Marijilda Canyon, Graham
Marjilda Wash	(T8S/R28E) See Marijilda Canyon, Graham
Marinette	See Youngtown, Maricopa
Marion Point	See Matkatamiba Mesa, Coconino (Grand Canyon), and Marion, Yavapai
Marjorie Wash	See Twin Buttes, Pima
Maroni, Fort	See Fort Valley, Coconino
Marquetta Pass	See Marquitta Pass, La Paz
Marsh	See Maish, Pima
Marshall Flat, Mountain	See Marshall Butte, Apache
Marsh Hill	(T21N/R7E; Elev. 7246') See Lowell Observatory, Coconino
Martin Spring	See Martin Mountain, Yavapai
Martinez	(T10N/R6W) See Congress Junction, Yavapai
Martinez Creek	(T9N/R5W) See Congress Junction, Yavapai
Martinez Hill Ruin	See Martinez Hill, Pima
Martinez Mountain	See Martinez Hill, Pima
Martinez Valley	See Congress Junction, Yavapai
Martinez Well	(T4N/R21W) See Martinez Lake, La Paz
Martires, Rio de Los	See Colorado River
Martyro River	See Colorado River
Mary Lake	See Lower Lake Mary, Coconino
Mary Spring	See White Horse Hills, Coconino
Marysville, Fort	See Maryville, Maricopa
Marysville Hill	See Maryville, Coconino
Masagnebe	See Mishongnovi, Navajo
Mascot Canyon	See Mascot, Cochise
Masies Canyon	See Massai Point, Cochise
Mason, Fort	See McKee, Camp, Santa Cruz
Massacre Cave	(T6N/R28E) See Muerto, Cañon del, Apache

Massai Canyon	See Massai Point, Cochise
Massissal Mountains	See Matzatal Mountains, Maricopa
Matawidika Canyon	See Meriwitica Canyon, Mohave
Matawidita Canyon	See Meriwitica Canyon, Mohave
Mathewson Wash	See Matthews, Graham
Mathewsville Wash	See Matthews, Graham
Matkatamiba Rapids	(T34N/R4W; Coconino) See Matkatamiba Canyon, Coconino/Mohave (Grand Canyon)
Mattatiwiddati Canyon	See Meriwitica Canyon, Mohave
Matthew (River)	See Salt River, Gila/Maricopa
Matthews	See Glenbar, Graham
Matthewsville	See Glenbar, Graham
Maverick Basin	See Maverick Hill, Greenlee
Maverick Lake	(T3N/R25E) See Maverick, Apache
Mawi	See Topawa, Pima
Max	See Venezia, Yavapai
Maxey	See Venezia, Yavapai
Maxton	See Venezia, Yavapai
Maxwell Reservoir	See Maxwell Lake, Maricopa
Mayeto	See Maito, Apache
Maysville	See Maryville, Maricopa
Mayswell Peak	(Elev. 5161') See Mayswell Canyon, Mohave
Maywell Wash	See Mayswell Canyon, Mohave
Maytank Canyon	(T19N/R2E) See Maytank Pocket, Coconino
Mazabyal Range	See Mazatzal Mountains, Maricopa/Gila
Mazatzal Peak	(T8N/R9E; Elev. 7888') See Mazatzal Mountains, Gila
Mazatzal Range	See Mazatzal Mountains, Gila/Maricopa
Mazatzal Wilderness	(T8N/R7E; Yavapai/Maricopa) See Mazatzal Mountains, Gila/Maricopa
McCarty Draw, Ridge	See McCarty Canyon, Coconino
McCauley Sinks	See Black Canyon, Navajo
McCleary Canyon	See McCleary Camp, Pima
McCleary Peak	(T19S/R15E; Elev. 8320'; Pima/Santa Cruz) See McCleary Camp, Pima
McClellan Wash	See McClellan Flats, Pinal
McClintock Canyon, Draw	See McClintock Ridge, Coconino
McClintock Spring	(T13N/R11E) See McClintock Ridge, Coconino
McCollum Ranch	See McCullum Ranch, Coconino
McCracken Mountains	See McCrackin Mine, Mohave
McCracken Peak	(Elev. 3529') See McCrackin Mine, Mohave
McDonald Mountain	See McDonald, Fort, Gila
McDonald Pocket	(T9N/R11E; Elev. 5621') See McDonald, Fort, Gila
McDougal Flat	See McDougal Spring, Coconino
McDowell, Mount	(T2N/R6E; Elev. 2828') See McDowell Mountains, Maricopa
McFadden Peak	(T7N/R13E; Elev. 7135') See McFadden Horse Mountain, Gila
McIntosh Spring	See Mesquite Spring, Gila
McKay Spring	(T9N/R25E) See McKay's Peak, Apache
McKenzie Tank	(T13S/R32E) See McKenzie Peak, Cochise
McKinnon Point, Trail	See Widforss Point, Coconino (Grand Canyon)
McKittrich Creek	See McKitrick Canyon, Greenlee
McLellan	See McClellan Tanks, Coconino
McLellan Dam, Reservoir	See McClellan Tanks, Coconino
McMillan	See McMillanville, Gila
McMullen Wash	(T1N/R15E) See McMillanville, Gila
McMullen Wells	See McMullen Valley, La Paz/Maricopa
McNutt, Mount	See Nutt, Mount, Mohave
McPherson, Camp	See Date Creek, Camp, Yavapai

Mead	See McDowell, Maricopa
Meath Dam	See Meath, Yavapai
Meath Wash	(T20N/R2W; Yavapai/Coconino) See Meath, Yavapai
Medicine Fort	(T23N/R8E) See Medicine Cave, Coconino
Medicine Valley	See Medicine Cave, Coconino
Medlar Wash	See Medlar Spring, Yavapai
Melendreth Pass	See Melendrez Pass, Pima
Mellen	See Topock, Mohave
Mellon	See Topock, Mohave
Menager's Dam	(T18S/R3W; Elev. 1732') See Artesa Mountain, Pima
Meneger's Dam	(T18S/R3W; Elev. 1732') See Artesa Mountain, Pima
Mercey Mine	See Copper Queen Mine, Cochise
Mericitica Canyon	See Meriwitica Canyon, Mohave
Meridian Butte	(T40N/R22E; Elev. 6221'; Navajo) See Meridian Butte, Apache
Merijilda Canyon	See Marijilda Canyon, Graham
Meriwhitac Canyon, Spring	See Meriwitica Canyon, Mohave
Merriam Mountain	See Merriam Crater, Coconino
Merrill Creek	See Merrill Peak, Graham
Merrill Mountain	See Merrill Crater, Coconino
Merritt Draw, Spring	See Merritt Cabin, Coconino
Mesa City	See Mesa, Maricopa
Mesaville	See Mesa, Maricopa
Metate, Cerro del	See Antelope Hill, Yuma
Metate Hill	See Antelope Hill, Yuma
Metates, Pichacho de	See Sentinel Peak, Pima
Meteor	See Meteor Crater, Coconino
Meteorite Mountain	See Meteor Crater, Coconino
Meteor Mountain	See Meteor Crater, Coconino
Methodist Creek	See Methodist Canyon, Gila
Methodist Mountain	(Elev. 5050') See Methodist Canyon, Gila, and Salome Mountain, Gila
Mexican Gulch	(T10N/R2E) See Boggs Ranch, Yavapai
Mexican Town	See Gold Road, Mohave
Miami Flat	(T1N/R15E; Elev. 3349') See Miami, Gila
Miami Wash	See Bloody Tanks Wash, Gila, and Miami, Gila
Michaels Lake, Saint	(T26N/R30E) See Michaels, Saint, Apache
Middelton	See Middleton, Yavapai
Middle Basin	See Virgin Basin, Mohave (Lake Mead)
Middle Crossing	See Pedro, San, Cochise
Middle Division	See Virgin Basin, Mohave (Lake Mead)
Middle Granite Gorge	(T34N/R2W) See Granite Gorge, Coconino (Grand Canyon)
Middle Lake	See Virgin Basin, Mohave (Lake Mead)
Middle Leonard Canyon	See Miller Canyon, Coconino
Middlemarch Canyon	(T18S/R23E) See Middlemarch, Cochise
Middle Pass	(T18S/R23E) See Dragoon Mountains, Cochise
Middleton Creek	(T10N/R1E) See Middleton, Yavapai
Midway Canyon	(T12S/R31E) See Midway, Cochise
Midway Grocery	See Paulden, Yavapai
Midway Peak	(T12S/R31E; Elev. 5651') See Midway, Cochise
Migley Ridge	See Midgley Canyon, Coconino
Miguel de San Jesus Guevavi, San	See Guevavi, Santa Cruz
Miguel of Sonitac, San	See Sonoita, Santa Cruz
Miguel Wash, San	See Miguel, San, Pima
Military Park	See Lowell, Fort, Pima
Milkweed Canyon, Creek	See Milkweed Spring, Mohave
Milkweed Tank	(T26N/R11W) See Milkweed Spring, Mohave
Milky House Ruin	(T16N/R25E) See Milky Wash, Apache

Milky Wash Ridge	(T16N/R24E) See Milky Wash, Apache
Mill City	See East Phoenix, Maricopa
Miller Creek	See McCarty Canyon, Coconino
Miller Creek	See Miller Valley, Yavapai
Miller Hill	(T23S/R24E) See Miller Canyon, Cochise
Miller Mountain	See Miller Valley, Yavapai
Miller Peak	(T23S/R20E; Elev. 9445') See Miller Canyon, Cochise
Miller Ranch	See Miller Valley, Yavapai
Miller Ridge	See Miller Canyon, Coconino
Millersburg	See Beaver Dam, Mohave, and Littlefield, Mohave
Miller Spring	See Miller Canyon, Coconino
Miller's Station	See Cienega, La, Pima
Miller Wash	See Miller Canyon, Coconino
Milligan, Fort	See Milligan Creek, Apache, and Round Valley, Apache
Milligan Lake	(T4N/R32E) See Milligan Peak, Greenlee
Milligan Ranch	See Whispering Pines, Greenlee
Mil-Li-Ket	See Castle Dome Mountains, La Paz
Milltown	See Flagstaff, Coconino
Millville	(Apache/Navajo) See Forestdale Creek, Navajo
Milpitas	See Hickiwan, Pima
Milton	See Flagstaff, Coconino, and Agassiz Peak, Coconino
Mineral Butte	See Mineral Creek, Pinal
Mineral City	See Ehrenberg, La Paz
Mineral Lake	(T21N/R3E) See Chalender Lake, Coconino
Mineral Mountain	(T3S/R11E; Elev. 3350') See Mineral Creek, Pinal/Gila
Mingkard Mountains	See Virgin River, Mohave
Mingus Lake	See Mingus Mountain, Yavapai
Miniature Grand Canyon	(T19N/R3E) See Sycamore Canyon, Coconino/Yavapai
Mining Mountain	(T7S/R17E; Elev. 3949') See Mineral Creek, Pinal
Minnehaha Flat	(T10N/R1W) See Minnehaha, Yavapai
Mint Creek, Wash	See Mint Valley, Yavapai
Miraflores, Brazo de	See Gila River
Mirror Mountain	See Glassford Hill, Yavapai
Misery, Fort	See Fort Valley, Coconino
Misery No. 2, Fort	See Misery, Fort, Yavapai
Mitchell Butte Wash	See Mitchell Butte, Navajo
Mitchell Mesa	(T41N/R21E; Elev. 6570') See Mitchell Butte, Navajo
Mitten Butte	See Pilot Rock, Navajo, and Mitten Peak, Navajo
Mitten, The	See Pilot Rock, Navajo, and Mitten Peak, Navajo
Mittry Lake Water Fowl Area	See Mittry Lake, Yuma
Mix Wash, Tom	See Tom Mix Wash, Pinal
Moa Ave	See Moenave, Coconino
Moa Ave Spring	See Moenave, Coconino
Mobile Valley	(T4S/R1W) See Mobile, Maricopa
Moccasin	See Moccasin Springs, Mohave
Moccasin Canyon	(T41N/R5W) See Moccasin Springs, Mohave
Moccasin Mountains	(T41N/R5W; Elev. 6506') See Moccasin Springs, Mohave
Mockingbird Wash	See Mockingbird Hill, Maricopa, or Mockingbird Mine, Mohave
Moen Avi	See Moenavi, Coconino
Moe Ave Spring	See Moenavi, Coconino
Moen Abi	See Moenavi, Coconino
Moencopi	See Moenkopi, Coconino
Moencopi Wash	See Moenkopi Wash, Coconino, and Moenkopi, Coconino
Moenkapi	See Moenkopi, Coconino
Moenkopi Plateau	(T28N/R12E; Elev. 5422') See Moenkopi, Coconino
Mogollon Buttes	See Mogollon Rim, Coconino/Navajo/Apache/Greenlee/Gila
Mogollon, Camp	See Apache, Fort, Apache

Mogollon Mesa	(T13N/R9E; Elev. c. 7000') See Mogollon Rim, Coconino/Navajo/Apache/Greenlee/Gila
Mogoyone, Sierra	See Mogollon Rim, Coconino/Navajo/Apache/Greenlee/ Gila
Mohatuk	(Maricopa) See Salt River, Gila
Mohave, Camp	See Mojave, Fort, Mohave
Mohave Canyon, City, Creek, Fort	See Mojave, Fort, Mohave
Mohave Peak	(T2S/R22W; Elev. 2771'; Yuma) See Mojave, Fort, Mohave
Mohave Point	See Paguekwash Point, Coconino (Grand Canyon)
Mohave Range	See Mohave Mountains, Mohave
Mohave Resort, Lake	See Katherine, Mohave
Mohave Rock	(T15N/R20W; Elev. 571') See Mojave, Fort, Mohave, and Castle Rock Bay, Mohave
Mohave Springs, Mesa	(T13N/R17W) See Mojave, Fort, Mohave
Mohave Wash	(T1S/R21W; Elev. 3700') SeeMojave, Fort, Mohave
Mohawk Gap	See Mohawk, Yuma
Mohawk Mine	See Mammoth, Pinal
Mohawk Pass	(T8S/R15W) See Mohawk, Yuma
Mohawk Peak	(T10S/R13W) See Mohawk, Yuma
Mohawk Range	See Mohawk, Yuma
Mohawk Stage Station	(T8S/R16W) See Mohawk, Yuma
Mohawk Summit	(T8S/R14W) See Mohawk, Yuma
Mohawk Valley	(T12S/R14W) See Mohawk, Yuma, and Roll Valley, Yuma
Mohon Mountain	(T18N/R10W; Mohave/Coconino) See Mahan Mountain, Coconino
Moivaxia	See Moivavi, Maricopa
Moki Buttes	See Hopi Buttes, Navajo
Molinton	See Stanshuatak, Pima
Molonitos	See Stanshuatak, Pima
Monitor	See Dome, Yuma, and Gila City, Yuma
Monitor Gulch	See Dome, Yuma
Monkey Canyon	(T21S/R16E) See Hughes Mountain, Santa Cruz
Monkey Spring	See Hughes Mountain, Santa Cruz, and Patagonia, Santa Cruz
Monkey Springs Ranch	See Hughes Mountain, Santa Cruz
Monroe Hot Springs	See Castle Creek, Yavapai, and Castle Hot Springs, Yavapai
Montana Camp	See Ruby, Santa Cruz
Montana Dam	(T23S/R11E; Elev. 5370') See Ruby, Santa Cruz
Montana Peak	See Ruby, Santa Cruz
Montezuma	See Jose, San, Graham, or Montezuma Well National Monument, Yavapai
Montezuma, Casa	See Casa Blanca, Pinal
Montezuma's Castle	See Casa Blanca, Pinal
Montezuma City	See Montezuma Well National Monument, Yavapai
Montezuma Lake	See Montezuma Castle National Monument, Yavapai
Montgomery Addition	See Montgomery, Maricopa
Montgomery's	See Tres Alamos, Cochise
Montrosa, Sierra	See Montoso, Cerro, Apache
Montrose, Sierra	See Montoso, Cerro, Apache
Moonlight Canyon, Valley	See Moonlight Creek, Navajo
Moonshine Hill	(T1N/R14E; Elev. 4018') See Inspiration, Gila
Moore, Camp	See Buchanan, Fort, Santa Cruz
Moore Camp	See Moore Gulch, Maricopa
Moo-Shah-Neh	See Mishongovi
Moqui (R. R. Siding)	(T30N/R22E; Elev. 6700') See Moqui Spring, Coconino
Moqui Buttes	See Hopi Buttes, Navajo
Mo-Quin-To-Ara, Sierra	See Castle Dome Mountains, La Paz
Moqui Draw	See Moqui Spring, Coconino

Moqui, Pozo de	See Moqui Spring, Coconino, and Shungopovi, Navajo
Moquitch Point, Spring	See Moquitch Canyon, Coconino
Moralita, La	See Stanshuatak, Pima
Moras Well, Las	See Moras, Las, Pima
Morenci Gulch	See Morenci, Greenlee
Morenci Hot Springs	(T5S/R29E) See Morenci, Greenlee
Moreno Mountains	See Morena Mountain, Pima
Morgan City Mine	See Morgan Mountain, Maricopa
Morin Inn (P.O.)	See Stoneman Lake, Coconino
Moritz Hill	(T23N/R4E) See Moritz Lake, Coconino
Moritz Ridge	See Moritz Lake, Coconino
Mormon Canyon	(T20N/R10E) See Mormon Mountain, Coconino
Mormon Dairy, Dairy Park, Dairy Spring	See Mormon Mountain, Coconino
Mormon Flat	See Mormon Flat Dam, Maricopa
Mormon Road	See House Rock, Coconino, and Mormon Ridge, Coconino
Moroni, Fort	See Fort Valley, Coconino
Mortenson Wash	See Mortensen Wash, Navajo
Morterson Wash	See Mortensen Wash, Navajo
Mortgage Draw	See Margs Draw, Coconino
Moritz Hill	See Moritz Lake, Coconino
Mortiz Lake	See Moritz Lake, Coconino
Mortz Lake	See Moritz Lake, Coconino
Moss Mine, Wash	(T20N/R20W) See Moss Hills, Mohave, and Goldroad, Mohave
Mountain Sheep Wash	See Mountain Sheep Spring, Mohave
Mountain Springs	See Mountain View, Pima
Mountain Springs Cave	See Colossal Cave, Pima
Mountain View	See Carriso, Apache
Mowry Flat	See Mowry Mine, Santa Cruz
Mowry Wash	See Mowry Mine, Santa Cruz
Mount Hope Wash	(T19N/R8W) See Hope, Mount, Yavapai
Moyencopi	See Moenkopi, Coconino
Muav Saddle	(Elev. 7050') See Muav Canyon, Coconino (Grand Canyon)
Muddy Creek	See Muddy Canyon, Yavapai
Mud Mountain	See Kofa Butte, Yuma
Mud Springs	See Navajo Spring, Apache, or Indian Hot Springs, Graham
Mud Springs Canyon	See Mud Springs, Cochise
Muencovi	See Moenkopi, Coconino
Mueykava	See Moivavi, Maricopa
Mu-Koon-Tu-Weap	See Toroweap Valley, Mohave
Mulden Spring	See Muldoon Canyon, Yavapai
Muldoon Spring	See Muldoon Gulch, Yavapai
Mule Canyon	See Parashant Canyon, Mohave
Mule Hoof Canyon	See Mule Hoof Bend, Gila
Mule Pass	(T23S/R24E) See Mule Mountains, Cochise
Mule Pass Gulch, Mountains	See Mule Gulch, Cochise, and Mule Mountains, Cochise
Mule Ridge	(T23S/R11E) See Montana Ridge, Santa Cruz
Mullen	See Topock, Mohave
Mullen Wash	See Mullen Mesa, Yavapai
Mulligan Canyon	See Mullican Canyon, Yavapai
Mummy House Ruins	See Mummy Cave Ruins, Apache
Munds	See Munds Draw, Yavapai
Munds Mountain	(T17N/R6E; Elev. 6812') See Munds Draw, Coconino
Munds Trail	(Coconino/Yavapai) See Munds Park, Coconino
Munsonville	See Jose, San, Graham
Murderer's Camp	See Black Jack Canyon, Greenlee
Murderer's Grave	See Kenyon Station, Maricopa

Murray Flat	See Frank Murray's Peak, Mohave
Murray's Spring	See Frank Murray's Peak, Mohave
Musina	(T7S/R12W) See Le Sage, Yuma
Mustang Peak	(T20S/R18E; Elev. 6317') See Mustang Mountains, Cochise/Santa Cruz
Mutt-A-Witt-A-Ka	See Meriwitica Canyon, Mohave
Muy Vavi	See Ajo, Pima
Myrtle Lake, Point	(T12N/R11E; Coconino) See Myrtle, Gila
Myrtle Trail	(Gila/Coconino) See Myrtle, Gila
Mystic Spring	(T33N/R1W) See Bass Canyon, Coconino
Mystic Spring Trail	See Bass Canyon, Coconino
Naakau Tó Hadaiiznili	See Mexican Water, Apache
Naanez'ash	See Francisco Peaks, San, Coconino
Na'ashóii'i	(T35N/R29E) See Big Lizard Creek, Apache
Naches	See Natchi Canyon, Coconino, and Naches, Graham
Naco Hills	(T23S/R23E; Elev. 5760') See Naco, Cochise
Nada	See Wittman, Maricopa
Nadaburg	See Wittman, Maricopa
Naegelin Canyon	See Naeglin Creek, Gila
Naeglin Rim, Spring Canyon	See Naeglin Creek, Gila
Na-Ettee	See Na Ah Tee Canyon, Navajo
Nagashi Bikin	See Baby Mummy Cave, Navajo
Nail's Crossing	(T40N/R3W) See Nail Canyon, Coconino
Naji Point	See Uncle Jim Point, Coconino (Grand Canyon)
Nakai Canyon, Creek	See Nokai Canyon, Navajo
Na'ni'ahstol	See Navajo Bridge, Coconino
Nancoweap	See Nankoweap Butte, Coconino (Grand Canyon)
Nankoweap Creek, Rapids, Trail	See Nankoweap Butte, Coconino (Grand Canyon)
Nankoweep	See Nankoweap Butte, Coconino (Grand Canyon)
Nantack Plateau	See Natanes Plateau, Gila
Nantac Rim	(T1S/R24E; Graham) See Natanes Plateau, Gila
Nantes Mountains	See Natanes Plateau, Gila, and Natanes Mountains, Gila/Graham
Napao, Sierra	See Francisco Mountains, San, Coconino
Napoc, Sierra	See Francisco Mountains, San, Coconino
Napoleon's Tomb	See Campanile, The, Mohave
Nariz, Nariz Flats	See Nariz, Sierra de la, Pima
Nash-Bito	See Lizard Spring, Apache
Nash Canyon	(T5N/R23E) See Nash Creek, Gila/Navajo
Naskline	See Nazlini, Apache
Naskline Creek	See Nazlini Creek, Apache
Natanes Butte	See Natanes Plateau, Graham/Gila, and Chiricahua Butte, Gila
Natanes Mountains	(T1N/R23E; Elev. 7520') See Natanes Plateau, Graham/Gila
Natanes Peak	See Natanes Plateau, Graham/Gila
Natchi Point	See Uncle Jim Point, Coconino (Grand Canyon)
Nat-Is-Ahn	See Navajo Mountain, Coconino
Nattbush Valley	See Nottbusch Butte, Yuma
Navajo Point	See Desert View Point, Coconino (Grand Canyon)
Nawt Vaya Pass	(T16S/R9E) See Nawt Vaya, Pima
Nazlini Canyon, Creek, Wash	See Nazlini, Apache
Neal	See Wikieup, Mohave
Neal Spring	(T9N/R10E) See Neal Mountain, Gila
Nee-Al-Neeng	See Navajo, Apache
Needle, The	See Needles Eye, Greenlee
Needle Rock	See Camp Creek, Maricopa

Needle Rock	See Agathla Needle, Navajo
Needles	See Topock, Mohave
Negrita River	See Black River, Apache
Negro, Rio	See Coyote Wash, Apache
Nehiegee	See Sawmill, Apache
Nelson Mesa	(T15N/R9W) See Nelson, Yavapai
Nero	See Richville, Apache
Nesheptanga	See Nesuftanga, Navajo
Neute Rosa	See Nutrioso, Apache
Nevills Rapids	See Seventy-five Mile Rapids, Coconino (Grand Canyon)
Newberry Point	See Newberry Mesa, Coconino (Grand Canyon)
Newberry Terrace	See Wotan's Throne, Coconino (Grand Canyon)
New Caves Acropolis	See O'Neal Spring, Coconino
New Creek	See Peach Springs, Mohave
New Kingdom of New Navarre	See New Philippines
Newman park	(T19N/R7E) See Newman Canyon, Coconino
New Oro Blanco	See Oro Blanco, Santa Cruz
New Osborne	See Bisbee Junction, Cochise
New Post	See Wallen, Camp, Cochise
New Post on the Gila	See Thomas, Fort, Gila/Graham
New River	(Maricopa/Yavapai) See New River Stage Station, Maricopa
New River Mesa	(T7N/R4E) See New River Stage Station, Maricopa
New River Mountains	(T7N/R3E; Elev. 4722'; Maricopa/Yavapai) See New River Stage Station, Maricopa
Newton Ranch	See Ellison, Gila
New Virginia	See Logan, Pima
New Water Mountains	(T3N/R16W; Elev. 2536') See New Water Pass, La Paz
Nexpa	See Pedro River, San, Cochise
Ni'anii'gi	See Window Rock, Apache
Nice Lake	See Nyce Lake, Navajo
Niegehe	See Sawmill, Apache
Niggertoe Peak	See Suwuk Tontk, Pima
Nigger Wash	See Negro Wash, Gila
Ninemile Ranch	See Ninemile Creek, Cochise
Nine Mile Station	See Laguna, Pima
Nine Mile Water	See Nine Mile State Station, Yuma
Nine Mile Water Hole	See Laguna, Pima
Ninety-Four Mile Creek	See Novinger Butte, Coconino (Grand Canyon)
Nipple, The	See College Peak, Cochise
Nish'e'clay'ze	See Verde, Camp, Yavapai
Nitsie Canyon	See Nitsi Canyon, Navajo
Nit Sin Canyon	See Nitsi Canyon, Navajo
Nizhaldzis	See Buell Mountain, Apache
Noah	See Tacna, Yuma
Noah (R.R. Stn.)	(T8S/R17W) See Tacna, Yuma
Noah's Ark	See Baboquivari Peak, Pima, or Tacna, Yuma
Noble Draw	See Noble Mountain, Apache
Nodman Canyon	See Nobman Canyon, Mohave
Nogales Pass, Wash	See Nogales, Santa Cruz
Noipa Kam Hills	See Noipa Kam, Pima
Noipa Kem	See Noipa Kam, Pima
Nokai Creek	See Nokai Canyon, Navajo
Nokai Mesa	(T41N/R17E) See Nokai Canyon, Navajo
Nokalto; Bench, Canyon	See Mexican Water, Apache
Noli	See Nolic, Pima
No Man's Land	See Diana Temple, Coconino (Grand Canyon)
Nombre de Jesus, Rio del	See Gila River
Noolick	See Nolic, Pima

Noon, Noon Camp	See Noonville, Santa Cruz
Noria	See Nolic, Pima
Noria, La	See Lochiel, Santa Cruz, or Nolic, Pima
Norlic	See Nolic, Pima
Norte, Rio del	See Colorado River
North Ajo	See Gibson, Pima
North Ajo Peak	(Elev. 2776') See Ajo, Pima
North Butte	See Double Peaks, Pinal
North Comobabi Mountains	(T15S/R5E; Elev. 4788') See Comobabi Mountains, Pima
North Creek	See North Canyon, Coconino
North Gila Bend	See Gila Bend, Maricopa
North Rim Run-Off	See North Rim, Coconino (Grand Canyon)
North Side Mountains	See Trumbull, Mount, Mohave
North Trigo Peaks	(T2N/R21W; Elev. 2170') See Trigo Mountains, La Paz
Norton	(T7S/R15W) See Norton Tank, Yuma
Nortvaya	See Nawt Vaya, Pima
N-O Spring	(13 S/R21E) See N-O Canyon, Cochise
Notovaxia	See Nawt Vaya, Pima
Nottbusch Mine	(T4S/R15W) See Nottbusch, Butte, Yuma
Nottbusch Valley	(T1S/R12W) See Nottbusch Butte, Yuma
Nottbusch Wash	(T5S/R10W; Maricopa) See Nottbusch Butte, Yuma
Nottbush Valley	See Nottbusch Butte, Yuma
Notvarja	See Nawt Vaya, Pima
Not Vaya	See Nawt Vaya, Pima
Not Vaya Pass	See Nawt Vaya Pass, Pima
No Water Mesa	See Dinne Mesa, Apache
Nuestra Señors de La Merced del Batqui	See Serafin, San, Pima
Nugales	See Nogales, Santa Cruz
Nugget	See Nugget Mine, Gila
Nuggetville	See Peach Orchard, Pinal
Numasitso Canyon	See Potato Canyon, Coconino
Number Two, Lake	See Carr Lake, Coconino
Nut Fall Canyon	See Nutall Canyon, Graham
Nutrioso Creek	(T8N/R30E) See Nutrioso, Apache
Nutrioso, Rio	(T5N/R27E) See Reservation Creek, Apache, and Nutrioso, Apache
Nuttle Canyon	See Nutall Canyon, Graham
Nuttles Creek	See Nuttall Canyon, Graham
Nuva-Takis-Ovi	See Francisco Peaks, San, Coconino
Nuvatiki Ovi	See Francisco Peaks, San Coconino, and Toreva, Apache
Nyerivi Ki	See Luis, San, Pima
Nyokikam	See Noipa Kam, Pima
Oakley Springs	(T32N/R9E) See Willow Springs, Coconino
Oatman Grove	(T5S/R9W) See Oatman Flat, Maricopa
Oatman Pass	See Sitgreaves Pass, Mohave
Obed Meadow, Spring	See Obed, Navajo
Obi Canyon	See Obi Point, Coconino (Grand Canyon)
Observation Plateau	See Huxley Terrace, Coconino (Grand Canyon)
Observation Point	See Obi Point, Coconino (Grand Canyon)
Observatory Hill	See Lowell Observatory, Coconino
Ocatila	See Ocotillo, Pinal
Ochoa	See Ochoaville, Santa Cruz
Ochoa, Mount	See Gavalan Peak, Maricopa
Octave Mine	See Octave, Yavapai
Odart Mountain	(T4N/R26E; Elev. 8524') See Odart Cienega, Apache
Oderville Canyon	See Orderville, Coconino
Ojio	See Winkelmann, Pinal

Ojo Alamo	See Kayenta, Navajo
Ojo Caliente	See Agua Caliente, Maricopa
Ojo de Casa	See Hogansaani Spring, Apache
Ojo del Agua de Sopore	See Sopori Ranch, Santa Cruz
Ojo de La Xara	See Tanner Springs, Apache
Ojo de Los Coyotes	See Pan Tak, Pima
Ojos de Los Osos	See Bear Springs, Cochise
Olalla	See Oraibi, Navajo
Old Ajo	See Ajo, Pima
Old Baldy	See Wrightson, Mount, Santa Cruz
Old Base Line	See Blue, Greenlee
Oldberg	See Olberg, Pinal
Old Brayton	See Bouse, La Paz
Old Camp Colorado	See Colorado, Camp, Yuma
Old Camp Date Creek	See Date Creek, Camp, Yavapai
Old Camp Grant	See Grant, Old Camp, Pinal
Old Dick Hill, Mine	See Helvetia, Pima
Old Fort Tyson	See Quartzsite, La Paz
Old Frijole Mine	See Helvetia, Pima
Old Glory Canyon	See Old Glory, Santa Cruz
Old Hance Trail	See Hance Creek, Coconino (Grand Canyon)
Old Maine	See Maine, Coconino
Old Mammoth Mine	See Mammoth, Pinal
Old Oraibi	(Elev. 6040') See Oraibi, Navajo
Old Palm Canyons	See Palm Canyon, Yuma
Old Pete Mountain	See Pete Mountain, Santa Cruz
Old Pueblo	See Tucson, Pima
Old Quijotoa Well	See Kaihon Kug, Pima
Old Reliable Mine	See Reliable, Yavapai
Old San Rafael Ruins	See Rafael de la Zanja Grant, San, Santa Cruz
Old Soldier Trail	See Soldier Camp, Pima
Old Stage Coach Tavern	See Rice, Apache
Old Summit	See Stockton Gap, Graham
Old Town; Spring	See Flagstaff, Coconino
Olgato Wash	See Oljeto Wash, Navajo
Olive Camp	See Olive, Santa Cruz
Oljeto	See Kayenta, Navajo
Oljeto Creek	See Oljeto Wash, Navajo
Ollie Oatman Spring	See Oatman, Mohave
Omer	See Eagar, Apache
Omer Ward	See Eagar, Apache, and Round Valley, Apache
O'Neal Hill	See O'Neal Spring, Coconino
150 Mile Canyon	(T34N/R4W; Mohave [Grand Canyon]) See 140 Mile Canyon, Coconino (Grand Canyon)
135 Mile Rapids	See 140 Mile Canyon, Coconino (Grand Canyon)
O'Neill Hills	See O'Neill Pass, Yuma
O'Neill Point	See Yavapai Point, Coconino (Grand Canyon)
Onion Creek	See Onion Saddle, Cochise
Onion Creek Saddle	See Onion Saddle, Cochise
Ookilsipava (or Ookilsipave) River	See Lynx Creek, Yavapai
Oonupin Pinabu	See Witch Water Pocket, Mohave
Oparsoitac	See Gila Bend, Maricopa
Opasoitac	See Gila Bend, Maricopa
Opdyke Tanks	See Rattlesnake Tank, Coconino
Oracle Camp	See Oracle, Pinal
Oracle Hill	(T10S/R15E; Elev. 5290') See Oracle, Pinal
Oracle Ridge	(T11S/R16E) See Oracle, Pinal
Orahai Mountain, Ridge	See Goldfield Mountains, Maricopa
Oraiba	See Oraibi, Navajo

Oraibe	See Oraibi, Navajo
Oraibi Butte	(T28N/R15E; Elev. 6561') See Oraibi, Navajo
Oraibi Wash	(T34N/R22E; Apache; T29N/R15E; Navajo; T24N/R15E; Coconino) See Oraibi, Navajo
Orange Peak	See Orange Butte, Cochise
Oraybe	See Oraibi, Navajo
Ord, Camp	See Apache, Fort, Apache
Ord Creek	(T7N/R26E) See Ord, Mount, Apache
Origin-Of-Life Cave	See Newpaper Rock, Apache
Ormejea	See Hormiguero, Pinal
Oro	See Burroville, Greenlee, and Oroville, Greenlee
Oro Belle Mine	See Oro, Yavapai
Oro Blanco Creek, Mountain	See Oro Blanco, Santa Cruz
Oro Blanco Peak	(T24S/R12E) See Pajarito Mountains, Santa Cruz, and Oro Blanco, Santa Cruz
Oro Blanco Wash	(T22S/R10E; Pima/Santa Cruz) See Oro Blanco, Santa Cruz
Oro, Canyon del	See Oro, Cañada del, Pinal/Pima
Oro Ranch	See Baca Float No. 5, Yavapai
Oro Wash, Cañada del	See Oro, Cañada del, Pima/Pinal
Orrville	See Centennial, La Paz, and Harrisburg, La Paz
Ortega Draw	(T10N/R24E) See Ortega Lake, Apache
Ortega Mountain	(T11N/R23E; Elev. 7007') See Ortega Lake, Apache
Ortega Sink	(T11N/R26E) See Ortega Lake, Apache
Ortega Spring	(T12N/R26E) See Ortega Lake, Apache
Orville	See Harrisburg, La Paz
Osa Wash, La	See Osa, La, Pima
Osborne	See Bisbee, Cochise
Osborne Spring Wash	See Osborne Spring, Yavapai
Osborne Wash	(T9N/R18W) See Clara Peak, La Paz
Osborne Well	(T9N/R17W; Elev. 1100') See Clara Peak, La Paz
Oso, Mesa La	See Osa, Mesa de la, Pima
Os Ka'kùmùk Tcótcikäm	See Pima Villages, Pinal/Maricopa
Os Kuk	See Pima Villages, Pinal/Maricopa, and Blackwater, Pinal
Osos Canellos, La Sierra de Las	See Canelo Hills, Santa Cruz
Otero Canyon	See Otero Creek, Maricopa
Otero (R.R. Stn.)	(T22S/R13E) See Oterno Land Grant, Santa Cruz
Otero Spring	See Otero Creek, Maricopa
Otey Spring	See Garden Spring, Coconino
Otoxakam	See Tule Tank, Yuma
Outlaw Springs	(T15S/R30E) See Outlaw Mountain, Cochise
Overton	See Garden Canyon, Cochise, and Sierra Vista, Cochise
Owatobi	See Awatobi, Navajo
Owen Mining District	See Owen, Mohave
Owens Lake	See Stoneman Lake, Coconino
Owens Mine	(T28N/R19W) See Owen, Mohave
Owens Peak	See Owen, Mohave
Owl Head Butte	(T9S/R12E) See Owls' Heads, Pinal
Oxbow; Mine	See Oxbow Hill, Gila
Oxbow Mountain	(T10N/R13E; Elev. 6448') See Oxbow Hill, Gila
Oxbow Yoke Hill, Yoke Mountain	See Oxbow Hill, Gila
Pa-A-Coon Spring	See Pahkoon Springs, Mohave
Pablo de Givuire	See Quiburi (Ruins), Cochise
Pablo de Quipuri, San	See Quiburi (Ruins), Cochise
Pabroach Spring	See Peach Springs, Mohave
Pacific	See Pacific City, Yuma
Packard's	See Punkin Center, Gila, and Tonto Basin, Gila
Packard Store	See Punkin Center, Gila, and Tonto Basin, Gila

Packard Wash	See Packard Spring, Gila
Packers Peak	See Parkers Peak, Pinal
Paddy Butte	See Paddy Creek, Apache
Paddy Cienega	(T4N/R26E) See Paddy Creek, Apache
Padricks	See Pedricks, Yuma
Page Springs Fish Cultural Station	See Page Springs, Yavapai
Pagoda Mountains	See Coronation Peak, Yuma
Pagoda Peak	See Coronation Peak, Yuma
Pa-Ha-Weap	See Colorado River
Pah-Coon Spring	See Pahkoon Springs, Mohave
Pah-Gaiv	See Colorado River
Pah-Guhn Springs	See Pahkoon Springs, Mohave
Pahreah Canyon	See Paria River, Coconino
Pahreah Crossing	See Lee's Ferry, Coconino
Pahreah Plateau	See Paria Plateau, Coconino
Pahreah River	See Paria River, Coconino
Pahreah Valley	See Paria River, Coconino
Pah-Roose	See Virgin River, Mohave
Pah Rute Canyon	See Piute Canyon, Navajo
Pah-Wash	See Peach Springs, Mohave
Paige Creek	(Cochise/Pima; T15S, R19E) See Paige Canyon, Cochise
Painted Desert Vista	(Coconino; T23N/R9E; Elev. 6415') See Painted Desert, Coconino/Navajo/Apache
Painted Rocks	See Painted Rock Mountains, Maricopa
Pais, Sierra del	See Guijas Mountains, Pima
Pa'it'spick'ine	See Moccasin Springs, Mohave
Paiute Canyon	See Piute Canyon, Navajo
Paute Creek	See Piute Canyon, Navajo
Pajarito Peak	(Elev. 4490') See Pajarito Mountains, Santa Cruz
Pajarito, Sierra de los, or Sierra del	See Pajarito Mountains, Santa Cruz
Pajaro Mountain	See Pajarito Mountains, Santa Cruz
Pakoon Springs, Wash	See Pahkoon Springs, Mohave
Palaco Canyon	See Peck Canyon, Santa Cruz
Palisade Spring	See Palisade Canyon, Pima
Palmerlee Canyon	See Palmerlee, Cochise
Palo Alto Valley	See Palo Alto, Pima
Palomas Mountains	(T5S/R13W; Elev. 1901') See Palomas, Yuma
Palomas Peak	See Nottbusch Peak, Yuma
Palo Verde Wash	(Mohave, T14N/R20W) See Palo Verde Mountains, Pinal
Panocha, Sierra	See Navajo Mountain, Coconino
Panoche, Sierra	See Navajo Mountain, Coconino, and Panoche Creek, Coconino
Pan Tak Mountains	See Coyote Mountains, Pima, and Pantak, Pima
Pan Tak Wash	See Pantak, Pima, and Pan Tak Pass, Pima
Pantano Creek	See Pantano, Pima
Papago Butte	(Pinal, T5S/R2E; Elev. 2079') See Papago Indian Reservation, Pima
Papago Canyon	(Pima, T18S/R16E) See Papago Indian Reservation, Pima
Papago Mountains	See Sauceda Mountains, Maricopa
Papago Park	See Papago (State) Park, Maricopa, or Baboquivari, Pima
Papago Well	(T15S/R10W) See Papago Indian Reservation, Pima
Papajuik	See Tonuk Vo, Pima
Paquette Canyon	See Quartzite Canyon, Apache
Parashant	(T41N/R5W; Elev. 5699') See Parashant Canyon, Mohave (Grand Canyon)

Paria Canyon	(T41N/R6E) See Paria River, Coconino (Grand Canyon)
Paria Valley	See Paria River, Coconino (Grand Canyon)
Parigua	See Hickiwan, Pima
Parishawampitts Canyon	See Parissawampitts Spring, Coconino
Parissawampitts Canyon, Point	See Parissawampitts Spring, Coconino
Park, The	(Yavapai, #1: T11N/R4W; #2: T9N/R8E) See Park, The, Coconino
Parker Butte	See Reno, Camp, Gila
Parker Canyon Wild Life Area	See Parker Canyon Lake, Santa Cruz, and Parker Canyon, Cochise/Santa Cruz
Parker Creek	(T5N/R13E) See Reno, Camp, Gila
Parker Dam Reservoir	See Havasu, Lake, Mohave/La Paz
Parker Valley	(T5N/R22W) See Parker (Town), La Paz
Parks Lake Water Fowl Area	See Parks Lake, Graham
Parsee Hill	See Poston Butte, Pinal
Parson Canyon	See Parson Peak, Graham
Partridge Ravine, Wash	See Partridge Creek, Coconino/Yavapai
Parusi-Wompats	See Parissawampitts Spring, Coconino
Pasqua Village	See Pascua Villa, Pima
Pass City	See Cactus, Maricopa
Pastura Peak	See Pastora Peak, Apache
Pasture Canyon Lake	(T32N/R11E) See Pasture Canyon, Coconino
Pasture Spring	See Cane Spring, Gila
Patagonia Mine	See Mowry Mine, Santa Cruz
Patagonia Mountains	(T23S/R16E; Elev. 7221') See Canelo, Santa Cruz
Patagonia Post Office (1866)	See Mowry Mine, Santa Cruz
Pat Burns Cienega	See Pat Hills, Cochise
Pat Mesa	See Pat Creek, Greenlee
Pat Mountain	(Elev. 6562') See Pat Creek, Greenlee
Pat Mullen Peak, Spring	See Pat Mullen Mountain, Navajo
Pato	See Kom Vo, Pima
Patos River, Los	See Francisco River, San, Greenlee
Patricks	See Pedricks, Yuma
Pattison (R.R. Siding)	See Amado, Santa Cruz
Paymaster Canyon	See Paymaster Wash, Graham
Paz Arroyo, La	(T3N/R21W) See Paz, La, La Paz
Paz Wash, La	(T4N/R21W; Elev. 1325') See Paz, La, La Paz, and Dome Rock Mountains, La Paz
Peach Orchard Spring	See Keams Canyon, Navajo
Peach Spring Canyon	See Peach Springs, Mohave
Peach Springs Draw	See Peach Springs, Mohave
Peach Spring Wash	See Peach Springs, Mohave
Peach Tree Spring	See Peach Springs, Mohave
Peachville	See Peach Orchard, Pinal
Peachville Mountain	See Peach Orchard, Pinal
Peachville Wash	See Peach Orchard, Pinal
Peacocke Spring	See Peacock Spring, Mohave
Peacock Mountains	(T23N/R14W; Elev. 6268') See Peacock Spring, Mohave
Peacock Ruin	See Lululongturqui, Navajo
Peale, Mount	See Peeley, Mount, Gila/Maricopa
Pearce Hill	(T18S/R25E; Elev. 4720') See Pearce, Cochise
Pearce Spring	See Pearce Mountain, Apache
Pearce Wash	(T35N/R10W) See Pearce Ferry, Mohave
Pecacho	See Picacho, Santa Cruz
Peck Basin	(T11N/R16E) See Peck Canyon, Santa Cruz
Peck Canyon	See Peck Mine, Yavapai
Peck Pass	See Peck Canyon, Santa Cruz

Peck Spring	See Peck Mine, Yavapai
Pedregosa Mountains	(T22S/R29E; Elev. 6541') See Swisshelm Mountains, Cochise
Pedrichs	See Pedricks, Yuma
Pedro, San	See Winkelman, Pinal, or Wellton, Yuma
Pedro Crossing, San	See Ohnesorgen Stage Station, Cochise
Pedro, Rio de San (1776)	See Little Colorado River
Pedro River Station, San	See Ohnesorgen Stage Station, Cochise
Pedro Settlement, San	See Ohnesorgen Stage Station, Cochise
Pedro, Sierra de San	See Dome Rock Mountains, Yuma
Peele, Mount	See Peeley, Mount, Gila/Maricopa
Peeples Creek	(T12N/R10W) See Peeples Ranch, Yavapai
Peeples Valley	See Peeples Ranch, Yavapai
Peeples Valley (Town)	See Yarnell, Yavapai
Pe-ep'tcïlt'k'	See Pima Villages, Pinal, and Pepchiltk, Pinal
Pele, Mount	See Peeley, Mount, Gila/Maricopa
Peer Mountain	See Quijotoa, Pima
Peloncillo Forest Reserve	See Coronado National Forest, Pima
Peloncillo Mountains	See Peloncillo, El, Cochise/Greenlee/Graham
Pelon Range	See Peloncillo, El, Cochise/Greenlee/Graham
Pelota, La	(Spanish = "big ball") See Castle Dome, Yuma
Pelton	See Silverbell, Pima
Peltonville	See Silverbell, Pima
Peña Blanca Dam	See Peña Blanca Canyon, Santa Cruz
Peña Blanca Spring	See Peña Blanca Canyon, Santa Cruz
Peña Blanca Wild Life Area	See Peña Blanca Lake, Santa Cruz
Penahachapi Pass	See Harquahala Mountains, La Paz
Penal Mountains	See Pinal Mountains, Gila/Pinal
Peñasco Canyon	See Peñasco Dam, Santa Cruz
Peñascos Blancos, Rio de Los	See Peña Blanca Creek, Apache
Penhatchapet Mountains	See Harquahala Mountains, La Paz
Pennsylvania Ranch	See Patagonia, Santa Cruz, and Hughes Mountain, Santa Cruz
Penrod	See Pinetop, Apache
Penrod Flat	See Pinetop, Apache
Peoples Ranch	See Peeples Ranch, Yavapai
Peoria Dam	See Gillespie Dam, Maricopa
Pepchalk	See Pepchiltk, Pinal
Peppersauce Canyon	See Peppersauce Wash, Pinal
Peppersauce Gulch	See Peppersauce Wash, Pinal
Percheron	See Pinedale, Navajo
Perhaps Mine	See Woolsey Peak, Maricopa
Peralta Canyon	See Peraltas Hill, Pinal
Peregua	See Hickiwan, Pima
Peria Mountains	See Perilla Mountains, Cochise
Peridot Hill	See Peridot, Gila
Peridot Ridge	See Peridot Creek, Gila
Perigua	See Hickiwan, Pima
Peri Mountains	See Perilla Mountains, Cochise
Perinimo	See Pisinimo, Pima
Periqua	See Hickiwan, Pima
Perky, The (River)	See Puerco River, Apache/Navajo
Perley Creek	See Pearly Creek, Gila
Perry Mesa	See Baby Canyon Indian Ruins, Yavapai
Pershing	See Ashurst, Graham
Pescado, Rio	See Zuñi River, Apache/New Mexico
Petà'íkuk	See Pima Villages, Pinal
Petato	See Gila Bend, Maricopa
Peterman's Station	See Mohawk, Yuma

Pete Smith Peak	See Smith Peak, Yuma
Peterson's Switch	See Kyrene, Maricopa
Petroglyph Wash	(Mohave, T31N/R21W) See Petroglyph, Maricopa
Phantom Camp	See Phantom Ranch, Coconino (Grand Canyon)
Phenix	See Phoenix, Maricopa
Phoenix Park Wash	(T11N/R17E) See Phoenix Park Canyon, Navajo
Pia Oik Pass	(T16S/R3W) See Pia Oik, Pima
Pia Oik Valley	(T17S/R2W) See Pia Oik, Pima
Pia Oik Wash	See Pia Oik, Pima
Picacho	See Topographical Hill, Coconino, or Picacho Butte, Pinal
Picacho City	See Picacho (town), Pinal
Picacho de Baboquivari	See Baboquivari Peak, Pima
Picacho de Calero	See Twin Peaks, Pima
Picacho del Diablo	See Pete Mountain, Santa Cruz
Picacho del Sentinela	See Sentinel Peak, Pima
Picacho de Metates	See Sentinel Peak, Pima
Picacho del Tucson	See Picacho Peak, Pinal
Picacho Lake	See Picacho Pass, Pinal, and Santa Cruz River, Santa Cruz
Picacho Peak Sahuaro Forest State Park	See Picacho Pass, Pinal
Picacho Peak State Park	See Picacho Pass, Pinal
Picacho Spring	See Picacho, Yavapai
Picacho Station	See Picacho Pass, Pinal
Picadilla Creek	See Otero Creek, Maricopa
Picinemoi	See Pisinimo, Pima
Picket Post	See Pinal, Pinal
Picket Post Butte	See Sentinel Mountain, Pima
Picket Post, Camp	See Pinal, Pinal, and Queen Creek, Pinal
Pico del Aguila	(Spanish = "eagle's point") See Aguila, Maricopa
Picture Rock	(Mohave, T15N/R20W) See Picture Rocks, Pima
Picture Rocks	See Painted Rocks, Maricopa, or Picture Rocks, Pima
Picture Rocks	(Pinal, T5S/R10E; Elev. 1937') See Picture Rocks, Pima
Piedra, Charco de La	See Hotasan Vo, Pima
Pierce Canyon	See Pearce Canyon, Mohave
Pierce Ferry, Fort, Mill Canyon	See Pearce Ferry, Mohave
Pierce Mountain	(T9N/R25E) See Pearce Wash, Navajo
Pierce Wash	(T11N/R17E) See Pearce Wash, Navajo
Pigeon Spring	See Pigeon Canyon, Mohave
Pigeon Spring	(Yavapai, T13N/R3W) See Pigeon Spring, Gila
Pigeon Wash	(T33N/R15W) See Pigeon Canyon, Mohave
Pigg Spring	See Pig Spring, Gila
Piloleno Mountain	See Pinaleno Mountains, Graham
Pilot Knob	See Pilot Rock, Mohave
Pilot Rock	See Mitten Peak, Navajo
Pima Agency	See Sacaton, Pinal
Pima Canyon	(T12S/R14E) See Pima County
Pima Gap	(T4S/R26E; Graham) See Pima County
Pimas Plain	See Forty Mile Desert
Pimas, Playa de Los	See Willcox Playa, Cochise
Pima-Sobaipuri River	See Pedro River, San, Cochise
Pima Spring	(T12S/R14E) See Pima Canyon, Pima
Pima Wash	See Pima Canyon, Pima
Pinacata Plain	See Pinacate Valley, Yuma
Pinal City	See Pinal, Pinal
Pinal Discovery	See Big Johnney Gulch, Gila
Pinal, Old Camp	See Pinal, Camp, Pinal

Pinal Point	See Pinal Peak, Greenlee
Pinal Ranch	See Pinal, Camp, Pinal
Pinaveta	See Pineveta, Yavapai
Pineair	See Reavis Ranch, Maricopa
Pine Canyon	(T12N/R9E; Gila) See Pine Butte, Gila
Pine Canyon	See Palisade Canyon, Pima
Pine Creek	See Pine Canyon, Cochise, or Turkey Creek, Coconino, or Reavis Creek, Pinal/Maricopa
Pine Flat	See Juniper Flat, Greenlee
Pine Flat Spring	See Pine Flat, Yavapai
Pine Hollow Canyon	See Pine Hollow, Coconino
Pine Mountain	See Pine Butte, Gila/Maricopa
Pine Mountain	(T11N/R5E; Elev. 6814') See Pine Flat, Yavapai
Pine Mountains	See Uinkaret Mountains, Mohave (Grand Canyon)
Pinedale Ridge, Wash	See Pinedale, Navajo
Pine Plain Mountains	See Pinaleno Mountains, Graham
Pine Ridge	See Pine Canyon, Cochise
Pinery Creek, Peak	See Pinery Canyon, Cochise
Pine Spring	(T12N/R9E) See Pine Canyon, Gila
Pine Spring	(T11N/R2W) See Dandy Wire Spring, Yavapai
Pine Springs Wash	(T2N/R25E) See Pine Springs, Apache
Pinetop Mountain, Springs	(T8N/R23E; Elev. 7385') See Pinetop, Navajo
Pinevela	See Pineveta, Yavapai
Pineveta Canyon	See Pineveta, Yavapai
Pinevita Mountain	See Pineveta, Yavapai
Pinnacle Mountain	See Pinnacle Peak, Maricopa
Pinnacle Peaks	See Chiricahua National Monument, Cochise
Piño Blanco Canyon	See Peña Blanca Canyon, Santa Cruz
Pinta	See Pinto, Apache
Pinta Mountains	See Pinta, Sierra, Yuma
Pinta Tank	See Heart Tank, Yuma
Pinto Mesa Spring	See Pinto Mesa, Yavapai
Pinto, Rio	See Pinto Creek, Gila
Pioneer Basin, Mountain, Pass	See Pioneer, Gila
Pipe Spring National Monument	See Pipe Spring, Mohave
Pipe Springs Wash	See Pipe Spring, Mohave
Pipestem Mountains	See Pipestem Creek, Greenlee
Pipe Valley Wash	See Pipe Spring, Mohave
Pipiaca	See Pipyak, Pima
Pipyak Valley	See Pipyak, Pima
Pirgua	See Hickiwan, Pima
Pirigua	See Hickiwan, Pima
Pirigua, Cerro de La	See Hickiwan, Pima
Piriqua	See Hickiwan, Pima
Pirtle	See Pirtleville, Cochise
Pisinemo	See Pisinimo, Pima
Pisinimo Valley	See Quijotoa Valley, Pima
Pisinimo Wash	See Pisinimo, Pima
Piskorski Canyon	See Peck Canyon, Santa Cruz
Pitchner Place	See Cornville, Yavapai
Pitote	See Castle Dome, Yuma
Pitsehytso Butte	See Bitsihuitsos Butte, Apache
Pittsburg Flat	See Pittsburg Landing, Mohave
Pitt Spring	See Pitt Tank, Coconino
Pius Farm Draw	See Pius Draw, Coconino
Pius Spring	See Pius Draw, Coconino
Piute Creek, Mesa	See Piute Canyon, Navajo
Pivotrock Spring	See Pivot Rock Canyon, Coconino
Placerita Gulch	See Placerita, Yavapai

Placeritas Creek	See Placerita, Yavapai
Placerville	See Willow Beach, Mohave (Lake Mead)
Plainview Point	See Plainview Peak, Graham
Planet Peak	See Planet, Mohave
Plateau of Arizona	See Coconino Plateau and Mogollon Plateau, Coconino/ Navajo
Plateau Point	See Poston Butte, Coconino (Grand Canyon)
Platos River, Los	See Francisco River, San, Greenlee
Platten Tank	(T2N/R4E) See Platten Springs, Coconino
Playa de Los Pimas	See Pedro Valley, San, Cochise
Playas	See Willcox, Cochise
Pleasant, Camp	See Carl Pleasant Lake, Maricopa
Pleasant Valley	See Mormon Lake, Coconino
Plomas Mountains	See Plomosa, La Paz
Plomo, El	See Alto, Santa Cruz
Plomosa Pass	(T4N/R17W) See Plomosa Mountains, La Paz
Plomosita Wash	(T3N/R18W) See Plomosa Mountains, La Paz
Plumas	See Plomosa, La Paz, and Harrisburg, La Paz
Plumosa Mountains	See Plomosa Mountains, La Paz
Plutonic Ridge	See Yuma, Yuma
Poachie Spring	(Elev. 3550') See Poachie Range, Mohave
Pochi Range	See Poachie Range, Mohave
Pocket Hill	(T41N/R13W; Mohave) See Pocket Creek, Gila
Pocket Lake	(T19N/R3E; Coconino) See Pocket Creek, Gila
Pocket Point	(T33N/R5W; Coconino) (Grand Canyon) See Pocket Creek, Gila
Pocket-To	See Colorado River
Pogue Butte	See Black Knob, Coconino
Pointer Mountain	See Point-of-Mountain, Pima
Point of Mountain	See Steele's Station, Cochise
Point of Pines Creek	(T1S/R24E) See Point of Pines (Ruins), Graham
Point of Rocks	See Granite Dells, Yavapai
Point of the Mountain Spring	See Point of the Mountain, Apache
Poison Canyon	(T12N/R9E) See Poison Spring, Gila
Poison Creek	(T9N/R2E; Yavapai) See Poison Spring, Gila
Poison Springs Wash	(T3N/R14E) See Poison Spring, Gila
Poker Canyon	(T3N/R24E) See Poker Mountain, Apache
Poker Gap Creek	(T2N/R24E) See Poker Mountain, Apache
Polaco	See Peck Canyon, Santa Cruz
Poland Creek	(T10N/R1E) See Poland, Yavapai
Poland Junction	(T12N/R1E) See Poland, Yavapai
Pole Bridge Canyon Natural Area	See Pole Bridge Canyon, Cochise
Pole Camp Canyon	See Pole Bridge Canyon, Cochise
Pomo, El	See Alto, Santa Cruz
Pond Canyon	(T33N/R2E) See Walla Valley, Coconino (Grand Canyon)
Porphyry Canyon	See Porphyry Mountain, Gila
Portal Peak	(T17S/R30E) See Portal, Cochise
Porter Canyon	See Porter Creek, Navajo
Porter Lake, Spring	(T9N/R25E) See Porter Creek, Navajo
Porter Mountain	(T9N/R23E; Elev. 7560') See Porter Creek, Navajo
Portrero	See Potrero Canyon, Santa Cruz
Posas Plain	See Posa Plain, La, Yuma
Poses, Los	See Posa Plain, La, Yuma
Poso Blanco	See Stoa Vaya, Pima
Postal's Ranch	See Del Rio Dam, Yavapai
Post Canyon	See Huachuca Canyon, Cochise/Santa Cruz
Postle Ranch	See Del Rio Dam, Yavapai
Post Office Canyon	See Post Office Hill, Navajo
Postvale	See Marana, Pima

Potato Ranch	See Tower Mountain, Yavapai
Pot Hole Peak	(Elev. 6880') See Pot Holes Canyon, Cochise
Potrero Creek	See Potrero Canyon, Santa Cruz
Potrero Ranch, El	(T23S/R13E) See Kitchen Ranch, Pete, Santa Cruz, and Potrero Canyon, Santa Cruz
Potter's Place Draw	(T17N/R26E) See Potter Mesa, Apache
Pottery Cave	See Harris Cave, Apache
Potts Tank	(Elev. 2000') See Potts Mountain, Mohave
Pounc A Gunt Creek	See Beaver Creek, Coconino, and Wall Creek, Coconino (Grand Canyon)
Poverty Mountain, Spring	(Elev. 6791') See Poverty Knoll, Mohave
Powell	See Needles, The, Mohave
Powell Island, Lake	See Antelope Island, Coconino
Powell Park	See Clay Park, Coconino
Powell (R. R. Stn.)	See Topock, Mohave
Powell Spring	See Powell Plateau, Coconino (Grand Canyon)
Powers	See Rucker, Cochise
Powmott	See Ruby, Santa Cruz
Poza, La	See Posa Plain, La, Yuma
Pozo Blanco	See Stoa Vaya, Pima
Pozo Bueno	See Posa Buena, Pima
Pozo Colorado	See Sauceda Mountains, Maricopa, and Vokivaxia (= "red well"), Pima
Pozo de Federico	See Kuakatch, Pima
Pozo de La Rosa	See Pine Springs, Coconino
Pozo de Santa Isabel	See Red Horse Wash, Coconino
Pozo Nuevo	See Poso Nuevo, Pima
Pozo Redondo, Mountains, Valley	See Sikort Chuapo, Pima
Pozos de San Basilio	See Pete Spring, Mohave
Pozos, Los	See Posos, Los, La Paz
Pozo Topado	See Covered Wells, Pima, and Maish Vaya, Pima
Pozo Verde	See Poso Verde, Pima
Pozo Verde Mountains	(T22S/R7E) See Poso Verde, Pima
Pozo Verde, Sierra del	See Poso Verde, Pima
Prado	See Valle, Coconino
Prairie Wash	(T31N/R2W; Coconino [Grand Canyon]) See Prairie Tank, Yavapai
Pranty Creek	See Lewis and Pranty Creek, Maricopa
Preciendo Canyon	See Presumido Pass, Pima
Prescimida Pass	See Presumido Pass, Pima
Prescimido Pass	See Presumido Pass, Pima
Prescott Barracks	See Whipple, Fort, Yavapai
Prescott Forest Preserve	See Prescott National Forest, Yavapai
Prescott Junction	See Seligman, Yavapai
President Mine	See President Canyon, Graham
President's Forest, The	See Kaibab National Forest, Coconino
Presidio de San Ignacio de Tubac	See Tubac, Santa Cruz
Presidio of San Pedro	See Pedro, San, Cochise
Presumido Canyon	See Presumido Pass, Pima
Presumido Peak	(Elev. 4806') See Presumido Pass, Pima
Price Canyon	(T19S/R30E) See Price, Camp, Cochise
Price Pocket	See Price Canyon, Mohave
Price Spring	(T19S/R30E) See Price, Camp, Cochise
Price's Spring	See Price Canyon, Mohave
Pridham Creek	See Pridham Canyon, Cochise
Prieta Range	See Prieta, Sierra, Yavapai
Prieta, Rio	See Black River, Apache
Prieta River	(Apache/Navajo/Gila/Graham) See Black River, Apache
Prieta, Sierra	See Granite Peak, Mohave, or Slate Mountains, Pinal

Prieto, Cerro	(T20S/R8E; Elev. 4665'; Pima) See Prieta Peak, Pinal
Prieto, Cerro	(T10S/R9E; Elev. 2688') See Prieta Peak, Pinal
Prieto Creek	See Eagle Creek, Greenlee
Prieto Mountains, San	See Prieta, Sierra, Yavapai
Prieto, Rio	See Salt River, Gila/Maricopa
Prieto River	See Little Colorado River, Coconino
Prieto Wash, Cerro	(T18S/R10E; Pima) See Prieto Peak, Pinal
Primrose Hill	See Poston Butte, Pinal
Pringle Ranch	See Slinkard Springs, Pinal, and Pringle Wash, Gila
Proctor Wash	(Pima/Santa Cruz) See Proctor Spring, Pima
Promontory Point	See Promontory Butte, Coconino/Gila
Prospect Point	(T30N/R8W) See Prospect Canyon, Coconino (Grand Canyon)
Prospect Ridge, Valley	(T30N/R8W) See Prospect Canyon, Coconino (Grand Canyon)
Providence Wells	See Sasabe, Pima
P S Ranch Wild Life Area	See P S Knoll, Apache
Pudre Canyon	See Padre, Canyon, Coconino
Pueblo Colorado	See Ganado, Apache, and Wukopakabi, Apache
Pueblo Colorado River, Wash	See Pueblo Colorado Valley, Apache/Navajo
Pueblo Creek	See Walnut Creek National Monument, Coconino
Pueblo de La Concepcion	See Yuma, Yuma
Pueblo Ganado	See Wukopakabi, Apache
Pueblo Mine	See Pueblo Canyon, Gila
Pueblo Viejo Valley	See Pueblo Viejo, Graham
Puerco del Oriente, Rio de	See Puerco River, Apache
Puerco del Ouest, Rio	See Puerco River, Apache
Puerco of the West, Rio	See Puerco River, Apache
Puerco Ridge	(T17N/R25; Elev. 5670') See Puerco River, Apache
Puerco, Rio	See Puerco River, Apache, or Pedro River, San, Cochise
Puerta de Las Mulas	See Mule Mountains, Cochise
Puerta Limita, La	See Marsh Pass, Navajo
Puerto de Los Muchachos	See Madera Canyon, Santa Cruz
Puerto Blanco	See Dripping Springs, Pima, and Puerto Blanco Mountains, Pima
Puerto de Dado	See Apache Pass, Cochise
Puerto de Los Cocomaricopas	See Estrella Mountains, Maricopa
Pulcifer Spring	See Pulcifer Creek, Apache
Pulpit Rock	See Castle Rock Bay, Mohave
Pumphouse	See Vainom Kug, Pima
Pumpkin Center	See Punkin Center, Gila
Pumpkin Flower Butte	See Sunflower Butte, Navajo
Pumpkinville	See Phoenix, Maricopa
Puntney	See Puntenney, Yavapai
Purdy	See Duncan, Greenlee
Purple Hills Pass	See Explorer's Pass, Yuma
Pusch Peak	See Pusch Ridge, Pima
Putman Wash	See Putman Spring, Mohave
Puzzles Mountains	See Tank Mountains, Yuma
Pymn Canyon Pond	(T33N/R11W) See Pymn Canyon, Mohave
Pyramid Mountain	See Pyramid Butte, Navajo
Pyramid Rock	See Pyramid Canyon, Mohave
Q Ranch	See Ellison, Gila
Quagunt Butte, Creek, Valley	See Kwagunt Butte, Coconino (Grand Canyon)
Quajata Creek	(T9S/R4E; Elev. 2700') See Green's Wash, Pinal
Quajota Wash	See Greene's Wash, Pinal
Quajote	See Kohatk, Pinal

Quaking Aspen Spring	(T34N/R1E; Mohave) See Quaking Aspen Canyon, Coconino
Quartermaster Falls	See Quartermaster Canyon, Mohave
Quartsite Canyon, Peak	See Quartzite Canyon, Gila
Quartsite Mountain	See Quartzite Mountain, Pinal
Quartzite Peak	(T2N/R15E) See Quartzite Canyon, Gila
Quartzite Peak	(T11S/R8E; Elev. 3160'; Pima) See Quartzite Canyon, Gila
Quartzite Peak	(T4S/R18E; Elev. 4869') See Quartzite Canyon, Gila, and Huggins Peak, Pinal
Quartzite Spring	(T11S/R15E; Pima) See Quartzite Canyon, Gila
Quartz Lead Wash	(T18N/R5W; Yavapai) See Quartzite Canyon, Gila
Quartz Ridge	(T17S/R31E; Cochise) See Quartz Mountain, Yavapai
Quartz Valley	See Quartzsite, La Paz
Queantoweap Valley	See Whitmore Canyon, Mohave
Quebabi	See Guebabi, Santa Cruz
Queen Creek Canyon	See Queen Creek, Pinal/Maricopa
Queen Creek Mine Canal	(T2S/R12E) See Queen Creek, Pinal/Maricopa
Queen Valley	(T1S/R10E; Elev. 2020') See Queen Creek, Pinal/Maricopa
Quejotoa	See Quijotoa, Pima
Quemada Canyon	See Posta Quemada Canyon, Pima
Quercus Canyon	See Texas Canyon, Cochise
Querhus Canyon	See Texas Canyon, Cochise
Querino (R.R. Stn.)	See Querino Canyon, Apache
Querous Canyon	See Texas Canyon, Cochise
Quibury	See Quiburi Ruins, Cochise
Quien Sabe Peak	(Elev. 4884') See Quien Sabe Creek, Maricopa
Quien Sabe Spring	See Quien Sabe Creek, Maricopa
Quihus Canyon	See Texas Canyon, Cochise
Quijotoa City	See Quijotoa, Pima
Quijotoa Draw	See Greene's Wash, Pinal
Quijotoa Mine	(T15S/R2E) See Quijotoa, Pima
Quijotoa Mountains, Pass, Range, Wash	See Quijotoa, Pima
Quinlin (Site)	See Quinlin Mountains, Pima
Quirino Canyon	See Querino Canyon, Apache
Quitoac	See Picacho Mountains, Pinal
Quitobaquito	(T17S/R8W) See Quitobaquito Springs, Pima
Quitobaquito Hills, Mountains	See Quitobaquito Springs, Pima
Quitovac	See Quitobaquito Springs, Pima
Quitovaquita	See Quitobaquito Springs, Pima
Quituna, La	See Serafin, San, Pima, and Quituni Valley, Pima
Quituni, La	See Serafin, San, Pima, and Artesia Mountain, Pima
Quituni Valley, La	(T18S/R2W) See Ali Ak Chin, Pima
Quijote	See Kohatk, Pinal
Quyotia	See Quijotoa, Pima
Rabbit Bill Tank	See Babbitt Bill Tank, Coconino
Rabbit Ear Butte, Mountain	See Hopi Buttes, Navajo
Rabbit Mountain	See Pilot Rock, Navajo
Rabbit, The	See Monument Pass, Navajo
Raccoon	See Coon Creek, Gila
Raccoon Creek	See Sycamore Creek, Gila
Racetrack Ridge	See Johnson Wash, Yavapai
Rafael, San	See Guevavi, Santa Cruz
Rafael del Actum Grande, San	See Serafin, San, Pima
Rafael de La Zanja Land Grant, San	See Rafael, San, Santa Cruz (P.O.)

Rafael Hotaigue, San	See Agua Caliente, Maricopa
Rafael Land Grant, San	See Lochiel, Santa Cruz, and Rafael, San, Santa Cruz
Rafael Otagui, San	See Agua Caliente, Maricopa
Rafael Ranch, San	See Rafael, San, Santa Cruz
Railroad Spring	See Gentile Spring, Mohave
Rainbow Forest	(T16N/R23E; Navajo/Apache) See Petrified Forest National Monument, and Giant Logs, Navajo/Apache
Rain Mountain	See Sasetanha Mesa, Apache
Rain Tank Flat	(T33N/R5E) See Rain Tank, Coconino
Rain Tank Wash	(T29N/R2E) See Rain Tank, Coconino
Ralph's Mill	See Tacna, Yuma
Ralph's Mill – Tacna (P.O.)	See Tacna, Yuma
Ramah City	See Joseph City, Navajo
Ramanote Peak	See Ramonote Peak, Santa Cruz
Rambo Wash	See Ramboz Wash, Gila
Ramboz Camp, Spring	See Ramboz Peak, Gila
Ramita, La	See Laramita, Cochise
Ramonote Canyon	See Ramonote Peak, Santa Cruz
Ramsey Peak	See Ramsey Canyon, Cochise
Ramsgate Spring	See Ramsgate (R.R. Siding), Yavapai
Ranchera de Los Gandules	See Moenkopi, Coconino
Rancheria de San Diego	See Kenyon Station, Maricopa
Rancho de Las Calabasas	See Calabasas, Santa Cruz
Ranegras Plain	See Ranegas Plain, La Paz
Ra Pyramid	See Ra, Tower of, Coconino (Grand Canyon)
Raspberry Basin	See Raspberry Creek, Greenlee
Raspberry Peak	(T3N/R30E; Elev. 8318') See Raspberry Creek, Greenlee
Raventon Ranch	See Reventon Ranch, Santa Cruz
Rawcom Tank	See Bawcom Tank, Coconino
Rawhide Canyon	(T2S/R13E; Pinal) See Rawhide Mountain, Graham/Pinal
Rawhide Mine, Wash	See Rawhide Mountains, Mohave
Ray Hill	See Ray, Pinal
Ray Junction	(T4S/R13E) See Kelvin, Pinal, and Ray, Pinal
Raymert, Raymert Wash	See Reymert, Pinal
Ray Mine	See Ray, Pinal
Rayner's	See Ramer Ranch, Gila
Redhead Wash	See Linden Draw, Navajo
Real Spring	See Beale Springs, Camp, Mohave
Reamer Draw, Peak	See Reimer Draw, Yavapai
Reavis Gap	See Reavis Ranch, Maricopa
Reavis Saddle Spring	(T1N/R11E) See Reavis Ranch, Pinal
Redland	See Ashhurst, Graham, and Cork, Graham
Redman Crossing, Flat	See Redman Mesa, Gila
Redondo Canyon	See Sikort Chuapo, Pima
Red Rooster Spring	See Red Rooster Mountain, Pinal
Reef	See Garces, Cochise
Reese Canyon	See Reese Peak, Coconino
Reevis Creek, Ranch, Saddle Spring, Trail Canyon	See Reavis Ranch, Pinal
Regal Creek, Mine Camp	See Regal Canyon, Gila
Reiley Canyon, Creek	(T12S/R22E) See Reilly Peak, Cochise
Reiley Hill	(T11S/R22E; Elev. 5485') See Reilly Peak, Cochise
Reiley Peak	See Reilly Peak, Cochise
Reimer Draw	See Reimer Peak, Yavapai
Reimer Spring	(T12N/R4E) See Reimer Peak, Yavapai
Renegade Ridge	See Greaterville, Pima
Reno Canyon	(T6N/R10E) See Reno, Camp, Gila
Reno Creek, Mount	See Reno, Camp, Gila
Reno Mountain	See Edwards' Peak, Gila

Represso	See Oracle Junction, Pinal
Reservation Flat	(T8N/R24) See Reservation Creek, Apache
Reservation Lake	(Elev. c. 9500') See Reservation Creek, Apache
Reservation Spring	(T9N/R24E) See Reservation Creek, Apache
Revantano	See Reventon Ranch, Santa Cruz
Reyes, Los	See Sonoita, Santa Cruz
Reyes, El Rio de Los	See Verde, Camp, Yavapai
Reyes de Sonoydag, Los	See Sonoita, Santa Cruz
Reymert Wash	See Reymert, Pinal
Rhoades, Rhoades Tank	See Parks, Coconino
Rhyolite Park	See Chiricahua National Monument, Cochise
Rice	See Carlos, San, Gila
Rice Canyon	(T12N/R4E) See Rice Peak, Yavapai
Rice Gulch	See Rice Peak, Yavapai, and Yellowjacket Gulch, Yavapai
Rice, Mount, Spring	See Rice Peak, Pima
Richey	See Richville, Apache
Rich Hill	See Antelope Peak, Yavapai
Richmond	See Tombstone, Cochise
Richmond Mountain	(T2N/R16E; Elev. 5836') See Richmond Basin, Gila
Richville Valley	See Richville, Apache
Rickerson, Fort	See Moroni, Fort, Coconino, and Fort Valley, Coconino
Rieletto	See Langhorne, Pima
Riggs Flat	(T8S/R23E) See Riggs, Camp, Graham
Riggs Flat Wild Life Area	See Riggs, Camp, Graham
Riggs Mesa	(T7S/R25E) See Riggs, Camp, Graham
Riggs Mountain	(T16S/R29E; Elev. 6153') See Ed Riggs Mountain, Cochise
Riggs Seep, Riggs Seep Spring	(T13S/R21E) See Ed Riggs Mountain, Cochise
Rim, The	See Mogollon Rim, Coconino
Rimmy Jims Tank	(T27N/R9E) See Rimmy Jims, Coconino
Rincon	See Lincon, Pima
Rincon, El	See Rincon Peak, Pima
Rinconada	See Aritutoc, Maricopa, and Gila Bend, Maricopa
Rincon Peak	(T15S/R18E; Elev. 8482') See Rincon Mountains, Pima
Rincon Range, Valley	See Rincon Mountains, Pima
Rincon, Sierra El	See Rincon Mountains, Pima
Ringon, Sierra del	See Rincon Mountains, Pima
Rio Rico	See Baca Float, Santa Cruz
Rioville	See Bonelli's Crossing, Mohave
Ripsey Peak	(T5S/R13E) See Ripsey Hill, Pinal
Ripsey Spring	See Ripsey Hill, Pinal
Ripsey Wash	(T4S/R13E) See Ripsey Hill, Pinal
Rita, Santa	See Greaterville, Pima
Rita Mountain, Santa	See Wrightson, Mount, Santa Cruz
Rita Peak, Santa	See Wrightson, Mount, Santa Cruz
Rita Range Reserve, Santa	See Rita Experimental Range and Wild Life Area, Santa, Pima/Santa Cruz
Ritter Mountain, Spring	See Ritter Butte, Coconino
Riverside	See Kelvin, Pinal
Riverton, El	See Reventon, Santa Cruz
Roade's Ranch	See Rhodes Ranch, Santa Cruz
Road Runner; Mountain	See Tatai Toak, Pima
Roberts Butte	See Robbins Butte, Maricopa
Robinson	See Pomerene, Cochise
Robinson Crater	(Elev. 7341') See Robinson Mountain, Coconino
Roblas Canyon	See Roblas Butte, Pinal
Robles Canyon	(T13S/R18E) See Robles Junction, Pima
Robles Pass	(Elev. 2650') See Robles Junction, Pima
Rockwood	See Hunt, Apache
Rocky Point	See Itak, Pima

Roddick Mountain	See Fraguita, Mount, Pima
Roden Crater	See Roden Spring, Coconino
Rodes Ranch	See Rhodes, La Paz
Rodick, Mount	See Fraquita Peak, Santa Cruz
Rodin's Cone	See Roden Spring, Coconino
Rodgers Tank	See Rogers Tank, Yavapai
Roggenstroh Mountains	See Rockinstraw Mountains, Gila
Rollen	See Patagonia, Santa Cruz
Rollin Town	See Patagonia, Santa Cruz
Roll Valley	(T14S/R9W) See Roll, Yuma
Romaine's Field	See Hoa Murk, Pima
Roods Ranch	See Rhodes Ranch, Santa Cruz
Roosevelt Camp	See Phantom Ranch, Coconino (Grand Canyon)
Roosevelt Dam, Lake	See Theodore Roosevelt Dam, Gila
Rooster Mesa	See Meridian Butte, Apache
Rooster Rock	(Elev. 5984') See Meridian Butte, Apache
Rosa del Achi, Santa	See Gu Achi, Pima
Rosa, Santa	See Gu Achi, Pima
Rosario	See Prospect, Cochise
Rosa Ranch, Santa	See Schuchk, Pima
Rosa, Sierra de Santa	(T18S/R3W; Elev. 2650'; Pima) See Ajo Range, Pima, and Rosa Mountains, Santa, Pima/Pinal
Rosa Valley, Santa	(T10S/R4E; Pima/Pinal) See Rosa Mountains, Santa, Pima/Pinal
Rosa Wash, Santa	(T9S/R4E; Pima/Pinal) See Rosa Mountains, Santa, Pima/Pinal, and Kohatk, Pinal
Rose Canyon, Rose Canyon Lake	See Rose Canyon Lake Wild Life Area, Pima
Rose Peak	See Rose Canyon Wild Life Area, Pima
Rosey Creek	See Benny Creek, Apache
Roth, Charco de	See Roche, Charco de, Pima
Round Tree Spring	See Roundtree Canyon, Yavapai
Roundy Crossing	(T11N/R21E; Navajo) See Roundy Creek, Coconino
Rousensock Canyon	See Rousensock Creek, Greenlee
Rover Mountain	See Rover Peak, Yavapai
Rowe Knob	See Rose's Well, Coconino (Grand Canyon), and Hopi Point, Coconino (Grand Canyon)
Rowe's Point	See Rose's Well, Coconino (Grand Canyon), and Hopi Point, Coconino (Grand Canyon)
Rowe's Station	See Maryville, Maricopa
Rowood	See Clarkstown, Pima, and Gibson, Pima
Royal Arches	(T35N/R5E) See Royal Arch Creek, Coconino (Grand Canyon)
Roy Spring	See Willow Spring (#1), Graham
Rsà'nûk	See Pima Villages, Pinal/Maricopa
Rsótûk	See Pima Villages, Pinal
Ruby Creek	See Ruby, Santa Cruz
Ruby Peak	(Elev. 5050') See Ruby, Santa Cruz
Ruby Trail Dam	(T23S/R11E) See Ruby, Santa Cruz
Rucker	See Rucker Canyon (P.O.), Cochise
Rucker, Camp, Canyon	See Rucker Canyon (P.O.), Cochise
Rucker Canyon Dam	See Fred Winn Falls, Cochise
Rucker Lake	See Rucker Canyon (P.O.), Cochise
Rudd Knoll, Spring	(T7N/R28E) See Rudd Creek, Apache
Rudd's Reservoir	(T7N/R28E) See Rudd Creek, Apache
Russell	See Russellville, Cochise
Russell Camp, City	See Russellville, Cochise
Russell Spring	See Russell, Yavapai
Russellville Peak	(T15S/R22E; Elev. 6616') See Russellville, Cochise
Russell Wash	See Russell Tank, Coconino

Rustle Gulch	See Russell Gulch, Gila
Rustler Canyon	(T20S/R29E) See Rustler Park, Cochise
Rustler Park Canyon	See Rustler Park, Graham
Rustler's Ranch	(T6S/R24E) See Rustler Park, Graham
Rust's Camp	See Phantom Ranch, Coconino (Grand Canyon)
Rusty Shovel	See Vakomak, Pima
Ryan Station Water Fowl Area	See Ryan, Coconino
S-a′al-kuig	See Salt River Indian Reservation, Maricopa
Saavedra Spring	See Saevedra Spring, Mohave
Sabino (R.R. Stn.)	(T12S/R12E) See Sabino Canyon, Pima (T12S/R15E)
Sabino Wash	See Sabino Canyon, Pima
Sacaton Butte	See Sacaton, Pinal
Sacaton Crossing	See Sacaton Ranch, Pinal
Sacaton Flats	(T4S/R8E; Elev. 1310′; Pinal/Maricopa) See Sacaton, Pinal
Sacaton Peak	(T5S/R7E; Elev. 2755′) See Sacaton, Pinal
Sacatones, Sierra	See Sacaton, Pinal
Sacaton Station	See Oatman Flat, Maricopa
Sacramento Hill, Mountain	See Sacramento Pit, Cochise
Sacramento (R.R. Siding)	See Griffith, Mohave
Sacramento Range	See Black Range, Mohave
Sacramento, Rio	See Verde River, Yavapai
Sacramento River	See Verde River
Sacramento Wash	(T23N/R18W) See Sacramento Valley, Mohave
Saddle, The	See Saddle Butte, Coconino
Saddle Back Mountain	See Saddle Mountain, Maricopa, or Saddle Mountain, Pinal
Saddle Canyon	(T34N/R1W) See Saddle Mountain, Coconino (Grand Canyon)
Saffell Canyon	See Saffel Knoll, Apache
Safford Peak	(T12S/R12E; Elev. 3565′; Pima) See Safford, Graham
Safford Valley	See Gila Valley, Graham
Sa-Gee-Ka	See Segeke Butte, Navajo
Sage Park	See Sage Peak, Cochise
Sagyatsosi Canyon	See Tsegihatosi Canyon, Apache
Sagy Canyon	See Tsegi Canyon, Navajo
Sahdii Bisi	See Petrified Forest National Monument
Sahili Creek	See Tsaile Creek, Apache
Sahotsaidbeazite Canyon	See Dennehotso Canyon, Apache
Sahuarita Butte	(T15S/R13E; Elev. 3850′) See Martinez Hill, Pima
Sahuarita Wash	(T11S/R14E) See Sahuarita, Pima
Sahuarito	See Sahuarita, Pima
Sahuarito Butte	See Martinez Hill, Pima
Sahuaro Gap Well	See Sahuaro Gap, Yuma
Sahuaro Lake	See Saguaro Lake, Maricopa
Sahwick	See Sawik, Maricopa
Sajini Butte	See Black Pinnacle Butte, Apache
Salado (Site)	(T12N/R28E) See Lyman Lake, Apache
Salado	See Salt River, Gila/Maricopa
Salado Reservoir	See Lyman Lake, Apache
Salado, Rio	See Salt River, Gila/Maricopa
Salado Spring	(T12N/R28E) See Lyman Lake, Apache
Salahkai Mesa, Point, Wash	See Balakai Mesa, Apache
Salceda Mountains	See Sauceda Mountains, Maricopa/Pima
Salee	See Tsehili, Apache, and Tsaile Creek, Apache
Salem	See Johns, Saint, Apache
Salero, Salero Hill	See Salero Mountain, Santa Cruz
Saletso Spring	See Setsiltso Spring, Apache

Salida Spring	See Salida Gulch, Yavapai
Salina Springs	See Salina, Apache
Salines, Rio	See Salt River, Gila/Maricopa
Salines River	See Salt River, Gila/Maricopa
Salitre Mountains	See Galiuro Mountains, Graham
Salitre Negro, El	See Black Creek, Apache
Salltso Spring	See Setsiltso Spring, Apache
Sally May Canyon	See Sally May Wash, Yavapai
Sally May Creek	See Salome Creek, Gila
Sally May Spring	See Sally May Wash, Yavapai
Salmon Lake Basin, Butte	See Salmon Lake, Coconino
Salome Mountain	(T15N/R11E; Elev. c. 5426') See Salome Creek, Gila
Salome Peak	(T6N/R14W; Elev. 3991') See Salome, La Paz
Salome Wash	See Salome, La Paz
Salt Banks	(Gila/Maricopa) See Salt River, Gila/Maricopa, and Salt River Draw, Navajo/Gila
Salt Canyon	(T10N/R13E; Gila) See Salt River, Gila/Maricopa
Salt Creek Rapids	See Salt Creek, Coconino (Grand Canyon)
Salt Lake	See Willcox, Cochise
Salt Mountain	(T2S/R20E) See Salt Creek, Gila
Salt Mountains	See Superstition Mountains, Pinal
Salt River Mountains	(T3N/R14E; Elev. 4857'; Gila) See Salt River, Gila/Maricopa, or South Mountains, Maricopa
Salt River National Wild Life Refuge	(T4N/R12E; Elev. c. 3000'; Gila) See Salt River, Gila/Maricopa
Salt River Peak	(T2N/R14E; Elev. 4857'; Gila) See Salt River, Gila/Maricopa
Salt River Range	See South Mountains, Maricopa
Salt River Valley	See Salt River, Gila/Maricopa
Salumay	See Salome Creek, Gila
Samaniego Hills	(T10S/R9E; Pinal) See Samaniego Peak, Pima
Samclark	See Clarkstown, Pima, and Rowood, Pima
Sand Creek	See Williams Fork, Mohave
Sand Wells	See Chot Vaya, Pima
Sanford	See Adamsville, Pinal
Santan Mountains	(T3S/R6E; Elev. 3093') See Santan, Pinal
Santiago, Sierra de	See Black Mountains, Mohave
Santos Angeles	See Guevavi, Santa Cruz
Santos Apostales San Simon Y Judas	See Gila Bend, Maricopa
Sanup Peak	See Sanup Plateau, Mohave
Sanur Plateau	See Shivwits Plateau, Mohave
S'a'opuk	See Pima Villages, Pinal/Maricopa
Sapori Ranch	See Sopori Ranch, Pima
Sarah Deming Trail	See Sarah Deming Canyon, Cochise
Saranake	See Sil Nakya, Pima
Sardina Canyon	(T20S/R11E) See Sardina Peak, Pima
Sardina Dam	See Sardina Peak, Santa Cruz
Sardine Falls, Saddle	See Sardine Creek, Greenlee
Sasabe, Arroyo del	See Sasabe, Pima
Sasabe Flat Valley	See Sasabe, Pima
Sasabi Flat	See Sasabe, Pima
Sasaby Falt	See Sasabe, Pima
Sastanha Mesa	See Sasetanha Mesa, Apache
Saurita	See Sahuarita, Pima
Sauz, Cienega	See Simon Valley, San, Cochise
Sauz, Rio	See Simon Valley, San, Cochise
Sauz, Valley del	See Simon Valley, San, Cochise
Savadras Spring	See Saevedra Spring, Mohave

Savedra Springs	See Saevedra Spring, Mohave
S B Canyon	See One Hundred and Fifty Mile Canyon, Mohave
Scanlon Ferry, Wash	See Greggs Ferry, Mohave
Scenic Divide	See Grand Scenic Divide, Coconino (Grand Canyon)
Scheelite Ridge	See Scheelite Canyon, Cochise
Schook Toahk Canal	See Slate Mountains, Pinal
Schuchli	See Gunsight Range, Pima, and Gunsight, Pima
Schuchk	See Schuck, Pima
Schuchuli	See Gunsight Range, Pima, and Gunsight, Pima
Schultz Mountain, Peak, Spring	See Schultz Pass, Coconino
Schunchule	See Gunsight Range, Pima, and Gunsight, Pima
Scull Valley	See Skull Valley, Yavapai
Sears Wash	See Salt Seeps Wash, Navajo
Seba Dalkai Wash	See Tees Toh Wash, Navajo
Sebi Dakai Butte	See Tees Toh Wash, Navajo
Second Forest	(T17N/R24E; Apache/Navajo) See Crystal Forest and Petrified National Forest, Apache/Navajo
Second Hollow	See First Hollow, Navajo
Second Knoll	See First Knoll, Navajo
Second Lagune (sic)	See Laguna, Yuma
Second Mesa	See Toreva, Navajo
Second Mesa Wash	See Second Mesa, Navajo
Secret Canyon	(Yavapai/Coconino) See Secret Mountain, Yavapai
Secret Hill; Pass Canyon; Pass Spring: Spring	See Secret Pass, Mohave
Secret Pass Wash	(T20N/R18W) See Secret Pass, Mohave
Sedro	See Johns, Saint, Apache
See-Cho-Maw-Wee	See Sichomovi, Navajo
Seecko-Wah-Wee	See Sikyatki, Navajo, and Sichomovi, Navajo
Seepage Canyon	See Seepage Mountain, Yavapai
See Spring	See See Canyon, Gila
Segatoa (Spring)	See Tsegitoa (Spring), Apache
Segetoa (Spring)	See Tsegitoe (Spring), Apache
Segihatsosi (Canyon)	See Tsegihatsosi (Canyon), Apache
Se-Gi-Ke Butte	See Segeka Butte, Navajo
Segi Mesas	See Tsegi Mesas, Navajo
Sehili Creek	See Tsaile (Creek), Apache
Seiber Point	See Sieber Point, Coconino (Grand Canyon)
Seligman Canyon	(T16N/R9W) See Seligman, Yavapai
Sells Agency	See Gu Achi, Pima, and Sells, Pima
Sells Valley	(T18S/R4E) See Sells, Pima
Senator	See Venezia, Yavapai, and Goodwin, Yavapai
Seneca Howland, Mount	See Navajo Mountain, Coconino
Sentinela, Picacho del	See Sentinel Peak, Pima
Sentinel Mountain	See Sentinel Peak, Pima
Sentinel Peak	(Elev. 1077') See Sentinel, Maricopa
Sentinel Peak	See Pete Mountain, Santa Cruz
Sentinel Plain	(T6S/R8W) See Sentinel, Maricopa
Sentinel Point	See Powell Memorial Point, Coconino (Grand Canyon)
Sentinel Wash	(T6S/R10W) See Sentinel, Maricopa
Separation Canyon	(T28N/R12W) See Separation Rapids, Mohave (Grand Canyon)
Sepori	See Sopori Ranch, Santa Cruz
Sepulveda Wash	See Sepulveda Creek, Apache
Serafin del Actum Grande, San	See Serafin, San, Pima
Serafino del Napcut, San	See Serafin, San, Pima
Seranake	See Sil Nakya, Pima
Serape	(T2S/R5E; Elev. 1220') See Tatkum Vo, Maricopa
Serguio, San	See Quito Baquito, Pima

Seri Point	See Pima Point, Coconino (Grand Canyon)
Serpentine Canyon, Rapids	See Shinumo Altar, Coconino (Grand Canyon)
Serventi Well	See Stanshuatak, Pima
Seven Cataracts	See Seven Falls, Pima
Seven Cities of Cibola	See Hopi Villages
Seven Mile Canyon	See Emigrant Canyon, Cochise, or Sevenmile Hill, Navajo
Seven Mile Canyon (#2)	See Sevenmile Wash, Gila
Sevenmile Creek, Crossing, Draw	See Sevenmile Wash, Gila
Sevenmile Mountain	(T3N/R17E) See Sevenmile Wash, Gila
Sevenmile Rim	(T5N/R24E; Elev. 6441') See Sevenmile Hill, Navajo
Seven Springs	See Seven Springs Wash, Apache
Seven Springs Wash	See Beaver Dam Wash, Mohave
Seventy-Five Mile Creek	See Seventy-Five Mile Rapid, Coconino (Grand Canyon)
Seymour	See Vulture, Maricopa
Sezhini Butte	See Black Rock Butte, Apache
Shaatikum	See Camote, Pima
Shaatkam	See Camote, Pima
Sháa Toho Ha Atiin	See Wild Cherry Canyon, Apache
Shaler Pyramid	See Shaler Plateau, Coconino (Grand Canyon), and Galahad Point, Coconino (Grand Canyon)
Shaleys Fork	See Bonita Creek, Graham
Shannon Hill	See Shannon Mountain, Greenlee
Shanto	See Shonto, Navajo
Shanto Spring	See Masipa Spring, Navajo
Shaotkam	See Camote, Pima
Sha-Pah-Lah-Wee	See Shipolovi, Navajo
Sharp Mountain	See Bangs, Mount, Mohave
Sharps	See Ray, Pinal
Sharp's Bar	See Willow Beach, Mohave (Lake Mead)
Shash Bitoo	See Bear Springs, Navajo
Shashdits'inih	See Black Rock Butte, Apache
Sha-To	See Masipa Spring, Navajo
Shato Canyon	See Shonto Spring, Navajo
Shato Plateau	See Shonto Spring, Navajo
Shato Wash	(Coconino/Navajo) See Shonto Spring, Navajo
Sheavwitz Plateau	See Shivwits Plateau, Mohave
Sheehy Spring	(T24S/R17E) See Sheehy Canyon, Santa Cruz
Sheldon Canyon	See Sheldon, Greenlee, and Ash Peak Canyon, Greenlee
Sheldon Mountain	(T7S/R36E; Elev. 5410') See Sheldon, Greenlee
Sheldon Mountain	(Elev. 2135') See Granite Reef Mountain, Maricopa
Sheno-Mo Canyon	See Shinumo Altar, Coconino (Grand Canyon)
Sheridan Hills, Lake	See Sheridan Mountains, Pima
Sherum Peak	See Cherum Peak, Mohave
Sheshe Canyon	See Sheehy Canyon, Santa Cruz
Shedelon Creek	See Chevelon Creek, Navajo
Shedlon's Fork	See Chevelon Creek, Navajo
Shewits Plateau	See Shivwits Plateau, Mohave
Shi-Mo-Pavi	See Shongopovi, Navajo
Shina-Bitz-Spits Spring	See Wolf Hole, Mohave
Shina-Bitz Spring	See Wolf Hole, Mohave
Shinarump Point	(T42N/R2W; Coconino) See Shinarump Cliffs, Coconino/Mohave
Shingle Mill Canyon	See Shingle Mill Mountain, Graham
Shinumo Amphitheater	(T33N/R1W) See Shinumo Altar, Coconino (Grand Canyon)
Shinumo Canyon, Creek, Garden, Rapids, Trail, Wash	See Shinumo Altar, Coconino (Grand Canyon)
Shi-Pau-I-Luvi	See Shipolovi, Navajo
Shipaulovi	See Shipolovi, Navajo

Shiwitz Plateau	See Shivwits Plateau, Mohave
Shoens Crossing	See Shones Crossing, Navajo
Shongopavi	See Shungopavy, Navajo
Shongopovi, Old (Site)	(T28N/R17E) See Shungopavy, Navajo
Shongopovi Spring	See Shungopavy, Navajo
Shonto Plateau, Wash	See Shonto Spring, Coconino/Navajo
Shopishk Valley	See Shopishk, Pinal
Short Creek	See Colorado City, Mohave
Short Horn Mountains	See S H Mountains, Yuma
Show Low Creek, Dam, Lake	See Show Low, Navajo
Showmowth-Pa	See Shungopavi, Navajo
Shultz Spring	See Shultz, Pinal
Shumuthpa	See Shungopavi, Navajo
Shumway Butte, Ruin	See Shumway, Navajo
Shungopa Spring	See Masipa Spring, Navajo
Shung-O-Pah-Wee	See Shungopavi, Navajo
Shungopovi Spring	See Shungopavi, Navajo
Shute Springs Creek	(T3N/R14E) See Shute Springs, Gila
Sibuóidah, El	See Kohatk, Pinal
Sibupic, Sierra	See Painted Rocks, Maricopa
Si-Chom-Ivi	See Sichomovi, Navajo
Siclehema	See Sikul Haimatk, Pima
Sidney	See Buckeye, Maricopa
Sieber Creek	(Elev. c. 5000'; Gila) See Sieber Point, Coconino (Grand Canyon)
Sieneguilla de Maria	See Michaels, Saint, Apache
Sierrita, Sierrita Prieta	See Slate Mountains, Pinal
Signal Peak	See Signal Mountain, Mohave, and Signal, Mohave
Siilimok	See Sil Murk, Maricopa
Sikort Chuapo Mountains	(Elev. 3603') See Sikort Chuapo, Pima
Sikort Chuapo Pass	See Sikort Chuapo, Pima
Sikort Chuapo Wash	(T12S/R4W) See Sikort Chuapo, Pima
Sikortjuupo	See Sikort Chuapo, Pima
Sikul Himatk Wash	See Sikul Himatk, Pima
Silinakik	See Sil Nakya, Pima
Silh-Tusayan	See Fluted Rock, Apache
Sil Nakya Hills	(Elev. 2846') See Sil Nakya, Pima
Sil Nakya Pass, Valley, Wash	See Sil Nakya, Pima
Silverbell Mountains	(T11S/R8E; Elev. 4261') See Silverbell, Pima
Silverbell Peak, Valley, Wash	See Silverbell, Pima
Silver Clip Claim	See Clip, Yuma
Silver Creek	See Lava Creek, Coconino (Grand Canyon)
Silver Creek	(T13N/R23E; Elev. c. 6100') See Silver Creek (Town), Navajo
Silver Creek Wash	See Silver Creek, Mohave
Silver Hill	See Abbie Waterman Peak, Pima
Silver King Wash	(T1S/R12E) See Silver King, Pinal
Silver Lake	See White Mountain Lake, Navajo
Silver Mountains, Range	See Bradshaw Mountains, Yavapai
Silver Reef Pass, Valley, Wash	See Silver Reef Mountains, Pinal
Silynarki	See Sil Nakya, Pima
Simmons Peak	(Elev. 5758') See Simmons, Yavapai
Simmons Valley	See Simmons, Yavapai
Simon, San	See Wahak Hotrontk, Pima
Simon Cienega, San	(T15S/R32E) See Simon River, San, Cochise/Graham
Simon Creek, San	See Simon River, San, Cochise/Graham
Simon Dam, San	(T11S/R29E; Graham) See Simon River, San, Cochise/Graham
Simon Head, San	(T16S/R30E) See Simon River, San, Cochise/Graham

Simon Peak, San	(T11S/R31E; Elev. 5325') See Simon River, San, Cochise/ Graham
Simon Valley, San	(T10S/R29E) See Simon River, San, Cochise/Graham
Simon Valley, San	(T14S/R1-E-2W; Elev. 1800-1945') See Quijotoa Valley, Pima
Simon Wash, San	See Simon River, San, Cochise/Graham
Simon Wash, San	See Quijotoa Valley, Pima
Sinagua, Sierra	See Francisco Peaks, San, Coconino, and Sinagua Valley, Coconino
Sinyala Butte, Canyon, Mesa, Mount, Rapids	See Sinyella, Mount, Coconino (Grand Canyon)
Siovaxia	See Bitter Well, Pinal
Siovi Shuatak	See Sweetwater, Pima
Siovi Shuatak Pass, Wash	See Sweetwater, Pima
Siovo Shuatak Pass, Wash	See Sweetwater, Pima
Sipaulovi	See Shipolovi, Navajo
Sisalatuk	See Gunsight, Pima
Sit-La-Lar-Te	See Grant, Camp/Fort, Graham
Siviuni	See Sichomovi, Navajo
Sivvaxia	See Sif Vaya, Pinal
Six Mile Hill	(T18S/R25E; Elev. 4898') See Pearce, Cochise
Sixteen Spring	(T15N/R11E) See Fain Mountain, Coconino
Sixty Mile Canyon, Rapids	See Sixtymile Creek, Coconino (Grand Canyon)
Skakaik	See Pima Villages, Pinal/Maricopa
Skeleton Cave	See Apache Cave, Maricopa
Skinner Pasture Tank	See Skinner Ridge, Coconino
Skinnerville	See Troy, Pinal
Skull Cave	See Apache Cave, Maricopa
Skull Mesa	(T7N/R4E; Elev. 4619') See Apache Cave, Maricopa
Skull Valley, Camp; Station; Wash	See Skull Valley, Yavapai
Slate Lakes	(T24N/R6E) See Slate Mountain, Coconino
Slate Lakes Cave	See Slate Mountain, Coconino
Sleeping Beauty Spring	See Sleeping Beauty Peak, Gila
Sleeping Woman	See Red Mountain, Santa Cruz
Sliker Tank	See Sliker Hill, Coconino
Slough Reservoir	See Lyman Lake, Apache
Small Akchin	See Serafin, San, Pima
Smetter's Ranch	See Agua Fria Ranch, Maricopa
Smith Creek	(T7N/R26E) See Smith Cienega, Apache
Smith Mesa	(T16N/R6W) See Smith Canyon, Yavapai
Smith Spring	See Black Rock Spring, Navajo
Smith Station	See Phoenix, Maricopa
Smithville	See Pima, Graham
Smuggler's Trail	See Dripping Springs, Yuma
Snake Creek	(T7N/R26E) See White River, Apache/Navajo
Snider Prairie	See Garland Prairie, Coconino
Snider's Station	See Bumble Bee, Yavapai
Snider's Waterhole	See Garland Prairie, Coconino
Snivelly's	See Gillette, Maricopa, and Dome, Yuma
Snowball	See Hart Prairie, Coconino
Snowball	See Germa, Mohave
Snow Lake	See Chavez Pass, Coconino
Snowshed	See Chiricahua Peak, Cochise
Snowstake Creek	(T7N/R25E; Elev. c. 8500') See Becker Creek, Apache
Snyder Gulch	See Chilito, Gila
Snyder Hole	See Garland Prairie, Coconino
Soacson	See Sacate, Pinal
Soap Creek Pasture	See Soap Creek #2, Coconino
Sobahipuri River	See Pedro River, San, Cochise

Sobaipuri-Pima (River)	See Cruz River, Santa, Santa Cruz
Socatoon	See Sacaton, Pinal
Stockton Pass Dam; Wash	(T8S/R26E) See Stockton Pass, Graham
Stockton Wash, Stockton Wash Dam	(T7S/R26E) See Stockton Pass, Graham
Stock Valley	See Empire Mountains, Pima, and Empire Valley, Pima
Soda Lake	See Willcox, Cochise
Solano Mission, San	See Topawa, Pima
Soldier Camp Creek	See Soldier Camp Wash, Gila
Soldier Camp Mountain	(T9N/R11E; Elev. 5200') See Soldier Camp Wash, Gila
Soldier Creek	See Soldier Camp Wash, Gila
Soldier Hole Ranch	See Soldier Hole, Cochise, and Brophy Well, Cochise
Soldiers Grave	See Sacaton Station, Pinal
Soldier Trail	See Soldier Camp, Pima
Solomonville	See Solomon, Graham
Solomonsville Pass	See Solomon Pass, Graham, and Solomon, Graham
Sombrero Butte	See Sombrero Peak, Gila
Sonoita Creek	(T22S/R15E) See Sonoita, Santa Cruz
Sonoita Land Grant	See Sonoita, Santa Cruz
Sonoita Mountains	(T17S/R6E; Elev. 1994') See Agua Dulce Mountains, Pima
Sonoita River, Valley	See Sonoita, Santa Cruz
Sonora Hill	(Elev. 2637') See Sonora, Pinal
Sonoyota	See Agua Dulce Mountains, Pima
Sonsala Buttes	See Sonsela Buttes, Apache
Sonsola Buttes	See Sonsela Buttes, Apache
Sopori Land Grant	See Sopori Ranch, Santa Cruz
Sopori Valley	See Sopori Ranch, Santa Cruz
Sopori Wash	(Santa Cruz/Pima) See Sopori Ranch, Santa Cruz
Sosile Butte	See Sonsela Buttes, Apache
Soto Wash	(T17S/R10E) See Soto Peak, Pima
Sounding Rocks	See Painted Rocks Mountains, Maricopa
South Canyon Spring	See South Canyon, Coconino
South College Peak	(Elev. 6385') See College Peak, Cochise
South Comobabi Mountains	See Comobavi, Pima
South Gila Bend	See Gila Bend, Maricopa
South Howland Cave	(T32N/R17W; Mohave) See Howlands Butte, Coconino (Grand Canyon)
Southerland Park	See Sutherland Peak, Cochise
South Pass	(T19S/R24E) See Dragoon Mountains, Cochise
South Peak	See South Butte, Pinal
South Rim	See Grand Canyon, Coconino/Mohave
South Trigo Peaks	(T1N/R21W; Elev. 2371') See Trigo Mountains, La Paz
South Well	See Vaya Chin, Pima
Southwestern Monuments	See Gila Pueblo, Gila
Sowats Point	(T36N/R2W) See Sowats Canyon, Coconino (Grand Canyon)
Sowats Spring	See Sowats Canyon, Coconino (Grand Canyon)
Soza Wash	(T12S/R19E) See Soza Mesa, Cochise
Spanish Ranch	See Robles Junction, Pima
Speaking Rock	See Monument Canyon, Apache
Specter Rapids, Terrace	See Specter Chasm, Coconino (Grand Canyon)
Spence Spring	(T14N/R3W) See Palace Station, Yavapai
Spion Kop	See Rawhide Mountains, Graham/Pinal
Spire Hills	See Spine, The, Pinal
Spitz Spring	See Spitz Hill, Coconino
Sponseller Mountain	(T10N//R23E; Elev. 7231') See Sponseller Lake, Navajo
Sponseller (R.R. Stn.)	(T9N/R23) See Sponseller Lake, Navajo
Spoonhead Butte	See Spoonhead, Mount, Coconino (Grand Canyon)
Springer's Store	See Springerville, Apache

Springlake	See Floy, Apache
Spruce Brook	See Tsehili, Apache, and Tsaile Creek, Apache
Spruce Canyon	See Tsaile Creek, Apache
Spruce Canyon	(T14N/R3W) See Spruce Mountain, Yavapai
Spruce Mountain	(T6N/R25E; Elev. 10,346'; Apache) See Spruce Mountain, Yavapai
Squash Blossom Butte	(T32N/R22E) See Squash Mountains, Navajo/Apache
Squeeze Canyon	See Vado Canyon, Coconino
Stage Coach, The	See Monument Pass, Navajo
Stanford, Fort	See Grant, Old Camp, Pinal
Stanford Ranch	See Kots Kug, Pima
Stanley Butte	(T5S/R19E; Elev. 7029') See Stanley, Graham
Stanton	(T10N/R5W; Elev. 3450') See Antelope Valley, Yavapai
Stanwix Flats	(T6S/R10W) See Stanwix, Maricopa
Stargo	(Elev. 4680') See Stargo Gulch, Greenlee
Stâ'tannyik	See Pima Villages, Pinal/Maricopa, and Hormiguero, Pinal
Steamboat Canyon	See Steamboat, Apache
Steamboat Wash	(T25N/R23E; Apache/Navajo) See Steamboat, Apache
Steam Pump Village	See Vainom Kug, Pima
Steele Canyon	(T22S/R24E) See Steele's Station, Cochise
Steele Hills	(T14S/R23E; Elev. 5270') See Steele's Station, Cochise
Stevens Ranch	See Eagle Creek, Greenlee
Stevens Ranch, Wash	See Stevens Mountain, Pima
Stewart Mountain Lake	See Stewart Mountain Dam, Maricopa
Stewart Pocket	See Steward Pocket, Gila
Stiles	See Dilkon, Navajo
Stiles Hill	See Boston Butte, Pinal
Stiles Ranch	See Castle Butte, Navajo
Stinking Springs Mountain	See Stinking Springs, Apache
Stinson Valley	See Stinson Wash, Navajo
Stjoekson	See Tucson, Pima
Stockton; Camp	See Stockton Hill, Mohave
Stockton Creek	See Stockton Pass, Graham
Stockton Draw	(T19S/R24E) See Stockton Hill, Cochise
Stockton Gap	(T4S/R31E; Greenlee) See Stockton Pass, Graham
Stoddard Spring	See Stoddard, Yavapai
Stone Cabin Gap; Wash	(T3S/R11W) See S H Mountains, Yuma
Stone Corral	See Hecla, Yavapai
Stone Corral Canyon	(T16N/R9W) See Hecla, Yavapai
Stone Corral Spring	(T16N/R10W) See Hecla, Yavapai
Stone House	See Chase Creek, Greenlee, or S H Mountains, Yuma
Stoneman Grade, The	See Pinal, Camp, Pinal
Stonewall	See Phoenix, Maricopa
Stonewall Jackson Mine	See McMillanville, Gila
Stontonyak	(T3S/R5E) See Stotonic, Pinal
Storey	See Perkinsville, Yavapai
Storm	See Storm Ranch, Yavapai
Stott Ranch Ruin	See Stott Canyon, Navajo
Stratton Gulch	See Stratton Canyon, Pima
Stratton Saddle	See Stratton Camp, Pima
Stratton Wash	(T11S/R17E; Pinal/Pima) See Stratton Camp, Pima
Strawberry Canyon, Creek, Hollow, Mountain, Valley	See Strawberry, Gila
Stray Horse Divide	See Stray Horse Creek, Greenlee
Stray Horse Spring	(T1N/R29E) See Stray Horse Creek, Greenlee
Strickland Wash	See Strickland Spring, Yavapai
Stringtown	See Alma, Maricopa
Sturges' Ranch	See Osa, La, Pima
Stycson	See Tucson, Pima

Suanca	See Simon Valley, San, Cochise
Submarine Rock	See Steamboat Rock, Gila
Sudacson	See Sacaton, Pinal
Sueltso	See Setsiltso Springs, Apache
Suffering Gulch	See Foreman Wash, Pinal
Sulfureo de Las Piramides, Rio	See Virgin River, Mohave
Sullivan Buttes	(T17N/R3W; Yavapai) See Sullivan Point, Coconino (Grand Canyon)
Sullivan Lake	(T17N/R2W; Elev. 4348'; Yavapai) See Sullivan Point, Coconino (Grand Canyon)
Sullivan Peak	See Sullivan Point, Coconino (Grand Canyon)
Sullivan Tank	(T20N/R7W; Yavapai) See Sullivan Point, Coconino (Grand Canyon)
Sulphur Draw	See Sulphur Springs, Cochise
Sulphur Hills	(T17S/R26E; Elev. 5120') See Sulphur Springs, Cochise
Sulphur Peak	(T18S/R31E; Elev. 8099'; Cochise) See Sulphur Springs, Cochise
Sulphur Springs Station	See Sulphur Springs, Cochise
Sumac Spring	See Chilchinbito (Spring), Navajo
Summerland	See Stanfield, Pima
Summer Point	See Summer Butte, Coconino
Summer's Amphitheater	See Summer Butte, Coconino (Grand Canyon)
Sumac Spring	See Chilchinbito (Spring), Navajo
Summit Peak	See Polaris Mountain, Yuma
Summit Spring	See Oracle, Pinal
Sumner Butte	See Summer Butte, Coconino (Grand Canyon)
Sunflower Creek	See Sunflower Mesa, Maricopa
Sunnyside Canyon	(T24S/R19E) See Sunnyside, Cochise
Sunnyside Spring	See Masipa Spring, Navajo
Sunrise	(T25N/R24E; Elev. 6200') See Sunrise Springs, Apache
Sunrise Trading Post	(T26N/R24) See Sunrise Springs, Apache
Sunset Canyon	See Jack's Canyon, Coconino
Sunset Crater	(Elev. 8000') See Sunset Crater National Monument, Coconino
Sunset Crossing, Mountain	See Sunset Pass, Coconino
Sunset Peak	See Sunset, Graham
Sunset Pass Spring	(T7N/R23E) See Sunset, Navajo
Sunset Rock	(T40N/R7E) See Cathedral Rock, Coconino
Sunshine	(T20N/R13E; Elev. c. 6000') See Meteor Crater, Coconino
Sunshine Trail	(T4N/R27E) See Wild Cherry Canyon, Apache
Supai Canyon	See Havasu Canyon, Coconino (Grand Canyon)
Supai Falls	(T33N/R4W; Elev. c. 3500') See Supai, Coconino (Grand Canyon)
Superstition Peak	(T1N/R9E) See Superstition Mountains, Pinal/Maricopa
Superstition Wilderness Area	(T2N/R10E) See Superstition Mountains, Pinal/Maricopa
Supolvre Creek	See Pulcifer Creek and Sepulveda, Apache
Supply, Camp	See Rucker, Camp, Cochise
Suprise Creek	See Surprise Valley, Apache, or Beaver Dam Wash, Mohave
Surprise Falls	(T35N/R1W) See Surprise Valley, Coconino (Grand Canyon)
Surprise Lookout	See Bass Camp, Coconino (Grand Canyon)
Sutaguison	See Sacaton, Pinal
Suwuki Vaya	See Chiulikam, Maricopa
Swamp Creek	(T10N/R15E) See Swamp Creek Mountain, Navajo
Sweet Creek	See Cruz River, Santa Cruz
Sweetwater	(T40N/R27E; Elev. 5360') See Totacon, Apache
Sweetwater Pass	(T16S/R4W) See Agua Dulce Pass, Pima
Sweetwater Wash	See Totacon, Apache

Swift Canyon Wash	(T8S/R25E) See Swift Trail, Graham
Swilling	See Phoenix, Maricopa, and Gillette, Maricopa
Swillings	See Gillette, Maricopa
Swilling's Ranch	See Gila City, Yuma
Swisshelm Peak	(T20S/R28E; Elev. 7185') See Swisshelm Mountains, Cochise
Switzer Canyon	(T21N/R7E) See Switzer Mesa, Coconino
Swiveller's Ranch	See Gila City, Yuma
Sydney	See Buckeye, Maricopa
Ta-Atukam	See Picacho Mountains, Pinal
Taazhibito	See Turkey Water, Navajo
Tabac Town	See Tubac, Santa Cruz
Tacca, Cerro de	See Picacho, Pinal
Tacca, Sierra de	See Picacho Mountains, Pinal
Taceo	See Picacho Mountains, Pinal
Tachitoa	See Hickiwan, Pima
Tachito Creek, Wash	See Polacca Wash, Apache/Navajo
Tachna	See Tacna, Yuma
Tadidiin Dzit	See Navajo Mountain, Coconino
Ta-enta Creek	See Tyende Creek, Navajo
Ta-enta Mesa	See Tyende Mesa, Navajo
Tahchito Creek	See Tah Chee Wash, Apache
Taht-Mahmeli	See Tat-momoli, Pinal
Tahuta Terrace	See Tahuta Point, Coconino (Grand Canyon)
Talahogan Spring, Wash	See Talahogan Canyon, Navajo
Talklai	See Carlos, San, Gila
Talkalai	See Rice, Gila, and Carlos, San, Gila
Ta-Lar-Che	See Thomas, Fort, Graham
Talla-Hogan	See Awatobi, Navajo, and Talahogan Canyon, Navajo
Tallyho Mine	See Helvetia, Pima
Tamar Mountain	See Wolf Mountain, Apache
Tangle Peak	(T9N/R6E; Elev. 3542') See Tangle Creek, Yavapai
Tanner Canyon	See Garden Canyon, Cochise
Tanner Canyon Rapids	See Tanner Canyon, Coconino (Grand Canyon)
Tanner Creek	See Roundy Creek, Coconino
Tanner-French Trail	See Tanner Canyon, Coconino (Grand Canyon)
Tanner Trail	See Tanner Canyon, Coconino (Grand Canyon)
Tanner Wash	See Roundup Creek, Navajo
Tanque Verde Canyon	(T13S/R17E) See Tanque Verde Ranch, Pima
Tanque Verde Creek	(T17S/R15E) See Tanque Verde Ranch, Pima
Tanque Verde Falls	See Tanque Verde Ranch, Pima
Tanque Verde Hot Springs	(T8S/R16E) See Tanque Verde Ranch, Pima
Tanque Verde Mountains	(T14S/R17E; Elev. 8666') See Tanque Verde Ranch, Pima
Tanque Verde Peak	(T14S/R17E; Elev. 7040') See Tanque Verde Ranch, Pima
Tanque Verde Wash	(T13S/R18E) See Tanque Verde Ranch, Pima
Tapeats Amphitheater, Cave	See Tapeats Creek, Coconino (Grand Canyon)
Tapeats Rapids	(T34N/R2W) See Tapeats Creek, Coconino (Grand Canyon)
Tapeats Spring	(T29N/R9E) See Tapeats Creek, Coconino (Grand Canyon)
Tapeats Terrace	(T34N/R1W) See Tapeats Creek, Coconino (Grand Canyon)
Tapeats Trail	See Tapeats Creek, Coconino (Grand Canyon)
Tapeets	See Tapeats Creek, Coconino (Grand Canyon)
Ta Pits	See Tapeats Creek, Coconino (Grand Canyon)
Tappan Spring Canyon	See Tappan Spring, Coconino
Tappan Wash	See Tappan Spring, Coconino
Tatia Toak	See Tatai Toak, Pima

Tatamumerikut	See Tat Momoli, Pinal
Tat Mahmeli	See Tat Momoli, Pinal
Tat Momoli Mountains	See Tat Momoli, Pinal
Tat Momoli Pass	(T9S/R4E) See Tat Momoli, Pinal
Tat Momoli Valley	(T9S/R5E) See Tat Momoli, Pinal
Tat Momoli Wash	(T10S/R5E; Pinal/Pima) See Tat Momoli, Pinal
Tatria Toak	See Tatai Toak, Pima
Tat'sïtûk^	See Pima Villages, Pinal/Maricopa
Taul Creek, Peak, Spring	See Towel Creek, Yavapai
Tautabit	See Totopitk, Pima
Tawaph	See Tawahpah, Navajo
Taylor Canyon	See Taylor Pass, Graham
Tcacca	See Picacho Mountains, Pinal
Tchensa Mountains	See Chuska Mountains, Apache
Teó-Ol-Tûk	See Casa Grande, Pinal
Tcóûtik Wútcik	See Pima Villages, Pinal/Maricopa
Tcupatak	See Pima Villages, Pinal/Maricopa
Tcu'wutukawutûk	See Pima Villages, Pinal/Maricopa
Tea Kettle Mountain	See Hat Mountain, Maricopa, or Teapot Mountain, Pinal
Teas Toh	See Tees Toh, Navajo
Teats, The	See Wrightson, Mount, Santa Cruz
Tecolate Valley	See Chukut Kuk, Pima
Tecolote, Plain	See Chukut Kuk, Pima
Tecolote Valley	(T19S/R3E) See Chukut Kuk, Pima
Tec Nos Pos, Tec Nos Pos Wash	See Four Corners, Apache, and Teec Nos Pos Trading Post, Apache
Teec Nos Pos Canyon; Teec Nos Pos Wash	See Four Corners, Apache, and Teec Nos Pos Trading Post, Apache
Tees Nos Pos	See Four Corners, Apache, and Teec Nos Pos Trading Post, Apache
Tees Toh Wash	(T24N/R18E) See Tees To, Navajo
Tegua Spring	See Tewa, Navajo
Telehogan Wash	See Talahogan Wash, Navajo
Telephone Wash	See Katherine Wash (Old), Mohave
Tempe Butte	(T1N/R4E; Elev. 1495') See Tempe, Maricopa
Temple Bar Wash	See Temple Wash, Mohave
Temple of Set	See Tower of Set, Coconino (Grand Canyon)
Temple Wash	(T30N/R19W) See Temple, The, Mohave
Tenahatchipi Pass	(T5N/R12W) See Harquahala Mountains, La Paz
Tenaja, Arroyo de La	See Paz, La, La Paz
Tenebito Spring	See Dinnebito, Coconino
Tenmile Wash	See Ten-Mile Camp, Maricopa, or Cornelia, Arroya, Pima
Ten Mile Well	See Batamote Mountains, Pima
Tennehleto Spring	See Moencopie, Coconino
Tennessee Wash	See Tennessee Gulch, Mohave
Tenney's Camp	See Woodruff, Navajo
Tenney's Spring	See Tenney's Gulch, Coconino
Tenny Mountain	(T5N/R30E; Elev. 9058'; Apache) See Tenny Flat, Navajo, and Woodruff, Navajo
Teresa, Rio Santa	See Paris River, Coconino (Grand Canyon)
Termacacori	See Tumacacori National Monument, Santa Cruz
Terrace of the Explorers	See Colonnade, The, Coconino (Grand Canyon)
Terrenate, El	(Sonora, Mexico) See Pedro River, San, Cochise
Terrenate, Rio	(Sonora, Mexico) See Pedro River, San, Cochise
Tes Nos Pas	See Teec Nos Pos Trading Post, Apache
Tesota	See Gila Bend, Maricopa
Tesotal	See Gila Bend, Maricopa
Teuwalanki	See Wupatki National Monument, Coconino
Teviston	See Bowie, Cochise

Tewa Spring	See Tewa, Navajo
Texas Hill	(T7S/R14W; Elev. 776') See Stoval, Yuma
Texas Hill Camp	See Stoval, Yuma
Tex Canyon (No. 2)	See Texas Canyon, Cochise
Te-Ye-Ba-A-Kit	See Debekid Lake, Navajo
Tezotal	See Gila Bend, Maricopa
Third Hollow	(T8N/R22E) See First Hollow, Navajo
Third Knoll	See First Knoll, Navajo
Thirteen Mile Spring	(T13N/R6E) See Thirteen Mile Rock, Yavapai
Thlo Hali	See Lohali Point, Apache
Thomas, Camp	See Thomas, Fort, Graham
Thomas, Mount	(T6N/R27E; Elev. 11,470') See Baldy, Mount, Apache
Thomas, Peak	(Elev. 11,470') See Baldy, Mount, Apache
Thompson Arboretum	See Boyce Thompson Southwestern Arboretum, Pinal
Thompson Spring	(T25N/R18W; Mohave) See Thompson Canyon, Coconino (Grand Canyon)
Thorburn	See Red Butte, Coconino
Thor's Hammer	See Chiracahua National Monument, Cochise
Thor Temple	(T32N/R4E; Elev. 6719') See Thor's Hammer, Coconino (Grand Canyon)
Thousand Wells	See Thousand Pockets, Coconino
Three Bridges	See Irene, Pima
Three Camp Mountain	See Timber Camp Mountain, Gila
Three Castles	See Sinking Ship, Coconino (Grand Canyon)
Three Peaks	See Triplets, Gila
Three R Gulch; Mountain	See Three R Canyon, Santa Cruz
Three Turkey House Ruins	See Three Turkey Canyon, Apache
Thunder Cave, River, Spring	See Tapeats Creek, Coconino (Grand Canyon)
Thunder River Trail	(T35N/R2W) See Tapeats Creek, Coconino (Grand Canyon)
Thurber	See Ray, Pinal
Thurso Valley	See Walla Valley, Coconino (Grand Canyon)
Tiger Canyon	(T9N/R1E) See Tiger, Yavapai
Tiger Creek	(T10N/R1W) See Tiger, Yavapai
T'its Bito	See Cottonwood Wash, Apache
Tiller Canyon	See Miller Canyon, Coconino
Tilted Peak	See Saddleback Mountain, Pinal
Tinaja Alta	See Tinajas Altas, Yuma
Tinaja de Corazon	See Heart Tank, Yuma
Tinaja Hills	See Tinaja Peak, Pima
Tinajas, Las	See Dripping Spring, La Paz
Tinajas de Candelaria	See Tinajas, Yuma, and Dripping Springs, Yuma
Tinajualto	See Tinajas Altas, Yuma
Tinaxa	See Tinajas, Yuma
Tinebito Spring	See Dinnebito Spring, Coconino
Tinechas	See Tinajas Altas, Yuma
Tinechas Altas	See Tinajas Altas, Yuma
Tinejas Altos Mountains	See Tinajas Altas Mountains, Yuma
Tinejas de Candelaria	See Tinajas, Yuma, and Dripping Springs, Yuma
Tinny Spring	See Tenney Spring, Coconino
Tip Over Canyon	(T34N/R2E) See Tipoff, The, Coconino (Grand Canyon)
Tip Over Spring	See Tipoff, The, Coconino (Grand Canyon)
Tisnasbas, Canyon, Creek	See Four Corners, Apache, and Teec Nos Pos Trading Post, Apache
Tison, Rio del	See Colorado River
Tiyo Point Trail	See Tiyo Point, Coconino (Grand Canyon)
Tjeavolitak	See Chiawuli Tak, Pima
Tjotom vaxia	See Bear: Bear's Wells, Pima
Tjuitjo	See Chiu Chuschu, Pinal

Tjuulik	See Choulic, Pima
Tnijotobar	See Quijotoa, Pima
Toapit	See Totopitk, Maricopa, or Stoa Pitk, Pima
Tobar	See Tovar Terrace, Coconino (Grand Canyon)
Tochinlini Canyon	See Walker Creek, Apache
Tocodoy Onigam	See Anegam, Pima
Todihi Biihili	See Snowflake, Navajo
Todokozh Spring	See Toh De Coz, Apache
Togai Spring	See Tuye Spring, Apache
Togay Spring	See Tuye Spring, Apache
Tohahadleeh	See Indian Wells, Navajo
To'hah'le'tes'ta	See Tohadistoa Spring, Navajo
Toh'atin Mesa	See Dinne Mesa, Apache
Tohatchi	See Toh Ah Chi, Navajo
Toh Chin Lini Mesa	(T40N/R29E; Elev. 6760') See Toh Chin Lini Canyon, Apache
Toison	See Tucson, Pima
Toko'nabi	See Navajo Mountain, Coconino/Utah
Tolacon	See Totacon, Apache
Tolchaco; Gap	See Tolchico, Coconino
Toledo	See York, Greenlee
Tollgate Canyon	See Tollhouse Canyon, Graham/Greenlee
Tollgate Camp	See Hualpai, Camp, Yavapai, and Toll Gate, Yavapai
Toltec Buttes, City	See Toltec, Pinal
Toltec Camp	See Salero Hill, Santa Cruz
Tombstone Canyon	(T23S/R24E) See Tombstone, Cochise
Tombstone Cemetery	See Boot Hill, Cochise
Tombstone Gulch, Hills	See Tombstone, Cochise
Tomocacari	See Tumacacori National Monument, Santa Cruz
Tompkins Valley	See Thompson Valley, Yavapai
Tondastya	See Kayenta, Navajo
Tonoco	See Tonoka, Pima
Tonoka Wash	See Tonoka, Pima
Tonolea	See Tonalea, Coconino
Tonopah Desert	See Tonopah, Maricopa
Tontobasin	See Punkin Center, Gila
Tonto Basin (Town)	See Punkin Center, Gila
Tonto Dam	See Theodore Roosevelt Dam, Gila
Tonto Forest Reserve	See Tonto National Forest, Gila, and Coconino National Forest, Coconino
Tonto Mountain	(T8N/R8E; Gila; T15N/R4W; Elev. 5631'; Yavapai) See Tonto Basin, Gila
Tonto Natural Bridge	(T11N/R9E) See Natural Bridge, Gila
Tonto Pasture Spring	(T15N/R4W; Yavapai) See Tonto Basin, Gila
Tonto Rim	(T3N/R24E) See Mogollon Rim, Apache
Tonto Settlement	See Gisela, Gila
Tonto Spring	(T10N/R12E; Gila; T15N/R4W; Yavapai) See Tonto Basin, Gila
Tonto (Stage) Station	See Tonto Spring Valley, Yavapai
Tonto Wash	(T14N/R4W; Yavapai) See Tonto Basin, Gila
Toothaker	See Liberty, Maricopa
Toot-Laden-Le	See Carlos, San, Gila, and Carlos Indian Reservation, San, Gila
Topacoba Spring	See Havasu Canyon, Coconino
Topahua	See Topawa, Pima
Topawa Hills	(T19S/R5E; Elev. 2775') See Topawa, Pima
Topawa Wash	(T19S/R6E) See Topawa, Pima
Topawo	See Topawa, Pima
Topeant	See Lopeant, Mohave

Topeat	See Lopeant, Mohave
Tope Kobe Gorge	See Topocoba Hilltop, Coconino (Grand Canyon)
Tope Kobe Spring	(T33N/R3W; Elev. 4975') See Topocoba Hilltop, Coconino (Grand Canyon), and Havasu Canyon, Coconino
Topocaba Trail	See Supai, Coconino (Grand Canyon), and Topocoba Hilltop, Coconino (Grand Canyon)
Topock Bay	(T16N/R21W) See Topock, Mohave
Topock Gorge	See Havasu National Wild Life Refuge, Mohave/La Paz
Topock Marsh	(T16N/R21W; Mohave/California) See Topock, Mohave, and Havasu National Wild Life Refuge, Mohave, La Paz
Topock Tract Water Fowl Area	(T16N/R21W) See Topock, Mohave
Topocoba Spring	See Topocoba Hilltop, Coconino (Grand Canyon)
Topocoba Trail	See Supai Trail, Coconino (Grand Canyon), and Topocoba Hilltop, Coconino (Grand Canyon)
Topocobya Canyon, Spring	See Topocoba Hilltop, Coconino (Grand Canyon), and Havasu Canyon, Coconino
Topowo	See Topawa, Pima
Tordillo Peak	See Picket Post Mountain, Pinal
Toreva Spring	See Toreva, Navajo
Tornado Valley	See Toroweap, Mohave
Toro Spring, Wash	(T20S/R12E) See Toro, Cañada del, Pima
Toroweap Lake, Trail	See Toroweap Valley, Mohave (Grand Canyon)
Toroweap Point	(T33N/R7W; Elev. 6393') See Toroweap Valley, Mohave (Grand Canyon)
Torowip Cliffs	See Toroweap Valley, Mohave (Grand Canyon)
Tortilato Mountains	See Tortilla Mountains, Pinal
Tortilla Butte	See Tortilla Mountains, Pinal
Tortilla Camapground	(T2N/R9E) See Tortilla Flat, Maricopa
Tortilla Mountain	(T2N/R10E; Elev. 4198') See Tortilla Flat, Maricopa
Tortilla Pass	(T1N/R11E) See Tortilla Mountains, Pinal
Tortillata, Sierra	See Tortolita Mountains, Pinal
Totabit	See Totopitk, Pima
Totec	See Toltec, Maricopa
Totem Pole	See Chiracahua National Monument, Cochise
Totlacon	See Totacon, Apache
Totobit	See Totopitk, Pima
Totobitk	See Totopitk, Pima
Thousand Wells	See Thousand Wells, Coconino
Tovar Amphitheater	(T31N/R2E) See Tovar Terrace, Coconino (Grand Canyon)
Tovar Hill, El	(T31N/R3E) See Tovar Terrace, Coconino (Grand Canyon)
Tovar Point, El	See Grandeur Point, Coconino (Grand Canyon)
Towel Peak, Spring	See Towel Creek, Yavapai
Tower Creek	(T10N/R1W) See Tower Mountain, Yavapai
Towers of Short Creek	See Vermillion Cliffs, Mohave
Tranquil Valley	(T33N/R2E) See Walla Valley, Coconino (Grand Canyon)
Travertine Creek	See Travertine Canyon, Coconino (Grand Canyon)
Travertine Falls, Rapids	(T27N/R11W; Mohave) See Travertine Canyon, Coconino (Grand Canyon)
Tres Alamos Wash	See Tres Alamos, Cochise
Tres Cebollas	See Bowie, Cochise
Trigo, Canyon	See Muerto, Canyon del, Apache
Trigo Pass	(T1N/R20W) See Trigo Mountains, La Paz
Trigo Wash	(T1N/R21W) See Trigo Mountains, La Paz
Triplet, Mount	See Triplets, The, Gila
Triplets Mountains, Peaks	See Tripletts, Gila
Tripp Canyon	See Bellows Canyon, Graham
Tritle Peak	(T33N/R4E; Elev. 6750'; Coconino [Grand Canyon]) See Tritle, Mount, Yavapai

Trout Spring	(T32N/R23E) See Lohali Point, Apache
Troy Mountain	(Elev. 4970') See Troy, Pinal
Truman Point	See Anderson Canyon, Coconino (Grand Canyon)
Truxton (P.O.)	See Valentine, Mohave, and Truxton Canyon, Mohave
Truxton Canyon (R.R. Stn.)	See Crozier, Mohave
Truxton Canyon Sub-Agency	See Truxton Canyon, Mohave, and Valentine, Mohave
Truxton Plateau, Valley	See Truxton Canyon, Mohave
Truxton Springs	See Truxton Canyon, Mohave; Valentine, Mohave; and Crozier, Mohave
Truxton Wash	(T25N/R10W) See Truxton Canyon, Mohave
Tsagy-At-Sosa Canyon	See Tsegihatsosi Canyon, Navajo
Tsalee Butte, Creek, Pinnacle	See Tsaile (Creek), Apache
Tsali Creek	See Tsaile (Creek), Apache
Tsa-Tsil-Too	See Setsiltso (Spring), Apache
Tschiulikam	See Chiulikam, Maricopa
Tschu'hutsho	See Chiu Chuschu, Pinal
Tschuski Mountains	See Chuska Mountains, Apache
Tse-A-Le	See Tsaile Creek, Apache
Tse-Ba-Ni-Zi-Ni Wash	See Balakai Mesa, Apache
Tsé Bii'ndesgaii	See Monument Valley, Navajo
Tsé Binni'I'	See Faith Rock, Apache
Tsebootsoe	See Bonito, Canyon, Apache
Tseghahoodzani	See Window Rock, Apache
Tsegi Branch, Laguna Canyon	See Betatakin, Navajo
Tsegi Point	See Tsegi Canyon, Navajo
Tsegi (Town)	(elev. 6200') See Tsegi Canyon, Navajo
Tsegihotsosi Canyon	See Tsegihatsosi Canyon, Navajo
Tsehili; Butte	See Tsaile, Apache
Tselani	See Salina, Apache
Tsel-ichii'dah'azkani	See Red Rock (Town), Apache
Tsenakahn Butte	See Round Rock (Town), Apache
Tse Nakani	See Round Rock (Town), Apache
Tsénástánii	See Petrified Forest National Monument, Apache
Tsetsiltso	See Setsiltso (Spring), Apache
Tsetsiltso (Spring)	See Setsiltso (Spring), Apache
Tseyi-Hatsosi	See Tsegihatsosi (Canyon), Apache
Tsezhini	See Black Pinnacle Butte, Apache
Tshiovo	See Tonuk Vo, Pima
Tshiuli	See Sweetwater, Pima
Tshiulikam	See Chiulikam, Maricopa
Tshiuliseik	See Sweetwater, Pima
Ts'ihootso	See Michaels, Saint, Apache
Tsiizizi	See Leupp, Coconino
Tsina'ee Dahsa'ash	See Lee's Ferry, Coconino
Tsinasbah	See Four Corners, Apache
Tsohotso Wash	(T26N/R30E See Michaels, Saint, Apache
Tuba Butte	(T32N/R10E; Elev. 5786') See Tuba City, Coconino
Tubac Creek	(T21S/R12E) See Tubac, Santa Cruz
Tubac Range	See Atascosa Mountains, Santa Cruz
Tuba Springs	See Tuba City, Coconino
Tubo	See Aravaipa Canyon, Pinal
Tucane	See Navajo Mountain, Coconino/Utah
Tucano	See Hopi Villages, Navajo
Tucker Spring	(T20N/R4W) See Tucker (R.R. Stn.), Yavapai
Tuckup Canyon; Tuck Up Point	See Tucket Canyon, Mohave (Grand Canyon)
Tuckup Rocky Point	(T34N/R6W; Elev. 5987') See Tucket Canyon, Mohave (Grand Canyon)
Tuckup Trail	See Tucket Canyon, Mohave (Grand Canyon)
Tucsoncito	See Ali Chukson, Pima

Tucson Wash	(T9S/R16E) See Tucson, Pima
Tucubavi	See Tubac, Santa Cruz
Tudacson	See Sacate, Pinal
Tudecoz Spring	See Toh De Coz Spring, Navajo
Tuesapit	See Totopitk, Maricopa
Tueson	See Tucson, Pima
Tuintsa Mountains	See Tunicha Mountains, Apache
Tulerosa Creek	See Goodwin, Camp, Graham
Tulip Point	See Swamp Point, Coconino (Grand Canyon)
Tully Peak	(T14S/R16E; Pima) See Tully, Cochise
Tullyville	See Tully, Cochise
Tumacacori	(T21S/R13E; Elev. 3275') See Tumacacori National Monument, Santa Cruz
Tumacacori Forest Reserve	See Coronado National Forest, Pima/Santa Cruz, and Tumacacori National Monument, Santa Cruz
Tumacacavori	See Tumacacori National Monument, Santa Cruz
Tumurru	See Vermillion Cliffs, Mohave
Tunechan Mountains	See Chuska Mountains, Apache
Tunecha, Sierra de	See Chusca Mountains, Apache
Tunecha Valley	See Tunitcha Mountains, Apache
Tunitcha Mountains	See Tunicha Mountains, Apache
Tuntsa Mountain	See Tunicha Mountains, Apache
Tuquison	See Tucson, Pima
Turnbull Mountains	See Teresa Mountains, Santa, Graham
Turner	(T20S/R19E) See Sierra Vista, Cochise
Turquoise	See Gleeson, Cochise
Turquoise Mountain	(T19S/R25E; Elev. 5400') See Gleeson, Cochise
Turret Butte	(T10N/R5E) See Turret Peak, Yavapai
Turret Mountain	See Turret Peak, Yavapai
Turtleback Mountain	See Burnt Mountain, Maricopa
Turtle Peak	See Turtle Mountain, Cochise
Turtle Tail Mountain	See Chupan Mountain, Pima
Tusayan Hill	See Tusayan Ruin, Coconino (Grand Canyon)
Tusayan Province	See Hopi Villages, Navajo, and Tusayan, Navajo
Tusayan Villages	See Hopi Villages, Navajo
Tuscumbia Creek	See Tuscumbia Mountain, Yavapai
Tuseral Mountains	See Tule Mountains, Yuma
Tusonimo	See Sacaton, Pinal
Tusonimon	See Sacaton, Pinal
Tuthill, Camp	See Tuthill, Fort, Coconino
Tu-Uk-So-On	See Tucson, Pima
Tuweap Valley	See Toroweap Valley, Mohave
Tuyey Spring	See Tuye Spring, Apache
Tuzigoot Hill	See Tuzigoot National Monument, Yavapai
Twenty-Five Mile Rapid	See Hansbrough-Richards Rapid, Coconino (Grand Canyon)
Twenty-Nine Mile Lake	(T13N/R8E) See Twenty-Nine Mile Butte, Coconino
209 Mile Canyon	(T29N/R11W) See Indian Canyon, Mohave
217 Mile Canyon; Rapids	See Road Runner Rapids, Coconino/Mohave (Grand Canyon)
237 Mile Rapids	See 140 Mile Canyon, Coconino/Mohave (Grand Canyon)
Txo'nilts'ili	(T4N/R30E) See Coyote Wash, Apache
T-Ye-Ba-A-Kit	See Debekid Lake, Navajo
Tyintcha Mountains	See Tunicha Mountains, Apache
Tyler	See Webb, Cochise
Tyrol	See Cave Creek, Maricopa
Tyson, Fort, Wash	See Quartzsite, La Paz
Tyson's Wells	See Quartzsite, La Paz
Tzlanapak	See Mormon Flat, Maricopa

Udall Draw Springs	See Udall Draw, Apache
Udall Park	See Udall Draw, Apache
Ugly Duckling	See Chiracahua National Monument, Cochise
Uhs Kug	See Blackwater, Pinal
Uhupat Oidak	See Gila Bend, Maricopa
Uinkaret Mountains	See Trumbull, Mount, Mohave
Ulcer Gulch	See Antelope Peak, Yavapai
Uncle Jims Buffalo Pasture	See Uncle Jim Point, Coconino (Grand Canyon)
Uncle Sam Gulch	(T23S/R24E) See Uncle Sam Hill, Cochise
Union	See Eagar, Apache
Union Hills	(T4N/R3E; Elev. 2383') See Union, Maricopa
Union Park	See Payson, Gila
Union Pass Station	See Union Pass, Mohave
Union Peak	See Davis, Mount, Yavapai
Union, Sierra de La	See Morena Mountain, Pima
Union Ward	See Eagar, Apache, and Round Valley, Apache
Unkar Creek Rapid	See Unkar Creek, Coconino (Grand Canyon)
Unpatoitak	See Tesota, Maricopa
Uparsoytac	See Gila Bend, Maricopa
Upasoitac	See Gila Bend, Maricopa
Updyke Tanks	See Rattlesnake Tanks, Yavapai
Upper Andrus Spring	See Andrus Canyon, Mohave
Upper Basin	See Gregg Basin, Mohave
Upper Crossing	See Pedro, San, Cochise
Upper Gila Valley	See Pueblo Viejo, Graham
Upper Goldwater Lake	(T13N/R2W) See Lower Goldwater Lake, Yavapai
Upper Laguna Creek	See Tsegi Canyon, Navajo
Upper Lake Mary	(T19N/R8E) See Horse Lake, Coconino
Upper Ruin	See Tonto National Monument, Gila
Utah, Camp; Fort	See Lehi, Maricopa
Utahville	See Lehi, Maricopa
Ute Ford	See Lee's Ferry, Coconino
Ute Mountain	(T18N/R19W; Elev. c. 4000') See Black Mesa, Mohave
Uturituc	See Sacaton, Pima
Uupatoitak	See Gila Bend, Maricopa
Va-Aki	See Casa Blanca, Pinal, and Pima Villages, Pinal/Maricopa
Vaca, Mesa La	See Black Mesa, Navajo
Vadito, El	See Johns, Saint, Apache
Vaheja	See Sikul Himatk, Pima
Vah Ki	See Casa Blanca, Pinal
Vail Trap Spring	(T16S/R18E) See Vail, Pima
Vaiva Hills	See Vaiva Vo, Pinal
Val de China	See Big Chino Valley, Yavapai
Val Chino	See Big Chino Valley, Yavapai
Valle de Las Playas	See Sulphur Springs Valley, Cochise
Valle del Lino	See Little Colorado River, Navajo
Valle de Los Sobaipuris	See Pedro Valley, San, Cochise
Valle Redondo	See Round Valley, Apache
Valley of Agalon	See Mormon Crossing, Coconino
Valley of Mystery	See House of Hands, Apache
Valley of the Ajo	See Ajo, Pima
Valley of the Sun	See Phoenix, Maricopa
Valshni Wash	See Vamori Wash, Pima, and Gu Oidak Wash, Pima
Valverde	See Humboldt, Yavapai
Vamori Valley	See Vamori, Pima
Vamori Wash	See Gu Oidak Wash, Pima
Vanarian	See Vanar, Cochise

Vanar Wash	(T13S/R32E) See Vanar, Cochise
Van Deren Spring	See Gash Mountain, Coconino
Vaquero Mesa	See Horse Mesa, Maricopa
Vatjeki	See Mesquite Charcos, Pima
Vavemo	See Itak, Pima
Veit, El	See Bates Well, Pima
Veit Ranch Wild Life Area	See Bates Well, Pima
Vekal Mountains, Valley	See Vekol, Pinal
Vekol Mountains	(T10S/R2E; Elev. 3625') See Vekol, Pinal
Vekol Valley	(Maricopa/Pinal) See Vekol, Pinal
Vekol Wash	See Vekol, Pinal
Verde	See Clemenceau, Yavapai
Verde Arroyo	See Lewis and Pranty Creek, Maricopa
Verde Forest Reserve	See Prescott, Yavapai
Verde National Forest	See Prescott National Forest, Yavapai/Coconino
Ventana Canyon	(No. 2) See Chiuli Shiak, Pima
Ventana Canyon Wash	(T13S/R15W) See Ventana Canyon, Pima (No. 1)
Ventana Pass	(T12S/R1E) See Ventana Canyon, Pima (No. 1)
Verde Reservation, Rio	See Verde, Camp, Yavapai
Verde, Sierra	See Poso Verde, Pima
Vergne Park, de La	See Fort Valley, Coconino
Vermejo, Rio	See Little Colorado River, and Zuñi River, Navajo/ Coconino
Vernon Creek	(T9N/R25E) See Vernon, Apache
Vesey's Paradise	See Vasey's Paradise, Coconino
Via Santee	See Viason Chin, Pima
Victor	See Vicksburg, La Paz
Victoria, La	See Winkelman, Pinal
Vinegaron Wash	(Yuma, T7S/R20W) See Vinegaron Well, La Paz
Vineyard Canyon	See Vineyard Mountain, Gila
Viopuli	See Pedro, San, Pima
Viopuli Wash	(T14S/R8E) See Pedro, San, Pima
Vipenak	See Nolia, Pima
Vi-Penor	See Nolia, Pima
Virgen, Rio	See Virgin River, Mohave (Lake Mead)
Virgin Bottoms	See Cane Beds, Mohave (Lake Mead)
Virginia City	See New Virginia, Mohave
Virgin Peak	(T1S/R13W; Elev. c. 2500') See Virgin Basin, Yuma
Vista Encantada	See Vista Encantadora, Coconino (Grand Canyon)
Vitty	See Simmons, Yavapai
Vivian	See Oatman, Mohave
Vock Spring	(T23N/R17W) See Vock Canyon, Mohave
Vogt Spring	See Vock Canyon, Mohave
Vokivaxia	See Chiulikam, Maricopa
Voltz Crossing	See Tolchico, Navajo
Volunteer Canyon	(T20N/R4E) See Volunteer Spring, Coconino
Volunteer Mountain	(Elev. 8047') See Volunteer Spring, Coconino
Volunteer Prairie	See Volunteer Spring, Coconino
Volunteer Wash	(T20N/R4E) See Volunteer Spring, Coconino
Vopelohavooka	See Vopolo Havoka, Pima
Votum	See Vaiva Vo, Pinal
Vought Spring	See Vock Spring, Mohave
V T Hill, Lake, Park	See De Motte Park, Coconino
Vturituc	See Sacaton, Pinal
Vulture Mine, Mountain, Peak, Range	See Vulture, Maricopa
Vulture Siding	See Morristown, Maricopa, and Vulture, Maricopa

Wachupe Mountains	See Huachuca, Fort, Cochise
Waddell Dam	See Carl Pleasant Lake, Maricopa
Wah-Poo-Ata	See Strawberry Valley, Gila
Wainwright, Mount	See Wing Mountain, Coconino
Wakefield Creek	(T17S/R19E) See Wakefield Canyon, Pima
Wakefield Spring	See Wakefield Canyon, Pima
Wakeup Wash	See Wikieup, Mohave
Walapai Indian Reservation	See Hualapai Indian Reservation, Mohave
Waldeck Peak, Mount	See Pete Mountain, Santa Cruz
Wales Arnold Ranch	See Montezuma Castle, Yavapai
Walhalla Glades, Plateau	(T32N/R4E) See Greenland Spring, Coconino (Grand Canyon)
Walker	See Taylor, Navajo
Walker Butte	(T39N/R27E; Elev. 6033') See Walker Creek, Apache
Walker Creek	(T14N/R6E) See Walker Basin, Yavapai
Walker Creek Reservoir	(T41N/R26E) See Walker Creek, Apache
Walker Creek Valley	See Walker Creek, Apache
Walker Diggings	See Walker, Yavapai
Walker Gulch	(T8N/R2W) See Walker, Yavapai
Walker Hill	(T22N/R5E; Elev. 7690') See Walker Lake, Coconino
Walker Mountain	(T14N/R6E; Elev. 5925') See Walker, Yavapai
Walker Tank	(T14N/R9E) See Walker Lake, Coconino
Wallace Plateau	See Wallace Butte, Coconino (Grand Canyon)
Wallapai Point	See Montezuma Point, Coconino (Grand Canyon)
Wallen, Fort	See Wallen, Camp, Cochise
Wall's Well	See Kuakatch, Pima
Walnut Grove	See Richville, Apache
Walpi Spring	See Walpi, Navajo
Waltenberg Canyon, Rapids	See Waltenburg Canyon, Coconino (Grand Canyon)
Walthenberg Canyon, Rapids	See Waltenburg Canyon, Coconino (Grand Canyon)
Ward Mesa	See Ward Terrace, Coconino
Ward Pocket Canyon	See Ward Pocket, Yavapai
Warner's Hill, Mountain	See Sentinel Peak, Pima
Warren Hill	See Warren, Cochise
Warrior (R.R. Siding), Mill	See Inspiration, Gila
Warsaw Canyon	See Warsaw, Santa Cruz
Washboard Creek	See Washboard Wash, Navajo
Wash de Flag	See Flagstaff, Coconino
Washington Gulch	See Washington Camp, Santa Cruz
Washington, Mount	(Elev. 7221') See Washington Camp, Santa Cruz
Wasson Peak	(T10N/R1W; Yavapai) See Wasson Peak, Pima
Waterman Pass	(T13S/R9E) See Waterman Mountains, Pima
Waterman Peak	(Elev. 3808') See Waterman Mountains, Pima
Waters Draw Spring	See Waters Draw, Coconino
Watervale	See Tombstone, Cochise
Waterville	See Tombstone, Cochise
Watohomigi Point	See Watahomigi Point, Coconino (Grand Canyon)
Watson Spring	(T12N/R1W) See Watson Lake, Yavapai
We-Al-Hus	See Estrella Mountains, Pinal
Weaver	See Octave, Yavapai
Weaver Creek	(T8N/R5W) See Octave, Yavapai, and Lion Canyon, Yavapai
Weaver Gulch	See Antelope Peak, Yavapai
Weaver Mountains	(T11N/R5W; Elev. 5300') See Octave, Yavapai, and Antelope Peak, Yavapai
Weaver Peak, Range	See Antelope Peak, Yavapai
Weaverville	See Antelope Peak, Yavapai, and Octave, Yavapai
Webb Valley, Well	See Webb Mountain, Maricopa
Weber Peak	See Webber Peak, Graham

Webster Gulch, Spring	See Webster Mountain, Gila
Welcome Creek	See Simon Valley, San, Cochise
Wells Ranch	See Oroville, Greenlee
Wellton Hills	(T10S/R18W; Elev. 1195') See Wellton, Yuma
Wellton Mesa	(T8S/R17W) See Wellton, Yuma
Wendendale	See Wenden, La Paz
Wepo Valley	See Wepo Spring, Navajo
Wepo Wash	(T29N/R20E) See Wepo Spring, Navajo
Web Bottom Mesa	(T10N/R6E) See Wet Bottom Creek, Gila
Wet Ass Creek	See Wet Bottom Creek, Gila
Wétcut	See Pima Villages, Pinal/Maricopa
Wheatfield Canyon	See Wheatfield Creek, Apache
Wheatfield Lake	(T6N/R30E; Elev. 7281') See Wheatfield Creek, Apache
Wheeler Lode	See Wheeler Wash, Mohave
Whetstone	(T17S/R20E) See Whetstone Mountains, Cochise
Whetstone Spring	See Whetstone Mountains, Cochise
Whipple; Barracks, Depot, Military Reservation	See Whipple, Fort, Yavapai
Whipple, Mount	See Cygnus Mountain, Mohave
Whipple Plateau	See Defiance Plateau, Apache
Whipple Valley	See Whipple, Fort, Yavapai
Whipsaw Creek	See Whipsau, Yavapai
White Cliff Creek	See Cottonwood Creek (#1), Mohave, and Knight Creek, Mohave
White Cone	See Mollie's Nipple, Mohave
White Cone Spring	See White Cone, Navajo
White Creek	See White Canyon, Coconino (Grand Canyon)
White Horse Knoll	(T20N/R4E) See White Horse Lake, Coconino
White House Canyon	See Madera Canyon, Pima/Santa Cruz
White House Lake	See White Horse Lake, Coconino
White Lake	See White Horse Lake, Coconino
Whitelock Cienega	See Whitlock Cienega, Graham
White Mesa Natural Bridge	See White Mesa Arch, Navajo
White Mountain Apache Indian Reservation	See Apache Indian Reservation, Fort, Apache
White Mountain Creek	See White River, Apache, or White River, Gila/Navajo
White Mountain River	See White River, Gila/Navajo
White Reed Mountains	See Lukachukai Mountains, Apache
White River	See Whitewater Draw, Cochise
White River Canyon	See Rucker Canyon, Cochise, and White Water Draw, Cochise
White Sage Wash	(T41N/R1E) See White Sage Flat, Coconino
White Spring	See Steamboat, Apache
White's Well	(T11S/R1E) See Ventana, Pima
Whitetail Creek	See White Tail Canyon, Cochise
Whitetail Pass	(T16S/R29E) See White Tail Canyon, Cochise
White Tank	See White Tank Mountains, Maricopa
White Tanks	See Chain Tanks, Yuma
White Top Butte	See White Top Mesa, Apache
White Water Canyon	See Rucker Canyon, Cochise
White Water Creek	See White Water Draw, Cochise
White Zigzags	See Hermit Trail, Coconino (Grand Canyon)
Whiting Knoll	(T9N/R26E; Elev. 9348'; Apache) See Whiting, Coconino
Whitlock Hills	See Whitlock Cienega, Graham
Whitlock Peak	(T9S/R31E; Elev. 6211'; Graham/Greenlee) See Whitlock Cienega, Graham
Whitlock Valley	See Whitlock Cienega, Graham
Whitlock Wash	(T9S/R24E; Graham/Pinal) See Whitlock Cienega, Graham

Whitlow's Ranch	(T1S/R11E) See Whitlow Canyon, Pinal
Whitmore Point	See Whitmore Pools, Mohave
Whitmore Rapids	(Coconino/Mohave) See Whitmore Pools, Coconino
Whitmore Spring	See Big Spring, Mohave, and Whitmore Pools, Coconino
Whitmore Wash	(T33N/R9W) See Whitmore Pools, Coconino
Whittman	See Wittman, Maricopa
Whittum	See Blue, Greenlee
Wickenburg Mountains	(T7N/R4W; Elev. 2736'; Yavapai/Maricopa) See Wickenburg, Maricopa
Wickenburg Ranch	See Wickenburg, Maricopa
Wickieup	See Wikieup, Mohave
Wickiup; Canyon	See Wikieup, Mohave
Wide Ruin Valley	(T21N/R24E; Apache/Navajo) See Wide Ruins, Apache
Wide Ruin Wash	See Wide Ruins, Apache
Widforss Trail	See Widforss Point, Coconino (Grand Canyon)
Widgé-E-Te-Ca-Pár	See Maricopa, Maricopa
Wilcox	See Willcox, Cochise
Wild Band Canyon	(T38N/R2W) See Wild Band Pocket, Mohave
Wild Band Pools	See Wild Band Pocket, Mohave
Wild Band Spring	(T38N/R2W; Coconino) See Wild Band Pocket, Mohave
Wild Band Valley	See Wild Band Pocket, Mohave
Wild Cherry Creek	See Cherry Creek, Yavapai
Wild Horse Band Pools	See Wild Band Pocket, Mohave
Wild Horse Spring	See Wild Horse Cienega, Apache
Wild Horse Wash	(T19N/R23E; Elev. 5500') See Wild Horse Cienega, Apache, and Digger Wash, Navajo
Wild Oak Creek Canyon	See Oak Creek Canyon, Coconino
Wild Rye Creek	See Rye, Gila
Wild Steer Mesa	See Wild Cow, Coconino
Wiley Camp	See North Rim, Coconino (Grand Canyon)
Willcox Playa	See Willcox, Cochise
Williams Canyon	See Banded Canyon, Mohave
Williams Creek	See Carlos River, San, Gila
Williams Fork	See Aubrey Landing, Mohave
Williams River	See Big Sandy River, Mohave
Williamson Valley, Williamson Valley Wash	See Simmons, Yavapai
Willow, Camp	See Willow Grove, Camp, Mohave
Wilson	See Simmons, Yavapai, and Vitty, Yavapai
Wilson Mountain	See Wilson Canyon, Coconino
Window, The	See Window Rock, Apache
Window Rock	See Window, The, Pima
Window Valley	(T13S/R2E) See Window Mountain, Pima
Windsor; Windsor Castle	See Pipe Spring, Mohave
Windsor Camp	See Windsor Spring, Gila
Wing, Mount	See Fort Valley, Coconino
Winn Falls	See Fred Winn Falls, Cochise
Winsor Castle	See Pipe Spring, Mohave
Winsor Springs	See Windsor Springs, Gila
Winter Camp	See Winsor Camp, Gila
Winters Wash; Well; Well Wash	See Wintersburg, Maricopa
Wipho	See Wepo, Navajo
Wi Sukohautave	See Aubrey Hills, Mohave
Witch Creek	See Fife Creek, Cochise
Witch Pool	See Witch Water Pocket, Mohave
Wittmore Spring	See Whitmore Pools, Coconino
Wolf Crossing	See Tolchico, Coconino
Wolf Hole Lake; Hole Mountain; Hole Spring	See Wolf Hole, Mohave

Wonderland of Rocks	See Riggs Canyon, Cochise, and Chiracahua National Monument, Cochise
Wonsits Plateau	See Uinkaret Plateau, Mohave/Utah
Wonsits Tiravu	(Coconino) See Uinkaret Plateau, Mohave/Utah
Wonsits Valley	See Antelope Valley, Mohave
Wood Mountain, Camp	See Wood, Camp, Yavapai
Wood Mountain Seep Spring, Camp	See Wood, Camp, Yavapai
	See Lakeside, Navajo
Woodruff Butte	(Elev. 5671') See Woodruff, Navajo
Woodruff Lake	See Woodruff, Navajo
Woods Canyon	See Wood Canyon, Cochise/Graham, or Wood, Camp, Yavapai
Woods Canyon Bridge	See Woods Canyon, Yavapai/Coconino
Woodside	See Prescott, Yavapai
Woods Spring	See Woods Canyon, Yavapai/Coconino
Woods Spring Wash	See Wood Springs, Gila
Woody Ridge, Spring	See Woody Mountain, Coconino
Woolf Ranch	See Reidhead Crossing, Navajo
Woolf's Crossing	See Tolchico, Coconino
Woolsey Butte, Ranch, Trail	See Woolsey Point, Coconino (Grand Canyon)
Woolsey Peak	(T3S/R6W; Elev. 3170'; Maricopa) See Woolsey Point, Coconino (Grand Canyon)
Woolsey Wash	(T5S/R7W) See Woolsey Tank, Maricopa
Woolsey Wash	(T14N/R4W; Yavapai) See Woolsey Point, Coconino (Grand Canyon)
Workman Creek Falls	See Workman Creek, Gila
W S Mountain	(Elev. 8430') See W S Lake, Greenlee
Wynola	See Wymola, Pinal
Xapupi'nc	See Agua Caliente, Maricopa
Xara, Rio de La	See Dead River Wash, Apache
Xara Spring, La	See Tanner Springs, Apache
Xavier, San, Mountain	See Xavier del Bac Mission, San, Pima
Xila River	See Gila River
Xongopavi	See Shungopavi, Navajo
Y, The	See Kimball Grove, Cochise
Yaeger Canyon; (R.R. Siding)	See Yaeger Spring, Yavapai
Yahdesut	See Chiricahua National Monument, Cochise
Yah'eh'ahi	See Desert View Point, Coconino (Grand Canyon)
Yaki Trail	See Phantom Ranch, Coconino (Grand Canyon)
Yampa Creek	See Truxton Canyon, Mohave
Yampai Cliffs, Creek, River	See Truxton Canyon, Mohave
Yampai Divide, (R.R. Stn.)	See Yampai, Mohave, and Truxton Canyon, Mohave
Yampay Creek	See Truxton Canyon, Mohave
Yaqui Canyon	(T24S/R20E; Cochise) See Yaki Point, Coconino (Grand Canyon)
Yaqui Spring	(Cochise) See Yaki Point, Coconino (Grand Canyon)
Yaqui Wash	(T2S/R16W) See Yaki Tanks, Yuma
Yarber Springs, Wash	See Yarbo Mine, Yavapai
Yarbo Spring, Wash	See Yarbo Mine, Yavapai
Yarnell Hill	See Yarnell, Yavapai, and Antelope Hill, Yavapai
Yarnell Spring	(T10N/R4W) See Yarnell, Yavapai
Yavapai Trail	(Gila/Maricopa) See Apache Trail, Gila
Yavapai Station	See Jacob's Pools, Coconino
Yava Supai	See Havasupai Point, Coconino (Grand Canyon)
Yeager Canyon, Lake	See Yaeger Canyon (#1), Coconino
Yellow Iron Mountains	See Goldfield Mountains, Maricopa

Yellow Rock Spring; Rock Water	See Pipe Spring National Monument, Mohave, and Pipe Spring, Mohave
Ygnacio de Tumacacori	See Tumacacori National Monument, Santa Cruz
Yonosi Point	See Yunosi Point, Coconino (Grand Canyon)
York Valley	See York, Greenlee
Youngs Lake	See Camel Francis Lake, Coconino
Youngs Spring	See Eskiminzen Spring, Pinal
Ysidro, San	See Havania Nakya, Pima
Yule Park	See Buell Park, Apache
Yuma Desert	See Yuma, Yuma
Yuma Mesa, Wash	(T9S/R22W) See Yuma, Yuma
Yuma Valley	(T9S/R24W) See Yuma, Yuma
Yumtheska Mesa	See Yumtheska Point, Coconino (Grand Canyon)

Zacatone, Camp	See Sacaton, Pinal
Zaguanos, Rio	See Colorado River
Zaguato	See Awatobi, Navajo
Zasabe	See Sasabe, Pima
Z'azabe	See Sasabe, Pima
Zeglar Spring	See Ziegler Mountain, Apache
Zegler Mountain	See Ziegler Mountain, Apache
Zenas	See Mesa, Maricopa
Zenos	See Mesa, Maricopa
Zihi-Dusk-Jhin	See Big Mountain, Navajo
Zildassaani	See Fluted Rocks, Apache
Zilditloi Mountain	See Chuska Mountains, Apache/New Mexico
Zilh-Le-Jini	See Black Mesa, Apache
Zilh-Nez-Mesa	See Zilnez Mesa, Apache
Zilh-Ta-Jini	See Big Mountain, Navajo
Zilh Tusayan	See Fluted Rock, Apache
Zill-Cle-Ki-Sa-On	See White Mountains, Apache/Navajo
Zillesa Mesa	See Little Black Spot Mountain, Navajo
Zill-Gish-Clar-Zhe	See Trumbull, Mount, Graham
Zil-In-Dil-Che-Deig-E-La	See Pinal Mountains, Gila
Zill Its-Us-Zill-In-Fale	See Four Peaks, Maricopa
Zilner Mesa	See Zilnez Mesa, Navajo
Zi'linitsai	See Big Mountain, Navajo
Zilth Nez Mesa	See Zilnez (Mesa), Navajo
Zuguato	See Awatobi, Navajo
Zuñi Mesas, Mountain	See Twin Buttes, Navajo

County Maps

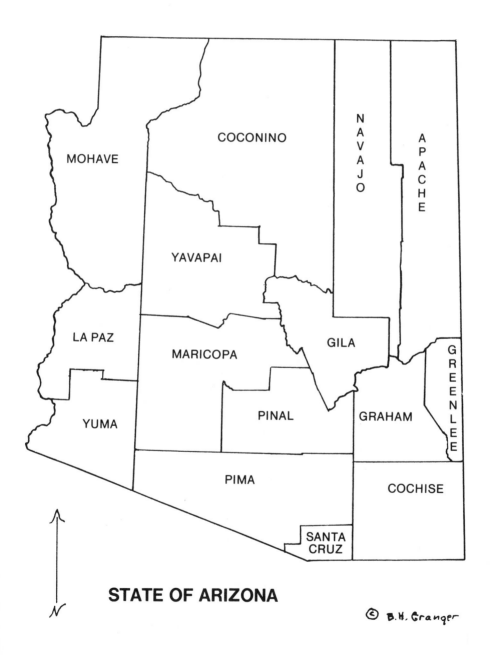

STATE OF ARIZONA

© B.H. Granger

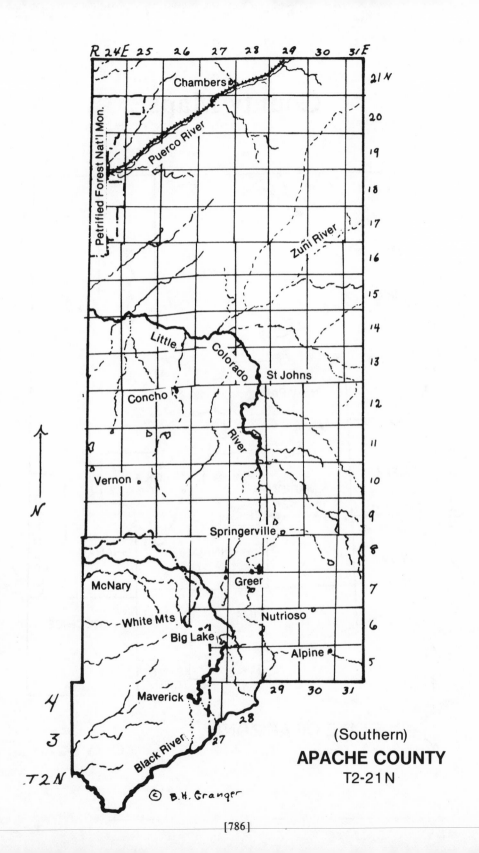

R 24E 25 26 27 28 29 30 31E

21 N
Chambers

20

Petrified Forest Nat'l Mon.

Puerco River

19

18

17

Zuñi River

16

15

14

Little

Colorado

13

St Johns

Concho

12

11

River

Vernon

10

N

9

Springerville

8

McNary

Greer

7

Nutrioso

White Mts

6

Big Lake

Alpine

5

4

Maverick

29 30 31

3

28

27

Black River

T 2 N

© B.H. Granger

(Southern)

APACHE COUNTY

T2-21 N

[786]

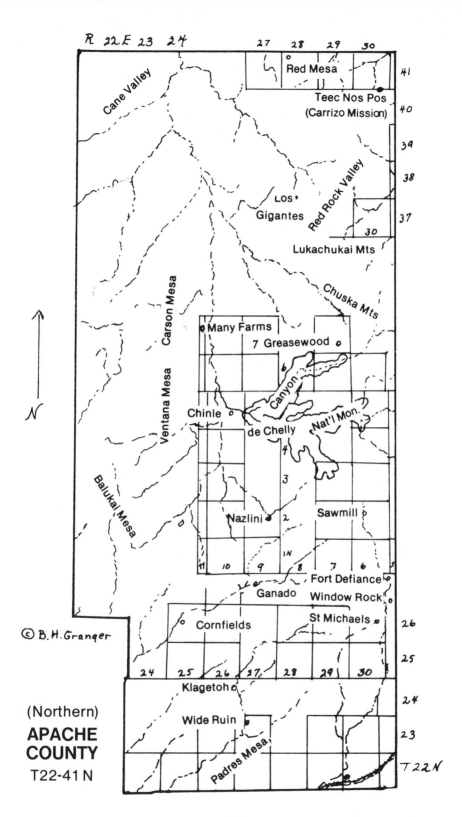

R 22 E 23 24   27   28   29   30

Red Mesa   41

Teec Nos Pos   40
(Carrizo Mission)

Cane Valley   39

                                                  38

Los   37
Gigantes   Red Rock Valley

                              30

Lukachukai Mts

Carson Mesa   Chuska Mts

Many Farms
7 Greasewood

Ventana Mesa   6

Chinle   Canyon

de Chelly   Nat'l Mon.

4

3

Balukai Mesa

Nazlini   2   Sawmill

1N
11 10   9   8   7   6

Fort Defiance

Ganado   Window Rock

© B. H. Granger

Cornfields   St Michaels   26

                                                  25

24   25   26   27   28   29   30

Klagetoh   24

(Northern)
Wide Ruin   23

APACHE
COUNTY   Padres Mesa   T 22 N

T 22-41 N

COCHISE COUNTY

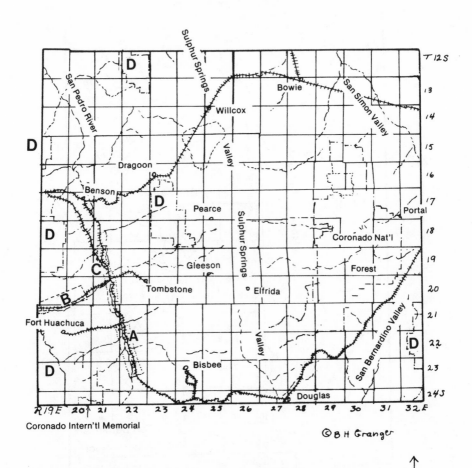

Coronado Intern'tl Memorial

© B H Granger

A. San Raphael del Valle Grant
B. San Ignacio del Babocomari Grant
C. San Juan de las Boquillas y Nogales Grant
D. Coronado Nat'l Forest

N

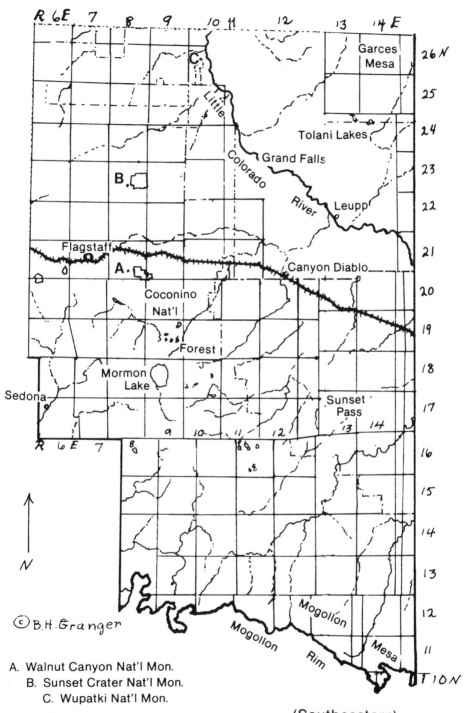

A. Walnut Canyon Nat'l Mon.
B. Sunset Crater Nat'l Mon.
C. Wupatki Nat'l Mon.

(Southeastern)
COCONINO COUNTY
T10-26N

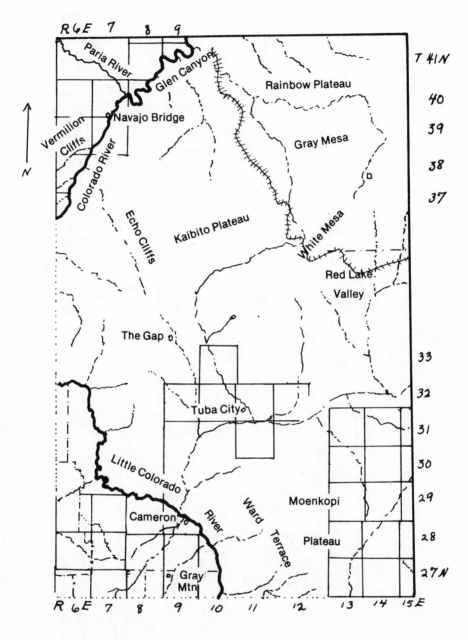

RGE 7 8 9

Paria River

Glen Canyon

Navajo Bridge

Vermilion Cliffs

Colorado River

Echo Cliffs

Kaibito Plateau

Rainbow Plateau

Gray Mesa

White Mesa

Red Lake Valley

The Gap

Tuba City

Little Colorado

Cameron

River

Ward Terrace

Moenkopi

Plateau

Gray Mtn

T 41 N

40

39

38

37

33

32

31

30

29

28

27 N

R 6 E 7 8 9 10 11 12 13 14 15 E

N

© B.H. Granger

(Northeastern)
COCONINO COUNTY
T27-41 N

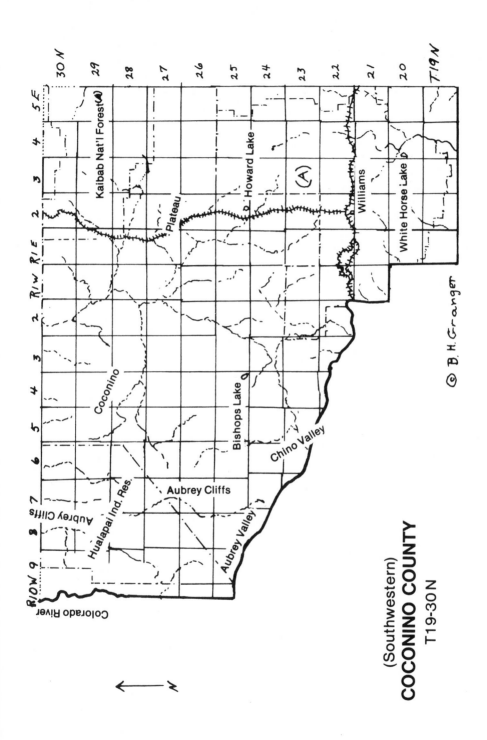

(Southwestern)
COCONINO COUNTY

T19-30N

© B.H.Granger

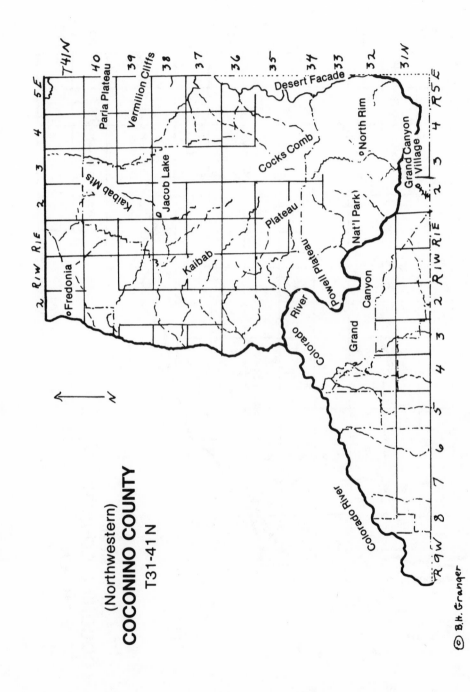

(Northwestern)
COCONINO COUNTY
T31-41N

© B.H. Granger

GILA COUNTY

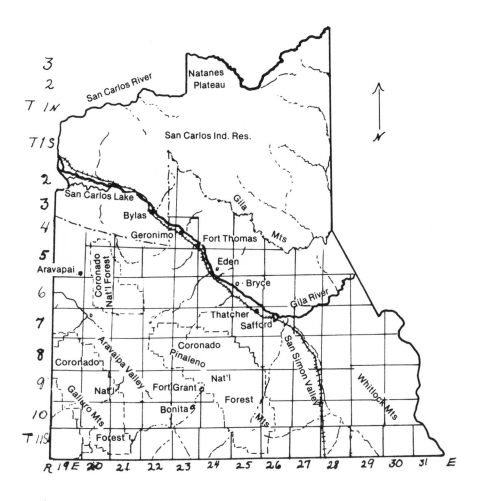

GRAHAM COUNTY

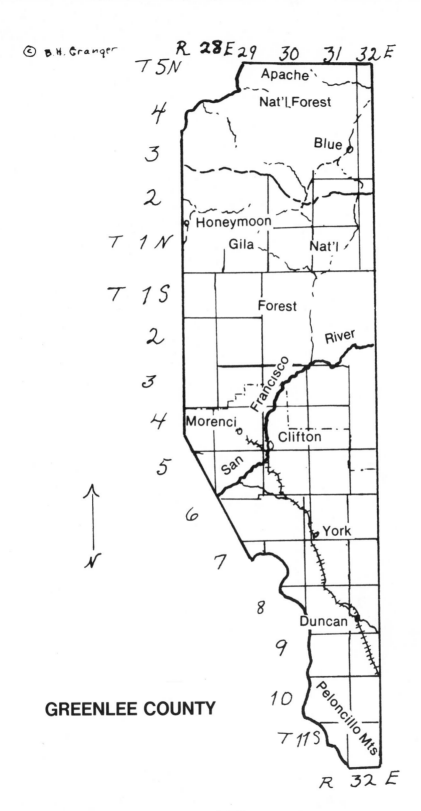

© B.H. Granger

R 28 E 29   30   31   32 E

T 5N

4

3

2

T 1N

T 1S

2

3

4

5

6

7

8

9

10

T 11S

Apache

Nat'l Forest

Blue

Honeymoon

Gila   Nat'l

Forest

River

Francisco

Morenci   Clifton

San

York

Duncan

Peloncillo Mts

R 32 E

N

GREENLEE COUNTY

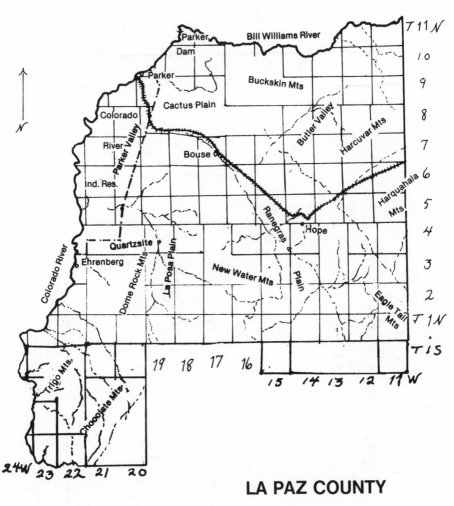

LA PAZ COUNTY

T1-11N

© B.H. Granger

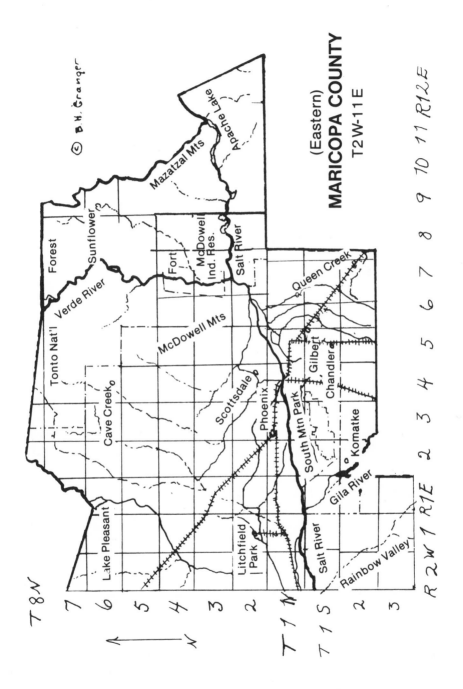

© B.H. Granger

(Eastern)
MARICOPA COUNTY
T2W-11E

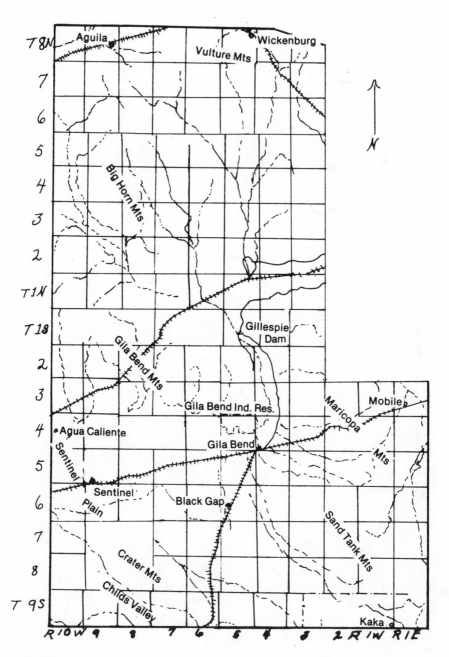

T8N — Aguila • — Wickenburg
Vulture Mts
7
N
6
5
4
Big Horn Mts
3
2
T1N
T1S
Gillespie Dam
2
Gila Bend Mts
3
Gila Bend Ind. Res.
Mobile •
Maricopa
4
• Agua Caliente
Gila Bend •
Mts
5
Sentinel
Sentinel
6
Plain
Black Gap •
Sand Tank Mts
7
8
Crater Mts
Childs Valley
T9S
Kaka •
R10W 9   8   7   6   5   4   3   2 R1W R1E

©B.H. Granger

(Western)
MARICOPA COUNTY
R1E-10W

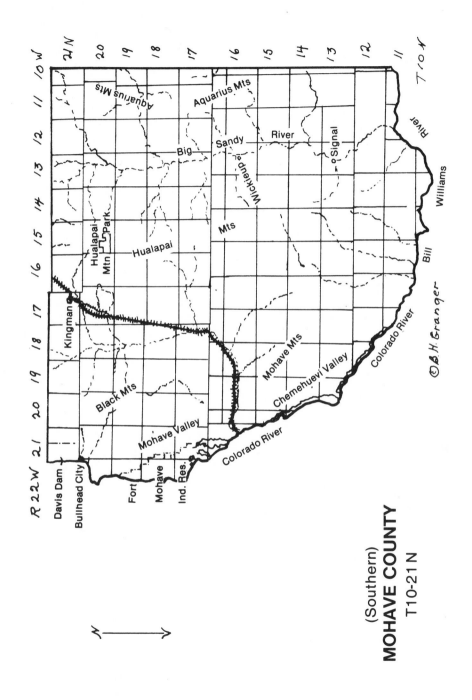

21 N
20
19
18
17
16
15
14
13
12
11
Tron

Aquarius Mts

Aquarius Mts

Sandy   River

Big

Signal

Williams

River

Wickenup

Mts

Hualapai

Park

Hualapai

Mtn

Kingman

©B.H.Granger

Bill

Mohave Mts

Colorado River

Black Mts

Chemehuevi Valley

Davis Dam

Bullhead City

Mohave Valley

Fort

Mohave

Ind. Res.

Colorado River

N →

(Southern)
MOHAVE COUNTY
T10-21 N

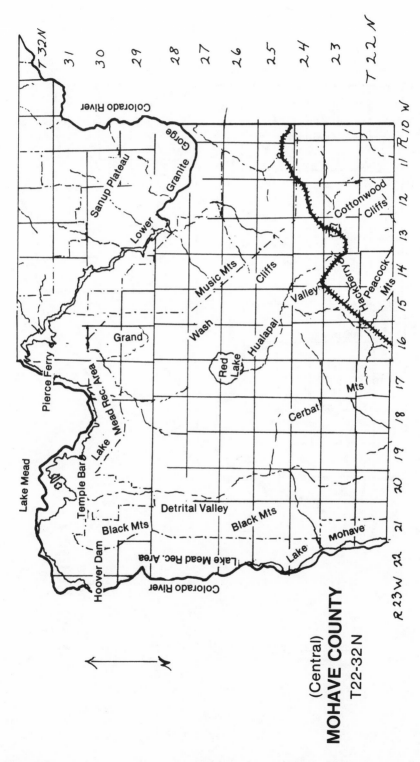

(Central)
MOHAVE COUNTY
T22-32N

© B.H.Granger

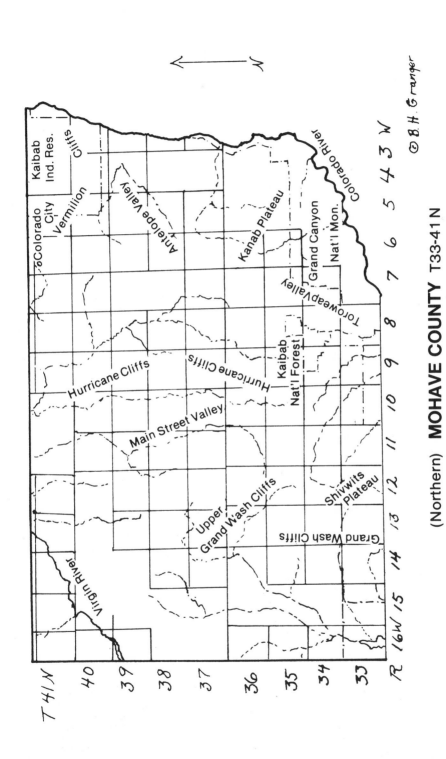

(Northern) **MOHAVE COUNTY** T33-41 N

© B. H. Granger

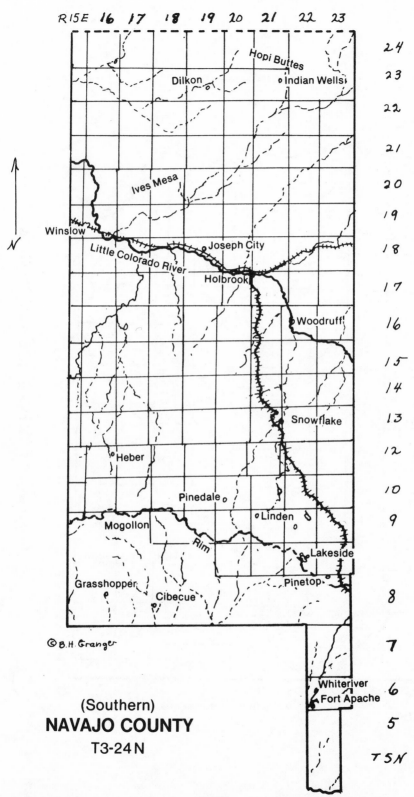

R15E 16 17 18 19 20 21 22 23

24
23
22
21
20
19
18
17
16
15
14
13
12
10
9
8
7
6
5
T5N

Hopi Buttes

Dilkon

Indian Wells

N

Ives Mesa

Winslow

Joseph City

Little Colorado River

Holbrook

Woodruff

Snowflake

Heber

Pinedale

Linden

Mogollon

Rim

Lakeside

Grasshopper

Pinetop

Cibecue

Whiteriver

Fort Apache

© B.H. Granger

(Southern)
NAVAJO COUNTY
T3-24 N

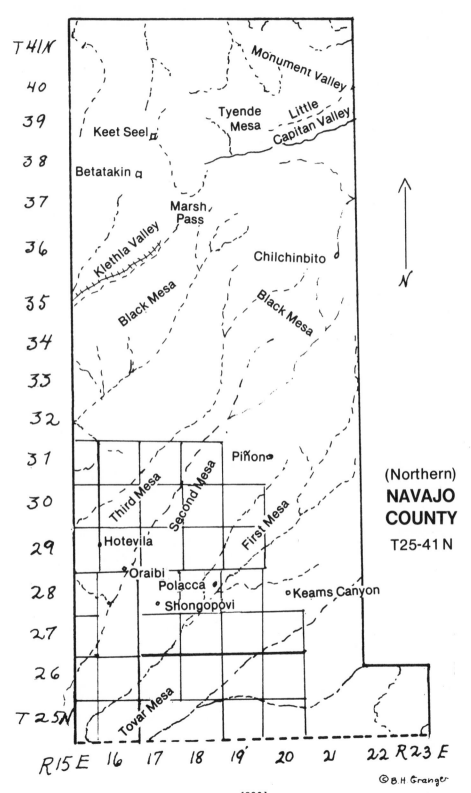

T 41 N
40
39
38
37
36
35
34
33
32
31
30
29
28
27
26
T 25 N

Monument Valley

Tyende
Mesa

Little
Capitan Valley

Keet Seel □

Betatakin ◻

Marsh
Pass

Chilchinbito ◗

Klethla Valley

Black Mesa

Black Mesa

Piñon ◗

Third Mesa

Second Mesa

First Mesa

(Northern)
**NAVAJO
COUNTY**
T25-41 N

Hotevila ◦

Oraibi ◦

Polacca ◦

Keams Canyon ◦

Shongopovi ◦

Tovar Mesa

N ↑

R 15 E   16   17   18   19   20   21   22 R 23 E

© B.H. Granger

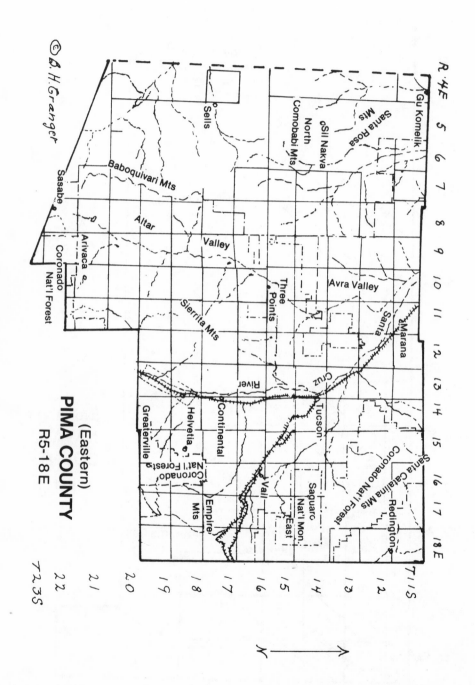

© B. H. Granger

(Eastern)
PIMA COUNTY
R5-18E

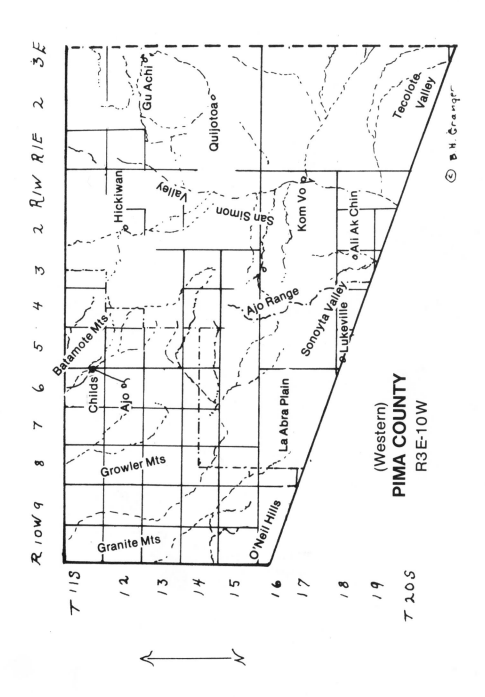

(Western)
PIMA COUNTY
R3E-10W

© B H. Granger

[805]

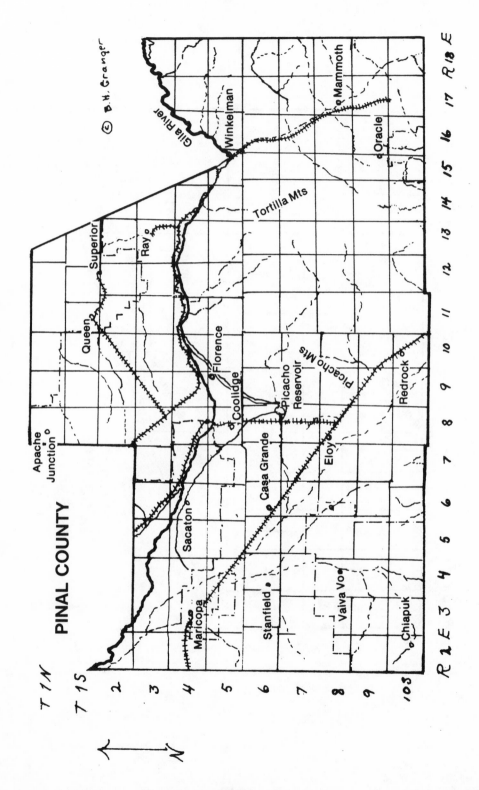

PINAL COUNTY

© B.H. Granger

SANTA CRUZ COUNTY

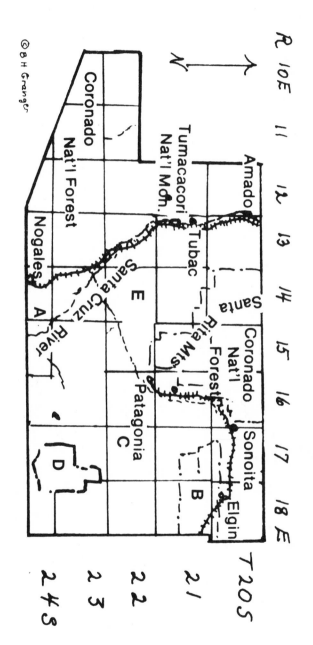

© B H Granger

A. Maria Santisima del Carmen Grant

B. San Ignacio del Babocomari Grant

C. San Jose de la Sonoita Grant

D. San Rafael de la Zanja Grant

E. Luis Maria Baca Float

(Eastern)
YAVAPAI COUNTY
R1W-8E

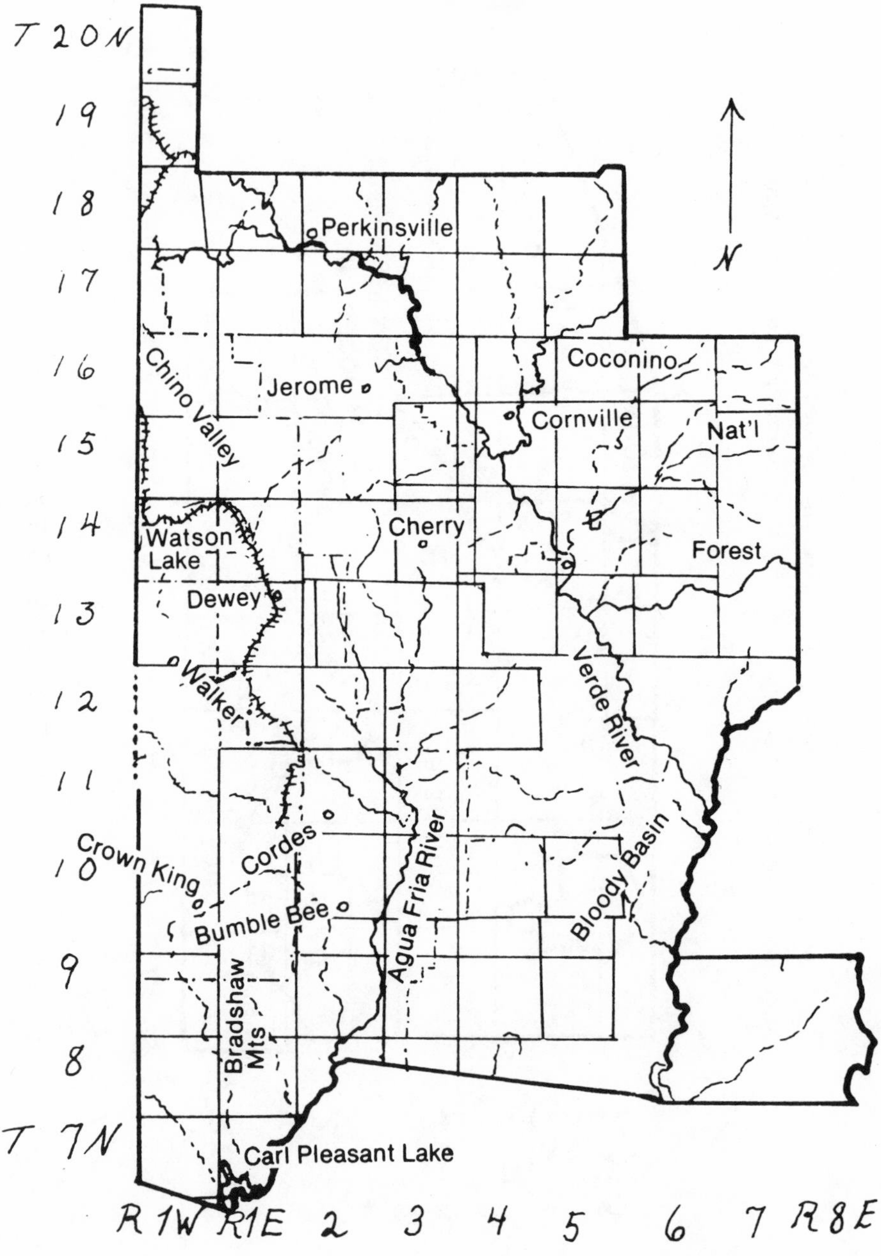

T 20 N
19
18 — Perkinsville
17
16 — Chino Valley — Jerome — Coconino
15 — Cornville — Nat'l
14 — Watson Lake — Cherry — Forest
13 — Dewey
12 — Walker — Verde River
11
10 — Crown King — Cordes — Agua Fria River — Bloody Basin
9 — Bumble Bee
8 — Bradshaw Mts
T 7 N — Carl Pleasant Lake

R1W R1E 2 3 4 5 6 7 R8E

N

© B.H. Granger

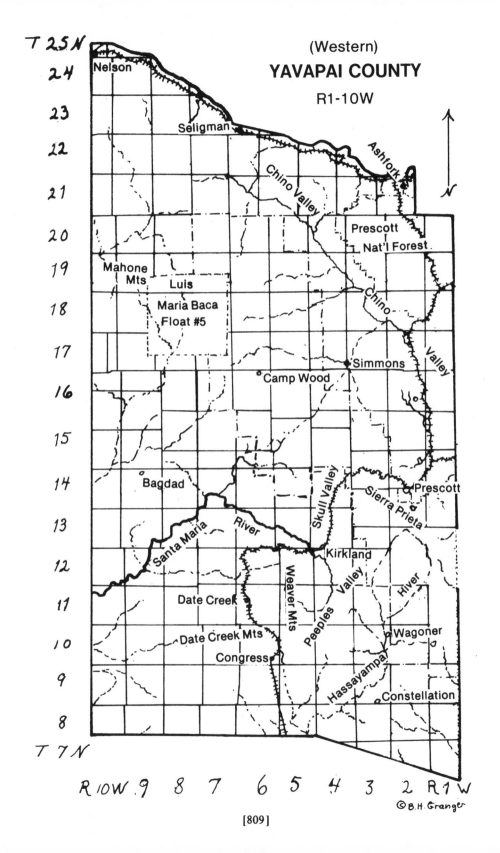

(Western)
YAVAPAI COUNTY
R1-10W

T 25N
24 — Nelson
23
22 — Seligman
21 — Chino Valley — Ashfork
20 — Prescott
19 — Mahone Mts — Nat'l Forest
18 — Luis — Chino
17 — Maria Baca Float #5 — Simmons
16 — Camp Wood — Valley
15
14 — Bagdad — Skull Valley — Prescott
13 — Santa Maria River — Sierra Prieta
12 — Kirkland
11 — Date Creek — Weaver Mts — Peeples Valley — River
10 — Date Creek Mts — Wagoner
9 — Congress — Hassayampa
8 — Constellation
T 7N

R 10W 9 8 7 6 5 4 3 2 R 1W

©B.H. Granger

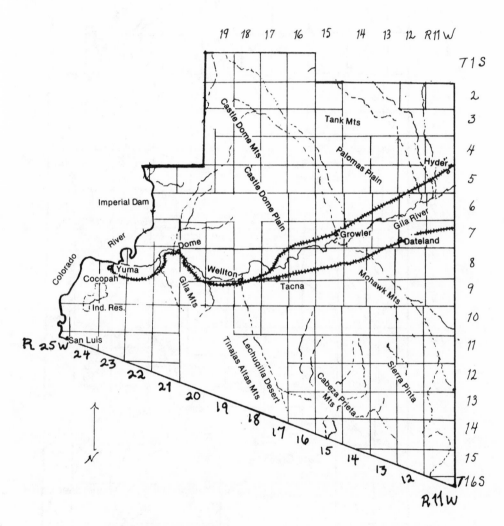

19 18 17 16 15 14 13 12 R11W

T1S

2

3

4

5

6

7

8

9

10

11

12

13

14

15

T16S

R11W

Tank Mts

Palomas Plain

Hyder

Castle Dome Mts

Castle Dome Plain

Imperial Dam

Gila River

Growler

Dateland

Colorado

River

Dome

Yuma

Cocopah

Wellton

Tacna

Mohawk Mts

Ind. Res.

Gila Mts

San Luis

R 25W 24 23 22 21 20 19 18 17 16 15 14 13 12

Tinajas Altas Mts

Lechuguilla Desert

Cabeza Prieta Mts

Sierra Pinta

N

© B.H. Granger

YUMA COUNTY

T1-16S

Contributors

ADAMS, W. G. (BILLY), and his wife set up a tourist camp at Winona in 1920. Mr. Adams also raised cattle.

ALLAN, HUGH, settled with his family on Cherry Creek, being among the earliest to do so. He carried mail between Dewey and outlying areas.

ALSDORF, JOHN (d. 1959), settled with two partners c. 1919 near what is now Eloy.

AMANN, ALMA K., prior to 1955 was acting postmistress at Black Canyon.

ANDERSON, MARGARET, in 1955 was one of the oldest pioneers still in Flagstaff.

ASHURST, HENRY FOUNTAIN, was the son of William Ashurst, among the first to settle in the Flagstaff area. The son served for many years as U.S. Senator.

BABCOCK, HENRY, lived in the Kingman area, arriving there c. 1900.

BARTLETT, KATHERINE, an archaeologist and historian, wrote many articles about Spanish exploration in Arizona. She was librarian at the Museum of Northern Arizona.

BECKER, JULIUS, spent his life in the Springerville region where his father (Gustav) and uncle c. 1880 established the Becker Mercantile Company.

BENHAM, H. L., a forest ranger, lived near Williams, arriving c. 1909.

BENNETT, FRED, came to Arizona in 1896 and worked as a cowboy and as a deputy sheriff.

BRANCH, WILLIAM B., in 1956 was Superintendent of the Petrified National Forest.

BROPHY, FRANK CULLEN, a leading banker was the son of a rancher who arrived in Arizona c. 1881, settling in Cochise County.

BRYANT, HAROLD C., was formerly Superintendent of Grand Canyon National Park.

BUNCH, ALMA, was the daughter of a pioneer who settled in southeastern Coconino County in the 1880s.

BURCARD (Fr. BURCARD FISHER), learned Navajo while at St. Michael's, where he served for many years.

BURGESS, OPIE RUNDLE, a long-time resident of Bisbee, was recognized as an authority on Cochise County history.

BURNS, ROBERT, was in 1956 a national park ranger at Katherine Boat Landing.

BURRALL, HARRY, an old-time ranger, spent more than fifty years in the Chiricahua Mountains and adjacent valleys.

BUTLER, MOLLY, was the daughter of Noah Butler, who settled in the Greer area in 1888.

BURNS, GENEVIEVE (b.c. 1880, near Globe) was born two years after her parents had arrived (in 1878).

CHUBB, MERRILL D., of the University of Kansas, climbed more buttes and temples in the Grand Canyon than any other person.

COLCORD, WILLIAM, was a pioneer rancher on the upper Gila River. (Interviewed by Mrs. Woody)

COLTON, HAROLD S., among other outstanding achievements founded the Museum of Northern Arizona.

CONRAD, JOHN F., was among the first to settle at Flagstaff.

COOPER, CHESTER (b.c. 1877), spent almost his entire life near Theodore Roosevelt Lake. His father arrived c. 1898 before the dam was constructed.

COREY, MARGARET LOUISE, for years was secretary and treasurer of the Northern Branch of the Arizona Historical Society.

COREY, BILL, a national forest ranger in Coconino County, with his wife Margaret Louise was devoted to historical matters.

CORRIGAN, THOMAS, was the son of the first postmaster at Piñon.

COSTER, BILL (b. 1874), in 1876 arrived in Arizona. He became a cattleman near Duncan.

CRAIG (Mrs. DUDLEY I. née Gerald), first saw Arizona in 1878 from her perch in front of her father on a horse. She spent her life at Pinal Ranch.

CROXEN, FRED W., served for many years as a forest ranger.

DARLING, CHARLES, in 1956 was with the Havasu Lake Wildlife Refuge.

DAVIS, SILAS O. (d. 1958), worked with and lived among Indians at the Fort Apache (Whiteriver) Reservation for years, helping to develop recreational enterprises.

DAVIS, WILLIAM W., was a pioneer in Thompson's Valley.

DEVORE, ALF, the son of a pioneer who settled in the Wheatfields District, later moved to Cherry Creek. (Interviewed by Mrs. Woody)

DOBYNS, HENRY F., an archaeologist, worked on Hualapai place names for Indian claims in connection with the Hualapai Reservation.

DUGAS, FRED (b. 1868), established his own ranch when he "was just a kid," and spent his life there.

EMPIE, HAL, born in Safford, moved to Duncan in 1934 and spent his life there.

ESCALANTE, CARLOS, and his wife built and owned the village of Sasabe on the international border.

FARMER, MALCOLM F., formerly was Assistant Director of the Museum of Northern Arizona.

FARNSWORTH, SOPHIE (b. Virginia City, Nevada), arrived in Clifton toward the end of 1898.

FERRA, EDITH (b. 1892), came to Union Pass in 1897. Except for thirteen years at Ajo, she spent her life in Mohave County.

FITZGERALD, ED C. (b. Solomonville), arrived in Clifton in 1903. He was treasurer of Greenlee County.

FORD, FRANK (b. 1888, Alcatraz Island), spent most of his life in the vicinity of Jerome and Williams.

FOSTER, GEORGE E., in 1956 was directing the management of affairs at Meteor Crater.

FRAZIER, (MRS. T.T., née Pemberton), in 1904 established a store at Roosevelt. Her father was George Pemberton, a pioneer in the region.

FRIER, DELLA POWELL, was the daughter of William Powell, who homesteaded on Cherry Creek. Her husband, Thomas Conway Frier, located in northern Arizona in 1884. He established a ranch near Marshall Lake in 1886, using the bar D T (Della and Tom) brand.

FRITZ, FRED, was a nationally known cattleman who lived near Clifton. (Interviewed by Elizabeth Shannon)

FUCHS, JAMES R., wrote his Master's thesis on the history of Williams.

GARDNER, GAIL I. (b. 1892, Prescott), for decades was a cattleman. He was postmaster at Prescott.

GARRETT, MRS. NORMAN, worked with Sen. Carl Hayden for years on pioneer history.

GILLETTE, VERNE, c. 1910 arrived in the Payson region, thereafter living for years near Globe. (Interviewed by Mrs. Woody)

GLANNON, THOMAS, lived in Nogales for decades.

GLASER, RAPHAEL M., in 1956 was stationed at the Truxton sub-agency for the Hualapai Indians.

GODDARD, JESS, a well known rancher, served as president of the Verde Historical Society.

GRAY, MRS. B.W., was a granddaughter of William Parker, who lived at Parker Canyon.

GRIGSBY, "UNCLE" DICK, an old-time cowman, ranged on either side of old Route 66 in eastern Arizona.

HARRIS, ASA ("ACE") (b. 1869, Oregon), ran away from home when ten and joined a stockman to drive cattle to the Colorado River. He led a venturesome life as a cowboy, ranger, deputy sheriff, and U.S. marshall.

HARRIS, W.M., when a boy discovered Harris Cave.

HART, LES (b. 1873), a pioneer rancher, had a ranch southwest of Flagstaff.

HAYES, CARL D.W., who lived in Columbus, N.M., traveled along the international border several times, and studied maps pertaining to it.

HENSEN, AL, helped search files at the Organ Pipe Cactus National Monument while he was visiting there during his assignment at Canyon de Chelly.

HEWARD, GLEN B., a resident of Holbrook, furnished information about his grandfather, Lehi Heward.

HICKS, MARK, arrived in Globe c. 1886. (Interviewed by Mrs. Woody)

HINCHLIFFE, LOUISE M., while on the Naturalist's staff at the Grand Canyon, was helpful in researching place names at the Canyon.

HOCKDERFER, GEORGE E., was the grandson of a man who in 1885 settled north of Flagstaff.

HOMER, PETER, was at the time of the interview, tribal council chairman for the Colorado Indian Agency at Parker.

HORNBUCKLE, DICK, at Davis Dam since 1945, was in charge of operations there.

HOUSHOLDER, E. ROSS, an engineer who prepared the official map of Mohave County, had lived in Kingman or nearby since 1916.

JACKSON, W.L., from 1930 on lived as a year-round resident at Groom Creek.

JENNING, C.A. (b.c. 1880), as a child was at both Fort Apache and Camp Grant, thereafter residing at Safford.

JOHNSON, BERT, in 1956 had lived in northern Arizona since 1874.

JOHNSON, HOWARD, and his wife in 1926 homesteaded at Aztec.

JONES, ADA E., a keen student of Santa Cruz County history, lived in Nogales for several decades.

JONES, ALDEN W., was in 1956 Assistant Superintendent of the Papago Indian Agency. He prepared a book on Papago place names.

JORDAN, FRANK (b. 1876), when ten years old went with his father to take up a homestead at Oatman Flat, where he spent most of his life.

KEENEY, K.A., in 1956 was Supervisor of the Coconino National Forest.

KELLAND, ROY, with his mother moved from Missouri to Tacna in 1936.

KELLY, LEO, a railroad engineer, had the run out of Ashfork for many years.

KENNEDY, JIM (b. 1871), a resident of Williams, was influential in Arizona highway development.

KETCHUM, ED., in 1956 a retired ranger, rode the international border country for many years.

KITT, EDITH O., for years secretary of the Arizona Historical Society, gave generously of her time as well as making her notes accessible. Although at her specific request her name is not cited, wherever the initials AHS occur without other information, Mrs. Kitt's name may be assumed.

KLINE, ADIE INGALLS, daughter of a well known pioneer (Frank Ingalls), was librarian of the Carnegie Library at Yuma.

KOLB, EMERY C. (b. 1881), arrived from Pittsburgh at the Grand Canyon in 1902. His rock home at the edge of the Canyon and his photographs are known to hundreds of thousands of Canyon visitors.

LARRIAU, JOHN (JUDGE) (b. 1880, Santa Fe), when barely six months old arrived with his parents at Contention near Tombstone. They moved soon to Fairbank where he spent most of his life.

LENON, ROBERT, an engineer, has prepared maps of both Santa Cruz and Yuma Counties. He has a wealth of knowledge about Arizona names.

MACIA, ETHEL (b. c. 1881, Tombstone), except for a brief stay with her motherless siblings at Pearce, and her attendance at the University of Arizona, spent her whole life at Tombstone, known to thousands of visitors as proprietor of the Rose Tree Inn.

MANUEL, MARK, in 1957 chairman of the Papago Tribal Council, made possible the taping of Papago pronunciation of place names.

McINTURFF, JEFF, arrived in the Pleasant Valley region in the early 1890s, moving much later to Globe. (Interviewed by Mrs. Woody)

MERCER, PRESTON M., as a sportsman, entomologist, and historian was a valuable source of information about names in Yuma County.

MERRITT, EVELYN B., a long-time resident of Prescott, is the author of a history of that locale.

MILLER, DICK, was a trapper in the Clifton area for many years. (Interviewed by Elizabeth Shannon)

MONSON, GALE, in Arizona since 1934, at the time of his interview was in charge of the Fish and Wildlife Service for the Kofa and Cabeza Prieta Game Ranges, developing both extensively.

MORRIS, EARL H., an archaeologist, has investigated Canyon de Chelly c. 1929.

MORSE, HELEN, was a life-time resident of the Seligman area.

NASH, W.B., JR., was the son of Lafayette P. Nash, who came to Arizona in 1881. (Interviewed by Mrs. Woody)

NETHERLAN, ALTON, was Deputy County Attorney when seen by the editor in Ajo in 1956.

NOBLE, LESLEY, was born at Alpine where his father was a pioneer.

NUTTAL, JEAN McCLELLAN, was born and raised near Dragoon, later becoming a resident of Tombstone.

OLLSEN, MRS. LOUIS (née Agnes Vineyard), was born in Greenback Valley. (Interviewed by Mrs. Woody)

PARKER, REV. CHARLES FRANKLIN a resident of Prescott, was a frequent contributor to *Arizona Highways*.

PARKMAN, I.H., inaugurated the Old Settlers Club and Museum at Buckeye, where he had lived since c. 1900.

PATEY, RALPH, of Kingman, when interviewed was in charge of the Chamber of Commerce.

PATTON, JAMES MONROE, in 1945 completed a Master's thesis on the history of Clifton, containing many interviews with pioneers.

PENROD, JOHN RALPH, and his wife were members of the Penrod family which located in the Pinetop area in 1897.

PERRY, EBEN P., was the son of a pioneer who arrived in Arizona in 1875. In 1929 the Perry family moved to Perryville.

PHILLIPS, W.S., former head of the Department of Botany at the University of Arizona, provided information on places of particular interest to botanists.

PIEPER, ERNEST (b. 1891, Globe), lived at Payson for nearly fifty years. (Interviewed by Mrs. Woody)

PLATTEN, MARY FORD ("Aunt Mary") (b. 1869, Kodiak Island, Alaska), recalled climbing on Gen. George Crook's knee and asking him about his beard. The widow of Fred Platten (who during Indian campaigns earned the Congressional Medal of Honor), many times accompanied her husband while he rode the ranges of northern Arizona.

POLLOCK, TOM E., a pioneer rancher, owned the Grapevine Canyon Ranch.

PRATHER, BESS, for years postmaster at Casa Grande, was prominent as a leader of women's activities in Arizona.

REILLY, PETER, became a resident of Clifton c. 1905 and spent his life there.

RICHARDS, J. MORRIS, well known as a newspaper man, was the grandson of Mormon Bishop J.W. Richards, assigned to Arizona c. 1877.

REILL, ROBERT, arrived in Globe in the 1890s. (Interviewed by Mrs. Woody)

RIGGS, LILLIAN, was the daughter of one pioneer – Neil Erickson – and the widow of another – Ed Riggs. She and her husband were the first to explore what became the Chiricahua National Monument.

ROSENBERGER, DOROTHY, a long-time resident of Prescott, supplied much information on places in Yavapai County.

ROTHWELL, LYNN, who lived on a ranch near Seligman, knew the area well.

SAVILLA, AGNES, as secretary for the Mohave Tribal Council supplied information about Poston and other places.

SCHELLBACH, LOUIS, a distinguished naturalist, provided access to his personal files at the Grand Canyon, where he was Chief Naturalist.

SCHMELZER, CHARLOTTE, now retired, taught for years on the staff of the Whiteriver (Apache) school, and furnished much information about that region.

SCHNEBLY, ELLSWORTH, was raised in the Oak Creek and Cottonwood areas. His family came to Oak Creek Canyon in 1912, and Sedona is named for his mother.

SCHROEDER, ALBERT H., when interviewed was associated with the Southwestern National Monuments at Globe. An archaeologist, he was helpful through his interest in early Spanish names and Arizona territorial history.

SCOTT, JAMES BOYCE, as Attorney for Greenlee County had investigated and made note of names in the Clifton area.

SECAKUKU, HALE, was formerly chairman of the Hopi Tribal Council.

SHANNON, ELIZABETH, whose uncle Charles M. Shannon was among the first to arrive in Clifton, not only supplied information, but also interviewed pioneers in the vicinity of Clifton.

SHREEVE, JIM, a former supervisor in Apache County, had a vital interest in St. Johns history.

SIMMONS, JESSE, came to Clifton in 1904. His wife was a native Arizonan.

SISK, HANSON R., editor and publisher of the *Nogales Herald,* was a source of much information about places in Santa Cruz County.

SLAMON, JOHN (JUDGE), lived in Ash Fork for nearly half a century.

SLIPHER, EARL O., associated for years with the Lowell Observatory in Flagstaff, and had a notable collection of helpful photographs.

SMITH, G.E.P., an authority on irrigation problems in Arizona, served as chairman of the Place Names Committee of the Arizona Historical Society and opened his files of the U.S. Geographic Board on Names.

SMITH, MARK (b. c. 1889), was a native of William and had lived there for sixty-seven years at the time he was interviewed in 1956.

SPAIN, MADELINE, provided information about names in Yuma County, where she lived for many years.

SPARKS, GRACE, a long-time resident of Yavapai County, moved to Santa Cruz County where she was a dynamic force in establishing and managing the Coronado International Monument.

SPROAT, JOHN (MRS.), and her husband arrived in Winona in 1912 and were for a time its only residents. Earlier she had worked for Ed and Lillian Riggs in Cochise County.

STANFIELD, W.A., a lawyer specializing in land matters near Eloy, clarified names in that vicinity.

STEMMER, CHARLES C., was a prominent businessman and cattleman.

STOUT, AL, in 1956 had lived near or in Casa Grande for over fifty years.

SUPERNAUGH, WILLIAM, in 1940 when names were being given to places in the Organ Pipe Cactus National Monument, was the monument Superintendent.

SWEETING, HARRIET (b. Frisco River, Greenlee County), was the daughter of Luther F. Sweeting, who bought the Mason Greenlee homestead and thereby acquired Evans Point.

SWITZER, W.H., was a leader in organizing and conducting the affairs of the Northern Branch of the Arizona Historical Society.

SYKES, STANLEY (d. 1956), an Englishman, en route to Australia stopped in Flagstaff and liked the area so well he spent his life there.

TERRY, SID, a railroad man, arrived in Williams in 1907.

THEOBALD, JOHN and his wife Lillian wrote histories of Arizona territorial post offices and Wells Fargo stations. Their knowledge of transportation and communication in pioneer Arizona was immensely helpful.

THOMPSON, WILLIAM M., was married to Mary Margaret Lockwood, daughter of pioneer historian Frank C. Lockwood. The Thompsons raised cattle near Dewey.

UPPLEGGER, REV. FRANZ (b.c. 1870), had been a missionary with the Apaches since 1919 and spoke their language well.

VARNEY, PHILIP, in the late 1970s visited Arizona ghost towns, thereafter publishing a book about them. He supplied contemporary information about such places.

WALKER, VIRGIL, was the son of William Walker, who came to Arizona in 1886. Mr. Walker lived in Nogales.

WARNER, BEN, since 1921 had lived at Rock Springs in Yavapai County.

WEBB, A.C., when a small boy c. 1890 arrived in Arizona where he became a rancher on Tonto Creek. (Interviewed by Mrs. Woody)

WENTZ, C.B., spent many years serving as a guide in White Mountain country.

WESTOVER, JOHN L., came to Joseph City in 1897.

WILLARD, C.A. (b. 1858), in 1956 had a clear and vivid memory of events in Arizona dating to the 1870s when he had arrived in Cottonwood.

WILLSON, ROSCOE G., was well known as the author of a weekly Arizona historical essay in the *Arizona Republic* ("Arizona Days and Ways").

WILSON, SID, was an old-time cowpoke who, among other adventures, traveled in the early 1900s to Europe with Buffalo Bill Cody's Wild West show. He had ranged Arizona all the way from the Mexican border to the Grand Canyon, setting in Tombstone where he was mayor in 1956.

WILTBANK, MILO, a life-long resident of Eagar, was a collector of rare books and manuscripts and an amateur historian of Arizona.

WINGFIELD, R.W., managed the Wingfield Commercial Company at Camp Verde. His father moved to that region in the late 1870s.

WOODY, CLARA (MRS.), traveled from one end of Gila County to the other and back again, amassing its history and interviewing pioneers. Her help on names in Gila County was immeasurable and invaluable.

YOUNG, ROBERT W., in 1956 was Assistant to the General Superintendent of the Navajo Indian Reservation. Thanks to his help, information on Navajo names in Arizona expanded considerably.

YOUNGGREN, JEANNE, who acted as research assistant for several years during the course of preparing this volume, became so interested that she button-holed and interviewed archaeologists, members of hiking clubs, botanists, geologists, and others, searching and finding substantiation for name information which had been in question.

Bibliography

1. Abert, J. W. *Examination of New Mexico in the Years 1846-1847*. Executive Document No. 23, 30th Congress, 1st Session.

2. Adams, Harriet Chalmer. "Grand Canyon Bridge." *National Geographic Magazine*, XXXIX (June 1921), 645-660.

3. Ames, Charles R. "A History of the Forest Service." *The Smoke Signal*. Tucson: The Westerners, n.d.

3a. Anderson, C. A., *et al. Geology and Ore Deposits of the Bagdad Area, Yavapai County* (G.S. Prof. Paper 278). Washington, D.C.: U.S. Government Printing Office, 1955.

4. Antisell, Thomas. *Exploration and Surveys for a Railroad Route from the Mississippi River to the Pacific Ocean, 1853-56, VII, Part 2*. Washington: 1857.

5. *Arizona: A State Guide.* "American Guide Series." New York: Hastings House, 1940.

6. *Arizona Business Atlas*. Chicago: Rand McNally & Co., 1893.

7. *Arizona: 1887-1950*. Phoenix: Bank of Douglas, 1949.

8. "Arizona Big Game Bulletin." N.p.: Arizona Game & Fish Department, n.d.

9. "Arizona Game and Fish Department List of Department-Managed Lands." N.p.: Arizona Game & Fish Department, n.d.

10. Arizona Geological Society. *Guide Book for Field Trip Excursions in Southern Arizona*. Tucson: Geological Society of America, 1952 (April).

11. *Arizona, the Grand Canyon State*. Westminster, CO: Western States Historical Society, 1975.

12. *Arizona, Her Great Mining, Agricultural, Stock-Raising and Lumber Interests: The Only Direct Route Via the Atchison, Topeka and Santa Fe Railroads*. N.p.: 1884 [?]. (Huntington Library)

13. *Arizona's National Monuments*. Santa Fe: Southwestern Monuments Association, 1945.

14. Baker, Arthur A. *Geology of the Monument Valley – Navajo Mountain Region, San Juan County, Utah*. Washington, D.C.: U.S. Government Printing Office, 1936.

15. Bancroft, Hubert Howe. *History of Arizona and New Mexico, II*. New York: The Bancroft Co., n.d. [1890?].

16. _____. *History of the North Mexican States and Texas*. San Francisco: A. L. Bancroft & Co., 1884.

17. Bandel, Eugene. *Frontier Life in the Army, 1854-1861*. Ralph Bieber, ed. Olga Bandel and Richard Jente, trans. Glendale, CA: The Arthur H. Clark Co., 1932.

18. Bank of Douglas. *Arizona 1887-1950*. Phoenix: Bank of Douglas, 1949.

18a. Barnes, Will C. *Arizona Place Names*. Tucson: University of Arizona, 1935.

19. Barringer, D. M. "Coon Mountain and Its Crater." *Proceedings of the Academy of Natural Sciences of Philadelphia* (December 1905).

20. Bartlett, John Russell. *Personal Narrative: or Exploration and Incidents in Texas, New Mexico, California, Sonora and Chihuahua, I, II*. New York: D. Appleton & Co., 1854.

21. Bartlett, Katherine. "How Don Pedro de Tovar Discovered the Hopi and Don Garcia Lopez de Cardenas Saw the Grand Canyon, With Notes Upon Their Probable Route." *Plateau*, XII (January 1940), 37 – 45.

22. _____. "Notes Upon the Routes of Espejo and Farfán to the Mines in the Sixteenth Century." *New Mexico Historical Review* (January 1942), pp. 21 – 36.

23. Beale, Edward Fitzgerald. *Wagon Road from Fort Defiance to the Colorado River*. Washington, D.C.: House Executive Document No. 124, 35th Congress, 1st Session, 1858.

24. Becker, Julius W. *Ms.*: "Statement by Julius W. Becker Relative to Highways Leading to and from Springerville, Arizona." Springerville, AZ: n.d.

25. "Becker's 75th Anniversary Number." *Apache County Independence News*, XXXIX (August 31, 1951).

26. Bell, James G. *Log of the Texas-California Cattle Trail*. Austin, TX: 1932. Reprinted from *The Southwestern Quarterly* 1932).

27. Bell, William J. *New Tracks in North America, I, II: Journal of Travel and Adventure Whilst Engaged in the Survey for a Southern Railroad to the Pacific Ocean*. London: 1869.

28. Bender, A. B. "Frontier Defense in the Territory of New Mexico, 1846-1853." *New Mexico Historical Review*, IX (July 1934), 249-272.

29. _____. "Government Explorations in the Territory of New Mexico." *New Mexico Historical Review*, IX (January 1934), 1–32.

30. Bender, Averam Burton. *March of Empire, The*. Lawrence, KS: University of Kansas Press, 1952.

31. Benson, Lyman, and Robert A. Darrow. *A Manual of Southwestern Desert Trees and Shrubs*. Tucson: University of Arizona Press, 1944.

32. Bentley, Harold Woodmansee. *A Dictionary of Spanish Terms, with Special Reference to the American Southwest*. New York: Columbia University Press, 1932.

33. Bents, Doris W. *The History of Tubac, 1752-1948*. Tucson: Master's Thesis, University of Arizona, 1949.

34. Bieber, Ralph P. *Exploring Southwestern Trails, 1846-1854*. Glendale, CA: 1938.

35. Billings, John S. *A Report of Barracks and Hospitals.* Washington, D.C.: U.S. Government Printing Office, 1870.

36. Birdseye, Claude H., and Raymond C. Moore. "A Boat Voyage Through the Grand Canyon of the Colorado." *The Geographical Review* (April 1924), pp. 177-196.

37. Birney, Hoffman. *Roads to Roam.* New York: The A. L. Burt Co., 1930.

38. Bishop, W. H. *Old Mexico and Her Lost Provinces.* 1883.

39. Blake, William P. "Geological Report." *Pacific Railroad Report,* V. Washington, D. C.: 1856.

40. Bloom, Lansing B., ed. "Bourke on the Southwest, II, III, IV, V." *New Mexico Historical Review,* IX (January 1934), 33-77; (April 1934), 159-183; (July 1934), 273-289; (October 1934), 375-435.

41. Bolton, Herbert Eugene. *Coronado on the Turquoise Trail.* Albuquerque: University of New Mexico Press, 1949.

42. _____. "Escalante in Dixie and the Arizona Strip." *New Mexico Historical Review,* III (January 1948), 41-72.

43. _____. *Kino's Historical Memoir of Pimeria Alta, I, II.* Berkeley, CA: University of California Press, 1948.

44. _____. *Padre on Horseback.* San Francisco: The Sonora Press, 1932.

45. _____. *Rim of Christendom: a Biography of Eusebio Francisco Kino, Pacific Coast Pioneer.* New York: The Macmillan Co., 1936.

46. _____. *Spanish Exploration in the Southwest (Original Narratives of Early American History), 1542-1706.* New York: Charles Scribner's Sons, 1916.

47. Bourke, John G., and George W. Baird. "Generals Crook and Miles in Arizona." *Smoke Signals.* Tucson: The Westerner, n.d.

48. Bourke, John G. *General Crook in the Indian Country.* Palmer Lake, CO: The Filter Press, 1974.

49. _____. *On the Border with Crook.* New York: Charles Scribner's Sons, 1891.

50. Bourne, Eulalia. *Ranch Schoolteacher.* Tucson: University of Arizona Press, c. 1974.

51. Box, Michael J. *Adventures and Explorations in New and Old Mexico.* New York: 1869.

52. Brandes, Raymond Stewart. *Frontier Military Posts in Arizona.* Globe, AZ: D. S. King, c. 1960.

53. Breed, Jack. "Land of the Havasupai." *The National Geographic Magazine,* XCIII (May 1948), 655 – 674.

54. Brinkerhoff, Sidney. "Camp Date Creek." *The Smoke Signal.* Tucson: The Westerners, 1964 (Fall).

55. Brown, Carl E. "Mapping Lake Mead." *The Geographical Review* (July 1941), pp. 385–403.

56. Browne, J. Ross. *A Tour Through Arizona, 1864.* New York: Harper & Bros., 1869.

57. Bryan, Kirk. *Papago Country of Arizona.* "Water Supply Paper 499, USGS, Dept. of the Interior." Washington, D.C.: U.S. Government Printing Office, 1925.

58. _____. "Personal Notes Taken While Studying Watering Places in Papago County, Arizona." Unpublished *ms.*

59. _____. *Routes to Desert Watering Places in the Papago Country, Arizona.* "Water Supply Paper 490-D, USGS, Dept. of the Interior." Washington, D.C.: U.S. Government Printing Office, 1922.

60. Burns, Walter Noble. *Tombstone, an Iliad of the Southwest.* New York: Grosset & Dunlap, 1929.

61. Cady, John H. *Arizona's Yesterdays: Being the Narrative of John H. Cady, Pioneer.* Basil Dillon, ed. N.p.: n.p., 1915.

62. *Census of the United States, 1870.*

63. *Census of the United States, 1880.*

64. Clifford, Josephine. "Crossing the Arizona Deserts." *Overland Monthly,* IV (1870), 537 – 544.

65. Clum, John P. "Es-Kim-In-Zin." *Arizona Historical Review* (April 1929), pp. 53 – 72; (July 1929), pp. 53 – 69.

66. _____. "San Carlos Blasted into Dust." *Arizona Historical Review,* III (April 1930), 59 – 70.

67. Clum, Woodworth. *Apache Agent: The Story of John P. Clum.* Boston: Houghton Mifflin Co., 1936.

68. Colquhoun, James. *Early History of Clifton-Morenci District.* London: William Clowes & Son, Ltd., 1935.

69. Colton, Harold S. "Grand Falls." *Museum Notes,* II (June 1930), 1 – 3.

70. _____. *The Sinagua.* Flagstaff, AZ: Museum of Northern Arizona, 1946.

71. Colton, Harold S., and Frank C. Baxter. *Days in the Painted Desert and the San Francisco Mountains.* Flagstaff, AZ: Coyote Range, 1927.

72. Conklin, E. *Picturesque Arizona: Being the Result of Travels and Observations in Arizona During the Fall and Winter of 1877.* New York: Continental Stereoscope Co. of New York, 1878.

73. Conkling, Roscoe P., and Margaret B. *The Butterfield Overland Mail, 1857 – 1869,* I, II. Glendale, CA: The Arthur H. Clark Co., 1947.

74. Cooke, Philip St. George. *Exploring Southwestern Trails.* Glendale, CA: The Arthur H. Clark Co., 1938.

75. Conway, Stevens Robert. *A History of Chandler, Arizona.* Tucson: Master's Thesis, University of Arizona, 1954.

76. *Coronado National Forest.* Forest Service, Southwestern Region, U.S. Dept. of Agriculture. Washington, D.C.: U.S. Government Printing Office, 1942.

77. Coues, Elliot, trans. *On the Trail of a Spanish Pioneer: The Diary and Itinerary of Francisco Garcès, 1775 – 1776.* New York: E. P. Harper, 1900.

78. Couts, Cave J. *From San Diego to the Colorado in 1849: The Journal and Maps of Cave J. Couts.* William McPherson, ed. Los Angeles: Arthur M. Ellis, 1932.

78a. Cox, Annie Mae. *A History of Bisbee.* Tucson: Master's Thesis, University of Arizona, 1938.

79. Crane, Leo. *Indians of the Enchanted Desert.* Boston: Little, Brown and Co., 1929.

80. Cremony, John C. *Life among the Apaches, 1849 – 1864.* San Francisco: A. Roman & Co., 1868.

81. Crofutt, George A. *Crofutt's New Overland Tourist and Pacific Coast Guide through Nebraska, Wyoming, Utah, Arizona . . . .* Omaha: Overland Publishing Co., 1883.

82. Crook, George. *General George Crook: His Autobiography.* Martin F. Schmitt, ed. Norman, OK: University of Oklahoma Press, 1946.

83. Cruse, Thomas. *Apache Days and After.* Caldwell, ID: The Caxton Printers, Ltd., 1941.

84. Cummings, Byron. "Turkey Hill Ruin." *Museum Notes,* II (May 1930), 6.

85. Darton, N. H. *Guidebook of the Western United States: Part C, The Santa Fe Route.* USGS (1915).

86. Davis, Alonzo E. Ms.: *Pioneer Days in Arizona.* Louise Davis Van Cleve and Jessie Davis White, eds. N.p.:n.p., 1915.

87. Dean, Jeffrey Stewart. *Chronological Analysis of Tsegi Phase Sites in Northeastern Arizona.* Tucson: University of Arizona Doctoral Dissertation, 1967.

88. Dellenbaugh, Frederick S. *A Canyon Voyage: The Narrative of the Second Powell Expedition down the Green-Colorado River from Wyoming and the Explorations on Land, in the Years 1871 and 1872.* New Haven: Yale University Press, 1926.

89. _____. *Romance of the Colorado River.* New York: G. P. Putnam's Sons, 1906.

90. Derby, George H. *Report to the Secretary of War, Communicating, in Compliance with a Resolution of the Senate, a Reconnaissance of the Gulf of California and the Colorado River, 1851.* Senate Executive Document 81, 32nd Congress, 1st Session. Washington, D.C.: 1852.

91. Diller, J. S., and J. S. Whitfield. "Mineralogical Notes: Dumortierite from Harlem, N.Y., and Clip, Arizona." *American Journal of Science,* XXXVII (1889), 216 – 219.

92. DiPeso, Charles C. *The Reeve Ruin of Southeastern Arizona.* Dragoon, AZ: The Amerind Foundation, 1958.

93. Dobyns, Henry F. "The Case of Paint vs. Garlic." *Arizona Quarterly,* XI (Summer 1955), 156 – 160.

94. Douglass, William A. "On the Naming of Arizona." *Names,* XXVII (December 1979), 217 – 231.

95. Dozier, Edward P. "The Hopi and Tewa." *Scientific American,* 196 (June 1957), 126 – 136.

96. _____. *The Hopi-Tewa of Arizona.* Berkeley, CA: University of California Press, 1954.

97. Drake, Robert J. "Mollusca in Alluvium, Buell Park, Apache County, Arizona." *Plateau,* XX (October 1949), 26 ff.

98. Dunlap, H. E. "Clay Beauford — Welford C. Bridwell." *Arizona Historical Review,* III (October 1930), 44 – 66.

99. _____. "Tom Horn, Chief of Scouts." *Arizona Historical Review* (April 1929), pp. 73–75.

100. Dutton, Clarence E. *Tertiary History of the Grand Cañon District, with Atlas.* Washington, D.C.: U.S. Government Printing Office, 1882.

101. Eccleston, Robert. *Overland to California on the Southwestern Trail: Diary of Robert Eccleston (1849).* George P. Hammond and Edward H. Howes, eds. Berkeley, CA: University of California Press, 1950.

102. Eddy, Frank Warren. *A Sequence of Cultural and Alluvial Deposits in the Cienega Creek Basin, Southeastern Arizona.* Tucson: Master's Thesis, University of Arizona, 1958.

103. Edmonson, Munro S. *Lore: An Introduction to the Science of Folklore and Literature.* New York: Holt, Rinehart & Winston, Inc., 1971.

104. Elliott, Wallace W. *History of Arizona Territory Showing Its Resources and Advantages with Illustrations.* San Francisco: Wallace W. Elliott Co., 1884.

105. Emory, William H. *Notes of a Military Reconnaissance from Fort Leavenworth, in Missouri, to San Diego, in California, Including Part of the Arkansas, Del Norte, and Gila Rivers.* Executive Document No. 41. Washington, D.C.: Wendell & Van Benthuysen, Printers, 1848.

106. _____. *Report on the United States and Mexican Boundary Survey, I.* Washington, D.C.: Cornelius Wendell, Printers, 1857.

107. Farish, Thomas Edwin. *History of Arizona,* I – VIII. Phoenix: c. Thomas Farish, 1915.

108. Farnsworth, Harriett. *Remnants of the Old West.* San Antonio: The Naylor Company, 1965.

109. Favour, Alpheus H. *Old Bill Williams, Mountain Man.* Chapel Hill, NC: University of North Carolina Press, 1936.

110. Ferguson, James. Ms., "The Mormon Battalion: A Lecture Delivered at Liverpool, November 7, 1855." (Huntington Library).

111. Fewkes, J. W. "Archaeological Expedition to Arizona in 1895." *17th Annual Report, Bureau of American Ethnology, Part II.* Washington, D.C.: 1900.

112. _____. "A Few Summer Ceremonies." *Journal of American Ethnology and Archaeology, II.* Boston: Houghton, Mifflin & Co., 1892.

113. _____. "Hopi Shrines Near the East Mesa, Arizona." *American Anthropology,* VII (April – June 1906), 346 – 375.

114. _____. "Tusayan Migration Traditions." *19th Annual Report, Bureau of American Ethnology, 1897 – 1898, Part II.* Washington, D.C.: U.S. Government Printing Office, 1900.

115. Figueroa, Francisco Garcia. *Documents Historical and Geographical Descriptions of Arizona & Sonora Translated Now for the First Time from the Original Manuscript of the Franciscan Father, Francisco Garcia Figueroa, by Frank de Thoma.* San Francisco: October 1899.

116. Fish, Joseph. Ms., *History of Arizona*, Parts I and II. (University of Arizona, Tucson)

117. Forbes, Robert H. *The Penningtons: Pioneers of Early Arizona.* N.p.: Arizona Archaeological and Historical Society, 1919.

118. Forrest, Earl R. *Arizona's Dark and Bloody Ground.* Caldwell, ID: Caxton Printers, Ltd., 1936.

119. _____. *Missions and Pueblos of the Old Southwest.* Cleveland, OH: Arthur H. Clark Co., 1929.

120. Forrest, Earle R., and Edwin B. Hill. *Lone War Trail of the Apache Kid.* Pasadena, CA: Trail's End Publishing Co., 1947.

121. Foster, George E. *Arizona's Meteorite Crater.* N.p.: n.p., c. 1951.

121a. Frazer, Robert Walter. *Forts of the West; Military Forts and Presidios and Posts, Commonly Called Forts, West of the Mississippi River, 1898.* Norman, OK: University of Oklahoma Press, 1965.

122. Freeman, Lewis R. *The Colorado River.* New York: Dodd Mead Co., 1923.

123. _____. "Surveying the Grand Canyon of the Colorado." *National Geographic Magazine*, XLV (May 1924), 471 – 548.

124. Fuchs, James R. *A History of Williams, Arizona, 1876 – 1951.* Tucson: Master's Thesis, University of Arizona, 1955.

125. Gatewood, Charles B., Jr. "Lieut. Charles B. Gatewood, 6th U.S. Cavalry, and the Surrender of Geronimo." *Arizona Historical Review*, IV (April 1931), 29 – 32.

126. Gatschet, A. S. "Words, Phrases and Paradigms of the Papago Language (July 1897)" *B.A.E. Ms. ±2502.* (Smithsonian Institution).

127. "General Scheme of Arizona." *U.S. Post Office Department Railway Mail Service Guide (August 1938).* Washington, D.C.: U.S. Government Printing Office, 1938.

128. Gilbert, J. K. *Report of the Geology of Portions of New Mexico and Arizona Examined in 1873: USGS Surveys West of the 100th Meridian: Geology*, III. Washington, D.C.: U.S. Government Printing Office, 1875.

129. Gillmor, Frances, and Louisa Wade Wetherill. *Trader to the Navajos.* Albuquerque, NM: University of New Mexico Press, 1934.

130. "Government Cave." *Museum Notes*, II (December 1, 1929), 1 – 3.

131. Graham, J. D. *3rd Report of Lt. Col. J. D. Graham.* Senate Congressional Document No. 121, First Session, 32nd Congress.

132. Granger, Byrd Howell. "Early Mormon Place Names in Arizona." *Western Folklore*, XVI (January 1957), 43 – 47.

133. _____, ed. "The Journal of Charles Debrille Poston." *Arizona Quarterly*, XIII (Summer 1957), 152 – 162; (Autumn 1957), 251 – 261; (Winter 1957), 353 – 362.

134. _____. *Grand Canyon Place Names.* Tucson: University of Arizona Press, 1960.

135. _____. *The True and Authentic History of Scottsdale.* Scottsdale, AZ: 1956.

136. _____. *Tucson: The Way It Was.* Tucson: IBM, 1980.

137. _____. *Will C. Barnes' Arizona Place Names, Revised and Enlarged by Byrd H. Granger.* Tucson: University of Arizona Press, 1960.

138. Gray, A. B. *Survey of a Route for the Southern Pacific Railroad, on the 32nd Parallel.* Cincinnati: 1856.

139. Greenslet, Ferris. *The Lowells and Their Seven Worlds.* Boston: Houghton Mifflin Co., 1946.

140. Gregory, Herbert E. *Geology and Geography of the Zion Park Region, Utah and Arizona.* "Geological Survey Professional Paper 220." Washington, D.C.: U.S. Government Printing Office, 1949.

141. _____. *The Navajo Country: A Geographic and Hydrographic Reconnaissance of Parts of Arizona, New Mexico, and Utah.* "Water Supply Paper 380." Washington, D.C.: U.S. Government Printing Office, 1916.

142. Guitéras, Eusebio, trans. *Rudo Ensayo: 1763: Records of the American Catholic Historical Society of Philadelphia, V, No. 2 (1894).* Tucson: Arizona Silhouettes, 1951.

143. Haile, Berard. *A Stem Vocabulary of the Navaho Language.* St. Michaels, AZ: St. Michaels Press, 1951.

144. Hall, Sharlot M. *First Citizen of Prescott: Pauline Weaver.* Prescott, AZ: n.p., 1929.

145. Hamersly, Thomas H.S., ed. *Complete Regular Army Register of the United States: For One Hundred Years (1779 to 1879).* Washington, D.C.: T. H. S. Hamersly, 1880.

146. Hamilton, Patrick. *The Resources of Arizona: A Manual of Reliable Information Concerning the Territory.* Prescott, AZ: State of Arizona, 1881.

147. Hand, George. Ms. *Diary.* (Tucson: Arizona Historical Society).

148. Hardy, R. W. H. *Travels in the Interior of Mexico in 1825 – 1828.* London: 1829.

149. Hargrave, Lyndon L. "Elden Pueblo." *Museum Notes*, II (November 1929), 1 – 3.

150. _____. "First Mesa." *Museum Notes*, III (February 1931), 1 – 6.

151. _____. "The Influence of Economic Geography upon the Rise and Fall of the Pueblo Culture in Arizona." *Museum Notes*, IV (December 1931), 1 – 3.

152. _____. "The Jeddito Valley and the First Pueblo Towns in Arizona to be Visited by

Europeans." *Museum Notes*, VIII (October 1935), 17 – 23.

153. _____. "Oraibi, A Brief History of the Oldest Inhabited Town in the United States." *Museum Notes*, IV (January 1932), 1–8.

154. _____. "Shungopovi." *Museum Notes*, II (April 1930), 1 – 4.

155. _____. "Sikyatki." *Museum Notes*, IX (June 1937), 63 – 66.

156. Hart, Herbert M. *Old Forts of the Southwest*. Seattle: Superior Publishing Co., 1964.

157. Hawkins, Helen B. *A History of Wickenburg to 1875*. Wickenburg, AZ: Maricopa County Historical Society, 1971.

158. Haws, Atella, and Milo C. Wiltbank and Twylah Hamblin. *Church of Jesus Christ of Latter Day Saints: Dedicatory Services, May 6, 1951*. Eagar, AZ: Eagar Ward, St. Johns Stake, 1951.

159. Heitman, Francis B. *Historical Register and Dictionary of the United States Army, from Its Organization, September 29, 1789, to March 2, 1903*. Washington, D.C.: U.S. Government Printing Office, 1903.

160. Hellenbeck, Cleve, and Juanita H. Williams. *Legends of the Spanish Southwest*. Glendale, CA: The Arthur H. Clark Co., 1938.

161. Hewett, Edgar L. "Origin of the Name Navajo." *American Anthropologist*, n.s. VIII (January – March 1906), 193.

162. Hill, Walter J. "Pioneer Coconino County, 1887." (Huntington Library).

163. Hinton, Richard J. *The Hand-book to Arizona*. San Francisco, CA: Payot, Upham and Co., n.d. Republished: Tucson, AZ: Arizona Silhouettes, 1954.

164. Hislop, Herbert R. *An Englishman's Arizona: 1876 – 1878: The Ranching Letters of Herbert R. Hislop*. Introduction by Bernard L. Fontana. Tucson: The Overland Press, 1965.

165. Hobbs, James. *Wild Life in the Far West*. Glorietta, NM: Rio Grande Press, 1969.

166. Hochderffer, George. *Flagstaff Whoa! The Autobiography of a Western Pioneer*. Flagstaff, AZ: Northland Press, 1965.

167. Hodge, Frederick W., ed. *Handbook of American Indians North of Mexico, I, II*. Washington, D.C.: 1907.

168. Hodge, Hiram C. *Arizona As It Is, or The Coming Country*. New York: Hurd and Houghton, 1877.

169. Hoffmeister, Donald Frederick, and Woodrow W. Goodpaster. *Mammals of the Huachuca Mountains*. Chicago: University of Illinois Press, 1954.

170. Holland, Melvin. *A History of Mesa*. Tucson, AZ: Master's Thesis, University of Arizona, 1933.

171. Hornaday, William T. *Campfires on Desert and Lava*, New York: Charles Scribner's Sons, 1908.

172. Hunter, Thomas Thompson. "Early Days in Arizona." *Arizona Historical Review*, III (April 1930), 105 – 120.

173. Huntington, Ellsworth. "The Desert Laboratory." *Harper's Magazine*, CXXII (April 1911), 651 – 662.

174. Ileff, Flora Gregg. *People of the Blue Water*. New York: Harper & Bros., 1954.

175. Ives, Joseph Christmas. *Report upon the Colorado River of the West, Explored in 1857 and 1858*. House Executive Document 90, 1st Session, 36th Congress. Washington, D.C.: 1861.

176. Jackson, Earl. *Your National Park System in the Southwest*. Globe, AZ: Southwest Parks and Monuments Association, 1976.

177. James, George Wharton. *Arizona the Wonderland*. Boston: The Page Co., 1917.

178. _____. *The Grand Canyon of Arizona: How to See It*. Boston: Little, Brown & Co., 1910.

179. _____. *Indians of the Painted Desert Region*. Boston: Little, Brown & Co., 1905.

180. Johnson, Charles Granville. *History of the Territory of Arizona and the Great Colorado of the Pacific*. San Francisco CA: n.p., 1868.

181. *Journal of the Advanced Party of the Mexican Boundary Commission, October 10 – November 13, 1890*. (Ms., Huntington Library).

182. Katchonga-dan. *Hopi: A Message for All People*. New York: Roosevelt Town, 1972.

183. Kelley, Isabel T. "Southern Piute Shamanism." *Anthropological Records, II, No. 4*. Berkeley, CA: University of California Press, 1939.

184. Kelly, Roger Edward. *Diminishing Returns: Twelfth and Thirteenth Century Sinagua Environmental Adaptation in North Central Arizona*. Tucson AZ: University of Arizona Doctoral Dissertation, 1971.

185. Kelm, Arnold E. *The History of Coolidge and Vicinity*. Tucson, AZ: Master's Thesis, University of Arizona, 1941.

186. Kern, Richard H. *Diary of His Trip with the Sitgreaves Expedition of 1851, August 13 – November 6*. (Facsimile, Huntington Library).

187. _____. *Notes of a Military Reconnaissance of Pais de Los Navajoes, Santa Fe to Albuquerque, August 17 to September 22, 1849*. (Facsimile, Huntington Library).

188. King, Clarence. Ms., "Reconnaissance in Arizona, Winter of 1865 and 1866 Under Order of Gen. McDowell." (Huntington Library).

189. Kitt, Edith O., and T. M. Pearce. "Arizona Place Name Records." *Western Folklore*, XI (October 1952), 284–287.

190. Kitt, Mrs. George F. "Reminiscences of Juan I. Tellez." *Arizona Historical Review*, VII (January 1936), 85–89.

191. Klinck, Richard E. *Land of Room Enough and Time Enough*. Albuquerque, NM: University of New Mexico Press, 1953.

192. Kolb, E. L. *Through the Grand Canyon from Wyoming to Mexico*. New York: Macmillan Co., 1920.

193. Kolb, Ellsworth, and Emery Kolb. "Experiences in the Grand Canyon." *National*

Geographic Magazine, XXVI (August 1914), 99–184.

194. Kroeber, A. L. "A Mohave Historical Epic." *Anthropological Records, XI, No. 2.* Berkeley, CA: University of California Press, 1951.

195. Kurath, William. "A Note on 'Arizone.'" *The Kiva,* XI (January 1946), 20 – 22.

196. Lage, Patricia. *History of Fort Huachuca, 1877 – 1913.* Tucson, AZ: Master's Thesis, University of Arizona, 1949.

197. "Land of Cochise, The." *The Pipeliner,* XV (Summer 1952), 56 – 67.

198. Lang, Walter B., ed. *The First Overland Mail. Butterfield Trail, San Francisco to Memphis, 1858 – 1861.* Washington, D.C.: n.p., 1945.

199. Lauver, Mary E. *History of the Use and Management of the Forested Lands of Arizona, 1862 – 1936.* Tucson, AZ. Master's Thesis, University of Arizona, 1938.

200 Lee, Willis T. *Geologic Reconnaissance of a Part of Western Arizona.* Washington, D.C.: U.S. Government Printing Office, 1908.

201. _____. *Underground Waters of Salt River Valley, Arizona.* Washington, D.C.: U.S. Government Printing Office, 1905.

202. Lesley, Lewis Burt. *Uncle Sam's Camels. The Journal of May Humphreys Stacey, Supplemented by the Report of Edward Fitzgerald Beale, 1857–1858.* Cambridge: Harvard University Press, 1929.

202a. Lingenfelter, Richard E. *Steamboats on the Colorado River, 1852–1916.* Tucson, AZ: The University of Arizona Press, 1978.

203. Lloyd, Elwood. *Arizonology. Knowledge of Arizona.* Flagstaff, AZ: The Coconino Sun, 1933.

204. Lockett, H. C. *Along the Beale Trail: A Photographic Account of Wasted Range Land.* Milton Snow, photographs. Willard W. Beatty, ed. Lawrence, KS: U.S. Office of Indian Affairs, 1938.

205. Lockwood, Frank C. *Life in Old Tucson, 1854 – 1864.* Tucson, AZ: Tucson Civic Committee, 1943.

206. _____. *Pioneer Days in Arizona.* New York: The Macmillan Co., 1932.

207. Lockwood, Frank C., and Donald W. Page. "Tucson, the Old Pueblo." *Arizona Historical Review,* III (April 1930), 16 – 58; (July 1930), 45 – 94.

208. Lumholtz, Carl. *New Trails in Mexico.* New York: Charles Scribner's Sons, 1912.

209. Lummis, Charles F. *Mesa, Canyon, and Pueblo.* New York: The Century Co., 1925.

210. _____. *Some Strange Corners of Our Country.* New York: The Century Co., 1898.

211. Luttrell, Estelle. *Newspapers and Periodicals of Arizona.* Tucson, AZ: University of Arizona Press, 1949.

212. MacDougal, D. T. "Across Papagueria." *American Geographic Society Bulletin,* XL (1908), 705 – 725.

213. "Madonna of the Trail, The." *Daughters of the American Revolution Magazine,* LXIII (July 1929), 399 – 404.

214. Maguire, Daniel. "First Arizona Expedition. 1883." (Facsimile of typescript, Huntington Library).

215. Malach, Roman. *Mohave County: Sketches of Early Days.* New York: Graphicopy, 1974.

216. Mangiante, Rosal. *History of Fort Defiance, 1851–1900.* Tucson, AZ: Master's Thesis, University of Arizona, 1950.

217. Marion, John H. *Notes of Travel Through the Territory of Arizona, Being an Account of the Trip Made by General George Stoneman and Others in the Autumn of 1870.* Prescott, AZ: Arizona Miner Office, 1870.

218. Marshall, James. *Santa Fe. The Railroad That Built an Empire.* New York: Random House, 1945.

219. Martin, Douglas. *Tombstone's Epitaph.* Albuquerque: University of New Mexico Press, 1951.

220. Matthes, Francois E. "Letter to Edward F. McKee, Park Naturalist, Grand Canyon, Relative to Place Names (February 17, 1936)." Grand Canyon, AZ: Naturalist Hq. Files.

221. _____. "Personal Papers (unpublished)." Grand Canyon, AZ: Naturalist Hq. Files.

222. Matthews, Washington. *Navaho Legends.* Boston: Houghton, Mifflin & Co., 1897.

223. Matthiesen, Peter. "Journeys to Hopi National Sacrifice Area." *Rocky Mountain Magazine* (July–August 1979), pp. 49–64.

223a. Mauer, Michael David. Tucson, AZ: *Cibecue Polychrome. Fourteenth Century Ceramic Type from East-Central Arizona,* Master's Thesis, University of Arizona, 1970.

224. McClintock, James H. *Arizona. Prehistoric, Aboriginal, Pioneer, Modern.* Chicago: S. J. Clarke Publishing Co., 1916.

225. _____. *Mormon Settlement in Arizona.* Phoenix, AZ: n.p., 1921.

226. McCormick, Richard. *Arizona. Its Resources and Prospects.* New York: 1865.

227. McGee, W. D. "The Old Yuma Trail." *National Geographic Magazine,* XII (March and April 1901), 103–107; 129–143.

228. McGee, W. J. "Papago Vocabulary [Collected at] San Xavier, Arizona, November 25, 1894." *Ms # 659* (Smithsonian Institution).

229. McGregor, John C. *Southwestern Archaeology.* Urbana, IL: University of Illinois Press, 1965.

230. Merrill, Frederick J. H. "Report on the Mining Property Known as *Planchas de Plata.*" New York: n.p., 1906.

231. Mirkowich, Nicholas. "A Note on Navajo Place Names." *American Anthropologist,* n.s., XXXXIII (April–June 1941), 313 – 314.

232. Möllhausen, Baldwin. *Diary of a Journey from the Mississippi to the Coasts of the*

Pacific with a United States Government Expedition, I, II. London: 1858.

233. Morgan, Learah Cooper, ed. Echoes of the Past. Tales of Old Yavapai. Prescott, AZ: Yavapai Cow Belles, 1955.

234. Morris, Earl H. "Exploring in the Canyon of Death." National Geographic Magazine, XLVIII (September 1925), 263–300.

235. Mott, Dorothy Challis. "Don Lorenzo Hubbell of Ganado." Arizona Historical Review, IV (April 1931), 45–51.

236. Mowry, Sylvester. The Geography and Resources of Arizona and Sonora. San Francisco, CA: A. Roman & Co., 1863.

237. _____. The Geography and Resources of Arizona, with Appendix. (3rd Edition) New York: 1864.

238. Muffley, Bernard W. The History of the Lower San Pedro Valley in Arizona. Tucson, AZ: Master's Thesis, University of Arizona, 1938.

239. Mulligan, R. A. "Apache Pass and Old Fort Bowie, 1850–1894." The Smoke Signal. Tucson: The Westerners, 1965.

240. Munk, Joseph A. Arizona Sketches. New York: The Graphton Press, 1905.

241. Myers, John Myers. The Last Chance: Tombstone's Early Years. New York: E. P. Dutton & Co., 1950.

242. National Archives of the United States, Washington, D.C.: Military and Postal Maps and Record Groups, including papers related to Surveys and Explorations, etc.

243. National Forest Facts: Southwestern Region. Albuquerque, NM: U.S. Dept. of Agriculture, Forest Service, 1955.

244. Nature Notes, No. 3 (June 30, 1929).

245. Newberry, John S. Report upon the Colorado River of the West, Explored in 1857–58 by Lt. J. C. Ives. Washington, D.C.: 1861.

246. Nichol, A. A. The Natural Vegetation of Arizona. Tucson, AZ: University of Arizona Technical Bulletin No. 68, 1937.

247. Oatman, Arizona: the New Gold Camp. Los Angeles: W. L. Wilson & Co., 1916.

248. Oblasser, Bonaventure. "Carnacion Tells Her Tale." Arizona Historical Review, IV (January 1931), 97–98.

249. Ogle, Ralph Hedrick. Federal Control of the Western Apaches, 1848–1886. Albuquerque, NM: University of New Mexico Press, 1940.

250. Oldaker, Elizabeth S. "Arizona Museum Notes." Arizona Historical Review, III (October 1930), 86–89; IV (January 1931), 106–107.

251. Opler, Morris Edward. Myths and Tales of the Chiricahua Apache Indians. Memoirs of the American Folklore Society, XXXVII, 1942.

252. Palmer, Edward. Unpublished Notes, 1866–1867. Tucson, AZ: University of Arizona Special Collections.

253. Papago Bulletin. Sells, AZ: 1965.

254. Parke, John G. "General Report of Explorations from the Pima Villages to the Rio Grande, 1854–55." Pacific Railroad Reports, VII, Part 1. Washington, D.C.: 1857.

255. Pattee, C. R. "Flagstaff, the Gateway to the Grand Cañon of the Colorado and other Scenic and Pre-Historic Attractions." Land of Sunshine (August 1897), pp. 10–12.

256. Pattie, James O. The Personal Narrative of James O. Pattie of Kentucky. Reuben Gold Thwaites, ed. Early Western Travels, XVIII. Cleveland, OH: Arthur H. Clark Co., 1905.

257. Patton, James Monroe. The History of Clifton. Tucson, AZ: Master's Thesis, University of Arizona, 1945.

258. Peattie, Roderick, ed. The Inverted Mountains. New York: The Vanguard Press, 1948.

259. Perkins, George E. Pioneers of the Western Desert. Los Angeles, CA: Wetzel Publishing Co., 1947.

260. Pickrell, Charles U. "A Rugged Son of Arizona." The Smoke Signal. Tucson, AZ: The Westerners, 1960 (May).

261. Pioneer Stories of Arizona's Verde Valley. N.p.. Verde Valley Pioneers Association, Inc., 1954.

262. Place Names on the Papago, Gila Bend, and San Xavier Indian Reservations, Approved for the Use and Guidance of the Indian Service. Sells, AZ: Sells Indian Agency, 1941 [?].

263. Polzer, Charles W. "Legends of Lost Mines and Missions." The Smoke Signal. Tucson, AZ: The Westerners, 1968 (Spring).

264. Post Office Department. 1903 U.S. Official Register, VII. Washington, D.C.: Post Office Department.

265. Powell, J. W. Canyons of the Colorado. Meadville, PA. Flood-Vincent, 1895.

266. Powell, John Wesley. Explorations of the Colorado River of the West and Its Tributaries. Explored in 1869, 1870, 1871, and 1872. Washington, D.C.: U.S. Government Printing Office, 1875.

267. _____. Report of Explorations in 1873 of the Colorado of the West and Its Tributaries. Washington, D.C.: 1874.

268. Prospectus. Salero Mining and Milling Company. N.p.: n.p., n.d. (Huntington Library).

269. Pumpelly, Raphael. Across America and Asia. Notes of a Five Years' Journey Around the World and of Residence in Arizona, Japan, and China. New York: Leypoldt and Holt, 1870.

270. Ransome, Frederick Leslie. Geology of the Globe Copper District, Arizona. Washington, D.C.: U.S. Government Printing Office, 1903.

271. "Record of Heber Ward, Luna, New Mexico." Ms.

272. Reid, John C. Reid's Tramp: or a Journal of the Incidents of Ten Months Travel Through Texas, New Mexico, Arizona, Sonora, and California. Selma, AL: John Hardy & Co., 1858; reprinted Austin, TX: The Steck Co., 1935.

273. Report of State Land Commission of Arizona to Governor and First State Legislature (Feb. 1, 1913). (Huntington Library).

274. Report of the Boundary Commission

upon the Survey and Re-Marking of the Boundary Between the United States and Mexico West of the Rio Grande, 1891–1896. Senate Document No. 247, 55th Congress, 2nd Session.

275. Riggs, Harvey D. "Arivaca Is Old Arizona." *The Arizona Publisher*, I (September 1955), 6.

276. Robinson, Henry Hollister. *San Francisco Volcanic Field, The*. U.S.G.S. Professional Paper 76. Washington, D.C.: 1913.

277. Rockfellow, John A. *Log of an Arizona Trail Blazer*. Tucson, AZ: Acme Printing Co., 1933.

278. Rolak, Bruno J. "History of Fort Huachuca, 1877–1890." *The Smoke Signal*. Tucson: The Westerners, 1974 (Spring).

279. Ross, Clyde P. *The Lower Gila Region, Arizona*. Water Supply Paper #498. Washington, D.C.: U.S. Government Printing Office, 1923.

280. _____. *Routes to Desert Watering Places*. Water Supply Paper #490-C. Washington, D.C.: U.S. Government Printing Office, 1922.

281. Russell, Frank. *The Pima Indians*. 26th Report of the Bureau of American Ethnology, 1904–05. Washington, D.C.: U.S. Government Printing Office, 1908.

282. Russell, Henry Norris. "Meteor Crater." *Museum Notes*, IV (September 1931), 1–3.

283. Saxton, Dean, and Lucille Saxton. *Dictionary: Papago and Pima to English (and Vice Versa)*. Tucson, AZ: University of Arizona Press, 1969.

284. Sain, Wilma Gray. *A History of the Miami Area, Arizona*. Tucson, AZ: Master's Thesis, University of Arizona, 1944.

285. "San Francisco Peaks." *Museum Note*, III (September 1930), 1–4.

286. Schrader, F. C. *Mineral Deposits of the Santa Rita and Patagonia Mountains, Arizona, with Contributions by J. M. Hill*. U.S.G.S. Bulletin 582. Washington, D.C.: n.d.

287. Sedelmayr, Jacobo. *Four Original Manuscript Narratives, 1744–1751*. Peter Masten Dunne, trans. Tucson, AZ: Arizona Pioneers Historical Society, 1955.

288. Seibold, Doris Katherine. *Folk Tales from the Patagonia Area*. Tucson, AZ: University of Arizona Bulletin No. 13 (October 1948).

289. Sharp, Robert L. *Big Outfit: Ranching on the Baca Float*. Tucson, AZ: University of Arizona Press, 1974.

290. Sherer, Lorraine M. *The Clan System of the Fort Mojave Indians*. Los Angeles, CA: Historical Society of Southern California, 1965.

291. Simpich, Frederick. "Along Our Side of the Border." *National Geographic Magazine*, XXXVIII (July 1920), 61–80.

292. Simpson, James H. *Journal of a Military Reconnaissance from Santa Fe, New Mexico, to the Navajo Country*. Philadelphia: Lippincott, Grambo and Co., 1852.

293. Sisk, Hanson Ray. *Historical Santa Cruz County*. Nogales, AZ: 1954.

294. Sitgreaves, Lorenzo. *Report of an Expedition Down the Zuni and Colorado Rivers*. Senate Executive Document 59, 33rd Congress, 1st Session, 1853. Washington, D.C.: Beverley Tucker, Senate Printer, 1854.

295. *Sixth Report of the United States Geographic Board: 1890 to 1932*. Washington, D.C.: U.S. Government Printing Office, 1933.

296. Slipher, V. M. "The Lowell Observatory." *Publications of the Astronomical Society of the Pacific*, XXXIX (June 1927), 143–154.

297. Sloan, Richard E. *Memories of an Arizona Judge*. Palo Alto, CA: Stanford University Press, 1932.

298. Smalley, George H. "The Spenazuma Mining Swindle." *Arizona Historical Review* (April 1929), pp. 86–102.

299. Smith, Gusse Thomas. "Arizona Names, Their Origin and Meaning." *Progressive Arizona and the Great Southwest* (March 1928), pp. 27–30.

300. Smith, T. B. *Grammar of the Pima or Nevome*. New York: Library of American Linguistics, 1860–1864.

301. Sorin, T. R. *Hand-book of Tucson and Surroundings, 1880*. Tucson, AZ: Tucson Citizen Printing, 1880.

302. Southworth, P. D. "Journal of a Trip on Examination of Certain Land in the Navajo Reservation, Being Portions of Letters Written from Winslow Arizona, to Mrs. Southworth at Phoenix, March 12 to April 9, 1914." Ms. photostat. (Huntington Library).

303. Spier, Leslie. *Havasupai Ethnology*. New York: American Museum Press, 1928.

304. _____. *Yuman Tribes of the Gila River*. Chicago: University of Chicago Press, 1933.

305. Stanley, David Sloane. *Diary of an Expedition Which Made a Journey Overland from Fort Smith, Arkansas, to San Diego, California, from July 24, 1853 to March 26, 1854 with Additional Diary Entries to April 9, 1854*. Ms. typewritten copy. (Huntington Library).

306. Stegner, Wallace. *Mormon Country*. New York: Duell, Sloan & Pearce, 1942.

307. Stephen, Alexander M. *Hopi Journal, Part II*. Elsie Clews Parsons, ed. New York: Columbia University Press, 1936.

308. Stephens, Bascom A. "Quijotoa Mining District." N.P.: n.p., 1884.

309. Stevens, Robert Conway. *A History of Chandler, Arizona*. Tucson, AZ: Master's Thesis, University of Arizona, 1954.

310. Stocker, Joseph. *Jewish Roots in Arizona*. Phoenix, AZ: Jewish Community Council, 1964.

311. Stone, Jerome. *The History of Fort Grant*. Tucson, AZ: Master's Thesis, University of Arizona, 1941.

312. Stoneman, George. *Report of Col. George Stoneman, October 31, 1870, U.S. Army*,

Department of Arizona. (Huntington Library).

313. Stoner, Victor R. *The Spanish Missions of the Santa Cruz Valley.* Tucson, AZ: Master's Thesis, University of Arizona, 1937.

314. Summerhayes, Martha. *Vanished Arizona: Recollections of My Army Life.* Chicago: The Lakeside Press, 1939.

315. Sweeny, Thomas W. *Journal of Lt. Thomas W. Sweeny, 1849–1853.* Arthur Woodward, ed. Los Angeles: Westernlore Press, 1956.

316. Sykes, Godfrey. "The Camino del Diablo." *Geographical Review*, XVII (1927), 62–74.

317. Tavernetti, Leonard Rex. *Spatial Organization and Economic Focus of the Arizona Strip.* Tucson, AZ: Master's Thesis, University of Arizona, 1971.

318. Tenney, Ammon M. *Diaries, 1887 – 1921.* (Huntington Library).

319. Tevis, James H. *Arizona in the '50's.* Albuquerque, NM: University of New Mexico Press, 1954.

320. Theobald, John Orr, and Lillian Theobald. *Arizona Territory: Post Offices and Postmasters.* Phoenix, AZ: Arizona Historical Foundation, 1961.

321. Theobald, John, and Lillian Theobald. *Wells Fargo in Arizona Territory.* Bert Fireman, ed. Tempe, AZ: Arizona Historical Foundation, 1978.

322. Thompson, Alisson Harris. "Diary." *Utah Historical Quarterly*, VII (January, April, July 1939).

323. Tillotson, Miner Raymond, and Horace M. Albright. *Grand Canyon Country.* Stanford, CA: Stanford University Press, c. 1935.

324. "Tuba City and the Charlie Day Spring." *Museum Notes*, III (May 1931), 1–4.

325. Udell, John. *Journal of John Udell.* Jefferson, OH: Ashtabula Sentinel Steam Press, 1868.

326. Underhill, Ruth M. *Here Come the Navaho!* Lawrence, KS: U.S. Indian Service, 1953.

327. U.S. Fish and Wildlife Service. Brochures on: Cabeza Prieta; Cibola; Havasu; and Imperial Game Refuges; and the Kofa Game Range. Albuquerque, NM: Bureau of Sport Fisheries and Wildlife, n.d.

328. _____. *Final Environmental Statement* (1975). N.p.: n.d.

329. United States Geological Survey. *Arizona Archives.* Reston, Virginia.

330. Vail, E. L. *Following the Trail of the Apaches: 1886.* (Ms., Arizona Historical Society, Tucson).

331. Van Valkenburgh, Richard; Lucy Wilcox, and John C. McPhee, eds. *diné bike'yah.* Window Rock, AZ: Office of Indian Affairs, 1941.

332. Van Valkenburgh, Richard. *The Ghost Towns.* Window Rock, AZ: Navajo Indian Service, 1941.

333. Verkamp, Margaret M. *History of Grand Canyon National Park.* Tucson, AZ: Master's Thesis, University of Arizona, 1940.

334. Wagoner, Jay J. *History of the Cattle Industry in Southern Arizona, 1540–1940.* Tucson, AZ: Master's Thesis, University of Arizona, 1949.

335. *Walapai Papers: Historical Reports, Documents, and Extracts from Publications Relating to the Walapai Indians of Arizona.* Senate Document No. 273, 74th Congress, 2nd Session. Washington, D.C.: U.S. Government Printing Office, 1936.

336. Wallace, Andrew. "Fort Whipple in the Days of Empire." *The Smoke Signal* (Fall 1972), pp. 114–137.

337. Wampler, Joseph. *Havasu Canyon.* Berkeley, CA: Howell-North Press, 1959.

338. Wayte, Harold C. *A History of Holbrook and the Little Colorado.* Tucson, AZ: Master's Thesis, University of Arizona, 1962.

339. Weaver, John Mason. *A History of Fort Lowell.* Tucson, AZ: Master's Thesis, University of Arizona, 1947.

340. Webber, Charles W. *The Gold Mines of the Gila: a Sequel to Old Hicks the Guide, I, II.* New York: Dewitt & Davenport, 1849.

341. Westover, Adele B., and J. Morris Richards. *A Brief History of Joseph City.* Winslow, AZ: The Winslow Mail, 1951.

342. Wheeler, George M. *Annual Report upon the Geographical Exploration and Surveys West of the 100th Meridian: Appendix of Annual Report of the Chief of Engineers for 1875.* Washington, D.C.: U.S. Government Printing Office, 1875.

343. _____. *Preliminary Report of Exploration and Surveys South of the Central Pacific R.R., Principally in Nevada and Arizona.* Washington, D.C.: 1872.

344. _____. *Progress Report upon Geographical and Geological Explorations and Surveys West of the One Hundreth Meridian in 1872.* Washington, D.C.: U.S. Government Printing Office, 1874.

345. _____. *Report upon Geographical and Geological Explorations and Surveys West of the One Hundreth Meridian, in Charge of First Lieutenant George M. Wheeler.* Washington, D.C.: U.S. Government Printing Office, 1875.

346. Whipple, Amiel W. *Itinerary: Exploration and Surveys for a Railroad Route from the Mississippi River to the Pacific Ocean: Route Near the 35th Parallel in 1853 and 1854.* Washington, D.C.: 1854.

347. _____. *The Itinerary of Lieutenant A. W. Whipple During His Explorations for a Railway Route from Fort Smith to Los Angeles in the Years 1853 and 1854*; published as *A Pathfinder in the Southwest.* Grant Foreman, ed. Norman, OK: University of Oklahoma Press, 1941.

348. _____. *Report of Explorations and Surveys to Ascertain the Most Practical and Economical Route for a Railroad from the Mississippi River to the Ocean, 1853-1854.* Washington, D.C.: 1854.

349. White, John B. Ms., *Names of the Different Tribes in Arizona and the Names by Which They are Called by the Apaches, c. 1875.* Bureau of American Ethnology. (Smithsonian Institution).

350. _____. Ms.#179. *A History of the Apache Indians of Arizona Territory. (Smithsonian Institution).*

351. _____. Ms. *Apache Place Names 1873–75.* (Smithsonian Institution).

352. *Wildlife Research in Arizona, 1969-1970.* Phoenix, AZ: Arizona Game and Fish Department, 1970.

353. Williams, Orean A. *Settlement and Growth of the Gila Valley as a Mormon Colony, 1879–1900.* Tucson, AZ: Master's Thesis, University of Arizona, 1937.

354. Williamson, Dan R. "Al Sieber, Famous Scout of the Southwest." *Arizona Historical Review,* IV (January 1931), 60–76.

355. Wilson, Eldred G. *Geology and Mineral Deposits of Southern Yuma County, Arizona.* Tucson, AZ: University of Arizona Bulletin IV, No. 2, Geological Series No. 7, Bulletin No. 134 (February 15, 1933).

356. _____. *A Resume of the Geology of Arizona.* Tucson, AZ: University of Arizona, 1971.

357. Winship, George Parker. *The Coronado Expedition, 1540–1542.* 14th Annual Report, Bureau of American Ethnology. Washington, D.C.: 1896.

358. Wisbey, Herbert A. *History of the Santa Fe Railroad in Arizona to 1917.* Tucson, AZ: Master's Thesis, University of Arizona, 1946.

359. Wolle, Muriel Vincent Sibell. *The Bonanza Trail: Ghost Towns and Mining Camps of the West.* Bloomington, IN: Indiana University Press, 1953.

360. Yount, Otis E. *The West of Philip St. George Cooke, 1809–1895.* Glendale, CA: Arthur H. Clark Co., 1955.

361. Young, Robert W. *The Navajo Yearbook of Planning in Action.* Window Rock, AZ: Navajo Agency, 1955.